The Oxford Russian Minidictionary

Edited by
Della Thompson

Oxford · New York
OXFORD UNIVERSITY PRESS

Oxford University Press, Walton Street, Oxford OX2 6DP

Oxford New York
Athens Auckland Bangkok Bombay
Calcutta Cape Town Dar es Salaam Delhi
Florence Hong Kong Istanbul Karachi
Kuala Lumpur Madras Madrid Melbourne
Mexico City Nairobi Paris Singapore
Taipei Tokyo Toronto
and associated companies in
Berlin Ibadan

Oxford is a trade mark of Oxford University Press

British Library Cataloguing in Publication Data

Data available

Library of Congress Cataloging in Publication Data

Data available
ISBN 0-19-864188-5

10 9 8 7 6 5 4 3

Printed in Great Britain by
Charles Letts (Scotland) Ltd.
Dalkeith, Scotland

math	mathematics	propr	proprietary term
med	medicine	psych	psychology
meteorol	meteorology		
mil	military	refl	reflexive
mus	music	rel	relative
		relig	religion; religious
n	noun		
naut	nautical	rly	railway
neg	negative		
neut	neuter	sb	substantive
nn	nouns	sg	singular
nom	nominative	sl	slang
		s.o.	someone
o.s.	oneself	sth	something
		superl	superlative
parl	parliamentary		
part	participle	tech	technical
partl	particle	tel	telephony
pers	person	theat	theatre
pf	perfective	theol	theology
philos	philosophy		
phon	phonetics	univ	university
phot	photography	usu	usually
phys	physics		
pl	plural	v	verb
polit	political	v aux	auxiliary verb
poss	possessive	vbl	verbal
predic	predicate; predicative	vi	intransitive verb
		voc	vocative
pref	prefix	vt	transitive verb
prep	preposition; prepositional	vulg	vulgar
		vv	verbs
pres	present (tense)		
pron, prons	pronoun(s)	zool	zoology

Abbreviations used in the Dictionary

abbr	abbreviation	eccl	ecclesiastical
abs	absolute	econ	economics
acc	accusative	electr	electricity
adj, adjs	adjective(s)	electron	electronics
adv, advs	adverb(s)	emph	emphatic
aeron	aeronautics	esp	especially
agric	agriculture	etc.	etcetera
anat	anatomy		
approx	approximate(ly)	f	feminine
archaeol	archaeology	fig	figurative
archit	architecture	fut	future (tense)
astron	astronomy		
attrib	attributive	gen	genitive
aux	auxiliary	geog	geography
		geol	geology
bibl	biblical	geom	geometry
biol	biology	gram	grammar
bot	botany		
		hist	historical
chem	chemistry		
cin	cinema(tography)	imper	imperative
coll	colloquial	impers	impersonal
collect	collective(ly)	impf	imperfective
comb	combination	indecl	indeclinable
comm	commerce	indef	indefinite
comp	comparative	indet	indeterminate
comput	computing	inf	infinitive
conj, conjs	conjunction(s)	instr	instrumental
cul	culinary	int	interjection
		interrog	interrogative
dat	dative		
def	definite	ling	linguistics
derog	derogatory	loc	locative
det	determinate		
dim	diminutive	m	masculine

If only one case-labelled form is given in the singular, it is an exception to the regular paradigm. If only one plural form is given (the nominative), the rest follow this. In other words, in this example, the accusative singular and all the plural forms have initial stress.

v) **скоба́** (*pl* -ы, -а́м)

In the plural, forms that are not shown (here instrumental and prepositional) are stressed like the last form given.

Proprietary terms

This dictionary includes some words which are, or are asserted to be, proprietary names or trade marks. Their inclusion does not imply that they have acquired for legal purposes a non-proprietary or general significance, nor is any other judgement implied concerning their legal status. In cases where the editor has some evidence that a word is used as a proprietary name or trade mark this is indicated by the label *propr*, but no judgement concerning the legal status of such words is made or implied thereby.

Both the comma and the ampersand (&) are used to show alternatives, e.g. **хоте́ть** + *gen*, *acc* means that the Russian verb may govern either the genitive or accusative; **сирота́** *m* & *f* orphan means that the Russian noun is treated as masculine or feminine according to the sex of the person denoted; **Cossack** *n* каза́к, -а́чка represents the masculine and feminine translations of Cossack; **dilate** *vt* & *i* расширя́ть(ся) means that the Russian verb forms cover both the transitive and intransitive English verbs.

Stress

The stress of Russian words is shown by an acute accent over the vowel of the stressed syllable. The vowel ё has no stress-mark since it is almost always stressed. The presence of two stress-marks indicates that either of the marked syllables may be stressed.

Changes of stress in inflexion are shown, e.g.

i) **предложи́ть** (-жу́, -жишь)

The absence of a stress-mark on the second person singular indicates that the stress is on the preceding syllable and that the rest of the conjugation is stressed in this way.

ii) **нача́ть** (.............; на́чал, -а́, -о)

The final form, на́чало, takes the stress of the first of the two preceding forms when these differ from each other. Forms that are not shown, here на́чали, are stressed like the last form given.

iii) **дождь** (-дя́)

The single form given in brackets is the genitive singular and all other forms have the same stressed syllable.

iv) **душа́** (*acc* -у; *pl* -и)

Introduction

In order to save space, related words are often grouped together in paragraphs, as are cross-references and compound entries.

The swung dash (~) and the hyphen are also used to save space. The swung dash represents the headword preceding it in bold, or the preceding Russian word, e.g. **Georgian** *n* грузи́н, ~ка. The hyphen is mainly used, in giving grammatical forms, to stand for part of the preceding, or (less often) following, Russian word, e.g. **приходи́ть** (-ожу́, -о́дишь).

Russian headwords are followed by inflexional information where considered necessary. So-called regular inflexions for the purpose of this dictionary are listed in the Appendices.

Where a noun ending is given but not labelled in the singular, it is the genitive ending; other cases are named; in the plural, where cases are identifiable by their endings, they are not labelled, e.g. **сестра́** (*pl* сёстры, сестёр, сёстрам). The gender of Russian nouns can usually be deduced from their endings and it is indicated only in exceptional cases (e.g. for masculine nouns in **-а, -я**, and **-ь**, neuter nouns in **-мя**, and all indeclinable nouns).

Verbs are labelled *impf* or *pf* to show their aspect. Where a perfective verb is formed by the addition of a prefix to the imperfective, this is shown at the headword by a light vertical stroke, e.g. **про|лепета́ть**. When a verb requires the use of a case other than the accusative, this is indicated, e.g. **маха́ть** *impf*, **махну́ть** *pf* + *instr* wave, brandish.

Contents

Preface

This is a completely new work in the Oxford Mini-dictionary range and is designed primarily for English-speaking users. It provides a handy yet extremely comprehensive reference work for students of Russian, tourists, and business people.

Particular attention has been given to the provision of inflected forms where these cause difficulty, and to showing the stressed syllable of every Russian word as well as changes in stress where they occur. Perfective and imperfective aspects are distinguished and both are given wherever appropriate.

Thanks are due to Alexander and Nina Levtov for their editorial help and valuable advice on contemporary Russian usage, and to Helen McCurdy for help with proof-reading.

D.J.T.

March 1995

accompanist. **аккомпани́ровать** *impf* +*dat* accompany.

акко́рд chord.

аккордео́н accordion.

аккордн|ый by agreement; **~ая рабо́та** piece-work.

аккредити́в letter of credit. **аккредитова́ть** *impf & pf* accredit.

аккумуля́тор accumulator.

аккура́тный neat, careful; punctual; exact, thorough.

акри́л acrylic. **акри́ловый** acrylic.

акроба́т acrobat.

аксессуа́р accessory; (stage) props.

аксио́ма axiom.

акт act; deed, document; **обвини́тельный ~** indictment.

актёр actor.

акти́в (*comm*) asset(s).

активиза́ция stirring up, making (more) active. **активизи́ровать** *impf & pf* make (more) active, stir up. **акти́вный** active.

активи́ровать *impf & pf* (*comp* *also* c~) register, record, presence or absence of; (*sl*) write off.

а́ктовый зал assembly hall.

актри́са actress.

актуа́льный topical, urgent.

аку́ла shark.

аку́стика acoustics. **акусти́ческий** acoustic.

акуше́р obstetrician. **акуше́рка** midwife.

акце́нт accent, stress. **акценти́ровать** *impf & pf* accent; accentuate.

акционе́р shareholder. **акционе́рный** joint-stock. **а́кция**[1] share; *pl* stock. **а́кция**[2] action.

а́лгебра algebra.

а́либи *neut indecl* alibi.

алиме́нты (*pl; gen* -ов) (*law*) maintenance.

алкоголи́зм alcoholism. **алкого́лик** alcoholic. **алкого́ль** *m* alcohol. **алкого́льный** alcoholic.

аллего́рия allegory.

аллерги́я allergy.

алле́я avenue; path, walk.

аллига́тор alligator.

алло́ hello! (*on telephone*).

алма́з diamond.

алта́рь (-я́) *m* altar; chancel, sanctuary.

алфави́т alphabet. **алфави́тный** alphabetical.

а́лчный greedy, grasping.

а́лый scarlet.

альбо́м album; sketch-book.

альмана́х literary miscellany; almanac.

альпи́йский Alpine. **альпини́зм** mountaineering. **альпини́ст, альпини́стка** (mountain-)climber.

альт (-á; *pl* -ы́) alto; viola.

альтернати́ва alternative. **альтернати́вный** alternative.

альтруисти́ческий altruistic.

алюми́ний aluminium.

амазо́нка Amazon; horse-woman; riding-habit.

амба́р barn; storehouse, warehouse.

амби́ция pride; arrogance.

амбулато́рия out-patients' department; surgery. **амбулато́рный больно́й** *sb* out-patient.

Аме́рика America. **америка́нец** (-нца), **америка́нка** American. **америка́нский** American; US.

аминокислота́ amino acid.

ами́нь *m* amen.

аммиа́к ammonia.

амни́стия amnesty.

амора́льный amoral; immoral.

амортиза́тор shock-absorber.

амортиза́ция depreciation; shock-absorption.

ампе́р (*gen pl* ампе́р) ampere.

ампута́ция amputation. **ампути́ровать** *impf & pf* amputate.

амфетами́н amphetamine.

амфи́бия amphibian.

амфитеа́тр amphitheatre; circle.

ана́лиз analysis; ~ кро́ви blood test. **анализи́ровать** *impf & pf* analyse. **анали́тик** analyst. **аналити́ческий** analytic(al).

анало́г analogue. **аналоги́чный** analogous. **анало́гия** analogy.

анана́с pineapple.

анархи́ст, ~ка anarchist. **анархи́ческий** anarchic. **ана́рхия** anarchy.

анатоми́ческий anatomical. **анато́мия** anatomy.

анахрони́зм anachronism. **анахрони́ческий** anachronistic.

анга́р hangar.

а́нгел angel. **а́нгельский** angelic.

анги́на sore throat.

англи́йский English; ~ая була́вка safety-pin. **англича́нин** (*pl* -ча́не, -ча́н) Englishman. **англича́нка** Englishwoman. **А́нглия** England, Britain.

анекдо́т anecdote, story; funny thing.

анеми́я anaemia.

анестезио́лог anaesthetist. **анестези́ровать** *impf & pf* anaesthetize. **анестези́рующее сре́дство** anaesthetic.

анестези́я anaesthesia.

анке́та questionnaire, form.

аннекси́ровать *impf & pf* annex. **анне́ксия** annexation.

аннули́ровать *impf & pf* annul; cancel, abolish.

анома́лия anomaly. **анома́льный** anomalous.

анони́мка anonymous letter. **анони́мный** anonymous.

анонси́ровать *impf & pf* announce.

анорекси́я anorexia.

анса́мбль *m* ensemble; company, troupe.

антагони́зм antagonism.

Анта́рктика the Antarctic.

анте́нна antenna; aerial.

антибио́тик antibiotic(s).

антидепресса́нт antidepressant.

антиква́р antiquary; antique-dealer. **антиквариа́т** antique-shop. **антиква́рный** antiquarian; antique.

антило́па antelope.

антипа́тия antipathy.

антисемити́зм anti-Semitism. **антисеми́тский** anti-Semitic.

антисе́птик antiseptic. **антисепти́ческий** antiseptic.

антите́зис (*philos*) antithesis.

антите́ло (*pl* -á) antibody.

антифри́з antifreeze.

анти́чность antiquity. **анти́чный** ancient, classical.

антоло́гия anthology.

антра́кт interval.

антраци́т anthracite.

антреко́т entrecôte, steak.

антрепренёр impresario.

антресо́ли (*pl; gen* -ей) mezzanine; shelf.

антропо́лог anthropologist. **антропологи́ческий** anthropological. **антрополо́гия** anthropology.

анфила́да suite (of rooms).

анчо́ус anchovy.

аншла́г 'house full' notice.

апарте́йд apartheid.

апати́чный apathetic. **апа́тия** apathy.

апелли́ровать *impf* & *pf* appeal. **апелляцио́нный суд** Court of Appeal. **апелля́ция** appeal.

апельси́н orange; orange-tree. **апельси́нный, апельси́новый** orange.

аплоди́ровать *impf* +*dat* applaud. **аплодисме́нты** *m pl* applause.

апло́мб aplomb.

Апока́липсис Revelation. **апока́липтический** apocalyptic.

апо́стол apostle.

апостро́ф apostrophe.

аппара́т apparatus; machinery, organs. **аппарату́ра** apparatus, gear; (*comput*) hardware. **аппара́тчик** operator; apparatchik.

аппе́ндикс appendix. **аппендици́т** appendicitis.

аппети́т appetite; прия́тного ~а! bon appétit! **аппети́тный** appetizing.

апре́ль *m* April. **апре́льский** April.

апте́ка chemist's. **апте́карь** *m* chemist. **апте́чка** medicine chest; first-aid kit.

ара́б, ара́бка Arab. **ара́бский** Arab, Arabic. **арави́йский** Arabian.

аранжи́ровать *impf* & *pf* (*mus*) arrange. **аранжиро́вка** (*mus*) arrangement.

ара́хис peanut.

арби́тр arbitrator. **арбитра́ж** arbitration.

арбу́з water-melon.

аргуме́нт argument. **аргу-**

мента́ция reasoning; arguments. **аргументи́ровать** *impf* & *pf* argue, (try to) prove.

аре́на arena, ring.

аре́нда lease. **аренда́тор** tenant. **аре́ндная пла́та** rent. **арендова́ть** *impf* & *pf* rent.

аре́ст arrest. **арестова́ть** *pf*, **аресто́вывать** *impf* arrest; seize, sequestrate.

аристокра́т, ~ка aristocrat. **аристократи́ческий** aristocratic. **аристокра́тия** aristocracy.

арифме́тика arithmetic. **арифмети́ческий** arithmetical.

а́рия aria.

а́рка arch.

А́рктика the Arctic. **аркти́ческий** arctic.

армату́ра fittings; reinforcement; armature. **армату́рщик** fitter.

арме́йский army.

Арме́ния Armenia.

а́рмия army.

армяни́н (*pl* -я́не, -я́н), **армя́нка** Armenian. **армя́нский** Armenian.

арома́т scent, aroma. **арома́тный** aromatic, fragrant.

арсена́л arsenal.

арте́ль artel.

арте́рия artery.

арти́куль *m* (*gram*) article.

артилле́рия artillery.

арти́ст, ~ка artiste, artist; expert. **артисти́ческий** artistic.

артри́т arthritis.

а́рфа harp.

архаи́ческий archaic.

арха́нгел archangel.

археоло́г archaeologist. **археологи́ческий** archaeological. **археоло́гия** archaeology.

архи́в archives. **архиви́ст**

archivist. **архи́вный** archive, archival.

архиепи́скоп archbishop. **архиере́й** bishop.

архипела́г archipelago.

архите́ктор architect. **архитекту́ра** architecture. **архитекту́рный** architectural.

арши́н arshin (71 cm.).

асбе́ст asbestos.

асимметри́чный asymmetrical. **асимметри́я** asymmetry.

аске́т ascetic. **аскети́зм** asceticism. **аскети́ческий** ascetic.

асоциа́льный antisocial.

аспира́нт, ~ка post-graduate student. **аспиранту́ра** post-graduate course.

аспири́н aspirin.

ассамбле́я assembly.

ассигна́ция banknote.

ассимиля́ция assimilation.

ассисте́нт assistant; junior lecturer, research assistant.

ассортиме́нт assortment.

ассоциа́ция association. **ассоции́ровать** impf & pf associate.

а́стма asthma. **астмати́ческий** asthmatic.

астро́лог astrologer. **астроло́гия** astrology.

астрона́вт astronaut. **астроно́м** astronomer. **астрономи́ческий** astronomical. **астроно́мия** astronomy.

асфа́льт asphalt.

ата́ка attack. **атакова́ть** impf & pf attack.

атама́н ataman (Cossack chieftain); (gang-)leader.

атеи́зм atheism. **атеи́ст** atheist.

ателье́ neut indecl studio; atelier.

а́тлас[1] atlas.

атла́с[2] satin. **атла́сный** satin.

атле́т athlete; strong man. **атле́тика** athletics. **атлети́ческий** athletic.

атмосфе́ра atmosphere. **атмосфе́рный** atmospheric.

а́том atom. **а́томный** atomic.

атташе́ m indecl attaché.

аттеста́т testimonial; certificate; pedigree. **аттестова́ть** impf & pf attest; recommend.

аттракцио́н attraction; sideshow; star turn.

ау́ int hi, cooee.

аудито́рия auditorium, lecture-room.

аукцио́н auction.

ау́л aul (Caucasian or Central Asian village).

аўто́псия autopsy.

афе́ра speculation, trickery. **афери́ст** speculator, trickster.

афи́ша placard, poster.

афори́зм aphorism.

А́фрика Africa. **африка́нец** (-нца), **африка́нка** African. **африка́нский** African.

аффе́кт fit of passion; temporary insanity.

ах int ah, oh. **а́хать** impf **а́хнуть** (pf) sigh; exclaim; gasp.

аэро|вокза́л air terminal. **~дина́мика** aerodynamics. **~дро́м** aerodrome, air-field. **~зо́ль** m aerosol. **~по́рт** (loc -ý) airport.

Б

б partl: see **бы**

ба́ба (coll) (old) woman; **сне́жная ~** snowman.

ба́бочка butterfly.

ба́бушка grandmother; grandma.

бага́ж (-á) luggage. **бага́жник**

carrier; luggage-rack; boot. **бага́жный ваго́н** luggage-van.

баго́р (-ра́) boat-hook.

багро́вый crimson, purple.

бадья́ (gen pl -де́й) tub.

ба́за base; depot; basis; ~ **да́нных** database.

база́р market; din.

ба́зис base; basis.

байда́рка canoe.

ба́йка flannelette.

бак[1] tank, cistern.

бак[2] forecastle.

бакала́вр (univ) bachelor.

бакале́йный grocery. **бакале́я** groceries.

ба́кен buoy.

бакенба́рды (pl; gen -ба́рд) side-whiskers.

баклажа́н (gen pl -ов or -жа́н) aubergine.

бакте́рия bacterium.

бал (loc -у́; pl -ы́) dance, ball.

балага́н farce.

балала́йка balalaika.

бала́нс (econ) balance.

баланси́ровать impf (pf c~) balance; keep one's balance.

балбе́с booby.

балдахи́н canopy.

балери́на ballerina. **бале́т** ballet.

ба́лка[1] beam, girder.

ба́лка[2] gully.

балко́н balcony.

балл mark (in school); degree; force; **ве́тер в пять ~ов** wind force 5.

балла́да ballad.

балла́ст ballast.

балло́н container, carboy, cylinder; balloon tyre.

баллоти́ровать impf vote; put to the vote; ~**ся** stand, be a candidate (**в** or **на**+acc for).

балова́ть impf (pf из~) spoil,

pamper; ~**ся** play about, get up to tricks; amuse o.s. **ба́ловство́** spoiling; mischief.

Балти́йское мо́ре Baltic (Sea).

бальза́м balsam; balm.

балюстра́да balustrade.

бамбу́к bamboo.

ба́мпер bumper.

бана́льность banality; platitude. **бана́льный** banal.

бана́н banana.

ба́нда band, gang.

банда́ж (-á) truss; belt, band.

бандеро́ль wrapper; printed matter, book-post.

ба́нджо neut indecl banjo.

банди́т bandit; gangster.

банк bank.

ба́нка jar; tin.

банке́т banquet.

банки́р banker. **банкно́та** banknote. **банкро́т** bankrupt. **банкро́тство** bankruptcy.

бант bow.

ба́ня bath; bath-house.

бар bar; snack-bar.

бараба́н drum. **бараба́нить** impf drum, thump. **бараба́нная перепо́нка** ear-drum. **бараба́нщик** drummer.

бара́к wooden barrack, hut.

бара́н ram; sheep. **бара́нина** mutton.

бара́нка ring-shaped roll; (steering-)wheel.

барахло́ old clothes, jumble; odds and ends. **барахо́лка** flea market.

бара́шек (-шка) young ram; lamb; wing nut; catkin. **бара́шковый** lambskin.

ба́ржа́ (gen pl барж(е́й)) barge.

ба́рин (pl -ре or -ры, бар) landowner; sir.

барито́н baritone.

бáрка barge.
бáрмен barman.
барóкко *neut indecl* baroque.
барóметр barometer.
барóн baron. **баронéсса** baroness.
барóчный baroque.
баррикáда barricade.
барс snow-leopard.
бáрский lordly; grand.
бархáн dune.
бáрхат (-у) velvet. **бáрхатный** velvet.
бáрыня landowner's wife; madam.
барыш (-á) profit. **барышник** dealer; (ticket) speculator.
барышня (*gen pl* -шень) young lady; miss.
барьéр barrier; hurdle.
бас (*pl* -ы́) bass.
баскетбóл basket-ball.
баснослóвный mythical, legendary; fabulous. **бáсня** (*gen pl* -сен) fable; fabrication.
басóвый bass.
бассéйн (*geog*) basin; pool; reservoir.
бастовáть *impf* be on strike.
батальóн battalion.
батарéйка, батарéя battery; radiator.
батóн long loaf; stick, bar.
бáтька *m*, **бáтя** *m* father; priest. **бáтюшки** *int* good gracious!
бах *int* bang!
бахвáльство bragging.
бахромá fringe.
бац *int* bang! crack!
бацилла bacillus. **бациллоноси́тель** *m* carrier.
бачóк (-чкá) cistern.
бáшка head.
башлы́к (-á) hood.
башмáк (-á) shoe; **под ~óм**

у+*gen* under the thumb of.
бáшня (*gen pl* -шен) tower; turret.
баю́кать *impf* (*pf* у~) sing lullabies (to). **баю́шки-баю́** *int* hushaby!
баян accordion.
бдéние vigil. **бди́тельность** vigilance. **бди́тельный** vigilant.
бег (*loc* -ý; *pl* -á) run, running; race. **бéгать** *indet* (*det* бежáть) *impf* run.
бегемóт hippopotamus.
беглéц (-á), **беглянка** fugitive. **бéглость** speed, fluency, dexterity. **бéглый** rapid, fluent; fleeting, cursory; *sb* fugitive, runaway. **беговóй** running; race. **бегóм** *adv* running, at the double. **беготня́** running about; bustle. **бéгство** flight; escape. **бегýн** (-á), **бегýнья** (*gen pl* -ний) runner.
бедá (*pl* -ы) misfortune; disaster; trouble; ~ **в том, что** the trouble is (that). **беднéть** *impf* (*pf* о~) grow poor. **бéдность** poverty; the poor. **бéдный** (-ден, -днá, -дно) poor. **бедня́га** *m*, **бедня́жка** *m & f* poor thing. **бедня́к** (-á), **бедня́чка** poor peasant; poor man, poor woman.
бедрó (*pl* бёдра, -дер) thigh; hip.
бéдственный disastrous. **бéдствие** disaster. **бéдствовать** *impf* live in poverty.
бежáть (бегý *det*; *indet* бéгать) *impf* (*pf* по~) run; flow; fly; boil over; *impf & pf* escape. **бéженец** (-нца), **бéженка** refugee.
без *prep*+*gen* without; ~ **пяти́**

(мину́т) три five (minutes) to three; ~ че́тверти a quarter to.

без-, безъ-, бес- *in comb* in-, un-; non-; -less. **без**алкого́льный non-alcoholic. ~апелляцио́нный peremptory, categorical. ~бо́жие atheism. ~бо́жный godless; shameless, outrageous. ~боле́зненный painless. ~бра́чный celibate. ~бре́жный boundless. ~ве́стный unknown; obscure. ~вку́сие lack of taste, bad taste. ~вку́сный tasteless. ~вла́стие anarchy. ~во́дный arid. ~возвра́тный irrevocable; irrecoverable. ~возме́здный free, gratis. ~во́лие lack of will. ~во́льный weak-willed. ~вре́дный harmless. ~вре́менный untimely. ~вы́ходный hopeless, desperate; uninterrupted. ~гла́зый one-eyed; eyeless. ~гра́мотный illiterate. ~грани́чный boundless, infinite. ~да́рный untalented. ~де́йственный inactive. ~де́йствие inertia, idleness; negligence. ~де́йствовать *impf* be idle, be inactive; idle, loaf. **безде́лица** trifle. **безде́лушка** knick-knack. **безде́льник** idler; ne'er-do-well. **безде́льничать** *impf* idle, loaf. **бе́здна** abyss, chasm; a huge number, a multitude.

без-. ~доказа́тельный unsubstantiated. ~до́мный homeless. ~до́нный bottomless; fathomless. ~доро́жье lack of (good) roads; season when roads are impassable. ~ду́мный unthinking. ~ду́шный heartless; inanimate; life-

less. ~жа́лостный pitiless, ruthless. ~жи́зненный lifeless. ~забо́тный carefree; careless. ~заве́тный selfless, wholehearted. ~зако́ние lawlessness; unlawful act. ~зако́нный illegal; lawless. ~засте́нчивый shameless, barefaced. ~защи́тный defenceless. ~зву́чный silent. ~зло́бный good-natured. ~ли́чный characterless; impersonal. ~лю́дный uninhabited; sparsely populated; lonely.

безме́н steelyard.

без-. ~ме́рный immense; excessive. ~мо́лвие silence. ~мо́лвный silent, mute. ~мяте́жный serene, placid. ~наде́жный hopeless. ~надзо́рный neglected. ~нака́занно *adv* with impunity. ~нака́занный unpunished. ~но́гий legless; one-legged. ~нра́вственный immoral.

безо *prep+gen* = **без** (*used before* весь *and* вся́кий).

безобра́зие ugliness; disgrace, scandal. **безобра́зничать** *impf* make a nuisance of o.s. **безобра́зный** ugly; disgraceful.

без-. ~огово́рочный unconditional. ~опа́сность safety; security. ~опа́сный safe; secure. ~ору́жный unarmed. ~основа́тельный groundless. ~остано́вочный unceasing; non-stop. ~отве́тный meek, unanswering; dumb. ~отве́тственный irresponsible. ~отка́зно *adv* without a hitch. ~отка́зный trouble-free, smooth-(running). ~отлага́тельный urgent. ~относи́-

тельно *adv*+**к**+*dat* irrespective of. **~отчётный** uncountable. **~оши́бочный** unerring; correct. **~рабо́тица** unemployment. **~рабо́тный** unemployed. **~разли́чие** indifference. **~разли́чно** *adv* indifferently; it is all the same. **~разли́чный** indifferent. **~рассу́дный** reckless, imprudent. **~ро́дный** alone in the world; without relatives. **~ро́потный** uncomplaining; meek. **~рука́вка** sleeveless pullover. **~ру́кий** armless; one-armed. **~уда́рный** unstressed. **~уде́ржный** unrestrained; impetuous. **~укори́зненный** irreproachable.

безу́мец (-мца) madman. **безу́мие** madness. **безу́мный** mad. **безу́мство** madness.

без-. **безупре́чный** irreproachable, faultless. **~усло́вно** *adv* unconditionally; of course, undoubtedly. **~усло́вный** unconditional, absolute; indisputable. **~успе́шный** unsuccessful. **~уста́нный** tireless. **~уте́шный** inconsolable. **~уча́стие** indifference, apathy. **~уча́стный** indifferent, apathetic. **~ымя́нный** nameless, anonymous; **~ымя́нный па́лец** ring-finger. **~ыску́сный** artless, ingenuous. **~ысхо́дный** irreparable; interminable.

бейсбо́л baseball.

бека́р (*mus*) natural.

бека́с snipe.

беко́н bacon.

Белару́сь Belarus.

беле́ть *impf* (*pf* по**~**) turn white; show white.

белизна́ whiteness. **бели́ла**

(*pl*; *gen* -и́л) whitewash; Tippex (*propr*). **бели́ть** (бели́шь) *impf* (*pf* вы**~**, на**~**, по**~**) whitewash; whiten; bleach.

бе́лка squirrel.

беллетри́ст writer of fiction. **беллетри́стика** fiction.

бело- *in comb* white-, leuco-. **белогварде́ец** (-е́йца) White Guard. **~кро́вие** leukaemia. **~ку́рый** fair, blonde. **~ру́с**, **~ру́ска**, **~ру́сский** Belorussian. **~сне́жный** snow-white.

белови́к (-а́) fair copy. **белово́й** clean, fair.

бело́к (-лка́) white (*of egg, eye*); protein.

белошве́йка seamstress. **белошве́йный** linen.

белу́га white sturgeon. **белу́ха** white whale.

бе́л|ый (бел, -а́, бе́ло) white; clean, blank; *sb* white person; **~ая берёза** silver birch; **~ое кале́ние** white heat; **~ый медве́дь** polar bear; **~ые но́чи** white nights, midnight sun.

бельги́ец, **-ги́йка** Belgian. **бельги́йский** Belgian. **Бе́льгия** Belgium.

бельё linen; bedclothes; underclothes; washing.

бельмо́ (*pl* -а́) cataract.

бельэта́ж first floor; dress circle.

бемо́ль *m* (*mus*) flat.

бенефи́с benefit (performance).

бензи́н petrol.

бензо- *in comb* petrol. **бензоба́к** petrol-tank. **~во́з** petrol tanker. **~запра́вочная** *sb* filling-station. **~коло́нка** petrol pump. **~прово́д** petrol pipe, fuel line.

берёг etc.: see **беречь.**

бе́рег (loc -ý; pl -á) bank, shore; coast; **на ~ý мо́ря** at the seaside. **берегово́й** coast; coastal.

бережёшь etc.: see **беречь.**

бережли́вый thrifty. **бе́режный** careful.

берёза birch. **Берёзка** hard-currency shop.

бере́менеть impf (pf за~) be(come) pregnant. **бере́менная** pregnant (+instr with). **бере́менность** pregnancy; gestation.

берёт beret.

бере́чь (-регу́, -режёшь; -рёг, -ла́) impf take care of; keep; cherish; husband; be sparing of; **~ся** take care; beware (+gen of).

берло́га den, lair.

беру́ etc.: see **брать.**

бес devil, demon.

бес-: see **без-.**

бесе́да talk, conversation. **бесе́дка** summer-house. **бесе́довать** impf talk, converse.

беси́ть (бешу́, бе́сишь) impf (pf вз~) enrage; **~ся** go mad; be furious.

бес-. **бесконе́чность** infinity; endlessness. **~коне́чный** endless. **~коры́стие** disinterestedness. **~коры́стный** disinterested. **~кра́йний** boundless.

бесо́вский devilish.

бес-. **беспа́мятство** unconsciousness. **~парти́йный** non-party. **~перспекти́вный** without prospects; hopeless. **~пе́чность** carelessness, unconcern. **~пла́тно** adv free. **~пла́тный** free. **~пло́дие** sterility, barren-

ness. **~пло́дность** futility. **~пло́дный** sterile, barren; futile. **~поворо́тный** irrevocable. **~подо́бный** incomparable. **~позвоно́чный** invertebrate.

беспоко́ить impf (pf o~, по~) disturb, bother; trouble; **~ся** worry; trouble. **беспоко́йный** anxious; troubled; fidgety. **беспоко́йство** anxiety.

бес-. **бесполе́зный** useless. **~помо́щный** helpless; feeble. **~поро́дный** mongrel, not thoroughbred. **~поря́док** (-дка) disorder; untidy state. **~поря́дочный** disorderly; untidy. **~поса́дочный** non-stop. **~по́чвенный** groundless. **~пошли́нный** duty-free. **~поща́дный** merciless. **~пра́вный** without rights. **~преде́льный** boundless. **~предме́тный** aimless; abstract. **~препя́тственный** unhindered; unimpeded. **~преры́вный** continuous. **~преста́нный** continual.

беспризо́рник, -ница waif, homeless child. **беспризо́рный** neglected; homeless; sb waif, homeless child.

бес-. **беспримме́рный** unparalleled. **~принци́пный** unscrupulous. **~пристра́стие** impartiality. **~пристра́стный** impartial. **~просве́тный** pitch-dark; hopeless; unrelieved. **~пу́тный** dissolute. **~свя́зный** incoherent. **~серде́чный** heartless. **~си́лие** impotence; feebleness. **~си́льный** impotent, powerless. **~сла́вный** inglorious. **~сле́дно** adv without trace. **~слове́сный** dumb; silent; meek; (theat) walk-on. **~сме́нный** permanent, continuous. **~сме́ртие** immortality. **~сме́ртный** immortal. **~смы́сленный** senseless; foolish; meaningless. **~смы́слица** nonsense. **~со́вестный** unscrupulous; shameless. **~созна́тельный** unconscious; involuntary. **~со́нница** insomnia. **~спо́рный** indisputable. **~сро́чный** indefinite; without a time limit. **~стра́стный** impassive. **~стра́шный** fearless. **~стыдный** shameless. **~та́ктный** tactless.

бестолко́вщина confusion, muddle-headedness. **бестолко́вый** muddle-headed, stupid; incoherent.

бес-. бесфо́рменный shapeless. **~хара́ктерный** weak, spineless. **~хи́тростный** artless; unsophisticated. **~хозя́йственный** improvident. **~цве́тный** colourless. **~це́льный** aimless; pointless. **~це́нный** priceless. **~це́нок: за ~це́нок** very cheap, for a song. **~церемо́нный** unceremonious; **~челове́чный** inhuman. **~че́стить** (-е́щу) *impf* (*pf* **o~че́стить**) dishonour. **~че́стный** dishonourable. **~числ́енный** innumerable, countless.

бесчу́вственный insensible; insensitive. **бесчу́вствие** insensibility; insensitivity.

бес-. бесшу́мный noiseless.

бето́н concrete. **бето́нный** concrete. **бетономеша́лка** concrete-mixer. **бето́нщик** concrete-worker.

бечева́ tow-rope; rope. **бечёвка** cord, string.

бе́шенство rabies; rage. **бе́**-

шеный rabid; furious.

бешу́ *etc.: see* **беси́ть**

библи́ческий biblical. **библиографи́ческий** bibliographical. **библиогра́фия** bibliography. **библиоте́ка** library. **библиоте́карь** *m*, **-те́карша** librarian. **би́блия** bible.

бива́к bivouac, camp.

би́вень (-вня) *m* tusk.

бигуди́ *pl indecl* curlers.

бидо́н can; churn.

бие́ние beating; beat.

бижуте́рия costume jewellery.

би́знес business. **бизнесме́н** businessman.

биле́т ticket; card; pass. **биле́тный** ticket.

биллио́н billion.

билья́рд billiards.

бино́кль *m* binoculars.

бинт (-á) bandage. **бинтова́ть** *impf* (*pf* **за~**) bandage. **бинто́вка** bandaging.

био́граф biographer. **биографи́ческий** biographical. **биогра́фия** biography. **биоло́г** biologist. **биологи́ческий** biological. **биоло́гия** biology. **биохи́мия** biochemistry.

би́ржа exchange.

би́рка name-plate; label.

бирюза́ turquoise.

бис *int* encore.

би́сер (*no pl*) beads.

бискви́т sponge cake.

би́та bat.

би́тва battle.

битко́м *adv*: **~ наби́т** packed.

биту́м bitumen.

бить (бью, бьёшь) *impf* (*pf* **за~, по~, про~, уда́рить**) beat; hit; defeat; sound; thump, bang; smash; **~ в цель** hit the target; **~ на**+*acc* strive for; **~ отбо́й** beat a retreat;

~ по+*dat* damage, wound; ~ся fight; beat; struggle; break; +*instr* knock, hit, strike; +*над*+*instr* struggle with, rack one's brains over.

бифштéкс beefsteak.

бич (-á) whip, lash; scourge; homeless person. **бичевáть** (-чýю) *impf* flog; castigate.

блáго good; blessing.

блáго- *in comb* well-, good-. **Благовéщение** Annunciation. ~**вúдный** plausible, specious. ~**волéние** goodwill; favour. ~**воспúтанный** well-brought-up.

благодарúть (-рю́) *impf* (*pf* по~) thank. **благодáрность** gratitude; не стóит благодáрности don't mention it. **благодáрный** grateful. **благодаря́** *prep*+*dat* thanks to, owing to.

благо-. благодéтель *m* benefactor. ~**дéтельница** benefactress. ~**дéтельный** beneficial. ~**дýшный** placid; good-humoured. ~**желáтель** *m* well-wisher. ~**желáтельный** well-disposed; benevolent. ~**звýчный** melodious, harmonious. ~**надёжный** reliable. ~**намéренный** well-intentioned. ~**получие** wellbeing; happiness. ~**получно** *adv* all right, well; happily; safely. ~**получный** happy, successful; safe. ~**приятный** favourable. ~**приятствовать** *impf* +*dat* favour. ~**разýмие** sense; prudence. ~**разýмный** sensible. ~**рóдие**: вáше ~рóдие Your Honour. ~**рóдный** noble. ~**рóдство** nobility. ~**склóнность** favour, good graces. ~**склóнный** favourable; gracious. ~**сло-**

вúть *pf*, **благословля́ть** *impf* bless. ~**состояние** prosperity. ~**творúтель** *m*, -**ница** philanthropist. ~**творúтельный** charitable, charity. ~**твóрный** salutary; beneficial; wholesome. ~**устрóенный** well-equipped, wellplanned; with all amenities.

блажéнный blissful; simpleminded. **блажéнство** bliss.

бланк form.

блат (*sl*) string-pulling; pull, influence. **блатнóй** criminal; soft, cushy.

бледнéть (-éю) *impf* (*pf* по~) (grow) pale. **блéдность** paleness, pallor. **блéдный** (-ден, -днá, -о) pale.

блеск brightness, brilliance, lustre; magnificence.

блеснýть (-нý, -нёшь) *pf* flash, gleam; shine. **блестéть** (-ещý, -стúшь *or* блéщешь) *impf* shine; glitter. **блёстка** sparkle; sequin. **блестя́щий** shining, bright; brilliant.

блéять (-éет) *impf* bleat.

ближáйший nearest, closest; next. **блúже** *comp of* **блúзкий, блúзко. ближнúй** near, close; neighbouring; *sb* neighbour. **близ** *prep*+*gen* near, by. **блúзкий** (-зок, -изкá, -о) near; close; imminent; ~**кие** *sb pl* one's nearest and dearest, close relatives. **блúзко** *adv* near (*of*+*gen* to). **близнéц** (-á) twin; *pl* Gemini. **близорýкий** short-sighted. **блúзость** closeness, proximity.

блик patch of light; highlight. **блин** (-á) pancake. **блиндáж** (-á) dug-out. **блистáть** *impf* shine; sparkle. **блок** block, pulley, sheave.

блока́да blockade. **блоки́ровать** *impf & pf* blockade; ~**ся** form a bloc. **блокно́т** writing-pad, note-book.

блонди́н, блонди́нка blond(e).

блоха́ (*pl* -и, -а́м) flea.

блуд lechery. **блудни́ца** whore.

блужда́ть *impf* roam, wander.

блу́за, блу́зка blouse.

блю́дечко saucer; small dish. **блю́до** dish; course. **блю́дце** saucer.

боб (-а́) bean. **бобо́вый** bean. **бобр** (-а́) beaver.

Бог (*voc* **Бо́же**) God; **дай** ~ God grant; ~ **его́ зна́ет** who knows? **не дай** ~ God forbid! **Бо́же (мой)!** my God! good God!; **ра́ди** ~**а** for God's sake; **сла́ва** ~**у** thank God.

богате́ть *impf* (*pf* раз~) grow rich. **бога́тство** wealth. **бога́тый** rich, wealthy; *sb* rich man. **бога́ч** (-а́) rich man.

богаты́рь (-я́) *m* hero; strong man.

боги́ня goddess. **Богома́терь** Mother of God. **Богомо́лец** (-льца), **богомо́лка** devout person; pilgrim. **богомо́лье** pilgrimage. **богомо́льный** religious, devout. **Богоро́дица** the Virgin Mary. **богосло́в** theologian. **богосло́вие** theology. **богослуже́ние** divine service. **боготвори́ть** *impf* idolize; deify. **богоху́льство** blasphemy.

бодри́ть *impf.* stimulate, invigorate; ~**ся** try to keep up one's spirits. **бо́дрость** cheerfulness, courage. **бо́дрствовать** be awake; stay awake; keep vigil. **бо́дрый** (бодр, -á, -о) cheerful, bright.

боеви́к (-а́) smash hit. **боево́й** fighting, battle. **боего-**

ло́вка warhead. **боеприпа́сы** (*pl*; *gen* -ов) ammunition. **боеспосо́бный** battle-worthy. **бое́ц** (бойца́) soldier; fighter, warrior.

Бо́же: *see* **Бог**. **бо́жеский** divine; just. **боже́ственный** divine. **божество́** deity; divinity. **бо́ж|ий** God's; ~**ья коро́вка** ladybird. **божо́к** (-жка́) idol.

бой (-ю; *loc* -ю́; *pl* -и́, -ёв) battle, action, fight; fighting; slaughtering; striking; breakage(s).

бо́йкий (бо́ек, бойка́, -о) smart, sharp; glib; lively.

бойко́т boycott.

бо́йня (*gen pl* бо́ен) slaughterhouse; butchery.

бок (*loc* -ý; *pl* -á) side; flank; ~ **о** ~ side by side; **на** ~ to the side; **на** ~ý on one side; **под** ~**ом** near by; **с** ~**у** from the side, from the flank; **с** ~**у на** ~ from side to side.

бока́л glass; goblet.

боково́й side; lateral. **бо́ком** *adv* sideways.

бокс boxing. **боксёр** boxer.

болва́н blockhead. **болва́нка** pig (*of iron etc.*).

болга́рин (*pl* -га́ры), **болга́рка** Bulgarian. **болга́рский** Bulgarian. **Болга́рия** Bulgaria.

бо́лее *adv* more; ~ **всего́** most of all; **тем** ~, **что** especially as.

боле́зненный sickly; unhealthy; painful. **боле́знь** illness; disease; abnormality.

боле́льщик, -щица fan, supporter. **боле́ть**[1] (-е́ю) *impf* be ill, suffer. **боле́ть**[2] (-ли́т) *impf* ache, hurt.

боло́тистый marshy. **боло́то** marsh, bog.

болта́ть[1] impf stir; shake; dangle; **~ся** dangle, swing; hang about.

болта́ть[2] impf chat, natter. **болтли́вый** talkative; indiscreet. **болтовня́** talk; chatter; gossip. **болту́н** (-а́), **болту́нья** chatterbox.

боль pain; ache. **больни́ца** hospital. **больни́чный** hospital; **~ листо́к** medical certificate. **бо́льно**[1] adv painfully, badly; predic+dat it hurts. **бо́льно**[2] adv very, terribly. **больно́й** (-лен, -льна́) ill, sick; diseased; sore; sb patient, invalid.

бо́льше comp of **большо́й**, **мно́го**; bigger, larger; greater; more; **~ не** not any more, no longer; **~ того́** and what is more; adv for the most part. **большеви́к** Bolshevik. **бо́льший** greater, larger; **~ей ча́стью** for the most part. **большинство́** majority. **большо́й** big, large; great; grown-up; **~а́я бу́ква** capital letter; **~о́й па́лец** thumb; big toe; **~и́е** sb pl grown-ups.

бо́мба bomb. **бомбарди́ровать** impf bombard; bomb. **бомбарди́ровка** bombardment, bombing. **бомбарди́ровщик** bomber. **бомбёжка** bombing. **бомби́ть** (-блю́) bomb. **бомбоубе́жище** bomb shelter.

бор (loc -у́; pl -ы́) coniferous forest.

бордо́вый wine-red.

бордю́р border.

боре́ц (-рца́) fighter; wrestler.

бо́рзый swift.

бормаши́на (dentist's) drill.

бормота́ть (-очу́, -о́чешь) impf (pf **про~**) mutter, mumble.

борода́ (acc бо́роду; pl бо́роды, -ро́д, -а́м) beard. **борода́вка** wart. **борода́тый** bearded.

борозда́ (pl бо́розды, -о́зд, -а́м) furrow; fissure. **бороздить** (-зжу́) impf (pf вз~) furrow; plough.

борона́ (acc бо́рону; pl бо́роны, -ро́н, -а́м) harrow. **борони́ть** impf (pf вз~) harrow.

боро́ться (-рю́сь, бо́решься) impf wrestle; struggle, fight.

борт (loc -у́; pl -а́, -о́в) side, ship's side; front; **за ~**, **за ~ом** overboard; **на ~**, **на ~у́** on board. **бортпроводни́к** (-а́) air steward. **бортпроводни́ца** air hostess.

борщ (-а́) borsch (beetroot soup).

борьба́ wrestling; struggle, fight.

босико́м adv barefoot.

босни́ец (-ийца), **босни́йка** Bosnian. **босни́йский** Bosnian. **Бо́сния** Bosnia.

босо́й (бос, -а́, -о) barefooted. **босоно́жка** sandal.

бот, **бо́тик** small boat.

бота́ник botanist. **бота́ника** botany. **ботани́ческий** botanical.

боти́нок (-нка) (ankle-high) boot.

бо́цман boatswain.

бо́чка barrel. **бочо́нок** (-нка) keg, small barrel.

боязли́вый timid, timorous. **боя́знь** fear, dread.

боя́рин (pl -я́ре, -я́р) boyar.

боя́рышник hawthorn.

боя́ться (бою́сь) impf +gen be afraid of; fear; dislike.

брак[1] marriage.

брак[2] defective goods; waste. **бракова́ть** impf (pf за~) reject.

браконьéр poacher.

браκοразвóдный divorce. **бракосочетáние** wedding.

бранúть impf (pf **вы~**) scold; abuse, curse. **~ся** (pf **по~**) swear, curse; quarrel. **брáнный** abusive; **~ое слóво** swear-word.

брань bad language; abuse.

браслéт bracelet.

брасс breast stroke.

брат (pl **-тья, -тьев**) brother; comrade; mate; lay brother, monk. **братáться** impf (pf **по~**) fraternize. **братоубийство** fratricide. **брáтский** brotherly, fraternal. **брáтство** brotherhood, fraternity.

брать (**беру́, -рёшь; брал, -á, -о**) impf (pf **взять**) take; obtain; hire; seize; demand, require; surmount, clear; work; +instr succeed by means of; **~ся** +acc touch; seize; get down to; +за+acc or inf undertake; appear, come.

брáчный marriage; mating.

бревéнчатый log. **бревнó** (pl **брёвна, -вен**) log, beam.

бред (loc **-ý**) delirium; raving(s). **брéдить** (**-éжу**) impf be delirious, rave; +instr rave about, be infatuated with. **брéдовый** delirious; fantastic, nonsensical.

бреду́ etc.: see **брести́**. **брéжу** etc.: see **брéдить**

брéзгать impf (pf **по~**) +inf or instr be squeamish about. **брезглúвый** squeamish.

брéзжить(ся impf dawn; gleam faintly, glimmer.

брезéнт tarpaulin.

брёл etc.: see **брести́**

брелóк charm, pendant. **бремени́ть** impf (pf **о~**) bur-

den. **брéмя** (**-мени**) neut burden; load.

бренчáть (**-чу́**) impf strum; jingle.

брести́ (**-еду́, -едёшь; брёл, -á**) impf stroll, go along.

бретéль, бретéлька shoulder strap.

брешь breach; gap.

брéю etc.: see **брить**

бригáда brigade; crew, team. **бригадúр** brigadier; team-leader; foreman.

бриллиáнт, брильáнт diamond.

бритáнец (**-нца**), **бритáнка** Briton. **бритáнский** British. **Б~ие острова́** the British Isles.

брúтва razor. **брúтвенный** shaving. **брúтый** shaved; clean-shaven. **брить** (**брéю**) impf (pf **по~**) shave; **~ся** shave (o.s.).

бровь (pl **-и, -éй**) eyebrow; brow.

брод ford.

бродúть (**-ожу́, -óдишь**) impf wander, roam, stroll; ferment. **бродя́га** m & f tramp, vagrant. **бродя́жничество** vagrancy. **бродя́чий** vagrant; wandering. **брожéние** ferment, fermentation.

броне- in comb armoured, armour. **броневúк** (**-á**) armoured car. **~вóй** armoured. **~нóсец** (**-сца**) battleship; armour.

брóнза bronze; bronzes. **брóнзовый** bronze; tanned.

бронирóванный armoured. **бронúровать** impf & pf (impf also **за~**) reserve, book.

бронхúт bronchitis.

брóня́[1] reservation; commandeering.

броня́[2] armour.

броса́ть *impf*, **бро́сить** (-óшу) *pf* throw (down); leave, desert; give up, leave off; ~**ся** throw o.s., rush; +*inf* begin; +*instr* squander; pelt one another with; ~**ся в глаза́** be striking. **бро́ский** striking; garish, glaring. **бросо́к** (-ска́) throw; bound, spurt.

бро́шка, брошь *pf* brooch.

брошю́ра pamphlet, brochure.

брус (*pl* -сья, -сьев) squared beam, joist; (**паралле́льные**) ~**ья** parallel bars.

брусни́ка red whortleberry; red whortleberries.

брусо́к (-ска́) bar; ingot.

бру́тто *indecl adj* gross.

бры́згать (-зжу *or* -гаю) *impf*, **бры́знуть** (-ну) *pf* splash; sprinkle. **бры́зги** (брызг) *pl* spray, splashes; fragments.

брыка́ть *impf*, **брыкну́ть** (-ну́, -нёшь) *pf* kick.

брюзга́ *m* & *f* grumbler. **брюзгли́вый** grumbling, peevish. **брюзжа́ть** (-жу́) *impf* grumble.

брю́ква swede.

брю́ки (*pl; gen* брюк) trousers.

брюне́т dark-haired man. **брюне́тка** brunette.

брю́хо (*pl* -и) belly; stomach. **брюшно́й** abdominal; ~ **тиф** typhoid. **брюшно́й** abdominal.

бряца́ть *impf* rattle; clank, clang.

бу́бен (-бна) tambourine. **бубене́ц** (-нца́) small bell. **бу́бны** (*pl; gen* -бён, *dat* -бна́м) (*cards*) diamonds. **бубно́вый** diamond.

буго́р (-гра́) mound, hillock; bump, lump.

будди́зм Buddhism. **будди́йский** Buddhist. **будди́ст** Buddhist.

бу́дет that will do; +*inf* it's time to stop.

буди́льник alarm-clock. **буди́ть** (бужу́, бу́дишь) *impf* (*pf* про~, раз~) wake; arouse.

бу́дка box, booth; hut; stall.

бу́дни (*pl; gen* -ней) *pl* week-days; working days; humdrum existence. **бу́дний, бу́дничный** weekday; everyday; humdrum.

бу́дто *conj* as if, as though; ~ (**бы**), (**как**) ~ apparently, ostensibly.

бу́ду *etc.: see* быть. **бу́дучи** being. **бу́дущий** *adj* future; next; ~**ее** *sb* future. **бу́дущность** future. **бу́дь(те)**: *see* быть

бужу́: *see* буди́ть

бузина́ (*bot*) elder.

буй (*pl* -и́, -ёв) buoy.

бу́йвол buffalo.

бу́йный (бу́ен, буйна́, -о) violent, turbulent; luxuriant, lush. **бу́йство** unruly behaviour. **бу́йствовать** *impf* create an uproar, behave violently.

бук beech.

бука́шка small insect.

бу́ква (*gen pl* букв) letter; ~ **в бу́кву** literally. **буква́льно** *adv* literally. **буква́льный** literal. **буква́рь** (-я́) *m* ABC. **букво́ед** pedant.

буке́т bouquet; aroma.

букини́ст second-hand bookseller.

бу́кля curl, ringlet.

бу́ковый beech.

букси́р tug-boat; tow-rope. **букси́ровать** *impf* tow. **буксова́ть** *impf* spin, slip.

була́вка pin.

бу́лка roll. **бу́лочная** *sb* baker's. **бу́лочник** baker.

булы́жник cobble-stone, cobbles.

бульва́р avenue; boulevard.

бульдо́г bulldog.

бульдо́зер bulldozer.

булька́ть *impf* gurgle.

бульо́н broth.

бум (*sport*) beam.

бума́га cotton; paper; document. бума́жка piece of paper; note. бума́жник wallet; paper-maker. бума́ж|ный cotton; paper; ~ змей kite.

бу́нкер bunker.

бунт (*pl* -ы́) rebellion; riot; mutiny. бунта́рь (-я́) *m* rebel; insurgent. бунтова́ть(ся *impf* (*pf* вз~) rebel; riot. бунтовщи́к (-а́), -щи́ца rebel, insurgent.

бур auger.

бура́в (-а́; *pl* -а́) auger; gimlet. бура́вить (-влю) *impf* (*pf* про~) bore, drill.

бура́н snowstorm.

буреве́стник stormy petrel.

буре́ние boring, drilling.

буржуа́ *m indecl* bourgeois. буржуази́я bourgeoisie. буржуа́зный bourgeois.

бури́льщик borer, driller. бури́ть *impf* (*pf* про~) bore, drill.

бурли́ть *impf* seethe.

буро́в|ой boring; ~áя вы́шка derrick; ~áя (сква́жина) borehole; ~óй стано́к drilling rig.

бу́рый (бур, -á, -о) brown.

бурья́н tall weeds.

бу́ря storm.

бу́сина bead. бу́сы (*pl*; *gen* бус) beads.

бутафо́рия (*theat*) props.

бутербро́д open sandwich.

буто́н bud.

бу́тсы (*pl*; *gen* -ов) *pl* football boots.

буты́лка bottle. буты́ль large bottle; carboy.

буфе́т snack bar; sideboard; counter. буфе́тчик barman. буфе́тчица barmaid.

бух *int* bang, plonk. бу́хать *impf* (*pf* бу́хнуть) thump, bang; bang down; thunder; thud; blurt out.

буха́нка loaf.

бухга́лтер accountant. бухгалте́рия accountancy; accounts department.

бу́хнуть (-ну) *impf* swell.

бу́хта bay.

бушева́ть (-шу́ю) *impf* rage, storm.

буя́н rowdy. буя́нить *impf* create an uproar.

бы, б *partl* I. +past tense or inf indicates the conditional or subjunctive. II. (+ни) forms indef prons and conjs.

быва́лый experienced; former; habitual, familiar. быва́ть *impf* be; happen; be inclined to be; **как ни в чём не быва́ло** as if nothing had happened; **быва́ло** *partl* used to; would; **ма́ть быва́ло ча́сто пе́ла э́ту пе́сню** my mother would often sing this song. бы́вший former, ex-.

бык (-á) bull, ox; pier.

были́на ancient Russian epic.

бы́л|о *partl* nearly, on the point of; (only) just. бы́л|ой past, bygone; ~óe *sb* the past. быль true story; fact.

быстрота́ speed. бы́стрый (быстр, -á, -о) fast, quick.

быт (*loc* -ý) way of life. бытие́ being, existence; objective reality; **кни́га Бытия́** Genesis. бытово́й everyday; social.

быть (*pres 3rd sg* есть, *pl* суть; *fut* бу́ду, *past* был, -á, -о; *imper*

бу́дь(те) *impf* be; be situated; happen. **бытьё** way of life.
бычо́к (-чка́) steer.
бью *etc.*: *see* **бить**
бюдже́т budget.
бюллете́нь *m* bulletin; ballot-paper; doctor's certificate.
бюро́ *neut indecl* bureau; office; writing-desk. **бюрокра́т** bureaucrat. **бюрократи́зм** bureaucracy. **бюрократи́ческий** bureaucratic. **бюрокра́тия** bureaucracy; bureaucrats.
бюст bust. **бюстга́льтер** bra.

В

в, во *prep* I. +*acc* into; to; on; at; within; through; **быть в** take after; **в два ра́за бо́льше** twice as big; **в на́ши дни** in our day; **войти́ в дом** go into the house; **в понеде́льник** on Monday; **в тече́ние**+*gen* during; **в четы́ре часа́** at four o'clock; **высото́й в три ме́тра** three metres high; **игра́ть в ша́хматы** play chess; **пое́хать в Москву́** go to Moscow; **сесть в ваго́н** get into the carriage; **смотре́ть в окно́** look out of the window. II. +*prep* in; at; **в двадца́том ве́ке** in the twentieth century; **в теа́тре** at the theatre; **в трёх киломе́трах от го́рода** three kilometres from the town; **в э́том году́** this year; **в январе́** in January.
ваго́н carriage; coach; ~-**рестора́н** restaurant car. **ваго́нетка** truck, trolley. **ваго́новожа́тый** *sb* tram-driver.
ва́жничать *impf* give o.s. airs; +*instr* plume o.s., pride o.s.,

on. **ва́жность** importance; pomposity. **ва́жный** (-жен, -жна́, -о) important; weighty; pompous.
ва́за vase, bowl.
вазели́н Vaseline (*propr*).
вака́нсия vacancy. **вака́нтный** vacant.
ва́кса (shoe-)polish.
ва́куум vacuum.
вакци́на vaccine.
вал[1] (*loc* -у́; *pl* -ы́) bank; rampart; billow, roller; barrage.
вал[2] (*loc* -у́; *pl* -ы́) shaft.
ва́ленок (-нка; *gen pl* -нок) felt boot.
вале́т knave, Jack.
ва́лик roller, cylinder.
вали́ть[1] *impf* flock, throng; **вали́(те)!** have a go!
вали́ть[2] (-лю́, -лишь) *impf* (*pf* по-~, с~) throw down, bring down; pile up; ~**ся** fall, collapse.
валово́й gross; wholesale.
валто́рна French horn.
валу́н (-а́) boulder.
вальс waltz. **вальси́ровать** *impf* waltz.
валю́та currency; foreign currency.
валя́ть *impf* (*pf* на-~, с~) drag; roll; shape; bungle; ~**дурака́** play the fool; **валя́й(те)!** go ahead!; ~**ся** lie, lie about; roll, wallow.
вам, ва́ми: *see* **вы**
вампи́р vampire.
ванда́л vandal. **вандали́зм** vandalism.
вани́ль vanilla.
ва́нна bath. **ва́нная** *sb* bathroom.
ва́рвар barbarian. **ва́рварский** barbaric. **ва́рварство** barbarity; vandalism.
ва́режка mitten.

варёный boiled. **варе́нье** jam. **вари́ть** (-рю́, -ришь) *impf* (*pf* c~) boil; cook; ~ся boil; cook.

вариа́нт version; option; scenario.

вас: *see* **вы**

василёк (-лька́) cornflower.

ва́та cotton wool; wadding.

ватерли́ния water-line. **ватерпа́с** (spirit-)level.

вати́н (sheet) wadding. **ва́тник** quilted jacket. **ва́тный** quilted, wadded.

ватру́шка cheese-cake.

ватт (*gen pl* ватт) watt.

ва́учер coupon (*exchangeable for government-issued share*).

ва́фля (*gen pl* -фель) wafer; waffle.

ва́хта (*naut*) watch. **вахтёр** janitor, porter.

ваш (-его) *m*, **ва́ша** (-ей) *f*, **ва́ше** (-его) *neut*, **ва́ши** (-их) *pl*, *pron* your, yours.

вбега́ть *impf*, **вбежа́ть** (вбегу́) *pf* run in.

вберу́ *etc.: see* **вобра́ть**

вбива́ть *impf of* **вбить**

вбира́ть *impf of* **вобра́ть**

вбить (вобью́, -бьёшь) *pf* (*impf* **вбива́ть**) drive in, hammer in.

вблизи́ *adv* (+от+*gen*) close (to), near by.

вбок *adv* sideways, to one side.

вброд *adv:* **переходи́ть** ~ ford, wade.

вва́ливать *impf*, **ввали́ть** (-лю́, -лишь) *pf* throw heavily, heave, bundle; ~ся fall heavily; sink, become sunken; burst in.

введе́ние introduction. **введу́** *etc.: see* **ввести́**

ввезти́ (-зу́, -зёшь; ввёз, -ла́) *pf* (*impf* **ввози́ть**) import; bring in.

вве́рить *pf* (*impf* **вверя́ть**) entrust, confide; ~ся +*dat* trust in, put one's faith in.

ввернуть (-ну́, -нёшь) *pf*, **ввёртывать** *impf* screw in; insert.

верх *adv* up, upward(s); ~**дном** upside down; ~ (по лестнице) upstairs. **вверху́** *adv* above, overhead.

вверя́ть(ся) *impf of* **вве́рить(ся)**

ввести́ (-еду́, -едёшь; ввёл, -а́) *pf* (*impf* **вводи́ть**) bring in; introduce.

ввиду́ *prep*+*gen* in view of.

ввинти́ть (-нчу́) *pf*, **ввинчи́вать** *impf* screw in.

ввод lead-in. **вводи́ть** (-ожу́, -о́дишь) *impf of* **ввести́**. **вво́дный** introductory; parenthetic.

ввожу́ *see* **вводи́ть**, **ввози́ть**

ввоз importation; import(s). **ввози́ть** (-ожу́, -о́зишь) *impf of* **ввезти́**

вво́лю *adv* to one's heart's content.

ввысь *adv* up, upward(s).

ввяза́ть (-яжу́, -я́жешь) *pf*, **ввя́зывать** *impf* knit in; involve; ~ся meddle, get or be mixed up (in).

вглубь *adv & prep*+*gen* deep (into), into the depths.

вгляде́ться (-яжу́сь) *pf*, **вгля́дываться** *impf* peer, look closely (в+*acc* at).

вгоня́ть *impf of* **вогна́ть**

вда́ваться (вдаю́сь, -ёшься) *impf of* **вда́ться**

вдави́ть (-авлю́, -а́вишь) *pf*, **вда́вливать** *impf* press in.

вдалеке́, вдали́ *adv* in the distance, far away. **вдаль**

into the distance.

вда́ться (-а́мся, -а́шься, -а́стся, -ади́мся; -а́лся, -ла́сь) *pf* (*impf* **вдава́ться**) jut out; penetrate, go in.

вдво́е *adv* twice; double; ~ **бо́льше** twice as big, as much, as many. **вдвоём** *adv* (the) two together, both. **вдвойне́** *adv* twice as much, double; doubly.

вдева́ть *impf of* **вдеть**

вде́лать *pf*, **вде́лывать** *impf* set in, fit in.

вдёргивать *impf*, **вдёрнуть** (-ну) *pf* в+*acc* thread through, pull through.

вдеть (-е́ну) *pf* (*impf* **вдева́ть**) put in, thread.

вдоба́вок *adv* in addition; besides.

вдова́ widow. **вдове́ц** (-вца́) widower.

вдо́воль *adv* enough; in abundance.

вдого́нку *adv* (за+*instr*) after, in pursuit (of).

вдоль *adv* lengthwise; ~ и **поперёк** far and wide; in detail; *prep*+*gen or* по+*dat* along.

вдох breath. **вдохнове́ние** inspiration. **вдохнове́нный** inspired. **вдохнови́ть** (-влю́) *pf*, **вдохновля́ть** *impf* inspire. **вдохну́ть** (-ну́, -нёшь) *pf* (*impf* **вдыха́ть**) breathe in.

вдре́безги *adv* to smithereens.

вдруг *adv* suddenly

вду́маться *pf*, **вду́мываться** *impf* ponder, meditate; +в+*acc* think over. **вду́мчивый** thoughtful.

вдыха́ние inhalation. **вдыха́ть** *impf of* **вдохну́ть**

вегетариа́нец (-нца), **-нка** vegetarian. **вегетариа́нский** vegetarian.

ве́дать *impf* know; +*instr* manage, handle. **ве́дение**[1] authority, jurisdiction.

веде́ние[2] conducting, conduct; ~ **книг** book-keeping.

ве́домость (*gen pl* -е́й) list, register. **ве́домственный** departmental. **ве́домство** department.

ведро́ (*pl* вёдра, -дер) bucket; vedro (*approx* 12 litres).

веду́ *etc.*: *see* **вести́**. **веду́щий** leading.

ведь *part* & *conj* you see, you know; isn't it? is it?

ве́дьма witch.

ве́ер (*pl* -а́) fan.

ве́жливость politeness. **ве́жливый** polite.

везде́ *adv* everywhere.

везе́ние luck. **везу́чий** lucky. **везти́** (-зу́, -зёшь; вёз, -ла́) *impf* (*pf* по~) convey; bring, take; *impers*+*dat* be lucky; **ему́ не везло́** he had no luck.

век (*loc* -у́; *pl* -а́) century; age; life, lifetime. **век** *adv* for ages.

ве́ко (*pl* -и, век) eyelid.

веково́й ancient, age-old.

ве́ксель (*pl* -я́, -е́й) *m* promissory note, bill (of exchange).

вёл *etc.*: *see* **вести́.**

веле́ть (-лю́) *impf & pf* order; не ~ forbid.

велика́н giant. **вели́кий** (-и́к, -а́ *or* -а́) great; big; large; too big; ~ **пост** Lent.

велико- *in comb* great. **Великобрита́ния** Great Britain. **великоду́шие** magnanimity. **~ду́шный** magnanimous. **~ле́пие** splendour. **~ле́пный** splendid.

велича́вый stately, majestic. **велича́йший** greatest, supreme. **вели́чественный**

majestic, grand. **вели́чество** Majesty. **вели́чие** greatness, grandeur. **величина́** (*pl* -и́ны, -а́м) size; quantity, magnitude; value; great figure.

велосипе́д bicycle. **велосипеди́ст** cyclist.

вельве́т velveteen; ~ в ру́бчик corduroy.

вельмо́жа *m* grandee.

ве́на vein.

венге́рец (-рца), **венге́рка** Hungarian. **венге́рский** Hungarian. **Ве́нгрия** Hungary.

венде́тта vendetta.

венери́ческий venereal.

вене́ц (-нца́) crown; wreath.

ве́ник besom; birch twigs.

вено́к (-нка́) wreath, garland.

ве́нтиль *m* valve.

вентиля́тор ventilator; extractor (fan). **вентиля́ция** ventilation.

венча́ние wedding; coronation. **венча́ть** *impf* (*pf* об~, по~, у~) crown; marry; ~ся be married, marry. **ве́нчик** halo; corolla; rim; ring, bolt.

ве́ра faith, belief.

вера́нда veranda.

ве́рба willow; willow branch. **ве́рбный**; ~ое воскресе́нье Palm Sunday.

верблю́д camel.

вербова́ть *impf* (*pf* за~) recruit; win over. **вербо́вка** recruitment.

верёвка rope; string; cord. **верёвочный** rope.

верени́ца row, file, line, string.

ве́реск heather.

веретено́ (*pl* -тёна) spindle.

вереща́ть (-щу́) *impf* squeal; chirp.

ве́рить *impf* (*pf* по~) believe,

have faith; +*dat* or в+*acc* believe (in), believe in.

вермише́ль vermicelli.

верне́е *adv* rather. **ве́рно** *partl* probably, I suppose. **ве́рность** faithfulness, loyalty.

верну́ть (-ну́, -нёшь) *pf* (*impf* **возвраща́ть**) give back, return; ~ся return.

ве́рный (-рен, -рна́, -о) faithful, loyal; true; correct; reliable.

ве́рование belief. **ве́ровать** *impf* believe. **вероиспове́дание** religion; denomination. **вероло́мный** treacherous, perfidious. **вероотсту́пник** apostate. **веротерпи́мость** (religious) toleration. **вероя́тно** *adv* probably. **вероя́тность** probability. **вероя́тный** probable.

ве́рсия version.

верста́ (*pl* вёрсты) verst (*1.06 km.*).

верста́к (-á) work-bench.

ве́ртел (*pl* -á) spit, skewer.

верте́ть (-чу́, -тишь) *impf* turn (round); twirl; ~ся turn (round), spin. **вертля́вый** fidgety; flighty.

вертика́ль vertical line. **вертика́льный** vertical.

вертолёт helicopter.

ве́ртушка flirt.

ве́рующий *sb* believer.

верфь shipyard.

верх (*loc* -у́; *pl* -и́) top; summit; height; *pl* upper crust, top brass; high notes. **ве́рхний** upper; top. **верхо́вный** supreme. **верхово́й** riding; *sb* rider. **верхо́вье** (*gen pl* -вьев) upper reaches. **верхола́з** steeple-jack. **верхо́м** *adv* on horseback; astride. **верху́шка** top, summit; apex; top brass.

верчу́ *etc.: see* **верте́ть**

верши́на top, summit; peak; apex. **верши́ть** *impf* +*instr* manage, control.

вершо́к vershok (*4.4 cm.*); smattering.

вес (*loc -у́; pl -а́*) weight.

весели́ть *impf* (*pf* раз~) cheer, gladden; ~ся enjoy o.s.; amuse o.s. **ве́село** *adv* merrily. **весёлый** (ве́сел, -а́, -о) merry; cheerful. **весе́лье** merriment.

весе́нний spring.

ве́сить (ве́шу) *impf* weigh. **ве́ский** weighty, solid.

весло́ (*pl* вёсла, -сел) oar.

весна́ (*pl* вёсны, -сен) spring. **весно́й** *adv* in (the) spring.

весну́шка freckle.

вест (*naut*) west; west wind.

вести́ (веду́, -дёшь; вёл, -а́) *impf* (*pf* по~) lead, take; conduct; drive; run; keep; ~ себя́ behave, conduct o.s.; ~сь be the custom.

вестибю́ль *m* (entrance) hall, lobby.

ве́стник herald; bulletin. **весть¹** (*gen pl -е́й*) news; без ве́сти without trace. **весть²**: Бог ~ God knows.

весы́ (*pl; gen -о́в*) scales, balance; Libra.

весь (всего́ *m*, вся, всей *f*, всё, всего́ *neut*, все, всех *pl*) *pron* all; *m* everything; *neut* everything; все everybody; всего́ хоро́шего! all the best!; всё everything; без всего́ without anything; все everybody.

весьма́ *adv* very, highly.

ветвь (*gen pl -е́й*) branch; bough.

ве́тер (-тра, *loc* -у́) wind. **ветеро́к** (-рка́) breeze.

ветера́н veteran.

ветерина́р vet.

ве́тка branch; twig.

ве́то *neut indecl* veto.

ве́тошь old clothes, rags.

ве́треный windy; frivolous. **ветрово́й** wind; ~ое стекло́ windscreen. **ветря́к** (-а́) wind turbine; windmill.

ве́тхий (ветх, -а́, -о) old; dilapidated; В~ заве́т Old Testament.

ветчина́ ham.

ветша́ть *impf* (*pf* об~) decay; become dilapidated.

ве́ха landmark.

ве́чер (*pl -а́*) evening; party. **вечери́нка** party. **вече́рний** evening. **вече́рня** (*gen pl -рен*) vespers. **ве́чером** *adv* in the evening.

ве́чно *adv* for ever, eternally. **вечнозелёный** evergreen. **ве́чность** eternity; ages. **ве́чный** eternal.

ве́шалка peg, rack; tab, hanger. **ве́шать** *impf* (*pf* взве́сить, пове́сить, све́шать) hang; weigh (out); ~ся hang o.s.; weigh o.s.

ве́шу *etc.: see* **ве́сить**

веща́ние broadcasting. **веща́ть** *impf* broadcast.

вещево́й clothing; ~ мешо́к hold-all, kit-bag. **веще́ственный** substantial, material, real. **вещество́** substance; matter. **вещь** (*gen pl -е́й*) thing.

ве́ялка winnowing-machine. **ве́яние** winnowing; blowing; trend. **ве́ять** (ве́ю) *impf* (*pf* про~) winnow; blow; flutter.

взад *adv* backwards; ~ и вперёд back and forth.

взаи́мность reciprocity. **взаи́мный** mutual, reciprocal.

взаимо- *in comb* inter-. **взаимоде́йствие** interaction; cooperation. **~де́йствовать** *impf* interact; cooperate. **~отноше́ние** interrelation; *pl* relations. **~по́мощь** mutual aid. **~понима́ние** mutual understanding. **~связь** interdependence, correlation.

взаймы́ *adv* : **взять** ~ borrow; **дать** ~ lend.

взаме́н *prep+gen* instead of; in return for.

взаперти́ *adv* under lock and key; in seclusion.

взба́лмошный unbalanced, eccentric.

взбега́ть *impf*, **взбежа́ть** (-егу́) *pf* run up.

взберу́сь *etc.*: *see* **взобра́ться**.

взбеси́ть(ся (-ешу́(сь, -е́сишь(ся) *pf*. **взбива́ть** *impf of* **взбить**. **взбира́ться** *impf of* **взобра́ться**

взби́тый whipped, beaten. **взбить** (взобью́, -бьёшь) *pf* (*impf* **взбива́ть**) beat (up), whip; shake up.

взборозди́ть (-зжу́) *pf*.

взбунтова́ть *pf*.

взбуха́ть *impf*, **взбу́хнуть** (-нет, -ух) *pf* swell (out).

взва́ливать *impf*, **взвали́ть** (-лю́, -лишь) *pf* load; +**на**+*acc* saddle with.

взве́сить (-ешу) *pf* (*impf* **ве́шать**, **взве́шивать**) weigh.

взвести́ (-еду́, -едёшь; -ёл, -а́) *pf* (*impf* **взводи́ть**) lead up; raise; cock; +**на**+*acc* impute to.

взве́шивать *impf of* **взве́сить** **взвива́ть(ся** *impf of* **взви́ть(ся**

взви́зг scream; yelp. **взви́згивать** *impf*, **взви́згнуть** (-ну) *pf* scream; yelp.

взвинти́ть (-нчу́) *pf*, **взви́нчивать** *impf* excite, work up;

inflate. **взви́нченный** worked up; nervy; inflated.

взвить (взовью́, -ёшь; -ил, -а́, -о) *pf* (*impf* **взвива́ть**) raise; **~ся** rise, be hoisted up; soar.

взво́д¹ platoon, troop.

взво́д² notch. **взводи́ть** (-ожу́, -о́дишь) *impf of* **взвести́**

взволно́ванный agitated; worried. **взволнова́ть(ся** (-ну́ю(сь) *pf*.

взгляд look; glance; opinion. **взгля́дывать** *impf*, **взгляну́ть** (-яну́, -я́нешь) *pf* look, glance.

взго́рье hillock.

вздёргивать *impf*, **вздёрнуть** (-ну) *pf* hitch up; jerk up; turn up.

вздор nonsense. **вздо́рный** cantankerous; foolish.

вздорожа́ние rise in price. **вздорожа́ть** *pf*.

вздох sigh. **вздохну́ть** (-ну́, -нёшь) *pf* (*impf* **вздыха́ть**) sigh.

вздра́гивать *impf* (*pf* **вздро́гнуть**) shudder, quiver.

вздремну́ть *pf* have a nap, doze.

вздро́гнуть (-ну) *pf* (*impf* **вздра́гивать**) start; wince.

вздува́ть(ся *impf of* **вздуть¹(ся**

взду́мать *pf* take it into one's head; **не взду́май(те)!** don't you dare!

взду́тие swelling. **взду́тый** swollen. **взду́ть¹** *pf* (*impf* **вздува́ть**) inflate; **~ся** swell.

взду́ть² *pf* thrash.

вздыха́ть *impf* (*pf* **вздохну́ть**) breathe; sigh.

взима́ть *impf* levy, collect.

взла́мывать *impf of* **взлома́ть**. **вз|леле́ять** *pf*.

взлёт flight; take-off. **взле-**

та́ть *impf*, взлете́ть (-лечу́) *pf* fly (up); take off. **взлёт-ный** take-off; **взлётно-поса́дочная полоса́** runway.

взлом breaking open, breaking in. **взлома́ть** *pf* (*impf* **взла́мывать**) break open; break up. **взло́мщик** burglar.

взлохма́ченный dishevelled.

взмах stroke, wave, flap. **взма́хивать** *impf*, **взмахну́ть** (-ну́, -нёшь) *pf* +*instr* wave, flap.

взмо́рье seaside; coastal waters.

вз|мути́ть (-учу́, -у́ти́шь) *pf*.

взнос payment; fee, dues.

взнузда́ть *pf*, **взну́здывать** *impf* bridle.

взобра́ться (взберу́сь, -ёшься; -а́лся, -ла́сь, -а́ло́сь) *pf* (*impf* **взбира́ться**) climb (up).

взобью etc.: see **взбить**. **взо-вью́** etc.: see **взвить**

взойти́ (-йду́, -йдёшь; -ошёл, -шла́) *pf* (*impf* **вос-, всхо-ди́ть**) rise, go up; на+*acc* mount.

взор look, glance.

взорва́ть (-ву́, -вёшь; -а́л, -а́, -о) *pf* (*impf* **взрыва́ть**) blow up; exasperate; **~ся** burst, explode.

взро́слый *adj & sb* adult.

взрыв explosion; outburst. **взрыва́тель** *m* fuse. **взрыва́ть** *impf*, **взрыть** (-ро́ю) *pf* (*pf also* **взорва́ть**) blow up; **~ся** explode. **взры́вчатый** explosive; blasting. **взрывча́тка** explosive. **взры́вчатый** explosive.

взъеро́шенный tousled, dishevelled. **взъеро́шивать** *impf*, **взъеро́шить** (-шу) *pf* tousle, rumple.

взыва́ть *impf* of **воззва́ть**

взыска́ние penalty; exaction.

взыска́тельный exacting. **взыска́ть** (-ыщу́, -ы́щешь) *pf*, **взы́скивать** *impf* exact, recover; call to account.

взя́тие taking, capture. **взя́тка** bribe. **взя́точничество** bribery. **взя́ть(ся** (возьму́(сь, -мёшь(ся; -я́л(ся, -а́(сь, -о(сь) *pf of* **бра́ть(ся**

вибра́ция vibration. **вибри́ровать** *impf* vibrate.

вивисе́кция vivisection.

вид[1] (*loc* -у́) look; appearance; shape, form; condition; view; prospect; sight; **де́лать вид** pretend; **име́ть в ~у́** intend; mean; bear in mind.

вид[2] kind; species.

вида́ться *impf* (*pf* по~) meet.

виде́ние[1] sight, vision. **виде́ние**[2] vision, apparition.

ви́део *neut indecl* video (cassette) recorder; video film; video cassette. **видеоигра́** video game. **видеока́мера** video camera. **видеокассе́та** video cassette. **видеомагнитофо́н** video (cassette) recorder.

ви́деть (ви́жу) *impf* (*pf* у~) see; **~ во сне** dream (of); **~ся** see one another; appear.

ви́димо *adv* evidently. **ви́димость** visibility; appearance. **ви́димый** visible; apparent, evident. **ви́дный** (-ден, -дна́, -о) visible; distinguished.

видоизмене́ние modification. **видоизмени́ть** *pf*, **видоизменя́ть** *impf* modify.

видоиска́тель *m* view-finder.

ви́жу see **ви́деть**

ви́за visa.

визг squeal; yelp. **визжа́ть** (-жу́) *impf* squeal, yelp, squeak.

визи́т visit. **визи́тка** business card.

викторина quiz.

ви́лка fork; plug. ви́лы (pl; gen вил) pitchfork.

вильну́ть (-ну́, -нёшь) pf, виля́ть impf twist and turn; prevaricate; +instr wag.

вина́ (pl ви́ны) fault, guilt; blame.

винегре́т Russian salad; medley.

вини́тельный accusative. вини́ть impf accuse; ~ся (pf по~) confess.

ви́нный wine; winy. вино́ (-а) wine.

винова́тый guilty. вино́вник initiator; culprit. вино́вный guilty.

виногра́д vine; grapes. виногра́дник vineyard. виногра́дный grape; wine. виноку́ренный заво́д distillery.

винт (-á) screw. винти́ть (-нчу́) impf screw up. винто́вка rifle. винтово́й screw; spiral.

виолонче́ль cello.

вира́ж (-á) turn; bend.

виртуо́з virtuoso. виртуо́зный masterly.

ви́рус virus. ви́русный virus.

ви́селица gallows. висе́ть (вишу́) impf hang. ви́снуть (-ну; вис(нул)) impf hang; droop.

ви́ски neut indecl whisky.

висо́к (-ска́) temple.

високо́сный год leap-year.

вист whist.

вися́чий hanging; ~ замо́к padlock; ~ мост suspension bridge.

витами́н vitamin.

витие́ватый flowery, ornate. вито́й twisted, spiral. вито́к (-тка́) turn, coil.

витра́ж (-á) stained-glass window. витри́на shop-window; showcase.

вить (вью, вьёшь; вил, -á, -о) impf (pf с~) twist, wind, weave; ~ся wind, twine; curl; twist; whirl.

вихо́р (-хра́) tuft. вихра́стый shaggy.

вихрь m whirlwind; vortex; снежный ~ blizzard.

ви́це- pref vice-. ви́це-адмира́л vice-admiral. ~президе́нт vice-president.

вицмунди́р (dress) uniform.

ВИЧ (abbr of ви́рус иммунодефици́та челове́ка) HIV.

вишнёвый cherry. ви́шня (gen pl -шен) cherry, cherries; cherry-tree.

вишу́: see висе́ть

вишь partl look, just look!

вка́лывать impf (sl) work hard; impf of вколо́ть

вка́пывать impf of вкопа́ть

вкати́ть (-ачу́, -а́тишь) pf, вка́тывать impf roll in; administer.

вклад deposit; contribution. вкла́дка supplementary sheet. вкладно́й лист loose leaf, insert. вкла́дчик depositor.

вкла́дывать impf of вложи́ть

вкле́ивать impf, вкле́ить pf stick in.

вкли́ниваться impf, вкли́ниться pf edge one's way in.

выключа́тель m switch. включа́ть impf, включи́ть (-чу́) pf include; switch on; plug in; ~ся в+acc join in, enter into.

включа́я including. включе́ние inclusion, insertion; switching on. включи́тельно adv inclusive.

вкола́чивать impf, вколоти́ть (-очу́, -о́тишь) pf hammer in, knock in.

вколо́ть (-олю́, -о́лешь) pf (impf вка́лывать) stick (in).

вкопа́ть pf (impf вка́пывать) dig in.

вкось adv obliquely.

вкра́дчивый ingratiating. вкра́дываться impf, вкра́сться (-аду́сь, -адёшься) pf creep in; insinuate o.s.

вкра́тце adv briefly, succinctly.

вкривь adv aslant; wrongly, perversely.

вкруг = вокру́г

вкруту́ю adv hard(-boiled).

вкус taste. вкуси́ть (-ушу́, -у́сишь) pf, вкуша́ть impf taste; partake of. вку́сный (-сен, -сна́, -о) tasty, nice.

вла́га moisture.

влага́лище vagina.

владе́лец (-льца), -лица owner. владе́ние ownership; possession; property. владе́тель m, -ница possessor; sovereign. владе́ть (-е́ю) impf +instr own, possess; control.

влады́ка m master, sovereign. влады́чество dominion, sway.

вла́жность humidity; moisture. вла́жный (-жен, -жна́, -о) damp, moist, humid.

вла́мываться impf of вломи́ться

вла́ствовать impf +(над+) instr rule, hold sway over. власте́лин ruler; master. вла́стный imperious, commanding; empowered, competent. власть (gen pl -е́й) power; authority.

вле́во adv to the left (от+gen of).

влеза́ть impf, влезть (-зу; влез) pf climb in; get in; fit in.

влёк etc.: see влечь

влета́ть impf, влете́ть (-ечу́) pf fly in; rush in.

влече́ние attraction; inclination. влечь (-еку́, -ечёшь; влёк, -ла́) impf draw; attract; ~ за собо́й involve, entail.

влива́ть impf, влить (волью́, -ёшь; влил, -а́, -о) pf pour in; instil.

влия́ние influence. влия́тельный influential. влия́ть impf (pf по~) на+acc influence, affect.

вложе́ние enclosure; investment. вложи́ть (-ожу́, -о́жишь) pf (impf вкла́дывать) put in, insert; enclose; invest.

вломи́ться (-млю́сь, -мишься) pf (impf вла́мываться) break in.

влюби́ть (-блю́, -бишь) pf, влюбля́ть impf make fall in love (в+acc with); ~ся fall in love. влюблённый (-лён, -а́) in love; sb lover.

вма́зать (-а́жу) pf, вма́зывать impf cement, putty in.

вмени́ть pf, вменя́ть impf impute; impose. вменя́емый (law) responsible; sane.

вме́сте adv together; ~ с тем at the same time, also.

вмести́лище receptacle. вмести́мость capacity; tonnage. вмести́тельный capacious. вмести́ть (-ещу́) pf (impf вмеща́ть) hold, accommodate; put; ~ся go in.

вме́сто prep+gen instead of.

вмеша́тельство interference; intervention. вмеша́ть pf, вме́шивать impf mix in; implicate; ~ся interfere, intervene.

вмеща́ть(ся impf of вмести́ть(ся

вмиг adv in an instant.

вмина́ть impf, **вмять** (вомну́, -нёшь) pf press in, dent. **вмя́тина** dent.

внаём, внаймы́ adv to let; for hire.

внача́ле adv at first.

вне +gen outside; ~ себя́ beside o.s.

вне- pref extra-; outside; -less. **внебра́чный** extra-marital; illegitimate. ~**вре́менный** timeless. ~**кла́ссный** extra-curricular. ~**очередно́й** out of turn; extraordinary. ~**шта́тный** freelance, casual.

внедре́ние introduction; inculcation. **внедри́ть** pf, **внедря́ть** impf inculcate; introduce; ~**ся** take root.

внеза́пно adv suddenly. **внеза́пный** sudden.

вне́млю etc.: see **внима́ть**

внесе́ние bringing in; deposit. **внести́** (-су́, -сёшь; внёс, -ла́) pf (impf **вноси́ть**) bring in; introduce; deposit; insert.

вне́шне adv outwardly. **вне́шний** outer; external; outside; foreign. **вне́шность** exterior; appearance.

вниз adv down(wards); ~ по+dat down. **внизу́** adv below; downstairs.

вника́ть impf, **вни́кнуть** (-ну; вник) pf +в+acc go carefully into, investigate thoroughly.

внима́ние attention. **внима́тельный** attentive. **внима́ть** impf (pf **внять**) listen to; heed.

вничью́ adv: око́нчиться ~ end in a draw; **сыгра́ть** ~ draw.

вновь adv anew, again.

вноси́ть (-ошу́, -о́сишь) impf of **внести́**

внук grandson; pl grandchildren, descendants.

вну́тренний inner; internal. **вну́тренность** interior; pl entrails; internal organs. **внутри́** adv & prep+gen inside. **внутрь** adv & prep+gen inside, in; inwards.

вну́ча́та (pl gen -ча́т) grandchildren. **внуча́тый** second, great-; ~ **брат** second cousin; ~ **племя́нник** great-nephew. **вну́чка** grand-daughter.

внуша́ть impf, **внуши́ть** (-шу́) pf instil; +dat inspire with. **внуше́ние** suggestion; reproof. **внуши́тельный** inspiring; imposing.

вня́тный distinct. **внять** (no fut; -ял, -á, -о) pf of **внима́ть**

во: see **в**

вобра́ть (вберу́, -рёшь; -а́л, -á, -о) pf (impf **вбира́ть**) absorb; inhale.

вобью́ etc.: see **вбить**

вовлека́ть impf, **вовле́чь** (-еку́, -ечёшь; -ёк, -екла́) pf draw in, involve.

во́время adv in time; on time.

во́все adv quite; ~ не not at all.

во-вторы́х adv secondly.

вогна́ть (вгоню́, -о́нишь; -гна́л, -á, -о) pf (impf **вгоня́ть**) drive in. **во́гнутый** concave. **вогну́ть** (-ну́, -нёшь) pf (impf **вгиба́ть**) bend or curve inwards.

вода́ (acc во́ду, gen -ы́; pl -ы) water; pl the waters; spa.

водворя́ть pf, **водворя́ть** impf settle, install; establish.

води́тель m driver. **води́ть** (вожу́, во́дишь; det **вести́**) lead; conduct; take; drive; ~**ся** be found; associate (with); be the custom.

во́дка vodka. **во́дн|ый** water; ~**ые лы́жи** water-skiing; water-skis.

водо- *in comb* water, water-; hydraulic; hydro-. **водобоя́знь** hydrophobia. **~воро́т** whirlpool; maelstrom. **~ём** reservoir. **~измеще́ние** displacement. **~ка́чка** watertower, pumping station. **~ла́з** diver. **~ле́й** Aquarius. **~непроница́емый** waterproof. **~отво́дный** drainage. **~па́д** waterfall. **~по́й** wateringplace. **~прово́д** water-pipe, water-main; water supply. **~прово́дчик** plumber. **~разде́л** watershed. **~ро́д** hydrogen. **во́доросль** water-plant; seaweed. **~снабже́ние** water supply. **~сто́к** drain, gutter. **~храни́лище** reservoir.

водружа́ть *impf*, **водрузи́ть** (-ужу́) *pf* hoist; erect.

водяни́стый watery. **водяно́й** water.

воева́ть (вою́ю) *impf* wage war. **воево́да** *m* voivode; commander.

воедино *adv* together.

военко́м military commissar.

военно- *in comb* military; war-. **вое́нно-возду́шный** air-, air-force. **вое́нно-морско́й** naval. **~пле́нный** *sb* prisoner of war. **вое́ннополево́й суд** court-martial. **~служащий** *sb* serviceman.

вое́нн|ый military; war; *sb* serviceman; **~ое положе́ние** martial law; **~ый суд** court-martial.

вожа́к (-á) guide; leader. **вожа́тый** *sb* guide; tram-driver.

вожделе́ние desire, lust.

вождь (-я́) *m* leader, chief.

вожжа́ (*pl* -и, -е́й) rein.

вожу́ *etc.*: *see* води́ть, вози́ть

воз (*loc* -ý; *pl* -ы́) cart; cartload.

возбуди́мый excitable. **возбуди́тель** *m* agent; instigator. **возбуди́ть** (-ужу́) *pf* **возбужда́ть** *impf* excite, arouse; incite. **возбужда́ющ|ий**: **~ее сре́дство** stimulant. **возбужде́ние** excitement. **возбуждённый** excited.

возвести́ть (-еду́, -дёшь; -вёл, -ла́) *pf* (*impf* **возводи́ть**) elevate; erect; level; +**к**+*dat* trace to.

возвести́ть (-ещу́) *pf*, **возвеща́ть** *impf* proclaim.

возводи́ть (-ожу́, -о́дишь) *impf* of **возвести́**

возвра́т return; repayment. **возврати́ть** (-ащу́) *pf*, **возвраща́ть** *impf* (*pf also* **верну́ть**) return, give back; **~ся** return; go back, come back. **возвра́тный** return; reflexive. **возвраще́ние** return.

возвы́сить *pf*, **возвыша́ть** *impf* raise; ennoble; **~ся** rise. **возвыше́ние** rise; raised place. **возвы́шенность** height; loftiness. **возвы́шенный** high; elevated.

возгла́вить (-влю) *pf*, **возглавля́ть** *impf* head.

во́зглас exclamation. **возгласи́ть** (-ашу́) *pf*, **возглаша́ть** *impf* proclaim.

возгора́емый inflammable. **возгора́ться** *impf*, **возгоре́ться** (-рю́сь) *pf* flare up; be seized (with).

воздава́ть (-даю́, -даёшь) *impf*, **возда́ть** (-а́м, -а́шь, -а́ст, -ади́м; -а́л, -á, -о) *pf* render.

воздвига́ть *impf*, **воздви́гнуть** (-ну; -дви́г) *pf* raise.

возде́йствие influence. **возде́йствовать** *impf & pf* +**на**+*acc* influence.

возде́лать *pf*, **возде́лывать**

impf cultivate, till.

воздержа́ние abstinence; abstention. **возде́ржанный** abstemious. **воздержа́ться** (-жу́сь, -жишься) *pf* refrain; abstain.

во́здух air. **воздухонепроница́емый** air-tight. **возду́ш|ный** air, aerial; airy; flimsy; ~ый змей kite; ~ый шар balloon.

воззва́ние appeal. **воззва́ть** (-зову́, -вёшь) *pf* (*impf* взыва́ть) appeal (o+*prep* for).

воззре́ние opinion, outlook.

вози́ть (вожу́, во́зишь) *impf* convey; carry; bring; take; ~ся romp play noisily; busy o.s.; potter about.

возлага́ть *impf of* возложи́ть

во́зле *adv* & *prep+gen* by, near; near by; past.

возложи́ть (-жу́, -жишь) *pf* (*impf* возлага́ть) lay; place.

возлю́бленный beloved; *sb* sweetheart.

возме́здие retribution.

возмести́ть (-ещу́) *pf*, **возмеща́ть** *impf* compensate for; refund. **возмеще́ние** compensation; refund.

возмо́жно *adv* possibly; +*comp* as ... as possible. **возмо́жность** possibility; opportunity. **возмо́жный** possible.

возмужа́лый mature; grown up. **возмужа́ть** *pf* grow up; gain strength.

возмути́тельный disgraceful. **возмути́ть** (-ущу́) *pf*, **возмуща́ть** *impf* disturb; stir up; rouse to indignation; ~ся be indignant. **возмуще́ние** indignation. **возмущённый** (-щён, -щена́) indignant.

вознагради́ть (-ажу́) *pf*, **вознагражда́ть** *impf* reward. **вознагражде́ние** reward; fee.

возненави́деть (-и́жу) *pf* conceive a hatred for.

вознесе́ние Ascension. **вознести́** (-су́, -сёшь; -нёс, -ла́) *pf* (*impf* возноси́ть) raise, lift up; ~сь rise; ascend.

возника́ть *impf*, **возни́кнуть** (-нет; -ник) *pf* arise, spring up. **возникнове́ние** rise, beginning, origin.

возни́ца *m* coachman.

возноси́ть(ся (-ошу́(сь, -о́сишь(ся) *impf of* вознести́(сь. **возноше́ние** raising; elevation.

возня́ row, noise; bother.

возобнови́ть (-влю́) *pf*, **возобновля́ть** *impf* renew; restore; ~ся begin again. **возобновле́ние** renewal; revival.

возража́ть *impf*, **возрази́ть** (-ажу́) *pf* object. **возраже́ние** objection.

во́зраст age. **возраста́ние** growth, increase. **возраста́ть** *impf*, **возрасти́** (-тёт; -рос, -ла́) *pf* grow, increase.

возроди́ть (-ожу́) *pf*, **возрожда́ть** *impf* revive; ~ся revive. **возрожде́ние** revival; Renaissance.

возро́с *etc.: see* возрасти́. **возро́сший** increased.

во́зчик carter, carrier.

возьму́ *etc.: see* взять.

во́ин warrior; soldier. **во́инск|ий** military; ~ая пови́нность conscription. **во́инственный** warlike. **во́инствующий** militant.

вой howl(ing); wail(ing).

войду́ *etc.: see* войти́

во́йлок felt. **во́йлочный** felt.

войнá (pl -ы) war.

войскó (pl -á) army; pl troops, forces. войсковóй military.

войти́ (-йду́, -йдёшь; вошёл, -шла́) pf (impf входи́ть) go in, come in, enter; get in(to).

вокзáл (railway) station.

вóкмен Walkman (propr), personal stereo.

вокрýг adv & prep+gen round, around.

вол (-á) ox, bullock.

волáн flounce; shuttlecock.

волды́рь (-я́) m blister; bump.

волево́й strong-willed.

волейбóл volleyball.

вóлей-нево́лей adv willy-nilly.

волк (-а, -óв) wolf. волкодáв wolf-hound.

волнá (pl -ы, во́лнáм) wave. волнéние choppiness; agitation; emotion. волни́стый wavy. волновáть impf (pf вз~) disturb; agitate; excite; ~ся be disturbed; worry, be nervous. волноло́м, волноре́з breakwater. волну́ющий disturbing; exciting.

волоки́та red tape; rigmarole.

волокни́стый fibrous, stringy. волокнó (pl -a) fibre, filament.

волокý etc.: see воло́чь

вóлос (pl -ы, -óс, -áм) pl hair. волосáтый hairy. волоснóй capillary.

вóлость (pl -и, -éй) volost (administrative division).

воло́чить (-очу́, -óчишь) impf drag; ~ся drag, trail; +за+instr run after, court. воло́чь (-окý, -очёшь; -óк, -лá) impf drag.

во́лчий wolf's; wolfish. волчи́ха, волчи́ца she-wolf.

волчóк (-чкá) top; gyroscope.

волчóнок (-нка; pl -чáта, -чáт) wolf cub.

волше́бник magician; wizard. волше́бница enchantress. волше́бный magic, magical; enchanting. волшебствó magic, enchantment.

вольнонаёмный civilian. во́льность liberty; license. во́льный (-лен, -льнá, -о, во́льны) free; free-style.

вольт[1] (gen pl вольт) volt. вольт[2] (loc -ý) vault.

вольфрáм tungsten.

вóля will; liberty.

вомну́ etc.: see вмять

вон adv out; off, away.

вон partl there, over there.

вонзáть impf, вонзи́ть (-нжý) pf plunge, thrust.

вонь stench. воню́чий stinking. воня́ть stink.

вообража́емый imaginary. вообража́ть impf, вообрази́ть (-ажý) pf imagine. воображе́ние imagination. вообрази́мый imaginable.

вообще́ adv in general; generally.

воодушеви́ть (-влю́) pf, воодушевля́ть impf inspire. воодушевле́ние inspiration; fervour.

вооружáть impf, вооружи́ть (-жý) pf arm, equip; ~ся arm o.s.; take up arms. вооруже́ние arming; arms; equipment. вооружённый (-жён, -á) armed; equipped.

вóочию adv with one's own eyes.

во-пéрвых adv first, first of all.

вопи́ть (-плю́) impf yell, howl. вопию́щий crying; scandalous.

воплоти́ть (-ощý) pf, воплощáть impf embody. воплоще́ние embodiment.

вопль *m* cry, wail; howling.

вопреки *prep+dat* in spite of.

вопрос question; problem. **вопросительный** interrogative; questioning; ~ знак question-mark.

вор (*pl* -ы, -ов) thief; criminal.

ворваться (-вусь, -вёшься; -ался, -лась, -алось) *pf* (*impf* **врываться**) burst in.

воркотня grumbling.

воробей sparrow.

вороватый thievish; furtive. **воровать** *impf* (*pf* с~) steal. **воровка** woman thief. **воровской** thieves'. **воровство** stealing; theft.

ворон raven. **ворона** crow.

воронка funnel; crater.

вороной black.

ворот[1] collar; neckband.

ворот[2] winch; windlass.

ворота (*pl*; *gen* -рот) gate(s); gateway; goal.

воротить (-очу, -отишь) *pf* bring back, get back; turn back; ~ся return.

воротник (-а) collar.

ворох (*pl* -а) heap, pile; heaps.

ворочать *impf* turn; move; +*instr* have control of; ~ся move, turn.

ворочу(сь *etc.*: *see* **воротиться**

ворошить (-шу) *impf* stir up; turn (over).

ворс nap, pile.

ворчать (-чу) *impf* grumble; growl. **ворчливый** peevish; grumpy.

восвояси *adv* home.

восемнадцатый eighteenth. **восемнадцать** eighteen. **восемь** (-сьми, *instr* -сьмью *or* -семью) eight. **восемьдесят** eighty. **восемьсот**

(-сьмисот, -стами) eight hundred. **восемью** *adv* eight times.

воск wax, beeswax.

воскликнуть (-ну) *pf*, **восклицать** *impf* exclaim. **восклицание** exclamation. **восклицательный** exclamatory; ~ знак exclamation mark.

восковой wax; waxy; waxed.

воскресать *impf*, **воскреснуть** (-ну; -éс) *pf* rise from the dead; revive. **воскресение** resurrection. **воскресенье** Sunday. **воскресить** (-ешу) *pf*, **воскрешать** *impf* resurrect; revive. **воскрешение** resurrection; revival.

воспаление inflammation. **воспалённый** (-лён, -á) inflamed. **воспалить** *pf*, **воспалять** *impf* inflame; ~ся become inflamed.

воспитание upbringing, education. **воспитанник, -ница** pupil. **воспитанный** well-brought-up. **воспитатель** *m* tutor; educator. **воспитательный** educational. **воспитать** *pf*, **воспитывать** *impf* bring up; foster; educate.

воспламенить *pf*, **воспламенять** *impf* ignite; fire; ~ся ignite; flare up. **воспламеняемый** inflammable.

вос|пользоваться *pf*.

воспоминание recollection, memory; *pl* memoirs; reminiscences.

вос|препятствовать *pf*.

воспретить (-ещу) *pf*, **воспрещать** *impf* forbid. **воспрещение** prohibition. **воспрещённый** (-щён, -á) prohibited.

восприимчивый impressionable; susceptible. **восприни-**

мать impf, **воспринять** (-иму, -имешь; -инял, -а, -о) pf perceive; grasp. **восприятие** perception.

воспроизведение reproduction. **воспроизвести** (-еду, -едешь; -вёл, -а) pf, **воспроизводить** (-ожу, -одишь) impf reproduce. **воспроизводительный** reproductive. **воспроизводство** reproduction.

вос|противиться (-влюсь) pf.

воссоединение reunification. **воссоединить** pf, **воссоединять** impf reunite.

восставать (-таю, -таёшь) impf of **восстать**.

восстание insurrection.

восстановить (-влю, -вишь) pf (impf **восстанавливать**) restore; reinstate; recall; ~ **против**+gen set against. **восстановление** restoration.

восстать (-áну) pf (impf **восставать**) rise (up).

восток east.

восторг delight, rapture. **восторгаться** +instr be delighted with, go into raptures over. **восторженный** enthusiastic.

восточный east, eastern; easterly; oriental.

востребование: до **востребования** to be called for; poste restante.

восхвалить (-лю, -лишь) pf, **восхвалять** impf praise, extol.

восхитительный entrancing; delightful. **восхитить** (-хищу) pf, **восхищать** impf enrapture; ~**ся** +instr be enraptured by. **восхищение** delight; admiration.

восход rising. **восходить** (-ожу, -одишь) impf of **взойти**; ~ **к**+dat go back to, date

from. **восхождение** ascent. **восходящий** rising.

восшествие accession.

восьмая sb eighth; octave. **восьмёрка** eight; figure eight; No. 8; figure of eight.

восьми- in comb eight-; octo-. **восьмигранник** octahedron. ~**десятый** eightieth. ~**летний** eight-year; eight-year-old. ~**сотый** eight-hundredth. ~**угольник** octagon. ~**угольный** octagonal.

восьмой eighth.

вот partl here (is), there (is); this (is); ~ **и всё** and that's all; ~ **как**! no! really? — **так**! that's right!; ~ **что**! no! not really? **вот-вот** adv just, on the point of; partl that's right!

воткнуть (-ну, -нёшь) pf, **втыкать** impf stick in, drive in.

вотру etc.: see **втереть**

воцариться pf, **воцаряться** impf come to the throne; set in.

вошёл etc.: see **войти**

вошь (вши; gen pl вшей) louse.

вошью etc.: see **вшить**

вою etc.: see **выть**

воюю etc.: see **воевать**

впадать impf, **впасть** (-аду) pf flow; lapse; fall in; +в+acc verge on, approximate to. **впадение** confluence, (river-)mouth. **впадина** cavity, hollow; socket. **впалый** sunken.

впервые adv for the first time.

вперёд adv forward(s), ahead; in future; in advance; (of clock) be fast. **впереди** adv in front, ahead; in (the) future; prep+gen in front of, before.

впечатление impression. **впечатлительный** impressionable.

вписáть (-ишý, -и́шешь) pf,
впи́сывать impf enter, insert; ~ся be enrolled, join.

впита́ть pf, впи́тывать impf
absorb, take in; ~ся soak.

впи́хивать impf, впи́хнуть
(-нý, -нёшь) pf cram in; shove.

вплавь adv (by) swimming.

вплести́ (-етý, -етёшь; -ёл, -á)
pf, вплета́ть impf plait in,
intertwine; involve.

вплотнýю adv close; in earnest.

вплоть adv; ~ до+gen (right)
up to.

вполго́лоса adv under one's
breath.

вполне́ adv fully, entirely; quite.

впопыха́х adv hastily; in
one's haste.

впо́ру adv at the right time;
just right, exactly.

впосле́дствии adv subse-
quently.

впотьма́х adv in the dark.

впра́ве adv: быть ~ have a
right.

впра́во adv to the right
(от+gen of).

впредь adv in (the) future; ~
до+gen until.

впро́голодь adv half starving.

впро́чем conj however, but;
though.

впры́скивание injection.
впры́скивать impf, впры́с-
нуть (-ну) pf inject.

впряга́ть impf впрячь (-ягý,
-яжёшь; -яг, -лá) pf harness.

впуск admittance. впуска́ть
impf, впусти́ть (-ущý, -ýстишь)
pf admit, let in.

впустýю adv to no purpose,
in vain.

впущý etc.: see впусти́ть

враг (-á) enemy. вражда́ enmity. вражде́бный hostile.
враждова́ть be at enmity.

вра́жеский enemy.

вразбро́д adv separately, dis-
unitedly.

вразре́з adv: идти́ ~ c+instr
go against.

вразуми́тельный intelligible,
clear; persuasive.

врасплóх adv unawares.

враста́ть impf, врасти́ (-тёт;
врос, -лá) pf grow in; take root.

врата́рь (-я́) m goalkeeper.

врать (вру, врёшь; -ал, -á, -о)
impf (pf на-, со-) lie, tell
lies; talk nonsense.

врач (-á) doctor. враче́бный
medical.

враща́ть impf rotate, revolve;
~ся revolve, rotate. враще́-
ние rotation, revolution.

вред (-á) harm; damage.
вреди́тель m pest; wrecker;
pl vermin. вреди́тельство
wrecking, (act of) sabotage.
вреди́ть (-ежý) impf (pf по-)
+dat harm; damage. вре́д-
ный (-ден, -днá, -о) harmful.

вре́зать (-е́жу) pf, вреза́ть
impf cut in; set in; (sl) ~ся
hit; cut (into); run (into);
be engraved; fall in love.

времена́ми adv at times. вре́-
менно adv temporarily. вре-
менно́й temporal. вре́мен-
ный temporary; provisional.
вре́мя (-мени; pl -менá, -мён,
-ам) neut time; tense; ~ го́да
season; ~ от вре́мени at times,
from time to time; на ~ for a
time; ско́лько вре́мени? what
is the time?; тем вре́менем
meanwhile.

вро́вень adv level, on a level.

вро́де prep+gen like; partl
such as, like; apparently.

врождённый (-дён, -á) innate.

врознь, врозь adv separately,
apart.

врос etc.: see врасти́. вру etc.: see врать

врун (-á), вру́нья liar.

вруча́ть impf, вручи́ть (-чу́) pf hand, deliver; entrust.

вручну́ю adv by hand.

врыва́ть(ся impf of во-рва́ться

вряд (ли) adv it's not likely; hardly, scarcely.

всади́ть (-ажу́, -а́дишь) pf, вса́живать impf thrust in; sink in. вса́дник rider, horseman. вса́дница rider, horsewoman.

вса́сывать impf of всоса́ть

все, все pron: see весь. все́ adv always, all the time; ~ (ещё) still; conj however, nevertheless; ~ же all the same.

все- in comb all-, omni-. все-возмо́жный of every kind; all possible. ~дозво́лен-ность permissiveness. ~ме́р-ный of every kind. ~ми́рный world, world-wide. ~могу́щий omnipotent. ~наро́дно adv publicly. ~наро́дный national; nation-wide. ~объе́млю-щий comprehensive, all-embracing. ~росси́йский All-Russian. ~си́льный omni-potent. ~сторо́нний all-round; comprehensive.

всегда́ always.

всего́ adv in all, all told; only.

вселе́нная sb universe.

всели́ть, вселя́ть impf in-stall, lodge; inspire; ~ся move in, install o.s.; be implanted.

все́нощная sb night service.

всео́бщий general, universal.

всерьёз adv seriously, in earnest.

всё-таки conj & partl all the same, still. всецело́ adv completely.

вска́кивать impf of вско-чи́ть

вскачь adv at a gallop.

вскипа́ть impf, вс|кипе́ть (-плю́) pf boil up; fig flare up.

вс|кипяти́ть(ся (-ячу́(сь)) pf

всколыхну́ть (-ну́, -нёшь) pf stir; stir up.

вскользь adv slightly; in passing.

вско́ре adv soon, shortly after.

вскочи́ть (-очу́, -о́чишь) pf (impf вска́кивать) jump up.

вскри́кивать impf, вскрик-нуть (-ну) pf shriek, scream.

вскрича́ть (-чу́) pf exclaim.

вскрыва́ть impf, вскрыть (-ро́ю) pf open; reveal; dissect. вскры́тие opening; revelation; post-mortem.

вслед adv & prep+dat after; ~ за+instr after, following. всле́дствие prep+gen in consequence of.

вслепу́ю adv blindly; blindfold.

вслух adv aloud.

вслу́шаться pf, вслу́шиваться impf listen attentively.

всма́триваться impf, всмо-тре́ться (-рю́сь, -ришься) pf look closely.

всмя́тку adv soft(-boiled).

всо́вывать impf of всу́нуть

всоса́ть (-су́, -сёшь) pf (impf вса́сывать) suck in; absorb; imbibe.

вс|паха́ть (-ашу́, -а́шешь) pf, вспа́хивать impf plough up. вспа́шка ploughing.

вс|пе́нить(ся pf

всплеск splash. всплёски-вать impf, всплесну́ть (-ну́, -нёшь) pf splash; ~ рука́ми throw up one's hands.

всплыва́ть impf, всплыть

(-ыву, -ывёшь; -ыл, -á, -о) pf rise to the surface; come to light.

вспоминать impf, вспомнить pf remember; ~ся impers +dat: мне вспомнилось I remembered.

вспомогательный auxiliary.

вс|потеть pf.

вспрыгивать impf, вспрыгнуть (-ну) pf jump up.

вспухать impf, вс|пухнуть (-нет; -ух) pf swell up.

вспылить pf flare up. вспыльчивый hot-tempered.

вспыхивать impf, вспыхнуть (-ну) pf blaze up; flare up. вспышка flash; outburst; outbreak.

вставать (-таю, -таёшь) impf of встать

вставить (-влю) pf, вставлять impf put in, insert. вставка insertion; framing, mounting; inset. вставной inserted; set in; ~ые зубы false teeth.

встать (-ану) pf (impf вставать) get up; stand up.

встревоженный adj anxious. вс|тревожить (-жу) pf.

встрепенуться (-нусь, -нёшься) pf rouse o.s.; start (up); beat faster.

встретить (-éчу) pf, встречать impf meet (with); ~ся meet; be found. встреча meeting. встречный coming to meet; contrary; head; counter; sb person met with; первый ~ the first person you meet, anybody.

встряска shaking; shock. встряхивать impf, встряхнуть (-ну, -нёшь) pf shake (up); rouse; ~ся shake o.s.; rouse o.s.

вступать impf, вступить (-плю, -пишь) pf +в+acc enter (into); join (in); ~ся intervene; +за+acc stand up for. вступительный introductory; entrance. вступление entry, joining; introduction.

всунуть (-ну) pf (impf всовывать) put in, stick in.

всхлипнуть (-ну) pf, всхлипывать impf sob.

всходить (-ожу, -одишь) impf of взойти. всходы (pl; gen -ов) (corn-)shoots.

всю: see весь

всюду adv everywhere.

вся: see весь

всяк|ий any; every, all kinds of; ~ом случае in any case; на ~ий случай just in case; pron anyone. всячески adv in every possible way.

втайне adv secretly.

вталкивать impf of втолкнуть. втаптывать impf of втоптать. втаскивать impf, втащить (-щу, -щишь) pf drag in.

втереть (вотру, вотрёшь; втёр) pf (impf втирать) rub in; ~ся insinuate o.s., worm o.s.

втирать(ся impf of втереть(ся

втискивать impf, втиснуть (-ну) pf squeeze in; ~ся squeeze (o.s.) in.

втихомолку adv surreptitiously.

втолкнуть (-ну, -нёшь) pf (impf вталкивать) push in.

втоптать (-пчу, -пчешь) pf (impf втаптывать) trample (in).

вторгаться impf, вторгнуться (-нусь; вторгся, -лась)

pf invade; intrude. **вторже́ние** invasion; intrusion.

вто́рить *impf* play or sing second part; +*dat* repeat, echo.

втори́чный second, secondary. **вто́рник** Tuesday. **вто́рос** second; ~**бе** *sb* second course. **второстепе́нный** secondary, minor.

второпя́х *adv* in haste.

в-тре́тьих *adv* thirdly. **втро́е** *adv* three times. **втроём** *adv* three (together). **втройне́** *adv* three times as much.

вту́лка plug.

втыка́ть *impf of* **воткну́ть**

втя́гивать *impf*, **втяну́ть** (-ну́, -нешь) *pf* draw in; ~**ся** +в+*acc* enter; get used to.

вуа́ль veil.

вуз *abbr (of* **вы́сшее уче́бное заведе́ние)** higher educational establishment; college.

вулка́н volcano.

вульга́рный vulgar.

вундерки́нд infant prodigy.

вход entrance; entry. **входи́ть** (-ожу́, -о́дишь) *impf of* **войти́. входно́й** entrance.

вхолосту́ю *adv* idle, free.

вцепи́ться (-плю́сь, -пишься) *pf*, **вцепля́ться** *impf* +в+*acc* clutch, catch hold of.

вчера́ *adv* yesterday. **вчера́шний** yesterday's.

вчерне́ in rough.

вче́тверо *adv* four times. **вчетверо́м** *adv* four (together).

вши *etc.: see* **вошь.**

вшива́ть *impf of* **вшить**

вши́вый lousy.

вширь *adv* in breadth; widely.

вшить (вошью́, -ьёшь) *pf* (*impf* **вшива́ть)** sew in.

въе́дливый corrosive; caustic.

въезд entry; entrance. **въе-**

зжа́ть *impf*, **въе́хать** (-е́ду, -е́дешь) *pf* (+в+*acc*) ride in(to); drive in(to); crash into.

вы (вас, вам, ва́ми, вас) *pron* you.

выбега́ть *impf*, **вы́бежать** (-ежи́м; -ежишь) *pf* run out.

вы́белить *pf*.

вы́беру *etc.: see* **вы́брать.**

выбива́ть(ся *impf of* **вы́бить(ся. выбира́ть(ся** *impf of* **вы́брать(ся**

вы́бить (-бью) *pf* (*impf* **выбива́ть)** knock out; dislodge; ~**ся** get out; break loose; come out; ~**ся из сил** exhaust o.s.

вы́бор choice; selection; *pl* election(s). **вы́борный** elective; electoral. **вы́борочный** selective.

вы́бранить *pf*. **выбра́сывать(ся** *impf of* **вы́бросить(ся**

вы́брать (-беру) *pf* (*impf* **выбира́ть)** choose; elect; take out; ~**ся** get out.

выбрива́ть *impf*, **вы́брить** (-рею) *pf* shave.

вы́бросить (-ошу) *pf* (*impf* **выбра́сывать)** throw out; throw away; ~**ся** throw o.s. out, leap out.

выбыва́ть *impf*, **вы́быть** (-буду) *pf* из+*gen* leave, quit.

выва́ливать *impf*, **вы́валить** *pf* throw out; pour out; ~**ся** tumble out.

вы́везти (-зу; -ез) *pf* (*impf* **вывози́ть)** take, bring, out; export; rescue.

вы́верить *pf* (*impf* **выверя́ть)** adjust, regulate.

вы́вернуть (-ну) *pf* (*impf* **вывёртывать)** turn inside out; unscrew; wrench.

выверя́ть *impf of* **вы́верить**

вывесить (-ешу) pf (impf вывешивать) weigh; hang out. **вывеска** sign; pretext.

вывести (-еду; -ел) pf (impf выводить) lead, bring, take, out; drive out; remove; exterminate; deduce; hatch; grow, breed; erect; depict; draw; ~ся go out of use; become extinct; come out; hatch out.

выветривание airing.

вывешивать impf of **вывесить**

вывих dislocation. **вывихивать** impf, **вывихнуть** (-ну) pf dislocate.

вывод conclusion; withdrawal. **выводить(ся** (-ожу(сь, -одишь(ся) impf of **вывести(сь**. **выводок** (-дка) brood; litter.

вывожу see **выводить**, **вывозить**

вывоз export; removal. **вывозить** (-ожу, -озишь) impf of **вывезти**. **вывозной** export.

выгадать pf, **выгадывать** impf gain, save.

выгиб curve. **выгибать** impf of **выгнуть**

выглаживать (-ажу) pf

выглядеть (-яжу) impf look, look like. **выглядывать** impf, **выглянуть** (-ну) pf look out; peep out.

выгнать (-гоню) pf (impf **выгонять**) drive out; distil.

выгнутый curved, convex. **выгнуть** (-ну) pf (impf выгибать) bend, arch.

выговаривать impf, **выговорить** pf pronounce, speak; +dat reprimand; ~ся speak out. **выговор** pronunciation; reprimand.

выгода advantage; gain. **выгодный** advantageous; profitable.

выгон pasture; common. **выгонять** impf of **выгнать**

выгорать impf, **выгореть** (-рит) pf burn down; fade.

выгравировать pf.

выгружать impf, **выгрузить** (-ужу) pf unload; disembark. **выгрузка** unloading; disembarkation.

выдавать (-даю, -даёшь) impf, **выдать** (-ам, -ашь, -аст, -адим) pf give (out), issue; betray; extradite; +за+acc pass off as; ~ся protrude; stand out; present itself. **выдача** issue; payment; extradition. **выдающийся** prominent.

выдвигать impf, **выдвинуть** (-ну) pf move out; pull out; put forward, nominate; ~ся move forward, move out; come out; get on (in the world). **выдвижение** nomination; promotion.

выделение secretion; excretion; isolation; apportionment. **выделить** pf, **выделять** impf pick out; detach; allot; secrete; excrete; isolate; ~ курсивом italicize; ~ся stand out, be noted (+instr for).

выдёргивать impf of **выдернуть**

выдержанный consistent; self-possessed; firm; matured, seasoned. **выдержать** (-жу) pf, **выдерживать** impf bear; endure; contain o.s.; pass (exam); sustain. **выдержка**[1] endurance; self-possession; exposure.

выдержка[2] excerpt.

выдернуть (-ну) pf (impf выдёргивать) pull out.

выдохнуть (-ну) pf (impf выдыхать) breathe out; ~ся

have lost fragrance or smell; be past one's best. **вы́дра** otter.

вы́драть (-деру) *pf.* **вы́**|дрессировать *pf.*

выдыха́ть *impf of* **вы́дуть**

вы́думанный made-up, fabricated. **выду́мать** *pf*, **выду́мывать** *impf* invent; fabricate. **вы́думка** invention; device; inventiveness.

вы́дуть *pf* (*impf also* выдува́ть) blow; blow out.

выдыха́ние exhalation. **выдыха́ть(ся** *impf of* **вы́дохнуть(ся**

вы́езд departure; exit. **вы́ездн(о́й** exit; **~ая се́ссия суда́** assizes. **выезжа́ть** *impf of* **вы́ехать**

вы́ехать (-еду) *pf* (*impf* выезжа́ть) go out, depart; drive out, ride out; move (house).

вы́жать (-жму, -жмешь) *pf* (*impf* выжима́ть) squeeze out; wring out.

вы́жечь (-жгу) *pf* (*impf* выжига́ть) burn out; cauterize.

выжива́ние survival. **выжива́ть** *impf of* **вы́жить**

выжига́ть *impf of* **вы́жечь**

выжида́тельный waiting; temporizing.

выжима́ть *impf of* **вы́жать**

вы́жить (-иву) *pf* (*impf* выжива́ть) survive; hound out; **~ из ума́** become senile.

вы́звать (-зову) *pf* (*impf* вызыва́ть) call (out); send for; challenge; provoke; **~ся** volunteer.

выздора́вливать *impf of* **вы́здороветь** (-ею) *pf* recover. **выздоровле́ние** recovery; convalescence.

вы́зов call; summons; challenge.

вызолоченный gilt.

вызу́бривать *impf*, **вы́|зубрить** *pf* learn by heart.

вызыва́ть(ся *impf of* **вы́звать(ся. вызыва́ющий** defiant; provocative.

вы́игрывать *pf*, **выи́грывать** *impf* win; gain. **вы́игрыш** win; gain; prize. **вы́игрышный** winning; lottery; advantageous.

вы́йти (-йду; -шел, -шла) *pf* (*impf* выходи́ть) go out; come out; get out; appear; turn out; be used up; have expired; **~ в свет** appear; **~ за́муж (за**+*acc*) marry; **~ из себя́** lose one's temper.

выка́лывать *impf of* **вы́колоть. выка́пывать** *impf of* **вы́копать**

выка́рмливать *impf of* **вы́кормить**

вы́качать *pf*, **выка́чивать** *impf* pump out.

выки́дывать *impf*, **вы́кинуть** *pf* throw out, reject; put out; miscarry, abort; **~ флаг** hoist a flag. **вы́кидыш** miscarriage, abortion.

вы́кладка laying out; lay-out; facing; kit; computation, calculation. **выкла́дывать** *impf of* **вы́ложить**

выключа́тель *m* switch. **выключа́ть** *impf*, **вы́ключить** (-чу) *pf* turn off, switch off; remove, exclude.

выкола́чивать *impf*, **вы́колотить** (-лочу) *pf* knock out, beat out; beat; extort, wring out

вы́колоть (-лю) *pf* (*impf* выка́лывать) put out; gouge out; tattoo.

вы́|копать *pf* (*impf also* **вы-ка́пывать**) dig; dig up, dig out; exhume; unearth.

вы́кормить (-млю) *pf* (*impf* **выка́рмливать**) rear, breed.

вы́корчевать (-чую) *pf*, **вы-корчёвывать** *impf* uproot, root out; eradicate.

выкра́ивать *impf of* **вы́кроить**

вы́|красить (-ашу) *pf*, **вы-кра́шивать** *impf* paint; dye.

выкри́кивать *impf*, **вы́крик-нуть** (-ну) *pf* cry out; yell.

вы́кроить (*impf* **выкра́ивать**) cut out; find (*time etc.*). **вы́кройка** pattern.

вы́крутить (-учу) *pf*, **выкру́-чивать** *impf* unscrew; twist; **∼ся** extricate o.s.

вы́куп ransom; redemption.

вы́|купать(ся *pf of* **купа́ть-(ся**

выкупа́ть² *impf*, **вы́купить** (-плю) ransom, redeem.

вы́лазка sally, sortie; excursion.

выла́мывать *impf of* **вы́ломать**

вылеза́ть *impf*, **вы́лезти** (-зу, -лез) *pf* climb out; come out.

вы́|лепить (-плю) *pf*

вы́лет flight; take-off. **вы́ле-тать** *impf*, **вы́лететь** (-ечу) *pf* fly out; take off.

вылечивать *impf*, **вы́ле-чить** (-чу) *pf* cure; **∼ся** recover, be cured.

выливать(ся *pf of* **вы́лить-(ся**

вы́|линять *pf*.

вы́лить (-лью) *pf* (*impf* **выли-ва́ть**) pour out; cast, found; **∼ся** flow out; be expressed.

вы́ложить (-жу) *pf* (*impf* **выкла́дывать**) lay out.

вы́ломать *pf*, **вы́ломить** (-млю) *pf* (*impf* **выла́мы-**

вать) break open.

вы́лупиться (-плюсь) *pf*, **вы-лупля́ться** *impf* hatch (out).

вы́лью *etc.*: *see* **вы́лить**

вы́|мазать (-мажу) *pf*, **выма́-зывать** *impf* smear, dirty.

выма́нивать *impf*, **вы́манить** *pf* entice; lure.

вы́мереть (-мрет; -мер) *pf* (*impf* **вымира́ть**) die out; become extinct. **вы́мерший** extinct.

вы́мести (-ету) *pf*, **вы́метать** *impf* sweep (out).

вымога́тельство blackmail, extortion. **вымога́ть** *impf* extort.

вымока́ть *impf*, **вы́мокнуть** (-ну; -ок) *pf* be drenched; soak; rot.

вы́молвить (-влю) *pf* say, utter.

вы́|мостить (-ощу) *pf*. **вы́-мою** *etc.*: *see* **вы́мыть**

вы́мпел pennant.

вы́мрет *see* **вы́мереть**. **вы-мыва́ть(ся** *impf of* **вы́-мыть(ся**

вы́мысел (-сла) invention, fabrication; fantasy.

вы́|мыть (-мою) *pf* (*impf also* **вымыва́ть**) wash; wash out; off; wash away; **∼ся** wash o.s.

вы́мышленный fictitious.

вы́мя (-мени) *neut* udder.

вына́шивать *impf of* **вы́но-сить²**

вы́нести (-су; -нес) *pf* (*impf* **выноси́ть¹**) carry out, take out; carry away; endure.

вынима́ть *impf of* **вы́нуть**

вы́нос carrying out. **выно-си́ть¹** (-ошу, -о́сишь) *impf of* **вы́нести**. **выноси́ть²** *pf* (*impf* **вына́шивать**) bear; nurture.

вы́носка carrying out; removal; footnote. **вынóсли-вость** endurance; hardiness. **вы́нудить** (-ужу) *pf*, **вынуж-да́ть** *impf* force, compel. **вы́нужденный** forced.

вы́нуть (-ну) *pf* (*impf* **вынимáть**) take out.

вы́пад attack; lunge. **выпа-да́ть** *impf of* **вы́пасть**

выпáливать *impf of* **вы́поло-ть**

выпáривать *impf*, **вы́па-рить** evaporate; steam. **выпáры-вать** *impf of* **вы́пороть²**

вы́пасть (-аду, -ал) *pf* (*impf* **выпадáть**) fall out; fall; oc-cur, turn out; lunge.

выпекáть *impf*, **вы́печь** (-еку, -ек) *pf* bake.

выпивáть *impf of* **вы́пить**; enjoy a drink. **вы́пивка** drink-ing bout; drinks.

выпи́ливать *impf*, **вы́пи-лить** *pf* saw, cut out.

вы́писать (-ишу) *pf*, **выпи́-сывать** *impf* copy out; write out; order; subscribe to; send for; ~ **из больни́цы** dis-charge from hospital; ~**ся** be discharged. **вы́писка** writing out; extract; ordering, sub-scription; discharge.

вы́пить (-пью) *pf* (*impf also* **выпивáть**) drink; drink up.

вы́плавить (-влю) *pf*, **выплав-ля́ть** *impf* smelt. **вы́плавка** smelting; smelted metal.

вы́плата payment. **вы́пла-тить** (-ачу) *pf*, **выплá-чивать** *impf* pay (out); pay off.

выплёвывать *impf of* **вы́плю-нуть**

выплывáть *impf*, **вы́плыть** (-ыву) *pf* swim out, sail out; emerge; crop up.

вы́плюнуть (-ну) *pf* (*impf* **выплёвывать**) spit out.

выполза́ть *impf*, **вы́ползти** (-зу, -олз) *pf* crawl out.

выполне́ние execution, car-rying out; fulfilment. **вы́полн-ить** *pf*, **выполня́ть** *impf* execute, carry out; fulfil.

вы́полоскать (-ощу) *pf*.

вы́полоть (-лю) *pf* (*impf also* **выпáлывать**) weed out; weed.

вы́пороть¹ (-рю) *pf*.

вы́пороть² (-рю) *pf* (*impf* **вы́пáрывать**) rip out, rip up.

вы́потрошить (-шу) *pf*.

вы́правка bearing; correction.

выпрáшивать *impf of* **вы́-просить**; solicit.

выпровá живать *impf*, **вы́-проводить** (-ожу) *pf* send packing.

вы́просить (-ошу) *pf* (*impf* **выпрáшивать**) (ask for and) get.

выпряга́ть *impf of* **вы́прячь**

вы́прямить (-млю) *pf*, **вы-прямля́ть** *impf* straighten (out); rectify; ~**ся** become straight; draw o.s. up.

вы́прячь (-ягу; -яг) *pf* (*impf* **выпряга́ть**) unharness.

вы́пуклый protuberant; bul-ging; convex.

вы́пуск output; issue; dis-charge; part, instalment; final-year students; omission. **выпуск-а́ть** *impf*, **вы́пустить** (-ущу) *pf* let out; issue; pro-duce; omit. **выпускни́к** (-á), **-и́ца** final-year student. **вы́-пускн|о́й** discharge; exhaust; ~**о́й экза́мен** finals, final ex-amination.

вы́путать *pf*, **выпу́тывать** *impf* disentangle; ~**ся** extri-cate o.s.

вы́пью *etc.: see* **вы́пить**

вырабатывать *impf*, выработать *pf* work out; work up; draw up; produce; earn. выработка manufacture; production; working out; drawing up; output; make.

выравнивать(ся *impf of* выровнять(ся

выражать *impf*, выразить (-ажу) *pf* express; ~ся express o.s. выражение expression. выразительный expressive.

вырастать *impf*, вырасти (-ту; -рос) *pf* grow, grow up; вырастить (-ащу) *pf*, выращивать *impf* bring up; breed; cultivate.

вырвать[1] (-ву) *pf* (*impf* вырывать[2]) pull out, tear out; extort; ~ся break loose, break free; escape; shoot.

вы|рвать[2] (-ву) *pf*.

вырез cut; décolletage. вырезать (-ежу) *pf*, вырезать *impf*, вырезывать *impf* cut (out); engrave. вырезка cutting out, excision; cutting; fillet.

выровнять *pf* (*impf* выравнивать) level; straighten (out); draw up; ~ся become level; equalize; catch up.

выродиться *pf*, вырождаться *impf* degenerate. выродок (-дка) degenerate; black sheep. вырождение degeneration.

выронить *pf* drop.

вырос *etc.*: *see* вырасти

выро́ю *etc.*: *see* вы́рыть

вырубать *impf*, вырубить (-блю) *pf* cut down; cut (out); carve out. вырубка cutting down; hewing out.

вы|ругать(ся *pf*.

выруливать *impf*, вы|рулить *pf* taxi.

выручать *impf*, выручить (-чу) *pf* help out; rescue; gain; make. выручка rescue; gain; proceeds; earnings.

вырывать[1] *impf*, вырыть (-рою) *pf* dig up, unearth.

вырывать[2](ся *impf of* вырвать(ся

высадить (-ажу) *pf*, высаживать *impf* set down; put ashore; transplant; smash; ~ся alight; disembark. высадка disembarkation; landing; transplanting.

высасывать *impf of* высосать

высвободить (-божу) *pf*, высвобождать *impf* free; release.

высекать *impf of* высечь. выселить *pf*, выселять *impf* evict; evacuate; move; ~ся move, remove.

вы|сечь[1] (-еку; -сек) *pf*. высечь[2] (-еку; -сек) (*impf* высекать) cut (out); carve.

высидеть (-ижу) *pf*, высиживать *impf* sit out; stay; hatch.

выситься *impf* rise, tower.

выскабливать *impf of* выскоблить

высказать (-ажу) *pf*, высказывать *impf* express; state; ~ся speak out. высказывание utterance; pronouncement.

выскакивать *impf of* выскочить

выскоблить *pf* (*impf* выскабливать) scrape out; erase; remove.

выскочить (-чу) *pf* (*impf* выскакивать) jump out; spring out; ~ c+*instr* come out with. выскочка upstart.

выслать (вышлю) *pf* (*impf*

высыла́ть send (out); exile; deport.

вы́следить (-ежу) *pf*, **высле́живать** *impf* trace; shadow.

выслу́живать(ся *impf*, **вы́служить** (-жу) *pf* qualify for; serve (out); ~**ся** gain promotion; curry favour.

вы́слушать *pf*, **выслу́шивать** *impf* hear out; sound; listen to.

высме́ивать *impf*, **вы́смеять** (-ею) *pf* ridicule.

вы́|сморкать(ся *pf*. **высо́вывать(ся** *impf of* **вы́сунуть(ся**

высо́кий (-о́к, -а́, -о́ко́) high; tall; lofty; elevated.

высоко́- *in comb* high-; highly. **высокоблагоро́дие** (your) Honour, Worship. ~**на́пряжённый** high-tension. ~**го́рный** mountain. ~**ка́чественный** high-quality. ~**квалифици́рованный** highly qualified. ~**ме́рие** haughtiness. ~**ме́рный** haughty. ~**па́рный** high-flown; bombastic. ~**часто́тный** high-frequency.

вы́сосать (-осу) *pf* (*impf* **выса́сывать**) suck out.

высота́ (*pl* -ы) height, altitude. **высо́тный** high-altitude; high-rise.

вы́|сохнуть (-ну, -ох) *pf* (*impf also* **высыха́ть**) dry (out); dry up; wither (away).

вы́спаться (-плюсь, -пишься) *pf* (*impf* **высыпа́ться²**) have a good sleep.

вы́ставить (-влю) *pf*, **выставля́ть** *impf* display, exhibit; post; put forward; set down; take out; +*instr* represent as; ~**ся** show off. **вы́ставка** exhibition.

выста́ивать *impf of* **вы́стоять**

вы́стегать *pf*. **вы́стирать** *pf*.

вы́стоять (-ою) *pf* (*impf* **выста́ивать**) stand; stand one's ground.

вы́страдать *pf* suffer; gain through suffering.

выстра́ивать(ся *impf of* **вы́строить(ся**

вы́стрел shot; report. **вы́стрелить** *pf* shoot, fire.

вы́строгать *pf*.

вы́строить *pf* (*impf* **выстра́ивать**) build; draw up, order, arrange; form up. ~**ся** form up.

вы́ступ protuberance, projection. **выступа́ть** *impf*, **вы́ступить** (-плю) *pf* come forward; come out; perform; speak; +**из**+*gen* go beyond. **выступле́ние** appearance, performance; speech; setting out.

вы́сунуть (-ну) *pf* (*impf* **высо́вывать**) put out, thrust out; ~**ся** show o.s., thrust o.s. forward.

вы́|сушить(ся (-шу(сь) *pf*.

вы́сший highest; high; higher.

высыла́ть *impf of* **вы́слать**. **вы́сылка** sending, dispatch; expulsion; exile.

вы́сыпать (-плю) *pf*, **высыпа́ть** *impf* pour out; spill; ~**ся¹** pour out; spill.

высыпа́ться² *impf of* **вы́спаться**

высыха́ть *impf of* **вы́сохнуть**

высь height; summit.

выта́лкивать *impf of* **вы́толкать, вы́толкнуть**. **выта́скивать** *impf of* **вы́тащить**. **выта́чивать** *impf of* **вы́точить**

вы́|тащить (-щу) *pf* (*impf also* **выта́скивать**) drag out; pull out.

вы́|твердить (-ржу) *pf*.

вытека́ть *impf* (*pf* **вы́течь**); ~ **из**+*gen* flow from, out of; result from.

вы́тереть (-тру, -тер) *pf* (*impf* **вытира́ть**) wipe (up); dry; wear out.

вы́терпеть (-плю) *pf* endure.

вы́тертый threadbare.

вы́теснить *pf*, **вытесня́ть** *impf* force out; oust; displace.

вы́течь (-чет; -ек) *pf* (*impf* **вытека́ть**) flow out, run out.

вытира́ть *impf of* **вы́тереть**

вы́толкать *pf*, **вы́толкнуть** (-ну) *pf* (*impf* **выта́лкивать**) throw out; push out.

вы́точенный turned. **вы́|точить** (-чу) *pf* (*impf also* **выта́чивать**) turn; sharpen; gnaw through.

вы́|травить (-влю) *pf*, **вы́|тра́вливать** *impf*, **вытравля́ть** *impf* exterminate, destroy; remove; etch; trample down; damage.

вытрезви́тель *m* detoxification centre. **вы́трезвить(ся** (-влю(сь)// *pf*, **вытрезвля́ть(ся** *impf* sober up.

вы́тру *etc.: see* **вы́тереть**

вы́|трясти (-су; -яс) *pf* shake out.

вытря́хивать *impf*, **вы́тряхнуть** (-ну) *pf* shake out.

выть (во́ю) *impf* howl; wail.

вытя́гивать *impf*, **вы́тянуть** (-ну) *pf* stretch (out); extend; extract; endure; ~**ся** stretch, stretch o.s.; shoot up; draw o.s. up. **вытя́жка** drawing out, extraction; extract.

вы́|утюжить (-жу) *pf*.

выу́чивать *impf*, **вы́|учить** (-чу) *pf* learn; teach; ~**ся** +*dat of* in+*loc* learn.

выха́живать *impf of* **выхо́дить²**

вы́хватить (-ачу) *pf*, **выхва́тывать** *impf* snatch out, up, away; pull out.

вы́хлоп exhaust. **выхлопно́й** exhaust, discharge.

вы́ход going out; departure; way out, exit; vent; appearance; yield; ~ **за́муж** marriage. **вы́ходец** (-дца) emigrant; immigrant. **выходи́ть¹** (-ожу́, -о́дишь) *impf of* **вы́йти**; **на**+*acc* look out on.

выходи́ть² (-ожу́) *pf* (*impf* **выха́живать**) nurse; rear, bring up.

вы́ходка trick; prank.

выходно́й exit; going-out, outgoing; discharge; ~**о́й день** day off; ~**о́й** *sb* person off duty; day off. **выхожу́** *etc.: see* **выходи́ть¹. выхожу́** *etc.: see* **выходи́ть²**

вы́цвести (-ветет) *pf*, **вы́цвета́ть** *impf* fade. **вы́цветший** faded.

вы́черкивать *impf*, **вы́черкнуть** (-ну) *pf* cross out.

вы́черпать *pf*, **выче́рпывать** *impf* bale out.

вы́честь (-чту, -чел, -чла) *pf* (*impf* **вычита́ть**) subtract. **вы́чет** deduction.

вычисле́ние calculation. **вычисли́тель** *m* calculator. **вычисли́тельн|ый** calculating, computing; ~**ая маши́на** computer. **вы́числить** *pf*, **вычисля́ть** *impf* calculate, compute.

вы́чистить (-ищу) *pf* (*impf also* **вычища́ть**) clean, clean up. **вычита́ние** subtraction. **вычита́ть** *impf of* **вы́честь. вычища́ть** *impf of* **вы́чистить. вы́чту** *etc.: see* **вы́честь**

вы́швырнуть (-ну) *pf*, **вы-**

швы́ривать impf chuck out.
вы́ше higher, taller; prep+gen beyond; over; adv above.
выше- in comb above-, afore-.
вышеизло́женный foregoing. **~на́званный** aforenamed. **~ска́занный**, **~ука́занный** aforesaid. **~упомя́нутый** afore-mentioned.
вы́шел etc.: see **вы́йти**
вышиба́ла m chucker-out.
вышиба́ть impf, **вы́шибить** (-бу; -иб) pf knock out; chuck out.
вышива́ние embroidery, needlework. **вышива́ть** impf of **вы́шить**. **вы́шивка** embroidery.
вышина́ height.
вы́шить (-шью) pf (impf вышива́ть) embroider. **вы́шитый** embroidered.
вы́шка tower; (бурова́я ~) derrick.
вы́шлю etc.: see **вы́слать**.
вы́шью etc.: see **вы́шить**
вы́явить (-влю) pf, **выявля́ть** impf reveal; make known; expose; **~ся** come to light, be revealed.
выясне́ние elucidation; explanation. **вы́яснить** pf, **выясня́ть** impf elucidate; explain; **~ся** become clear; turn out.
Вьетна́м Vietnam. **вьетна́мец** -мка Vietnamese. **вьетна́мский** Vietnamese.
вью etc.: see **вить**
вью́га snow-storm, blizzard.
вьюно́к (-нка) bindweed.
вью́чн|ый pack; **~ое живо́тное** beast of burden.
вью́щийся climbing; curly.
вяжу́ etc.: see **вяза́ть**. **вя́жущий** binding; astringent.
вяз elm.
вяза́ние knitting, crocheting;

binding, tying. **вя́занка**[1] knitted garment. **вяза́нка**[2] bundle. **вя́заный** knitted, crocheted. **вяза́нье** knitting; crochet(-work). **вяза́ть** (вяжу́, вя́жешь) impf (pf c~) tie, bind; knit, crochet; be astringent; **~ся** accord; tally. **вя́зка** tying; knitting, crocheting; bunch.
вя́зкий (-зок, -зка́, -о) viscous; sticky; boggy. **вя́знуть** (-ну; вяз(нул), -зла) impf (pf за~, у~) stick, get stuck.
вя́зовый elm.
вязь ligature; arabesque.
вя́леный dried; sun-cured.
вя́лый limp; sluggish; slack. **вя́нуть** (-ну; -нул, вял) impf (pf за~, у~) fade, wither; flag.

Г

г. abbr (of **год**) year; (of **го́род**) city; (of **господи́н**) Mr.
г abbr (of **грамм**) gram.
га abbr (of **гекта́р**) hectare.
га́вань harbour.
гага́чий пух eiderdown.
гад reptile; repulsive person; pl vermin.
гада́лка fortune-teller. **гада́ние** fortune-telling; guesswork. **гада́ть** impf (pf по~) tell fortunes; guess.
га́дина reptile; repulsive person; pl vermin. **га́дить** (га́жу) impf (pf на~) +в+prep, на+acc, prep foul, dirty, defile. **га́дкий** (-док, -дка́, -о) nasty, vile repulsive. **га́дость** filthy, muck; dirty trick; pl filthy expressions. **гадю́ка** adder, viper; repulsive person.
га́ечный ключ spanner, wrench.
газ[1] gauze.

газ² gas; wind; **дать ~** step on the gas; **сбáвить ~** reduce speed.

газéта newspaper. **газéтчик** journalist; newspaper-seller.

газирóванный aerated. **газóвый** gas.

газóн lawn. **газонокосúлка** lawn-mower.

газопровóд gas pipeline; gas-main.

гáйка nut; female screw.

галáктика galaxy.

галантерéйный магазúн haberdasher's. **галантерéя** haberdashery.

галáнтный gallant.

галерéя gallery. **галёрка** gallery, gods.

галифé *indecl pl* riding-breeches.

гáлка jackdaw.

галлюцинáция hallucination.

галóп gallop. **гáлочка** tick.

гáлстук tie; neckerchief.

галýшка dumpling.

гáлька pebble; pebbles, shingle.

гам din, uproar.

гамáк (-á) hammock.

гáмма scale; gamut; range.

гангрéна gangrene.

гáнгстер gangster.

гантéль dumb-bell.

гарáж (-á) garage.

гарантúровать *impf & pf* guarantee. **гарáнтия** guarantee.

гардерóб wardrobe; cloak-room. **гардерóбщик, -щица** cloakroom attendant.

гардúна curtain.

гармонизúровать *impf & pf* harmonize.

гармóника accordion, concertina. **гармонúческий, гармонúчный** harmonious. **гармóния** harmony; concord. **гар-**

мóнь accordion, concertina.

гарнизóн garrison.

гарнúр garnish; vegetables.

гарнитýр set; suite.

гарь burning; cinders.

гасúтель *m* extinguisher; suppressor. **гасúть (гашý, гáсишь)** *impf (pf* **за~, по~)** extinguish; suppress. **гáснуть (-ну; гас)** *impf (pf* **за~, по~, у~)** be extinguished, go out; grow feeble.

гастрóли *f pl* tour; guest-appearance, performance. **гастролúровать** *impf* (be on) tour.

гастронóм gourmet; provision shop. **гастрономúческий** gastronomic; provision. **гастронóмия** gastronomy; provisions; delicatessen.

гауптвáхта guardroom.

гашúш hashish.

гвардéец (-éйца) guardsman. **гвардéйский** guards'. **гвáрдия** Guards.

гвоздúк tack. **гвоздúка** pink('s), carnation(s); cloves. **гвóздики (-ов)** *pl* stilettos. **гвоздь (-я; *pl* -и, -éй)** *m* nail; tack; crux; highlight, hit.

гг. *abbr (of* **гóды)** years.

где *adv* where; **~ бы ни** wherever. **гдé-либо** *adv* anywhere. **гдé-нибудь** *adv* somewhere; anywhere. **гдé-то** *adv* somewhere.

ректáр hectare.

гéлий helium.

гемоглобúн haemoglobin.

геморрóй haemorrhoids. **гемофилúя** haemophilia.

ген gene.

гéнезис origin, genesis.

генерáл general. **генерáльный** general; **~ая репетúция** dress rehearsal.

генера́тор generator.

генера́ция generation; oscillation.

гене́тика genetics. **генети́ческий** genetic.

генеа́льный brilliant. **ге́ний** genius.

гео- in comb geo-. **гео́граф** geographer. ~**графи́ческий** geographical. ~**гра́фия** geography. **гео́лог** geologist. ~**логи́ческий** geological. ~**ло́гия** geology. ~**метри́ческий** geometric. ~**ме́трия** geometry.

георги́н dahlia.

геофи́зика geophysics.

гепа́рд cheetah.

гепати́т hepatitis.

гера́нь geranium.

герб arms, coat of arms. **ге́рбовый** heraldic; ~**ая печа́ть** official stamp.

геркуле́с Hercules; rolled oats.

герма́нец (-нца) ancient German. **Герма́ния** Germany. **герма́нский** Germanic.

гермафроди́т hermaphrodite.

гермети́ческий hermetic, hermetically sealed; air-tight.

герои́зм heroism. **герои́ня** heroine. **герои́ческий** heroic. **геро́й** hero. **геро́йский** heroic.

герц (gen pl герц) hertz.

ге́рцог duke. **герцоги́ня** duchess.

г-жа abbr (of госпожа́) Mrs.; Miss.

гиаци́нт hyacinth.

ги́бель death; destruction; ruin; loss; wreck; downfall. **ги́бельный** disastrous, fatal.

ги́бкий (-бок, -бка́, -бко) flexible, adaptable, versatile; supple. **ги́бкость** flexibility; suppleness.

ги́бнуть (-ну; ги́б(нул)) impf (pf по~) perish.

гибри́д hybrid.

гига́нт giant. **гига́нтский** gigantic.

гигие́на hygiene. **гигиени́ческий**, **-и́чный** hygienic, sanitary.

гид guide.

гидра́влический hydraulic.

ги́дро- pref hydro-. ~**электроста́нция** hydro-electric power-station.

гие́на hyena.

ги́льза cartridge-case; sleeve; (cigarette-)wrapper.

гимн hymn.

гимна́зия grammar school, high school.

гимна́ст gymnast. **гимна́стика** gymnastics. **гимнасти́ческий** gymnastic.

гинеко́лог gynaecologist. **гинеколо́гия** gynaecology.

гипе́рбола hyperbola.

гипно́з hypnosis. **гипнотизёр** hypnotist. **гипнотизи́ровать** impf (pf за~) hypnotize. **гипноти́ческий** hypnotic.

гипо́теза hypothesis. **гипотети́ческий** hypothetical.

гиппопота́м hippopotamus.

гипс gypsum, plaster (of Paris); plaster cast. **ги́псовый** plaster.

гирля́нда garland.

ги́ря weight.

гистерэктоми́я hysterectomy.

гита́ра guitar.

гл. abbr (of глава́) chapter.

глав- abbr in comb head, chief, main.

глава́ (pl -ы) head; chief; chapter; cupola. **глава́рь** (-я́) m leader, ring-leader. **главк** central directorate. **главнокома́ндующий** sb commander-in-chief. **гла́вный** chief, main;

~ым о́бразом chiefly, mainly, for the most part; ~ое *sb* the main thing; the essentials.

глаго́л verb.

гла́|дить (-а́жу) *impf* (*pf* вы́-, по-) stroke; iron. гла́дкий smooth; plain. гла́дко *adv* smoothly. гладь smooth surface.

глаз (*loc* -у́; *pl* -а́, глаз) eye; в ~а́ to one's face; за ~а́+*gen* behind the back of; смотре́ть во все ~а́ be all eyes.

глазиро́ванный glazed; glossy; iced; glacé.

глазни́ца eye-socket. глазно́й eye; optic; ~ врач oculist. глазо́к (-зка́) peephole.

глазу́нья fried eggs.

глазу́рь glaze; syrup; icing.

гла́нды (гланд) *pl* tonsils.

гла́сность publicity; glasnost, openness. гла́сный public; vowel; *sb* vowel.

гли́на clay. гли́нистый clayey. гли́няный clay; earthenware; clayey.

гли́ссер speed-boat.

глист (*intestinal*) worm.

глицери́н glycerine.

гло́бус globe.

глота́ть *impf* swallow. гло́тка gullet; throat. глото́к (-тка́) gulp; mouthful.

гло́х|нуть (-ну; глох) *impf* (*pf* за-, о-) become deaf; die away, subside; grow wild.

глубина́ (*pl* -ы) depth; heart; interior. глубо́кий (-о́к, -а́, -о́ко) deep; profound; late, advanced, extreme. глубокомы́слие profundity. глубокоуважа́емый (*in formal letters*) dear.

глуми́ться (-млю́сь) *impf* mock, jeer (над+*instr*). глумле́ние mockery.

глупе́ть (-е́ю) *impf* (*pf* по-)

grow stupid. глупе́ц (-пца́) fool. глу́пость stupidity. глу́пый (глуп, -а́, -о) stupid.

глуха́рь (-я́) *m* capercaillie.

глух|о́й (глух, -а́, -о) deaf; muffled; obscure, vague; dense; wild; remote; deserted; sealed; blank; ~о́й, ~а́я *sb* deaf man, woman. глухонемо́й deaf and dumb; *sb* deaf mute. глухота́ deafness. глуши́тель *m* silencer. глуши́ть (-шу́) *impf* (*pf* за-, о-) stun; muffle; dull; jam; extinguish; stifle; suppress. глушь backwoods.

глы́ба clod; lump, block.

глюко́за glucose.

гляде́ть (-яжу́) *impf* (*pf* по-, гля́нуть) look, gaze, peer; ~ в о́ба be on one's guard; (того́ и) гляди́ it looks as if; I'm afraid; гля́дя по+*dat* depending on.

гля́нец (-нца) gloss, lustre; polish.

гля́нуть (-ну) *pf* (*impf* гляде́ть) glance.

гм *int* hm!

г-н *abbr* (*of* господи́н) Mr.

гнать (гоню́, го́нишь; гнал, -а́, -о) *impf* drive; urge (on); hunt, chase; persecute; distil; ~ся *за+instr* pursue.

гнев anger, rage. гне́ваться *impf* (*pf* раз~) be angry. гне́вный angry.

гнедо́й bay.

гнездо́ (*pl* гнёзда) nest.

гнёт weight; oppression. гнету́щий oppressive.

гни́да nit.

гние́ние decay, putrefaction, rot. гнило́й (-и́л, -а́, -о) rotten; muggy. гнить (-ию́, -иёшь; -и́л, -а́, -о) *impf* (*pf* с~) rot.

гное́ние suppuration. гно́иться *impf* (*pf* с~) suppurate, discharge matter. **гной** pus. **гно́йник** abscess; ulcer. **гно́йный** purulent.

гну́сный (-сен, -сна́, -о) vile, foul.

гнуть (гну, гнёшь) *impf* (*pf* со~) bend; aim at; ~ся bend; stoop.

гнуша́ться *impf* (*pf* по~) disdain; +*gen or instr* shun; abhor.

гобеле́н tapestry.

гобо́й oboe.

гове́ть (-е́ю) *impf* fast.

говно́ (*vulg*) shit.

говори́ть *impf* (*pf* по~, сказа́ть) speak, talk; say; tell; ~ся: как говоря́т as they say.

говя́дина beef. **говя́жий** beef.

го́гот cackle; loud laughter. **гогота́ть** (-очу́, -о́чешь) *impf* cackle; roar with laughter.

год (*loc* -у́; *pl* -ы *or* -á, *gen* -о́в *or* лет) year. **года́ми** *adv* for years (on end).

годи́ться, (-жу́сь) *impf* be fit, suitable; serve.

годи́чный a year's; annual.

го́дный (-ден, -дна́, -о, -ы *or* -ы́) fit, suitable; valid.

годово́й one-year-old. **годово́й** annual. **годовщи́на** anniversary.

гожу́сь *etc.: see* **годи́ться**

гол goal.

голени́ще (boot-)top. **го́лень** shin.

голла́ндец (-дца) Dutchman. **Голла́ндия** Holland. **голла́ндка** Dutchwoman; Dutch stove. **голла́ндский** Dutch.

голова́ (*acc* го́лову; *pl* го́ловы, - о́в, -а́м) head. **голова́стик** tadpole. **голо́вка** head; cap; nose, tip. **головно́й** head; leading; ~**áя боль** headache; ~**о́й мозг** brain, cerebrum.

~**о́й убо́р** headgear, headdress. **головокруже́ние** giddiness, dizziness. **головоло́мка** puzzle. **головоре́з** cut-throat; rascal.

го́лод hunger; famine; acute shortage. **голода́ние** starvation; fasting. **голода́ть** *impf* go hungry, starve; fast. **голо́дный** (го́лоден, -дна́, -о, -ы *or* -ы́) hungry. **голо́дка** hunger-strike.

гололёд (period of) black ice.

го́лос (*pl* -á) voice; part; vote. **голоси́ть** (-ошу́) *impf* sing loudly; cry; wail.

голосло́вный unsubstantiated, unfounded.

голосова́ние voting; poll. **голосова́ть** *impf* (*pf* про~) vote; vote on.

голу́бка pigeon; (my) dear, darling. **голубо́й** light blue.

голу́бчик my dear (fellow); darling. **го́лубь** *m* pigeon, dove. **голубя́тня** (*gen pl* -тен) dovecot, pigeon-loft.

го́лый (гол, -ла́, -ло) naked, bare.

гомоге́нный homogeneous.

го́мон hubbub.

гомосексуали́ст homosexual. **гомосексуа́льный** homosexual.

гондо́ла gondola.

гоне́ние persecution. **го́нка** race; dashing; haste.

гонора́р fee.

го́ночный racing.

гонча́р (-á) potter.

го́нщик racer. **гоню́** *etc.: see* **гнать. гоня́ть** *impf* drive; send on errands; ~ся +за+*instr* chase, hunt.

гора́ (*acc* го́ру, *pl* го́ры, -а́м) mountain; hill; **в го́ру** uphill; **под го́ру** downhill.

гора́здо adv much, far, by far.

горб (-а́, loc -у́) hump; bulge. **горба́тый** hunchbacked. **горбить** (-блю) impf (pf c~) arch, hunch; ~ся stoop. **горбу́н** (-а́) m, **горбу́нья** (gen pl -ний) hunchback. **горбу́шка** (gen pl -шек) crust (of loaf).

горди́ться (-ржу́сь) impf put on airs; +instr be proud of. **го́рдость** pride. **го́рдый** (горд, -а́, -о, го́рды) proud. **горды́ня** arrogance.

го́ре grief, sorrow; trouble. **горева́ть** (-рю́ю) impf grieve. **горе́лка** burner. **горе́лый** burnt. **горе́ние** burning, combustion; enthusiasm.

го́рестный sad; sorrowful. **го́ресть** sorrow; pl misfortunes. **горе́ть** (-рю́) impf (pf c~) burn.

горе́ц (-рца́) mountain-dweller. **го́речь** bitterness; bitter taste.

горизо́нт horizon. **горизонта́ль** horizontal. **горизонта́льный** horizontal.

гори́стый mountainous, hilly. **го́рка** hill; hillock; steep climb.

го́рло throat; neck. **горлови́й** throat; guttural; raucous. **го́рлышко** neck.

гормо́н hormone.

горн[1] furnace, forge.

горн[2] bugle.

го́рничная sb maid, chambermaid.

горнорабо́чий sb miner.

горноста́й ermine.

го́рный mountain; mountainous; mineral; mining. **горня́к** (-а́) miner.

го́род (pl -а́) town; city. **городо́к** (-дка́) small town. **городско́й** urban; city; municipal. **горожа́нин** (pl -а́не, -а́н)

m, **-жа́нка** town-dweller.

гороско́п horoscope.

горо́х pea, peas. **горо́шек** (-шка) spots, spotted pattern; душистый ~ sweet peas; зелёный ~ green peas. **горо́шина** pea.

горсове́т abbr (of городско́й сове́т) city soviet, town soviet.

горсть (gen pl -е́й) handful.

горта́нный guttural. **горта́нь** larynx.

горчи́ца mustard. **горчи́чник** mustard plaster.

горшо́к (-шка́) flowerpot; pot; potty; chamber-pot.

го́рький (-рек, -рька́, -о) bitter.

горю́чий combustible; ~ee sb fuel. **горя́чий** (-ря́ч, -а́) hot; passionate; ardent. **горячи́ться** (-чу́сь) impf (pf раз~) get excited. **горя́чка** fever; feverish haste. **горя́чность** zeal.

гос- abbr in comb (of госуда́рственный) state.

го́спиталь m (military) hospital.

го́споди int good heavens! **господи́н** (pl -ода́, -о́д, -а́м) master; gentleman; Mr; pl ladies and gentlemen. **госпо́дство** supremacy. **госпо́дствовать** impf hold sway; prevail. **Госпо́дь** (Го́спода, voc Го́споди) m God, the Lord. **госпожа́** lady; Mrs.

гостеприи́мный hospitable. **гостеприи́мство** hospitality. **гости́ная** sb drawing-room, sitting-room. **гости́ница** hotel. **гости́ть** (гощу́) impf stay, be on a visit. **гость** (gen pl -е́й) m, **го́стья** (gen pl -ий) guest, visitor.

государственный State, public. **государство** State. **государыня, государь** *m* sovereign; Your Majesty.

готический Gothic.

готовить (-влю) *impf* (*pf* с~) prepare; ~ся prepare (o.s.); be at hand. **готовность** readiness, willingness. **готовый** ready.

гофрированный corrugated; waved; pleated.

грабёж robbery; pillage. **грабитель** *m* robber. **грабительский** predatory; exorbitant. **грабить** (-блю) *impf* (*pf* о~) rob, pillage.

грабли (-бель *or* -блей) *pl* rake.

гравёр, гравировщик engraver.

гравий gravel. **гравировать** *impf* (*pf* вы~) engrave; etch. **гравировка** engraving.

гравитационный gravitational.

гравюра engraving, print; etching.

град[1] city, town.

град[2] hail; volley. **градина** hailstone.

градус degree. **градусник** thermometer.

гражданин (*pl* граждане, -дан) **гражданка** citizen. **гражданский** civil; civic; civilian. **гражданство** citizenship.

грамзапись (gramophone) recording.

грамм gram.

грамматика grammar. **грамматический** grammatical. **грамота** reading and writing; official document; deed. **грамотность** literacy. **грамотный** literate; competent. **грампластинка** (gramo-

phone) record.

гранат pomegranate; garnet. **граната** shell, grenade.

грандиозный grandiose.

гранёный cut, faceted; cut-glass.

гранит granite.

граница border; boundary; limit; **за границей**, **за границу** abroad. **граничить** *impf* border.

грань border, verge; side, facet.

граф count; earl. **графа** column. **график** graph; chart; schedule; graphic artist. **графика** drawing; graphics; script.

графин carafe; decanter. **графиня** countess.

графит graphite.

графический graphic. **графлёный** ruled. **графство** county.

грациозный graceful. **грация** grace.

грач (-á) rook.

гребёнка comb. **гребень** (-бня) *m* comb; crest. **гребец** (-бца) rower, oarsman. **гребной** rowing. **гребу** *etc.: see* **грести**

грёза day-dream, dream. **грезить** (-éжу) *impf* dream.

грек Greek.

грелка hot-water bottle.

греметь (*impf* про~) thunder, roar; rattle; resound. **гремучая змея** rattlesnake.

грести (-ебу, -ебёшь; грёб, -бла) *impf* row; rake.

греть (-éю) *impf* warm, heat; ~ся warm o.s., bask.

грех (-á) sin. **греховный** sinful. **грехопадение** the Fall; fall.

Греция Greece. **грецкий орех** walnut. **гречанка** Greek. **греческий** Greek, Grecian.

гречи́ха buckwheat. **гре́чневый** buckwheat.

греши́ть (-шу́) *impf* (*pf* по~, со~) sin. **гре́шник, -ница** sinner. **гре́шный** (-шен, -шна́, -о) sinful.

гриб (-а́) mushroom. **грибно́й** mushroom.

гри́ва mane.

гри́венник ten-copeck piece.

грим make-up; grease-paint. **гримирова́ть** *impf* (*pf* за~) make up; +*instr* make up as.

грипп flu.

гриф neck (of violin etc.).

гри́фель *m* pencil lead.

гроб (*loc* -у́, *pl* -ы́ *or* -а́) coffin; grave. **гробни́ца** tomb. **гробово́й** coffin; deathly. **гробовщи́к** (-а́) coffin-maker; undertaker.

гроза́ (*pl* -ы) (thunder-)storm.

гроздь (*pl* -ди *or* -дья, -дей *or* -дьев) cluster, bunch.

грози́ть(ся (-ожу́(сь) *impf* (*pf* по~, при~) threaten. **гро́зный** (-зен, -зна́, -о) menacing; terrible; severe.

гром (*pl* -ы, -о́в) thunder.

грома́да mass; bulk, pile. **грома́дный** huge, colossal.

громи́ть (-млю́) *impf* destroy; smash, rout.

гро́мкий (-мок, -мка́, -о) loud; famous; notorious; fine-sounding. **гро́мко** *adv* loud(ly); aloud. **громкоговори́тель** *m* loud-speaker. **громово́й** thunder; thunderous; crushing. **громогла́сный** loud; public.

громозди́ть (-зжу́) *impf* (*pf* на~) pile up; ~**ся** tower; clamber up. **громо́здкий** cumbersome.

гро́мче *comp of* **гро́мкий, гро́мко**

гроссме́йстер grand master. **гроте́скный** grotesque.

грохот crash, din.

грохота́ть (-очу́, -о́чешь) *impf* (*pf* про~) crash; rumble; roar.

грош (-а́) half-copeck piece; farthing. **грошо́вый** cheap; trifling.

грубе́ть (-е́ю) *impf* (*pf* за~, о~, по~) grow coarse. **груби́ть** (-блю́) *impf* (*pf* на~) be rude. **грубия́н** boor. **гру́бость** rudeness; coarseness; rude remark. **гру́бый** (груб, -а́, -о) coarse; rude.

гру́да heap, pile.

груди́на breastbone. **груди́нка** brisket; breast. **грудно́й** breast, chest; pectoral. **грудь** (*gen* & *i, instr* -ю, *loc* -и́; *pl* -и, -е́й) breast; chest.

груз load; burden.

грузи́н (*gen pl* -и́н), **грузи́нка** Georgian. **грузи́нский** Georgian.

грузи́ть (-ужу́, -у́зишь) *impf* (*pf* за~, на~, по~) load, lade, freight; ~**ся** load, take on cargo.

Гру́зия Georgia.

гру́зный (-зен, -зна́, -о) weighty; bulky. **грузови́к** lorry, truck. **грузово́й** goods, cargo. **гру́зчик** stevedore; loader.

грунт ground, soil; priming. **грунтова́ть** *impf* (*pf* за~) prime. **грунтово́й** soil; earth; priming.

гру́ппа group. **группирова́ть** *impf* (*pf* с~) group; ~**ся** group, form groups. **группиро́вка** grouping. **группово́й** group; team.

грусти́ть (-ущу́) *impf* grieve, mourn; +*по*+*dat* pine for. **гру́стный** (-тен, -тна́, -о) sad. **грусть** sadness.

гру́ша pear.

грыжа hernia, rupture.

грызть (-зу́, -зёшь, грыз) *impf* (*pf* раз~) gnaw; nag; **~ся** fight; squabble. **грызу́н** (-а́) rodent.

гряда́ (*pl* -ы, -а́м) ridge; bed; row, series; bank. **гря́дка** (flower-)bed.

гряду́щий approaching; future.

гря́зный (-зен, -зна́, -о) muddy; dirty. **грязь** (*loc* -и́) mud; dirt, filth; *pl* mud-cure.

гря́нуть (-ну) *pf* ring out, crash in; strike up.

губа́ (*pl* -ы, -а́м) lip; *pl* pincers.

губерна́тор governor. **губе́рния** province. **губе́рнский** provincial.

губи́тельный ruinous; pernicious. **губи́ть** (-блю́, -бишь) *impf* (*pf* по~) ruin; spoil.

гу́бка sponge.

губна́я пома́да lipstick.

гу́бчатый porous, spongy. **гуверна́нтка** governess. **гуверна́р** tutor.

гуде́ть (гужу́) *impf* (*pf* про~) hum; drone; buzz; hoot. **гудо́к** (-дка́) hooter, siren, horn, whistle; hoot.

гудро́н tar. **гудро́нный** tar, tarred.

гул rumble. **гу́лкий** (-лок, -лка́, -о) resonant; booming.

гуля́нье (*gen pl* -ний) walk; fête; outdoor party. **гуля́ть** *impf* (*pf* по~) stroll; go for a walk; have a good time.

гуманита́рный of the humanities; humane. **гума́нный** humane.

гумно́ (*pl* -а, -мен *or* -мён, -ам) threshing-floor; barn.

гурт (-а́) herd; flock. **гуртовщи́к** (-а́) herdsman. **гурто́м**
adv wholesale; en masse.

гуса́к (-а́) gander.

гу́сеница caterpillar; (caterpillar) track. **гу́сеничный** caterpillar.

гусёнок (-нка; *pl* -ся́та, -ся́т) gosling. **гуси́ный** goose; **~ая ко́жа** goose-flesh.

густе́ть (-е́ет) *impf* (*pf* за~) thicken. **густо́й** (густ, -а́, -о) thick, dense; rich. **густота́** thickness, density; richness.

гусы́ня goose. **гусь** (*pl* -и, -е́й) *m* goose. **гусько́м** *adv* in single file.

гутали́н shoe-polish.

гу́ща grounds, sediment; thicket; thick. **гу́ще** *comp of* густо́й.

ГЭС *abbr (of* гидроэлектроста́нция*)* hydro-electric power station.

Д

д. *abbr (of* дере́вня*)* village; *(of* дом*)* house.

да *conj* and; but.

да *partl* yes; really? well; +*3rd pers of v*, may, let; **да здра́вствует**...! long live ..!

дава́ть (даю́, -ёшь) *impf of* **дать; дава́й(те)** let us be, come on; **~ся** yield; come easy.

дави́ть (-влю́, -вишь) *impf* (*pf* за~, по~, раз~, у~) press; squeeze; crush; oppress; **~ся** choke; hang o.s. **да́вка** crushing; crush. **давле́ние** pressure.

да́вний ancient; of long standing. **давно́** *adv* long ago; for a long time. **да́вность** antiquity; remoteness; long standing. **давны́м-давно́** *adv* long long ago.

дади́м etc.: see **дать**. **даю́** etc.: see **дава́ть**.

да́же even.

да́лее adv further; **и так ~** and so on, etc. **далёкий** (-ёк, -á, -ёко) distant, remote; far (away). **далеко́** adv far; far off; by a long way; **~ за** long after; **~ не** far from. **даль** (loc -и́) distance. **дальне́йший** further. **да́льний** distant, remote; long; **Восто́к** the Far East. **дальнозо́ркий** long-sighted. **да́льность** distance; range. **да́льше** adv further; then, next; longer.

дам etc.: see **дать**

да́ма lady; partner; queen.

да́мба dike; dam.

да́мский ladies'.

Да́ния Denmark.

да́нные sb pl data; facts. **да́нный** given, present. **дань** tribute; debt.

дантист dentist.

дар (pl -ы́) gift. **дари́ть** (-рю́, -ришь) impf (pf по~) +dat give, make a present.

дарова́ние talent. **дарова́ть** impf & pf grant, confer. **дарови́тый** gifted. **даровóй** free (of charge). **да́ром** adv free, gratis; in vain.

да́та date.

да́тельный dative.

дати́ровать impf & pf date.

да́тский Danish. **датча́нин** (pl -áне, -áн), **датча́нка** Dane.

дать (дам, дашь, даст, дади́м; дал, -á, да́ло) pf (impf дава́ть) give; grant; let; **~ взаймы́** lend; **~ся** pf of **дава́ться**

да́ча dacha; **на да́че** in the country. **да́чник** (holiday) visitor.

два m & neut, **две** f (двух, -ум,

-умя́, -ух) two. **двадцатиле́тний** twenty-year; twenty-year-old. **двадца́тый** twentieth; **~ые го́ды** the twenties. **два́дцать** (-и, instr -ью́) twenty. **два́жды** adv twice; double. **двена́дцатый** twelfth. **двена́дцать** twelve.

дверь (loc -и́; pl -и, -ей, instr -я́ми or -ьми́) door.

две́сти (двухсо́т, -умста́м, -умяста́ми, -ухста́х) two hundred.

дви́гатель m engine; motor; motive force. **дви́гать** (-аю or -и́жу) impf, **дви́нуть** (-ну) pf move; set in motion; advance; **~ся** advance; get started. **движе́ние** movement; motion; exercise; traffic. **дви́жимость** chattels; personal property. **дви́жимый** movable; moved. **дви́жущий** motive.

двóе (-и́х) two; two pairs.

двое- in comb two-; double(-). **двоебóрье** biathlon. **~женец** (-нца) bigamist. **~жёнство** bigamy. **~тóчие** colon.

двои́ться impf divide in two; appear double; **у негó двои́лось в глаза́х** he saw double. **двойно́й** binary. **двóйка** two; figure 2; No. 2. **двойни́к** (-á) double. **двойнóй** double, twofold; binary. **двóйня** (gen pl -óен) twins. **двóйственный** two-faced; dual.

двор (-á) yard; courtyard; homestead; court. **дворéц** (-рцá) palace. **двóрник** yard caretaker; windscreen-wiper. **двóрня** servants. **дворо́вый** yard, courtyard; sb house-serf. **дворяни́н** (pl -я́не, -я́н), **дворя́нка** member of the nobility or gentry. **дворя́нство**

nobility, gentry;

двоюродн|ый: ~ый брат, ~ая сестра (first) cousin; ~ый дядя, ~ая тётка first cousin once removed. **двоякий** double; two-fold.

дву-, двух- in comb two-; by-; double. **двубортный** double-breasted. ~личный two-faced. ~ногий two-legged. ~ручный two-handed; two-handled; ~рушник double-dealer. ~смысленный ambiguous. ~(х)спальный double. ~сторонний double-sided; two-way; bilateral. ~хгодичный two-year. ~хлетний two-year; two-year-old; biennial. ~хместный two-seater; two-berth. ~хмоторный twin-engined. ~хсотлетие bicentenary. ~хсотый two-hundredth. ~хтактный two-stroke. ~хэтажный two-storey. ~язычный bilingual.

дебаты (-ов) pl debate. **дебет** debit. **дебетовать** impf & pf debit. **дебит** yield, output.

дебри (-ей) pl jungle; thickets; the wilds. **дебют** début.

дева maid, maiden; Virgo. **девальвация** devaluation. **деваться** impf of **деться**. **девиз** motto; device.

девица spinster; girl. **девичий** girlish, maidenly; ~ья фамилия maiden name. **девка** wench, lass; tart. **девочка** (little) girl. **девственник, -ица** virgin. **девственный** virgin; innocent. **девушка** girl. **девчонка** girl.

девяносто ninety. **девяностостый** ninetieth. **девятка** nine; figure 9; No. 9. **девятна́дца-** тый nineteenth. **девятна́дцать** nineteen. **девятый** ninth. **девять** (-й, instr -ью) nine. **девятьсо́т** (-тисо́т, -тиста́м, -тьюста́ми, -тиста́х) nine hundred.

дегенери́ровать impf & pf degenerate.

дёготь (-гтя) tar.

дегуста́ция tasting.

дед grandfather; grandad. **де́душка** grandfather; grandad.

дееприча́стие adverbial participle.

дежу́рить impf be on duty. **дежу́рный** duty; on duty; sb person on duty. **дежу́рство** (being on) duty.

дезерти́р deserter. **дезерти́ровать** impf & pf desert. **дезинфе́кция** disinfection. **дезинфици́ровать** impf & pf disinfect. **дезодора́нт** deodorant; air-freshener.

дезориента́ция disorientation. **дезориенти́ровать** impf & pf disorient; ~ся lose one's bearings.

де́йственный efficacious; effective. **де́йствие** action; operation; effect; act. **действи́тельно** adv really; indeed. **действи́тельность** reality; validity; efficacy. **действи́тельный** actual; valid; efficacious; active. **де́йствовать** impf (pf по~) affect, have an effect; act; work. **де́йствующий** active; in force; working; ~ее лицо́ character; ~ие ли́ца cast.

декабри́ст Decembrist. **дека́брь** (-я́) m December. **дека́брьский** December.

дека́да ten-day period or festival.

декáн dean. деканáт office of dean.

деклáмация recitation, declamation. деклами́ровать *impf (pf* про~) recite, declaim.

деклара́ция declaration.

декорати́вный decorative. декора́тор scene-painter. декора́ция scenery.

декрéт decree; maternity leave. декрéтный óтпуск maternity leave.

дéланный artificial; affected. дéлать *impf (pf* с~) make; do; ~ вид pretend; ~ся become; happen.

делегáт delegate. делегáция delegation; group.

делёж (-á), делёжка sharing; partition. делéние division; point *(on a scale).*

делéц (-льца́) smart operator.

делика́тный delicate.

дели́мое *sb* dividend. дели́мость divisibility. дели́тель *m* divisor. дели́ть (-лю́, -лишь) *impf (pf* по~, раз~) divide; share; ~ шесть на три divide six by three; ~ся divide; be divisible; +*instr* share.

дéло (*pl* -á) business; affair; matter; deed; thing; case; в сáмом дéле really, indeed; ~ в том the point is; как (вáши) делá? how are things?; на сáмом дéле in actual fact; по дéлу, по делáм on business. делови́тый business-like, efficient. делово́й business; business-like. дéльный efficient; sensible.

дéльта delta.

дельфи́н dolphin.

демаго́г demagogue.

демобилиза́ция demobilization. демобилизова́ть *impf & pf* demobilize.

демокра́т democrat. демократиза́ция democratization. демократизи́ровать *impf & pf* democratize. демократи́ческий democratic. демокра́тия democracy.

дéмон demon.

демонстра́ция demonstration. демонстри́ровать *impf & pf* demonstrate.

дéнежный monetary; money; ~ перево́д money order.

денýсь *etc.: see* дéться

день (дня) *m* day; afternoon; днём in the afternoon; на днях the other day; one of these days; чéрез ~ every other day.

дéньги (-нег, -ньгáм) *pl* money.

департáмент department.

депó *neut indecl* depot.

депорта́ция deportation. депорти́ровать *impf & pf* deport.

депутáт deputy; delegate.

дёргать *impf (pf* дёрнуть) pull, tug; pester; ~ся twitch; jerk.

деревéнский village; rural. дерéвня (*pl* -и, -вéнь, -вня́м) village; the country. дéрево (*pl* -éвья, -ьев) tree; wood. деревя́нный wood; wooden.

держáва power. держáть (-жý, -жишь) *impf* hold; support; keep; ~ пари́ bet; ~ себя́ behave; ~ся hold; be held up; hold o.s.; hold out; +*gen* keep to.

дерзáние daring. дерзáть *impf,* дерзнýть (-нý, -нёшь) *pf* dare. дéрзкий impudent; daring. дéрзость impertinence; daring.

дёрн turf.

дёрнуть(ся (-ну(сь) *pf of* дёргать(ся

деру́ etc.: see **драть**

деса́нт landing; landing force.

де́скать partl indicating reported speech.

десна́ (pl дёсны, -сен) gum.

де́спот despot.

десятиле́тие decade; tenth anniversary. **десятиле́тка** ten-year (secondary) school. **десятиле́тний** ten-year; ten-year-old. **деся́тичный** decimal. **деся́тка** ten; figure 10; No. 10; tenner (10-rouble note). **деся́ток** (-тка) ten; decade. **деся́тый** tenth. **де́сять** (-и, instr -ью) ten.

детдо́м children's home. **детса́д** kindergarten.

дета́ль detail; part, component. **дета́льный** detailed; minute.

детекти́в detective story.

детёныш young animal; pl young. **де́ти** (-те́й, -тям, -тьми, -тях) pl children.

де́тская sb nursery. **де́тский** children's; childish. **де́тство** childhood.

де́ться (де́нусь) pf (impf дева́ться) get to, disappear to.

дефе́кт defect.

дефи́с hyphen.

дефици́т deficit; shortage. **дефици́тный** scarce.

дешеве́ть (-е́ет) impf (pf по~) fall in price. **дешевле** comp of **дёшево, деше́вый**. **дёшево** adv cheap, cheaply. **деше́вый** (дёшев, -á, -о) cheap; empty, worthless.

де́ятель m: **госуда́рственный** ~ statesman; **обще́ственный** ~ public figure. **де́ятельность** activity; work. **де́ятельный** active, energetic.

джаз jazz.

дже́мпер pullover.

джентельме́н gentleman.

джинсо́вый denim. **джи́нсы** (-ов) pl jeans.

джо́йстик joystick.

джу́нгли (-ей) pl jungle.

диабе́т diabetes.

диа́гноз diagnosis.

диагона́ль diagonal.

диагра́мма diagram.

диале́кт dialect. **диале́ктика** dialectics.

диало́г dialogue.

диа́метр diameter.

диапазо́н range; band.

диапозити́в slide, transparency.

диафра́гма diaphragm.

дива́н sofa; divan.

диверса́нт saboteur. **диве́рсия** sabotage.

диви́зия division.

диви́ться (-влю́сь) impf (pf по~) marvel (at + dat).

ди́вный marvellous. **ди́во** wonder, marvel.

дида́ктика didactics.

дие́з (mus) sharp.

дие́та diet. **диети́ческий** dietetic.

ди́зель m diesel; diesel engine. **ди́зельный** diesel.

дика́рь (-я́) m, **дика́рка** savage. **ди́кий** wild; savage; queer; preposterous. **дикобра́з** porcupine. **дикорасту́щий** wild. **ди́кость** wildness, savagery; absurdity.

дикта́нт dictation. **дикту́ра** dictatorship.

диктова́ть impf (pf про~) dictate. **ди́ктор** announcer. **ди́кция** diction.

диле́мма dilemma.

дилета́нт dilettante.

дина́мика dynamics.
динами́т dynamite.
динами́ческий dynamic.
дина́стия dynasty.
диноза́вр dinosaur.
дипло́м diploma; degree; degree work. **диплома́т** diplomat. **дипломати́ческий** diplomatic.
директи́ва instructions; directives. **дире́ктор** (*pl* ~á) director; principal. **дире́кция** management.
дирижа́бль *m* airship, dirigible.
дирижёр conductor. **дирижи́ровать** *impf* +*instr* conduct.
диск disc, disk; dial; discus.
ди́скант treble.
дискоте́ка discotheque.
дискре́тный discrete; digital.
дискримина́ция discrimination.
диску́ссия discussion, debate.
диспансе́р clinic.
диспе́тчер controller.
ди́спут public debate.
диссерта́ция dissertation, thesis.
дистанцио́нный distance, distant; remote; remote-control. **диста́нция** distance; range; region.
дисципли́на discipline.
дитя́ (-я́ти; *pl* де́ти, -е́й) *neut* child; baby.
дифтери́т diptheria.
дифто́нг diphthong.
диффама́ция libel.
дичь game.
длина́ length. **дли́нный** (-нен, -нна́, -о) long. **дли́тельность** duration. **дли́тельный** long, protracted. **дли́ться** *impf* (*pf* про-) last.
для *prep*+*gen* for; for the sake of; ~ того́, что́бы... in order to.

днев́а́льный *sb* orderly, man on duty. **дневни́к** (-á) diary, journal. **дневно́й** day; daily. **днём** *adv* in the day time; in the afternoon. **дни** *etc.*: see **день**
дни́ще bottom.
ДНК *abbr* (*of* дезоксирибонуклеи́новая кислота́) DNA.
дно (дна; *pl* до́нья, -ьев) bottom.
до *prep*+*gen* (up) to; as far as; until; before; to the point of; до на́шей э́ры ВС; до сих пор till now; до тех пор till then; before; до того́, как before; до того́, что to such an extent that, to the point where; мне не до Гm not in the mood for
доба́вить (-влю) *pf*, **добавля́ть** *impf* (+*acc or gen*) add. **доба́вка** addition; second helping. **добавле́ние** addition; supplement; extra. **доба́вочный** additional.
добега́ть *impf*, **добежа́ть** (-егу́) *pf* +до+*gen* run to, as far as; reach.
добива́ть *impf*, **доби́ть** (-бью, -бьёшь) *pf* finish (off); ~ся +*gen* get, obtain; ~ся своего́ get one's way.
добира́ться *impf of* добра́ться
до́блесть valour.
добра́ться (-беру́сь, -ёшься; -а́лся, -ла́сь, -а́лось) *pf* (*impf* добира́ться) +до+*gen* get to, reach.
добро́ good; э́то не к добру́ it is a bad sign.
добро- *in comb* good-, well-. **доброво́лец** (-льца) volunteer. ~во́льно *adv* voluntarily. ~во́льный voluntary. ~де́тель virtue. ~де́тель-

ный virtuous. **~душие** good nature. **~душный** good-natured. **~желательный** benevolent. **~качественный** of good quality; benign. **~совестный** conscientious.

доброта goodness, kindness. **добротный** of good quality. **добрый** (добр, -а, -о, -ы) good; kind; **будьте добры** +*imper*. please; would you be kind enough to.

добывать *impf*, **добыть** (-буду; добыл, -а, -о) *pf* get, obtain, procure; mine. **добыча** output; mining; booty.

добью *etc*.: *see* **добить**. **доведу** *etc*.: *see* **довести**

довезти (-езу, -езёшь; -вёз, -ла) *pf* (*impf* **довозить**) take (to), carry (to), drive (to).

доверенность warrant; power of attorney. **доверенный** trusted; *sb* agent, proxy. **доверие** trust, confidence. **доверить** *pf* (*impf* **доверять**); **~ся** +*dat* trust in; confide in.

доверху *adv* to the top. **доверчивый** trustful, credulous. **доверять** *impf* of **доверить**; (+*dat*) to trust.

довесок (-ска) makeweight.

довести (-еду, -едёшь; -вёл, -а) *pf*, **доводить** (-ожу, -одишь) *impf* lead, take (to); bring, drive (to). **довод** argument, reason.

довоенный pre-war.

довозить (-ожу, -озишь) *impf* of **довезти**

довольно *adv* enough; quite, fairly. **довольный** satisfied; pleased. **довольство** contentment. **довольствоваться** *impf* (*pf* у**~**) be content.

догадаться *pf*, **догады-**

-ваться *impf* guess; suspect. **догадка** surmise, conjecture. **догадливый** quick-witted.

догма dogma.

догнать (-гоню, -гонишь; -гнал, -á, -о) *pf* (*impf* **догонять**) catch up (with).

договариваться *impf*, **договориться** *pf* come to an agreement; arrange. **договор** (*pl* -ы *or* -á, -ов) agreement; contract; treaty. **договорный** contractual; agreed.

догонять *impf of* **догнать**

догорать *impf*, **догореть** (-рит) *pf* burn out, burn down.

доеду *etc*.: *see* **доехать**. **доезжать** *impf of* **доехать**

доехать (-еду) *pf* (*impf* **доезжать**) +**до**+*gen* reach, arrive at.

дождаться (-дусь, -дёшься; -áлся, -лась, -áлóсь) *pf* +*gen* wait for, wait until.

дождевик (-á) raincoat. **дождевой** rain(y). **дождливый** rainy. **дождь** (-я) *m* rain; **~ идёт** it is raining.

доживать *impf*, **дожить** (-иву, -ивёшь; дожил, -á, -о) *pf* live out; spend. **дожидаться** *impf* +*gen* wait for.

доза dose.

дозволить *pf*, **дозволять** *impf* permit.

дозвониться *pf* get through, reach by telephone.

дозор patrol.

дозревать *impf*, **дозреть** (-éет) *pf* ripen.

доисторический prehistoric.

доить *impf* (*pf* по**~**). milk.

дойти (дойду, -дёшь; дошёл, -шла) *pf* (*impf* **доходить**) +**до**+*gen* reach; get through to.

док dock.

доказа́тельный conclusive. **доказа́тельство** proof, evidence. **доказа́ть** (-ажу́) *pf*, **дока́зывать** *impf* demonstrate, prove.

докати́ться (-ачу́сь, -а́тишься) *pf*, **дока́тываться** *impf* roll; boom; **~до**+*gen* sink into.

докла́д report; lecture. **докладна́я (запи́ска)** report; memo. **докла́дчик** speaker, lecturer. **докла́дывать** *impf of* **доложи́ть**

докрасна́ *adv* to red heat; to redness.

до́ктор (*pl* -а́) doctor. **до́кторский** doctoral. **до́кторша** woman doctor; doctor's wife.

доктри́на doctrine.

докуме́нт document; deed. **документа́льный** documentary. **документа́ция** documentation; documents.

долби́ть (-блю́) *impf* hollow; chisel; repeat; swot up.

долг (*loc* -у́, *pl* -и́) duty; debt; **взять в ~** borrow; **дать в ~** lend.

до́лгий (до́лог, -лга́, -о) long. **до́лго** *adv* long, (for) a long time. **долгове́чный** lasting; durable. **долгожда́нный** long-awaited. **долгоигра́ющая пласти́нка** LP.

долголе́тие longevity. **долголе́тний** of many years; longstanding. **долгосро́чный** long-term.

долгота́ (*pl* -ы) length; longitude.

долево́й lengthwise. **до́лее** *adv* longer.

должа́ть *impf* (*pf* за**~**) borrow.

до́лжен (-жна́) *predic+dat* in debt to; +*inf* obliged; bound; likely; must, have to, ought to;

должно́ быть probably. **должни́к** (-а́), **-ни́ца** debtor. **до́лжное** *sb* due. **должностно́й** official. **до́лжность** (*gen pl* -е́й) post, office; duties. **до́лжный** due, fitting.

доли́на valley.

до́ллар dollar.

доложи́ть¹ (-ожу́, -о́жишь) *pf* (*impf* **докла́дывать**) add.

доложи́ть² (-ожу́, -о́жишь) *pf* (*impf* **докла́дывать**) +*acc or* о+*prep* report; announce.

доло́й *adv* away, off; +*acc* down with!

долото́ (*pl* -а) chisel.

до́лька segment; clove.

до́льше *adv* longer.

до́ля (*gen pl* -е́й) portion; share; lot, fate.

дом (*loc* -у́; *pl* -а́) house; home. **до́ма** *adv* at home. **дома́шн|ий** house; home; domestic; home-made; **~яя хозя́йка** housewife.

до́менн|ый blast-furnace; **~ая печь** blast-furnace.

домини́ровать *impf* dominate, predominate.

домкра́т jack.

до́мна blast-furnace.

домовладе́лец (-льца), **-ли́ца** house-owner; landlord. **домово́дство** housekeeping; domestic science. **домово́й** house; household; housing.

домога́тельство solicitation; bid. **домога́ться** *impf* +*gen* solicit, bid for.

домо́й *adv* home, homewards.

домохозя́йка housewife. **домрабо́тница** domestic servant, maid.

доне́льзя *adv* in the extreme.

донесе́ние dispatch, report. **донести́** (-су́, -сёшь; -нёс, -сла́) *pf* (*impf* **доноси́ть**) report, announce; +*dat* inform; **на**+*acc* inform; ~**сь** be heard; +**до**+*gen* reach.

до́низу *adv* to the bottom; **све́рху** ~ from top to bottom.

до́нор donor.

доно́с denunciation, information. **доноси́ть(ся** (-ношу́(сь, -но́сишь(ся) *impf of* **донести́(сь**

доно́счик informer.

донско́й Don.

доны́не *adv* hitherto.

до́нья *etc.*: *see* дно

до н.э. *abbr* (*of* до на́шей э́ры) ВС.

допла́та additional payment, excess fare. **доплати́ть** (-ачу́, -а́тишь) *pf*, **допла́чивать** *impf* pay in addition; pay the rest.

допо́длинно *adv* for certain. **допо́длинный** authentic, genuine.

дополне́ние supplement, addition; (*gram*) object. **дополни́тельно** *adv* in addition. **дополни́тельный** supplementary, additional. **допо́лнить** *pf*, **дополня́ть** *impf* supplement.

допра́шивать *impf*, **допроси́ть** (-ошу́, -о́сишь) *pf* interrogate. **допро́с** interrogation.

до́пуск right of entry, admittance. **допуска́ть** *impf*, **допусти́ть** (-ущу́, -у́стишь) *pf* admit; permit; tolerate; suppose. **допусти́мый** permissible, acceptable. **допуще́ние** assumption.

дореволюцио́нный pre-revolutionary.

доро́га road; way; journey; route; **по доро́ге** on the way.

до́рого *adv* dear, dearly. **дорогови́зна** high prices.

дорого́й (до́рог, -а́, -о) dear.

доро́дный portly.

дорожа́ть *impf* (*pf* вз~, по~) rise in price, go up. **доро́же** *comp of* до́рого, до́рого́й. **дорожи́ть** (-жу́) *impf* +*instr* value.

доро́жка path; track; lane; runway; strip, runner; stair-carpet. **доро́жный** road; high-way; travelling.

доса́да annoyance. **досади́ть** (-ажу́) *pf*, **досажда́ть** *impf* +*dat* annoy. **доса́дный** annoying. **доса́довать** be annoyed (**на**+*acc* with).

доска́ (*acc* до́ску) *pl* -и, -со́к, -ска́м) board; slab; plaque.

досло́вный literal; word-for-word.

досмо́тр inspection.

доспе́хи *pl* armour.

досро́чный ahead of time, early.

достава́ть(ся (-таю́(сь, -ёшь(ся) *impf of* доста́ть(ся

доста́вить (-влю) *pf*, **доставля́ть** *impf* deliver; supply; cause, give. **доста́вка** delivery.

доста́ну *etc.*: *see* доста́ть

доста́ток (-тка) sufficiency; prosperity. **доста́точно** *adv* enough, sufficiently. **доста́точный** sufficient; adequate. **доста́ть** (-а́ну) *pf* (*impf* **достава́ть**) take (out); get, obtain; +*gen* or до+*gen* touch; reach; *impers* suffice; ~**ся** +*dat* be inherited by; fall to the lot of; **ему́ доста́нется** he'll catch it.

достига́ть *impf*, **дости́гнуть, дости́чь** (-и́гну -сти́г) *pf* +*gen* reach, achieve; attain or до+*gen* reach. **достиже́ние** achievement.

досто́верный reliable, trustworthy; authentic.

досто́инство dignity; merit; value. **досто́йный** deserved; suitable; worthy; +*gen* worthy of.

достопримеча́тельность sight, notable place.

достоя́ние property.

до́ступ access. **досту́пный** accessible; approachable; reasonable; available.

досу́г leisure, (spare) time. **досу́жий** leisure; idle.

до́сыта *adv* to satiety.

досье́ *neut indecl* dossier.

досяга́емый attainable.

дота́ция grant, subsidy.

дотла́ utterly; to the ground.

дотра́гиваться *impf*, **дотро́нуться** (-нусь) *pf* +**до**+*gen* touch.

дотя́гивать *impf*, **дотяну́ть** (-яну́, -я́нешь) *pf* draw, drag, stretch out; hold out; live; put off; **~ся** stretch, reach; drag on.

до́хлый dead; sickly. **до́хнуть**[1] (-нет; дох) *pf* из~, по~, с~) die; kick the bucket. **дохну́ть**[2] (-ну́, -нёшь) *pf* draw a breath.

дохо́д income; revenue. **доходи́ть** (-ожу́, -о́дишь) *impf of* **дойти́**. **дохо́дный** profitable. **дохо́дчивый** intelligible.

доце́нт reader, senior lecturer.

до́чиста *adv* clean; completely.

до́чка daughter. **дочь** (-чери, *instr* -черью; *pl* -чери, -чере́й, *instr* -черьми́) daughter.

дошёл *etc.: see* **дойти́**

дошко́льник, **-ница** child under school age. **дошко́льный** pre-school.

доща́тый plank, board. **доще́чка** small plank, board; plaque.

доя́рка milkmaid.

драгоце́нность jewel; treasure; *pl* jewellery; valuables. **драгоце́нный** precious.

дразни́ть (-ню́, -нишь) *impf* tease.

дра́ка fight.

драко́н dragon.

дра́ма drama. **драмати́ческий** dramatic. **драмату́рг** playwright. **драматурги́я** dramatic art; plays.

драп thick woollen cloth.

драпиро́вка draping; curtain; hangings. **драпиро́вщик** upholsterer.

драть (деру́, -рёшь; драл, -а́, -о) *impf* (*pf* вы~, за~, со~) tear (up); irritate; make off; flog; **~ся** fight.

дребезги́; **в ~** to smithereens. **дребезжа́ть** (-жи́т) *impf* jingle, tinkle.

древеси́на wood; timber. **древе́сный** wood; **~ у́голь** charcoal.

дре́вко (*pl* -и, -ов) pole, staff; shaft.

древнегре́ческий ancient Greek. **древнеевре́йский** Hebrew. **древнеру́сский** Old Russian. **дре́вний** ancient; aged. **дре́вность** antiquity.

дрейф drift; leeway. **дрейфова́ть** *impf* drift.

дрема́ть (-млю́, -млешь) *impf* doze; slumber. **дремо́та** drowsiness.

дрему́чий dense.

дрессиро́ванный trained; performing. **дрессирова́ть** *impf* (*pf* вы~) train; school. **дрессиро́вка** training. **дрессиро́вщик** trainer.

дроби́ть (-блю́) *impf* (*pf* раз~) break up, smash; crush;

~ся break to pieces, smash.
дробови́к (-á) shot-gun.
дробь (small) shot; drumming; fraction. **дро́бный** fractional.

дрова́ (дров) *pl* firewood.

дрогну́ть (-ну) *pf*, **дрожа́ть** (-жу́) *impf* tremble; shiver; quiver.

дро́жжи (-éй) *pl* yeast.

дрожь shivering, trembling.

дрозд (-á) thrush.

дро́ссель *m* throttle, choke.

дро́тик javelin, dart.

друг[1] (*pl* -узья́, -зе́й) friend. **друг**[2] (*gen* друга (дру́гу)) each other, one another. **друго́й** other, another; different; **на ~ день** (the) next day. **дру́жба** friendship. **дружелю́бный**, **дру́жеский**, **дру́жественный** friendly. **дружи́ть** (-жу́, -у́жишь) *impf* be friends; **~ся** (*pf* по~ся) make friends. **дру́жный** (-жен, -жна́, -о) amicable, harmonious; simultaneous, concerted.

дря́блый (дрябл, -á, -о) flabby.

дря́зги (-зг) *pl* squabbles.

дрянно́й worthless; good-for-nothing. **дрянь** rubbish.

дряхле́ть (-éю) *impf* (*pf* o~) become decrepit. **дря́хлый** (-хл, -лá, -о) decrepit, senile.

дуб (*pl* -ы́) oak; blockhead. **дуби́на** club, cudgel; blockhead. **дуби́нка** truncheon, baton.

дублёнка sheepskin coat.

дублёр understudy. **дублика́т** duplicate. **дубли́ровать** duplicate; understudy; dub.

дубо́вый oak; coarse; clumsy.

дуга́ (*pl* -и) arc; arch.

ду́дка pipe, fife.

ду́ло muzzle; barrel.

ду́ма thought; Duma; council.

ду́мать *impf* (*pf* по~) think; **+inf** think of, intend. **~ться** *impf* (*impers* +*dat*) seem.

дунове́ние puff, breath. **ду́нуть** (-ну) *pf* of **дуть**

дупло́ (*pl* -а, -пел) hollow; hole; cavity.

ду́ра, дура́к (-á) fool. **дура́чить** (-чу) *impf* (*pf* o~) fool, dupe; **~ся** play the fool. **дуре́ть** (-е́ю) *impf* (*pf* o~) grow stupid.

дурма́н narcotic; intoxicant. **дурма́нить** *impf* (*pf* o~) stupefy.

дурно́й (-рен, -рнá, -о) bad; evil; ugly; **мне ду́рно** I feel faint, sick. **дурнота́** faintness; nausea.

ду́тый hollow; inflated. **дуть** (ду́ю) *impf* (*pf* вы́~, по~, ду́нуть) blow; **ду́ет** there is a draught. **дутьё** glass-blowing. **ду́ться** (ду́юсь) *impf* pout; sulk.

дух spirit; spirits; heart; mind; breath; ghost; smell; **в ~е** in a good mood; **не в моём ~е** not to my taste; **ни слу́ху ни ~у** no news, not a word. **духи́** (-о́в) *pl* scent, perfume. **Ду́хов день** Whit Monday. **духове́нство** clergy. **духови́дец** (-дца) clairvoyant; medium. **духо́вка** oven. **духо́вный** spiritual; ecclesiastical. **духово́й** wind. **духота́** stuffiness, closeness.

душ shower(-bath).

душа́ (*acc* -у; *pl* -и) soul; heart; feeling; spirit; inspiration; **в душе́** inwardly; at heart; **от всей души́** with all one's heart. **душева́я** *sb* shower-room.

душевнобольно́й mentally ill, insane; *sb* mental patient.

lunatic. **душе́вный** mental; sincere, cordial.

души́стый fragrant; ~ горо́шек sweet pea(s).

души́ть (-шу́, -шишь) *impf* (*pf* за~) strangle; stifle, smother.

души́ться (-шу́сь, -шишься) *impf* (*pf* на~) use, put on, perfume.

ду́шный (-шен, -шна́, -о) stuffy, close.

дуэ́ль duel.

дуэ́т duet.

ды́бом *adv* on end; **у меня́ во́лосы вста́ли** ~ my hair stood on end. **дыбы́: станови́ться** на ~ rear; resist.

дым (*loc* -у́, *pl* -ы́) smoke. **дыми́ть** (-млю́) *impf* (*pf* на~) smoke; ~**ся** smoke, steam, billow. **ды́мка** haze. **ды́мный** smoky. **дымово́й** smoke; ~**ая труба́** flue, chimney. **дымо́к** (-мка́) puff of smoke. **дымохо́д** flue.

ды́ня melon.

дыра́ (*pl* -ы), **ды́рка** (*gen pl* -рок) hole; gap.

дыха́ние breathing; breath. **дыха́тельн|ый** respiratory; breathing; ~**ое го́рло** windpipe. **дыша́ть** (-шу́, -шишь) *impf* breathe.

дья́вол devil. **дья́вольский** devilish, diabolical.

дьяко́н (*pl* -а́) deacon.

дю́жина dozen.

дюйм inch.

дю́на dune.

дя́дя (*gen pl* -ей) *m* uncle.

дя́тел (-тла) woodpecker.

Е

ева́нгелие gospel; the Gospels.

евангели́ческий evangelical.

евре́й, евре́йка Jew; Hebrew. **евре́йский** Jewish.

Евро́па Europe. **европе́ец** (-е́йца) European. **европе́йский** European.

Еги́пет Egypt. **еги́петский** Egyptian. **египтя́нин** (*pl* -я́не, -я́н) **египтя́нка** Egyptian.

его́ *see* **он, оно́**; *pron* his; its.

еда́ food; meal.

едва́ *adv & conj* hardly; just; scarcely; ~ **ли** hardly; ~ **(ли) не** almost, all but.

еди́м etc.: *see* **есть**[1]

едине́ние unity. **едини́ца** (figure) one; unit; individual. **еди́ничный** single; individual.

едино- *in comb* mono-, uni-; one; co-. **единобра́чие** monogamy. ~**вла́стие** autocracy. ~**вре́менно** *adv* only once; simultaneously. ~**гла́сие, ~ду́шие** unanimity. ~**гла́сный, ~ду́шный** unanimous. ~**кро́вный брат** half-brother. ~**мы́слие** like-mindedness; agreement. ~**мы́шленник** like-minded person. ~**утро́бный брат** half-brother.

еди́нственно *adv* only. **еди́нственный** only, sole. **еди́нство** unity. **еди́ный** one; single; united.

е́дкий (е́док, едка́, -о) caustic; pungent.

едо́к (-а́) mouth, head; eater.

е́ду *see* **е́хать**.

её *see* **она́**; *pron* her, hers; its.

ёж (ежа́) hedgehog.

еже- *in comb* every; -ly. **ежего́дник** annual, year-book. ~**го́дный** annual. ~**дне́вный** daily. ~**ме́сячник** monthly. ~**ме́сячный** monthly. ~**неде́льник, ~неде́льный** weekly.

ежеви́ка (*no pl; usu collect*)

blackberry; blackberries; black-berry bush.

ёжели *conj* if.

ёжиться (ёжусь) *impf* (*pf* съ~) huddle up; shrink away.

езда́ ride, riding; drive, driving; journey. **éздить** (éзжу) *impf* go; ride, drive; ~ верхóм ride. **ездóк** (-á) rider.

ей *see* онá

ей-бóгу *int* really! truly!

ел *etc.: see* есть[1]

éле *adv* scarcely; only just. **éле-éле** *emphatic variant of* éле

ёлка fir-tree, spruce; Christmas tree. **ёлочка** herringbone pattern. **ёлочный** Christmas-tree. **ель** fir-tree; spruce.

ем *etc.: see* есть[1]

ёмкий capacious. **ёмкость** capacity.

ему́ *see* он, онó

епи́скоп bishop.

éресь heresy. **ерети́к** (-á) heretic. **ерети́ческий** heretical.

ёрзать *impf* fidget.

ероши́ть (-шу) *impf* (*pf* взъ~) ruffle, rumple.

ерунда́ nonsense.

éсли *conj* if; ~ бы if only; ~ бы не but for, if it were not for; ~ не unless.

ест *see* есть[1]

есте́ственно *adv* naturally. **есте́ственный** natural. **есте́ство** nature; essence. **естествозна́ние** (natural) science.

есть[1] (ем, ешь, ест, еди́м; ел) *impf* (*pf* съ~) eat; corrode, eat away.

есть[2] *see* быть; is, are; there is, there are; у меня́ ~ I have.

ефре́йтор lance-corporal.

éхать (éду) *impf* (*pf* по~) go; ride, drive; travel; ~ верхóм ride.

ехи́дный malicious, spiteful.

ешь *see* есть[1]

ещё *adv* still; yet; (some) more; any more; yet, further; again; +*comp* still; even; всё ~ still; ~ бы! of course! oh yes! can you ask?; ~ не, нет ~ not yet; ~ раз once more, again; покá ~ for the present, for the time being.

ею́ *see* онá

Ж

ж *conj: see* же

жáба toad.

жáбра (*gen pl* -бр) gill.

жáворонок (-нка) lark.

жáдничать *impf* be greedy; be mean. **жáдность** greed; meanness. **жáдный** (-ден, -дна́, -о) greedy; avid; mean.

жáжда thirst; +*gen* thirst, craving for. **жáждать** (-ду) *impf* thirst, yearn.

жаке́т, жаке́тка jacket.

жале́ть (-éю) *impf* (*pf* по~) pity, feel sorry for; regret; +*acc or gen* grudge.

жáлить (*pf* у~) sting, bite.

жáлкий (-лок, -лка́, -о) pitiful. **жáлко** *predic: see* жаль

жáло sting.

жáлоба complaint. **жáлобный** plaintive.

жáлованье salary. **жáловать** *impf* (*pf* по~) +*acc or dat* of person, *instr or acc* of thing grant, bestow on; ~ся complain (на+*acc* of, about).

жáлостливый compassionate. **жáлостный** piteous, compassionate. **жáлость** pity. **жаль, жáлко** *predic, impers* (it is) a pity; +*dat* it grieves;

+*gen* grudge; **как ~** what a pity; **мне ~ его́** I'm sorry for him.

жалюзи́ *neut indecl* Venetian blind.

жанр genre.

жар (*loc* -ý) heat; heat of the day; fever; (high) temperature; ardour. **жара́** heat; hot weather.

жарго́н slang.

жа́реный roast; grilled; fried. **жа́рить** *impf* (*pf* за~, из~) roast; grill; fry; scorch, burn; **~ся** roast, fry. **жа́рк|ий** (-рок, -рка́, -о) hot; passionate; **~ое** *sb* roast (meat). **жаро́вня** (*gen pl* -вен) brazier. **жар-пти́ца** Firebird. **жа́рче** *comp of* **жа́ркий**

жа́тва harvest. **жать**[1] (жну, жнёшь) *impf* (*pf* с~) reap, cut.

жать[2] (жму, жмёшь) *impf* press, squeeze; pinch; oppress. *see* **жечь**

жва́чка chewing, rumination; cud; chewing-gum. **жва́чн|ый** ruminant; **~ое** *sb* ruminant.

жгу *etc.: see* **жечь**

жгут (-á) plait; tourniquet.

жгу́чий burning. **жёг** *etc.: see* **жечь**

ждать (жду, ждёшь; -ал, -á, -о) *impf* +*gen* wait (for); expect.

же, ж *conj* but; and; however; also; *partl* giving emphasis or expressing identity; **мне же ка́жется** it seems to me, however; **сего́дня же** this very day; **что же ты де́лаешь?** what on earth are you doing?

жева́тельная рези́нка chewing-gum. **жева́ть** (жую́, жуёшь) *impf* chew; ruminate.

жезл (-á) rod; staff.

жела́ние wish, desire. **жела́нный** longed-for; beloved.

жела́тельный desirable; advisable. **жела́ть** *impf* (*pf* по~) +*gen* wish for; desire; want.

желе́ *neut indecl* jelly.

железа́ (*pl* желе́зы, -лёз, -за́м) gland; *pl* tonsils.

железнодоро́жник railwayman. **железнодоро́жный** railway. **желе́зн|ый** iron; **~ая доро́га** railway. **желе́зо** iron.

железобето́н reinforced concrete.

жёлоб (*pl* -á) gutter. **желобо́к** (-бка́) groove, channel, flute.

желте́ть (-е́ю) *impf* (*pf* по~) turn yellow; be yellow. **желто́к** (-тка́) yolk. **желту́ха** jaundice. **жёлтый** (жёлт, -á, жёлто) yellow.

желу́док (-дка) stomach. **желу́дочный** stomach; gastric.

жёлудь (*gen pl* -е́й) *m* acorn.

жёлчный bilious; gall; irritable. **жёлчь** bile, gall.

жема́ниться *impf* mince, put on airs. **жема́нный** mincing, affected. **жема́нство** affectedness.

же́мчуг (*pl* -á) pearl(s). **жемчу́жина** pearl. **жемчу́жный** pearl(y).

жена́ (*pl* жёны) wife. **жена́тый** married.

жени́ть (-ню́, -нишь) *impf & pf* (*pf* по~) marry. **жени́тьба** marriage. **жени́ться** (-ню́сь, -нишься) *impf & pf* (+**на**+*prep*) marry, get married (to). **жени́х** (-á) fiancé; bridegroom.

же́нский women's; feminine; female. **же́нственный** womanly, feminine. **же́нщина** woman.

жердь (*gen pl* -е́й) pole; stake.

жеребёнок (-нка; *pl* -бя́та,

-бя́т) foal. **жеребе́ц** (-бца́) stallion.

жеребьёвка casting of lots.

жерло́ (pl -a) muzzle; crater.

жёрнов (pl -á, -о́в) millstone.

же́ртва sacrifice; victim. **же́ртвенный** sacrificial. **же́ртвовать** impf (pf по∼) present, make a donation (of); +instr sacrifice.

жест gesture. **жестикули́ровать** impf gesticulate.

жёсткий (-ток, -тка́, -о) hard, tough; rigid, strict.

жесто́кий (-то́к, -á, -о) cruel; severe. **жесто́кость** cruelty.

жесть tin(-plate). **жестяно́й** tin.

жето́н medal; counter; token.

жечь (жгу, жжёшь; жёг, жгла) impf (pf с∼) burn; ∼ся burn, sting; burn o.s.

живи́тельный invigorating. **жи́вность** poultry, fowl. **живо́й** (жив, -á, -о) living, alive; lively; vivid; brisk; animated; poignant; bright; **на ∼у́ю ни́тку** hastily, anyhow; **шить на ∼у́ю ни́тку** tack. **живопи́сец** (-сца) painter. **живопи́сный** picturesque. **живопись** painting. **жи́вость** liveliness.

живо́т (-á) abdomen; stomach. **животново́дство** animal husbandry. **живо́тное** sb animal. **живо́тный** animal.

живу́ etc.: see **жить**. **живу́чий** hardy. **живьём** adv alive.

жи́дкий (-док, -дка́, -о) liquid; watery; weak; sparse; ∼ий криста́лл liquid crystal. **жи́дкость** liquid, fluid; wateriness, weakness. **жи́жа** sludge; slush; liquid. **жи́же** comp of **жи́дкий**

жи́зненный life, of life; vital;

living; ∼ у́ровень standard of living. **жизнеописа́ние** biography. **жизнера́достный** cheerful. **жизнеспосо́бный** capable of living; viable. **жизнь** life.

жи́ла vein; tendon, sinew.

жиле́т, жиле́тка waistcoat.

жиле́ц (-льца́), **жили́ца** lodger; tenant; inhabitant.

жили́ще dwelling, abode. **жили́щный** housing; living.

жи́лка vein; fibre; streak.

жило́й dwelling; habitable; ∼о́й дом dwelling house; block of flats; ∼а́я пло́щадь, жилпло́щадь floor-space; housing, accommodation. **жильё** habitation; dwelling.

жир (loc -ý, pl -ы́) fat; grease. **жире́ть** (-е́ю) impf (pf по∼, раз∼) grow fat. **жи́рный** (-рен, -рна́, -о) fatty; greasy; rich. **жирово́й** fatty; fat.

жира́ф giraffe.

жите́йский worldly; everyday. **жи́тель** m inhabitant; dweller. **жи́тельство** residence. **жи́тница** granary. **жи́то** corn, cereal. **жить** (живу́, -вёшь; жил, -á, -о) impf live. **житьё** life; existence; habitation.

жму etc.: see **жать[2]**

жму́риться impf (pf за∼) screw up one's eyes, frown.

жни́вье (pl -ья, -ьев) stubble (-field). **жну** etc.: see **жать[1]**

жоке́й jockey.

жонглёр juggler.

жрать (жру, жрёшь; -ал, -á, -о) guzzle.

жре́бий lot; fate, destiny; ∼ бро́шен the die is cast.

жрец priest. **жри́ца** priestess.

жужжа́ть (-жжу́) hum, buzz; drone; whiz(z).

жук (-á) beetle.

жу́лик petty thief; cheat. **жу́льничать** *impf* (*pf* с~) cheat.

жура́вль (-я́) *m* crane.

жури́ть *impf* reprove.

журна́л magazine, periodical. **журнали́ст** journalist. **журнали́стика** journalism.

журча́ние babble; murmur. **журча́ть** (-чи́т) *impf* babble, murmur.

жу́ткий (-ток, -тка́, -о) uncanny; terrible, terrifying. **жу́тко** *adv* terrifyingly; terribly, awfully.

жую́ *etc.*: *see* жева́ть

жюри́ *neut indecl* judges.

З

за *prep* **I.** +*acc* (*indicating motion or action*) *or instr* (*indicating rest or state*) behind; beyond; across, the other side of; at; to; **за́ город, за́ городом** out of town; **за рубежо́м** abroad; **сесть за роя́ль** sit down at the piano; **сиде́ть за роя́лем** sit at the piano; **за у́гол, за угло́м** round the corner. **II.** +*acc* after; over; during, in the space of; by; for; to; **за ва́ше здоро́вье!** your health!; **вести́ за́ руку** lead by the hand; **далеко́ за́ полночь** long after midnight; **за два дня до**+*gen* two days before; **за́ три киломе́тра от дере́вни** three kilometres from the village; **плати́ть за биле́т** pay for a ticket; **за после́днее вре́мя** lately. **III.** +*instr* after; for, because of; at, during; **год за го́дом** year after year; **идти́ за молоко́м**

go for milk; **за обе́дом** at dinner.

заба́ва amusement; game; fun. **забавля́ть** *impf* amuse; ~ся amuse o.s. **заба́вный** amusing, funny.

забасто́вать *pf* strike; go on strike. **забасто́вка** strike. **забасто́вщик** striker.

забве́ние oblivion.

забе́г heat, race. **забега́ть** *impf*, **забежа́ть** (-егу́) *pf* run up; +к+*dat* drop in on; ~ вперёд run ahead; anticipate. **за|бере́менеть** (-ею) *pf* become pregnant.

заберу́ *etc.*: *see* забра́ть

забива́ние jamming. **забива́ть(ся** *impf of* заби́ть(ся¹

забинтова́ть *pf*, **забинто́вывать** *impf* bandage.

забира́ть(ся *impf of* забра́ть(ся

заби́тый downtrodden. **заби́ть**¹ (-бью́, -бьёшь) *pf* (*impf* забива́ть) drive in, hammer in; score; seal, block up; obstruct; choke; jam; cram; beat up; beat; ~ся hide, take refuge; become cluttered *or* clogged; +в+*acc* get into, penetrate. **за|би́ть(ся²** *pf* begin to beat. **забия́ка** *m* & *f* squabbler; bully.

заблаговре́менно *adv* in good time; well in advance. **заблаговре́менный** timely.

заблесте́ть (-ещу́, -ести́шь *or* -е́щешь) *pf* begin to shine, glitter, glow.

заблуди́ться (-ужу́сь, -у́дишься) *pf* get lost. **заблу́дший** lost, stray. **заблужда́ться** *impf* be mistaken. **заблужде́ние** error; delusion.

забо́й (pit-)face.

заболева́емость sickness

rate. **заболева́ние** sickness, illness; falling ill. **заболева́ть**[1] *impf*, **заболе́ть**[1] (-е́ю) *pf* fall ill; +*instr* go down with. **заболева́ть**[2] (-ли́т) *pf* (begin to) ache, hurt.

забо́р[1] fence.

забо́р[2] taking away; obtaining on credit.

забо́та concern; care; trouble(s). **забо́тить** (-о́чу) *impf* (*pf* о~) trouble, worry; ~**ся** *impf* (*pf* по~) worry; take care (о+*prep* of); take trouble; care. **забо́тливый** solicitous, thoughtful.

за|брако́вать *pf*.

забра́сывать *impf of* **забро́-**
сать, забро́сить

забра́ть (-беру́, -берёшь; -а́л, -а́, -о) *pf* (*impf* **забира́ть**) take; take away; seize; appropriate; ~**ся** climb; get to, into.

забреда́ть *impf*, **забрести́** (-еду́, -едёшь; -ёл, -а́) *pf* stray, wander; drop in.

за|брони́ровать *pf*.

забро́сать *pf* (*impf* **забра́-**
сывать) fill up; bespatter, deluge. **забро́сить** (-о́шу) *pf* (*impf* **забра́сывать**) throw; abandon; neglect. **забро́-**
шенный neglected; deserted.

забры́згать *pf*, **забры́згивать** *impf* splash, bespatter.

забыва́ть *impf*, **забы́ть** (-бу́ду) *pf* forget; ~**ся** forget o.s.; lose consciousness; forget o.s. **забы́вчивый** forgetful. **за-**
бытьё oblivion; drowsiness.

забью́ *etc.*: *see* **забить**

зава́ливать *impf*, **завали́ть** (-лю́, -лишь) *pf* block up; pile; cram; overload; knock down; make a mess of; ~**ся** fall; collapse; tip up.

зава́ривать *impf*, **завари́ть**

(-арю́, -а́ришь) *pf* make; brew; weld. **зава́рка** brewing; brew; welding.

заведе́ние establishment. **за-**
ве́довать *impf* +*instr* manage.

заве́домо *adv* wittingly. **за-**
ве́домый *notorious*, undoubted.

заведу́ *etc.*: *see* **завести́**

заве́дующий *sb* (+*instr*) manager; head.

завезти́ (-зу́, -зёшь; -ёз, -ла́) *pf* (*impf* **завози́ть**) convey, deliver.

за|вербова́ть *pf*.

заве́ритель *m* witness. **заве́-**
рить *pf* (*impf* **заверя́ть**) assure; certify; witness.

заверну́ть (-ну́, -нёшь) *pf* (*impf* **завёртывать, завора́-**
чивать) wrap, wrap up; roll up; screw tight, screw up; (off); drop in, call in.

заверте́ться (-рчу́сь, -ртишь-**
ся**) *pf* begin to turn *or* spin; lose one's head.

завёртывать *impf of* **за-**
верну́ть

заверша́ть *impf*, **заверши́ть** (-шу́) *pf* complete, conclude. **заверше́ние** completion; end.

заверя́ть *impf of* **заве́рить**

заве́са veil, screen. **заве́сить** (-е́шу) *pf* (*impf* **заве́шивать**) curtain (off).

завести́ (-еду́, -ёшь; -вёл, -а́) *pf* (*impf* **заводи́ть**) take, bring; drop off; start up; acquire; introduce; wind (up), crank; ~**сь** *pf*; appear; be established; start.

заве́т behest, bidding, ordinance; Testament. **заве́тный** cherished; secret.

заве́шивать *impf of* **заве́сить**

завеща́ние will, testament.

завеща́ть bequeath.

завзя́тый inveterate, out-and-out.

завива́ть(ся *impf of* зави́ть(ся. зави́вка waving; curling; wave.

зави́дно *impers+dat*: мне ~ I feel envious. зави́дный enviable. зави́довать *impf* (*pf* по~) +*dat* envy.

завинти́ть (-нчу́) *pf*, зави́нчивать screw up.

зави́сеть (-и́шу) *impf* +от+*gen* depend on. зави́симость f dependence. в зави́симости от depending on, subject to. зави́симый dependent.

зави́стливый envious. за́висть f envy.

завито́й (за́вит, -а́, -о) curled, waved. завито́к (-тка́) curl, lock; flourish. зави́ть (-вью́, -вьёшь; -и́л, -а́, -о) *pf* (*impf* завива́ть) curl, wave; twine; ~ся curl, wave, twine; have one's hair curled.

завладева́ть *impf*, завладе́ть (-е́ю) *pf* +*instr* take possession of; seize.

завлека́тельный alluring; fascinating. завлека́ть *impf*, завле́чь (-еку́, -ечёшь; -лёк, -ла́) *pf* lure; fascinate.

заво́д[1] factory; works; stud-farm.

заво́д[2] winding mechanism. заводи́ть(ся (-ожу́(сь, -о́дишь(ся) *impf of* завести́. заво́дный clockwork; winding; cranking.

заводско́й factory; *sb* factory worker. заво́дчик factory owner.

за́водь f backwater.

завоева́ние winning; conquest; achievement. завоева́тель *m* conqueror. завое-

ва́ть (-оюю) *pf*, завоёвывать *impf* conquer; win, gain; try to get.

завожу́ *etc.: see* заводи́ть, завози́ть

заво́з delivery; carriage. завози́ть (-ожу́, -о́зишь) *impf of* завезти́

завора́чивать *impf of* заверну́ть. заворо́т turn, turning; sharp bend.

завою́ *etc.: see* завы́ть.

завсегда́ *adv* always. завсегда́тай habitué, frequenter.

за́втра tomorrow. за́втрак breakfast; lunch. за́втракать *impf* (*pf* по~) have breakfast; have lunch. за́втрашний tomorrow's; ~ день tomorrow.

завыва́ть *impf*, завы́ть (-во́ю) *pf* (begin to) howl.

завяза́ть (-яжу́, -я́жешь) *pf* (*impf* завя́зывать) tie, tie up; start; ~ся start; arise; (*of fruit*) set. завя́зка string, lace; start; opening.

за|вя́знуть (-ну; -я́з) *pf*. завя́зывать(ся *impf of* завяза́ть(ся

за|вя́нуть (-ну; -я́л) *pf*.

загада́ть (-а́ю) *pf*, зага́дывать *impf* think of; plan ahead; guess at the future; ~ зага́дку ask a riddle. зага́дка riddle; enigma. зага́дочный enigmatic, mysterious.

зага́р sunburn, tan.

за|гаси́ть (-ашу́, -а́сишь) *pf*. за|га́снуть (-ну) *pf*.

загво́здка snag; difficulty.

заги́б fold; exaggeration. загиба́ть *impf of* загну́ть. за|гипнотизи́ровать *pf*.

загла́вие title; heading. загла́вный title; ~ая бу́ква capital letter.

загла́дить (-а́жу) *pf*, загла́-

живáть *impf* iron, iron out; make up for; expiate; **~ся** iron out, become smooth; fade.

за|глóхнуть (-ну; -глóх) *pf.*

заглушáть *impf*, заглушúть (-шý) *pf* drown, muffle; jam; suppress, stifle; alleviate.

заглядéнье lovely sight. за|глядéться (-яжýсь) *pf*, заглядываться *impf* на+*acc* stare at; be lost in admiration of. заглядывать *impf*, заглянýть (-нý, -нешь) *pf* peep; drop in.

загнáть (-гоню, -гóнишь; -áл, -á, -о) *pf* (*impf* загонять) drive in, drive home; drive; exhaust.

загнивáние decay; suppuration. загнивáть *impf*, загнúть (-ию, -иёшь; -úл, -á, -о) *pf* rot; decay; fester.

загнýть (-нý, -нёшь) *pf* (*impf* загибáть) turn up, turn down; bend.

заговáривать *impf*, заговорúть *pf* begin to speak; tire out with talk; cast a spell over; protect with a charm (*от* against). зáговор plot; spell. заговóрщик conspirator.

заголóвок (-вка) title; heading; headline.

загóн enclosure, pen; driving in. загонять¹ *impf* of загнáть. загонять² *pf* tire out; work to death.

загорáживать *impf* of загородúть.

загорáть *impf*, загорéть (-рю) *pf* become sunburnt; **~ся** catch fire; blaze; *impers*+*dat* want very much. загорéлый sunburnt.

загородúть (-рожý, -рóдишь) *pf* (*impf* загорáживать) enclose, fence in; obstruct. загорóдка fence, enclosure.

зáгородный suburban; country.

заготáвливать *impf*, заготовлять *impf*, заготóвить (-влю) *pf* lay in (a stock of); store; prepare. заготóвка (State) procurement, purchase; laying in.

заградúть (-ажý) *pf*, загражáть *impf* block, obstruct; bar. заграждéние obstruction; barrier.

заграницa abroad, foreign parts. заграничный foreign.

загребáть *impf*, загрестú (-ебý, -ебёшь; -ёб, -лá) *pf* rake up, gather; rake in.

загрúвок (-вка) withers; nape (of the neck).

за|гримировáть *pf.*

загромождáть *impf*, загромоздúть (-зжý) *pf* block up, encumber; cram.

загружáть *impf*, за|грузúть (-ужý, -ýзишь) *pf* load; feed; **~ся** load up with, take on. загрýзка loading, feeding; charge, load, capacity.

за|грунтовáть *pf.*

загрустúть (-ущý) *pf* grow sad.

загрязнéние pollution. за|грязнúть *pf*, загрязнять *impf* soil; pollute; **~ся** become dirty.

зáгс *abbr* (*of* (отдéл) зáписи áктов граждáнского состоя́ния) registry office.

загубúть (-блю, -бишь) *pf* ruin; squander, waste.

загуля́ть *pf*, загýливать *impf* take to drink.

за|густéть *pf.*

зад (*loc* -ý; *pl* -ы́) back; hindquarters; buttocks; **~ом** наперёд back to front.

задавáть(ся (-даю́(сь) *impf* of задáть(ся

задави́ть (-влю́, -вишь) *pf* crush; run over.

задади́м *etc.*, **зада́м** *etc.*: *see* **зада́ть**

зада́ние task, job.

зада́тки (-тков) *pl* abilities, promise.

зада́ток (-тка) deposit, advance.

зада́ть (-а́м, -а́шь, -а́ст, -ади́м; за́дал, -á, -о) *pf* (*impf* **задава́ть**) set; give; ~ **вопро́с** ask a question; ~**ся** turn out well; succeed; ~**ся мы́слью, це́лью** make up one's mind. **зада́ча** problem; task.

задвига́ть *impf*, **задви́нуть** (-ну) *pf* bolt; bar; push; ~**ся** shut; slide. **задви́жка** bolt; catch.

задво́рки (-рок) *pl* back yard; backwoods.

задева́ть *impf of* **заде́ть**

заде́лать *pf*, **заде́лывать** *impf* do up; block up, close up.

заде́ну *etc.*: *see* **заде́ть**. **заде́рживать** *impf of* **задерну́ть**

задержа́ние detention. **задержа́ть** (-жу́, -жишь) *pf*, **заде́рживать** *impf* delay; withhold; arrest; ~**ся** stay too long; be delayed. **заде́ржка** delay.

задёрнуть (-ну) *pf* (*impf* **задёргивать**) pull; draw.

задеру́ *etc.*: *see* **задра́ть**

заде́ть (-е́ну) *pf* (*impf* **задева́ть**) brush (against); graze; offend; catch (against).

задира́ *m & f* bully; troublemaker. **задира́ть** *impf of* **задра́ть**

за́дн|**ий** back, rear; **дать** ~**ий ход** reverse; ~**яя мысль** ulterior motive; ~**ий план** background; ~**ий прохо́д** anus.

за́дник back; backdrop.

задо́лго *adv* +**до**+*gen* before.

задолжа́ть *pf*. **задо́лженность** debts.

задо́р fervour. **задо́рный** provocative; fervent.

задохну́ться (-ну́сь, -нёшься; -о́хся *or* -у́пся) *pf* (*impf* **задыхáться**) suffocate; choke; pant.

за|**дра́ть** (-деру́, -дерёшь; -áл, -á, -о) *pf* (*impf also* **задира́ть**) tear to pieces; kill; lift up; break; provoke; insult.

задрема́ть (-млю́ -млешь) *pf* doze off.

задрожа́ть (-жу́) *pf* begin to tremble.

задува́ть *impf of* **заду́ть**

заду́мать *pf*, **заду́мывать** *impf* plan; intend; think of; ~**ся** become thoughtful; meditate. **заду́мчивость** reverie. **заду́мчивый** pensive.

заду́ть (-у́ю) *pf* (*impf* **задува́ть**) blow out; begin to blow.

заду́шевный sincere; intimate.

за|**души́ть** (-ушу́, -у́шишь) *pf*

задыха́ться *impf of* **задохну́ться**

заеда́ть *impf of* **зае́сть**

зае́зд calling in; lap, heat. **зае́здить** (-зжу) *pf* override; wear out. **заезжа́ть** *impf of* **зае́хать**. **зае́зженный** hackneyed; worn out. **зае́зжий** visiting.

заём (за́йма) loan.

зае́сть (-е́м, -е́шь, -е́ст, -еди́м) *pf* (*impf* **заеда́ть**) torment; jam; entangle.

зае́хать (-е́ду) *pf* (*impf* **зае́зжать**) call in; enter, ride in, drive in; reach; +**за**+*acc* go past; +**за**+*instr* call for, fetch.

за|**жа́рить(ся** *pf*

зажа́ть (-жму́, -жмёшь) *pf*

(impf **зажима́ть**) squeeze; grip; suppress.
заже́чь (-жгу, -жжёшь; -жёг, -жгла) pf (impf **зажига́ть**) set fire to; kindle; light; ∼ся catch fire.

зажива́ть impf of **зажи́ть**. **заживи́ть** (-влю́) pf, **заживля́ть** impf heal. **за́живо** adv alive.

зажига́лка lighter. **зажига́ние** ignition. **зажига́тельный** inflammatory; incendiary. **зажига́ть(ся** impf of **заже́чь(ся**

зажи́м clamp; terminal; suppression. **зажима́ть** impf of **зажа́ть**. **зажимно́й** tight-fisted.

зажи́точный prosperous. **зажи́ть** (-иву́, -ивёшь; -ил, -а́, -о) pf (impf **зажива́ть**) heal; begin to live.

зажму́ etc.: see **зажа́ть**. **за|жму́риться** pf.

зазвене́ть (-и́т) pf begin to ring.

зазелене́ть (-е́ет) pf turn green.

землё́ние earthing; earth. **заземли́ть** pf, **заземля́ть** impf earth.

зазнава́ться (-наю́сь, -наёшься) impf, **зазна́ться** pf give o.s. airs.

зазу́брина notch. **за|зубри́ть** (-рю́, -у́бри́шь) pf.

заи́грывать impf flirt.

за́йка m & f stammerer. **заика́ние** stammer. **заика́ться** impf, **заикну́ться** (-ну́сь, -нёшься) pf stammer, stutter; +o+prep mention.

заи́мствование borrowing. **заи́мствовать** impf & pf (pf also **по∼**) borrow.

заинтересо́ванный inter-

ested. **заинтересова́ть** pf, **заинтересо́вывать** impf interest; ∼ся +instr become interested in.

заи́скивать impf ingratiate o.s.

зайду́ etc.: see **зайти́**. **займу́** etc.: see **заня́ть**

зайти́ (-йду́, -йдёшь; зашёл, -шла́) pf (impf **заходи́ть**) call; drop in; set; +в+acc reach; +за+acc go behind, turn; +за +instr call for, fetch.

за́йчик little hare (esp. as endearment); reflection of sunlight. **за́йчиха** doe hare.

закабали́ть pf, **закабаля́ть** impf enslave.

закады́чный intimate, bosom.

зака́з order; на ∼ to order. **заказа́ть** (-ажу́, -а́жешь) pf, **зака́зывать** impf order; book. **заказн|о́й** made to order; ∼о́е (письмо́) registered letter. **зака́зчик** customer, client.

зака́л temper; cast. **зака́ливать** impf, **закали́ть** (-лю́) pf (impf also **закаля́ть**) temper; harden. **зака́лка** tempering, hardening.

зака́лывать impf of **заколо́ть**. **закаля́ть** impf of **закали́ть**. **зака́нчивать(ся** impf of **зако́нчить(ся**

зака́пать pf, **зака́пывать**[1] impf begin to drip; rain; spot.

зака́пывать[2] impf of **закопа́ть**

зака́т sunset. **закати́ть** pf, **зака́тывать**[1] impf begin to roll; roll up; roll out. **закати́ть** (-ачу́, -а́тишь) pf, **зака́тывать**[2] impf roll; ∼ся roll; set.

заква́ска ferment; leaven.

заки́дывать[1] impf of **закида́ть**[1] impf shower; bespatter.

заки́дывать[2] impf, **заки́нуть** (-ну) pf throw (out, away).

закипа́ть *impf*, закипе́ть (-пи́т) *pf* begin to boil.

закиса́ть *impf*, заки́снуть (-ну, -ис, -ла) *pf* turn sour; become apathetic. заки́сь oxide.

закла́д pawn; pledge; bet; би́ться об ~ bet; в ~е in pawn. закла́дка laying; bookmark. закладно́й pawn. закла́дывать *impf of* заложи́ть

закле́ивать *impf*, закле́ить *pf* glue up.

за|клейми́ть (-млю́) *pf*.

заклёпывать *pf*, заклёпывать *impf* rivet. заклёпка rivet; riveting.

заклина́ние incantation; spell. заклина́ть *impf* invoke; entreat.

заключа́ть *impf*, заключи́ть (-чу́) *pf* conclude; enter into; contain; confine. заключа́ться consist; lie, be. заключе́ние conclusion; decision; confinement. заключённый *sb* prisoner. заключи́тельный final, concluding.

закля́тие pledge. закля́тый sworn.

закова́ть (-кую́, -куёшь) *pf*, зако́вывать *impf* chain; shackle.

зака́лывать *impf of* заколоти́ть

заколдо́ванный bewitched; ~ круг vicious circle. заколдова́ть *pf* bewitch; lay a spell on.

зако́лка hair-grip; hair-slide. заколоти́ть (-лочу́, -ло́тишь) *pf* (*impf* зака́лывать) board up; knock in; knock insensible.

за|коло́ть (-олю́, -о́лешь) *pf* (*impf also* зака́лывать) stab;

pin up; (*impers*) у меня́ заколо́ло в боку́ I have a stitch.

зако́н law. законнорождённый legitimate. зако́нность legality. зако́нный lawful; legitimate.

зако́но- *in comb* law, legal. законове́дение law, jurisprudence. ~да́тельный legislative. ~да́тельство legislation. ~ме́рность regularity, normality. ~ме́рный regular, natural. ~прое́кт bill.

за|консерви́ровать *pf*. за|ко́нспекти́ровать *pf*.

зако́нченность completeness. зако́нченный finished; accomplished. зако́нчить (-чу) *pf* (*impf* зака́нчивать) end, finish; ~ся end, finish.

закопа́ть *pf* (*impf* зака́пывать²) begin to dig; bury.

закопте́лый sooty, smutty. за|копти́ть (-пчу́) *pf*. за|копти́ть (-пчу́) *pf*.

закорене́лый deep-rooted; inveterate.

закосне́лый incorrigible.

закочене́лый numb with cold. за|коченеть (-е́ю) *pf*.

закра́дываться *impf of* закра́сться

закра́сить (-а́шу) *pf* (*impf* закра́шивать) paint over. закра́сться (-аду́сь, -адёшься) *pf* (*impf* закра́дываться) steal in, creep in.

закра́шивать *impf of* закра́сить

закрепи́тель *m* fixative. закрепи́ть (-плю́) *pf*, закрепля́ть *impf* fasten; fix; consolidate; (*+instr* assign to; ~ за собо́й secure.

закрепости́ть (-ощу́) *pf*, крепоща́ть *impf* enslave.

закрепоще́ние enslavement; slavery; serfdom.

закрича́ть (-чу́) *pf* cry out; begin to shout.

закро́йщик cutter.

закро́ю *etc.: see* **закры́ть**

закругле́ние rounding; curve. **закругли́ть** (-лю́) *pf*, **закругля́ть** *impf* make round; round off; ~**ся** become round; round off.

закружи́ться (-ужу́сь, -у́жи́шься) *pf* begin to whirl *or* go round.

за|крути́ть (-учу́, -у́тишь) *pf*, **закру́чивать** *impf* twist, twirl; wind round; turn; screw in; turn the head of; ~**ся** twist, twirl, whirl; wind round.

закрыва́ть *impf*, **закры́ть** (-ро́ю) *pf* close, shut; turn off; close down; cover; ~**ся** close, shut; end; close down; cover o.s.; shelter. **закры́тие** closing; shutting; closing down; shelter. **закры́тый** closed, shut; private.

закули́сный behind the scenes; backstage.

закупа́ть *impf*, **закупи́ть** (-плю́, -пишь) *pf* buy up; stock up with. **заку́пка** purchase.

заку́поривать *impf*, **заку́порить** *pf* cork; stop up; coop up. **заку́порка** corking; thrombosis.

заку́почный purchase. **заку́пщик** buyer.

заку́ривать *impf*, **закури́ть** (-рю́, -ришь) *pf* light up; begin to smoke.

закуси́ть (-ушу́, -у́сишь) *pf*, **заку́сывать** *impf* have a snack; bite. **заку́ска** hors-d'œuvre; snack. **заку́сочная** *sb* snack-bar.

за|ку́тать *pf*, **заку́тывать** *impf*

wrap up; ~**ся** wrap o.s. up.

зал hall; ~ **ожида́ния** waiting-room.

залега́ть *impf of* **зале́чь**

за|ледене́ть (-е́ю) *pf*.

залежа́лый stale, long unused. **залежа́ться** (-жу́сь) *pf*, **залёживаться** *impf* lie too long; find no market; become stale. **за́лежь** deposit, seam; stale goods.

залеза́ть *impf*, **зале́зть** (-зу; -ез) *pf* climb, climb up; get in; creep in.

за|лепи́ть (-плю́, -пишь) *pf*, **залепля́ть** *impf* paste over; glue up.

залета́ть *impf*, **залете́ть** (-ечу́) *pf* fly; +**в**+*acc* fly into.

зале́чивать *impf*, **залечи́ть** (-чу́, -чишь) *pf* heal, cure; ~**ся** heal (up).

зале́чь (-ля́гу, -ля́жешь, -ля́г) *pf* (*impf* **залега́ть**) lie down; lie low; lie, be deposited.

зали́в bay, gulf. **залива́ть** *impf*, **зали́ть** (-лью́, -льёшь; за́лил, -á, -о) *pf* flood, inundate; spill on; extinguish; spread; ~**ся** be flooded; pour, spill; +*instr* break into.

зало́г deposit; pledge; security, mortgage; token; voice. **заложи́ть** (-жу́, -жишь) *pf* (*impf* **закла́дывать**) lay; put; mislay; pile up; pawn, mortgage; harness; lay in. **зало́жник** hostage.

залп volley, salvo; ~**ом** without pausing for breath.

залью́ *etc.: see* **зали́ть**. **заля́гу** *etc.: see* **зале́чь**

зам *abbr* (*of* **замести́тель**) assistant, deputy. **зам-** *abbr in comb* (*of* **замести́тель**) assistant, deputy, vice-.

за|ма́зать (-а́жу) *pf*, **зама́зывать** *impf* paint over; putty.

smear; soil; **~ся** get dirty.
зама́зка putty; puttying.
зама́лчивать impf of **замолча́ть**
зама́нивать impf, **замани́ть** (-ню́, -нишь) pf entice; decoy. **зама́нчивый** tempting.
за|маринова́ть pf.
за|маскирова́ть pf, **замаскиро́вывать** impf mask; disguise; **~ся** disguise o.s.
замах threatening gesture. **зама́хиваться** impf, **замахну́ться** (-ну́сь, -нёшься) pf +instr raise threateningly.
зама́чивать impf of **замочи́ть**
замедле́ние slowing down, deceleration; delay. **заме́длить** (-лю) pf, **замедля́ть** impf slow down; slacken; delay; **~ся** slow down.
замёл etc.: see **замести́**
заме́на substitution; substitute. **заме́нимый** replaceable. **замени́тель** m (+gen) substitute (for). **замени́ть** (-ню́, -нишь) pf, **заменя́ть** impf replace; be a substitute for.
замере́ть (-мру́, -мрёшь; за́мер, -ла́, -о) pf (impf **замира́ть**) stand still; freeze; die away.
замерза́ние freezing. **замерза́ть** impf, **замёрзнуть** (-ну) pf freeze (up); freeze to death.
заме́рить pf (impf **замеря́ть**) measure, gauge.
замеси́ть (-ешу́, -е́сишь) pf (impf **заме́шивать**²) knead.
замести́ (-ету́, -етёшь; -мёл, -а́) pf (impf **замета́ть**) sweep up; cover.
замести́тель m substitute, assistant, deputy, vice-. **замести́ть** (-ещу́) pf (impf **замеща́ть**) replace; deputize for.
замета́ть impf of **замести́**
заме́тить (-е́чу) pf (impf за-

меча́ть) notice; note; remark.
заме́тка mark; note. **заме́тный** noticeable; outstanding.
замеча́ние remark; reprimand. **замеча́тельный** remarkable; splendid. **замеча́ть** impf of **заме́тить**
замеша́тельство confusion; embarrassment. **заме́шивать**¹ impf mix up, entangle. **заме́шивать**² impf of **замеси́ть**
замеща́ть impf of **замести́ть**. **замеще́ние** substitution; filling.
зами́нка hitch; hesitation.
замира́ть impf of **замере́ть**
за́мкнутый reserved; closed, exclusive. **замкну́ть** (-ну́, -нёшь) pf (impf **замыка́ть**) lock; close; **~ся** close; shut o.s. up; become reserved.
замо́к¹ (-мка) castle.
замо́к² (-мка́) lock; padlock; clasp.
замолка́ть impf, **замо́лкнуть** (-ну; -мо́лк) pf fall silent; stop.
замолча́ть (-чу́) pf (impf **зама́лчивать**) fall silent; cease corresponding; hush up.
замора́живать impf, **заморо́зить** (-о́жу) pf freeze. **заморо́женный** frozen; iced. **за́морозки** (-ов) pf (slight) frosts.
замо́рский overseas.
за|мочи́ть (-чу́, -чишь) pf (impf also **зама́чивать**) wet; soak; ret.
замо́чная сква́жина keyhole.
замру́ etc.: see **замере́ть**
за́муж adv: **вы́йти ~** (за+acc) marry. **за́мужем** adv married (за+instr to).
за|му́чить (-чу) pf torment; wear out; bore to tears. **за|му́читься** (-чусь) pf.

за́мша suede.

замыка́ние locking; short circuit. **замыка́ть(ся** *impf of* **замкну́ть(ся**.

за́мысел (-сла) project, plan. **замы́слить** *pf*, **замышля́ть** *impf* plan; contemplate.

за́навес, занаве́ска curtain.

занести́ (-су́, -сёшь; -ёс, -ла́) *pf* (*impf* **заноси́ть**) bring; note down; (*impers*) cover with snow etc.; (*impers*) skid.

занима́ть *impf* (*pf* **заня́ть**) occupy; interest; engage; borrow; **~ся** +*instr* be occupied with; study.

зано́за splinter. **заноз́и́ть** (-ожу́) *pf* get a splinter in.

зано́с snow-drift; skid. **заноси́ть** (-ошу́, -о́сишь) *impf of* **занести́**. **зано́счивый** arrogant.

заня́тие occupation; *pl* studies. **заня́тóй** busy. **за́нятый** (-нят, -á, -о) occupied; taken; engaged. **заня́ть(ся** (займу́(сь, -мёшь(ся; за́нял(ся, -á(сь, -о(сь) *pf of* **занима́ть(ся**.

заодно́ *adv* in concert; at one; at the same time.

заостри́ть *pf*, **заостря́ть** *impf* sharpen; emphasize.

зао́чник, -ница student taking correspondence course; external student. **зао́чно** *adv* in one's absence; by correspondence course. **зао́чный курс** correspondence course.

за́пад west. **за́падный** west, western; westerly.

западня́ (*gen pl* -не́й) trap; pitfall, snare.

за|накова́ть *pf*, **запако́вывать** *impf* pack; wrap up.

запа́л ignition; fuse. **запа́ливать** *impf*, **запали́ть** *pf* light, kindle; set fire to. **запа́льная**

свеча́ (spark-)plug.

запа́с reserve; supply; hem. **запаса́ть** *impf*, **запасти́** (-су́, -сёшь; -ác, -лá) *pf* store, store; lay in a stock of; **~ся** +*instr* provide o.s. with; stock up with. **запасно́й** *sb* reservist. **запасно́й, запа́сный** spare; reserve; **~ вы́ход** emergency exit.

за́пах smell.

запа́хивать *impf*, **запахну́ть**[2] (-ну́, -нёшь) *pf* wrap up.

запа́хнуть[1] (-ну; -áх) *pf* begin to smell.

за|па́чкать(ся *pf*.

запека́ть(ся *impf of* **запе́чь-(ся**. **запеку́** *etc.*: *see* **запе́чь**

за|пелена́ть *pf*.

запере́ть (-пру́, -прёшь; за́пер, -ла́, -ло) *pf* (*impf* **запира́ть**) lock; lock in; bar; **~ся** lock o.s. in.

запеча́тать *pf*, **запеча́тывать** *impf* seal. **запечатлева́ть** *impf*, **запечатле́ть** (-е́ю) *pf* imprint, engrave.

запе́чь (-еку́, -ечёшь; -пёк, -лá) *pf* (*impf* **запека́ть**) bake; **~ся** bake; become parched; clot, coagulate.

запива́ть *impf of* **запи́ть**

запина́ться *impf of* **запну́ть-ся**. **запи́нка** hesitation.

запира́ть(ся *impf of* **запере́ть(ся**

записа́ть (-ишу́, -и́шешь) *pf*, **запи́сывать** *impf* note; take down; record; enter; **~ся** register, enrol (**в**+*acc* in; in). **запи́ска** note. **записно́й** note; inveterate; **~ая кни́жка** notebook. **за́пись** recording; registration; record.

запи́ть (-пью́, -пьёшь; за́пил, -á, -о) *pf* (*impf* **запива́ть**) begin drinking; wash down (with).

запиха́ть *pf*, **запи́хивать** *impf*, **запихну́ть** (-ну́, -нёшь) *pf* push in, cram in.

запишу́ *etc.: see* **записа́ть**

запла́кать (-а́чу) *pf* begin to cry.

за|плани́ровать *pf*.

запла́та patch.

за|плати́ть (-ачу́, -а́тишь) *pf* pay (**за**+*acc* for).

заплачу́ *etc.: see* **запла́кать**

заплачу́ *see* **заплати́ть**

заплести́ (-ету́, -етёшь; -ёл, -а́) *pf*, **заплета́ть** *impf* plait.

за|пломбирова́ть *pf*.

заплы́в heat, round. **заплыва́ть** *impf*, **заплы́ть** (-ыву́, -ывёшь; -ы́л, -а́, -о) *pf* swim in, sail in; swim out, sail out; be bloated.

запну́ться (-ну́сь, -нёшься) *pf* (*impf* **запина́ться**) hesitate; stumble.

запове́дник reserve; preserve; **госуда́рственный ~** national park. **запове́дный** prohibited. **за́поведь** precept; commandment.

заподо́зривать *impf*, **заподо́зрить** *pf* suspect (**в**+*prep* of).

запозда́лый belated; delayed. **запозда́ть** *pf* (*impf* **запа́здывать**) be late.

запо́й hard drinking.

заполза́ть *impf*, **заползти́** (-зу́, -зёшь; -о́лз, -зла́) creep, crawl.

запо́лнить *pf*, **заполня́ть** *impf* fill (in, up).

запомина́ть *impf*, **запо́мнить** *pf* remember; memorize; **~ся** stay in one's mind.

запо́нка cuff-link; stud.

запо́р bolt; lock; constipation.

за|поте́ть (-е́ет) *pf* mist over.

запою́ *etc.: see* **запе́ть**

запра́вить (-влю) *pf*, **за-**

правля́ть *impf* tuck in; prepare; refuel; season, dress; mix in; **~ся** refuel. **запра́вка** refuelling; seasoning, dressing.

запра́шивать *impf of* **запроси́ть**

запре́т prohibition, ban. **запрети́ть** (-ещу́) *pf*, **запреща́ть** *impf* prohibit, ban. **запре́тный** forbidden. **запреще́ние** prohibition.

за|программи́ровать *pf*.

запро́с inquiry; overcharging; *pl* needs. **запроси́ть** (-ошу́, -о́сишь) *pf* (*impf* **запра́шивать**) inquire.

за́просто *adv* without ceremony.

запрошу́ *etc.: see* **запроси́ть**.

запру́ *etc.: see* **запере́ть**

запру́да dam, weir; mill-pond.

запряга́ть *impf*, **запря́чь** (-яту́, -яжёшь; -я́г, -ла́) *pf* harness; yoke.

запуга́ть *pf*, **запу́гивать** *impf* cow, intimidate.

за́пуск launching. **запуска́ть** *impf*, **запусти́ть** (-ущу́, -у́стишь) *pf* thrust (in); start; launch; (+*acc or instr*) neglect.

запу́щенный neglected; desolate. **запусте́ние** neglect; desolation.

за|пу́тать *pf*, **запу́тывать** *impf* tangle; confuse; **~ся** get tangled; get involved.

запущу́ *etc.: see* **запусти́ть**

запча́сть (*gen pl* -е́й) *abbr* (*of* **запасна́я часть**) spare part.

запыха́ться *pf* be out of breath.

запью́ *etc.: see* **запи́ть**

запя́стье wrist.

запята́я *sb* comma.

за|пятна́ть *pf*.

зараба́тывать *impf*, **зараба́-**

ботн|ый: ~ая пла́та wages; pay. **за́работок** (-тка) earnings.

заража́ть impf, **зарази́ть** (-ажу́) pf infect; ~ся +instr be infected with, catch. **зара́за** infection. **зарази́тельный** infectious. **зара́зный** infectious.

зара́нее adv in good time; in advance.

зараста́ть impf, **зарасти́** (-ту́, -тёшь; -ро́с, -ла́) pf be overgrown; heal.

за́рево glow.

за|**регистри́ровать(ся** pf.

за|**ре́зать** (-е́жу) pf kill, knife; slaughter.

зарека́ться impf of **заре́чься**

зарекомендова́ть pf: ~ себя́ +instr show o.s. to be.

заре́чься (-еку́сь, -ечёшься; -ёкся, -екла́сь) pf (impf **зарека́ться**) +inf renounce.

за|**ржа́веть** (-еет) pf.

зарисо́вка sketching; sketch.

зароди́ть (-ожу́) pf, **зарожда́ть** impf generate; ~ся be born; arise. **заро́дыш** foetus; embryo. **зарожде́ние** conception; origin.

заро́к vow, pledge.

заро́с etc.: see **зарасти́**

заро́ю etc.: see **зары́ть**

зарпла́та abbr (of **за́работная пла́та**) wages; pay.

заруба́ть impf of **заруби́ть**

зарубе́жный foreign.

заруби́ть (-блю́, -бишь) pf (impf **заруба́ть**) kill, cut down; notch. **зару́бка** notch.

заруча́ться impf, **заручи́ться** (-учу́сь) pf +instr secure.

зарыва́ть impf, **зары́ть** (-ро́ю) pf bury.

заря́ (pl зо́ри, зорь) dawn; sunset.

заря́д charge; supply. **заряди́ть** (-яжу́, -я́дишь) pf, **заряжа́ть** impf load; charge; stoke; ~ся be loaded; be charged. **заря́дка** loading; charging; exercises.

заса́да ambush. **засади́ть** (-ажу́, -а́дишь) pf, **заса́живать** impf plant; drive; set (за+acc to); ~ (в тюрьму́) put in prison. **заса́живаться** impf of **засе́сть**

заса́ливать impf of **засоли́ть**

засвети́ть (-ечу́, -е́тишь) pf light; ~ся light up.

за|**свиде́тельствовать** pf.

засева́ть impf of **засе́ять**

заседа́ние meeting; session. **заседа́ть** impf sit, be in session.

засе́ивать impf of **засе́ять**. **засе́к** etc.: see **засе́чь**. **засека́ть** impf of **засе́чь**

засекре́тить (-е́чу) pf, **засекре́чивать** impf classify as secret; clear; give access to secret material.

засеку́ etc.: see **засе́чь**. **засе́л** etc.: see **засе́сть**

заселе́ние settlement. **засели́ть** pf, **заселя́ть** impf settle; colonize; populate.

засе́сть (-ся́ду, -сёл) pf (impf **заса́живаться**) sit down; sit tight; settle; lodge in.

засе́чь (-еку́, -ечёшь; -ёк, -ла́) pf (impf **засека́ть**) flog to death; notch.

засе́ять (-е́ю) pf (impf **засева́ть**, **засе́ивать**) sow.

засили́е dominance, sway.

заслони́ть pf, **заслоня́ть** impf cover, screen; push into the background. **засло́нка** (furnace, oven) door.

заслу́га merit, desert; service.

заслу́женный deserved, merited; Honoured; time-honoured. **заслужи́ть** (-ужу́, -у́жишь) pf deserve; earn; +gen be worthy of.

засмея́ться (-éюсь, -еёшься) begin to laugh.

заснима́ть impf of **засня́ть**

засну́ть (-ну́, -нёшь) pf (impf **засыпа́ть**) fall asleep.

засня́ть (-ниму́, -и́мешь; -я́л, -á, -о) pf (impf **заснима́ть**) photograph.

засо́в bolt, bar.

засо́вывать impf of **засу́нуть**

засо́л salting, pickling. **засоли́ть** (-олю́, -о́лишь) pf (impf **заса́ливать**) salt, pickle.

засоре́ние littering; contamination; obstruction. **засори́ть** pf, **засоря́ть** impf litter; get dirt into; clog.

засо́хнуть (-ну; -со́х) pf (impf also **засыха́ть**) dry (up); wither.

заста́ва gate; outpost.

заставá́ть (-таю́, -таёшь) impf of **заста́ть**

заста́вить (-влю) pf, **заставля́ть** impf make; compel.

заста́иваться impf of **застоя́ться**. **застану́** etc.: see **заста́ть**

заста́ть (-а́ну) pf (impf **застава́ть**) find; catch.

застёгивать impf, **застегну́ть** (-ну́, -нёшь) pf fasten, do up. **застёжка** fastening; clasp, buckle; **~мо́лния** zip.

застекли́ть pf, **застекля́ть** impf glaze.

засте́нок (-нка) torture chamber.

засте́нчивый shy.

застига́ть impf, **засти́гнуть, засти́чь** (-и́гну; -сти́г) pf catch; take unawares.

засти́чь see **засти́гнуть**

засто́й stagnation. **засто́йный** stagnant.

застопо́риться pf.

застоя́ться (-и́тся) pf (impf **заста́иваться**) stagnate; stand too long.

застра́ивать impf of **застро́ить**

застрахо́ванный insured. **застрахова́ть** pf, **застрахо́вывать** impf insure.

застрева́ть impf of **застря́ть**

застрели́ть (-елю́, -е́лишь) pf shoot (dead); **~ся** shoot o.s.

застро́ить (-о́ю) pf (impf **застра́ивать**) build over, on, up. **застро́йка** building.

застря́ть (-я́ну) pf (impf **застрева́ть**) stick; get stuck.

за́ступ spade.

заступа́ться impf, **заступи́ться** (-плю́сь, -пишься) +за+acc stand up for. **засту́пник** defender. **засту́пничество** protection; intercession.

застыва́ть impf, **засты́ть** (-ы́ну) pf harden, set; become stiff; freeze; be petrified.

засу́нуть (-ну) pf (impf **засо́вывать**) thrust in, push in.

засу́ха drought.

засыпа́ть[1] (-плю) pf, **засыпа́ть** impf fill up; strew.

засыпа́ть[2] impf of **засну́ть**

засыха́ть impf of **засо́хнуть**.

зася́ду etc.: see **засе́сть**

затаённый (-ён, -ена́) secret; repressed. **зата́ивать** impf, **затаи́ть** pf suppress; conceal; harbour; **~ дыха́ние** hold one's breath.

зата́пливать impf of **затопи́ть**. **зата́птывать** impf of **затопта́ть**

зата́скивать impf, **затащи́ть** (-щу́, -щишь) pf drag in; drag off; drag away.

затвердевáть impf, **за|тверде́ть** (-е́ет) pf become hard; set. **затверде́ние** hardening; callus.

затво́р bolt; lock; shutter; flood-gate. **затвори́ть** (-рю́, -ришь) pf, **затворя́ть** impf shut, close; **~ся** shut o.s. up, lock o.s. in. **затво́рник** hermit, recluse.

затева́ть impf of **зате́ять**

затёк etc.: see **зате́чь**. **зате|ка́ть** impf of **зате́чь**

зате́м adv then, next; ~ что because.

затемне́ние darkening, obscuring; blacking out; blackout. **затемни́ть** pf, **затемня́ть** impf darken, obscure; black out.

зате́ривать impf, **затеря́ть** pf lose, mislay; **~ся** be lost; be mislaid; be forgotten.

зате́чь (-ечёт, -еку́т; -тёк, -кла́) pf (impf **затека́ть**) pour, flow; swell up; become numb.

зате́я undertaking, venture; escapade; joke. **зате́ять** pf (impf **затева́ть**) undertake, venture.

затиха́ть impf, **зати́хнуть** (-ну; -ти́х) pf die down, abate; fade. **зати́шье** calm; lull.

заткну́ть (-ну́, -нёшь) pf (impf **затыка́ть**) stop up; stick, thrust.

затмева́ть impf, **затми́ть** (-ми́шь) pf darken; eclipse; overshadow. **затме́ние** eclipse.

зато́ conj but then, but on the other hand.

затону́ть (-о́нет) pf sink, be submerged.

затопи́ть¹ (-плю́, -пишь) pf (impf **зата́пливать**) light; turn on the heating.

затопи́ть² (-плю́, -пишь) pf,

затопля́ть impf flood, submerge; sink.

затопта́ть (-пчу́, -пчешь) pf (impf **зата́птывать**) trample (down).

зато́р obstruction, jam; congestion.

за|тормози́ть (-ожу́) pf.

заточа́ть impf, **заточи́ть** (-чу́) pf incarcerate. **заточе́ние** incarceration.

затра́гивать impf of **затро́нуть**

затра́та expense; outlay. **затра́тить** (-а́чу) pf, **затра́чивать** impf spend.

затре́бовать pf request, require; ask for.

затро́нуть (-ну) pf (impf **затра́гивать**) affect; touch (on).

затрудне́ние difficulty. **затрудни́тельный** difficult. **затрудни́ть** pf, **затрудня́ть** impf trouble; make difficult; hamper; **~ся** +inf or instr find difficulty in.

за|туши́ться (-пи́тся) pf.

за|туши́ть (-шу́, -шишь) pf extinguish; suppress.

за́тхлый musty, mouldy; stuffy.

затыка́ть impf of **заткну́ть**

заты́лок (-лка) back of the head; scrag-end.

затя́гивать impf, **затяну́ть** (-ну́, -нешь) pf tighten; cover; close, heal; spin out; **~ся** be covered; close; be delayed; drag on; inhale. **затя́жка** inhaling; prolongation; delaying; putting off; lagging. **затяжно́й** long-drawn-out.

заура́дный ordinary; mediocre.

зау́треня morning service.

зау́чивать impf, **заучи́ть** (-чу́, -чишь) pf learn by heart.

за|фарширова́ть pf. **за|фикси́-**
ровать pf. **за|фрахт-**
ова́ть pf.

захва́т seizure, capture. **за-**
хвати́ть (-ачу́, -а́тишь) pf
seize; thrill. **захва́тывать** impf take;
seize; thrill. **захвати́ческий** aggressive. **захва́тчик**
aggressor. **захва́тывающий**
gripping.

захлебну́ться (-ну́сь, -нёшь-
ся) pf, **захлёбываться** impf
choke (**от**+gen with).

захлестну́ть (-ну́, -нёшь) pf,
захлёстывать impf flow
over, swamp, overwhelm.

захло́пнуть (-ну) pf, **захло́-**
пывать impf slam, bang;
~ся slam to.

захо́д sunset; calling in. **за-**
ходи́ть (-ожу́, -о́дишь) impf
of **зайти́**

захолу́стный remote, provincial. **захолу́стье** backwoods.

за|хорони́ть (-ню́, -нишь) pf.
за|хоте́ть(ся) (-очу́(сь), -о́чешь-
(ся, -о́тим(ся) pf.

зацвести́ (-ете́т; -вёл, -а́) pf,
зацвета́ть impf come into
bloom.

зацепи́ть (-плю́, -пишь) pf,
зацепля́ть impf hook; engage; sting (**за**+acc on);
~ся **за**+acc catch on; catch
hold of.

зачасту́ю adv often.

зача́тие conception. **зача́ток**
(-тка) embryo; rudiment;
germ. **зача́точный** rudimentary. **зача́ть** (-чну́, -чнёшь;
-ча́л, -а́, -о) pf (impf **зачи-**
на́ть) conceive.

зачёл etc.: see **заче́сть**

заче́м adv why; what for.
заче́м-то adv for some reason.

зачёркивать impf, **зачерк-**

ну́ть (-ну́, -нёшь) pf cross out.

зачерпну́ть (-ну́, -нёшь) pf,
заче́рпывать impf scoop up;
draw up.

за|черстве́ть (-е́ет) pf.

заче́сть (-чту́, -чтёшь; -чёл,
-чла́) pf (impf **зачи́тывать**)
take into account, reckon as
credit. **зачёт** test; получи́ть
~, сдать **~ по**+dat pass a test;
поста́вить **~ по**+dat pass in.
зачётная кни́жка (student's)
record book.

зачина́ть impf of **зача́ть**.
зачи́нщик instigator.

зачи́слить, **зачисля́ть** impf
include; enter; enlist; **~ся**
join, enter.

зачи́тывать impf of **заче́сть**.
зачту́ etc.: see **заче́сть**. **за-**
шёл etc.: see **зайти́**

зашива́ть impf, **заши́ть** (-шью́,
-шьёшь) pf sew up.

за|шифрова́ть pf, **зашифро́-**
вывать impf encipher, encode.

за|шнурова́ть pf, **зашнуро́-**
вывать impf lace up.

за|шпаклева́ть (-лю́ю) pf.
за|штопа́ть pf. **за|штрихо-**
ва́ть pf. **зашью́** etc.: see **за-**
ши́ть

защи́та defence; protection.
защити́ть (-ищу́) pf, **защи-**
ща́ть pf defend, protect.
защи́тник defender. **защи́т-**
ный protective.

заяви́ть (-влю́, -вишь) pf, **за-**
явля́ть impf announce, declare; **~ся** turn up. **зая́вка**
claim; demand. **заявле́ние**
statement; application.

за́яц (за́йца) hare; stowaway.
е́хать за́йцем travel without a ticket.

зва́ние rank; title. **зва́ный** in-
vited; **~ обе́д** banquet, dinner.

зва́тельный vocative. **звать** (зову́, -вёшь; звал, -á, -о) *impf* (*pf* по~) call; ask, invite; **как вас зову́т?** what is your name? ~**ся** be called.

звезда́ (*pl* звёзды) star. **звёздный** star; starry; star-lit; stellar. **звёздочка** little star; asterisk.

звене́ть (-ню́) *impf* ring; +*instr* jingle, clink.

звено́ (*pl* зве́нья, -ьев) link; team, section; unit; component. **звеньево́й** *sb* section leader.

звери́нец (-нца) menagerie. **зверово́дство** fur farming. **зве́рский** brutal; terrific. **зве́рство** atrocity. **зве́рствовать** *impf* commit atrocities. **зверь** (*pl* -и, -éй) *m* wild animal.

звон ringing (sound); peal, chink, clink. **звони́ть** *impf* (*pf* по~) ring; ring up; ~ **кому́-нибудь (по телефо́ну)** ring s.o. up. **зво́нкий** (-нок, -нка́, -о) ringing, clear. **звоно́к** (-нка́) bell; (*telephone*) call.

звук sound. **звуко-** *in comb* sound. **звукоза́пись** (sound) recording. ~**изоля́ция** sound-proofing. ~**непроница́емый** sound-proof. ~**снима́тель** *m* pick-up. **звуково́й** audio; acoustic. **звуча́ние** sound(ing); vibration. **звуча́ть** (-чи́т) *impf* (*pf* про~) be heard; sound. **зву́чный** (-чен, -чна́, -о) sonorous.

зда́ние building.

здесь *adv* here. **зде́шний** local; **не** ~ a stranger here.

здоро́ваться *impf* (*pf* по~) exchange greetings. **здо́рово** *adv* splendidly; very (much);

well done!; great! **здоро́вый** healthy, strong; well; whole-some, sound. **здоро́вье** health; **за ва́ше** ~? your health! **как ва́ше** ~? how are you? **здравница** sanatorium. **здравомы́слящий** sensible, judicious. **здравоохране́ние** public health.

здра́вствовать *impf* be healthy; prosper. **здра́вствуй(те)** how do you do?; hello! **да здра́вствует!** long live! **здра́вый** sensible; ~ **смысл** common sense.

зе́бра zebra.

зева́ть *impf*, **зевну́ть** (-ну́, -нёшь) *pf* yawn; gape; (*pf* про~) miss, let slip; lose. **зево́к** (-вка́), **зево́та** yawn.

зелене́ть (-éет) *impf* (*pf* по~) turn green; show green. **зелёный** (зе́лен, -á, -о) green; ~ **лук** spring onions. **зе́лень** green; greenery; greens.

земе́льный land.

земле- *in comb* land; earth. **землевладе́лец** (-льца) land-owner. ~**де́лец** (-льца) farm-er. ~**де́лие** farming, agriculture. ~**де́льческий** agricultural. ~**ко́п** navvy. ~**ро́йный** excavating. ~**трясе́ние** earthquake.

земля́ (*acc* -ю; *pl* -и, земе́ль, -ям) earth; land; soil. **земля́к** (-á) fellow-countryman. **земляни́ка** (*no pl; usu collect*) wild strawberry; wild strawberries. **земля́нка** dug-out; mud hut. **земляно́й** earthen; earthy. **земля́чка** country-woman. **земно́й** earthly; terrestrial; ground; mundane; ~ **шар** the globe.

зени́т zenith. **зени́тный** ze-nith; anti-aircraft.

зе́ркало (pl -á) mirror. зерка́льный mirror; smooth; plate-glass.

зерни́стый grainy. зерно́ (pl зёрна, зёрен) seed; kernel, core; ко́фе в зёрнах coffee beans. зерново́й grain. зерновы́е sb pl cereals. зернохрани́лище granary.

зигза́г zigzag.

зима́ (acc -у; pl -ы) winter. зи́мний winter, wintry. зимова́ть impf (pf пере~, про~) spend the winter; hibernate. зимо́вка wintering; hibernation. зимо́вье winter quarters. зимо́й adv in winter.

зия́ть impf gape, yawn.

злак grass; cereal.

злить (злю) impf (pf обо~, о~, разо~) anger; irritate; ~ся be angry, be in a bad temper; rage. зло (gen зол) evil; harm; misfortune; malice. зло- in comb evil, harm, malice. злове́щий ominous. ~во́ние stink. ~во́нный stinking. ~ка́чественный malignant; pernicious. ~па́мятный rancorous, unforgiving. ~ра́дный malevolent, gloating. ~сло́вие malicious gossip. ~умы́шленник malefactor; plotter. ~язы́чный slanderous.

зло́ба spite; anger; ~ дня topic of the day, latest news. зло́бный malicious. злободне́вный topical. злоде́й villain. злоде́йский villainous. злоде́йство villainy; crime, evil deed. злодея́ние crime, evil deed. злой (зол, зла) evil; wicked; malicious; vicious; bad-tempered; severe. зло́стный malicious; intentional. зло́сть malice; fury.

злоупотреби́ть (-блю) pf, злоупотребля́ть impf +instr abuse. злоупотребле́ние +instr abuse of.

змеи́ный snake; cunning. змей snake; dragon; kite. змея́ (pl -и) snake.

знак sign; mark; symbol.

знако́мить (-млю) impf (pf о~, по~) acquaint; introduce; ~ся become acquainted; get to know; +с+instr meet, make the acquaintance of. знако́мство acquaintance; (circle of) acquaintances. знако́мый familiar; быть ~ым с+instr be acquainted with, know; ~ый, ~ая sb acquaintance.

знамена́тель m denominator. знамена́тельный significant. знаме́ние sign. знамени́тость celebrity. знамени́тый celebrated, famous. зна́мя (-мени; pl -мёна) neut banner; flag.

зна́ние knowledge.

зна́тный (-тен, -тна́, -о) distinguished; aristocratic; splendid.

знато́к (-á) expert; connoisseur. знать impf know; дать ~ inform, let know.

значе́ние meaning; significance; importance. зна́чит then; that means. значи́тельный considerable; important; significant. зна́чить (-чу) impf mean; signify; be of importance; ~ся be mentioned, appear. значо́к (-чка́) badge; mark.

зна́ющий expert; learned.

знобить impf, impers+acc: меня́, etc., зноби́т I feel shivery.

зной intense heat. **зно́йный** hot; burning.

зов call, summons. **зову́** etc.: see **звать**

зо́дчество architecture. **зо́дчий** sb architect.

зол see **зло**, **злой**

зола́ ashes, cinders.

золо́вка sister-in-law (husband's sister).

золоти́стый golden. **зо́лото** gold. **золото́й** gold; golden. **золочёный** gilt, gilded.

зо́на zone; region.

зонд probe. **зонди́ровать** impf sound, probe.

зонт (-а́), **зо́нтик** umbrella.

зоо́лог zoologist. **зоологи́ческий** zoological. **зооло́гия** zoology. **зоопа́рк** zoo. **зоотехник** livestock specialist.

зо́ри etc.: see **заря́**

зо́ркий (-рок, -рка́, -о) sharpsighted; perspicacious.

зрачо́к (-чка́) pupil (of the eye).

зре́лище sight; spectacle.

зре́лость ripeness; maturity; **аттеста́т зре́лости** school-leaving certificate. **зре́лый** (зрел, -а́, -о) ripe, mature.

зре́ние (eye)sight, vision; **то́чка зре́ния** point of view.

зреть (-е́ю) impf (pf **со-**) ripen; mature.

зри́мый visible.

зри́тель m spectator, observer; pl audience. **зри́тельный** visual; optic; **~ зал** hall, auditorium.

зря adv in vain.

зуб (pl -ы or -бья, -о́в or -бьев) tooth; cog. **зуби́ло** chisel. **зубно́й** dental; tooth; **~ врач** dentist. **зубовраче́бный** dentists', dental; **~ кабине́т** dental surgery. **зубочи́стка** toothpick.

зубр (European) bison; diehard.

зубри́ть (-рю́, зубри́шь) impf (pf **вы-**, **за-**) cram.

зубча́тый toothed; serrated.

зуд itch. **зуде́ть** (-и́т) itch.

зы́бкий (-бок, -бка́, -о) unsteady, shaky; vacillating. **зыбь** (gen pl -е́й) ripple, rippling.

зюйд (naut) south; south wind.

зя́блик chaffinch.

зя́бнуть (-ну; зяб) impf suffer from cold, feel the cold.

зябь land ploughed in autumn for spring sowing.

зять (pl -тья́, -тьёв) son-in-law; brother-in-law (sister's husband or husband's sister's husband).

И, Й

и conj and; even; too; (with neg) either; **и... и** both ... and.

и́бо conj for.

и́ва willow.

игла́ (pl -ы) needle; thorn; spine; quill. **иглоука́лывание** acupuncture.

игнори́ровать impf & pf ignore.

и́го yoke.

иго́лка needle.

иго́рный gaming, gambling. **игра́** (pl -ы) play, playing; game; hand; turn; **~ слов** pun. **игра́льный** playing; **~ые ко́сти** dice. **игра́ть** impf (pf **сыгра́ть**) play; act; **~ в**+acc play (game); **~ на**+prep play (an instrument). **игри́вый** playful. **игро́к** (-а́) player; gambler. **игру́шка** toy.

идеа́л ideal. **идеали́зм** idealism. **идеа́льный** ideal.

идейный high-principled; acting on principle; ideological.

идеологический ideological. **идеология** ideology.

идёт *etc.: see* идти

идея idea; concept.

идиллия idyll.

идиот idiot.

идол idol.

идти (иду, идёшь; шёл, шла) *impf* (*pf* пойти) go; come; run, work; pass; go on, be in progress; be on; fall; +(к+)*dat* suit.

иерей priest.

иждивенец (-нца), **-венка** dependant. **иждивение** maintenance; **на иждивении** at the expense of.

из, изо *prep+gen* from, out of, of.

изба (*pl* -ы) izba (hut).

избавить (-влю) *pf*, **избавлять** *impf* save, deliver; ~ся be saved, escape; ~ся от get rid of; get out of.

избалованный spoilt.

избегать *impf*, **избегнуть** (-ну; -бег(нул)) *pf*, **избежать** (-егу) *pf +gen or inf* avoid; escape, evade.

изберу *etc.: see* избрать

избивать *impf of* избить. **избиение** slaughter, massacre; beating, beating-up.

избиратель *m*, **-ница** elector, voter. **избирательный** electoral; election. **избирать** *impf of* избрать

избитый trite, hackneyed. **избить** (изобью, -бьёшь) *pf* (*impf* избивать) beat unmercifully, beat up; massacre.

избранн|ый selected; select; ~ые *sb pl* the élite. **избрать** (-беру, -берёшь; -ал, -а, -о) *pf* (*impf* избирать) elect; choose.

избыток (-тка) surplus; abundance. **избыточный** surplus; abundant.

изверг monster. **извержение** eruption; expulsion; excretion.

извернуться (-нусь, -нёшься) *pf* (*impf* изворачиваться) dodge, be evasive.

известие news; information; *pl* proceedings. **известить** (-ещу) *pf* (*impf* извещать) inform, notify.

известка lime.

известно it is (well) known; of course, certainly. **известность** fame, reputation. **известный** known; well-known, famous; notorious; certain.

известняк (-á) limestone. **известь** lime.

извещать *impf of* известить. **извещение** notification; advice.

извиваться *impf* coil; writhe; twist, wind; meander. **извилина** bend, twist. **извилистый** winding; meandering.

извинение excuse; apology. **извинить** *pf*, **извинять** *impf* excuse; извини(те) (меня) excuse me, (I'm) sorry; ~ся apologize; excuse o.s.

извиться (изовьюсь, -вьёшься; -ился, -ась, -ось) *pf* coil; writhe.

извлекать *impf*, **извлечь** (-еку, -ечёшь; -ёк, -ла) *pf* extract; derive; elicit.

извне *adv* from outside.

извозчик cabman; carrier.

изворачиваться *impf of* извернуться. **изворот** bend, twist; *pl* tricks, wiles. **изворотливый** resourceful; shrewd.

извратить (-ащу) *pf*, **извращать** *impf* distort; pervert. **извращение** perversion; distortion. **извращённый** perverted, unnatural.

изги́б bend, twist. изгиба́ть(ся *impf of* изогну́ть(ся

изгна́ние banishment; exile. изгна́нник exile. изгна́ть (-гоню́, -го́нишь; -а́л, -á, -о) *pf* (*impf* изгоня́ть) banish; exile.

изголо́вье bed-head. изголода́ться be famished, starve; +по+*dat* yearn for.

изгоню́ *etc.: see* изгна́ть. изгоня́ть *impf of* изгна́ть

и́згородь fence, hedge.

изгота́вливать *impf*, изгото́вить (-влю) *pf*, изготовля́ть *impf* make, manufacture; ~ся get ready; ~вле́ние making, manufacture.

издава́ть (-даю́, -даёшь) *impf of* изда́ть

и́здавна *adv* from time immemorial; for a very long time.

издаду́т *etc.: see* изда́ть

издалека́, и́здали *advs* from afar.

изда́ние publication; edition; promulgation. изда́тель *m* publisher. изда́тельство publishing house. изда́ть (-áм, -áшь, -áст, -ади́м; и́здал, -á, -о) *pf* (*impf* издава́ть) publish; promulgate; produce; emit; ~ся be published.

издева́тельство mockery; taunt. издева́ться *impf* (+над+*instr*) mock (at).

изде́лие work; make; article; *pl* wares.

изде́ржки (-жек) *pl* expenses; costs; cost.

издо́хнуть *pf.*

изжа́рить(ся *pf.*

изжо́га heartburn.

из-за *prep+gen* from behind; because of.

излага́ть *impf of* изложи́ть

излече́ние treatment; recovery;

cure. излечи́ть (-чу́, -чишь) cure; ~ся be cured; +от+*gen* rid o.s. of.

изли́шек (-шка) surplus; excess. изли́шество excess; over-indulgence. изли́шний (-шен, -шня) superfluous.

изложе́ние exposition; account. изложи́ть (-жу́, -жишь) *pf* (*impf* излага́ть) expound; set forth; word.

изло́м break, fracture; sharp bend. излома́ть *pf* break; smash; wear out; warp.

излуча́ть *impf* radiate, emit. излуче́ние radiation; emanation.

изма́зать (-áжу) *pf* dirty, smear all over; use up; ~ся get dirty, smear o.s. all over.

изме́на betrayal; treason; infidelity.

измене́ние change, alteration; inflection. измени́ть[1] (-ню́, -нишь) *pf* (*impf* изменя́ть[1]) change, alter; ~ся change.

измени́ть[2] (-ню́, -нишь) *pf* (*impf* изменя́ть[2]) +*dat* betray; be unfaithful to. изме́нник, -ица traitor.

изменя́емый variable. изменя́ть[1,2] *impf of* измени́ть[1,2](ся

измере́ние measurement; measuring. изме́рить *pf*, измеря́ть *impf* measure, gauge.

измождённый (-ён, -á) worn out.

изму́чить (-чу) *pf* torment; tire out, exhaust; ~ся be exhausted. изму́ченный worn out.

измышле́ние fabrication; invention.

измя́тый crumpled, creased; haggard, jaded. изм[я́ть (изомну́(сь, -нёшь(ся) *pf.*

изна́нка wrong side; seamy side.

из|наси́ловать pf rape, assault.

изна́шивание wear (and tear). изна́шивать(ся impf of износи́ть(ся

изне́женный pampered; delicate; effeminate.

изнемога́ть impf, изнемо́чь (-огу́, -о́жешь; -о́г, -ла́) pf be exhausted. изнеможе́ние exhaustion.

изно́с wear; wear and tear; deterioration. износи́ть (-ошу́, -о́сишь) pf (impf изна́шивать) wear out; use up. изно́шенный worn out; threadbare.

изнуре́ние exhaustion. изнурённый (-ён, -ена́) exhausted, worn out; jaded. изнури́тельный exhausting.

изнутри́ adv from inside, from within.

изо see из

изоби́лие abundance, plenty. изоби́ловать impf +instr abound in, be rich in. изоби́льный abundant.

изоблича́ть impf, изобличи́ть (-чу́) pf expose; show. изобличе́ние exposure; conviction.

изобража́ть impf, изобрази́ть (-ажу́) pf represent, depict, portray (+instr as); ~ из себя́+acc make o.s. out to be. изображе́ние image; representation; portrayal. изобрази́тельный graphic; decorative; ~ые иску́сства fine arts.

изобрести́ (-ету́, -ете́шь; -ёл, -а́) pf, изобрета́ть impf invent; devise. изобрета́тель m inventor. изобрета́тельный inventive. изобрете́ние

invention.

изобью́ etc.: see изби́ть. изовью́сь etc.: see изви́ться

изо́гнутый bent, curved; winding. изогну́ть (-ну́(сь, -нёшь(ся) pf (impf изгиба́ть(ся) bend, curve.

изоли́ровать impf & pf isolate; insulate. изоля́тор insulator; isolation ward; solitary confinement cell. изоля́ция isolation; quarantine; insulation.

изомну́ etc.: see измя́ть

изо́рванный tattered, torn. изорва́ть (-ву́, -вёшь; -а́л, -а́, -о) pf tear, tear to pieces; ~ся be in tatters.

изощрённый (-рён, -а́) refined; keen. изощри́ться pf, изощря́ться impf acquire refinement; excel.

из-под prep+gen from under.

Изра́иль m Israel. изра́ильский Israeli.

из|расхо́довать(ся pf.

и́зредка adv now and then.

изреза́ть (-е́жу) pf cut up.

изрече́ние dictum, saying.

изры́ть (-ро́ю) pf dig up, plough up; ~тый pitted.

изря́дно adv fairly, pretty. изря́дный fair, handsome; fairly large.

изуве́чить (-чу) pf maim, mutilate.

изуми́тельный amazing. изуми́ть (-млю́) pf, изумля́ть impf amaze; ~ся be amazed. изумле́ние amazement.

изумру́д emerald.

изуро́дованный maimed; disfigured. из|уро́довать pf.

изуча́ть impf, изучи́ть (-чу́, -чишь) pf learn, study. изуче́ние study.

изъе́здить (-зжу) pf travel all

over; wear out.

изъяви́ть (-влю́, -вишь) *pf*, **изъявля́ть** *impf* express.

изъя́н defect, flaw.

изъя́тие withdrawal; removal; exception. **изъя́ть** (изыму́, -мешь) *pf*. **изыма́ть** *impf* withdraw.

изыска́ние investigation, research; prospecting; survey. **изы́сканный** refined. **изыска́ть** (-ыщу́, -ы́щешь) *pf*, **изы́скивать** *impf* search out; (try to) find.

изю́м raisins.

изя́щество elegance, grace. **изя́щный** elegant, graceful.

ика́ть *impf*, **икну́ть** (-ну́, -нёшь) *pf* hiccup.

ико́на icon.

ико́та hiccup, hiccups.

икра́[1] (hard) roe; caviare.

икра́[2] (*pl* -ы) calf (*of leg*).

ил silt; sludge.

и́ли *conj* or; ~... ~ either ... or.

и́листый muddy, silty.

иллюзиони́ст illusionist. **иллю́зия** illusion.

иллюмина́тор porthole. **иллюмина́ция** illumination.

иллюстра́ция illustration. **иллюстри́ровать** *impf & pf* illustrate.

им see **он**, **они́**, **оно́**.

им. *abbr* (*of* и́мени) named after.

и́мени *etc.*: see **и́мя**

име́ние estate.

имени́ны (-и́н) *pl* name-day (party). **имени́тельный** nominative. **и́менно** *adv* namely; exactly, precisely; **вот** ~ ! exactly!

име́ть (-е́ю) *impf* have; ~ де́ло c+*instr* have dealings with, have to do with; ~

ме́сто take place; ~**ся** be; be available.

и́ми see **они́**

имита́ция imitation. **имити́ровать** *impf* imitate.

иммигра́нт, ~**ка** immigrant.

импера́тор emperor. **импера́торский** imperial. **императри́ца** empress. **империали́зм** imperialism. **империали́ст** imperialist. **империалисти́ческий** imperialist(ic). **импе́рия** empire.

и́мпорт import. **импорти́ровать** *impf & pf* import. **и́мпортный** import(of).

импровиза́ция improvisation. **импровизи́ровать** *impf & pf* improvise.

и́мпульс impulse.

иму́щество property.

и́мя (и́мени; *pl* имена́, -ён) *neut* name; first name; noun; ~ прилага́тельное adjective; ~ существи́тельное noun; ~ числи́тельное numeral.

и́наче *adv* differently, otherwise; так и́ли ~ in any event; *conj* otherwise, or else.

инвали́д disabled person; invalid. **инвали́дность** disablement, disability.

инвента́рь (-я́) *m* stock; equipment; inventory.

инде́ец (-е́йца) (American) Indian. **инде́йка** (*gen pl* -е́ек) turkey(-hen). **инде́йский** (American) Indian.

и́ндекс index; code.

индиа́нка (-нок) Indian; American Indian. **инди́ец** (-и́йца) Indian.

индивидуали́зм individualism. **индивидуа́льность** individuality. **индивидуа́льный** individual. **индивиду́ум** individual.

инди́йский Indian. **И́ндия** India. **инду́с, инду́ска** Hindu. **инду́сский** Hindu.

индустриализа́ция industrialization. **индустриализи́ровать** *impf & pf* industrialize. **индустриа́льный** industrial. **инду́стрия** industry.

индю́к, индю́шка turkey.

и́ней hoar-frost.

ине́ртность inertia; sluggishness. **ине́рция** inertia.

инжене́р engineer; ~-меха́ник mechanical engineer; ~-строи́тель *m* civil engineer.

инжи́р fig.

инициа́л initial.

инициати́ва initiative. **инициа́тор** initiator.

инквизи́ция inquisition.

инкруста́ция inlaid work, inlay.

инкуба́тор incubator.

ино- *in comb* other, different; hetero-. **иногоро́дний** of, from, another town. ~**ро́дец** (-дца) non-Russian. ~**ро́дный** foreign. ~**сказа́тельный** allegorical. ~**стра́нец** (-нца), ~**стра́нка** (*gen pl* -нок) foreigner. ~**стра́нный** foreign. ~**язы́чный** speaking, of, another language; foreign.

иногда́ *adv* sometimes.

ино́й different; other; some; ~ раз sometimes.

и́нок monk. **и́нокиня** nun.

инотде́л foreign department.

инсектици́д insecticide.

инспе́ктор inspector. **инспе́кция** inspection; inspectorate.

инста́нция instance.

инсти́нкт instinct. **инстинкти́вный** instinctive.

институ́т institute.

инстру́ктор instructor. **инстру́кция** instructions.

инструме́нт instrument; tool.

инсули́н insulin.

инсцениро́вка dramatization, adaptation; pretence.

интегра́ция integration.

интелле́кт intellect. **интеллектуа́льный** intellectual.

интеллиге́нт intellectual. **интеллиге́нтный** cultured, educated. **интеллиге́нция** intelligentsia.

интенси́вность intensity. **интенси́вный** intensive.

интерва́л interval.

интерве́нция intervention.

интервью́ *neut indecl* interview.

интере́с interest. **интере́сный** interesting. **интересова́ть** *impf* interest; ~**ся** be interested (+*instr* in).

интерна́т boarding-school.

интернациона́льный international.

интерни́ровать *impf & pf* intern.

интерпрета́ция interpretation. **интерпрети́ровать** *impf & pf* interpret.

интерье́р interior.

инти́мный intimate.

интона́ция intonation.

интри́га intrigue; plot. **интригова́ть** *impf*, (*pf* за~) intrigue.

интуи́ция intuition.

инфа́ркт infarct; coronary (thrombosis), heart attack.

инфекцио́нный infectious. **инфе́кция** infection.

инфля́ция inflation.

информа́ция information.

инфракра́сный infra-red.

йо́д *etc.: see* йод

ио́н ion.

ипохо́ндрик hypochondriac. **ипохо́ндрия** hypochondria.

ипподро́м racecourse.

Ира́к Iraq. **ира́ец** (-кца) Iraqi. **ира́кский** Iraqi.

Ира́н Iran. **ира́нец** (-нца), **ира́нка** Iranian. **ира́нский** Iranian.

ирла́ндец (-дца) Irishman. **Ирла́ндия** Ireland. **ирла́ндка** Irishwoman. **ирла́ндский** Irish.

ирони́ческий ironic. **иро́ния** irony.

иррига́ция irrigation.

иск suit, action.

искажа́ть impf, **исказа́ть** (-ажу́) pf distort, pervert; misrepresent. **искаже́ние** distortion, perversion.

искале́ченный crippled, maimed. **искале́чить** (-чу) pf cripple, maim; break.

иска́ть (ищу́, и́щешь) impf (+acc or gen) seek, look for.

исключа́ть impf, **исключи́ть** (-чу́) pf exclude; eliminate; expel. **исключа́я** prep+gen except. **исключе́ние** exception; exclusion; expulsion; elimination; **за исключе́нием** +gen with the exception of. **исключи́тельно** adv exceptionally; exclusively. **исключи́тельный** exceptional; exclusive.

иско́нный primordial.

ископа́емое sb mineral; fossil. **ископа́емый** fossilized, fossil.

искорени́ть pf, **искореня́ть** impf eradicate.

и́скоса adv askance; sidelong.

и́скра spark.

и́скренний sincere. **и́скренность** sincerity.

искривле́ние bend; distortion, warping.

ис|купа́ть¹(ся pf.

искупа́ть² impf, **искупи́ть**

(-плю́, -пишь) pf atone for; make up for. **искупле́ние** redemption, atonement.

искуси́ть (-ушу́) pf of искуша́ть

иску́сный skilful; expert. **иску́сственный** artificial; feigned. **иску́сство** art; skill. **искусствове́д** art historian.

искуша́ть impf (pf искуси́ть) tempt; seduce. **искуше́ние** temptation, seduction.

испа́нец (-нца) Spaniard. **Испа́ния** Spain. **испа́нка** Spanish woman. **испа́нский** Spanish.

испаре́ние evaporation; pl fumes. **испари́ться** pf, **испаря́ться** impf evaporate.

ис|па́чкать pf. **ис|пе́чь** (-еку́, -ечёшь) pf.

испове́довать impf & pf confess; profess; **~ся** confess; make one's confession; **+в**prep unburden o.s. of. **и́споведь** confession.

исподтишка́ adv in an underhand way; on the quiet.

исполи́н giant. **исполи́нский** gigantic.

исполко́м abbr (of исполни́тельный комите́т) executive committee.

исполне́ние fulfilment, execution. **исполни́тель** m, **~ница** executor; performer. **исполни́тельный** executive. **испо́лнить** pf, **исполня́ть** impf carry out, execute; fulfil; perform; **~ся** be fulfilled.

испо́льзование utilization. **испо́льзовать** impf & pf make (good) use of, utilize.

ис|по́ртить(ся (-рчу(сь) pf. **испо́рченный** depraved; spoiled; rotten.

исправи́тельный correctional; corrective. испра́вить (-влю) pf, исправля́ть impf rectify, correct; mend; reform; ~ся improve, reform. исправле́ние repairing; improvement; correction. испра́вленный improved, corrected; revised; reformed. испра́вный in good order; punctual; meticulous.

ис|про́бовать pf.

испу́г fright. ис|пуга́ть(ся) pf.

испуска́ть impf, испусти́ть (-ущу́, -у́стишь) pf emit, let out.

испыта́ние test, trial; ordeal. испыта́ть impf, испы́тывать impf test; try; experience.

иссле́дование investigation; research. иссле́дователь m researcher; investigator. иссле́довательский research. иссле́довать impf & pf investigate, examine; research into.

истаска́ться pf, иста́скиваться impf wear out; be worn out.

истека́ть impf of исте́чь. исте́кший past.

исте́рика hysterics. истери́ческий hysterical. истери́я hysteria.

истече́ние outflow; expiry. исте́чь (-чёт, -тёк, -ла́) pf (impf истека́ть) elapse; expire.

и́стина truth. и́стинный true.

истлева́ть impf, истле́ть (-е́ю) pf rot, decay; be reduced to ashes.

исто́к source.

истолкова́ть pf, истолко́вывать impf interpret; comment on. ис|толо́чь (-лку́, -лчёшь; -ло́к, -лкла́) pf.

исто́ма languor.

исторга́ть impf, исто́ргнуть (-ну; -о́рг) pf throw out.

исто́рик historian. истори́ческий historical; historic. исто́рия history; story; incident.

исто́чник spring; source.

истоща́ть impf, истощи́ть (-щу́) pf exhaust; emaciate. истоще́ние emaciation; exhaustion.

ис|тра́тить (-а́чу) pf.

истреби́тель m destroyer; fighter. истреби́ть (-блю́) pf, истребля́ть impf destroy; exterminate.

ис|тупи́ть (-пится) pf.

истяза́ние torture. истяза́ть impf torture.

исхо́д outcome; end; Exodus. исходи́ть (-ожу́, -о́дишь) impf (+из со от+gen) issue (from), come (from); proceed (from). исхо́дный initial; departure.

исхуда́лый undernourished, emaciated.

исцеле́ние healing; recovery. исцели́ть pf, исцеля́ть impf heal, cure.

исчеза́ть impf, исче́знуть (-ну; -е́з) pf disappear, vanish. исчезнове́ние disappearance.

исче́рпать pf, исче́рпывать impf exhaust; conclude. исче́рпывающий exhaustive.

исчисле́ние calculation; calculus.

ита́к conj thus; so then.

Ита́лия Italy. италья́нец (-нца), италья́нка Italian. италья́нский Italian.

ИТАР-ТАСС abbr (of Информацио́нное телегра́фное аге́нтство Росси́и; see ТАСС) ITAR-Tass.

и т.д. abbr (of и так да́лее) etc., and so on.

ито́г sum; total; result. ито́го

adv in all, altogether.

и т.п. *abbr* (*of* и тому подо́бное) etc., and so on.

иуде́й, иуде́йка Jew. **иуде́йский** Judaic.

их their, theirs; *see* они́.

иша́к (-á) donkey.

ище́йка bloodhound; police dog.

ищу́ *etc.*: *see* иска́ть.

ию́ль *m* July. **ию́льский** July.

ию́нь *m* June. **ию́ньский** June.

йо́га yoga.

йод iodine.

йо́та iota.

К

к, ко *prep+dat* to, towards; by; for; on; on the occasion of; **к пе́рвому января́** by the first of January; **к тому́ вре́мени** by then; **к тому́ же** besides, moreover; **к чему́?** what for?

-ка *partl* modifying force of *imper or expressing decision or intention*; **да́йте-ка пройти́** let me pass, please; **скажи́-ка** мне do tell me.

каба́к (-á) tavern.

кабала́ servitude.

каба́н (-á) wild boar.

кабаре́ *neut indecl* cabaret.

кабачо́к (-чка́) marrow.

ка́бель *m* cable. **ка́бельтов** cable, hawser.

каби́на cabin; booth; cockpit; cubicle; cab. **кабине́т** study; surgery; room; office; Cabinet.

каблу́к (-á) heel.

кабота́ж coastal shipping. **кабота́жный** coastal.

кабы́ if.

кавале́р knight; partner, gentleman. **кавалери́йский** cavalry. **кавалери́ст** cavalryman.

кавале́рия cavalry.

ка́верзный tricky.

Кавка́з the Caucasus. **кавка́зец** (-зца) **кавка́зка** Caucasian. **кавка́зский** Caucasian.

кавы́чки (-чек) *pl* inverted commas, quotation marks.

каде́т cadet. **каде́тский ко́рпус** military school.

ка́дка tub, vat.

кадр frame, still; close-up; cadre; *pl* establishment; staff; personnel; specialists. **ка́дровый** (*mil*) regular; skilled, trained.

кады́к (-á) Adam's apple.

каждодне́вный daily, everyday. **ка́ждый** each, every; everybody.

ка́жется *etc.*: *see* каза́ться.

каза́к (-á; *pl* -áки, -áков). **каза́чка** Cossack.

каза́рма barracks.

каза́ться (кажу́сь, ка́жешься) *impf* (*pf* по~) seem, appear; *impers* ка́жется, каза́лось apparently; каза́лось бы it would seem; +*dat*: мне ка́жется it seems to me; I think.

Казахста́н Kazakhstan. **каза́чий** Cossack.

каземат casemate.

казённый State; government; fiscal; public; formal; banal, conventional. **казна́** Exchequer, Treasury; public purse; the State. **казначе́й** treasurer, bursar; paymaster.

казино́ *neut indecl* casino.

казни́ть *impf & pf* execute; punish; castigate. **казнь** execution.

кайма́ (*gen pl* каём) border, edging.

как *adv* how; what; **вот** ~! you don't say!; ~ **вы ду́маете**

what do you think?; ~ его зовут? what is his name?; ~ же naturally, of course; ~ же так? how is that?; ~ ни however. как conj as; like; when; since; +neg but, except, than; в то время ~ while, whereas; ~ можно, ~ нельзя+comp as ... as possible; ~ можно скорее as soon as possible; нельзя лучше as well as possible; ~ только as soon as, when; между тем, ~ while, whereas. как будто conj as if; partl apparently. как бы how; as if; как бы... не as if, supposing; как бы... не however. как-либо adv somehow. как-нибудь adv somehow; anyhow. как раз adv just, exactly. как-то adv somehow; once.

какао neut indecl cocoa.

каков (-á, -ó, -ы) pron what, what sort (of); ~ он? what is he like?; ~ собой? what does he look like?; погода-то какова! what weather! каково adv how. какой pron what; (such) as; which; ~... ни whatever, whichever. какой-либо, какой-нибудь prons some; any; only. какой-то pron some; a kind of.

как раз, как-то see как

кактус cactus.

кал faeces, excrement.

каламбур pun.

калека m & f cripple.

календарь (-я) m calendar.

каление incandescence.

калечить impf (pf ис-, по-) cripple, maim; ~ся become a cripple.

калибр calibre; bore; gauge.

калий potassium.

калитка (wicket-)gate.

каллиграфия calligraphy.

калория calorie.

калоша galosh.

калька tracing-paper; tracing.

калькуляция calculation.

кальсоны (-н) pl long johns.

кальций calcium.

камбала flat-fish; plaice; flounder.

каменистый stony, rocky. каменноугольный coal; ~ бассейн coal-field. каменный stone; rock; stony; hard, immovable; ~ век Stone Age; ~ уголь coal. каменоломня (gen pl -мен) quarry. каменщик (stone)mason; bricklayer. камень (-мня; pl -мни, -мней) m stone.

камера chamber; cell; camera; inner tube, (football) bladder; ~ хранения cloak-room, left-luggage office. камерный chamber. камертон tuning-fork.

камин fireplace; fire.

камкордер camcorder.

каморка closet, very small room.

кампания campaign; cruise.

камыш (-á) reed, rush; cane.

канава ditch; gutter.

Канада Canada. канадец (-дца) Canadian. канадка Canadian. канадский Canadian.

канал canal; channel. канализация sewerage (system).

канарейка canary.

канат rope; cable.

канва canvas; groundwork; outline, plan.

кандалы (-ов) pl shackles.

кандидат candidate; ~ наук person with higher degree. кандидатура candidature.

каникулы (-ул) pl vacation; holidays.

кани́стра can, canister.

канони́ческий canon(ical).

кано́э neut indecl canoe.

кант edging; mount. **канто-ва́ть** impf; «не ~» 'this way up'.

кану́н eve.

ка́нуть (-ну) pf drop, sink; **как в во́ду** ~ vanish into thin air.

канцеля́рия office. **канцеля́рский** clerical. **канцеля́рщина** red-tape.

ка́нцлер chancellor.

ка́пать (-аю or -плю) impf (pf **ка́пнуть, на~**) drip, drop; trickle; +instr spill.

капе́лла choir; chapel.

ка́пелька small drop; a little; ~ **росы́** dew-drop.

капельме́йстер conductor; bandmaster.

капилля́р capillary.

капита́л capital. **капитали́зм** capitalism. **капитали́ст** capitalist. **капиталисти́ческий** capitalist. **капита́льный** capital; main, fundamental; major.

капита́н captain; skipper.

капитули́ровать impf & pf capitulate. **капитуля́ция** capitulation.

капка́н trap.

ка́пля (gen pl -пель) drop; bit, scrap. **ка́пнуть** (-ну) pf of **ка́пать**

капо́т hood, cowl, cowling; bonnet; house-coat.

капри́з caprice. **капри́зничать** impf play up. **капри́зный** capricious.

капу́ста cabbage.

капюшо́н hood.

ка́ра punishment.

кара́бкаться impf (pf вс~) clamber.

карава́н caravan; convoy.

кара́кули f pl scribble.

караме́ль caramel; caramels.

каранда́ш (-á) pencil.

каранти́н quarantine.

кара́т carat.

кара́тельный punitive. **кара́ть** impf (pf по~) punish.

карау́л guard; watch; ~! help! **карау́лить** impf guard; lie in wait for. **карау́льный** guard; sb sentry, sentinel, guard.

карбюра́тор carburettor.

каре́та carriage, coach.

ка́рий brown; hazel.

карикату́ра caricature; cartoon.

карка́с frame; framework.

ка́ркать impf, **ка́ркнуть** (-ну) pf caw, croak.

ка́рлик, ка́рлица dwarf; pygmy. **ка́рликовый** dwarf; pygmy.

карма́н pocket. **карма́нник** pickpocket. **карма́нный** adj pocket.

карни́з cornice; ledge.

карп carp.

ка́рта map; (playing-)card.

карта́вить (-влю) impf burr.

картёжник gambler.

карте́чь case-shot, grape-shot.

карти́на picture; scene. **карти́нка** picture; illustration. **карти́нный** picturesque; picture.

карто́н cardboard. **карто́нка** cardboard box.

картоте́ка card-index.

карто́фель m potatoes; potato(-plant). **карто́фельный** potato; ~ое пюре́ mashed potatoes.

ка́рточка card; season ticket; photo. **ка́рточный** card.

карто́шка potatoes; potato.

карусе́ль merry-go-round.

ка́рцер cell, lock-up.

карье́р[1] full gallop.

карье́р² quarry; sand-pit.

карье́ра career. **карьери́ст** careerist.

каса́ние contact. **каса́тельная** *sb* tangent. **каса́ться** *impf* (*pf* **косну́ться**) +*gen* or до+*gen* touch; touch on; concern; **что каса́ется** as regards.

ка́ска helmet.

каска́д cascade.

каспи́йский Caspian.

ка́сса till; cash-box; booking-office; box-office; cash-desk; cash.

кассе́та cassette. **кассе́тный магнитофо́н** cassette recorder.

касси́р, касси́рша cashier.

кастра́т eunuch. **кастра́ция** castration. **кастри́ровать** *impf* & *pf* castrate, geld.

кастрю́ля saucepan.

катало́г catalogue.

ката́ние rolling; driving; **~ верхо́м** riding; **~ на конька́х** skating.

катапу́льта catapult. **катапульти́ровать(ся** *impf* & *pf* catapult.

ката́р catarrh.

катара́кта cataract.

катастро́фа catastrophe. **катастрофи́ческий** catastrophic.

ката́ть *impf* (*pf* вы́~, с~) roll; (take for a) drive; **~ся** roll, roll about; go for a drive; **~ся верхо́м** ride, go riding; **~ся на конька́х** skate, go skating.

категори́ческий categorical. **катего́рия** category.

ка́тер (*pl* -á) cutter; launch.

кати́ть (-ачу́, -а́тишь) *impf* bowl along, rip, tear; **~ся** rush, tear; flow, stream, roll; **кати́сь, кати́тесь** get out! clear off! **като́к** (-тка́) skating-rink; roller.

като́лик, католи́чка Catholic. **католи́ческий** Catholic.

ка́торга penal servitude, hard labour. **ка́торжник** convict. **ка́торжный** penal; **~ые рабо́ты** hard labour; drudgery.

кату́шка reel, bobbin; spool; coil.

каучу́к rubber.

кафе́ *neut indecl* café.

ка́федра pulpit; rostrum; chair; department.

ка́фель *m* Dutch tile.

кача́лка rocking-chair. **кача́ние** rocking, swinging; pumping. **кача́ть** *impf* (*pf* качну́ть) +*acc* or *instr* rock, swing; shake; **~ся** rock, swing; roll; reel. **каче́ли** (-ей) *pl* swing.

ка́чественный qualitative; high-quality. **ка́чество** quality; **в ка́честве**+*gen* as, in the capacity of.

ка́чка rocking; tossing.

качну́ть(ся (-ну́(сь, -нёшь(ся) *pf* of **кача́ть(ся. качу́** *etc.: see* кати́ть

ка́ша gruel, porridge; **завари́ть ка́шу** stir up trouble.

ка́шель (-шля) cough. **ка́шлянуть** (-ну) *pf*, **ка́шлять** *impf* (have a) cough.

кашта́н chestnut. **кашта́новый** chestnut.

каю́та cabin, stateroom.

ка́ющийся penitent. **ка́яться** (ка́юсь) *impf* (*pf* по~, рас~) repent; confess; **ка́юсь** I (must) confess.

кв. *abbr* (*of* квадра́тный) square; (*of* кварти́ра) flat.

квадра́т square; quad; **в квадра́те** squared; **возвести́ в ~** square. **квадра́тный** square; quadratic.

ква́кать *impf*, **ква́кнуть** (-ну) *pf* croak.

квалифика́ция qualification.
квалифици́рованный qualified, skilled.

квант, ква́нта quantum. **ква́нтовый** quantum.

кварта́л block; quarter. **кварта́льный** quarterly.

кварте́т quartet.

кварти́ра flat; apartment(s); quarters. **квартира́нт, -ра́нтка** lodger; tenant. **кварти́рная пла́та, квартпла́та** rent.

кварц quartz.

квас (pl ~ы́) kvass. **ква́сить** (-а́шу) impf sour; pickle. **ква́шеная капу́ста** sauerkraut.

кве́рху adv up, upwards.

квит, кви́ты quits.

квита́нция receipt. **квито́к** (-тка́) ticket, check.

КГБ abbr (of Комите́т госуда́рственной безопа́сности) KGB.

ке́гля skittle.

кедр cedar.

ке́ды (-ов) pl trainers.

кекс (fruit-)cake.

ке́лья (gen pl -лий) cell.

кем see кто

ке́мпинг campsite.

кенгуру́ m indecl kangaroo.

ке́пка cloth cap.

кера́мика ceramics.

кероси́н stove. **кероси́нка** paraffin stove.

ке́та Siberian salmon. **ке́товый** ; **~ая икра́** red caviare.

кефи́р kefir, yoghurt.

киберне́тика cybernetics.

кива́ть impf, **кивну́ть** (-ну́, -нёшь) pf (голово́й) nod (one's head); (+на+acc) motion (to). **киво́к** (-вка́) nod.

кида́ть impf (кину́ть throw, fling; **~ся** fling o.s.; rush; +instr throw.

кий (-я́; pl -и́, -ёв) (billiard) cue.

киле́вой keel; **~ая ка́чка** pitching.

кило́ neut indecl kilo. **килова́тт** kilowatt. **килогра́мм** kilogram. **киломе́тр** kilometre.

киль m keel; fin. **кильва́тер** wake.

ки́лька sprat.

кинжа́л dagger.

кино́ neut indecl cinema.

кино- in comb film-, cine-. **киноаппара́т** cinecamera. **~арти́ст, ~арти́стка** film actor, actress. **~журна́л** newsreel. **~за́л** cinema; auditorium. **~звезда́** film-star. **~зри́тель** m film-goer. **~карти́на** film. **~опера́тор** camera-man. **~плёнка** film. **~режиссёр** film director. **~теа́тр** cinema. **~хро́ника** news-reel.

ки́нуть(ся (-ну(сь) pf of **кида́ть(ся**

кио́ск kiosk, stall.

ки́па pile, stack; bale.

кипари́с cypress.

кипе́ние boiling. **кипе́ть** (-плю́) impf (pf вс~) boil, seethe.

кипу́чий boiling, seething, ebullient. **кипяти́льник** kettle, boiler. **кипяти́ть** (-ячу́) impf (pf вс~) boil; **~ся** boil; get excited. **кипято́к** (-тка́) boiling water. **кипячёный** boiled.

Кирги́зия Kirghizia.

кирка́ pick(axe).

кирпи́ч (-а́) brick; bricks. **кирпи́чный** brick; brick-red.

кисе́ль m kissel, blancmange.

кисе́т tobacco-pouch.

кисея́ muslin.

кислоро́д oxygen. **кислота́**

(*pl* -ы) acid; acidity. **кисло́тный** acid. **ки́слый** sour; acid. **ки́снуть** (-ну; кис) *impf* (*pf* про~) turn sour.

ки́сточка brush; tassel. **кисть** (*gen pl* -е́й) cluster, bunch; brush; tassel; hand.

кит (-á) whale.

кита́ец (-а́йца; *pl* -цы, -цев) Chinese. **Кита́й** China. **кита́йский** Chinese. **китая́нка** Chinese (woman).

китобо́й whaler. **кито́вый** whale.

кичи́ться (-чу́сь) *impf* plume o.s.; strut. **кичли́вость** conceit. **кичли́вый** conceited.

кише́ть (-ши́т) *impf* swarm, teem.

кише́чник bowels, intestines. **кише́чный** intestinal. **кишка́** gut, intestine; hose.

клавеси́н harpsichord. **клавиату́ра** keyboard. **кла́виша** key. **кла́вишный:** ~ **инструме́нт** keyboard instrument.

клад treasure. **кла́дбище** cemetery; graveyard. **кла́дка** laying; masonry. **кладова́я** *sb* pantry; store-room. **кладовщи́к** (-á) storeman. **кладу́** *etc.:* *see* **класть**

кла́няться *impf* (*pf* поклони́ться) +*dat* bow to; greet.

кла́пан valve; vent.

кларне́т clarinet.

класс class; class-room. **кла́ссик** classic. **кла́ссика** the classics. **классифици́ровать** *impf* & *pf* classify. **класси́ческий** classical. **кла́ссный** class; first-class. **кла́ссовый** class.

класть (-аду́, -адёшь; -ал) *impf* (*pf* положи́ть, сложи́ть) lay; put.

клева́ть (клюю́, клюёшь) *impf* peck; bite.

кле́вер (*pl* -á) clover.

клевета́ slander; libel. **клевета́ть** (-ещу́, -е́щешь) *impf* (*pf* на~) +на+*acc* slander; libel. **клеветни́к** (-á), -**ни́ца** slanderer. **клеветни́ческий** slanderous; libellous.

клеёнка oilcloth. **кле́ить** *impf* (*pf* с~) glue; stick; ~ся stick; become sticky. **клей** (*loc* -ю́; *pl* -и́) glue, adhesive. **кле́йкий** sticky.

клейми́ть (-млю́) *impf* (*pf* за~) brand; stamp; stigmatize. **клеймо́** (*pl* -а) brand; stamp; mark.

кле́йстер paste.

клён maple.

клепа́ть *impf* rivet.

кле́тка cage; check; cell. **кле́точка** cellule. **кле́точный** cellular. **клетча́тка** cellulose. **кле́тчатый** checked.

клёш flare.

клешня́ (*gen pl* -е́й) claw.

кле́щи (-е́й) pincers, tongs.

клие́нт client. **клиенту́ра** clientèle.

кли́зма enema.

клик cry, call. **кли́кать** (-и́чу) *impf*, **кли́кнуть** (-ну) *pf* call.

кли́макс menopause. **кли́мат** climate. **климати́ческий** climatic.

клин (*pl* -нья, -ньев) wedge. **клино́к** (-нка́) blade.

кли́ника clinic. **клини́ческий** clinical.

клипс clip-on ear-ring.

кли́ч call. **кли́чка** name; nickname. **кли́чу** *etc.:* *see* **кли́кать**

клок (-á; *pl* -о́чья, -ьев *or* -и́, -о́в) rag, shred; tuft.

КЛО́КОТ bubbling; gurgling.

клокота́ть (-о́чет) *impf* bubble; gurgle; boil up.

клони́ть (-ню́, -нишь) *impf* bend; incline; +к+*dat* drive at; ~**ся** bow, bend; +к+*dat* near, approach.

клоп (-á) bug.

кло́ун clown.

клочо́к (-чка́) scrap, shred. **кло́чья** *etc.*: *see* клок

клуб[1] club.

клуб[2] (*pl* -ы́) puff; cloud.

клу́бень (-бня) *m* tuber.

клуби́ться *impf* swirl; curl.

клубни́ка (*no pl*; *usu collect*) strawberry; strawberries.

клубо́к (-бка́) ball; tangle.

клу́мба (flower-)bed.

клык (-á) fang; tusk; canine (*tooth*).

клюв beak.

клю́ква cranberry; cranberries.

клю́нуть (-ну) *pf of* клева́ть

ключ[1] (-á) key; clue; keystone; clef; wrench; spanner.

ключ[2] (-á) spring; source.

ключево́й key. **ключи́ца** collarbone.

клю́шка (hockey) stick; (golf-) club.

клюю́ *etc.*: *see* клева́ть

кля́кса blot, smudge.

кляну́ *etc.*: *see* клясть

кля́нчить (-чу) *impf* (*pf* вы́~) beg.

кляп gag.

клясть (-яну́, -янёшь; -ял, -á, -о) *impf* curse; ~**ся** (*pf* по~ся) swear, vow. **кля́тва** oath, vow. **кля́твенный** on oath.

кни́га book.

книго- *in comb* book, biblio-. **книгове́дение**[1] bibliography. ~**ве́дение**[2] book-keeping. ~**изда́тель** *m* publisher. ~**лю́б** bibliophile, book-lover. ~**храни́лище** library;

book-stack.

книже́чка booklet. **кни́жка** book; note-book; bank-book. **кни́жный** book; bookish.

кни́зу *adv* downwards.

кно́пка drawing-pin; press-stud; (push)button, knob.

кнут (-á) whip.

княги́ня princess. **кня́жество** principality. **княжна́** (*gen pl* -жо́н) princess. **князь** (*pl* -зья́, -зе́й) *m* prince.

ко *see* к *prep*.

коали́ция coalition.

кобура́ holster.

кобы́ла mare; (vaulting-)horse.

ко́ваный forged; wrought; terse.

кова́рный insidious, crafty; perfidious. **кова́рство** insidiousness, craftiness; perfidy.

кова́ть (кую́, -ёшь) *impf* (*pf* под~) forge; hammer; shoe.

ковёр (-вра́) carpet; rug; mat.

коверка́ть *impf* (*pf* ис~) distort, mangle, ruin.

ко́вка forging; shoeing.

коври́жка honeycake, gingerbread.

ко́врик rug; mat.

ковче́г ark.

ковш (-á) scoop, ladle.

ковы́ль *m* feather-grass.

ковыля́ть *impf* hobble.

ковыря́ть (-ну́, -нёшь) *pf*, **ковыря́ть** *impf* dig into; tinker; +в+*prep* pick (at); ~**ся** rummage; tinker.

когда́ *adv* when; ~ (бы) ни whenever; *conj* when; while, as; if. **когда́-либо**, **когда́-нибудь** *advs* some time; ever. **когда́-то** *adv* once; formerly; some time.

кого́ *see* кто

ко́готь (-гтя; *pl* -гти, -гте́й) *m* claw; talon.

код code.
кодеи́н codeine.
ко́декс code.
ко́е-где́ *adv* here and there.
ко́е-ка́к *adv* anyhow; somehow (or other). **ко́е-како́й** *pron* some. **ко́е-кто́** *pron* somebody; some people. **ко́е-что́** (-чего́) *pron* something; a little.
ко́жа skin; leather; peel. **ко́жанка** leather jacket. **ко́жаный** leather; tanning. **ко́жевенный** leather; tanning. **ко́жный** skin. **кожура́** rind, peel, skin.
коза́ (*pl* -ы) goat, nanny-goat. **козёл** (-зла́) billy-goat. **козеро́г** ibex; Capricorn. **ко́зий** goat; ~ **пух** angora. **козлёнок** (-нка; *pl* -ля́та, -ля́т) kid. **ко́злы** (-зел) *pl* coach driver's seat; trestle(s); saw-horse. **ко́зни** (-ей) *pl* machinations. **козырёк** (-рька́) peak. **козырно́й** trump. **козырну́ть** (-ну́, -нёшь) *pf*, **козыря́ть** *impf* lead trumps; trump; play one's trump card; salute. **ко́зырь** (*pl* -и, -ей) *m* trump.
ко́йка (*gen pl* ко́ек) berth; bunk; bed.
кока́ин cocaine.
ко́ка-ко́ла Coca-Cola (*propr*).
коке́тка coquette. **коке́тство** coquetry.
коклю́ш whooping-cough.
ко́кон cocoon.
коко́с coconut.
кокс coke.
кокте́йль *m* cocktail.
кол (-á; *pl* -лья, -ьев) stake, picket.
ко́лба retort.
колбаса́ (*pl* -ы) sausage.
колго́тки (-ток) *pl* tights.
колдова́ть *impf* practise witchcraft. **колдовство́** sorcery. **колду́н** (-á) sorcerer,

wizard. **колду́нья** (*gen pl* -ний) witch, sorceress.
колеба́ние oscillation; variation; hesitation. **колеба́ть** (-блю) *impf* (*pf* по~) shake; ~**ся** oscillate; fluctuate; hesitate.
коле́но (*pl* -и, -ей, -ям) knee; (*in pl*) lap. **коле́нчатый** crank, cranked; bent; ~ **вал** crankshaft.
колесни́ца chariot. **колесо́** (*pl* -ёса) wheel.
колея́ rut; track, gauge.
ко́лика (*usu pl*) colic; stitch.
коли́чественный quantitative; ~**ое числи́тельное** cardinal number. **коли́чество** quantity; number.
колле́га *m & f* colleague. **колле́гия** board; college.
коллекти́в collective. **коллективиза́ция** collectivization. **коллекти́вный** collective. **коллекционе́р** collector. **колле́кция** collection.
колли́зия clash, conflict.
коло́да block; pack (*of cards*).
коло́дец (-дца) well.
ко́локол (*pl* -á, -о́в) bell. **колоко́льный** bell. **колоко́льня** bell-tower. **колоко́льчик** bell; bluebell.
колониали́зм colonialism. **колониа́льный** colonial. **колониза́тор** colonizer. **колониза́ция** colonization. **колонизова́ть** *impf & pf* colonize. **коло́ния** colony.
коло́нка geyser; (*street*) water fountain; stand-pipe; column; **бензи́новая** ~ petrol pump. **коло́нна** column.
колори́т colouring, colour. **колори́тный** colourful, graphic.
ко́лос (-о́сья, -ьев) *pl* ear. **коло́ситься** *impf* form ears.

колосса́льный huge; terrific.

колоти́ть (-очу́, -о́тишь) *impf* (*pf* по~) beat; pound; thrash; smash; ~ся pound, thump; shake.

коло́ть[1] (-лю́, -лешь) *impf* (*pf* рас~) break, chop.

коло́ть[2] (-лю́, -лешь) *impf* (*pf* за~, кольну́ть) prick; stab; sting; slaughter; ~ся prick.

колпа́к (-а́) cap; hood, cowl.

колхо́з *abbr* (*of* коллекти́вное хозя́йство) kolkhoz, collective farm. **колхо́зник, ~ица** kolkhoz member. **колхо́зный** kolkhoz.

колыбе́ль cradle.

колыха́ть (-ы́шу) *impf*, **колыхну́ть** (-ну́, -нёшь) *pf* sway, rock; ~ся sway; flutter.

кольну́ть (-ну́, -нёшь) *pf of* коло́ть

кольцо́ (*pl* -а, -ле́ц, -льцам) ring.

колю́ч|ий prickly; sharp; ~ая про́волока barbed wire. **колю́чка** prickle; thorn.

коля́ска carriage; pram; sidecar.

ком (*pl* -мья, -мьев) lump; ball.

ком *see* кто

кома́нда command; order; detachment; crew; team. **команди́р** commander. **командирова́ть** *impf & pf* post, send on a mission. **командиро́вка** posting; mission, business trip. **командиро́вочные** *sb pl* travelling expenses. **кома́ндование** command. **кома́ндовать** *impf* (*pf* с~) give orders; be in command; +*instr* command. **кома́ндующий** *sb* commander.

кома́р (-а́) mosquito.

комба́йн combine harvester.

комбина́т industrial complex.

комбина́ция combination; manoeuvre; slip. **комбинезо́н** overalls, boiler suit; dungarees. **комбини́ровать** *impf* (*pf* с~) combine.

коме́дия comedy.

коменда́нт commandant; manager; warden. **комендату́ра** commandant's office.

коме́та comet.

ко́мик comic actor; comedian. **ко́микс** comic, comic strip.

комисса́р commissar.

комиссионе́р (commission-) agent, broker. **комиссио́нный** commission; ~ый магази́н second-hand shop; ~ые *sb pl* commission. **коми́ссия** commission; committee.

комите́т committee.

коми́ческий comic; comical. **коми́чный** comical, funny.

кома́ть *impf* (*pf* с~) crumple.

коммента́рий commentary; *pl* comment. **коммента́тор** commentator. **комменти́ровать** *impf & pf* comment (on).

коммерса́нт merchant; businessman **комме́рция** commerce. **комме́рческий** commercial.

коммивояжёр commercial traveller.

комму́на commune. **комму́нальный** communal; municipal. **коммуни́зм** communism. **коммуника́ция** communication.

коммуни́ст, ~ка communist. **коммунисти́ческий** communist.

коммута́тор switchboard.

коммюнике́ *neut indecl* communiqué.

ко́мната room. **ко́мнатный** room; indoor.

комо́д chest of drawers.

комо́к (-мка́) lump.

компа́кт-ди́ск compact disc. **компа́ктный** compact.

компа́ния company. **компаньо́н**, **~ка** companion; partner.

компа́ртия Communist Party.

ко́мпас compass.

компенса́ция compensation. **компенси́ровать** *impf & pf* compensate.

ко́мплекс complex. **ко́мплексный** complex, compound, composite; combined. **компле́кт** (complete) set; complement; kit. **комплектова́ть** *impf* (*pf* c~, y~) complete; bring up to strength. **компле́кция** build; constitution.

комплиме́нт compliment.

компози́тор composer. **компози́ция** composition.

компоне́нт component.

компо́ст compost.

компо́стер punch. **компости́ровать** *impf* (*pf* про~) punch.

компо́т stewed fruit.

компре́ссор compressor.

компромети́ровать *impf* (*pf* c~) compromise. **компроми́сс** compromise.

компью́тер computer.

комсомо́л Komsomol. **комсомо́лец** (-льца), **-лка** Komsomol member. **комсомо́льский** Komsomol.

кому́ *see* кто

комфо́рт comfort.

конве́йер conveyor.

конве́рт envelope; sleeve.

конвои́р escort. **конвои́ровать** *impf* escort. **конво́й** escort, convoy.

конгре́сс congress.

конденса́тор condenser.

конди́терская *sb* confectioner's, cake shop.

кондиционе́р air-conditioner. **кондицио́нный** air-conditioning.

конду́ктор (*pl* -á), **-торша** conductor; guard.

конево́дство horse-breeding. **конёк** (-нька́) *dim of* конь; hobby(-horse).

коне́ц (-нца́) end; **в конце́ концо́в** in the end, after all. **коне́чно** *adv* of course. **коне́чность** extremity. **коне́чный** final, last; ultimate; finite.

кони́ческий conic, conical.

конкре́тный concrete.

конкуре́нт competitor. **конкуре́нция** competition. **конкури́ровать** *impf* compete. **ко́нкурс** competition; contest.

ко́нница cavalry. **ко́нный** horse; mounted; equestrian; ~ **заво́д** stud.

конопля́ hemp.

консервати́вный conservative. **консерва́тор** Conservative.

консервато́рия conservatoire.

консерви́ровать *impf & pf* (*pf also* за~) preserve; can, bottle. **консе́рвный** preserving; ~**ая ба́нка** tin; ~**ый нож** tin-opener. **консерво-откры́ватель** *m* tin-opener. **консе́рвы** (-ов) *pl* tinned goods.

конси́лиум consultation.

конспе́кт synopsis, summary. **конспекти́ровать** *impf* (*pf* за~, про~) make an abstract of.

конспирати́вный secret, clandestine. **конспира́ция** security.

констата́ция ascertaining; establishment. **констати́ровать**

impf & pf ascertain; establish.
конституцио́нный constitutional. **конститу́ция** constitution.

констру́ировать *impf & pf* (*pf also* **с~**) construct; design. **конструкти́вный** structural; constructional; constructive. **констру́ктор** designer, constructor. **констру́кция** construction; design.

ко́нсул consul.

консульта́ция consultation; advice; clinic; tutorial. **консульти́ровать** *impf* (*pf* **про~**) advise; *+instr* consult; **~ся** obtain advice; *+instr* consult.

конта́кт contact. **конта́ктные ли́нзы** *f pl* contact lenses.

конте́йнер container.

конте́кст context.

контине́нт continent.

конто́ра office. **конто́рский** office.

контраба́нда contraband. **контрабанди́ст** smuggler.

контраба́с double-bass.

контраге́нт contractor. **контра́кт** contract.

контра́льто *neut/fem indecl* contralto (*voice/person*).

контрама́рка complimentary ticket.

контрапу́нкт counterpoint.

контра́ст contrast.

контрибу́ция indemnity.

контрнаступле́ние counter-offensive.

контролёр inspector; ticket-collector. **контроли́ровать** *impf* (*pf* **про~**) check; check. **контро́ль** *m* control; check; inspection. **контро́льн|ый** control; **~ая рабо́та** test.

контрразве́дка counter-in-

telligence; security service. **контрреволю́ция** counter-revolution.

конту́зия bruising; shell-shock. **ко́нтур** contour, outline; circuit.

конура́ kennel.

ко́нус cone.

конфедера́ция confederation.

конфере́нция conference.

конфе́та sweet.

конфискова́ть *impf & pf* confiscate.

конфли́кт conflict.

конфо́рка ring (*on stove*).

конфу́з discomfort, embarrassment, embarrassment. **конфу́зить** (-**у́жу**) *impf* (*pf* **с~**) confuse, embarrass; **~ся** feel embarrassed.

концентра́т concentrate. **концентрацио́нный** concentration. **концентра́ция** concentration. **концентри́ровать** (**-ся**) *impf* (*pf* **с~**) concentrate.

конце́пция conception.

конце́рт concert; concerto. **концертме́йстер** leader; soloist. **конце́ртный** concert.

концла́герь *abbr* (*of* концентрацио́нный ла́герь) concentration camp.

конча́ть *impf*, **ко́нчить** *pf* finish; end; *+inf* stop; **~ся** end, finish; expire. **ко́нчик** tip. **кончи́на** decease.

конь (-**я́**, *pl* **-и**, **-е́й**) *m* horse; knight. **коньки́** (-**о́в**) *pl* skates; **~ на ро́ликах** roller skates. **конькобе́жец** (-**жца**) skater.

конья́к (-**а́**) cognac.

ко́нюх groom, stable-boy. **коню́шня** (*gen pl* -**шен**) stable.

кооперати́в cooperative. **кооперати́вный** cooperative. **коопера́ция** cooperation.

координа́та coordinate. **координа́ция** coordination.

копа́ть *impf* (*pf* копну́ть, вы́~); dig; dig up, dig out; ~ся rummage.

копе́йка copeck.

ко́пи (-ей) *pl* mines.

копи́лка money-box.

копирова́льный carbon paper. копи-рова́ние copying. копи-рова́ть *impf* (*pf* c~) copy; imitate.

копи́ть (-плю́, -пишь) *impf* (*pf* на~) save (up); accumulate; ~ся accumulate.

ко́пия copy.

копна́ (*pl* -ы, -пён) shock, stook.

копну́ть (-ну́, -нёшь) *pf of* копа́ть

ко́поть hoof.

копте́ть (-пчу́) *impf* swot; vegetate. копти́ть (-пчу́) *impf* (*pf* за~, на~) smoke, cure; blacken with smoke. копче́-ние smoking; smoked foods. копчёный smoked.

копы́то hoof.

копьё (*pl* -я, -пий) spear, lance.

кора́ bark, rind; cortex; crust.

кора́бельный ship; naval. кораблевожде́ние navigation. кораблекруше́ние shipwreck. кораблестрое́ние shipbuilding. кора́бль (-я́) *m* ship, vessel; nave.

кора́лл coral.

коре́йский Korean. Коре́я Korea.

корена́стый thickset. коре-ни́ться *impf* be rooted. коренно́й radical, fundamental; native. ко́рень (-рня, *pl* -и, -е́й) *m* root. корешо́к (-шка́) root(let); spine; counterfoil.

корзи́на, корзи́нка basket.

коридо́р corridor.

кори́ца cinnamon.

кори́чневый brown.

ко́рка crust; rind, peel.

корм (*loc* -у́; *pl* -а́) fodder.

корма́ stern.

корми́лец (-льца) bread-win-ner. корми́ть (-млю́, -мишь) *impf* (*pf* на~, по~, про~) feed; ~ся feed; +*instr* live on, make a living by; кормле́ние feeding. кормово́й¹ fodder.

кормово́й² stern.

корнево́й root; radical. корне-плоды́ (-ов) root-crops.

коро́бить (-блю) *impf* (*pf* по~) warp; jar upon; ~ся (*pf also* с~ся) warp.

коро́бка box.

коро́ва cow.

короле́ва queen. короле́в-ский royal. короле́вство kingdom. коро́ль (-я́) *m* king.

коромы́сло yoke; beam; rocking shaft.

коро́на crown.

коронаротромбо́з coronary (thrombosis).

коро́нка crown. коронова́ть *impf & pf* crown.

коро́ткий (коро́ток, -тка́, коро́тко́, коро́тки́) short; intimate. ко́ротко *adv* briefly; inti-mately. коротково́лновый short-wave. коро́че *comp of* коро́ткий, ко́ротко

корпора́ция corporation.

ко́рпус (*pl* -ы, -ов *or* -а́, -о́в) corps; services; building; hull; housing, case; body.

корректи́ровать *impf* (*pf* про~, с~) correct, edit. корре́ктный correct, proper. корре́ктор (*pl* -а́) proof-reader. корректу́ра proof-reading; proof.

корреспонде́нт correspond-ent. корреспонде́нция cor-respondence.

корро́зия corrosion.

коррупция corruption.

корт (tennis-)court.

кортеж cortège; motorcade.

кортик dirk.

корточки (-чек) *pl*: **сидеть на корточках** squat.

корчевать (-чую) *impf* root out.

корчить (-чу) *impf* (*pf* с~) contort; *impers* convulse; ~ **из себя** pose as; ~**ся** writhe.

коршун kite.

корыстный mercenary. **корысть** avarice; profit.

корыто trough; wash-tub.

корь measles.

коса[1] (*acc* сý, *pl* -ы) plait, tress.

коса[2] (*acc* косý, *pl* -ы) spit.

коса[3] (*acc* косý, *pl* -ы) scythe.

косвенный indirect.

косилка mowing-machine, mower. **косить** (кошý, косишь) *impf* (*pf* с~) cut; mow (down).

косить[2] (кошý) *impf* (*pf* по~, с~) squint; be crooked; ~**ся** slant; look sideways; look askance.

косметика cosmetics, make-up. **космический** cosmic; space. **космодром** spacecraft launching-site. **космонавт, -навтка** cosmonaut, astronaut. **космос** cosmos; (outer) space.

косноязычный tongue-tied.

коснуться (-нýсь, -нёшься) *pf of* касаться

косоглазие squint. **косой** (кос, -á, -о) slanting; oblique; sidelong; squinting, cross-eyed.

костёр (-трá) bonfire; camp-fire.

костлявый bony. **костный** bone; stone. **косточка** (small) bone; stone.

костыль (-я) *m* crutch.

кость (*loc* -ú, *pl* -и, -éй) bone; die.

костюм clothes; suit. **костюмированный** fancy-dress.

костяной bone; ivory.

косынка (*triangular*) head-scarf, shawl.

кот (-á) tom-cat.

котёл (-тлá) boiler; copper, cauldron. **котелок** (-лкá) pot; mess-tin; bowler (hat). **котельная** *sb* boiler-room, -house.

котёнок (-нка; *pl* -тята, -тят) kitten. **котик** fur-seal; sealskin.

котлета rissole; burger; **отбивная** ~ chop.

котлован foundation pit, trench.

котомка knapsack.

который *pron* which, what; who; that; ~ **час?** what time is it?

котята *etc.*: *see* **котёнок**

кофе *m indecl* coffee. **кофеварка** percolator. **кофеин** caffeine.

кофта, кофточка blouse, top.

кочан (-á *or* -чнá) (cabbage-) head.

кочевать (-чую) *impf* be a nomad; wander; migrate. **кочевник** nomad. **кочевой** nomadic.

кочегар stoker, fireman. **кочегарка** stokehold, stokehole.

коченеть *impf* (*pf* за~, о~) grow numb.

кочерга (*gen pl* -рёг) poker.

кочка hummock.

кошелёк (-лькá) purse.

кошка cat.

кошмар nightmare. **кошмарный** nightmarish.

кошý *etc.*: *see* **косить**

кощунство blasphemy.

коэффициент coefficient.

КП *abbr* (*of* Коммунистическая партия) Communist

Party. **КПСС** abbr (of Коммунисти́ческая па́ртия Сове́тского Сою́за) Communist Party of the Soviet Union, CPSU.
краб crab.

кра́деный stolen. **краду́** etc.: see **красть**

кра́жа theft; ~ со взло́мом burglary.

край (loc -ю́; pl -я́, -ёв) edge; brink; land; region. **кра́йне** adv extremely. **кра́йний** extreme; last; outside; wing; по кра́йней ме́ре at least. **кра́йность** extreme; extremity.

крал etc.: see **красть**

кран tap; crane.

крапи́ва nettle.

краса́вец (-вца) handsome man. **краса́вица** beauty. **краси́вый** beautiful; handsome.

краси́тель m dye. **кра́сить** (-а́шу) impf (pf вы́~, о~, по~) paint; colour; dye; stain; ~ся (pf на~) make-up. **кра́ска** paint, dye; colour.

красне́ть (-е́ю) impf (pf по~) blush; redden; show red.

красноарме́ец (-е́йца) Red Army man. **красноарме́йский** Red Army. **красноречи́вый** eloquent.

краснота́ redness. **красну́ха** German measles. **кра́сн|ый** (-сен, -сна́, -о) red; beautiful; fine; ~ое де́рево mahogany; ~ая сморо́дина (no pl; usu collect) redcurrant; redcurrants; (~ая строка́ (first line of) new paragraph.

красова́ться impf impress by one's beauty; show off.
красота́ (pl -ы) beauty. **кра́сочный** paint; ink; colourful.

красть (-аду́, -адёшь; крал)

---

impf (pf у~) steal; ~ся creep.

кра́тер crater.

кра́ткий (-ток, -тка́, -о) short; brief. **кратковре́менный** brief; transitory. **кратко-сро́чный** short-term.

кра́тное sb multiple.

кратча́йший superl of **кра́ткий**. **кра́тче** comp of **кра́ткий**, **кра́тко**

крах crash; failure.

крахма́л starch. **крахма́лить** impf (pf на~) starch.

кра́ше comp of **краси́вый**, **краси́во**

кра́шеный painted; coloured; dyed; made up. **кра́шу** etc.: see **кра́сить**

креве́тка shrimp; prawn.

креди́т credit. **креди́тный** credit. **кредитоспосо́бный** solvent.

кре́йсер (pl -а́, -о́в) cruiser.

крем cream.

кремато́рий crematorium.

креме́нь (-мня́) m flint.

кремль (-я́) m citadel; Kremlin.

кре́мниевый silicon.

кре́мовый cream.

крен list, heel; bank. **кре́ниться** impf (pf на~) heel over, list; bank.

крепи́ть (-плю́) impf strengthen; support; make fast; constipate; ~ся hold out; brace. **кре́пк|ий** (-пок, -пка́, -о) strong; firm; ~ие напи́тки spirits. **крепле́ние** strengthening; fastening.

кре́пнуть (-ну, -еп) impf (pf о~) get stronger.

крепостни́чество serfdom. **крепостн|о́й** serf; ~о́е пра́во serfdom; ~о́й sb serf. **кре́пость** fortress; strength. **кре́пче** comp of **кре́пкий**, **кре́пко**

кресло (gen pl -сел) armchair; stall.

крест (-á) cross. **крести́ны** (-и́н) pl christening. **крести́ть** (крещу́, -ести́шь) impf & pf (pf also о∼, пере∼) christen; make sign of the cross over; ∼ся cross o.s.; be christened. **крест-на́крест** adv crosswise. **кре́стник**, **кре́стница** god-child. **крёстн|ый**; ∼ая (мать) godmother; ∼ый **оте́ц** godfather. **кресто́вый похо́д** crusade. **крестоно́сец** (-сца) crusader.

крестья́нин (pl -я́не, -я́н), **крестья́нка** peasant. **крестья́нский** peasant. **крестья́нство** peasantry.

креще́ние christening; Epiphany. **крещён|ый** (-ён, -ена́) baptized; sb Christian. **крещу́** etc.: see **крести́ть**

крива́я sb curve. **кривизна́** crookedness; curvature. **криви́ть** (-влю́) impf (pf по∼, с∼) bend, distort; ∼ душо́й go against one's conscience; ∼ся become crooked or bent; make a wry face. **кривля́ться** impf give o.s. airs. **криво́й** (крив, -á, -о) crooked; curved; one-eyed.

кри́зис crisis.

крик cry, shout.

кри́кет cricket.

кри́кнуть (-ну) pf of **крича́ть**

крими́нальный criminal.

криста́лл crystal. **кристалли́ческий** crystal.

крите́рий criterion.

кри́тик critic. **кри́тика** criticism; critique. **критикова́ть** impf criticize. **крити́ческий** critical.

крича́ть (-чу́) impf (pf кри́кнуть) cry, shout.

кров roof; shelter.

крова́вый bloody.

крова́тка, **крова́ть** bed.

кровено́сный blood-; circulatory.

кро́вля (gen pl -вель) roof.

кро́вный blood; thoroughbred; vital, intimate.

крово- in comb blood. **кровожа́дный** bloodthirsty. ∼**изли́яние** haemorrhage. ∼**обраще́ние** circulation. ∼**проли́тие** bloodshed. ∼**проли́тный** bloody. ∼**смеше́ние** incest. ∼**тече́ние** bleeding; haemorrhage. ∼**точи́ть** (-чи́т) impf bleed.

кровь (loc -и́) blood. **кровяно́й** blood.

крои́ть (крою́) impf (pf с∼) cut (out). **кро́йка** cutting out.

крокоди́л crocodile.

кро́лик rabbit.

кроль m crawl(-stroke).

крольчи́ха she-rabbit, doe.

кро́ме prep+gen except; besides; ∼ **того́** besides, moreover.

кро́мка edge.

кро́на crown; top.

кронште́йн bracket; corbel.

кропотли́вый painstaking; laborious.

кросс cross-country race.

кроссво́рд crossword (puzzle).

крот (-á) mole.

кро́ткий (-ток, -тка́, -тко) meek, gentle. **кро́тость** gentleness; mildness.

кро́хотный, **кро́шечный** tiny.

кро́шка crumb; a bit.

круг (loc -ý, pl -и́) circle; circuit; sphere. **круглосу́точный** round-the-clock. **кру́глый** (кру́гл, -á, -о) round; complete; ∼ **год** all the year round. **кругово́й** circular;

all-round. **кругозо́р** prospect; outlook. **круго́м** adv around; prep+gen round. **кругосве́тный** round-the-world.

кружевно́й lacy. **кру́жево** (pl -á, -ев, -áм) lace.

кружи́ть (-ужу́, -у́жи́шь) impf (pf за~, с~) whirl, spin round; **~ся** whirl, spin round.

кру́жка mug.

кружо́к (-жка́) circle, group.

круи́з cruise.

крупа́ (pl -ы) groats; sleet. **крупи́ца** grain.

кру́пный large, big; great; coarse; ~ый план close-up.

крутизна́ steepness.

крути́ть (-учу́, -у́тишь) impf (pf за~, с~) twist, twirl; roll; turn, wind; ~ся turn, spin; whirl.

круто́й (крут, -á, -о) steep; sudden; sharp; severe; drastic. **кру́ча** steep slope. **кру́че** comp of **круто́й, кру́то**

кручу́ etc.: see **крути́ть**

круше́ние crash; ruin; collapse.

крыжо́вник gooseberries; gooseberry bush.

крыла́тый winged. **крыло́** (pl -лья, -льев) wing; vane; mudguard.

крыльцо́ (pl -a, -лéц, -цáм) porch; (front, back) steps.

Крым the Crimea. **кры́мский** Crimean.

кры́са rat.

крыть (кро́ю) impf cover; roof; trump; ~ся be, lie; be concealed. **кры́ша** roof. **кры́шка** lid.

крюк (-á; pl -ки́, -ко́в or -ю́чья, -чьев) hook; detour. **крючо́к** (-чка́) hook.

кря́ду adv in succession.

кряж ridge.

кря́кать impf, **кря́кнуть** (-ну) pf quack.

кряхте́ть (-хчу́) impf groan.

кста́ти adv to the point; opportunely; at the same time; by the way.

кто (кого́, кому́, кем, ком) pron who; anyone; ~ (бы) ни whoever. **кто́-либо, кто́-нибудь** prons anyone; someone. **кто́-то** pron someone.

куб (pl -ы́) cube; boiler; в ~е cubed.

ку́бик brick, block.

куби́нский Cuban.

куби́ческий cubic; cube.

ку́бок (-бка) goblet; cup.

кубоме́тр cubic metre.

кувши́н jug; pitcher. **кувши́нка** water-lily.

кувырка́ться impf, **кувыркну́ться** (-ну́сь) pf turn somersaults. **кувырко́м** adv head over heels; topsy-turvy.

куда́ adv where (to); what for; +comp much, far; ~ (бы) ни wherever. **куда́-либо, куда́-нибудь** adv anywhere, somewhere. **куда́-то** adv somewhere.

ку́дри (-éй) pl curls. **кудря́вый** curly; florid.

кузне́ц (-á) blacksmith. **кузне́чик** grasshopper. **ку́зница** forge, smithy.

ку́зов (pl -á) basket; body.

ку́кла doll; puppet. **ку́колка** dolly; chrysalis. **ку́кольный** doll's; puppet.

кукуру́за maize.

куку́шка cuckoo.

кула́к (-á) fist; kulak. **кула́цкий** kulak. **кула́чный** fist.

куле́к (-лька́) bag.

кули́к (-á) sandpiper.

кулина́рия cookery. **кулина́рный** culinary.

кули́сы (-ис) wings; за кули́сами behind the scenes.

кули́ч (-á) Easter cake.

кулуа́ры (-ов) pl lobby.

культива́ция culmination.

культ cult. культиви́ровать impf cultivate.

культу́ра culture; standard; cultivation. культури́зм body-building. культу́рно adv in a civilized manner. культу́рный cultured; cultivated; cultural.

куми́р idol.

кумы́с koumiss (fermented mare's milk).

куни́ца marten.

купа́льный bathing. купа́льня bathing-place. купа́ть impf (pf вы́~, ис~) bathe; bath; ~ся bathe; take a bath.

купе́ neut indecl compartment.

купе́ц (-пца́) merchant. купе́ческий merchant. купи́ть (-плю́, -пишь) pf (impf покупа́ть) buy.

ку́пол (pl -á) cupola, dome.

купо́н coupon.

купоро́с vitriol.

купчи́ха merchant's wife; female merchant.

кура́нты (-ов) pl chiming clock; chimes.

курга́н barrow; tumulus.

куре́ние smoking. кури́льщик, -щица smoker.

кури́ный hen's; chicken's.

кури́ть (-рю́, -ришь) impf (pf по~) smoke; ~ся burn; smoke.

ку́рица (pl ку́ры, кур) hen, chicken.

куро́к (-рка́) cocking-piece; взвести́ ~ cock a gun; спусти́ть ~ pull the trigger.

куропа́тка partridge.

куро́рт health-resort; spa.

курс course; policy; year; exchange rate. курса́нт student.

курси́в italics.

курси́ровать impf ply.

ку́ртка jacket.

курча́вый curly(-headed).

ку́ры etc.: see ку́рица

курье́за a funny thing. курьёзный curious.

курье́р messenger; courier. курье́рский express.

куря́тник hen-house.

куря́щий sb smoker.

куса́ть impf bite; sting; ~ся bite.

кусо́к (-ска́) piece; lump. ку́со́чек (-чка) piece.

куст (-á) bush, shrub. куста́рник bush(es), shrub(s).

куста́рный hand-made; handicrafts; primitive; ~ая промы́шленность cottage industry. куста́рь (-я́) m craftsman.

ку́тать (impf за~) wrap up; ~ся muffle o.s. up.

кути́ть (кучу́, ку́тишь) impf, кутну́ть (-ну́, -нёшь) pf carouse; go on a binge.

куха́рка cook. ку́хня (gen pl -хонь) kitchen; cuisine. ку́хонный kitchen.

ку́ча heap; heaps.

ку́чер (pl -á) coachman.

ку́чка small heap or group.

кучу́ see кути́ть

куша́к (-á) sash; girdle.

ку́шанье food; dish. ку́шать impf (pf по~, с~) eat.

куше́тка couch.

кую́ etc.: see кова́ть

Л

лабора́нт, -а́нтка laboratory assistant. лаборато́рия laboratory.

ла́ва lava.

лави́на avalanche.

ла́вка bench; shop. ла́вочка

small shop.

лавр bay tree, laurel.

ла́герный camp. **ла́герь** (*pl* -я́ *or* -и, -ей *or* -ей) *m* camp; campsite.

лад (*loc* -у́; *pl* -ы́, -о́в) harmony; manner, way; stop, fret.

ла́дан incense.

ла́дить (ла́жу) *impf* get on, be on good terms. **ла́дно** *adv* all right; very well! **ла́дный** fine, excellent; harmonious.

ладо́нь palm.

ладья́ rook, castle; boat.

ла́жу *etc.: see* **ла́дить, ла́зить**

лазаре́т field hospital; sick-bay.

ла́зать *see* **ла́зить. лазе́йка** hole; loop-hole.

ла́зер laser.

ла́зить (ла́жу), **ла́зать** *impf* climb, clamber.

лазу́рный sky-blue, azure. **лазу́рь** azure.

лазу́тчик scout; spy.

лай bark, barking. **ла́йка**[1] (Siberian) husky, laika.

ла́йка[2] kid. **ла́йковый** kid; kidskin.

ла́йнер liner; airliner.

лак varnish, lacquer.

лака́ть *impf* (*pf* вы́~) lap.

лаке́й footman, man-servant; lackey.

лакирова́ть *impf* (*pf* от~) varnish; lacquer.

ла́кмус litmus.

ла́ковый varnished, lacquered.

ла́комиться (-млюсь) *impf* (*pf* по~) +*instr* treat o.s. to. **ла́комка** *m & f* gourmand. **ла́комство** delicacy. **ла́комый** dainty, tasty; +до fond of.

лакони́чный laconic.

ла́мпа lamp; valve, tube. **лампа́да** icon-lamp. **ла́мпочка**

lamp; bulb.

ландша́фт landscape.

ла́ндыш lily of the valley.

лань fallow deer; doe.

ла́па paw; tenon.

ла́поть (-птя; *pl* -и, -ей) *m* bast shoe.

ла́почка pet, sweetie.

лапша́ noodles; noodle soup.

ларёк (-рька́) stall. **ларь** (-я́) *m* chest; bin.

ла́ска[1] caress.

ла́ска[2] weasel.

ласка́ть *impf* caress, fondle; ~ся +к+*dat* make up to; fawn upon. **ла́сковый** affectionate, tender.

ла́сточка swallow.

латви́ец (-и́йца), **-и́йка** Latvian. **латви́йский** Latvian. **Ла́твия** Latvia.

лати́нский Latin.

лату́нь brass.

ла́ты (лат) *pl* armour.

латы́нь Latin.

латы́ш, латы́шка Latvian, Lett. **латы́шский** Latvian, Lett.

лауреа́т prize-winner.

ла́цкан lapel.

лачу́га hovel, shack.

ла́ять (ла́ю) *impf* bark.

лба *etc.: see* **лоб**

лгать (лгу, лжёшь; лгал, -а́, о́) *impf* (*pf* на~, со~) lie; tell lies; +на+*acc* slander. **лгун** (-а́), **лгу́нья** liar.

лебеди́ный swan. **лебёдка** swan, pen; winch. **ле́бедь** (-я) *m* swan, cob.

лев (льва) lion.

левобере́жный left-bank. **левша́** (*gen pl* -е́й) *m & f* left-hander. **ле́вый** *adj* left; left-hand; left-wing.

лёг *etc.: see* **лечь**

лега́льный legal.

леге́нда legend. **легенда́рный** legendary.

лёгк|ий (-гок, -гка́, лёгки) light; easy; slight, mild; **~ая атле́тика** field and track events. **легко́** adv easily, lightly, slightly.

легко- in comb light; easy, easily. **легкове́рный** credulous. **~ве́с** light-weight. **~мы́сленный** thoughtless; flippant, frivolous, superficial. **~мы́слие** flippancy, frivolity.

легков|о́й: ~а́я маши́на (private) car. **лёгкое** sb lung. **лёгкость** lightness; easiness. **ле́гче** comp of лёгкий, легко́

лёд (льда, loc -у́) ice. **ледене́ть** (-е́ю) impf (pf за~, о~) freeze; grow numb with cold. **ледене́ц** (-нца́) fruit-drop. **леденя́щий** chilling, icy.

ле́ди f indecl lady.

ле́дник¹ ice-box; refrigerator van. **ледни́к²** (-а́) glacier. **леднико́вый** glacial; **~ пери́од** Ice Age. **~ ice. ледоко́л** ice-breaker. **ледяно́й** ice; icy.

лежа́ть (-жу́) impf lie; be, be situated. **лежа́чий** lying (down).

ле́звие (cutting) edge; razor-blade.

лезть (-зу; лез) impf (pf по~) climb; clamber, crawl; get, go; fall out.

лейбори́ст Labourite.

ле́йка watering-can.

лейтена́нт lieutenant.

лека́рство medicine.

ле́ксика vocabulary. **лексико́н** lexicon; vocabulary.

ле́ктор lecturer. **ле́кция** lecture.

леле́ять (-е́ю) impf (pf вз~) cherish, foster.

лён (льна) flax.

лени́вый lazy.

ленингра́дский (of) Leningrad. **ле́нинский** (of) Lenin; Leninist.

лени́ться (-ню́сь, -нишься) impf (pf по~) be lazy; +inf be too lazy to.

ле́нта ribbon; band; tape.

ленти́й, -я́йка lazy-bones. **лень** laziness.

лепесто́к (-тка́) petal. **лепета́ть** (-ечу́, -е́чешь) impf (pf про~) babble, prattle.

лепёшка scone; tablet, pastille.

лепи́ть (-плю́, -пишь) impf (pf вы́~, за~, с~) model, fashion; mould; **~ся** cling; crawl. **ле́пка** modelling. **лепно́й** modelled, moulded.

лес (loc -у́, pl -а́) forest, wood; pl scaffolding.

леса́ (pl ле́сы) fishing-line.

лесни́к (-а́) forester. **лесни́чий** sb forestry officer; forest warden. **лесно́й** forest.

лесо- in comb wood, forest, forestry; timber wood. **лесово́дство** forestry. **~заготовка** logging. **~пи́лка, ~пи́льня** (gen pl -лен) sawmill. **~ру́б** woodcutter.

ле́стница stairs, staircase; ladder.

ле́стный flattering. **лесть** flattery.

лёт (loc -у́) flight, flying.

лета́ (лет) pl years; age; **ско́лько вам лет?** how old are you?

лета́тельный flying. **лета́ть** impf, **лете́ть** (лечу́) impf (pf полете́ть) fly; rush; fall.

ле́тний summer.

лётный flying, flight.

лето (pl -á) summer; pl years. **летом** adv in summer.

летопись chronicle.

летосчисление chronology.

летуч|ий flying; passing; brief; volatile; **~ая мышь** bat. **лётчик, -чица** pilot.

лечебница clinic. **лечебный** medical; medicinal. **лечение** (medical) treatment. **лечить** (-чу, -чишь) impf treat (**от** for); **~ся** be given, have treatment (**от** for).

лечу etc.: see **лететь, лечить**

лечь (ля́гу, ля́жешь; лёг, -ла́) pf (impf **ложиться**) lie, lie down; go to bed.

лещ (-á) bream.

лжесвидетельство false witness.

лжец (-á) liar. **лживый** lying; deceitful.

ли, ль interrog partl & conj whether, if; **ли,... ли** whether ... or; **рано ли, поздно ли** sooner or later.

либерал liberal. **либеральный** liberal.

либо conj or; **~... ~** either ... or.

ливень (-вня) m heavy shower, downpour. **ливрея** livery.

лига league.

лидер leader. **лидировать** impf & pf be in the lead.

лизать (лижу, -ешь) impf, **лизнуть** (-ну, -нёшь) pf lick. **ликвидация** liquidation; abolition. **ликвидировать** impf & pf liquidate; abolish.

ликёр liqueur.

ликование rejoicing. **ликовать** impf rejoice.

лилия lily.

лиловый lilac, violet.

лиман estuary.

лимит limit.

лимон lemon. **лимонад** lemonade; squash. **лимонный** lemon.

лимфа lymph.

лингвист linguist. **лингвистика** linguistics. **лингвистический** linguistic.

линейка ruler; line. **линейный** linear; **~ корабль** battleship.

линза lens.

линия line.

линолеум lino(leum).

линять impf (pf **вы~, по~, с~**) fade; moult.

липа lime tree.

липкий (-пок, -пка́, -о) sticky. **липнуть** (-ну; лип) impf stick. **липовый** lime.

лира lyre. **лирик** lyric poet. **лирика** lyric poetry. **лирический** lyric; lyrical.

лиса (pl -ы), **-сица** fox.

лист (-á; pl -ы or -ья, -óв or -ьев) leaf; sheet; page; form; **играть с ~á** play at sight. **листать** impf leaf through. **листва** foliage. **лиственница** larch **лиственный** deciduous. **листовка** leaflet. **листовой** sheet, plate; leaf. **листок** (-тка́) dim of **лист**; leaflet; form, pro-forma.

Литва Lithuania.

литейный founding, casting. **литератор** man of letters. **литература** literature. **литературный** literary.

литовец (-вца), **литовка** Lithuanian. **литовский** Lithuanian.

литой cast.

литр litre.

лить (лью, льёшь; лил, -á, -о) impf (pf **с~**) pour; shed; cast;

mould. **литьё** founding, casting, moulding; castings, mouldings. **ли́ться** (льётся, ли́лся, -а́сь, ли́ло́сь) *impf* flow; pour.

лиф bodice. **ли́фчик** bra.

лифт lift.

лихо́й[1] (лих, -а́, -о) dashing, spirited.

лихо́й[2] (лих, -а́, -о, ли́хи́) evil.

лихора́дка fever. **лихора́дочный** feverish.

лицево́й facial; exterior; front.

лицеме́р hypocrite. **лицеме́рие** hypocrisy. **лицеме́рный** hypocritical.

лицо́ (*pl* -a) face; exterior; right side; person; **быть к лицу́** +*dat* suit, befit; **ли́чно** *adv* personally, in person. **ли́чность** personality; person. **ли́чный** personal; private; ~ **соста́в** staff, personnel.

лиша́й lichen; herpes; shingles. **лиша́йник** lichen.

лиша́ть(ся) *impf of* **лиши́ть(ся)**

лише́ние deprivation; privation. **лишённый** (-ён, -ена́) +*gen* lacking in, devoid of. **лиши́ть** (-шу́) *pf* (*impf* **лиша́ть**) +*gen* deprive of; ~**ся** +*gen* lose, be deprived of. **ли́шний** superfluous; unnecessary; spare; ~ **раз** once more; **с** ~**им** odd, and more.

лишь *adv* only; *conj* as soon as; ~ **бы** if only, provided that.

лоб (лба, *loc* лбу) forehead.

ло́бзик fret-saw.

лови́ть (-влю́, -вишь) *impf* (*pf* **пойма́ть**) catch, try to catch. **ло́вкий** (-вок, -вка́, -о) adroit, cunning. **ло́вкость** adroitness; cunning.

ло́вля (*gen pl* -вель) catching,

hunting; fishing-ground. **ло́вушка** trap.

ло́вче *comp of* **ло́вкий**

логари́фм logarithm.

ло́гика logic. **логи́ческий, логи́чный** logical.

ло́говище, ло́гово den, lair.

ло́дка boat.

лоды́рничать *impf* loaf, idle about. **ло́дырь** *m* loafer, idler.

ло́жа box; (masonic) lodge.

ложби́на hollow.

ло́же couch; bed.

ложи́ться (-жу́сь) *impf of* **лечь**

ло́жка spoon.

ло́жный false. **ложь** (лжи) *f* lie, falsehood.

лоза́ (*pl* -ы) vine.

ло́зунг slogan, catchword.

лока́тор radar *or* sonar apparatus.

локомоти́в locomotive.

ло́кон lock, curl.

ло́коть (-ктя; *pl* -и, -е́й) *m* elbow.

лом (*pl* -ы, -о́в) crowbar; scrap, waste. **ло́маный** broken. **лома́ть** *impf* (*pf* по~, с~) break; cause to ache; ~**ся** break; crack; put on airs; be obstinate.

ломба́рд pawnshop.

ло́мберный стол card-table.

ломи́ть (ло́мит) *impf* break; break through, rush; *impers* cause to ache; ~**ся** be (near to) breaking. **ло́мка** breaking; *pl* quarry. **ло́мкий** (-мок, -мка́, -о) fragile, brittle.

ломо́ть (-мтя́; *pl* -мти́) *m* large slice; hunk; chunk. **ло́мтик** slice.

ло́но bosom, lap.

лопа́сть (*pl* -и, -е́й) blade; fan, vane; paddle.

лопа́та spade; shovel. **лопа́тка** shoulder-blade; shovel; trowel.

ло́паться *impf*, **ло́пнуть** (-ну) *pf* burst; split; break; fail; crash.

лопу́х (-á) burdock.

лорд lord.

лоси́на elk-skin, chamois leather; elk-meat.

лоск lustre, shine.

лоску́т (-á; *pl* -ы́ *or* -ья, -о́в *or* -ьев) rag, shred, scrap.

лосни́ться *impf* be glossy, shine.

ло́сось *m* salmon.

лось (*pl* -и, -е́й) *m* elk.

лосьо́н lotion; aftershave; cream.

лот lead, plummet.

лотере́я lottery, raffle.

лото́к (-тка́) hawker's stand *or* tray; chute; gutter; trough.

лохма́тый shaggy, dishevelled.

лохмо́тья (-ьев) *pl* rags.

ло́цман pilot.

лошади́ный horse; equine. **ло́шадь** (*pl* -и, -е́й, *instr* -дьми́ *or* -дя́ми) horse.

лощёный glossy, polished.

лощи́на hollow, depression.

лоя́льный fair, honest; loyal.

лубо́к (-бка́) splint; popular print.

луг (*loc* -ý; *pl* -á) meadow.

лу́жа puddle.

лужа́йка lawn, glade.

лужёный tin-plated.

лук¹ onions.

лук² bow.

лука́вить (-влю) *impf* (*pf* с~) be cunning. **лука́вство** craftiness. **лука́вый** crafty, cunning.

лу́ковица onion; bulb

луна́ (*pl* -ы) moon. **луна́тик** sleep-walker.

лу́нка hole; socket.

лу́нный moon; lunar.

лу́па magnifying-glass.

лупи́ть (-плю́, -пишь) *impf* (*pf*

от~) flog.

луч (-á) ray; beam. **лучево́й** ray, beam; radial; radiation. **лучеза́рный** radiant.

лучи́на splinter.

лу́чше better; ~ всего́, ~ всех best of all. **лу́чший** better; best; в ~ем слу́чае at best; всего́ ~его! all the best!

лы́жа ski. **лы́жник** skier. **лы́жный спорт** skiing. **лыжня́** ski-track.

лы́ко bast.

лысе́ть (-е́ю) *impf* (*pf* об~, по~) grow bald. **лы́сина** bald spot; blaze. **лы́сый** (лыс, -á, -о) bald.

ль *see* ли

льва *etc.*: *see* лев. **льви́ный** lion, lion's. **льви́ца** lioness.

льго́та privilege; advantage. **льго́тный** privileged; favourable.

льда *etc.*: *see* лёд. **льди́на** block of ice; ice-floe.

льна *etc.*: *see* лён. **льново́дство** flax-growing.

льнуть (-ну, -нёшь) *impf* (*pf* при~) +к+*dat* cling to; have a weakness for; make up to.

льняно́й flax, flaxen; linen; linseed.

льстец (-á) flatterer. **льсти́вый** flattering; smooth-tongued. **льстить** (льщу) *impf* (*pf* по~) +*dat* flatter.

лью *etc.*: *see* лить

любе́зность courtesy; kindness; compliment. **любе́зный** courteous; obliging; kind; бу́дьте ~ы be so kind as (to).

люби́мец (-мца), **-мица** pet, favourite. **люби́мый** beloved; favourite. **люби́тель** *m*, **-ница** lover; amateur. **люби́тельский** amateur. **люби́ть** (-блю́, -бишь) *impf* love; like.

любова́ться *impf* (*pf* по~) +*instr* or на+*acc* admire.
любо́вник lover. любо́вница mistress. любо́вный love-; loving. любо́вь (-бви́, *instr* -бо́вью) love.
любозна́тельный inquisitive.
любо́й any; either; *sb* anyone.
любопы́тный curious; inquisitive. любопы́тство curiosity.
любя́щий loving.
лю́ди (-е́й, -ям, -дьми́, -ях) *pl* people. лю́дный populous; crowded. людое́д cannibal; ogre. людско́й human.
люк hatch(way); trap; manhole.
лю́лька cradle.
люминесце́нтный luminescent. люминесце́нция luminescence.
лю́стра chandelier.
лю́тня (*gen pl* -тен) lute.
лю́тый (лют, -á, -o) ferocious.
ляга́ть *impf*, лягну́ть (-ну́, -нёшь) *pf* kick; ~ся kick.
ля́гу *etc.*: *see* лечь
лягу́шка frog.
ля́жка thigh, haunch.
ля́згать *impf* clank; +*instr* rattle.
ля́мка strap; тяну́ть ля́мку toil.

M

мавзоле́й mausoleum.
мавр, маврита́нка Moor. маврита́нский Moorish.
магази́н shop.
маги́стр (holder of) master's degree.
магистра́ль main; main line, main road.
маги́ческий magic(al). ма́гия magic.

магнети́зм magnetism.
ма́гний magnesium.
магни́т magnet. магни́тный magnetic. магнитофо́н tape-recorder.
мада́м *f indecl* madam, madame.
мажо́р major (key); cheerful mood. мажо́рный major; cheerful.
ма́зать (ма́жу) *impf* (*pf* вы́~, за~, из~, на~, по~, про~) oil, grease; smear, spread; soil; ~ся get dirty; make up. мазо́к (-зка́) touch, dab; smear. мазу́т fuel oil. мазь ointment; grease.
маи́с maize.
май May. ма́йский May.
ма́йка T-shirt.
майо́р major.
мак poppy, poppy-seeds.
макаро́ны (-н) *pl* macaroni.
мака́ть *impf* (*pf* макну́ть) dip.
маке́т model; dummy.
макну́ть (-ну́, -нёшь) *pf of* мака́ть
макре́ль mackerel.
максима́льный maximum. ма́ксимум maximum; at most.
макулату́ра waste paper; pulp literature.
маку́шка top; crown.
мал *etc.*: *see* ма́лый
малахи́т malachite.
мале́йший least, slightest. ма́ленький little; small.
мали́на (*no pl*; *usu collect*) raspberry; raspberries; raspberry-bush. мали́новый raspberry.
ма́ло *adv* little, few; not enough; ~ того́ moreover; ~ того́ что... not only ...
мало- *in comb* (too) little. малова́жный of little importance. ~вероя́тный unlikely. ~гра́мотный semi-literate.

crude. ~ду́шный faint-hearted. ~иму́щий needy. ~кро́вие anaemia. ~ле́тний young; juvenile; minor. ~о́пытный inexperienced. ~чи́сленный small (in number), few.

мало-ма́льски adv in the slightest degree; at all. ма́ло-пома́лу adv little by little.

ма́л|ый (мал, -а́) little, (too) small; са́мое ~oe at the least; sb fellow; lad. малы́ш (-а́) kiddy; little boy. ма́льчик boy. мальчи́шка m urchin, boy. мальчуга́н little boy. малю́тка m & f baby, little one.

маля́р (-а́) painter, decorator.

маля́рия malaria.

ма́ма mother, mummy. ма́маша mummy. ма́мин mother's.

ма́монт mammoth.

мандари́н mandarin, tangerine.

манда́т warrant; mandate.

мане́вр manoeuvre; shunting. маневри́ровать impf (pf c~) manoeuvre; shunt; +instr make good use of.

мане́ж riding-school.

манеке́н dummy; mannequin. манеке́нщик, -щица model.

мане́ра manner; style. мане́рный affected.

манже́та cuff.

маникю́р manicure.

манипули́ровать impf manipulate. манипуля́ция manipulation; machination.

мани́ть (-ню́, -нишь) impf (pf по~) beckon; attract; lure.

манифе́ст manifesto. манифеста́ция demonstration.

мани́шка (false) shirt-front.

ма́ния mania; ~ величия megalomania.

ма́нная ка́ша semolina.

мано́метр pressure-gauge.

ма́нтия cloak; robe, gown.

мануфакту́ра manufacture; textiles.

манья́к maniac.

марафо́нский бег marathon.

ма́рганец (-нца) manganese.

маргари́н margarine.

маргари́тка daisy.

марино́ванный pickled. мариновать impf (pf за~) pickle; put off.

марионе́тка puppet.

ма́рка stamp; counter; brand, trade-mark; grade; reputation.

ма́ркий easily soiled.

маркси́зм Marxism. маркси́ст Marxist. маркси́стский Marxist.

ма́рлевый gauze. ма́рля gauze; cheesecloth.

мармела́д fruit jellies.

ма́рочный high-quality.

Марс Mars.

март March. ма́ртовский March.

марты́шка marmoset; monkey.

марш march.

ма́ршал marshal.

марширова́ть impf march.

маршру́т route, itinerary.

ма́ска mask. маскара́д masked ball; masquerade. маскирова́ть impf (pf за~) disguise; camouflage. маскиро́вка disguise; camouflage.

Ма́сленица Shrovetide. масле́нка butter-dish; oil-can. масли́на olive. ма́сло (pl -á, ма́сел, -слам) butter; oil; oil paints. маслобо́йка churn. маслобо́йня (gen pl -бен) dairy. масля́нистый oily. масля́ный oily. масляный oil.

ма́сса mass; a lot, lots.

масса́ж massage. масси́ровать impf & pf massage.

масси́в massif; expanse, tract. масси́вный massive.

ма́ссовый mass.

ма́стер (*pl* -á), мастери́ца foreman, forewoman; (master) craftsman; expert. мастери́ть *impf* (*pf* c~) make, build. мастерска́я *sb* workshop. мастерско́й masterly. мастерство́ craft; skill.

масти́ка mastic; putty; floorpolish.

масти́тый venerable.

масть (*pl* -и, -éй) colour; suit.

масшта́б scale.

мат¹ checkmate.

мат² mat.

мат³ foul language.

матема́тик mathematician. матема́тика mathematics. математи́ческий mathematical.

материа́л material. материали́зм materialism. материалисти́ческий materialist. материа́льный material.

матери́к (-á) continent; mainland. материко́вый continental.

матери́нский maternal, motherly. матери́нство maternity.

мате́рия material; pus; topic.

ма́тка womb; female.

ма́товый matt; frosted.

матра́с, матра́ц mattress.

матрёшка Russian doll.

ма́трица matrix; die, mould.

матро́с sailor, seaman.

матч match.

мать (ма́тери, *instr* -рью; *pl* -тери, -рéй) mother.

ма́фия Mafia.

мах swing, stroke. маха́ть (машу́, ма́шешь) *impf*, махну́ть (-ну́, -нёшь) *pf* +*instr* wave; brandish; wag; flap; go; rush.

махина́ция machinations.

махови́к (-á) fly-wheel.

махро́вый dyed-in-the-wool; terry.

ма́чеха stepmother.

ма́чта mast.

маши́на machine; car. маши́на́льный mechanical. маши́ни́ст operator; engine-driver; scene-shifter. машини́стка typist; ~-стенографи́стка shorthand-typist. маши́нка machine; typewriter; sewing-machine. маши́нопи́сный typewritten. маши́нопись typing; typescript. машино-строе́ние mechanical engineering.

мая́к (-á) lighthouse; beacon.

ма́ятник pendulum. ма́яться *impf* toil; suffer; languish.

мгла haze; gloom.

мгнове́ние instant, moment. мгнове́нный instantaneous, momentary.

ме́бель furniture. меблиро́ванный furnished. меблиро́вка furnishing; furniture.

мегава́тт (*gen pl* -а́тт) megawatt. мего́м megohm. мега́-то́нна megaton.

мёд (*loc* -ý; *pl* -ы́) honey.

меда́ль medal. медальо́н medallion.

медве́дица she-bear. медве́дь *m* bear. медве́жий bear('s). медвежо́нок (-нка; *pl* -жа́та, -жа́т) bear cub.

ме́дик medical student; doctor. медикаме́нты (-ов) *pl* medicines.

медици́на medicine. меди-ци́нский medical.

ме́дленный slow. медли́тельный sluggish; slow. ме́длить *impf* linger; be slow.

ме́дный copper; brass.

медо́вый honey; ~ **ме́сяц** honeymoon.

медосмо́тр medical examination, check-up. **медпу́нкт** first aid post. **медсестра́** (-сестры́, -сестёр, -сёстрам) nurse.

меду́за jellyfish.

медь copper.

меж prep+instr between.

меж- in comb inter-.

межа́ (pl -и, меж, -ам) boundary.

междоме́тие interjection.

ме́жду prep+instr between; among; ~ **про́чим** incidentally, by the way; ~ **тем** meanwhile; ~ **тем, как** while.

ме́жду- in comb inter-. **междугоро́дный** inter-city. ~**наро́дный** international.

межконтинента́льный intercontinental. **межплане́тный** interplanetary.

мезони́н attic (storey); mezzanine (floor).

Ме́ксика Mexico.

мел (loc -у́) chalk.

мёл etc.: see **мести́**

меланхо́лия melancholy.

меле́ть (-е́ет) impf (pf об~) grow shallow.

мелиора́ция land improvement.

ме́лкий (-лок, -лка́, -о) small; shallow; fine; petty. **ме́лко** adv fine, small. **мелкобуржуа́зный** petty bourgeois. **мелково́дный** shallow.

мелоди́чный melodious, melodic. **мело́дия** melody.

ме́лочный petty. **ме́лочь** (-и, -ей) small items; (small) change; pl trifles, trivialities.

мель (loc -и́) shoal; bank; **на мели́** aground.

мелька́ть impf, **мелькну́ть** (-ну́, -нёшь) pf be glimpsed fleetingly. **мелько́м** adv in passing; fleetingly.

ме́льник miller. **ме́льница** mill.

мельча́йший superl of **ме́лкий**. **ме́льче** comp of **ме́лкий**, **ме́лко**. **мелюзга́** small fry.

мелю́ etc.: see **моло́ть**

мембра́на membrane; diaphragm.

мемора́ндум memorandum.

мемуа́ры (-ов) pl memoirs.

ме́на exchange, barter.

ме́неджер manager.

ме́нее adv less; **тем не** ~ none the less.

мензу́рка measuring-glass.

меново́й exchange; barter.

менуэ́т minuet.

ме́ньше smaller; less. **меньшеви́к** (-á) Menshevik. **ме́ньший** lesser, smaller; younger. **меньшинство́** minority.

меню́ neut indecl menu.

меня́ see **я** pron

меня́ть impf (pf об~, по~) change; exchange; ~**ся** change; +instr exchange.

ме́ра measure.

мере́щиться (-щусь) impf (pf по~) seem, appear.

мерза́вец (-вца) swine, bastard. **ме́рзкий** (-зок, -зка́, -о) disgusting.

мерзлота́: **ве́чная** ~ permafrost. **мёрзнуть** (-ну; мёрз) impf (pf за~) freeze.

ме́рзость vileness; abomination.

меридиа́н meridian.

мери́ло standard, criterion.

ме́рин gelding.

ме́рить impf (pf по~, с~) measure; try on. **ме́рка** measure.

ме́рный measured; rhythmical. **мероприя́тие** measure.

мертве́ть (-е́ю) *impf* (*pf* о~, по~) grow numb; be benumbed. **мертве́ц** (-á) corpse, dead man. **мёртвый** (мёртв, -á, мёртво) dead.

мерца́ть *impf* twinkle; flicker.

меси́ть (мешу́, ме́сишь) *impf* (*pf* с~) knead.

ме́сса Mass.

места́ми *adv* here and there. **месте́чко** (*pl* -и, -чек) small town.

мести́ (мету́, метёшь; мёл, -á) *impf* sweep; whirl.

ме́стность locality; area. **ме́стный** local; locative. **-ме́стный** *in comb* -berth, -seater. **ме́сто** (*pl* -á) place; site; seat; room; job. **местожи́тельство** (place) of residence. **местоиме́ние** pronoun. **местонахожде́ние** location, whereabouts. **месторожде́ние** deposit; layer.

месть vengeance, revenge.

ме́сяц month; moon. **ме́сячный** monthly; *sb pl* period.

мета́лл metal. **металли́ческий** metal, metallic. **металлу́ргия** metallurgy.

мета́н methane.

мета́ние throwing, flinging. **мета́ть**[1] (мечу́, ме́чешь) *impf* (*pf* метну́ть) throw, fling; ~ся rush about; toss (and turn).

мета́ть[2] *impf* (*pf* на~, с~) tack.

метафи́зика metaphysics.

мета́фора metaphor.

метёлка panicle.

мете́ль snow-storm.

мете́ор meteor. **метеори́т** meteorite. **метеоро́лог** meteorologist. **метеорологи́ческий** meteorological. **метеороло́гия** meteorology.

метеосво́дка weather report. **метеоста́нция** weather-station.

ме́тить[1] (ме́чу) *impf* (*pf* на~, по~) mark.

ме́тить[2] (ме́чу) *impf* (*pf* на~) aim; mean.

ме́тка marking, mark.

ме́ткий (-ток, -тка́, -о) well-aimed, accurate.

метла́ (*pl* мётлы, -тел) broom.

метну́ть (-ну́, -нёшь) *pf of* мета́ть[1]

ме́тод method. **мето́дика** method(s); methodology. **методи́ческий** methodical. **методоло́гия** methodology.

метр metre.

ме́трика birth certificate. **метри́ческ|ий**[1]: ~ое свиде́тельство birth certificate.

метри́ческий[2] metric; metrical.

метро́ *neut indecl*, **метрополите́н** Metro; underground.

мету́ *etc.: see* мести́

мех[1] (*loc* -ý; *pl* -á) fur.

мех[2] (*pl* -и) wine-skin, water-skin; *pl* bellows.

механиза́ция mechanization. **механи́зм** mechanism; gear(ing). **меха́ник** mechanic. **меха́ника** mechanics; trick; knack. **механи́ческий** mechanical; mechanistic.

мехово́й fur.

меч (-á) sword.

ме́ченый marked.

мече́ть mosque.

мечта́ (day-)dream. **мечта́тельный** dreamy. **мечта́ть** *impf* dream.

мечу́ *etc.: see* ме́тить. **мечу́** *etc.: see* мета́ть

меша́лка mixer.

меша́ть[1] *impf* (*pf* по~) +*dat* hinder; prevent; disturb.

меша́ть[2] *impf* (*pf* по~, с~)

stir; mix; mix up; **~ся** (в+*acc*) interfere (in), meddle (with).

мешо́к (-шка́) bag; sack. **меш-кови́на** sacking, hessian.

меща́н|ин (*pl* -а́не, -а́н) petty bourgeois; Philistine. **меща́нский** bourgeois, narrow-minded; Philistine. **меща́нство** petty bourgeoisie; philistinism, narrow-mindedness.

миг moment, instant.

мига́ть *impf*, **мигну́ть** (-ну́, -нёшь) *pf* blink; wink, twinkle.

ми́гом *adv* in a flash.

мигра́ция migration.

мигре́нь migraine.

мизантро́п misanthrope.

мизи́нец (-нца) little finger; little toe.

микро́б microbe.

микроволно́вая печь microwave oven.

микро́н micron.

микроорган́изм microorganism.

микроско́п microscope. **микроскопи́ческий** microscopic.

микросхе́ма microchip.

микрофо́н (*gen pl* -н) microphone.

ми́ксер (*cul*) mixer, blender.

миксту́ра medicine, mixture.

ми́ленький pretty; nice; sweet; dear.

милитари́зм militarism.

милиционе́р militiaman, policeman. **мили́ция** militia, police force.

миллиа́рд billion, a thousand million. **миллиме́тр** millimetre. **миллио́н** million. **миллионе́р** millionaire.

милосе́рдие mercy, charity. **милосе́рдный** merciful, charitable.

ми́лостивый gracious, kind.

ми́лостыня alms. **ми́лость** favour, grace. **ми́лый** (мил -á, -о) nice; kind; sweet; dear.

ми́ля mile.

ми́мика (facial) expression; mimicry.

ми́мо *adv* & *prep* +*gen* by; past. **мимолётный** fleeting. **мимохо́дом** *adv* in passing.

ми́на¹ mine; bomb.

ми́на² expression, mien.

минда́ль (-я́) *m* almond(-tree); almonds.

минера́л mineral. **минерало́гия** mineralogy. **минера́льный** mineral.

миниатю́ра miniature. **миниатю́рный** miniature; tiny.

минима́льный minimum. **ми́нимум** minimum.

министе́рство ministry. **мини́стр** minister.

минова́ть *impf* & *pf* pass; *impers*+*dat* escape.

миномёт mortar. **миноно́сец** (-сца) torpedo-boat.

мино́р minor (key); melancholy.

мину́вш|ий past; **~ee** *sb* the past.

ми́нус minus.

мину́та minute. **мину́тный** minute; momentary.

мину́ть (-нешь; ми́ну́л) *pf* pass.

мир¹ (*pl* -ы́) world.

мир² peace.

мира́ж mirage.

мири́ть *impf* (*pf* по~, при~) reconcile; **~ся** be reconciled.

ми́рный peaceful; peace.

мировоззре́ние (world-)outlook; philosophy. **мирово́й** world. **мирозда́ние** universe

миролюби́вый peace-loving.

ми́ска basin, bowl.

мисс *f indecl* Miss.

миссионе́р missionary.

ми́ссия mission.

ми́стер Mr.

ми́стика mysticism.

мистифика́ция hoax, leg-pull.

ми́тинг mass meeting; rally.

митрополи́т metropolitan.

миф myth. **мифи́ческий** mythical. **мифологи́ческий** mythological. **мифоло́гия** mythology.

ми́чман warrant officer.

мише́нь target.

ми́шка (Teddy) bear.

младе́нец (-нца) baby; infant. **мла́дший** younger; youngest; junior.

млекопита́ющие sb pl mammals. **Мле́чный Путь** Milky Way.

мне see **я** pron

мне́ние opinion.

мни́мый imaginary; sham. **мни́тельный** hypochondriac; mistrustful. **мнить** (мню) impf think.

мно́гие sb pl many (people); ~ое sb many, a great deal. **мно́го** adv+gen much; many; на ~ by far.

много- in comb many-, poly-, multi-, multiple-. **многобо́рье** combined event. **~гра́нный** polyhedral; many-sided. **~де́тный** having many children. **~же́нство** polygamy. **~зна-чи́тельный** significant. **~кра́тный** repeated; frequentative. **~ле́тний** lasting, living, many years; of many years' standing; perennial. **~лю́д-ный** crowded. **~национа́ль-ный** multi-national. **~обе-ща́ющий** promising. **~обра́-зие** diversity. **~сло́вный** verbose. **~сторо́нний** multi-lateral; many-sided; versatile.

~то́чие dots, omission points. **~уважа́емый** respected; Dear. **~уго́льный** polygonal. **~цве́тный** multi-coloured; multifarious. **~чи́сленный** numerous. **~эта́жный** many-storeyed. **~язы́чный** polyglot.

мно́жественный plural. **мно́-жество** great number. **мно́-жить** (-жу) impf (pf у~) multiply; increase.

мной, мно́ю: see **я** pron. **мну** etc.: see **мять**

мобилиза́ция mobilization. **мобилизова́ть** impf & pf mobilize.

мог etc.: see **мочь**

моги́ла grave. **моги́льный** (of the) grave; sepulchral.

могу́ etc.: see **мочь**. **могу́чий** mighty. **могу́щественный** powerful. **могу́щество** power, might.

мо́да fashion.

модели́ровать impf & pf design. **моде́ль** model; pattern. **модельер** fashion designer. **моде́льный** model; fashion-able.

модернизи́ровать impf & pf modernize.

моди́стка milliner.

модифика́ция modification. **модифици́ровать** impf & pf modify.

мо́дный (-ден, -дна́, -о) fash-ionable; fashion.

мо́жет see **мочь**

можжеве́льник juniper.

мо́жно one may, one can; it is permissible; it is possible; **как ~**+comp as ... as possible; **как ~ скоре́е** as soon as possible.

моза́ика mosaic; jigsaw.

мозг (loc -ý, pl -и́) brain; marrow. **мозгово́й** cerebral.

мозо́ль corn; callus.

мой (моего́) *m*, **моя́** (мое́й) *f*, **моё** (моего́) *neut*, **мои́** (-и́х) *pl pron* my; mine; **по-мо́ему** in my opinion; in my way.

мо́йка washing.

мо́кнуть (-ну; мок) *impf* get wet; soak. **мокро́та** phlegm. **мо́крый** wet, damp.

мол (*loc* -у́) mole, pier.

молва́ rumour, talk.

моле́бен (-бна) church service.

моле́кула molecule. **молекуля́рный** molecular.

моли́тва prayer. **моли́ть** (-лю́, -лишь) *impf* pray; beg; **~ся** (*pf* по~ся) pray.

моллю́ск mollusc.

молниено́сный lightning. **мо́лния** lightning; zip(-fastener).

молодёжь youth, young people. **молоде́ть** (-е́ю) *impf* (*pf* по~) get younger, look younger. **молоде́ц** (-дца́) fine fellow *or* girl; **~!** well done! **молодожёны** (-ов) *pl* newly-weds. **молодо́й** (мо́лод, -а́, -о) young. **мо́лодость** youth. **молоко́** milk.

мо́лот hammer. **молоти́ть** (-очу́, -о́тишь) *impf* (*pf* с~) thresh; hammer. **молото́к** (-тка́) hammer. **мо́лотый** ground. **моло́ть** (мелю́, ме́лешь) *impf* (*pf* с~) grind, mill.

моло́чная *sb* dairy. **моло́чный** milk; dairy; milky.

мо́лча *adv* silently, in silence. **молчали́вый** silent, taciturn; tacit. **молча́ние** silence. **молча́ть** (-чу́) *impf* be *or* keep silent.

моль moth.

мольба́ entreaty.

мольбе́рт easel.

моме́нт moment; feature. **момента́льно** *adv* instantly. **момента́льный** instantaneous.

мона́рх monarch. **монархи́ст** monarchist.

монасты́рь (-я́) *m* monastery; convent. **мона́х** monk. **мона́хиня** nun.

монго́л, **~ка** Mongol.

моне́та coin.

моногра́фия monograph.

моноли́тный monolithic.

моноло́г monologue.

монопо́лия monopoly.

моното́нный monotonous.

монта́ж (-а́) assembling, mounting; editing. **монта́жник** rigger, fitter. **монтёр** fitter, mechanic. **монти́ровать** *impf* (*pf* с~) mount; install; fit; edit.

монуме́нт monument. **монумента́льный** monumental.

мора́ль moral; morals, ethics. **мора́льный** moral; ethical.

морг morgue.

морга́ть *impf*, **моргну́ть** (-ну́, -нёшь) *pf* blink; wink.

мо́рда snout, muzzle; (ugly) mug.

мо́ре (*pl* -я́, -е́й) sea.

морепла́вание navigation. **морепла́ватель** *m* seafarer. **морехо́дный** nautical.

морж (-а́), **моржи́ха** walrus.

Мо́рзе *indecl* Morse; **а́збука ~** Morse code.

мори́ть *impf* (*pf* у~) exhaust; **~ го́лодом** starve.

морко́вка carrot. **морко́вь** carrots.

моро́женое *sb* ice-cream. **моро́женый** frozen, chilled. **моро́з** frost; *pl* intensely cold weather. **моро́зилка** freezer compartment; freezer. **моро́зильник** deep-freeze.

моро́сить (-о́жу) freeze.
моро́зный frosty.
мороси́ть *impf* drizzle.
морск|о́й sea; maritime; marine, nautical; **~а́я сви́нка** guinea-pig; **~о́й флот** navy, fleet.
мо́рфий morphine.
морщи́на wrinkle; crease.
мо́рщить (-щу) *impf* (*pf* на~, по~, с~) wrinkle; pucker; **~ся** knit one's brow; wince; crease, wrinkle.
моря́к (-á) sailor, seaman.
москви́ч (-á), **~ка** Muscovite.
моско́вский (of) Moscow.
мост (мо́ста́, *loc* -ý; *pl* -ы́) bridge. **мо́стик** bridge. **мости́ть** (-ощу́) *impf* (*pf* вы́~) pave. **мостки́** (-о́в) *pl* planked footway. **мостова́я** *sb* roadway; pavement. **мостово́й** bridge.
мота́ть[1] *impf* (*pf* мотну́ть, на~) wind, reel.
мота́ть[2] *impf* (*pf* про~) squander.
мота́ться *impf* dangle; wander; rush about.
моти́в motive; reason; tune; motif. **мотиви́ровать** *impf* & *pf* give reasons for, justify. **мотиви́ровка** reason(s); justification.
мотну́ть (-ну́, -нёшь) *pf of* мота́ть
мото- in comb motor-, engine-. **мотого́нки** (-нок) *pl* motorcycle races. **~пехо́та** motorized infantry. **~ро́ллер** (motor-)scooter. **~ци́кл** motor cycle.
мото́к (-тка́) skein, hank.
мото́р motor, engine. **мото-ри́ст** motor-mechanic. **мото́рный** motor; engine.
моты́га hoe, mattock.

мотылёк (-лька́) butterfly, moth.
мох (мха *or* мо́ха, *loc* мху; *pl* мхи, мхов) moss. **мохна́тый** hairy, shaggy.
моча́ urine.
моча́лка loofah.
мочево́й пузы́рь bladder.
мочи́ть (-чу́, -чишь) *impf* (*pf* за~, на~) wet, moisten; soak; **~ся** (*pf* по~) urinate.
мо́чка ear lobe.
мочь (могу́, мо́жешь; мог, -ла́) *impf* (*pf* с~) be able; **мо́жет (быть)** perhaps.
моше́нник rogue. **моше́нничать** *impf* (*pf* с~) cheat, swindle. **моше́ннический** rascally.
мо́шка midge. **мошкара́** (swarm of) midges.
мо́щность power; capacity. **мо́щный** (-щен, -щна́, -о) powerful.
мощу́ *etc.: see* мости́ть
мощь power.
мою́ *etc.: see* мыть. **мо́ющий** washing; detergent.
мрак darkness, gloom. **мрако́бес** obscurantist.
мра́мор marble. **мра́морный** marble.
мра́чный dark; gloomy.
мсти́тельный vindictive. **мстить** (мщу) *impf* (*pf* ото~) take vengeance on; +за+*acc* avenge.
мудре́ц (-á) sage, wise man. **му́дрость** wisdom. **му́дрый** (-др, -á, -о) wise, sage.
муж (*pl* -жья́ *or* -и́) husband. **муж́ать** *impf* grow up; mature; **~ся** take courage. **мужеподо́бный** mannish; masculine. **му́жественный** manly, steadfast. **му́жество**

мужи́к (-á) peasant; fellow.

мужско́й masculine; male. **мужчи́на** *m* man.

му́за muse.

музе́й museum.

му́зыка music. **музыка́льный** musical. **музыка́нт** musician.

му́ка[1] torment.

мука́[2] flour.

мультипли ка́ция, мульт-фи́льм cartoon film.

му́мия mummy.

мунди́р (full-dress) uniform.

мундшту́к (-á) mouthpiece; cigarette-holder.

муниципа́льный municipal.

мураве́й (-вья́) ant. **мура-ве́йник** ant-hill.

мурлы́кать (-ы́чу *or* -каю) *impf* purr.

муска́т nutmeg.

му́скул muscle. **му́скульный** muscular.

му́сор refuse; rubbish. **му́сор-ный я́щик** dustbin.

мусульма́нин (*pl* -ма́не, -ма́н), -а́нка Muslim.

мути́ть (мучу́, му́ти́шь) *impf* (*pf* вз~) make muddy; stir up, upset. **му́тный** (-тен, -тна́, -о) turbid, troubled; dull. **муть** sediment; murk.

му́ха fly.

муче́ние torment, torture. **му́ченик, му́ченица** martyr. **мучи́тельный** agonizing. **му́-чить** (-чу) *impf* (*pf* за~, из~) torment; harass; ~**ся** torment o.s.; suffer agonies.

мучно́й flour, meal; starchy.

мха *etc.*: *see* **мох**

мчать (мчу) *impf* rush along, whirl along; ~**ся** rush.

мщу *etc.*: *see* **мстить**

мы (нас, нам, на́ми, нас) *pron* we; **мы с ва́ми** you and I.

мы́лить (*pf* на~) soap;

~**ся** wash o.s. **мы́ло** (*pl* -á) soap. **мы́льница** soap-dish. **мы́льный** soap, soapy.

мыс cape, promontory.

мы́сленный mental. **мы́сли-мый** conceivable. **мысли́тель** *m* thinker. **мы́слить** *impf* think; conceive. **мысль** thought; idea. **мы́слящий** thinking.

мыть (мо́ю) *impf* (*pf* вы́~, по~) wash; ~**ся** wash (o.s.).

мыча́ть (-чу́) *impf* (*pf* про~) low, moo; bellow; mumble.

мышело́вка mousetrap.

мы́шечный muscular.

мышле́ние thinking, thought.

мы́шца muscle.

мышь (*gen pl* -е́й) mouse.

мэр mayor. **мэ́рия** town hall.

мя́гкий (-гок, -гка́, -о) soft; mild; ~ **знак** soft sign, the let-ter ь. **мя́гче** *comp of* **мя́гкий, мя́гко**. **мя́коть** fleshy part; flesh; pulp.

мяси́стый fleshy; meaty. **мяс-ни́к** (-á) butcher. **мясно́й** meat. **мя́со** meat; flesh. **мясо-ру́бка** mincer.

мя́та mint; peppermint.

мяте́ж (-á) mutiny, revolt. **мя-те́жник** mutineer, rebel. **мя-те́жный** rebellious; restless.

мя́тный mint, peppermint.

мять (мну, мнёшь) *impf* (*pf* из~, раз~, с~) work up; knead; crumple; ~**ся** become crumpled; crush (easily).

мяу́кать *impf* miaow.

мяч (-á), **мя́чик** ball.

Н

на[1] *prep* **I.** +acc on; on to, to, into; at; till, until; for; by. **II.** +prep on, upon; in; at.

на[2] *partl* here; here you are.

наба́вить (-влю) *pf*, **набавля́ть** *impf* add (to), increase.

наба́т alarm-bell.

набе́г raid, foray.

набекре́нь *adv* aslant.

на|бели́ть (-е́лишь) *pf*. **на́бело** *adv* without corrections.

на́бережная *sb* embankment, quay.

наберу́ *etc.: see* **набра́ть**

набива́ть(ся *impf of* **наби́ть(ся. наби́вка** stuffing, padding; (textile) printing.

набира́ть(ся *impf of* **набра́ть(ся**

наби́тый packed, stuffed; crowded. **наби́ть** (-бью, -бьёшь) *pf* (*impf* **набива́ть**) stuff, pack, fill; smash; print; hammer, drive; ~ся crowd in.

наблюда́тель *m* observer. **наблюда́тельный** observant; observation. **наблюда́ть** *impf* observe, watch; +**за**+*instr* look after; supervise. **наблюде́ние** observation; supervision.

набо́жный devout, pious.

на́бок *adv* on one side, crooked.

наболе́вший sore, painful.

набо́р recruiting; collection, set; type-setting.

набра́сывать(ся *impf of* **набро́сить(ся, набро́сить(ся**

набра́ть (-беру́, -берёшь; -а́л, -а́, -о) *pf* (*impf* **набира́ть**) gather; enlist; compose, set up; ~ **но́мер** dial a number; ~ся assemble, collect; +**ся сме́лости** pluck up courage.

набрести́ (-еду́, -дёшь; -ёл, -ела́) *pf* +**на**+*acc* come across.

набро́сать *pf* (*impf* **набра́сывать**) throw (down); sketch; jot down. **набро́сить** (-о́шу) *pf*

(*impf* **набра́сывать**) throw; ~ся throw o.s.; ~ся на attack. **набро́сок** (-ска) sketch, draft.

набуха́ть *impf*, **набу́хнуть** (-нет; -у́х) *pf* swell.

набью́ *etc.: see* **наби́ть**

наважде́ние delusion.

нава́ливать *impf*, **навали́ть** (-лю́, -лишь) *pf* heap, pile up; load; ~ся lean; +**на**+*acc* fall (up)on.

наведе́ние laying (on); placing.

наведу́ *etc.: see* **навести́**

наве́к, наве́ки *adv* for ever.

навёл *etc.: see* **навести́**

наве́рно, наве́рное *adv* probably. **наверняка́** *adv* certainly, for sure.

наверста́ть *pf*, **навёрстывать** *impf* make up for.

наве́рх *adv* up(wards); upstairs. **наверху́** *adv* above; upstairs.

наве́с awning.

наве́сить (-е́шу) *pf* (*impf* **наве́шивать**) hang (up). **навесно́й** hanging.

навести́ (-еду́, -едёшь; -вёл, -á) *pf* (*impf* **наводи́ть**) direct; aim; cover (with); spread; introduce, bring; make.

навести́ть (-ещу́) *pf* (*impf* **навеща́ть**) visit.

наве́шать *pf*, **наве́шивать**[1] *impf* hang (out); weigh out.

наве́шивать[2] *impf of* **наве́сить. навеща́ть** *impf of* **навести́ть**

на́взничь *adv* backwards, on one's back.

навзры́д *adv:* **пла́кать ~** sob.

навига́ция navigation.

нависа́ть *impf*, **нави́снуть** (-нет; -вис) *pf* overhang, hang (over); threaten. **нави́сший** beetling.

навлека́ть impf, навле́чь (-еку́, -ечёшь; -ёк, -ла́) pf bring, draw; incur.

наводи́ть (-ожу́, -о́дишь) impf of навести́. наводя́щий вопро́с leading question. наво́дка aiming; applying.

наводне́ние flood. наводни́ть pf, наводня́ть impf flood; inundate.

наво́з dung, manure.

на́волочка pillowcase.

на|вра́ть (-ру́, -рёшь; -а́л, -а́, -о) pf tell lies, romance; talk nonsense; +в+prep make mistake(s) in.

навреди́ть (-ежу́) pf +dat harm.

навсегда́ adv for ever.

навстре́чу adv to meet; идти́ ~ go to meet; meet halfway.

на́выворот adv inside out; back to front.

на́вык experience, skill.

на́вынос adv to take away.

на́выпуск adv worn outside.

навью́чивать impf, на|вью́чить (-чу) pf load.

навяза́ть (-яжу́, -я́жешь) pf, навя́зывать impf tie, fasten; thrust, foist; ~ся thrust o.s. навя́зчивый importunate; obsessive.

на|га́дить (-а́жу) pf.

нага́н revolver.

нагиба́ть(ся impf of нагну́ть(ся

нагишо́м adv stark naked.

нагле́ц (-а́) impudent fellow. на́глость impudence. на́глый (нагл, -а́, -о) impudent.

нагля́дный clear, graphic; visual.

нагна́ть (-гоню́, -го́нишь; -а́л, -а́, -о) pf (impf нагоня́ть) overtake, catch up (with); inspire, arouse.

нагнести́ (-ету́, -етёшь) pf,

нагнета́ть impf compress; supercharge.

нагное́ние suppuration. нагнои́ться pf suppurate.

нагну́ть (-ну́, -нёшь) pf (impf нагиба́ть) bend; ~ся bend, stoop.

нагова́ривать impf, наговори́ть pf slander; talk a lot (of); record.

наго́й (наг, -а́, -о) naked, bare.

на́голо adv naked, bare.

нагоня́ть impf of нагна́ть

нагора́ть impf, нагоре́ть (-ри́т) pf be consumed; impers+dat be scolded.

наго́рный upland, mountain; mountainous.

нагота́ nakedness, nudity.

награ́бить (-блю) pf amass by dishonest means.

награ́да reward; decoration; prize. награди́ть (-ажу́) pf, награжда́ть impf reward; decorate; award prize to.

нагрева́тельный heating. нагрева́ть impf, нагре́ть (-е́ю) pf warm, heat; ~ся get hot, warm up.

нагроможда́ть impf, на|громозди́ть (-зжу́) pf heap up, pile up. нагроможде́ние heaping up; conglomeration.

на|груби́ть (-блю́) pf.

нагружа́ть impf, на|грузи́ть (-ужу́, -у́зишь) pf load; ~ся load o.s. нагру́зка loading; load; work; commitments.

нагря́нуть (-ну) pf appear unexpectedly.

над, на́до prep+instr over, above; on; at.

надави́ть (-влю́, -вишь) pf, нада́вливать impf press; squeeze out; crush.

надба́вка addition, increase.

надвига́ть impf, надви́нуть

(-ну) *pf* move, pull, push; ~ся approach.

на́двое *adv* in two.

надгро́бие epitaph. **надгро́бный** (on or over a) grave.

надева́ть *impf of* **наде́ть**

наде́жда hope. **надёжность** reliability. **надёжный** reliable.

наде́л allotment.

наде́лать *pf* make; cause; do. **надели́ть** (-лю́, -ли́шь) *pf*, **наделя́ть** *impf* endow, provide.

наде́ть (-е́ну) *pf* (*impf* **надева́ть**) put on.

наде́яться (-е́юсь) *impf* (*pf* **по~**) hope; rely.

надзира́тель *m* overseer, supervisor. **надзира́ть** *impf* +за+*instr* supervise, oversee. **надзо́р** supervision; surveillance.

надла́мывать(ся *impf of* **надломи́ть(ся**

надлежа́щий fitting, proper, appropriate. **надлежи́т** (-жа́ло) *impers* (+*dat*) it is necessary, required.

надло́м break; crack; breakdown. **надломи́ть** (-млю́, -мишь) *pf* (*impf* **надла́мывать**) break; crack; breakdown. ~**ся** break, crack, breakdown. **надло́мленный** broken.

надме́нный haughty, arrogant.

на́до[1] (+*dat*) it is necessary; I (*etc.*) need, ought to; I (*etc.*) need. **на́добность** necessity, need.

на́до[2]: *see* **над**.

надоеда́ть *impf*, **надое́сть** (-е́м, -е́шь, -е́ст, -еди́м) *pf* +*dat* bore, pester. **надое́дливый** boring, tiresome.

надо́лго *adv* for a long time.

надорва́ть (-ву́, -вёшь; -а́л, -а́, -о) *pf* (*impf* **надрыва́ть**) tear;

strain; ~ся tear; overstrain o.s.

на́дпись inscription.

надре́з cut, incision. **надре́зать** (-е́жу) *pf*, **надреза́ть** *impf*, **надре́зывать** *impf* make an incision in.

надруга́тельство outrage. **надруга́ться** *pf* +над+*instr* outrage, insult.

надры́в tear; strain; breakdown; outburst. **надрыва́ть(ся** *impf of* **надорва́ть(ся**. **надры́вный** hysterical; heartrending.

надста́вить (-влю) *pf*, **надставля́ть** *impf* lengthen.

надстра́ивать *impf*, **надстро́ить** (-о́ю) *pf* build on top; extend upwards. **надстро́йка** building upwards; superstructure.

надува́тельство swindle. **надува́ть(ся** *impf of* **наду́ть(ся. надувно́й** pneumatic, inflatable.

наду́манный far-fetched.

наду́тый swollen; haughty; sulky. **наду́ть** (-у́ю) *pf* (*impf* **надува́ть**) inflate; swindle; ~**ся** swell out; sulk.

на|души́ть(ся (-шу́(сь, -шишь(ся) *pf*

наеда́ться *impf of* **нае́сться**

наедине́ *adv* privately, alone.

нае́зд flying visit; raid. **нае́здник, -ица** rider. **наезжа́ть** *impf of* **нае́здить, нае́хать**; pay occasional visits.

наём (на́йма) hire; renting; **взять в ~** rent; **сдать в ~** let. **наёмник** hireling; mercenary. **наёмный** hired, rented.

нае́сться (-е́мся, -е́шься, -е́стся, -еди́мся) *pf* (*impf* **наеда́ться**) eat one's fill; stuff o.s.

нае́хать (-е́ду) *pf* (*impf* **наезжа́ть**) arrive unexpectedly;

+**на́**+*acc* run into, collide with.

нажа́ть (-жму́, -жмёшь) *pf* (*impf* **нажима́ть**) press; put pressure (on).

наждак (-а́) emery. **нажда́ч- ная бума́га** emery paper.

нажи́ва profit, gain.

наживать(ся *impf of* **нажи́ть(ся**

нажи́м pressure; clamp. **нажи- ма́ть** *impf of* **нажа́ть**.

нажи́ть (-иву́, -ивёшь; на́жил, -а́, -о) *pf* (*impf* **нажива́ть**) acquire; contract, incur; ~**ся** (-жи́лся, -а́сь) get rich.

нажму́ *etc.: see* **нажа́ть**

наза́втра *adv* (the) next day.

наза́д *adv* back(wards); **(тому́)** ~ ago.

назва́ние name; title. **назва́ть** (-зову́, -зовёшь; -а́л, -а́, -о) *pf* (*impf* **называ́ть**) call, name; ~**ся** be called.

назе́мный ground, surface.

назло́ *adv* out of spite; to spite.

назнача́ть *impf*, **назна́чить** (-чу) *pf* appoint; fix, set; pre- scribe. **назначе́ние** appoint- ment; fixing, setting; prescrip- tion.

назову́ *etc.: see* **назва́ть**

назо́йливый importunate.

назрева́ть *impf*, **назре́ть** (-е́ет) *pf* ripen, mature; become im- minent.

называ́емый: так ~ so- called. **называ́ть(ся** *impf of* **назва́ть(ся**.

наибо́лее *adv* (the) most. **наи- бо́льший** greatest, biggest.

наи́вный naive.

наивы́сший highest.

наигра́ть *pf*, **наи́грывать** *impf* win; play, pick out.

наизна́нку *adv* inside out.

наизу́сть *adv* by heart.

наилу́чший best.

наименова́ние name; title.

наи́скось *adv* obliquely.

найму́ *etc.: see* **наня́ть**

найти́ (-йду́, -йдёшь; нашёл, -шла́, -шло́) *pf* (*impf* **нахо- ди́ть**) find; ~**сь** be found; be, be situated.

наказа́ние punishment. **наказа́ть** (-ажу́, -а́жешь) *pf*, **нака́- зывать** *impf* punish.

нака́л incandescence. **нака́- ливать** *impf*, **накали́ть** *pf*, **накаля́ть** *impf* heat; make red-hot; strain, make tense; ~**ся** glow, become incandes- cent; become strained.

нака́лывать(ся *impf of* **на- коло́ть(ся**

накану́не *adv* the day before. ~ *prep*+*gen*.

нака́пливать(ся *impf of* **на- копи́ть(ся**

накача́ть *pf*, **нака́чивать** *impf* pump (up).

наки́дка cloak, cape; extra charge. **наки́нуть** (-ну) *pf*, **наки́дывать** *impf* throw; throw on; ~**ся** throw o.s.; ~**ся на** attack.

на́кипь scum; scale.

накладна́я *sb* invoice. **на- кладно́й** laid on; false; ~**ые расхо́ды** overheads. **накла́- дывать** *impf of* **наложи́ть**

наклевета́ть (-ещу́, -е́щешь) *pf*.

накле́ивать *impf*, **накле́ить** *pf* stick on. **накле́йка** stick- ing (on, up); label.

накло́н slope, incline. **на- клоне́ние** inclination; mood. **наклони́ть** (-ню́, -нишь) *pf*, **наклоня́ть** *impf* incline, bend; ~**ся** stoop, bend. **накло́нный** inclined, sloping.

нако́лка pinning; (*pinned-on*) ornament for hair; tattoo. **наколо́ть**[1] (-лю́, -лешь)

(*impf* нака́лывать) prick;
pin; ~ся prick o.s.

наколо́ть² (-лю́, -лешь) *pf*
(*impf* нака́лывать) chop.

наконе́ц *adv* at last. нако-
не́чник tip, point.

на|копи́ть (-плю́, -пишь) *pf*,
накопля́ть *impf* (*impf also*
нака́пливать) accumulate;
~ся accumulate. нако-
пле́ние accumulation.

на|копти́ть (-пчу́) *pf.* на|кор-
ми́ть (-млю́, -мишь) *pf.*

накра́сить (-а́шу) *pf*. paint;
make up. на|кра́ситься
(-а́шусь) *pf.*

на|крахма́лить *pf.*

на|крени́ть *pf.* накрени́ться
(-ни́тся) *pf*, накреня́ться
impf tilt; list.

накрича́ть (-чу́) *pf* (+на+*acc*)
shout (at).

накро́ю *etc.: see* накры́ть

накрыва́ть *impf*, накры́ть
(-ро́ю) *pf* cover; catch; ~ на
стол lay the table; ~ся cover
o.s.

накури́ть (-рю́, -ришь) *pf* fill
with smoke.

налага́ть *impf of* наложи́ть

нала́|дить (-а́жу) *pf*, нала́-
живать *impf* regulate, adjust;
repair; organize; ~ся come
right; get going.

на|лга́ть (-лгу́, -лжёшь; -а́л,
-а́, -о) *pf.*

нале́во *adv* to the left.

налёг *etc.: see* нале́чь. нале-
га́ть *impf of* нале́чь

налегке́ *adv* lightly dressed;
without luggage.

налёт flight; thin coating.
налета́ть¹ *pf* have flown.
налета́ть² *impf*, налете́ть
(-лечу́) *pf* swoop down; come
flying; spring up.

нале́чь (-ля́гу, -ля́жешь; -лёг,

-ла́) *pf* (*impf* налега́ть) lean,
apply one's weight, lie; apply
o.s.

налжёшь *etc.: see* налга́ть

налива́ть(ся *impf of* нали́ть-
(ся. нали́вка fruit liqueur.

нали́ть (-лью́, -льёшь; на́лил,
-а́, -о) *pf* (*impf* налива́ть) pour
(out), fill; ~ся (-и́лся, -а́сь,
-и́лось) pour in; ripen.

налицо́ *adv* present; available.
нали́чие presence. нали́ч|ный
on hand; cash; ~ые (де́ньги)
ready money.

нало́г tax. налогоплате́ль-
щик taxpayer. нало́женн|ый:
~ым платежо́м C.O.D. на-
ложи́ть (-жу́, -жишь) *pf*
(*impf* накла́дывать, нала-
га́ть) lay (in, on), put (in, on);
apply; impose.

налью́ *etc.: see* нали́ть

наля́гу *etc.: see* нале́чь

нам *etc.: see* мы

на|ма́зать (-а́жу) *pf*, нама́-
зывать *impf* oil, grease;
smear, spread.

нама́тывать *impf of* намо-
та́ть. нама́чивать *impf of*
намочи́ть

намёк hint. намека́ть *impf*,
намекну́ть (-ну́, -нёшь) *pf*
hint.

намерева́ться *impf* +*inf* intend to. наме́рен *predic*: я
~(а)+*inf* I intend to. наме́-
рение intention. наме́рен-
ный intentional.

на|мета́ть *pf.* на|ме́тить¹ (-е́чу)
pf.

наме́тить² (-е́чу) *pf* (*impf* на-
меча́ть) plan; outline; nominate; ~ся be outlined, take
shape.

намно́го *adv* much, far.

намока́ть *impf*, намо́кнуть
(-ну) *pf* get wet.

намо́рдник muzzle.

на|мо́рщить(ся) pf (-щу(сь)) pf.

на|мота́ть (impf also нама́тывать) wind, reel.

на|мочи́ть (-очу́, -о́чишь) pf (impf also нама́чивать) wet; soak; splash, spill.

намыли́вать impf, на|мы́лить pf soap.

нанести́ (-су́, -сёшь; -ёс, -ла́) pf (impf наноси́ть) carry, bring; draw, plot; inflict.

на|низа́ть (-ижу́, -и́жешь) pf (impf нани́зывать) string, thread.

нанима́тель m tenant; employer. нанима́ть(ся impf of наня́ть(ся

наноси́ть (-ошу́, -о́сишь) impf of нанести́

наня́ть (найму́, -мёшь; на́нял, -а́, -о) pf (impf нанима́ть) hire; rent; ~ся get a job.

наоборо́т adv on the contrary; back to front; the other, the wrong, way (round); vice versa.

наотма́шь adv violently.

наотре́з adv flatly, point-blank.

напада́ть impf of напа́сть. напада́ющий sb forward. нападе́ние attack; forwards.

напа́рник co-driver, (work)-mate.

напа́сть (-аду́, -адёшь; -а́л) pf (impf напада́ть) на+acc attack; descend on; seize; come upon. напа́сть misfortune.

напе́в tune. напева́ть impf of напе́ть

напереби́й adv interrupting, vying with, one another.

наперёд adv in advance.

напереко́р adv+dat in defiance of, counter to.

напёрсток (-тка) thimble.

напе́ть (-по́ю, -поёшь) pf (impf напева́ть) sing; hum, croon.

на|печа́тать(ся pf. напива́ться impf of напи́ться

напи́льник file.

на|писа́ть (-ишу́, -и́шешь) pf.

напи́ток (-тка) drink. напи́ться (-пью́сь, -пьёшься; -и́лся, -ась, -и́лось) pf (impf напива́ться) quench one's thirst, drink; get drunk.

напиха́ть pf, напи́хивать impf cram, stuff.

на|плева́ть (-люю́, -люёшь) pf; ~! to hell with it! who cares?

наплы́в influx; accumulation; canker.

наплюю́ etc.: see наплева́ть

напова́л outright.

наподо́бие prep+gen like, not unlike.

на|по́йть (-ою́, -о́йшь) pf.

напока́з adv for show.

наполни́тель m filler. на|по́лнить(ся pf, наполня́ть(ся impf) fill.

наполови́ну adv half.

напомина́ние reminder. напомина́ть impf, напо́мнить pf (+dat) remind.

напо́р pressure. напо́ристый energetic, pushing.

напосле́док adv in the end; after all.

напою́ etc.: see напе́ть, напо́йть

напр. abbr (of наприме́р) e.g., for example.

напра́вить (-влю) pf, направля́ть impf direct; send; sharpen; ~ся make (for), go (towards). направле́ние direction; trend; warrant; order. напра́вленный purposeful.

напра́во adv to the right.

напра́сно adv in vain, for nothing; unjustly, mistakenly.

напра́шиваться impf of напроси́ться

напримёр for example.

на|проказничать pf.

напрока́т adv for, on, hire.

напролёт adv through, without a break.

напроло́м adv straight, regardless of obstacles.

напроси́ться (-ошу́сь, -о́сишься) pf (impf **напра́шиваться**) thrust o.s.; suggest itself; ~ на ask for, invite.

напро́тив adv opposite; on the contrary. **напро́тив** prep+gen opposite.

напряга́ть impf of на|прячь(ся. **напряже́ние** tension; exertion; voltage. **на|пряжённый** tense; intense; intensive.

напрями́к adv straight (out).

напря́чь (-ягу́, -яжёшь; -я́г, -ла́) pf (impf **напряга́ть**) strain; ~ся strain o.s.

на|пуга́ть(ся pf. **на|пу́дрить-ся** pf.

напуска́ть impf, **напусти́ть** (-ущу́, -у́стишь) pf let in; let loose; ~ся +на+acc fly at, go for.

напу́тать pf +в+prep make a mess of.

на|пыли́ть pf.

напью́сь etc.: see **напи́ться**

наравне́ adv equally; equally.

нараспа́шку adv unbuttoned.

нараста́ние growth, accumulation. **нараста́ть** impf, **нарасти́** (-тёт; -ро́с, -ла́) pf grow; increase.

нарасхва́т adv very quickly, like hot cakes.

нарва́ть[1] (-рву́, -рвёшь; -а́л, -а́, -о) pf (impf **нарыва́ть**) pick; tear up.

нарва́ть[2] (-вёт; -а́л, -а́, -о) pf (impf **нарыва́ть**) gather.

нарва́ться (-ву́сь, -вёшься;

-а́лся, -ала́сь, -а́лось) pf (impf **нарыва́ться**) +на+acc run into, run up against.

наре́зать (-е́жу) pf, **наре́за́ть** impf cut (up), slice, carve; thread, rifle.

наре́чие[1] dialect.

наре́чие[2] adverb.

на|рисова́ть pf.

нарко́з narcosis. **наркома́н, -ма́нка** drug addict. **наркома́ния** drug addiction. **нарко́тик** narcotic.

наро́д people. **наро́дность** nationality; national character. **наро́дный** national; folk; popular; people's.

наро́с etc.: see **нарасти́**

наро́чно adv on purpose, deliberately. **на́рочный** sb courier.

нару́жность exterior. **нару́жный** external, outward. **нару́жу** adv outside.

нару́чник handcuff. **нару́чный** wrist.

наруше́ние breach; infringement. **нару́шитель** m transgressor. **нару́шить** (-шу) pf, **наруша́ть** impf break; disturb, infringe, violate.

нарци́сс narcissus; daffodil.

на́ры (нар) pl plank-bed.

нары́в abscess, boil. **нарыва́ть(ся** impf of нарва́ть(ся

наря́д[1] order, warrant.

наря́д[2] attire; dress. **наряди́ть** (-яжу́) pf (impf **наряжа́ть**) dress (up); ~ся dress up. **наря́дный** well-dressed.

наряду́ adv alike; equally; side by side.

наряжа́ть(ся impf of наряди́ть(ся. **нас** see **мы**

насади́ть (-ажу́, -а́дишь) pf, **насажда́ть** impf (impf also **наса́живать**) plant; propagate; implant. **насáдка** setting, fixing. **насаждéние** planting; plantation; propagation. **насáживать** impf of **насадить**

насекóмое sb insect.

населéние population. **населённость** density of population. **населённый** populated; ~ пункт settlement; built-up area. **населить** pf, **населять** impf settle, people.

насилие violence, force. **насиловать** (pf из~) coerce; rape. **насилу** adv with difficulty. **насильник** aggressor; rapist; violator. **насильно** adv by force. **насильственный** violent, forcible.

наскáкивать impf of **наскочить**

насквóзь adv through, throughout.

наскóлько adv how much?, how far?; as far as.

нáскоро adv hastily.

наскочить (-очу, -óчишь) pf (impf **наскáкивать**) +на+acc run into, collide with; fly at.

наскучить (-чу) pf bore.

насладиться (-ажусь) pf, **наслаждáться** impf (+instr) enjoy, take pleasure. **наслаждéние** pleasure, enjoyment.

наслéдие legacy; heritage. **наслéдить** (-ежу) pf. **наслéдник** heir; successor. **наслéдница** heiress. **наслéдный** next in succession. **наслéдовать** impf & pf (pf also y~) inherit, succeed to. **наслéдственность** heredity. **наслéдственный** hereditary, inherited. **наслéдство** inheritance; heritage. **нáсмерть** adv to (the) death. **на|смешить** (-шý) pf. **насмéшка** mockery; gibe. **на|смешливый** mocking.

нáсморк runny nose; cold.

на|сорить pf.

насóс pump.

нáспех adv hastily.

на|сплетничать pf. **наставáть** (-таёт) impf of **настáть**

наставлéние exhortation; directions, manual.

настáвник tutor, mentor.

настаивать[1] impf of **настоять**[1]. **настáивать**[2](ся impf of **настоять**[2](ся

настáть (-áнет) pf (impf **наставáть**) come, begin, set in.

нáстежь adv wide (open).

настелю etc.: see **настлать**

настигáть impf, **настигнуть**, **настичь** (-игну; -иг) pf catch up with, overtake.

настил flooring, planking. **настилáть** impf of **настлáть**

настичь see **настигáть**

настлáть (-телю, -тéлешь) pf (impf **настилáть**) lay, spread.

настóйка liqueur, cordial. **настóйчивый** persistent; urgent.

настóлько adv so, so much.

настóльный table, desk; reference.

насторáживать impf, **насторожить** (-жу) pf set; prick up; ~ся prick up one's ears. **настороженный** (-ен, -енна) guarded; alert.

настоятельный insistent; urgent. **настоять**[1] (-ою) pf (impf **настáивать**[1]) insist.

настоять[2] (-ою) pf (impf **настáивать**[2]) brew; ~ся draw, stand.

настоящее sb the present. **настоящий** (the) present, this; real, genuine.

на|страивать(ся impf of **на|строить(ся**

настри́чь (-игу́, -ижёшь; -и́г) *pf* shear, clip.

настро́ение mood. **настро́ить** (-о́ю) *pf* (*impf* **настра́ивать**) tune (in); dispose; ~**ся** dispose o.s. **настро́йка** tuning. **настро́йщик** tuner.

на|стро́ить(-чу) *pf*.

наступа́тельный offensive. **наступа́ть¹** *impf of* **наступи́ть¹**

наступа́ть² *impf of* **наступи́ть²**. **наступа́ющий¹** coming.

наступа́ющий² *sb* attacker.

наступи́ть¹ (-плю́, -пишь) *pf* (*impf* **наступа́ть¹**) tread; attack; advance.

наступи́ть² (-у́пит) *pf* (*impf* **наступа́ть²**) come, set in. **наступле́ние¹** coming.

наступле́ние² offensive, attack.

насу́питься (-плюсь) *pf*, **насу́пливаться** *impf* frown.

на́сухо *adv* dry. **насуши́ть** (-шу́, -шишь) *pf* dry.

насу́щный urgent, vital; **хлеб** ~ daily bread.

насчёт *prep+gen* about, concerning; as regards. **насчита́ть** *pf*, **насчи́тывать** *impf* count; hold; ~**ся** *+gen* number.

насыпа́ть (-плю) *pf*, **насыпа́ть** *impf* pour in, on; fill; spread; heap up. **на́сыпь** embankment.

насы́тить (-ы́щу) *pf*, **насыща́ть** *impf* satiate; saturate; ~**ся** be full; be saturated.

ната́лкивать(ся *impf of* **натолкну́ть(ся**. **ната́пливать** *impf of* **натопи́ть**

ната́скать *pf*, **ната́скивать** *impf* train; coach, cram; bring in, lay in.

натвори́ть *pf* do, get up to.

натере́ть (-тру́, -трёшь; -тёр) *pf* (*impf* **натира́ть**) rub on, in; polish; chafe; grate; ~**ся** rub o.s.

на́тиск onslaught.

наткну́ться (-ну́сь, -нёшься) *impf* **натыка́ться**) **+на**+*acc* run into; strike, stumble on.

натолкну́ть (-ну́, -нёшь) *pf* (*impf* **ната́лкивать**) push; lead; ~**ся** run against, across.

натопи́ть (-плю́, -пишь) *pf* (*impf* **ната́пливать**) heat (up); stoke up; melt.

ната́щак *adv* on an empty stomach.

натра́вить (-влю́, -вишь) *pf* (*impf* **натра́вливать** *impf*, **натравля́ть**) *pf* set (on); stir up.

на|трениро́вать(ся *pf*.

на́трий sodium.

нату́ра nature. **натура́льный** natural; genuine. **нату́рщик, -щица** artist's model.

натыка́ться *impf of* **наткну́ться(ся**

натюрмо́рт still life.

натя́гивать *impf*, **натяну́ть** (-ну́, -нешь) *pf* stretch; draw; pull (on); ~**ся** stretch. **натя́нутость** tension. **натя́нутый** tight; strained.

науга́д *adv* at random.

нау́ка science; learning.

нау́тро *adv* (the) next morning.

на|учи́ть (-чу́, -чишь) *pf*.

нау́чный scientific; ~**ая фанта́стика** science fiction.

нау́шник ear-flap; ear-phone; informer.

нафтали́н naphthalene.

наха́л, -ха́лка impudent creature. **наха́льный** impudent. **наха́льство** impudence.

нахвата́ть *pf*, **нахва́тывать**

impf pick up, get hold of; **~ся** +*gen* pick up.

нахлебник hanger-on.

нахлынуть (-нет) *pf* well up; surge; gush.

на|хмурить(ся *pf*.

находить (-ожу(сь, -одишь(ся) *impf of* найти(сь. на|ходка find. находчивый resourceful, quick-witted.

нацеливать *impf*, на|целить *pf* aim; **~ся** (take) aim.

наценка extra, addition; additional charge.

нацизм Nazism. национализация nationalization. национализировать *impf & pf* nationalize. национализм nationalism. националистический nationalist(ic). национальность nationality; ethnic group. национальный national. нацист, -истка Nazi. нация nation. нацмен, -менка *abbr* member of a national minority.

начало beginning; origin; principle, basis. начальник head, chief; boss. начальный initial; primary. начальство the authorities; command. начать (-чну, -чнёшь; начал, -á, -о) *pf* (*impf* начинать) begin; **~ся** begin.

начертать *pf* trace, inscribe. на|чертить (-рчу, -ртишь) *pf*.

начинание undertaking. начинать(ся *impf of* начать(ся. начинающий *sb* beginner.

начинить *pf*, начинять *impf* stuff, fill. начинка stuffing, filling.

начистить (-ищу) *pf* (*impf* начищать) clean. начисто *adv* clean; flatly, decidedly; openly, frankly. начистоту

adv openly, frankly.

начитанность learning; wide reading. начитанный well-read.

начищать *impf of* начистить

наш (-его) *m*, наша (-ей) *f*, наше (-его) *neut*, наши (-их) *pl*, *pron* our, ours.

нашатырный спирт ammonia. нашатырь (-я) *m* salammoniac; ammonia.

нашёл *etc.: see* найти

нашествие invasion.

нашивать *impf*, нашить (-шью, -шьёшь) *pf* sew on. нашивка stripe, chevron; tab.

нашлёпать *impf* slap.

нашуметь (-млю) *pf* make a din; cause a sensation.

нашью *etc.: see* нашить

нащупать *pf*, нащупывать *impf* grope for.

на|электризовать *pf*.

наяву *adv* awake; in reality.

не *partl* not.

не- *pref* un-, in-, non-, mis-, dis-; -less; not. неаккуратный careless; untidy; unpunctual. небезразличный not indifferent. небезызвестный not unknown; notorious; well-known.

небеса *etc.: see* небо[2]. небесный heavenly; celestial.

не- неблагодарный ungrateful; thankless. неблагонадёжный unreliable. неблагополучный unsuccessful, bad, unfavourable. неблагоприятный unfavourable. неблагоразумный imprudent. неблагородный ignoble, base.

нёбо[1] palate.

нёбо[2] (*pl* -беса, -бёс) sky; heaven.

не-. небогатый of modest

means, modest. **небольшо́й** small, not great; **с небольши́м** a little over.

небосво́д firmament. **небосклон** horizon. **небоскрёб** skyscraper.

небо́сь adv I dare say; probably.

не-. небре́жный careless. **небыва́лый** unprecedented; fantastic. **небыли́ца** fable, cock-and-bull story. **небытие́** non-existence. **небью́щийся** unbreakable. **нева́жно** adv not too well, indifferently. **нева́жный** unimportant; indifferent. **невдалеке́** adv not far away. **неве́дение** ignorance. **неве́домый** unknown; mysterious. **неве́жа** m & f boor, lout. **неве́жда** m & f ignoramus. **неве́жественный** ignorant. **неве́жество** ignorance. **неве́жливый** rude.

невели́кий (-и́к, -а́, -и́ко́) small. **неве́рие** unbelief, atheism; scepticism. **неве́рный** (-рен, -рна́, -о) incorrect, wrong; inaccurate, unsteady; unfaithful. **невероя́тный** improbable; incredible. **неве́рующий** unbelieving; sb atheist. **невесёлый** joyless, sad. **невесо́мый** weightless; imponderable.

неве́ста fiancée; bride. **неве́стка** daughter-in-law; brother's wife, sister-in-law.

не-. невзгода adversity. **невзира́я на** prep+acc regardless of. **невзнача́й** adv by chance. **невзра́чный** unattractive, plain. **невида́нный** unprecedented, unheard-of. **неви́димый** invisible. **неви́нность** innocence. **неви́нный** innocent. **не-**

вменя́емый irresponsible. **невмеша́тельство** non-intervention; non-interference. **невмоготу́, невмочь** advs unbearable, too much (for). **невнима́тельный** inattentive, thoughtless. **нево́д** seine(-net).

не-. невозврати́мый, невозвра́тный irrevocable, irrecoverable. **невозмо́жный** impossible. **невозмути́мый** imperturbable. **нево́льник, -ница** slave. **нево́льный** involuntary; unintentional; forced. **нево́ля** captivity; necessity.

не-. невообрази́мый unimaginable, inconceivable. **невооружённый** unarmed; ~ным гла́зом with the naked eye. **невоспи́танный** ill-bred, bad-mannered. **невоспламеня́ющийся** non-flammable. **невосприи́мчивый** unreceptive; immune.

невралги́я neuralgia. **невреди́мый** safe, unharmed. **невро́з** neurosis. **невроло́гический** neurological. **невроти́ческий** neurotic.

не-. невы́годный disadvantageous; unprofitable. **невы́держанный** lacking self-control; unmatured. **невыноси́мый** unbearable. **невыполни́мый** impracticable. **невысо́кий** (-со́к, -а́, -о́ко́) low; short. **не́га** luxury; bliss.

негати́вный negative.

не́где adv (there is) nowhere.

не-. неги́бкий (-бок, -бка́, -о) inflexible, stiff. **негла́сный** secret. **неглубо́кий** (-бо́к, -а́, -о) shallow. **неглу́пый** (-у́п, -а́, -о) sensible, quite intelligent.

него́дный (-ден, -дна́, -о) unfit, unsuitable; worthless. **не-годова́ние** indignation. **не-годова́ть** *impf* be indignant. **него́дяй** scoundrel. **него-степрии́мный** inhospitable.

негр Negro, black man.

негра́мотность illiteracy. **не-гра́мотный** illiterate.

негритя́нка Negress, black woman. **негритя́нский** Negro.

не-. **негро́мкий** (-мок, -мка́, -о) quiet. **неда́вний** recent. **неда́вно** *adv* recently. **неда-лёкий** (-ёк, -á, -ёко) near; short; not bright, dull-witted. **недалеко́** *adv* not far, near. **неда́ром** *adv* not for nothing, not without reason. **не-дви́жимость** real estate. **не-дви́жимый** immovable. **не-двусмы́сленный** unequivocal. **недействи́тельный** ineffective; invalid. **недели́мый** indivisible.

неде́льный of a week, week's. **неде́ля** week.

не-. **недёшево** *adv* dear(ly). **недоброжела́тель** *m* ill-wisher. **недоброжела́тель-ность** hostility. **недоброка́-чественный** of poor quality. **недобросо́вестный** unscrupulous; careless. **недо́брый** (-обр, -обра́, -о) unkind; bad. **недове́рие** distrust. **недо-ве́рчивый** distrustful. **недо-во́льный** dissatisfied. **недо-во́льство** dissatisfaction. **недо-еда́ние** malnutrition. **недо-еда́ть** *impf* be undernourished.

не-. **недо́лгий** (-лог, -лга́, -о) short, brief. **недо́лго** *adv* not long. **недолгове́чный** short-lived. **недомога́ние** indisposition. **недомога́ть** *impf* be

unwell. **недомы́слие** thoughtlessness. **недоно́шенный** premature. **недооце́нивать** *impf*, **недооцени́ть** (-ню, -нишь) *pf* underestimate; underrate. **не-дооце́нка** underestimation. **недопусти́мый** inadmissible, intolerable. **недоразуме́ние** misunderstanding. **не-дорого́й** (-до́рог, -á, -о) inexpensive. **недосмотре́ть** (-рю́,-ришь) *pf* overlook. **не-доспа́ть** (-плю́; -ал, -á, -о) *pf* (*impf* **недосыпа́ть**) not have enough sleep.

недостава́ть (-таёт) *impf*, **недоста́ть** (-а́нет) *pf impers* be missing, be lacking. **не-доста́ток** (-тка) shortage, deficiency. **недоста́точный** insufficient, inadequate. **недо-ста́ча** lack, shortage.

не-. **недостижи́мый** unattainable. **недосто́йный** unworthy, **недосту́пный** inaccessible. **недосчита́ться** *pf*, **недосчи́тываться** *impf* miss, find missing, be short (of). **недосыпа́ть** *impf of* недоспа́ть. **недосяга́емый** unattainable.

недоумева́ть *impf* be at a loss, be bewildered. **недо-уме́ние** bewilderment.

не-. **недоу́чка** *m & f* half-educated person. **недочёт** deficit; defect.

не́дра (недр) *pl* depths, heart, bowels.

не-. **не́друг** enemy. **недру-желю́бный** unfriendly.

неду́г illness, disease.

недурно́й not bad; not bad-looking.

не-. **неесте́ственный** unnatural. **нежда́нный** unexpected. **нежела́ние** unwillingness. **нежела́тельный** undesirable.

не́жели than.

нежена́тый unmarried.

не́женка *m & f* mollycoddle.

нежи́ло́й uninhabited; uninhabitable.

не́житься (-жусь) *impf* luxuriate, bask. **не́жность** tenderness; *pl* endearments. **не́жный** tender; affectionate.

не-. незабве́нный unforgettable. **незабу́дка** forget-me-not. **незабыва́емый** unforgettable. **незави́симость** independence. **незави́симый** independent. **незадо́лго** *adv* not long. **незаконнорождённый** illegitimate. **незако́нный** illegal, illicit; illegitimate. **незако́нченный** unfinished. **незамени́мый** irreplaceable. **незамерза́ющий** ice-free; anti-freeze. **незаме́тный** imperceptible. **незаму́жняя** unmarried. **незапа́мятный** immemorial. **незаслу́женный** unmerited. **незауря́дный** uncommon, outstanding.

не́зачем *adv* there is no need.

не-. незащищённый unprotected. **незва́ный** uninvited. **нездоро́виться** *impf, impers* +*dat*: мне нездоро́вится I don't feel well. **нездоро́вый** unhealthy. **нездоро́вье** ill health. **незнако́мец** (-мца), **незнако́мка** stranger. **незнако́мый** unknown, unfamiliar. **незна́ние** ignorance. **незначи́тельный** insignificant. **незре́лый** unripe, immature. **незри́мый** invisible. **незы́блемый** unshakable, firm. **неизбе́жность** inevitability. **неизбе́жный** inevitable. **не-**

изве́данный unknown. **неизве́стность** uncertainty; ignorance; obscurity. **неизве́стный** unknown; *sb* stranger.

не-. неизлечи́мый incurable. **неизме́нный** unchanging; devoted. **неизменя́емый** unalterable. **неизмери́мый** immeasurable, immense. **неизу́ченный** unstudied; unexplored. **неиму́щий** poor. **неинтере́сный** uninteresting. **неи́скренний** insincere. **неискушённый** inexperienced, unsophisticated. **неисполни́мый** impracticable. **неисправи́мый** incorrigible; irreparable. **неиспра́вный** out of order, defective; careless. **неиссле́дованный** unexplored. **неисся́каемый** inexhaustible. **неи́стовый** fury, frenzy; atrocity. **нейстовый** furious, frenzied; uncontrolled. **неистощи́мый**, **неисчерпа́емый** inexhaustible. **неисчисли́мый** innumerable.

нейло́н, нейло́новый nylon. **нейро́н** neuron.

нейтрализа́ция neutralization. **нейтрализова́ть** *impf & pf* neutralize. **нейтралите́т** neutrality. **нейтра́льный** neutral. **нейтро́н** neutron.

неквалифици́рованный unskilled.

не́кий *pron* a certain, some.

не́когда[1] *adv* once, formerly.

не́когда[2] *adv* there is no time; мне ~ I have no time.

не́кого (не́кому, не́кем, не́ о ком) *pron* there is nobody.

некомпете́нтный not competent, unqualified.

не́котор|ый *pron* some; **~ые** *sb pl* some (people).

некраси́вый plain, ugly; not nice.

некроло́г obituary.

некста́ти *adv* at the wrong time, out of place.

не́кто *pron* somebody; a certain.

не́куда *adv* there is nowhere.

не-. некульту́рный uncivilized, uncultured. **некуря́щий** *sb* non-smoker. **нела́дный** wrong. **нелега́льный** illegal. **нелёгкий** not easy; heavy. **неле́пость** absurdity, nonsense. **неле́пый** absurd. **нело́вкий** awkward. **нело́вкость** awkwardness.

нельзя́ *adv* it is impossible; it is not allowed.

не-. нелюби́мый unloved. **нелюди́мый** unsociable. **нема́ло** *adv* quite a lot (of). **нема́лый** considerable. **неме́дленно** *adv* immediately. **неме́дленный** immediate.

неме́ть (-е́ю) *impf* (*pf* о~) become dumb. **не́мец** (-мца) German. **неме́цкий** German.

неминуемый inevitable.

не́мка German woman.

немно́гие *sb pl* a few. **немно́го** *adv* a little; some; a few. **немно́жко** *adv* a little.

немо́й (нем, -а́, -о) dumb, mute, silent. **немота́** dumbness.

не́мощный feeble.

немы́слимый unthinkable.

ненави́деть (-и́жу) *impf* hate. **ненави́стный** hated; hateful. **не́нависть** hatred.

не-. ненагля́дный beloved. **ненадёжный** unreliable. **ненадо́лго** *adv* for a short time. **нена́стье** bad weather. **ненасы́тный** insatiable. **ненор-**

ма́льный abnormal. **нену́жный** unnecessary, unneeded. **необду́манный** thoughtless, hasty. **необеспе́ченный** without means, unprovided for. **необита́емый** uninhabited. **необозри́мый** boundless, immense. **необосно́ванный** unfounded, groundless. **необрабо́танный** uncultivated; crude; unpolished. **необразо́ванный** uneducated. **необходи́мость** necessity. **необходи́мый** necessary. **не-. необъясни́мый** inexplicable. **необъя́тный** immense. **необыкнове́нный** unusual. **необыча́йный** extraordinary. **необы́чный** unusual. **необяза́тельный** optional. **неограни́ченный** unlimited. **неоднокра́тный** repeated. **неодобри́тельный** disapproving. **неодушевлённый** inanimate.

неожи́данность unexpectedness. **неожи́данный** unexpected, sudden.

неокласси́цизм neoclassicism. **не-. неоко́нченный** unfinished. **неопла́ченный** unpaid. **неопра́вданный** unjustified. **неопределённый** indefinite; infinitive; vague. **неопровержи́мый** irrefutable. **неопублико́ванный** unpublished. **нео́пытный** inexperienced. **неоргани́ческий** inorganic. **неоспори́мый** incontestable. **неосторо́жный** careless. **неосуществи́мый** impracticable. **неотврати́мый** inevitable. **нео́ткуда** *adv* there is nowhere.

не-. неотло́жный urgent. **неотрази́мый** irresistible. **неот-**

сту́пный persistent. **неотъ-
е́млемый** inalienable. **не-
официа́льный** unofficial.
неохо́та reluctance. **неохо́т-
но** adv reluctantly. **неоцени́-
мый** inestimable, invaluable. **непарти́йный** non-party;
unbefitting a member of
the (Communist) Party. **не-
переводи́мый** untranslatable. **непереходный** intransitive. **неплатёжеспосо́б-
ный** insolvent.

не-. непло́хо adv not badly,
quite well. **неплохо́й** not bad,
quite good. **непобеди́мый**
invincible. **неповинове́ние**
insubordination. **непово́рот-
ливый** clumsy. **неповтори́-
мый** inimitable, unique. **непого́да** bad weather. **непо-
греши́мый** infallible. **непо-
далёку** adv not far (away).
неподви́жный motionless,
immovable; fixed. **непод-
де́льный** genuine; sincere.
непо́дкупный incorruptible.
неподража́емый inimitable.
неподходя́щий unsuitable,
inappropriate. **непоколеби́-
мый** unshakable, steadfast.
непоко́рный recalcitrant,
unruly.

не-. непола́дки (-док) pl de-
fects. **неполноце́нность**
ко́мплекс неполноце́нности
inferiority complex. **неполно-
це́нный** defective; inadequate.
непо́лный incomplete; not (a)
full. **непоме́рный** excessive.
непонима́ние incomprehen-
sion, lack of understanding.
непоня́тный incomprehensible. **непоправи́мый** irreparable. **непоря́док** (-дка) disorder. **непоря́дочный** dishonourable. **непосе́да** m &

f fidget. **непоси́льный** beyond one's strength. **непо-
сле́довательный** inconsistent. **непослуша́ние** disobedience. **непослу́шный** disobedient. **непосре́дствен-
ный** immediate; spontaneous.
непостижи́мый incomprehensible. **непостоя́нный** in-
constant, changeable. **непо-
хо́жий** unlike; different.

не-. непра́вда untruth. **не-
правдоподо́бный** improbable. **непра́вильно** adv
wrong. **непра́вильный** irregular; wrong. **непра́вый**
wrong. **непракти́чный** un-
practical. **непревзойдённый** unsurpassed. **непред-
ви́денный** unforeseen. **непредубеждённый** unpreju-
diced. **непредусмо́тренный**
unforeseen. **непредусмо-
три́тельный** short-sighted.
непрекло́нный inflexible;
adamant. **непрело́жный** immutable.

не-. непреме́нно adv without
fail. **непреме́нный** indispensable. **непреодоли́мый** insuperable. **непререка́емый**
unquestionable. **непреры́в-
но** adv continuously. **непре-
ры́вный** continuous. **непре-
ста́нный** incessant. **непри-
ве́тливый** unfriendly; bleak.
непривлека́тельный unattractive. **непривы́чный** unaccustomed. **непригля́дный**
unattractive. **неприго́дный**
unfit, useless. **неприе́мле-
мый** unacceptable. **непри-
коснове́нность** inviolabil-
ity, immunity. **неприкосно-
ве́нный** inviolable; reserve.
неприли́чный indecent. **не-
примири́мый** irreconcilable.

непринуждённый unconstrained; relaxed. **неприспосо́бленный** unadapted; maladjusted. **непристо́йный** obscene. **непристу́пный** inaccessible. **непритяза́тельный**, **неприхотли́вый** unpretentious, simple. **неприя́зненный** hostile, inimical. **неприя́знь** hostility. **неприя́тель** *m* enemy. **неприя́тельский** enemy. **неприя́тность** unpleasantness; trouble. **неприя́тный** unpleasant.

не-. непрове́ренный unverified. **непрогля́дный** pitch-dark. **непрое́зжий** impassable. **непрозра́чный** opaque. **непроизводи́тельный** unproductive. **непроизво́льный** involuntary. **непромока́емый** waterproof. **непроница́емый** impenetrable. **непрости́тельный** unforgivable. **непроходи́мый** impassable. **непро́чный** (-чен, -чна́) fragile, flimsy.

не прочь *predic* not averse.

не-. непро́шеный uninvited, unsolicited. **нерабоспосо́бный** disabled. **нерабо́чий**: ~ день day off. **нера́венство** inequality. **неравноме́рный** uneven. **нера́вный** unequal. **неради́вый** lackadaisical. **неразбери́ха** muddle. **неразбо́рчивый** not fastidious; illegible. **неразвито́й** (-ра́звит, -á, -о) undeveloped; backward. **неразгово́рчивый** taciturn. **неразделённый**: ~ая любо́вь unrequited love. **неразличи́мый** indistinguishable. **неразлу́чный** inseparable. **неразрешённый** unsolved; forbidden. **неразреши́мый** insoluble. **неразры́вный** indissoluble. **неразу́мный** unwise; unreasonable. **нераствори́мый** insoluble.

нерв nerve. **не́рвничать** *impf* fret, be nervous. **нервнобольно́й** *sb* neurotic. **не́рвный** (-вен, -вна́, -о) nervous; nerve; irritable. **нерво́зный** nervy, irritable.

не-. нереа́льный unreal; unrealistic. **нере́дкий** (-док, -дка́, -о) not infrequent, not uncommon. **нереши́тельность** indecision. **нереши́тельный** indecisive, irresolute. **нержаве́ющая сталь** stainless steel. **неро́вный** (-вен, -вна́, -о) uneven, rough; irregular. **неруши́мый** inviolable.

неря́ха *m & f* sloven. **неря́шливый** slovenly.

не-. несбы́точный unrealizable. **несваре́ние желу́дка** indigestion. **несве́жий** (-éж, -á) not fresh; tainted; weary. **несвоевре́менный** ill-timed; overdue. **несво́йственный** not characteristic. **несгора́емый** fireproof. **несерьёзный** not serious. **несессе́р** case. **несимметри́чный** asymmetrical.

нескла́дный incoherent; awkward. **несклоня́емый** indeclinable. **не́сколько** (-их) *pron* some, several; *adv* somewhat.

не-. несконча́емый interminable. **нескро́мный** (-мен, -мна́, -о) immodest; indiscreet. **несло́жный** simple. **неслы́ханный** unprecedented. **неслы́шный** inaudible. **несме́тный** countless, incalculable. **несмолка́емый** ceaseless.

несмотря́ на *prep+acc* in spite of.

не-. несно́сный intolerable. несоблюде́ние non-observance. несовершенноле́тний under-age; *sb* minor. несоверше́нный imperfect; incomplete; imperfective. несоверше́нство imperfection. несовмести́мый incompatible. несогла́сие disagreement. несогласо́ванный uncoordinated. несозна́тельный irresponsible. несоизмери́мый incommensurable. несокруши́мый indestructible. несомне́нный undoubted, unquestionable. несообра́зный incongruous. несоотве́тствие disparity. несостоя́тельный insolvent; of modest means; untenable. неспе́лый unripe. неспоко́йный restless; uneasy. неспосо́бный not bright; incapable. несправедли́вость injustice. несправедли́вый unjust, unfair; incorrect. несравне́нный (-е́нен, -е́нна) incomparable. несравни́мый incomparable. нестерпи́мый unbearable.

нести́ (-су́, -сёшь; нёс, -ла́) *impf* (*pf* по-), carry; bear; bring, take; suffer; incur; lay; ~сь rush, fly; float, be carried.

не-. несто́йкий unstable. несуще́ственный immaterial, inessential.

несу́ *etc.: see* нести́

несхо́дный unlike, dissimilar. несчастли́вый unfortunate, unlucky; unhappy. несча́стный unhappy, unfortunate; ~ слу́чай accident. несча́стье misfortune; к несча́стью un-

fortunately. несчётный innumerable.

нет *partl* no, not; nothing. нет, не́ту there is not, there are not.

не-. нетакти́чный tactless. нетвёрдый (-ёрд, -а́, -о) unsteady, shaky. нетерпели́вый impatient. нетерпе́ние impatience. нетерпи́мый intolerable, intolerant. неторопли́вый leisurely. нето́чный (-чен, -чна́, -о) inaccurate, inexact. нетре́звый drunk. нетро́нутый untouched; chaste, virginal. нетрудово́й дохо́д unearned income. нетрудоспосо́бность disability.

не́тто *indecl adj & adv* net(t).

не́ту *see* нет

не-. неубеди́тельный unconvincing. неуваже́ние disrespect. неуве́ренность uncertainty. неуве́ренный uncertain. неувяда́ющий unfading. неугомо́нный indefatigable. неуда́ча failure. неуда́чливый unlucky. неуда́чник, -ница unlucky person, failure. неуда́чный unsuccessful, unfortunate. неуде́ржимый irrepressible. неудо́бный uncomfortable; inconvenient; embarrassing. неудо́бство discomfort; inconvenience; embarrassment. неудовлетворе́ние dissatisfaction. неудовлетворённый dissatisfied. неудовлетвори́тельный unsatisfactory. неудово́льствие displeasure.

неуже́ли? *partl* really?

не-. неузнава́емый unrecognizable. неукло́нный steady; undeviating. неуклю́жий clumsy. **неулови́мый** elusive; subtle. **неуме́лый** inept; clumsy. **неуме́ренный** immoderate. **неуме́стный** inappropriate; irrelevant. **неумоли́мый** implacable, inexorable. **неумы́шленный** unintentional.

не-. неупла́та non-payment. **неуравнове́шенный** unbalanced. **неурожа́й** bad harvest. **неуро́чный** untimely, inopportune. **неуря́дица** disorder, mess. **неуспева́емость** poor progress. **неусто́йка** forfeit. **неусто́йчивый** unstable; unsteady. **неусту́пчивый** unyielding. **неуте́шный** inconsolable. **неутоми́мый** unquenchable. **неутоми́мый** tireless. **неу́ч** ignoramus. **неучти́вый** discourteous. **неуязви́мый** invulnerable.

нефри́т jade.

не́фте- *in comb* oil, petroleum. **нефтено́сный** oil-bearing. ~**перего́нный заво́д** oil refinery. ~**прово́д** (oil) pipeline. ~**проду́кты** (-ов) *pl* petroleum products. **нефть** oil, petroleum. **нефтяно́й** oil, petroleum.

не-. нехва́тка shortage. **нехорошо́** *adv* badly. **нехоро́ший** (-о́ш, -а́) bad; ~**о́** it is bad, it is wrong. **нехотя́** *adv* unwillingly; unintentionally. **нецелесообра́зный** inexpedient; pointless. **нецензу́рный** unprintable. **неча́янный** unexpected; accidental. **не́чего** (не́чему, -чем, не́ о чем) *pron* (*with separable pref*) (there is) nothing. **нечелове́ческий** inhuman, superhuman.

нече́стный dishonest, unfair. **нечётный** odd.

нечистопло́тный dirty; slovenly; unscrupulous. **нечистота́** (*pl* -о́ты, -о́т) dirtiness; filth; *pl* sewage. **нечи́стый** (-и́ст, -а́, -о) dirty, unclean; impure; unclear. **не́чисть** evil spirits; scum.

нечленоразде́льный inarticulate.

не́что *pron* something.

не-. неэконо́мили́чный uneconomical. **неэффекти́вный** ineffective; inefficient. **нея́вка** failure to appear. **нея́ркий** dim, faint; dull, subdued. **нея́сный** (-сен, -сна, -о) not clear; vague.

ни *partl* not a; **ни оди́н** (одна́, одно́) not a single; (*with prons and pronominal advs*) -ever; **кто...** whoever. **ни** *conj*: **ни... ни** neither ... nor; **ни то ни** neither one thing nor the other.

ни́ва cornfield, field.

нивели́р level.

нигде́ *adv* nowhere.

нидерла́ндец (-дца; *gen pl* -дцев) Dutchman. **нидерла́ндка** Dutchwoman. **нидерла́ндский** Dutch. **Нидерла́нды** (-ов) *pl* the Netherlands.

ни́же *adj* lower, humbler; *adv* below; *prep+gen* below, beneath. **нижесле́дующий** following. **ни́жний** lower, under-; ~**ее бельё** underclothes; ~**ий эта́ж** ground floor. **низ** (*loc* -у́; *pl* -ы́) bottom; *pl* lower classes; low notes.

низа́ть (нижу́, ни́жешь) *impf* (*pf* на-) string, thread. **низверга́ть** *impf*, **низверг-**

ну́ть (-ну́; -ёрг) *pf* throw down, overthrow; ~ся come down; be overthrown. низверже́ние overthrow.

низи́на low-lying place. ни́зкий (-зок, -зка́, -о) low, mean. низкопокло́нство servility. низкопро́бный base; low-grade. низкоро́слый undersized. низкосо́ртный low-grade.

ни́зменность lowland; baseness. ни́зменный low-lying; base.

низо́вье (*gen pl* -ьев) the lower reaches. ни́зость baseness, meanness. ни́зший lower, lowest; ~ее образова́ние primary education.

ника́к *adv* in no way. ника-ко́й *pron* no; no ... whatever

ни́кель *m* nickel.

нике́м *see* никто́. никогда́ *adv* never. никто́ (-ого́, -ому́, -ке́м, ни о ко́м) *pron* (*with separable pref*) nobody, no one. никуда́ *adv* nowhere. ни-кче́мный useless. нима́ло *adv* not in the least.

нимб halo, nimbus.

ни́мфа nymph; pupa.

ниотку́да *adv* from nowhere. нипочём *adv* it is nothing; dirt cheap; in no circumstances.

ниско́лько *adv* not at all.

ниспроверга́ть *impf*, ниспрове́ргнуть (-ну; -ёрг) *pf* overthrow. ниспроверже́ние overthrow.

нисходя́щий descending.

ни́тка thread; string; до ни́тки to the skin; на живу́ю ни́тку hastily, anyhow. ни́точка thread. нить thread; filament.

ничего́ *etc.*: *see* ничто́. ничего́ *adv* all right; it doesn't mat-

ter, never mind; *as indecl adj* not bad, pretty good. ниче́й (-чья, -чьё) *pron* nobody's; ничья́ земля́ no man's land. ничья́ *sb* draw; tie.

ничко́м *adv* face down, prone. ничто́ (-чего́, -чему́, -чём, ни о чём) *pron* (*with separable pref*) nothing. ничто́жество nonentity, nobody. ничто́ж-ный insignificant; worthless.

ничу́ть *adv* not a bit.

ничьё *etc.*: *see* ниче́й

ни́ша niche, recess.

ни́щенка beggar-woman. ни́-щенский beggarly. нищета́ poverty. ни́щий (нищ, -а́, -е) destitute, poor; *sb* beggar.

но *conj* but; still.

нова́тор innovator. нова́тор-ский innovative. нова́тор-ство innovation.

Но́вая Зела́ндия New Zealand.

нове́йший newest, latest.

нове́лла short story.

но́венький brand-new.

новизна́ novelty; newness. нови́нка novelty. новичо́к (-чка́) novice.

ново- *in comb* new(ly). ново-бра́нец (-нца) new recruit. ~бра́чный *sb* newly-wed. ~введе́ние innovation. ~го́дний new year's. ~зе-ла́ндец (-дца; *gen pl* -дцев) ~зела́ндка New-Zealander. ~зела́ндский New Zealand. ~лу́ние new moon. ~при-бы́вший newly-arrived; *sb* newcomer. ~рождённый newborn. ~сёл new settler. ~се́лье new home; house-warming. новостро́йка new building.

но́вость news; novelty. но́в-шество innovation, novelty.

но́вый (нов, -á, -о) new; modern; ~ **год** New Year's Day.

нога́ (acc но́гу; pl но́ги, ног, нога́м) foot, leg.

но́готь (-гтя; pl -и) m fingernail, toe-nail.

нож (-á) knife.

но́жка small foot or leg; leg; stem, stalk.

но́жницы (-иц) pl scissors, shears.

но́жны (-жен) pl sheath, scabbard.

ножо́вка saw, hacksaw.

ноздря́ (pl -и, -éй) nostril.

нока́ут knock-out. **нокаути́ровать** impf & pf knock out.

ноле́во́й, нуле́во́й zero. **ноль** (-я́), **нуль** (-я́) m nought, zero, nil.

номенклату́ра nomenclature; top positions in government.

но́мер (pl -á) number; size; (hotel-)room; item; trick. **номеро́к** (-рка́) tag; label, ticket.

номина́л face value. **номина́льный** nominal.

нора́ (pl -ы) burrow, hole.

Норве́гия Norway. **норве́жец** (-жца), **норве́жка** Norwegian. **норве́жский** Norwegian.

норд (naut) north; north wind. **но́рка** mink.

но́рма standard, norm; rate. **нормализа́ция** standardization. **нормализова́ть** impf & pf standardize. **норма́льно** all right, OK. **норма́льный** normal; standard. **нормирова́ние**, **нормиро́вка** regulation; rate-fixing; rationing. **норми́рова́ть** impf & pf regulate, standardize; ration.

нос (loc -ý; pl -ы́) nose; beak; bow, prow. **но́сик** (small) nose; spout.

носи́лки (-лок) pl stretcher; litter. **носи́льщик** porter. **носи́тель** m, **~ница** (fig) bearer; (med) carrier. **носи́ть** (-ошу́, -о́сишь) impf carry, bear, wear; **~ся** rush, tear along, fly; float, be carried; wear. **но́ска** carrying, wearing. **но́ский** hard-wearing.

носово́й nose; nasal; ~ **плато́к** (pocket) handkerchief. **носо́к** (-ска́) little nose; toe; sock. **носоро́г** rhinoceros.

но́та note; pl music. **нота́ция** notation; lecture, reprimand.

нота́риус notary.

ночева́ть (-чу́ю) impf (pf пере~) spend the night. **ночёвка** spending the night. **ночле́г** place to spend the night; passing the night. **ночле́жка** doss-house. **ночни́к** (-á) night-light. **ночно́й** night, nocturnal; **~ая руба́шка** nightdress; **~о́й горшо́к** potty; chamber-pot. **ночь** (loc -и́; gen pl -éй) night. **но́чью** adv at night.

но́ша burden. **но́шеный** worn; second-hand.

но́ю etc.: see **ныть**

ноя́брь (-я́) m November. **ноя́брьский** November.

нрав disposition; temper; pl customs, ways. **нра́виться** (-влюсь) impf (pf по~) +dat please; **мне нра́вится** I like. **нра́вственность** morality, morals. **нра́вственный** moral.

ну int & partl well, well then.

ну́дный tedious.

нужда́ (pl -ы) need. **нужда́ться** impf be in need; +в+prep need, require. **ну́жный** (-жен, -жна́, -о, ну́жны) necessary; ~о it is necessary; +dat I, etc., must, ought to need.

нулево́й, нуль *see* нолево́й, ноль

нумера́ция numeration; numbering. **нумерова́ть** *impf* (*pf* **про~**) number.

нутро́ inside, interior; instinct(s).

ны́не *adv* now; today. **ны́нешний** present; today's. **ны́нче** *adv* today; now.

нырну́ть (-ну́, -нёшь) *pf*, **ныря́ть** *impf* dive.

ныть (но́ю) *impf* ache; whine. **ны́тьё** whining.

н.э. *abbr* (*of* на́шей э́ры) AD.

нюх smell; flair. **ню́хать** *impf* (*pf* **по~**) smell, sniff.

ня́нчить (-чу) *impf* nurse, look after; **~ся** *c+instr* nurse; fuss over. **ня́нька** nanny. **ня́ня** (*children's*) nurse, nanny.

О

о, об, о́бо *prep* I. +*prep* of, about, concerning. II. +*acc* against; on, upon.

о *int* oh!

оа́зис oasis.

об *see* о *prep*.

о́ба (обо́их) *m & neut*, о́бе (обе́их) *f* both.

обалдева́ть *impf*, обалде́ть (-е́ю) *pf* go crazy; become dulled; be stunned.

обанкро́титься (-о́чусь) *pf* go bankrupt.

обая́ние fascination, charm. **обая́тельный** fascinating, charming.

обва́л fall(ing); crumbling; collapse; caving-in; landslide; (сне́жный) ~ avalanche. **обвали́ть** (-лю́, -лишь) *pf* (*impf* **обва́ливать**) cause to fall *or* collapse; crumble; heap round;

~ся collapse, cave in; crumble. **обва́ливать** *pf* (*impf* **обва́ливать**) roll.

обва́ривать *impf*, **обвари́ть** (-рю́, -ришь) *pf* pour boiling water over; scald; **~ся** scald oneself.

обведу́ *etc.*: *see* обвести́. **об|ве́л** *etc.*: *see* обвести́. **об|венча́ть(ся** *pf*.

обверну́ть (-ну́, -нёшь) *pf*, **обвёртывать** *impf* wrap, wrap up.

обве́с short weight. **обве́сить** (-е́шу) *pf* (*impf* **обве́шивать**) cheat in weighing.

обвести́ (-еду́, -еде́шь; -ёл, -ела́) *pf* (*impf* **обводи́ть**) lead round, take round; encircle; surround; outline; dodge.

обве́тренный weather-beaten.

обветша́лый decrepit. **об|ветша́ть** *pf*.

обве́шивать *impf* of обве́сить. **обвива́ть(ся** *impf* of обви́ть(ся

обвине́ние charge, accusation; prosecution. **обвини́тель** *m* accuser; prosecutor. **обвини́тельный** accusatory; ~ акт indictment; ~ пригово́р verdict of guilty. **обвини́ть** *pf*, **обвиня́ть** *impf* prosecute, indict; +в+*prep* accuse of, charge with. **обвиня́емый** *sb* the accused; defendant.

обви́ть (обовью́, обовьёшь; обви́л, -á, -о) *pf* (*impf* **обвива́ть**) wind round; **~ся** wind round.

обводи́ть (-ожу́, -о́дишь) *impf* of обвести́

обвора́живать *impf*, **обворожи́ть** (-жу́) *pf* charm, enchant. **обворожи́тельный** charming, enchanting.

обвяза́ть (-яжу́, -я́жешь) pf, обвя́зывать impf tie round; ~ся +instr tie round o.s.

обго́н passing. обгоня́ть impf of обогна́ть

обгора́ть impf, обгоре́ть (-рю́) pf be burnt, be scorched. обгоре́лый burnt, charred, scorched.

обде́лать pf (impf обде́лывать) finish; polish; set; manage, arrange.

обдели́ть (-лю́, -лишь) pf (impf обделя́ть) +instr do out of one's (fair) share of.

обде́лывать impf of обде́лать. обделя́ть impf of обдели́ть

обдеру́ etc.: see ободра́ть. обдира́ть impf of ободра́ть

обду́манный deliberate, well-considered. обду́мать pf, обду́мывать impf consider, think over.

о́бе: see о́ба. обега́ть impf of обежа́ть. обегу́ etc.: see обежа́ть

обе́д dinner, lunch. обе́дать impf (pf по~) have dinner, dine. обе́денный dinner.

обедне́вший impoverished. обедне́ние impoverishment. о|бедне́ть (-е́ю) pf.

обе́дня (gen pl -ден) mass.

обежа́ть (-егу́) pf (impf обега́ть) run round; run past; outrun.

обезбо́ливание anaesthetization. обезбо́ливать impf, обезбо́лить (-лю) pf anaesthetize.

обезвре́дить (-е́жу) pf, обезвре́живать impf render harmless.

обездо́ленный unfortunate, hapless.

обеззара́живающий disinfectant.

обезли́ченный depersonalized; robbed of individuality.

обезобра́живать impf, о|безобра́зить (-а́жу) pf disfigure.

обезопа́сить (-а́шу) pf secure.

обезору́живать impf, обезору́жить (-жу) pf disarm.

обезу́меть (-ею) pf lose one's senses, lose one's head.

обезья́на monkey; ape.

обели́ть pf, обеля́ть impf vindicate; clear of blame.

оберега́ть impf, обере́чь (-егу́, -ежёшь; -рёг, -ла́) pf guard; protect.

оберну́ть (-ну́, -нёшь) pf, обёртывать impf (impf also обора́чивать) twist; wrap up; turn; ~ся turn (round); turn out; +instr or в+acc turn into. обёртка wrapper; (dust-) jacket, cover. обёрточный wrapping.

оберу́ etc.: see обобра́ть

обескура́живать impf, обескура́жить (-жу) pf discourage; dishearten.

обескро́вить (-влю) pf, обескро́вливать impf drain of blood, bleed white; render lifeless.

обеспе́чение securing, guaranteeing; ensuring; provision; guarantee; security. обеспе́ченность security; +instr provision of. обеспе́ченный well-to-do; well provided for. обеспе́чивать impf, обеспе́чить (-чу) pf provide for; secure; ensure; protect; +instr provide with.

о|беспоко́ить(ся pf.

обесси́леть (-ею) pf grow weak, lose one's strength. обесси́ливать impf, обес-

си́лить pf weaken.
о|бессла́вить (-влю) pf.
обессме́ртить (-рчу) pf immortalize.
обесцене́ние depreciation.
обесце́нивать impf, обесце́нить pf depreciate; cheapen; ~ся depreciate.
о|бесче́стить (-е́щу) pf.
обе́т vow, promise. обето-ва́нный promised. обеща́-ние promise. обеща́ть impf & pf (pf also по~) promise.
обжа́лование appeal. об-жа́ловать pf appeal against.
обже́чь (обожгу́, обожжёшь; обжёг, обожгла́) pf, обжи-га́ть impf burn; scorch; bake; ~ся burn o.s.; burn one's fingers.
обжо́ра m & f glutton. об-жо́рство gluttony.
обзавести́сь (-еду́сь, -еде́шь-ся; -вёлся, -ла́сь) pf, обза-води́ться (-ожу́сь, -о́дишь-ся) impf +instr provide o.s. with; acquire.
обзову́ etc.: see обозва́ть
обзо́р survey, review.
обзыва́ть impf of обозва́ть
обива́ть impf of оби́ть. оби́в-ка upholstering; upholstery.
оби́да offence, insult; nui-sance. оби́деть (-и́жу) pf, обижа́ть impf offend; hurt, wound; ~ся take offence; feel hurt. оби́дный offensive; an-noying. оби́дчивый touchy. оби́женный offended.
оби́лие abundance. оби́ль-ный abundant.
обира́ть impf of обобра́ть
обита́емый inhabited. оби-та́тель m inhabitant. оби-та́ть impf live.
оби́ть (обобью́, -ьёшь) pf (impf обива́ть) upholster; knock off.

обихо́д custom, (general) use, practice. обихо́дный every-day.
обкла́дывать(ся impf of об-ложи́ть(ся
обкра́дывать(ся impf of обо-кра́сть
обла́ва raid; cordon, cordon-ing off.
облага́емый taxable. обла-га́ть(ся impf of обложи́ть (ся: ~ся нало́гом be liable to tax.
облада́ние possession. обла-да́тель m possessor. обла-да́ть impf +instr possess.
о́блако (pl -á, -о́в) cloud.
обла́мывать(ся impf of об-лома́ть(ся, обломи́ться
областно́й regional. о́бласть (gen pl -е́й) region; field, sphere.
обла́чность cloudiness. о́б-лачный cloudy.
облёг etc.: see обле́чь. об-лега́ть impf of обле́чь
облега́ть impf, облегчи́ть (-чу́) pf lighten; relieve; alle-viate; facilitate. облегче́ние relief.
обледене́лый ice-covered. обледене́ть (-е́ет) pf be-come covered with ice.
облёзлый shabby; mangy.
облека́ть(ся impf of обле́чь[2](ся. облеку́ etc.: see обле́чь[2]
облепи́ть (-плю́, -пишь) pf, облепля́ть impf stick to, cling to; throng round; plaster.
облета́ть(ся impf of обле-те́ть (-лечу́) fly (round); spread (all over); fall.
обле́чь[1] (-ля́жет; -лёг, -ла́) pf (impf облега́ть) cover, en-velop; fit tightly.

обле́чь[2] (-еку́, -ечёшь; -ёк, -кла́) *pf* (*impf* **облека́ть**) clothe, invest; **~ся** clothe o.s.; +*gen* take the form of.

облива́ть(ся *impf of* **обли́ть(ся**

облига́ция bond.

облиза́ть (-ижу́, -и́жешь) *pf*, **обли́зывать** *impf* lick (all over); **~ся** smack one's lips.

о́блик look, appearance.

обли́тый (обли́т, -а́, -о) covered, enveloped. **обли́ть** (оболью́, -льёшь; о́бли́л, -ила́, -о) *pf* (*impf* **облива́ть**) pour, sluice, spill; **~ся** sponge down, take a shower; pour over o.s.

облицева́ть (-цу́ю) *pf*, **облицо́вывать** *impf* face. **облицо́вка** facing; lining.

облича́ть *impf*, **обличи́ть** (-чу́) *pf* expose; reveal; point to. **обличе́ние** exposure, denunciation. **обличи́тельный** denunciatory.

обложе́ние taxation; assessment. **обложи́ть** (-жу́, -жишь) *pf* (*impf* **обкла́дывать, облага́ть**) edge; face; cover; surround; assess; **круго́м обложи́ло** (**не́бо**) the sky is completely overcast; **~ нало́гом** tax; **~ся** +*instr* surround o.s. with. **обло́жка** (dust-)cover; folder.

облока́чиваться *impf*, **облокоти́ться** (-очу́сь, -о́ти́шься) *pf* на+*acc* lean one's elbows on.

облома́ть (*impf* **обла́мывать**) break off; **~ся** break off. **обломи́ться** (-ло́мится) *pf* (*impf* **обла́мываться**) break off. **обло́мок** (-мка) fragment.

облу́пленный chipped.

облучи́ть (-чу́) *pf*, **облуча́ть** *impf* irradiate. **облуче́ние** irradiation.

об|лысе́ть (-е́ю) *pf*.

обля́жет *etc.: see* **обле́чь**[1]

обма́зать (-а́жу) *pf*, **обма́зывать** *impf* coat; putty; besmear; **обма́зка** +*instr* get covered with.

обма́кивать *impf*, **обмакну́ть** (-ну́, -нёшь) *pf* dip.

обма́н deceit; illusion; **~ зре́ния** optical illusion. **обма́нный** deceitful. **обману́ть** (-ну́, -нешь) *pf*, **обма́нывать** *impf* deceive; cheat; **~ся** be deceived. **обма́нчивый** deceptive. **обма́нщик** deceiver; fraud.

обма́тывать(ся *impf of* **обмота́ть(ся**

обма́хивать *impf*, **обмахну́ть** (-ну́, -нёшь) *pf* brush off; fan; **~ся** fan o.s.

обме́л *etc.: see* **обмести́**

обмеле́ние shallowing. **об|меле́ть** (-е́ет) *pf* become shallow.

обме́н exchange; barter; **в ~ за**+*acc* in exchange for; **~ веще́ств** metabolism. **обме́нивать** *impf*, **обмени́ть** (-ню́, -нишь) *pf*, **обменя́ть** *pf* exchange; **~ся** +*instr* exchange. **обме́нный** exchange.

обме́р measurement; false measure.

обмере́ть (обомру́, -рёшь; о́бмер, -ла́, -ло) *pf* (*impf* **обмира́ть**) faint; **~ от у́жаса** be horror-struck.

обмеря́ть *impf* **обме́рить** *pf* measure; cheat in measuring.

обмести́ (-ету́, -етёшь; -мёл, -а́) *pf*, **обмета́ть**[1] *impf* sweep off, dust.

обмета́ть[2] (-ечу́ *or* -а́ю, -е́чешь

or -áешь) *pf* (*impf* обмётывать) oversew.

обметý *etc.: see* обмести. обмётываться *impf of* обметáть.

обмирáть *impf of* обмерéть

обмóлвиться (-влюсь) *pf* make a slip of the tongue; +*instr* say, utter. обмóлвка slip of the tongue.

обморóженный frost-bitten.

óбморок fainting-fit, swoon.

обмотáть (*impf* обмáтывать) wind round; ~ся +*instr* wrap o.s. in. обмóтка winding; *pl* puttees.

обмóю *etc.: see* обмыть

обмундировáние fitting out (with uniform); uniform. обмундировáть, обмундирóвывать *impf* fit out (with uniform).

обмывáть *impf*, обмыть (-мóю) *pf* bathe, wash; ~ся wash, bathe.

обмякáть *impf*, обмякнуть (-ну; -мяк) *pf* become soft or flabby.

обнадёживать *impf*, обнадёжить (-жу) *pf* reassure.

обнажáть *impf*, обнажить (-жý) *pf* bare, uncover; reveal. обнажённый (-ён, -енá) naked, bare; nude.

обнарóдовать *impf & pf* promulgate.

обнаружéние revealing; discovery; detection. обнарýживать *impf*, обнарýжить (-жу) *pf* display; reveal; discover; ~ся come to light.

обнести (-сý, -сёшь; -нёс, -лá) *pf* (*impf* обносить) enclose; +*instr* serve round; pass over, leave out.

обнимáть(ся *impf of* обнять(ся. обнимý *etc.: see* обнять

обнищáние impoverishment

обновить (-влю) *pf*, обновлять *impf* renovate; renew. обновка new acquisition; new garment. обновлéние renovation, renewal.

обносить (-ошý, -óсишь) *impf of* обнести; ~ся *pf* have worn out one's clothes.

обнять (-ниму, -нимешь; óбнял, -á, -о) *pf* (*impf* обнимáть) embrace; clasp; ~ся embrace; hug one another.

обо *see o prep.*

обобрáть (оберý, -рёшь; обобрáл, -á, -о) *pf* (*impf* обирáть) rob; pick.

обобщáть *impf*, обобщить (-щý) *pf* generalize. обобщéние generalization. обобществить (-влю) *pf*, обобществлять *impf* socialize; collectivize. обобществлéние socialization; collectivization.

обобью *etc.: see* обить. обовью *etc.: see* обвить

обогатить (-ащý) *pf*, обогащáть *impf* enrich; enrich o.s. обогащéние enrichment.

обогнáть (обгоню, -óнишь; обогнáл, -á, -о) *pf* (*impf* обгонять) pass; outstrip.

обогнуть (-нý, -нёшь) *pf* (*impf* огибáть) round, skirt; bend round.

обогревáтель *m* heater. обогревáть *impf*, обогрéть (-éю) *pf* heat, warm; ~ся warm up.

óбод (*pl* -óдья, -ьев) rim. ободóк (-дкá) thin rim, narrow border.

обóдранный ragged. ободрáть (обдерý, -рёшь; -áл, -á, -о) *pf* (*impf* обдирáть) skin, flay; peel; fleece.

ободре́ние encouragement, reassurance. ободри́тельный encouraging, reassuring. ободри́ть pf, ободря́ть impf encourage, reassure; ~ся cheer up, take heart.

обожа́ть impf adore.

обожгу́ etc.: see обже́чь

обожестви́ть (-влю́) pf, обожествля́ть impf deify.

обожжённый (-ён, -ена́) burnt, scorched.

обо́з string of vehicles; transport.

обозва́ть (обзову́, -вёшь; -а́л, -а́, -о) pf (impf обзыва́ть) call; call names.

обозлённый (-ён, -а́) angered; embittered. обозли́ть pf, озли́ть pf anger; embitter; ~ся get angry.

обозна́ться pf mistake s.o. for s.o. else.

обознача́ть impf, обозна́чить (-чу) pf mean; mark; ~ся appear, reveal o.s. обозначе́ние sign, symbol.

обозрева́тель m reviewer; columnist. обозрева́ть impf, обозре́ть (-рю́) pf survey. обозре́ние survey; review; revue. обозри́мый visible.

обо́и (-ев) pl wallpaper.

обо́йма (gen pl -о́йм) cartridge clip.

обойти́ (-йду́, -йдёшь; -ошёл, -ошла́) pf (impf обходи́ть) go round; pass; avoid; pass over; ~сь manage, make do; +c+instr treat.

обокра́сть (обкраду́, -дёшь) pf (impf обкра́дывать) rob.

оболо́чка casing; membrane; cover, envelope, jacket; shell.

обольсти́тель m seducer. обольсти́тельный seductive. обольсти́ть (-льщу́) pf,

обольща́ть impf seduce. обольще́ние seduction; delusion.

оболью́ etc.: see обли́ть

обомру́ etc.: see обмере́ть

обоня́ние (sense of) smell. обоня́тельный olfactory.

обопру́ etc.: see опере́ть

обора́чивать(ся impf of оберну́ть(ся, обороти́ть(ся

обо́рванный torn, ragged. оборва́ть (-ву́, -вёшь; -а́л, -а́, -о) pf (impf обрыва́ть) tear off; break; snap; cut short; ~ся break; snap; fall; stop suddenly.

обо́рка frill, flounce.

оборо́на defence. оборони́тельный defensive. обороня́ть pf, обороня́ть impf defend; ~ся defend o.s. оборо́нный defence, defensive.

оборо́т turn; revolution; circulation; turnover; back; ~ ре́чи turn of phrase; смотри́ на ~е P.T.O. оборо́ти́ть (-рочу́, -ро́тишь) pf (impf обора́чивать) turn; ~ся turn (round) +instr or в+acc turn into. оборо́тный circulating; reverse; ~ капита́л working capital.

обору́дование equipping; equipment. обору́довать impf & pf equip.

обоснова́ние basing; basis; ground. обосно́ванный wellfounded. обоснова́ть, обосно́вывать impf ground, base; substantiate; ~ся settle down.

обосо́бленный isolated, solitary.

обостре́ние aggravation. обострённый keen; strained; sharp, pointed. обостри́ть pf, обостря́ть impf sharpen.

strain; aggravate; ~ся become strained; be aggravated; become acute.

оботру́ etc.: see **обтере́ть**

обо́чина verge; shoulder, edge.

обошёл etc.: see **обойти́**. **обо́шью** etc.: see **обши́ть**

обою́дный mutual, reciprocal.

обраба́тывать impf, **обрабо́тать** pf till, cultivate; work, work up; treat, process. **обрабо́тка** working (up); processing; cultivation.

об|ра́доваться etc.: see **радова́ть(ся** pf.

о́браз shape, form; image; manner; way; icon; **гла́вным ~ом** mainly; **таки́м ~ом** thus. **образе́ц** (-зца́) pattern; sample. **о́бразный** graphic; figurative. **образова́ние** formation; education. **образо́ванный** educated. **образова́тельный** educational. **образова́ть** impf & pf, **образо́вывать** impf form; ~ся form; arise; turn out well.

образу́мить (-млю) pf bring to reason; ~ся see reason.

образцо́вый model. **образчик** specimen, sample.

обра́мить (-млю) pf, **обрамля́ть** impf frame.

обраста́ть impf, **обрасти́** (-ту́, -тёшь; -ро́с, -ла́) pf be overgrown.

обрати́мый reversible, convertible. **обрати́ть** (-ащу́) pf, **обраща́ть** impf turn; convert; **~ внима́ние на**+acc pay or draw attention to; ~ся turn; appeal; apply; address; +в+acc turn into; +c+instr treat; handle. **обра́тно** adv back; backwards; conversely; **~ пропорциона́льный** inversely proportional. **обра́тный** reverse; return; opposite; inverse. **обраще́ние** appeal, address; conversion; (+c+instr) treatment (of); handling (of); use (of).

обре́з edge; sawn-off gun; **в ~+**gen only just enough. **обре́зать** (-е́жу) pf, **обреза́ть** impf cut (off); clip, trim; pare; prune; circumcise; ~ся cut o.s. **обре́зок** (-зка) scrap; pl ends; clippings.

обрека́ть impf of **обре́чь**. **обреку́** etc.: see **обре́чь**. **обрёл** etc.: see **обрести́**

обремени́тельный onerous. **о|бремени́ть** pf, **обременя́ть** impf burden.

обрести́ (-ету́, -етёшь; -рёл, -а́) pf, **обрета́ть** impf find. **обрече́ние** doom. **обречённый** doomed. **обре́чь** (-еку́, -ечёшь; -ёк, -ла́) pf (impf **обрека́ть**) doom.

обрисова́ть pf, **обрисо́вывать** impf outline, depict; ~ся appear (in outline).

оброни́ть (-ню́, -нишь) pf drop; let drop.

обро́с etc.: see **обрасти́**.

обруба́ть impf, **обруби́ть** (-блю́, -бишь) pf chop off; cut off. **обру́бок** (-бка) stump.

об|руга́ть pf.

о́бруч (pl -и, -е́й) hoop. **обруча́льн|ый** engagement; **~ое кольцо́** betrothal ring, wedding ring. **обруча́ть** impf, **обручи́ть** (-чу́) betroth; ~ся +c+instr become engaged to. **обруче́ние** engagement.

обру́шивать impf, **об|ру́шить** (-шу) pf bring down; ~ся come down, collapse.

обры́в precipice. **обрыва́ть(ся** impf of **оборва́ть(ся**. **обры́вок** (-вка) scrap; snatch.

обры́згать *pf*, обры́згивать *impf* splash; sprinkle.

обрю́зглый flabby.

обря́д rite, ceremony.

обсервато́рия observatory.

обслу́живание service; maintenance. обслу́живать *impf*, обслужи́ть (-жу́, -жи́шь) *pf* serve; operate.

обсле́дование inspection. обсле́дователь *m* inspector. обсле́довать *impf & pf* inspect.

обсо́хнуть (-ну; -о́х) *pf* (*impf* обсыха́ть) dry (off).

обста́вить (-влю) *pf*, обставля́ть *impf* surround; furnish; arrange. обстано́вка furniture; situation, conditions; set.

обстоя́тельный thorough, reliable; detailed. обстоя́тельство circumstance. обстоя́ть (-ои́т) *impf* be; go; как обстои́т де́ло? how is it going?

обстре́л fire, fire; под ~ом under fire. обстре́ливать *impf*, обстреля́ть *impf* fire at; bombard.

обступа́ть *impf*, обступи́ть (-у́пит) *pf* surround.

обсуди́ть (-ужу́, -у́дишь) *pf*, обсужда́ть *impf* discuss. обсужде́ние discussion.

обсчита́ть *pf*, обсчи́тывать *impf* shortchange; ~ся miscount, miscalculate.

обсы́пать (-плю) *pf*, обсыпа́ть *impf* strew; sprinkle.

обсыха́ть *impf of* обсо́хнуть.

обта́чивать *impf of* обточи́ть

обтека́емый streamlined.

обтере́ть (оботру́, -трёшь; обтёр) *pf* (*impf* обтира́ть) wipe; rub; ~ся dry o.s.; sponge down.

о(б)теса́ть (-ешу́, -е́шешь) *pf*, о(б)тёсывать *impf* roughhew; teach good manners to; trim.

обтира́ние sponge-down. обтира́ть(ся *impf of* обтере́ть(ся

обточи́ть (-чу́, -чишь) *pf* (*impf* обта́чивать) grind; machine.

обтрёпанный frayed; shabby.

обтя́гивать *impf*, обтяну́ть (-ну́, -нешь) *pf* cover; fit close. обтя́жка cover; skin; в обтя́жку close-fitting.

обува́ть(ся *impf of* обу́ть(ся. о́бувь footwear; boots, shoes.

обу́гливать *impf*, обу́глить *pf* char; carbonize; ~ся char, become charred.

обу́за burden.

обузда́ть *pf*, обу́здывать *impf* bridle, curb.

обурева́ть *impf* grip; possess.

обусло́вить (-влю) *pf*, обусло́вливать *impf* cause; +*instr* make conditional on; ~ся +*instr* be conditional on; depend on.

обу́тый shod. обу́ть (-у́ю) *pf* (*impf* обува́ть) put shoes on; ~ся put on one's shoes.

обу́х butt, back.

обуча́ть *impf*, об|учи́ть (-чу́, -чишь) *pf* teach; train; ~ся +*dat or inf* learn. обуче́ние teaching; training.

обхва́т girth; в ~е in circumference. обхвати́ть (-ачу́, -а́тишь) *pf*, обхва́тывать *impf* embrace; clasp.

обхо́д round(s); roundabout way; bypass. обходи́тельный courteous; pleasant. обходи́ть (-ожу́(сь, -о́дишь (ся) *impf of* обойти́(сь. обхо́дный roundabout.

обша́ривать *impf*, обша́рить *pf* rummage through, ransack.

обшива́ть *impf of* **обши́ть**.
обши́вка edging; trimming;
boarding, panelling; plating.
обши́рный extensive; vast.
обши́ть (обошью́, -шьёшь) *pf*
(*impf* **обшива́ть**) edge; trim;
make outfit(s) for; plank.
обшла́г (-á; *pl* -á, -óв) cuff.
обща́ться *impf* associate.
обще- *in comb* common(ly),
general(ly). **общедосту́пный**
moderate in price; popular.
~жи́тие hostel. **~изве́стный**
generally known. **~наро́д-
ный** national, public. **~образо-
ва́тельный** of general
education. **~при́нятый** generally accepted. **~сою́зный**
All-Union. **~челове́ческий**
common to all mankind; universal.
обще́ние contact; social intercourse. **обще́ственность** (the)
public; public opinion; community. **обще́ственный** social, public; voluntary. **о́бще-
ство** society; company. **о́бщий** general; common; **в
~ем** on the whole, in general.
общи́на community; commune.
общи́пать (-плю́, -плешь) *pf*.
общи́тельный sociable. **о́бщ-
ность** community.
объеда́ть(ся *impf of* **объе́сть-
(ся**
объедине́ние unification;
merger; union, association.
объединённый (-ён, -á)
united. **объедини́тельный**
unifying. **объедини́ть** *pf*,
объединя́ть *impf* unite; join;
combine; **~ся** unite.
объе́дки (-ов) *pl* leftovers,
scraps.
объе́зд riding round; detour.
объе́здить (-зжу, -здишь) *pf*

(*impf* **объезжа́ть**) travel over;
break in.
объезжа́ть *impf of* **объе́здить,
объе́хать**
объе́кт object; objective; establishment, works. **объекти́в**
lens. **объекти́вность** objectivity. **объекти́вный** objective.
объём volume; scope. **объём-
ный** by volume, volumetric.
объе́сть (-ем, -ешь, -ест, -еди́м)
pf (*impf* **объеда́ть**) gnaw
(round), nibble; **~ся** overeat.
объе́хать (-е́ду) *pf* (*impf*
объезжа́ть) drive or go
round; go past; travel over.
объяви́ть (-влю́, -вишь) *pf*,
объявля́ть *impf* declare, announce; **~ся** turn up; *instr*
declare o.s. **объявле́ние**
declaration, announcement;
advertisement.
объясне́ние explanation.
объясни́мый explainable.
объясни́ть *pf*, **объясня́ть**
impf explain; **~ся** be explained; make o.s. understood;
+*c*+*instr* have it out with.
объя́тие embrace.
обыва́тель *m* Philistine. **обы-
ва́тельский** narrow-minded.
обыгра́ть *pf*, **обы́грывать**
impf beat (*in a game*).
обы́денный ordinary; everyday.
обыкнове́ние habit. **обыкно-
ве́нно** *adv* usually. **обыкно-
ве́нный** usual; ordinary.
о́быск search. **обыска́ть** (-ыщу́,
-ы́щешь) *pf*, **обы́скивать** *impf*
search.
обы́чай custom; usage. **обы́ч-
но** *adv* usually. **обы́чный**
usual.
обя́занность duty; responsibility. **обя́занный** (+*inf*)

obliged; +*dat* indebted to (+*instr* for). **обяза́тельно** *adv* without fail. **обяза́тельный** obligatory. **обяза́тельство** obligation; commitment. **обяза́ть** (-яжу́, -я́жешь) *pf*, **обя́зывать** *impf* bind; commit; oblige; ~**ся** pledge o.s.; undertake.

ова́л oval. **ова́льный** oval.

ова́ция ovation.

овдове́ть (-е́ю) *pf* become a widow, widower.

ове́с (овса́) oats.

ове́чка *dim of* **овца́**; harmless person.

овладева́ть *impf*, **овладе́ть** (-е́ю) *pf* +*instr* seize; capture; master.

о́вод (*pl* -ы *or* -á) gadfly.

о́вощ (*pl* -и, -е́й) vegetable. **овощно́й** vegetable.

овра́г ravine, gully.

овся́нка oatmeal; porridge. **овся́ный** oat, oatmeal.

овца́ (*pl* -ы, ове́ц, о́вцам) sheep; ewe. **овча́рка** sheepdog. **овчи́на** sheepskin.

ога́рок (-рка) candle-end.

огиба́ть *impf of* **обогну́ть**

оглавле́ние table of contents.

огласи́ть (-ашу́) *pf*, **огла-ша́ть** *impf* announce; fill (with sound); ~**ся** resound. **огла́ска** publicity. **оглаше́ние** publication.

огло́бля (*gen pl* -бель) shaft.

о|гло́хнуть (-ну, -ох) *pf*.

оглуша́ть *impf*, **о|глуши́ть** (-шу́) *pf* deafen; stun. **оглуши́тельный** deafening.

огляде́ть (-яжу́) *pf*, **огля́ды-вать** *impf*, **огляну́ть** (-ну́, -нешь) *pf* look round; look over; ~**ся** look round; look back. **огля́дка** looking back.

огнево́й fire; fiery. **о́гненный** fiery. **огнеопа́сный** inflammable. **огнеприпа́сы** (-ов) *pl* ammunition. **огнесто́йкий** fire-proof. **огнестре́льный**: ~**ое ору́жие** firearm(s). **огне-туши́тель** *m* fire-extinguisher. **огнеупо́рный** fire-resistant.

ого́ *int* oho!

огова́ривать *impf*, **огово-ри́ть** *pf* slander; stipulate (for); ~**ся** make a proviso; make a slip (of the tongue). **огово́р** slander. **огово́рка** reservation, proviso; slip of the tongue.

оголённый bare, nude. **оголи́ть** *pf* (*impf* **оголя́ть**) bare; strip; ~**ся** strip o.s.; become exposed.

оголя́ть(ся *impf of* **оголи́ть(ся**

огонёк (-нька́) (*small*) light; zest. **ого́нь** (огня́) *m* fire; light.

огора́живать *impf*, **огоро-ди́ть** (-рожу́, -ро́дишь) *pf* fence in, enclose; ~**ся** fence o.s. in. **огоро́д** kitchen-garden. **огоро́дный** kitchen-garden.

огорча́ть *impf*, **огорчи́ть** (-чу́) *pf* grieve, pain; ~**ся** grieve, be distressed. **огорче́ние** grief; chagrin.

о|гра́бить (-блю) *pf*. **огра-бле́ние** robbery; burglary.

огра́да fence. **огради́ть** (-ажу́) *pf*, **огражда́ть** *impf* guard, protect.

ограниче́ние limitation, restriction. **ограни́ченный** limited. **ограни́чивать** *impf*, **ограни́чить** (-чу) *pf* limit, restrict; ~**ся** +*instr* limit or confine o.s. to; be limited to.

огро́мный huge; enormous.

о|грубе́ть (-е́ю) *pf*.

огры́зок (-зка) bit, end; stub.

огуре́ц (-рца́) cucumber.

ода́лживать *impf of* **одолжи́ть**

одарённый gifted. **ода́ривать** *impf*, **одари́ть**, **одаря́ть** *impf* give presents (to); +*instr* endow with.

одева́ть(ся *impf of* **оде́ть(ся**

оде́жда clothes; clothing.

одеколо́н eau-de-Cologne.

одели́ть *pf*, **оделя́ть** *impf* (+*instr*) present (with); endow (with).

оде́ну *etc.: see* **оде́ть. одёргивать** *impf of* **одёрнуть**

о|деревене́ть (-ею) *pf*.

одержа́ть (-жу́, -жишь) *pf*, **оде́рживать** *impf* gain. **одержи́мый** possessed.

одёрнуть (-ну) *pf* (*impf* **одёргивать**) pull down, straighten.

оде́тый dressed; clothed. **оде́ть** (-е́ну) *pf* (*impf* **одева́ть**) dress; clothe; **~ся** dress (o.s.). **одея́ло** blanket. **одея́ние** garb, attire.

оди́н (одного́), **одна́** (одно́й); **одно́** (одного́); *pl* **одни́** (одни́х) one; a, an; a certain; alone; only; nothing but; same; **одно́ и то же** the same thing; **оди́н на оди́н** in private; **оди́н раз** once; **одни́м сло́вом** in a word; **по одному́** one by one.

одина́ковый identical, the same, equal.

оди́ннадцатый eleventh. **оди́ннадцать** eleven.

одино́кий solitary; lonely; single. **одино́чество** solitude; loneliness. **одино́чка** *m & f* (one) person alone. **одино́чный** individual; one-man; single; **~ое заключе́ние** solitary confinement.

одича́лый wild.

одна́жды *adv* once; one day; once upon a time.

одна́ко *conj* however.

одно- *in comb* single, one; uni-, mono-, homo-. **~бо́кий** one-sided. **~вре́менно** *adv* simultaneously, at the same time. **~вре́менный** simultaneous. **~зву́чный** monotonous. **~знача́щий** synonymous. **~зна́чный** synonymous; one-digit. **~имённый** of the same name. **~кла́ссник** classmate. **~кле́точный** unicellular. **~кра́тный** single. **~ле́тний** one-year; annual. **~ме́стный** single-seater. **~обра́зие**, **~обра́зность** monotony. **~обра́зный** monotonous. **~ро́дность** homogeneity, uniformity. **~ро́дный** homogeneous; similar. **~сторо́нний** one-sided; unilateral; one-way. **~фами́лец** (-льца) person of the same surname. **~цве́тный** one-colour; monochrome. **~эта́жный** one-storeyed.

одобре́ние approval. **одобри́тельный** approving. **одо́брить** *pf*, **одобря́ть** *impf* approve (of).

одолева́ть *impf*, **одоле́ть** (-е́ю) *pf* overcome.

одолжа́ть *impf*, **одолжи́ть** (-жу́) *pf* lend; +*y*+*gen* borrow from. **одолже́ние** favour.

о|дряхле́ть (-е́ю) *pf*.

одува́нчик dandelion.

оду́маться *pf*, **оду́мываться** *impf* change one's mind.

одуре́лый stupid. **о|дуре́ть** (-е́ю) *pf*.

одурма́нивать *impf*, **о|дурма́нить** *pf* stupefy. **одуря́ть** *impf* stupefy.

одухотворённый inspired; spiritual. одухотворить *pf*, одухотворять *impf* inspire.

одушеви́ть (-влю) *pf*, одушевля́ть *impf* animate. одушевле́ние animation.

одышка shortness of breath.

ожере́лье necklace.

ожесточи́ть (-чу) *pf* embitter, harden. ожесточе́ние bitterness. ожесточённый bitter; hard.

ожива́ть *impf of* ожи́ть

оживи́ть (-влю) *pf*, оживля́ть *impf* revive; enliven; ~ся become animated. оживле́ние animation; reviving; enlivening. оживлённый animated, lively.

ожида́ние expectation; waiting. ожида́ть *impf* + *gen or* [*acc*] wait for; expect.

ожире́ние obesity. о|жире́ть (-ею) *pf*.

ожи́ть (-иву́, -ивёшь; о́жил, -á, -о) *pf* (*impf* ожива́ть) come to life, revive.

ожо́г burn, scald.

озабо́ченность preoccupation; anxiety. озабо́ченный preoccupied; anxious.

озагла́вить (-лю) *pf*, озагла́вливать *impf* entitle; head.

озада́чивать *impf*, озада́чить (-чу) *pf* perplex, puzzle.

озари́ть *pf*, озаря́ть *impf* light up, illuminate; ~ся light up.

оздорови́тельный бег jogging. оздоровле́ние sanitation.

озелени́ть *pf*, озеленя́ть *impf* plant (with trees etc.). óзеро (*pl* озёра) lake.

ози́мые *sb* winter crops. ози́мый winter. óзимь winter crop.

озира́ться *impf* look round; look back.

о|зли́ть(ся: see обозли́ть(ся ozлобить (-блю) *pf*, озлобля́ть *impf* embitter; ~ся grow bitter. озлобле́ние bitterness, animosity. озло́бленный embittered.

о|знако́мить (-млю) *pf*, ознакомля́ть *impf* c + *instr* acquaint with; ~ся c + *instr* familiarize o.s. with.

ознаменова́ть *pf*, ознамено́вывать *impf* mark; celebrate.

означа́ть *impf* mean, signify. озно́б shivering, chill.

озо́н ozone.

озо́рник (-á) mischief-maker. озорно́й naughty, mischievous. озо́рство mischief.

озя́бнуть (-ну; озя́б) *pf* be cold, be freezing.

ой *int* oh.

оказа́ть (-ажу́, -а́жешь) *pf* (*impf* ока́зывать) render, provide, show; ~ся turn out, prove; find o.s., be found.

ока́зия unexpected event, funny thing.

ока́зывать(ся *impf of* оказа́ть(ся

окамене́лость fossil. окамене́лый fossilized; petrified. о|камене́ть (-е́ю) *pf*.

оканто́вка mount.

ока́нчивать(ся *impf*, око́нчить(ся. ока́пывать(ся *impf of* окопа́ть(ся

окая́нный damned, cursed.

океа́н ocean. океа́нский ocean; oceanic.

оки́дывать *impf*, оки́нуть (-ну) *pf*; ~ взгля́дом take in at a glance, glance over.

óкисел (-сла) oxide. окисле́ние oxidation. óкись oxide.

оккупа́нт invader. **оккупа́ция** occupation. **оккупи́ровать** *impf & pf* occupy.

окла́д salary scale; (basic) pay.

оклевета́ть (-ещу́, -е́щешь) *pf* slander.

окле́ивать *impf*, **окле́ить** *pf* cover; paste over; ~ **обо́ями** paper.

окно́ (*pl* о́кна) window.

о́ко (*pl* о́чи, оче́й) eye.

око́вы (око́в) *pl* fetters.

околдова́ть *pf*, **околдо́вывать** *impf* bewitch.

о́коло *adv & prep+gen* by; close (to), near; around; about.

око́льный roundabout.

око́нный window.

оконча́ние end; conclusion; termination; ending. **оконча́тельный** final. **око́нчить** (-чу) *pf* (*impf* ока́нчивать) finish, end; ~**ся** finish, end.

око́п trench. **окопа́ть** *pf* (*impf* ока́пывать) dig round; ~**ся** entrench o.s., dig in. **око́пный** trench.

о́корок (*pl* -а́, -о́в) ham, gammon.

окочене́лый stiff with cold. **о|кочене́ть** (-е́ю) *pf*.

око́шечко, око́шко (*small*) window.

окра́ина outskirts, outlying districts.

о|кра́сить (-а́шу) *pf*, **окра́шивать** *impf* paint, colour; dye. **окра́ска** painting; colouring; dyeing; colouration.

о|кре́пнуть (-ну) *pf*. **о|крести́ть(ся** (-ещу́(сь, -е́стишь(ся) *pf*.

окре́стность environs. **окре́стный** neighbouring.

о́крик hail; shout. **окри́кивать** *impf*, **окри́кнуть** (-ну) *pf* hail, call, shout to.

окрова́вленный blood-stained.

о́круг (*pl* ~а́) district. **окру́га** neighbourhood. **округли́ть** *pf*, **округля́ть** *impf* round; round off. **окру́глый** rounded. **окружа́ть** *impf*, **окружи́ть** (-жу́) *pf* surround; encircle. **окружа́ющий** surrounding; ~**ее** *sb* environment; ~**ие** *sb pl* associates. **окруже́ние** encirclement; environment. **окружно́й** district. **окру́жность** circumference.

окрыли́ть *pf*, **окрыля́ть** *impf* inspire, encourage.

окта́ва octave.

окта́н octane.

октя́брь (-я́) *m* October. **октя́брьский** October.

окули́ст oculist.

окуна́ть *impf*, **окуну́ть** (-ну́, -нёшь) *pf* dip; ~**ся** dip; plunge; become absorbed.

о́кунь (*pl* -и, -е́й) *m* perch.

окупа́ть *impf*, **окупи́ть** (-плю́, -пишь) *pf* compensate, repay; ~**ся** be repaid, pay for itself.

оку́рок (-рка) cigarette-end.

оку́тать *pf*, **оку́тывать** *impf* wrap up; shroud, cloak.

окучивать *impf*, **оку́чить** (-чу) *pf* earth up.

ола́дья (*gen pl* -ий) fritter; drop-scone.

оледене́лый frozen. **о|ледене́ть** (-е́ю) *pf*.

оле́ний deer, deer's; reindeer. **оле́нина** venison. **оле́нь** *m* deer; reindeer.

оли́ва olive. **оли́вковый** olive; olive-coloured.

олига́рхия oligarchy.

олимпиа́да olympiad; Olympics. **олимпи́йск|ий** Olympic; Olympian; ~**ие и́гры** Olympic games.

олифа drying oil (*e.g. linseed oil*).

олицетворение personification; embodiment. **олицетворить** *pf*, **олицетворять** *impf* personify, embody.

олово tin. **оловянный** tin.

ом ohm.

омар lobster.

омерзение loathing. **омерзительный** loathsome.

омертвелый stiff, numb; necrotic. **о|мертветь** (-ею) *pf*.

омлет omelette.

омоложение rejuvenation.

омоним homonym.

омою *etc.: see* **омыть**

омрачать *impf*, **омрачить** (-чу) *pf* darken, cloud.

омут whirlpool; maelstrom.

омывать *impf*, **омыть** (омою) *pf* wash; ~ся be washed.

он (его, ему, им, о нём) *pron* he. **она** (её, ей, ей (ею), о ней) *pron* she.

ондатра musk-rat.

онеметь numb. **о|неметь** (-ею) *pf*.

они (их, им, ими, о них) *pron* they. **оно** (его, ему, им, о нём) *pron* it; this, that.

опадать *impf of* **опасть**.

опаздывать *impf of* **опоздать**

опала disgrace.

о|палить *pf*.

опаловый opal.

опалубка casing.

опасаться *impf +gen* fear; avoid, keep off. **опасение** fear; apprehension.

опасность danger; peril. **опасный** dangerous.

опека guardianship; trusteeship. **опекаемый** *sb* ward. **опе-**

кать *impf* be guardian of; take care of. **опекун** (-а), **-унша** guardian; tutor; trustee.

опера opera.

оперативный efficient; operative, surgical; operational. **оператор** operator; cameraman. **операционный** operating; **~ая** *sb* operating theatre. **операция** operation.

опередить (-режу) *pf*, **опережать** *impf* outstrip, leave behind.

оперение plumage.

оперетта, **-етка** operetta.

опереть (обопру, -прёшь; опёр, -ла) *pf* (*impf* **опирать**) +о+*acc* lean against; ~ся на *or* о+*acc* lean on, lean against.

оперировать *impf & pf* operate on; operate, act; +*instr* use.

оперный opera; operatic.

о|печалить(ся *pf*.

опечатать *pf* (*impf* **опечатывать**) seal up.

опечатка misprint.

опечатывать *impf of* **опечатать**

опешить (-шу) *pf* be taken aback.

опилки (-лок) *pl* sawdust; filings.

опирать(ся *impf of* **опереть(ся**

описание description. **описательный** descriptive. **описать** (-ишу, -ишешь) *pf*, **описывать** *impf* describe; ~ся make a slip of the pen. **описка** slip of the pen. **опись** inventory.

опиум opium.

оплакать (-ачу) *pf*, **оплакивать** *impf* mourn for; bewail.

оплата payment. **оплатить** (-ачу, -атишь) *pf*, **оплачи-**

вать *impf* pay (for).

оплака́ть *etc.: see* **опла́кать**. **оплачу́** *etc.: see* **оплати́ть**

оплеу́ха slap in the face.

оплодотвори́ть *pf*, **оплодотворя́ть** *impf* impregnate; fertilize.

о|пломбирова́ть *pf*.

опло́т stronghold, bulwark.

опло́шность blunder, mistake.

оповести́ть (-ещу́) *pf*, **оповеща́ть** *impf* notify. **оповеще́ние** notification.

опозда́вший *sb* late-comer. **опозда́ние** lateness; delay. **опозда́ть** *pf* (*impf* **опа́здывать**) be late; +**на**+*acc* miss.

опознава́тельный distinguishing; ~ **знак** landmark. **опознава́ть** (-наю́, -наёшь) *impf*, **опозна́ть** *pf* identify. **опозна́ние** identification.

о|позо́рить(ся *pf*.

оползать́, **оползти́** (-зёт; -о́лз, -ла́) *pf* slip, slide. **о́ползень** (-зня) *m* landslide.

ополче́ние militia.

опо́мниться *pf* come to one's senses.

опо́р: во весь ~ at full speed. **опо́ра** support; pier; **то́чка опо́ры** fulcrum, foothold.

опора́жнивать *impf of* **опоро́жнить**

опо́рный support, supporting, supported; bearing.

опорожни́ть, **опорожня́ть** *impf* (*impf also* **опора́жнивать**) empty.

о|поро́чить (-чу) *pf*.

опохмели́ться, **опохмеля́ться** *impf* take a hair of the dog that bit you.

опошли́ть, **опошля́ть** *impf* vulgarize, debase.

опоя́сать (-я́шу), **опоя́-**

сывать *impf* gird; girdle.

оппозицио́нный opposition. **оппози́ция** opposition.

оппортуни́зм opportunism.

опра́ва setting, mounting; spectacle frames.

оправда́ние justification; excuse; acquittal. **оправда́тельный пригово́р** verdict of not guilty. **оправда́ть** *pf*, **опра́вдывать** *impf* justify; excuse; acquit; ~**ся** justify o.s.; be justified.

опра́вить (-влю) *pf*, **оправля́ть** *impf* set right, adjust; mount; ~**ся** put in order; recover; +**от**+*gen* get over.

опра́шивать *impf of* **опроси́ть**

определе́ние definition; determination; decision. **определённый** definite; certain. **определи́мый** definable. **определи́ть** *pf*, **определя́ть** *impf* define; determine; appoint; ~**ся** be formed; be determined; find one's position.

опроверга́ть *impf*, **опрове́ргнуть** (-ну; -ве́рг) *pf* refute, disprove. **опроверже́ние** refutation; denial.

опроки́дывать *impf*, **опроки́нуть** (-ну) *pf* overturn; topple; ~**ся** overturn; capsize.

опроме́тчивый rash, hasty.

опро́с (cross-)examination; (opinion) poll. **опроси́ть** (-ошу́, -о́сишь) *pf* (*impf* **опра́шивать**) question; (cross-)examine. **опро́сный лист** questionnaire.

опры́скать, **опры́скивать** *impf* sprinkle; spray.

опря́тный neat, tidy.

óптик optician. **óптика** опtics. **опти́ческий** optic, optical.

оптима́льный optimal. **оптими́зм** optimism. **оптими́ст** optimist. **оптимисти́ческий** optimistic.

опто́вый wholesale. **о́птом** adv wholesale.

опубликова́ние publication; promulgation. **о|публикова́ть** pf, **опублико́вывать** impf publish; promulgate.

опуска́ть(ся impf of опусти́ть(ся

опусте́лый deserted. **о|пусте́ть** (-е́ет) pf.

опусти́ть (-ущу́, -у́стишь) pf (impf **опуска́ть**) lower; let down; turn down; omit; post; ~ся lower o.s.; sink; fall; go down; go to pieces.

опусто́шать impf, **опусто-ши́ть** (-шу́) pf devastate. **опусто-ше́ние** devastation. **опусто-ши́тельный** devastating.

опу́тать pf, **опу́тывать** impf entangle; ensnare.

опуха́ть impf, **о|пу́хнуть** (-ну; опу́х) pf swell, swell up. **опу́холь** swelling; tumour.

опу́шка edge of a forest; trimming.

опущу́ etc.: see **опусти́ть**

опыле́ние pollination. **опыли́ть** pf, **опыля́ть** impf pollinate.

о́пыт experience; experiment. **о́пытный** experienced; experimental.

опьяне́ние intoxication. **о|пьяне́ть** (-е́ю) pf, **о|пьяни́ть** pf, **опьяня́ть** impf intoxicate, make drunk.

опя́ть adv again.

ора́ва crowd, horde.

ора́кул oracle.

орангута́нг orangutan.

ора́нжевый orange. **оран-же́рея** greenhouse, conservatory.

ора́тор orator. **орато́рия** oratorio.

ора́ть (ору́, орёшь) impf yell.

орби́та orbit; (eye-)socket.

о́рган¹ organ; body. **орга́н**² (mus) organ. **организа́тор** organizer. **организацио́н-ный** organization(al). **организа́ция** organization. **орга-ни́зм** organism. **организо́-ванный** organized. **организо-ва́ть** impf & pf (pf also c~) organize; ~ся be organized; organize. **органи́че-ский** organic.

о́ргия orgy.

орда́ (pl -ы) horde.

о́рден (pl -á) order.

о́рдер (pl -á) order; warrant; writ.

ордина́та ordinate.

ордина́тор house-surgeon.

орёл (орла́) eagle; ~ и́ли ре́шка? heads or tails?

орео́л halo.

оре́х nut, nuts; walnut. **оре́хо-вый** nut; walnut. **оре́шник** hazel; hazel-thicket.

оригина́л original; eccentric. **оригина́льный** original.

ориента́ция orientation. **ориен-ти́р** landmark; reference point. **ориенти́роваться** impf & pf orient o.s.; +на+acc head for; aim at. **ориенти-ро́вка** orientation. **ориенти-ро́вочный** reference; tentative; approximate.

орке́стр orchestra.

орли́ный eagle; aquiline.

орна́мент ornament; ornamental design.

о|робе́ть (-е́ю) pf.

ороси́тельный irrigation.

ороси́ть (-ошу́) *pf*, ороша́ть *impf* irrigate; ороше́ние irrigation; поля́ ороше́ния sewage farm.

ору́ *etc.*: *see* ора́ть

ору́дие instrument; tool; gun. ору́дийный gun. ору́довать *impf* +*instr* handle; run. оруже́йный arms; gun. ору́жие arm, arms; weapons.

орфографи́ческий orthographic(al). орфогра́фия orthography, spelling.

оса́ (*pl* -ы) wasp.

оса́да siege. осади́ть[1] (-ажу́) *pf* (*impf* осажда́ть) besiege.

осади́ть[2] (-ажу́, -а́дишь) *pf* (*impf* оса́живать) check; force back; rein in; take down a peg.

оса́дный siege.

оса́док (-дка) sediment; fallout; after-taste; *pl* precipitation, fall-out. оса́дочный sedimentary.

осажда́ть *impf of* осади́ть[1] оса́живать *impf of* осади́ть[2]. осажу́ *see* осади́ть[1,2]

оса́нка carriage, bearing.

осва́ивать(ся *impf of* осво́ить(ся

осведоми́тельный informative; information. осве́домить (-млю) *pf*, осведомля́ть *impf* inform; ~ся о+*prep* inquire about, ask after. осведомле́ние notification. осведомлённый well-informed, knowledgeable.

освежа́ть *impf*, освежи́ть (-жу́) *pf* refresh; air. освежи́тельный refreshing.

освети́тельный illuminating. освети́ть (-ещу́) *pf*, освеща́ть *impf* light up; illuminate; throw light on; ~ся light up. освеще́ние lighting, illumi-

nation. освещённый (-ён, -á) lit.

о|свиде́тельствовать *pf*.

освиста́ть (-ищу́, -и́щешь) *pf*, осви́стывать *impf* hiss (off); boo.

освободи́тель *m* liberator. освободи́тельный liberation, emancipation. освободи́ть (-ожу́) *pf*, освобожда́ть *impf* liberate; emancipate; dismiss; vacate; empty; ~ся free o.s.; become free. освобожде́ние liberation; release; emancipation; vacation. освобождённый (-ён, -á) freed, free; exempt.

осво́ение mastery; opening up. осво́ить *pf* (*impf* осва́ивать) master; become familiar with; ~ся familiarize o.s.

освящённый (-ён, -ена́) consecrated; sanctified; ~ века́ми time-honoured.

о|седла́ть *pf*, осёдлывать *impf* saddle.

осе́длый settled.

осека́ться *impf of* осе́чься

осёл (-сла́) donkey; ass.

осело́к (-лка́) touchstone; whetstone.

осени́ть *pf* (*impf* осеня́ть) overshadow; dawn upon.

осе́нний autumn(al). о́сень autumn. о́сенью *adv* in autumn.

осеня́ть *impf of* осени́ть

осе́сть (ося́ду; осе́л) *pf* (*impf* оседа́ть) settle; subside.

осётр (-á) sturgeon. осетри́на sturgeon.

осе́чка misfire. осе́чься (-еку́сь, -ечёшься; -ёкся, -екла́сь) *pf* (*impf* осека́ться) stop short.

оси́ливать *impf*, оси́лить *pf* overpower; master.

оси́на aspen.

о|си́пнуть (-ну; оси́п) get hoarse.

осироте́лый orphaned. осироте́ть (-е́ю) pf be orphaned.

оска́ливать impf, о|ска́лить pf; ~ зу́бы, ~ся bare one's teeth.

о|сканда́лить(ся pf.

оскверни́ть pf, оскверня́ть impf profane; defile.

оско́лок (-лка) splinter; fragment.

оско́мина bitter taste (in the mouth); наби́ть оско́мину set the teeth on edge.

оскорби́тельный insulting, abusive. оскорби́ть (-блю́) pf, оскорбля́ть impf insult; offend; ~ся take offence. оскорбле́ние insult. оскорблённый (-ён, -á) insulted.

ослабева́ть impf, о|слабе́ть (-е́ю) pf weaken; slacken. осла́бить (-блю) pf, ослабля́ть impf weaken; slacken. ослабле́ние weakening; slackening, relaxation.

ослепи́тельный blinding, dazzling. ослепи́ть (-плю́) pf, ослепля́ть impf blind, dazzle. ослепле́ние blinding, dazzling; blindness. о|сле́пнуть (-ну; -е́п) pf.

осли́ный donkey; asinine. осли́ца she-ass.

осложне́ние complication. осложни́ть pf, осложня́ть impf complicate; ~ся become complicated.

ослы́шаться (-шусь) pf mishear.

осма́тривать(ся impf of осмотре́ть(ся.

осме́ивать impf of осмея́ть

о|смеле́ть (-е́ю) pf. осме́ли-

ва́ться impf, осме́литься pf dare; venture.

осмея́ть (-ею́, -еёшь) pf (impf осме́ивать) ridicule.

осмо́тр examination, inspection. осмотре́ть (-рю́, -ришь) pf (impf осма́тривать) examine, inspect; look round; ~ся look round. осмотри́тельный circumspect.

осмы́сленный sensible, intelligent. осмы́сливать impf, осмы́слить pf, осмысля́ть impf interpret; comprehend.

оснасти́ть (-ащу́) pf, оснаща́ть impf fit out, equip. осна́стка rigging. оснаще́ние fitting out; equipment.

осно́ва base, basis, foundation; pl fundamentals; stem (of a word). основа́ние founding, foundation; base; basis; reason; на како́м основа́нии? on what grounds? основа́тель m founder. основа́тельный well-founded; solid; thorough. основа́ть pf, осно́вывать impf found; base; ~ся settle; be founded, be based. основно́й fundamental, basic; main; в основно́м in the main, on the whole. основополо́жник founder.

осо́ба person. осо́бенно adv especially. осо́бенность peculiarity; в осо́бенности in particular. осо́бенный special, particular, peculiar. особня́к (-á) private residence; detached house. особняко́м adv by o.s. осо́бо adv apart; especially. осо́бый special; particular.

осознава́ть (-наю́, -наёшь) impf, осозна́ть pf realize.

осо́ка sedge.

о́спа smallpox; pock-marks.

оспа́рива|ть *impf*, **оспо́рить** *pf* dispute; contest.

о|срами́ть(ся -млю́(сь) *pf*.

оставаться -таю́сь, -таёшься *impf of* **оста́ться**

ост (*naut*) east; east wind.

оста́в|ить -влю) *pf*, **оставля́ть** *impf* leave; abandon; reserve.

остальн|о́й the rest of; ~ое *sb* the rest; ~ы́е *sb pl* the others.

остана́влива|ть(ся *impf of* **останови́ть(ся**

оста́нки (-ов) *pl* remains.

останов|и́ть -влю́, -вишь) *pf* (*impf* **остана́вливать**) stop; restrain; ~ся stop, halt; stay; +на+*prep* dwell on; settle on. **остано́вка** stop.

оста́ток (-тка) remainder; rest; residue; *pl* remains; leftovers. **оста́ться** (-а́нусь) *pf* (*impf* **оставаться**) remain; stay; *impers* it remains, it is necessary; **нам не остаётся ничего́ друго́го, как** we have no choice but.

остекли́ть *pf*, **остекля́ть** *impf* glaze.

остервене́ть *pf* become enraged.

остерега́ть *impf*, **остере́чь** (-регу́, -режёшь; -рёг, -ла́) *pf* warn; ~ся (+*gen*) beware (of).

о́стов frame, framework; skeleton.

о|столбене́ть -е́ю) *pf*.

осторо́жно *adv* carefully; ~! look out! **осторо́жность** care, caution. **осторо́жный** careful, cautious.

острига́|ть(ся *impf of* **остри́чь(ся**

остриё point; spike; (cutting) edge. **остри́ть**[1] *impf* sharpen. **остри́ть**[2] *impf* (*pf* с~) be

witty.

о|стри́чь -игу́, -ижёшь; -йг) *pf* (*impf also* **острига́ть**) cut, clip; ~ся have one's hair cut.

о́стров (*pl* -а́) island. **острово́к** (-вка́) islet; ~ безопа́сности (traffic) island.

острота́[1] witticism, joke. **острота́**[2] sharpness; keenness; pungency.

остроу́мие wit. **остроу́мный** witty.

о́стрый (остр, -а́, -о) sharp; pointed; acute; keen. **остря́к** (-а́) wit.

о|студи́ть -ужу́, -удишь) *pf*, **остужа́ть** *impf* cool.

оступа́ться *impf*, **оступи́ться** *pf* stumble.

остыва́ть *impf*, **остыть** (-ы́ну) *pf* get cold; cool down.

осуди́ть -ужу́, -у́дишь) *pf*, **осужда́ть** *impf* condemn; convict. **осужде́ние** condemnation; conviction. **осуждё́нный** (-ён, -а́) condemned, convicted; *sb* convict.

осу́нуться -нусь) *pf* grow thin, become drawn.

осуша́ть *impf*, **осуши́ть** (-шу́, -шишь) *pf* drain; dry. **осуше́ние** drainage.

осуществи́мый feasible. **осуществи́ть** -влю́) *pf*, **осуществля́ть** *impf* realize, bring about; accomplish; ~ся be fulfilled; come true. **осуществле́ние** realization; accomplishment.

осчастли́вить (-влю) *pf*, **осчастли́вливать** *impf* make happy.

осыпа́ть (-плю) *pf*, **осыпа́ть** *impf* strew; shower; ~ся crumble; fall. **о́сыпь** scree.

ось (*gen pl* -е́й) axis; axle.

осьмино́г octopus.

ося́ду *etc.: see* **осе́сть**

осяза́емый tangible. **осяза́ние** touch. **осяза́тельный** tactile; tangible. **осяза́ть** *impf* feel.

от, ото *prep+gen* from; of; against.

ота́пливать *impf of* **отопи́ть**

ота́ра flock (*of sheep*).

отба́вить (-влю) *pf*, **отбавля́ть** *impf* pour off; **хоть отбавля́й** more than enough.

отбега́ть *impf*, **отбежа́ть** (-егу́) *pf* run off.

отберу́ *etc.: see* **отобра́ть**

отбива́ть(ся *impf of* **отби́ть(ся**

отбивна́я котле́та cutlet, chop.

отбира́ть *impf of* **отобра́ть**

отби́ть (отобью́, -ёшь) *pf* (*impf* **отбива́ть**) beat (off), repel; win over; break off; **~ся** break off; drop behind; **+от**+*gen* defend o.s. against.

о́тблеск reflection.

отбо́й repelling; retreat; ringing off; **бить ~** beat a retreat; **дать ~** ring off.

отбо́йный молото́к (-тка́) pneumatic drill.

отбо́р selection. **отбо́рный** choice, select(ed).

отбра́сывать *impf*, **отбро́сить** (-о́шу) *pf* throw off or away; hurl back; reject; **~ тень** cast a shadow. **отбро́сы** (-ов) *pl* garbage.

отбыва́ть *impf*, **отбы́ть** (-бу́ду; о́тбыл, -а́, -о) *pf* depart; serve (*a sentence*).

отва́га courage, bravery.

отва́живаться *impf*, **отва́житься** (-жусь) *pf* dare. **отва́жный** courageous.

отва́л dump, slag-heap; casting off; **до ~a** to satiety.

отва́ливать *impf*, **отвали́ть** (-лю́, -лишь) *pf* push aside; cast off; fork out.

отва́р broth; decoction. **отва́ривать** *impf*, **отвари́ть** (-рю́, -ришь) *pf* boil. **отварно́й** boiled.

отве́дать *pf* (*impf* **отве́дывать**) taste, try.

отведу́ *etc.: see* **отвести́**

отве́дывать *impf of* **отве́дать**

отвезти́ (-зу́, -зёшь; -вёз, -ла́) *pf* (*impf* **отвози́ть**) take or cart away.

отвёл *etc.: see* **отвести́**

отверга́ть *impf*, **отве́ргнуть** (-ну; -ве́рг) *pf* reject; repudiate.

отве́рженный outcast.

отверну́ть (-ну́, -нёшь) *pf* (*impf* **отвёртывать**, **отвора́чивать**) turn aside; turn down; turn on; unscrew; screw off; **~ся** turn away; come unscrewed.

отве́рстие opening; hole.

отверте́ть (-рчу́, -ртишь) *pf* (*impf* **отвёртывать**) unscrew; twist off; **~ся** come unscrewed; get off. **отвёртка** screwdriver.

отвёртывать(ся *impf of* **отверну́ть(ся**, **отверте́ть(ся**

отве́с plumb; vertical slope. **отве́сить** (-е́шу) *pf* (*impf* **отве́шивать**) weigh out. **отве́сный** perpendicular, sheer.

отвести́ (-еду́, -едёшь; -вёл, -а́) *pf* (*impf* **отводи́ть**) lead; take; draw or take aside; deflect; draw off; reject; allot.

отве́т answer.

отве́тить *pf*, **отвеча́ть** *impf* branch off. **ответвле́ние** branch, off-shoot.

отве́тить (-е́чу) *pf*, **отвеча́ть** *impf* answer; **+на**+*acc* reply to; **+за**+*acc* answer for. **отве́тный** in reply, return. **отве́тственность** responsibility. **отве́тственный** responsible. **отве́тчик** defendant.

отве́шивать *impf of* **отве́сить**. **отве́шу** *etc.: see* **отве́сить**

отвинти́ть (-нчу́) *pf*, **отви́нчивать** *impf* unscrew.

отвиса́ть *impf*, **отви́снуть** (-нет; -ис) *pf* hang down, sag. **отви́слый** hanging, baggy.

отвлека́ть (-еку́, -ечёшь; -влёк, -ла́) *pf* distract, divert; **~ся** be distracted. **отвлечённый** abstract.

отво́д taking aside; diversion; leading, taking; rejection; allotment. **отводи́ть** (-ожу́, -о́дишь) *impf of* **отвести́**.

отвоева́ть (-оюю) *pf*, **отвоёвывать** *impf* win back; spend in fighting.

отвози́ть (-ожу́, -о́зишь) *impf of* **отвезти́**. **отвора́чивать(ся** *impf of* **отверну́ть(ся**

отвори́ть (-рю́, -ришь) *pf* (*impf* **отворя́ть**) open; **~ся** open.

отворя́ть(ся *impf of* **отвори́ть(ся**. **отворю́ю** *etc.: see* **отвоева́ть**

отврати́тельный disgusting. **отвраще́ние** disgust, repugnance.

отвыка́ть *impf*, **отвы́кнуть** (-ну; -ык) *pf* **+от** *or inf* lose the habit of; grow out of.

отвяза́ть (-яжу́, -я́жешь) *pf*, **отвя́зывать** *impf* untie, unfasten; **~ся** come untied, come loose; **+от**+*gen* get rid of; leave alone.

отгада́ть *pf*, **отга́дывать** *impf* guess. **отга́дка** answer.

отгиба́ть(ся *impf of* **отогну́ть(ся**

отгла́дить (-а́жу) *pf*, **отгла́живать** *impf* iron (out).

отгова́ривать *impf*, **отговори́ть** *pf* dissuade; **~ся** +*instr* plead, pretext. **отгово́рка** excuse, pretext.

отголо́сок (-ска) echo.

отгоня́ть *impf of* **отогна́ть**

отгора́живать *impf*, **отгороди́ть** (-ожу́, -о́дишь) *pf* fence off; partition off; **~ся** shut o.s. off.

отдава́ть¹(ся (-даю́(сь) *impf of* **отда́ть(ся**. **отдава́ть²** (-аёт) *impf impers*+*instr* taste of; smell of; smack of; **от него́** отдаёт во́дкой he reeks of vodka.

отдале́ние removal; distance. **отдалённый** remote. **отдали́ть** (-лю́) *pf*, **отдаля́ть** *impf* remove; estrange; postpone; **~ся** move away; digress.

отда́ть (-а́м, -а́шь, -а́ст, -ади́м; о́тдал, -а́, -о) *pf* (*impf* **отдава́ть¹**) give back, return; give; give up; give away; recoil; cast off; **~ся** give o.s. (up); resound. **отда́ча** return; payment; casting off; efficiency; output; recoil.

отде́л department; section. **отде́лать** *pf* (*impf* **отде́лывать**) finish, put the finishing touches to; trim; **~ся** **+от**+*gen* get rid of; +*instr* get off with.

отделе́ние separation; department; compartment; section. **отдели́ть** (-елю́, -е́лишь) *pf* (*impf* **отделя́ть**) separate; detach; **~ся** separate; detach o.s.; get detached.

отде́лка finishing; finish,

decoration. **отде́лывать(ся** *impf of* **отде́лать(ся**

отде́льно separately; apart. **отде́льный** separate. **отделя́ть(ся** *impf of* **отдели́ть(ся**

отдёргивать *impf*, **отдёрнуть** (-ну) *pf* draw *or* pull aside *or* back.

отдеру́ *etc.: see* **отодра́ть. отдира́ть** *impf of* **отодра́ть**

отдохну́ть (-ну́, -нёшь) *pf (impf* **отдыха́ть**) rest.

отду́шина air-hole, vent.

о́тдых rest. **отдыха́ть** *impf (pf* **отдохну́ть**) rest; be on holiday.

отдыша́ться (-шу́сь, -шишься) *pf* recover one's breath.

отека́ть *impf of* **оте́чь. о|те-ли́ться** (-е́лится) *pf.*

оте́ль *m* hotel.

отеса́ть *etc.: see* **обтеса́ть**

оте́ц (отца́) father. **оте́ческий** fatherly, paternal. **оте́чественный** home, native. **оте́чество** native land, fatherland.

оте́чь (-еку́, -ечёшь; отёк, -ла́) *pf (impf* **отека́ть**) swell (up).

отжива́ть *impf*, **отжи́ть** (-иву́, -ивёшь; о́тжил, -а́, -о) *pf* become obsolete *or* outmoded. **отжи́вший** obsolete; outmoded.

о́тзвук echo.

о́тзыв[1] opinion; reference; review; response. **отзы́в**[2] recall. **отзыва́ть(ся** *impf of* **отозва́ть(ся. отзы́вчивый** responsive.

отка́з refusal; repudiation; failure; natural. **отказа́ть** (-ажу́, -а́жешь) *pf*, **отка́зывать** *impf* break down; (+*dat* +*prep*) refuse, deny (*s.o. sth*); **~ся** (+*от*+*gen* +*inf*) refuse; turn down; renounce, give up.

отка́лывать(ся *impf of* **отколо́ть(ся. отка́пывать** *impf of* **откопа́ть. отка́рмливать** *impf of* **откорми́ть**

откати́ть (-ачу́, -а́тишь) *pf*, **отка́тывать** *impf* roll away; **~ся** roll away *or* back; be forced back.

откача́ть *pf*, **отка́чивать** *impf* pump out; give artificial respiration to.

отка́шливаться *impf*, **отка́шляться** *pf* clear one's throat.

откидно́й folding, collapsible. **отки́дывать** *impf*, **отки́нуть** (-ну) *pf* fold back; throw aside.

откла́дывать *impf of* **отложи́ть**

откле́ивать *impf*, **откле́ить** (-е́ю) *pf* unstick; **~ся** come unstuck.

о́тклик response; comment; echo. **откли́каться** *impf*, **откли́кнуться** (-нусь) *pf* answer; respond.

отклоне́ние deviation; declining, refusal; deflection. **отклони́ть** (-ню́, -нишь) *pf*, **отклоня́ть** *impf* deflect; decline; **~ся** deviate; diverge.

отключи́ть (-чу́) *pf* cut off, disconnect.

отколоти́ть (-очу́, -о́тишь) *pf* knock off; beat up.

отколо́ть (-лю́, -лешь) *pf (impf* **отка́лывать**) break off; chop off; unpin; **~ся** break off; come unpinned; break away.

откопа́ть *pf (impf* **отка́пывать**) dig up; exhume.

откорми́ть (-млю́, -мишь) *pf (impf* **отка́рмливать**) fatten.

отко́с slope.

открепи́ть (-плю́) *pf*, **открепля́ть** *impf* unfasten; **~ся**

become unfastened.

откровéние revelation. **откровéнный** frank; outspoken; unconcealed. **откро́ю** *etc.*: *see* **открыть**

открути́ть (-учу́, -у́тишь) *pf*, **откру́чивать** *impf* untwist, unscrew.

открыва́ть *impf*, **открыть** (-ро́ю) *pf* open; reveal; discover; turn on; **~ся** open; come to light, be revealed. **откры́тие** discovery; revelation; opening. **откры́тка** postcard, card. **откры́то** openly. **откры́тый** open.

отку́да *adv* from where; from which; how; **~ ни возьми́сь** from out of nowhere. **отку́да-либо**, **-нибудь** from somewhere or other. **отку́да-то** from somewhere.

отку́поривать *impf*, **отку́порить** *pf* uncork.

откуси́ть (-ушу́, -у́сишь) *pf*, **отку́сывать** *impf* bite off.

отлага́тельство delay. **отлага́ть** *impf of* **отложи́ть**

от|лакирова́ть *pf.* **отла́мывать** *impf of* **отломáть**, **отломи́ть**

отлепи́ть (-плю́, -пишь) *pf* unstick, take off; **~ся** come unstuck, come off.

отлёт flying away; departure. **отлета́ть** *impf*, **отлете́ть** (-лечу́) *pf*, fly, fly away, fly off; rebound.

отли́в ebb, ebb-tide; tint; play of colours. **отлива́ть** *impf*, **отли́ть** (отолью́; о́тлил, -á, -o) *pf* pour off; pump out; cast, found; (*no pf*) +*instr* be shot with. **отли́вка** casting; moulding.

отлича́ть *impf*, **отличи́ть** (-чу́) *pf* distinguish; **~ся** distin-

guish o.s.; differ; +*instr* be notable for. **отли́чие** difference; distinction; **знак отли́чия** order, decoration; **с отли́чием** with honours. **отли́чник** outstanding student, worker, etc. **отличи́тельный** distinctive; distinguishing. **отли́чный** different; excellent.

отло́гий sloping.

отложе́ние sediment; deposit. **отложи́ть** (-ожу́, -о́жишь) *pf* (*impf* **откла́дывать**, **отлага́ть**) put aside; postpone; deposit.

отломáть, **отломи́ть** (-млю́, -мишь) *pf* (*impf* **отла́мывать**) break off.

от|лупи́ть *pf.*

отлуча́ть *impf*, **отлучи́ть** (-чу́) *pf* (**от цéркви**) excommunicate; **~ся** absent o.s. **отлу́чка** absence.

отлы́нивать *impf* +**от**+*gen* shirk.

отма́хиваться *impf*, **отмахну́ться** (-ну́сь, -нёшься) *pf* +**от**+*gen* brush off; brush aside.

отмежева́ться (-жу́юсь) *pf*, **отмежёвываться** *impf* +**от**+*gen* dissociate o.s. from.

о́тмель (sand-)bank.

отме́на abolition; cancellation. **отмени́ть** (-ню́, -нишь) *pf*, **отменя́ть** *impf* repeal; abolish; cancel.

отмере́ть (отомрёт; о́тмер, -лá, -ло) *pf* (*impf* **отмира́ть**) die off; die out.

отме́ривать *impf*, **отме́рить** *pf*, **отмеря́ть** *impf* measure off.

отмести́ (-ету́, -етёшь; -ёл, -á) *pf* (*impf* **отмета́ть**) sweep aside.

отмета́ть *impf of* **отмести́**

отме́тить (-е́чу) *pf*, **отмеча́ть**

impf mark, note; celebrate; **~ся** sign one's name; sign out. **отмéтка** note; mark.

отмирáть *impf of* **отмерéть**

отморáживать *impf,* **отморóзить** (-óжу) *pf* injure by frost-bite. **отморóжение** frost-bite. **отморóженный** frost-bitten.

отмóю *etc.: see* **отмы́ть**

отмывáть *impf,* **отмы́ть** (-мóю) *pf* wash away; wash off; **~ся** wash o.s. clean; come out.

отмыкáть *impf of* **отомкнýть**

отмы́чка master key.

отнести́ (-сý, -сёшь; -нёс, -лá) *pf* (*impf* **относи́ть**) take; carry away; ascribe, attribute; **~сь к+**dat treat; regard; apply to; concern, have to do with.

отнимáть(ся *impf of* **отня́ть(ся**

относи́тельно *adv* relatively; *prep+*gen concerning. **относи́тельность** relativity. **относи́тельный** relative. **относи́ть(ся** (-ошý(сь, -óсишь(ся) *impf of* **отнести́(сь. отношéние** attitude; relation; respect; ratio; **в отношéнии+**gen, **по отношéнию к+**dat with regard to; **в прямóм (обрáтном) отношéнии** in direct (inverse) ratio.

отны́не *adv* henceforth.

отню́дь not at all.

отня́тие taking away; amputation. **отня́ть** (-нимý, -ни́мешь; óтнял, -á, -о) *pf* (*impf* **отнимáть**) take (away); amputate; **~ от грýди** wean; **~ся** be paralysed.

ото: *see* **от**

отображáть *impf,* **отобрази́ть** (-ажý) *pf* reflect; represent. **отображéние** reflec-

tion; representation.

отобрáть (отберý, -рёшь; отобрáл, -á, -о) *pf* (*impf* **отбирáть**) take (away); select.

отобью́ *etc.: see* **отби́ть**

отовсю́ду *adv* from everywhere.

отогнáть (отгоню́, -óнишь; отогнáл, -á, -о) *pf* (*impf* **отгоня́ть**) drive away, off.

отогнýть (-нý, -нёшь) *pf* (*impf* **отгибáть**) bend back; bend.

отогревáть *impf,* **отогрéть** (-éю) *pf* warm.

отодвигáть *impf,* **отодви́нуть** (-ну) *pf* move aside; put off.

отодрáть (отдерý, -рёшь; отодрáл, -á, -о) *pf* (*impf* **отдирáть**) tear off, rip off.

отож(д)ествить (-влю́) *pf,* **отож(д)ествля́ть** *impf* identify.

отозвáть (отзовý, -вёшь; отозвáл, -á, -о) *pf* (*impf* **отзывáть**) take aside; recall; **~ся на+**acc answer; **на+**acc or *prep* tell on; have an affect on.

отойти́ (-йдý, -йдёшь; отошёл, -шлá) *pf* (*impf* **отходи́ть**) move away; depart; withdraw; digress; come out; recover.

отолью́ *etc.: see* **отли́ть**. **отомрёт** *etc.: see* **отмерéть**.

ото|**мсти́ть** (-мщý) *pf.*

отомкнýть (-нý, -нёшь) *pf* (*impf* **отмыкáть**) unlock, unbolt.

отопи́тельный heating. **отопи́ть** (-плю́, -пишь) *pf* (*impf* **отáпливать**) heat. **отоплéние** heating.

отопрý *etc.: see* **отперéть**. **отопью́** *etc.: see* **отпи́ть**.

отóрванный cut off, isolated. **оторвáть** (-вý, -вёшь)

(*impf* **отрыва́ть**) tear off; tear away; ~**ся** come off, be torn off; be cut off, lose touch; break away; tear o.s. away; ~**ся от земли́** take off.

оторопе́ть (-е́ю) *pf* be struck dumb.

отосла́ть (-ошлю́, -ошлёшь) *pf* (*impf* **отсыла́ть**) send (off); send back; +к+*dat* refer to.

отоспа́ться (-сплюсь, -я́лся, -ала́сь, -ось) *pf* (*impf* **отсыпа́ться**) catch up on one's sleep.

отошёл *etc.*: *see* **отойти́. отошлю́** *etc.*: *see* **отосла́ть**

отпада́ть *impf of* **отпа́сть.**

от|пари́ровать *pf.* **отпа́рывать** *impf of* **отпоро́ть**

отпа́сть (-адёт) *pf* (*impf* **отпада́ть**) fall off; fall away; pass.

отпева́ние funeral service.

отпере́ть (отопру́, -прёшь; о́тпер, -ла́, -ло) *pf* (*impf* **отпира́ть**) unlock; ~**ся** open; +**от**+*gen* deny; disown.

от|печа́тать *pf,* **отпеча́тывать** *impf* print (off); type (out); imprint. **отпеча́ток** (-тка) imprint, print.

отпива́ть *impf of* **отпи́ть**

отпи́ливать *impf,* **отпили́ть** (-лю́, -лишь) *pf* saw off.

от|пира́тельство denial. **отпира́ть(ся** *impf of* **отпере́ть(ся**

отпи́ть (отопью́, -пьёшь; о́тпил, -á, -о) *pf* (*impf* **отпива́ть**) take a sip of.

отпи́хивать *impf,* **отпихну́ть** (-ну́, -нёшь) *pf* push off; shove aside.

отплати́ть (-ачу́, -а́тишь) *pf,* **отпла́чивать** *impf* +*dat* pay back.

отплыва́ть *impf,* **отплы́ть**

(-ыву́, -ывёшь; -ы́л, -á, -о) *pf* (set) sail; swim off. **отплы́тие** sailing, departure.

о́тповедь rebuke.

отполза́ть *impf,* **отползти́** (-зу́, -зёшь; -о́лз, -ла́) *pf* crawl away.

от|полирова́ть *pf.* **от|полоска́ть** (-ощу́) *pf.*

отпо́р repulse; rebuff.

отпоро́ть (-рю́, -решь) *pf* (*impf* **отпа́рывать**) rip off.

отправи́тель *m* sender. **отпра́вить** (-влю) *pf,* **отправля́ть** *impf* send, dispatch; ~**ся** set off, start. **отпра́вка** dispatch. **отправле́ние** sending; departure; performance. **отправн|о́й**: ~**о́й пункт,** ~**я́я то́чка** starting-point.

от|пра́здновать *pf.*

отпра́шиваться *impf,* **отпроси́ться** (-ошу́сь, -о́сишься) *pf* ask for leave; get leave.

отпры́гивать *impf,* **отпры́гнуть** (-ну) *pf* jump or spring back or aside.

о́тпрыск offshoot; scion.

отпряга́ть *impf of* **отпря́чь отпря́нуть** (-ну) *pf* recoil, start back.

отпря́чь (-ягу́, -яжёшь; -я́г, -ла́) *pf* (*impf* **отпряга́ть**) unharness.

отпу́гивать *impf,* **отпугну́ть** (-ну́, -нёшь) *pf* frighten off.

о́тпуск (*pl* -á) leave, holiday(s). **отпуска́ть** *impf,* **отпусти́ть** (-ущу́, -у́стишь) *pf* let go, let off; set free; release; slacken; (let) grow; allot; remit. **отпускни́к** (-á) person on leave. **отпускно́й** holiday; leave. **отпуще́ние** remission; **козёл отпуще́ния** scapegoat.

отраба́тывать *impf,* **отрабо́тать** *pf* work off; master;

отрабо́танный worked out; waste, spent, exhaust.

отра́ва poison. **отрави́ть** (-влю́, -вишь) *pf*, **отравля́ть** *impf* poison.

отра́да joy, delight. **отра́дный** gratifying, pleasing.

отража́тель *m* reflector; scanner. **отража́ть** *impf*, **отрази́ть** (-ажу́) *pf* reflect; repulse; ~ся be reflected; **+на**+*prep* affect. **отраже́ние** reflection; repulse.

о́трасль branch.

отраста́ть *impf*, **отрасти́** (-тёт; отро́с, -ла́) *pf* grow. **отрасти́ть** (-ащу́) *pf*, **отра́щивать** *impf* (let) grow.

от|**реаги́ровать** *pf*. **от**|**регули́ровать** *pf*. **от**|**редакти́ровать** *pf*.

отре́з cut; length. **отре́зать** (-е́жу) *pf*, **отреза́ть** *impf* cut off; snap.

о|**трезве́ть** (-е́ю) *pf*. **отрезви́ть** (-влю́, -ви́шь) *pf*, **отрезвля́ть** *impf* sober; ~ся sober up.

отре́зок (-зка) piece; section; segment.

отрека́ться *impf of* **отре́чься**

от|**рекомендова́ть**(**ся**) *pf*. **отрёкся** *etc.: see* **отре́чься**. **от**|**ремонти́ровать** *pf*. **от**|**репети́ровать** *pf*.

отре́пье, отре́пья (-ьев) *pl* rags.

от|**реставри́ровать** *pf*.

отрече́ние renunciation; ~ от престо́ла abdication. **отре́чься** (-еку́сь, -ечёшься) *pf* (*impf* **отрека́ться**) renounce.

отреша́ться *impf*, **отреши́ться** (-шу́сь) *pf* renounce; get rid of.

отрица́ние denial; negation. **отрица́тельный** negative.

отрица́ть *impf* deny.

отро́с *etc.: see* **отрасти́**. **отро́сток** (-тка) shoot, sprout; appendix.

о́трочество adolescence.

о́труби (-е́й) *pl* bran.

отруби́ть (-блю́, -бишь) *pf* (*impf* **отруба́ть**) chop off; snap back.

от|**руга́ть** *pf*.

отры́в tearing off; alienation, isolation; в ~е от+*gen* out of touch with; ~ (от земли́) take-off. **отрыва́ть**(**ся** *impf of* **оторва́ть**(**ся**. **отры́вистый** staccato; disjointed. **отрывно́й** tear-off. **отры́вок** (-вка) fragment, excerpt. **отры́вочный** fragmentary, scrappy.

отры́жка belch; throw-back.

отря́д detachment; order.

отря́хивать *impf*, **отряхну́ть** (-ну́, -нёшь) *pf* shake down or off.

от|**салютова́ть** *pf*.

отса́сывание suction. **отса́сывать** *impf of* **отсоса́ть**

отсве́чивать *impf* be reflected; **+instr** shine with.

отсе́в sifting, selection; dropping out. **отсева́ть**(**ся**, **отсе́ивать**(**ся** *impf of* **отсе́ять**(**ся**

отсе́к compartment. **отсека́ть** *impf*, **отсе́чь** (-еку́, -ечёшь; -се́к, -ла́) *pf* chop off.

отсе́ять (-е́ю) *pf* (*impf* **отсева́ть, отсе́ивать**) sift; screen; eliminate; ~ся drop out.

отсиде́ть (-ижу́) *pf*, **отси́живать** *impf* make numb by sitting; sit through; serve out.

отска́кивать *impf*, **отскочи́ть** (-чу́, -чишь) *pf* jump aside or away; rebound; come off.

отслу́живать *impf*, отслужи́ть (-жу́, -жишь) *pf* serve one's time; be worn out.

отсоса́ть (-осу́, -осёшь) *pf* (*impf* отса́сывать) suck off, draw off.

отсо́хнуть (-ну) *pf* (*impf* отсыха́ть) wither.

отсро́чивать *impf*, отсро́чить *pf* postpone, defer. отсро́чка postponement, deferment.

отстава́ние lag; lagging behind. отстава́ть (-таю́, -аёшь) *impf of* отста́ть

отста́вить (-влю) *pf*, отставля́ть *impf* set *or* put aside. отста́вка resignation; retirement; в отста́вке retired; вы́йти в отста́вку resign, retire. отставно́й retired.

отста́ивать(ся *impf of* отстоя́ть(ся

отста́лость backwardness. отста́лый backward. отста́ть (-а́ну) *pf* (*impf* отстава́ть) fall behind; lag behind; become detached; lose touch; break (off); be slow. отста́ющий *sb* backward pupil.

от|стега́ть

отстёгивать *impf*, отстегну́ть (-ну́, -нёшь) *pf* unfasten, undo; ~ся come unfastened *or* undone.

отстоя́ть¹ (-ою́) *pf* (*impf* отста́ивать) defend; stand up for. отстоя́ть² (-ои́т) *на+acc* be ... distant (от+*gen* from). отстоя́ться (*impf* отста́иваться) settle; become stabilized.

отстра́ивать(ся *impf of* отстро́ить(ся

отстране́ние pushing aside; dismissal. отстрани́ть *pf*, отстраня́ть *impf* push aside;

remove; suspend; ~ся move away; keep aloof; ~ся *or* dodge.

отстре́ливаться *impf*, отстреля́ться *pf* fire back.

отстрига́ть *impf*, отстри́чь (-игу́, -ижёшь; -ри́г) *pf* cut off.

отстро́ить *pf* (*impf* отстра́ивать) finish building; build up.

отступа́ть *impf*, отступи́ть (-плю́, -пишь) *pf* step back; recede; retreat; back down; ~ от+*gen* give up; deviate from; ~ся от+*gen* give up; go back on. отступле́ние retreat; deviation; digression. отступно́й: ~ые де́ньги, ~о́е *sb* indemnity, compensation. отступя́ *adv* (farther) off, away (от+*gen* from).

отсу́тствие absence; lack. отсу́тствовать *impf* be absent. отсу́тствующий absent; *sb* absentee.

отсчита́ть *pf*, отсчи́тывать *impf* count off.

отсыла́ть *impf of* отосла́ть отсы́пать (-плю) *pf*, отсыпа́ть *impf* pour out; measure off.

отсыпа́ться *impf of* отоспа́ться

отсыре́лый damp. от|сыре́ть (-ет) *pf*.

отсыха́ть *impf of* отсо́хнуть отсю́да *adv* from here; hence.

оття́гивать *impf of* оття́нуть отта́лкивать *impf of* оттолкну́ть. отта́лкивающий repulsive, repellent.

отта́чивать *impf of* отточи́ть оття́ять (-а́ю) *pf* (*impf* отта́ивать) thaw out.

отте́нок (-нка) shade, nuance; tint.

о́ттепель thaw.

оттесня́ть *impf*, оттесни́ть

impf drive back; push aside.

óттиск impression; off-print, reprint.

оттого́ *adv* that is why; ~, **что** because.

оттолкну́ть (-ну́, -нёшь) *pf* (*impf* **отта́лкивать**) push away; antagonize; ~**ся** push off.

оттопы́ренный protruding.
оттопы́ривать *impf*, **оттопы́рить** *pf* stick out; ~**ся** protrude; bulge.

отточи́ть (-чу́, -чишь) *pf* (*impf* **отта́чивать**) sharpen.

отту́да *adv* from there.

оття́гивать *impf*, **оттяну́ть** (-ну́, -нешь) *pf* draw out; draw off; delay. **оття́жка** *f* delay.

отупе́ние stupefaction. **о|тупе́ть** (-е́ю) *pf* sink into torpor.

от|утю́жить (-жу) *pf*.

отуча́ть *impf*, **отучи́ть** (-чу́, -чишь) *pf* break (of); ~**ся** break o.s. (of).

отха́ркать *pf*, **отха́ркивать** *impf* expectorate.

отхвати́ть (-чу́, -а́тишь) *pf*, **отхва́тывать** *impf* snip or chop off.

отхлебну́ть (-ну́, -нёшь) *pf*, **отхлёбывать** *impf* sip, take a sip of.

отхлы́нуть (-нет) *pf* flood or rush back.

отхо́д departure; withdrawal. **отходи́ть** (-ожу́, -о́дишь) *impf* of **отойти́. отхо́ды** (-ов) *pl* waste.

отцвести́ (-сту́, -стёшь; -ёл, -á) *pf*, **отцвета́ть** *impf* finish blossoming, fade.

отцепи́ть (-плю́, -пишь) *pf*, **отцепля́ть** *impf* unhook; uncouple.

отцо́вский father's; paternal.

отча́иваться *impf* of **отча́яться**

отча́ливать *impf*, **отча́лить** *pf* cast off.

отча́сти *adv* partly.

отча́яние despair. **отча́янный** desperate. **отча́яться** (-а́юсь) *pf* (*impf* **отча́иваться**) despair.

отчего́ *adv* why. **отчего́-либо, -нибудь** *adv* for some reason or other. **отчего́-то** *adv* for some reason.

от|чека́нить *pf*.

о́тчество patronymic.

отчёт account; **отда́ть себе́ ~ в+***prep* be aware of, realize. **отчётливый** distinct; clear. **отчётность** book-keeping; accounts. **отчётный** *adj*: **~ год** financial year, current year; **~ докла́д** report.

отчи́зна native land. **отчим** paternal. **о́тчим** step-father.

отчисле́ние deduction; dismissal. **отчи́слить** *pf*, **отчисля́ть** *impf* deduct; dismiss.

отчита́ть *pf*, **отчи́тывать** *impf*, tell off; ~**ся** report back.

отчужде́ние alienation; estrangement.

отшатну́ться (-ну́сь, -нёшься) *pf*, **отша́тываться** *impf* start back, recoil; **+от+***gen* give up forsake.

отшвы́ривать *impf*, **отшвырну́ть** (-ну́, -нёшь) *pf* fling away; throw off.

отше́льник hermit; recluse.

от|шлёпать *pf* spank.

от|шлифова́ть *pf*. **от|штукату́рить** (-рю) *pf*.

отщепе́нец (-нца) renegade.

отъе́зд departure. **отъезжа́ть** *impf*, **отъе́хать** (-е́ду) *pf* drive off, go off.

отъя́вленный inveterate.

отыгра́ть, **оты́грывать** *impf* win back; ~**ся** win back what one has lost.

отыска́ть (-ыщу́, -ы́щешь) pf, оты́скивать impf find; look for; ~ся turn up, appear.

отяготи́ть (-ощу́) pf, отягоща́ть impf burden.

офице́р officer. офице́рский officer's, officers'.

официа́льный official.

официа́нт waiter. официа́нтка waitress.

официо́з semi-official organ. официо́зный semi-official.

оформи́тель m designer; stage-painter. офо́рмить (-млю) pf, оформля́ть impf put into shape; make official; process; ~ся take shape; go through the formalities. оформле́ние design; mounting; staging; processing.

ох int oh! ah!

оха́пка armful.

охарактеризова́ть pf.

о́хать impf (pf о́хнуть) moan; sigh.

охва́т scope; inclusion; outflanking. охвати́ть (-ачу́, -а́тишь) pf, охва́тывать impf envelop; seize; comprehend.

охладева́ть impf, охладе́ть (-е́ю) pf grow cold. охлади́ть (-ажу́) pf, охлажда́ть impf cool; ~ся become cool, cool down. охлажде́ние cooling; coolness.

охмеле́ть (-е́ю) pf, о́хнуть (-ну) pf of о́хать

охо́та¹ hunt, hunting; chase. охо́та² wish, desire. охо́титься (-о́чусь) impf hunt. охо́тник¹ hunter.

охо́тник² volunteer; enthusiast. охо́тничий hunting.

охо́тно adv willingly, gladly.

о́хра ochre.

охра́на guarding; protection; guard. охрани́ть pf, охра-

ня́ть impf guard, protect.

охри́плый, охри́пший hoarse. охри́пнуть (-ну; охри́п) pf become hoarse.

оцара́пать(ся pf.

оцени́ть (-ню́, -нишь) pf estimate; appraise. оце́нка estimation; appraisal; estimate. оце́нщик valuer.

оцепене́ть (-е́ю) pf.

оцепи́ть (-плю́, -пишь) pf, оцепля́ть impf surround; cordon off.

оча́г (-а́) hearth; centre; breeding ground; hotbed.

очарова́ние charm, fascination. очарова́тельный charming. очарова́ть pf, очаро́вывать impf charm, fascinate.

очеви́дец (-дца) eye-witness. очеви́дно adv obviously, evidently. очеви́дный obvious.

о́чень adv very; very much.

очередно́й next in turn; usual, regular; routine. о́чередь (gen pl -е́й) turn; queue.

о́черк essay, sketch.

очерне́ть (-е́ю) pf.

очерстве́ть (-е́ю) pf.

очерта́ние outline(s), contour(s). очерти́ть (-рчу́, -ртишь) pf, оче́рчивать impf outline.

о́чи etc.: see о́ко

очисти́тельный cleansing. очи́стить (-и́щу) pf, очища́ть impf clean; refine; clear; peel; ~ся clear up; become clear (от+gen of). очи́стка cleaning; purification; clearance. очи́стки (-ов) pl peelings. очище́ние cleansing; purification.

очки́ (-о́в) pl spectacles. очко́ (gen pl -о́в) pip; point. очко́вая змея́ cobra.

очну́ться (-ну́сь, -нёшься) pf wake up; regain consciousness.

óчн|ый: ~ое обуче́ние classroom instruction; ~ая ста́вка confrontation.

очути́ться (-у́тишься) *pf* find o.s.

оше́йник collar.

ошеломи́тельный stunning. **ошеломи́ть** (-млю́) *pf*, **ошеломля́ть** *impf* stun.

ошиба́ться *impf*, **ошиби́ться** (-бу́сь, -бёшься -и́бся) be mistaken, make a mistake; be wrong. **оши́бка** *f* error. **оши́бочный** erroneous.

ошпа́ривать *impf*, **о**|**шпа́рить** *pf* scald.

о|**штрафова́ть** *pf*. **о**|**штукату́рить** *pf*.

ощети́ниваться *impf*, **о**|**щети́ниться** *pf* bristle (up).

о|**щипа́ть** (-плю́, -плешь) *pf*, **ощи́пывать** *impf* pluck.

ощу́пать *pf*, **ощу́пывать** *impf* feel; grope about. **о́щупь:** на ~ to the touch; by touch. **о́щупью** *adv* gropingly; by touch.

ощути́мый, ощути́тельный perceptible; appreciable. **ощути́ть** (-ущу́) *pf*, **ощуща́ть** *impf* feel, sense. **ощуще́ние** sensation; feeling.

П

па *neut indecl* dance step.

павильо́н pavilion; film studio.

павли́н peacock.

па́водок (-дка) (sudden) flood.

па́вший fallen.

па́губный pernicious, ruinous.

па́даль carrion.

па́дать *impf* (*pf* пасть, упа́сть) fall; ~ ду́хом lose heart. **паде́ж** (-á) case. **паде́ние** fall; degradation; incidence. **па́дкий** на+*acc or* до+*gen* hav-

ing a weakness for.

па́дчерица step-daughter.

паёк (пайка́) ration.

па́зуха bosom; sinus; axil.

пай (*pl* -и́, -ёв) share. **па́йщик** shareholder.

паке́т package; packet; paper bag.

Пакиста́н Pakistan. **пакиста́не|ц** (-нца), **-а́нка** Pakistani. **пакиста́нский** Pakistani.

па́кля tow; oakum.

пакова́ть *impf* (*pf* за~, у~) pack.

па́костный dirty, mean. **па́кость** dirty trick; obscenity.

пакт pact.

пала́та chamber, house. **пала́тка** tent; stall, booth.

пала́ч (-á) executioner.

па́лец (-льца) finger; toe.

палиса́дник (*small*) front garden.

палиса́ндр rosewood.

пали́тра palette.

пали́ть[1] *impf* (*pf* о~, с~) burn; scorch.

пали́ть[2] *impf* (*pf* вы́~, пальну́ть) fire, shoot.

па́лка stick; walking-stick.

пало́мник pilgrim. **пало́мничество** pilgrimage.

па́лочка stick; bacillus; wand; baton.

па́луба deck.

пальба́ fire.

па́льма palm(-tree). **па́льмовый** palm.

пальну́ть (-ну́, -нёшь) *pf of* пали́ть

пальто́ *neut indecl* (over)coat.

паля́щий burning, scorching.

па́мятник monument; memorial. **па́мятный** memorable; memorial. **па́мять** memory; consciousness; на ~ as a keepsake.

панацея panacea.

панель footpath; panel(ling); wainscot(ing). **панельный** panelling.

паника panic. **паникёр** alarmist.

панихида requiem.

панический panic; panicky.

панно *neut indecl* panel.

панорама panorama.

пансион boarding-house; board and lodging. **пансионат** holiday hotel. **пансионер** boarder, guest.

панталоны (-он) *pl* knickers.

пантера panther.

пантомима mime.

панцирь *m* armour, coat of mail.

папа¹ *m* pope.

папа² *m*, **папаша** *m* daddy.

папаха tall fur cap.

папироса (*Russian*) cigarette.

папка file; folder.

папоротник fern.

пар¹ (*loc* -ý, *pl* -ы́) steam.

пар² (*loc* -ý, *pl* -ы́) fallow.

пара pair; couple; (two-piece) suit.

параграф paragraph.

парад parade; review. **парадный** parade; gala; main, front; **~ая форма** full dress (uniform).

парадокс paradox. **парадоксальный** paradoxical.

паразит parasite.

парализовать *impf & pf* paralyse. **паралич** (-á) paralysis.

параллель parallel. **параллельный** parallel.

параметр parameter.

паранойя paranoia.

парашют parachute.

парение soaring.

парень (-рня; *gen pl* -рней) *m* lad; fellow.

пари *neut indecl* bet; **держать**

~ bet, lay a bet.

парик (-á) wig. **парикмахер** hairdresser. **парикмахерская** *sb* hairdresser's.

парировать *impf & pf* (*pf also* от~) parry, counter.

паритет parity.

парить¹ *impf* soar, hover.

парить² *impf* steam; stew; *impers* **парит** it is sultry; **~ся** (*pf* по~ся) steam, sweat, stew.

парк park; depot; stock.

паркет parquet.

парламент parliament. **парламентарий** parliamentarian. **парламентёр** envoy; bearer of flag of truce. **парламентский** parliamentary; **~ закон** Act of Parliament.

парник (-á) hotbed; seed-bed. **парниковый** *adj*: **~ые растения** hothouse plants.

парнишка *m* boy, lad.

парной fresh; steamy.

парный (forming a pair); twin.

паро- *in comb* steam-. **паровоз** (steam-)engine, locomotive. **~образный** vaporous. **~ход** steamer; steamship. **~ходство** steamship-line.

паровой steam; steamed.

пародия parody.

пароль *m* password.

паром ferry(-boat).

парт- *abbr in comb* Party. **партбилет** Party (membership) card. **~ком** Party committee. **~организация** Party organization.

парта (*school*) desk.

партер stalls; pit.

партизан (*gen pl* -áн) partisan; guerilla. **партизанский** partisan, guerilla; unplanned.

партийный party; Party; *sb* Party member.

партиту́ра (*mus*) score.

па́ртия party; group; batch; game, set; part.

партнёр partner.

па́рус (*pl* -á, -óв) sail. **паруси́на** canvas. **па́русник** sailing vessel. **па́русный** sail; ~ спорт sailing.

парфюме́рия perfumes.

парча́ (*gen pl* -е́й) brocade. **парчо́вый** brocade.

па́сека apiary, beehive.

пасётся *see* пасти́сь

па́сквиль *m* lampoon; libel.

па́смурный overcast; gloomy.

па́спорт (*pl* -á) passport.

пасса́ж passage; arcade.

пассажи́р passenger.

пасси́вный passive.

па́ста paste.

па́стбище pasture.

па́ства flock.

пасте́ль pastel.

пастерна́к parsnip.

пасти́ (-су́, -сёшь; пас, -ла́) *impf* graze; tend.

пасти́сь (-сётся; па́сся, -ла́сь) *impf* graze. **пасту́х** (-á) shepherd. **па́стырь** *m* pastor.

пасть¹ mouth; jaws.

пасть² (паду́, -дёшь; пал) *pf of* па́дать

Па́сха Easter; Passover.

па́сынок (-нка) stepson, stepchild.

пат stalemate.

пате́нт patent.

патети́ческий passionate.

пато́ка treacle; syrup.

патоло́гия pathology.

патриа́рх patriarch.

патрио́т patriot. **патриоти́зм** patriotism. **патриоти́ческий** patriotic.

патро́н cartridge; chuck; lamp-socket.

патру́ль (-я́) *m* patrol.

па́уза pause; (*also mus*) rest.

пау́к (-á) spider. **паути́на** cobweb; gossamer; web.

па́фос zeal, enthusiasm.

пах (*loc* -ý) groin.

па́харь *m* ploughman. **паха́ть** (пашу́, па́шешь) *impf* (*pf* вс~) plough.

па́хнуть¹ (-ну; пах) *impf* smell (+*instr*).

пахну́ть² (-нёт) *pf* puff, blow.

па́хота ploughing. **па́хотный** arable.

паху́чий odorous, strong-smelling.

пацие́нт, ~ка patient.

пацифи́зм pacificism. **пацифи́ст** pacifist.

па́чка bundle; packet, pack; tutu.

па́чкать *impf* (*pf* за~, ис~) dirty, soil, stain.

пашу́ *etc.*: *see* паха́ть. **па́шня** (*gen pl* -шен) ploughed field.

паште́т pâté.

пая́льная ла́мпа blow-lamp. **пая́льник** soldering iron. **пая́ть** (-я́ю) *impf* solder.

пая́ц clown, buffoon.

певе́ц (-вца́) **певи́ца** singer. **певу́чий** melodious. **пе́вчий** singing; *sb* chorister.

пе́гий piebald.

педаго́г teacher; pedagogue. **педаго́гика** pedagogy. **педагоги́ческий** pedagogical; educational; ~ институ́т (teachers') training college.

педа́ль pedal.

педиа́тр paediatrician. **педиатри́ческий** paediatric.

пейза́ж landscape; scenery.

пёк *see* печь. **пека́рный** baking. **пека́рня** (*gen pl* -рен) bakery. **пе́карь** (*pl* -я, -е́й) *m* baker. **пе́кло** scorching heat; hell-fire. **пеку́** *etc.*: *see* печь

пелена́ (*gen pl* -лён) shroud. **пелена́ть** *impf* (*pf* за~) swaddle; put a nappy on.

пе́ленг bearing. **пеленгова́ть** *impf & pf* take the bearings of.

пелёнка nappy.

пельме́нь *m* meat dumpling.

пе́на foam; scum; froth.

пена́л pencil-case.

пе́ние singing.

пе́нистый foamy; frothy. **пе́ниться** *impf* (*pf* вс~) foam.

пе́нка skin. **пенопла́ст** plastic foam.

пеницилли́н penicillin.

пенсионе́р, пенсионе́рка pensioner. **пенсио́нный** pensionable. **пе́нсия** pension.

пень (пня) *m* stump, stub.

пенька́ hemp.

пе́пел (-пла) ash, ashes. **пе́пельница** ashtray.

перве́йший the first; first-class. **пе́рвенец** (-нца) first-born. **пе́рвенство** first place; championship. **пе́рвенствовать** *impf* take first place; take priority. **перви́чный** primary.

перво- *in comb* first; prime. **первобы́тный** primitive; primeval. **~исто́чник** source; origin. **~кла́ссный** first-class. **~ку́рсник** first-year student. **~нача́льный** original; primary. **~со́ртный** best-quality; first-class. **~сте́пенный** paramount.

пе́рвое *sb* first course. **пе́рвый** first; former.

перга́мент parchment.

перебега́ть *impf*, **перебежа́ть** (-бегу́) *pf* cross, run across; desert. **перебе́жчик** deserter; turncoat.

переберу́ *etc.*: *see* **перебра́ть**

перебива́ть(ся *impf of* **переби́ть(ся**

перебира́ть(ся *impf of* **перебра́ть(ся**

переби́ть (-бью́, -бьёшь) *pf* (*impf* **перебива́ть**) interrupt; slaughter; beat; break; re-upholster; **~ся** break; make ends meet. **перебо́й** interruption; stoppage; irregularity.

переборо́ть sorting out; partition; bulkhead.

переборо́ть (-рю́, -решь) *pf* overcome.

переборщи́ть (-щу́) *pf* go too far; overdo it.

перебра́сывать(ся *impf of* **переброси́ть(ся**

перебра́ть (-беру́, -берёшь; -а́л, -а́, -о) *pf* (*impf* **перебира́ть**) sort out; look through; turn over in one's mind; finger; **~ся** get over, cross; move.

переброси́ть (-о́шу) *pf* (*impf* **перебра́сывать**) throw over; transfer; **~ся** fling o.s.; spread. **перебро́ска** transfer.

перебью́ *etc.*: *see* **переби́ть**

перева́л crossing; pass. **перева́ливать** *impf*, **перевали́ть** (-лю́, -лишь) *pf* transfer, shift; cross; pass.

перева́ривать *impf*, **перевари́ть** (-рю́, -ришь) *pf* reheat; overcook; digest; tolerate.

переведу́ *etc.*: *see* **перевести́**

перевезти́ (-зу́, -зёшь; -вёз, -ла́) *pf* (*impf* **перевози́ть**) take across; transport; (re)move.

переверну́ть (-ну́, -нёшь) *pf*, **перевёртывать** *impf* (*impf also* **перевора́чивать**) turn (over); upset; turn inside out; **~ся** turn (over).

переве́с preponderance; advantage. **переве́сить** (-е́шу) *pf* (*impf* **переве́шивать**) re-weigh; outweigh; tip the scales; hang elsewhere.

перевести́ (-веду́, -веде́шь; -ве́л, -а́) *pf* (*impf* **переводи́ть**) take across; lead, move, shift; translate; convert; ~сь be transferred; run out; become extinct.

переве́шивать *impf of* **переве́сить. перевира́ть** *impf of* **перевра́ть**

перево́д transfer, move, shift; translation; conversion; waste. **переводи́ть(ся** (-ожу́(сь, -о́дишь(ся) *impf of* **перевести́(сь. переводно́й** (*adj*): ~**áя бума́га** carbon paper; ~**áя карти́нка** transfer. **перево́дный** transfer; translated. **перево́дчик**, ~**ица** translator; interpreter.

перево́з transporting, ferry. **перевози́ть** (-ожу́, -о́зишь) *impf of* **перевезти́. перево́зка** conveyance. **перево́зчик** ferryman; removal man.

перевооружа́ть *impf*, **перевооружи́ть** (-жу́) *pf* rearm; ~**ся** rearm. **перевооруже́ние** rearmament.

перевоплоти́ть (-ощу́) *pf*, **перевоплоща́ть** *impf* reincarnate; ~**ся** be reincarnated. **перевоплоще́ние** reincarnation.

перевора́чивать(ся *impf of* **перевернуть(ся. переворо́т** revolution; overturn; cataclysm; **госуда́рственный** ~ coup d'état.

перевоспита́ние re-education. **перевоспита́ть** *pf*, **перевоспи́тывать** *impf* re-educate.

перевра́ть (-ру́, -рёшь; -а́л,

-á, -о) *pf* (*impf* **перевира́ть**) garble; misquote.

перевыполне́ние over fulfilment. **перевы́полнить** *pf*, **перевыполня́ть** *imp* over-fulfil.

перевяза́ть (-яжу́, -я́жешь) *p* **перевя́зывать** *impf* band age; tie up; re-tie. **перевя́зк** dressing, bandage.

переги́б bend; excess, ex treme. **перегиба́ть(ся** *imp of* **перегну́ть(ся**

перегля́дываться *impf* **перегляну́ться** (-ну́сь, -неш ся) *pf* exchange glances.

перегна́ть (-гоню́, -го́нишь; -á -á, -о) *pf* (*impf* **перегоня́ть**) outdistance; surpass; drive distil.

перегно́й humus.

перегну́ть (-ну́, -нёшь) *pf* (*impf* **перегиба́ть**) bend; ~ **па́лку** go too far; ~**ся** bend; lea over.

перегова́ривать *impf*, **пере говори́ть** *pf* talk; out-talk ~**ся** (c+*instr*) exchange re marks (with). **перегово́ры** (-ов) *pl* negotiations, parley **перегово́рный** *adj*: ~ **пунк** public call-boxes; trunk-call of fice.

перего́н driving; stage. **пере го́нка** distillation. **перего́н ный** distilling, distillation **перегоню́** *etc.*: *see* **перегна́ть перегоня́ть** *impf of* **пере гна́ть**

перегора́живать *impf o* **перегороди́ть**

перегора́ть *impf*, **перего ре́ть** (-ри́т) *pf* burn out, fuse **перегороди́ть** (-рожу́, -ро́дишь) *pf* (*impf* **перегора́живать**) partition off; block. **перего ро́дка** partition.

перегрев overheating. **перегревать** *impf*, **перегреть** (-éю) *pf* overheat; **~ся** overheat.

перегружать *impf*, **перегрузить** (-ужу, -узишь) *pf* overload; transfer. **перегрузка** overload; transfer.

перегрызать *impf*, **перегрызть** (-зу, -зёшь; -грыз) *pf* gnaw through.

перед, **передо**, **пред**, **предо** *prep+instr* before; in front of; compared to. **перёд** (перёда; *pl* -á) front, forepart.

передавать (-даю, -даёшь) *impf*, **передать** (-ám, -áшь, -áст, -адим; передал, -á, -о) *pf* pass, hand, hand over; transfer; hand down; make over; tell; communicate; convey; give too much; **~ся** pass; be transmitted; be communicated; be inherited. **передатчик** transmitter. **передача** passing; transmission; communication; transfer; broadcast; drive; gear, gearing.

передвигать *impf*, **передвинуть** (-ну) *pf* move, shift; **~ся** move, shift. **передвижение** movement; transportation. **передвижка** movement; *in comb* travelling; itinerant. **передвижной** movable, mobile.

переделать *pf*, **переделывать** *impf* alter; refashion. **переделка** alteration.

передёргивать(ся *impf of* **передёрнуть(ся**

передержать (-жу, -жишь) *pf*, **передерживать** *impf* overdo; overcook; overexpose.

передёрнуть (-ну) *pf* (*impf* **передёргивать**) pull aside or across; cheat; distort;

~ся wince.

передний front; **~ план** foreground. **передник** apron. **передняя** *sb* (entrance) hall, lobby. **передо**: *see* **перед**. **передовик** *pl* exemplary worker. **передовица** leading article. **передовой** advanced; foremost; leading.

передохнуть (-ну, -нёшь) *pf* pause for breath.

передразнивать *impf*, **передразнить** (-ню, -нишь) *pf* mimic.

передумать *pf*, **передумывать** *impf* change one's mind.

передышка respite.

переезд crossing; move. **переезжать** *impf*, **переехать** (-éду) *pf* cross; run over, knock down; move (house).

пережаривать *impf*, **пережарить** *pf* overdo, overcook.

пережидать (-жду, -ждёшь; -ал, -á, -о) *pf* (*impf* **пережидать**) wait for the end of.

пережёвывать *impf* chew; repeat over and over again.

переживание experience. **переживать** *impf of* **пережить**

пережидать *impf of* **переждать**

пережитое *sb* the past. **пережиток** (-тка) survival; vestige. **пережить** (-иву, -ивёшь; пережил, -á, -о) *pf* (*impf* **переживать**) experience; go through; endure; outlive.

перезарядить (-яжу, -ядишь) *pf*, **перезаряжать** *impf* recharge, reload.

перезванивать *impf*, **перезвонить** *pf+dat* ring back.

перезимовать *pf*

перезрелый overripe.

переиграть *pf*, **переигры-**

вать *impf* play again; overact.

переизбира́ть *impf*, **переизбра́ть** (-беру́, -берёшь; -бра́л, -а́, -о) *pf* re-elect. **переизбра́ние** re-election.

переиздава́ть (-даю́, -даёшь) *impf*, **переизда́ть** (-а́м, -а́шь, -а́ст, -ади́м; -а́л, -а́, -о) *pf* republish, reprint. **переизда́ние** republication; new edition.

переименова́ть *pf*, **переимено́вывать** *impf* rename.

перейму́ *etc.: see* **переня́ть**

перейти́ (-йду́, -йдёшь; перешёл, -шла́) *pf* (*impf* **переходи́ть**) cross; pass; turn (**в**+*acc* to, into).

перекантова́ть *pf* transfer (*a load*).

перека́пывать *impf of* **перекопа́ть**

перекати́ть (-чу́, -тишь) *pf*, **перека́тывать** *impf* roll; ~**ся** roll.

перекача́ть *pf*, **перека́чивать** *impf* pump (across).

переквалифици́роваться *impf & pf* retrain.

переки́дывать *impf*, **переки́нуть** (-ну) *pf* throw over; ~**ся** leap.

переки́сь peroxide.

перекла́дина cross-beam; joist; horizontal bar.

перекла́дывать *impf of* **переложи́ть**

перекли́чка roll-call.

переключа́тель *m* switch. **переключа́ть** *impf*, **переключи́ть** (-чу́) *pf* switch (over); ~**ся** switch (over).

перекова́ть (-кую́, -куёшь) *pf*, **переко́вывать** *impf* re-shoe; re-forge.

перекопа́ть *pf* (*impf* **перека́пывать**) dig (all of); dig again.

перекоси́ть (-ошу́, -о́сишь) *pf* warp; distort; ~**ся** warp; become distorted.

перекочева́ть (-чу́ю) *pf*, **перекочёвывать** *impf* migrate.

переко́шенный distorted, twisted.

перекра́ивать *impf of* **перекро́ить**

перекра́сить (-а́шу) *pf*, **перекра́шивать** *impf* (re-)paint; (re-)dye; ~**ся** change colour; turn one's coat.

пере|крести́ть (-ещу́, -е́стишь) *pf*, **перекре́щивать** *impf* cross; ~**ся** cross, intersect; cross o.s. **перекре́стный** cross; ~**ый допро́с** crossexamination; ~**ый ого́нь** cross-fire; ~**ая ссы́лка** crossreference. **перекрёсток** (-тка) cross-roads, crossing.

перекри́кивать *impf*, **перекрича́ть** (-чу́) *pf* shout down.

перекро́ить (-ою́) *pf* (*impf* **перекра́ивать**) cut out again; reshape.

перекрыва́ть *impf*, **перекры́ть** (-ро́ю) *pf* re-cover; exceed. **перекры́тие** ceiling.

перекую́ *etc.: see* **перекова́ть**

перекупа́ть *impf*, **перекупи́ть** (-плю́, -пишь) *pf* buy by outbidding s.o. **переку́пщик** second-hand dealer

перекуси́ть (-ушу́, -у́сишь) *pf*, **переку́сывать** *impf* bite through; have a snack.

перелага́ть *impf of* **переложи́ть**

перела́мывать *impf of* **переломи́ть**

перелеза́ть *impf*, **переле́зть** (-зу; -ез) *pf* climb over.

переле́сок (-ска) copse.

перелёт migration; flight

перелета́ть *impf*, переле-те́ть (-лечу́) *pf* fly over. перелётный migratory.

перелива́ние decanting; transfusion. перелива́ть *impf* of перели́ть. перелива́ться *impf* of перели́ться; gleam; modulate.

перелиста́ть *pf*, перели́стывать *impf* leaf through.

перели́ть (-лью́, -льёшь; -и́л, -а́, -о) *pf* (*impf* перелива́ть) pour; decant; let overflow; transfuse. перели́ться (-льётся; -и́лся, -ила́сь, -ило́сь) *pf* (*impf* перелива́ться) flow; overflow.

перелицева́ть (-цу́ю) *pf*, перелицо́вывать *impf* turn; have turned.

переложе́ние arrangement. переложи́ть (-жу́, -жишь) *pf* (*impf* перекла́дывать, перелага́ть) put elsewhere; shift; transfer; interlay; put in too much; set; arrange; transpose.

перело́м breaking; fracture; turning-point, crisis; sudden change. перелома́ть *pf* break; ~ся break, be broken. переломи́ть (-млю́, -мишь) *pf* (*impf* перела́мывать) break in two; master. перело́мный critical.

перелью́ *etc.*: see перели́ть

перема́нивать *impf*, перемани́ть (-ню́, -нишь) *pf* win over; entice.

перемежа́ться *impf* alternate.

переме́на change; break. перемени́ть (-ню́, -нишь) *pf*, переменя́ть *impf* change; ~ся change. переме́нный variable; ~ ток alternating current. переме́нчивый change-

переме́стить (-ещу́) *pf* (*impf* переме́щать) move; transfer; ~ся move.

переме́шать *pf*, переме́шивать *impf* mix; mix up; shuffle; ~ся get mixed (up).

перемеща́ть(ся *impf* of переме́стить(ся. переме́щение transference; displacement. переме́щенный displaced; ~ые ли́ца displaced persons.

переми́рие armistice, truce.

перемыва́ть *impf*, перемы́ть (-мо́ю) *pf* wash (up) again.

перенапряга́ть *impf*, перенапря́чь (-ягу́, -яжёшь: -я́г, -ла́) *pf* overstrain.

переселе́ние overpopulation. переселённый (-лён, -а́) overpopulated; overcrowded.

перенести́ (-су́, -сёшь; -нёс, -ла́) *pf* (*impf* переноси́ть) carry, move, take; transfer; take over; postpone; endure, bear; ~сь be carried; be carried away.

перенима́ть *impf* of переня́ть

перено́с transfer; word division; знак ~а end-of-line hyphen. перено́симый endurable. переноси́ть(ся (-ошу́(сь, -о́сишь(ся) *impf* of перенести́(сь

перено́сица bridge (*of the nose*).

перено́ска carrying over; transporting; carriage. перено́сный portable; figurative. перено́счик carrier.

пере|ночева́ть (-чу́ю) *pf*. переношу́ *etc.*: see переноси́ть

переня́ть (-ейму́, -еймёшь; пе́реня́л, -а́, -о) *pf* (*impf* перенима́ть) imitate; adopt.

переоборудовать *impf & pf* re-equip.

переобуваться *impf*, **переобуться** (-уюсь, -уёшься) *pf* change one's shoes.

переодеваться *impf*, **переодеться** (-енусь) *pf* change (one's clothes).

переосвидетельствовать *impf & pf* re-examine.

переоценивать *impf*, **переоценить** (-ню, -нишь) *pf* overestimate; revalue. **переоценка** overestimation; revaluation.

перепачкать *pf* make dirty; **~ся** get dirty.

перепел (*pl* -á) quail.

перепеленать *pf* change (a baby).

перепечатать *pf*, **перепечатывать** *impf* reprint. **перепечатка** reprint.

перепиливать *impf*, **перепилить** (-лю, -лишь) *pf* saw in two.

переписать (-ишу, -ишешь) *pf*, **переписывать** *impf* copy; rewrite; make a list of. **переписка** copying; correspondence. **переписываться** *impf* correspond. **перепись** census.

переплавить (-влю) *pf*, **переплавлять** *impf* smelt.

переплатить (-ачу, -атишь) *pf*, **переплачивать** *impf* overpay.

переплести (-лету, -летёшь; -лёл, -á) *pf*, **переплетать** *impf* bind; interlace, intertwine; re-plait; **~ся** interlace, interweave; get mixed up. **переплёт** binding. **переплётчик** bookbinder.

переплывать *impf*, **переплыть** (-ыву, -ывёшь; -ыл, -á, -о) *pf* swim *or* sail across.

переподготовка further training; refresher course.

переползать *impf*, **переползти** (-зу, -зёшь; -олз, -олзла) *pf* crawl *or* creep across.

переполнение overfilling; overcrowding. **переполненный** overcrowded; too full. **переполнить** *pf*, **переполнять** *impf* overfill; overcrowd.

переполох commotion.

перепонка membrane; web.

переправа crossing; ford.

переправить (-влю) *pf*, **переправлять** *impf* convey; take across; forward; **~ся** cross, get across.

перепродавать (-даю, -даёшь) *impf*, **перепродать** (-ám, -áшь, -áст, -адим; -продал, -á, -о) *pf* re-sell. **перепродажа** re-sale.

перепроизводство overproduction.

перепрыгивать *impf*, **перепрыгнуть** (-ну) *pf* jump (over).

перепугать *pf* frighten, scare; **~ся** get a fright.

перепутать *pf*, **перепутывать** *impf* tangle; confuse, mix up.

перепутье cross-roads.

перерабатывать *impf*, **переработать** *pf* convert; treat; re-make; re-cast; process; work overtime; overwork; **~ся** overwork. **переработка** processing; reworking; overtime work.

перераспределение redistribution. **перераспределить** *pf*, **перераспределять** *impf* redistribute.

перерастание outgrowing; escalation; development (into). **перерастать** *impf*, **пере-**

расти́ (-ту́, -тёшь; -ро́с, -ла́) pf outgrow; develop.

перерасхо́д over-expenditure; overdraft. перерасхо́довать impf & pf expend too much of.

перерасчёт recalculation.

перерва́ть (-ву́, -вёшь; -а́л, -а́, -о) pf (impf перерыва́ть) break, tear asunder; ~ся break, come apart.

перере́зать (-е́жу) pf, перере́зать impf, переро́зывать impf cut off; kill.

перероди́ть (-ожу́) pf, перерожда́ть impf regenerate; ~ся be reborn; be regenerated; degenerate. перерожде́ние regeneration; degeneration.

перерос etc.: see перерасти́.

перерою etc.: see перерыть.

переруба́ть impf, переруби́ть (-блю́, -бишь) pf chop in two.

перерыв break; interruption; interval.

перерыва́ть[1](ся impf of перерва́ть(ся

перерыва́ть[2] impf, перерыть (-ро́ю) pf dig up; rummage through.

пересади́ть (-ажу́, -а́дишь) pf, переса́живать impf transplant; graft; seat somewhere else. переса́дка transplantation; grafting; change.

переса́живаться impf of пересе́сть. переса́ливать impf of пересоли́ть

пересдава́ть (-даю́сь) impf, пересда́ть (-а́м, -а́шь, -а́ст, -адим; -да́л, -а́, -о) pf sublet; re-sit.

пересека́ть(ся impf of пересе́чь(ся

переселе́нец (-нца) settler;

immigrant. переселе́ние migration; immigration; resettlement; moving. переселя́ть pf, переселя́ть impf move; ~ся move; migrate.

пересе́сть (-ся́ду) pf (impf переса́живаться) change one's seat; change (trains etc.).

пересече́ние crossing, intersection. пересе́чь (-секу́, -сечёшь; -сёк, -ла́) pf (impf пересека́ть) cross; intersect; ~ся cross, intersect.

переси́ливать impf, переси́лить pf overpower.

переска́з (re)telling; exposition. пересказа́ть (-ажу́, -а́жешь) pf, переска́зывать impf retell.

переска́кивать impf, перескочи́ть (-чу́, -чишь) pf jump or skip (over).

пересла́ть (-ешлю́, -шлёшь) pf (impf пересыла́ть) send; forward.

пересма́тривать impf, пересмотре́ть (-трю́, -тришь) pf look over; reconsider. пересмо́тр revision; reconsideration; review.

пересоли́ть (-олю́, -о́лишь) pf (impf переса́ливать) oversalt; overdo it.

пересо́хнуть (-нет; -о́х) pf (impf пересыха́ть) dry up, become parched.

переспа́ть (-плю́; -а́л, -а́, -о) pf oversleep; spend the night. переспе́лый overripe.

переспра́шивать impf, переспроси́ть (-ошу́, -о́сишь) pf ask again.

перестава́ть (-таю́, -таёшь) impf of переста́ть

переста́вить (-влю) pf, переставля́ть impf move; rearrange; transpose. переста-

новка rearrangement; transposition.

перестать (-а́ну) *pf* (*impf* **переставать**) stop, cease.

перестрада́ть *pf* have suffered.

перестра́ивать(ся *impf of* **перестро́ить(ся**

перестрахо́вка re-insurance; overcautiousness.

перестре́лка exchange of fire. **перестреля́ть** *pf* shoot (down).

перестро́ить *pf* (*impf* **перестра́ивать**) rebuild; reorganize; retune; re-form; reorganize o.s.; switch over (**на**+*acc* to). **перестро́йка** reconstruction; reorganization; retuning; perestroika.

переступа́ть *impf*, **переступи́ть** (-плю́, -пишь) *pf* step over; cross; overstep.

пересчита́ть *pf*, **пересчи́тывать** *impf* (*pf also* **пересче́сть**) re-count; count.

пересыла́ть *impf of* **пересла́ть**. **пересы́лка** sending, forwarding.

пересыпа́ть *impf*, **пересы́пать** (-плю, -плешь) *pf* pour; sprinkle; pour too much.

пересыха́ть *impf of* **пересо́хнуть**. **перея́ду** *etc.: see* **пересе́сть**. **перета́пливать** *impf of* **перетопи́ть**

перета́скивать *impf*, **перетащи́ть** (-щу́, -щишь) *pf* drag (over, through); move.

перетере́ть (-тру́, -трёшь; -тёр) *pf*, **перетира́ть** *impf* wear out, wear down; grind; wipe; **~ся** wear out or through.

перетопи́ть (-плю́, -пишь) *pf* (*impf* **перета́пливать**) melt. **перетру́** *etc.: see* **перетере́ть**. **перете́ть** (пру, прёшь; пёр, -ла)

impf go; make or force one's way; haul; come out.

перетя́гивать *impf*, **перетяну́ть** (-ну́, -нешь) *pf* pull, draw; win over; outweigh.

переубеди́ть *pf*, **переубежда́ть** *impf* make change one's mind.

переу́лок (-лка) side street, alley, lane.

переустро́йство reconstruction, reorganization.

переутоми́ть (-млю́) *pf*, **переутомля́ть** *impf* overtire; **~ся** overtire o.s. **переутомле́ние** overwork.

переучёт stock-taking.

переу́чивать *impf*, **переучи́ть** (-чу́, -чишь) *pf* teach again.

перефрази́ровать *impf & pf* paraphrase.

перехвати́ть (-ачу́, -а́тишь) *pf*, **перехва́тывать** *impf* intercept; snatch a bite (of); borrow.

перехитри́ть *pf* outwit.

перехо́д transition; crossing; conversion. **переходи́ть** (-ожу́, -о́дишь) *impf of* **перейти́**. **перехо́дный** transitional; transitive. **переходя́щий** transient; intermittent; brought forward.

пе́рец (-рца) pepper.

перече́нь *etc.: see* **пересче́сть**. **пе́речень** (-чня) *m* list, enumeration.

перечёркивать *impf*, **перечеркну́ть** (-ну́, -нёшь) *pf* cross out, cancel.

перече́сть (-чту́, -чтёшь; -чёл, -чла́) *pf: see* **пересчита́ть**, **перечита́ть**

перечисле́ние enumeration; transfer. **перечи́слить** *pf*, **перечисля́ть** *impf* enumerate; transfer.

перечита́ть pf, **перечи́тывать** impf (pf also **перече́сть**) re-read.

пере́чить (-чу) impf contradict; cross, go against.

пе́речница pepper-pot.

перечту́ etc.: see **перече́сть**.

перечу́ etc.: see **пере́чить**.

переша́гивать impf, **перешагну́ть** (-ну́, -нёшь) pf step over.

переше́ек (-е́йка) isthmus; neck.

перешёл etc.: see **перейти́**

переши́вать impf, **переши́ть** (-шью, -шьёшь) pf alter; have altered.

перешлю́ etc.: see **пересла́ть**

переэкзамено́вывать pf, **переэкзамено́вывать** impf re-examine; ~ся retake an exam.

пери́ла (-и́л) pl railing(s); banisters.

пери́на feather-bed.

пери́од period. **перио́дика** periodicals. **периоди́ческий** periodical; recurring.

пери́стый feathery; cirrus.

перифери́я periphery.

перламу́тр mother-of-pearl. **перламу́тровый** mother-of-pearl. **перло́в|ый**: ~ая крупа́ pearl barley.

перма́не́нт perm. **перманентный** permanent.

перна́тый feathered. **перна́тые** sb pl birds. **перо́** (pl **пе́рья**, -ьев) feather; pen. **перо́чинный нож, но́жик** penknife.

перпендикуля́рный perpendicular.

перро́н platform.

перс Persian. **перси́дский** Persian.

пе́рсик peach.

персия́нка Persian woman.

персо́на person; со́бственной персо́ной in person. **персона́ж** character; personage. **персона́л** personnel, staff. **персона́льный** personal.

перспекти́ва perspective; vista; prospect. **перспекти́вный** perspective; long-term; promising.

пе́рстень (-тня) m ring.

перфока́рта punched card.

пе́рхоть dandruff.

перча́тка glove.

пе́рчить (-чу) impf (pf по~) pepper.

пёс (пса) dog.

пе́сенник song-book; (choral) singer; song-writer. **пе́сенный** song; of songs.

песе́ц (-сца́) (polar) fox.

песнь (gen pl -ей) song; canto. **пе́сня** (gen pl -сен) song.

песо́к (-ска́) sand. **песо́чный** sand; sandy.

пессими́зм pessimism. **пессими́ст** pessimist. **пессимисти́ческий** pessimistic.

пестрота́ diversity of colours; diversity. **пёстрый** variegated; diverse; colourful.

песча́ник sandstone. **песча́ный** sandy. **песчи́нка** grain of sand.

петербу́ргский (of) St Petersburg.

пети́ция petition.

петли́ца buttonhole; tab. **пе́тля** (gen pl -тель) loop; noose; stitch; hinge.

петру́шка¹ parsley.

петру́шка² m Punch; f Punch-and-Judy show.

пету́х (-а́) cock. **петушо́к** (-шка́) cockerel.

петь (пою́, поёшь) impf (pf про~, с~) sing.

пехо́та infantry, foot. **пехоти́нец** (-нца) infantryman. **пехо́тный** infantry.

печа́лить *impf* (*pf* o~) sadden; ~ся grieve, be sad. **печа́ль** sorrow. **печа́льный** sad.

печа́тать *impf* (*pf* на~, от~) print; ~ся write, be published; be at the printer's. **печа́тн|ый** printing; printer's; printed; ~ые бу́квы block capitals; ~ый стано́к printing-press. **печа́ть** seal, stamp; print; printing; press.

пече́ние baking.

печёнка liver.

печёный baked.

пе́чень liver.

пече́нье pastry; biscuit. **пе́чка** stove. **печно́й** stove; oven; kiln. **печь** (*loc* -и́, *gen pl* -е́й) stove; oven; kiln. **печь** (пеку́, -чёшь; пёк, -ла́) *impf* (*pf* ис~) bake; ~ся bake.

пешехо́д pedestrian. **пешехо́дный** pedestrian; foot-. **пе́ший** pedestrian; foot. **пе́шка** pawn. **пешко́м** *adv* on foot. ~ челове́к cave-dweller.

пеще́ра cave. **пеще́рный** cave;

пиани́но *neut indecl* (upright) piano. **пиани́ст**, ~ка pianist.

пивна́я *sb* pub. **пивно́й** beer. **пи́во** beer. **пивова́р** brewer.

пигме́й pygmy.

пиджа́к (-а́) jacket.

пижа́ма pyjamas.

пижо́н dandy.

пик peak; часы́ пик rush-hour.

пи́ка lance.

пика́нтный piquant; spicy.

пика́п pick-up (van).

пике́ *neut indecl* dive.

пике́т picket. **пике́тчик** picket.

пи́ки (пик) *pl* (*cards*) spades.

пики́ровать *impf* & *pf* (*pf also* с~) dive.

пики́ровщик, пики́рующий бомбардиро́вщик dive-bomber.

пикни́к (-а́) picnic.

пи́кнуть (-ну) *pf* squeak; make a sound.

пи́ковый of spades.

пила́ (*pl* -ы) saw; nagger. **пилёный** sawed, sawn. **пили́ть** (-лю́, -лишь) *impf* saw; nag (at). **пи́лка** sawing; fret-saw; nail-file.

пило́т pilot.

пило́тка forage-cap.

пилоти́ровать *impf* pilot.

пилю́ля pill.

пина́ть *impf* (*pf* пнуть) kick. **пино́к** (-нка́) kick.

пингви́н penguin.

пинце́т tweezers.

пио́н peony.

пионе́р pioneer. **пионе́рский** pioneer.

пипе́тка pipette.

пир (*loc* -у́; *pl* -ы́) feast, banquet. **пирова́ть** *impf* feast.

пирами́да pyramid.

пира́т pirate.

пиро́г (-а́) pie. **пиро́жное** *sb* cake, pastry. **пирожо́к** (-жка́) pasty.

пирс pier.

пируэ́т pirouette.

пи́ршество feast; celebration.

пи́саный handwritten. **пи́сарь** (*pl* -я́) *m* clerk. **писа́тель** *m*, **писа́тельница** writer, author. **писа́ть** (пишу́, пи́шешь) *impf* (*pf* на~) write; paint; ~ся be spelt. ~ма́слом paint in oils; ~ся be spelt.

писк squeak, chirp. **писклявый** squeaky. **пи́скнуть** (-ну) *pf of* пища́ть

писто́н (percussion-)cap; piston.

пистоле́т pistol; gun; ~-пулемёт sub-machine gun.

писчебума́жный stationery. **пи́счая бума́га** writing paper. **пи́сьменно** adv in writing. **пи́сьменность** literature. **пи́сьменный** writing, written. **письмо́** (pl -а, -сем) letter.

пита́ние nourishment; feeding. **пита́тельный** nutritious; alimentary; feed. **пита́ть** impf feed; nourish; supply; **~ся** be fed, eat; +instr feed on.

пито́мец (-мца) charge; pupil; alumnus. **пито́мник** nursery.

пить (пью, пьёшь; пил, -а́, -о) impf (pf вы́~) drink. **питьё** (pl -тья, -тьёв) drinking; drink. **питьево́й** drinkable; drinking.

пиха́ть impf, **пихну́ть** (-ну́, -нёшь) pf push, shove.

пи́хта (silver) fir.

пи́чкать impf (pf на~) stuff.

пи́шущий writing; **~ая маши́нка** typewriter.

пи́ща food.

пища́ть (-щу́) impf (pf пи́скнуть) squeak; cheep.

пищеваре́ние digestion. **пищево́д** oesophagus, gullet. **пищево́й** food.

пия́вка leech.

пла́вание swimming; sailing; voyage. **пла́вательный** swimming; **~ бассе́йн** swimmingpool. **пла́вать** impf swim; float; sail. **плавба́за** depot ship, factory ship.

плави́льный melting, smelting. **плави́льня** foundry. **пла́вить** (-влю) impf (pf рас~) melt, smelt; **~ся** melt. **пла́вка** fusing; melting.

пла́вки (-вок) pl bathing trunks.

пла́вкий fusible; fuse. **плавле́ние** melting.

плавни́к (-á) fin; flipper. **пла́вный** smooth, flowing; liquid. **плаву́чий** floating.

плагиа́т plagiarism. **плагиа́тор** plagiarist.

пла́зма plasma.

плака́т poster; placard.

пла́кать (-а́чу) impf cry, weep; **~ся** complain, lament; +на+acc complain of; bemoan.

пла́кса cry-baby. **пла́ксивый** whining. **плаку́чий** weeping.

пла́менный flaming; ardent. **пла́мя** (-мени) neut flame; blaze.

план plan.

планёр glider. **планери́зм** gliding. **планери́ст** gliderpilot.

плане́та planet. **плане́тный** planetary.

плани́рование[1] planning. **плани́рование**[2] gliding; glide. **плани́ровать**[1] impf (pf за~) plan. **плани́ровать**[2] impf (pf с~) glide (down).

пла́нка lath, slat.

пла́новый planned, systematic; planning. **планоме́рный** systematic, planned.

планта́ция plantation.

пласт (-á) layer; stratum. **пласти́на** plate. **пласти́нка** plate; (gramophone) record. **пласти́ческий, пласти́чный** plastic. **пластма́сса** plastic. **пластма́ссовый** plastic.

пла́стырь m plaster.

пла́та pay; charge; fee. **платёж** (-á) payment. **платёжеспосо́бный** solvent. **платёжный** pay.

пла́тина platinum. **пла́тиновый** platinum.

плати́ть (-ачу́, -а́тишь) impf (pf за~, у~) pay; **~ся**

по~ся) за+acc pay for. **плат-
ный** paid; requiring payment.
платок (-тка) shawl; head-
scarf; handkerchief.
платонический platonic.
платформа platform; truck.
платье (gen pl -ьев) clothes,
clothing; dress; gown. **платя-
ной** clothes.
плафон ceiling; lamp shade.
плацдарм bridgehead, beach-
head; base; springboard.
плацкарта reserved-seat ticket.
плач weeping. **плачевный**
lamentable. **плачу** etc.: see
плакать
плачу etc.: see **платить**
плашмя adv flat, prone.
плащ (-а́) cloak; raincoat.
плебей plebeian.
плевательница spittoon.
плевать (плюю, плюёшь)
impf (pf на~, плюнуть) spit;
inf+dat: мне ~ I don't give a
damn (на+acc about); ~ся spit.
плевок (-вка) spit, spittle.
плеврит pleurisy.
плед rug; plaid.
плёл etc.: see **плести**
племенной tribal; pedigree.
племя (-мени; pl -мена, -мён)
neut tribe. **племянник** nephew.
племянница niece.
плен (loc -у́) captivity.
пленарный plenary.
пленительный captivating.
пленить pf (impf **пленять**)
captivate; ~ся be captivated.
плёнка film; tape; pellicle.
пленник prisoner. **пленный**
captive.
пленум plenary session.
пленять(ся impf of **пленить-
(ся**
плесень mould.
плеск splash, lapping. **плескать** (-ещу́, -е́щешь) impf

(pf плеснуть) splash; lap;
~ся splash; lap.
плесневеть (-еет) impf (pf
за~) go mouldy, grow musty.
плеснуть (-ну́, -нёшь) pf of
плескать
плести (-ету́, -етёшь; плёл,
-а́) impf (pf с~) plait; weave;
~сь trudge along. **плетение**
plaiting; wickerwork. **плетёный** wattled; wicker. **пле-
тень** (-тня) m wattle fencing.
плётка, плеть (gen pl -ей)
lash.
плечико (pl -и, -ов) shoulder-
strap; pl coat-hanger. **плечи-
стый** broad-shouldered. **пле-
чо́** (pl -и, -а́м) shoulder.
плешивый bald. **плешина**,
плешь bald patch.
плещу́ etc.: see **плескать**
плинтус plinth; skirting-board.
плис velveteen.
плиссированный pleat.
плита́ (pl -ы) slab; flag-
(stone); stove, cooker; моги́-
льная ~ gravestone. **пли́тка**
tile; (thin) slab; stove, cooker;
~ шокола́да bar of choc-
olate. **пли́точный** tiled.
пловец (-вца́), **пловчиха**
swimmer. **пловучий** floating;
buoyant.
плод (-а́) fruit. **плоди́ть**
(-ожу́) impf (pf рас~) produce, procreate; ~ся propagate.
плодо- in comb fruit-. **пло-
дови́тый** fruitful, prolific;
fertile. ~**во́дство** fruit-grow-
ing. ~**но́сный** fruit-bearing,
fruitful. ~**овощной** fruit and
vegetable. ~**ро́дный** fertile.
~**тво́рный** fruitful.
пло́мба seal; filling. **пломби-
рова́ть** impf (pf за~, о~)
fill; seal.

пло́ский (-сок, -ска́, -о) flat; trivial.

пло́ско- in comb flat. **плоского́рье** plateau. **~гу́бцы** (-ев) pl pliers. **~до́нный** flat-bottomed.

пло́скость (gen pl -е́й) flatness; plane; platitude.

плот (-а́) raft.

плоти́на dam; weir; dyke.

пло́тник carpenter.

пло́тность solidity; density. **пло́тный** (-тен, -тна́, -о) thick; compact; dense; solid, strong; hearty.

плотоя́дный carnivorous.

плоть flesh.

плохо́й bad; poor.

площа́дка area, (sports) ground, court, playground; site; landing; platform. **пло́щадь** (gen pl -е́й) area; space; square.

плуг (pl -и́) plough.

плут (-а́) cheat, swindler; rogue. **плутова́тый** cunning. **плутовско́й** roguish; picaresque. **плуто́ний** plutonium.

плыть (-ыву́, -ывёшь; плыл, -а́, -о) impf swim; float; sail.

плю́нуть (-ну) pf of плева́ть

плюс plus; advantage.

плющ (-а́) ivy.

плюю́ etc.: see плева́ть

пляж beach.

пляса́ть (-яшу́, -я́шешь) impf (pf c~) dance. **пля́ска** dance; dancing.

пневмати́ческий pneumatic.

пневмони́я pneumonia.

пнуть (пну, пнёшь) pf of пина́ть

пня etc.: see пень

по prep I. +dat on; along; round, about; by; over; according to; in accordance with; for; in; at; by (reason of);

on account of; from; **по понеде́льникам** on Mondays; **по профе́ссии** by profession; **по ра́дио** over the radio. II. +dat or acc of cardinal number, forms distributive number: **по́ два, по два** in twos, by two; **по пять рубле́й шту́ка** at five roubles each. III. +acc to, up to; for, to get; **идти́ по во́ду** go to get water; **по пе́рвое сентября́** up to (and including) 1st September. IV. +prep on, (immediately) after; **по прибы́тии** on arrival.

по- pref I. in comb +dat of adjs, with an advs in -и, indicates manner, use of a named language, or accordance with the opinion or wish of: **говори́ть по-ру́сски** speak Russian; **жить по-ста́рому** live in the old style; **по-мо́ему** in my opinion. II. in comb with adjs and nn, indicates situation along or near a thing: **помо́рье** seaboard, coastal region. III. in comb with comp of adjs indicates a smaller degree of comparison: **поме́ньше** a little less.

поба́иваться impf be rather afraid.

побе́г[1] flight; escape.

побе́г[2] shoot; sucker.

побегу́шки: **быть на побегу́шках** run errands.

побе́да victory. **победи́тель** m victor; winner. **победи́ть** pf (impf побежда́ть) conquer; win. **победо́носный**, **побе́дный** victorious, triumphant.

по|**бежа́ть** pf.

побежда́ть impf of победи́ть

по|**беле́ть** (-е́ю) pf. **по**|**бели́ть** pf. **побе́лка** whitewashing.

побере́жный coastal. побере́жье (sea-)coast.

по|беспоко́ить(ся *pf*.

побира́ться *impf* beg; live by begging.

по|би́ть(ся (-бью(сь, -бьёшь(ся) *pf*. по|благодари́ть *pf*.

побла́жка indulgence.

по|бледне́ть (-е́ю) *pf*.

поблёскивать *impf* gleam. поблизости *adv* nearby.

побо́и (-ев) *pl* beating. побо́ище *pl* slaughter; bloody battle.

побо́рник champion, advocate. поборо́ть (-рю́, -решь) *pf* overcome.

побо́чный secondary; done on the side; ~ проду́кт by-product.

по|брани́ться *pf*.

по|брата́ться *pf* побрати́м twin town.

по|бре́згать *pf*. по|бри́ть(ся (-бре́ю(сь) *pf*.

побуди́тельный stimulating. побуди́ть (-ужу́) *pf*, побужда́ть *impf* induce, prompt. побужде́ние motive; inducement.

побыва́ть *pf* have been, have visited; look in, visit. побы́вка leave. побы́ть (-бу́ду, -дешь; по́был, -а, -о) *pf* stay (for a short time).

побью́(сь *etc.: see* поби́ть(ся

пова́диться (-а́жусь) get into the habit (of). пова́дка habit.

по|вали́ть(ся (-лю́(сь, -лишь(ся) *pf*.

пова́льно *adv* without exception. пова́льный general, mass.

по́вар (*pl* -а́) cook, chef. пова́ренный culinary; cookery, cooking.

по-ва́шему *adv* in your opinion.

пове́дать *pf* disclose; relate.

поведе́ние behaviour.

поведу́ *etc.: see* повести́

по|везти́ (-зу́, -зёшь; -вёз, -ла́) *pf*. повёл *etc.: see* повести́

повелева́ть *impf* +*instr* rule (over); +*dat* command. повеле́ние command. повели́тельный imperious; imperative.

по|венча́ть(ся *pf*.

поверга́ть *impf*, пове́ргнуть (-ну; -ве́рг) *pf* throw down; plunge.

пове́ренная *sb* confidante. пове́ренный *sb* attorney; confidant; ~ в дела́х chargé d'affaires. по|ве́рить[1] *pf*.

пове́рить[2] (*pf* поверя́ть) check; confide. пове́рка check; roll-call.

поверну́ть (-ну́, -нёшь) *pf*, повёртывать *impf* (*impf also* повора́чивать) turn; ~ся turn.

пове́рх *prep*+*gen* over. пове́рхностный surface, superficial. пове́рхность surface.

пове́рье (*gen pl* -ий) popular belief, superstition. поверя́ть *impf of* пове́рить[2]

пове́са playboy.

по|весели́ть (-е́ю) *pf*.

повесели́ть *pf* cheer (up); amuse; ~ся have fun.

пове́сить(ся (-е́шу(сь) *pf of* ве́шать(ся

повествова́ние narrative, narration. повествова́тельный narrative. повествова́ть *impf* +*o*+*prep* narrate, relate.

по|вести́ (-еду́, -едёшь; -вёл, -а́) *pf* (*impf* поводи́ть) +*instr* move.

пове́стка notice; summons; ~ (дня) agenda.

по́весть (gen pl -е́й) story, tale.

пове́трие epidemic; craze.

повешу etc.: see **пове́сить**.

по|вздо́рить pf.

повзросле́ть (-е́ю) pf grow up.

по-ви́димому apparently.

пови́дло jam.

по|вини́ться pf.

пови́нность duty, obligation; **во́инская ~** conscription. **пови́нный** guilty.

повинова́ться impf & pf obey. **повинове́ние** obedience.

повиса́ть impf, **по|ви́снуть** (-ну; -ви́с) pf hang (on); hang down, hang.

повле́чь (-еку́, -ечёшь; -ёк, -ла́) pf (**за собо́й**) entail, bring in its train.

по|влия́ть pf.

по́вод[1] occasion, cause; **по ~у**+gen as regards, concerning.

по́вод[2] (loc -ý; pl -о́дья, -ьев) rein; **быть на ~ý у**+gen be under the thumb of. **поводи́ть** (-ожу́, -о́дишь) impf of **повести́**. **поводо́к** (-дка́) leash. **поводы́рь** (-я́) m guide.

пово́зка f vehicle.

повора́чивать(ся impf of **поверну́ть(ся, повороти́ть(ся; повора́чивайся, -айтесь** get a move on!

поворо́т turn, turning; bend; turning-point. **повороти́ть(ся** (-очу́(сь, -о́тишь(ся) pf (impf **повора́чивать(ся**) turn. **поворо́тливый** agile, nimble; manoeuvrable. **поворо́тный** turning; rotary; revolving.

по|вреди́ть (-ежу́) pf. **повре-жда́ть** impf damage; injure; **~ся** be damaged; be injured. **поврежде́ние** damage, injury.

повремени́ть pf wait a little; **+c**+instr delay over.

повседне́вный daily; everyday.

повсеме́стно adv everywhere. **повсеме́стный** universal, general.

повста́нец (-нца) rebel, insurgent. **повста́нческий** rebel; insurgent.

повсю́ду adv everywhere.

повторе́ние repetition. **по-вторить** pf, **повторя́ть** impf repeat; **~ся** repeat o.s.; be repeated; recur. **повто́рный** repeated.

повы́сить (-ы́шу) pf, **повы-ша́ть** impf raise, heighten; **~ся** rise. **повыше́ние** rise; promotion. **повы́шенный** heightened, high.

повяза́ть (-яжу́, -я́жешь) pf, **повя́зывать** impf tie. **повя́зка** band; bandage.

по|гада́ть pf.

пога́нка toadstool. **пога́ный** foul; unclean.

погаса́ть impf, **по|га́снуть** (-ну) pf go out, be extinguished. **по|гаси́ть** (-ашу́, -а́сишь) pf. **погаша́ть** impf liquidate, cancel. **пога́шен-ный** used, cancelled, cashed.

погиба́ть impf, **по|ги́бнуть** (-ну; -ги́б) pf perish; be lost. **поги́бель** ruin. **поги́бший** lost; ruined; killed.

по|гла́дить (-а́жу) pf.

по|глоти́ть (-ощу́, -о́тишь) pf, **поглоща́ть** impf swallow up; absorb. **поглоще́ние** absorption.

по|глупе́ть (-е́ю) pf.

по|гляде́ть (-яжу́) pf. **погля́-дывать** impf glance (from time to time); **+за**+instr keep an eye on.

погна́ть (-гоню́, -го́нишь; -гна́л, -á, -о) *pf* drive; **~ся за**+*instr* run after; start in pursuit of.

по|гну́ть(ся (-ну́(сь, -нёшь(ся) *pf*. **погну́шаться** *pf*.

поговори́ть *pf* have a talk.

погово́рка saying, proverb.

пого́да weather.

погоди́ть (-ожу́) *pf* wait a little; **немно́го погодя́** a little later.

поголо́вно *adv* one and all. **поголо́вный** general; capitation. **поголо́вье** number.

пого́н (*gen pl* -о́н) shoulder-strap.

пого́нщик driver. **погоню́** *etc.*: *see* **погна́ть**. **пого́ня** pursuit, chase. **погоня́ть** *impf* urge on, drive.

погорячи́ться (-чу́сь) *pf* get worked up.

пого́ст graveyard.

пограни́чник frontier guard. **пограни́чный** frontier.

по́греб (*pl* -á) cellar. **погреба́льный** funeral. **погреба́ть** *impf of* **погрести́**. **погребе́ние** burial.

погрему́шка rattle.

погрести́[1] (-ебу́, -ебёшь; -рёб, -лá) *pf* (*погреба́ть*) bury.

погрести́[2] (-ебу́, -ебёшь; -рёб, -лá) *pf* row for a while.

погре́ть (-е́ю) *pf* warm; **~ся** warm o.s.

по|греши́ть (-шу́) *pf* sin; err. **погре́шность** error, mistake.

по|грози́ть(ся (-ожу́(сь) *pf*. **по|грубе́ть** (-е́ю) *pf*.

погружа́ть *impf*, **по|грузи́ть** (-ужу́, -у́зишь) *pf* load; ship; dip, plunge, immerse; **~ся** sink, plunge; dive; be plunged absorbed. **погруже́ние** submergence; immersion; dive.

погру́зка loading; shipment.

погряза́ть *impf*, **по|гря́знуть** (-ну; -яз) *pf* be bogged down; wallow.

по|губи́ть (-блю́, -бишь) *pf*. **по|гуля́ть** *pf*.

под, подо *prep* I. +*acc* or *instr* under; near, close to; take; **взять по́д руку**+*acc* take the arm of; **~ ви́дом**+*gen* under the guise of; **по́д го́ру** downhill; **~ Москво́й** in the environs of Moscow. II. +*instr* occupied by, used as; (meant, implied) by; in, with; **говя́дина ~ хре́ном** beef with horse-radish. III. +*acc* towards; to (the accompaniment of); in imitation of; on; for, to serve as; **ему́ ~ пятьдеся́т (лет)** he is getting on for fifty.

подава́ть(ся (-даю́(сь, -даёшь(ся) *impf of* **пода́ть(ся**

подави́ть (-влю́, -вишь) *pf*, **подавля́ть** *impf* suppress; depress; overwhelm. **по|дави́ться** (-влю́сь, -вишься) *pf*. **подавле́ние** suppression; repression. **пода́вленность** depression. **пода́вленный** suppressed; depressed. **подавля́ющий** overwhelming.

пода́вно *adv* all the more.

пода́гра gout.

пода́льше *adv* a little further.

по|дари́ть (-рю́, -ришь) *pf*. **пода́рок** (-рка) present.

пода́тливый pliant, pliable.

пода́ть (*gen pl* -е́й) tax. **пода́ть** (-áм, -áшь, -áст, -ади́м; по́дал, -á, -о) *pf* (*impf* **подава́ть**) serve; give; put, move, turn; put forward, present, hand in; **~ся** give way; yield; +**на**+*acc* set out for. **пода́ча** giving, presenting; serve; feed, supply. **пода́чка** handout, crumb. **подаю́** *etc.*:

see подава́ть. подая́ние alms.
подбега́ть *impf*, подбежа́ть (-егу́) *pf* come running (up).
подбива́ть *impf of* подби́ть
подберу́ *etc.*: *see* подбира́ть.
подбира́ть(ся *impf of* подобра́ть(ся
подби́ть (-добью́, -добьёшь) *pf* (*impf* подбива́ть) line; re-sole; bruise; put out of action; incite.
подбодря́ть *pf*, подбодря́ть *impf* cheer up, encourage; ~ся cheer up, take heart.
подбо́р selection, assortment.
подборо́док (-дка) chin.
подбоче́нившись *adv* with hands on hips.
подбра́сывать *impf*, подбро́сить (-ро́шу) *pf* throw up.
подва́л cellar; basement. подва́льный basement, cellar.
подведу́ *etc.*: *see* подвести́
подвезти́ (-зу́, -зёшь, -вёз, -ла́) *pf* (*impf* подвози́ть) bring, take; give a lift.
подвене́чный wedding.
подверга́ть *impf*, подве́ргнуть (-ну; -ве́рг) *pf* subject; expose; ~ся +dat undergo. подве́рженный subject, prone.
подверну́ть (-ну́, -нёшь) *pf*, подвёртывать *impf* turn up; tuck under; sprain; tighten; ~ся be sprained; be turned up; be tucked under.
подве́сить (-е́шу) *pf* (*impf* подве́шивать) hang up, suspend. подвесно́й hanging, suspended.
подвести́ (-еду́, -едёшь; -вёл, -а́) *pf* (*impf* подводи́ть) lead up, bring up; place (under); bring under, subsume; let down; ~ ито́ги reckon up; sum up.
подве́шивать *impf of* подве́сить
по́двиг exploit, feat.

подвига́ть(ся *impf of* подви́нуть(ся
подви́жник religious ascetic; champion.
подвижно́й mobile; ~ соста́в rolling-stock. подви́жность mobility. подви́жный mobile; lively; agile.
подвиза́ться *impf* (в *or* на+prep) work (in).
подви́нуть (-ну) *pf* (*impf* подвига́ть) move; push; advance; ~ся move; advance.
подвла́стный +dat subject to; under the control of.
подво́да cart. подводи́ть (-ожу́, -о́дишь) *impf of* подвести́
подво́дный submarine; underwater; ~ая скала́ reef.
подво́з transport; supply. подвози́ть (-ожу́, -о́зишь) *impf of* подвезти́
подворо́тня (*gen pl* -тен) gateway.
подво́х trick.
подвы́пивший tipsy.
подвяза́ть (-яжу́, -я́жешь) *pf*, подвя́зывать *impf* tie up. подвя́зка garter; suspender.
подгиба́ть *impf of* подогну́ть
подгляде́ть (-яжу́) *pf*, подгля́дывать *impf* peep; spy.
подгова́ривать *impf*, подговори́ть *pf* incite.
подгоню́ *etc.*: *see* подогна́ть.
подгоня́ть *impf of* подогна́ть
подгора́ть *impf*, подгоре́ть (-ри́т) *pf* get a bit burnt. подгоре́лый slightly burnt.
подготови́тельный preparatory. подгото́вить (-влю) *pf*, подготовля́ть *impf* prepare; ~ся prepare, get ready. подгото́вка preparation, training.

поддава́ться (-даю́сь, -даёшься) *impf of* **подда́ться**

подда́кивать *impf* agree, assent.

по́дданный *sb* subject; citizen. **по́дданство** citizenship.

подда́ться (-а́мся, -а́шься, -а́стся, -ади́мся, -а́лся, -а́лась) *pf* (*impf* **поддава́ться**) yield, give way.

подде́лать *pf*, **подде́лывать** *impf* counterfeit; forge. **подде́лка** falsification; forgery; imitation. **подде́льный** false, counterfeit.

поддержа́ть (-жу́, -жишь) *pf*, **подде́рживать** *impf* support; maintain. **подде́ржка** support.

по|де́йствовать *pf*.

поде́лать *pf* do; **ничего́ не поде́лаешь** it can't be helped. **по|дели́ть(ся** (-лю́(сь, -лишь(ся) *pf*.

поде́лка *pl* small (handmade) articles.

поде́лом *adv:* ~ **ему́** (*etc.*) it serves him (*etc.*) right.

подённый by the day. **подёнщик, -ица** day-labourer.

подёргиваться *impf* twitch.

поде́ржанный second-hand.

подёрнуть (-нет) *pf* cover.

подеру́ *etc.*: *see* **подра́ть**

по|деше́веть (-éет) *pf*.

поджа́ривать(ся *impf*, **поджа́рить(ся** *pf* fry, roast, grill; toast. **поджа́ристый** brown(ed).

поджа́рый lean, wiry.

поджа́ть (-дожму́, -дожмёшь) *pf* (*impf* **поджима́ть**) draw in, draw under; ~ **гу́бы** purse one's lips.

поджечь (-дожгу́, -ожжёшь -жёг, -дожгла́) *pf*, **поджига́ть** *impf* set fire to; burn.

поджига́тель *m* arsonist;

instigator.

поджида́ть *impf* (+*gen*) wait (for).

поджо́г arson.

подзаголо́вок (-вка) sub-title, sub-heading.

подзащи́тный *sb* client.

подземе́лье (*gen pl* -лий) cave; dungeon. **подзе́мный** underground.

подзову́ *etc.*: *see* **подозва́ть**

подзо́рная труба́ telescope.

подзыва́ть *impf of* **подозва́ть**

по|диви́ться (-влю́сь) *pf*.

подка́пывать(ся *impf of* **подкопа́ть(ся**

подкара́уливать *impf*, **подкара́улить** *pf* be on the watch (for).

подкати́ть (-ачу́, -а́тишь) *pf*, **подка́тывать** *impf* roll up, drive up; roll.

подка́шивать(ся *impf of* **подкоси́ть(ся**

подки́дывать *impf*, **подки́нуть** (-ну) *pf* throw up. **подки́дыш** foundling.

подкла́дка lining. **подкла́дывать** *impf of* **подложи́ть**

подкле́ивать *impf*, **подкле́ить** *pf* glue (up); mend.

подко́ва (horse-)shoe. **подкова́ть** (-кую́, -ёшь) *pf*, **подко́вывать** *impf* shoe.

подко́жный hypodermic.

подкоми́ссия, подкомите́т sub-committee.

подко́п undermining; underground passage. **подкопа́ть** *pf* (*impf* **подка́пывать**) undermine; **~ся под+**acc undermine; burrow under.

подкоси́ть (-ошу́, -о́сишь) *pf* (*impf* **подка́шивать**) cut down; **~ся** give way.

подкра́дываться *impf of* подкра́сться

подкра́сить (-а́шу) *pf* (*impf* подкра́шивать) touch up; ~ся make up lightly.

подкра́сться (-аду́сь, -адёшься) *pf* (*impf* подкра́дываться) sneak up.

подкра́шивать(ся *impf of* подкра́сить(ся. подкра́шу *etc.: see* подкра́сить

подкрепи́ть (-плю́) *pf*, подкрепля́ть *impf* reinforce; support; corroborate; fortify; ~ся fortify o.s. подкрепле́ние confirmation; sustenance; reinforcement.

подкрути́ть (-учу́, -у́тишь) *pf* (*impf* подкру́чивать) tighten up.

подку́п bribery. подкупа́ть *impf*, подкупи́ть (-плю́, -пишь) *pf* bribe; win over.

подла́живаться (-а́жусь) *pf*, подла́живаться *impf* +к+dat adapt o.s. to; make up to.

подла́мываться *impf of* подломи́ться

по́дле *prep+gen* by the side of, beside.

подлежа́ть (-жу́) *impf* +dat be subject to; не подлежи́т сомне́нию it is beyond all doubt. подлежа́щее *sb* subject. подлежа́щий+dat subject to.

подлеза́ть *impf*, подле́зть (-зу, -зешь) *pf* crawl (under).

подле́сок (-ска) undergrowth.

подле́ц (-а́) scoundrel.

подлива́ть *impf of* подли́ть. подли́вка sauce, dressing; gravy.

подли́за *m & f* toady. подлиза́ться (-ижу́сь, -и́жешься) *pf*, подли́зываться *impf* +к+dat suck up to.

подли́нник original. по́длин-

но *adv* really. по́длинный genuine; authentic; original; real.

подли́ть (-долью́, -дольёшь; по́длил, -а́, -о) *pf* (*impf* подлива́ть) pour; add.

подло́г forgery.

подло́дка submarine.

подложи́ть (-жу́, -жишь) *pf* (*impf* подкла́дывать) add; +под+acc lay under; line.

подло́жный false, spurious; counterfeit, forged.

подлоко́тник arm (of chair).

подломи́ться (-о́мится) *pf* (*impf* подла́мываться) break; give way.

по́длость meanness, baseness; mean trick. по́длый (подл, -а́, -о) mean, base.

подма́зать (-а́жу) *pf*, подма́зывать *impf* grease; bribe.

подмасте́рье (*gen pl* -ьев) *m* apprentice.

подме́н, подме́на replacement. подме́нивать *impf*, подмени́ть (-ню́, -нишь) *pf*, подменя́ть *impf* replace.

подмести́ (-ету́, -етёшь; -мёл, -а́) *pf*, подмета́ть[1] sweep.

подмета́ть[2] *pf* (*impf* подмётывать) tack.

подме́тить (-е́чу) *pf* (*impf* подмеча́ть) notice.

подмётка sole.

подмётывать *impf of* подмета́ть[2]. подмеча́ть *impf of* подме́тить

подмеша́ть *pf*, подме́шивать *impf* mix in, stir in.

подми́гивать *impf*, подмигну́ть (-ну́, -нёшь) *pf* +dat wink at.

подмо́га help.

подмока́ть *impf*, подмо́кнуть (-нет; -мо́к) *pf* get damp, get wet.

подмора́живать *impf*, подморо́зить (-о́жу) *pf* freeze.

подмоско́вный (situated) near Moscow.

подмо́стки (-ов) *pl* scaffolding; stage.

подмо́ченный damp; tarnished.

подмы́ть (-мо́ю) *impf*, подмы́ть (-о́ю) *pf* wash; wash away; его́ так и подмыва́ет he feels an urge (to).

подмы́шка armpit.

поднево́льный dependent; forced.

поднести́ (-су́, -сёшь; -ёс, -ла́) *pf* (*impf* подноси́ть) present; take, bring.

поднима́ть(ся *impf of* подня́ть(ся

поднови́ть (-влю́) *pf*, подновля́ть *impf* renew, renovate.

подного́тная *sb* ins and outs.

подно́жие foot; pedestal. подно́жка running-board. подно́жный корм pasture.

подно́с tray. подноси́ть (-ошу́, -о́сишь) *impf of* поднести́. подноше́ние giving; present.

подня́тие raising. подня́ть (-ниму́, -ни́мешь; по́днял, -а́, -о) *pf* (*impf* поднима́ть, подыма́ть) raise; lift (up); rouse; ~ся rise; go up.

подо *see* под

подоба́ть *impf* befit, become. подоба́ющий proper.

подо́бие likeness; similarity. подо́бн|ый like, similar; и тому́ ~ое and so on, and such like; ничего́ ~ого! nothing of the sort!

подобостра́стие servility. подобостра́стный servile.

подобра́ть (-беру́, -берёшь; -бра́л, -а́, -о) *pf* (*impf* подбира́ть) pick up; tuck up,

put up; pick; ~ся steal up.

подо́бью *etc.*: *see* подби́ть

подогна́ть (-гоню́, -го́нишь; -а́л, -а́, -о) *pf* (*impf* подгоня́ть) drive; urge on; adjust.

подогну́ть (-ну́, -нёшь) *pf* (*impf* подгиба́ть) tuck in; bend under.

подогрева́ть *impf*, подогре́ть (-е́ю) *pf* warm up.

пододвига́ть *impf*, пододви́нуть (-ну) *pf* move up.

пододея́льник blanket cover; top sheet.

подожгу́ *etc.*: *see* поджечь

подожда́ть (-ду́, -дёшь; -а́л, -а́, -о) *pf* wait (+*gen or acc* for).

подожму́ *etc.*: *see* поджа́ть

подозва́ть (-дзову́, -дзовёшь; -а́л, -а́, -о) *pf* (*impf* подзыва́ть) call to; beckon.

подозрева́емый suspected; suspect. подозрева́ть *impf* suspect. подозре́ние suspicion. подозри́тельный suspicious.

по|до́ить (-ою́, -о́ишь) *pf*.

подойти́ (-йду́, -йдёшь; -ошёл, -шла́) *pf* (*impf* подходи́ть) approach; come up; +*dat* suit, fit.

подоко́нник window-sill.

подо́л hem.

подо́лгу *adv* for ages; for hours (*etc.*) on end.

подолью́ *etc.*: *see* подли́ть

подо́нки (-ов) *pl* dregs; scum.

подоплёка underlying cause.

подопру́ *etc.*: *see* подпере́ть

подо́пытный experimental.

подорва́ть (-рву́, -рвёшь; -а́л, -а́, -о) *pf* (*impf* подрыва́ть) undermine; blow up.

по|дорожа́ть *pf*.

подоро́жник plantain. подоро́жный roadside.

подосла́ть (-ошлю́, -ошлёшь) pf (impf **подсыла́ть**) send (secretly).

подоспева́ть impf, **подоспе́ть** (-е́ю) pf arrive, appear (in time).

подостла́ть (-стелю́, -сте́лешь) pf (impf **подстила́ть**) lay under.

подотде́л section, subdivision.

подотру́ etc.: see **подтере́ть**.

подотчётный accountable.

по|до́хнуть (-ну) pf (impf also **подыха́ть**).

подохо́дный нало́г income-tax.

подо́шва sole; foot.

подошёл etc.: see **подойти́**. **подошлю́** etc.: see **подосла́ть**. **подошью́** etc.: see **подши́ть**.

подпада́ть impf, **подпа́сть** (-аду́, -адёшь; -а́л) pf +acc fall under.

подпева́ть impf (+dat) sing along (with).

подпере́ть (-допру́; -пёр) pf (impf **подпира́ть**) prop up.

подпи́ливать impf, **подпили́ть** (-лю́, -лишь) pf saw; saw a little off.

подпира́ть impf of **подпере́ть**.

подписа́ние signing. **подписа́ть** (-ишу́, -и́шешь) pf, **подпи́сывать** impf sign; ~ся sign; subscribe. **подписно́й** subscription. **подписно́й** subscriber. **по́дпись** signature.

подпла́вывать (-ываю, -ываешь)-плыл, -а́, -о) pf к+dat swim or sail up to.

подполза́ть impf, **подползти́** (-зу́, -зёшь; -по́лз, -ла́) pf creep up (к+dat to); ~под+acc crawl under.

подполко́вник lieutenant-colonel.

подпо́лье cellar; underground. **подпо́льный** underfloor; underground.

подпо́ра, **подпо́рка** prop, support.

подпо́чва subsoil.

подпра́вить (-влю) pf, **подправля́ть** impf touch up, adjust.

подпры́гивать impf, **подпры́гнуть** (-ну) pf jump up (and down).

подпуска́ть impf, **подпусти́ть** (-ущу́, -у́стишь) pf allow to approach.

подраба́тывать impf, **подрабо́тать** pf earn on the side; work up.

подра́внивать impf of **подровня́ть**.

подража́ние imitation. **подража́ть** impf imitate.

подразделе́ние subdivision. **подраздели́ть** pf, **подразделя́ть** impf subdivide.

подразумева́ть impf imply, mean; ~ся be meant, be understood.

подраста́ть impf, **подрасти́** (-ту́, -тёшь; -ро́с, -ла́) pf grow.

по|дра́ть(ся (-деру́(сь, -дерёшь(ся, -а́л(ся, -ла́(сь, -о́(сь or -о(сь) pf.

подреза́ть (-е́жу) pf, **подреза́ть** impf cut; clip, trim.

подро́бно adv in detail. **подро́бность** detail. **подро́бный** detailed.

подровня́ть pf (impf **подра́внивать**) level, even; trim.

подро́с etc.: see **подрасти́**. **подро́сток** (-тка) adolescent; youth.

подро́ю etc.: see **подры́ть**.

подруба́ть¹ *impf*, **подруби́ть** (-блю́, -бишь) *pf* chop down; cut short(er).

подруба́ть² *impf*, **подруби́ть** (-блю́, -бишь) *pf* hem.

подру́га friend. **подру́жески** *adv* in a friendly way. **по|дружи́ться** (-жу́сь) *pf*.

по-друго́му *adv* in a different way.

подру́чный at hand; improvised; *sb* assistant.

подры́в undermining; injury. **подрыва́ть¹** *impf of* подорва́ть

подрыва́ть² *impf*, **подры́ть** (-ро́ю) *pf* undermine, sap. **подрывно́й** blasting, demolition; subversive.

подря́д¹ *adv* in succession.

подря́д² contract. **подря́дчик** contractor.

подса́живаться *impf of* подсе́сть

подса́ливать *impf of* подсоли́ть

подсве́чник candlestick.

подсе́сть (-ся́ду, -ся́дешь; -се́л) *pf* (*impf* **подса́живаться**) sit down (к+*dat* near).

подсказа́ть (-ажу́, -а́жешь) *pf*, **подска́зывать** *impf* prompt; suggest. **подска́зка** prompting.

подска́кивать *impf*, **подскочи́ть** (-чу́, -чишь) *pf* jump (up); soar; come running.

подсласти́ть (-ащу́) *pf*, **подсла́щивать** *impf* sweeten.

подсле́дственный under investigation.

подслу́шать *pf*, **подслу́шивать** *impf* overhear; eavesdrop, listen.

подсма́тривать *impf*, **подсмотре́ть** (-рю́, -ришь) *pf* spy (on).

подсне́жник snowdrop.

подсо́бный subsidiary; auxiliary.

подсо́вывать *impf of* подсу́нуть

подсозна́ние subconscious (mind). **подсозна́тельный** subconscious.

подсоли́ть (-со́лишь) *pf* (*impf* **подса́ливать**) add salt to.

подсо́лнечник sunflower. **подсо́лнечный** sunflower.

подсо́хнуть (-ну) *pf* (*impf* **подсыха́ть**) dry out a little.

подспо́рье help.

подста́вить (-влю) *pf*, **подставля́ть** *impf* put (under); bring up; expose; ~ **но́жку** +*dat* trip up. **подста́вка** stand; support. **подставно́й** false.

подстака́нник glass-holder.

подстелю́ *etc.*: *see* подостла́ть

подстерега́ть *impf*, **подстере́чь** (-егу́, -ежёшь; -рёг, -ла́) *pf* lie in wait for.

подстила́ть *impf of* подостла́ть. **подсти́лка** litter.

подстра́ивать *impf of* подстро́ить

подстрека́тель *m* instigator. **подстрека́тельство** instigation. **подстрека́ть** *impf*, **подстрекну́ть** (-ну́, -нёшь) *pf* instigate, incite.

подстре́ливать *impf*, **подстрели́ть** (-лю́, -лишь) *pf* wound.

подстрига́ть *impf*, **подстри́чь** (-игу́, -ижёшь; -иг) *pf* cut; clip, trim; ~**ся** have a hair-cut.

подстро́ить *pf* (*impf* подстра́ивать) build on; cook up.

подстро́чн|ый literal; ~ое примеча́ние footnote.

по́дступ approach. **подступа́ть** *impf*, **подступи́ть** (-плю́, -пишь) *pf* approach; **~ся к**+*dat* approach.

подсуди́мый *sb* defendant; the accused. **подсу́дный**+*dat* under the jurisdiction of.

подсу́нуть (-ну) *pf* (*impf* **подсо́вывать**) put, shove; palm off.

подсчёт calculation; count. **подсчита́ть** *pf*, **подсчи́тывать** *impf* count (up); calculate.

подсыла́ть *impf of* **подосла́ть**. **подсыха́ть** *impf of* **подсо́хнуть**. **подся́ду** etc.: *see* **подсе́сть**. **подта́лкивать** *impf of* **подтолкну́ть**

подта́скивать *impf of* **подтащи́ть**

подтасова́ть *pf*, **подтасо́вывать** *impf* shuffle unfairly; juggle with.

подта́чивать *impf of* **подточи́ть**

подтащи́ть (-щу́, -щишь) *pf* (*impf* **подта́скивать**) drag up

подтверди́ть (-ржу́) *pf*, **подтвержда́ть** *impf* confirm; corroborate. **подтвержде́ние** confirmation, corroboration.

подтёк bruise. **подтека́ть** *impf of* **подте́чь**; leak.

подтере́ть (-дотру́, -дотрёшь; подтёр) *pf* (*impf* **подтира́ть**) wipe (up).

подте́чь (-ечёт; -тёк, -ла́) *pf* (*impf* **подтека́ть**) **под**+*acc* flow under.

подтира́ть *impf of* **подтере́ть** **подтолкну́ть** (-ну́, -нёшь) *pf* (*impf* **подта́лкивать**) push; urge on.

подточи́ть (-чу́, -чишь) *pf* (*impf* **подта́чивать**) sharpen; eat away; undermine.

подтру́нивать *impf*, **подтруни́ть** *pf* **над**+*instr* tease.

подтя́гивать *impf*, **подтяну́ть** (-ну́, -нешь) *pf* tighten; pull up; move up; **~ся** tighten one's belt etc.; move up; pull o.s. together. **подтя́жки** (-жек) *pl* braces, suspenders. **подтя́нутый** smart.

поду́мать *pf* think (for a while). **поду́мывать** *impf*+*inf* or о+*prep* think about.

поду́ть (-у́ю) *pf* blow.

поду́шка pillow; cushion.

подхали́м *m* toady. **подхали́мство** grovelling.

подхвати́ть (-ачу́, -а́тишь) *pf*, **подхва́тывать** *impf* catch (up), pick up; take up.

подхлестну́ть (-ну́, -нёшь) *pf*, **подхлёстывать** *impf* whip up.

подхо́д approach. **подходи́ть** (-ожу́, -о́дишь) *impf of* **подойти́**. **подходя́щий** suitable.

подцепи́ть (-плю́, -пишь) *pf*, **подцепля́ть** *impf* hook on; pick up

подча́с *adv* sometimes.

подчёркивать *impf*, **подчеркну́ть** (-ну́, -нёшь) *pf* underline; emphasize.

подчине́ние subordination; submission. **подчинённый** subordinate. **подчини́ть** *pf*, **подчиня́ть** *impf* subordinate, subject; **~ся** +*dat* submit to.

подшива́ть *impf of* **подши́ть**. **подши́вка** hemming; lining; soling.

подши́пник bearing.

подши́ть (-дошью́, -дошьёшь) *pf* (*impf* **подшива́ть**) hem, line; sole.

подшути́ть (-учу́, -у́тишь) *pf*,

подшу́чивать *impf* над+*instr* mock; play a trick on.

подъе́ду *etc.: see* подъе́хать

подъе́зд entrance, doorway; approach. подъезжа́ть *impf of* подъе́хать

подъём lifting; raising; ascent; climb; enthusiasm; instep; reveille. подъёмник lift, elevator, hoist. подъёмный lifting; ~ кран crane; ~ мост drawbridge.

подъе́хать (-е́ду) *pf* (*impf* подъезжа́ть) drive up.

подыма́ть(ся *impf of* подня́ть(ся

подыска́ть (-ыщу́, -ы́щешь) *pf*, поды́скивать *impf* seek (out).

подыто́живать *impf*, подыто́жить (-жу) *pf* sum up.

подыха́ть *impf of* подо́хнуть подыша́ть (-шу́, -шишь) *pf* breathe.

поеда́ть *impf of* пое́сть

поеди́нок (-нка) duel.

по́езд (*pl* -á) train. пое́здка trip.

пое́сть (-е́м, -е́шь, -е́ст, -еди́м; -е́л) *pf* (*impf* поеда́ть) eat, eat up; have a bite to eat.

по́|е́хать (-е́ду) *pf* go; set off.

по|жале́ть (-е́ю) *pf*.

пожа́луй *adv* perhaps. пожа́луй-ста *partl* please; you're welcome.

пожа́р fire. пожа́рище scene of a fire. пожа́рник, пожа́рный *sb* fireman. пожа́рный fire; ~ая кома́нда fire-brigade; ~ая ле́стница fire-escape; ~ая маши́на fire-engine.

пожа́тие handshake. пожа́ть[1] (-жму́, -жмёшь) *pf* (*impf* пожима́ть) press; ~ ру́ку+*dat*

shake hands with; ~ плеча́ми shrug one's shoulders.

пожа́ть[2] (-жну́, -жнёшь) *pf* (*impf* пожина́ть) reap.

пожела́ние wish, desire.

по|жела́ть (-е́ю) *pf*.

по|желте́ть (-е́ю) *pf*.

по|жени́ть (-ню́, -нишь) *pf*. пожени́ться (-же́нимся) *pf* get married.

поже́ртвование donation.

по|же́ртвовать *pf*.

пожива́ть *impf* live; как (вы) пожива́ете? how are you (getting on)? пожи́зненный life(long). пожило́й elderly.

пожима́ть *impf of* пожа́ть[1] пожина́ть *impf of* пожа́ть[2] пожира́ть *impf of* пожра́ть

пожи́тки (-ов) *pl* belongings.

пожи́ть (-иву́, -ивёшь; по́жил, -á, -о) *pf*. live for a while; stay.

пожму́ *etc.: see* пожа́ть[1].

пожну́ *etc.: see* пожа́ть[2]

пожра́ть (-ру́, -рёшь; -áл, -á, -о) *pf* (*impf* пожира́ть) devour.

по́за pose.

по|забо́титься (-о́чусь) *pf*.

позабыва́ть *impf*, позабы́ть (-у́ду) *pf* forget all about.

по|зави́довать *pf*. по|за́втракать *pf*.

позавчера́ *adv* the day before yesterday.

позади́ *adv & prep+gen* behind.

по|займствовать *pf*.

позапро́шлый before last.

по|зва́ть (-зову́, -зовёшь; -áл, -á, -о) *pf*.

позволе́ние permission. позволи́тельный permissible. позво́лить (-лю) *pf*, позволя́ть *impf* + *dat* allow, permit; позво́ль(те)allow me; excuse me.

по|звони́ть *pf.*

позвоно́к (-нка́) vertebra. по-звоно́чник spine. позвоно́чный spinal; vertebrate; ~ые *sb pl* vertebrates.

поздне́е *adv* later. по́здний late; по́здно it is late.

по|здоро́ваться *pf.* поздра́-вить (-влю) *pf,* поздравля́ть *impf* с+*instr* congratulate on. поздравле́ние congratulation.

по|зелене́ть (-е́ет) *pf.*

по́зже *adv* later of day.

пози́ровать *impf* pose.

позити́в positive. позити́вный positive.

пози́ция position.

познава́тельный cognitive. познава́ть (-наю́, -наёшь) *impf of* позна́ть

по|знако́мить(ся) (-млю(сь)) *pf.*

позна́ние cognition. позна́ть *pf (impf* познава́ть) get to know.

позоло́та gilding. по|золоти́ть (-лочу́) *pf.*

позо́р shame, disgrace. позо́-рить *impf (pf* о~) disgrace; ~ся disgrace o.s. позо́рный shameful.

позы́в urge; inclination.

поигра́ть *pf* play (for a while).

поимённо *adv* by name.

по́имка capture.

поинтересова́ться *pf* be curious.

поиска́ть (-ищу́, -и́щешь) *pf* look for. по́иски (-ов) *pl* search.

пои́стине *adv* indeed.

пои́ть (пою́, по́ишь) *impf (pf* на~) give something to drink; water.

пойду́ *etc.: see* пойти́

по́йло swill.

пойма́ть *pf of* лови́ть. пойму́

etc.: see поня́ть

пойти́ (-йду́, -йдёшь; пошёл, -шла́) *pf of* идти́, ходи́ть; go, walk; begin to walk; +*inf* begin; пошёл! off you go! I'm off; пошёл вон! be off!

пока́ *adv* for the present; cheerio; ~ что in the meanwhile. пока́ *conj* while; ~ не until.

пока́з showing, demonstration. показа́ние testimony, evidence; reading. показа́-тель *m* index. показа́тельный significant; model; demonstration. показа́ть (-ажу́, -а́жешь) *pf,* пока́зывать *impf* show. показа́ться (-ажу́сь, -а́жешься) *pf,* пока́зываться *impf* show o.s.; appear. показно́й for show; ostentatious. показу́ха show.

по|кале́чить(ся) (-чу(сь)) *pf.*

пока́мест *adv & conj* for the present; while; meanwhile.

по|кара́ть *pf.*

покати́ть (-чу́, -тишь) *pf* start (rolling); ~ся start rolling.

пока́тый sloping; slanting.

покача́ть *pf* rock, swing; ~ голово́й shake one's head. пока́чивать rock slightly; ~ся rock; stagger. покачну́ть (-ну́, -нёшь) *pf* shake; rock; ~ся sway, totter, lurch.

пока́шливать *impf* have a slight cough.

покая́ние confession; repentance. по|ка́яться *pf.*

поквита́ться *pf* be quits; get even.

покида́ть *impf,* поки́нуть (-ну) *pf* leave; abandon. поки́ну-тый deserted.

покладая́: не ~ рук untiringly.

покла́дистый complaisant, obliging.

покло́н bow; greeting; regards. поклоне́ние worship. поклони́ться (-ню́сь, -нишься) pf of кла́няться. покло́нник admirer; worshipper. поклоня́ться impf +dat worship.

по|кля́сться (-яну́сь, -нёшься; -я́лся, -ла́сь) pf.

покои́ться impf rest, repose. поко́й rest, peace; room. поко́йник, -ица де-ceased. поко́йный calm, quiet; deceased.

по|колеба́ть(ся) (-е́блю(сь)) pf. поколе́ние generation.

по|колоти́ться (-очу́(сь), -о́тишь(ся)) pf.

поко́нчить (-чу) pf c+instr fin-ish; put an end to; ~ с собо́й commit suicide.

покоре́ние conquest. покори́ть pf (impf покоря́ть) sub-due; conquer; ~ся submit.

по|корми́ть(ся) (-млю́(сь), -мишь(ся)) pf.

поко́рный humble; submis-sive, obedient.

по|коро́бить(ся) (-блю(сь)) pf. покоря́ть(ся) impf of покори́ть(ся)

поко́с mowing; meadow(-land). покоси́вшийся rickety, ram-shackle. по|коси́ться (-ошу́(сь)) pf.

по|кра́сить (-а́шу) pf. покра́ска painting, colouring.

по|красне́ть (-е́ю) pf. по|криви́ться (-влю́(сь)) pf.

покро́в cover. покрови́тель m, покрови́тельница patron; sponsor. покрови́тельствен-ный protective; patronizing. покрови́тельство protec-tion, patronage. покрови́-тельствовать impf +dat protect, patronize.

покро́й cut.

покроши́ть (-шу́, -шишь) pf crumble; chop.

покрути́ть (-учу́, -у́тишь) pf twist.

покрыва́ло cover; bedspread; veil. покрыва́ть impf, по|кры́ть (-ро́ю) pf cover; ~ся cover o.s.; get covered. покры́тие covering; surfac-ing; payment. покры́шка cover; tyre.

покупа́тель m buyer; cus-tomer. покупа́ть impf of купи́ть. поку́пка purchase. покупно́й bought, pur-chased; purchase.

по|кури́ть (-рю́, -ришь) pf have a smoke.

по|ку́шать pf.

покуше́ние +на+acc attempted assassination of.

пол¹ (loc -у́, pl -ы́) floor.

пол² sex.

пол- in comb with n in gen, in oblique cases usu полу-, half.

пола́ (pl -ы) flap; из-под полы́ on the sly.

полага́ть impf suppose, think. полага́ться impf of положи́ться; полага́ется impers one is supposed to; +dat it is due to.

по|ла́комить(ся) (-млю(сь)) pf.

полго́да (полуго́да) m half a year.

по́лдень (-дня or -лу́дня) m noon. полдне́вный adj.

по́ле (pl -я́, -е́й) field; ground; margin; brim. полево́й field; ~ые цветы́ wild flowers.

полежа́ть (-жу́) pf lie down for a while.

поле́зный useful; helpful; good, wholesome; ~ая нагру́з-ка payload.

по|ле́зть (-зу; -ле́з) pf.

полемизи́ровать impf debate, engage in controversy. **поле́мика** controversy; polemics. **полеми́ческий** polemical.

по|лени́ться (-ню́сь, -нишься) *pf.*

поле́но (*pl* -е́нья, -ьев) log.

полёт flight. **по|лете́ть** (-лечу́) *pf.*

по́лзать *indet impf.* **ползти́** (-зу́, -зёшь; полз, -ла́) *det impf* crawl, creep; ooze; fray. **ползу́чий** creeping.

поли- *in comb* poly-.

полива́ть(ся *impf of* **поли́ть(ся. поли́вка** watering.

полига́мия polygamy.

полигло́т polyglot.

полиграфи́ческий printing. **полиграфи́я** printing.

полиго́н range.

поликли́ника polyclinic.

полиме́р polymer.

поли́ня́лый faded. **по|линя́ть** *pf.*

полиомиели́т poliomyelitis

полирова́льный polishing. **полирова́ть** *impf* (*pf* от~) polish. **полиро́вка** polishing; polish. **полиро́вщик** polisher.

полит- *abbr in comb* (*of* **полити́ческий**) political. **~бюро́** *neut indecl* Politburo. **~заключённый** *sb* political prisoner.

политехни́ческий polytechnic.

поли́тик politician. **поли́тика** policy; politics. **полити́ческий** political.

поли́ть (-лью́, -льёшь; по́лил, -а́, -о) *pf* (*impf* **полива́ть**) pour over; water; **~ся** +*instr* pour over o.s.

полице́йский police; *sb* policeman. **поли́ция** police.

поли́чн|ое *sb:* с ~ым red-handed.

полк (-а́, *loc* -у́) regiment.

по́лка shelf; berth.

полко́вник colonel. **полково́дец** (-дца) commander; general. **полково́й** regimental.

пол-ли́тра half a litre.

полне́ть (-е́ю) *impf* (*pf* по~) put on weight.

по́лно *adv* that's enough! stop it!

полно- *in comb* full; completely. **полнолу́ние** full moon. **~метра́жный** full-length. **~пра́вный** enjoying full rights; competent. **~це́нный** of full value.

полномо́чие (*usu pl*) authority, power. **полномо́чный** plenipotentiary.

по́лностью *adv* in full; completely. **полнота́** completeness; corpulence.

по́лночь (-л(у́)ночи) midnight. **по́лный** (-лон, -лна́, по́лно́) full; complete; plump.

полови́к (-а́) mat, matting.

полови́на half; два с полови́ной two and a half; ~ шесто́го half-past five. **полови́нка** half.

полови́ца floor-board.

полово́дье high water.

полово́й[1] floor.

полово́й[2] sexual.

поло́гий gently sloping.

положе́ние position; situation; status; regulations; thesis; provisions. **поло́женный** agreed; determined. **положи́м** let us assume; suppose. **положи́тельный** positive. **положи́ть** (-жу́, -жишь) *pf* (*impf* **класть**) put; lay (down); **~ся** (*impf* **полага́ться**) rely.

по́лоз (pl -о́зья, -ьев) runner.
по|лома́ть(ся pf. поло́мка breakage.

полоса́ (acc полосу́; pl по́лосы, -ло́с, -а́м) stripe; band; region; belt; period. полоса́тый striped.

полоска́ть (-ощу́, -о́щешь impf (pf вы~, от~, про~) rinse; ~ го́рло gargle; ~ся paddle; flap.

по́лость¹ (gen pl -е́й) cavity.
по́лость² (gen pl -е́й) travelling rug.

полоте́нце (gen pl -нец) towel.
полоте́р floor-polisher.
поло́тнище width; panel. полотно́ (pl -а, -тен) linen; canvas. полотня́ный linen.

поло́ть (-лю́, -лешь) impf (pf вы~) weed.

полощу́ etc.: see полоска́ть
полти́нник fifty copecks.

полтора́ (-лу́тора) m & neut, полторы́ (-лу́тора) f one and a half. полтора́ста (полу́т-) a hundred and fifty.

полу-¹ see пол-
полу-² in comb half-, semi-, demi-. полуботи́нок (-нка; gen pl -нок) shoe. ~го́дие half a year. ~годи́чный six months', lasting six months. ~годова́лый six-month-old. ~годово́й half-yearly, six-monthly. ~гра́мотный semi-literate. ~защи́тник half-back. ~круг semicircle. ~кру́глый semicircular. ~ме́сяц crescent (moon). ~мра́к semi-darkness. ~но́чный midnight. ~о́стров peninsula. ~откры́тый ajar. ~прово́дник (-а́) semi-conductor, transistor. ~ста́нок (-нка) halt. ~тьма́ semi-darkness. ~фабрика́т semi-finished

product, convenience food. ~фина́л semi-final. ~часово́й half-hourly. ~ша́рие hemisphere. ~шу́бок (-бка) sheepskin coat.

полу́денный midday.
получа́тель m recipient.
получа́ть impf, получи́ть (-чу́, -чишь) pf get, receive, obtain; ~ся turn up; turn out; из э́того ничего́ не получи́лось nothing came of it. получе́ние receipt. полу́чка receipt; pay-(packet).

полу́чше adv a little better.
получаса́ (получаса́) m half an hour.

по́лчище horde.
по́лый hollow; flood.
по|лысе́ть (-е́ю) pf.
по́льза use; benefit, profit; в по́льзу+gen in favour of, on behalf of. по́льзование use.
по́льзоваться impf (pf вос~) +instr make use of, utilize; profit by; enjoy.

по́лька Pole; polka. по́льский Polish; sb polonaise.
по|льсти́ть(ся (-льщу́(сь) pf.
по́лью etc. see поли́ть
По́льша Poland.

полюби́ть (-блю́, -бишь) pf come to like; fall in love with.
по|любова́ться (-бу́юсь) pf.
полюбо́вный amicable.
по|любопы́тствовать pf.
по́люс pole.
поля́к Pole.
поля́на glade, clearing.
поляриза́ция polarization.
поля́рник polar explorer.
поля́рный polar; ~ая звезда́ pole-star.

пом- abbr in comb of помо́щник) assistant. ~на́ч assistant chief, assistant head.
пома́да pomade; lipstick.

помаза́ние anointment. **по|ма́-
зать(ся** (-а́жу(сь) pf. **пома-
зо́к** (-зка́) small brush.
помале́ньку adv gradually;
gently; modestly; so-so.
пома́лкивать impf hold one's
tongue.
по|мани́ть (-ню́, -нишь) pf.
пома́рка blot; pencil mark;
correction.
по|ма́слить pf.
помаха́ть (-машу́, -ма́шешь) pf,
пома́хивать impf +instr wave;
wag.
поме́длить pf +c+instr delay.
поме́ньше a little smaller; a
little less.
по|меня́ть(ся pf.
помере́ть (-мру́, -мрёшь; -мер,
-ла́, -ло) pf (impf **помира́ть**)
die.
по|мере́щиться (-щусь) pf.
по|ме́рить pf.
помертве́лый deathly pale.
по|мертве́ть (-е́ю) pf.
помести́ть (-ещу́) pf (impf **по-
меща́ть**) accommodate; place,
locate; invest; **~ся** lodge; find
room. **поме́стье** (gen pl -тий,
-тьям) estate.
по́месь cross-(breed), hybrid.
помёт dung; droppings; litter,
brood.
поме́та, поме́тка mark, note.
по|ме́тить (-е́чу) pf (impf
also **помеча́ть**) mark; date; **~
га́лочкой** tick.
поме́ха hindrance; obstacle; pl
interference.
помеча́ть impf of **поме́тить**
поме́шанный mad; sb lunatic.
помеша́тельство madness;
craze. **по|меша́ть** pf. **поме-
ша́ться** pf go mad.
помеща́ть impf of **помести́ть**.
помеща́ться impf of помести́ться; be (situated); be ac-

commodated, find room.
помеще́ние premises; apartment, room, lodging; location;
investment. **поме́щик** landowner.
помидо́р tomato.
поми́лование forgiveness. **по-
ми́ловать** pf forgive.
помимо prep+gen apart from;
besides; without the knowledge of.
помина́ть impf of **помяну́ть**;
не ~ ли́хом remember kindly.
поми́нки (-нок) pl funeral re-
past.
помира́ть impf of **помере́ть**
по|мири́ть(ся pf.
по́мнить impf remember.
помога́ть impf of **помо́чь**
по-мо́ему adv in my opinion.
помо́и (-ев) pl slops. **помо́й-
ка** (gen pl -о́ек) rubbish dump.
помо́йный slop.
помо́л grinding.
помо́лвка betrothal.
по|моли́ться (-лю́сь, -лишься)
pf. **по|молоде́ть** (-е́ю) pf.
помолча́ть (-чу́) pf be silent
for a time.
помо́рье: see по- II.
по|мо́рщиться (-щусь) pf.
помо́ст dais; rostrum.
по|мо́чи́ться (-чу́сь, -чишься)
pf.
помо́чь (-огу́, -о́жешь; -о́г, -ла́)
pf (impf **помога́ть**) (+dat) help.
помо́щник, помо́щница
assistant. **по́мощь** help; на ~!
help!
помо́ю etc.: see **помы́ть**
по́мпа pump.
помутне́ние dimness, cloud-
ing.
помча́ться (-чу́сь) pf rush; dart
off.
помыка́ть impf +instr order
about.

по́мысел (-сла) intention; thought.

по|мы́ть(ся (-мо́ю(сь) pf.

помяну́ть (-ну́, -нёшь) pf (impf помина́ть) mention; pray for

помя́тый crumpled. по|мя́ть-ся (-мну́(сь) pf.

по|наде́яться (-е́юсь) pf count, rely.

понадо́биться (-блюсь) pf be or become necessary; е́сли пона́добится if necessary.

понапра́сну adv in vain.

понаслы́шке adv by hearsay.

по-настоя́щему adv properly, truly.

понача́лу adv at first.

понево́ле adv willynilly; against one's will.

понеде́льник Monday.

понемно́гу, понемно́жку adv little by little.

по|нести́(сь (-су́(сь, -сёшь(ся; -нёс(ся, -ла́(сь) pf.

понижа́ть impf, пони́зить (-и́жу) pf lower; reduce; ~ся fall, drop, go down. пониже́-ние fall; lowering; reduction.

поника́ть impf, по|ни́кнуть (-ну; -ни́к) pf droop, wilt.

понима́ние understanding. понима́ть impf of поня́ть

по-но́вому adv in a new fashion.

поно́с diarrhoea.

поноси́ть[1] (-ошу́, -о́сишь) pf carry; wear.

поноси́ть[2] (-ошу́, -о́сишь) impf abuse (verbally).

поно́шенный worn; threadbare.

по|нра́виться (-влюсь) pf.

понто́н pontoon.

понуди́ть (-у́жу) pf, понужда́ть impf compel.

понука́ть impf urge on.

по|ну́рить pf: ~ го́лову hang

one's head. пону́рый downcast.

по|ню́хать pf. поню́шка: ~ табаку́ pinch of snuff.

поня́тие concept; notion, idea.

поня́тливый bright, quick.

поня́т|ный understandable, comprehensible; clear; ~о naturally; ~о? do you see? поня́ть (пойму́, -мёшь; по́нял, -а́, -о) pf (impf понима́ть) understand; realize.

по|обе́дать pf. по|обеща́ть pf.

пода́ль adv at some distance.

поодино́чке adv one by one.

поочерёдно adv in turn.

поощре́ние encouragement.

поощри́ть pf, поощря́ть impf encourage.

поп (-а́) priest.

попада́ние hit. попада́ть(ся impf of попа́сть(ся

попадья́ priest's wife.

попа́ло: see попа́сть. по|па́-риться pf.

попа́рно adv in pairs, two by two.

попа́сть (-аду́, -адёшь; -а́л) pf (impf попада́ть) +в+acc hit; get (into); find o.s. in; +на+acc hit upon, come on; не туда́ ~ get the wrong number; ~ся be caught; find o.s.; turn up; что попадётся anything. попа́ло with prons & advs: где ~ anywhere; как ~ anyhow; что ~ the first thing to hand.

попере́к adv & prep+gen across.

попереме́нно adv in turns.

попере́чник diameter. попере́чный transverse, diametrical, cross; ~ый разре́з, ~ое сече́ние cross-section.

поперхну́ться (-ну́сь, -нёшься) *pf* choke.

по|пе́рчить (-чу) *pf*.

попече́ние care; charge; **на попече́нии**+*gen* in the care of. **попечи́тель** *m* guardian, trustee.

попира́ть *impf* (*pf* **попра́ть**) trample on; flout.

попи́ть (-пью́, -пьёшь; по́пил, -ла́, по́пило) *pf* have a drink.

поплаво́к (-вка́) float.

попла́кать (-а́чу) *pf* cry a little.

по|плати́ться (-чу́сь, -ти́шься) *pf*.

поплы́ть (-ыву́, -ывёшь; -ы́л, -ыла́, -о) *pf* start swimming.

попо́йка drinking-bout.

попола́м *adv* in two, in half; half-and-half.

поползнове́ние half a mind; pretension(s).

пополне́ние replenishment; reinforcement. **по|полне́ть** (-е́ю) *pf*. **попо́лнить** *pf*, **пополня́ть** *impf* replenish; re-stock; reinforce.

пополу́дни *adv* in the afternoon; p.m.

попо́на horse-cloth.

по|по́тчевать (-чую) *pf*.

поправи́мый rectifiable. **по|пра́вить** (-влю) *pf*, **поправля́ть** *impf* repair; correct, put right; set straight; **~ся** correct o.s.; get better, recover; improve. **попра́вка** correction; repair; adjustment; recovery.

попра́ть *pf of* попира́ть

по-пре́жнему *adv* as before.

попрёк reproach. **попрека́ть** *impf*, **попрекну́ть** (-ну́, -нёшь) *pf* reproach.

по́прище field; walk of life.

по|про́бовать *pf*. **по|проси́ть** (-ся (-ошу́(сь, -о́сишь(ся) *pf*.

по́просту *adv* simply; without ceremony.

попроша́йка *m & f* cadger. **по|проша́йничать** *impf* cadge.

попроща́ться *pf* (+*c*+*instr*) say goodbye (to).

попры́гать *pf* jump, hop.

попуга́й parrot.

популя́рность popularity. **популя́рный** popular.

попусти́тельство connivance.

по-пусто́му, **по́пусту** *adv* in vain.

попу́тно *adv* at the same time; in passing. **попу́тный** passing. **попу́тчик** fellow-traveller.

по|пыта́ться *pf*. **попы́тка** attempt.

по|пяти́ться (-я́чусь) *pf*. **попя́тный** backward; **идти́ на ~** go back on one's word.

по́ра[1] pore.

пора́[2] (*acc* -у; *pl* -ы, пор, -а́м) time; it is time; **до каки́х пор?** till when?; **до сих пор** till now; **с каки́х пор?** since when?

порабо́тать *pf* do some work.

порабо́тить (-ощу́) *pf*, **порабоща́ть** *impf* enslave. **порабоще́ние** enslavement.

поравня́ться *pf* come alongside.

по|ра́довать(**ся** *pf*.

поража́ть *impf*, **по|рази́ть** (-ажу́) *pf* hit; strike; defeat; affect; astonish; **~ся** be astounded. **пораже́ние** defeat. **порази́тельный** striking; astonishing.

по-ра́зному *adv* differently.

пора́нить *pf* wound; injure.

порва́ть (-ву́, -вёшь; -ва́л, -а́, -о) *pf* (*impf* **порыва́ть**) tear (up); break, break off; **~ся** tear; break (off).

по|реде́ть (-е́ет) *pf*.

порéз cut. **порéзать** (-éжу) *pf* cut; ~ся cut o.s.

порéй leek.

по|рекомендовáть *pf.* **по|ржáветь** (-еет) *pf.*

пóристый porous.

порицáние censure; blame. **порицáть** *impf* blame; censure.

пóрка flogging.

пóровну *adv* equally.

порóг threshold; rapids.

порóда breed, race, species. **породистый** thoroughbred. **породить** (-ожу) *pf* (*impf* **порождáть**) give birth to; give rise to.

по|роднить(ся *pf.* **порóдный** pedigree.

порождáть *impf of* **породить**

порóжний empty.

пóрознь *adv* separately, apart.

порóй, порóю *adv* at times.

порóк vice; defect.

поросёнок (-нка; *pl* -сята, -сят) piglet.

пóросль shoots; young wood. **порóть**[1] (-рю, -решь) *impf* (*pf* вы~) thrash; whip.

порóть[2] (-рю, -решь) *impf* (*pf* рас~) undo, unpick; ~ся come unstitched.

пóрох (*pl* ~á) gunpowder, powder. **порохово́й** powder.

порóчить (-чу) *impf* (*pf* о~) discredit; smear. **порóчный** vicious, depraved; faulty.

порошить (-шит) *impf* snow slightly.

порошóк (-шкá) powder.

порт (*loc* -ý; *pl* -ы, -óв) port.

портативный portable.

портвéйн port (wine).

пóртик portico.

пóртить (-чу) *impf* (*pf* ис~) spoil; mar; ~ся deteriorate; go bad.

портниха dressmaker. **порт-**

нóвский tailor's. **портнóй** *sb* tailor.

портóвый port.

портрéт portrait.

портсигáр cigarette-case.

португáлец (-льца), **-лка** Portuguese. **Португáлия** Portugal. **португáльский** Portuguese.

портфéль *m* brief-case; portfolio.

портьéра curtain(s), portière.

портя́нка foot-binding.

поругáние desecration; humiliation.

порýганный desecrated; outraged. **поругáть** *pf* scold, swear at; ~ся swear; fall out.

порýка bail; guarantee; surety; **на порýки** on bail.

по-рýсски *adv* (in) Russian.

поручéние assignment; errand; message.

пóручень (-чня) *m* handrail.

поручительство guarantee; bail.

поручить (-чу, -чишь) *pf* (*impf* **поручáть**) entrust; instruct. **поручиться** (-чýсь, -чишься) *pf of* **ручáться**

порхáть *impf*, **порхнýть** (-нý, -нёшь) *pf* flutter, flit.

пóрция portion; helping.

пóрча spoiling; damage; curse.

пóршень (-шня) *m* piston.

порыв[1] gust; rush; fit

порыв[2] breaking. **порывáть(ся**[1] *impf of* **порвáть(ся**

порывáться[2] *impf* make jerky movements; endeavour. **порывистый** gusty; jerky; impetuous; fitful.

порядковый ordinal. **поря́док** (-дка) order; sequence; manner, way; procedure; **всё в поря́дке** everything is alright; ~ дня agenda, order of the day. поря́дочный decent; honest; respectable; fair, considerable.

посади́ть (-ажу́, -а́дишь) pf of сади́ть, сажа́ть. поса́дка planting; embarkation; boarding; landing. поса́дочный planting; landing.

посажу́ etc.: see посади́ть.

по|сва́тать(ся pf. по|све|же́ть (-е́ет) pf. по|свети́ть (-ечу́, -е́тишь) pf. по|светле́ть (-е́ет) pf.

посви́стывать impf whistle.

по-сво́ему adv (in) one's own way.

посвяти́ть (-ящу́) pf, посвяща́ть impf devote; dedicate; let in; ordain. посвяще́ние dedication; initiation; ordination.

посе́в sowing; crops. посевно́й sowing; ~а́я пло́щадь area under crops.

по|седе́ть (-е́ю) pf.

поселе́нец (-нца) settler; exile. поселе́ние settlement; exile. по|сели́ть pf, поселя́ть impf settle; lodge; arouse; ~ся settle, take up residence. посёлок (-лка) settlement; housing estate.

посеребрённый (-ён, -а́) silver-plated. по|серебри́ть pf.

посереди́не adv & prep+gen in the middle of.

посети́тель m visitor. посети́ть (-ещу́) pf (impf посеща́ть) visit; attend.

по|се́товать pf.

посеща́емость attendance. посеща́ть impf of посети́ть. посеще́ние visit.

по|се́ять (-е́ю) pf.

посиде́ть (-ижу́) pf sit (for a while).

поси́льный within one's powers; feasible.

по|сине́лый gone blue. по|сине́ть (-е́ю) pf.

по|скака́ть (-ачу́, -а́чешь) pf.

поскользну́ться (-ну́сь, -нёшься) pf slip.

поско́льку conj as far as, (in) so far as.

по|скро́мничать pf. по|скупи́ться (-плю́сь) pf.

посла́нец (-нца) messenger, envoy. посла́ние message; epistle. посла́нник envoy, minister. посла́ть (-шлю́, -шлёшь) pf (impf посыла́ть) send.

по́сле adv & prep+gen after; afterwards.

по́сле- in comb post-; after-. послевое́нный post-war. ~за́втра adv the day after tomorrow. ~родово́й postnatal. ~сло́вие epilogue; concluding remarks.

после́дний last; recent; latest; latter. после́дователь m follower. после́довательность sequence; consistency. после́довательный consecutive; consistent. по|сле́довать pf. после́дствие consequence. после́дующий subsequent; consequent.

посло́вица proverb, saying.

по|служи́ть (-жу́, -жишь) pf. послужно́й service.

послуша́ние obedience. по|слу́шать(ся pf. послу́шный obedient.

по|слы́шаться (-шится) pf.

посма́тривать impf look from time to time.

по|смея́ться impf chuckle.

посме́ртный posthumous.

по|сме́ть (-е́ю) pf.

посмея́ние ridicule. посмея́ться (-ею́сь, -еёшься) pf.

laugh; +над+*instr* laugh at.
по|смотре́ть(ся (-рю́(сь, -ришь(ся) *pf*.
посо́бие aid; allowance; benefit; textbook. посо́бник accomplice.
по|сове́товать(ся *pf*. по|со|де́йствовать *pf*.
посо́л (-сла́) ambassador.
по|соли́ть (-олю́, -о́лишь) *pf*.
посо́льство embassy.
поспа́ть (-сплю; -а́л, -а́, -о) *pf* sleep; have a nap.
поспева́ть[1] *impf*, по|спе́ть[1] (-е́ет) *pf* ripen.
поспева́ть[2], поспе́ть[2] (-е́ю) *pf* have time; be in time (к+*dat*, +*acc* for); +за+*instr* keep up with.
по|спеши́ть (-шу́) *pf*. поспе́шный hasty, hurried.
по|спо́рить *pf*. по|спосо́бствовать *pf*.
посрами́ть (-млю́) *pf*, посрамля́ть impf disgrace.
посреди́, посреди́не *adv* & *prep*+*gen* in the middle (of). посре́дник mediator. посре́дничество mediation. посре́дственный mediocre. посре́дством *prep*+*gen* by means of.
по|ссо́рить(ся *pf*.
пост[1] (-а́, *loc* -у́) post.
пост[2] (-а́, *loc* -у́) fast(ing).
по|ста́вить[1] (-влю) *pf*.
поста́вить[2] (-влю) *pf*, поставля́ть impf supply. поста́вка delivery. поставщи́к (-а́) supplier.
постаме́нт pedestal.
постанови́ть (-влю́, -вишь) *pf* (*impf* постановля́ть) decree; decide.
постано́вка production; arrangement; putting, placing.
постановле́ние decree; decision. постановля́ть *impf of*

постанови́ть
постано́вщик producer; (film) director.
по|старе́ть *pf*.
по|старе́ть (-е́ю) *pf* age. по ста́рому *adv* as before.
посте́ль bed. посте́лю *etc*.: *see* постла́ть
посте́пенный gradual.
по|стесня́ться *pf*.
постига́ть *impf of* пости́чь. пости́гнуть: *see* пости́чь. постиже́ние comprehension, grasp. постижи́мый comprehensible.
постила́ть *impf of* постла́ть
по|стира́ть *pf* do some washing.
по|сти́ться (-щусь) *impf* fast.
пости́чь, пости́гнуть (-и́гну; -и́г(нул) *pf* (*impf* постига́ть) comprehend, grasp; befall.
по|стла́ть (-стелю́, -сте́лешь) (*impf also* постила́ть) spread; make (*bed*).
по́стный lenten; lean; glum; ~ое ма́сло vegetable oil.
постово́й on point duty.
посто́й billeting.
посто́льку: ~, поско́льку *conj* to that extent, insofar as.
по|сторони́ться (-ню́сь, -ни́шься) *pf*. посторо́нний strange; foreign; extraneous; outside; *sb* stranger, outsider.
постоя́нный permanent; constant; continual; ~ый ток direct current. постоя́нство constancy.
по|стоя́ть (-ою́) *pf* stand (for a while); +за+*acc* stand up for.
пострада́вший *sb* victim. по|страда́ть *pf*.
постри́чься *impf*, по|стри́чься (-игу́сь, -ижёшься, -и́гся) *pf* take monastic vows; get one's hair cut.

построе́ние construction; building; framing. по|стро́ить(ся) (-о́ю(сь)) pf. постро́й ка building.

постскри́птум postscript.

постули́ровать impf & pf postulate.

поступа́тельный forward. поступа́ть impf, поступи́ть (-плю́, -пишь) pf act; do; be received; +в or на+acc enter, join; +с+instr treat; ~ся +instr waive, forgo. поступле́ние entering, joining; receipt. посту́пок (-пка) act, deed. по́ступь gait; step.

по|стуча́ть(ся) (-чу́(сь)) pf.

по|стыди́ться (-ыжу́сь) pf. посты́дный shameful.

посу́да crockery; dishes. посу́дный china; dish.

по|сули́ть pf.

посчастли́виться pf impers (+dat) be lucky; ей посчастли́вилось +inf she had the luck to.

посчита́ть pf count (up). по|счита́ться pf.

посыла́ть impf of посла́ть. посы́лка sending; parcel; errand; premise. посы́льный sb messenger.

посыпа́ть (-плю, -плешь) pf, посыпа́ть impf strew. посы́паться (-плется) pf begin to fall; rain down.

посяга́тельство encroachment; infringement. посяга́ть impf, посягну́ть (-ну́, -нёшь) pf encroach, infringe.

пот (loc -у́; pl -ы́) sweat.

пота́йно́й secret.

потака́ть impf +dat indulge.

потасо́вка brawl.

пота́ш (-а́) potash.

по-тво́ему adv in your opinion.

потво́рствовать impf (+dat) be indulgent (towards), pander (to).

потёк damp patch.

потёмки (-мок) pl darkness. по|темне́ть (-е́ет) pf.

потенциа́л potential. потенциа́льный potential.

по|тепле́ть (-е́ет) pf.

потерпе́вший sb victim. по|терпе́ть (-плю́, -пишь) pf.

поте́ря loss; waste; pl casualties. по|теря́ть(ся) pf.

по|тесни́ть pf. по|тесни́ться pf sit closer, squeeze up.

поте́ть (-е́ю) impf (pf вс~, за~) sweat; mist over.

поте́ха fun. по|те́шить(ся) (-шу(сь)) pf. поте́шный amusing.

поте́чь (-чёт, -тёк, -ла́) pf begin to flow.

потира́ть impf rub.

потихо́ньку adv softly; secretly; slowly.

по́тный (-тен, -тна́, -тно) sweaty.

пото́к stream; torrent; flood.

потоло́к (-лка́) ceiling.

по|толсте́ть (-е́ю) pf.

пото́м adv later (on); then. пото́мок (-мка) descendant. пото́мство posterity.

потому́ adv that is why; ~ что conj because.

по|тону́ть (-ну́, -нешь) pf. по|топи́ть flood, deluge. по|топи́ть (-плю́, -пишь) pf, потопля́ть impf sink.

по|топта́ть (-пчу́, -пчешь) pf. по|торопи́ть(ся) (-плю́(сь), -пишь(ся)) pf.

пото́чный continuous; production-line.

по|трати́ть (-а́чу) pf.

потреби́тель m consumer, user. потреби́тельский consumer; consumers'. потреби́ть (-блю́) pf, потребля́ть *impf* consume. **потребле́ние** consumption. **потре́бность** need, requirement. **потре́бовать(ся** *pf.*

по|трево́жить(ся (-жу(сь) *pf.* **потрёпанный** shabby; tattered. **по|трепа́ть(ся** (-плю́(сь, -плешь(ся) *pf.*

по|тре́скаться *pf.* **потре́скивать** *impf* crackle.

потро́гать *pf.* touch, feel, finger.

потроха́ (-о́в) *pl* giblets. **потроши́ть** (-шу́) *impf* (*pf* вы́~) disembowel, clean.

потряса́ть *impf*, **потрясти́** (-су́, -сёшь; -я́с, -ла́) *pf* shake; rock; stagger; +*acc* or *instr* brandish, shake. **потряса́ющий** staggering, tremendous. **потрясе́ние** shock.

поту́ги *f pl* vain attempts; ро-дово́е ~ labour. **поту́пить** (-плю) *pf*, **потупля́ть** *impf* lower; ~ся look down.

по|тускне́ть (-е́ет) *pf.*

потусторо́нний мир the next world.

потуха́ть *impf*, **по|ту́хнуть** (-нет, -ух) *pf* go out; die out. **поту́хший** extinct; lifeless. **по|туши́ть** (-шу́, -шишь) *pf.*

по́тчевать (-чую) *impf* (*pf* по~) +*instr* treat to.

потя́гиваться *impf*, **по|тяну́ться** (-ну́сь, -нешься) *pf* stretch o.s. **по|тяну́ть** (-ну́, -нешь) *pf.*

по|у́жинать *pf.* **по|умне́ть** (-е́ю) *pf.*

поуча́ть *impf* preach at. **поучи́тельный** instructive. **поха́бный** obscene.

похвала́ praise. **по|хва-**

по|ли́ть(ся (-лью́(сь, -льёшь(ся) *pf.* **похва́льный** laudable; laudatory.

по|хва́стать(ся *pf.*

похити́тель *m* kidnapper; abductor; thief. **похи́тить** (-и́щу) *pf*, **похища́ть** *impf* kidnap; abduct; steal. **похище́ние** theft; kidnapping; abduction.

похлёбка broth, soup.

по|хло́пать *pf* slap; clap.

по|хлопота́ть (-очу́, -о́чешь) *pf.*

похо́д campaign; march; hike; excursion.

по|хода́тайствовать *pf.*

походи́ть (-ожу́, -о́дишь) *impf* на+*acc* resemble.

похо́дка gait, walk. **похо́дный** mobile, field; marching. **похожде́ние** adventure.

похо́жий alike; ~ на like.

похолода́ние drop in temperature.

по|хорони́ть (-ню́, -нишь) *pf.* **похоро́нный** funeral. **по́хо-роны** (-ро́н) *pl* funeral. **по|хороше́ть** (-е́ю) *pf.*

по́хоть lust.

по|худе́ть (-е́ю) *pf.*

по|целова́ть (-ова́(ся *pf.* **поцелу́й** kiss.

поча́ток (-тка) ear; (corn) cob. **по́чва** soil; ground; basis. **по́ч-венный** soil; ~ покро́в top-soil.

почём *adv* how much; how; ~ знать? who can tell? ~ я зна́ю? how should I know?

почему́ *adv* why. **почему́-либо**, **~-нибудь** *advs* for some reason or other. **почему́-то** *adv* for some reason.

по́черк hand(writing).

почерне́лый blackened; darkened. **по|черне́ть** (-е́ю) *pf.*

почерпну́ть (-ну́, -нёшь) *pf*

draw, scoop up; glean.

по|черстве́ть (-е́ю) pf. по|чеса́ть(ся (-ешу́(сь, -е́шешь(ся pf.

почёсть honour. почёт honour; respect. почётный of honour; honourable; honorary.

по́чечный renal; kidney.

почива́ть impf of почи́ть

почи́н initiative.

по|чини́ть (-ню́, -нишь) pf, починя́ть impf repair, mend. почи́нка repair.

по|чи́стить(ся (-и́щу(сь) pf.

почита́ть¹ impf honour; revere.

почита́ть² pf read for a while.

почи́ть (-и́ю, -и́ешь) pf (impf почива́ть) rest; pass away; на ла́врах rest on one's laurels.

по́чка¹ bud.

по́чка² kidney.

по́чта post, mail; post-office. почтальо́н postman. почта́мт (main) post-office.

почте́ние respect. почте́нный venerable; considerable.

почти́ adv almost.

почти́тельный respectful. почти́ть (-чту́) pf honour.

почто́в|ый postal; ~ая ка́рточка postcard; ~ый перево́д postal order; ~ый я́щик letter-box.

по|чу́вствовать pf.

по|чу́диться (-ишься) pf.

пошатну́ть (-ну́, -нёшь) pf shake; ~ся shake; stagger.

по|шевели́ть(ся (-елю́(сь, -е́ли́шь(ся) pf. пошёл etc.: see пойти́

поши́вочный sewing.

по́шлина duty.

по́шлость vulgarity; banality. по́шлый vulgar; banal.

поштучный by the piece.

по|шути́ть (-учу́, -у́тишь) pf. поща́да mercy. по|щади́ть (-ажу́) pf.

по|щекота́ть (-очу́, -о́чешь) pf.

пощёчина slap in the face.

по|щу́пать pf.

поэ́зия poetry. поэ́ма poem. поэ́т poet. поэти́ческий poetic.

поэ́тому adv therefore.

пою́ etc.: see петь, пойть

появи́ться (-влю́сь, -вишься) pf, появля́ться impf appear. появле́ние appearance.

по́яс (pl -а́) belt; girdle; waistband; waist; zone.

поясне́ние explanation. поясни́тельный explanatory. поясни́ть (-ню́) pf (impf поясня́ть) explain, elucidate.

поясни́ца small of the back. поясно́й waist; to the waist; zonal.

поясня́ть impf of поясни́ть

пра- pref first; great-. прабабушка great-grandmother.

пра́вда (the) truth. правди́вый true; truthful. правдоподо́бный likely; plausible. пра́ведный righteous; just.

пра́вило rule; principle.

пра́вильн|ый right, correct; regular; ~о! that's right!

прави́тель m ruler. прави́тельственный government(al). прави́тельство government.

пра́вить¹ (-влю) +instr rule, govern; drive.

пра́вить² (-влю) impf correct. пра́вка correcting.

правле́ние board; administration; government.

пра́|внук, ~вну́чка great-grandson, -granddaughter.

пра́во¹ (pl -а́) law; right; (pl -ди́тельские) права́ driving licence; на права́х+gen in the capacity of, as.

пра́во² *adv* really.

пра́во-¹ *in comb* law; right. правове́рный orthodox. ~ме́рный lawful, rightful. ~мо́чный competent. ~наруше́ние infringement of the law, offence. ~наруши́тель *m* offender, delinquent. ~писа́ние spelling, orthography. ~сла́вный orthodox; *sb* member of the Orthodox Church. ~су́дие justice.

пра́во-² *in comb* right, right-hand. правосторо́нний right; right-hand.

правово́й legal.

правота́ rightness; innocence.

пра́вый¹ right; right-hand; right-wing.

пра́вый² (прав, -á, -о) right, correct; just.

пра́вящий ruling.

пра́дед great-grandfather; *pl* ancestors. праде́душка *m* great-grandfather.

пра́здник (public) holiday. пра́здничный festive. пра́зднование celebration. пра́здновать *impf* (*pf* от~) celebrate. пра́здность idleness. пра́здный idle; useless.

пра́ктика practice; practical work. практикова́ть *impf* practise; ~ся (*pf* на~)ся be practised; +в+*prep* practise. практи́ческий, практи́чный practical.

пра́отец (-тца) forefather.

пра́порщик ensign.

прапра́дед great-great-grandfather. прароди́тель *m* forefather.

прах dust; remains. пра́чечная *sb* laundry. пра́чка laundress.

пребыва́ние stay. пребы-

ва́ть *impf* be; reside.

превзойти́ (-йду́, -йдёшь; -ошёл, -шла́) *pf* (*impf* превосходи́ть) surpass; excel.

превозмога́ть *impf*, превозмо́чь (-огу́, -о́жешь; -ог, -ла́) *pf* overcome.

превознести́ (-су́, -сёшь; -ёс, -ла́) *pf*, превозноси́ть (-ошу́, -о́сишь) *impf* extol, praise.

превосходи́тельство Excellency. превосходи́ть (-ожу́, -о́дишь) *impf of* превзойти́. превосхо́дный superlative; superb, excellent. превосхо́дство superiority. превосходя́щий superior.

преврати́ть (-ащу́) *pf*, превраща́ть *impf* convert, turn, reduce; ~ся turn, change. превра́тный wrong; changeful. превраще́ние transformation.

превы́сить (-ы́шу) *pf*, превыша́ть *impf* exceed. превыше́ние exceeding, excess.

прегра́да obstacle; barrier. прегради́ть (-ажу́) *pf*, прегражда́ть *impf* bar, block.

пред *prep*+*instr*: *see* пе́ред

предава́ть(ся (-даю́(сь, -даёшь(ся) *impf of* преда́ть(ся

преда́ние legend; tradition; handing over, committal. пре́данность devotion. пре́данный devoted. преда́тель *m*, ~ница betrayer, traitor. преда́тельский treacherous. преда́тельство treachery. преда́ть (-а́м, -а́шь, -а́ст, -ади́м; пре́дал, -á, -о) *pf* (*impf* предава́ть) hand over, commit; betray; ~ся abandon o.s.; give way, indulge.

предаю́ *etc.*: *see* предава́ть

предвари́тельный preliminary; prior. предвари́ть *pf*,

предваря́ть *impf* forestall, anticipate.

предвéстник forerunner; harbinger. **предвеща́ть** *impf* portend; augur.

предвзя́тый preconceived; biased.

предви́деть (-и́жу) *impf* foresee.

предвкуси́ть (-ушу́, -у́сишь) *pf*, **предвкуша́ть** *impf* look forward to.

предводи́тель *m* leader. **предводи́тельствовать** *impf* +*instr* lead.

предвоéнный pre-war.

предвосхи́тить (-и́щу) *pf*, **предвосхища́ть** *impf* anticipate.

предвы́борный (pre-)election.

предго́рье foothills.

преддвéрие threshold.

предéл limit; bound. **предéльный** boundary; maximum; utmost.

предзнаменова́ние omen, augury.

предисло́вие preface.

предлага́ть *impf of* предложи́ть. **предло́г**[1] pretext.

предло́г[2] preposition.

предложéние[1] sentence; clause.

предложéние[2] offer; proposition; proposal; motion; suggestion; supply. **предложи́ть** (-жу́, -жишь) *pf* (*impf* предлага́ть) offer; propose; suggest; order.

предло́жный prepositional.

предмéстье suburb.

предмéт object; subject.

предназнача́ть *impf*, **предназна́чить** (-чу) *pf* destine; intend; earmark.

преднамéренный premeditated.

предо: *see* перед

прéдок (-дка) ancestor.

предопределéние predetermination. **предопредели́ть** *pf*, **предопределя́ть** *impf* predetermine, predestine.

предоста́вить (-влю) *pf*, **предоставля́ть** *impf* grant; leave; give.

предостерега́ть *impf*, **предостерéчь** (-егу́, -ежёшь; -ёг, -ла́) *pf* warn. **предостережéние** warning. **предосторо́жность** precaution.

предосуди́тельный reprehensible.

предотврати́ть (-ащу́) *pf*, **предотвраща́ть** *impf* avert, prevent.

предохранéние protection; preservation. **предохрани́тель** *m* guard; safety device, safety-catch; fuse. **предохрани́тельный** preservative; preventive; safety. **предохрани́ть** *pf*, **предохраня́ть** *impf* preserve, protect.

предписа́ние order; *pl* directions, instructions. **предписа́ть** (-ишу́, -и́шешь) *pf*, **предпи́сывать** *impf* order, direct; prescribe.

предплéчье forearm.

предполага́емый supposed. **предполага́ется** *impers* it is proposed. **предполага́ть** *impf*, **предположи́ть** (-жу́, -о́жишь) *pf* suppose, assume. **предположéние** supposition, assumption. **предположи́тельный** conjectural; hypothetical.

предпослéдний penultimate, last-but-one.

предпосы́лка precondition; premise.

предпочéсть (-чту́, -чтёшь; -чёл,

-чла́) pf, предпочита́ть impf prefer. предпочте́ние preference. предпочти́тельный preferable.

предприи́мчивый enterprising.

предпринима́тель m owner; entrepreneur; employer. предпринима́тельство: свобо́дное ~ free enterprise. предпринима́ть impf, предприня́ть (-иму́, -и́мешь; -и́нял, -á, -о) pf undertake. предприя́тие undertaking, enterprise.

предрасположе́ние predisposition.

предрассу́док (-дка) prejudice.

предрека́ть impf, предре́чь (-еку́, -ечёшь; -рёк, -лá) pf foretell.

предреша́ть impf, предреши́ть (-шу́) pf decide beforehand; predetermine.

председа́тель m chairman.

предсказа́ние prediction. предсказа́ть (-ажу́, -áжешь) pf, предска́зывать impf predict; prophesy.

предсме́ртный dying.

представа́ть (-таю́, -таёшь) impf of предста́ть

представи́тель m representative. представи́тельный representative; imposing. представи́тельство representation.

предста́вить (-влю) pf, представля́ть impf present; submit; introduce; represent; ~ себе́ imagine; represent; ~ собо́й represent, be; ~ся present itself, occur; seem; introduce o.s.; +instr pretend to be. представле́ние presentation; performance; idea, notion.

предста́ть (-áну) pf (impf

представа́ть) appear.

предстоя́ть (-ои́т) impf be in prospect; lie ahead. предстоя́щий forthcoming; imminent.

предте́ча m & f forerunner, precursor.

предубежде́ние prejudice.

предугада́ть pf, предуга́дывать impf guess; foresee.

предупреди́тельный preventive; warning; courteous, obliging. предупреди́ть (-ежу́) pf, предупрежда́ть impf warn; give notice; prevent; anticipate. предупрежде́ние notice; warning; prevention.

предусма́тривать impf, предусмотре́ть (-рю́, -ришь) pf envisage, foresee; provide for. предусмотри́тельный prudent; far-sighted.

предчу́вствие presentiment; foreboding. предчу́вствовать impf have a presentiment (about).

предше́ственник predecessor. предше́ствовать impf +dat precede.

предъяви́тель m bearer. предъяви́ть (-влю́, -вишь) pf, предъявля́ть impf show, produce; bring (lawsuit); ~ пра́во на+acc lay claim to.

предыду́щий previous.

прее́мник successor. прее́мственность succession; continuity.

пре́жде adv first; formerly; prep+gen before; ~ всего́ first of all; first and foremost; ~ чем conj before. преждевре́менный premature. пре́жний previous, former.

презервати́в condom.

президе́нт president. президе́нтский presidential. прези́диум presidium.

презира́ть *impf* despise. **презре́ние** contempt. **презре́нный** contemptible. **презри́тельный** scornful.

преиму́щественно *adv* mainly, chiefly, principally. **преиму́щественный** main, primary; preferential. **преиму́щество** advantage; preference; **по преиму́ществу** for the most part.

преиспо́дняя *sb* the underworld.

прейскура́нт price list, catalogue.

преклони́ть *pf*, **преклоня́ть** *impf* bow, bend; **~ся** bow down; +*dat* or **пе́ред**+*instr* admire, worship. **прекло́нный**: **~ во́зраст** old age.

прекра́сный beautiful; fine; excellent.

прекрати́ть (-ащу́) *pf*, **прекраща́ть** *impf* stop, discontinue; **~ся** cease, end. **прекраще́ние** halt; cessation.

преле́стный delightful. **пре́лесть** charm, delight.

преломи́ть (-млю́, -мишь) *pf*, **преломля́ть** *impf* refract. **преломле́ние** refraction.

прельсти́ть (-льщу́) *pf*, **прельща́ть** *impf* attract; entice; **~ся** be attracted; fall (+*instr* for).

прелюбодея́ние adultery. **прелю́дия** prelude.

премину́ть (-ну) *pf* with neg not fail.

премирова́ть *impf* & *pf* award a prize to; give a bonus. **пре́мия** prize; bonus; premium.

премье́р prime minister; lead(ing actor). **премье́ра** première. **премье́р-мини́стр** prime minister. **премье́рша**

leading lady.

пренебрега́ть *impf*, **пренебре́чь** (-егу́, -ежёшь; -ёг, -ла́) *pf* +*instr* scorn; neglect. **пренебреже́ние** scorn; neglect. **пренебрежи́тельный** scornful.

пре́ния (-ий) *pl* debate.

преоблада́ние predominance. **преоблада́ть** *impf* predominate; prevail.

преобража́ть *impf*, **преобрази́ть** (-ажу́) *pf* transform. **преображе́ние** transformation; Transfiguration. **преобразова́ние** transformation; reform. **преобразова́ть** *pf*, **преобразо́вывать** *impf* transform; reform, reorganize.

преодолева́ть *impf*, **преодоле́ть** (-е́ю) *pf* overcome.

препара́т preparation.

препина́ние: зна́ки препина́ния punctuation marks.

препира́тельство altercation, wrangling.

преподава́ние teaching. **преподава́тель** *m*, **~ница** teacher. **преподава́тельский** teaching. **преподава́ть** (-даю́, -даёшь) *impf* teach.

преподнести́ (-су́, -сёшь; -ёс, -ла́) *pf*, **преподноси́ть** (-ошу́, -о́сишь) present with, give.

препроводи́ть (-вожу́, -во́дишь) *pf*, **препровожда́ть** *impf* send, forward.

препя́тствие obstacle; hurdle. **препя́тствовать** *impf* (*pf* вос~) +*dat* hinder.

прерва́ть (-ву́, -вёшь; -а́л, -а, -о) *pf* (*impf* **прерыва́ть**) interrupt; break off; **~ся** be interrupted; break.

перека́ние argument. **перека́ться** *impf* argue.

прерыва́ть(ся *impf of* **прерва́ть(ся**

пресека́ть *impf*, пресе́чь (-еку́, -ечёшь; -е́к, -екла́) *pf* stop; put an end to; ~ся stop; break.

пресле́дование pursuit; persecution; prosecution. пресле́довать *impf* pursue; haunt; persecute; prosecute.

пресло́вутый notorious.

пресмыка́ться *impf* grovel. пресмыка́ющееся *sb* reptile.

пресново́дный freshwater. пре́сный fresh; unleavened; insipid; bland.

пресс press. пре́сса the press. пресс-конфере́нция press-conference.

престаре́лый aged.

прести́ж prestige.

престо́л throne.

преступле́ние crime. престу́пник criminal. престу́пность criminality; crime, delinquency. престу́пный criminal.

пресы́титься (-ы́щусь) *pf*, пресыща́ться *impf* be satiated. пресыще́ние surfeit, satiety.

претвори́ть *pf*, претворя́ть *impf* (в+*acc*) turn, change, convert; ~ в жизнь realize, carry out.

претенде́нт claimant; candidate; pretender. претендова́ть *impf* на+*acc* lay claim to; have pretensions to. прете́нзия claim; pretension; быть в прете́нзии на+*acc* have a grudge, a grievance, against.

претерпева́ть *impf*, претерпе́ть (-плю́, -пишь) *pf* undergo; suffer.

преть (пре́ет) *impf* (*pf* со~) rot.

преувеличе́ние exaggeration. преувели́чивать *impf*, преувели́чить (-чу) *pf* exaggerate.

преуменьша́ть *impf*, преуме́ньшить (-е́ньшу) *pf* underestimate; understate.

преуспева́ть *impf*, преуспе́ть (-е́ю) *pf* be successful; thrive.

преходя́щий transient.

прецеде́нт precedent.

при *prep* +*prep* by, at; in the presence of; attached to, affiliated to; with; about; on; in the time of; under; during; when, in case of; ~ всём том for all that.

приба́вить (-влю) *pf*, прибавля́ть *impf* add; increase; ~ся increase; rise; день приба́вился the days are getting longer. приба́вка addition; increase. прибавле́ние addition; supplement; appendix. приба́вочный additional; surplus.

Приба́лтика the Baltic States.

прибау́тка humorous saying.

прибега́ть[1] *impf of* прибежа́ть

прибега́ть[2] *impf*, прибе́гнуть (-ну; -бе́г) *pf* к+*dat* resort to.

прибежа́ть (-егу́) *pf* (*impf* прибега́ть) come running.

прибе́жище refuge.

прибере́гать *impf*, прибере́чь (-егу́, -ежёшь; -ёг, -ла́) *pf* save (up), reserve.

приберу́ *etc.*: *see* прибра́ть. прибива́ть *impf of* приби́ть. прибира́ть *impf of* прибра́ть

приби́ть (-бью́, -бьёшь) *pf* (*impf* прибива́ть) nail; flatten; drive.

приближа́ть *impf*, прибли́зить (-и́жу) *pf* bring *or* move nearer; ~ся approach; draw nearer. приближе́ние approach. приблизи́тельный approximate.

прибо́й surf, breakers.

прибо́р instrument, device, apparatus; set. **прибо́рная доска́** instrument panel; dashboard.

прибра́ть (-беру́, -берёшь; -а́л, -а́, -о) *pf* (*impf* **прибира́ть**) tidy (up); put away.

прибре́жный coastal; offshore.

прибыва́ть *impf*, **прибы́ть** (-бу́ду; при́был, -а́, -о) *pf* arrive; increase, grow; rise; wax. **при́быль** profit, gain; increase, rise. **при́быльный** profitable. **прибы́тие** arrival.

прибы́ю etc.: see **прибы́ть**

привал halt.

прива́ривать *impf*, **прива-ри́ть** (-рю́, -ришь) *pf* weld on.

приватиза́ция privatization. **приватизи́ровать** *impf & pf* privatize.

приведу́ etc.: see **привести́**

привезти́ (-зу́, -зёшь; -ёз, -ла́) (*impf* **привози́ть**) bring.

привере́дливый pernickety.

приве́рженец (-нца) adherent. **приве́рженный** devoted.

приве́сить (-е́шу) *pf* (*impf* **приве́шивать**) hang up, suspend.

привести́ (-еду́, -едёшь; -ёл, -а́) *pf* (*impf* **приводи́ть**) bring; lead; take; reduce; cite; put in(to), set.

приве́т greeting(s); regards; hi! **приве́тливый** friendly; affable. **приве́тствие** greeting; speech of welcome. **приве́тствовать** *impf & pf* greet, salute; welcome.

приве́шивать *impf of* **приве́сить**

привива́ть(ся *impf of* **приви́ть(ся. приви́вка** inoculation.

привиде́ние ghost; apparition. **при|ви́деться** (-дится) *pf*.

привилегиро́ванный privileged. **привиле́гия** privilege.

привинти́ть (-нчу́) *pf*, **приви́нчивать** *impf* screw on.

приви́ть (-вью, -вьёшь; -и́л, -а́, -о) *pf* (*impf* **привива́ть**) inoculate; graft; inculcate; foster; ~**ся** take; become established.

при́вкус after-taste; smack.

привлека́тельный attractive. **привлека́ть** *impf*, **привле́чь** (-еку́, -ечёшь; -ёк, -ла́) *pf* attract; draw; draw in, win over; (*law*) have up; ~ **к суду́** sue. **привлече́ние** attraction.

приво́д drive, gear. **приво-ди́ть** (-ожу́, -о́дишь) *impf of* **привести́. приводно́й** driving.

привожу́ etc.: see **приводи́ть, привози́ть**

приво́з bringing; importation; load. **привози́ть** (-ожу́, -о́зишь) *impf of* **привезти́. привозно́й, приво́зный** imported.

приво́льный free.

привстава́ть (-таю́, -таёшь) *impf*, **привста́ть** (-а́ну) *pf* half-rise; rise.

привыка́ть *impf*, **привы́к-нуть** (-ну; -ы́к) *pf* get accustomed. **привы́чка** habit. **привы́чный** habitual, usual.

привью́ etc.: see **приви́ть**

привя́занность attachment; affection. **привяза́ть** (-яжу́, -я́жешь) *pf*, **привя́зывать** *impf* attach; tie, bind; ~**ся** become attached; attach o.s.; +к+*dat* pester. **привя́зчивый** annoying; affectionate. **при́вязь** tie; lead, leash; tether.

пригиба́ть *impf of* пригну́ть

пригласи́ть (-ашу́) *pf*, приглаша́ть *impf* invite. приглаше́ние invitation.

пригляде́ться (-яжу́сь) *pf*, пригля́дываться *impf* look closely; +к+*dat* scrutinize; get used to.

пригна́ть (-гоню́, -го́нишь; -а́л, -а́, -о) *pf* (*impf* пригоня́ть) bring in; fit, adjust.

пригну́ть (-ну́, -нёшь) *pf* (*impf* пригиба́ть) bend down.

пригова́ривать¹ *impf* keep saying.

пригова́ривать² *impf*, приговори́ть *pf* sentence, condemn. пригово́р verdict, sentence.

пригоди́ться (-ожу́сь) *pf* prove useful. приго́дный fit, suitable.

пригоня́ть *impf of* пригна́ть

пригора́ть *impf*, пригоре́ть (-ри́т) *pf* be burnt.

при́город suburb. при́городный suburban.

приго́рок (-рка) hillock.

при́горшня (*gen pl* -ей) handful.

приготови́тельный preparatory. пригото́вить (-влю) *pf*, приготовля́ть *impf* prepare; ~ся prepare. приготовле́ние preparation.

пригрева́ть *impf*, пригре́ть (-е́ю) *pf* warm; cherish.

при|грози́ть (-ожу́) *pf*.

придава́ть (-даю́, -даёшь) *impf*, прида́ть (-а́м, -а́шь, -а́ст, -ади́м; при́дал, -а́, -о) *pf* add; give; attach. прида́ча adding; addition; в прида́чу into the bargain.

придави́ть (-влю́, -вишь) *pf*, прида́вливать *impf* press (down).

прида́ное *sb* dowry. прида́-

ток (-тка) appendage.

придвига́ть *impf*, придви́нуть (-ну) *pf* move up, draw up; ~ся move up, draw near.

придво́рный court.

приде́лать *pf*, приде́лывать *impf* attach.

приде́рживаться *impf* hold on, hold; +*gen* keep to.

придеру́сь *etc.: see* придра́ться. придира́ться *impf of* придра́ться. приди́рка quibble; fault-finding. приди́рчивый fault-finding.

придоро́жный roadside.

придра́ться (-деру́сь, -дерёшься; -а́лся, -а́сь, -а́ло́сь) *pf* (*impf* придира́ться) find fault.

приду́ *etc.: see* прийти́

приду́мать *pf*, приду́мывать *impf* think up, invent.

прие́ду *etc.: see* прие́хать

прие́зд arrival. приезжа́ть *impf of* прие́хать. прие́зжий newly arrived; *sb* newcomer.

приём receiving; reception; surgery; welcome; admittance; dose; go; movement; method, way; trick. прие́млемый acceptable. приёмная *sb* waiting-room; reception room. приёмник (radio) receiver. приёмный receiving; reception; entrance; foster, adopted.

прие́хать (-е́ду) *pf* (*impf* приезжа́ть) arrive, come.

прижа́ть (-жму́, -жмёшь) *pf* (*impf* прижима́ть) press; clasp; ~ся nestle up.

приже́чь (-жгу́, -жжёшь; -жёг, -жгла́) *pf* (*impf* прижига́ть) cauterize.

прижива́ться *impf of* прижи́ться

прижига́ние cauterization. прижига́ть *impf of* приже́чь

прижима́ть(ся *impf of*

прижа́ть(ся

прижи́ться (-иву́сь, -иве́шься; -жи́лся, -а́сь) pf (impf прижива́ться) become acclimatized.

прижму́ etc.: see прижа́ть

приз (pl -ы́) prize.

призва́ние vocation. призва́ть (-зову́, -зове́шь; -а́л, -а́, -о) pf (impf призыва́ть) call; call upon; call up.

приземи́стый stocky, squat.

приземле́ние landing. приземли́ться pf, приземля́ться impf land.

призёр prizewinner.

при́зма prism.

признава́ть (-наю́, -наёшь) impf, призна́ть pf recognize; admit; ~ся confess. при́знак sign, symptom; indication. призна́ние confession, declaration; acknowledgement; recognition. при́знанный acknowledged, recognized. призна́тельный grateful.

призову́ etc.: see призва́ть

при́зрак spectre, ghost. при́зрачный ghostly; illusory, imagined.

призы́в call, appeal; slogan; call-up. призыва́ть impf of призва́ть. призывно́й conscription.

при́иск mine.

прийти́ (приду́, -дёшь; пришёл, -шла) pf (impf приходи́ть) come; arrive; ~ в себя́ regain consciousness; ~сь +по+dat fit; impers+dat have to; happen (to), fall to the lot (of).

прика́з order, command. прика́зание order, command. приказа́ть (-ажу́, -а́жешь) pf, прика́зывать impf order, command.

прика́лывать impf of приколо́ть. прикаса́ться impf of прикосну́ться

прика́нчивать impf of прико́нчить

прикати́ть (-ачу́, -а́тишь) pf, прика́тывать impf roll up.

прики́дывать impf, прики́нуть (-ну) pf throw in, add; weigh; estimate; ~ся +instr pretend (to be).

прикла́д[1] butt.

прикла́д[2] trimmings. прикладно́й applied. прикла́дывать(ся impf of приложи́ть(ся

прикле́ивать impf, прикле́ить pf stick; glue.

приключа́ться impf, приключи́ться pf happen, occur. приключе́ние adventure. приключе́нческий adventure.

прикова́ть (-кую́, -куёшь), прико́вывать impf chain; rivet.

прикола́чивать impf, приколоти́ть (-очу́, -о́тишь) pf nail. приколо́ть (-лю́, -лешь) pf (impf прика́лывать) pin; stab.

прикомандирова́ть pf, прикомандиро́вывать impf attach.

прико́нчить (-чу) pf (impf прика́нчивать) use up; finish off.

прикоснове́ние touch; concern. прикосну́ться (-ну́сь, -нёшься) pf (impf прикаса́ться) к+dat touch.

прикрепи́ть (-плю́) pf, прикрепля́ть impf fasten, attach. прикрепле́ние fastening; registration.

прикрыва́ть impf, прикры́ть (-ро́ю) pf cover; screen; shelter. прикры́тие cover; escort.

прику́ривать impf, прику́-

ри́ть (-рю́, -ри́шь) *pf* get a light.

прикуси́ть (-ушу́, -у́сишь) *pf*, прику́сывать *impf* bite.

прила́вок (-вка) counter.

прилага́тельное *sb* adjective. прилага́ть *impf* of приложи́ть

прила́дить (-а́жу) *pf*, прила́живать *impf* fit, adjust.

приласка́ть *pf* caress, pet; ~ся snuggle up.

прилега́ть *impf* (*pf* приле́чь) к+*dat*; adjoin. прилега́ющий close-fitting; adjoining, adjacent.

приле́жный diligent.

прилепи́ть(ся -плю́(сь, -пишь(ся) *pf*, прилепля́ть(ся *impf* stick.

прилёт arrival. прилета́ть *impf*, прилете́ть (-ечу́) *pf* arrive, fly in; come flying.

приле́чь (-ля́гу, -ля́жешь; -ёг, -гла́) *pf* (*impf* прилега́ть) lie down.

прили́в flow, flood; rising tide; surge. прилива́ть *impf* of прили́ть. прили́вный tidal.

прилипа́ть *impf*, прили́пнуть (-нет; -ли́п) *pf* stick.

прили́ть (-льёт; -и́л, -а́, -о) *pf* (*impf* прилива́ть) flow; rush.

прили́чие decency. прили́чный decent.

приложе́ние application; enclosure; supplement; appendix.

приложи́ть (-жу́ -жишь) *pf* (*impf* прикла́дывать, прилага́ть) put; apply; affix; add; enclose; ~ся take aim; +*instr* put, apply; +к+*dat* kiss.

прильёт *etc.*: see прили́ть.

при́льну(сь (-ну́, -нёшь) *pf*.

приля́гу *etc.*: see приле́чь

прима́нивать *impf*, прима́нить (-ню́, -нишь) *pf* lure, en-

tice. прима́нка bait, lure.

примене́ние application; use. примени́ть (-ню́, -нишь) *pf*, применя́ть *impf* apply; use; ~ся adapt o.s., conform.

приме́р example.

при|ме́рить *pf* (*impf also* примеря́ть) try on. приме́рка fitting.

приме́рно *adv* approximately. приме́рный exemplary; approximate.

примеря́ть *impf of* приме́рить

при́месь admixture.

приме́та sign, token. приме́тный perceptible; conspicuous.

примеча́ние note, footnote; *pl* comments. примеча́тельный notable.

примеша́ть *pf*, приме́шивать *impf* add, mix in.

примина́ть *impf of* примя́ть

примире́ние reconciliation. примири́тельный conciliatory. при|мири́ть *pf*, примиря́ть *impf* reconcile; conciliate; ~ся be reconciled.

примити́вный primitive.

примкну́ть (-ну́, -нёшь) *pf* (*impf* примыка́ть) join; fix, attach.

примну́ *etc.*: see примя́ть

примо́рский seaside; maritime. примо́рье seaside.

примо́чка wash, lotion.

приму́ *etc.*: see приня́ть

примча́ться (-чу́сь) *pf* come tearing along.

примыка́ть *impf of* примкну́ть; +к+*dat* adjoin. примыка́ющий affiliated.

примя́ть (-мну́, -мнёшь) *pf* (*impf* примина́ть) crush; trample down.

принадлежа́ть (-жу́) *impf* belong. принадле́жность belonging; membership; *pl* cessories; equipment.

принести́ (-су́, -сёшь) *pf* (*impf* **приноси́ть**) bring; fetch.

принима́ть *impf*, **принижа́ть** (-ижу́) *pf* humiliate; belittle.

принима́ть(ся *impf of* **приня́ть(ся**

приноси́ть (-ошу́, -о́сишь) *impf of* принести́. **приноше́ние** gift, offering.

при́нтер (*comput*) printer.

принуди́тельный compulsory. **прину́дить** (-у́жу) *pf*, **принужда́ть** *impf* compel. **принужде́ние** compulsion, coercion. **принуждённый** constrained, forced.

принц prince. **принце́сса** princess.

при́нцип principle. **принципиа́льно** *adv* on principle; in principle. **принципиа́льный** of principle; general.

приня́тие taking; acceptance; admission. it is accepted, it is usual; **не ~** it is not done. **приня́ть** (-иму́, -и́мешь; при́нял, -á, -о) *pf* (*impf* **принима́ть**) take; accept; take over; receive; **+за**+*acc* take for; **~ уча́стие** take part; **~ся** begin; take; take root; **~ за рабо́ту** set to work.

приободри́ть *pf*, **приободря́ть** *impf* cheer up; **~ся** cheer up.

приобрести́ (-ету́, -етёшь; -рёл, -á) *pf*, **приобрета́ть** *impf* acquire. **приобрете́ние** acquisition.

приобща́ть *impf*, **приобщи́ть** (-щу́) *pf* join, attach, unite; **~ся к**+*dat* join in.

приорите́т priority.

приостана́вливать *impf*, **приостанови́ть** (-влю́, -вишь) *pf* stop, suspend; **~ся** stop.

приостано́вка halt, suspension.

приоткрыва́ть *impf*, **приоткры́ть** (-ро́ю) *pf* open slightly.

припа́док (-дка) fit; attack.

припа́сы (-ов) *pl* stores, supplies.

припе́в refrain.

приписа́ть (-ишу́, -и́шешь) *pf*, **припи́сывать** *impf* add; attribute. **припи́ска** postscript; codicil.

припло́д offspring; increase.

приплыва́ть *impf*, **приплы́ть** (-ыву́, -ывёшь; -ы́л, -á, -о) *pf* swim up; sail up.

приплю́снуть (-ну) *pf*, **приплю́щивать** *impf* flatten.

приподнима́ть *impf*, **приподня́ть** (-ниму́, -ни́мешь; -о́днял, -á, -о) *pf* raise (a little); **~ся** raise o.s. (a little).

припо́й solder.

приполза́ть *impf*, **приползти́** (-зу́, -зёшь; -полз, -лá) *pf* creep up, crawl up.

припомина́ть *impf*, **припо́мнить** *pf* recollect.

припра́ва seasoning, flavouring. **припра́вить** (-влю) *pf*, **приправля́ть** *impf* season, flavour.

припря́тать (-я́чу) *pf*, **припря́тывать** *impf* secrete, put by.

припу́гивать *impf*, **припугну́ть** (-ну́, -нёшь) *pf* scare.

прираба́тывать *impf*, **прирабо́тать** *pf* earn ... extra. **при́работок** (-тка) additional earnings.

прира́внивать *impf*, **приравня́ть** *pf* equate (with к+*dat*).

прираста́ть *impf*, **прирасти́** (-тёт; -ро́с, -лá) *pf* adhere; take; increase; accrue.

приро́да nature. приро́дный natural; by birth; innate. прирождённый innate; born.

прирост etc.: see прирасти́. прирост increase.

приручать impf, приручи́ть (-чу́) pf tame; domesticate.

приса́живаться impf of присе́сть

присва́ивать impf, присво́ить pf appropriate; award.

приседать impf, присе́сть (-ся́ду) pf (impf also приса́живаться) sit down, take a seat.

прискакать (-ачу́, -а́чешь) pf come galloping.

приско́рбный sorrowful.

присла́ть (-ишлю́, -ишлёшь) pf (impf присыла́ть) send.

прислони́ть(ся (-оню́(сь, -о́ни́шь(ся) pf, прислоня́ть(ся impf lean, rest.

прислу́га servant; crew. прислу́живать impf (к+dat) wait (on), attend.

прислу́шаться pf, прислу́шиваться impf listen; +к+dat listen to; heed.

присма́тривать impf, присмотре́ть (-рю́, -ришь) pf +за+instr look after, keep an eye on; ~ся (к+dat) look closely (at). присмо́тр supervision.

при|сни́ться pf.

присоедине́ние joining; addition; annexation. присоедини́ть pf, присоединя́ть impf join; add; annex; ~ся (к+dat) join; subscribe to (an opinion).

приспосо́бить (-блю) pf, приспособля́ть impf fit, adjust, adapt; ~ся adapt o.s. приспособле́ние adaptation; device; appliance. приспосо́бля́емость adaptability.

пристава́ть (-таю́, -таёшь)

impf of приста́ть

приста́вить (-влю) pf (impf приставля́ть) к+dat place, set, or lean against; add; appoint to look after.

приста́вка prefix.

приставля́ть impf of приста́вить

приста́льный intent.

прист́анище refuge, shelter.

при́стань (gen pl -е́й) landing-stage; pier; wharf.

приста́ть (-а́ну) pf (impf пристава́ть) stick, adhere (к+dat to); pester.

пристёгивать impf, пристегну́ть (-ну́, -нёшь) pf fasten.

присто́йный decent, proper.

пристра́ивать(ся impf of пристро́ить(ся

пристра́стие predilection; passion; bias. пристра́стный biased.

пристре́ливать impf, пристрели́ть pf shoot (down).

пристро́ить (-о́ю) pf (impf пристра́ивать) add, build on; fix up; ~ся be fixed up, get a place. пристро́йка annexe, extension.

при́ступ assault; fit, attack. приступа́ть impf, приступи́ть (-плю́, -пишь) pf к+dat set about, start.

при|стыди́ть (-ыжу́) pf.

при|стыкова́ться pf.

присуди́ть (-ужу́, -у́дишь) pf, присужда́ть impf sentence, condemn; award; confer. присужде́ние awarding; conferment.

прису́тствие presence. прису́тствовать impf be present, attend. прису́тствующие sb pl those present.

прису́щий inherent; characteristic.

присыла́ть *impf of* присла́ть

прися́га oath. присяга́ть *impf*, присягну́ть (-ну́, -нёшь) *pf* swear.

прися́ду *etc.: see* присе́сть

прися́жный *sb* juror.

притаи́ть *pf* hide.

прита́птывать *impf of* притопта́ть

прита́скивать *impf*, притащи́ть (-ащу́, -а́щишь) *pf* bring, drag, haul; ~ся drag o.s.

притвори́ться *pf*, притворя́ться *impf +instr* pretend to be. притво́рный pretended, feigned. притво́рство pretence, sham. притво́рщик sham; hypocrite.

притека́ть *impf of* прите́чь

притесне́ние oppression. притесни́ть *pf*, притесня́ть *impf* oppress.

прите́чь (-ечёт, -еку́т; -ёк, -ла́) *pf* (*impf* притека́ть) pour in.

притиха́ть *impf*, прити́хнуть (-ну; -их) *pf* quiet down.

прито́к tributary; influx.

прито́лока lintel.

прито́м *conj* (and) besides.

прито́н den, haunt.

притопта́ть (-пчу́, -пчешь) *pf* (*impf* прита́птывать) trample down.

прито́рный sickly-sweet, luscious, cloying.

притра́гиваться *impf*, притро́нуться (-нусь) *pf* touch.

притупля́ть *impf* blunt, dull; deaden; ~ся become blunt or dull.

при́тча parable.

притя́гивать *impf of* притяну́ть

притяга́тельный attractive, magnetic. притя́гивать *impf of* притяну́ть

притяжа́тельный possessive.

притяже́ние attraction.

притяза́ние claim, pretension.

притяза́тельный demanding.

притя́нутый far-fetched. притяну́ть (-ну́, -нешь) *pf* (*impf* притя́гивать) attract; drag (up).

приуро́чивать *impf*, приуро́чить (-чу) *pf* к+*dat* time to.

приуса́дебный: ~ уча́сток individual plot (*in kolkhoz*).

приуча́ть *impf*, приучи́ть (-чу́, -чишь) *pf* train, school.

прихлеба́тель *m* sponger.

прихо́д coming, arrival; receipts; parish. приходи́ть(ся (-ожу́(сь, -о́дишь(ся) *impf of* прийти́(сь. прихо́дный receipt. приходя́щий non-resident; ~ больно́й outpatient.

прихожа́нин (*pl* -а́не, -а́н), -а́нка parishioner.

прихо́жая *sb* hall, lobby.

прихотли́вый capricious; fanciful, intricate. при́хоть whim, caprice.

прихра́мывать limp (slightly).

прице́л sight; aiming. прице́ливаться *impf*, прице́литься *pf* take aim.

прице́ниваться *impf*, прицени́ться (-ню́сь, -ни́шься) *pf* к+*dat* ask the price (of).

прице́п trailer. прицепи́ть (-плю́, -пишь) *pf*, прицепля́ть *impf* hitch, hook on; ~ся к+*dat* stick to, cling to. прице́пка hitching, hooking on; quibble. прицепно́й: ~ ваго́н trailer.

прича́л mooring; mooring line. прича́ливать *impf*, прича́лить *pf* moor.

прича́стие[1] participle. прича́стие[2] communion. причасти́ть (-ащу́) *pf* (*impf* причаща́ть) give communion to; ~ся receive communion.

прича́стный[1] participial. при-

ча́стный[2] concerned; privy.

причаща́ть *impf of* **причасти́ть**

причём *conj* moreover, and.

причеса́ть (-ешу́, -е́шешь) *pf*, **причёсывать** *impf* comb; do the hair (of); **~ся** do one's hair, have one's hair done. **причёска** hair-do; haircut.

причи́на cause; reason. **причини́ть** *pf*, **причиня́ть** *impf* cause.

причи́слить *pf*, **причисля́ть** *impf* number, rank (к+*dat* among); add on.

причита́ние lamentation. **причита́ть** *impf* lament.

причита́ться *impf* be due.

причмо́кивать *impf*, **причмо́кнуть** (-ну) *pf* smack one's lips.

причу́да caprice, whim.

при|чу́диться *pf*.

причу́дливый odd; fantastic; whimsical.

при|швартова́ть *pf*. **пришёл** *etc.: see* **прийти́**

прише́лец (-льца) newcomer.

прише́ствие coming; advent.

пришива́ть *impf*, **приши́ть** (-шью́, -шьёшь) *pf* sew on.

пришлю́ *etc.: see* **присла́ть**

пришпи́ливать *impf*, **пришпи́лить** *pf* pin on.

пришпо́ривать *impf*, **пришпо́рить** *pf* spur (on).

прищеми́ть (-млю́) *pf*, **прищемля́ть** *impf* pinch.

прище́пка clothes-peg.

прищу́риваться *impf*, **прищу́риться** *pf* screw up one's eyes.

прию́т shelter, refuge. **прию́ти́ть** (-ючу́) *pf* shelter; **~ся** take shelter.

прия́тель *m*, **прия́тельница** friend. **прия́тельский** friendly. **прия́тный** nice, pleasant.

про *prep+acc* about; for; ~ себя́ to o.s.

проанализи́ровать *pf*.

про́ба trial, test; hallmark; sample.

пробе́г run; race. **пробега́ть** *impf*, **пробежа́ть** (-егу́) *pf* run; cover; run past.

пробе́л blank, gap; flaw.

пробе́ру *etc.: see* **пробра́ть**.

пробива́ть(ся *impf of* **проби́ть(ся**. **пробира́ть(ся** *impf of* **пробра́ть(ся**

пробирка test-tube. **проби́ровать** *impf* test, assay.

про|би́ть (-бью́, -бьёшь) *pf* (*impf also* **пробива́ть**) make a hole in; pierce; punch; **~ся** force, make, one's way.

про́бка cork; stopper; fuse; (traffic) jam, congestion. **про́бковый** cork.

пробле́ма problem.

про́блеск flash; gleam, ray.

про́бный trial, test; ~ ка́мень touchstone. **про́бовать** *impf* (*pf* ис~, по~) try; attempt.

пробо́ина hole.

пробо́р parting.

про|бормота́ть (-очу́, -о́чешь) *pf*.

пробра́ть (-беру́, -берёшь; -а́л, -а́, -о) *pf* (*impf* **пробира́ть**) penetrate; scold; **~ся** make or force one's way.

пробу́ду *etc.: see* **пробы́ть**

про|буди́ть (-ужу́, -у́дишь) *pf*, **пробужда́ть** *impf* wake (up); arouse; **~ся** wake up. **пробужде́ние** awakening.

про|бура́вить (-влю) *pf*, **пробура́вливать** *impf* bore (through), drill.

про|бури́ть *pf*.

пробы́ть (-бу́ду; про́бы́л, -а́, -о) *pf* stay; be.

пробью́ *etc.: see* **проби́ть**

провал failure; downfall; gap.

прова́ливать *impf*, **прова-ли́ть** (-лю́, -лишь) *pf* bring down; ruin; reject, fail; **~ся** collapse; fall in; fail; disappear.

прове́дать *pf*, **прове́дывать** *impf* call on; learn.

проведе́ние conducting; construction; installation.

провезти́ (-зу́; -зёшь; -ёз, -ла́) *pf* (*impf* **провози́ть**) convey, transport.

прове́рить *pf*, **проверя́ть** *impf* check; test. **прове́рка** checking, check; testing.

про|вести́ (-еду́, -едёшь; -ёл, -а́) *pf* (*impf also* **проводи́ть**) lead, take; build; install; carry out; conduct; pass; draw; spend; +*instr* pass over.

прове́тривать *impf*, **про-ве́трить** *pf* air.

про|ве́ять (-е́ю) *pf*.

провиде́ние Providence.

прови́зия provisions.

провини́ться *pf* be guilty; do wrong.

провинциа́льный provincial. **прови́нция** province; the provinces.

про́вод (*pl* -а́) wire, lead, line. **проводи́мость** conductivity. **проводи́ть**[1] (-ожу́, -о́дишь) *impf of* **провести́**; conduct.

проводи́ть[2] (-ожу́, -о́дишь) *pf* (*impf* **провожа́ть**) accompany; see off.

прово́дка leading, taking; building; installation; wiring, wires.

проводни́к[1] (-а́) guide; conductor.

проводни́к[2] (-а́) conductor; bearer; transmitter.

про́воды (-ов) *pl* send-off. **провожа́тый** *sb* guide, escort. **провожа́ть** *impf of*

проводи́ть

прово́з conveyance, transport.

провозгласи́ть (-ашу́) *pf*, **провозглаша́ть** *impf* proclaim; propose. **провозглаше́ние** proclamation.

провози́ть (-ожу́, -о́зишь) *impf of* **провезти́**

провока́тор agent provocateur. **провока́ция** provocation.

про́волока wire. **про́волочный** wire.

прово́рный quick; agile. **прово́рство** quickness; agility.

провоци́ровать *impf & pf* (*pf* с~) provoke.

прогада́ть *pf*, **прога́дывать** *impf* miscalculate.

прога́лина glade; space.

прогиба́ть(ся *impf of* **прогну́ть(ся**

прогла́тывать *impf*, **проглоти́ть** (-очу́, -о́тишь) *pf* swallow.

прогляде́ть (-яжу́) *pf*, **про-гля́дывать**[1] *impf* overlook; look through. **прогляну́ть** (-я́нет) *pf*, **прогля́дывать**[2] *pf* show, peep through, appear.

прогна́ть (-гоню́, -го́нишь; -а́л, -а́, -о) *pf* (*impf* **прогоня́ть**) drive away; banish; drive; sack.

прогнива́ть *impf*, **прогни́ть** (-иёт; -и́л, -а́, -о) *pf* rot through.

прогно́з prognosis; (weather) forecast.

прогну́ть (-ну́, -нёшь) *pf* (*impf* **прогиба́ть**) cause to sag; **~ся** sag, bend.

прогова́ривать *impf*, **проговори́ть** *pf* say, utter; talk; **~ся** let the cat out of the bag.

проголода́ться *pf* get hungry.

про|голосова́ть *pf*.

прого́н purlin; girder; stairwell.

прогоня́ть impf of **прогна́ть**

прогора́ть impf, **прогоре́ть** (-рю́) pf burn (through); burn out; go bankrupt.

прого́рклый rancid, rank.

програ́мма programme; syllabus. **программи́ровать** impf (pf за-) programme.

прогрева́ть impf, **прогре́ть** (-е́ю) pf heat; warm up; **~ся** warm up.

про|греме́ть (-млю́) pf. **про|грохота́ть** (-очу́, -о́чешь) pf.

прогре́сс progress. **прогресси́вный** progressive. **прогресси́ровать** impf progress.

прогрыза́ть impf, **прогры́зть** (-зу́, -зёшь; -ы́з) pf gnaw through.

про|гуде́ть (-гужу́) pf.

прогу́л truancy; absenteeism. **прогу́ливать** impf, **прогуля́ть** pf play truant, be absent, (from); miss; take for a walk; **~ся** take a walk. **прогу́лка** walk, stroll; outing. **прогу́льщик** absentee, truant.

продава́ть (-даю́, -даёшь) impf, **прода́ть** (-а́м, -а́шь, -а́ст, -ади́м; про́дал, -á, -о) pf sell. **продава́ться** (-даётся) impf be for sale; sell. **продаве́ц** (-вца́) seller, vendor; salesman. **продавщи́ца** seller, vendor; saleswoman. **прода́жа** sale. **прода́жный** for sale; corrupt.

продвига́ть impf, **продви́нуть** (-ну) pf move on, push forward; advance; **~ся** move forward; push on. **продвиже́ние** advancement.

продева́ть impf of **проде́ть**

про|деклами́ровать pf.

проде́лать pf, **проде́лывать** impf do, perform, make. **проде́лка** trick; prank.

продемонстри́ровать pf

demonstrate, show.

продёргивать impf of **продёрнуть**

продержа́ть (-жу́, -жишь) pf hold; keep; **~ся** hold out.

продёрнуть (-ну, -нешь) pf (impf **продёргивать**) pass, run; criticize severely.

проде́ть (-е́ну) pf (impf **продева́ть**) pass; **~ ни́тку в иго́лку** thread a needle.

продешеви́ть (-влю́) pf sell too cheap.

про|диктова́ть pf.

продлева́ть impf, **продли́ть** pf prolong. **продле́ние** extension. **про|дли́ться** pf.

продма́г grocery. **продово́льственный** food. **продово́льствие** food; provisions.

продолгова́тый oblong.

продолжа́тель m continuer. **продолжа́ть** impf, **продо́лжить** (-жу) pf continue; prolong; **~ся** continue, last, go on. **продолже́ние** continuation; sequel; **в ~+gen** in the course of. **продолжи́тельность** duration. **продолжи́тельный** long; prolonged.

продо́льный longitudinal.

продро́гнуть (-ну; -óг) pf be chilled to the bone.

продтова́ры (-ов) pl food products.

продува́ть impf of **проду́ть**

проду́кт product; pl food-stuffs. **продукти́вность** productivity. **продукти́вный** productive. **проду́ктовый** food. **проду́кция** production.

проду́манный well thought-out; considered. **проду́мать** pf, **проду́мывать** impf think over; think out.

проду́ть (-у́ю, -у́ешь) pf (impf **продува́ть**) blow through.

продыря́вить (-влю) *pf* make a hole in.

проеда́ть *impf of* **прое́сть**.

прое́ду *etc.: see* **прое́хать**

прое́зд passage, thoroughfare; trip. **прое́здить** (-зжу) *pf* (*impf* **проезжа́ть**) spend travelling. **прое́здно́й** travelling; ~**о́й биле́т** ticket; ~**а́я пла́та** fare; ~**ы́е** *sb pl* travelling expenses. **проезжа́ть** *impf of* **прое́здить, прое́хать**. **прое́зжий** passing (by); *sb* passer-by.

прое́кт project, plan, design; draft. **проекти́ровать** *impf* (*pf* **с~**) project; plan. **прое́ктный** planning; planned. **прое́ктор** projector.

проекцио́нный фона́рь *m* projector. **прое́кция** projection.

прое́сть (-е́м, -е́шь, -е́ст, -еди́м; -е́л) *pf* (*impf* **проеда́ть**) eat through, corrode; spend on food.

прое́хать (-е́ду) *pf* (*impf* **проезжа́ть**) pass, ride, drive (by, through); cover.

прожа́ренный (*cul*) well-done.

прожева́ть (-жую́, -жуёшь) *pf*, **прожёвывать** *impf* chew well.

проже́ктор (*pl* -ы *or* -а́) searchlight.

проже́чь (-жгу́, -жжёшь; -жёг, -жгла́) *pf* (*impf* **прожига́ть**) burn (through).

прожива́ть *impf of* **прожи́ть**. **прожига́ть** *impf of* **проже́чь** **прожи́точный ми́нимум** living wage. **прожи́ть** (-иву́, -ивёшь; -о́жи́л, -а́, -о) *pf* (*impf* **прожива́ть**) live; spend.

прожо́рливый gluttonous.

про́за prose. **проза́ический** prose; prosaic.

прозва́ние, про́звище nickname. **прозва́ть** (-зову́, -зо-

вёшь; -а́л, -а́, -о) *pf* (*impf* **прозыва́ть**) nickname, name.

про|звуча́ть *pf*.

про|зева́ть *pf*. **про|зимова́ть** *pf*. **прозо́вы** *etc.: see* **прозва́ть**

прозорли́вый perspicacious.

прозра́чный transparent.

прозрева́ть *impf*, **прозре́ть** *pf* regain one's sight; see clearly. **прозре́ние** recovery of sight; insight.

прозыва́ть *impf of* **прозва́ть** **прозяба́ние** vegetation. **прозяба́ть** *impf* vegetate.

проигра́ть *pf*, **прои́грывать** *impf* lose; play; ~**а** gamble away all one's money. **прои́грыватель** *m* record-player. **про́игрыш** *m* loss.

произведе́ние work; production; product. **произвести́** (-еду́, -едёшь; -ёл, -а́) *pf*, **производи́ть** (-ожу́, -о́дишь) *impf* make; carry out; produce; **+в**+*acc/nom pl* promote to (the rank of). **производи́тель** *m* producer. **производи́тельность** productivity. **производи́тельный** productive. **произво́дный** derivative. **произво́дственный** industrial; production. **произво́дство** production.

произво́л arbitrariness; arbitrary rule. **произво́льный** arbitrary.

произнести́ (-су́, -сёшь; -ёс, -ла́) *pf*, **произноси́ть** (-ошу́, -о́сишь) *impf* pronounce; utter. **произноше́ние** pronunciation. **произойти́** (-ойдёт; -ошёл, -шла́) *pf* (*impf* **происходи́ть**) happen, occur; result; be descended.

произраста́ть *impf*, **произрасти́** (-ту́; -тёшь; -рос, -ла́) *pf* sprout; grow.

про́иски (-ов) *pl* intrigues.

проистека́ть *impf*, **происте́чь** (-ечёт; -ёк, -ла́) *pf* spring, result.

происходи́ть (-ожу́, -о́дишь) *impf of* **произойти́**; **происхожде́ние** origin; birth.

происше́ствие event, incident.

пройдо́ха *m & f* sly person.

пройти́ (-йду́, -йдёшь; -ошёл, -шла́) *pf* (*impf* **проходи́ть**) pass; go; go past; cover; study; get through; ~сь (*impf* **проха́живаться**) take a stroll.

прок use, benefit.

прокажённый *sb* leper. **прока́за**[1] leprosy.

прока́за[2] mischief; prank. **прока́зничать** *impf* (*pf* **на**~) be up to mischief. **прока́зник** prankster.

прока́лывать *impf of* **проколо́ть**

прока́пывать *impf of* **прокопа́ть**

прока́т hire.

прокати́ться (-ачу́сь, -а́тишься) *pf* roll; for a drive. **прока́тный** rolling; rolled.

прокипяти́ть (-ячу́) *pf* boil (thoroughly).

прокиса́ть *impf*, **про**|**ки́снуть** (-нет) *pf* turn (sour).

прокла́дка laying; construction; washer; packing. **прокла́дывать** *impf of* **проложи́ть**

проклама́ция leaflet.

проклина́ть *impf*, **прокля́сть** (-яну́, -янёшь; -оклял, -а́, -о) *pf* curse, damn. **прокля́тие** curse; damnation. **прокля́тый** (-ят, -а́, -о) damned.

проко́л puncture.

проколо́ть (-лю́, -лешь) *pf* (*impf* **прока́лывать**) prick, pierce.

прокомменти́ровать *pf* comment (upon).

про|**компости́ровать** *pf*. **про**|**конспекти́ровать** *pf*. **про**|**консульти́ровать**(**ся** *pf*. **про**|**контроли́ровать** *pf*.

прокопа́ть *pf* (*impf* **прока́пывать**) dig, dig through.

проко́рм nourishment, sustenance. **про**|**корми́ть**(**ся** (-млю́(сь, -мишь(ся) *pf*.

про|**корректи́ровать** *pf*.

прокра́дываться *impf*, **прокра́сться** (-аду́сь, -адёшься) *pf* steal in.

прокурату́ра office of public prosecutor. **прокуро́р** public prosecutor.

прокуси́ть (-ушу́, -у́сишь) *pf*, **проку́сывать** *impf* bite through.

прокути́ть (-учу́, -у́тишь) *pf*, **проку́чивать** *impf* squander; go on a binge.

пролага́ть *impf of* **проложи́ть**

прола́мывать *impf of* **проломи́ть**

пролега́ть *impf* lie, run.

пролеза́ть *impf*, **проле́зть** (-зу; -лез) *pf* get through, climb through.

про|**лепета́ть** (-ечу́, -е́чешь) *pf*.

пролёт span; stairwell; bay. **пролетариа́т** proletariat. **пролета́рий** proletarian. **пролета́рский** proletarian.

пролета́ть *impf*, **пролете́ть** (-ечу́) *pf* fly; cover; fly by, past, through.

проли́в strait. **пролива́ть** *impf*, **проли́ть** (-лью, -льёшь; -о́лил, -а́, -о) *pf* spill, shed; ~ся be spilt.

проло́г prologue.

проложи́ть (-жу́, -жишь) *pf* (*impf* **прокла́дывать**, **прола-**

ráть lay; build; interlay.

пролóм breach, break. **проломáть, проломить** (-млю, -мишь) *pf* (*impf* **проламывать**) break (through).

пролью *etc.*: see **пролить**

про|мáзать (-áжу) *pf*. **промáтывать(ся** *impf of* **промотáть(ся**

прóмах miss; slip, blunder. **промáхиваться** *impf*, **промахнýться** (-нýсь, -нёшься) *pf* miss; make a blunder.

промáчивать *impf of* **промочить**

промедлéние delay. **промéдлить** *pf* delay; procrastinate.

промежýток (-тка) interval; space. **промежýточный** intermediate

промелькнýть (-нý, -нёшь) *pf* flash (past, by).

промéнивать *impf*, **променять** *pf* exchange.

промерзáть *impf*, **промёрзнуть** (-ну; -ёрз) *pf* freeze through. **промёрзлый** frozen.

промокáть *impf*, **промóкнуть** (-ну; -мóк) *pf* get soaked; let water in.

промóлвить (-влю) *pf* say, utter.

промолчáть (-чý) *pf* keep silent.

про|мотáть *pf* (*impf also* **промáтывать**) squander.

промочить (-чý, -чишь) *pf* (*impf* **промáчивать**) soak, drench.

промóю *etc.*: see **промыть**

промтовáры (-ов) *pl* manufactured goods.

промчáться (-чýсь) *pf* rush by.

промывáть *impf of* **промыть**

прóмысел (-сла) trade, business; *pl* works. **промыслóвый** producers'; business; game.

промыть (-мóю) *pf* (*impf* **промывáть**) wash (thoroughly); bathe; ∼ мозг+*dat* brain-wash.

про|мычáть (-чý) *pf*.

промышленник industrialist. **промышленность** industry. **промышленный** industrial.

пронести (-сý, -сёшь; -ёс, -лá) *pf* (*impf* **проносить**) carry (past, through); pass (over); ∼сь rush past, through; scud (past); fly; spread.

пронзáть *impf*, **пронзить** (-нжý) *pf* pierce, transfix. **пронзительный** piercing.

пронизáть (-ижý, -ижешь) *pf*, **пронизывать** *impf* pierce; permeate.

проникáть *impf*, **проникнуть** (-ну; -ик) *pf* penetrate; percolate; ∼ся be imbued. **проникновéние** penetration; feeling. **проникновéнный** heartfelt.

проницáемый permeable. **проницáтельный** perspicacious.

проносить(ся (-ошý(сь, -óсишь(ся) *impf of* **пронести(сь.**

про|нумеровáть *pf*.

пронюхать *pf*, **пронюхивать** *impf* smell out, get wind of.

прообраз prototype.

пропагáнда propaganda. **пропагандист** propagandist.

пропадáть *impf of* **пропáсть.**

пропáжа loss.

пропáлывать *impf of* **прополóть**

прóпасть precipice; abyss; lots of.

пропáсть (-адý, -адёшь) *pf* (*impf* **пропадáть**) be missing; be lost; disappear; be done for, die; be wasted. **пропáщий** lost; hopeless.

пропекáть(ся *impf of* **пропéчь(ся. про|пéть** (-пою, -поёшь) *pf*.

пропечь (-еку́, -ечёшь; -ёк, -ла́) *pf* (*impf* **пропека́ть**) bake thoroughly; ~ся get baked through.

пропива́ть *impf of* **пропи́ть**

прописа́ть (-ишу́, -и́шешь) *pf*, **пропи́сывать** *impf* prescribe; register; ~ся register. **пропи́ска** registration; residence permit. **прописн|о́й**: ~а́я бу́ква capital letter; ~а́я и́стина truism. **про́писью** *adv* in words.

пропита́ние subsistence, sustenance. **пропита́ть** *pf*, **пропи́тывать** *impf* impregnate, saturate.

пропи́ть (-пью́, -пьёшь; -о́пи́л, -а́, -о) *pf* (*impf* **пропива́ть**) spend on drink.

проплыва́ть *impf*, **проплы́ть** (-ыву́, -ывёшь; -ы́л, -а́, -о) *pf* swim, sail, *or* float past *or* through.

пропове́дник preacher; advocate. **пропове́довать** *impf* preach; advocate. **про́поведь** sermon; advocacy.

проползти́ *impf*, **проползти́** (-зу́, -зёшь; -по́лз, -ла́) *pf* crawl, creep.

пропо́лка weeding. **прополо́ть** (-лю́, -лешь) *pf* (*impf* **пропа́лывать**) weed.

про|полоска́ть (-ощу́, -о́щешь) *pf*.

пропорциона́льный proportional, proportionate. **пропо́рция** proportion.

про́пуск (*pl* -а́ *or* -и, -о́в *or* -ов) pass, permit; password; admission; omission; non-attendance; blank, gap. **пропуска́ть** (-у́щу́, -у́стишь) *impf*, **пропусти́ть** (-ущу́, -у́стишь) *pf* let pass; let in; pass; leave out; miss. **про́пускн|о́й**: ~а́я спосо́бность

capacity.

пропью́ *etc.*: *see* **пропи́ть**

прора́б works superintendent. **прораба́тывать** *impf*, **прорабо́тать** *pf* work (through, at); study; pick holes in.

прораста́ние germination; sprouting. **прораста́ть** *impf*, **прорасти́** (-тёт; -ро́с, -ла́) germinate, sprout.

прорва́ть (-ву́, -вёшь; -а́л, -а́, -о) *pf* (*impf* **прорыва́ть**) break through; ~ся burst open; break through.

про|реаги́ровать *pf*.

проредить (-ежу́) *pf*, **проре́живать** *impf* thin out.

про́рез cut; slit, notch. **про|ре́зать** (-е́жу) *pf*, **прореза́ть** *impf* (*impf also* **проре́зывать**) cut through; ~ся be cut, come through.

проре́зывать(ся *impf of* **проре́зать(ся. про|репети́ровать** *pf*.

проре́ха tear, slit; flies; deficiency.

про|рецензи́ровать *pf*.

проро́к prophet.

пророни́ть *pf* utter.

проро́с *etc.*: *see* **прорасти́**

проро́ческий prophetic. **проро́чество** prophecy.

проро́ю *etc.*: *see* **проры́ть**

проруба́ть *impf*, **проруби́ть** (-блю́, -бишь) *pf* cut *or* hack through. **про́рубь** ice-hole.

проры́в break; break-through; hitch. **прорыва́ть¹(ся** *impf of* **прорва́ть(ся**

прорыва́ть² *impf*, **проры́ть** (-ро́ю) *pf* dig through; ~ся dig one's way through.

проса́чиваться *impf of* **просочи́ться**

просве́рливать *impf*, **просверли́ть** *pf* drill, bore;

perforate.

просвет (clear) space; shaft of light; ray of hope; opening. **просветительный** educational. **просветить**[1] (-ещу) *pf* (*impf* **просвещать**) enlighten.

просветить[2] (-ечу, -етишь) *pf* (*impf* **просвечивать**) X-ray.

просветление brightening (up); lucidity. **про|светлеть** (-еет) *pf*.

просвечивание radioscopy. **просвечивать** *impf of* **просветить**; be translucent; be visible.

просвещать *impf of* **просветить**. **просвещение** enlightenment.

просвира communion bread.

проседь streak(s) of grey.

просеивать *impf of* **просеять**.

просека cutting, ride.

проселок (-лка) country road.

просеять (-ею) *pf* (*impf* **просеивать**) sift.

про|сигнализировать *pf*.

просидеть (-ижу) *pf*, **про|сиживать** (*impf*) sit.

просительный pleading. **просить** (-ошу, -осишь) *impf* (*pf* **по∼**) ask; beg; invite; **∼ся** ask; apply.

проскакивать *impf of* **проскочить**

проскальзывать *impf of*, **проскользнуть** (-ну, -нёшь) *pf* slip, creep.

проскочить (-чу, -чишь) *pf* (*impf* **проскакивать**) rush by; slip through; creep in.

прославить (-влю) *pf*, **про|славлять** *impf* glorify; make famous; **∼ся** become famous. **прославленный** renowned.

проследить (-ежу) *pf*, **про|слеживать** *impf* track

(down); trace.

прослезиться (-ежусь) *pf* shed a few tears.

прослойка layer, stratum.

прослужить (-жу, -жишь) *pf* serve (for a certain time).

про|слушать *pf*, **прослушивать** *impf* hear; listen to; miss, not catch.

про|слыть (-ыву, -ывешь; -ыл, -а, -о) *pf*.

просматривать *impf*, **просмотреть** (-рю, -ришь) *pf* look over; overlook. **просмотр** survey; view, viewing; examination.

проснуться (-нусь, -нёшься) *pf* (*impf* **просыпаться**) wake up.

просо millet.

просовывать(ся *impf of* **просунуть(ся**

про|сохнуть (-ну; -ох) *pf* (*impf also* **просыхать**) dry out.

просочиться (-ится) *pf* (*impf* **просачиваться**) percolate; seep (out); leak (out).

проспать (-плю; -ал, -а, -о) *pf* (*impf* **просыпать**) sleep (through); oversleep.

проспект avenue.

про|спрягать *pf*.

просроченный overdue; expired. **просрочить** (-чу) *pf* allow to run out; be behind with; overstay. **просрочка** delay; expiry of time limit.

простаивать *impf of* **простоять**

простак (-á) simpleton.

простенок (-нка) pier (between windows).

простереться (-трётся; -тёрся) *pf*, **простираться** *impf* extend.

простительный pardonable, excusable. **простить** (-ощу) *pf* (*impf* **прощать**) forgive;

excuse; ~ся (c+*instr*) say goodbye (to).

проститу́тка prostitute. **проститу́ция** prostitution.

про́сто *adv* simply.

простоволо́сый bare-headed. **простоду́шный** simple-hearted; ingenuous.

просто́й[1] downtime.

прост|о́й[2] simple; plain; mere; ~ым гла́зом with the naked eye; ~бе число́ prime number. **простоква́ша** thick sour milk. **про́сто-на́просто** *adv* simply. **простонаро́дный** of the common people.

просто́р spaciousness; space. **просто́рный** spacious.

просторе́чие popular speech. **простосерде́чный** simple-hearted.

простота́ simplicity.

просто|я́ть (-ою́) *pf* (*impf* **проста́ивать**) stand (idle).

простра́нный extensive, vast. **простра́нственный** spatial. **простра́нство** space.

простре́л lumbago. **простре́л|ивать** *impf*, **простре́лить** (-лю́, -лишь) *pf* shoot through.

про|стро́чить (-очу́, -о́чишь) *pf.*

просту́да cold. **простуди́ть|ся** (-ужу́сь, -у́дишься) *pf*, **простужа́ться** *impf* catch (a) cold.

простyпа́ть *impf*, **простyпи́ть** (-ит) *pf* appear.

просту́пок (-пка) misdemeanour.

простыня́ (*pl* просты́ни, -ы́нь, -ня́м) sheet.

про|сты́ть (-ы́ну) *pf* get cold.

просу́нуть (-ну) *pf* (*impf* **просо́вывать**) push, thrust.

просу́шивать *impf*, **просуши́ть** (-шу́, -шишь) *pf* dry out;

~ся (get) dry.

просущество́вать *pf* exist; endure.

просчёт error. **просчита́ть|ся**, **просчи́тываться** *impf* miscalculate.

просы|па́ть (-плю) *pf*, **сыпа́ть**[1] *impf* spill; ~ся get spilt.

просыпа́ть[2] *impf* of **проспа́ть**. **просыпа́ться** *impf* of **просну́ться**. **просыха́ть** *impf* of **просо́хнуть**.

про́сьба request.

прота́лкивать *impf* of **протолкну́ть**. **прота́пливать** *impf* of **протопи́ть**. **прота́птывать** *impf* of **протопта́ть**.

прота́скивать *impf*, **протащи́ть** (-щу́, -щишь) *pf* drag, push (through).

проте́з artificial limb, prosthesis; зубно́й ~ denture.

протеи́н protein.

протека́ть *impf* of **проте́чь**.

проте́кция patronage.

протере́ть (-тру́, -трёшь; -тёр) *pf* (*impf* **протира́ть**) wipe (over); wear (through).

проте́ст protest. **протеста́нт**, ~ка Protestant. **протестова́ть** *impf* protest.

проте́чь (-ечёт; -тёк, -ла́) *pf* (*impf* **протека́ть**) flow; leak; seep; pass; take its course.

про́тив *prep*+*gen* against; opposite; contrary to, as against.

проти́вень (-вня) *m* baking-tray; meat-pan.

проти́в|иться (-влюсь) *impf* (*pf* вос~) +*dat* oppose; resist. **проти́вник** opponent; the enemy. **проти́вный**[1] opposite; contrary. **проти́вный**[2] nasty, disgusting.

противо- *in comb* anti-, contra-.

counter-. **противове́с** counter-balance. **~возду́шный** anti-aircraft. **~га́з** gas-mask. **~де́йствие** opposition. **~де́йствовать** *impf* +*dat* oppose; counteract. **~есте́ственный** unnatural. **~зако́нный** illegal.

~зача́точный contraceptive. **~поло́жность** opposite; opposition, contrast. **~поло́жный** opposite; contrary. **~поста́вить** (-влю) *pf*, **~поставля́ть** *impf* oppose; contrast. **~речи́вый** contradictory; conflicting. **~ре́чие** contradiction. **~ре́чить** (-чу) *impf* +*dat* contradict. **~сто́ять** (-ою́) *impf* +*dat* resist, withstand. **~та́нковый** anti-tank. **~я́дие** antidote.

протира́ть *impf of* протере́ть

проти́скивать *impf*, **проти́снуть** (-ну) *pf* force, squeeze (through, into).

проткну́ть (-ну́, -нёшь) *pf* (*impf* протыка́ть) pierce; skewer.

протоко́л minutes; report; protocol.

протолкну́ть (-ну́, -нёшь) *pf* (*impf* прота́лкивать) push through.

прото́н proton.

протопи́ть (-плю́, -пишь) *pf* (*impf* прота́пливать) heat (thoroughly).

протопта́ть (-пчу́, -пчешь) *pf* (*impf* прота́птывать) tread; wear out.

протоптанный beaten, well-trodden.

прототи́п prototype.

прото́чный flowing, running.

про|тра́вить *pf*, функ *etc.*: *see* протере́ть. **про|труби́ть** (-блю́) *pf*.

протрезви́ться (-влю́сь) *pf*,

протрезвля́ться *impf* sober up.

протуха́ть *impf*, **проту́хнуть** (-нет; -ух) *pf* become rotten; go bad.

протыка́ть *impf of* проткну́ть

протя́гивать *impf*, **протяну́ть** (-ну́, -нешь) *pf* stretch; extend; hold out; **~ся** stretch out; extend; last. **протяже́ние** extent, stretch; period. **протя́жный** long-drawn-out; drawling.

проу́чивать *impf*, **проучи́ть** (-чу́, -чишь) *pf* study; teach a lesson.

профа́н ignoramus.

профана́ция profanation.

профессиона́л professional. **профессиона́льный** professional; occupational. **профе́ссия** profession. **профе́ссор** (*pl* -а́) professor.

профила́ктика prophylaxis; preventive measures.

про́филь *m* profile; type.

про|фильтрова́ть *pf*.

профсою́з trade-union.

проха́живаться *impf of* пройти́сь

прохво́ст scoundrel.

прохла́да coolness. **прохлади́тельный** refreshing, cooling. **прохла́дный** cool, chilly. **прохо́д** passage; gangway, aisle; duct. **проходи́мец** (-мца) rogue. **проходи́мый** passable. **проходи́ть** (-ожу́, -о́дишь) *impf of* пройти́. **проходно́й** entrance; communicating. **проходя́щий** passing. **прохо́жий** passing, in transit; *sb* passer-by.

процвета́ние prosperity. **процвета́ть** *impf* prosper, flourish.

процеди́ть (-ежу́, -е́дишь) *pf* (*impf* **проце́живать**) filter, strain.

процеду́ра procedure; (*usu in pl*) treatment.

проце́живать *pf of* процеди́ть

проце́нт percentage; per cent; interest.

проце́сс process; trial; legal proceedings. **проце́ссия** procession.

про|цити́ровать *pf*.

прочёска screening; combing.

проче́сть (-чту́, -чтёшь; -чёл, -чла́) *pf of* чита́ть

про́чий other.

прочи́стить (-и́щу) *pf* (*impf* **прочища́ть**) clean; clear.

про|чита́ть *impf*, **прочи́тывать** *impf* read (through).

прочища́ть *pf of* прочи́стить

про́чность firmness, stability, durability. **про́чный** (-чен, -чна́, -о) firm, sound, solid; durable.

прочте́ние reading. **прочту́** *etc.: see* **проче́сть**

прочу́вствовать *pf* feel deeply; experience, go through.

прочь *adv* away, off; averse to. **проше́дший** past; last. **про-шёл** *etc.: see* пройти́

проше́ние application, petition.

прошепта́ть (-пчу́, -пчешь) *pf* whisper.

проше́ствие: по проше́ствии +*gen* after.

прошива́ть *impf*, **проши́ть** (-шью́, -шьёшь) *pf* sew, stitch.

прошлого́дний last year's. **про́шл|ый** past; last; ~**ое** *sb* the past.

про|шнурова́ть *pf*. **про|што-пать** *pf*. **прошью́** *etc.: see* проши́ть

проща́й(те) goodbye. **про-ща́льный** parting; farewell. **проща́ние** farewell; parting.

проща́ть(ся *impf of* прости́ть(ся

про́ще simpler, plainer.

проще́ние forgiveness, pardon.

прощу́пать *pf*, **прощу́пы-вать** *impf* feel.

про|экзаменова́ть *pf*.

прояви́тель *m* developer. **прояви́ть** (-влю́, -вишь) *pf*, **проявля́ть** *impf* show, display; develop; ~**ся** reveal itself. **проявле́ние** display; manifestation; developing.

проясни́ться *pf*, **проясня́ться** (*impf* clear, clear up.

пруд (-á, *loc* -ý) pond. **пруди́ть** (-ужу́, -у́дишь) *impf* (*pf* за~) dam.

пружи́на spring. **пружи́ни-стый** springy. **пружи́нный** spring.

пру́сский Prussian.

прут (-а *or* -á; *pl* -тья) twig.

пры́гать *impf*, **пры́гнуть** (-ну) *pf* jump, leap; bounce; ~ **с шесто́м** pole-vault. **прыгу́н** (-á), **прыгу́нья** (*gen pl* -ний) jumper. **прыжо́к** (-жка́) jump; leap; **прыжки́** jumping; **прыж-ки́ в во́ду** diving; ~ **в высоту́** high jump; ~ **в длину́** long jump.

пры́скать *impf*, **пры́снуть** (-ну) *pf* spurt; sprinkle; burst out laughing.

прыть speed; energy.

прыщ (-á), **пры́щик** pimple.

пряди́льный spinning. **пря-ди́льня** (*gen pl* -лен) (spin-ning-)mill. **пряди́льщик** spin-ner. **пряду́** *etc.: see* **прясть**. **прядь** lock; strand. **пря́жа** yarn, thread.

пряжка buckle, clasp.

прялка distaff; spinning-wheel.

прямая *sb* straight line. **прямо** *adv* straight; straight on; frankly; really.

прямодушие directness, straightforwardness. **~душный** direct, straightforward.

прямой (-ям, -á, -о) straight; upright, erect; through; direct; straightforward; real.

прямолинейный rectilinear; straightforward. **прямоугольник** rectangle. **прямоугольный** rectangular.

пряник spice cake. **пряность** spice. **пряный** spicy; heady.

прясть (-яду, -ядёшь; -ял, -яла, -о) *impf* (*pf* с~) spin.

прятать (-ячу) *impf* (*pf* с~) hide; **~ся** hide. **прятки** (-ток) *pl* hide-and-seek.

пса *etc.*: *see* пёс

псалóм (-лмá) psalm. **псалтырь** *f* Psalter.

псевдоним pseudonym.

псих madman, lunatic. **психиатрия** psychiatry. **психика** psyche; psychology. **психический** mental, psychical. **психоанализ** psychoanalysis. **психóз** psychosis. **психолог** psychologist. **психологический** psychological. **психология** psychology. **психопат** psychopath. **психопатический** psychopathic. **психосоматический** psychosomatic. **психотерапéвт** psychotherapist. **психотерапия** psychotherapy. **психотический** psychotic.

птенец (-нцá) nestling; fledgling. **птица** bird. **птицеферма** poultry-farm. **птичий** bird, bird's; poultry. **птичка** bird; tick.

публика public; audience. **публикация** publication; notice, advertisement. **публиковать** *impf* (*pf* о~) publish. **публицистика** writing on current affairs. **публичность** publicity. **публичный** public; ~ **дом** brothel.

пугало scarecrow. **пугать** *impf* (*pf* ис~, на~) frighten; scare; **~ся** (+*gen*) be frightened (of). **пугач** (-á) toy pistol. **пугливый** fearful.

пуговица button.

пуд (*pl* -ы́) pood (= 16.38 kg).

пудовый, пудóвый one pood in weight.

пудель *m* poodle.

пудинг blancmange.

пудра powder. **пудреница** powder compact. **пудреный** powdered. **пудриться** *impf* (*pf* на~) powder one's face.

пузатый pot-bellied.

пузырёк (-рькá) vial; bubble. **пузырь** (-я́) *m* bubble; blister; bladder.

пук (*pl* -и́) bunch, bundle; tuft.

пукать *impf*, **пукнуть** *pf* fart.

пулемёт machine-gun. **пулемётчик** machine-gunner. **пуленепробиваемый** bulletproof.

пульверизатор atomizer; spray.

пульс pulse. **пульсар** pulsar. **пульсировать** *impf* pulsate. **пульт** desk, stand; control panel.

пуля bullet.

пункт point; spot; post; item. **пунктир** dotted line. **пунктирный** dotted, broken.

пунктуальный punctual. **пунктуация** punctuation. **пунцóвый** crimson.

пуп (-á) navel. **пуповина** umbilical cord. **пупо́к** (-пка́) navel; gizzard.

пурга́ blizzard.

пурита́нин (pl -та́не, -та́н), -а́нка Puritan.

пу́рпур purple, crimson. **пурпу́р|ный**, -**овый** purple.

пуск starting (up). **пуска́й** see пусть. **пуска́ть(ся** impf of пусти́ть(ся. **пусково́й** starting.

пусте́ть (-е́ет) impf (pf о~) empty; become deserted.

пусти́ть (пущу́, пу́стишь) pf (impf пуска́ть) let go; let in; let; start; send; set in motion; throw; put forth; ~**ся** set out; start.

пустова́ть impf be or stand empty. **пусто́й** (-ст, -а́, -о) empty; idle; shallow. **пустота́** (pl -ы) emptiness; void; vacuum; futility. **пустоте́лый** hollow.

пусты́нный uninhabited; deserted; desert. **пусты́ня** desert. **пусты́рь** (-я́) m waste land; vacant plot.

пусты́шка blank; hollow object; dummy.

пусть, пуска́й partl let; all right; though, even if.

пустя́к (-а́) trifle. **пустяко́вый** trivial.

пу́таница muddle, confusion. **пу́таный** muddled, confused. **пу́тать** (impf за~, пере~, с~) tangle; confuse; mix up; ~**ся** get confused or mixed up.

путёвка pass; place on a group tour. **путеводи́тель** m guide, guide-book. **путево́й** travelling; road. **путём** prep+gen by means of. **путеше́ственник** traveller. **путеше́ствие** journey; voyage. **путеше́ствовать** impf travel; voyage.

пу́ты (пут) pl shackles.

путь (-и́, instr -ём, prep -и́) way; track; path; course; journey; voyage; means; **в пути́** en route, on the way.

пух (loc -у́) down; fluff.

пу́хлый (-хл, -а́, -о) plump.

пу́хнуть (-ну; пух) impf (pf вс~, о~) swell.

пухови́к (-а́) feather-bed. **пухо́вка** powder-puff. **пухо́вый** downy.

пучи́на abyss; the deep.

пучо́к (-чка́) bunch, bundle.

пу́шечный gun, cannon.

пуши́нка bit of fluff. **пуши́стый** fluffy.

пу́шка gun, cannon.

пушни́на furs, pelts. **пушно́й** fur; fur-bearing.

пу́ще adv more; ~ **всего́** most of all.

пущу́ etc.: see пусти́ть

пчела́ (pl -ёлы) bee. **пчели́ный** bee, bees'. **пчелово́д** bee-keeper. **пче́льник** apiary.

пшени́ца wheat. **пшени́чный** wheat(en).

пшённый millet. **пшено́** millet.

пыл (loc -у́) heat, ardour.

пыла́ть impf blaze; burn.

пылесо́с vacuum cleaner. **пылесо́сить** impf vacuum (-clean).

пыли́нка speck of dust. **пыли́ть** impf (pf за~, на~) raise a dust; cover with dust; ~**ся** get dusty.

пы́лкий ardent; fervent.

пыль (loc -и́) dust. **пы́льный** (-лен, -льна́, -о) dusty. **пыльца́** pollen.

пыре́й couch grass.

пырну́ть (-ну́, -нёшь) pf jab.

пыта́ть impf torture. **пыта́ться** impf (pf по~) try. **пы́тка** torture, torment. **пытли́вый** inquisitive.

пыхте́ть (-хчу́) *impf* puff, pant.

пы́шка bun.

пы́шность splendour. **пы́шный** (-шен, -шна́, -шно) splendid; lush.

пьедеста́л pedestal.

пье́са play; piece.

пью *etc.*: see **пить**.

пьяне́ть (-е́ю) *impf* (*pf* o~) get drunk. **пьяни́ть** *impf* (*pf* o~) intoxicate, make drunk. **пья́ница** *m & f* drunkard. **пья́нство** drunkenness. **пья́нствовать** *impf* drink heavily. **пья́ный** drunk.

пюпи́тр lectern; stand.

пюре́ *neut indecl* purée.

пядь (*gen pl* -е́й) span; ни пя́ди not an inch.

пя́льцы (-лец) *pl* embroidery frame.

пята́ (*pl* -ы, -а́м) heel.

пята́к (-а́), **пятачо́к** (-чка́) five-copeck piece. **пятёрка** five; figure 5; No. 5; fiver (5-rouble note).

пяти- *in comb* five; penta-. **~бо́рье** pentathlon. **~десятиле́тие** fifty years; fiftieth anniversary; birthday. П~**деся́тница** Pentecost. **~деся́тый** fiftieth; **~деся́тые го́ды** the fifties. **~коне́чный** five-pointed. **~ле́тие** five years; fifth anniversary. **~ле́тка** five-year plan. **~со́тый** five-hundredth. **~уго́льник** pentagon. **~уго́льный** pentagonal.

пяти́ться (пячу́сь) *impf* (*pf* по~) move backwards; back.

пя́тка heel.

пятна́дцатый fifteenth. **пятна́дцать** fifteen.

пятна́ть *impf* (*pf* за~) spot, stain. **пятна́шки** (-шек) *pl* tag. **пятни́стый** spotted.

пя́тница Friday.

пятно́ (*pl* -а, -тен) stain; spot; blot; **роди́мое ~** birth-mark.

пя́тый fifth. **пять** (-и́, *instr* -ью́) five. **пятьдеся́т** (-и́десяти, *instr* -ью́десятью) fifty. **пятьсо́т** (-тисо́т, -тиста́м) five hundred. **пя́тью** *adv* five times.

Р

раб (-а́), **раба́** slave. **рабовладе́лец** (-льца) slave-owner. **раболе́пие** servility. **раболе́пный** servile. **раболе́пствовать** *impf* cringe, fawn.

рабо́та work; job; functioning. **рабо́тать** *impf* work; function; be open; **~ над** work on. **рабо́тник**, **-ица** worker. **работоспосо́бность** capacity for work, efficiency. **работоспосо́бный** able-bodied, hardworking. **рабо́тящий** hardworking. **рабо́чий** *sb* worker. **рабо́чий** worker's; working; **~ая си́ла** manpower.

ра́бский slave; servile. **ра́бство** slavery. **рабы́ня** female slave.

равви́н rabbi.

ра́венство equality. **равне́ние** alignment. **равни́на** plain. **равно́** *adv* alike; equally; **как ~ как** as well as. **равно́** *predic*: see **ра́вный**

равно- *in comb* equi-, iso-. **равнобе́дренный** isosceles. **~ве́сие** equilibrium; balance. **~де́нствие** equinox. **~ду́шие** indifference. **~ду́шный** indifferent. **~ме́рный** even; uniform. **~пра́вие** equality of rights. **~пра́вный** having equal rights. **~си́льный**

equal strength; equal, equivalent, tantamount. ~сторо́нний equilateral. ~це́нности of equal value; tantamount.

ра́вный (-вен, -вна́) equal. **равно́** *predic* make(s), equals; **всё** ~о́ (it is) all the same. **равня́ть** *impf* (*pf* с~) make even; treat equally; +c+*instr* compare with, treat as equal to; ~ся compare, compete; be equal; be tantamount.

рад (-а, -о) *predic* glad.

рада́р radar.

ра́ди *prep+gen* for the sake of.

радиа́тор radiator. **радиа́ция** radiation.

ра́дий radium.

радика́льный radical.

ра́дио *neut indecl* radio.

радио- *in comb* radio-; radioactive. **радиоакти́вный** radioactive. **~веща́ние** broadcasting. **~волна́** radio-wave. **~гра́мма** radio-telegram. **радио́лог** radiologist. **~ло́гия** radiology. **~лока́тор** radar (set). **~люби́тель** *m* radio amateur, ham. **~ма́як** (-á) radio beacon. **~переда́тчик** transmitter. **~переда́ча** broadcast. **~приёмник** radio (set). **~связь** radio communication. **~слу́шатель** *m* listener. **~ста́нция** radio station. **~электро́ника** radio-electronics.

радио́ла radiogram.

ради́ровать *impf* & *pf* radio. **ради́ст** radio operator.

ра́диус radius.

ра́довать *impf* (*pf* об~, по~) gladden, make happy; ~ся be glad, rejoice. **ра́достный** joyful. **ра́дость** gladness, joy.

ра́дуга rainbow. **ра́дужный** iridescent; cheerful; **ра́ду-** оболо́чка iris.

раду́шие cordiality. **раду́шный** cordial.

ражу́ *etc.*: *see* рази́ть

раз (*pl* -ы́, раз) time, occasion; one; ещё ~ (once) again; как ~ just, exactly; не ~ more than once; ни ~у not once. **раз** *adv* once, one day. **раз** *conj* if; since.

разба́вить (-влю) *pf*, **разбавля́ть** *impf* dilute.

разбаза́ривать *impf*, **разбаза́рить** *pf* squander.

разба́лтывать(ся *impf of* разболта́ть(ся

разбе́г running start. **разбе-га́ться** *impf*, **разбежа́ться** (-éгусь) *pf* take a run, run up; scatter.

разберу́ *etc.*: *see* разобра́ть

разбива́ть(ся *impf of* разби́ть(ся. **разби́вка** laying out; spacing (out).

разбинтова́ть *pf*, **разбинто́вывать** *impf* unbandage.

разбира́тельство investigation. **разбира́ть** *impf of* разобра́ть; ~ся *impf of* разобра́ться

разби́ть (-зобью́, -зобьёшь) *pf* (*impf* **разбива́ть**) break; smash; divide (up); damage; defeat; mark out; space (out); ~ся break, get broken; hurt o.s. **разби́тый** broken; jaded.

раз|бога́теть (-е́ю) *pf*.

разбо́й robbery. **разбо́йник** robber. **разбо́йничий** robber.

разболе́ться¹ (-ли́тся) *pf* begin to ache badly.

разболе́ться² (-е́юсь) *pf* become ill.

разболта́ть¹ *pf* (*impf* разба́лтывать) divulge, give away.

разболта́ть² *pf* (*impf* раз-

ба́лтывать) shake up; loosen; **~ся** work loose; get out of hand.

разбомби́ть (-блю́) *pf* bomb, destroy by bombing.

разбо́р analysis; critique; discrimination; investigation. **разбо́рка** sorting out; dismantling. **разбо́рный** collapsible. **разбо́рчивый** legible; discriminating.

разбра́сывать *impf of* **разброса́ть**

разбреда́ться *impf*, **разбрести́сь** (-еде́тся; -е́лся, -ла́сь) *pf* disperse; straggle. **разбро́д** disorder. **разбро́санный** scattered; disconnected, incoherent. **разброса́ть** *pf* (*impf* **разбра́сывать**) throw about; scatter.

разбуди́ть (-ужу́, -у́дишь) *pf*

разбуха́ть *impf*, **разбу́хнуть** (-нет, -бу́х) *pf* swell.

разбушева́ться (-шу́юсь) *pf* fly into a rage; blow up; rage.

разва́л breakdown, collapse. **разва́ливать** *impf*, **развали́ть** (-лю́, -лишь) *pf* pull down; mess up; **~ся** collapse; go to pieces; tumble down; sprawl. **разва́лина** ruin; wreck.

ра́зве *partl* really?; **~ (то́лько), ~ (что)** except that, only.

развева́ться *impf* fly, flutter.

разве́дать *pf* (*impf* **разве́дывать**) find out; reconnoitre.

разведе́ние breeding; cultivation.

разведённ|ый divorced; **~ый, ~ая** *sb* divorcee.

разве́дка intelligence (service); reconnaissance; prospecting. **разве́дочный** prospect-

ing, exploratory.

разведу́ *etc.: see* **развести́**

разве́дчик intelligence officer; scout; prospector. **разве́дывать** *impf of* **разве́дать**

развезти́ (-зу́, -зёшь; -ёз, -ла́) *pf* (*impf* **развози́ть**) convey, transport; deliver.

разве́ивать(ся *impf of* **разве́ять(ся. развёл** *etc.: see* **развести́**

развенча́ть *pf*, **развенчи́вать** dethrone; debunk.

развёрнутый extensive, all-out; detailed. **развернуть** (-ну́, -нёшь) *pf* (*impf* **развёртывать, развора́чивать**) unfold, unwrap; unroll; unfurl; deploy; expand; develop; turn; scan; display; **~ся** unfold, unroll, come unwrapped; deploy; develop; spread; turn.

развёрстка allotment, apportionment.

развёртывать(ся *impf of* **развернуть(ся**

раз|весели́ть *pf* cheer up; amuse; **~ся** cheer up.

разве́сить¹ (-е́шу) *pf* (*impf* **разве́шивать**) spread; hang (out).

разве́сить² (-е́шу) *pf* (*impf* **разве́шивать**) weigh out. **разве́ска** weighing. **разве́сной** sold by weight.

развести́ (-еду́, -еде́шь; -ёл, -а́) *pf* (*impf* **разводи́ть**) take; separate; divorce; dilute; dissolve; start; breed; cultivate; **~сь** be divorced; breed, multiply.

разветви́ться (-ви́тся) *pf*, **разветвля́ться** *impf* branch, fork. **разветвле́ние** branching, forking; branch; fork.

разве́шать *pf*, **разве́шивать** *impf* hang.

развёшивать *impf of* разве́сить, разве́шать. разве́шу *etc.: see* разве́сить

разве́ять (-е́ю) *pf* (*impf* разве́ивать) scatter, disperse; dispel; ~ся disperse; be dispelled

развива́ть(ся) *impf of* разви́ть(ся)

разви́лка fork.

развинти́ть (-нчу́) *pf*, разви́нчивать *impf* unscrew

разви́тие development. разви́той (ра́звит, -а́, -о) developed; mature. разви́ть (-зовью́; -зовьёшь; -и́л, -а́, -о) *pf* (*impf* развива́ть) develop; unwind; ~ся develop.

развлека́ть *impf*, развле́чь (-еку́, -ечёшь; -ёк, -ла́) *pf* entertain, amuse; ~ся have a good time; amuse o.s. развлече́ние entertainment, amusement.

разво́д divorce. разводи́ть(ся (-ожу́(сь, -о́дишь(ся) *impf of* развести́(сь. разво́дка separation. разводно́й: ~ ключ adjustable spanner; ~ мост drawbridge.

развози́ть (-ожу́, -о́зишь) *impf of* развезти́

разволнова́ть(ся *pf* get excited; be agitated.

развора́чивать(ся *impf of* развернуть(ся

разворова́ть *pf*, разворо́вывать *impf* loot; steal.

разворо́т U-turn; turn; development.

развра́т depravity, corruption. разврати́ть (-ащу́) *pf*, развраща́ть *impf* corrupt; deprave. развра́тничать *impf* lead a depraved life. развра́тный debauched, corrupt. развращённый (-ён, -а́) corrupt.

развяза́ть (-яжу́, -я́жешь) *pf*, развя́зывать *impf* untie; unleash; ~ся come untied; ~ся с+*instr* rid o.s. of. развя́зка dénouement; outcome. развя́зный overfamiliar.

разга́дывать *pf*, разга́дывать *impf* solve, guess, interpret. разга́дка solution.

разга́р height, climax.

разгиба́ть(ся *impf of* разогну́ть(ся

разглаго́льствовать *impf* hold forth.

разгла́дить (-а́жу) *pf*, разгла́живать *impf* smooth out; iron (out).

разгласи́ть (-ашу́) *pf*, разглаша́ть *impf* divulge; +о+*prep* trumpet. разглаше́ние disclosure.

разгляде́ть (-яжу́) *pf*, разгля́дывать *impf* make out, discern.

разгне́вать *pf* anger. раз|гне́ваться *pf*.

разгова́ривать *impf* talk, converse. разгово́р conversation. разгово́рник phrase-book. разгово́рный colloquial. разгово́рчивый talkative.

разго́н dispersal; running start; distance. разгоня́ть(ся *impf of* разогна́ть(ся

разгора́живать *impf of* разгороди́ть

разгора́ться *impf*, разгоре́ться (-рю́сь) *pf* flare up.

разгороди́ть (-ожу́, -о́дишь) *pf* (*impf* разгора́живать) partition off.

раз|горячи́ться (-чу́(сь) *pf*.

разгра́бить (-блю) *pf* plunder, loot. разграбле́ние plunder, looting.

разграниче́ние demarcation; differentiation. разграничивать *impf*, разграни́чить (-чу) *pf* delimit; differentiate.

разгреба́ть *impf*, разгрести́ (-ебу́, -ебёшь; -ёб, -ла́) *pf* rake *or* shovel (away).

разгро́м crushing defeat; devastation; havoc. разгроми́ть (-млю́) *pf* rout, defeat.

разгружа́ть *impf*, разгрузи́ть (-ужу́, -у́зи́шь) *pf* unload; relieve; ~ся unload; be relieved. разгру́зка unloading; relief.

разгрыза́ть *impf*, разгры́зть (-зу́, -зёшь; -ы́з) *pf* crack.

разгу́л revelry; outburst. разгу́ливать *impf* stroll about. разгуля́ться *pf* spread o.s.; become wide awake; clear up. разгу́льный wild, rakish.

раздава́ть(ся (-даю́сь, -даёшься) *impf of* разда́ть(ся

раздави́ть (-влю́, -вишь) *pf* crush; run over.

разда́вливать *impf* crush; run over.

разда́ть (-ám, -áшь, -áст, -ади́м; роз- *or* разда́л, -á, -о) *pf* (*impf* раздава́ть) distribute, give out; ~ся be heard; resound; ring out; make way; expand; put on weight. разда́ча distribution. раздаю́ *etc.: see* раздава́ть

раздва́ивать(ся *impf of* раздво́ить(ся

раздвига́ть *impf*, раздви́нуть (-ну) *pf* move apart; ~ся move apart. раздвижно́й expanding; sliding.

раздвое́ние division; split; ~ ли́чности split personality. раздво́енный forked; cloven; split. раздво́ить *pf* (*impf* раздва́ивать) divide into two; bisect; ~ся fork; split.

раздева́лка cloakroom. разде-

ва́ть(ся *impf of* разде́ть(ся

разде́л division; section. разде́латься *pf* +с+*instr* finish with; settle accounts with.

разделе́ние division. разделя́мый divisible. раздели́ть (-лю́, -лишь) *pf*, разделя́ть *impf* divide; separate; share; ~ся divide; be divided; be divisible; separate. разде́льный separate.

разде́ну *etc.: see* разде́ть.

раздеру́ *etc.: see* разодра́ть

разде́ть (-де́ну) *pf* (*impf* раздева́ть) undress; ~ся undress; take off one's coat.

раздира́ть *impf of* разодра́ть

раздобыва́ть *impf*, раздобы́ть (-бу́ду) *pf* get, get hold of.

раздо́лье expanse; liberty. раздо́льный free.

раздо́р discord.

раздоса́довать *pf* vex.

раздража́ть *impf*, раздражи́ть (-жу́) *pf* irritate; annoy; ~ся get annoyed. раздраже́ние irritation. раздражи́тельный irritable.

раздроби́ть (-блю́) *pf*, раздробля́ть *impf* break; smash to pieces.

раздува́ть(ся *impf of* разду́ть(ся

разду́мать *pf*, разду́мывать *impf* change one's mind; ponder. разду́мье meditation; thought.

разду́ть (-у́ю) *pf* (*impf* раздува́ть) blow; fan; exaggerate; whip up; swell; ~ся swell.

развева́ть *impf of* разви́нь

разжа́лобить (-блю) *pf* move (to pity).

разжа́ловать *pf* demote.

разжа́ть (-зожму́, -мёшь) *pf*

(*impf* **разжима́ть**) unclasp, open; release.

разжева́ть (-жую́, -жуёшь) *pf*, **разжёвывать** *impf* chew.

разже́чь (-зожгу́, -зожжёшь; -жёг, -зожгла́) *pf*, **разжига́ть** *impf* kindle; rouse.

разжима́ть *impf of* **разжа́ть**.

раз|жире́ть (-е́ю) *pf*.

рази́нуть (-ну) *pf* (*impf* **разева́ть**) open; ~ **рот** gape. **рази́ня** *m* & *f* scatter-brain.

рази́тельный striking. **рази́ть** (ра́жу́) *pf* (*pf* **по~**) strike.

разлага́ть(ся *impf of* **разложи́ть(ся**

разла́д discord; disorder.

разла́мывать(ся *impf of* **разломи́ть(ся, разлома́ть(ся.**

разлёгся *etc.: see* **разле́чься**

разлеза́ться *impf*, **разле́зться** (-зется; -ле́зся) *pf* come to pieces; fall apart.

разлета́ться *impf*, **разлете́ться** (-лечу́сь) *pf* fly away; scatter; shatter; rush.

разле́чься (-ля́гусь, -лёгся, -гла́сь) *pf* stretch out.

разли́в bottling; flood; overflow. **разлива́ть** *impf*, **разли́ть** (-золью́, -зольёшь; -и́л, -а́, -о) *pf* pour out; spill; flood (with); ~**ся** spill; overflow; spread. **разливно́й** draught.

различа́ть *impf*, **различи́ть** (-чу́) *pf* distinguish; discern; ~**ся** differ. **разли́чие** distinction; difference. **различи́тельный** distinctive, distinguishing. **разли́чный** different.

разложе́ние decomposition; decay; disintegration. **разложи́ть** (-жу́, -жишь) *pf* (*impf* **разлага́ть, раскла́дывать**) put away; spread (out); distribute; break down; decom-

pose; resolve; corrupt; ~**ся** decompose; become demoralized; be corrupted; disintegrate, go to pieces.

разло́м breaking; break. **разлома́ть, разломи́ть** (-млю́, -мишь) *pf* (*impf* **разла́мывать**) break to pieces; pull down; ~**ся** break to pieces.

разлу́ка separation. **разлуча́ть** *impf*, **разлучи́ть** (-чу́) *pf* separate, part; ~**ся** separate, part.

разлюби́ть (-блю́, -бишь) *pf* stop loving *or* liking.

разля́гусь *etc.: see* **разле́чься**

разма́зать (-а́жу) *pf*, **разма́зывать** *impf* spread, smear.

разма́лывать *impf of* **размоло́ть**

разма́тывать *impf of* **размота́ть**

разма́х sweep; swing; span; scope. **разма́хивать** *impf* +*instr* swing; brandish. **разма́хиваться** *impf*, **размахну́ться** (-ну́сь, -нёшься) *pf* swing one's arm. **разма́шистый** sweeping.

размежева́ние demarcation, delimitation. **размежева́ть** (-жую́) *pf*, **размежёвывать** *impf* delimit.

размёл *etc.: see* **размести́**

размельча́ть *impf*, **размельчи́ть** (-чу́) *pf* crush, pulverize.

размелю́ *etc.: see* **размоло́ть**

разме́н exchange. **разме́нивать** *impf*, **разменя́ть** *pf* change; ~**ся** +*instr* exchange; dissipate. **разме́нная моне́та** (small) change.

разме́р size; measurement; amount; scale; extent; *pl* proportions. **разме́ренный** measured. **разме́рить** *pf*, **размеря́ть** *impf* measure.

размести́ (-ету́, -ете́шь; -мёл, -а́) pf (impf **размета́ть**) sweep clear; sweep away.

размести́ть (-ещу́) pf (impf **размеща́ть**) place, accommodate; distribute; **~ся** take one's seat.

размета́ть impf of **размести́**

разме́тить (-е́чу) pf, **разме-ча́ть** impf mark.

размеша́ть pf, **разме́шивать** impf stir in.

размеща́ть(ся impf of **размести́ть(ся. размеще́ние** placing; accommodation; distribution. **размещу́** etc.: see **размести́ть**

размина́ть(ся impf of **размя́ть(ся**

разми́нка limbering up.

размину́ться (-ну́сь, -нёшься) pf pass; +c+instr pass; miss.

размножа́ть impf, **размно́жить** (-жу) pf multiply, duplicate; breed; **~ся** multiply; breed.

размозжи́ть (-жу́) pf smash.

размо́лвка tiff.

размоло́ть (-мелю́, -ме́лешь) pf (impf **разма́лывать**) grind.

размора́живать impf, **разморо́зить** (-о́жу) pf unfreeze, defrost; **~ся** unfreeze; defrost.

размота́ть pf (impf **разма́тывать**) unwind.

размыва́ть impf, **размы́ть** (-о́ет) pf wash away; erode.

размыка́ть(ся impf of **разомкну́ть**

размышле́ние reflection; meditation. **размышля́ть** impf reflect, ponder.

размягча́ть impf, **размягчи́ть** (-чу́) pf soften; **~ся** soften.

размяка́ть impf, **размя́к-**

-ну́ть (-ну; -мя́к) pf soften.

раз|мя́ть (-зомну́, -зомнёшь) pf (impf also **размина́ть**) knead; mash; **~ся** stretch one's legs; limber up.

разна́шивать impf of **разно-си́ть**

разнести́ (-су́, -сёшь; -ёс, -ла́) pf (impf **разноси́ть**) carry; deliver; spread; note down; smash; scold; scatter; impers make puffy, swell.

разнима́ть impf of **разня́ть**

разни́ться impf differ. **ра́зница** difference.

разно- in comb different, vari-, hetero-. **разнобо́й** lack of co-ordination; difference. **~ви́д-ность** variety. **~гла́сие** disagreement; discrepancy. **~обра́зие** variety, diversity. **~обра́зный** various, diverse. **~речи́вый** contradictory; **~ро́дный** heterogeneous; **~сторо́нний** many-sided; versatile. **~цве́тный** variegated. **~шёрстный** of different colours; ill-assorted.

разноси́ть[1] (-ошу́, -о́сишь) pf (impf **разна́шивать**) wear in.

разноси́ть[2] (-ошу́, -о́сишь) impf of **разнести́. разно́ска** delivery.

ра́зность difference.

разно́счик pedlar.

разносу́ etc.: see **разноси́ть**

разну́зданный unbridled.

ра́зн|ый different; various; **~ое** sb various things.

разню́хать pf, **разню́хивать** impf smell out.

разня́ть (-ниму́, -ни́мешь; ро́-зор разня́л, -а́, -о) pf (impf **разнима́ть**) take to pieces; separate.

разоблача́ть impf, **разо-блачи́ть** (-чу́) pf expose.

разоблачéние exposure.

разобрáть (-зберý, -рёшь; -áл, -á, -о) *pf* (*impf* **разбирáть**) take to pieces; buy up; sort out; investigate; analyse; understand; **~ся** sort things out; +в+*prep* investigate, look into; understand.

разобщáть *impf*, **разобщи́ть** (-щý) *pf* separate; estrange, alienate.

разобью́ etc.: *see* **разби́ть**. **разовью́** etc.: *see* **разви́ть**. **рáзовый** single.

разогнáть (-згоню́, -óнишь; -гнáл, -á, -о) *pf* (*impf* **разгоня́ть**) scatter; disperse; dispel; drive fast; **~ся** gather speed.

разогнýть (-нý, -нёшь) *pf* (*impf* **разгибáть**) unbend, straighten; **~ся** straighten up.

разогревáть *impf*, **разогрéть** (-éю) *pf* warm up.

разодéть(ся (-éну(сь) *pf* dress up.

разодрáть (-здерý, -рёшь; -áл, -á, -о) *pf* (*impf* **раздирáть**) tear (up); lacerate.

разожгý etc.: *see* **разжéчь**. **разожмý** etc.: *see* **разжáть**. **разо|зли́ть** *pf*.

разойти́сь (-йдýсь, -йдёшься, -ошёлся, -ошлáсь) *pf* (*impf* **расходи́ться**) disperse; diverge; radiate; differ; conflict; part; be spent; be sold out.

разолью́ etc.: *see* **разли́ть** **рáзом** *adv* at once, at one go. **разомкнýть** (-нý, -нёшь) *pf* (*impf* **размыкáть**) open; break. **разомнý** etc.: *see* **размя́ть**.

разорвáть (-вý, -вёшь; -áл, -á, -о) *pf* (*impf* **разрывáть**) tear; break (off); blow up; **~ся** tear; break; explode.

разорéние ruin; destruction.

разори́тельный ruinous, wasteful. **разори́ть** *pf* (*impf* **разоря́ть**) ruin; destroy; **~ся** ruin o.s.

разоружáть *impf*, **разоружи́ть** (-жý) *pf* disarm; **~ся** disarm. **разоружéние** disarmament.

разоря́ть(ся *impf of* **разори́ть(ся**

разослáть (-ошлю́, -ошлёшь) *pf* (*impf* **рассылáть**) distribute, circulate.

разостлáть, расстели́ть (-сстелю́, -тéлешь) *pf* (*impf* **расстилáть**) spread (out); lay; **~ся** spread.

разотрý etc.: *see* **растерéть** **разочаровáние** disappointment.

разочаровáть *pf*, **разочарóвывать** *impf* disappoint **~ся** be disappointed.

разочтý etc.: *see* **расчéсть** **разошéлся** etc.: *see* **разойти́сь**. **разошлю́** etc.: *see* **разослáть** etc.: *see* **расши́ть**

разрабáтывать *impf*, **разрабóтать** *pf* cultivate; work, exploit; work out; develop. **разрабóтка** cultivation; exploitation; working out; mining; quarry.

разражáться *impf*, **разрази́ться** (-ажýсь) *pf* break out; burst out.

разрастáться *impf*, **разрасти́сь** (-тётся; -рóсся, -лáсь) *pf* grow; spread.

разрежённый (-ён, -á) rarefied.

разрéз cut; section; point of view. **разрéзать** (-éжу) *pf*, **разрезáть** *impf* cut; slit.

разрешáть *impf*, **разреши́ть** (-шý) *pf* (+*dat*) allow; solve;

...ettle; ~ся be allowed; be ...olved; be settled. **разреше́-** ...ие permission; permit; solu... ...ion; settlement. **разреши́-** ...ый solvable.

...азрóзненный uncoordinated; ...dd; incomplete.

разрóсся etc.: see **разра-** ...ти́сь. **разрóю** etc.: see **разрыть**.

разруба́ть impf, **разруби́ть** ...блю́, -бишь) pf cut; chop up.

разру́ха ruin, collapse. **раз-** ...уша́ть impf, **разру́шить** ...шу) pf destroy; demolish; ...uin; ~ся go to ruin, collapse. **азруше́ние** destruction. **раз-** ...уши́тельный destructive.

...азры́в break; gap; rupture; ...urst. **разрыва́ть**[1] (ся ...f разорва́ть(ся

азрыва́ть[2] impf of **разры́ть** ...азрывнóй explosive.

...азрыда́ться pf burst into ...ears.

азры́ть (-рóю) pf (impf **раз-** ...ыва́ть) dig (up).

...азрыхли́ть pf, **разрых-** ...ля́ть impf loosen; hoe.

азря́д[1] category; class.

азря́д[2] discharge. **разря-** ...и́ть (-яжу́, -яди́шь) pf (impf ...аряжа́ть) discharge; dis... ...harge; space out; ~ся run ...own; clear, ease. **разря́дка** ...pacing (out); discharging; un... ...oading; relieving.

...азряжа́ть(ся impf of **разря-** ...и́ть(ся

...азубеди́ть (-ежу́) pf, **раз-** ...убежда́ть impf dissuade; ...ся change one's mind.

...азува́ть(ся impf of **разу́ться** ...азуве́рить pf, **разуверя́ть** ...mpf dissuade, undeceive; ...ся (в+prep) lose faith (in).

...азузнава́ть (-наю́, -наёшь)

impf, **разузна́ть** pf (try to) find out.

разукра́сить (-а́шу) pf, **раз-** **украши́вать** impf adorn, embellish.

ра́зум reason; intellect. **раз-** **уме́ться** (-е́ется) impf be understood, be meant; (само́ собо́й) разуме́ется of course; it goes without saying. **разу́м-** **ный** rational, intelligent; sensible; reasonable; wise.

разу́ться (-у́юсь) pf (impf **разу-** **ва́ться**) take off one's shoes.

разу́чивать impf, **разучи́ть** (-чу́, -чишь) pf learn (up). **разу́чиваться** impf, **раз-** **учи́ться** (-чу́сь, -чишься) pf forget (how to).

разъеда́ть impf of **разъе́сть разъедини́ть** pf, **разъеди-** **ня́ть** impf separate; disconnect.

разъе́дусь etc.: see **разъ-** **е́хаться**

разъе́зд departure; siding (track); mounted patrol; pl travel; journeys. **разъездно́й** travelling. **разъезжа́ть** impf drive or ride about; travel; ~ся impf of **разъе́хаться**

разъе́сть (-е́ст, -едя́т; -е́л) pf (impf **разъеда́ть**) eat away; corrode.

разъе́хаться (-е́дусь) pf (impf **разъезжа́ться**) depart; separate; pass (one another); miss one another.

разъярённый (-ён, -а́) furious. **разъяри́ть** pf, **разъ-** **яря́ть** impf infuriate; ~ся get furious.

разъясне́ние explanation; interpretation. **разъясни́тель-** **ный** explanatory.

разъясни́ть pf, **разъясня́ть** impf explain; interpret; ~ся become clear, be cleared up.

разыгрáть pf, **разы́грывать** impf perform; draw; raffle; play a trick on; **~ся** get up; run high.

разыскáть (-ыщу́, -ы́щешь) pf find. **разы́скивать** impf search for.

рай (loc -ю́) paradise; garden of Eden.

райкóм district committee.

райóн region. **райóнный** district.

рáйский heavenly.

рак crayfish; cancer; Cancer.

ракéта¹, **ракéтка** racket.

ракéта² rocket; missile; flare.

рáковина shell; sink.

рáковый cancerous.

ракýшка cockle-shell, mussel.

рáма frame. **рáмка** frame; pl framework.

рáмпа footlights.

рáна wound. **ранéние** wounding; wound; injury. **рáненый** wounded; injured.

ранг rank.

рáнец (-нца) knapsack; satchel.

рáнить impf & pf wound; injure.

рáнний early. **рáно** adv early. **рáньше** adv earlier; before; formerly.

рапи́ра foil.

рáпорт report. **рапортовáть** impf & pf report.

рáса race. **раси́зм** racism. **раси́стский** racist.

раскáиваться impf of **раскáяться**

раскалённый (-ён, -á) scorching; incandescent. **раскали́ть** pf (impf **раскаля́ть**) make red-hot; **~ся** become red-hot.

раскáлывать(ся impf of **расколóть(ся**. **раскаля́ть(ся** impf of **раскали́ть(ся**. рас-

кáпывать impf of раскопáт

раскáт roll, peal. **раскатá** pf, **раскáтывать** impf ro (out), smooth out; level; driv or ride (about). **раскáтисты** rolling, booming. **раскá** ти́ться (-ачусь, -áтишься) p **раскáтываться** impf gathe speed; roll away; peal, boom rock.

раскáчивать pf, **раскáчиват** impf swing; rock; **~ся** swing rock.

раскáяние repentance. **рас|кá** яться pf (impf also **раскá** иваться) repent.

расквитáться pf settle ac counts.

раски́дывать impf, **раски́** нуть (-ну) pf stretch (out spread; pitch; **~ся** sprea out; sprawl.

раскладнóй folding. **раскла** душка camp-bed. **раскла** дывать impf of разложи́ть

раскланяться pf bow; tak leave.

расклéивать impf, **расклé** ить pf unstick; stick (up); **~с** come unstuck.

раскóл split; schism. **рас|кó** лóть (-лю́, -лешь) pf (imp also раскáлывать) split; break disrupt; **~ся** split. **раскóль** ник dissenter.

раскопáть pf (impf also раско пывать) dig up, unearth, ex cavate. **раскóпки** (-пок) p excavations.

раскóсый slanting.

раскрáивать impf of рас кройть.

раскрáсить (-áшу) pf, imp **раскрáшивать** paint, colour

раскрепости́ть (-ощу́) pf, **раскрепощáть** impf liber ate. **раскрепощéние** eman cipation.

раскритикова́ть pf criticize harshly.

раскро́ить pf (impf **раскра́ивать**) cut out.

раскро́ю etc.: see **раскры́ть**

раскрути́ть (-учу́, -у́тишь) pf, **раскру́чивать** impf untwist; **~ся** come untwisted.

раскрыва́ть impf, **раскры́ть** (-бю) pf open; expose; reveal; discover; **~ся** open; uncover o.s.; come to light.

раскупа́ть impf, **раскупи́ть** (-у́пит) pf buy up.

раску́поривать impf, **раску́порить** pf uncork, open.

раскуси́ть (-ушу́, -у́сишь) pf, **раску́сывать** impf bite through; see through.

ра́совый racial.

распа́д disintegration; collapse. **распада́ться** impf of **распа́сться**

распакова́ть pf, **распако́вывать** impf unpack.

распа́рываться impf of **распоро́ть(ся**

распа́сться (-адётся) pf (impf **распада́ться**) disintegrate, fall to pieces.

распаха́ть (-ашу́, -а́шешь) pf, **распа́хивать**[1] impf plough up.

распа́хивать[2] impf, **распахну́ть** (-ну́, -нёшь) pf throw open; **~ся** fly open, swing open.

распашо́нка baby's vest.

распева́ть impf sing.

распеча́тать pf, **распеча́тывать** impf unseal.

распи́ливать impf, **распили́ть** (-лю́, -лишь) pf saw up.

распина́ть impf of **распя́ть**

расписа́ние time-table. **расписа́ть** (-ишу́, -и́шешь) pf, **распи́сывать** impf enter; assign; paint; **~ся** sign; register

one's marriage; +**в**+prep sign for; acknowledge. **распи́ска** receipt. **расписно́й** painted, decorated.

распиха́ть pf, **распи́хивать** impf push, shove, stuff.

рас|**пла́вить** (-влю) pf, **расплавля́ть** impf melt, fuse. **распла́вленный** molten.

распла́каться (-а́чусь) pf burst into tears.

распласта́ть pf, **распла́стывать** impf spread; flatten; split; **~ся** sprawl.

распла́та payment; retribution. **расплати́ться** (-ачу́сь, -а́тишься) pf, **распла́чиваться** impf (+**с**+instr) pay off; get even; +**за**+acc pay for.

расплеска́ть(ся (-ещу́(сь, -е́щешь(ся) pf, **распле́скивать(ся** impf spill.

расплести́ (-ету́, -етёшь; -ёл, -а́) pf, **расплета́ть** impf unplait; untwist.

рас|**плоди́ть(ся** (-ожу́(сь) pf.

расплыва́ться impf, **расплы́ться** (-ывётся; -ы́лся, -а́сь) pf run. **расплы́вчатый** indistinct; vague.

расплю́щивать impf, **расплю́щить** (-щу) pf flatten out, hammer out.

распну́ etc.: see **распя́ть**

распознава́ть (-наю́, -наёшь) impf, **распозна́ть** pf recognize, identify; diagnose.

располага́ть impf (pf **расположи́ть**) +instr have at one's disposal. **располага́ться** impf of **расположи́ться**

располза́ться impf, **расползти́сь** (-зётся; -о́лзся, -зла́сь) pf crawl (away); give at the seams.

расположе́ние disposition; arrangement; situation; ten-

dency; liking; mood. **располо́-
женный** disposed, inclined.
расположи́ть (-жу́, -жишь)
pf (*impf* **располага́ть**) dispose; set out; win over; **~ся**
settle down.

распо́рка cross-bar, strut.

рас|поро́ть (-рю́, -решь) *pf*
(*impf also* **распа́рывать**) unpick, rip; **~ся** rip, come undone.

распоряди́тель *m* manager.
распоряди́тельный capable; efficient. **распоряди́ть-
ся** (-яжу́сь) *pf*, **распоря-
жа́ться** *impf* order, give orders; see; +*instr* manage, deal
with. **распоря́док** (-дка) order; routine. **распоряже́ние**
order; instruction; disposal,
command.

распра́ва violence; reprisal.
распра́вить (-влю) *pf*, **рас-
правля́ть** *impf* straighten;
smooth out; spread.
распра́виться (-влюсь) *pf*,
расправля́ться *impf* с+*instr*
deal with severely; make short
work of.

распределе́ние distribution;
allocation. **распредели́тель**
m distributor. **распредели́-
тельный** distributing; **~ щит** switchboard.
распредели́ть (-лю́) *pf*, **распре-
деля́ть** *impf* distribute; allocate.

распродава́ть (-даю́, -даёшь)
impf, **распрода́ть** (-а́м, -а́шь,
-а́ст, -ади́м; -о́дал, -а́, -о) *pf*
sell off; sell out of. **распро-
да́жа** (clearance) sale.
распростёртый outstretched;
prostrate.
распростране́ние spreading;
dissemination. **распространённый** (-ён, -а́) widespread,

prevalent. **распространи́ть**
pf, **распространя́ть** *imp*f
spread; **~ся** spread.

распря (*gen pl* -ей) quarrel.

распряга́ть *impf*, **распря́чь**
(-ягу́, -яжёшь; -яг, -ла́) *pf* unharness.

распрями́ться *pf*, **распрям-
ля́ться** *impf* straighten up.

распуска́ть *impf*, **распу-
сти́ть** (-ущу́, -у́стишь) *pf* dismiss; dissolve; let out; relax; let
get out of hand; melt; spread
~ся open; come loose; dissolve; melt; get out of hand
let o.s. go.

распу́тать *pf* (*impf* **распу́-
тывать**) untangle; unravel.

распу́тица season of bad
roads.

распу́тный dissolute. **рас
пу́тство** debauchery. **рас
пу́тывать** *impf* of **распу́-
тать**

распу́тье crossroads.

распуха́ть *impf*, **распу́хнуть**
(-ну; -у́х) *pf* swell (up).

распу́щенный undisciplined
spoilt; dissolute.

распыли́тель *m* spray, atomizer. **распыли́ть** *pf*, **распы-
ля́ть** *impf* spray; pulverize
disperse.

распя́тие crucifixion; crucifix
распя́ть (-пну́, -пнёшь) *p*f
(*impf* **распина́ть**) crucify.

расса́да seedlings. **расса-
ди́ть** (-ажу́, -а́дишь) *pf* **рас-
са́живать** *impf* plant out
seat; separate, seat separately

расса́живаться *impf* o
**рассе́сться. расса́сывать-
ся** *impf of* **рассоса́ться**

рассвести́ (-етёт; -ело́) *pf*
рассвета́ть *impf* dawn
рассве́т dawn.

рас|свирипе́ть (-е́ю) *pf*.

расседла́ть pf unsaddle.

рассе́ивание dispersal, scattering. **рассе́ивать(ся** impf of **рассе́ять(ся**

рассека́ть impf of **рассе́чь**

расселе́ние settling, resettlement; separation.

рассе́лина cleft, fissure.

рассели́ть pf, **расселя́ть** impf settle, resettle; separate. **рас|серди́ть(ся** (-жу(сь, -рди́шь(ся) pf.

рассе́сться (-ся́дусь, -ся́дешься pf (impf **расса́живаться**) take seats; sprawl.

рассе́чь (-еку́, -ечёшь, -ёк, -ла́) pf (impf **рассека́ть**) cut (through); cleave.

рассе́янность absent-mindedness; dispersion. **рассе́янный** absent-minded; diffused; scattered. **рассе́ять** (-ёю) pf (impf **рассе́ивать**) scatter; dispel; ~ся disperse, scatter; clear; divert o.s.

расска́з story; account. **рассказа́ть** (-ажу́, -а́жешь) pf, **расска́зывать** impf tell, recount. **расска́зчик** storyteller, narrator.

рассла́бить (-блю) pf, **расслабля́ть** impf weaken.

рассла́ивать(ся impf of **рассло́ить(ся**

рассле́дование investigation, examination; inquiry; **произвести́** ~+gen hold an inquiry into. **рассле́довать** impf & pf investigate, look into, hold an inquiry into.

рассло́ить pf (impf **рассла́ивать**) divide into layers; ~ся become stratified; flake off.

рассл́ышать (-шу) pf catch.

рассма́тривать impf of **рассмотре́ть** examine; consider.

рас|смеши́ть (-шу́) pf.

рассмея́ться (-е́юсь, -еёшься) pf burst out laughing.

рассмотре́ние examination; consideration. **рассмотре́ть** (-рю́, -ришь) pf (impf **рассма́тривать**) examine, consider; discern, make out.

рассова́ть (-су́ю, -суёшь) pf, **рассо́вывать** impf по+dat shove into.

рассо́л brine; pickle.

рассо́риться pf c+instr fall out with.

рас|сортирова́ть pf, **рассортиро́вывать** impf sort out.

рассоса́ться (-сётся) pf (impf **рассоса́ться**) resolve.

рассо́хнуться (-нется; -о́хся) pf (impf **рассыха́ться**) crack.

расспра́шивать impf, **расспроси́ть** (-ошу́, -о́сишь) pf question; make inquiries of.

рассро́чить (-чу) pf spread (over a period). **рассро́чка** instalment.

расстава́ние parting. **расстава́ться** (-таю́сь, -таёшься) impf of **расста́ться**

расста́вить (-влю) pf, **расставля́ть** impf place, arrange; move apart. **расстано́вка** arrangement; pause.

расста́ться (-а́нусь) pf (impf **расстава́ться**) part, separate.

расстёгивать impf, **расстегну́ть** (-ну́, -нёшь) pf undo, unfasten; ~ся come undone; undo one's coat.

расстели́ть(ся, etc.: see **разостла́ть(ся. расстила́ть(ся, -а́ю(сь** impf of **разостла́ть(ся**

расстоя́ние distance.

расстра́ивать(ся impf of **расстро́ить(ся**

расстре́л execution by firing squad. **расстре́ливать** impf расстреля́ть *pf* shoot.

расстро́енный disordered; upset; out of tune. расстро́ить *pf* (*impf* расстра́ивать) upset; thwart; disturb; throw into confusion; put out of tune; ~ся be upset; get out of tune; fall into confusion; fall through.

расстро́йство upset; disarray; confusion; frustration.

расступа́ться *impf*, расступи́ться (-у́пится) *pf* part, make way.

рассуди́тельный reasonable, sensible. рассуди́ть (-ужу́, -у́дишь) *pf* judge; think; decide. рассу́док (-дка) reason; intellect. рассужда́ть *impf* reason; 0+*prep* discuss. рассужде́ние reasoning; discussion; argument.

рассую́ *etc.*: *see* рассова́ть.

рассчи́танный deliberate; intended. рассчита́ть *pf*, рассчи́тывать *impf*, расче́сть (разочту́, -тёшь; расчёл, разочла́) *pf* calculate; count; depend; ~ся settle accounts.

рассыла́ть *impf of* разосла́ть. рассы́лка distribution. рассы́льный *sb* delivery man.

рассы́пать (-плю) *pf*, рассыпа́ть *impf* spill; scatter; ~ся spill, scatter; spread out; crumble. рассы́пчатый friable; crumbly.

рассыха́ться *impf of* рассо́хнуться. рассяду́сь *etc.*: *see* рассе́сться. раста́лкивать *impf of* растолка́ть. раста́пливать(ся *impf of* растопи́ть(ся

растаска́ть *pf*, раста́скивать *impf*, растащи́ть (-щу́, -щишь) *pf* pilfer; filch.

растащи́ть *see* растаска́ть.

рас|та́ять (-а́ю) *pf*.

раство́р[2] opening, span. раство́р[1] solution; mortar. раствори́мый soluble. раствори́тель *m* solvent. раствори́ть[1] *pf* (*impf* растворя́ть) dissolve; ~ся dissolve.

раствори́ть[2] (-рю́, -ришь) *pf* (*impf* растворя́ть) open; ~ся open.

растворя́ть(ся *impf of* раствори́ть(ся. растека́ться *impf of* расте́чься

расте́ние plant.

растере́ть (разотру́, -трёшь; растёр) *pf* (*impf* растира́ть) grind; spread; rub; massage.

растерза́ть *pf*, расте́рзывать *impf* tear to pieces.

расте́рянность confusion, dismay. расте́рянный confused, dismayed. растеря́ть *pf* lose; ~ся get lost; lose one's head.

расте́чься (-ечётся, -еку́тся; -тёкся, -ла́сь) *pf* (*impf* растека́ться) run; spread.

расти́ (-ту́; рос, -ла́) *impf* grow; grow up.

растира́ние grinding; rubbing, massage. растира́ть(ся *impf of* растере́ть(ся

расти́тельность vegetation; hair. расти́тельный vegetable. расти́ть (ращу́) *impf* bring up; train; grow.

растлева́ть *impf*, растли́ть *pf* seduce; corrupt.

растолка́ть *pf* (*impf* раста́лкивать) push apart; shake.

растолкова́ть *pf*, растолко́вывать *impf* explain.

рас|толо́чь (-лку́, -лчёшь; -ло́к -лкла́) *pf*.

растолсте́ть (-е́ю) *pf* put on weight.

растопи́ть[1] (-плю́, -пишь) *pf*

(*impf* **раста́пливать**) melt; thaw; **~ся** melt.

растопи́ть[2] (-плю́, -пишь) *pf* (*impf* **раста́пливать**) light, kindle; **~ся** begin to burn.

растопта́ть (-пчу́, -пчешь) *pf* trample, stamp on.

расторга́ть *impf*, **расто́ргнуть** (-ну; -орг) *pf* annul, dissolve. **расторже́ние** annulment, dissolution.

расторо́пный quick; efficient.

расточа́ть *impf*, **расточи́ть** (-чу́) *pf* squander, dissipate. **расточи́тельный** extravagant, wasteful.

растра́вить (-влю́, -вишь) *pf*, **растравля́ть** *impf* irritate.

растра́та spending; waste; embezzlement. **растра́тить** (-а́чу) *pf*, **растра́чивать** *impf* spend; waste; embezzle.

растрёпанный dishevelled; tattered. **рас|трепа́ть** (-плю́, -плешь) *pf* disarrange; tatter.

растре́скаться *pf*, **растрёскиваться** *impf* crack, chap.

растро́гать *pf* move, touch; **~ся** be moved.

расту́щий growing.

растя́гивать *impf*, **растяну́ть** (-ну́, -нешь) *pf* stretch (out); strain, sprain; drag out; **~ся** stretch; drag on; sprawl. **растяже́ние** tension; strain, sprain. **растяжи́мый** tensile; stretchable. **растя́нутый** stretched; long-winded.

рас|фасова́ть *pf*.

расформирова́ть *pf*, **расформиро́вывать** *impf* break up; disband.

расха́живать *impf* walk about; pace up and down.

расхва́ливать *impf*, **расхвали́ть** (-лю́, -лишь) *pf* lavish praises on.

расхвата́ть *pf*, **расхва́тывать** *impf* seize on, buy up.

расхити́тель *m* embezzler. **расхи́тить** (-и́щу) *pf*, **расхища́ть** *impf* steal, misappropriate. **расхище́ние** misappropriation.

расхля́банный loose; lax.

расхо́д expenditure; consumption; *pl* expenses; outlay. **расходи́ться** (-ожу́сь, -о́дишься) *impf of* **разойти́сь**. **расхо́дование** expense, expenditure. **расхо́довать** *impf* (*pf* **из~**) spend; consume. **расхожде́ние** divergence.

расхола́живать *impf*, **расхолоди́ть** (-ожу́) *pf* damp the ardour of.

расхоте́ть (-очу́, -о́чешь, -оти́м) *pf* no longer want.

расхохота́ться (-очу́сь, -о́чешься) *pf* burst out laughing.

расцара́пать *pf* scratch (all over).

расцвести́ (-ету́, -етёшь; -ёл, -á) *pf*, **расцвета́ть** *impf* blossom; flourish. **расцве́т** blossoming (out); flowering, heyday.

расцве́тка colours; colouring.

расце́нивать *impf*, **расцени́ть** (-ню́, -нишь) *pf* estimate, value; consider. **расце́нка** valuation; price; (wage-)rate.

расцепи́ть (-плю́, -пишь) *pf*, **расцепля́ть** *impf* uncouple, unhook.

расчеса́ть (-ешу́, -ешешь) *pf* (*impf* **расчёсывать**) comb; scratch. **расчёска** comb.

расче́сть *etc.: see* **рассчита́ть**. **расчёсывать** *impf of* **расчеса́ть**

расчёт[1] calculation; estimate; gain; settlement. **расчётливый** thrifty; careful. **расчёт-**

ный calculation; pay; accounts; calculated.

расчи́стить (-и́щу) *pf*, **расчища́ть** *impf* clear; ~**ся** clear. **расчи́стка** clearing.

расчлени́ть *pf*, **расчленя́ть** *impf* dismember; divide.

расшата́ть *pf*, **раша́тывать** *impf* shake loose, make rickety; impair.

расшевели́ть (-лю́, -ели́шь) *pf* stir; rouse.

расшиба́ть *impf*, **расшиби́ть** (-бу́, -бёшь; -и́б) *pf* smash to pieces; hurt; stub; ~**ся** hurt o.s.

расшива́ть *impf* of **расши́ть**

расшире́ние widening; expansion; dilation, dilatation.

расши́рить *pf*, **расширя́ть** *impf* widen; enlarge; expand; ~**ся** broaden, widen; expand, dilate.

расши́ть (разошью́, -шьёшь) *pf* (*impf* **расшива́ть**) embroider; unpick.

расшифрова́ть *pf*, **расшифро́вывать** *impf* decipher.

расшнурова́ть *pf*, **расшнуро́вывать** *impf* unlace.

расще́лина crevice.

расщепи́ть (-плю́) *pf*, **расщепля́ть** *impf* split; ~**ся** split. **расщепле́ние** splitting; fission.

ратифици́ровать *impf* & *pf* ratify.

рать army, battle.

ра́унд round.

рафини́рованный refined.

рацио́н ration.

рационализа́ция rationalization. **рационализи́ровать** *impf* & *pf* rationalize. **рациона́льный** rational; efficient. **ра́ция** walkie-talkie.

рвану́ться (-ну́сь, -нёшься) *pf* dart, dash.

рва́ный torn; lacerated. **рвать**[1] (рву, рвёшь; рвал, -á, -о) *impf* tear (out); pull out; pick; blow up; break off; ~**ся** break; tear; burst, explode; be bursting.

рвать[2] (рвёт; рва́ло) *impf* (*pf* **вы́**~) *impers+acc* vomit.

рвач (-á) self-seeker.

рве́ние zeal.

рво́та vomiting.

реабилита́ция rehabilitation. **реабилити́ровать** *impf* & *pf* rehabilitate.

реаги́ровать *impf* (*pf* **от**~, **про**~) react.

реакти́в reagent. **реакти́вный** reactive; jet-propelled. **реа́ктор** reactor.

реакционе́р reactionary. **реакцио́нный** reactionary. **реа́кция** reaction.

реализа́ция realization. **реали́зм** realism. **реализова́ть** *impf* & *pf* realize. **реали́ст** realist. **реалисти́ческий** realistic.

реа́льность reality; practicability. **реа́льный** real; practicable.

ребёнок (-нка; *pl* ребя́та, -я́т and де́ти, -éй) child; infant.

ребро́ (*pl* рёбра, -бер) rib; edge.

ребя́та (-я́т) *pl* children; guys; lads. **ребя́ческий** child's; childish. **ребя́чество** childishness. **ребя́читься** (-чусь) *impf* be childish.

рёв roar; howl.

рева́нш revenge; return match.

ревера́нс curtsey.

реве́ть (-ву́, -вёшь) *impf* roar; bellow; howl.

ревизио́нный inspection; auditing. **реви́зия** inspection; audit; revision. **ревизо́р** inspector.

ревмати́зм rheumatism.

ревни́вый jealous. **ревнова́ть** *impf* (*pf* при~) be jealous. **ре́вностный** zealous. **ре́вность** jealousy.

револьве́р revolver.

революционе́р revolutionary. **революцио́нный** revolutionary. **револю́ция** revolution.

рега́та regatta.

ре́гби *neut indecl* rugby.

ре́гент regent.

регио́н region. **региона́льный** regional.

регистра́тор registrar. **регистрату́ра** registry. **регистра́ция** registration. **регистри́ровать** *impf & pf* (*pf also* за~) register, record; ~ся register; register one's marriage.

регла́мент standing orders; time-limit. **регламента́ция** regulation. **регламенти́ровать** *impf & pf* regulate.

регресси́ровать *impf* regress.

регули́ровать *impf* (*pf* от~, у~) regulate; adjust. **регулиро́вщик** traffic controller. **регуля́рный** regular. **регуля́тор** regulator.

редакти́ровать *impf* (*pf* от~) edit. **реда́ктор** editor. **реда́кторский** editorial. **редакцио́нный** editorial, editing. **реда́кция** editorial staff; editorial office; editing.

реде́ть (-е́ет) *impf* (*pf* по~) thin (out).

реди́с radishes. **реди́ска** radish.

ре́дкий (-док, -дка́, -о) thin; sparse; rare. **ре́дко** *adv* sparsely; rarely, seldom. **ре́дкость** rarity.

редколле́гия editorial board.

рее́стр register.

режи́м régime; routine; procedure; regimen; conditions.

режиссёр-(постано́вщик) producer; director.

ре́жущий cutting, sharp. **ре́зать** (ре́жу) *impf* (*pf* за~, про~, с~) cut; engrave; kill, slaughter.

резви́ться (-влю́сь) *impf* gambol, play. **ре́звый** frisky, playful.

резе́рв reserve. **резе́рвный** reserve; back-up.

резервуа́р reservoir.

резе́ц (-зца́) cutter; chisel; incisor.

резиде́нция residence.

рези́на rubber. **рези́нка** rubber; elastic band. **рези́новый** rubber.

ре́зкий sharp; harsh; abrupt; shrill. **резно́й** carved. **резня́** carnage.

резолю́ция resolution.

резона́нс resonance; response.

результа́т result.

резьба́ carving, fretwork.

резюме́ *neut indecl* résumé.

рейд[1] roads, roadstead.

рейд[2] raid.

ре́йка lath, rod.

рейс trip; voyage; flight.

рейту́зы (-у́з) *pl* leggings; riding breeches.

река́ (*acc* ре́ку; *pl* -и, -река́м) river.

ре́квием requiem.

реквизи́т props.

рекла́ма advertising, advertisement. **реклами́ровать** *impf & pf* advertise. **рекла́мный** publicity.

рекоменда́тельный of recommendation. **рекоменда́ция** recommendation; reference. **рекомендова́ть** *impf* & *pf* (*also* от~, по~) recommend; ~ся introduce o.s.; be advisable.

реконструи́ровать *impf* & *pf* reconstruct. **реконстру́кция** reconstruction.

реко́рд record. **реко́рдный** record, record-breaking. **рекордсме́н, -éнка** record-holder.

ре́ктор principal (*of university*).

реле́ (*electr*) *neut indecl* relay.

религио́зный religious. **рели́гия** religion.

рели́квия relic.

релье́ф relief. **релье́фный** relief; raised, bold.

рельс rail.

рема́рка stage direction.

реме́нь (-мня́) *m* strap; belt.

реме́сленник artisan, craftsman. **реме́сленный** handicraft; mechanical. **ремесло́** (*pl* -ёсла, -ёсел) craft; trade.

ремо́нт repair(s); maintenance. **ремонти́ровать** *impf* & *pf* (*pf also* от~) repair; recondition. **ремо́нтный** repair.

ре́нта rent; income. **рента́бельный** paying, profitable.

рентге́н X-rays. **рентге́новский** X-ray. **рентгено́лог** radiologist. **рентгеноло́гия** radiology.

реorganиза́ция reorganization. **реorganизова́ть** *impf* & *pf* reorganize.

ре́па turnip.

репатрии́ровать *impf* & *pf* repatriate.

репертуа́р repertoire.

репети́ровать *impf* (*pf* от~, про~, с~) rehearse; coach. **репети́тор** coach. **репети́ция** rehearsal.

ре́плика retort; cue.

репорта́ж report; reporting. **репортёр** reporter.

репре́ссия repression.

репроду́ктор loud-speaker. **репроду́кция** reproduction.

репута́ция reputation.

ресни́ца eyelash.

респу́блика republic. **республика́нский** republican.

рессо́ра spring.

реставра́ция restoration. **реставри́ровать** *impf* & *pf* (*pf also* от~) restore.

рестора́н restaurant.

ресу́рс resort; *pl* resources.

ретрансля́тор (radio-)relay.

рефера́т synopsis, abstract; paper, essay.

рефере́ндум referendum.

рефле́кс reflex. **рефле́ктор** reflector.

рефо́рма reform. **реформи́ровать** *impf* & *pf* reform.

рефрижера́тор refrigerator.

рецензи́ровать *impf* (*pf* про~) review. **реце́нзия** review.

реце́пт prescription; recipe.

рециди́в relapse. **рецидиви́ст** recidivist.

речево́й speech; vocal.

ре́чка river. **речно́й** river.

речь (*gen pl* -éй) speech.

реша́ть(ся *impf* *of* **реши́ть(ся. реша́ющий** decisive, deciding. **реше́ние** decision; solution.

решётка grating; grille, railing; lattice; trellis; fender, (fire)guard; (fire-)grate; tail. **решето́** (*pl* -ёта) sieve. **решётчатый** lattice, latticed.

реши́мость resoluteness; resolve. **реши́тельно** *adv* resolutely; definitely; absolutely. **реши́тельность** determination. **реши́тельный** definite;

decisive. **решить** (-шу́) pf (impf **реша́ть**) decide; solve; ~ся make up one's mind.

ржаветь (-еет) impf (pf за~, по~) rust. **ржа́вчина** rust. **ржа́вый** rusty.

ржаной rye.

ржать (ржу, ржёшь) impf neigh.

римлянин (pl -яне, -ян), **римля́нка** Roman. **ри́мский** Roman.

ринг boxing ring.

ри́нуться (-нусь) pf rush, dart.

рис rice.

риск risk. **риско́ванный** risky; risqué. **рискова́ть** impf run risks; +instr or inf risk.

рисова́ние drawing. **рисова́ть** impf (pf на~) draw; paint, depict; ~ся be silhouetted; appear; pose.

ри́совый rice.

рису́нок (-нка) drawing; figure; pattern, design.

ритм rhythm. **ритми́ческий, ритми́чный** rhythmic.

ритуа́л ritual.

риф reef.

ри́фма rhyme. **рифмова́ть** impf rhyme; ~ся rhyme.

робе́ть (-е́ю) impf (pf о~) be timid. **ро́бкий** (-бок, -бка́, -о) timid, shy. **ро́бость** shyness.

ро́бот robot.

ров (рва, loc -у́) ditch.

рове́сник coeval. **ро́вно** adv evenly; exactly; absolutely. **ро́вный** flat; even; level; equal; exact; equal. **ровня́ть** impf (pf с~), even, level.

рог (pl -á, -о́в) horn; antler. **рога́тка** catapult. **рога́тый** horned. **рогови́ца** cornea. **рогово́й** horn; horny; horn-rimmed.

рого́жа bast mat(ting).

род (loc -у́; pl -ы́) family, kin, clan; birth, origin, stock; generation; genus; sort; kind. **роди́льный** maternity. **ро́дина** native land; homeland. **ро́динка** birth-mark. **роди́тели** (-ей) pl parents. **роди́тельный** genitive. **роди́тельский** parental. **роди́ть** (рожу́, -и́л, -и́ла́, -о) impf & pf (impf also **рожа́ть, рожда́ть**) give birth to; ~ся be born.

родни́к (-á) spring.

родни́ть (pf по~) make related, link; ~ся become related. **родно́й** own; native; home; ~о́й брат brother; ~ы́е sb pl relatives. **родня́** relative('s); kinsfolk. **родово́й** tribal; ancestral; generic; gender. **родонача́льник** ancestor; father. **родосло́вн|ый** genealogical; ~ая sb genealogy, pedigree. **ро́дственник** relative. **ро́дственный** related; kinship. **родство́** relationship. **ро́ды** (-ов) pl childbirth; labour.

ро́жа (ugly) mug.

рожа́ть, рожда́ть(ся impf of **роди́ть(ся. рожда́емость** birth-rate. **рожде́ние** birth. **рожде́ственский** Christmas. **Рождество́** Christmas.

рожь (ржи) rye.

ро́за rose.

ро́зга (gen pl -зог) birch.

ро́здал etc.: see **разда́ть**

розе́тка electric socket; rosette.

ро́зница retail; в ~у retail. **ро́зничный** retail. **рознь** difference; dissension. **ро́знял** etc.: see **разня́ть**

ро́зовый pink.

ро́зыгрыш draw; drawn game.

ро́зыск search; inquiry.

ро́йться swarm. **рой** (loc -ю́; pl -и́, -ёв) swarm.

рок fate.

рокиро́вка castling.

рок-му́зыка rock music.

роково́й fateful; fatal.

ро́кот roar, rumble. **рокота́ть** (-о́чет) impf roar, rumble.

ро́лик roller; castor; pl roller skates.

роль (gen pl -е́й) role.

ром rum.

рома́н novel; romance. **рома-ни́ст** novelist.

рома́нс (mus) romance.

рома́нтик romantic. **рома́нтика** romance. **романти́ческий, романти́чный** romantic.

рома́шка camomile.

ромб rhombus.

роня́ть impf (pf **урони́ть**) drop.

ро́пот murmur, grumble. **ропта́ть** (-пщу́, -пщешь) impf murmur, grumble.

рос etc.: see **расти́**

роса́ (pl -ы) dew. **роси́стый** dewy.

роско́шный luxurious; luxuriant. **ро́скошь** luxury; luxuriance.

ро́слый strapping.

ро́спись painting(s), mural(s).

ро́спуск dismissal; disbandment.

росси́йский Russian. **Росси́я** Russia.

ро́ссыпи f pl deposit.

рост growth; increase; height, stature.

ро́стбиф roast beef.

ростовщи́к (-а́) usurer, money-lender.

росто́к (-тка́) sprout, shoot.

ро́счерк flourish.

рот (рта, loc рту) mouth.

ро́та company.

рота́тор duplicator.

ро́тный company; sb company commander.

ротозе́й, -зе́йка gaper, rubberneck; scatter-brain.

ро́ща grove.

ро́ю etc.: see **рыть**

роя́ль m (grand) piano.

ртуть f mercury.

руба́нок (-нка) plane.

руба́ха, руба́шка shirt.

рубе́ж (-а́) boundary, border(-line); line; **за ~о́м** abroad.

рубе́ц (-бца́) scar; weal; hem; tripe.

руби́н ruby. **руби́новый** ruby; ruby-coloured.

руби́ть (-блю́, -бишь) impf (pf **с~**) fell; hew, chop; mince; build (of logs).

ру́бище rags.

ру́бка¹ felling; chopping; mincing.

ру́бка² deck house; **боева́я ~** conning-tower; **рулева́я ~** wheelhouse.

рубле́вка one-rouble note. **рублёвый** (one-)rouble note.

ру́бленый minced, chopped; of logs.

рубль (-я́) m rouble.

ру́брика rubric, heading.

ру́бчатый ribbed. **ру́бчик** scar; rib.

ру́гань abuse, swearing. **руга́тельный** abusive. **руга́тельство** oath, swear-word. **руга́ть** impf (pf **вы~, об~, от~**) curse, swear at; abuse; **~ся** curse, swear; swear at one another.

руда́ (pl -ы) ore. **рудни́к** (-а́) mine, pit. **рудни́чный** mine; pit; **~ газ** fire-damp. **рудоко́п** miner.

руже́йный rifle, gun. **ружьё** (pl -ья, -жей, -жьям) gun, rifle.

руйна *usu pl* ruin.

рука́ (*acc* -у, *gen pl* -и, рук, -а́м) hand; arm; **идти́ по́д руку с**+*instr* walk arm in arm with; **под руко́й** at hand; **руко́й пода́ть** a stone's throw away; **э́то мне не с руку́** that suits me.

рука́в (-а́; *pl* -а́, -о́в) sleeve.

рукави́ца mitten; gauntlet.

руководи́тель *m* leader; manager; instructor; guide. **руководи́ть** (-ожу́) *impf* +*instr* lead; guide; direct, manage.

руково́дство leadership; guidance; direction; guide; handbook, manual; leaders. **руково́дствоваться**+*instr* follow; be guided by. **руководя́щий** leading; guiding.

рукоде́лие needlework.

рукомо́йник washstand.

рукопа́шный hand-to-hand.

рукопи́сный manuscript. **ру́копись** manuscript.

рукоплеска́ние applause. **рукоплеска́ть** (-ещу́, -е́щешь) *impf* +*dat* applaud.

рукопожа́тие handshake.

рукоя́тка handle.

рулево́й steering; *sb* helmsman.

руле́тка tape-measure; roulette.

рули́ть *impf* (*pf* вы́~) taxi.

руль (-я́) *m* rudder; helm; (steering-)wheel; handlebar.

румы́н (*gen pl* -ын), **-ка** Romanian. **Румы́ния** Romania. **румы́нский** Romanian.

румя́на (-я́н) *pl* rouge. **румя́нец** (-нца) (high) colour; flush; blush. **румя́ный** rosy, ruddy.

ру́пор megaphone; mouth-piece.

руса́к (-а́) hare.

руса́лка mermaid.

русифици́ровать *impf & pf* Russify.

ру́сло river-bed, channel; course.

ру́сский Russian; *sb* Russian.

ру́сый light brown.

Русь (*hist*) Russia.

рути́на routine.

рухля́дь junk.

ру́хнуть (-ну) *pf* crash down.

руча́тельство guarantee. **руча́ться** *impf* (*pf* поручи́ться) **+за**+*acc* vouch for, guarantee.

руче́й (-чья́) brook.

ру́чка handle; (door-)knob; (chair-)arm; pen; **ручно́й** hand; arm; manual; tame; **~ы́е часы́** wrist-watch.

ру́шить (-у) *impf* (*pf* об~) pull down; **~ся** collapse.

ры́ба fish. **рыба́к** (-а́) fisherman. **рыба́лка** fishing. **рыба́цкий**, **рыба́чий** fishing. **ры́бий** fish; fishy; **~ жир** cod-liver oil. **ры́бный** fish. **рыболо́в** fisherman. **рыболо́вный** fishing.

рыво́к (-вка́) jerk.

рыда́ние sobbing. **рыда́ть** *impf* sob.

ры́жий (рыж, -а́, -е) red, red-haired; chestnut.

ры́ло snout; mug.

ры́нок (-нка) market; market-place. **ры́ночный** market.

рыса́к (-а́) trotter.

рысь[1] (*loc* -и́) trot; **~ю, на рыся́х** at a trot.

рысь[2] lynx.

рытви́на rut, groove. **ры́ть(ся** (ро́ю(сь) *impf* (*pf* вы́~, от~) dig; rummage.

рыхли́ть *impf* (*pf* вз~, раз~) loosen. **ры́хлый** (-л, -а́, -о) friable; loose.

ры́царский chivalrous. **ры́царь** *m* knight.

рыча́г (-а́) lever.

рыча́ть (-чу́) *impf* growl, snarl.

рья́ный zealous.

рюкза́к rucksack.

рю́мка wineglass.

ряби́на¹ rowan, mountain ash.

ряби́на² pit, pock. **ряби́ть** (-и́т) *impf* ripple; *impers*: у меня́ ряби́т в глаза́х I am dazzled. **рябо́й** pock-marked. **ря́бчик** hazel hen, hazel grouse. **рябь** ripples; dazzle.

ря́вкать *impf*, **ря́вкнуть** (-ну) *pf* bellow, roar.

ряд (*loc* -у́; *pl* -ы́) row; line; file, rank; series; number. **рядово́й** ordinary; common; ~ соста́в rank and file; *sb* private. **ря́дом** *adv* alongside; close by; +с+*instr* next to.

ря́са cassock.

С

с, со *prep* **I.** +*gen* from; since; off; for, with; on; by; **с ра́дости** for joy; **с утра́** since morning. **II.** +*acc* about; the size of; **с неде́лю** for about a week. **III.** +*instr* with; and; **мы с ва́ми** you and I; **что с ва́ми?** what is the matter?

са́бля (*gen pl* -бель) sabre.

сабота́ж sabotage. **саботи́ровать** *impf & pf* sabotage.

са́ван shroud; blanket.

с|агити́ровать *pf*.

сад (*loc* -у́; *pl* -ы́) garden. **сади́ть** (сажу́, са́дишь) *impf* (*pf* по~) plant. **сади́ться** (сажу́сь) *impf* (*pf* сесть). **садо́вник, -ница** gardener. **садово́дство** gardening; horticulture. **садо́вый** garden; cultivated.

сади́зм sadism. **сади́ст** sadist. **сади́стский** sadistic.

са́жа soot.

сажа́ть *impf* (*pf* посади́ть) plant; seat; set, put. **са́женец** (-нца) seedling; sapling.

са́жень (*pl* -и, -жен *or* -же́ней) sazhen (2.13 metres).

сажу́ *etc.: see* сади́ть

са́йка roll.

с|активи́ровать *pf*.

сала́зки (-зок) *pl* toboggan.

сала́т lettuce; salad.

са́ло fat, lard; suet; tallow.

сало́н saloon; salon.

салфе́тка napkin.

са́льный greasy; tallow; obscene.

салю́т salute. **салютова́ть** *impf & pf* (*pf also* от~) +*dat* salute.

сам (-ого́) *m*, **сама́** (-о́й, *acc* -о́ё) *f*, **само́** (-ого́) *neut*, **са́ми** (-и́х) *pl*, *pron* -self, -selves; myself, *etc.*, ourselves, *etc.*; ~ себе́ in itself; by o.s.; ~ собо́й of itself, of its own accord; ~ собо́й (разуме́ется) of course; it goes without saying.

са́мбо *neut indecl abbr* (*of* самозащи́та без ору́жия) unarmed combat.

саме́ц (-мца́) male. **са́мка** female.

само- *in comb* self-, auto-. **самобы́тный** original, distinctive. **~внуше́ние** auto-suggestion. **~возгора́ние** spontaneous combustion. **~во́льный** wilful; unauthorized. **~де́льный** home-made. **~держа́вие** autocracy. **~держа́вный** autocratic. **~де́ятельность** amateur work, amateur performance; initiative. **~дово́льный** self-satisfied. **~ду́р** petty tyrant. **~ду́рство** highhandedness. **~забве́ние** selflessness. **~забве́нный** selfless. **~защи́та** self-defence. **~зва́нец** (-нца) impostor.

pretender. **~ка́т** scooter. **~кри́тика** self-criticism. **~люби́вый** proud; touchy. **~лю́бие** pride, self-esteem. **~мне́ние** conceit, self-importance. **~надёянный** presumptuous. **~облада́ние** self-control. **~обма́н** self-deception. **~оборо́на** self-defence. **~образова́ние** self-education. **~обслу́живание** self-service. **~определе́ние** self-determination. **~отве́рженность** selflessness. **~отве́рженный** selfless. **~поже́ртвование** self-sacrifice. **~ро́док** (-дка) nugget; person with natural talent. **~сва́л** tip-up lorry. **~созна́ние** (self-)consciousness. **~сохране́ние** self-preservation. **~стоя́тельность** independence. **~стоя́тельный** independent. **~су́д** lynch law, mob law. **~тёк** drift. **~тёком** adv by gravity; of its own accord. **~уби́йственный** suicidal. **~уби́йство** suicide. **~уби́йца** m & f suicide. **~уваже́ние** self-respect. **~увере́нность** self-confidence. **~увере́нный** self-confident. **~униже́ние** self-abasement. **~управле́ние** self-government. **~управля́ющийся** self-governing. **~упра́вный** arbitrary. **~учи́тель** m self-instructor, manual. **~у́чка** m & f self-taught person. **~хо́дный** self-propelled. **~чу́вствие** general state; **как ва́ше ~чу́вствие?** how do you feel?

самова́р samovar.
самого́н home-made vodka.
самолёт aeroplane.
самоцве́т semi-precious stone.

са́мый pron (the) very, (the) right; (the) same; (the) most.
сан dignity, office.
санато́рий sanatorium.
санда́лия sandal.
са́ни (-е́й) pl sledge, sleigh.
санита́р medical orderly; stretcher-bearer. **санита́рия** sanitation. **санита́рка** nurse. **санита́рн|ый** medical; health; sanitary; **~ая маши́на** ambulance; **~ый у́зел = санузе́л.**
са́нки (-нок) pl sledge; toboggan.
санкциони́ровать impf & pf sanction. **са́нкция** sanction.
са́новник dignitary.
санпу́нкт medical centre.
санскри́т Sanskrit.
санте́хник plumber.
сантиме́тр centimetre; tape-measure.
сану́зел (-зла́) sanitary arrangements; WC.
санча́сть (gen pl -е́й) medical unit.
сапёр sapper.
сапо́г (-а́; gen pl -о́г) boot.
сапо́жник shoemaker; cobbler. **сапо́жный** shoe.
сапфи́р sapphire.
сара́й shed; barn.
саранча́ locust(s).
сарафа́н sarafan; pinafore dress.
сарде́лька small fat sausage.
сарди́на sardine.
сарка́зм sarcasm. **саркасти́ческий** sarcastic.
сатана́ m Satan. **сатани́нский** satanic.
сателли́т satellite.
сати́н sateen.
сати́ра satire. **сати́рик** satirist. **сатири́ческий** satirical.
Сау́довская Ара́вия Saudi Arabia.
сафья́н morocco. **сафья́новый** morocco.

са́хар sugar. **сахари́н** saccharine. **са́харистый** sugary. **са́харница** sugar-basin. **са́харный** sugar; sugary; ~ый заво́д sugar-refinery; ~ый песо́к granulated sugar; ~ая пу́дра castor sugar; ~ая свёкла sugar-beet.

сачо́к (-чка́) net.

сба́вить (-влю) pf, **сбавля́ть** impf take off; reduce.

с|баланси́ровать pf.

сбега́ть[1] impf run; +за+instr run for. **сбега́ть**[2] impf, **сбежа́ть** (-егу́) pf run down (from); run away; disappear; ~ся come running.

сберега́тельная ка́сса savings bank. **сберега́ть** impf, **сбере́чь** (-егу́, -ежёшь; -ёг, -ла́) pf save up; preserve. **сбереже́ние** economy; saving; savings. **сберка́сса** savings bank.

сбива́ть impf, **с|бить** (собью́, -бьёшь) pf bring down, knock down; knock off; distract; wear down; knock together; churn; whip, whisk; ~ся be dislodged; slip; go wrong; be confused; ~ся с пути́ lose one's way; ~ся с ног be run off one's feet. **сби́вчивый** confused; inconsistent.

сближа́ть impf, **сбли́зить** (-и́жу) pf bring (closer) together, draw together; ~ся draw together; become good friends. **сближе́ние** rapprochement; closing in.

сбо́ку adv from one side; on one side.

сбор collection; duty; fee, toll; takings; gathering. **сбо́рище** crowd, mob. **сбо́рка** assembling, assembly; gather. **сбо́рник** collection. **сбо́рный**

assembly; mixed, combined; prefabricated; detachable. **сбо́рочный** assembly. **сбо́рщик** collector; assembler.

сбра́сывать(ся impf of сбро́сить(ся

сбрива́ть impf, **сбрить** (сбре́ю) pf shave off.

сброд riff-raff.

сброс fault, break. **сбро́сить** (-о́шу) pf (impf сбра́сывать) throw down, drop; throw off; shed; discard.

сбру́я (collect) (riding) tack.

сбыва́ть impf, **сбыть** (сбу́ду, сбыл, -а́, -о) pf sell, market; get rid of; ~ся come true, be realized. **сбыт** (no pl) sale; market.

св. abbr (of **свято́й**) Saint.

сва́дебный wedding. **сва́дьба** (gen pl -деб) wedding.

сва́ливать impf, **с|вали́ть** (-лю́, -лишь) pf throw down; overthrow; pile up; ~ся fall (down), collapse. **сва́лка** dump; scuffle.

с|вали́ть pf.

сва́ривать impf, **с|вари́ть** (-рю́, -ришь) pf boil; cook; weld. **сва́рка** welding.

сварли́вый cantankerous.

сварно́й welded. **сва́рочный** welding. **сва́рщик** welder.

сва́стика swastika.

сва́тать impf (pf по~, со~) propose as a husband or wife; propose to; ~ся к+dat or за+acc propose to.

сва́я pile.

све́дение piece of information; knowledge; pl information, intelligence; knowledge. **све́дущий** knowledgeable; versed.

сведу́ etc.: see **свести́**

свежезаморо́женный fresh-frozen; chilled. **све́жесть**

freshness. **свеже́ть** (-е́ет) *impf* (*pf* по~) become cooler; freshen. **све́жий** (-еж, -а́) fresh; new.

свезти́ (-зу́, -зёшь; свёз, -ла́) *pf* (*impf* **свози́ть**) take; bring or take down or away.

свёкла beet, beetroot.

свёкор (-кра) father-in-law. **свекро́вь** mother-in-law.

свёл *etc.*: *see* **свести́**

сверга́ть *impf*, **све́ргнуть** (-ну; сверг) *pf* throw down, overthrow. **сверже́ние** overthrow.

све́рить *pf* (*impf* **сверя́ть**) collate.

сверка́ть *impf* sparkle, twinkle; glitter; gleam. **сверкну́ть** (-ну́, -нёшь) *pf* flash.

сверли́льный drill, drilling; boring. **сверли́ть** *impf* (*pf* про~) drill; bore (through); nag. **сверло́** drill. **сверля́щий** gnawing, piercing.

сверну́ть (-ну́, -нёшь) *pf* (*impf* **свёртывать, свора́чивать**) roll (up); turn; curtail, cut down; ~ ше́ю+*dat* wring the neck of; ~ся roll up, curl up; curdle, coagulate; contract.

све́рстник contemporary.

свёрток (-тка) package, bundle. **свёртывание** rolling (up); curdling; coagulation; curtailment, cuts. **свёртывать(ся** *impf of* **сверну́ть(ся**

сверх *prep*+*gen* over, above, on top of; beyond; in addition to; ~ того́ moreover.

сверх- *in comb* super-, over-, hyper-. **сверхзвуково́й** supersonic. ~**пла́новый** over and above the plan. ~**при́быль** excess profit. ~**проводни́к** (-а́) superconductor. ~**секре́тный** top secret. ~**уро́чный**

overtime. ~**уро́чные** *sb pl* overtime. ~**челове́к** superman. ~**челове́ческий** superhuman. ~**есте́ственный** supernatural.

све́рху *adv* from above; ~ донизу from top to bottom.

сверчо́к (-чка́) cricket.

сверше́ние achievement.

све́сить (-е́шу) *pf* (*impf* **све́шивать**) let down, lower; ~**ся** hang over, lean over.

свести́ (-еду́, -едёшь; -ёл, -а́) *pf* (*impf* **своди́ть**) take; take down; take away; remove; bring together; reduce; bring; cramp.

свет[1] light; daybreak.

свет[2] world; society.

света́ть *impers* dawn. **свети́ло** luminary. **свети́ть** (-ечу́, -е́тишь) *impf* (*pf* по~) shine; +*dat* light; light the way for; ~**ся** shine, gleam. **светле́ть** (-е́ет) *impf* (*pf* по~, про~) brighten (up); grow lighter. **све́тлость** brightness; Grace. **све́тлый** light; bright; joyous. **светлячо́к** (-чка́) glow-worm.

свето- *in comb* light, photo-. **светонепроница́емый** lightproof. ~**фи́льтр** light filter. ~**фо́р** traffic light(s).

светово́й light; luminous; ~ **день** daylight hours.

светопреставле́ние end of the world.

све́тский fashionable; refined; secular.

светя́щийся luminous, fluorescent. **свеча́** (*pl* -и, -е́й) candle; (spark-)plug. **свече́ние** luminescence, fluorescence. **све́чка** candle. **свечу́** *etc.*: *see* **свети́ть**

с|ве́шать *pf*, све́шивать(ся *impf of* све́сить(ся. сва́ивать *impf of* свить

свида́ние meeting; appointment; до свида́ния! goodbye!

свиде́тель *m*, -ница witness. свиде́тельство evidence; testimony; certificate. свиде́тельствовать *impf* (*pf* за~, о~) give evidence, testify; be evidence (of); witness.

свина́рник pigsty.

свине́ц (-нца́) lead.

свини́на pork. сви́нка mumps. свино́й pig; pork. сви́нство despicable act; outrage; squalor.

свинцо́вый lead; leaden.

свинья́ (*pl* -и́нья, -е́й, -ья́м) pig, swine.

свире́ль (reed-)pipe.

свирепе́ть (-е́ю) *impf* (*pf* рас~) grow savage; become violent. свире́пствовать *impf* rage; be rife. свире́пый fierce, ferocious.

свиса́ть *impf*, сви́снуть (-ну, -ис) *pf* hang down, dangle; trail.

свист whistle; whistling. свиста́ть (-ищу́, -и́щешь) *impf* whistle. свисте́ть (-ищу́) *impf*, сви́стнуть (-ну *pf* whistle; hiss. свисто́к (-тка́) whistle.

сви́та suite; retinue.

сви́тер sweater.

сви́ток (-тка) roll, scroll. с|вить (совью́, совьёшь; -ил, -а́, о~) *pf* (*impf also* сви́вать) twist, wind; ~ся roll up.

свихну́ться (-ну́сь, -нёшься) *impf* go mad; go astray.

свищ (-а́) flaw; (knot-)hole; fistula.

свищу́ *etc.*: *see* свиста́ть, свисте́ть

свобо́да freedom. свобо́дно *adv* freely; easily; fluently; loose(ly). свобо́дный free; easy; vacant; spare; loose; flowing. свободолюби́вый freedom-loving. свободо-мы́слие free-thinking.

свод code; collection; arch, vault.

сводить (-ожу́, -о́дишь) *impf of* свести

сво́дка summary; report. сво́дный composite; step-.

сво́дчатый arched, vaulted.

своево́лие self-will, wilfulness. своево́льный wilful.

своевре́менно *adv* in good time; opportunely. своевре́менный timely, opportune.

своенра́вие capriciousness. своенра́вный wilful, capricious.

своеобра́зие originality; peculiarity. своеобра́зный original; peculiar.

свожу́ *etc.*: *see* сводить, свозить. свозить (-ожу́, -о́зишь) *impf of* свезти

свой (своего́) *m*, своя́ (свое́й) *f*, своё (своего́) *neut*, свои́ (свои́х) *pl*, *pron* one's (own); my, his, her, its; our, your, their. сво́йственный peculiar, characteristic. сво́йство property, attribute, characteristic.

сво́лочь swine; riff-raff.

сво́ра pack; leash.

свора́чивать *impf of* сверну́ть, свороти́ть. с|ворова́ть *pf*.

свороти́ть (-очу́, -о́тишь) *pf* (*impf* свора́чивать) dislodge; shift; turn; twist.

своя́к brother-in-law (*husband of wife's sister*). своя́ченица sister-in-law (*wife's sister*).

свыка́ться *impf*, свы́кнуться (-нусь; -ыкся) pf get used.

свысока́ adv haughtily. свы́ше adv from above. свы́ше prep+gen over; beyond.

свя́занный constrained; combined; bound. свя́за́ть (-яжу́, -я́жешь) pf, свя́зывать impf tie, bind; connect; ~ся get in touch; get involved. связи́ст, -и́стка signaller; worker in communication services. свя́зка sheaf, bundle; ligament. свя́зный connected, coherent. связь (loc -и́) connection; link, bond; liaison; communication(s).

святи́лище sanctuary. свя́тки (-ток) pl Christmas-tide. свя́то adv piously; religiously. свято́й (-ят, -а́, -о) holy; ~о́й, -а́я sb saint. святы́ня sacred object or place. свя́ще́нник priest. свяще́нный sacred.

сгиб bend. сгиба́ть impf of согну́ть

сгла́дить (-а́жу) pf, сгла́живать impf smooth out; smooth over, soften.

сгла́зить (-а́жу) pf put the evil eye on.

сгнива́ть impf, сгнить (-ию́, -иёшь; -ил, -а́, -о) pf rot.

сгно́иться pf.

сгова́риваться impf, сгово́ри́ться pf come to an arrangement; arrange. сго́вор agreement. сгово́рчивый compliant.

сгоня́ть impf of согна́ть

сгора́ние combustion; дви́гатель вну́треннего сгора́ния internal-combustion engine. сгора́ть impf of сгоре́ть

сго́рбить(ся (-блю(сь) pf.

сгоре́ть (-рю́) pf (impf also сгора́ть) burn down; be burnt

down; be used up; burn; burn o.s. out. сгоряча́ adv in the heat of the moment.

с|гото́вить (-влю(сь) pf.

сгреба́ть impf, сгрести́ (-ебу́, -ебёшь; -ёб, -ла́) pf rake up, rake together.

сгружа́ть impf, сгрузи́ть (-ужу́, -у́зишь) pf unload.

с|группирова́ть pf.

сгусти́ть (-ущу́) pf, сгуща́ть impf thicken; condense; ~ся thicken; condense; clot. сгу́сток (-тка) clot. сгуще́ние thickening, condensation; clotting.

сдава́ть (сдаю́, сдаёшь) impf of сдать; ~ экза́мен take an examination; ~ся give in. сда́ться

сда́вить (-влю́, -вишь) pf, сда́вливать impf squeeze.

сдать (-ам, -ашь, -аст, -ади́м; -ал, -а́, -о) pf (impf сдава́ть) hand over; pass; let, hire out; surrender, give up; deal; ~ся surrender, yield. сда́ча handing over; hiring out; surrender; change; deal.

сдвиг displacement; fault; change, improvement. сдвига́ть impf, сдви́нуть (-ну) pf shift, move; move together; ~ся move, budge; come together.

с|де́лать pf. сде́лка transaction; deal, bargain. сде́льный piece-work; ~ая рабо́та piece-work. сде́льщина piece-work.

сде́рживать impf of сдёрнуть сде́ржанный restrained, reserved. сдержа́ть (-жу́, -жишь) pf, сде́рживать impf hold back; restrain; keep.

сдёрнуть (-ну) pf (impf сдёргивать) pull off.

сдеру́ etc.: see **содра́ть.**

сдира́ть impf of **содра́ть**

сдо́ба shortening; fancy bread, bun(s). **сдо́бный** (-бен, -бна́, -о) rich, short.

с|до́хнуть (-нет; сдох) pf die; kick the bucket.

сдружи́ться (-жу́сь) pf become friends.

сду́вать impf, **сду́нуть** (-ну) pf, **сдуть** (-у́ю) pf blow away or off.

сеа́нс performance; showing; sitting.

себесто́имость prime cost; cost (price).

себя́ (dat & prep себе́, instr собо́й or собо́ю) refl pron oneself; myself, yourself, himself, etc.; **ничего́ себе́** not bad; **собо́й** -looking, in appearance.

себялю́бие selfishness.

сев sowing.

се́вер north. **се́верный** north, northern; northerly. **се́веро-восто́к** north-east **се́веро-восто́чный** north-east(ern). **се́веро-за́пад** north-west. **се́веро-за́падный** north-west(ern). **северя́нин** (pl -я́не, -я́н) northerner.

севооборо́т crop rotation.

сего́ see **сей. сего́дня** adv today. **сего́дняшний** of today, today's.

седе́ть (-е́ю) impf (pf по~) turn grey. **седина́** (pl -ы) grey hair(s).

седла́ть impf (pf о~) saddle. **седло́** (pl сёдла, -дел) saddle.

седоборо́дый grey-bearded. **седоволо́сый** grey-haired. **седо́й** (сед, -а́, -о) grey(-haired).

седо́к (-а́) passenger; rider.

седьмо́й seventh.

сезо́н season. **сезо́нный** seasonal.

сей (сего́) m, **сия́** (сей) f, **сие́** (сего́) neut, **сии́** (сих) pl, pron this; these; **сию́ мину́ту** at once, instantly.

сейсми́ческий seismic.

сейф safe.

сейча́с adv (just) now; soon; immediately.

сёк etc.: see **сечь**

секре́т secret.

секретариа́т secretariat.

секрета́рский secretarial. **секрета́рша, секрета́рь** (-я́) m secretary.

секре́тный secret.

секс sex. **сексуа́льный** sexual; sexy.

сексте́т sextet.

се́кта sect. **секта́нт** sectarian.

се́ктор sector.

секу́ etc.: see **сечь**

секуляриза́ция secularization.

секу́нда second. **секунда́нт** second. **секу́ндный** second. **секундоме́р** stop-watch.

секцио́нный sectional. **се́кция** section.

селёдка herring.

селезёнка spleen.

се́лезень (-зня) m drake.

селе́кция breeding.

селе́ние settlement, village.

сели́тра saltpetre, nitre.

сели́ть(ся impf (pf по~) settle. **село́** (pl сёла) village.

сельдере́й celery.

сельдь (pl -и, -е́й) herring.

се́льск|ий rural; village; ~ое хозя́йство agriculture. **сельскохозя́йственный** agricultural.

сельсове́т village soviet.

сема́нтика semantics. **семанти́ческий** semantic.

семафо́р semaphore; signal.

сёмга (smoked) salmon.

семе́йный family; domestic;

семейство family.

семени *etc.: see* семя

семенить *impf* mince.

семенник (-á) testicle; seed-vessel. семенной seed; seminal.

семёрка seven; figure 7; No. 7. семеро (-ых) seven.

семестр term, semester.

семечко (*pl* -и) seed; *pl* sunflower seeds.

семидесятилетие seventy years; seventieth anniversary, birthday. семидесятый seventieth; ~ые годы the seventies. семилетка seven-year school. семилетний seven-year; seven-year-old.

семинар seminar. семинария seminary.

семисотый seven-hundredth. семнадцатый seventeenth. семнадцать seventeen. семь (-ми, -мью) seven. семьдесят (-мидесяти, -мьюдесятью) seventy. семьсот (-мисот, *instr* -мьюстами) seven hundred. семью *adv* seven times.

семья (*pl* -и, -ей, -ям) family. семьянин family man.

семя (-мени; *pl* -менá, -мян, -менáм) seed; semen, sperm.

сенат senate. сенатор senator.

сени (-ей) *pl* (entrance-)hall.

сено hay. сеновал hayloft. сенокос haymaking; hayfield. сенокосилка mowing-machine.

сенсационный sensational. сенсация sensation.

сентенция maxim.

сентиментальный sentimental.

сентябрь (-я) *m* September. сентябрьский September.

сепсис sepsis.

сера sulphur; ear-wax.

серб, ~ка Serb. Сербия Serbia. сербский Serb(ian). сербскохорватский Serbo-Croat(ian).

сервант sideboard.

сервиз service, set. сервировать *impf & pf* serve; lay (a table). сервировка laying; table lay-out.

сердечник core. сердечность cordiality; warmth. сердечный heart; cardiac; cordial; warm(-hearted). сердитый angry. сердить (-ржу, -рдишь) *impf* (*pf* рас~) anger; ~ся be angry. сердобольный tender-hearted. сердце (*pl* -á, -дéц) heart; в сердцах in anger; от всего сердца from the bottom of one's heart. сердцебиение palpitation. сердцевидный heart-shaped. сердцевина core, pith, heart.

серебрёный silver-plated. серебристый silvery. серебрить *impf* (*pf* по~) silver, silver-plate; ~ся become silvery. серебро silver. серебряный silver.

середина middle.

серёжка earring; catkin.

серенада serenade.

серенький grey; dull.

сержант sergeant.

серийный serial; mass. серия series; part.

серный sulphur; sulphuric.

сероглазый grey-eyed.

серость uncouthness; ignorance.

серп (-á) sickle; ~ луны crescent moon.

серпантин streamer.

сертификат certificate.

серый (сер, -á, -о) grey; dull; uneducated.

серьга́ (*pl* -и, -рёг) earring.

серьёзность seriousness. **серьёзный** serious.

се́ссия session.

сестра́ (*pl* сёстры, сестёр, сёстрам) sister.

сесть (ся́ду) *pf* (*impf* сади́ться) sit down; land; set; shrink; +на+*acc* board, get on.

се́тка net, netting; (luggage-)rack; string bag; grid.

се́товать *impf* (*pf* по~) complain.

сетча́тка retina. **сеть** (*loc* -и́, *pl* -и, -е́й) net; network.

сече́ние section. **сечь** (секу́, сечёшь; сёк) *impf* (*pf* вы́~) cut to pieces; flog; ~ся split.

се́ялка seed drill. **се́ять** (се́ю) *impf* (*pf* по~) sow.

сжа́литься *pf* take pity (над+*instr*) on.

сжа́тие pressure; grasp, grip; compression. **сжа́тый** compressed; compact; concise.

с|жать[1] (сожму́, -нёшь) *pf*.

сжать[2] (сожму́, -мёшь) (*impf* сжима́ть) squeeze; compress; grip; clench; ~ся tighten; shrink; contract.

с|жечь (сожгу́, сожжёшь; сжёг, сожгла́) *pf* (*impf* сжига́ть) burn (down); cremate.

сжива́ться *impf* of сжи́ться

сжига́ть *impf* of сжечь

сжима́ть(ся *impf* of сжать[2]

сжи́ться (-иву́сь, -ивёшься; -и́лся, -ась) *pf* (*impf* сжива́ться) с+*instr* get used to.

с|жу́льничать *pf*.

сза́ди *adv* from behind; behind. **сза́ди** *prep*+*gen* behind.

сзыва́ть *impf* of созва́ть

сиби́рский Siberian. **Сиби́рь** Siberia. **сибиря́к** (-а́), **сибиря́чка** Siberian.

сига́ра cigar. **сигаре́та** cigarette.

сигна́л signal. **сигнализа́ция** signalling. **сигнализи́ровать** *impf* & *pf* (*pf* also про~) signal. **сигна́льный** signal. **сигна́льщик** signalman.

сиде́лка sick-nurse. **сиде́нье** sitting. **сиде́нье** seat. **сиде́ть** (-ижу́) *impf* sit; be; fit. **сидя́чий** sitting; sedentary.

сие́ *etc.*: *see* сей

си́ла strength; force; power; в си́лу +*gen* on the strength of, because of; не по ~ам beyond one's powers; си́лой by force. **сила́ч** (-а́) strong man. **си́литься** *impf* try, make efforts. **силово́й** power; of force.

сило́к (-лка́) noose, snare. **си́лос** silo; silage.

силуэ́т silhouette.

си́льно *adv* strongly, violently; very much, greatly. **си́льный** (-лен *or* -лён, -льна́, -о) strong; powerful; intense, hard.

симбио́з symbiosis.

си́мвол symbol. **символизи́ровать** *impf* symbolize. **символи́зм** symbolism. **символи́ческий** symbolic.

симме́трия symmetry.

симпатизи́ровать *impf* +*dat* like, sympathize with. **симпати́чный** likeable, nice. **симпа́тия** liking; sympathy.

симпо́зиум symposium.

симпто́м symptom.

симули́ровать *impf* & *pf* simulate, feign. **симуля́нт** malingerer, sham. **симуля́ция** simulation, pretence.

симфони́ческий symphony. **симфо́ния** symphony.

синаго́га synagogue.

синева́ blue. **синева́тый** bluish. **синегла́зый** blue-eyed.

синеть (-éю) *impf* (*pf* по~) turn blue; show blue. **синий** (синь, -ня, -не) (dark) blue.

синица titmouse.

синод synod. синоним synonym. синтаксис syntax.

синтез synthesis. синтезировать *impf & pf* synthesize. синтетический synthetic.

синус sine; sinus.

синхронизировать *impf & pf* synchronize.

синь¹ blue. синь² *see* синий.

синька blueing; blue-print.

синяк (-á) bruise.

сионизм Zionism.

сиплый hoarse, husky. сипнуть (-ну; сип) *impf* (*pf* о~) become hoarse, husky.

сирена siren; hooter.

сиреневый lilac(-coloured). сирень lilac.

Сирия Syria.

сироп syrup.

сирота (*pl* -ы) *m & f* orphan. сиротливый lonely. сиротский orphan's, orphans'.

система system. систематизировать *impf & pf* systematize. систематический, систематичный systematic.

ситец (-тца) (printed) cotton; chintz.

сито sieve.

ситуация situation.

ситцевый print, chintz.

сифилис syphilis.

сифон siphon.

сия *see* сей

сияние radiance. сиять *impf* shine, beam.

сказ tale. сказание story, legend. сказать (-ажу, -ажешь) *pf* (говорить), say; speak; tell. сказаться (-ажусь, -ажешься) *pf*, сказываться *impf* tell (on); declare o.s. сказитель *m*

story-teller. сказка (fairy-)tale; fib. сказочный fairy-tale; fantastic. сказуемое *sb* predicate.

скакалка skipping-rope. скакать (-ачу, -ачешь) *impf* (*pf* по~), skip; jump; gallop. скаковой race, racing.

скала (*pl* -ы) rock face; cliff. скалистый rocky.

скалить *impf* (*pf* о~); ~ зубы bare one's teeth; grin; ~ся bare one's teeth.

скалка rolling-pin.

скалолаз rock-climber.

скалывать *impf of* сколоть

скальп scalp.

скальпель *m* scalpel.

скамеечка footstool; small bench. скамейка bench. скамья (*pl* скамьи, -ей) bench; ~ подсудимых dock.

скандал scandal; brawl, rowdy scene. скандалист trouble-maker. скандалиться *impf* (*pf* о~) disgrace o.s. скандальный scandalous.

скандинавский Scandinavian.

скандировать *impf & pf* declaim.

скапливать(ся *impf of* скопить(ся

скарб goods and chattels.

скаредный stingy.

скарлатина scarlet fever.

скат slope; pitch.

с|катать *pf* (*impf* скатывать) roll (up).

скатерть (*pl* -и, -ей) table-cloth.

скатить (-ачу, -атишь) *pf*, скатывать¹ *impf* roll down; ~ся roll down; slip, slide. скатывать² *impf of* скатать

скафандр diving-suit; space-suit.

скачка gallop, galloping. скачки (-чек) *pl* horse-race; races.

скачо́к (-чка́) jump, leap.

скашивать *impf of* **скоси́ть**

сква́жина slit, chink; well.

сквер public garden.

скве́рно badly; bad. **скверно-**
сло́вить (-влю) *impf* use foul
language. **скве́рный** (-рен, -рна́, -о) foul; bad.

сквози́ть *impf* be transparent;
show through; **сквози́т** *impers*
there is a draught. **сквозно́й**
through; transparent. **сквоз-**
ня́к (-а́) draught. **сквозь**
prep+gen through.

скворе́ц (-рца́) starling.

скеле́т skeleton.

ске́птик sceptic. **скептици́зм**
scepticism. **скепти́ческий**
sceptical.

скетч sketch.

ски́дка reduction. **ски́ды-**
вать *impf*, **ски́нуть** (-ну) *pf*
throw off or down; knock off.

скипетр sceptre.

скипида́р turpentine.

скирд (-а́, *pl* -ы́), **скирда́** (*pl*
-ы, -а́м) stack, rick.

скиса́ть *impf*, **ски́снуть** (-ну;
скис) *pf* go sour.

скита́лец (-льца) wanderer.
скита́ться *impf* wander.

скиф Scythian.

склад[1] depot; store.

склад[2] mould; turn; logical
connection; ~ **ума́** mentality.

скла́дка fold; pleat; crease;
wrinkle.

скла́дно smoothly.

складно́й folding, collapsible.

скла́дный (-ден, -дна́, -о) well-
knit, well-built; smooth, coherent.

скла́дчина: в скла́дчину by
clubbing together. **скла́ды-**
вать(ся *impf of* **сложи́ть(ся**

скле́ивать *impf*, **скле́ить**
pf stick together; ~**ся** stick
together.

склеп (burial) vault, crypt.

склепа́ть *pf*, **склёпывать**
impf rivet. **склёпка** riveting.

склеро́з sclerosis.

скло́ка squabble.

склон slope; **на ~е лет** in one's
declining years. **склоне́ние**
inclination; declension. **склон-**
и́ть (-оню́, -нишь) *pf*, **склоня́ть**
impf incline; bow; win over; decline; ~**ся** bend, bow; yield; be
declined. **скло́нность** inclination; tendency. **скло́нный** (-нен,
-нна́, -о) inclined, disposed.
склоня́емый declinable.

скля́нка phial; bottle; (*naut*)
bell.

ско́ба (*pl* -ы, -а́м) cramp, clamp,
staple.

ско́бка *dim of* **скоба́**; bracket;
pl parenthesis, parentheses.

скобли́ть (-облю́, -о́блишь)
impf scrape, plane.

ско́ванность constraint. **ско́-**
ванный constrained; bound.
скова́ть (скую́, скуёшь) *pf*
(*impf* **ско́вывать**) forge; chain;
fetter; pin down, hold, contain.

сковорода́ (*pl* ско́вороды, -ро́д,
-а́м), **сковоро́дка** frying-pan.
ско́вывать *impf of* **скова́ть**

скола́чивать *impf*, **сколо-**
ти́ть (-очу́, -о́тишь) *pf* knock
together.

сколо́ть (-лю́, -лешь) *pf* (*impf*
ска́лывать) chop off; pin together.

скольже́ние sliding, slipping;
glide. **скользи́ть** (-льжу́) *impf*,
скользну́ть (-ну́, -нёшь) *pf*
slide; slip; glide. **ско́льзкий**
(-зок, -зка́, -о) slippery. **сколь-**
зя́щий sliding.

ско́лько *adv* how much; how
many; as far as.

с|кома́ндовать *pf*. с|комби́-

ни́ровать *pf.* с|ко́мкать *pf.*
с|комплектова́ть *pf.*
с|компромети́ровать *pf.*
с|конструи́ровать *pf.*
сконфу́женный embarrassed, confused, disconcerted. с|конфу́зить(ся (-у́жу(сь) *pf.*
с|концентри́ровать *pf.*
сконча́ться *pf* pass away, die.
с|копи́ровать *pf.*
скопи́ть (-плю́, -пишь) *pf* (*impf* ска́пливать) save (up); amass; ~ся accumulate. скопле́ние accumulation; crowd.
ско́пом *adv* in a crowd, en masse.
скорбе́ть (-блю́) *impf* grieve.
ско́рбный sorrowful. скорбь (*pl* -и, -е́й) sorrow.
скоре́е, скоре́й *comp of* ско́ро, ско́рый; *adv* rather, sooner; как мо́жно ~ as soon as possible; ~ всего́ most likely.
скорлупа́ (*pl* -ы) shell.
скорня́к (-а́) furrier.
ско́ро *adv* quickly; soon.
ско́ро- *in comb* quick-, fast-. скорова́рка pressure-cooker. ~гово́рка patter; tongue-twister. ско́ропись cursive; shorthand. ~по́ртящийся perishable. ~пости́жный sudden. ~спе́лый early; fast-ripening; premature; hasty. ~сшива́тель *m* binder, file. ~те́чный transient, short-lived.
скоростно́й high-speed. ско́рость (*gen pl* -е́й) speed; gear.
скорпио́н scorpion; Scorpio.
с|корректи́ровать *pf.* с|ко́рчить(ся (-чу(сь) *pf.*
ско́рый (скор, -а́, -о) quick, fast; near; forthcoming; ~ая по́мощь first-aid; ambulance.
с|коси́ть[1] (-ошу́, -о́сишь) *pf*

(*impf also* ска́шивать) mow.
с|коси́ть[2] (-ошу́) *pf* (*impf also* ска́шивать) squint; cut on the cross.
скот (-а́), скоти́на cattle; livestock; beast. ско́тный cattle.
ското- *in comb* cattle. ското-бо́йня (*gen pl* -оен) slaughter-house. ~вод cattle-breeder. ~во́дство cattle-raising.
ско́тский cattle; brutish. ско́тство brutish condition; brutality.
с|кра́сить (-а́шу) *pf*, скра́шивать *impf* smooth over; relieve.
скребо́к (-бка́) scraper. скребу́ *etc.: see* скрести́
скре́жет grating; gnashing. скрежета́ть (-ещу́, -е́щешь) *impf* grate; +*instr* gnash.
скре́па clamp, brace; counter-signature.
скрепи́ть (-плю́) *pf*, скрепля́ть *impf* fasten (together), make fast; clamp; countersign, ratify; скрепя́ се́рдце reluctantly. скре́пка paper-clip. скрепле́ние fastening; clamping; tie, clamp.
скрести́ (-ебу́, -ебёшь; -ёб, -ла́) *impf* scrape; scratch; ~сь scratch.
скрести́ть (-ещу́) *pf*, скре́щивать *impf* cross; interbreed. скреще́ние crossing. скре́щивание crossing; interbreeding.
с|криви́ть(ся (-влю́(сь) *pf.*
скрип squeak, creak. скрипа́ч (-а́) violinist. скрипе́ть (-плю́) *impf*, скри́пнуть (-ну) *pf* squeak, creak; scratch. скрипи́чный violin; ~ ключ treble clef. скри́пка violin. скрипу́чий squeaky, creaking.

с|кро́ить *pf.*

скро́мничать *impf (pf* по~**)** be (too) modest. **скро́мность** modesty. **скро́мный** (-мен, -мна́, -о) modest.

скрою́ *etc.*: see **скрыть**. **скро́ю** *etc.*: see **скрои́ть**

скрупулёзный scrupulous.

с|крути́ть (-учу́, -у́тишь) *pf,* **скру́чивать** *impf* twist; roll; tie up.

скрыва́ть *impf,* **скрыть** (-о́ю) .*pf* hide, conceal; ~**ся** hide, go into hiding, be hidden; steal away; disappear. **скры́тничать** *impf* be secretive. **скры́тный** secretive. **скры́тый** secret, hidden; latent.

скря́га *m & f* miser.

ску́дный (-ден, -дна́, -о) scanty; meagre. **ску́дость** scarcity, paucity.

ску́ка boredom.

скула́ (*pl* -ы) cheek-bone. **скула́стый** with high cheek-bones.

скули́ть *impf* whine, whimper.

ску́льптор sculptor. **скульпту́ра** sculpture.

ску́мбрия mackerel.

скунс skunk.

скупа́ть *impf of* **скупи́ть**

скупе́ц (-пца́) miser.

скупи́ть (-плю́, -пишь) *pf* (*impf* скупа́ть) buy (up).

скупи́ться (-плю́сь) *impf* (*pf* по~) be stingy; skimp; be sparing of (+на+*acc*).

ску́пка buying (up).

ску́по *adv* sparingly. **скупо́й** (-п, -а́, -о) stingy, meagre. **ску́пость** stinginess. **ску́пщик** buyer(-up).

ску́тер (*pl* -а́) outboard speed-boat.

скуча́ть *impf* be bored; ~**по** +*dat* miss, yearn for.

ску́ченность density, over-

crowding. **ску́ченный** dense, overcrowded. **ску́чить** (-чу) *pf* crowd (together); ~**ся** cluster; crowd together.

ску́чный (-чен, -чна́, -о) boring; **мне ску́чно** I'm bored.

с|ку́шать *pf.* **скую́** *etc.*: see **скова́ть**

слабе́ть (-е́ю) *impf (pf* о~**)** weaken, grow weak. **слаби́тельный** laxative; ~**ое** *sb* laxative. **сла́бить** *impers:* **его́ сла́бит** he has diarrhoea.

слабо- *in comb* weak, feeble, slight. **слабово́лие** weakness of will. **~во́льный** weak-willed. **~не́рвный** nervy, nervous. **~разви́тый** under-developed. **~у́мие** feeble-mindedness. **~у́мный** feeble-minded.

сла́бость weakness. **сла́бый** (-б, -а́, -о) weak.

сла́ва glory; fame; **на сла́ву** wonderfully well. **сла́вить** (-влю) *impf* celebrate, sing the praises of; ~**ся** (+*instr*) be famous (for). **сла́вный** glorious, renowned; nice.

славяни́н (*pl* -я́не, -я́н) Slav. **славя́нка** Slav. **славянофи́л** Slavophil(e). **славя́нский** Slav, Slavonic.

слага́емое *sb* component, term, member. **слага́ть** *impf of* **сложи́ть**

сла́дить (-а́жу) *pf* с+*instr* cope with, handle; arrange.

сла́дкий (-док, -дка́, -о) sweet; ~**ое** *sb* sweet course. **сладостра́стник** voluptuary. **сладостра́стный** voluptuous. **сла́дость** joy; sweetness; *pl* sweets.

сла́женность harmony. **сла́женный** co-ordinated, harmonious.

сла́мывать impf of **сломи́ть**

сла́нец (-нца) m shale, slate.

сластёна m & f person with a sweet tooth.

сласть (pl -и, -е́й) delight; pl sweets, sweet things.

слать (шлю, шлёшь) impf send.

слаща́вый sugary, sickly-sweet. **сла́ще** comp of **сла́дкий**

сле́ва adv from or on the left. ~ напра́во from left to right.

слёг etc.: see **слечь**

слегка́ adv slightly; lightly.

след (следа́, dat -у, loc -у́; pl -ы́) track; footprint; trace.

следи́ть[1] (-ежу́) impf +за+instr watch; follow; keep up with; look after; keep an eye on. **следи́ть**[2] (-ежу́) impf (pf на-) leave footprints. **сле́дование** movement. **сле́дователь** m investigator. **сле́довательно** adv consequently. **сле́довать** impf (pf по-) I. +dat or за+instr follow; go, be bound; II. impers ought; be owing, be owed; вам сле́дует +inf you ought to; как сле́дует properly; as it should be; ско́лько с меня́ сле́дует? how much do I owe (you)? **сле́дом** adv (за+instr) immediately after, close behind. **сле́дственный** investigation, inquiry. **сле́дствие**[1] consequence. **сле́дствие**[2] investigation. **сле́дующий** following, next.

слёжка shadowing.

слеза́ (pl -ёзы, -а́м) tear.

слеза́ть impf of **слезть**

слеза́ться (-и́тся) impf water.

слезли́вый tearful. **слёзный** tear; tearful. **слезоточи́вый** watering. ~ газ tear-gas.

слезть (-зу; слез) pf (impf

слеза́ть) climb or get down; dismount; get off; come off.

слепе́нь (-пня́) m horse-fly.

слепе́ц (-пца́) blind man.

слепи́ть[1] impf blind; dazzle.

с|лепи́ть[2] (-плю́, -пишь) pf stick together.

слепну́ть (-ну; слеп) impf (pf о-) go blind. **слепо́** adv blindly. **слеп|о́й** (-п, -а́, -о) blind; ~ы́е sb pl the blind.

слепо́к (-пка) cast.

слепота́ blindness.

сле́сарь (pl -я́ or -и) m metalworker; locksmith.

слёт gathering; rally. **слета́ть** impf, **слете́ть** (-ечу́) pf fly down or away; fall down or off; ~ся fly together; congregate.

слечь (сля́гу, -я́жешь; слёг, -ла́) pf take to one's bed.

сли́ва plum; plum-tree.

слива́ть(ся impf of **слить(ся**. **сли́вки** (-вок) pl cream. **сли́вочный** cream; creamy; ~ое ма́сло butter; ~ое моро́женое dairy ice-cream.

сли́зистый slimy. **слизня́к** (-а́) slug. **слизь** mucus; slime.

с|линя́ть pf.

слипа́ться impf, **сли́пнуться** (-нется, -ипся) pf stick together.

сли́тно together, as one word. **сли́ток** (-тка) ingot, bar. **с|лить** (солью́, -ьёшь; -ил, -а́, -о) pf (impf also **слива́ть**) pour, pour out or off; fuse, amalgamate; ~ся flow together; blend; merge.

слича́ть impf, **сличи́ть** (-чу́) pf collate; check. **сличе́ние** collation, checking.

сли́шком adv too; too much.

слия́ние confluence; merging; merger.

слова́к, -а́чка Slovak. **слова́цкий** Slovak.

слова́рный lexical; dictionary. **слова́рь (-я́)** *m* dictionary; vocabulary. **слове́сность** literature; philology. **слове́сный** verbal, oral. **сло́вно** *conj* as if; like, as. **сло́во** (*pl* **-а́**) word; **одни́м ~м** in a word. **сло́вом** *adv* in a word. **словообразова́ние** word-formation. **словоохо́тливый** talkative. **словосочета́ние** word combination, phrase. **словоупотребле́ние** usage.

слог[1] style.

слог[2] (*pl* **-и, -о́в**) syllable.

слоёный flaky.

сложе́ние composition; addition; build, constitution. **сложи́ть (-жу́, -жишь)** *pf* (*impf* **класть** *or* **сла-га́ть**) put *or* lay (together); pile, stack; add, add up; fold (up); compose; take off, put down; lay down; **~ся** turn out; take shape; arise; club together. **сло́жность** complication; complexity. **сло́жный** (**-жен, -жна́, -о**) complicated; complex; compound.

сло́истый stratified; flaky. **слой** (*pl* **-и́, -ёв**) layer; stratum.

слом demolition, pulling down. **с|лома́ть(ся** *pf.* **сломи́ть (-млю́, -мишь)** *pf* (*impf* **сла́мывать**) break (off); overcome; **сломя́ го́лову** at breakneck speed; **~ся** break.

слон (-а́) elephant; bishop. **слони́ха** she-elephant. **слоно́вый** elephant; **~ая кость** ivory.

слоня́ться *impf* loiter, mooch (about).

слуга́ (*pl* **-и**) *m* (man) serv-

ant. **служа́нка** servant, maid. **слу́жащий** *sb* employee. **слу́жба** service; work. **служе́бный** office; official; auxiliary; secondary. **служе́ние** service, serving. **служи́ть (-жу́, -жишь)** *impf* (*pf* **по~**) serve; work.

с|лука́вить (-влю) *pf.*

слух hearing; ear; rumour; **по ~у** by ear. **слухово́й** acoustic, auditory, aural; **~о́й аппара́т** hearing aid; **~о́е окно́** dormer (window).

слу́чай incident, event; case; opportunity; chance; **ни в ко́ем слу́чае** in no circumstances. **случа́йно** by chance, accidentally; by any chance. **случа́йность** chance; chance; accident. **случа́йный** accidental; chance; incidental. **случа́ться** *impf*, **случи́ться** *pf* happen.

слу́шание listening; hearing. **слу́шатель** *m* listener; student; *pl* audience. **слу́шать** *impf* (*pf* **по~, про~**) listen (to); hear; attend lectures on; (**я) слу́шаю!** hello!; very well; **~ся** +*gen* obey, listen to.

слыть (**-ыву́, -ывёшь; -ыл, -а́, -о**) *impf* (*pf* **про~**) have the reputation (+*instr or* **за**+*acc* for).

слыха́ть *impf*, **слы́шать (-шу)** *impf* (*pf* **у~**) hear; sense. **слы́шаться** (**-шится**) *impf* (*pf* **по~**) be heard. **слы́шимость** audibility. **слы́шимый** audible. **слы́шный** audible.

слюда́ mica.

слюна́ (*pl* **-и, -ёй**) saliva; spit; *pl* spittle. **слюня́вый** dribbling.

сля́гу *etc.: see* **слечь**

сля́коть slush.

см. abbr (of **смотри́**) see, vide.

сма́зать (-а́жу) pf, **сма́зывать** impf lubricate; grease; slur over. **сма́зка** lubrication; greasing; grease. **сма́зочный** lubricating.

смак relish. **смакова́ть** impf relish; savour.

с|**маневри́ровать** pf.

сма́нивать impf, **смани́ть** (-ню́, -нишь) pf entice.

с|**мастери́ть** pf. **сма́тывать** impf of смота́ть

сма́хивать impf, **смахну́ть** (-ну́, -нёшь) pf brush away or off.

сма́чивать impf of смочи́ть

сме́жный adjacent.

смека́лка native wit.

смёл etc.: see смести́

смеле́ть (-е́ю) impf (pf о~) grow bolder. **сме́лость** boldness, courage. **сме́лый** bold, courageous. **смельча́к** (-а́) daredevil.

смелю́ etc.: see смоло́ть

сме́на changing; change; replacement(s); relief; shift. **смени́ть** (-ню́, -нишь) pf, **сменя́ть**[1] impf change; replace; relieve; take turns; +instr give place to. **сме́нный** shift; changeable. **сме́нщик** relief; pl new shift. **сменя́ть**[2] pf exchange.

с|**ме́рить** pf.

смерка́ться impf, **смёркнуться** (-нется) pf get dark.

смерте́льный mortal, fatal; death; extreme. **сме́ртность** mortality. **сме́ртный** mortal; death; deadly, extreme. **смерть** (gen pl -е́й) death.

смерч whirlwind; waterspout; sandstorm.

смеси́тельный mixing. **сме-**

си́ть (-ешу́, -е́сишь) pf.

смести́ (-ету́, -етёшь; -ёл, -а́) pf (impf **смета́ть**) sweep off, away.

смести́ть (-ещу́) pf (impf **смеща́ть**) displace; remove.

смесь mixture; medley.

сме́та estimate.

смета́на sour cream.

с|**мета́ть**[1] pf (impf also **смё-тывать**) tack (together).

смета́ть[2] impf of смести́

сметли́вый quick, sharp.

смету́ etc.: see смести́. **смё-тывать** impf of смета́ть

сметь (-е́ю) impf (pf по~) dare.

смех laughter; laugh. **смехотво́рный** laughable.

сме́шанный mixed; combined. **с**|**меша́ть**[1] pf, **сме́шивать** impf mix, blend; confuse; ~**ся** mix, (inter)blend; get mixed up. **смеше́ние** mixture; mixing up.

смеши́ть (-шу́) impf (pf на~, рас~) make laugh. **смешли́вый** given to laughing. **смешно́й** funny; ridiculous.

смешу́ etc.: see смеси́ть, смеши́ть

смеща́ть(**ся** impf of смести́ть**(ся**. **смеще́ние** displacement, removal. **смещу́** etc.: see сместить

смея́ться (-ею́сь, -еёшься) impf laugh (at +над+instr).

смире́ние humility, meekness. **смире́нный** humble, meek. **смири́тельный**: ~**ая руба́шка** straitjacket. **смири́ть** pf, **смиря́ть** impf restrain, subdue; ~**ся** submit; resign o.s. **смирно** adv quietly; ~! attention! **смирный** quiet; submissive.

смогУ́ etc.: see смочь

смола́ (pl -ы) resin; pitch, tar; rosin. смоли́стый resinous.

смолка́ть impf, смо́лкнуть (-ну; -олк) pf fall silent.

смо́лоду adv from one's youth.

с|молоти́ть (-очу́, -о́тишь) pf.

с|моло́ть (смелю́, сме́лешь) pf.

смоляно́й pitch, tar, resin.

с|монти́ровать pf.

сморка́ть impf (pf вы́-) blow; ~ся blow one's nose.

сморо́дина (no pl; usu collect) currant; currants; currant-bush.

смо́рщенный wrinkled. с|мо́рщить(ся (-щу(сь) pf.

смота́ть pf (impf сма́тывать) wind, reel.

смотр (loc -ý; pl -о́тры) review, inspection. смотре́ть (-рю́, -ришь) impf (pf по-) look (at на+acc); see; watch; look through; examine; +за+instr look after; +в+acc, на+acc look on to; +instr look (like); смотри́(те)! take care!; смотря́ it depends; смотря́ по+dat depending on; ~ся look at o.s. смотрово́й observation, inspection.

смочи́ть (-чу́, -чишь) pf (impf сма́чивать) moisten.

с|мочь (-огу́, -о́жешь; смог, -ла́) pf.

с|моше́нничать pf. смою etc.: see смыть

смрад stench. сма́дный stinking.

сму́глый (-гл, -а́, -о) dark-complexioned, swarthy.

смути́ть (-ущу́) pf, смуща́ть impf embarrass, confuse; ~ся be embarrassed, be confused.

сму́тный vague; dim; troubled.

смуще́ние embarrassment,

confusion. смущённый (-ён, -á) embarrassed, confused.

смыва́ть impf of смыть

смыка́ть(ся impf of сомкну́ть(ся

смысл sense; meaning. смы́слить impf understand. смыслово́й semantic.

смыть (смо́ю) pf (impf смыва́ть) wash off, away.

смычо́к (-чка́) bow.

смышлёный clever.

смягча́ть impf, смягчи́ть (-чу́) pf soften; alleviate; ~ся soften; relent; grow mild.

смяте́ние confusion; commotion. с|мять(ся (сомну́, -нёшь(ся) pf.

снабди́ть (-бжу́) pf, снабжа́ть impf +instr supply with. снабже́ние supply, supplying.

сна́йпер sniper.

снару́жи adv on or from (the) outside.

снаря́д projectile, missile; shell; contrivance; tackle, gear. снаряди́ть (-яжу́) pf, снаряжа́ть impf equip, fit out. снаряже́ние equipment, outfit.

снасть (gen pl -е́й) tackle; rigging.

снача́ла adv at first; all over again.

сна́шивать impf of сноси́ть

СНГ abbr (of Содру́жество незави́симых госуда́рств) CIS.

снег (loc -ý; pl -á) snow.

снеги́рь (-я́) bullfinch.

снегово́й snow. снегопа́д snowfall. Снегу́рочка Snow Maiden. снежи́нка snowflake. сне́жный snow(y); ~ая ба́ба snowman. снежо́к (-жка́) light snow; snowball.

снести́[1] (-су́, -сёшь; -ёс, -ла́) pf (impf сноси́ть) take down, together; bring *or* fetch down; carry away; blow off; demolish; endure; **~сь** communicate (c+*instr* with).

с|нести́[2](сь -су́(сь, -сёшь(ся; снёс(ся, -сла́(сь) *pf*

снижа́ть *impf*, **сни́зить** (-и́жу) *pf* lower; bring down; reduce; **~ся** come down; fall. **сниже́ние** lowering; loss of height.

снизойти́ (-йду́, -йдёшь; -ошёл, -шла́) *pf* (*impf* **снисходи́ть**) condescend.

сни́зу *adv* from below.

снима́ть(ся *impf of* **снять(ся.**

сни́мок (-мка) photograph. **сниму́** *etc.: see* **снять**

снискать (-ищу́, -и́щешь) *pf*, **сни́скивать** *impf* gain, win.

снисходи́тельность condescension; leniency. **снисходи́тельный** condescending; lenient. **снисходи́ть** (-ожу́, -о́дишь) *impf of* **снизойти́**. **снисхожде́ние** indulgence, leniency.

сни́ться *impf* (*pf* **при~**) *impers*+*dat* dream.

снобизм snobbery.

сно́ва *adv* again, anew.

снова́ть (сную, снуёшь) *impf* rush about.

сновиде́ние dream.

сноп (-а́) sheaf.

сноро́вка knack, skill.

снос demolition; drift; wear. **сноси́ть**[1] (-ошу́, -о́сишь) *pf* (*impf* **сна́шивать**) wear out. **сноси́ть**[2](ся (-ошу́(сь, -о́сишь(ся) *impf of* **снести́(сь.** **сно́ска** footnote. **сно́сно** *adv* tolerably, so-so. **сно́сный** tolerable; fair.

снотво́рный soporific.

сноха́ (*pl* -и) daughter-in-law.

сноше́ние intercourse; relations, dealings.

сношу́ *etc.: see* **сноси́ть**

сня́тие taking down; removal; making. **снять** (сниму́, -и́мешь; -ял, -а́, -о) *pf* (*impf* **снима́ть**) take off; take down; gather in; remove; rent; take; make; photograph; **~ся** come off; move off; be photographed.

со *see* **с** *prep*.

со- *pref* co-, joint. **соа́втор** co-author.

соба́ка dog. **соба́чий** dog's; canine. **соба́чка** little dog; trigger.

соберу́ *etc.: see* **собра́ть**

собе́с *abbr* (*of* **социа́льное обеспе́чение**) social security (department).

собесе́дник interlocutor, companion. **собесе́дование** conversation.

собира́тель *m* collector. **собира́ть(ся** *impf of* **собра́ть(ся**

собла́зн temptation. **соблазни́тель** *m*, **~ница** tempter; seducer. **соблазни́тельный** tempting; seductive. **соблазни́ть** *pf*, **соблазня́ть** *impf* tempt; seduce.

соблюда́ть *impf*, **со|блюсти́** (-юду́, -дёшь; -ёл, -а́) *pf* observe; keep (to). **соблюде́ние** observance; maintenance.

собо́й, собо́ю *see* **себя́**

соболе́знование sympathy, condolence(s). **соболе́зновать** *impf* +*dat* sympathize *or* commiserate with.

со́боль (*pl* -и *or* -я́) *m* sable.

собо́р cathedral; council, synod. **собо́рный** cathedral.

собра́ние meeting; assembly; collection. **со́бранный** collected; concentrated.

собра́т (*pl* -ья, -ьев) colleague.

собрáть (-берý, -берёшь; -áл, -á, -о) pf (impf собирáть) gather; collect; ~ся gather; prepare; intend, be going; +c+instr collect.

сóбственник owner, proprietor. сóбственнический proprietary; proprietorial. сóбственно adv: ~ (говоря) strictly speaking, as a matter of fact. собственнорýчно adv personally, with one's own hand. сóбственность property; ownership. сóбственный (one's) own; proper; true; имя ~ое proper name; ~ой персóной in person.

собы́тие event.

собью́ etc.: see сбить

совá (pl -ы) owl.

совáть (сую́, -ёшь) impf (pf сýнуть) thrust, shove; ~ся push, push in; butt in.

совершáть impf, совершить (-шý) pf accomplish; carry out; commit; complete; ~ся happen; be accomplished. совершéние accomplishment; perpetration. совершéнно adv perfectly; absolutely, completely. совершеннолéтие majority. совершеннолéтний of age. совершéнный[1] perfect; absolute, complete. совершéнный[2] perfective. совершéнство perfection. совершéнствование perfecting; improvement. совершéнствовать impf (pf у~) perfect; improve; ~ся в+instr perfect o.s. in; improve.

сóвестливый conscientious. сóвестно impers+dat be ashamed. сóвесть conscience.

совéт advice, counsel; opinion; council; soviet, Soviet. совéтник adviser. совéто-

вать impf (pf по~) advise; ~ся c+instr consult, ask advice of. совéтолог Kremlinologist. совéтский Soviet; ~ая власть the Soviet regime; ~ий Сою́з the Soviet Union. совéтчик adviser.

совещáние conference. совещáтельный consultative, deliberative. совещáться impf deliberate; consult.

совладáть pf c+instr control, cope with.

совмести́мый compatible. совмести́тель m person holding more than one office. совмести́ть (-ещý) pf, совмещáть impf combine; ~ся coincide; be combined, combine. совмéстно jointly. совмéстный joint, combined.

совóк (-вкá) shovel; scoop; dust-pan.

совокупи́ться (-плю́сь) pf, совокупля́ться impf copulate. совокуплéние copulation. совокýпно adv jointly. совокýпность aggregate, sum total.

совпадáть impf, совпáсть (-адёт) pf coincide; agree, tally. совпадéние coincidence.

соврати́ть (-ащý) pf (impf совращáть) pervert, seduce.

со|врáть (-врý, -врёшь; -áл, -á, -о) pf

совращáть(ся impf of соврати́ть(ся. совращéние perverting, seduction.

совремéнник contemporary. совремéнность the present (time); contemporaneity. совремéнный contemporary; modern.

соврý etc.: see соврáть

совсéм adv quite; entirely.

совхóз State farm.

совью *etc.: see* **свить**

согла́сие consent; assent; agreement; harmony. **согласи́ться** (-ашу́сь) *pf* (*impf* **соглаша́ться**) consent; agree. **согла́сно** *adv* in accord, in harmony; *prep*+*dat* in accordance with. **согла́сный**[1] agreeable (to); in agreement; harmonious. **согла́сный**[2] consonant(al); *sb* consonant.

согласова́ние co-ordination; agreement. **согласо́ванность** co-ordination. **согласова́ть** *pf*, **согласо́вывать** *impf* co-ordinate; make agree; **~ся** conform; agree.

соглаша́ться *impf of* **согласи́ться**. **соглаше́ние** agreement. **соглашу́** *etc.: see* **согласи́ть**

согна́ть (сгоню́, сго́нишь; -а́л, -а́, -о) *pf* (*impf* **сгоня́ть**) drive away; drive together.

со|гну́ть (-ну́, -нёшь) *pf* (*impf also* **сгиба́ть**) bend, curve; **~ся** bend (down).

согрева́ть *impf*, **согре́ть** (-е́ю) *pf* warm, heat; **~ся** get warm; warm o.s.

со|греши́ть (-шу́) *pf*.

со́да soda.

соде́йствие assistance. **соде́йствовать** *impf & pf* (*pf also* **по~**) +*dat* assist; promote; contribute to.

содержа́ние maintenance, upkeep; content(s); pay. **содержа́тельный** rich in content; pithy. **содержа́ть** (-жу́, -жишь) *impf* keep; maintain; contain; **~ся** be kept; be maintained; be; be contained. **содержи́мое** *sb* contents.

со|дра́ть (сдеру́, -рёшь; -а́л, -а́, -о) *pf* (*impf also* **сдира́ть**) tear off, strip off; fleece.

содрога́ние shudder. **содро-**

га́ться *impf*, **содрогну́ться** (-ну́сь, -нёшься) *pf* shudder.

содру́жество concord; commonwealth.

соедине́ние joining, combination; joint; compound; formation. **Соединённое Короле́вство** United Kingdom. **Соединённые Шта́ты (Аме́рики)** *m pl* United States (of America). **соединённый** (-ён, -а́) united, joint. **соедини́тельный** connective, connecting. **соедини́ть** *pf*, **соединя́ть** *impf* join, unite; connect; combine; unite; **~ся** unite; combine.

сожале́ние regret; pity; **к сожале́нию** unfortunately. **сожале́ть** (-е́ю) *impf* regret, deplore.

сожгу́ *etc.: see* **сжечь**. **сожже́ние** burning; cremation.

сожи́тель *m*, **~ница** roommate, flat-mate; lover. **сожи́тельство** co-habitation.

сожму́ *etc.: see* **сжать**[2]. **сожну́** *etc.: see* **сжать**[1]. **созва́ниваться** *impf of* **созвони́ться**

созва́ть (-зову́, -зовёшь; -а́л, -а́, -о) *pf* (*impf* **сзыва́ть**, **созыва́ть**) call together; call; invite.

созве́здие constellation.

созвони́ться *pf* (*impf* **созва́ниваться**) ring up; speak on the telephone.

созву́чие accord; assonance. **созву́чный** harmonious; +*dat* in keeping with.

создава́ть (-даю́, -даёшь) *impf*, **созда́ть** (-а́м, -а́шь, -а́ст, -ади́м; со́здал, -а́, -о) *pf* create; establish; **~ся** be created; arise, spring up. **созда́ние** creation; work; creature. **созда́тель** *m* creator; originator.

созерца́ние contemplation. **созерца́тельный** contemplative. **созерца́ть** impf contemplate.

созида́ние creation. **созида́тельный** creative.

сознава́ть (-наю́, -наёшь) impf, **созна́ть** pf be conscious of, realize; acknowledge; ~**ся** confess. **созна́ние** consciousness; acknowledgement; confession. **созна́тельность** awareness, consciousness. **созна́тельный** conscious; deliberate.

созову́ etc.: see **созва́ть**

созрева́ть impf, **со|зре́ть** (-е́ю) pf ripen, mature.

созы́в summoning, calling. **созыва́ть** impf of **созва́ть**

соизмери́мый commensurable.

соиска́ние competition. **со|иска́тель** m, ~**ница** m competitor, candidate.

сойти́ (-йду́, -йдёшь; сошёл, -шла́) pf (impf **сходи́ть**) go or come down; get off; leave; come off; pass. leave; ~ **с ума́** go mad, go out of one's mind; ~**сь** meet; gather; become friends; become intimate; agree.

сок (loc (-ý) juice.

со́кол falcon.

сократи́ть (-ащу́) pf, **сокраща́ть** impf reduce; abbreviate; reduce; contract; ~**ся** grow shorter; decrease; contract. **сокраще́ние** shortening; abridgement; abbreviation; reduction.

сокрове́нный secret; innermost. **сокро́вище** treasure. **сокро́вищница** treasure-house.

сокруша́ть impf, **сокруши́ть** (-шу́) pf shatter; smash; distress; ~**ся** grieve, be distressed. **сокруше́ние** smash-ing; grief. **сокрушённый** (-ён, -á) grief-stricken. **сокруши́тельный** shattering.

скры́тие concealment.

со|лга́ть (-лгу́, -лжёшь; -áл, -á, -о) pf.

солда́т (gen pl -áт) soldier. **солда́тский** soldier's.

соле́ние salting; pickling. **солёный** (со́лон, -á, -о) salt(y); salted; pickled. **соле́нье** salted food(s); pickles.

соли́дность solidarity. **соли́дный** solid; strong; reliable; respectable; sizeable.

соли́ст, соли́стка soloist.

соли́ть (-лю́, со́лишь) impf (pf по~) salt; pickle.

со́лнечный sun; solar; sunny; ~ **свет** sunlight; sunshine; ~ **уда́р** sunstroke. **со́лнце** sun. **солнцепёк: на ~е** in the sun. **солнцестоя́ние** solstice.

со́ло neut indecl solo; adv solo.

солове́й (-вья́) nightingale.

со́лод malt.

солодко́вый liquorice.

соло́ма straw; thatch. **соло́менный** straw; thatch. **соло́минка** straw.

со́лон etc.: see **солёный**. **солони́на** corned beef. **соло́нка** salt-cellar. **солонча́к** (-á) saline soil; pl salt marshes. **соль** (pl -и, -е́й) salt.

со́льный solo.

солью́ etc.: see **слить**

соля́ной, соля́ный salt, saline; **соля́ная кислота́** hydrochloric acid.

со́мкнутый close. **сомкну́ть** (-ну́, -нёшь) pf (impf **смыка́ть**) close; ~**ся** close.

сомнева́ться impf doubt, have doubts. **сомне́ние** doubt. **сомни́тельный** doubtful.

сомну́ etc.: see **смять**

сон (сна) sleep; dream. **сонли́вость** sleepiness; somnolence. **сонли́вый** sleepy. **со́нный** sleepy; sleeping.

сона́та sonata.

сонет sonnet.

сообража́ть impf, **сообрази́ть** (-ажу́) pf consider, think out; weigh; understand. **соображе́ние** consideration; understanding; notion. **сообрази́тельный** quick-witted. **сообра́зный** c+instr conforming to, in keeping with.

сообща́ adv together. **сообща́ть** impf, **сообщи́ть** (-щу́) pf communicate, impart, announce; impart; +dat inform. **сообще́ние** communication, report; announcement. **сообще́ство** association. **сообщник** accomplice.

сооруди́ть (-ужу́) pf, **сооружа́ть** impf build, erect. **сооруже́ние** building; structure.

соотве́тственно adv accordingly, correspondingly; prep +dat according to, in accordance with. **соотве́тственный** corresponding. **соотве́тствие** accordance, correspondence. **соотве́тствовать** impf correspond, conform. **соотве́тствующий** corresponding; suitable.

соотéчественник fellow-countryman.

соотноше́ние correlation. **сопе́рник** rival. **сопе́рничать** impf compete, vie. **сопе́рничество** rivalry.

сопе́ть (-плю́) impf wheeze; snuffle.

со́пка hill, mound.

сопли́вый snotty.

сопоста́вить (-влю) pf, **со-** поставля́ть impf compare. **сопоставле́ние** comparison.

сопреде́льный contiguous.

со|пре́ть pf.

соприкаса́ться impf, **соприкосну́ться** (-ну́сь, -нёшься) pf adjoin; come into contact. **соприкоснове́ние** contact.

сопроводи́тельный accompanying. **сопроводи́ть** (-ожу́) pf, **сопровожда́ть** impf accompany; escort. **сопровожде́ние** accompaniment; escort.

сопротивле́ние resistance. **сопротивля́ться** impf +dat resist, oppose.

сопу́тствовать impf +dat accompany.

сопью́сь etc.: see **спи́ться**

сор litter, rubbish.

соразме́рить pf, **соразмеря́ть** impf balance, match. **соразме́рный** proportionate, commensurate.

сора́тник comrade-in-arms.

сорва́ть (-ву́, -вёшь; -а́л, -а́, -о) pf (impf **срыва́ть**) tear off, away, down; break off; pick; break; ruin, spoil; vent; ~**ся** break away, break loose; fall, come down; fall through.

с|организова́ть pf.

соревнова́ние competition; contest. **соревнова́ться** impf compete.

сори́ть impf (pf **на~**) +acc or instr litter; throw about. **со́рный** rubbish, refuse; ~**ая трава́** weed(s). **сорня́к** (-á) weed.

со́рок (-á) forty.

соро́ка magpie.

сороков|о́й fortieth; ~**ые го́ды** the forties.

соро́чка shirt; blouse; shift.

сорт (*pl* -á) grade, quality; sort. **сортировáть** *impf* (*pf* рас∼) sort, grade. **сортирóвка** sorting. **сортирóвочный** sorting; ∼ая *sb* marshalling-yard. **сортирóвщик** sorter. **сóртный** high quality.

сосáть (-сý, -сёшь) *impf* suck. **сосáть** *pf*.

сосéд (*pl* -и), **сосéдка** neighbour. **сосéдний** neighbouring; adjacent, next. **сосéдский** neighbour's. **сосéдство** neighbourhood. **сосúска** frankfurter, sausage.

сóска (*baby's*) dummy.

соскáкивать *impf of* соскочúть

соскáльзывать *impf*, **соскользнýть** (-нý, -нёшь) *pf* slide down, slide off.

соскочúть (-чý, -чишь) *pf* (*impf* соскáкивать) jump off *or* down; come off.

соскýчиться (-чусь) *pf* get bored; ∼ по+*dat* miss.

сослагáтельный subjunctive.

сослáть (сошлю, -лёшь) *pf* (*impf* ссылáть) exile, deport; ∼ся на+*acc* refer to; cite; plead, allege.

сослóвие estate; class.

сослужúвец (-вца) colleague.

соснá (*pl* -ы, -сен) pine(-tree). **соснóвый** pine; deal.

сосóк (-скá) nipple, teat.

сосредотóченный concentrated. **сосредотóчивать** *impf*, **сосредотóчить** (-чу) *pf* concentrate; focus; ∼ся concentrate.

состáв composition; structure; compound; staff; strength; train; в ∼е+*gen* consisting of. **составúтель** *m* compiler. **составúть** (-влю) *pf*, **составлять** *impf* put together;

make (up); draw up; compile; be, constitute; total; ∼ся form, be formed. **составнóй** compound; component, constituent.

состáриться *pf*.

состояние state, condition; fortune. **состоятельный** well-to-do; well-grounded. **состоять** (-ою) *impf* be; +из+*gen* consist of; +в+*prep* consist in, be. **состояться** (-оится) *pf* take place.

страдáние compassion. **сострадáтельный** compassionate.

состóрить *pf*. **состряпать** *pf*.

состыкóвывать *impf*, **состыковáть** *pf*, dock; ∼ся dock.

состязáние competition, contest. **состязáться** *impf* compete.

сосýд vessel.

сосýлька icicle.

сосуществовáние co-existence.

сосчитáть *pf*. сот *see* сто.

сотворéние creation. **сотворúть** *pf*.

соткáть (-кý, -кёшь; -áл, -áлá, -о) *pf*.

сóтня (*gen pl* -тен) a hundred.

сотрý *etc.*: *see* стерéть

сотрýдник collaborator; colleague; employee. **сотрýдничать** *impf* collaborate; +в+*prep* contribute to. **сотрýдничество** collaboration.

сотрясáть *impf*, **сотрястú** (-сý, -сёшь; -яс, -ла) *pf* shake; ∼ся tremble. **сотрясéние** shaking; concussion.

сóты (-ов) *pl* honeycomb.

сóтый hundredth.

соумышленник accomplice.

сóус sauce; gravy; dressing.

соучáстие participation; complicity. **соуча́стник** participant; accomplice.

софа́ (*pl* -ы) sofa.

соха́ (*pl* -и) (wooden) plough.

со́хнуть (-ну; сох) *impf* (*pf* **вы́~, за~, про~**) (get) dry; wither.

сохране́ние preservation; conservation; (safe)keeping; retention. **сохрани́ть** *pf*, **сохраня́ть** *impf* preserve, keep; ~ся remain (intact); last out; be well preserved. **сохра́нный** safe.

социа́л-демокра́т Social Democrat. **социа́л-демократи́ческий** Social Democratic. **социали́зм** socialism. **социали́ст** socialist. **социалисти́ческий** socialist. **социа́льный** social; ~ое обеспе́чение social security. **социо́лог** sociologist. **социоло́гия** sociology.

соцреали́зм socialist realism.

сочета́ние combination. **сочета́ть** *impf & pf* combine; ~ся combine; harmonize; match.

сочи́ние composition; work. **сочини́ть** (-ню́), **сочиня́ть** *impf* compose; write; make up.

сочи́ться (-и́тся) *impf* ooze (out), trickle; ~ кро́вью bleed.

со́чный (-чен, -чна́, -о) juicy; rich.

сочту́ etc.: *see* **счесть**

сочу́вствие sympathy. **сочу́вствовать** *impf* +*dat* sympathize with.

сошёл etc.: *see* **сойти́. сошлю́** etc.: *see* **сосла́ть. сошью́** etc.: *see* **сшить**

сощу́ривать *impf*, **сощу́рить** *pf* screw up, narrow; ~ся screw up one's eyes; narrow.

сою́з¹ union; alliance; league.

сою́з² conjunction. **сою́зник**

ally. **сою́зный** allied; Union.

спад recession; abatement. **спада́ть** *impf of* **спасть**

спазм spasm.

спа́ивать *impf of* **спая́ть, спои́ть**

спа́йка soldered joint; solidarity, unity.

спали́ть *pf*.

спа́льн|ый sleeping; ~ый ваго́н sleeping car; ~ое ме́сто berth. **спа́льня** (*gen pl* -лен) bedroom.

спа́ржа asparagus.

спартакиа́да sports meeting. **спаса́тельн|ый** rescue; ~ жиле́т life jacket; ~ круг lifebuoy; ~ по́яс lifebelt. **спаса́ть(ся** *impf of* **спасти́(сь. спасе́ние** rescue, escape; salvation. **спаси́бо** thank you. **спаси́тель** *m* rescuer; saviour. **спаси́тельный** saving; salutary.

спасти́ (-су́, -сёшь; спас, -ла́) *pf* (*impf* **спаса́ть**) save; rescue; ~сь escape; be saved. **спасть** (-адёт) *pf* (*impf* **спада́ть**) fall (down); abate.

спать (сплю; -ал, -а́, -о) sleep; **лечь ~** go to bed.

спа́янность cohesion, unity. **спа́янный** united. **спая́ть** *pf* (*impf* **спа́ивать**) solder, weld; unite.

спекта́кль *m* performance; show.

спектр spectrum.

спекули́ровать *impf* speculate. **спекуля́нт** speculator, profiteer. **спекуля́ция** speculation; profiteering.

спе́лый ripe.

сперва́ *adv* at first; first.

спе́реди *adv* in front, from the front; *prep*+*gen* (from) in front of.

спёртый close, stuffy.

спеси́вый arrogant, haughty. спесь arrogance, haughtiness.

спеть¹ (-е́ет) *impf* (*pf* по-) ripen.

с|петь² (спою́, споёшь) *pf*.

спец- *abbr in comb* (*of* специа́льный) special. спецко́р special correspondent. ~оде́жда protective clothing; overalls.

специализа́ция specialization. специализи́роваться *impf & pf* specialize. специали́ст a specialist, expert. специа́льность speciality; profession. специа́льный special; specialist.

специ́фика specific character. специфи́ческий specific.

спе́ция spice.

спецо́вка protective clothing; overall(s).

спеши́ть (-шу́) *impf* (*pf* по-) hurry, be in a hurry; be fast. спе́шка hurry, haste. спе́шный urgent.

спива́ться *impf of* спи́ться

СПИД *abbr* (*of* синдро́м приобретённого иммуноде́фицита) Aids.

с|пики́ровать *pf*.

спи́ливать *impf*, спили́ть (-лю́, -лишь) *pf* saw down, off.

спина́ (*acc* -у; *pl* -ы) back. спи́нка back. спинно́й spinal; ~ мозг spinal cord.

спира́ль spiral.

спирт alcohol, spirit(s). спиртно́й alcoholic; ~о́е *sb* alcohol. спиртовка spirit-stove. спиртово́й spirit, alcoholic.

списа́ть (-ишу́, -и́шешь) *pf*, спи́сывать *impf* copy; ~ся exchange letters. спи́сок (-ска) list; record.

спи́ться (сопью́сь, -ьёшься; -и́лся -а́сь) *pf* (*impf* спива́ться)

take to drink.

спи́хивать *impf*, спихну́ть (-ну́, -нёшь) *pf* push aside, down.

спи́ца knitting-needle; spoke.

спи́чечн|ый match; ~ая коро́бка match-box. спи́чка match.

спишу́ *etc.: see* списа́ть

сплав¹ floating. сплав² alloy.

спла́вить¹ (-влю) *pf*, сплавля́ть¹ *impf* float; raft; get rid of. спла́вить² (-влю) *pf*, сплавля́ть² *impf* alloy; ~ся fuse.

с|плани́ровать *pf*. спла́чивать(ся) *impf of* сплоти́ть(ся)

сплёвывать *impf of* сплю́нуть

с|плести́ (-ету́, -етёшь; -ёл, -а́) *pf*, сплета́ть *impf* weave; plait; interlace. сплете́ние interlacing; plexus.

спле́тник, -ница gossip, scandalmonger. спле́тничать *impf* (*pf* на-) gossip. спле́тня (*gen pl* -тен) gossip, scandal.

сплоти́ть (-очу́) *pf* (*impf* спла́чивать) join; unite, rally; close ranks. сплоче́ние uniting. сплочённость cohesion, unity. сплочённый (-ён, -á) united; firm; unbroken.

сплошно́й solid; complete; continuous; utter. сплошь *adv* all over; completely; ~ да ря́дом pretty often.

сплю *see* спать

сплю́нуть (-ну) *pf* (*impf* сплёвывать) spit; spit out.

сплю́щивать *impf*, сплю́щить (-щу) *pf* flatten; ~ся become flat.

с|пляса́ть (-яшу́, -я́шешь) *pf*.

сподви́жник comrade-in-arms.

спои́ть (-ою́, -о́ишь) *pf* (*impf* спа́ивать) make a drunkard of.

споко́йн|ый quiet; calm;

но́чи good night! **споко́йствие** quiet; calm, serenity.
спола́скивать *impf of* **сполосну́ть**
сполза́ть *impf*, **сползти́** (-зу́, -зёшь; -о́лз, -ла́) *pf* climb down; slip (down); fall away.
сполна́ *adv* in full.
сполосну́ть (-ну́, -нёшь) *pf* (*impf* **спола́скивать**) rinse.
спо́нсор sponsor, backer.
спор argument; controversy; dispute. **спо́рить** *impf* (*pf* **по~**) argue; dispute; debate. **спо́рный** debatable, questionable; disputed; moot.
спо́ра spore.
спорт sport. **спорти́вный** sports; ~ **зал** gymnasium. **спортсме́н**, ~**ка** athlete, player.
спо́соб way, method; **таки́м ~ом** in this way. **спосо́бность** ability, aptitude; capacity. **спосо́бный** able; clever; capable. **спосо́бствовать** *impf* (*pf* **по~**) +*dat* assist; further.
споткну́ться (-ну́сь, -нёшься) *pf*, **спотыка́ться** *impf* stumble.
спохвати́ться (-ачу́сь, -а́тишься) *pf*, **спохва́тываться** *impf* remember suddenly.
спою́ *etc.: see* **спеть, спои́ть**
спра́ва *adv* from *or* on the right.
справедли́вость justice; fairness; truth. **справедли́вый** just; fair; justified.
спра́вить (-влю) *pf*, **справля́ть** *impf* celebrate. **спра́виться**[1] (-влюсь) *pf*, **справля́ться** *impf* +*instr* cope with, manage. **спра́виться**[2] (-влюсь) *pf*, **справля́ться** *impf* inquire; +**в**+*prep* consult.

спра́вка information; reference; certificate; **наводи́ть ~** make inquiries. **спра́вочник** reference-book, directory. **спра́вочный** inquiry, information.
спра́шивать(ся) *impf of* **спроси́ть(ся)**
спринт sprint. **спри́нтер** sprinter.
с|провоци́ровать *pf*. **с|проекти́ровать** *pf*.
спрос demand; asking; **без ~у** without permission. **спроси́ть** (-ошу́, -о́сишь) *pf* (*impf* **спра́шивать**) ask (for); inquire; ~**ся** ask permission.
спрут octopus.
спры́гивать *impf*, **спры́гнуть** (-ну) *pf* jump off, jump down.
спры́скивать *impf*, **спры́снуть** (-ну) *pf* sprinkle.
спряга́ть *impf* (*pf* **про~**) conjugate. **спряже́ние** conjugation.
с|прясть (-яду́, -ядёшь; -ял, -яла́, -о) *pf*. **с|пря́тать(ся)** (-я́чу(сь)) *pf*.
спу́гивать *impf*, **спугну́ть** (-ну́, -нёшь) *pf* frighten off.
спуск lowering; descent; slope. **спуска́ть** *impf*, **спусти́ть** (-ущу́, -у́стишь) *pf* let down, lower; let go, release; let out; send out; go down; forgive; squander; ~ **кора́бль** launch a ship; ~ **куро́к** pull the trigger; ~ **пе́тлю** drop a stitch; ~**ся** go down, descend. **спускно́й** drain. **спусково́й** trigger.
спустя́ *prep*+*acc* after; later.
с|пу́тать(ся) *pf*.
спу́тник satellite, sputnik; (travelling) companion.
спущу́ *etc.: see* **спусти́ть**
спя́чка hibernation; sleepiness.

ср. *abbr* (*of* сравни) cf.

срабатывать *impf*, **сработать** *pf* make; work, operate.

сравнение comparison; simile. **сравнивать** *impf of* сравнить, сравнять. **сравнимый** comparable. **сравнительно** *adv* comparatively. **сравнительный** comparative. **сравнить** *pf* (*impf* сравнивать) compare; ~ся c+*instr* compare with. **с|равнять** *pf* (*impf also* сравнивать) make even, equal; level.

сражать *impf*, **сразить** (-ажу) *pf* strike down; overwhelm, crush; ~ся fight. **сражение** battle.

сразу *adv* at once.

срам shame. **срамить** (-млю) *impf* (*pf* о~) shame; ~ся cover o.s. with shame. **срамота** shame.

срастание growing together. **срастаться** *impf*, **срастись** (-тётся; сросся, -лась) *pf* grow together; knit.

среда¹ (*pl* -ы) environment, surroundings; medium. **среда²** (*acc* -у; *pl* -ы, -ам *or* -ам) Wednesday. **среди** *prep*+*gen* among; in the middle of; ~ бела дня in broad daylight. **средиземноморский** Mediterranean. **средне** *adv* so-so. **средневековый** medieval. **средневековье** the Middle Ages. **средний** middle; medium; mean; average; middling; secondary; neuter; ~ее *sb* mean, average. **средоточие** focus. **средство** means; remedy.

срез cut; section; slice. **срезать** (-ежу) *pf*, **срезать** *impf* cut off; slice; fail; ~ся fail.

с|репетировать *pf*.

срисовать *pf*, **срисовывать** *impf* copy.

с|ровнять *pf*.

сродство affinity.

срок date; term; time, period; в ~, к ~у in time, to time.

сросся *etc.*: *see* срастись

срочно *adv* urgently. **срочность** urgency. **срочный** urgent; for a fixed period.

срою *etc.*: *see* срыть

сруб felling; framework. **срубать** *impf*, **с|рубить** (-блю, -бишь) *pf* cut down; build (*of* logs).

срыв disruption; breakdown; ruining. **срывать¹(ся** *impf of* сорвать(ся

срывать² *impf*, **срыть** (срою) *pf* raze to the ground.

сряду *adv* running.

ссадина scratch. **ссадить** (-ажу, -адишь) *pf*, **ссаживать** *impf* set down; help down; turn off.

ссора quarrel. **ссорить** *impf* (*pf* по~) cause to quarrel; ~ся quarrel.

СССР *abbr* (*of* Союз Советских Социалистических Республик) USSR.

ссуда loan. **ссудить** (-ужу, -удишь) *pf*, **ссужать** *impf* lend, loan.

ссылать(ся *impf of* сослать(ся. **ссылка¹** exile. **ссылка²** reference. **ссыльный, ссыльный** *sb* exile.

ссыпать (-плю) *pf*, **ссыпать** *impf* pour.

стабилизатор stabilizer; tailplane. **стабилизировать(ся** *impf & pf* stabilize. **стабильность** stability. **стабильный** stable, firm.

ставень (-вня; *gen pl* -вней) **ставня** (*gen pl* -вен) shutter.

ста́вить (-влю) *impf* (*pf* по~) put, place, set; stand; station; erect; install; apply; present, stage. **ста́вка**[1] rate; stake. **ста́вка**[2] headquarters.

ста́вня *see* **ста́вень**

стадио́н stadium.

ста́дия stage.

ста́дность herd instinct. **ста́дный** gregarious. **ста́до** (*pl* -á) herd, flock.

стаж length of service; probation. **стажёр** probationer; student on a special non-degree course. **стажиро́вка** period of training.

стака́н glass.

сталелите́йный steel-founding; ~ заво́д steel foundry. **сталеплави́льный** steelmaking; ~ заво́д steel works. **сталепрока́тный** steel-(roll-)ing; ~ стан rolling-mill.

ста́лкивать(ся *impf of* **столкну́ть(ся**

ста́ло быть *conj* consequently. **сталь** steel. **стально́й** steel.

стаме́ска chisel.

стан[1] figure, torso.

стан[2] camp.

стан[3] mill.

станда́рт standard. **станда́ртный** standard.

стани́ца Cossack village.

станкострое́ние machine-tool engineering.

станови́ться (-влю́сь, -ви́шься) *impf of* **стать**[1]

стано́к (-нка́) machine tool, machine.

ста́ну *etc.*: *see* **стать**[2]

станцио́нный station. **ста́нция** station.

ста́пель (*pl* -я) *m* stocks.

ста́птывать(ся *impf of* **стопта́ть(ся**

стара́ние effort. **стара́тель-** **ность** diligence. **стара́тельный** diligent. **стара́ться** *impf* (*pf* по~) try.

старе́ть *impf* (*pf* по~, у~) grow old. **ста́рец** (-рца) elder, (*venerable*) old man. **стари́к** (-á) old man. **стари́на** antiquity, olden times; antique(s); old fellow. **стари́нный** ancient; old; antique. **ста́рить** (*impf* (*pf* со~) age, make old; ~ся age, grow old.

старо- *in comb* old. **старове́р** Old Believer. **~жи́л** old resident. **~мо́дный** old-fashioned. **~славя́нский** Old Slavonic.

ста́роста head; monitor; churchwarden. **ста́рость** old age.

старт start; на ~! on your marks! **ста́ртер** starter. **стартова́ть** *impf & pf* start. **ста́ртовый** starting.

стару́ха, стару́шка old woman. **ста́рческий** old man's; senile. **ста́рше** *comp of* **ста́рый**. **ста́рш|ий** oldest, eldest; senior; head; ~ие *sb pl* (one's) elders; ~ий *sb* chief; man in charge. **старшина́** *m* sergeant-major; petty officer; leader, senior representative. **ста́рый** (-ар, -á, -о) old. **старьё** old things, junk.

ста́скивать *impf of* **стащи́ть**

с|тасова́ть *pf*.

стати́ст extra.

стати́стика statistics. **статисти́ческий** statistical.

ста́тный stately.

ста́тский civil, civilian.

ста́тус status. **ста́тус-кво́** *neut indecl* status quo. **статуэ́тка** statuette.

ста́туя statue.

стать¹ (-а́ну) *pf* (*impf* станови́ться) stand; take up position; stop; cost; begin; +*instr* become; +*c*+*instr* become of; не ~ *impers*+*gen* cease to be; disappear; его́ не ста́ло he is no more; ~ на коле́ни kneel.

стать² physique, build.

ста́ться (-а́нется) *pf* happen.

статья́ (*gen pl* -е́й) article; clause; item; matter.

стациона́р permanent establishment; hospital. **стациона́рный** stationary; permanent; ~ больно́й in-patient.

ста́чечник striker. **ста́чка** strike.

с|тащи́ть (-щу́, -щишь) *pf* (*impf also* ста́скивать) drag off, pull off.

ста́я flock; school, shoal; pack.

ствол (-а́) trunk; barrel.

ство́рка leaf, fold.

сте́бель (-бля; *gen pl* -бле́й) *m* stem, stalk.

стёган|ый quilted; ~ое одея́ло quilt. **стега́ть¹** *impf* (*pf* вы́-) quilt.

стега́ть² *impf*, **стегну́ть** (-ну́) *pf also* от~) whip, lash.

стежо́к (-жка́) stitch.

стезя́ path, way.

стёк *etc.*: *see* стечь. **стека́ть(ся** *impf of* стечь(ся

стекло́ (*pl* -ёкла, -кол) glass; lens; (window-)pane.

стекло́- *in comb* glass. **стекло-волокно́** glass fibre. ~очисти́тель *m* windscreen-wiper. ~ре́з glass-cutter. ~тка́нь fibreglass.

стекля́нный glass; glassy. **стеко́льщик** glazier.

стели́ть *see* стлать

стелла́ж (-а́) shelves, shelving.

сте́лька insole.

стелю́ *etc.*: *see* стлать

с|темне́ть (-е́ет) *pf*.

стена́ (*acc* -у; *pl* -ы, -а́м) wall. **стенгазе́та** wall newspaper. **стенд** stand. **сте́нка** wall; side. **стенно́й** wall.

стеногра́мма shorthand record. **стено́граф, стено-графи́ст,** ~ка stenographer. **стенографи́ровать** *impf & pf* take down in shorthand. **стенографи́ческий** shorthand. **стеногра́фия** shorthand.

стенокарди́я angina.

степе́нный staid; middle-aged. **сте́пень** (*gen pl* -е́й) degree; extent; power.

степно́й steppe. **степь** (*loc* -и́; *gen pl* -е́й) steppe.

стервя́тник vulture.

стерегу́ *etc.*: *see* стере́чь

сте́рео *indecl adj* stereo. **сте́рео-** *in comb* stereo. **стерео-ти́п** stereotype. **стереоти́пный** stereotype(d). **стерео-фони́ческий** stereo(phonic). ~фо́ния stereo(phony).

стере́ть (сотру́, сотрёшь; стёр) *pf* (*impf* стира́ть¹) wipe off; rub out, rub sore; efface; ~ся rub off; wear down; be effaced.

стере́чь (-регу́, -режёшь; -ёг, -ла́) *impf* guard; watch for.

сте́ржень (-жня) *m* pivot; rod; core.

стерилизова́ть *impf & pf* sterilize. **стери́льный** sterile.

сте́рлинг sterling.

сте́рлядь (*gen pl* -е́й) sterlet.

стерпе́ть (-плю́, -пишь) *pf* bear, endure.

стёртый worn, effaced.

стесне́ние constraint. **стесни́тельный** shy; inconvenient. **с|тесни́ть** *pf*, **стесня́ть** *impf* constrain; hamper; inhibit;

с|тесни́ться *pf*, стесня́ться *impf* (*pf also* по~) +*inf* feel too shy (to), be ashamed to.

стече́ние confluence; gathering; combination. стечь (-чёт; -ёк, -ла́) *pf* (*impf* стека́ть) flow down; ~ся flow together; gather.

стилисти́ческий stylistic. стиль *m* style. сти́льный stylish; period.

сти́мул stimulus, incentive. стимули́ровать *impf* & *pf* stimulate.

стипе́ндия grant.

стира́льный washing. стира́ть¹(ся *impf of* стере́ть(ся

стира́ть² *impf* (*pf* вы́~) wash, launder; ~ся wash. сти́рка washing, wash, laundering.

сти́скивать *impf*, сти́снуть (-ну) *pf* squeeze; clench; hug.

стих (-а́) verse; line; *pl* poetry.

стиха́ть *impf of* сти́хнуть

стихи́йный elemental; spontaneous. стихи́я element.

сти́хнуть (-ну; стих) *pf* (*impf* стиха́ть) subside; calm down.

стихотворе́ние poem. стихотво́рный in verse form.

стлать, стели́ть (стелю́, сте́лешь) *impf* (*pf* по~) spread; ~ посте́ль make a bed; ~ся spread; creep.

сто (ста; *gen pl* сот) a hundred.

стог (*loc* -е & -у́, *pl* -а́) stack, rick.

сто́имость cost; value. сто́ить *impf* cost; be worth(while); deserve.

стой *see* стоя́ть

сто́йка counter, bar; prop; upright; strut. сто́йкий firm; stable; steadfast. сто́йкость firmness, stability; steadfastness. сто́йло stall. стойма́

adv upright.

сток flow; drainage; drain, gutter; sewer.

стол (-а́) table; desk; cuisine.

столб (-а́) post, pole, pillar, column. столбене́ть (-е́ю) *impf* (*pf* о~) be rooted to the ground. столбня́к (-а́) stupor; tetanus.

столе́тие century; centenary. столе́тний hundred-year-old; of a hundred years.

столи́ца capital; metropolis. столи́чный (of the) capital.

столкнове́ние collision; clash. столкну́ть (-ну́, -нёшь) *pf* (*impf* ста́лкивать) push off, away; cause to collide; bring together; ~ся collide, clash; +*c*+*instr* run into.

столо́вая *sb* dining-room; canteen. столо́вый table.

столп (-а́) pillar.

столпи́ться *pf* crowd.

столь *adv* so. сто́лько *adv* so much, so many.

столя́р (-а́) joiner, carpenter. столя́рный joiner's.

стомато́лог dentist.

стометро́вка (the) hundred metres.

стон groan. стона́ть (-ну́, -нешь) *impf* groan.

стоп! *int* stop!

стопа́¹ foot.

стопа́² (*pl* -ы) ream; pile.

сто́пка¹ pile.

сто́пка² small glass.

сто́пор stop, catch. сто́пори́ться *impf* (*pf* за~) come to a stop.

стопроце́нтный hundred-per-cent.

стоп-сигна́л brake-light.

стопта́ть (-пчу́, -пчешь) *pf* (*impf* ста́птывать) wear down; ~ся wear down.

с|торгова́ть(ся pf.

сто́рож (pl -á) watchman, guard. сторожево́й watch; patrol-. сторожи́ть (-жу́) impf guard, watch (over).

сторона́ (acc сто́рону; pl сто́роны, -ро́н, -она́м) side; direction; hand; feature; part; land; в сто́рону aside; с мое́й стороны́ for my part; с одно́й стороны́ on the one hand. сторони́ться (-ню́сь, -нишься) impf (pf по~) stand aside; +gen avoid. сторо́нник supporter, advocate.

сто́чный sewage, drainage.

стоя́нка stop; parking; stopping place, parking space; stand; rank. стоя́ть (-ою́) impf (pf по~) stand; be; stay; stop; have stopped; +за+acc stand up for; ~ на коле́нях kneel. стоя́чий standing; upright; stagnant.

стоя́щий deserving; worthwhile.

стр. abbr (of страни́ца) page.

страда́ (pl -ды) (hard work at) harvest time.

страда́лец (-льца) sufferer. страда́ние suffering. страда́тельный passive. страда́ть (-а́ю or -а́жду) impf (pf по~) suffer; ~ за +gen feel for.

стра́жа guard, watch; под стра́жей under arrest, in custody; стоя́ть на стра́же +gen guard.

страна́ (pl -ны) country; land; ~ све́та cardinal point.

страни́ца page.

стра́нник, стра́нница wanderer.

стра́нно adv strangely. стра́нность strangeness; eccentricity. стра́нный (-а́нен, -анна́, -о) strange.

стра́нствие wandering. стра́нствовать impf wander.

Страстно́й of Holy Week; ~ая пя́тница Good Friday.

стра́стный (-тен, -тна́, -о) passionate. страсть¹ (gen pl -е́й) passion. страсть² adv awfully, frightfully.

стратеги́ческий strategic(al). страте́гия strategy.

стратосфе́ра stratosphere.

стра́ус ostrich.

страх fear.

страхова́ние insurance; ~ жи́зни life insurance. страхова́ть (-у́ю) impf (pf за~) insure (от+gen against); ~ся insure o.s. страхо́вка insurance.

страши́ть (-шу́) impf +gen be afraid of. стра́шно adv awfully. стра́шный (-шен, -шна́, -о) terrible, awful.

стрекоза́ (pl -зы) dragonfly. стрекота́ть (-очу́, -о́чешь) impf chirr.

стрела́ (pl -ы) arrow; shaft; boom. стреле́ц (-льца́) Sagittarius. стре́лка pointer; hand; needle; arrow; spit; points. стрелко́вый rifle; shooting; infantry. стрело́к (-лка́) shot; rifleman, gunner. стре́лочник pointsman. стрельба́ (pl -ы) shooting, firing. стре́льчатый lancet; arched. стреля́ть impf shoot; fire; ~ся shoot o.s.; fight a duel.

стремгла́в adv headlong.

стреми́тельный swift; impetuous. стреми́ться (-млю́сь) impf strive. стремле́ние striving, aspiration. стремни́на rapid(s).

стре́мя (-мени; pl -мена́, -мя́н, -а́м) neut stirrup. стремя́нка step-ladder.

стресс stress.

стри́женый short; short-haired, cropped; shorn. **стри́жка** hair-cut; shearing. **стричь** (-игу́, -ижёшь; -иг) *impf* (*pf* о~) cut, clip; cut the hair of; shear; ~ся have one's hair cut.

строга́ть *impf* (*pf* вы́~) plane, shave.

стро́гий strict; severe. **стро́гость** strictness.

строево́й combatant; line; drill. **строе́ние** building; structure; composition.

строжа́йший, стро́же *superl & comp of* **стро́гий**

строи́тель *m* builder. **строи́тельный** building, construction. **строи́тельство** building, construction; building site. **стро́ить** *impf* (*pf* по~) build; construct; make; draw up; ~ся be built, be under construction; draw up. **стро́йка** fall in! **строй** (*loc* -ю́; *pl* -и́ *or* -и́, -ёв *or* -ёв) system; régime; structure; pitch; formation. **стро́йка** building; building-site. **стро́йность** proportion; harmony; balance, order. **стро́йный** (-о́ен, -ойна́, -о) harmonious, orderly, well-proportioned, shapely.

строка́ (*acc* -о́ку́; *pl* -и, -а́м) line; **кра́сная** ~ new paragraph.

строп, стро́па sling; shroud line.

стропи́ло rafter, beam. **стропти́вый** refractory. **строфа́** (*pl* -ы, -а́м) stanza. **строчи́ть** (-чу́, -о́чи́шь) *impf* (*pf* на~, про~) stitch; scribble, dash off. **стро́чка** stitch; line.

стро́ю *etc.: see* **стро́ить**

струга́ть *impf* (*pf* вы́~) plane. **стру́жка** shaving.

струи́ться *impf* stream.

структу́ра structure.

струна́ (*pl* -ы) string. **стру́нный** stringed.

струп (*pl* -пья, -пьев) scab.

с|тру́сить (-у́шу) *pf*.

стручо́к (-чка́) pod.

струя́ (*pl* -и, -уй) jet, spurt, stream.

стря́пать *impf* (*pf* со~) cook; concoct. **стря́пня** cooking.

стря́хивать *impf*, **стряхну́ть** (-ну́, -нёшь) *pf* shake off.

студени́ческий jelly-like.

студе́нт, студе́нтка student. **студе́нческий** student.

сту́день (-дня) *m* jelly; aspic.

студи́ть (-ужу́, -у́дишь) *impf* (*pf* о~) cool.

сту́дия studio.

сту́жа severe cold, hard frost.

стук knock; clatter. **сту́кать** *impf*, **сту́кнуть** (-ну) *pf* knock; bang; strike; ~ся knock (o.s.), bang. **стука́ч** (-а́) *informer*.

стул (*pl* -лья, -льев) chair. **стульча́к** (-а́) (*lavatory*) seat. **сту́льчик** stool.

сту́па mortar.

ступа́ть *impf*, **ступи́ть** (-плю́, -пишь) *pf* step; tread. **ступе́нчатый** stepped, graded. **ступе́нь** (*gen pl* -е́ней) step, rung; stage, grade. **ступе́нька** step. **ступня́** foot; sole.

стуча́ть (-чу́) *impf* (*pf* по~) knock; chatter; pound; ~ся в+*acc* knock at.

стушева́ться (-шу́юсь) *pf*, **стушёвываться** *impf* efface o.s.

с|туши́ть (-шу́, -шишь) *pf*.

стыд (-а́) shame. **стыди́ть** (-ыжу́) *impf* (*pf* при~) put to shame; ~ся (*pf* по~ся) be ashamed. **стыдли́вый** bashful. **стыдн|ый** shameful; ~о! shame! ~о impers+*dat* ему́

~o he is ashamed; **как тебе не** ~o! you ought to be ashamed of yourself!

стык joint; junction. **стыкова́ть** impf (pf co~) join end to end; (pf при́~ся) dock. **стыко́вка** docking.

сты́нуть, стыть (-ину; стыл) impf cool; get cold.

сты́чка skirmish; squabble. **стюарде́сса** stewardess.

стя́гивать impf, **стяну́ть** (-ну́, -нешь) pf tighten; pull together; assemble; pull off; steal; ~**ся** tighten; assemble.

стяжа́тель (-я) m money-grubber. **стяжа́ть** impf & pf gain, win.

суббо́та Saturday.

субсиди́ровать impf & pf subsidize. **субси́дия** subsidy.

субъе́кт subject; ego; person; character, type. **субъекти́вный** subjective.

сувени́р souvenir.

суверените́т sovereignty. **сувере́нный** sovereign.

сугли́нок (-нка) loam.

сугро́б snowdrift.

сугу́бо adv especially.

суд (-а́) court; trial; verdict.

суда́ etc.: see **суд**, **су́дно**[1]

суда́к (-а́) pike-perch.

суде́бный judicial; legal; forensic. **суде́йский** judge's; referee's, umpire's. **суди́мость** previous convictions.

суди́ть (сужу́, су́дишь) impf judge; try; referee; foreordain; ~**ся** go to law.

су́дно[1] (pl -да́, -о́в) vessel, craft.

су́дно[2] (gen pl -ден) bed-pan.

судово́й ship's; marine.

судомо́йка kitchen-maid; scullery.

судопроизво́дство legal

proceedings.

су́дорога cramp, convulsion. **су́дорожный** convulsive.

судостро́ение shipbuilding. **судостро́ительный** ship-building. **судохо́дный** navigable; shipping.

судьба́ (pl -ы, -де́б) fate, destiny.

судья́ (pl -и, -е́й, -ям) m judge; referee; umpire.

суеве́рие superstition. **суеве́рный** superstitious.

суета́ bustle, fuss. **суети́ться** (-ечу́сь) impf bustle, fuss. **суетли́вый** fussy, bustling.

сужде́ние opinion; judgement

суже́ние narrowing; constriction. **сужива́ть** impf, **су́зить** (-у́жу) pf narrow, contract; ~**ся** narrow; taper.

сук (-а́, loc -у́, pl су́чья, -ьев or -и́, -о́в) bough.

су́ка bitch. **су́кин** adj: ~ **сын** son of a bitch.

сукно́ (pl -а, -кон) cloth; положи́ть под ~ shelve. **суко́нный** cloth; clumsy, crude.

сули́ть impf (pf по~) promise

султа́н plume.

сумасбро́д, сумасбро́дка nutcase. **сумасбро́дный** wild mad. **сумасбро́дство** wild behaviour. **сумасше́дший** mad; ~**ий** sb, ~**ая** sb lunatic. **сумасше́ствие** madness

сумато́ха turmoil; bustle.

сумбу́р confusion. **сумбу́рный** confused.

су́мерки (-рек) pl twilight, dusk.

суме́ть (-е́ю) pf +inf contrive to, manage to.

су́мка bag.

су́мма sum. **сумма́рный** summary; total. **сумми́ровать** impf & pf add up; summarize

су́мрак twilight; murk. **су́мрачный** gloomy.

су́мчатый marsupial.

сунду́к (-á) trunk, chest.

су́нуть(ся (-ну(сь) *pf of* **сова́ть(ся**

суп (*pl* -ы́) soup.

суперма́ркет supermarket.

суперобло́жка dust-jacket.

супру́г husband, spouse; *pl* husband and wife, (*married*) couple. **супру́га** wife, spouse. **супру́жеский** conjugal. **супру́жество** matrimony.

сурга́ч (-á) sealing-wax.

сурди́нка mute; **под сурди́нку** on the sly.

суро́вость severity, sternness. **суро́вый** severe, stern; bleak; unbleached.

суро́к (-рка́) marmot.

суррога́т substitute.

су́слик ground-squirrel.

суста́в joint, articulation.

су́тки (-ток) *pl* twenty-four hours; a day.

су́толока commotion.

су́точный round-the-clock; **~ые** *sb pl* per diem allowance.

суту́литься *impf* stoop. **суту́лый** round-shouldered.

суть essence, main point.

суфлёр prompter. **суфли́ровать** *impf +dat* prompt.

су́ффикс suffix.

суха́рь (-я́) *m* rusk; *pl* breadcrumbs. **су́хо** *adv* drily; coldly.

сухожи́лие tendon.

сухо́й (сух, -á, -о) dry; cold. **сухопу́тный** land. **су́хость** dryness; coldness. **сухоща́вый** lean, skinny.

сучкова́тый knotty; gnarled. **сучо́к** (-чка́) twig; knot.

су́ша (dry) land. **су́ше** *comp of* **сухо́й**. **сушёный** dried.

суши́лка dryer; drying-room.

суши́ть (-шу́, -шишь) *impf* (*pf* **вы́~**) dry, dry out, up; **~ся** (get) dry.

суще́ственный essential, vital. **существи́тельное** *sb* noun. **существо́** being, creature; essence. **существова́ние** existence. **существова́ть** *impf* exist. **су́щий** absolute, downright. **су́щность** essence.

сую́ *etc.*: *see* **сова́ть**. **с|фабрикова́ть** *pf.* **с|фальши́вить** (-влю) *pf.*

с|фантази́ровать *pf.*

сфе́ра sphere. **сфери́ческий** spherical.

сфинкс sphinx.

с|формирова́ть(ся *pf.* **с|формова́ть** *pf.* **с|формули́ровать** *pf.* **с|фотографи́ровать(ся** *pf.*

схвати́ть (-ачу́, -а́тишь) *pf,* **схва́тывать** *impf* (*impf also* **хвата́ть**) seize; catch; grasp; **~ся** snatch; grapple. **схва́тка** skirmish; *pl* contractions.

схе́ма diagram; outline, plan; circuit. **схемати́ческий** schematic; sketchy. **схемати́чный** sketchy.

с|хитри́ть *pf.*

схлы́нуть (-нет) *pf* (break and) flow back; subside.

сход coming off; descent; gathering. **сходи́ть**[1]**(ся** (-ожу́(сь, -о́дишь(ся) *impf of* **сойти́(сь**. **сходи́ть**[2] (-ожу́, -о́дишь) *pf* go; **+за**+*instr* go to fetch. **схо́дка** gathering, meeting. **схо́дный** (-ден, -дна́, -о) similar; reasonable. **схо́дня** (*gen pl* -ей) (*usu pl*) gangplank. **схо́дство** similarity.

с|хорони́ть(ся (-ню́(сь, -ни́шь(ся) *pf.*

сцеди́ть (-ежу́, -е́дишь) *pf*, **сце́живать** *impf* strain off, decant.

сце́на stage; scene. **сцена́рий** scenario; script. **сцена́рист** script-writer. **сцени́ческий** stage.

сцепи́ть (-плю́, -пишь) *pf*, **сцепля́ть** *impf* couple; ~**ся** be coupled; grapple. **сце́пка** coupling. **сцепле́ние** coupling; clutch.

счастли́вец (-вца), **счастли́вчик** lucky man. **счастли́вица** lucky woman. **счастли́вый** (сча́стлив -а) happy; lucky; ~о! all the best!; ~ого пути́ bon voyage. **сча́стье** happiness; good fortune.

счесть(ся (сочту́(сь, -тёшь(ся; счёл(ся, сочла́(сь) *pf of* **счита́ть(ся**. **счёт** (*loc* -ý; *pl* -á) bill; account; counting, calculation; score; expense. **счётный** calculating; accounts. **счетово́д** book-keeper. **счётчик** counter; meter. **счёты** (-ов) *pl* abacus.

счи́стить (-и́щу) *pf* (*impf* **счища́ть**) clean off; clear away.

счита́ть *impf* (*pf* **со~**, **счесть**) count; reckon; consider; ~**ся** (*pf also* **по~ся**) settle accounts; be considered; +с+*instr* take into consideration; reckon with.

счища́ть *impf of* **счи́стить**

США *pl indecl abbr* (*Со-еди́ненные Шта́ты Аме́рики*) USA.

сшиба́ть *impf*, **сшиби́ть** (-бу́, -бёшь; сшиб) *pf* strike, hit, knock (off); ~ **с ног** knock down; ~**ся** collide; come to blows.

сшива́ть *impf*, **сшить** (сошью́, -ьёшь) *pf* sew (together).

съеда́ть *impf of* **съесть**. **съе-**

до́бный edible; nice.

съе́ду *etc.*: *see* **съе́хать**

съёживаться *impf*, **съёжиться** (-жусь) *pf* shrivel, shrink.

съезд congress; conference; arrival. **съе́здить** (-зжу) *pf* go, drive, travel.

съезжа́ть *impf of* **съе́хать(ся. съел, съем** *etc.*: *see* **съесть**

съёмка removal; survey, surveying; shooting. **съёмный** detachable, removable. **съёмщик, съёмщица** tenant; surveyor.

съестно́й food; ~**о́е** *sb* food (supplies). **съесть** (-ем, -ешь, -ест, -еди́м; съел) *pf* (*impf also* **съеда́ть**)

съе́хать (-е́ду) *pf* (*impf* **съезжа́ть**) go down; come down; move; ~**ся** meet; assemble.

съязви́ть (-влю́) *pf*.

сы́воротка whey; serum.

сыгра́ть *pf of* **игра́ть**; ~**ся** play (well) together.

сын (*pl* сыновья́, -е́й *or* -ы́, -о́в) son. **сыно́вний** filial. **сыно́к** (-нка́) little son; sonny.

сы́пать (-плю) *impf* pour; pour forth; ~**ся** fall; pour out; rain down; fray. **сыпно́й тиф** typhus. **сыпу́чий** friable; free-flowing; shifting. **сыпь** rash, eruption.

сыр (*loc* -ý; *pl* -ы́) cheese. **сыре́ть** (-е́ю) *pf* **от~**) become damp.

сыре́ц (-рца́) raw product.

сыро́й (сыр, -á, -о) damp; raw; uncooked, unboiled; unfinished; unripe. **сы́рость** dampness. **сырьё** raw material(s).

сыска́ть (сыщу́, сы́щешь) *pf* find.

сы́тный (-тен, -тна́, -о) filling. **сы́тость** satiety. **сы́тый** (сыт, -á, -о) full.

сыч (-а́) little owl.

сы́щик detective.

с|эконо́мить (-млю) *pf.*

сэр sir.

сюда́ *adv* here, hither.

сюже́т subject; plot; topic. **сюже́тный** subject; having a theme.

сюи́та suite.

сюрпри́з surprise.

сюрреали́зм surrealism. **сюрреалисти́ческий** surrealist.

сюрту́к (-а́) frock-coat.

сяк *adv*: *see* **так**. **сям** *adv*: *see* **там**

Т

та *see* **тот**

таба́к (-а́) tobacco. **табаке́рка** snuff-box. **таба́чный** tobacco.

та́бель (-я; *pl* -и, -ей *or* -я́, -е́й) *m* table, list. **та́бельный** table; time.

табле́тка tablet.

табли́ца table; ~ умноже́ния multiplication table.

та́бор (gipsy) camp.

табу́н (-а́) herd.

табуре́т, табуре́тка stool.

тавро́ (*pl* -а, -а́м) brand.

тавтоло́гия tautology.

таджи́к, -и́чка Tadzhik. **Таджикиста́н** Tadzhikistan.

таёжный taiga.

таз (*loc* -у́; *pl* -ы́) basin; pelvis. **тазобе́дренный** hip. **та́зовый** pelvic.

таи́нственный mysterious; secret. **таи́ть** *impf* hide, harbour; ~ся hide; lurk.

Тайва́нь *m* Taiwan.

тайга́ taiga.

тайко́м *adv* secretly, surreptitiously; ~ от+*gen* behind the

back of.

тайм half; period of play.

та́йна secret; mystery. **тайни́к** (-а́) hiding-place; *pl* recesses. **та́йный** secret; privy.

тайфу́н typhoon.

так so; like this; as it should be; just like that; и ~ even so; as it is; и ~ да́лее and so on; и ~ и сяк this way and that; не ~ wrong; ~ же in the same way; ~ же... как as ... as; и есть I thought so!; ~ ему́ и на́до serves him right; ~ и́ли ина́че one way or another; ~ себе́ so-so. **так** *conj* then; so; ~ как as, since.

такела́ж rigging.

та́кже *adv* also, too, as well.

тако́в *m* (-а́ *f*, -о́ *neut*, -ы́ *pl*) *pron* such.

тако́й *pron* such (a); в ~о́м слу́чае in that case; кто он ~о́й? who is he?; ~о́й же the same; ~и́м о́бразом in this way; что э́то ~о́е? what is this? **тако́й-то** *pron* so-and-so; such-and-such.

та́кса fixed or statutory price; tariff.

таксёр taxi-driver. **такси́** *neut indecl* taxi. **такси́ст** taxi-driver. **таксопа́рк** taxi depot.

такт time; bar; beat; tact.

та́к-таки after all, really.

та́ктика tactics. **такти́ческий** tactical.

такти́чность tact. **такти́чный** tactful.

та́ктов|ый time, timing; ~ая черта́ bar-line.

тала́нт talent. **тала́нтливый** talented.

талисма́н talisman.

та́лия waist.

тало́н, тало́нчик coupon.

та́лый thawed, melted.

тальк talc; talcum powder.

там *adv* there; ~ **и сям** here and there; ~ **же** in the same place; ibid.

тамада́ *m* toast-master.

та́мбур[1] tambour; lobby; platform. **та́мбур**[2] chain-stitch.

тамо́женник customs official. **тамо́женный** customs. **тамо́жня** custom-house.

та́мошний of that place, local.

тампо́н tampon.

та́нгенс tangent.

та́нго *neut indecl* tango.

та́нец (-нца) dance; dancing.

тани́н tannin.

танк tank. **та́нкер** tanker. **танки́ст** member of a tank crew. **та́нковый** tank, armoured.

танцева́льный dancing; ~ **ве́чер** dance. **танцева́ть** (-цу́ю) *impf* dance. **танцо́вщик**, **танцо́вщица** (ballet) dancer. **танцо́р**, **танцо́рка** dancer.

та́пка, **та́почка** slipper.

та́ра packing; tare.

тарака́н cockroach.

тара́н battering-ram.

тара́нтул tarantula.

таре́лка plate; cymbal; satellite dish.

тари́ф tariff.

таска́ть *impf* drag, lug; carry; pull; take; pull out; sweep; wear; ~**ся** drag; hang about.

тасова́ть (-су́ю) *impf* (*pf* **с**~) shuffle.

ТАСС *abbr* (*of* Телегра́фное аге́нтство Сове́тского Сою́за) Tass (Telegraph Agency of the Soviet Union).

тата́рин, **тата́рка** Tatar.

татуиро́вка tattooing, tattoo.

тафта́ taffeta.

тахта́ ottoman.

та́чка wheelbarrow.

тащи́ть (-щу́, -щишь) *impf* (*pf*

вы́~, **с**~) pull; drag; lug; carry; take; pull out; swipe; ~**ся** drag o.s. along; drag.

та́ять (та́ю) *impf* (*pf* **рас**~) melt; thaw; dwindle.

тварь creature(s); wretch.

тверде́ть (-е́ет) *impf* (*pf* **за**~) harden, become hard. **тверди́ть** (-ржу́) *impf* (*pf* **вы́**~) repeat, say again and again; memorize. **твёрдо** *adv* hard; firmly, firm. **твердоло́бый** thick-skulled; diehard. **твёрдый** hard; firm; solid; steadfast; ~ **знак** hard sign, ъ; ~**ое те́ло** solid. **тверды́ня** stronghold.

твой (-его́) *m*, **твоя́** (-ей) *f*, **твоё** (-его́) *neut*, **твои́** (-и́х) *pl* your, yours.

творе́ние creation, work; creature. **творе́ц** (-рца́) creator. **твори́тельный** instrumental. **твори́ть** *impf* (*pf* **со**~) create; do; make; ~**ся** happen.

творо́г (-а́) curds; cottage cheese.

тво́рческий creative. **тво́рчество** creation; creative work; works.

те *see* **тот**

т.е. *abbr* (*of* **то есть**) that is, i.e.

теа́тр theatre. **театра́льный** theatre; theatrical.

тебя́ *etc.*: *see* **ты**

те́зис thesis.

тёзка *m & f* namesake.

тёк *see* **течь**

текст text; libretto, lyrics.

тексти́ль *m* textiles. **тексти́льный** textile.

тексту́ра texture.

теку́чий fluid; unstable. **теку́щий** current; routine.

теле- *in comb* tele-; television.

телеателье́ *neut indecl* television maintenance workshop.

~ви́дение television. ~визио́нный television. ~визор television (set). ~гра́мма telegram. ~граф telegraph (office). ~графи́ровать *impf & pf* telegraph. ~гра́фный telegraph(ic). ~зри́тель *m* (television) viewer. ~объекти́в telephoto lens. ~пати́ческий telepathic. ~па́тия telepathy. ~ско́п telescope. ~ста́нция television station. ~сту́дия television studio. ~фо́н telephone; (telephone) number; (по)звони́ть по ~фо́ну +*dat* ring up. ~фон-автома́т public telephone, call-box. ~фони́ст, -и́стка (telephone) operator. ~фо́нный telephone; ~фо́нная кни́га telephone directory; ~фо́нная ста́нция telephone exchange; ~фо́нная тру́бка receiver. ~фон-отве́тчик answering machine. ~фотогра́фия telephotography. ~центр television centre.

теле́га cart, wagon. теле́жка small cart; trolley.

телёнок (-нка; *pl* -я́та, -я́т) calf.

теле́сн|ый bodily; corporal; ~ого цве́та flesh-coloured.

Теле́ц (-льца́) Taurus.

тели́ться *impf* (*pf* о~) calve.

тёлка heifer.

те́ло (*pl* -а́) body. телогре́йка padded jacket. телосложе́ние build. телохрани́тель *m* bodyguard.

теля́та *etc.*: *see* телёнок. теля́тина veal. теля́чий calf; veal.

тем *conj* (so much) the; ~ лу́чше so much the better; ~ не ме́нее nevertheless.

тем *see* тот, тьма

те́ма subject; theme. тема́тика subject-matter; themes. темати́ческий subject; thematic.

тембр timbre.

темне́ть (-е́ет) *impf* (*pf* по~, с~) become dark. темни́ца dungeon. темно́ *predic* it is dark. темноко́жий dark-skinned, swarthy. тёмноси́ний dark blue. темнота́ darkness. тёмный dark.

темп tempo; rate.

темпера́мент temperament. темпера́ментный temperamental.

температу́ра temperature.

те́мя (-мени) *neut* crown, top of the head.

тенде́нция tendency; bias.

теневой, тени́стый shady.

те́ннис tennis. тенниси́ст, -и́стка tennis-player. те́ннисн|ый tennis; ~ая площа́дка tennis-court.

те́нор (*pl* -а́) tenor.

тент awning.

тень (*loc* -и́; *pl* -и, -е́й) shade; shadow; phantom; ghost; particle, vestige; atom; suspicion; те́ни для век *pl* eyeshadow.

тео́лог theologian. теологи́ческий theological. теоло́гия theology.

теоре́ма theorem. теоре́тик theoretician. теорети́ческий theoretical. тео́рия theory.

тепе́решн|ий present. тепе́рь *adv* now; today.

тепли́ть (-е́ет) *impf* (*pf* по~) get warm. тепли́ться (-ится) *impf* flicker; glimmer. тепли́ца greenhouse, conservatory. тепли́чный hothouse. тепло́ heat; warmth. тепло́ *adv* warmly; *predic* it is warm. тепло- *in comb* heat; thermal;

thermo-. **тепловоз** diesel locomotive. **~ёмкость** thermal capacity. **~кровный** warmblooded. **~обмен** heat exchange. **~проводный** heatconducting. **~стойкий** heatresistant. **~ход** motor ship. **~централь** heat and power station.

тепловой heat; thermal. **теплота** heat; warmth. **тёплый** (-пел, -пла, тёпло) warm.

терапевт therapeutist. **терапия** therapy.

теребить (-блю) *impf* pull (at); pester.

тереть (тру, трёшь; тёр) *impf* rub; grate; **~ся** rub o.s.; **~ся около**+*gen* hang about, hang around; **~ся среди** +*gen* mix with.

терзать *impf* tear to pieces; torment; **~ся** +*instr* suffer; be a prey to.

тёрка grater.

термин term. **терминология** terminology.

термический thermic, thermal. **термометр** thermometer. **термос** thermos (flask). **термостат** thermostat. **термоядерный** thermonuclear.

терновник sloe, blackthorn. **терновый** thorny.

терпеливый patient. **терпение** patience. **терпеть** (-плю, -пишь) *impf* (*pf* по~) suffer; bear, endure. **терпеться** (-пится) *impf impers*+*dat*: ему не терпится +*inf* he is impatient to. **терпимость** tolerance. **терпимый** tolerant; tolerable.

терпкий (-пок, -пка, -о) astringent; tart.

терраса terrace.

территориальный territorial.

территория territory.

террор terror. **терроризировать** *impf & pf* terrorize. **террорист** terrorist.

тёртый grated; experienced.

терьер terrier.

терять *impf* (*pf* по~, у~) lose; shed; **~ся** get lost; disappear; fail, decline; become flustered.

тёс boards, planks. **тесать** (тешу, тешешь) *impf* cut, hew.

тесёмка ribbon, braid.

теснить *impf* (*pf* по~, с~) crowd; squeeze, constrict; be too tight; **~ся** press through; move up; crowd, jostle. **теснота** crowded state; crush. **тесный** crowded; (too) tight; close; compact; **~о** it is crowded.

тесовый board, plank.

тест test.

тесто dough; pastry.

тесть *m* father-in-law.

тесьма ribbon, braid.

тетерев (*pl* -а) black grouse. **тетёрка** grey hen.

тётка aunt.

тетрадка, тетрадь exercise book.

тётя (*gen pl* -ей) aunt.

тех- *abbr in comb* (*of* технический) technical.

техник technician. **техника** technical equipment; technology; technique. **техникум** technical college. **технический** technical; **~ие условия** specifications. **технолог** technologist. **технологический** technological. **технология** technology. **техперсонал** technical personnel.

течение flow; course; current stream; trend.

течь[1] (-чёт; тёк, -ла) *impf* flow; stream; leak. **течь**[2] leak

тешить (-шу) *impf* (*pf* по~

amuse; gratify; **~ся** (+*instr*)
amuse, gratify (with).

тешу́ etc.: see **теса́ть**

тёща mother-in-law.

тигр tiger. **тигри́ца** tigress.

тик[1] tic.

тик[2] teak.

ти́на slime, mud.

тип type. **типи́чный** typical.
типово́й standard; model.
типогра́фия printing-house,
press. **типогра́фский** typo-
graphical.

тир shooting-range, -gallery.

тира́ж (-á) draw; circulation;
edition.

тира́н tyrant. **тира́нить** *impf*
tyrannize. **тирани́ческий** tyrannical. **тира́ния** tyranny.

тире́ *neut indecl* dash.

ти́скать *impf*, **ти́снуть** (-ну)
pf press, squeeze. **тиски́** (-о́в)
pl vice; **в тиска́х** +*gen* in the
grip of. **тисне́ние** stamping;
imprint; design. **тиснёный**
stamped.

тита́н[1] titanian.

тита́н[2] boiler.

тита́н[3] titan.

титр sub-title.

ти́тул title; title-page. **ти́туль-
ный** title.

тиф (*loc* -ý) typhus.

ти́хий (тих, -á, -о) quiet; silent;
calm; slow. **тихоокеа́нский**
Pacific. **ти́ше** *comp of* **ти́хий**,
ти́хо; *int* **ти́ше!** quiet! **тишина́**
quiet, silence.

т. к. *abbr* (*of* **так как**) as, since.

тка́ный woven fabric,
cloth; tissue. **ткать** (тку,
ткёшь; -ал, -ала́, -о) *impf* (*pf*
со~) weave. **тка́цкий** weav-
ing; **~ стано́к** loom. **ткач**,
ткачи́ха weaver.

ткнуть(ся (-у(сь, -ёшь(ся) *pf
of* **ты́кать(ся**

тле́ние decay; smouldering.
тлеть (-éет) *impf* rot, decay;
smoulder; **~ся** smoulder.

тля aphis.

тмин caraway(-seeds).

то *pron* that; **а не то́** or else,
otherwise; (**да**) **и то́** and even
then, and that; **то́ есть** that is
(to say); **то и де́ло** every now
and then. **то** *conj* then; **не
то́...**, **не то** either ... or; half
..., half ...; **то ..., то** now ..., now;
то ли..., **то ли** whether ... or.
-то *partl* just, exactly; **в то́м-
то и де́ло** that's just it.

тобо́й see **ты**

това́р goods; commodity.

това́рищ comrade; friend; colleague. **това́рищеский** com-
radely; friendly.

това́рищество comradeship;
company; association.

това́рный goods; commodity.

товаро- *in comb* commodity;
goods. **товарообме́н** barter.
~оборо́т (sales) turnover.
~отправи́тель *m* consignor.
~получа́тель *m* consignee.

тогда́ *adv* then; **~ как** whereas.
тогда́шний of that time.

того́ see **тот**

тожде́ственный identical.
тожде́ство identity.

то́же *adv* also, too.

ток (*pl* -и) current.

тока́рный turning; **~ стано́к**
lathe. **тока́рь** (*pl* -я́, -е́й *or* -и,
-ей) *m* turner, lathe operator.

токси́ческий toxic.

толк sense; use; **бе́з ~у** sense-
lessly; **знать ~ в**+*prep* know
well; **сбить с ~у** confuse; **с
~ом** intelligently.

толка́ть *impf* (*pf* **толкну́ть**)
push, shove; jog; **~ся** jostle.

то́лки (-ов) *pl* rumours, gossip.

толкну́ть(ся (-ну́(сь, -нёшь(-ся) *pf of* **толка́ть(ся**

толкова́ние interpretation; *pl* commentary. **толкова́ть** *impf* interpret; explain; talk. **толко́вый** intelligent; clear; ~ **слова́рь** defining dictionary. **то́лком** *adv* plainly; seriously.

толкотня́ crush, squash.

толку́ *etc.: see* **толо́чь**

толку́чка crush, squash; second-hand market.

толокно́ oatmeal.

толо́чь (-лку́, -лчёшь; -ло́к, -лкла́) *impf* (*pf* ис~, рас~) pound, crush.

толпа́ (*pl* -ы) crowd. **толпи́ться** *impf* crowd; throng.

толсте́ть (-е́ю) *impf* (*pf* по~) grow fat; put on weight. **толстоко́жий** thick-skinned; pachydermatous. **то́лстый** (-á, -о) fat; thick. **толстя́к** (-á) fat man *or* boy.

толчёный crushed; ground. **толчёт** *etc.: see* **толо́чь**

толчея́ crush, squash.

толчо́к (-чка́) push, shove; (*sport*) put; jolt; shock, tremor.

то́лща thickness; thick. **то́лще** *comp of* **то́лстый**. **толщина́** thickness; fatness.

толь *m* roofing felt.

то́лько *adv* only, merely; ~ **что** (only) just; *conj* only but; (**как**) ~, (**лишь**) ~ as soon as; ~ **бы** if only.

том (*pl* ~á) volume. **то́мик** small volume.

тома́т tomato. **тома́тный** tomato.

томи́тельный tedious, wearing; agonizing. **томи́ть** (-млю́) *impf* (*pf* ис~) tire; torment; ~**ся** languish; be tormented. **томле́ние** languor. **то́мный**

(-мен, -мна́, -о) languid, languorous.

тон (*pl* -á *or* -ы, -ов) tone; note; shade; form. **тона́льность** key.

то́ненький thin; slim. **то́нкий** (-нок, -нка́, -о) thin; slim; fine; refined; subtle; keen. **то́нкость** thinness; slimness; fineness; subtlety.

то́нна ton.

тонне́ль *see* **тунне́ль**

то́нус tone.

тону́ть (-ну́, -нешь) *impf* (*pf* по~, у~) sink; drown.

то́ньше *comp of* **то́нкий**.

то́пать *impf* (*pf* **то́пнуть**) stamp.

топи́ть[1] (-плю́, -пишь) *impf* (*pf* по~, у~) sink; drown; ruin; ~**ся** drown o.s.

топи́ть[2] (-плю́, -пишь) *impf* stoke; heat; melt (down); ~**ся** burn; melt. **то́пка** stoking; heating; melting (down); furnace.

то́пкий boggy, marshy.

то́пливный fuel. **то́пливо** fuel.

то́пнуть (-ну) *pf of* **то́пать**

топографи́ческий topographical. **топогра́фия** topography.

то́поль (*pl* -я́ *or* -и) *m* poplar.

топо́р (-á) axe. **топо́рик** hatchet. **топо́рище** axe-handle. **топо́рный** axe; clumsy; crude.

то́пот tramp; clatter. **топта́ть** (-пчу́, -пчешь) *impf* (*pf* за~) trample (down); ~**ся** stamp ~**ся на ме́сте** mark time.

топча́н (-á) trestle-bed.

топь bog, marsh.

торг (*loc* -ý; *pl* -и́) trading; bargaining; *pl* auction. **торго-ва́ть** *impf* (*pf* c~) trade ~**ся** bargain, haggle. **торго́вец** (-вца) merchant; tradesman. **торго́вка** market woman; stall-holder. **торго́вля** trade. **торго́вый** trade, commercial; merchant. **торгпре́д** *abbr* trade representative.

торе́ц (-рца́) butt-end; wooden paving-block.

торже́ственный solemn; ceremonial. **торжество́** celebration; triumph. **торжество-ва́ть** *impf* celebrate; triumph.

торможе́ние braking. **тор-мо́з** (*pl* -á *or* -ы) brake. **тормози́ть** (-ожу́) *impf* (*pf* за~) brake; hamper.

тормоши́ть (-шу́) *impf* pester; bother.

торопи́ть (-плю́, -пишь) *impf* (*pf* по~) hurry; hasten; ~ся hurry. **торопли́вый** hasty.

торпе́да torpedo.

торс torso.

торт cake.

торф peat. **торфяно́й** peat.

торча́ть (-чу́) *impf* stick out; protrude; hang about.

торше́р standard lamp.

тоска́ melancholy; boredom; nostalgia; ~ по+*dat* longing for. **тоскли́вый** melancholy; depressed; dreary. **тоскова́ть** *impf* be melancholy, depressed; long; ~ по+*dat* miss.

тост toast.

тот *m* (та *f*, то *neut*, те *pl*) *pron* that; the former; the other; the one; the same; the right; **и ~ и друго́й** both; **к тому́ же** moreover; **не ~** the wrong; **ни ~ ни друго́й** neither; **тот, кто** the one who, the person who. **то́тчас** *adv* immediately.

тоталитари́зм totalitarianism. **тоталита́рный** totalitarian. **тота́льный** total.

точи́лка sharpener; pencil-sharpener. **точи́ло** whetstone, grindstone. **точи́льный** grind-ing, sharpening; ~ ка́мень whetstone, grindstone. **точи́ль-щик** (knife-)grinder. **точи́ть** (-чу́, -чишь) *impf* (*pf* вы́~, на~) sharpen; hone; turn; eat away; gnaw at.

то́чка spot; dot; full stop; point; ~ зре́ния point of view; **~ с запято́й** semicolon. **то́чно[1]** *adv* exactly, precisely; punctually. **то́чно[2]** *conj* as though, as if. **то́чность** punctuality; precision; accuracy; **в то́чности** exactly, precisely. **то́чный** (-чен, -чна́, -о) exact, precise; accurate; punctual. **точь-в-то́чь** *adv* exactly; word for word.

тошни́ть *impf impers*: **меня́ тошни́т** I feel sick. **тошнота́** nausea. **тошнотво́рный** sickening, nauseating.

то́щий (тощ, -á, -е) gaunt, emaciated; skinny; empty; poor.

трава́ (*pl* -ы) grass; herb. **тра-ви́нка** blade of grass.

трави́ть (-влю́, -вишь) *impf* (*pf* вы́~, за~) poison; exterminate, destroy; etch; hunt; torment; badger. **травле́ние** extermination; etching. **тра́вля** hunting; persecution; badgering.

тра́вма trauma, injury.

травоя́дный herbivorous. **тра-вяни́стый**, **травяно́й** grass; herbaceous; grassy.

траге́дия tragedy. **тра́гик** tragedian. **траги́ческий**, **траги́ч-ный** tragic.

традицио́нный traditional. **тради́ция** tradition.

траекто́рия trajectory.

тракта́т treatise; treaty.

тракти́р inn, tavern.

трактова́ть *impf* interpret; treat, discuss. **трактова́-**

treatment; interpretation.

тра́ктор tractor. **тракто́рист** tractor driver.

трал trawl. **тра́лить** *impf* (*pf* про~) trawl; sweep. **тра́льщик** trawler; mine-sweeper.

трамбова́ть *impf* (*pf* y~) ram, tamp.

трамва́й tram. **трамва́йный** tram.

трампли́н spring-board; ski-jump.

транзи́стор transistor; transistor radio.

транзи́тный transit.

транс trance.

трансатланти́ческий transatlantic.

трансли́ровать *impf* & *pf* broadcast, transmit. **трансляцио́нный** broadcasting. **трансля́ция** broadcast, transmission.

тра́нспорт transport; consignment. **транспортёр** conveyor. **транспорти́р** protractor. **транспорти́ровать** *impf* & *pf* transport. **тра́нспортный** transport.

трансформа́тор transformer.

транше́я trench.

трап ladder.

тра́пеза meal.

трапе́ция trapezium; trapeze.

тра́сса line, course, direction; route, road.

тра́та expenditure; waste. **тра́тить** (-а́чу) *impf* (*pf* ис~, по~) spend, expend; waste.

тра́улер trawler.

тра́ур mourning. **тра́урный** mourning; funeral; mournful.

трафаре́т stencil; stereotype; cliché. **трафаре́тный** stencilled; conventional, stereotyped.

тра́чу *etc.*: see **тра́тить**

тре́бование demand; request, requirement; requisition, order; *pl* needs. **тре́бовательный** demanding. **тре́бовать** *impf* (*pf* по~) summon; +*gen* demand, require; need; ~ся be needed, be required.

трево́га alarm; anxiety. **трево́жить** (-жу) *impf* (*pf* вс~, по~) alarm; disturb; worry; ~ся worry, be anxious; trouble o.s. **трево́жный** worried anxious; alarming; alarm.

тре́звенник teetotaller. **трезве́ть** (-е́ю) *impf* (*pf* о~) sober up.

трезво́н peal (*of bells*); rumours; row.

тре́звость sobriety. **тре́звый** (-зв, -а́, -о) sober; teetotal.

тре́йлер trailer.

трель trill; warble.

тре́нер trainer, coach.

тре́ние friction.

трениро́вать *impf* (*pf* на~) train, coach; ~ся be in training. **трениро́вка** training, coaching. **трениро́вочный** training.

трепа́ть (-плю, -плешь) *impf* (*pf* ис~, по~, рас~) blow about; dishevel; wear out; pat; ~ся fray; wear out; flutter.

тре́пет trembling; trepidation.

трепета́ть (-ещу́, -е́щешь) *impf* tremble; flicker; palpitate. **тре́петный** trembling; flickering; palpitating; timid.

треск crack; crackle; fuss.

треска́ cod.

тре́скаться¹ *impf* (*pf* по~) crack; chap.

тре́скаться² *impf of* тре́снуться

тре́снуть (-нет) *pf* snap, crackle; crack; chap; bang; ~ся bang. **тре́скаться** +*instr* bang.

трест trust.

тре́т|ий (-ья, -ье) third; ~**ье** sb sweet (course).

трети́ровать impf slight.

тре́тить (gen pl -е́й) third.

тре́тье etc.: see **тре́тий**.

треуго́льник triangle. **треуго́льный** triangular.

тре́фы (треф) pl clubs.

трёх- in comb three-, tri-. **трёхго́дичный** three-year. ~**голо́сный** three-part. ~**гра́нный** three-edged; trihedral. ~**колёсный** three-wheeled. ~**ле́тний** three-year; three-year old. ~**ме́рный** three-dimensional. ~**ме́сячный** three-month; quarterly; three-month-old. ~**по́лье** three-field system. ~**со́тый** three-hundredth. ~**сторо́нний** three-sided; trilateral; tripartite. ~**эта́жный** three-storeyed.

треща́ть (-щу́) impf crack; crackle; creak; chirr; crack up; chatter. **тре́щина** crack, split; fissure; chap.

три (трёх, -ём, -емя́, -ёх) three. **трибу́на** platform, rostrum; stand. **трибуна́л** tribunal.

тригономе́трия trigonometry. **тридцатиле́тний** thirty-year; thirty-year old. **тридца́тый** thirtieth. **три́дцать** (-и́, instr -ью́) thirty. **три́жды** adv three times; thrice.

трико́ neut indecl tricot; tights; knickers. **трикота́ж** knitted fabric; knitwear. **трикота́жный** jersey, tricot; knitted.

трина́дцатый thirteenth. **трина́дцать** thirteen. **трио́ль** triplet.

три́ппер gonorrhoea.

три́ста (трёхсо́т, -ёмста́м, -емя́ста́ми, -ёхста́х) three hundred.

трито́н zool triton.

триу́мф triumph.

тро́гательный touching, moving. **тро́гать(ся** impf of **тро́нуть(ся**

тро́е (-и́х) pl three. **трое-бо́рье** triathlon. **троекра́тный** thrice-repeated. **Тро́ица** Trinity; **тро́ица** trio. **Тро́ицын день** Whit Sunday.

тро́йка three; figure 3; troika; No. 3; three-piece suit. **тройно́й** triple, treble; three-ply. **тро́йственный** triple; tripartite.

тролле́йбус trolley-bus.

тромб blood clot.

тромбо́н trombone.

трон throne.

тро́нуть (-ну) pf (impf тро́гать) touch; disturb; affect; ~**ся** start, set out; be touched: be affected.

тропа́ path.

тро́пик tropic.

тропи́нка path.

тропи́ческий tropical.

трос rope, cable.

тростни́к (-а́) reed, rush. **тро́сточка**, **трость** (gen pl -е́й) cane, walking-stick.

тротуа́р pavement.

трофе́й trophy; pl spoils (of war), booty.

трою́родн|ый: ~**ый брат**, ~**ая сестра́** second cousin.

тру etc.: see **тере́ть**

труба́ (pl -ы) pipe; chimney; funnel; trumpet; tube. **труба́ч** (-а́) trumpeter; trumpet-player. **труби́ть** (-блю́) impf (pf про-) blow, sound; blare. **тру́бка** tube; pipe; (telephone) receiver. **трубопрово́д** pipe-line; piping; manifold. **трубочи́ст** chimney-sweep. **тру́бочный** pipe. **тру́бчатый** tubular.

труд (-á) labour; work; effort; с ~о́м with difficulty. **труди́ться** (-ужу́сь, -у́дишься) *impf* toil, labour; work; trouble. **тру́дно** *predic* it is difficult; hard. **тру́дность** (-деи, -днá, -о) difficult; hard.

трудо- *in comb* labour, work. **трудоде́нь** (-дня́) *m* workday (unit). ~ёмкий labour-intensive. ~люби́вый industrious. ~любие industry. ~спосо́бность ability to work. ~спосо́бный able-bodied; capable of working.

трудово́й work; working; earned; hard-earned. **трудя́щийся** working; ~иеся *sb pl* the workers. **тру́женик, тру́женица** toiler.

труп corpse; carcass.

тру́ппа troupe, company.

трус coward.

тру́сики (-ов) *pl* shorts; trunks; pants.

труси́ть[1] (-ушу́) *impf* trot, jog along.

тру́сить[2] (-ушу) *impf* (*pf* с~) be a coward; lose one's nerve; be afraid. **трусли́вa** coward. **трусли́вый** cowardly. **тру́сость** cowardice.

трусы́ (-о́в) *pl* shorts; trunks; pants.

труха́ dust; trash.

тру́шу *etc.*: see **труси́ть**[1], **тру́сить**[1].

трущо́ба slum; godforsaken hole.

трюк stunt; trick.

трюм hold.

трюмо́ *neut indecl* pier-glass.

трю́фель (*gen pl* -лей) *m* truffle.

тря́пка rag; spineless creature; *pl* clothes. **тря́пье** rags; clothes.

тряси́на quagmire. **тря́ска** shaking, jolting. **трясти́** (-су́, -сёшь; -яс, -лá) *impf*, **тряхну́ть** (-ну́, -нёшь) *pf* (*pf also* вы~) shake; shake out; jolt; ~сь shake; tremble, shiver; jolt.

тсс *int* sh! hush!

туале́т dress; toilet. **туале́тный** toilet.

туберкулёз tuberculosis.

ту́го *adv* tight(ly), taut; with difficulty. **туго́й** (туг, -á, -о) tight; taut; tightly filled; difficult.

туда́ *adv* there, thither; that way; to the right place; ни ~ ни сюда́ neither one way nor the other; ~ и обра́тно there and back.

ту́же *comp of* **ту́го, туго́й**

тужу́рка (double-breasted) jacket.

туз (-á, *acc* за) ace; bigwig.

тузе́мец (-мца), **-мка** native.

ту́ловище trunk; torso.

тулу́п sheepskin coat.

тума́н fog; mist; haze. **тума́нить** *impf* (*pf* за~) dim, cloud, obscure; ~ся grow misty; be befogged. **тума́нность** fog, mist; nebula; obscurity. **тума́нный** foggy; misty; hazy; obscure, vague.

ту́мба post; bollard; pedestal. **ту́мбочка** bedside table.

ту́ндра tundra.

туне́ядец (-дца) sponger.

туни́ка tunic.

тунне́ль *m*, **тонне́ль** *m* tunnel.

тупе́ть (-е́ю) *impf* (*pf* о~) become blunt; grow dull. **тупи́к** (-á) cul-de-sac, dead end; im passe; поста́вить в ~ stump; nonplus. **тупи́ться** (-пится *impf* (*pf* за~, ис~) become blunt. **тупи́ца** *m & f* block head, dimwit. **тупо́й** (туп, -а́, -о) blunt; obtuse; dull; vacant, stupid. **ту́пость** bluntness; vacancy; dullness; slowness.

тур turn; round.

тура́ rook, castle.

турба́за holiday village, campsite.

турби́на turbine.

туре́цкий Turkish; ~ **бараба́н** bass drum.

тури́зм tourism. **тури́ст, -и́стка** tourist. **тури́ст(и́че)ский** tourist.

туркме́н (gen pl -ме́н), ~**ка** Turkmen. **Туркмениста́н** Turkmenistan.

турне́ neut indecl tour.

турне́пс swede.

турни́р tournament.

туро́к (-рка) Turk. **турча́нка** Turkish woman. **Ту́рция** Turkey.

ту́склый dim, dull; lacklustre. **тускне́ть** (-е́ет) impf (pf **по~**) grow dim.

тут adv here; now; ~ **же** there and then.

ту́фля shoe.

ту́хлый rotten, bad. **ту́хнуть**[1] (-нет; тух) go bad. **ту́хнуть**[2] (-нет; тух) impf (pf **по~**) go out.

ту́ча cloud; storm-cloud.

ту́чный (-чен, -чна́, -чно) fat; rich, fertile.

туш flourish.

ту́ша carcass.

тушева́ть (-шу́ю) impf (pf **за~**) shade.

тушёный stewed. **туши́ть**[1] (-шу́, -шишь) impf (pf **с~**) stew.

туши́ть[2] (-шу́, -шишь) impf (pf **за~, по~**) extinguish.

тушу́ю etc.: see **тушева́ть**.

тушь Indian ink; ~ **(для ресни́ц)** mascara.

щта́тельность care. **щта́тельный** careful; painstaking.

щтеду́шный feeble, frail.

щтесла́вие vanity, vainglory. **щтесла́вный** vain. **щтета́** vanity. **щте́тный** vain, futile.

ты (тебя́, тебе́, тобо́й, тебе́) you; thou; **быть на ты** c+instr be on intimate terms with.

ты́кать (ты́чу) impf (pf ткнуть) poke; prod; stick.

ты́ква pumpkin; gourd.

тыл (loc -ý; pl -ы́) back; rear. **ты́льный** back; rear.

тын paling; palisade.

ты́сяча (instr -ей or -ью) thousand. **тысячеле́тие** millennium; thousandth anniversary. **ты́сячный** thousandth; of (many) thousands.

тычи́нка stamen.

тьма[1] dark, darkness.

тьма[2] host, multitude.

тюбете́йка skull-cap.

тю́бик tube.

тюк (-á) bale, package.

тюле́нь m seal.

тюльпа́н tulip.

тюре́мный prison. **тюре́мщик** gaoler. **тюрьма́** (pl -ы, -рем) prison, gaol.

тюфя́к (-á) mattress.

тя́га traction; thrust; draught; attraction; craving. **тяга́ться** impf vie, contend. **тяга́ч** (-á) tractor.

тя́гостный burdensome; painful. **тя́гость** burden. **тяготе́ние** gravity, gravitation; bent, inclination. **тяготе́ть** (-е́ю) impf gravitate; be attracted; ~ **над** hang over. **тяготи́ть** (-ощу́) impf be a burden on; oppress.

тягу́чий malleable, ductile; viscous; slow.

тя́жба lawsuit; competition;

тяжело́ *adv* heavily; seriously. **тяжело́** *predic* it is hard; it is painful. **тяжелоатле́т** weight-lifter. **тяжелове́с** heavyweight. **тяжелове́сный** heavy; ponderous. **тяжёлый** (-ёл, -а́) heavy; hard; serious; painful. **тя́жесть** gravity; weight; heaviness; severity. **тя́жкий** heavy; severe; grave.

тяну́ть (-ну́, -нешь) *impf* (*pf* по~) pull; draw; drag; drag out; weigh; *impers* attract; be tight; ~ся stretch; extend; stretch out; stretch o.s.; drag on; crawl; drift; move along one after another; last out; reach.

тяну́чка toffee.

У

у *prep+gen* by; at; with; from; of; belonging to; **у меня́ (есть)** I have; **у нас** at our place; in our country.

уба́вить (-влю) *pf*, **убавля́ть** *impf* reduce, diminish.

у|ба́юкать *pf*, **убаю́кивать** *impf* lull (to sleep).

убега́ть *impf of* **убежа́ть**

убеди́тельный convincing; earnest. **убеди́ть** (-и́шь) *pf* (*impf* **убежда́ть**) convince; persuade; ~ся be convinced; make certain.

убежа́ть (-егу́) *pf* (*impf* **убега́ть**) run away; escape; boil over.

убежда́ть(ся *impf of* **убеди́ть(ся. убежде́ние** persuasion; conviction, belief. **убеждённость** conviction. **убеждённый** (-ён, -а́) convinced; staunch.

убе́жище refuge, asylum; shelter.

уберега́ть *impf*, **убере́чь** (-регу́, -режёшь; -рёг, -гла́) *pf* preserve, protect; ~ся от+*gen* protect o.s. against.

уберу́ *etc.: see* **убра́ть**

убива́ть(ся *impf of* **уби́ть(ся. уби́йственный** deadly; murderous; killing. **уби́йство** murder. **уби́йца** *m & f* murderer.

убира́ть(ся *impf of* **убра́ть(ся; убира́йся!** clear off!

уби́тый killed; crushed; *sb* dead man. **уби́ть** (убью́, -бьёшь) *pf* (*impf* **убива́ть**) kill; murder; ~ся hurt o.s.

убо́гий wretched. **убо́жество** poverty; squalor.

убо́й slaughter.

убо́р dress, attire.

убо́рка harvesting; clearing up. **убо́рная** *sb* lavatory; dressing-room. **убо́рочн|ый** harvesting; ~**ая маши́на** harvester. **убо́рщик, убо́рщица** cleaner. **убра́нство** furniture.

убра́ть (уберу́, -рёшь; -а́л, -а́, -о) *pf* (*impf* **убира́ть**) remove; take away; put away; harvest; clear up; decorate; ~ **посте́ль** make a bed; ~ **со стола́** clear the table; ~ся tidy up, clean up; clear off.

убыва́ть *impf*, **убы́ть** (убу́ду убы́л, -а́, -о) *pf* diminish; subside; wane; leave. **убы́ль** diminution; casualties. **убы́ток** (-тка) loss; *pl* damages. **убы́точный** unprofitable.

убью́ *etc.: see* **уби́ть**

уважа́емый respected; dear. **уважа́ть** *impf* respect. **уваже́ние** respect; **с ~м** your sincerely. **уважи́тельный** valid; respectful.

уве́домить (-млю) *pf*, **уве́домля́ть** *impf* inform. **уве́домле́ние** notification.

уведу́ *etc.: see* **увести́**

увезти́ (-зу́, -зёшь; увёз, -ла́) *pf* (*impf* **увози́ть**) take (away); steal; abduct.

увеко́вечивать *impf*, **увеко́вечить** (-чу) *pf* immortalize; perpetuate.

увёл *etc.: see* **увести́**

увеличе́ние increase; magnification; enlargement. **увели́чивать** *impf*, **увели́чить** (-чу) *pf* increase; magnify; enlarge; **~ся** increase, grow. **увеличи́тель** *m* enlarger. **увеличи́тельн|ый** magnifying; enlarging; **~ое стекло́** magnifying glass.

у|венча́ть *pf*, **уве́нчивать** *impf* crown; **~ся** be crowned.

увере́нность confidence; certainty. **уве́ренный** confident; sure; certain. **уве́рить** *pf* (*impf* **уверя́ть**) assure; convince; **~ся** satisfy o.s.; be convinced.

уверну́ться (-ну́сь, -нёшься) *pf*, **увёртываться** *impf* **от**+*gen* evade. **уве́ртка** dodge, evasion; subterfuge; *pl* wiles. **уве́ртливый** evasive, shifty.

увертю́ра overture.

уверя́ть(ся *impf of* **уве́рить(ся**

увеселе́ние amusement, entertainment. **увесели́тельный** entertainment; pleasure. **увеселя́ть** *impf* amuse, entertain.

уве́систый weighty.

увести́ (-еду́, -едёшь; -ёл, -а́) *pf* (*impf* **уводи́ть**) take (away); walk off with.

уве́чить (-чу) *impf* maim, cripple. **уве́чный** maimed, crippled; *sb* cripple. **уве́чье** maiming; injury.

уве́шать *pf*, **уве́шивать** *impf* hang (+*instr* with).

увеща́ть *impf*, **увещева́ть** *impf* exhort, admonish.

у|ви́дать(ся *see*. **у|ви́деть(ся** (-ижу(сь) *pf*.

уви́ливать *impf*, **увильну́ть** (-ну́, -нёшь) *pf* **от**+*gen* dodge; evade.

увлажни́ть *pf*, **увлажня́ть** *impf* moisten.

увлека́тельный fascinating. **увлека́ть** *impf*, **увле́чь** (-еку́, -ечёшь; -ёк, -ла́) *pf* carry away; fascinate; **~ся** be carried away; become mad (+*instr* about). **увлече́ние** animation; passion; crush.

уво́д withdrawal; stealing. **уводи́ть** (-ожу́, -о́дишь) *impf of* **увести́**

увози́ть (-ожу́, -о́зишь) *impf of* **увезти́**

уво́лить *pf*, **увольня́ть** *impf* discharge, dismiss; retire; **~ся** be discharged, dismiss, retire. **увольне́ние** discharge, dismissal.

увы́ *int* alas!

увяда́ть *impf of* **увя́нуть**. **увя́дший** withered.

увяза́ть[1] *impf of* **увя́знуть**.

увяза́ть[2] (-яжу́, -я́жешь) *pf* (*impf* **увя́зывать**) tie up; pack up; co-ordinate; **~ся** pack; tag along. **увя́зка** tying up; co-ordination.

у|вя́знуть (-ну; -я́з) *pf* (*impf also* **увяза́ть**) get bogged down.

увя́зывать(ся *impf of* **увяза́ть(ся**

у|вя́нуть (-ну) *pf* (*impf also* **увяда́ть**) fade, wither.

угада́ть *pf*, **уга́дывать** *impf* guess.

уга́р carbon monoxide (poisoning); ecstasy. **уга́рный газ** carbon monoxide.

угаса́ть *impf*, **у|га́снуть** (-нет;

-ác) *pf* go out; die down.

угле- in *comb* coal; charcoal; carbon. **углево́д** carbohydrate. ~**водоро́д** hydrocarbon. ~**добы́ча** coal extraction. ~**кислота́** carbonic acid; carbon dioxide. ~**ки́слый** carbonate (of). ~**ро́д** carbon.

углово́й corner; angular.

углуби́ть (-блю́) *pf*, **углубля́ть** *impf* deepen; ~**ся** deepen; delve deeply; become absorbed. **углубле́ние** depression, dip; deepening. **углублённый** deepened; profound; absorbed.

угна́ть (угоню́, -о́нишь; -а́л, -а́, -о) *pf* (*impf* **угоня́ть**) drive away; despatch; steal; ~**ся за**+*instr* keep pace with.

угнета́тель *m* oppressor. **угнета́ть** *impf* oppress; depress. **угнете́ние** oppression; depression. **угнетённый** oppressed; depressed.

угова́ривать *impf*, **уговори́ть** *pf* persuade; ~**ся** arrange, agree. **угово́р** persuasion; agreement.

уго́да: в уго́ду +*dat* to please. **угоди́ть** (-ожу́) *pf*, **угожда́ть** *impf* fall; get; bang; (+*dat*) hit; +*dat* or **на**+*acc* please. **уго́дливый** obsequious. **уго́дно** *predic*+*dat*: **как вам** ~ as you wish; **что вам** ~? what would you like?; *partl* **кто** ~ anyone (you like); **что** ~ anything (you like).

уго́дье (*gen pl* -ий) land.

у́гол (угла́, *loc* -у́) corner; angle.

уголо́вник criminal. **уголо́вный** criminal.

уголо́к (-лка́, *loc* -у́) corner.

у́голь (у́гля́; *pl* у́гли, -ей *or* -е́й) *m* coal; charcoal.

у́го́льник set square.

у́го́льный coal; carbon(ic).

угомони́ть *pf* calm down; ~**ся** calm down.

уго́н driving away; stealing. **угоня́ть** *impf of* **угна́ть**

угора́ть *impf*, **угоре́ть** (-рю́) *pf* get carbon monoxide poisoning; be mad. **угоре́лый** mad; possessed.

у́горь[1] (угря́) *m* eel.

у́горь[2] (угря́) *m* blackhead.

угости́ть (-ощу́) *pf*, **угоща́ть** *impf* entertain; treat. **угоще́ние** entertaining, treating; refreshments.

угрожа́ть *impf* threaten. **угро́за** threat, menace.

угро́зыск *abbr* criminal investigation department.

угрызе́ние pangs.

угрю́мый sullen, morose.

удава́ться (удаётся) *impf o,*

удави́ться

у|**дави́ть**(**ся** (-влю́(сь, -ви́шь(ся) *pf*. **уда́вка** running-knot half hitch.

удале́ние removal; sending away; moving off. **удали́ть** *pf* (*impf* **удаля́ть**) remove; send away; move away; ~**ся** move off, away; retire.

удало́й, уда́лый (-а́л, -а́, -о) daring, bold. **у́даль, уда́ль**(**ство́** daring, boldness.

удаля́ть(**ся** *impf of* **удали́ть**(**ся**

уда́р blow; stroke; attack; kick; thrust; seizure; bol **ударе́ние** accent; stress; emphasis. **уда́рить** *pf*, **ударя́т** *impf* (*impf also* **бить**) strike; hit; beat; ~**ся** strike, h +**в**+*acc* break into; burst in to. **уда́рник, -ница** shock worker. **уда́рный** percussion shock; stressed; urgent.

уда́ться (-а́стся; -аду́тся; -а́лся; -ла́сь) *pf* (*impf* **удава́ться**) succeed, be a success; *impers* +*dat* +*inf* succeed, manage; мне удало́сь найти́ рабо́ту I managed to find a job. **уда́ча** good luck; success. **уда́чный** successful; felicitous.

удва́ивать *impf*, **удво́ить** (-о́ю) *pf* double, redouble. **удвое́ние** (re)doubling.

уде́л lot, destiny.

удели́ть *pf* (*impf* **уделя́ть**) spare, give.

уделя́ть *impf of* **удели́ть**

удержа́ние deduction; retention, keeping. **удержа́ть** (-жу́, -жишь) *pf*, **уде́рживать** *impf* hold (on to); retain; restrain; suppress; deduct; ~ся hold out; stand firm; refrain (from).

удеру́ *etc.: see* **удра́ть**

удешеви́ть (-влю́) *pf*, **удешевля́ть** *impf* reduce the price of.

удиви́тельный surprising; amazing; wonderful. **удиви́ть** (-влю́) *pf*, **удивля́ть** *impf* surprise, amaze; ~ся be surprised, be amazed. **удивле́ние** surprise, amazement.

удила́ (-и́л) *pl* bit.

удилище fishing-rod.

удира́ть *impf of* **удра́ть**

уди́ть (ужу́, у́дишь) *impf* fish for; ~ ры́бу fish; ~ся bite.

удлине́ние lengthening; extension. **удлини́ть** *pf*, **удлиня́ть** *impf* lengthen; extend; ~ся become longer; be extended.

удо́бно *adv* comfortably; conveniently. **удо́бный** comfortable; convenient.

удобова́римый digestible.

удобре́ние fertilization; fertilizer. **удо́брить** *pf*, **удобря́ть** *impf* fertilize.

удо́бство comfort; convenience.

удовлетворе́ние satisfaction; gratification. **удовлетворён-ный** (-рён, -а́) satisfied. **удовлетвори́тельный** satisfactory. **удовлетвори́ть** *pf*, **удовлетворя́ть** *impf* satisfy; +*dat* meet; +*instr* supply with; ~ся be satisfied.

удово́льствие pleasure. **у|до-во́льствоваться** *pf*.

удо́й milk-yield; milking.

удостове́рение certification; certificate; ~ ли́чности identity card. **удостове́рить** *pf*, **удостоверя́ть** *impf* certify, witness; ~ся make sure (в+*prep* of), assure o.s.

удосто́ить *pf* (*impf* **удоста́ивать**) make an award to; +*gen* award; +*instr* favour with; ~ся +*gen* be awarded; be favoured with.

у́дочка (fishing-)rod.

удра́ть (удеру́, -ёшь; удра́л, -а́, -о) *pf* (*impf* **удира́ть**) make off.

удруча́ть *impf*, **удручи́ть** (-чу́) *pf* depress. **удручён-ный** (-чён, -а́) depressed.

удуша́ть *impf*, **удуши́ть** (-шу́, -шишь) *pf* stifle, suffocate. **удуше́ние** suffocation. **уду́-шливый** stifling. **уду́шье** asthma; asphyxia.

уедине́ние solitude; seclusion. **уединённый** secluded; lonely. **уедини́ться** *pf*, **уединя́ться** *impf* seclude o.s.

уе́зд uyezd, District.

уезжа́ть *impf*, **уе́хать** (уе́ду) *pf* go away, depart.

уж[1] (-á) grass-snake.

уж[2]: *see* **уже́**[2]. **уж**[3], **уже́**[3] *partl* indeed; really.

у|жа́лить *pf*.

ужа́с horror, terror; *predic* it is awful. ужаса́ть *impf*, ужасну́ть (-ну́, -нёшь) *pf* horrify; ~ся be horrified, be terrified. ужа́сно *adv* terribly; awfully. ужа́сный awful, terrible.

уже́[1] *comp of* у́зкий

уже́[2], уж[2] *adv* already; ~ не no longer. уже́[3]: *see* уж[3]

уже́ние fishing.

ужива́ться *impf of* ужи́ться. ужи́вчивый easy to get on with.

ужи́мка grimace.

у́жин supper. у́жинать *impf* (*pf* по~) have supper.

ужи́ться (-иву́сь, -ивёшься; -и́лся, -ла́сь) *pf* (*impf* ужива́ться) get on.

ужу́ *see* уди́ть

узако́нивать *impf*, узако́нить *pf* legalize.

узбе́к, -е́чка Uzbek. Узбекиста́н Uzbekistan.

узда́ (*pl* -ы) bridle.

у́зел (узла́) knot; junction; centre; node; bundle.

у́зкий (у́зок, узка́, -о) narrow; tight; narrow-minded. узкоколе́йка narrow-gauge railway.

узлова́тый knotty. узлов|о́й junction; main, key; ~а́я ста́нция junction.

узнава́ть (-наю́, -наёшь) *impf*, узна́ть *pf* recognize; get to know; find out.

у́зник, у́зница prisoner.

узо́р pattern, design. узо́рчатый patterned.

у́зость narrowness; tightness.

узурпа́тор usurper. узурпи́ровать *impf & pf* usurp.

у́зы (уз) *pl* bonds, ties.

уйду́ *etc.*: *see* уйти́

у́йма lots (of).

уйму́ *etc.*: *see* уня́ть

уйти́ (уйду́, -дёшь; ушёл, ушла́) *pf* (*impf* уходи́ть) go away, leave, depart; escape; retire; bury o.s.; be used up; pass away.

ука́з decree; edict. указа́ние indication; instruction. ука́занный appointed, stated. указа́тель *m* indicator; gauge; index; directory. указа́тельный indicating; demonstrative; ~ па́лец index finger. указа́ть (-ажу́, -а́жешь) *pf*, ука́зывать *impf* show; indicate; point; point out. ука́зка pointer; orders.

ука́лывать *impf of* уколо́ть

ука́та́ть *pf*, ука́тывать[1] *impf* roll; flatten; wear out. укати́ть (-ачу́, -а́тишь) *pf*, ука́тывать[2] *impf* roll away; drive off; ~ся roll away.

укача́ть *pf*, ука́чивать *impf* rock to sleep; make sick.

укла́д structure; style; organization. укла́дка packing; stacking; laying; setting. укла́дчик packer; layer. укла́дывать(ся)[1] *impf of* уложи́ть(ся

укла́дываться[2] *impf o*· улечься

укло́н slope; incline; gradient; bias; deviation. уклоне́ние deviation; digression. уклони́ться *pf*, уклоня́ться *impf* deviate; ~от+*gen* turn (off aside); avoid; evade. укло́нчивый evasive.

уклю́чина rowlock.

уко́л prick; injection; thrust· уколо́ть (-лю́, -лешь) *pf* (*imp*· ука́лывать) prick; wound.

у|комплектова́ть *pf*, уком плекто́вывать *impf* com· plete; bring up to (ful· strength; man; +*instr* equi· with.

уко́р reproach.

укора́чивать *impf of* **укоро́тить**

укорени́ть *pf,* **укореня́ть** *impf* implant, inculcate; **~ся** take root.

укори́зна reproach. **укори́зненный** reproachful. **укори́ть** *pf (impf* **укоря́ть**) reproach (**в**+*prep* with).

укороти́ть (-очу́) *pf (impf* **укора́чивать**) shorten.

укоря́ть *impf of* **укори́ть**

уко́с (hay-)crop.

укра́дкой *adv* stealthily. **украду́** *etc.: see* **украсть**

Украи́на Ukraine. **украи́нец** (-нца) **украи́нка** Ukrainian. **украи́нский** Ukrainian.

укра́сить (-а́шу) *pf (impf* **украша́ть**) adorn, decorate; **~ся** be decorated; adorn o.s.

у|кра́сть (-аду́, -дёшь) *pf.*

украша́ть(ся) *impf of* **украсить(ся)**. **украше́ние** decoration; adornment.

укрепи́ть (-плю́) *pf,* **укрепля́ть** *impf* strengthen; fix; fortify; **~ся** become stronger; fortify one's position. **укрепле́ние** strengthening; reinforcement; fortification.

укро́мный secluded, cosy.

укро́п dill.

укроти́тель *m* (animal-)tamer. **укроти́ть** (-ощу́) *pf,* **укроща́ть** *impf* tame; curb; **~ся** become tame; calm down. **укроще́ние** taming.

укро́ю *etc.: see* **укрыть**

крупне́ние enlargement; amalgamation. **укрупни́ть** *pf,* **укрупня́ть** *impf* enlarge; amalgamate.

крыва́тель *m* harbourer. **укрыва́тельство** harbouring; receiving. **укрыва́ть** *impf,*

укры́ть (-ро́ю) *pf* cover; conceal, harbour; shelter; receive; **~ся** cover o.s.; take cover. **укры́тие** cover; shelter.

у́ксус vinegar.

уку́с bite; sting. **укуси́ть** (-ушу́, -у́сишь) *pf* bite; sting.

уку́тать (-а́ю) *pf,* **уку́тывать** *impf* wrap up; **~ся** wrap o.s. up.

укушу́ *etc.: see* **укусить**

ул. *abbr (of* у́лица) street, road.

ула́вливать *impf of* **улови́ть**

ула́дить (-а́жу) *pf,* **ула́живать** *impf* settle, arrange.

у́лей (у́лья) (bee)hive.

улета́ть *impf,* **улете́ть** (улечу́) *pf* fly (away). **улету́читься, улету́чиваться** (-чусь) *pf* evaporate; vanish.

уле́чься (уля́гусь, -я́жешься; улёгся, -гла́сь) *pf (impf* **укла́дываться**) lie down; settle; subside.

ули́ка clue; evidence.

ули́тка snail.

у́лица street; **на у́лице** in the street; outside.

улича́ть *impf,* **уличи́ть** (-чу́) *pf* establish the guilt of.

у́личный street.

уло́в catch. **улови́мый** perceptible; audible. **улови́ть** (-влю́, -вишь) *pf (impf* **ула́вливать**) catch; seize. **уло́вка** trick, ruse.

уложе́ние code. **уложи́ть** (-жу́, -жишь) *pf (impf* **укла́дывать**) lay; pack; pile; **~ спать** put to bed; **~ся** pack (up); fit in.

улуча́ть *impf,* **улучи́ть** (-чу́) *pf* find, seize.

улу́чшить *impf,* **улу́чшить** (-шу) *pf* improve; better; **~ся** improve; get better. **улучше́ние** improvement.

улыба́ться *impf,* **улыбну́ть-**

ся (-ну́сь, -нёшься) *pf* smile. **улы́бка** smile.

ультима́тум ultimatum.

ультра- *in comb* ultra-. **ультразвуково́й** supersonic. **~фиоле́товый** ultra-violet.

уля́гусь *etc.*: *see* **уле́чься**

ум (-а́) mind, intellect; head; **сойти́ с ~а́** go mad.

умали́ть *pf* (*impf* **умаля́ть**) belittle.

умалишённый mad; *sb* lunatic.

ума́лчивать *impf of* **умолча́ть**

умаля́ть *impf of* **умали́ть**

уме́лец (-льца) skilled craftsman. **уме́лый** able, skilful. **уме́ние** ability, skill.

уменьша́ть *impf*, **уме́ньшить** (-шу) *pf* reduce, diminish, decrease; **~ся** diminish, decrease, abate. **уменьше́ние** decrease, reduction; abatement. **уменьши́тельный** diminutive.

уме́ренность moderation. **уме́ренный** moderate; temperate.

умере́ть (умру́, -рёшь; у́мер, -ла́, -о) *pf* (*impf* **умира́ть**) die.

уме́рить *pf* (*impf* **умеря́ть**) moderate; restrain.

умертви́ть (-рщвлю́, -ртви́шь) *pf*, **умерщвля́ть** *impf* kill, destroy; mortify. **у́мерший** dead; *sb* the deceased. **умерщвле́ние** killing, destruction; mortification.

умеря́ть *impf of* **уме́рить**

умести́ть (-ещу́) *pf* (*impf* **умеща́ть**) fit in, find room for; **~ся** fit in, go in. **уме́стный** appropriate; pertinent; timely.

уме́ть (-е́ю) *impf* be able, know how.

умеща́ть(ся *impf of* **умести́ть(ся**

умиле́ние tenderness; emotion. **умили́ть** *pf*, **умиля́ть** *impf* move, touch; **~ся** be moved.

умира́ние dying. **умира́ть** *impf of* **умере́ть**. **умира́ющий** dying; *sb* dying person.

умиротворе́ние pacification; appeasement. **умиротвори́ть** *pf*, **умиротворя́ть** *impf* pacify; appease.

умне́ть (-е́ю) *impf* (*pf* **по~**) grow wiser. **у́мница** good girl; *m & f* clever person.

умножа́ть *impf*, **у|мно́жить** (-жу) *pf* multiply; increase; **~ся** increase, multiply. **умноже́ние** multiplication; increase. **умножи́тель** *m* multiplier.

у́мный (умён, умна́, у́мно́) clever, wise, intelligent. **умозаключе́ние** deduction; conclusion.

умоли́ть *pf* (*impf* **умоля́ть**) move by entreaties.

умолка́ть *impf*, **умо́лкнуть** (-ну; -о́лк) *pf* fall silent; stop. **умолча́ть** (-чу́) *pf* (*impf* **ума́лчивать**) fail to mention; hush up.

умоля́ть *impf of* **умоли́ть** beg, entreat.

умопомеша́тельство derangement.

умори́тельный incredibly funny, killing. **у|мори́ть** *pf* kill; exhaust.

умо́ю *etc.*: *see* **умы́ть. умр** *etc.*: *see* **умере́ть**

у́мственный mental, intellectual.

умудри́ть *pf*, **умудря́ть** *impf* make wiser; **~ся** contrive.

умыва́льная *sb* wash-room. **умыва́льник** wash-stand, wash-basin. **умыва́ть(ся** *impf of* **умы́ть(ся**

у́мысел (-сла) design, intention.

умы́ть (умо́ю) *pf* (*impf* **умыва́ть**) wash; **~ся** wash (o.s.).

умы́шленный intentional.

у|насле́довать *pf*.

унести́ (-су́, -сёшь; -ёс, -ла́) *pf* (*impf* **уноси́ть**) take away; carry off, make off with; **~сь** speed away; fly by; be carried (away).

универма́г *abbr* department store. **универса́льный** universal; all-round; versatile; all-purpose; **~ магази́н** department store; **~ое сре́дство** panacea. **универса́м** *abbr* supermarket.

университе́т university. **университе́тский** university.

унижа́ть *impf*, **уни́зить** (-и́жу) *pf* humiliate; **~ся** humble o.s.; stoop. **униже́ние** humiliation. **уни́женный** humble. **унизи́тельный** humiliating.

уника́льный unique.

унима́ть(ся *impf of* **уня́ть(ся**

унисо́н unison.

унита́з lavatory pan.

унифици́ровать *impf* & *pf* standardize.

уничижи́тельный pejorative.

уничтожа́ть *impf*, **уничто́жить** (-жу) *pf* destroy, annihilate; abolish; do away with. **уничтоже́ние** destruction, annihilation; abolition.

уноси́ть(ся (-ошу́(сь, -о́сишь(ся) *impf of* **унести́(сь**

у́нция ounce.

уныва́ть *impf* be dejected. **уны́лый** dejected; doleful, cheerless. **уны́ние** dejection, despondency.

уня́ть (уйму́, -мёшь; -я́л, -а́, -о) *pf* (*impf* **унима́ть**) calm, soothe; **~ся** calm down.

упа́док (-дка) decline; decay; **~ ду́ха** depression. **упа́дочнический** decadent. **упа́дочный** depressive; decadent.

у|пакова́ть *pf*, **упако́вывать** *impf* pack (up). **упако́вка** packing; wrapping. **упако́вщик** packer.

упа́сть (-аду́, -адёшь) *pf of* **па́дать**

упере́ть (упру́, -рёшь; -ёр) *pf*, **упира́ть** *impf* rest, lean; **~ на**+*acc* stress; **~ся** rest, lean; resist; +**в**+*acc* come up against.

упи́танный well-fed; fattened.

упла́та payment. **у|плати́ть** (-ачу́, -а́тишь) *pf*, **упла́чивать** *impf* pay.

уплотне́ние compression; condensation; consolidation; sealing. **уплотни́ть** *pf*, **уплотня́ть** *impf* condense; compress; pack more into.

уплыва́ть *impf*, **уплы́ть** (-ыву́, -ывёшь; -ыл, -а́, -о) *pf* swim or sail away; pass.

упова́ть *impf* +**на**+*acc* put one's trust in.

уподо́бить (-блю) *pf*, **уподобля́ться** *impf* +*dat* become like.

упое́ние ecstasy, rapture. **упои́тельный** intoxicating, ravishing.

уполза́ть *impf*, **уползти́** (-зу́, -зёшь; -о́лз, -зла́) *pf* creep away, crawl away.

уполномо́ченный *sb* (authorized) agent, representative; proxy. **уполномо́чивать**, **уполномо́чивать** *impf*, **уполномо́чить** (-чу) *pf* authorize, empower.

упомина́ние mention. **упомина́ть** *impf*, **упомяну́ть** (-ну́, -нешь) *pf* mention, refer to.

упо́р prop, support; в ~ point-blank; сде́лать ~ на+acc or prep lay stress on. упо́рный stubborn; persistent. упо́рство stubbornness; persistence. упо́рствовать impf be stubborn; persist (в+prep in).

упоря́дочивать impf, упоря́дочить (-чу) pf regulate, put in order.

употреби́тельный (widely-)used; common. употреби́ть (-блю́) pf, употребля́ть impf use. употребле́ние use; usage.

упра́ва justice.

управдо́м abbr manager (of block of flats). упра́виться (-влюсь) pf, управля́ться impf cope, manage; +c+instr deal with. управле́ние management; administration; direction; control; driving, steering; government. управля́емый снаря́д guided missile. управля́ть impf +instr manage, direct, run; govern; be in charge of; operate; drive. управля́ющий sb manager.

упражне́ние exercise. упражня́ть impf exercise, train; ~ся practise, train.

упраздни́ть pf, упраздня́ть impf abolish.

упра́шивать impf of упроси́ть

упрёк reproach. упрека́ть impf, упрекну́ть (-ну́, -нёшь) pf reproach.

упроси́ть (-ошу́, -о́сишь) pf (impf упра́шивать) entreat; prevail upon.

упрости́ть (-ощу́) pf (impf упроща́ть) (over-)simplify.

упро́чивать impf, упро́чить (-чу) pf strengthen, consolidate; ~ся be firmly established.

упрошу́ etc.: see упроси́ть

упроща́ть impf of упрости́ть. упрощённый (-щён, -а́) (over-)simplified.

упру́ etc.: see упере́ть

упру́гий elastic; springy. упру́гость elasticity; spring. упру́же comp of упру́гий

упря́жка harness; team. упряжно́й draught. у́пряжь harness.

упря́миться (-млюсь) impf be obstinate; persist. упря́мство obstinacy; persistence. упря́мый obstinate; persistent.

упуска́ть impf, упусти́ть (-ущу́, -у́стишь) pf let go, let slip; miss. упуще́ние omission; slip; negligence.

ура́ int hurrah!

уравне́ние equalization; equation. ура́внивать impf, уравня́ть pf equalize. уравни́тельный equalizing, levelling. уравнове́сить (-е́шу) pf, уравнове́шивать impf balance; counterbalance. уравнове́шенность composure уравнове́шенный balanced composed.

урага́н hurricane; storm.

ура́льский Ural.

ура́н uranium; Uranus. ура́новый uranium.

урва́ть (-ву́, -вёшь; -а́л, -а́, -о pf (impf урыва́ть) snatch.

урегули́рование regulation settlement. у|регули́роват pf.

уре́зать (-е́жу) pf, уреза́ть уре́зывать impf cut of shorten; reduce.

у́рка m & f (sl) lag, convict.

у́рна urn; litter-bin.

у́ровень (-вня) m level; stand ard.

уро́д freak, monster.

уроди́ться (-ожу́сь) *pf* ripen; grow.

уро́дливость deformity; ugliness. **уро́дливый** deformed; ugly; bad. **уро́довать** *impf* (*pf* **из~**) disfigure; distort. **уро́дство** disfigurement; ugliness.

урожа́й harvest; crop; abundance. **урожа́йность** yield; productivity. **урожа́йный** productive, high-yield.

урождённый née. **уроже́нец** (-нца) **уроже́нка** native. **урожу́сь** *see* **уроди́ться**

уро́к lesson.

уро́н loss; damage. **урони́ть** (-ню́, -нишь) *pf of* **роня́ть**

урча́ть (-чу́) *impf* rumble.

урыва́ть *impf of* **урва́ть**. **уры́вками** *adv* in snatches, by fits and starts.

ус (*pl* -ы́) whisker; tendril; moustache.

усади́ть (-ажу́, -а́дишь) *pf*, **уса́живать** *impf* seat, offer a seat; plant. **уса́дьба** (*gen pl* -деб *or* -дб) country estate; farmstead. **уса́живаться** *impf of* **усе́сться**

уса́тый moustached; whiskered.

усва́ивать *impf*, **усво́ить** *pf* master; assimilate; adopt. **усвое́ние** mastering; assimilation; adoption.

усе́рдие zeal; diligence. **усе́рдный** zealous; diligent.

усе́сться (уся́дусь, -е́лся) *pf* (*impf* **уса́живаться**) take a seat; settle down (to).

усиде́ть (-ижу́) *pf* remain seated; hold down a job. **уси́дчивый** assiduous.

у́сик tendril; runner; antenna; *pl* small moustache.

усиле́ние strengthening; reinforcement; intensification; am-

plification. **уси́ленный** intensified, increased; earnest. **уси́ливать** *impf*, **уси́лить** *pf* intensify, increase; amplify; strengthen, reinforce; **~ся** increase, intensify; become stronger. **уси́лие** effort. **усили́тель** *m* amplifier; booster.

ускака́ть (-ачу́, -а́чешь) *pf* skip off; gallop off.

ускольза́ть *impf*, **ускользну́ть** (-ну́, -нёшь) *pf* slip off; steal away; escape.

ускоре́ние acceleration. **ускоренный** accelerated; rapid; crash. **ускори́тель** accelerator. **ускорить** *pf*, **ускоря́ть** *impf* quicken; accelerate; hasten; **~ся** accelerate, be accelerated; quicken.

усло́вие condition. **усло́виться** (-влюсь) *pf*, **усло́вливаться**, **усла́вливаться** *impf* agree; arrange. **усло́вленный** agreed, fixed. **усло́вность** convention. **усло́вный** conditional; conditioned; conventional; agreed; relative.

усложне́ние complication. **усложни́ть** *pf*, **усложня́ть** *impf* complicate; **~ся** become complicated.

услу́га service; good turn. **услу́жливый** obliging.

услыха́ть (-ышу) *pf*, **услы́шать** (-ышу) *pf* hear; sense; scent.

усма́тривать *impf of* **усмотре́ть**

усмеха́ться *impf*, **усмехну́ться** (-ну́сь, -нёшься) *pf* smile; grin; smirk. **усме́шка** smile; grin; sneer.

усмире́ние pacification; suppression. **усмири́ть** *pf*, **усмиря́ть** *impf* pacify; calm; suppress.

усмотре́ние discretion, judgement. усмотре́ть (-рю, -ришь) pf (impf усма́тривать) perceive; see; regard; +за+instr keep an eye on.

усну́ть (-ну́, -нёшь) pf go to sleep.

усоверше́нствование advanced studies; improvement, refinement. у|соверше́нствовать(ся pf.

усомни́ться pf doubt.

успева́емость progress. успева́ть impf, успе́ть (-е́ю) pf have time; manage; succeed. успе́х success; progress. успе́шный successful.

успока́ивать impf, успоко́ить pf calm, quiet, soothe; ~ся calm down; abate. успока́ивающий calming, sedative. успокое́ние calming, soothing; calm; peace. успокои́тельн|ый calming; reassuring; ~ое sb sedative, tranquillizer.

уста́ (-т, -та́м) pl mouth.

уста́в regulations, statutes; charter.

уставля́ть (-та́ю, -ёшь) impf of уста́ть; не устава́я incessantly.

уста́вить (-влю) pf, уставля́ть impf set, arrange; cover, fill; direct; ~ся find room, go in; stare.

уста́лость tiredness. уста́лый tired.

устана́вливать impf, установи́ть (-влю, -вишь) pf put, set up; install; set; establish; fix; ~ся dispose o.s.; be established; set in. устано́вка putting, setting up; setting; plant, unit; directions. установле́ние establishment. устано́вленный

established, prescribed.

устану́ etc.: see уста́ть

устарева́ть impf, у|старе́ть (-е́ю) pf become obsolete; become antiquated. устаре́лый obsolete; antiquated, out-of-date.

уста́ть (-а́ну) pf (impf устава́ть) get tired.

устила́ть impf, устла́ть (-телю́, -те́лешь) pf cover; pave.

у́стный oral, verbal.

усто́й abutment; foundation; support. усто́йчивость stability, steadiness. усто́йчивый stable, steady. устоя́ть (-ою́) pf keep one's balance; stand firm; ~ся settle; become fixed.

устра́ивать(ся impf of устро́ить(ся

устране́ние removal, elimination. устрани́ть pf, устраня́ть impf remove; eliminate; ~ся resign, retire.

устраша́ть impf, устраши́ть (-шу́) pf frighten; ~ся be frightened.

устреми́ть (-млю́) pf, устремля́ть impf direct, fix; ~ся rush; be directed; concentrate. устремле́ние rush; aspiration.

у́стрица oyster.

устрои́тель m, ~ница organizer. устро́ить pf (impf устра́ивать) arrange, organize; make; cause; settle; put in order; place, fix up; get; suit; ~ся work out; manage; settle down; be found, get fixed up. устро́йство arrangement; construction; mechanism, device; system.

усту́п shelf, ledge. уступа́ть impf, уступи́ть (-плю́, -пишь) pf yield; give up; ~ доро́гу make way. **усту́пка** concession. **усту́пчивый** pliable; compliant.

устыди́ться (-ыжу́сь) *pf* (+*gen*) be ashamed (of).

усугу́бить (-блю) *pf*, **усугубля́ть** *impf* increase; aggravate.

усы́ *see* **ус**

усынови́ть (-влю́) *pf*, **усыновля́ть** *impf* adopt. **усыновле́ние** adoption.

усы́пать (-плю) *pf*, **усыпа́ть** *impf* strew, scatter.

усыпи́тельный soporific.

усыпи́ть (-плю́) *pf*, **усыпля́ть** *impf* put to sleep; lull; weaken.

уся́дусь *etc.*: *see* **усе́сться**

ута́ивать *impf*, **утаи́ть** *impf* conceal; keep secret.

ута́птывать *impf* *see* **утопта́ть**

ута́скивать *impf*, **утащи́ть** (-щу́, -щишь) *pf* drag off.

у́тварь utensils.

утверди́тельный affirmative. **утверди́ть** (-ржу́) *pf*, **утвержда́ть** *impf* confirm; approve; ratify; establish; assert; ~ся gain a foothold; become established; be confirmed. **утвержде́ние** approval; confirmation; ratification; assertion; establishment.

утека́ть *impf* *of* **уте́чь**

утёнок (-нка; *pl* утя́та, -я́т) duckling.

утепли́ть *pf*, **утепля́ть** *impf* warm.

утере́ть (утру́, -рёшь; утёр) *pf* (*impf* **утира́ть**) wipe (off, dry).

утерпе́ть (-плю́, -пишь) *pf* restrain o.s.

утёс cliff, crag.

уте́чка leak, leakage; escape;

loss. **уте́чь** (-еку́, -ечёшь; утёк, -ла́) *pf* (*impf* **утека́ть**) leak, escape; pass.

утеша́ть *impf*, **уте́шить** (-шу) *pf* console; ~ся console o.s. **утеше́ние** consolation. **утеши́тельный** comforting.

утилизи́ровать *impf* & *pf* utilize.

ути́ль *m*, **утильсырьё** scrap.

ути́ный duck, duck's.

утира́ть(ся *impf* *of* **утере́ть(ся**

утиха́ть *impf*, **ути́хнуть** (-ну; -их) *pf* abate, subside; calm down.

у́тка duck; canard.

уткну́ть (-ну́, -нёшь) *pf* bury; fix; ~ся bury o.s.

утоли́ть *pf* (*impf* **утоля́ть**) quench; satisfy; relieve.

утолще́ние thickening; bulge.

утоля́ть *impf* *of* **утоли́ть**

утоми́тельный tedious; tiring. **утоми́ть** (-млю́) *pf*, **утомля́ть** *impf* tire, fatigue; ~ся get tired. **утомле́ние** weariness. **утомлённый** weary.

у|**тону́ть** (-ну́, -нешь) *pf* drown, be drowned; sink.

утончённый refined.

у|**топи́ть(ся** (-плю́(сь, -пишь(ся) *pf*. **уто́пленник** drowned man.

утопи́ческий utopian. **уто́пия** Utopia.

утопта́ть (-пчу́, -пчешь) *pf* (*impf* **ута́птывать**) trample down.

уточне́ние more precise definition; amplification. **уточни́ть** *pf*, **уточня́ть** *impf* define more precisely; amplify.

утра́ивать *impf* *of* **утро́ить**

у|**трамбова́ть** *pf*, **утрамбо́вывать** *impf* ram, tamp; ~ся become flat.

утра́та loss. **утра́тить** (-а́чу) *pf*, **утра́чивать** *impf* lose.

у́тренний morning. **у́тренник** morning performance; early-morning frost.

утри́ровать *impf & pf* exaggerate.

у́тро (-а *or* -á, -у *or* -ý; *pl* -а, -ам *or* -ám) morning.

утро́ба womb; belly.

утро́ить *pf* (*impf* **утра́ивать**) triple, treble.

утру́ *etc.: see* **утере́ть**, **у́тро**

утружда́ть *impf* trouble, tire.

утю́г (-á) iron. **утю́жить** (-жу) *impf* (*pf* **вы́~**, **от~**) iron.

ух *int* oh, ooh, ah.

уха́ fish soup.

уха́б pot-hole. **уха́бистый** bumpy.

уха́живать *impf* за+*instr* tend; look after; court.

ухвати́ть (-ачу́, -а́тишь) *pf*, **ухва́тывать** *impf* seize; grasp; **~ся** за+*acc* grasp, lay hold of; set to; seize; jump at.

ухва́тка grip; skill; trick; manner.

ухитри́ться *pf*, **ухитря́ться** *impf* manage, contrive. **ухищре́ние** device, trick.

ухмы́лка smirk. **ухмыльну́ться** (-ну́сь, -нёшься) *pf*, **ухмыля́ться** *impf* smirk.

у́хо (*pl* у́ши, уше́й) ear; ear-flap.

ухо́д[1] за+*instr* care of; tending, looking after.

ухо́д[2] leaving, departure. **уходи́ть** (-ожу́, -о́дишь) *impf of* **уйти́**

ухудша́ть *impf*, **уху́дшить** (-шу) *pf* make worse; **~ся** get worse. **ухудше́ние** deterioration.

уцеле́ть (-е́ю) *pf* remain intact; survive.

уце́нивать *impf*, **уцени́ть** (-ню́, -нишь) *pf* reduce the price of.

уцепи́ть (-плю́, -пишь) *pf* catch hold of, seize; **~ся** за+*acc* catch hold of, seize; jump at.

уча́ствовать *impf* take part; hold shares. **уча́ствующий** *sb* participant. **уча́стие** participation; share; sympathy.

участи́ть (-ащу́) *pf* (*impf* **учаща́ть**) make more frequent; **~ся** become more frequent, quicken.

участли́вый sympathetic. **уча́стник** participant. **уча́сток** (-тка) plot; part, section; sector; district; field, sphere. **у́часть** lot, fate.

учаща́ть(ся *impf of* **участи́ть(ся**

уча́щийся *sb* student; pupil.

учёба studies; course; training. **уче́бник** text-book. **уче́бный** educational; school; training. **уче́ние** learning; studies; apprenticeship; teaching; doctrine; exercise.

учени́к (-á), **учени́ца** pupil; apprentice; disciple. **учени́ческий** pupil's(s); apprentice('s); unskilled; crude. **учёность** learning, erudition. **учёный** learned; scholarly; academic; scientific; **~ая сте́пень** (*university*) degree; **~ый** *sb* scholar; scientist.

уче́сть (учту́, -тёшь; учёл, учла́) *pf* (*impf* **учи́тывать**) take stock of; take into account; discount. **учёт** stock-taking; calculation; taking into account; registration; discount; **без ~а** +*gen* disregarding; **взять на ~** register. **учётный** registration; discount.

учи́лище (*specialist*) school.

у|чини́ть *pf,* **учиня́ть** *impf* make; carry out; commit.

учи́тель (*pl* -я́) *m,* **учи́тельница** teacher. **учи́тельск|ий** teacher's; teachers'; **~ая** *sb* staff-room.

учи́тывать *impf of* **уче́сть**

учи́ть (учу́, у́чишь) *impf* (*pf* **вы́~, на~, об~**) teach; be a teacher; learn; **~ся** be a student; +*dat or inf* learn, study.

учреди́тельный constituent. **учреди́ть** (-ежу́) *pf,* **учрежда́ть** *impf* found, establish. **учрежде́ние** founding; establishment; institution.

учти́вый civil, courteous.

учту́ *etc.: see* **уче́сть**

уша́нка hat with ear-flaps.

ушёл *etc.: see* **уйти́. у́ши** *etc.: see* **у́хо**

уши́бо injury; bruise. **ушиба́ть** *impf,* **ушиби́ть** (-бу́, -бёшь; ушиб) *pf* injure; bruise; hurt; **~ся** hurt o.s.

ушко́ (*pl* -и́, -о́в) eye; tab.

ушно́й ear, aural.

уще́лье ravine, gorge, canyon.

ущеми́ть (-млю́) *pf,* **ущемля́ть** *impf* pinch, jam; limit; encroach on; hurt. **ущемле́ние** pinching, jamming; limitation; hurting.

уще́рб detriment; loss; damage; prejudice. **уще́рбный** waning.

ущипну́ть (-ну́, -нёшь) *pf of* **щипа́ть**

Уэ́льс Wales. **уэ́льский** Welsh.

ую́т cosiness, comfort. **ую́тный** cosy, comfortable.

уязви́мый vulnerable. **уязви́ть** (-влю́) *pf,* **уязвля́ть** *impf* wound, hurt.

уясни́ть *pf,* **уясня́ть** *impf* understand, make out.

Ф

фа́брика factory. **фабрика́нт** manufacturer. **фабрика́т** finished product, manufactured product. **фабрикова́ть** *impf* (*pf* с~) fabricate, forge. **фабри́чн|ый** factory; manufacturing; factory-made; **~ая ма́рка, ~ое клеймо́** trade-mark.

фа́була plot, story.

фаго́т bassoon.

фа́за phase; stage.

фаза́н pheasant.

фа́зис phase.

файл (*comput*) file.

фа́кел torch, flare.

факс fax.

факси́миле *neut indecl* facsimile.

факт fact; **соверши́вшийся ~** fait accompli. **факти́чески** *adv* virtually; virtually. **факти́ческий** actual; real; virtual.

фа́ктор factor.

факту́ра texture; style, execution.

факультати́вный optional. **факульте́т** faculty, department.

фа́лда tail (*of coat*).

фальсифика́тор falsifier, forger. **фальсифика́ция** falsification; adulteration; forgery. **фальсифици́ровать** *impf* & *pf* falsify; forge; adulterate. **фальши́вить** (-влю) *impf* (*pf* с~) be a hypocrite; sing or play out of tune. **фальши́вка** forged document. **фальши́вый** false; spurious; forged; artificial; out of tune. **фальшь** deception; falseness.

фами́лия surname. **фамилья́рничать** be over-familiar. **фамилья́рность** (over-)familiarity. **фамилья́рный** (over-)familiar; unceremonious.

фанати́зм fanaticism. **фана́тик** fanatic.

фане́ра veneer; plywood.

фанта́зёр dreamer, visionary. **фантази́ровать** impf (pf c~) dream; make up, dream up; improvise. **фанта́зия** fantasy; fancy; imagination; whim. **фанта́стика** fiction, fantasy. **фантасти́ческий, фантасти́чный** fantastic.

фа́ра headlight.

фарао́н pharaoh; faro.

фарва́тер fairway, channel.

фармазо́н freemason.

фармаце́вт pharmacist.

фарс farce.

фа́ртук apron.

фарфо́р china; porcelain. **фарфо́ровый** china.

фарцо́вщик currency speculator.

фарш stuffing; minced meat. **фарширова́ть** impf (pf за~) stuff.

фаса́д façade.

фасова́ть impf (pf рас~) package.

фасо́ль kidney bean(s), French bean(s); haricot beans.

фасо́н cut; fashion; style; manner. **фасо́нный** shaped.

фата́ veil.

фатали́зм fatalism. **фата́льный** fatal.

фаши́зм Fascism. **фаши́ст** Fascist. **фаши́стский** Fascist.

фая́нс faience, pottery.

февра́ль (-я́) m February. **февра́льский** February.

федера́льный federal. **федера́ция** federation.

фееру́чес fairy-tale.

фейерве́рк firework(s).

фельдше́р (pl -á) -**ше́рица** (partly-qualified) medical assistant.

фельето́н feuilleton, feature.

фемини́зм feminism. **феминисти́ческий, фемини́стский** feminist.

фен (hair-)dryer.

феноме́н phenomenon. **феномена́льный** phenomenal.

феода́л feudal lord. **феодали́зм** feudalism. **феода́льный** feudal.

ферзь (-я́) m queen.

фе́рма[1] farm.

фе́рма[2] girder, truss.

ферма́та (mus) pause.

ферме́нт ferment.

фе́рмер farmer.

фестива́ль m festival.

фетр felt. **фе́тровый** felt.

фехтова́льщик, -щица fencer. **фехтова́ние** fencing. **фехтова́ть** impf fence.

фе́я fairy.

фиа́лка violet.

фиа́ско neut indecl fiasco.

фи́бра fibre.

фигля́р buffoon.

фигу́ра figure; court-card; (chess-)piece. **фигура́льный** figurative, metaphorical. **фигури́ровать** impf figure, appear. **фигури́ст, -и́стка** figure-skater. **фигу́рка** figurine, statuette; figure. **фигу́рный** figured; ~**ое ката́ние** figure-skating.

фи́зик physicist. **фи́зика** physics. **физио́лог** physiologist. **физиологи́ческий** physiological. **физиоло́гия** physiology. **физионо́мия** physiognomy; face, expression. **физиотерапе́вт** physiotherapist. **фи́зи́ческий** physical; physics.

физкульту́ра abbr P.E., gymnastics. **физкульту́рный** *abbr* gymnastic; athletic; ~ зал gymnasium.

фикса́ж fixer. **фикса́ция** fixing. **фикси́ровать** *impf & pf (pf also* за~) fix; record.

фикти́вный fictitious. ~ брак marriage of convenience. **фи́кция** fiction.

филантро́п philanthropist. **филантро́пия** philanthropy.

филармо́ния philharmonic society; concert hall.

филатели́ст philatelist.

филе́ *neut indecl* sirloin; fillet.

филиа́л branch.

фили́стер philistine.

фило́лог philologist. **филологи́ческий** philological. **филоло́гия** philology.

фило́соф philosopher. **филосо́фия** philosophy. **филосо́фский** philosophical.

фильм film. **фильмоско́п** projector.

фильтр filter. **фильтрова́ть** *impf (pf* про~) filter.

фина́л finale; final. **фина́льный** final.

финанси́ровать *impf & pf* finance. **фина́нсовый** financial. **фина́нсы** (-ов) *pl* finance, finances.

фи́ник date.

фи́ниш finish; finishing post.

фи́нка Finn. **Финля́ндия** Finland. **финля́ндский** Finnish.

финн Finn. **фи́нский** Finnish.

фиоле́товый violet.

фи́рма firm; company. **фи́рменное блю́до** speciality of the house.

фисгармо́ния harmonium.

фити́ль (-я́) *m* wick; fuse.

флаг flag. **фла́гман** flagship.

флако́н bottle, flask.

фланг flank; wing.

флане́ль flannel.

флегмати́чный phlegmatic.

фле́йта flute.

фле́ксия inflexion. **флекти́вный** inflected.

фли́гель (*pl* -я́) *m* wing; annexe.

флирт flirtation. **флиртова́ть** *impf* flirt.

флома́стер felt-tip pen.

фло́ра flora.

флот fleet. **фло́тский** naval.

флю́гер (*pl* -á) weather-vane.

флюоресце́нтный fluorescent.

флюс[1] gumboil, abscess.

флюс[2] (*pl* -ы) flux.

фля́га flask; churn. **фля́жка** flask.

фойе́ *neut indecl* foyer.

фо́кус[1] trick.

фо́кус[2] focus. **фокуси́ровать** *impf* focus.

фо́кусник conjurer, juggler.

фолиа́нт folio.

фольга́ foil.

фолькло́р folklore.

фон background.

фона́рь small lamp; torch. **фона́рный** lamp; ~ столб lamp-post. **фона́рь** (-я́) *m* lantern; lamp; light.

фонд fund; stock; reserves.

фоне́тика phonetics. **фонети́ческий** phonetic.

фонта́н fountain.

форе́ль trout.

фо́рма form; shape; mould; cast; uniform. **форма́льность** formality. **форма́льный** formal. **форма́т** format. **форма́ция** structure; stage; formation; mentality. **фо́рменный** uniform; proper, regular. **формирова́ние** forming; unit, formation. **формирова́ть** *impf (pf* с~) form; organize; ~ся form, develop.

формова́ть *impf (pf* с~)

form, shape; mould, cast.
фо́рмула formula. **формули́ровать** impf & pf (pf also c~) formulate. **формули́ровка** formulation; wording; formula. **формуля́р** logbook; library card.

форси́ровать impf & pf force; speed up.

форсу́нка sprayer; injector.

фортепья́но neut indecl piano.

фо́рточка small hinged (window)pane.

форту́на fortune.

фо́рум forum.

фо́сфор phosphorus.

фо́то neut indecl photo(graph).

фото- in comb photo-, photoelectric. **фотоаппара́т** camera. **~бума́га** photographic paper. **~гени́чный** photogenic. **фото́граф** photographer. **~графи́ровать** impf (pf c~) photograph. **~графи́роваться** be photographed, have one's photograph taken. **~графи́ческий** photographic. **~гра́фия** photography; photograph; photographer's studio. **~ко́пия** photocopy. **~люби́тель** m amateur photographer. **~объекти́в** (camera) lens. **~репортёр** press photographer. **~хро́ника** news in pictures. **~элеме́нт** photoelectric cell.

фрагме́нт fragment.

фра́за sentence; phrase. **фразеоло́гия** phraseology.

фрак tail-coat, tails.

фракцио́нный fractional; factional. **фра́кция** fraction; faction.

франк franc.

франкмасо́н Freemason.

франт dandy.

Фра́нция France. **францу́-**

же́нка Frenchwoman. **францу́з** Frenchman. **францу́зский** French.

фрахт freight. **фрахтова́ть** impf (pf за~) charter.

фрега́т frigate.

фрезеро́вщик milling machine operator.

фре́ска fresco.

фронт (pl -ы́, -о́в) front. **фронтови́к** (-á) front-line soldier. **фронтово́й** front(-line).

фронто́н pediment.

фрукт fruit. **фрукто́вый** fruit; **~ сад** orchard.

фтор fluorine. **фто́ристый** fluorine; fluoride. **~ ка́льций** calcium fluoride.

фу int ugh! oh!

фуга́нок (-нка) smoothing-plane.

фуга́с landmine. **фуга́сный** high-explosive.

фундаме́нт foundation. **фундамента́льный** solid, sound; main; basic.

функциона́льный functional. **функциони́ровать** impf function. **фу́нкция** function.

фунт pound.

фура́ж (-á) forage, fodder. **фура́жка** peaked cap, forage-cap.

фурго́н van; caravan.

фут foot; foot-rule. **футбо́л** football. **футболи́ст** footballer. **футбо́лка** football jersey, sports shirt. **футбо́льный** football; **~ мяч** football.

футля́р case, container.

футури́зм futurism.

фуфа́йка jersey; sweater.

фы́ркать impf, **фы́ркнуть** (-ну) pf snort.

фюзеля́ж fuselage.

X

халат dressing-gown. **халат-ный** careless, negligent.

халтура pot-boiler; hackwork; money made on the side. **халтурщик** hack.

хам boor, lout. **хамский** boorish, loutish. **хамство** boorishness, loutishness.

хамелеон chameleon.

хан khan.

хандра depression. **хандрить** (*pf* be depressed.

ханжа hypocrite. **ханжеский** sanctimonious, hypocritical.

хаос chaos. **хаотичный** chaotic.

характер character. **характеризовать** *impf & pf* (*pf* also **о~**) describe; characterize; **~ся** be characterized. **характеристика** reference; description. **характерный** characteristic; distinctive; character.

харкать *impf*, **харкнуть** (-ну) *pf* spit.

хартия charter.

хата peasant hut.

хвала praise. **хвалебный** laudatory. **хвалёный** highly-praised. **хвалить** (-лю, -лишь) *impf* (*pf* по~) praise; **~ся** boast.

хвастать(ся *impf* (*pf* по~) boast. **хвастливый** boastful. **хвастовство** boasting. **хвастун** (-а) boaster.

хватать[1] *impf*, **хватить** (-ачу, -атишь) *pf* (*pf also* **схватить**) snatch, seize; grab; **~ся** remember; +*gen* realize the absence of; +**за**+*acc* snatch at, clutch at; take up.

хватать[2] *impf*, **хватить** (-атит) *pf*, *impers* (+*gen*) suffice, be

enough; last out; **времени не хватало** there was not enough time; **у нас не хватает денег** we haven't enough money; **хватит!** that will do! **ещё не хватало!** that's all we needed! **хватка** grasp, grip; method; skill.

хвойный coniferous; **~ые** *sb pl* conifers.

хворать *impf* be ill.

хворост brushwood; (*pastry*) straws. **хворостина** stick, switch.

хвост (-а) tail; tail-end. **хвостик** tail. **хвостовой** tail.

хвоя needle(s); (*coniferous*) branch(es).

херувим cherub.

хибар(к)а shack, hovel.

хижина shack, hut.

хилый (-л, -á, -о) sickly.

химера chimera.

химик chemist. **химикат** chemical. **химический** chemical. **химия** chemistry.

химчистка dry-cleaning; dry-cleaner's.

хина, хинин quinine.

хирург surgeon. **хирургический** surgical. **хирургия** surgery.

хитрец (-а) cunning person. **хитрить** *impf* (*pf* с~) use cunning; be crafty. **хитрость** cunning; ruse; skill; intricacy. **хитрый** cunning; skilful; intricate.

хихикать *impf*, **хихикнуть** (-ну) *pf* giggle, snigger.

хищение theft; embezzlement. **хищник** predator, bird *or* beast of prey. **хищнический** predatory; rapacious; **~ые птицы** birds of prey.

хладнокровие coolness, composure. **хладнокровный** cool, composed.

хлам rubbish.

хлеб (pl -ы, -ов or -á, -óв) bread; loaf; grain. **хлеба́ть** impf, **хлебну́ть** (-ну́, -нёшь) pf gulp down; baker's. **хле́бный** bread; baker's; grain. **хлебозаво́д** (gen pl -рен) bakery. **хлебопека́рня** (gen pl -рен) bakery.

хлев (loc -ý, pl -á) cow-shed.

хлеста́ть (-ещу́, -е́щешь) impf, **хлестну́ть** (-ну́, -нёшь) pf lash; whip.

хлоп int bang! **хло́пать** impf (pf **хло́пнуть**) bang; slap; ~ (в ладо́ши) clap.

хлопково́дство cotton-growing. **хло́пковый** cotton.

хло́пнуть (-ну) pf of **хло́пать**

хлопо́к[1] (-пка́) clap.

хло́пок[2] (-пка) cotton.

хлопота́ть (-очу́, -о́чешь) impf (pf по~) busy o.s.; bustle about; take trouble; +о+prep or за+acc petition for. **хлопотли́вый** troublesome; exacting; busy, bustling. **хло́поты** (-о́т) pl trouble; efforts.

хлопчатобума́жный cotton.

хло́пья (-ьев) pl flakes.

хлор chlorine. **хло́ристый, хло́рный** chlorine; chloride. **хло́рка** bleach. **хлорофи́лл** chlorophyll. **хлорофо́рм** chloroform.

хлы́нуть (-нет) pf gush, pour.

хлыст (-á) whip, switch.

хмеле́ть (-е́ю) impf (pf за~, о~) get tipsy. **хмель** (loc -ю́) m hop, hops; drunkenness; во хмелю́ tipsy. **хмельно́й** (-лён, -льна́) drunk; intoxicating.

хму́рить impf (pf на~): ~ бро́ви knit one's brows; ~ся frown; become gloomy; be overcast. **хму́рый** gloomy; overcast.

хны́кать (-ы́чу or -аю) impf whimper, snivel.

хо́бби neut indecl hobby.

хо́бот trunk. **хобото́к** (-тка́) proboscis.

ход (loc -ý, pl -ы, -ов or -ы́ or -á, -óв) motion; going; speed; course; operation; stroke; move; manoeuvre; entrance; passage; в ~ý in demand; дать за́дний ~ reverse; пусти́ть в ~ set in motion; на ~ý in transit, on the move; in motion; in operation; по́лным ~ом at full speed; пусти́ть в ~ start, set in motion; три часа́ ~у three hours' journey. **хода́тайство** petitioning; application. **хода́тайствовать** impf (pf по~) petition, apply. **ходи́ть** (хожу́, хо́дишь) impf walk; go; run; pass; go round; lead; play; move; wear; +в+prep wear; +за+instr look after. **хо́дкий** (-док, -дка́, -о) fast; marketable; popular. **ходьба́** walking; walk. **ходя́чий** walking; able to walk; popular; current.

хозрасчёт abbr (of хозя́йственный расчёт) self-financing system.

хозя́ин (pl -я́ева, -я́ев) owner, proprietor; master; boss; landlord; host; хозя́ева по́ля home team. **хозя́йка** owner; mistress; hostess; landlady. **хозя́йничать** impf keep house; be in charge; lord it. **хозя́йственник** financial manager. **хозя́йственный** economic; household; economical. **хозя́йство** economy; housekeeping; equipment; farm; дома́шнее ~ housekeeping; се́льское ~ agriculture.

хоккеи́ст (ice-)hockey-player. **хокке́й** hockey, ice-hockey.

холе́ра cholera.

холестери́н cholesterol.

холл hall, vestibule.

холм (-á) hill. **холми́стый** hilly.

хо́лод (pl -á, -óв) cold; coldness; cold weather. **хо́лодно** adv coldly. **хо́лодный** (хо́лоден, -дна́, -о) cold; inadequate, thin; ~ое ору́жие cold steel.

холо́п serf.

холосто́й (хо́лост, -á) unmarried, single; bachelor; idle; blank. **холостя́к** (-á) bachelor.

холст (-á) canvas; linen.

холу́й (-луя́) m lackey.

хому́т (-á) (horse-)collar; burden.

хомя́к (-á) hamster.

хор (pl хо́ры) choir; chorus.

хорва́т, ~ка Croat. **Хорва́тия** Croatia. **хорва́тский** Croatian.

хорёк (-рька́) polecat.

хореографи́ческий choreographic. **хореогра́фия** choreography.

хори́ст member of a choir or chorus.

хорони́ть (-ню́, -нишь) impf (pf за~, по~, с~) bury.

хоро́шенький pretty; nice. **хороше́нько** adv properly, thoroughly. **хороше́ть** (-е́ю) impf (pf по~) grow prettier. **хоро́ший** (-óш, -á, -о́) good; nice; pretty, nice-looking; ~о́ adv well; nicely; all right! good.

хо́ры (хор or -óв) pl gallery.

хоте́ть (хочу́, хо́чешь, хоти́м) impf (pf за~) wish; +gen, acc want; ~ пить be thirsty; ~ сказа́ть mean; ~ся impers +dat want; мне хоте́лось бы I should like; мне хо́чется I want.

хоть conj although; even if; partl at least, if only; for example; ~ бы if only. **хотя́** conj although; ~ бы even if; if only.

хо́хот loud laugh(ter). **хохота́ть** (-очу́, -о́чешь) impf laugh loudly.

хочу́ etc.: see **хоте́ть**

храбре́ц (-á) brave man. **храбри́ться** make a show of bravery; pluck up courage. **хра́брость** bravery. **хра́брый** brave.

храм temple, church.

хране́ние keeping; storage; **ка́мера хране́ния** cloakroom, left-luggage office. **храни́лище** storehouse, depository. **храни́тель** m keeper, custodian; curator. **храни́ть** impf keep; preserve; ~ся be kept.

храпе́ть (-плю́) impf snore; snort.

хребе́т (-бта́) spine; (mountain) range; ridge.

хрен horseradish.

хрестома́тия reader.

хрип wheeze. **хрипе́ть** (-плю́) impf wheeze. **хри́плый** (-пл, -á, -о) hoarse. **хри́пнуть** (-ну; хрип) impf (pf о~) become hoarse. **хрипота́** hoarseness.

христиани́н (pl -áне, -áн), **христиа́нка** Christian. **христиа́нский** Christian. **христиа́нство** Christianity. **Христо́с** (-истá) Christ.

хром chromium; chrome. **хромати́ческий** chromatic. **хрома́ть** impf limp; be poor. **хромо́й** (хром, -á, -о) lame; sb lame person.

хромосо́ма chromosome. **хромота́** lameness.

хро́ник chronic invalid. **хро́ника** chronicle; news items; news-

reel. **хрони́ческий** chronic.
хронологи́ческий chronological. **хроноло́гия** chronology.
хру́пкий (-пок, -пка́, -о) fragile; frail. **хру́пкость** fragility; frailness.
хруст crunch; crackle.
хруста́ль (-я́) m cut glass; crystal. **хруста́льный** cut-glass; crystal; crystal-clear.
хрусте́ть (-ущу́) impf, **хру́стнуть** (-ну) pf crunch; crackle.
хрю́кать impf, **хрю́кнуть** (-ну) pf grunt.
хрящ (-а́) cartilage, gristle. **хрящево́й** cartilaginous, gristly.
худе́ть (-е́ю) impf (pf по~) grow thin.
ху́до harm; evil. **ху́до** adv ill, badly.
худоба́ thinness.
худо́жественный art, arts; artistic; ~ **фильм** feature film. **худо́жник** artist.
худо́й[1] (худ, -а́, -о) thin, lean.
худо́й[2] (худ, -а́, -о) bad; full of holes; worn; **ему́ ху́до** he feels bad.
худоща́вый thin, lean.
ху́дший superl of **худо́й, плохо́й** (the) worst. **ху́же** comp of **худо́й, ху́до, плохо́й, пло́хо** worse.
хула́ abuse, criticism.
хулига́н hooligan. **хулига́нить** impf behave like a hooligan. **хулига́нство** hooliganism.
ху́нта junta.
ху́тор (pl -а́) farm; small village.

Ц

ца́пля (gen pl -пель) heron.
цара́пать impf, **цара́пнуть** (-ну) pf (also на~) scratch; scribble; ~**ся** scratch; scratch one another. **цара́-**

пина scratch. **цари́зм** tsarism. **цари́ть** impf reign, prevail. **цари́ца** tsarina; queen. **ца́рский** tsar's; royal; tsarist; regal. **ца́рство** kingdom; realm; reign. **ца́рствование** reign. **ца́рствовать** impf reign. **царь** (-я́) m tsar; king.
цвести́ (-ету́, -ете́шь; -ёл, -а́) impf flower, blossom; flourish.
цвет[1] (pl -а́) colour; ~ **лица́** complexion.
цвет[2] (loc -у́; pl -ы́) flower; prime; **в цвету́** in blossom.
цветни́к (-а́) flower-bed, flower-garden.
цветно́й coloured; colour; non-ferrous; ~**ая капу́ста** cauliflower; ~**о́е стекло́** stained glass.
цвето́во́й colour; ~**а́я слепота́** colour-blindness.
цвето́к (-тка́; pl цветы́ or цветки́, -о́в) flower. **цвето́чный** flower. **цвету́щий** flowering; prosperous.
цеди́ть (цежу́, це́дишь) impf strain, filter.
целе́бный curative, healing.
целево́й earmarked for a specific purpose. **целенапра́вленный** purposeful. **целесообра́зный** expedient. **целеустремлённый** (-ён, -ённа or -ена́) purposeful.
целико́м adv whole; entirely.
целина́ virgin lands, virgin soil. **цели́нный** virgin; ~**ые зе́мли** virgin lands.
цели́тельный healing, medicinal.
це́лить(ся impf (pf на~) aim, take aim.
целлофа́н cellophane.
целова́ть impf (pf по~) kiss; ~**ся** kiss.
це́лое sb whole; integer. **целому́дренный** chaste. **цело-**

му́дрие chastity. це́лостность integrity. це́лый (цел, -á, -о) whole; safe, intact.

цель target; aim, object, goal. це́льный (-лен, -льна́, -о) of one piece, solid; whole; integral; single. це́льность wholeness.

цеме́нт cement. цементи́ровать impf & pf cement. цеме́нтный cement.

цена́ (acc -у; pl -ы) price, cost; worth.

ценз qualification. це́нзор censor. цензу́ра censorship.

цени́тель m judge, connoisseur. цени́ть (-ню́, -нишь) impf value; appreciate. це́нность value; price; pl valuables; values. це́нный valuable.

цент cent. це́нтнер centner (100kg).

центр centre. централиза́ция centralization. централизова́ть impf & pf centralize. центра́льный central. центробе́жный centrifugal.

цепене́ть (-е́ю) impf (pf о~) freeze; become rigid. це́пкий tenacious; prehensile; sticky; obstinate. це́пкость tenacity.

цепля́ться impf за+acc clutch at; cling to.

цепно́й chain. цепо́чка chain; file. цепь (loc -и́; gen pl -е́й) chain; series; circuit.

церемо́ниться impf (pf по~) stand on ceremony. церемо́ния ceremony.

церковнославя́нский Church Slavonic. церко́вный ecclesiastical; church (-кви; gen pl -е́й) church.

цех (loc -у́; pl -и or -á) shop; section; guild.

цивилиза́ция civilization. цивилизо́ванный civilized. цивилизова́ть impf & pf

civilize.

циге́йка beaver lamb.

цикл cycle.

цико́рий chicory; top hat.

цили́ндр cylinder; top hat. цили́ндрический cylindrical.

цимба́лы (-áл) pl cymbals.

цинга́ scurvy.

цини́зм cynicism. ци́ник cynic. цини́чный cynical.

цинк zinc. ци́нковый zinc.

цино́вка mat.

цирк circus.

циркули́ровать impf circulate. ци́ркуль m (pair of) compasses; dividers. циркуля́р circular. циркуля́ция circulation.

цисте́рна cistern, tank.

цитаде́ль citadel.

цита́та quotation. цити́ровать impf (pf про~) quote.

ци́трус citrus. ци́трусовый citrous; ~ые sb pl citrus plants.

циферблат dial, face.

ци́фра figure; number, numeral. цифрово́й numerical, digital.

цо́коль m socle, plinth.

цыга́н (pl -е, -áн or -ы, -ов), -ráнка gipsy. цыга́нский gipsy.

цыплёнок (-нка pl -ля́та, -ля́т) chicken; chick.

цы́почки: на ~, на цы́почках on tip-toe.

Ч

чаба́н (-á) shepherd.

чад (loc -у́) fumes, smoke.

чадра́ yashmak.

чай (pl -и́, -ёв) tea. чаевы́е (-ы́х) sb pl tip.

ча́йка (gen pl чáек) (sea-)gull.

ча́йная sb tea-shop. ча́йник teapot; kettle. ча́йный tea. чайхана́ tea-house.

чалма́ turban.

чан (loc -ý; pl -ы́) vat, tub.

чарова́ть impf bewitch; charm.

час (with numerals -á, loc -ý, pl -ы́) hour; pl guard-duty; **кото́рый час?** what's the time? ~ **one o'clock; в два** ~á at two o'clock; **стоя́ть на** ~áх stand guard; ~ы́ **пик** rush-hour. **часо́вня** (gen pl -вен) chapel. **часово́й** sb sentry. **часово́й** clock, watch; of one hour, hour-long. **часовщи́к** (-á) watchmaker.

части́ца small part; particle. **части́чно** adv partly, partially. **части́чный** partial.

ча́стник private trader.

ча́стность detail; **в ча́стности** in particular. **ча́стный** private; personal; particular, individual.

ча́сто adv often; close, thickly. **частоко́л** paling, palisade. **частота́** (pl -ы) frequency. **часто́тный** frequency. **часту́шка** ditty. **ча́стый** (част, -á, -о) frequent; close (together); dense; close-woven; rapid.

часть (gen pl -ей) part; department; field; unit.

часы́ (-о́в) pl clock, watch.

ча́хлый stunted; sickly, puny. **чахо́тка** consumption.

ча́ша bowl; chalice; ~ **весо́в** scale, pan. **ча́шка** cup; scale, pan.

ча́ща thicket.

ча́ще comp of **ча́сто**, **ча́стый**; ~ **всего́** most often, mostly.

ча́яние expectation; hope. **ча́ять** (ча́ю) impf hope, expect.

чего́ see **что**

чей m, **чья** f, **чьё** neut, **чьи** pl

pron whose. **чей-либо**, **чей-нибудь** anyone's. **чей-то** someone's.

чек cheque; bill; receipt.

чека́нить impf (pf **вы**~, **от**~) mint, coin; stamp, engrave; enunciate. **чека́нка** coinage, minting. **чека́нный** stamping, engraving, stamped, engraved; precise, expressive.

чёлка fringe; forelock.

чёлн (-á; pl **чёлны́**) dug-out (canoe); boat. **челно́к** (-á) dug-out (canoe); shuttle.

челове́к (pl **лю́ди**; with numerals, gen -ве́к, -ам) man, person.

челове́ко- in comb man, anthropo-. **человеколюби́вый** philanthropic. ~**лю́бие** philanthropy. ~**ненави́стнический** misanthropic. **челове́ко-ча́с** (-ы́) man-hour.

челове́чек (-чка) little man. **челове́ческий** human; humane. **челове́чество** mankind. **челове́чность** humaneness. **челове́чный** humane.

че́люсть jaw(-bone); dentures, false teeth.

чем, чём see **что**. **чем** conj than; ~..., **тем**...+comp the more..., the more...

чемода́н suitcase.

чемпио́н, ~**ка** champion, title-holder. **чемпиона́т** championship.

чему́ see **что**

чепуха́ nonsense; trifle.

чепе́ц cap; bonnet.

че́рви (-ей), **че́рвы** (черв) pl hearts. **черво́нн|ый** of hearts; ~**ое зо́лото** pure gold.

червь (-я́; pl -и, -е́й) m worm; bug. **червя́к** (-á) worm.

черда́к (-á) attic, loft.

черёд (-á, loc -ý) turn; **идти́**

свои́м ~о́м take its course.
чередова́ние alternation.
чередова́ть *impf* alternate;
~ся alternate, take turns.
че́рез, чрез *prep+acc* across;
over; through; via; in; after;
every other.
черёмуха bird cherry.
черено́к (-нка́) handle; graft,
cutting.
че́реп (*pl* -а́) skull.
черепа́ха tortoise; turtle; tortoiseshell. черепа́ховый tortoise; turtle; tortoiseshell. чере-
па́ший tortoise, turtle; very
slow.
черепи́ца tile. черепи́чный
tile; tiled.
черепо́к (-пка́) potsherd, fragment of pottery.
чересчу́р *adv* too; too much.
чере́шневый cherry. чере́шня
(*gen pl* -шен) cherry(-tree).
черке́с, черке́шенка Circas-
sian.
черкну́ть (-ну́, -нёшь) *pf* scrape;
leave a mark on; scribble.
черне́ть (-е́ю) *impf* (*pf* по~)
turn black; show black. чер-
ни́ка (*no pl*; *usu collect*) bilberry; bilberries. черни́ла
(-и́л) *pl* ink. черни́льный
ink. черни́ть *impf* (*pf* о~)
blacken; slander.
черно- *in comb* black; unskilled; rough. чёрно-бе́лый
black-and-white. ~бу́рый
dark-brown; ~бу́рая лиса́
silver fox. ~воло́сый black-
haired. ~гла́зый black-eyed.
~зём chernozem, black earth.
~ко́жий black; *sb* black. ~
мо́рский Black-Sea. ~ра-
бо́чий *sb* unskilled worker,
labourer. ~сли́в prunes. ~смо-
ро́динный blackcurrant.

черновик (-а́) rough copy,
draft. черново́й rough; draft.

чернота́ blackness; darkness.
чёрн|ый (-рен, -рна́) black;
back; unskilled; ferrous;
gloomy; *sb* (*derog*) black person; ~ая сморо́дина (*no pl*;
usu collect) blackcurrant(s).
черпа́к (-а́) scoop. черпа́ть
impf, черпну́ть (-ну́, -нёшь)
pf draw; scoop; extract.
черстве́ть (-е́ю) *impf* (*pf* за~,
о~, по~) get stale; become
hardened. чёрствый (чёрств,
-а́, -о) stale; hard.
чёрт (*pl* че́рти, -е́й) devil.
черта́ line; boundary; trait,
characteristic. чертёж (-а́)
drawing; blueprint, plan. чер-
тёжник draughtsman. чертё-
жный drawing. черти́ть (-рчу́,
-ртишь) *impf* (*pf* на~) draw.
чёртов *adj* devil's; devilish.
черто́вский devilish.
чертополо́х thistle.
чёрточка line; hyphen. чер-
че́ние drawing. черчу́ *etc*.:
see черти́ть
чеса́ть (чешу́, -шешь) *impf* (*pf*
по~) scratch; comb; card;
~ся scratch o.s.; itch; comb
one's hair.
чесно́к (-а́) garlic.
чествова́ние celebration.
че́ствовать *impf* celebrate;
honour. че́стность honesty.
че́стный (-тен, -тна́, -о) honest. честолюби́вый ambi-
tious. честолю́бие ambition.
честь (*loc* -и́) honour; от-
да́ть ~ *+dat* salute.
чета́ pair, couple.
четве́рг (-а́) Thursday. чет-
вере́ньки: на ~, на четве-
ре́ньках on hands and knees.
четвёрка four; figure 4;
No. 4. четве́ро (-ы́х) four.
четвероно́г|ий four-legged;
~ое *sb* quadruped. четверо-
сти́шие quatrain. четвёр-

тый fourth. **че́тверть** (gen pl -е́й) quarter; quarter of an hour; **без че́тверти часа** a quarter to one. **четверть-фина́л** quarter-final.

чёткий (-ток, -тка́, -о) precise; clear-cut; clear; distinct. **чёткость** precision; clarity; distinctness.

чётный even.

четы́ре (-рёх, -рьмя́, -рёх) four. **четы́реста** (-рёхсо́т, -мьюста́ми, -ёхста́х) four hundred. **четырёх-** in comb four-, tetra-. **четырёхкра́тный** fourfold. **~ме́стный** four-seater. **~со́тый** four-hundredth. **~уго́льник** quadrangle. **~уго́льный** quadrangular.

четы́рнадцатый fourteenth. **четы́рнадцать** fourteen.

чех Czech.

чехо́л (-хла́) cover, case.

чечеви́ца lentil; lens.

че́шка Czech. **че́шский** Czech.

чешу́ etc.: see **чеса́ть**

чешу́йка scale. **чешуя́** scales.

чиж (-а́) siskin.

чин (pl -ы́) rank.

чини́ть[1] (-ню́, -нишь) impf (pf по~) repair, mend.

чини́ть[2] impf (pf у~) carry out; cause; **~ препя́тствия** +dat put obstacles in the way of.

чино́вник civil servant; official.

чип (micro)chip.

чи́псы (-ов) pl (potato) crisps.

чири́кать impf, **чири́кнуть** (-ну) pf chirp.

чи́ркать impf, **чи́ркнуть** (-ну) pf +instr strike.

чи́сленность numbers; strength. **чи́сленный** numerical. **числи́тель** m numerator. **числи́тельное** sb numeral. **чи́слить** impf count, reckon; **~ся** be; +instr be reckoned. **число́**

(pl -а, -сел) number; date; day; **в числе́** +gen among; **в том числе́** including; **еди́нственное ~** singular; **мно́жественное ~** plural. **числово́й** numerical.

чи́стилище purgatory.

чи́стильщик cleaner. **чи́стить** (чи́щу) impf (pf вы~, о~, по~) clean; peel; clear. **чи́стка** cleaning; purge. **чи́сто** adv cleanly, clean; purely; completely. **чистово́й** fair, clean. **чистокро́вный** thoroughbred. **чистописа́ние** calligraphy. **чистопло́тный** neat; decent. **чистосерде́чный** frank, sincere. **чистота́** cleanness; neatness; purity. **чи́стый** clean; neat; pure; complete.

чита́емый widely-read, popular. **чита́льный** reading. **чита́тель** m reader. **чита́ть** impf (pf про~, проче́сть) read; recite; **~ ле́кции** lecture; **~ся** be legible; be discernible. **чи́тка** reading.

чиха́ть impf, **чихну́ть** (-ну́, -нёшь) pf sneeze.

чи́ще comp of **чи́сто**, **чи́стый**. **чи́щу** etc.: see **чи́стить**

член member; limb; term; part; article. **члени́ть** impf (pf рас~) articulate. **член-корреспонде́нт** corresponding member, associate. **членоразде́льный** articulate. **чле́нский** membership. **чле́нство** membership.

чмо́кать impf, **чмо́кнуть** (-ну) pf smack; squelch; kiss noisily; **~ губа́ми** smack one's lips.

чо́каться impf, **чо́кнуться** (-нусь) pf clink glasses.

чо́порный prim; standoffish.

чопорный prim; standoffish.

чревоу́гольный +instr fraught with. **чре́во** belly, womb. **чревовеща́тель** m ventriloquist.

чревоуго́дие gluttony.

чрез *see* **че́рез. чрезвыча́й-Н|ый** extraordinary; extreme; **~ое положе́ние** state of emergency. **чрезме́рный** excessive.

чте́ние reading. **чтец** (-á) reader; reciter.

чтить (чту) *impf* honour.

что, чего́, чему́, чем, о чём *pron* what; how?; why?; how much?; which, what, who; anything; **в чём де́ло?** what is the matter? **для чего́?** what ... for? why?; **~ ему́ до э́то-го?** what does it matter to him?; **~ с тобо́й?** what's the matter (with you)?; **~ за** what? what sort of?; что ..!; **что** *conj* that. **что (бы) ни** *pron* whatever, no matter what.

чтоб, чтобы *conj* in order (to), so as; that; to. **что́-либо, что́-нибудь** *prons* anything. **что́-то¹** *pron* something. **что́-то²** *adv* for somewhat, slightly; somehow, for some reason.

чу́вственность sensuality. **чувстви́тельность** sensitivity; perceptibility; sentimentality. **чувстви́тельный** sensitive; perceptible; sentimental. **чу́вство** feeling; sense; senses; **прийти́ в ~** come round. **чу́вствовать** *impf* (*pf* по~) feel; realize; appreciate; **~ся** be perceptible; make itself felt.

чугу́н (-á) cast iron. **чугу́нный** cast-iron.

чуда́к (-á), **чуда́чка** eccentric, crank. **чуда́чество** eccentricity.

чудеса́ *etc.: see* **чу́до. чуде́сный** miraculous; wonderful.

чу́диться (-ишься) *impf* (*pf* при~) seem.

чу́дно *adv* wonderfully; wonderful! **чудно́й** (-де́н, -дна́)

odd, strange. **чу́дный** wonderful; magical. **чу́до** (*pl* -деса́) miracle; wonder. **чудо́вище** monster. **чудо́вищный** monstrous. **чудоде́йственный** miracle-working; miraculous. **чу́дом** *adv* miraculously. **чудотво́рный** miraculous, miracle-working.

чужби́на foreign land. **чужда́ться** *impf* +*gen* avoid; stand aloof from. **чу́ждый** (-жд, -á, -о) alien (to); +*gen* free from, devoid of. **чуже-зе́мец** (-мца), **-зе́мка** foreigner. **чужезе́мный** foreign. **чужо́й** someone else's, others'; strange, alien; foreign.

чула́н store-room; larder.

чуло́к (-лка́; *gen pl* -ло́к) stocking.

чума́ plague.

чума́зый dirty.

чурба́н block. **чу́рка** block, lump.

чу́ткий (-ток, -тка́, -о) keen; sensitive; sympathetic; delicate. **чу́ткость** keenness; delicacy.

чу́точка: ни чу́точки not in the least; **чу́точку** a little (bit).

чу́тче *comp of* **чу́ткий**

чуть *adv* hardly; just; very slightly; **~ не** almost, **~чуть** a tiny bit.

чутьё scent; flair.

чу́чело stuffed animal, stuffed bird; scarecrow.

чушь nonsense.

чу́ять (чу́ю) *impf* scent; sense.

чьё *etc.: see* **чей**

Ш

ша́баш sabbath.

шабло́н template; mould, stencil; cliché. **шабло́нный** stencil; trite; stereotyped.

шаг (with numerals -á, *loc* -ý; *pl* -и́) step; footstep; pace. **шага́ть** *impf*, **шагну́ть** (-ну́, -нёшь) *pf* step; stride; pace; make progress. **ша́гом** *adv* at walking pace.

ша́йба washer; puck.

ша́йка[1] tub.

ша́йка[2] gang, band.

шака́л jackal.

шала́ш (-á) cabin, hut.

шали́ть *impf* be naughty; play up. **шаловли́вый** mischievous, playful. **ша́лость** prank; *pl* mischief. **шалу́н** (-á), **шалу́нья** (*gen pl* -ний) naughty child.

шаль shawl.

шально́й mad, crazy.

ша́мкать *impf* mumble.

шампа́нское *sb* champagne.

шампиньо́н field mushroom.

шампу́нь *m* shampoo.

шанс chance.

шанта́ж (-á) blackmail. **шантажи́ровать** *impf* blackmail.

ша́пка hat; banner headline. **ша́почка** hat.

шар (with numerals -á; *pl* -ы́) sphere; ball; balloon.

шара́хать *impf*, **шара́хнуть** (-ну) *pf*; ~**ся** dash; shy.

шарж caricature.

ша́рик ball; corpuscle. **ша́риковый**: ~**ая** (**а́вто)ру́чка** ball-point pen; ~**ый** подши́пник ball-bearing. **шарикоподши́пник** ball-bearing.

ша́рить *impf* grope; sweep.

ша́ркать *impf*, **ша́ркнуть** (-ну) *pf* shuffle; scrape.

шарлата́н charlatan.

шарма́нка barrel-organ. **шарма́нщик** organ-grinder.

шарни́р hinge, joint.

шарова́ры (-áр) *pl* (*wide*) trousers.

шарови́дный spherical. **шаро-** **во́й** ball; globular. **шарообра́зный** spherical.

шарф scarf.

шасси́ *neut indecl* chassis.

шата́ть *impf* rock, shake; *impers* +*acc* его́ шата́ет he is reeling; ~**ся** sway; reel, stagger; come loose, be loose; be unsteady; loaf about.

шатёр (-трá) tent; marquee.

ша́ткий unsteady; shaky.

шату́н (-á) connecting-rod.

ша́фер (*pl* -á) best man.

шах check; ~ **и мат** checkmate.

шахмати́ст chess-player. **ша́хматы** (-ат) *pl* chess; chessmen.

ша́хта mine, pit; shaft. **шахтёр** miner. **шахтёрский** miner's; mining.

ша́шка[1] draught; *pl* draughts.

ша́шка[2] sabre.

шашлы́к (-á) kebab; barbecue.

шва *etc.*: *see* шов

шва́бра mop.

шваль rubbish; riff-raff.

швартóв mooring-line; *pl* moorings. **швартова́ть** *impf* (*pf* при~) moor; ~**ся** moor.

швед, ~**ка** Swede. **шве́дский** Swedish.

швейн|**ый** sewing; ~**ая маши́на** sewing-machine.

швейца́р porter, doorman. **швейца́рец** (-рца), ~**ца́рка** Swiss. **Швейца́рия** Switzerland. **швейца́рский** Swiss.

Шве́ция Sweden.

швея́ seamstress.

швырну́ть (-ну́, -нёшь) *pf*, **швыря́ть** *impf* throw, fling; ~**ся** +*instr* throw (about); treat carelessly.

шевели́ть (-елю́, -е́ли́шь) *impf*, **шевельну́ть** (-ну́, -нёшь) *pf* (*pf also* по~) (+*instr*) move, stir; ~**ся** move, stir, stir.

шеде́вр masterpiece.

ше́йка (*gen pl* ше́ек) neck.

шёл see идти́

шелесте́ть rustle. **шелесте́ть** (-сти́шь) *impf* rustle.

шёлк (*loc* -у́; *pl* -а́) silk. **шелкови́стый** silky. **шелкови́ца** mulberry(-tree). **шелкови́чный** mulberry; ~ **червь** silk-worm. **шёлковый** silk.

шелохну́ть (-ну́, -нёшь) *pf* stir, agitate; ~**ся** stir, move.

шелуха́ skin; peelings; pod. **шелуши́ть** (-шу́) peel; shell; ~**ся** peel (off), flake off.

шепеля́вить (-влю) *impf* lisp. **шепеля́вый** lisping.

шепну́ть (-ну́, -нёшь) *pf*, **шепта́ть** (-пчу́, -пчешь) *impf* whisper; ~**ся** whisper (together).

шёпот whisper. **шёпотом** *adv* in a whisper.

шере́нга rank; file.

шерохова́тый rough; uneven.

шерсть wool; hair, coat. **шерстяно́й** wool(len).

шерша́вый rough.

шест (-а́) pole; staff.

ше́ствие procession. **ше́ствовать** process; march.

шестёрка six; figure 6; No. 6. **шестерня́** (*gen pl* -рён) gear-wheel, cogwheel.

ше́стеро (-ры́х) six.

шести- in comb six-, hexa-, sex(i)-. **шестигра́нник** hexahedron. ~**дне́вка** six-day (*working*) week. ~**деся́тый** sixtieth. ~**ме́сячный** six-month; six-month-old. ~**со́тый** six-hundredth. ~**уго́льник** hexagon.

шестнадцатиле́тний sixteen-year; sixteen-year-old. **шестна́дцатый** sixteenth. **шестна́дцать** sixteen. **шесто́й** sixth. **шесть** (-и́, *instr* -ью́) six. **шестьдеся́т** (-и́десяти, *instr* -ью́десятью) sixty. **шестьсо́т** (-исо́т, -иста́м, -ьюста́ми, -иста́х)

six hundred. **ше́стью** *adv* six times.

шеф boss, chief; patron, sponsor. **шеф-по́вар** chef. **ше́фство** patronage, adoption. **ше́фствовать** *impf* +над+ *instr* adopt; sponsor.

ше́я neck.

шиворо́т collar.

шика́рный chic, smart; splendid.

ши́ло (*pl* -ья, -ьев) awl.

шимпанзе́ *m indecl* chimpanzee.

ши́на tyre; splint.

шине́ль overcoat.

шинкова́ть *impf* shred, chop.

ши́нный tyre.

шип (-а́) thorn, spike, crampon; pin; tenon.

шипе́ние hissing; sizzling. **шипе́ть** (-плю́) *impf* hiss; sizzle; fizz.

шипо́вник dog-rose.

шипу́чий sparkling; fizzy. **шипу́чка** fizzy drink. **шипя́щий** sibilant.

ши́ре *comp of* широ́кий, широ́ко. **ширина́** width; gauge. **ши́рить** *impf* extend, expand; ~**ся** spread, extend.

ши́рма screen.

широ́к|ий (-о́к, -а́, -о́ко) wide, broad; **това́ры** ~**ого** потребле́ния consumer goods. **широ́ко** *adv* wide, widely, broadly.

широко- in comb wide-, broad-. **широкове́щание** broadcasting. ~**веща́тельный** broadcasting. ~**экра́нный** wide-screen.

широта́ (*pl* -ы) width, breadth; latitude. **широ́тный** of latitude; latitudinal. **широча́йший** *superl of* широ́кий. **ширпотре́б** *abbr* consumption; consumer goods. **ширь**

(wide) expanse.

шить (шью, шьёшь) *impf* (*pf* с~) sew; make; embroider. **шитьё** sewing; embroidery.

ши́фер slate.

шифр cipher, code; shelf-mark. **шифро́ванный** in cipher, coded. **шифрова́ть** *impf* (*pf* за~) encipher. **шифро́вка** enciphering; coded communication.

ши́шка cone; bump; lump; (*sl*) big shot.

шкала́ (*pl* -ы) scale; dial.

шкату́лка box, casket, case.

шкаф (*loc* -ý; *pl* -ы́) cupboard; wardrobe. **шка́фчик** cupboard, locker.

шквал squall.

шкив (*pl* -ы́) pulley.

шко́ла school. **шко́льник** schoolboy. **шко́льница** schoolgirl. **шко́льный** school.

шку́ра skin, hide, pelt. **шку́рка** skin; rind; emery paper, sandpaper.

шла *see* идти́

шлагба́ум barrier.

шлак slag; dross; clinker. **шлакобло́к** breeze-block.

шланг hose.

шлейф train.

шлем helmet.

шлёпать *impf*, **шлёпнуть** (-ну) *pf* smack, spank; shuffle; tramp; ~**ся** fall flat, plop down.

шли *see* идти́

шлифова́льный polishing; grinding. **шлифова́ть** *impf* (*pf* от~) polish; grind. **шлифо́вка** polishing.

шло *see* идти́. **шлю** *etc.: see* слать

шлюз lock, sluice.

шлю́пка boat.

шля́па hat. **шля́пка** hat; head.

шмель (-я́) *m* bumble-bee.

шмон *sl* search, frisking.

шмы́гать *impf*, **шмыгну́ть** (-ыгну́, -ыгнёшь) *pf* dart, rush; +*instr* rub, brush; ~ **но́сом** sniff.

шни́цель *m* schnitzel.

шнур (-á) cord; lace; flex, cable. **шнурова́ть** *impf* (*pf* за~, про~) lace up; tie. **шнуро́к** (-рка́) lace.

шов (шва) seam; stitch; joint.

шовини́зм chauvinism. **шовини́ст** chauvinist. **шовинисти́ческий** chauvinistic.

шок shock. **шоки́ровать** *impf* shock.

шокола́д chocolate. **шокола́дка** chocolate, bar of chocolate. **шокола́дный** chocolate.

шо́рох rustle.

шо́рты (шорт) *pl* shorts.

шо́ры (шор) *pl* blinkers.

шоссе́ *neut indecl* highway.

шотла́ндец (-дца) Scotsman, Scot. **Шотла́ндия** Scotland. **шотла́ндка**[1] Scotswoman. **шотла́ндка**[2] tartan. **шотла́ндский** Scottish, Scots.

шофёр driver; chauffeur. **шофёрский** driver's; driving.

шпа́га sword.

шпага́т cord; twine; string; splits.

шпаклева́ть (-лю́ю) *impf* (*pf* за~) caulk; fill, putty. **шпаклёвка** filling, puttying. putty.

шпа́ла sleeper.

шпана́ (*sl*) hooligan(s); riff-raff.

шпарга́лка crib.

шпа́рить *impf* (*pf* о~) scald.

шпат spar.

шпиль *m* spire; capstan. **шпи́лька** hairpin; hat-pin; tack; stiletto heel.

шпина́т spinach.

шпинга́лет (vertical) bolt; catch, latch.

шпио́н spy. **шпиона́ж** espionage. **шпио́нить** *impf* spy (за+*instr* on). шпио́нский spy's; espionage.

шпо́ра spur.

шприц syringe.

шпро́та sprat.

шпу́лька spool, bobbin.

шрам scar.

шрапне́ль shrapnel.

шрифт (*pl* -ы́) type, print.

шт. *abbr* (*of* шту́ка) item, piece.

штаб (*pl* -ы́) staff; headquarters.

шта́бель (*pl* -я́) *m* stack.

штабно́й staff; headquarters.

штамп die, punch; stamp; cliché. штампо́ванный stamped, pressed; trite; stock.

шта́нга bar, rod, beam; weight. штанги́ст weight-lifter.

штани́шки (-шек) *pl* (*child's*) shorts. штаны́ (-о́в) trousers.

штат¹ State.

штат², шта́ты (-ов) *pl* staff, establishment.

штати́в tripod, base, stand.

шта́тный staff; established. шта́тск|ий civilian; ~ое (пла́тье) civilian clothes; ~ий *sb* civilian.

ште́мпель (*pl* -я́) *m* stamp; почто́вый ~ postmark.

ште́псель (*pl* -я́) *m* plug, socket.

штиль *m* calm.

штифт (-а́) pin, dowel.

што́льня (*gen pl* -лен) gallery.

што́пать *impf* (*pf* за~) darn. што́пка darning; darning wool.

што́пор corkscrew; spin.

што́ра blind.

шторм gale.

штраф fine. штрафно́й penal; penalty. штрафова́ть *impf* (*pf* о~) fine.

штрих (-а́) stroke; feature. штрихова́ть *impf* (*pf* за~) shade, hatch.

штуди́ровать *impf* (*pf* про~) study.

шту́ка item, one; piece; trick.

штукату́р plasterer. штукату́рить *impf* (*pf* от~, о~) plaster. штукату́рка plastering; plaster.

штурва́л (steering-)wheel, helm.

штурм storm, assault.

шту́рман (*pl* -ы *or* -а́) navigator.

штурмова́ть *impf* storm, assault. штурмов|о́й assault; storming; ~а́я авиа́ция ground-attack aircraft. штурмовщи́на rushed work.

шту́чный piece, by the piece.

штык (-а́) bayonet.

штырь (-я́) *m* pintle, pin.

шу́ба fur coat.

шу́лер (*pl* -а́) card-sharper.

шум noise; uproar; racket; stir. шуме́ть (-млю́) *impf* make a noise; row; make a fuss. шу́мный (-мен, -мна́, -о) noisy; loud; sensational.

шумов|о́й sound; ~ые эффе́кты sound effects. шумо́к (-мка́) noise; под ~ on the quiet.

шу́рин brother-in-law (*wife's brother*).

шурф prospecting shaft.

шурша́ть (-шу́) *impf* rustle.

шу́стрый (-тёр, -тра́, -о) smart, bright, sharp.

шут (-а́) fool; jester. шути́ть (-чу́, -тишь) *impf* (*pf* по~) joke; play, trifle; +над+*instr* make fun of. шу́тка joke, jest. шутли́вый humorous; joking, light-hearted. шу́точный comic; joking. шутя́ *adv* for fun, in jest; easily.

шушу́каться *impf* whisper together.

шху́на schooner.

шью etc.: see шить

Щ

щаве́ль (-я́) *m* sorrel.

щади́ть (щажу́) *impf* (*pf* по~) spare.

щебёнка, ще́бень (-бня) *m* crushed stone, ballast; road-metal.

ще́бет twitter, chirp. **щебета́ть** (-ечу́, -е́чешь) *impf* twitter, chirp.

щего́л (-гла́) goldfinch.

щёголь *m* dandy, fop. **щего́льный** (-ну́, -нёшь) *pf*, **щего-ля́ть** *impf* dress fashionably; strut about; +*instr* show off, flaunt. **щего́льско́й** foppish.

ще́дрость generosity. **ще́д-рый** (-др, -á, -о) generous; liberal.

щека́ (*acc* щёку; *pl* щёки, -áм) cheek.

щеко́лда latch, catch.

щекота́ть (-очу́, -о́чешь) *impf* (*pf* по~) tickle. **щеко́тка** tickling, tickle. **щекотли́вый** ticklish, delicate.

щёлкать *impf*, **щёлкнуть** (-ну) *pf* crack; flick; trill; +*instr* click, snap, pop.

щёлок bleach. **щелочно́й** alkaline. **щёлочь** (*gen pl* -éй) alkali.

щелчо́к (-чка́) flick; slight; blow.

щель (*gen pl* -éй) crack; chink; slit; crevice; slit trench.

щеми́ть (-млю́) *impf* constrict; ache; oppress.

щено́к (-нка́; *pl* -нки́, -óв *or* -ня́та, -я́т) pup; cub.

щепа́ (*pl* -ы, -áм), **ще́пка** splinter, chip; kindling.

щепети́льный punctilious.

ще́пка *see* щепа́

щепо́тка, щепо́ть pinch.

щети́на bristle; stubble. **щети́-нистый** bristly. **щети́ниться** *impf* (*pf* о~) bristle. **щётка** brush; fetlock.

щи (щей *or* щец, щам, ща́ми) *pl* shchi, cabbage soup.

щи́колотка ankle.

щипа́ть (-плю́, -плешь) *impf*, **щипну́ть** (-ну́, -нёшь) *pf* (*pf also* об~, о~, ущипну́ть) pinch, nip; sting, bite; burn; pluck; nibble; ~**ся** pinch.

щипко́м *adv* pizzicato. **щип-по́к** (-пка́) pinch, nip. **щип-цы́** (-о́в) *pl* tongs, pincers, pli-ers; forceps.

щит (-á) shield; screen; sluice-gate; (tortoise-)shell; board; panel. **щитови́дный** thyroid. **щито́к** (-тка́) dashboard.

щу́ка pike.

щуп probe. **щу́пальце** (*gen* -лец) tentacle; antenna. **щу́пать** *impf* (*pf* по~) feel, touch.

щу́плый (-пл, -á, -о) weak, puny.

щу́рить *impf* (*pf* со~) screw up, narrow; ~**ся** screw up one's eyes; narrow.

Э

эбе́новый ebony.

эвакуа́ция evacuation. **эва-куи́рованный** *sb* evacuee. **эвакуи́ровать** *impf & pf* evacuate.

эвкали́пт eucalyptus.

эволюциони́ровать *impf & pf* evolve. **эволюцио́нный** evo-lutionary. **эволю́ция** evolution.

эги́да aegis.

эгои́зм egoism, selfishness. **эго-и́ст, ~ка** egoist. **эгоисти́-ческий, эгоисти́чный** ego-istic, selfish.

эй *int* hi! hey!

эйфори́я euphoria.

эква́тор equator.

эквивале́нт equivalent.

экзальта́ция exaltation.

экза́мен examination; **вы́держать, сдать** ∼ pass an examination. **экзамена́тор** examiner. **экзаменова́ть** impf (pf про∼) examine; ∼**ся** take an examination.

экзеку́ция (corporal) punishment.

экзе́ма eczema.

экземпля́р specimen; copy.

экзистенциали́зм existentialism.

экзоти́ческий exotic.

э́кий what (a).

экипа́ж[1] carriage.

экипа́ж[2] crew. **экипирова́ть** impf & pf equip. **экипиро́вка** equipping; equipment.

эклекти́зм eclecticism.

экле́р éclair.

экологи́ческий ecological. **эколо́гия** ecology.

эконо́мика economics; economy. **экономи́ст** economist. **эконо́мить** (-млю) impf (pf c∼) use sparingly; save; economize. **экономи́ческий** economic; economical. **эконо́мия** economy; saving. **эконо́мка** housekeeper. **эконо́мный** economical; thrifty.

экра́н screen. **экраниза́ция** filming; film version.

экскава́тор excavator.

экскурса́нт tourist. **экскурсио́нный** excursion. **экску́рсия** (conducted) tour; excursion. **экскурсово́д** guide.

экспанси́вный effusive.

экспатриа́нт expatriate. **экспатрии́ровать** impf & pf expatriate.

экспеди́ция expedition; dispatch; forwarding office.

экспериме́нт experiment. **эксперимента́льный** experimental. **эксперименти́ровать** impf experiment.

экспе́рт expert. **эксперти́за** (expert) examination; commission of experts.

эксплуата́тор exploiter. **эксплуатацио́нный** operating. **эксплуата́ция** exploitation; operation. **эксплуати́ровать** impf exploit; operate, run.

экспози́ция lay-out; exposition; exposure. **экспона́т** exhibit. **экспоно́метр** exposure meter.

э́кспорт export. **экспорти́ровать** impf & pf export. **экспо́ртный** export.

экспре́сс express (train etc.).

экспро́мт impromptu. **экспро́мтом** adv impromptu.

экспроприа́ция expropriation. **экспроприи́ровать** impf & pf expropriate.

экста́з ecstasy.

экстравага́нтный eccentric, bizarre.

экстра́кт extract.

экстреми́ст extremist. **экстреми́стский** extremist.

э́кстренный urgent; emergency; special.

эксцентри́чный eccentric.

эксце́сс excess.

эласти́чный elastic; supple.

элева́тор grain elevator; hoist.

элега́нтный elegant, smart.

эле́гия elegy.

электризова́ть impf (pf на∼) electrify. **эле́ктрик** electrician. **электрифика́ция** electrification. **электрифици́ровать** impf & pf electrify. **электри́ческий** electric(al). **электри́чество** electricity. **электри́чка** electric train.

электро- in comb electro-, electric, electrical. электробытовой electrical. ~воз electric locomotive. ~двигатель m electric motor. электролиз electrolysis. ~магнитный electromagnetic. ~монтёр electrician. ~одеяло electric blanket. ~поезд electric train. ~прибор electrical appliance. ~провод (pl -á) electric cable. ~проводка electric wiring. ~станция power-station. ~техник electrical engineer. ~техника electrical engineering. ~шок electric-shock treatment. ~энергия electrical energy.

электрод electrode.

электрон electron. электроника electronics.

электронный electron; electronic.

элемент element; cell; character. элементарный elementary.

элита élite.

эллипс ellipse.

эмалевый enamel. эмалировать impf enamel. эмаль enamel.

эмансипация emancipation.

эмбарго neut indecl embargo.

эмблема emblem.

эмбрион embryo.

эмигрант emigrant, émigré. эмиграция emigration. эмигрировать impf & pf emigrate.

эмоциональный emotional. эмоция emotion.

эмпирический empirical.

эмульсия emulsion.

эндшпиль m end-game.

энергетика power engineering. энергетический energy. энергичный energetic. энергия energy.

энтомология entomology.

энтузиазм enthusiasm. энтузиаст enthusiast.

энциклопедический encyclopaedic. энциклопедия encyclopaedia.

эпиграмма epigram. эпиграф epigraph.

эпидемия epidemic.

эпизод episode. эпизодический episodic; sporadic.

эпилепсия epilepsy. эпилептик epileptic.

эпилог epilogue. эпитафия epitaph. эпитет epithet. эпицентр epicentre.

эпопея epic.

эпоха epoch, era.

эра era; до нашей эры BC; нашей эры AD.

эрекция erection.

эрозия erosion.

эротизм eroticism. эротика sensuality. эротический, эротичный erotic, sensual.

эрудиция erudition.

эскадра (naut) squadron. эскадрилья (gen pl -лий) (aeron) squadron. эскадрон (mil) squadron. эскадронный squadron.

эскалатор escalator. эскалация escalation.

эскиз sketch; draft. эскизный sketch; draft.

эскимос, эскимоска Eskimo.

эскорт escort.

эсминец (-нца) abbr (of эскадренный миноносец) destroyer.

эссенция essence.

эстакада trestle bridge; overpass; pier, boom.

эстамп print, engraving, plate.

эстафета relay race; baton.

эстетика aesthetics. эстетический aesthetic.

эстонец (-нца), эстонка Estonian. **Эсто́ния** Estonia. **эсто́нский** Estonian.

эстра́да stage, platform; variety. **эстра́дный** stage; variety; ~ конце́рт variety show.

эта́ж (-а́) storey, floor. **этажёрка** shelves.

э́так adv so, thus; about. **э́такий** such (a), what (a).

этало́н standard.

эта́п stage; halting-place.

э́тика ethics.

этике́т etiquette.

этике́тка label.

эти́л ethyl.

этимоло́гия etymology.

эти́ческий, эти́чный ethical.

этни́ческий ethnic. **этногра́фия** ethnography.

э́то part1 this (is), that (is), it (is). **э́тот** m, **э́та** f, **э́то** neut, **э́ти** pl pron this, these.

этю́д study, sketch; étude.

эфеме́рный ephemeral.

эфио́п, ~ка Ethiopian. **эфио́пский** Ethiopian.

эфи́р ether; air. **эфи́рный** ethereal; ether, ester.

эффе́кт effect. **эффекти́вность** effectiveness. **эффекти́вный** effective. **эффе́ктный** effective; striking.

эх int eh! oh!

э́хо echo.

эшафо́т scaffold.

эшело́н echelon; special train.

Ю

юбиле́й anniversary; jubilee. **юбиле́йный** jubilee.

ю́бка skirt. **ю́бочка** short skirt.

ювели́р jeweller. **ювели́рный** jeweller's, jewellery; fine, intricate.

юг south; на ~е in the south. **юго-восто́к** south-east. **юго-**

за́пад south-west. **югосла́в,** ~ка Yugoslav. **Югосла́вия** Yugoslavia. **югосла́вский** Yugoslav.

юдофо́б anti-Semite. **юдо́фобство** anti-Semitism.

южа́нин (pl -а́не, -а́н), **южа́нка** southerner. **ю́жный** south, southern; southerly.

юла́ top; fidget. **юли́ть** impf fidget.

ю́мор humour. **юмори́ст** humourist. **юмористи́ческий** humorous.

ю́ность youth. **ю́ноша** (gen pl -шей) m youth. **ю́ношеский** youthful. **ю́ношество** youth; young people. **ю́ный** (юн, -а́, -о) young; youthful.

юпи́тер floodlight.

юриди́ческий legal, juridical. **юриско́нсульт** legal adviser. **юри́ст** lawyer.

ю́ркий (-рок, -рка́, -рко) quick-moving, brisk; smart. **юрода́вый** crazy.

ю́рта yurt, nomad's tent.

юсти́ция justice.

юти́ться (ючу́сь) impf huddle (together).

Я

я (меня́, мне, мной (-о́ю), (обо) мне) pron I.

я́беда m & f, tell-tale; informer.

я́блоко (pl -и, -ок) apple; глазно́е ~ eyeball. **я́блоневый, я́блочный** apple. **я́блоня** apple-tree.

яви́ться (явлю́сь, я́вишься) pf, **явля́ться** impf appear; arise; +instr be, serve as. **я́вка** appearance; attendance; secret rendez-vous. **явле́ние** phenomenon; appearance; occurrence; scene. **я́вный** obvious; overt. **я́вствовать** be clear, be obvious.

ягнёнок (-нка; *pl* -ня́та, -я́т) lamb.

я́года berry; berries.
я́годица buttock(s).
ягуа́р jaguar.
яд poison; venom.
я́дерный nuclear.
ядови́тый poisonous; venomous.

ядрёный healthy; bracing; juicy. **ядро́** (*pl* -а, я́дер) kernel, core; nucleus; (cannon-)ball; shot.

я́зва ulcer, sore. **я́звенн**|**ый** ulcerous; ~**ая боле́знь** ulcers.
язви́тельный caustic, sarcastic. **язви́ть** (-влю́) *impf* (*pf* **съ~**) be sarcastic.

язы́к (-а́) tongue; language. **языкове́д** linguist. **языкове́дение, языкозна́ние** linguistics. **языково́й** linguistic. **язы́ковый** tongue; lingual. **язычо́к** reed.
язы́чник heathen, pagan.
язычо́к (-чка́) tongue; reed; catch.

яи́чко (*pl* -и, -чек) egg; testicle. **яи́чник** ovary. **яи́чница** fried eggs. **яйцо́** (*pl* я́йца, яи́ц) egg; ovum.

я́кобы *conj* as if; *partl* supposedly.

я́корн|**ый** anchor; ~**ая стоя́нка** anchorage. **я́корь** (*pl* -я́) *m* anchor.

я́лик skiff.
я́ма pit, hole.
ямщи́к (-а́) coachman.

январский January. **янва́рь** (-я́) *m* January.
янта́рный amber. **янта́рь** (-я́) *m* amber.
япо́нец (-нца), **япо́нка** Japanese. **Япо́ния** Japan. **япо́нский** Japanese.
ярд yard.
я́ркий (-рок, ярка́, -о) bright; colourful, striking.
ярлы́к (-а́) label; tag.
я́рмарка fair.
ярмо́ (*pl* -а) yoke.
ярово́й spring.
я́ростный furious, fierce.
я́рость fury.
я́рус circle; tier; layer.
я́рче *comp of* я́ркий
я́рый fervent; furious; violent.
я́сень *m* ash(-tree).
я́сли (-ей) *pl* manger; crèche; day nursery.
ясне́ть (-е́ет) *impf* become clear, clear. **я́сно** *adv* clearly. **яснови́дение** clairvoyance. **яснови́дец** (-дца), **яснови́дица** clairvoyant. **я́сность** clarity; clearness. **я́сный** (я́сен, ясна́, -о) clear; bright; fine.
я́ства (яств) *pl* victuals.
я́стреб (*pl* -а́) hawk.
я́хта yacht.
яче́йка cell.
ячме́нь[1] (-я́) *m* barley.
ячме́нь[2] (-я́) *m* stye.
я́щерица lizard.
я́щик box; drawer.

A

a, an *indef article, not usu translated;* **twice a week** два ра́за в неде́лю.

aback *adv:* **take ~** озада́чивать *impf,* озада́чить *pf.*

abacus *n* счёты *m pl.*

abandon *vt* покида́ть *impf,* поки́нуть *pf;* (give up) отка́зываться *impf,* отказа́ться *pf* от+*gen:* **~ o.s. to** предава́ться *impf,* преда́ться *pf* +*dat.* **abandoned** *adj* поки́нутый; (profligate) распу́тный.

abase *vt* унижа́ть *impf,* уни́зить *pf.* **abasement** *n* униже́ние.

abate *vi* затиха́ть *impf,* зати́хнуть *pf.*

abattoir *n* скотобо́йня.

abbey *n* абба́тство.

abbreviate *vt* сокраща́ть *impf,* сократи́ть *pf.* **abbreviation** *n* сокраще́ние.

abdicate *vi* отрека́ться *impf,* отре́чься *pf* от престо́ла. **abdication** *n* отрече́ние (от престо́ла).

abdomen *n* брюшна́я по́лость. **abdominal** *adj* брюшно́й.

abduct *vt* похища́ть *impf,* похи́тить *pf.* **abduction** *n* похище́ние.

aberration *n* (mental) помутне́ние рассу́дка.

abet *vt* подстрека́ть *impf,* подстрека́ть *pf* (к соверше́нию преступле́ния *etc.*).

abhor *vt* ненави́деть *impf.* **abhorrence** *n* отвраще́ние.

abhorrent *adj* отврати́тельный.

abide *vt* (tolerate) выноси́ть *impf,* вы́нести *pf;* **~ by** (rules *etc.*) сле́довать *impf,* по~ *pf.* **ability** *n* спосо́бность.

abject *adj* (wretched) жа́лкий; (humble) уни́женный; **~ poverty** кра́йняя нищета́.

ablaze *predic* охва́ченный огнём.

able *adj* спосо́бный, уме́лый; **be ~ to** мочь *impf,* с~ *pf;* (know how to) уме́ть *impf,* с~ *pf.*

abnormal *adj* ненорма́льный. **abnormality** *n* ненорма́льность.

aboard *adv* на борт(у́); (train) в по́езд(е).

abode *n* жили́ще; **of no fixed ~** без постоя́нного местожи́тельства.

abolish *vt* отменя́ть *impf,* отмени́ть *pf.* **abolition** *n* отме́на.

abominable *adj* отврати́тельный. **abomination** *n* ме́рзость.

aboriginal *adj* коренно́й; *n* абориге́н, коренно́й жи́тель *m.* **aborigine** *n* абориге́н, коренно́й жи́тель *m.*

abort *vi* (med) выки́дывать *impf,* вы́кинуть *pf; vt* (terminate) прекраща́ть *impf,* прекрати́ть *pf.* **abortion** *n* або́рт; **have an ~** де́лать *impf,* с~ *pf* або́рт. **abortive**

adj безуспе́шный.

abound *vi* быть в изоби́лии; **~ in** изоби́ловать *impf* +*instr*.

about *adv & prep* (*approximately*) о́коло+*gen*; (*concerning*) о+*prep*, насчёт+*gen*; (*up and down*) по+*dat*; (*in the vicinity*) круго́м; **be ~ to** собира́ться *impf*, собра́ться *pf* +*inf*.

above *adv* наверху́; (*higher up*) вы́ше; **from ~** све́рху; свы́ше; *prep* над+*instr*; (*more than*) свы́ше+*gen*. **aboveboard** *adj* че́стный. **abovementioned** *adj* вышеупомя́нутый.

abrasion *n* истира́ние; (*wound*) сса́дина. **abrasive** *adj* абрази́вный; (*manner*) колю́чий; *n* абрази́вный материа́л.

abreast *adv* в ряд; **keep ~ of** идти́ в но́гу с+*instr*.

abridge *vt* сокраща́ть *impf*, сократи́ть *pf*. **abridgement** *n* сокраще́ние.

abroad *adv* за грани́цей, за грани́цу; **from ~** из-за грани́цы.

abrupt *adj* (*steep*) круто́й; (*sudden*) внеза́пный; (*curt*) ре́зкий.

abscess *n* абсце́сс.

abscond *vi* скрыва́ться *impf*, скры́ться *pf*.

absence *n* отсу́тствие. **absent** *adj* отсу́тствующий; **be ~** отсу́тствовать *impf*; *vt*: **~ o.s.** отлуча́ться *impf*, отлучи́ться *pf*. **absentee** *n* отсу́тствующий *sb*. **absenteeism** *n* прогу́л. **absent-minded** *adj* рассе́янный.

absolute *adj* абсолю́тный; (*complete*) по́лный, соверше́нный.

absolution *n* отпуще́ние гре-

хо́в. **absolve** *vt* проща́ть *impf*, прости́ть *pf*.

absorb *vt* впи́тывать *impf*, впита́ть *pf*. **absorbed** *adj* поглощённый. **absorbent** *adj* вса́сывающий. **absorption** *n* впи́тывание; (*mental*) погружённость.

abstain *vi* возде́рживаться *impf*, воздержа́ться *pf* (**from** от+*gen*). **abstemious** *adj* возде́ржанный. **abstention** *n* воздержа́ние; (*person*) воздержа́вшийся *sb*. **abstinence** *n* воздержа́ние.

abstract *adj* абстра́ктный, отвлечённый; *n* рефера́т. **absurd** *adj* абсу́рдный. **absurdity** *n* абсу́рд.

abundance *n* оби́лие. **abundant** *adj* оби́льный.

abuse *vt* (*insult*) руга́ть *impf*, вы́-, об~, от~ *pf*; (*misuse*) злоупотребля́ть *impf*, злоупотреби́ть *pf*; *n* (*curses*) руга́нь, руга́тельства *neut pl*; (*misuse*) злоупотребле́ние. **abusive** *adj* оскорби́тельный, руга́тельный.

abut *vi* примыка́ть *impf* (**on** к+*dat*).

abysmal *adj* (*extreme*) безграни́чный; (*bad*) ужа́сный. **abyss** *n* бе́здна.

academic *adj* академи́ческий. **academician** *n* акаде́мик. **academy** *n* акаде́мия.

accede *vi* вступа́ть *impf*, вступи́ть *pf* (**to** в, на+*acc*); (*assent*) соглаша́ться *impf*, согласи́ться *pf*.

accelerate *vt & i* ускоря́ть(ся) *impf*, уско́рить(ся) *pf*; (*motoring*) дава́ть *impf*, дать *pf* газ. **acceleration** *n* ускоре́ние. **accelerator** *n* ускори́тель *m*; (*pedal*) акселера́тор.

accent n акцéнт; (*stress*) ударéние; *vt* дéлать *impf*, c~ *pf* ударéние на+*acc*. **accentuate** *vt* акцентúровать *impf* & *pf*.

accept *vt* принимáть *impf*, приня́ть *pf*. **acceptable** *adj* приéмлемый. **acceptance** n приня́тие.

access n дóступ. **accessible** *adj* достýпный. **accession** n вступлéние (на престóл). **accessories** n принадлéжности f pl. **accessory** n (*accomplice*) соучáстник, -ица.

accident n (*chance*) случáйность; (*mishap*) несчáстный случáй; (*crash*) авáрия; by ~ случáйно. **accidental** *adj* случáйный.

acclaim *vt* (*praise*) восхваля́ть *impf*, восхвали́ть *pf*; n восхвалéние.

acclimatization n акклиматизáция. **acclimatize** *vt* акклиматизúровать *impf* & *pf*.

accommodate *vt* помещáть *impf*, помести́ть *pf*; (*hold*) вмещáть *impf*, вмести́ть *pf*. **accommodating** *adj* услýжливый. **accommodation** n (*hotel*) нóмер; (*home*) жильé.

accompaniment n сопровождéние; (*mus*) аккомпанемéнт. **accompanist** n аккомпаниáтор. **accompany** *vt* сопровождáть *impf*, сопроводи́ть *pf*; (*escort*) провожáть *impf*, проводи́ть *pf*; (*mus*) аккомпани́ровать *impf* +*dat*.

accomplice n соучáстник, -ица.

accomplish *vt* совершáть *impf*, соверши́ть *pf*. **accomplished** *adj* закóнченный. **accomplishment** n выполнéние; (*skill*) совершéнство.

accord n соглáсие; of one's own ~ добровóльно; of its own ~ сам собóй, сам по себé. **accordance** n: in ~ with в соотвéтствии с+*instr*, соглáсно+*dat*. **according** *adv*: ~ to по+*dat*, ~ to him по егó словáм. **accordingly** *adv* соотвéтственно.

accordion n аккордеóн.

accost *vt* пристава́ть *impf*, приста́ть *pf* к+*dat*.

account n (*comm*) счёт; (*report*) отчёт; (*description*) описáние; on no ~ ни в кóем слýчае; in ~ в счёт причитáющейся сýммы; on ~ of из-за+*gen*, по причи́не+*gen*; take into ~ принимáть *impf*, приня́ть *pf* в расчёт; *vi*: ~ for объясня́ть *impf*, объясни́ть *pf*. **accountable** *adj* отвéтственный.

accountancy n бухгалтéрия. **accountant** n бухгáлтер.

accrue *vi* нараста́ть *impf*, нарасти́ *pf*.

accumulate *vt* & *i* накáпливать(ся) *impf*, копи́ть(ся) *impf*, на~ *pf*. **accumulation** n накоплéние. **accumulator** n аккумуля́тор.

accuracy n тóчность. **accurate** *adj* тóчный.

accusation n обвинéние. **accusative** *adj* (n) вини́тельный (падéж). **accuse** *vt* обвиня́ть *impf*, обвини́ть *pf* (of в+*prep*); the ~d обвиня́емый sb.

accustom *vt* приучáть *impf*, приучи́ть *pf* (to к+*dat*). **accustomed** *adj* привы́чный; be, get ~ привыкáть *impf*, привы́кнуть *pf* (to к+*dat*).

ace n туз; (*pilot*) ас.

ache n боль; *vi* болéть *impf*.

achieve *vt* достигáть *impf*,

дости́чь & дости́гнуть *pf* +*gen*.
achievement *n* достиже́ние.
acid *n* кислота́; *adj* ки́слый;
~ **rain** кисло́тный дождь.
acidity *n* кислота́.
acknowledge *vt* признава́ть *impf*, призна́ть *pf*; (*receipt of*) подтвержда́ть *impf*, подтверди́ть *pf* получе́ние +*gen*.
acknowledgement *n* призна́ние; подтвержде́ние.
acne *n* прыщи́ *m pl*.
acorn *n* жёлудь *m*.
acoustic *adj* акусти́ческий.
acoustics *n pl* аку́стика.
acquaint *vt* знако́мить *impf*, по~ *pf*. **acquaintance** *n* знако́мство; (*person*) знако́мый *sb*. **acquainted** *adj* знако́мый.
acquiesce *vi* соглаша́ться *impf*, согласи́ться *pf*. **acquiescence** *n* согла́сие.
acquire *vt* приобрета́ть *impf*, приобрести́ *pf*. **acquisition** *n* приобрете́ние. **acquisitive** *adj* стяжа́тельский.
acquit *vt* опра́вдывать *impf*, оправда́ть *pf*; ~ **o.s.** вести́ *impf* себя́. **acquittal** *n* оправда́ние.
acre *n* акр.
acrid *adj* е́дкий.
acrimonious *adj* язви́тельный.
acrobat *n* акроба́т. **acrobatic** *adj* акробати́ческий.
across *adv* & *prep* че́рез+*acc*; (*athwart*) поперёк (+*gen*); (*to, on, other side*) на ту сто́рону (+*gen*), на той стороне́ (+*gen*); (*crosswise*) крест-на́крест.
acrylic *n* акри́л; *adj* акри́ловый.
act *n* (*deed*) акт, посту́пок; (*law*) акт, зако́н; (*of play*) де́йствие; (*item*) но́мер; *vi* поступа́ть *impf*, поступи́ть

pf; де́йствовать *impf*, по~ *pf*; *vt* игра́ть *impf*, сыгра́ть *pf*. **acting** *n* игра́; (*profession*) актёрство; *adj* исполня́ющий обя́занности+*gen*.
action *n* де́йствие, посту́пок; (*law*) иск, проце́сс; (*battle*) бой; ~ **replay** повто́р; **be out of** ~ не рабо́тать *impf*.
activate *vt* приводи́ть *impf*, привести́ *pf* в де́йствие. **active** *adj* акти́вный; ~ **service** действи́тельная слу́жба; ~ **voice** действи́тельный зало́г. **activity** *n* де́ятельность.
actor *n* актёр. **actress** *n* актри́са.
actual *adj* действи́тельный. **actuality** *n* действи́тельность. **actually** *adv* на са́мом де́ле, факти́чески.
acumen *n* проница́тельность.
acupuncture *n* иглоука́лывание.
acute *adj* о́стрый.
AD *abbr* н.э. (на́шей э́ры).
adamant *adj* непрекло́нный.
adapt *vt* приспособля́ть *impf*, приспосо́бить *pf*; (*theat*) инсцени́ровать *impf* & *pf*; ~ **o.s.** приспособля́ться *impf*, приспосо́биться *pf*. **adaptable** *adj* приспособля́ющийся. **adaptation** *n* приспособле́ние; (*theat*) инсцени́ровка. **adapter** *n* ада́птер.
add *vt* прибавля́ть *impf*, приба́вить *pf*; (*say*) добавля́ть *impf*, доба́вить *pf*; ~ **together** скла́дывать *impf*, сложи́ть *pf*; ~ **up** сумми́ровать *impf* & *pf*; ~ **up to** соста́вить *pf*; (*fig*) своди́ться *impf*, свести́сь *pf* к+*dat*. **addenda** *n* приложе́ния *pl*.
adder *n* гадю́ка.

addict *n* наркома́н, ~ка. **addicted** *adj*: **be** ~ to быть рабо́м+*gen*; **become** ~ to пристрасти́ться *pf* к+*dat*. **addiction** *n* (*passion*) пристра́стие; (*to drugs*) наркома́ния.

addition *n* прибавле́ние; дополне́ние; (*math*) сложе́ние; **in** ~ вдоба́вок, кро́ме того́. **additional** *adj* доба́вочный. **additive** *n* доба́вка.

address *n* а́дрес; (*speech*) речь; ~ **book** записна́я кни́жка; *vt* адресова́ть *impf* & *pf*; (*speak to*) обраща́ться *impf*, обрати́ться *pf* к+*dat*; **a meeting** выступа́ть *impf*, вы́ступить *pf* на собра́нии. **addressee** *n* адреса́т.

adept *adj* све́дущий; *n* ма́стер.

adequate *adj* доста́точный.

adhere *vi* прилипа́ть *impf*, прили́пнуть *pf* (**to** к+*dat*); (*fig*) приде́рживаться *impf* +*gen*. **adherence** *n* приве́рженность. **adherent** *n* приве́рженец. **adhesive** *adj* ли́пкий; *n* кле́йкое вещество́.

ad hoc *adj* специа́льный.

ad infinitum *adv* до бесконе́чности.

adjacent *adj* сме́жный.

adjective *n* (и́мя) прилага́тельное.

adjoin *vt* прилега́ть *impf* к+*dat*.

adjourn *vt* откла́дывать *impf*, отложи́ть *pf*; *vi* объявля́ть *impf*, объяви́ть *pf* переры́в; (*move*) переходи́ть *impf*, перейти́ *pf*.

adjudicate *vt* выноси́ть *impf*, вы́нести *pf* реше́ние (**in** по+*dat*); суди́ть *impf*.

adjust *vt* & *i* приспособля́ть(ся) *impf*, приспосо́бить(ся) *pf*; *vt* пригоня́ть

impf, пригна́ть *pf*; (*regulate*) регули́ровать *impf*, от~ *pf*. **adjustable** *adj* регули́руемый. **adjustment** *n* регули́рование, подго́нка.

ad lib *vt* & *i* импровизи́ровать *impf*, сымпровизи́ровать *pf*.

administer *vt* (*manage*) управля́ть *impf* +*instr*; (*give*) дава́ть *impf*, дать *pf*. **administration** *n* управле́ние; (*government*) прави́тельство. **administrative** *adj* администрати́вный. **administrator** *n* администра́тор.

admirable *adj* похва́льный.

admiral *n* адмира́л.

admiration *n* восхище́ние.

admire *vt* (*look at*) любова́ться *impf* +*pf* +*instr*, на+*acc*; (*respect*) восхища́ться *impf*, восхити́ться *pf* +*instr*. **admirer** *n* покло́нник.

admissible *adj* допусти́мый. **admission** *n* (*access*) до́ступ; (*entry*) вход; (*confession*) призна́ние. **admit** *vt* (*allow in*) впуска́ть *impf*, впусти́ть *pf*; (*confess*) признава́ть *impf*, призна́ть *pf*. **admittance** *n* до́ступ. **admittedly** *adv* призна́ться.

admixture *n* при́месь.

adolescence *n* о́трочество. **adolescent** *adj* подро́стковый; *n* подро́сток.

adopt *vt* (*child*) усыновля́ть *impf*, усынови́ть *pf*; (*thing*) усва́ивать *impf*, усво́ить *pf*; (*accept*) принима́ть *impf*, приня́ть *pf*. **adoptive** *adj* приёмный. **adoption** *n* усыновле́ние; приня́тие.

adorable *adj* преле́стный. **adoration** *n* обожа́ние. **adore** *vt* обожа́ть *impf*.

adorn vt украша́ть impf, укра́сить pf. **adornment** n украше́ние.

adrenalin n адренали́н.

adroit adj ло́вкий.

adulation n преклоне́ние.

adult adj & n взро́слый (sb).

adulterate vt фальсифици́ровать impf & pf.

adultery n супру́жеская изме́на.

advance n (going forward) продвиже́ние (вперёд); (progress) прогре́сс; (mil) наступле́ние; (of pay etc.) ава́нс; in ~ зара́нее; pl (overtures) ава́нсы m pl; vi (go forward) продвига́ться impf, продви́нуться pf вперёд; идти́ impf вперёд; (mil) наступа́ть impf; vt продви́га́ть impf, продви́нуть pf; (put forward) выдвига́ть impf, вы́двинуть pf. **advanced** adj (modern) передово́й. **advancement** n продвиже́ние.

advantage n преиму́щество; (profit) вы́года, по́льза; take ~ of по́льзоваться impf, вос~ pf +instr. **advantageous** adj вы́годный.

adventure n приключе́ние. **adventurer** n иска́тель m приключе́ний. **adventurous** adj предприи́мчивый.

adverb n наре́чие.

adversary n проти́вник. **adverse** adj неблагоприя́тный. **adversity** n несча́стье.

advertise vt (publicize) реклами́ровать impf & pf; vt & i (~ for) дава́ть impf, дать pf объявле́ние о+prep. **advertisement** n объявле́ние, рекла́ма.

advice n сове́т. **advisable** adj жела́тельный. **advise** vt сове́товать impf, по~ pf +dat & inf; (notify) уведомля́ть impf, уве́домить pf. **advisedly** adv наме́ренно. **adviser** n сове́тник. **advisory** adj совеща́тельный.

advocate n (supporter) сторо́нник; vt выступа́ть impf, вы́ступить pf за+acc; (advise) сове́товать impf, по~ pf.

aegis n эги́да.

aerial n анте́нна; adj возду́шный.

aerobics n аэро́бика.

aerodrome n аэродро́м. **aerodynamics** n аэродина́мика. **aeroplane** n самолёт. **aerosol** n аэрозо́ль m.

aesthetic adj эстети́ческий. **aesthetics** n pl эсте́тика.

afar adv: from ~ издалека́.

affable adj приве́тливый.

affair n (business) де́ло; (love) рома́н.

affect vt влия́ть impf, по~ pf на+acc; (touch) тро́гать impf, тро́нуть pf; (concern) затра́гивать impf, затро́нуть pf; **affectation** n жема́нство. **affected** adj жема́нный. **affection** n привя́занность. **affectionate** adj не́жный.

affiliated adj свя́занный (to c+instr).

affinity n (relationship) родство́; (resemblance) схо́дство; (attraction) влече́ние.

affirm vt утвержда́ть impf. **affirmation** n утвержде́ние. **affirmative** adj утверди́тельный.

affix vt прикрепля́ть impf, прикрепи́ть pf.

afflict vt постига́ть impf, пости́чь pf; **be afflicted with** страда́ть impf +instr. **affliction** n боле́знь.

affluence *n* бога́тство. **affluent** *adj* бога́тый.

afford *vt* позволя́ть *impf*, позво́лить *pf* себе́; (*supply*) предоставля́ть *impf*, предоста́вить *pf*.

affront *n* оскорбле́ние; *vt* оскорбля́ть *impf*, оскорби́ть *pf*.

afield *adv*: far ~ далеко́; farther ~ да́льше.

afloat *adv & predic* на воде́.

afoot *predic*: be ~ гото́виться *impf*.

aforesaid *adj* вышеупомя́нутый.

afraid *predic*: be ~ боя́ться *impf*.

afresh *adv* сно́ва.

Africa *n* А́фрика. **African** *n* африка́нец, -ка́нка; *adj* африка́нский.

after *adv* пото́м; *prep* по́сле +*gen*; (*time*) че́рез+*acc*; (*behind*) за+*acc*, *instr*; ~ all в конце́ концо́в; *conj* по́сле того́, как.

aftermath *n* после́дствия *neut pl*. **afternoon** *n* втора́я полови́на дня; in the ~ днём. **aftershave** *n* лосьо́н по́сле бритья́. **afterthought** *n* запозда́лая мысль.

afterwards *adv* пото́м.

again *adv* опя́ть; (*once more*) ещё раз; (*anew*) сно́ва.

against *prep* (*opposing*) про́тив+*gen*; (*touching*) к+*dat*; (*hitting*) о+*acc*.

age *n* во́зраст; (*era*) век, эпо́ха; *vt* ста́рить *impf*, со~ *pf*; *vi* старе́ть *impf*, по~ *pf*. **aged** *adj* престаре́лый.

agency *n* аге́нтство. **agenda** *n* пове́стка дня. **agent** *n* аге́нт.

aggravate *vt* ухудша́ть *impf*,

уху́дшить *pf*; (*annoy*) раздража́ть *impf*, раздражи́ть *pf*.

aggregate *adj* совоку́пный; *n* совоку́пность.

aggression *n* агре́ссия. **aggressive** *adj* агресси́вный. **aggressor** *n* агре́ссор.

aggrieved *adj* оби́женный.

aghast *predic* в у́жасе (at *at* +*gen*).

agile *adj* прово́рный. **agility** *n* прово́рство.

agitate *vt* волнова́ть *impf*, вз~ *pf*; *vi* агити́ровать *impf*. **agitation** *n* волне́ние; агита́ция.

agnostic *n* агно́стик. **agnosticism** *n* агностици́зм.

ago *adv* (тому́) наза́д; long ~ давно́.

agonize *vi* му́читься *impf*. **agonizing** *adj* мучи́тельный. **agony** *n* аго́ния.

agrarian *adj* агра́рный.

agree *vi* соглаша́ться *impf*, согласи́ться *pf*; (*arrange*) догова́риваться *impf*, договори́ться *pf*. **agreeable** *adj* (*pleasant*) прия́тный. **agreement** *n* согла́сие; (*treaty*) соглаше́ние; in ~ согла́сен (-сна).

agricultural *adj* сельскохозя́йственный. **agriculture** *n* се́льское хозя́йство.

aground *predic* на мели́; *adv*: run ~ сади́ться *impf*, сесть *pf* на мель.

ahead *adv* (*forward*) вперёд; (*in front*) впереди́; ~ of time досро́чно.

aid *vt* помога́ть *impf*, помо́чь *pf* +*dat*; *n* (*help*) по́мощь; (*teaching*) посо́бие; in ~ of в по́льзу +*gen*.

Aids *n* СПИД.

ailing *adj* (*ill*) больно́й. **ailment** *n* неду́г.

aim n цель, намере́ние; take ~ прице́ливаться impf, прице́литься pf (at в+acc); vi це́литься impf, на~ pf (at в+acc); (also fig) ме́тить impf, на~ pf (at в+acc); (also fig) наце́ливать impf, наце́лить pf; (also fig) наводи́ть impf, навести́ pf. **aimless** adj бесце́льный.

air n во́здух; (look) вид; by ~ самолётом; on the ~ в эфи́ре; attrib возду́шный; vt (ventilate) прове́тривать impf, прове́трить pf; (make known) выставля́ть impf, вы́ставить pf напока́з. **air-conditioning** n кондициони́рование во́здуха. **aircraft** n самолёт. **aircraft-carrier** n авиано́сец. **airfield** n аэродро́м. **air force** n ВВС (вое́нно-возду́шные си́лы) f pl. **air hostess** n стюарде́сса. **airless** adj ду́шный. **airlift** n возду́шные перево́зки f pl; vt перевози́ть impf, перевезти́ pf по во́здуху. **airline** n авиали́ния. **airlock** n возду́шная про́бка. **airmail** n а́виа(по́чта). **airman** n лётчик. **airport** n аэропо́рт. **air raid** n возду́шный налёт. **airship** n дирижа́бль m. **airstrip** n взлётно-поса́дочная полоса́. **airtight** adj гермети́чный. **air traffic controller** n диспе́тчер. **airwaves** n pl радиово́лны f pl.

aisle n боковой неф; (passage) прохо́д.

ajar adj приоткры́тый.

akin predic (similar) похо́жий; be ~ to быть сродни́ к+dat.

alabaster n алеба́стр.

alacrity n быстрота́.

alarm n трево́га; vt трево́жить impf, вс~ pf; ~ clock буди́льник. **alarming** adj трево́жный. **alarmist** n паникёр; adj паникёрский.

alas int увы́!

album n альбо́м.

alcohol n алкого́ль m, спирт; спиртны́е напи́тки m pl. **alcoholic** adj алкого́льный; n алкого́лик, -и́чка.

alcove n алько́в.

alert adj бди́тельный; n трево́га; vt предупрежда́ть impf, предупреди́ть pf.

algebra n а́лгебра.

alias adv ина́че (называ́емый); n кли́чка, вы́мышленное и́мя neut.

alibi n а́либи neut indecl.

alien n иностра́нец, -нка; adj иностра́нный; ~ to чу́ждый +dat. **alienate** vt отчужда́ть impf. **alienation** n отчужде́ние.

alight[1] vi сходи́ть impf, сойти́ pf; (bird) сади́ться impf, сесть pf.

alight[2] predic: be ~ горе́ть impf; (shine) сия́ть impf.

align vt выра́внивать impf, вы́ровнять pf. **alignment** n выра́внивание.

alike predic похо́ж; adv одина́ково.

alimentary adj: ~ canal пищевари́тельный кана́л.

alimony n алиме́нты m pl.

alive predic жив, в живы́х.

alkali n щёлочь. **alkaline** adj щелочно́й.

all adj весь n всё, pl все; adv совсе́м, соверше́нно; n всё ~ along всё вре́мя; ~ right хорошо́, ла́дно; (not bad) та́к себе; непло́хо; ~ the same всё равно́; in ~ всего́; two ~ два; not at ~ ниско́лько.

allay vt успока́ивать impf,

успокóить *pf.*

allegation *n* утверждéние. **allege** *vt* утверждáть *impf.* **allegedly** *adv* якобы.

allegiance *adv* вéрность.

allegorical *adj* аллегори́ческий. **allegory** *n* аллегóрия.

allergic *adj* аллерги́ческий; **be ~ to** имéть аллерги́ю к+*dat.* **allergy** *n* аллерги́я.

alleviate *vt* облегчáть *impf,* облегчи́ть *pf.* **alleviation** *n* облегчéние.

alley *n* переýлок.

alliance *n* союз. **allied** *adj* сою́зный.

alligator *n* аллигáтор.

allocate *vt* (*distribute*) распределя́ть *impf,* распредели́ть *pf;* (*allot*) выделя́ть *impf,* вы́делить *pf.* **allocation** *n* распределéние; выделéние.

allot *vt* выделя́ть *impf,* вы́делить *pf;* (*distribute*) распределя́ть *impf,* распредели́ть *pf.* **allotment** *n* выделéние; (*land*) учáсток.

allow *vt* разрешáть *impf,* разреши́ть *pf;* (*let happen; concede*) допускáть *impf,* допусти́ть *pf;* **~ for** учи́тывать *impf,* учéсть *pf.* **allowance** *n* (*financial*) посóбие; (*deduction, also fig*) ски́дка; **make ~(s) for** учи́тывать *impf,* учéсть *pf.*

alloy *n* сплав.

all-round *adj* разносторóнний.

allude *vi* ссылáться *impf,* сосслáться *pf* (**to** на+*acc*).

allure *vt* замáнивать *impf,* замани́ть *pf.* **allure(ment)** *n* примáнка. **alluring** *adj* замáнчивый.

allusion *n* ссы́лка.

ally *n* сою́зник; *vt* соединя́ть *impf,* соедини́ть *pf;* **~ one-**

self with вступáть *impf,* вступи́ть *pf* в сою́з с+*instr.*

almighty *adj* всемогýщий.

almond *n* (*tree; pl collect*) миндáль *m;* (*nut*) миндáльный орéх.

almost *adv* почти́, едвá не.

alms *n pl* ми́лостыня.

aloft *adv* навéрх(-ý).

alone *predic* оди́н; (*lonely*) одинóк; *adv* тóлько; **leave ~** оставля́ть *impf,* остáвить *pf* в покóе; **let ~** не говоря́ уже о+*prep.*

along *prep* по+*dat,* (*position*) вдоль+*gen;* (*onward*) дáльше; **all ~** всё врéмя; **~ with** вмéсте с+*instr.* **alongside** *adv & prep* ря́дом (с +*instr*).

aloof *predic & adv* (*distant*) сдéржанный; (*apart*) в сторонé.

aloud *adv* вслух.

alphabet *n* алфави́т. **alphabetical** *adj* алфави́тный.

alpine *adj* альпи́йский.

already *adv* ужé.

also *adv* тáкже, тóже.

altar *n* алтáрь *m.*

alter *vt* (*modify*) передéлывать *impf,* передéлать *pf; vt & i* (*change*) изменя́ть(ся) *impf,* измени́ть(ся) *pf.* **alteration** *n* передéлка; изменéние.

alternate *adj* череду́ющийся; *vt & i* череду́ть(ся) *impf.* **alternating current** переме́нный ток; **on ~ days** чéрез день. **alternation** *n* чередовáние. **alternative** *n* альтернати́ва; *adj* альтернати́вный.

although *conj* хотя́.

altitude *n* высотá.

alto *n* альт.

altogether *adv* (*fully*) совсéм;

(in total) всего́.

altruistic *adj* альтруисти́ческий.

aluminium *n* алюми́ний.

always *adv* всегда́; *(constantly)* постоя́нно.

Alzheimer's disease *n* боле́знь Альцге́ймера.

a.m. *abbr (morning)* утра́; *(night)* но́чи.

amalgamate *vt & i* слива́ть(ся) *impf*, слить(ся) *pf*; *(chem)* амальгами́ровать(ся) *impf & pf.* **amalgamation** *n* слия́ние; *(chem)* амальгами́рование.

amass *vt* копи́ть *impf*, на~ *pf*.

amateur *n* люби́тель *m*, ~ница; *adj* люби́тельский.

amateurish *adj* дилета́нтский.

amaze *vt* изумля́ть *impf*, изуми́ть *pf.* **amazement** *n* изумле́ние. **amazing** *adj* изуми́тельный.

ambassador *n* посо́л.

amber *n* янта́рь *m*.

ambience *n* среда́; атмосфе́ра.

ambiguity *n* двусмы́сленность. **ambiguous** *adj* двусмы́сленный.

ambition *n (quality)* честолю́бие; *(aim)* мечта́. **ambitious** *adj* честолюби́вый.

amble *vi* ходи́ть *indet*, идти́ *det* неторопли́вым ша́гом.

ambulance *n* маши́на ско́рой по́мощи.

ambush *n* заса́да; *vt* напада́ть *impf*, напа́сть *pf* из заса́ды на+*acc*.

ameliorate *vt & i* улучша́ть(ся) *impf*, улу́чшить(ся) *pf.* **amelioration** *n* улучше́ние.

amen *int* ами́нь!

amenable *adj* сгово́рчивый

(to +dat)

amend *vt (correct)* исправля́ть *impf*, испра́вить *pf*; *(change)* вноси́ть *impf*, внести́ *pf* попра́вки в+*acc*. **amendment** *n* попра́вка, исправле́ние. **amends** *n pl:* make ~ for загла́живать *impf*, загла́дить *pf*.

amenities *n pl* удо́бства *neut pl.*

America *n* Аме́рика. **American** *adj* америка́нский; *n* америка́нец, -нка. **americanism** *n* американи́зм.

amiable *adj* любе́зный. **amicable** *adj* дружелю́бный.

amid(st) *prep* среди́+*gen.*

amino acid *n* аминокислота́.

amiss *adv* нела́дный; take ~ обижа́ться *impf*, оби́деться *pf* на+*acc*.

ammonia *n* аммиа́к; *(liquid* ~) нашаты́рный спирт.

ammunition *n* боеприпа́сы *m pl.*

amnesia *n* амнези́я.

amnesty *n* амни́стия.

among(st) *prep (amidst)* среди́+*gen*, *(between)* ме́жду+*instr*.

amoral *adj* амора́льный.

amorous *adj* влюбчивый.

amorphous *adj* бесфо́рменный.

amortization *n* амортиза́ция.

amount *n* коли́чество; *vi:* ~ to составля́ть *impf*, соста́вить *pf*; *(be equivalent to)* быть равноси́льным+*dat*.

ampere *n* ампе́р.

amphetamine *n* амфетами́н.

amphibian *n* земново́дное. **amphibious** *adj* земново́дный; *(mil)* плаваю́щий.

amphitheatre *n* амфитеа́тр.

ample *adj* доста́точный. **amplification** *n* усиле́ние.

plifier *n* усили́тель *m*. **amplify** *vt* уси́ливать *impf*, уси́лить *pf*. **amply** *adv* доста́точно.

amputate *vt* ампути́ровать *impf* & *pf*. **amputation** *n* ампута́ция.

amuse *vt* забавля́ть *impf*; развлека́ть *impf*, развле́чь *pf*. **amusement** *n* заба́ва, развлече́ние; *pl* аттракцио́ны *m pl*. **amusing** *adj* заба́вный; *(funny)* смешно́й.

anachronism *n* анахрони́зм. **anachronistic** *adj* анахрони́ческий.

anaemia *n* анеми́я. **anaemic** *adj* анеми́чный.

anaesthesia *n* анестези́я. **anaesthetic** *n* обезбо́ливающее сре́дство. **anaesthetist** *n* анестезио́лог. **anaesthetize** *vt* анестези́ровать *impf* & *pf*.

anagram *n* анагра́мма.

analogous *adj* аналоги́чный. **analogue** *n* ана́лог. **analogy** *n* анало́гия.

analyse *vt* анализи́ровать *impf* & *pf*. **analysis** *n* ана́лиз. **analyst** *n* анали́тик, психоанали́тик. **analytical** *adj* анали́тический.

anarchic *adj* анархи́ческий. **anarchist** *n* анархи́ст, ~ка; *adj* анархи́стский. **anarchy** *n* ана́рхия.

anathema *n* ана́фема.

anatomical *adj* анатоми́ческий. **anatomy** *n* анато́мия.

ancestor *n* пре́док. **ancestry** *n* происхожде́ние.

anchor *n* я́корь *m*; *vt* ста́вить *impf*, по~ *pf* на я́корь, *vi* станови́ться *impf*, стать *pf* на я́корь. **anchorage** *n* я́корная стоя́нка.

anchovy *n* анчо́ус.

ancient *adj* дре́вний, стари́нный.

and *conj* и, (*but*) а; с+*instr*; **you ~ I** мы с ва́ми; **my wife ~ I** мы с жено́й.

anecdote *n* анекдо́т.

anew *adv* сно́ва.

angel *n* а́нгел. **angelic** *adj* а́нгельский.

anger *n* гнев; *vt* серди́ть *impf*, рас~ *pf*.

angina *n* стенокарди́я.

angle¹ *n* у́гол; *(fig)* то́чка зре́ния.

angle² *vi* уди́ть *impf* ры́бу. **angler** *n* рыболо́в.

angry *adj* серди́тый.

anguish *n* страда́ние, му́ка. **anguished** *adj* отча́янный.

angular *adj* углово́й; *(sharp)* углова́тый.

animal *n* живо́тное *sb*; *adj* живо́тный. **animate** *adj* живо́й. **animated** *adj* оживлённый; **~ cartoon** мультфи́льм. **animation** *n* оживле́ние.

animosity *n* вражде́бность.

ankle *n* лоды́жка.

annals *n pl* ле́топись *n*.

annex *vt* аннекси́ровать *impf* & *pf*. **annexation** *n* анне́ксия. **annexe** *n* пристро́йка.

annihilate *vt* уничтожа́ть *impf*, уничто́жить *pf*. **annihilation** *n* уничтоже́ние.

anniversary *n* годовщи́на.

annotate *vt* комменти́ровать *impf* & *pf*. **annotated** *adj* снабжённый коммента́риями. **annotation** *n* анната́ция.

announce *vt* объявля́ть *impf*, объяви́ть *pf*; заявля́ть *impf*, заяви́ть *pf*; *(radio)* сообща́ть *impf*, сообщи́ть *pf*. **announcement** *n* объявле́ние; сообще́-

ние. **announcer** n ди́ктор.

annoy vt досажда́ть impf, досади́ть pf; раздража́ть impf, раздражи́ть pf. **annoyance** n доса́да. **annoying** adj доса́дный.

annual adj ежего́дный, (of a given year) годово́й; n (book) ежего́дник, (bot) одноле́тник. **annually** adv ежего́дно. **annuity** n (ежего́дная) ре́нта.

annul vt аннули́ровать impf & pf. **annulment** n аннули́рование.

anoint vt пома́зывать impf, пома́зать pf.

anomalous adj анома́льный. **anomaly** n анома́лия.

anonymous adj анони́мный. **anonymity** n анони́мность.

anorak n ку́ртка.

anorexia n анорекси́я.

another adj, pron друго́й; ~ one ещё (оди́н); in ~ ten years ещё че́рез де́сять лет.

answer n отве́т; vt отвеча́ть impf, отве́тить pf (person) +dat, (question) на+acc; ~ the door отворя́ть impf, отвори́ть pf дверь; ~ the phone подходи́ть impf, подойти́ pf к телефо́ну. **answerable** adj отве́тственный. **answering machine** n телефо́н-отве́тчик.

ant n мураве́й.

antagonism n антагони́зм. **antagonistic** adj антагонисти́ческий. **antagonize** vt настра́ивать impf, настро́ить pf про́тив себя́.

Antarctic n Анта́рктика.

antelope n антило́па.

antenna n у́сик; (also radio) анте́нна.

anthem n гимн.

anthology n антоло́гия.

anthracite n антраци́т.

anthropological adj антрополологи́ческий. **anthropologist** n антропо́лог. **anthropology** n антрополо́гия.

anti-aircraft adj зени́тный. **antibiotic** n антибио́тик. **antibody** n антите́ло. **anticlimax** n разочарова́ние. **anticlockwise** adj & adv про́тив часово́й стре́лки. **antidepressant** n антидепресса́нт. **antidote** n противоя́дие. **antifreeze** n антифри́з. **antipathy** n антипа́тия. **antiSemitic** adj антисеми́тский. **anti-Semitism** n антисемити́зм. **antiseptic** adj antисепти́ческий; n антисе́птик. **antisocial** adj асоциа́льный. **anti-tank** adj противота́нковый. **antithesis** n противополо́жность; (philos) анти́тезис.

anticipate vt ожида́ть impf +gen; (with pleasure) предвкуша́ть impf, предвкуси́ть pf; (forestall) предупрежда́ть impf, предупреди́ть pf. **anticipation** n ожида́ние; предвкуше́ние; предупрежде́ние.

antics n вы́ходки f pl.

antiquarian adj антиква́рный. **antiquated** adj устаре́лый. **antique** adj стари́нный; n антиква́рная вещь; ~ shop антиква́рный магази́н. **antiquity** n дре́вность.

antler n оле́ний рог.

anus n за́дний прохо́д.

anvil n накова́льня.

anxiety n беспоко́йство.

anxious adj беспоко́йный; be ~ беспоко́иться impf; трево́житься impf.

any adj, pron (some) како́й-нибудь; ско́лько-нибудь; (every) вся́кий, любо́й; (anybody) кто́-нибудь, (anything) что́-нибудь; (with neg) никако́й, ни оди́н; ниско́лько; никто́, ничто́; adv ско́лько-нибудь; (with neg) ниско́лько, ничу́ть.

anybody, anyone pron кто́-нибудь; (everybody) вся́кий, любо́й; (with neg) никто́. **anyhow** adv ка́к-нибудь; (be) как; (with neg) ника́к; conj во вся́ком слу́чае; всё равно́. **anyone** see **anybody**. **anything** pron что́-нибудь; всё (что уго́дно); (with neg) ничего́. **anyway** adv во вся́ком слу́чае; как бы то ни было. **anywhere** adv где́/куда́ уго́дно; (with neg, interrog) где́-нибудь, куда́-нибудь.

apart adv (aside) в стороне́, в сто́рону; (separately) врозь; (distant) друг от дру́га; (into pieces) на ча́сти; ~ **from** кро́ме+gen.

apartheid n апарте́ид.
apartment n (flat) кварти́ра.
apathetic adj апати́чный. **apathy** n апа́тия.
ape n обезья́на; vt обезья́нничать impf, с~ pf c+gen.
aperture n отве́рстие.
apex n верши́на.
aphorism n афори́зм.
apiece adv (per person) на ка́ждого; (per thing) за шту́ку; (amount) по+dat or acc with numbers.
aplomb n апло́мб.
Apocalypse n Апока́липсис.
apocalyptic adj апокали́птический.
apologetic adj извиня́ющийся; be ~ извиня́ться impf.
apologize vi извиня́ться impf, извини́ться pf (to пе́ред +instr,

for за+acc). **apology** n извине́ние.
apostle n апо́стол.
apostrophe n апостро́ф.
appal vt ужаса́ть impf, ужасну́ть pf. **appalling** adj ужа́сный.
apparatus аппара́т; прибо́р; (gymnastic) гимнасти́ческие снаря́ды m pl.
apparel n оде́ние.
apparent adj (seeming) ви́димый; (manifest) очеви́дный. **apparently** adv ка́жется, по-ви́димому.
apparition n виде́ние.
appeal n (request) призы́в, обраще́ние; (law) апелля́ция, обжа́лование; (attraction) привлека́тельность; ~ **court** апелляцио́нный суд; vi (request) взыва́ть impf, воззва́ть pf (to к+dat; for o+prep); обраща́ться impf, обрати́ться pf (с призы́вом); (law) апелли́ровать impf & pf; ~ **to** (attract) привлека́ть impf, привле́чь pf.
appear vi появля́ться impf, появи́ться pf; (in public) выступа́ть impf, вы́ступить pf; (seem) каза́ться impf, по~ pf. **appearance** n появле́ние; выступле́ние; (aspect) вид.
appease vt умиротворя́ть impf, умиротвори́ть pf.
append vt прилага́ть impf, приложи́ть pf. **appendicitis** n аппендици́т. **appendix** n приложе́ние; (anat) аппе́ндикс.
appertain vi: ~ **to** относи́ться impf +dat.
appetite n аппети́т. **appetizing** adj аппети́тный.
applaud vt аплоди́ровать impf +dat. **applause** n апло-

дисме́нты *m pl.*

apple *n* я́блоко; *adj* я́блочный; ~ **tree** я́блоня.

appliance *n* прибо́р. **applicable** *adj* примени́мый. **applicant** *n* кандида́т. **application** *n* (*use*) примене́ние; (*putting on*) наложе́ние; (*request*) заявле́ние. **applied** *adj* прикладно́й. **apply** *vt* (*use*) применя́ть *impf*, примени́ть *pf*; (*put on*) накла́дывать *impf*, наложи́ть *pf*; *vi* (*request*) обраща́ться *impf*, обрати́ться *pf* (**to** к+*dat*; **for** за+*acc*); ~ **for** (*job*) подава́ть *impf*, пода́ть *pf* заявле́ние на+*acc*; ~ **to** относи́ться *impf* к+*dat*.

appoint *vt* назнача́ть *impf*, назна́чить *pf*. **appointment** *n* назначе́ние; (*job*) до́лжность; (*meeting*) свида́ние.

apposite *adj* уме́стный.

appraise *vt* оце́нивать *impf*, оцени́ть *pf*.

appreciable *adj* заме́тный; (*considerable*) значи́тельный. **appreciate** *vt* цени́ть *impf*; (*understand*) понима́ть *impf*, поня́ть *pf*; *vi* повыша́ться *impf*, повы́ситься *pf* в цене́. **appreciation** *n* (*estimation*) оце́нка; (*gratitude*) призна́тельность; (*rise in value*) повыше́ние цены́. **appreciative** *adj* призна́тельный (**of** за+*acc*).

apprehension *n* (*fear*) опасе́ние. **apprehensive** *adj* опаса́ющийся.

apprentice *n* учени́к; *vt* отдава́ть *impf*, отда́ть *pf* в уче́ние. **apprenticeship** *n* учени́чество.

approach *vt & i* подходи́ть *impf*, подойти́ *pf* (к+*dat*); приближа́ться *impf*, прибли́зиться *pf* (к+*dat*); *vt* (*apply to*) обраща́ться *impf*, обрати́ться *pf* к+*dat*; *n* приближе́ние; подхо́д; подъе́зд; (*access*) до́ступ.

approbation *n* одобре́ние.

appropriate *adj* подходя́щий; *vt* присва́ивать *impf*, присво́ить *pf*. **appropriation** *n* присвое́ние.

approval *n* одобре́ние; **on** ~ на про́бу. **approve** *vt* утвержда́ть *impf*, утверди́ть *pf*; *vt & i* (~ **of**) одобря́ть *impf*, одо́брить *pf*.

approximate *adj* приблизи́тельный; *vi* приближа́ться *impf* (**to** к+*dat*). **approximation** *n* приближе́ние.

apricot *n* абрико́с.

April *n* апре́ль *m; adj* апре́льский.

apron *n* пере́дник.

apropos *adv*: ~ **of** по по́воду+*gen*.

apt *adj* (*suitable*) уда́чный; (*inclined*) скло́нный. **aptitude** *n* спосо́бность.

aqualung *n* аквала́нг. **aquarium** *n* аква́риум. **Aquarius** *n* Водоле́й. **aquatic** *adj* водяно́й; (*of sport*) во́дный. **aqueduct** *n* акведу́к.

aquiline *adj* орли́ный.

Arab *n* ара́б, ~ка; *adj* ара́бский. **Arabian** *adj* арави́йский. **Arabic** *adj* ара́бский.

arable *adj* па́хотный.

arbitrary *adj* произво́льный. **arbitrate** *vi* де́йствовать *impf* в ка́честве трете́йского судьи́. **arbitration** *n* арбитра́ж, трете́йское реше́ние. **arbitrator** *n* арби́тр, трете́йский судья́ *m.*

arc *n* дуга́. **arcade** *n* арка́да; (*shops*) пасса́ж.

arch[1] *n* а́рка, свод; (*of foot*) свод стопы́; *vt & i* выгиба́ть(ся) *impf*, вы́гнуть(ся) *pf*.

arch[2] *adj* игри́вый.

archaeological *adj* археологи́ческий. **archaeologist** *n* архео́лог. **archaeology** *n* археоло́гия.

archaic *adj* архаи́ческий.

archangel *n* арха́нгел.

archbishop *n* архиепи́скоп.

arched *adj* сво́дчатый.

arch-enemy *n* закля́тый враг. **archer** *n* стрело́к из лу́ка. **archery** *n* стрельба́ из лу́ка. **archipelago** *n* архипела́г.

architect *n* архите́ктор. **architectural** *adj* архитекту́рный. **architecture** *n* архитекту́ра.

archive(s) *n* архи́в.

archway *n* сво́дчатый прохо́д.

Arctic *adj* аркти́ческий; *n* А́рктика.

ardent *adj* горя́чий. **ardour** *n* пыл.

arduous *adj* тру́дный.

area *n* (*extent*) пло́щадь; (*region*) райо́н; (*sphere*) о́бласть.

arena *n* аре́на.

argue *vt* (*maintain*) утвержда́ть *impf*; дока́зывать *impf*; *vi* спо́рить *impf*, по~ *pf*. **argument** *n* (*dispute*) спор; (*reason*) до́вод. **argumentative** *adj* лю́бящий спо́рить.

aria *n* а́рия.

arid *adj* сухо́й.

Aries *n* Ове́н.

arise *vi* возника́ть *impf*, возни́кнуть *pf*.

aristocracy *n* аристокра́тия. **aristocrat** *n* аристокра́т, ~ка. **aristocratic** *adj* аристократи́ческий.

arithmetic *n* арифме́тика. ar-

ithmetical *adj* арифмети́ческий.

ark *n* (Но́ев) ковче́г.

arm[1] *n* (*of body*) рука́; (*of chair*) ру́чка; **in ~** по́д руку; **at ~'s length** (*fig*) на почти́тельном расстоя́нии; **with open ~s** с распростёртыми объя́тиями.

arm[2] *n pl* (*weapons*) ору́жие; *pl* (*coat of ~s*) герб; *vt* вооружа́ть *impf*, вооружи́ть *pf*. **armaments** *n pl* вооруже́ние.

armchair *n* кре́сло.

Armenia *n* Арме́ния. **Armenian** *n* армяни́н, армя́нка; *adj* армя́нский.

armistice *n* переми́рие.

armour *n* (*for body*) доспе́хи *m pl*; (*for vehicles; fig*) броня́. **armoured** *adj* брониро́ванный; (*vehicles etc.*) брета́нковый, броне-; **~ car** броневи́к. **armoury** *n* арсена́л.

armpit *n* подмы́шка.

army *n* а́рмия; *adj* арме́йский.

aroma *n* арома́т. **aromatic** *adj* аромати́чный.

around *adv* круго́м; *prep* вокру́г+*gen*; **all ~** повсю́ду.

arouse *vt* (*wake up*) буди́ть *impf*, раз~ *pf*; (*stimulate*) возбужда́ть *impf*, возбуди́ть *pf*.

arrange *vt* расста́вить *impf*, расста́вить *pf*; (*plan*) устра́ивать *impf*, устро́ить *pf*; (*mus*) аранжи́ровать *impf & pf*; *vi* **~ to** договора́ться *impf*, договори́ться *pf* +*inf*. **arrangement** *n* расположе́ние; устро́йство; (*agreement*) соглаше́ние; (*mus*) аранжиро́вка; *pl* приготовле́ния *neut pl*.

array *vt* выставля́ть *impf*, вы́ставить *pf*; *n* (*dress*) нарядъ; (*display*) колле́кция.

arrears *n pl* задо́лженность.

arrest *vt* аресто́вывать *impf*, арестова́ть *pf* и аре́ст.

arrival *n* прибы́тие, прие́зд; (*new ~*) вновь прибы́вший *sb*. **arrive** *vi* прибыва́ть *impf*, прибы́ть *pf*; приезжа́ть *impf*, прие́хать *pf*.

arrogance *n* высокоме́рие. **arrogant** *adj* высокоме́рный.

arrow *n* стрела́; (*pointer*) стре́лка.

arsenal *n* арсена́л.

arsenic *n* мышья́к.

arson *n* поджо́г.

art *n* иску́сство; *pl* гуманита́рные нау́ки *f pl*; *adj* худо́жественный.

arterial *adj*: ~ **road** магистра́ль. **artery** *n* арте́рия.

artful *adj* хи́трый.

arthritis *n* артри́т.

article *n* (*literary*) статья́; (*clause*) пункт; (*thing*) предме́т; (*gram*) арти́кль *m*.

articulate *vt* произноси́ть *impf*, произнести́ *pf*; (*express*) выража́ть *impf*, вы́разить *pf*; *adj* (*of speech*) членоразде́льный; **be** ~ чётко выража́ть *impf* свои́ мы́сли. **articulated lorry** *n* грузово́й автомоби́ль с прице́пом.

artifice *n* хи́трость. **artificial** *adj* иску́сственный.

artillery *n* артилле́рия.

artisan *n* реме́сленник.

artist *n* худо́жник. **artiste** *n* арти́ст, ~ка. **artistic** *adj* худо́жественный.

artless *adj* простоду́шный.

as *adv* как; *conj* (*when*) когда́; в то вре́мя как; (*because*) так как; (*manner*) как; (*though, however*) как ни; *rel pron* ка-

ко́й; кото́рый; что; **as ... as** так (же)... как; **as for**, то относи́тельно+*gen*; что каса́ется+*gen*; **as if** как бу́дто; **as it were** как бы; так сказа́ть; **as soon as** как то́лько; **as well** та́кже; то́же.

asbestos *n* асбе́ст.

ascend *vt* (*go up*) поднима́ться *impf*, подня́ться *pf* по+*dat*; (*throne*) восходи́ть *impf*, взойти́ *pf* на+*acc*; *vi* возноси́ться *impf*, вознести́сь *pf*. **ascendancy** *n* власть. **Ascension** *n* (*eccl*) Вознесе́ние. **ascent** *n* восхожде́ние (**of** на+*acc*).

ascertain *vt* устана́вливать *impf*, установи́ть *pf*.

ascetic *adj* аскети́ческий; *n* аске́т. **asceticism** *n* аскети́зм.

ascribe *vt* припи́сывать *impf*, приписа́ть *pf* (**to** +*dat*).

ash[1] *n* (*tree*) я́сень *m*.

ash[2], **ashes** *n* зола́, пе́пел; (*human remains*) прах. **ashtray** *n* пе́пельница.

ashamed *predic*: **he is** ~ ему́ сты́дно; **be, feel,** ~ стыди́ться *impf* и по~ *pf* +*gen*.

ashen *adj* (*pale*) мертве́нно-бле́дный.

ashore *adv* на бе́рег(у́).

Asia *n* А́зия. **Asian, Asiatic** *adj* азиа́тский; *n* азиа́т, ~ка.

aside *adv* в сто́рону.

ask *vt* и *i* (*enquire of*) спра́шивать *impf*, спроси́ть *pf*; (*request*) проси́ть *impf*, по~ *pf* (**for** *acc, gen*, о+*prep*); (*invite*) приглаша́ть *impf*, пригласи́ть *pf*; (*demand*) тре́бовать *impf* +*gen* (**of** от+*gen*); ~ **after** осведомля́ться *impf*, осве́домиться *pf* о+*prep*; ~ **a question** задава́ть *impf*, зада́ть *pf* вопро́с.

askance *adv* ко́со.

askew *adv* кри́во.

asleep *predic & adv:* be ~ спать *impf,* fall ~ засыпа́ть *impf,* засну́ть *pf.*

asparagus *n* спа́ржа.

aspect *n* вид; *(side)* сторона́.

aspersion *n* клевета́.

asphalt *n* асфа́льт.

asphyxiate *vt* удуша́ть *impf,* удуши́ть *pf.*

aspiration *n* стремле́ние. **aspire** *vi* стреми́ться *impf* (to к+*dat*).

aspirin *n* аспири́н; *(tablet)* табле́тка аспири́на.

ass *n* осёл.

assail *vt* напада́ть *impf,* напа́сть *pf* на+*acc*; *(with questions)* забра́сывать *impf,* заброса́ть *pf* вопро́сами. **assailant** *n* напада́ющий *sb.*

assassin *n* уби́йца *m & pf.* **assassinate** *vt* убива́ть *impf,* уби́ть *pf.* **assassination** *n* уби́йство.

assault *n* нападе́ние; *(mil)* штурм; ~ and battery оскорбле́ние де́йствием; *vt* напада́ть *impf,* напа́сть *pf* на+*acc*.

assemblage *n* сбо́рка. **assemble** *vt & i* собира́ть(ся) *impf,* собра́ть(ся) *pf.* **assembly** *n* собра́ние; *(of machine)* сбо́рка.

assent *n* согласие. **assent** *vi* соглаша́ться *impf,* согласи́ться *pf* (to на+*acc*); *n* согла́сие.

assert *vt* утвержда́ть *impf;* ~ o.s. отста́ивать *impf,* отстоя́ть *pf* свои́ права́. **assertion** *n* утвержде́ние. **assertive** *adj* насто́йчивый.

assess *vt (amount)* определя́ть *impf,* определи́ть *pf; (value)* оце́нивать *impf,* оце-

ни́ть *pf.* **assessment** *n* определе́ние; оце́нка.

asset *n* це́нное ка́чество; *(comm; also pl)* акти́в.

assiduous *adj* приле́жный.

assign *vt (appoint)* назнача́ть *impf,* назна́чить *pf; (allot)* отводи́ть *impf,* отвести́ *pf.* **assignation** *n* свида́ние. **assignment** *n (task)* зада́ние; *(mission)* командиро́вка.

assimilate *vt* усва́ивать *impf,* усво́ить *pf.* **assimilation** *n* усвое́ние.

assist *vt* помога́ть *impf,* помо́чь *pf* +*dat*. **assistance** *n* по́мощь. **assistant** *n* помо́щник, ассисте́нт.

associate *vt* ассоции́ровать *impf & pf; vi* обща́ться *impf* (with c+*instr*); *n* колле́га *m & f.* **association** *n* о́бщество, ассоциа́ция.

assorted *adj* ра́зный. **assortment** *n* ассортиме́нт.

assuage *vt (calm)* успока́ивать *impf,* успоко́ить *pf; (alleviate)* смягча́ть *impf,* смягчи́ть *pf.*

assume *vt (take on)* принима́ть *impf,* приня́ть *pf; (suppose)* предполага́ть *impf,* предположи́ть *pf;* ~d name вы́мышленное и́мя *neut;* let us ~ предполо́жим. **assumption** *n (taking on)* приня́тие на себя́; *(supposition)* предположе́ние.

assurance *n* заве́рение; *(self-~)* самоуве́ренность; *(insurance)* страхова́ние. **assure** *vt* уверя́ть *impf,* уве́рить *pf.*

asterisk *n* звёздочка.

asthma *n* а́стма. **asthmatic** *adj* астмати́ческий.

astonish *vt* удивля́ть *impf,* удиви́ть *pf.* **astonishing** *adj*

удиви́тельный. **astonishment**
n удивле́ние.

astound vt изумля́ть impf,
изуми́ть pf. **astounding** adj
изуми́тельный.

astray adv: go ~ сбива́ться
impf, сби́ться pf с пути́; lead
~ сбива́ть impf, сбить pf с
пути́.

astride prep верхо́м на+prep.

astringent adj вя́жущий;
те́рпкий.

astrologer n астро́лог. **astrology** n астроло́гия. **astronaut** n астрона́вт. **astronomer** n астроно́м. **astronomical** adj астрономи́ческий.
astronomy n астроно́мия.

astute adj прони́цательный.

asunder adv (apart) врозь; (in
pieces) на ча́сти.

asylum n сумасше́дший дом;
(refuge) убе́жище.

asymmetrical adj асимметри́-
чный. **asymmetry** n асим-
ме́трия.

at prep (position) на+prep,
в+prep, y+gen: **at a concert** на
конце́рте; **at the cinema** в
кино́; **at the window** y окна́;
(time) в+acc: **at two o'clock** в
два часа́; на+acc: **at Easter** на
Па́сху; (price) по+dat: **at 5p
a pound** по пяти́ пе́нсов за
фунт; (speed): **at 60 mph** со
ско́ростью 60 миль в час; ~
first снача́ла, сперва́; ~
home до́ма; ~ **last**
наконе́ц; ~ **least** по кра́йней
ме́ре; ~ **that** на том; (moreover) к тому́ же.

atheism n атеи́зм. **atheist** n
атеи́ст, ~ка.

athlete n спортсме́н, ~ка.
athletic adj атлети́ческий.
athletics n (лёгкая) атле́-
тика.

atlas n а́тлас.

atmosphere n атмосфе́ра. **atmospheric** adj атмосфе́р-
ный.

atom n а́том; ~ **bomb** а́том-
ная бо́мба. **atomic** adj а́том-
ный.

atone vi искупа́ть impf, ис-
купи́ть pf (for +acc). **atonement** n искупле́ние.

atrocious adj ужа́сный. **atrocity** n зве́рство.

attach vt (fasten) прикреп-
ля́ть impf, прикрепи́ть pf;
(append) прилага́ть impf,
приложи́ть pf; (attribute) при-
дава́ть impf, прида́ть pf; **attached to** (devoted) привя́-
занный к+dat. **attaché** n
атташе́ n indecl. **attachment**
n прикрепле́ние; привя́зан-
ность; (tech) принадле́ж-
ность.

attack vt напада́ть impf, на-
па́сть pf на+acc; n нападе́-
ние; (of illness) припа́док.

attain vt достига́ть impf, до-
сти́чь & дости́гнуть pf (+gen).
attainment n достиже́ние.

attempt vt пыта́ться impf,
по~ pf +inf; n попы́тка.

attend vt & i (be present at) при-
су́тствовать impf (на+prep);
vt (accompany) сопровож-
да́ть impf, сопроводи́ть pf;
(go to regularly) посеща́ть
impf, посети́ть pf; ~ **to** за-
нима́ться impf, заня́ться pf.
attendance n (presence) при-
су́тствие; (number) посеща́е-
мость. **attendant** adj сопро-
вожда́ющий; n дежу́рный sb;
(escort) провожа́тый sb.

attention n внима́ние; **pay** ~
обраща́ть impf, обрати́ть pf
внима́ние (**to** на+acc); (mil)
смирно! **attentive** adj

внима́тельный; (solicitous) забо́тливый.

attest vt & i (also ~ to) заверя́ть impf, завери́ть pf; свиде́тельствовать impf, за~ pf (o+prep).

attic n черда́к.

attire vt наряжа́ть impf, наряди́ть pf; n наря́д.

attitude n (posture) по́за; (opinion) отноше́ние (towards k+dat).

attorney n пове́ренный sb; **power of ~** дове́ренность.

attract vt привлека́ть impf, привле́чь pf. **attraction** n привлека́тельность; (entertainment) аттракцио́н. **attractive** adj привлека́тельный.

attribute vt припи́сывать impf, приписа́ть pf; (quality) сво́йство. **attribution** n припи́сывание. **attributive** adj атрибути́вный.

attrition n: war of ~ война́ на истоще́ние.

aubergine n баклажа́н.

auburn adj тёмно-ры́жий.

auction n аукцио́н; vt продава́ть impf, прода́ть pf с аукцио́на. **auctioneer** n аукциони́ст.

audacious adj (bold) сме́лый; (impudent) де́рзкий. **audacity** n сме́лость; де́рзость.

audible adj слы́шный. **audience** n пу́блика, аудито́рия; (listeners) слу́шатели m pl; (viewers, spectators) зри́тели m pl; (interview) аудие́нция.

audit n прове́рка счето́в, реви́зия; vt прове́рить impf, прове́рить pf (счета́+gen). **audition** n про́ба; vt устра́ивать impf, устро́ить pf про́бу +gen. **auditor** n реви́зор. **auditorium** n зри́тельный зал.

augment n увели́чивать impf, увели́чить pf.

augur vt & i предвеща́ть impf.

August n а́вгуст; adj а́вгустовский. **august** adj вели́чественный.

aunt n тётя, тётка.

au pair n домрабо́тница иностра́нного происхожде́ния.

aura n орео́л.

auspices n pl покрови́тельство. **auspicious** adj благоприя́тный.

austere adj стро́гий. **austerity** n стро́гость.

Australia n Австра́лия. **Australian** n австрали́ец, -и́йка; adj австрали́йский.

Austria n А́встрия. **Austrian** n австри́ец, -и́йка; adj австри́йский.

authentic adj по́длинный. **authenticate** vt устана́вливать impf, установи́ть pf по́длинность+gen. **authenticity** n по́длинность.

author, authoress n а́втор.

authoritarian adj авторита́рный. **authoritative** adj авторите́тный. **authority** n (power) власть, полномо́чие; (weight, expert) авторите́т; (source) авторите́тный исто́чник. **authorization** n уполномо́чивание; (permission) разреше́ние. **authorize** vt (action) разреша́ть impf, разреши́ть pf; (person) уполномо́чивать impf, уполномо́чить pf. **authorship** n а́вторство.

autobiographical adj автобиографи́ческий. **autobiography** n автобиогра́фия. **autocracy** n автокра́тия. **autocrat** n автокра́т. **autocratic** adj автократи́ческий. **autograph** n авто́граф. **automatic** adj автомати́ческий. **automation** *n* автоматиза́ция. **automaton** *n* автома́т. **automobile** *n* автомоби́ль *m*. **autonomous** *adj* автоно́мный. **autonomy** *n* автоно́мия. **autopilot** *n* автопило́т. **autopsy** *n* вскры́тие; ауто́псия.

autumn *n* о́сень. **autumn(al)** *adj* осе́нний.

auxiliary *adj* вспомога́тельный; *n* помо́щник, -ица.

avail *n*: to no ~ напра́сно; ~ o.s. of по́льзоваться *impf*, вос~ *pf* +*instr*. **available** *adj* досту́пный, нали́чный.

avalanche *n* лави́на.

avant-garde *n* аванга́рд; *adj* аванга́рдный.

avarice *n* жа́дность. **avaricious** *adj* жа́дный.

avenge *vt* мстить *impf*, ото~ *pf* за+*acc*. **avenger** *n* мсти́тель *m*.

avenue *n* (of trees) алле́я; (wide street) проспе́кт; (means) путь *m*.

average *n* сре́днее число́, сре́днее *sb*; on ~ в сре́днем; *adj* сре́дний; *vt* де́лать *impf* в сре́днем; *vt & i*: ~ (out at) составля́ть *impf*, соста́вить *pf* в сре́днем.

averse *adj*: not ~ to не прочь +*inf*, не про́тив+*gen*. **aversion** *n* отвраще́ние. **avert** *vt* (ward off) предотвраща́ть *impf*, предотврати́ть *pf*; (turn away) отводи́ть *impf*, отвести́ *pf*.

aviary *n* пти́чник.

aviation *n* авиа́ция.

avid *adj* жа́дный; (keen) стра́стный.

avocado *n* авока́до *neut indecl*.

avoid *vt* избега́ть *impf*, избежа́ть *pf* +*gen*; (evade) укло-

ня́ться *impf*, уклони́ться *pf* от+*gen*. **avoidance** *n* избежа́ние, уклоне́ние.

avowal *n* призна́ние. **avowed** *adj* при́знанный.

await *vt* ждать *impf* +*gen*.

awake *predic*: be ~ не спать *impf*. **awake(n)** *vt* пробужда́ть *impf*, пробуди́ть *pf*; *vi* просыпа́ться *impf*, просну́ться *pf*.

award *vt* присужда́ть *impf*, присуди́ть *pf* (person dat, thing acc); награжда́ть *impf*, награди́ть *pf* (person acc, thing instr); *n* награ́да.

aware *predic*: be ~ of сознава́ть *impf*; know *impf*, знать *impf*. **awareness** *n* созна́ние.

away *adv* прочь; be ~ отсу́тствовать *impf*; far ~ (from) далеко́ (от+*gen*); 5 miles ~ в пяти́ ми́лях отсю́да; ~ game игра́ на чужо́м по́ле.

awe *n* благогове́йный страх. **awful** *adj* ужа́сный. **awfully** *adv* ужа́сно.

awhile *adv* не́которое вре́мя.

awkward *adj* нело́вкий. **awkwardness** *n* нело́вкость.

awning *n* наве́с, тент.

awry *adv* ко́со.

axe *n* топо́р; *vt* уре́зывать, уре́зать *impf*, уре́зать *pf*.

axiom *n* аксио́ма. **axiomatic** *adj* аксиомати́ческий.

axis, axle *n* ось.

ay *int* да!; *n* (in vote) го́лос „за“.

Azerbaijan *n* Азербайджа́н. **Azerbaijani** *n* азербайджа́нец (-нца), -а́нка; *adj* азербайджа́нский.

azure *n* лазу́рь; *adj* лазу́рный.

B

BA *abbr* (*univ*) бакала́вр.

babble *n* (*voices*) болтовня́; (*water*) журча́ние; *vi* болта́ть *impf*; (*water*) журча́ть *impf*.

baboon *n* павиа́н.

baby *n* младе́нец; ~**-sit** присма́тривать за детьми́ в отсу́тствие роди́телей; ~**-sitter** приходя́щая ня́ня.

babyish *adj* ребя́ческий.

bachelor *n* холостя́к; (*univ*) бакала́вр.

bacillus *n* баци́лла.

back *n* (*of body*) спина́; (*rear*) за́дняя часть; (*reverse*) оборо́т; (*of seat*) спи́нка; (*sport*) защи́тник; *adj* за́дний; *vt* (*support*) поддержа́ть *impf*, поддержа́ть *pf*; (*car*) отодвига́ть *impf*, отодви́нуть *pf*; (*horse*) ста́вить *impf*, по- *pf* на+*acc*; (*finance*) финанси́ровать *impf* & *pf*; *vi* отодвига́ться *impf*, отодви́нуться *pf* наза́д; **~ed out of the garage** вы́ехал за́дом из гаража́; **~ down** уступа́ть *impf*, уступи́ть *pf*; **~ out** уклоня́ться *impf*, уклони́ться *pf* (**of** от+*gen*); **~ up** (*support*) подде́рживать *impf*, поддержа́ть *pf*; (*confirm*) подкрепля́ть *impf*, подкрепи́ть *pf*. **backbiting** *n* спле́тня. **backbone** *n* позвоно́чник; (*support*) гла́вная опо́ра; (*firmness*) твёрдость ха́рактера. **backcloth**, **backdrop** *n* за́дник; (*fig*) фон. **backer** *n* спо́нсор; (*supporter*) сторо́нник. **backfire** *vi* дава́ть *impf*, дать *pf* отсе́чку. **background**

n фон, за́дний план; (*person's*) происхожде́ние. **backhand(er)** *n* уда́р сле́ва. **backhanded** *adj* (*fig*) сомни́тельный. **backhander** *n* (*bribe*) взя́тка. **backing** *n* подде́ржка. **backlash** *n* реа́кция. **backlog** *n* задо́лженность. **backside** *n* зад. **backstage** *adv* за кули́сами; *adj* закули́сный. **backstroke** *n* пла́вание на спине́. **back-up** *n* подде́ржка; (*copy*) резе́рвная ко́пия; *adj* вспомога́тельный. **backward** *adj* отста́лый. **backward(s)** *adv* наза́д. **backwater** *n* заво́дь. **back yard** *n* за́дний двор.

bacon *n* беко́н.

bacterium *n* бакте́рия. **bad** *adj* плохо́й; (*food etc.*) испо́рченный; (*language*) гру́бый; **~-mannered** неви́спитанный; **~ taste** безвку́сица; **~-tempered** раздражи́тельный.

badge *n* значо́к.

badger *n* барсу́к; *vt* трави́ть *impf*, за-~ *pf*.

badly *adv* пло́хо; (*very much*) о́чень.

badminton *n* бадминто́н.

baffle *vt* озада́чивать *impf*, озада́чить *pf*.

bag *n* (*handbag*) су́мка; (*plastic* ~, *sack*, *under eyes*) мешо́к; (*paper* ~) бума́жный паке́т; *pl* (*luggage*) бага́ж.

baggage *n* бага́ж.

baggy *adj* мешкова́тый.

bagpipe *n* волы́нка.

bail[1] *n* (*security*) поручи́тельство; **release on** ~ отпуска́ть *impf*, отпусти́ть *pf* на пору́ки; *vt* (~ **out**) брать *impf*, взять *pf* на пору́ки; (*help*) выруча́ть *impf*, вы́ручить *pf*.

bail², **bale²** vt вычерпывать impf, вычерпнуть pf (воду из+gen); ~ **out** vi выбрасываться impf, выброситься pf с парашютом.

bailiff n судебный исполнитель.

bait n наживка; приманка (also fig); vt (torment) травить impf, за~ pf.

bake vt & i печь(ся) impf, ис~ pf. **baker** n пекарь m, булочник. **bakery** n пекарня; (shop) булочная sb.

balalaika n балалайка.

balance n (scales) весы m pl; (equilibrium) равновесие; (econ) баланс; (remainder) остаток; ~ **sheet** баланс; vt (make equal) уравновешивать impf, уравновесить pf; vt & i (econ; hold steady) балансировать impf, c~ pf.

balcony n балкон.

bald adj лысый; ~ **patch** лысина. **balding** adj лысеющий. **baldness** n плешивость.

bale¹ n (bundle) кипа.

bale² see **bail²**

balk vi артачиться impf, за~ pf; **she balked at the price** цена её испугала.

ball¹ n (in games) мяч; (sphere; billiards) шар; (wool) клубок; ~**-bearing** шарикоподшипник; ~**point (pen)** шариковая ручка.

ball² n (dance) бал.

ballad n баллада.

ballast n балласт.

ballerina n балерина.

ballet n балет. **ballet-dancer** n артист, ~ка, балета.

balloon n воздушный шар.

ballot n голосование. **ballot-paper** n избирательный бюл-

летень m; vt держать impf голосование между+instr.

balm n бальзам. **balmy** adj (soft) мягкий.

Baltic n Балтийское море; ~ **States** прибалтийские государства, Прибалтика.

balustrade n балюстрада.

bamboo n бамбук.

bamboozle vt надувать impf, надуть pf.

ban n запрет; vt запрещать impf, запретить pf.

banal adj банальный. **banality** n банальность.

banana n банан.

band n (stripe, strip) полоса; (braid, tape) тесьма; (category) категория; (of people) группа; (gang) банда; (mus) оркестр; (radio) диапазон; vi: ~ **together** объединяться impf, объединиться pf.

bandage n бинт; vt бинтовать impf, за~ pf.

bandit n бандит.

bandstand n эстрада для оркестра.

bandwagon n: **jump on the** ~ пользоваться impf, вос~ pf благоприятными обстоятельствами.

bandy-legged adj кривоногий.

bane n отрава.

bang n (blow) удар; (noise) стук; (of gun) выстрел; vt (strike) ударять impf, ударить pf; vi хлопать impf, хлопнуть pf; (slam shut) захлопывать impf, захлопнуть pf; ~ **one's head** удариться impf, удариться pf головой; ~ **the door** хлопать impf, хлопнуть pf дверью.

bangle n браслет.

banish vt изгоня́ть impf, изгна́ть pf.

banister n пери́ла neut pl.

banjo n ба́нджо neut indecl.

bank¹ n (of river) бе́рег; (of earth) вал; vt сгреба́ть impf, сгрести́ pf в ку́чу; vi (aeron) накреня́ться impf, накрени́ться pf.

bank² n (econ) банк; ~ **account** счёт в ба́нке; ~ **holiday** устано́вленный пра́здник; vi (keep money) держа́ть impf де́ньги (в ба́нке); vt (put in ~) класть impf, положи́ть pf в ба́нк; vi полага́ться impf, положи́ться pf на+acc. **banker** n банки́р. **banknote** n банкно́та.

bankrupt n банкро́т; adj обанкро́тившийся; vt доводи́ть impf, довести́ pf до банкро́тства. **bankruptcy** n банкро́тство.

banner n зна́мя neut.

banquet n банке́т, пир.

banter n подшу́чивание.

baptism n креще́ние. **baptize** vt крести́ть impf, о~ pf.

bar n (beam) брус; (of cage) решётка; (of chocolate) плитка; (of soap) кусо́к; (barrier) прегра́да; (law) адвокату́ра; (counter) сто́йка; (room) бар; (mus) такт; vt (obstruct) прегражда́ть impf, прегради́ть pf; (prohibit) запреща́ть impf, запрети́ть pf.

barbarian n ва́рвар. **barbaric**, **barbarous** adj ва́рварский.

barbecue n (party) шашлы́к; vt жа́рить impf, за~ pf на ве́ртеле.

barbed wire n колю́чая про́волока.

barber n парикма́хер. ~'s **shop** парикма́херская sb.

bar code n маркиро́вка.

bard n бард.

bare adj (naked) го́лый; (empty) пусто́й; (small) минима́льный; vt обнажа́ть impf, обнажи́ть pf; ~ **one's teeth** ска́лить impf, о~ pf зу́бы. **barefaced** adj на́глый. **barefoot** adj босо́й. **barely** adv едва́.

bargain n (deal) сде́лка; (good buy) вы́годная сде́лка; vi торгова́ться impf, с~ pf; ~ **for**, **on** (expect) ожида́ть impf +gen.

barge n ба́ржа; vi: ~ **into** (room etc.) вырыва́ться impf, ворва́ться pf в+acc.

baritone n барито́н.

bark¹ n (of dog) лай; vi ла́ять impf.

bark² n (of tree) кора́.

barley n ячме́нь n.

barmaid n буфе́тчица. **barman** n буфе́тчик.

barmy adj тро́нутый.

barn n амба́р.

barometer n баро́метр.

baron n баро́н. **baroness** n бароне́сса.

baroque n баро́кко neut indecl; adj баро́чный.

barrack¹ n каза́рма.

barrack² vt освиста́ивать impf, освиста́ть pf.

barrage n (in river) запру́да; (gunfire) огнево́й вал; (fig) град.

barrel n бо́чка; (of gun) ду́ло.

barren adj беспло́дный.

barricade n баррика́да; vt баррикади́ровать impf, за~ pf.

barrier n барье́р.

barring prep исключа́я.

barrister n адвока́т.

barrow n теле́жка.

barter n товарообмéн; vi обмéниваться impf, обменя́ться pf товáрами.

base[1] adj нúзкий; (metal) неблагорóдный.

base[2] n оснóва; (also mil) бáза; vt оснóвывать impf, основáть pf. **baseball** n бейсбóл.

baseless adj необоснóванный. **basement** n подвáл.

bash vt трéснуть pf; n: have a ~! попрóбуй(те)!

bashful adj застéнчивый.

basic adj оснóвнóй. **basically** adv в оснóвном.

basin n таз; (geog) бассéйн.

basis n оснóва, бáзис.

bask vi грéться impf; (fig) наслаждáться impf, наслади́ться pf (in +instr).

basket n корзи́на. **basketball** n баскетбóл.

bass n бас; adj басóвый.

bassoon n фагóт.

bastard n (sl) негодя́й.

baste vt (cul) полива́ть impf, поли́ть pf жи́ром.

bastion n бастиóн.

bat[1] n (zool) летýчая мышь.

bat[2] n (sport) бита́; vi бить impf, по~ pf по мячý.

bat[3] vt: he didn't ~ an eyelid он и глáзом не моргнýл.

batch n пáчка; (of loaves) вы́печка.

bated adj: with ~ breath зата́ив дыха́ние.

bath n (vessel) вáнна; pl плáвательный бассéйн; have a bath принимáть impf, приня́ть pf вáнну; vt купáть impf, вы́~, ис~ pf. **bathe** vi купáться impf, вы́~, ис~ pf; vt купáть impf, вы́~, ис~ pf. **bather** n купáльщик, -ица. **bath-house** n бáня. **bathing** n: ~ cap купáльная шапóч-

ка; ~ costume купáльный костю́м. **bathroom** n вáнная sb.

baton n (staff of office) жезл; (sport) эстафéта; (mus) (дирижёрская) пáлочка.

battalion n батальóн.

batten n рéйка.

batter n взби́тое тéсто; vt колоти́ть impf, по~ pf.

battery n батарéя.

battle n би́тва, (fig) борьбá; vi боро́ться impf. **battlefield** n пóле би́твы. **battlement** n зубчáтая стенá. **battleship** n линéйный корáбль m.

bawdy adj непристóйный.

bawl vi орáть impf.

bay[1] n (bot) лавр; adj лáвровый.

bay[2] n (geog) зали́в.

bay[3] n (recess) пролёт; ~ window фонáрь m.

bay[4] vi (bark) ля́ять impf; (howl) выть impf.

bay[5] adj (colour) гнедóй.

bayonet n штык.

bazaar n базáр.

BC abbr до н.э. (до нáшей эры).

be v 1. быть: usually omitted in pres: he is a teacher он учи́тель. 2. (exist) существовáть impf. 3. (frequentative) бывáть impf. 4. (~ situated) находи́ться impf; (stand) стоя́ть impf; (lie) лежáть impf. 5. (in general definitions) явля́ться impf +instr. Moscow is the capital of Russia столи́цей Росси́и явля́ется гóрод Москвá. 6.: there is, there are имéются; (emph) есть.

be[2] v aux 1. be+inf, expressing duty, plan: дóлжен+inf. 2. be+past participle passive, expressing passive: быть+past *participle passive in short form:* **it was done** бы́ло сде́лано; *impers construction of 3 pl+past:* **I was beaten** меня́ би́ли; *reflexive construction: music was heard* слы́шалась му́зыка. **3.** *be+pres participle active, expressing continuous tenses:* imperfective aspect: **I am reading** я чита́ю.

beach *n* пляж.

beacon *n* ма́як, сигна́льный ого́нь *m*.

bead *n* бу́сина; *(drop)* ка́пля; *pl* бу́сы *f pl*.

beak *n* клюв.

beaker *n* *(child's)* ча́шка с но́сиком; *(chem)* мензу́рка.

beam *n* ба́лка; *(ray)* луч; *vi (shine)* сия́ть *impf*.

bean *n* фасо́ль, боб.

bear¹ *n* медве́дь *m*.

bear² *vt (carry)* носи́ть *indet*, нести́ *det*, по~ *pf*; *(endure)* терпе́ть *impf*; *(child)* роди́ть *impf & pf*; ~ **out** подтвержда́ть *impf*, подтверди́ть *pf*; ~ **up** держа́ться *impf*. **bearable** *adj* терпи́мый.

beard *n* борода́. **bearded** *adj* борода́тый.

bearer *n* носи́тель *m*; *(of cheque)* предъяви́тель *m*; *(of letter)* пода́тель *m*.

bearing *n (deportment)* оса́нка; *(relation)* отноше́ние; *(position)* пе́ленг; *(tech)* подши́пник; **get one's ~s** ориенти́роваться *impf & pf*; **lose one's ~** потеря́ть *pf* ориентиро́вку.

beast *n* живо́тное *sb*; *(fig)* скоти́на *m & f.* **beastly** *adj (coll)* проти́вный.

beat *n* бой; *(round)* обхо́д; *(mus)* такт; *vt* бить *impf*, по~ *pf*; *(cul)* взбива́ть *impf*,

взбить *pf*; *vi* би́ться *impf*, ~ **off** отбива́ть *impf*, отбить *pf*; ~ **up** избива́ть *impf*, изби́ть *pf*. **beating** *n* битьё; *(defeat)* пораже́ние; *(of heart)* бие́ние.

beautiful *adj* краси́вый. **beautify** *vt* украша́ть *impf* укра́сить *pf*. **beauty** *n* красота́; *(person)* краса́вица.

beaver *n* бобр.

because *conj* потому́, что; так как; *adv:* ~ **of** из-за+*gen*.

beckon *vt* мани́ть *impf*, по~ *pf* к себе́.

become *vi* станови́ться *impf*, стать *pf* +*instr*; ~ **of** ста́ться *pf* c+*instr*. **becoming** *adj (dress)* иду́щий к лицу́+*dat*.

bed *n* крова́ть, посте́ль; *(garden)* гря́дка; *(sea)* дно; *(river)* ру́сло; *(geol)* пласт; **go to** ~ ложи́ться *impf*, лечь *pf* спать; **make the** ~ стели́ть *impf*, по~ *pf* посте́ль. **bed and breakfast** *n (hotel)* ма́ленькая гости́ница. **bedclothes** *n pl*, **bedding** *n* посте́льное бельё. **bedridden** *adj* прико́ванный к посте́ли. **bedroom** *n* спа́льня. **bedside table** *n* ту́мбочка. **bedsitter** *n* однокомнатная кварти́ра. **bedspread** *n* покрыва́ло. **bedtime** *n* вре́мя *neut* ложи́ться спать.

bedevil *vt* му́чить *impf*, за~ *pf*.

bedlam *n* бедла́м.

bedraggled *adj* растрёпанный.

bee *n* пчела́. **beehive** *n* у́лей.

beech *n* бук.

beef *n* говя́дина. **beefburger** *n* котле́та.

beer *n* пи́во.

beetle *n* жук.

beetroot *n* свёкла.

befall vt & i случа́ться impf, случи́ться pf (+dat).

befit vt подходи́ть impf, подойти́ pf +dat.

before adv ра́ньше; prep пе́ред+instr, до+gen; conj до того́ как; пре́жде чем; (rather than) скоре́е чем; **the day ~ yesterday** позавчера́. **beforehand** adv зара́нее.

befriend vt дружи́ться impf, по~ pf c+instr.

beg vt (ask) о́чень проси́ть impf, по~ pf (person+acc; thing+acc or gen); vi ни́щенствовать impf; (of dog) служи́ть impf; ~ for проси́ть impf, по~ pf +acc or gen; ~ **pardon** проси́ть impf проще́ние.

beggar n ни́щий sb.

begin vt (& i) начина́ть(ся) impf, нача́ть(ся) pf. **beginner** n начина́ющий sb. **beginning** n нача́ло.

begrudge vt (give reluctantly) жале́ть impf, co~ pf o+prep.

beguile vt (charm) очаро́вывать impf, очарова́ть pf; (seduce, delude) обольща́ть impf, обольсти́ть pf.

behalf n: on ~ of от и́мени +gen; (in interest of) в по́льзу +gen.

behave vi вести́ impf себя́. **behaviour** n поведе́ние.

behest n заве́т.

behind adv, prep сза́ди (+gen), позади́ (+gen), за (+acc, instr); n зад; **be, fall, ~** отстава́ть impf, отста́ть pf.

behold vt смотре́ть impf, по~ pf. **beholden** predic: ~ **to** обя́зан+dat.

beige adj бе́жевый.

being n (existence) бытие́; (creature) существо́.

Belarus n Белару́сь.

belated adj запозда́лый.

belch vi рыга́ть impf, рыгну́ть pf, vt изверга́ть impf, изве́ргнуть pf.

beleaguer vt осажда́ть impf, осади́ть pf.

belfry n колоко́льня.

Belgian n белги́ец, -ги́йка; adj бельги́йский. **Belgium** n Бе́льгия.

belie vt противоре́чить impf +dat.

belief n (faith) ве́ра; (confidence) убежде́ние. **believable** adj правдоподо́бный. **believe** vt ве́рить impf, по~ pf +dat; ~ **in** ве́рить impf в+acc. **believer** n ве́рующий sb.

belittle vt умаля́ть impf, умали́ть pf.

bell n ко́локол; (doorbell) звоно́к; ~ **tower** колоко́льня.

bellicose adj вои́нственный. **belligerence** n вои́нственность. **belligerent** adj вою́ющий; (aggressive) вои́нственный.

bellow vt & i реве́ть impf.

bellows n pl мехи́ m pl.

belly n живо́т.

belong vi принадлежа́ть impf (**to** (k)+dat). **belongings** n pl пожи́тки (-ков) pl.

Belorussian n белору́с, ~ка; adj белору́сский.

beloved adj & sb возлю́бленный.

below adv (position) вниз, (place) внизу́, ни́же; prep ни́же+gen.

belt n (strap) по́яс, (zone) зо́на, полоса́; ремень, (also tech) ремень.

bench n скаме́йка; (for work) стано́к.

bend n изги́б; vt (& i, also ~ down) сгиба́ть(ся) impf,

гну́ть(ся) *pf*; ~ **over** склоня́ться *impf*, склони́ться *pf* над+*instr*.

beneath *prep* под+*instr*.

benediction *n* благослове́ние.

benefactor *n* благоде́тель *m*. **benefactress** *n* благоде́тельница.

beneficial *adj* поле́зный. **beneficiary** *n* получа́тель *m*; (*law*) насле́дник. **benefit** *n* по́льза; (*allowance*) посо́бие; (*theat*) бенефи́с; *vt* приноси́ть *impf*, принести́ *pf* по́льзу +*dat*; извлека́ть *impf*, извле́чь *pf* вы́году.

benevolence *n* благожела́тельность. **benevolent** *adj* благожела́тельный.

benign *adj* до́брый, мя́гкий; (*tumour*) доброка́чественный.

bent *n* скло́нность.

bequeath *vt* завеща́ть *impf* & *pf* (**to**+*dat*). **bequest** *n* посме́ртный дар.

berate *vt* руга́ть *impf*, вы́~ *pf*.

bereave *vt* лиша́ть *impf*, лиши́ть *pf* (**of** +*gen*). **bereavement** *n* тяжёлая утра́та.

berry *n* я́года.

berserk *adj*: **go** ~ взбеси́ться *pf*.

berth *n* (*bunk*) ко́йка; (*naut*) стоя́нка; *vi* прича́ливать *impf*, прича́лить *pf*.

beseech *v* умоля́ть *impf*, умоли́ть *pf*.

beset *vt* осажда́ть *impf*, осади́ть *pf*.

beside *prep* о́коло+*gen*, ря́дом с+*instr*; ~ **the point** некста́ти; ~ **o.s.** вне себя́. **besides** *adv* кро́ме того́; *prep* кро́ме+*gen*.

besiege *vt* осажда́ть *impf*, осади́ть *pf*.

besotted *adj* одурма́ненный.

bespoke *adj* сде́ланный на зака́з.

best *adj* лу́чший, са́мый лу́чший; *adv* лу́чше всего́, бо́льше всего́; **all the** ~! всего́ наилу́чшего! **do one's** ~ де́лать *impf*, с~ *pf* всё возмо́жное; ~ **man** ша́фер.

bestial *adj* зве́рский. **bestiality** *n* зве́рство.

bestow *vt* дарова́ть *impf* & *pf*.

bestseller *n* бестсе́ллер.

bet *n* пари́ *neut indecl*; (*stake*) ста́вка; *vi* держа́ть *impf* пари́ (**on** на+*acc*); *vt* (*stake*) ста́вить *impf*, по~ *pf*; **he bet me £5** он поспо́рил со мной 5 фу́нтов.

betray *vt* изменя́ть *impf*, измени́ть *pf*+*dat*. **betrayal** *n* изме́на.

better *adj* лу́чший; *adv* лу́чше; (*more*) бо́льше; *vt* улучша́ть *impf*, улу́чшить *pf*; **all the** ~ тем лу́чше; ~ **off** бо́лее состоя́тельный; ~ **o.s.** выдвига́ться *impf*, вы́двинуться *pf*; **get** ~ (*health*) поправля́ться *impf*, попра́виться *pf*; **get the** ~ **of** брать *impf*, взять *pf* верх над+*instr*; **had** ~: **you had** ~ **go** вам (*dat*) лу́чше бы пойти́; **think** ~ **of** переду́мать *impf*, переду́мать *pf*. **betterment** *n* улучше́ние.

between *prep* ме́жду+*instr*.

bevel *vt* ска́шивать *impf*, скоси́ть *pf*.

beverage *n* напи́ток.

bevy *n* ста́йка.

beware *vi* остерега́ться *impf*, остере́чься *pf* (**of** +*gen*).

bewilder *vt* сбива́ть *impf*, сбить *pf* с то́лку. **bewildered** *adj* озада́ченный. **bewilder-**

ment *n* замеша́тельство.

bewitch *vt* заколдо́вывать *impf*, заколдова́ть *pf*; (*fig*) очаро́вывать *impf*, очарова́ть *pf*. **bewitching** *adj* очарова́тельный.

beyond *prep* за+*acc* & *instr*; по ту сто́рону+*gen*; (*above*) сверх+*gen*; (*outside*) вне+*gen*; **the back of ~** край све́та.

bias *n* (*inclination*) укло́н; (*prejudice*) предубежде́ние. **biased** *adj* предубежде́нный.

bib *n* нагру́дник.

Bible *n* Би́блия. **biblical** *adj* библе́йский.

bibliographical *adj* библиографи́ческий. **bibliography** *n* библиогра́фия.

bicarbonate (of soda) *n* питьева́я со́да.

biceps *n* би́цепс.

bicker *vi* пререка́ться *impf*.

bicycle *n* велосипе́д.

bid *n* предложе́ние цены́; (*attempt*) попы́тка; *vt* & *i* предлага́ть *impf*, предложи́ть *pf* (це́ну) (**for** за+*acc*); *vt* (*command*) прика́зывать *impf*, приказа́ть *pf* +*dat*. **bidding** *n* предложе́ние цены́; (*command*) приказа́ние.

bide *vt*: **~ one's time** ожида́ть *impf* благоприя́тного слу́чая.

biennial *adj* двухле́тний, двухле́тника.

bier *n* катафа́лк.

bifocals *n pl* бифока́льные очки́ *pl*.

big *adj* большо́й; (*also important*) кру́пный.

bigamist *n* (*man*) двоеже́нец; (*woman*) двуму́жница. **bigamy** *n* двубра́чие.

bigwig *n* ши́шка.

bike *n* велосипе́д. **biker** *n*

мотоцикли́ст.

bikini *n* бики́ни *neut indecl*.

bilateral *adj* двусторо́нний.

bilberry *n* черни́ка (*no pl; usu collect*).

bile *n* жёлчь. **bilious** *adj* жёлчный.

bilingual *adj* двуязы́чный.

bill[1] *n* счёт; (*parl*) законопрое́кт; (**~ of exchange**) ве́ксель; (*poster*) афи́ша; *vt* (*announce*) объявля́ть *impf*, объяви́ть *pf* в афи́шах; (*charge*) присыла́ть *impf*, присла́ть *pf* счёт+*dat*.

bill[2] *n* (*beak*) клюв.

billet *vt* расквартиро́вывать *impf*, расквартирова́ть *pf*.

billiards *n* билья́рд.

billion *n* биллио́н.

billow *n* вал; *vi* вздыма́ться *impf*.

bin *n* му́сорное ведро́; (*corn*) закро́м.

bind *vt* (*tie*) свя́зывать *impf*, связа́ть *pf*; (*oblige*) обя́зывать *impf*, обяза́ть *pf*; (*book*) переплета́ть *impf*, переплести́ *pf*. **binder** *n* (*person*) переплётчик; (*agric*) вяза́льщик; (*for papers*) па́пка. **binding** *n* переплёт.

binge *n* кутёж.

binoculars *n pl* бино́кль *m*.

biochemistry *n* биохи́мия. **biographer** *n* био́граф. **biographical** *adj* биографи́ческий. **biography** *n* биогра́фия. **biological** *adj* биологи́ческий. **biologist** *n* био́лог. **biology** *n* биоло́гия.

bipartisan *adj* двухпарти́йный.

birch *n* берёза; (*rod*) ро́зга.

bird *n* пти́ца; **~ of prey** хи́щная пти́ца.

birth *n* рожде́ние; (*descent*)

происхождéние; ~ **certi-
cate** мéтрика; ~ **control** про-
тивозачáточные мéры *f pl*.
birthday *n* день *m* рождéния; **fourth** ~ четырёхлéтие.
birthplace *n* мéсто рождéния. **birthright** *n* прáво по рождéнию.
biscuit *n* печéнье.
bisect *vt* разрезáть *impf*, разрéзать *pf* попопáм.
bisexual *adj* бисексуáльный.
bishop *n* епúскоп; (*chess*) слон.
bit[1] *n* (*piece*) кусóчек; **a** ~ немнóго; **not a** ~ ничýть.
bit[2] *n* (*tech*) сверлó; (*bridle*) удилá (-л) *pl*.
bitch *n* (*coll*) стéрва. **bitchy** *adj* стервóзный.
bite *n* укýс; (*snack*) закýска; (*fishing*) клёв; *vt* кусáть *impf*, укусúть *pf*; *vi* (*fish*) клевáть *impf*, клюнýть *pf*. **biting** *adj* éдкий.
bitter *adj* гóрький. **bitterness** *n* гóречь.
bitumen *n* битýм.
bivouac *n* бивáк.
bizarre *adj* стрáнный.
black *adj* чёрный; ~ **eye** подбúтый глаз; ~ **market** чёрный рынок; *v*: ~ **out** затемнять *impf*, затемнить *pf*; (*vi*) сознáние; *n* (*colour*) чёрный цвет; (~ *person*) негр, (~ *-итянка*; (*mourning*) трáур. **blackberry** *n* ежевúка (*no pl*; *usu collect*). **blackbird** *n* чёрный дрозд. **blackboard** *n* доскá. **blackcurrant** *n* чёрная сморóдина (*no pl*; *usu collect*). **blacken** *vt* чернúть *impf*, о~ *pf*. **blackleg** *n* штрейкбрéхер. **blacklist** *n* вносúть *impf*, внестú *pf*

в чёрный спúсок. **blackmail** *n* шантáж; *vt* шантажúровать *impf*. **blackout** *n* затемнéние; (*faint*) потéря сознáния. **blacksmith** *n* кузнéц.
bladder *n* пузýрь *m*.
blade *n* (*knife*) лéзвие; (*oar*) лóпасть; (*grass*) былúнка.
blame *n* винá, порицáние; *vt* винúть *impf* (**for** в+*prep*); **be to** ~ быть виновáтым. **blameless** *adj* безупрéчный.
blanch *vt* (*vegetables*) ошпáривать *impf*, ошпáрить *pf*; *vi* бледнéть *impf*, по~ *pf*.
bland *adj* мягкий; (*dull*) прéсный.
blandishments *n pl* лесть.
blank *adj* (*look*) отсýтствующий; (*paper*) чúстый; *n* (*space*) прóпуск; (*form*) бланк; (*cartridge*) холостóй патрóн; ~ **cheque** незапóлненный чек.
blanket *n* одеялó.
blare *vi* трубúть *impf*, про~ *pf*.
blasé *adj* пресýщенный.
blasphemous *adj* богохýльный. **blasphemy** *n* богохýльство.
blast *n* (*wind*) порýв вéтра; (*explosion*) взрыв; *vt* взрывáть *impf*, взорвáть *pf*; ~ **off** стартовáть *impf & pf*. **blast-furnace** *n* дóмна.
blatant *adj* явный.
blaze *n* (*flame*) плáмя *neut*; (*fire*) пожáр; *vi* пылáть *impf*.
blazer *n* лёгкий пиджáк.
bleach *n* хлóрка, отбéливатель *m*; *vt* отбéливать *impf*, отбелúть *pf*.
bleak *adj* пустýнный; (*dreary*) унýлый.
bleary-eyed *adj* с затумáненными глазáми.
bleat *vi* блéять *impf*.

bleed vi кровоточи́ть impf.

bleeper n персона́льный сигнализа́тор.

blemish n пятно́.

blend n смесь; vt сме́шивать impf, смеша́ть pf; vi гармони́ровать impf. **blender** n ми́ксер.

bless vt благословля́ть impf, благослови́ть pf. **blessed** adj благослове́нный. **blessing** n (action) благослове́ние; (object) бла́го.

blight vt губи́ть impf, по~ pf.

blind adj слепо́й; ~ **alley** тупи́к; n што́ра; vt ослепля́ть impf, ослепи́ть pf. **blindfold** vt завя́зывать impf, завяза́ть pf глаза́+dat. **blindness** n слепота́.

blink vi мига́ть impf, мигну́ть pf. **blinkers** n pl шо́ры (-р) pl.

bliss n блаже́нство. **blissful** adj блаже́нный.

blister n пузы́рь m, волды́рь m.

blithe adj весёлый; (carefree) беспе́чный.

blitz n бомбёжка.

blizzard n мете́ль.

bloated adj взду́тый.

blob n (liquid) ка́пля; (colour) кля́кса.

bloc n блок.

block n (wood) чурба́н; (stone) глы́ба; (flats) жило́й дом; vt прегражда́ть impf, прегради́ть pf; ~ **up** забива́ть impf, заби́ть pf.

blockade n блока́да; vt блоки́ровать impf & pf.

blockage n зато́р.

bloke n па́рень m.

blond n блонди́н, ~ка; adj белоку́рый.

blood n кровь; ~ **donor** до́нор; ~**-poisoning** n зараже́ние кро́ви; ~ **pressure** кровяно́е давле́ние; ~ **relation** бли́зкий ро́дственник, -ая ро́дственница; ~ **transfusion** перелива́ние кро́ви. **bloodhound** n ище́йка. **bloodshed** n кровопроли́тие. **bloodshot** adj нали́тый кро́вью. **bloodthirsty** adj кровожа́дный. **bloody** adj крова́вый.

bloom n расцве́т; vi цвести́ pf.

blossom n цвет; in ~ в цвету́.

blot n кля́кса; пятно́; vt (dry) промока́ть impf, промокну́ть pf; (smudge) па́чкать impf, за~ pf.

blotch n пятно́.

blotting-paper n промока́тельная бума́га.

blouse n ко́фточка, блу́зка.

blow[1] n уда́р.

blow[2] vt & i дуть impf; ~ **away** сноси́ть impf, снести́ pf; ~ **down** вали́ть impf, по~ pf; ~ **one's nose** сморка́ться impf, сморкну́ться pf; ~ **out** задува́ть impf, заду́ть pf; ~ **over** (fig) проходи́ть impf, пройти́ pf; ~ **up** взрыва́ть impf, взорва́ть pf; (inflate) надува́ть impf, наду́ть pf. **blow-lamp** n пая́льная ла́мпа.

blubber[1] n ворва́нь.

blubber[2] vi реве́ть impf.

bludgeon n дуби́нка; vt (compel) вынужда́ть impf, вы́нудить pf.

blue adj (dark) си́ний; (light) голубо́й; n си́ний, голубо́й, цвет. **bluebell** n колоко́льчик. **bluebottle** n си́няя му́ха. **blueprint** n си́нька, светоко́пия; (fig) прое́кт.

bluff n блеф; vi блефова́ть impf.

blunder n опло́шность; vi опло́шать pf.

blunt adj тупо́й; (person) прямо́й; vt тупи́ть impf, за~, ис~ pf.

blur vt затума́нивать impf, затума́нить pf. **blurred** adj расплы́вчатый.

blurt vt: ~ **out** выба́лтывать impf, вы́болтать pf.

blush vi красне́ть impf, по~ pf.

bluster vi бушева́ть impf; n пусты́е слова́ neut pl.

boar n бо́ров; (wild) каба́н.

board n доска́; (committee) правле́ние, сове́т; **on** ~ на борт(у́); (ship) сесть pf (на кора́бль, в по́езд и т.д.); ~ **up** забива́ть impf, заби́ть pf. **boarder** n пансионе́р. **boarding-house** n пансио́н. **boarding-school** n интерна́т.

boast vi хва́статься impf, по~ pf; vt горди́ться impf +instr. **boaster** n хвасту́н. **boastful** adj хвастли́вый.

boat n (small) ло́дка; (large) кора́бль m.

bob vi подпры́гивать impf, подпры́гнуть pf.

bobbin n кату́шка.

bobsleigh n бо́бслей.

bode vt: ~ **well/ill** предвеща́ть impf хоро́шее/недо́брое.

bodice n лиф, корса́ж.

bodily adv целико́м; adj теле́сный.

body n те́ло, ту́ловище; (corpse) труп; (group) о́рган; (main part) основна́я часть. **bodyguard** n телохрани́тель m. **bodywork** n ку́зов.

bog n боло́то; **get** ~**ged down** увяза́ть impf, увя́знуть pf. **boggy** adj боло́тистый.

bogus adj подде́льный.

boil[1] n (med) фуру́нкул.

boil[2] vi кипе́ть impf, вс~ pf; vt кипяти́ть impf, с~ pf; (cook) вари́ть impf, с~ pf; ~ **down to** сходи́ться impf, сойти́сь pf к тому́, что; ~**over** выкипа́ть impf, вы́кипеть pf; n кипе́ние; **bring to the** ~ доводи́ть impf, довести́ pf до кипе́ния. **boiled** adj варёный. **boiler** n котёл; ~ **suit** комбинезо́н. **boiling** adj кипя́щий; ~ **point** то́чка кипе́ния; ~ **water** кипято́к.

boisterous adj шумли́вый.

bold adj сме́лый; (type) жи́рный.

bollard n (in road) столб; (on quay) пал.

bolster n ва́лик; vt: ~ **up** подпира́ть impf, подпере́ть pf.

bolt n засо́в; (tech) болт; vt запира́ть impf, запере́ть pf на засо́в; скрепля́ть impf, скрепи́ть pf болта́ми; vi (flee) удира́ть impf, удра́ть pf; (horse) понести́ pf.

bomb n бо́мба; vt бомби́ть impf. **bombard** vt бомбарди́ровать impf. **bombardment** n бомбардиро́вка. **bomber** n бомбардиро́вщик.

bombastic adj напы́щенный.

bond n (econ) облига́ция; (link) связь; pl око́вы (-в) pl, (fig) у́зы (уз) pl.

bone n кость.

bonfire n костёр.

bonnet n ка́пор; (car) капо́т.

bonus n пре́мия.

bony adj кости́стый.

boo vt осви́стывать impf, освиста́ть pf; vi улюлю́кать impf.

booby trap n лову́шка.

book n кни́га; vt (order) зака́зывать impf, заказа́ть pf.

(*reserve*) брони́ровать *impf*, за~ *pf*. **bookbinder** *n* переплётчик. **bookcase** *n* кни́жный шкаф, кни́жный шкаф; ~ **office** ка́сса. **bookkeeper** *n* бухга́лтер. **bookmaker** *n* букме́кер. **bookshop** *n* кни́жный магази́н.

boom[1] *n* (*barrier*) бон.

boom[2] *n* (*sound*) гул; (*econ*) бум; *vi* гуде́ть *impf*; (*fig*) процвета́ть *impf*.

boon *n* бла́го.

boor *n* хам. **boorish** *adj* ха́мский.

boost *n* соде́йствие; *vt* увели́чивать *impf*, увели́чить *pf*.

boot *n* боти́нок; (*high*) сапо́г; (*football*) бу́тса; (*car*) бага́жник.

booth *n* кио́ск, бу́дка; (*polling*) каби́на.

booty *n* добы́ча.

booze *n* вы́пивка; *vi* выпива́ть *impf*.

border *n* (*frontier*) грани́ца; (*trim*) кайма́; (*gardening*) бордю́р; *vi* грани́чить *impf* (**on** с +*instr*). **borderline** *n* грани́ца.

bore[1] *n* (*calibre*) кана́л (ствола́); *vt* сверли́ть *impf*, про~ *pf*.

bore[2] *n* (*thing*) ску́ка; (*person*) ску́чный челове́к; *vt* надоеда́ть *impf*, надое́сть *pf*. **boredom** *n* ску́ка. **boring** *adj* ску́чный.

born *adj* прирождённый; **be** ~ роди́ться *impf* & *pf*.

borough *n* райо́н.

borrow *vt* одолжа́ть *impf*, одолжи́ть *pf* (**from** у+*gen*).

Bosnia *n* Бо́сния. **Bosnian** *n* босни́ец, -и́йка; *adj* босни́йский.

bosom *n* грудь.

boss *n* нача́льник; *vt* кома́ндовать *impf*, с~ *pf* +*instr*. **bossy** *adj* команди́рский.

botanical *adj* ботани́ческий. **botanist** *n* бота́ник. **botany** *n* бота́ника.

botch *vt* зала́тывать *impf*, залата́ть *pf*.

both *adj* & *pron* о́ба *m* & *neut*, о́бе *f*; ~ **... and** и... и.

bother *n* доса́да; *vt* беспоко́ить *impf*.

bottle *n* буты́лка; ~**neck** суже́ние; *vt* разлива́ть *impf*, разли́ть *pf* по буты́лкам; ~ **up** сде́рживать *impf*, сдержа́ть *pf*.

bottom *n* ни́жняя часть; (*river etc.*) дно; (*buttocks*) зад; **at the** ~ **of** (*stairs*) внизу́ +*gen*; **get to the** ~ **of** добира́ться *impf*, добра́ться *pf* до су́ти +*gen*; *adj* са́мый ни́жний. **bottomless** *adj* бездо́нный.

bough *n* сук.

boulder *n* валу́н.

bounce *vi* подпры́гивать *impf*, подпры́гнуть *pf*; (*cheque*) верну́ться *pf*.

bound[1] *n* (*limit*) преде́л; *vt* ограни́чивать *impf*, ограни́чить *pf*.

bound[2] *n* (*spring*) прыжо́к; *vi* пры́гать *impf*, пры́гнуть *pf*.

bound[3] *adj*: **he is** ~ **to be there** он обяза́тельно там бу́дет.

bound[4] *adj*: **to be** ~ **for** напра́вля́ться *impf*, напра́виться *pf* в+*acc*.

boundary *n* грани́ца.

boundless *adj* безграни́чный.

bountiful *adj* (*generous*) ще́дрый; (*ample*) оби́льный.

bounty *n* ще́дрость; (*reward*) пре́мия.

bouquet *n* буке́т.

bourgeois *adj* буржуа́зный.

bourgeoisie *n* буржуази́я.
bout *n* (*med*) при́ступ; (*sport*) схва́тка.
bow[1] *n* (*weapon*) лук; (*knot*) бант; (*mus*) смычо́к.
bow[2] *n* (*obeisance*) покло́н; *vi* кла́няться *impf*, поклони́ться *pf*; *vt* склоня́ть *impf*, склони́ть *pf*.
bow[3] *n* (*naut*) нос.
bowel *n* кишка́; (*depths*) не́дра (-р) *pl*.
bowl[1] *n* ми́ска.
bowl[2] *n* (*ball*) шар; *vi* подава́ть *impf*, пода́ть *pf* мяч. **bowler** *n* подаю́щий *sb* мяч; (*hat*) котело́к. **bowling-alley** *n* кегельба́н. **bowls** *n* игра́ в шары́.
box[1] *n* коро́бка, я́щик; (*theat*) ло́жа; ~ **office** ка́сса.
box[2] *vi* боксирова́ть *impf*. **boxer** *n* боксёр. **boxing** *n* бокс. **Boxing Day** *n* второ́й день Рождества́.
boy *n* ма́льчик. **boyfriend** *n* молодо́й челове́к. **boyhood** *n* о́трочество. **boyish** *adj* мальчи́шеский.
boycott *n* бойко́т; *vt* бойкоти́ровать *impf* & *pf*.
bra *n* ли́фчик.
brace *n* (*clamp*) скре́па; *pl* подтя́жки *f pl*; (*dental*) ши́на; *vt* скрепля́ть *impf*, скрепи́ть *pf*; ~ **o.s.** собира́ться *impf*, собра́ться *pf* с си́лами.
bracelet *n* брасле́т.
bracing *adj* бодря́щий.
bracket *n* (*support*) кронште́йн; *pl* ско́бки *f pl*; (*category*) катего́рия.
brag *vi* хва́статься *impf*, по~ *pf*.
braid *n* тесьма́.
braille *n* шрифт Бра́йля.
brain *n* мозг. **brainstorm** *n*

припа́док безу́мия. **brainwash** *vt* промыва́ть *impf*, промы́ть *pf* мозги́+*dat*. **brainwave** *n* блестя́щая иде́я.
braise *vt* туши́ть *impf*, с~ *pf*.
brake *n* то́рмоз; *vt* тормози́ть *impf*, за~ *pf*.
bramble *n* ежеви́ка.
bran *n* о́труби (-бе́й) *pl*.
branch *n* ве́тка; (*fig*) о́трасль; (*comm*) филиа́л; *vi* разветвля́ться *impf*, разветви́ться *pf*; ~ **out** (*fig*) расширя́ть *impf*, расши́рить *pf* де́ятельность.
brand *n* (*mark*) клеймо́; (*make*) ма́рка; (*sort*) сорт; *vt* клейми́ть *impf*, за~ *pf*.
brandish *vt* разма́хивать *impf* +*instr*.
brandy *n* конья́к.
brash *adj* наха́льный.
brass *n* лату́нь, жёлтая медь; (*mus*) ме́дные инструме́нты *m pl*; *adj* лату́нный, ме́дный; ~ **band** ме́дный духово́й орке́стр; **top** ~ вы́сшее нача́льство.
brassière *n* бюстга́льтер.
brat *n* чертёнок.
bravado *n* брава́да.
brave *adj* хра́брый; *vt* покоря́ть *impf*, покори́ть *pf*. **bravery** *n* хра́брость.
bravo *int* бра́во!
brawl *n* сканда́л; *vi* дра́ться *impf*, по~ *pf*.
brawny *adj* му́скулистый.
bray *n* крик осла́; *vi* крича́ть *impf*.
brazen *adj* бессты́дный.
brazier *n* жаро́вня.
breach *n* наруше́ние; (*break*) проло́м; (*mil*) брешь; *vt* прорыва́ть *impf*, прорва́ть *pf*; (*rule*) наруша́ть *impf*, нару́шить *pf*.

bread n хлеб; (white) бу́лка.
breadcrumb n кро́шка.
breadwinner n корми́лец.
breadth n ширина́; (fig) широта́.
break n проло́м, разры́в; (pause) переры́в, па́уза; vt (& i) лома́ть(ся) impf, с~ pf; разби́ть(ся) impf, раз-би́ть(ся) pf; vt (violate) наруша́ть impf, нару́шить pf; ~ **away** вырыва́ться impf, вы́рваться pf; ~ **down** (vi) (tech) лома́ться impf, с~ pf; (talks) срыва́ться impf, сорва́ться pf; (vt) (door) выла́мывать impf, вы́ломать pf; ~ **in(to)** вла́мываться impf, вломи́ться pf в+acc; ~ **off** (vt & i) отла́мывать(ся) impf, отломи́ть(ся) pf; (vt) (speaking) замолча́ть pf; (vt) (relations) порыва́ть impf, порва́ть pf; ~ **out** вырыва́ться impf, вы́рваться pf; (fire, war) вспы́хнуть pf; ~ **through** пробива́ться impf, проби́ться pf; ~ **up** (vi) (marriage) распада́ться impf, распа́сться pf; (meeting) прерыва́ться impf, прерва́ться pf; (vt) (disperse) разгоня́ть impf, разогна́ть pf; (vt & i) разбива́ть(ся) impf, раз-би́ть(ся) pf; ~ **with** порыва́ть impf, порва́ть pf c+instr. **breakage** n поло́мка. **break-down** n поло́мка; (med) не́рвный срыв. **breaker** n буру́н. **breakfast** n за́втрак; vi за́втракать impf, по~ pf. **break-neck** adj: at ~ speed сломя́ го́лову. **breakthrough** n проры́в. **breakwater** n волноре́з. **breast** n грудь; ~-**feeding** n кормле́ние гру́дью; ~ **stroke** n брасс.

breath n дыха́ние; **be out of ~** запыха́ться impf & pf. **breathe** vi дыша́ть impf; ~ **in** вдыха́ть impf, вдохну́ть pf; ~ **out** выдыха́ть impf, вы́дохнуть pf. **breather** n переды́шка. **breathless** adj запыха́вшийся.
breeches n pl бри́джи (-жей) pl.
breed n поро́да; vi размножа́ться impf, размножи́ться pf; vt разводи́ть impf, раз-вести́ pf. **breeder** n -во́д: **cat-tle** ~ скотово́д. **breeding** n разведе́ние, -во́дство; (up-bringing) воспита́нность.
breeze n ветеро́к; (naut) бриз. **breezy** adj све́жий.
brevity n кра́ткость.
brew n (beer) вари́ть impf, с~ pf; (tea) зава́ривать impf, завари́ть pf; (beer) ва́рка; (tea) зава́рка. **brewer** n пивова́р. **brewery** n пивова́ренный заво́д.
bribe n взя́тка; vt подкупа́ть impf, подкупи́ть pf. **bribery** n подкуп.
brick n кирпи́ч; adj кирпи́ч-ный. **bricklayer** n ка́мень-щик.
bridal adj сва́дебный. **bride** n неве́ста. **bridegroom** n жени́х. **bridesmaid** n подру́жка неве́сты.
bridge¹ n (of nose) перено́сица; vt (gap) заполня́ть impf, запо́лнить pf; (over-come) преодолева́ть impf, преодоле́ть pf.
bridge² n (cards) бридж.
bridle n узда́; vi возмуща́ться impf, возмути́ться pf.
brief adj недо́лгий; (concise) кра́ткий; n инстру́кция; vt инструкти́ровать impf & pf.

briefcase n портфе́ль m.

briefing n инструкта́ж.

briefly adv кра́тко. **briefs** n pl трусы́ (-со́в) pl.

brigade n брига́да. **brigadier** n генера́л-майо́р.

bright adj я́ркий. **brighten** (also ~ up) vi проясня́ться impf, проясни́ться pf; vt оживля́ть impf, оживи́ть pf. **brightness** n я́ркость.

brilliant adj блестя́щий.

brim n край; (hat) поля́ (-ле́й) pl.

brine n рассо́л.

bring vt (carry) приноси́ть impf, принести́ pf; (lead) приводи́ть impf, привести́ pf; (transport) привози́ть impf, привезти́ pf; ~ **about** приноси́ть impf, принести́ pf; ~ **back** возвраща́ть impf, возврати́ть pf; ~ **down** сва́ливать impf, свали́ть pf; ~ **round** (unconscious person) приводи́ть impf, привести́ pf в себя́; (deliver) привози́ть impf, привезти́ pf; ~ **up** (educate) воспи́тывать impf, воспита́ть pf; (question) поднима́ть impf, подня́ть pf.

brink n край.

brisk adj (lively) оживлённый; (air etc.) све́жий; (quick) бы́стрый.

bristle n щети́на; vi щети́ниться impf, o~ pf.

Britain n Великобрита́ния, А́нглия. **British** adj брита́нский, англи́йский; ~ **Isles** Брита́нские острова́ m pl. **Briton** n брита́нец, -нка; англича́нин, -а́нка.

brittle adj хру́пкий.

broach vt затра́гивать impf, затро́нуть pf.

broad adj широ́кий; in ~ day-

light средь бе́ла дня; in ~ outline в о́бщих черта́х. **broad-minded** adj с широ́кими взгля́дами. **broadly** adv: ~ speaking вообще́ говоря́.

broadcast n переда́ча; vt передава́ть impf, переда́ть pf по ра́дио, по телеви́дению; (seed) се́ять impf, по~ pf вразбро́с. **broadcaster** n ди́ктор. **broadcasting** n ра́дио-, теле-, веща́ние.

brocade n парча́.

broccoli n бро́кколи neut indecl.

brochure n брошю́ра.

broke predic без гроша́. **broken** adj сло́манный; ~-hearted с разби́тым се́рдцем.

broker n комиссионе́р.

bronchitis n бронхи́т.

bronze n бро́нза; adj бро́нзовый.

brooch n брошь, бро́шка.

brood n вы́водок; vi мра́чно размышля́ть impf.

brook[1] n ручёй.

brook[2] vt терпе́ть impf.

broom n метла́. **broomstick** n (witches') помело́.

broth n бульо́н.

brothel n публи́чный дом.

brother n брат; ~-in-law (sister's husband) зять; (husband's brother) де́верь; (wife's brother) шу́рин; (wife's sister's husband) своя́к. **brotherhood** n бра́тство. **brotherly** adj бра́тский.

brow n (eyebrow) бровь; (forehead) лоб; (of hill) гре́бень m. **browbeaten** adj запу́ганный.

brown adj кори́чневый; (eyes) ка́рий; n кори́чневый цвет; vt (cul) подрумя́нивать impf, подрумя́нить pf.

browse vi (look around) осма́триваться impf, осмотре́ться pf; (in book) просма́тривать impf просмотре́ть pf кни́гу.

bruise n синя́к; vt ушиба́ть impf, ушиби́ть pf.

brunette n брюне́тка.

brunt n основна́я тя́жесть.

brush n щётка; (paint) кисть; vt (clean) чи́стить impf, вы́~, по~ pf (щёткой); (touch) легко́ каса́ться impf, косну́ться pf +gen; (hair) расчёсывать impf, расчеса́ть pf щёткой; ~ aside, off отма́хиваться impf, отмахну́ться pf от+gen; ~ up смета́ть impf, смести́ pf; (renew) подчища́ть impf, подчи́стить pf.

brushwood n хво́рост.

Brussels sprouts n pl брюссе́льская капу́ста.

brutal adj жесто́кий. **brutality** n жесто́кость. **brutalize** vt ожесточа́ть impf, ожесточи́ть pf. **brute** n живо́тное sb; (person) скоти́на. **brutish** adj ха́мский.

B.Sc. abbr бакала́вр нау́к.

bubble n пузы́рь m; vi пузы́риться impf; кипе́ть impf, вс~ pf.

buck n саме́ц оле́ня, кро́лика etc.; vi брыка́ться impf.

bucket n ведро́.

buckle n пря́жка; vt застёгивать impf, застегну́ть pf (пря́жкой); vi (warp) коро́биться impf, по~, с~ pf.

bud n по́чка.

Buddhism n будди́зм. **Buddhist** n будди́ст; adj будди́йский.

budge vt & i шевели́ть(ся) impf, по~ pf.

budget n бюдже́т; vi: ~ for

предусма́тривать impf, предусмотре́ть pf в бюдже́те.

buff adj све́тло-кори́чневый.

buffalo n бу́йвол.

buffet[1] n буфе́т.

buffet[2] vt броса́ть impf (impers).

buffoon n шут.

bug n (insect) бука́шка; (germ) инфе́кция; (in computer) оши́бка в програ́мме; (microphone) потайно́й микрофо́н; vt (install) ~ устана́вливать impf, установи́ть pf аппарату́ру для подслу́шивания в+prep; (listen) подслу́шивать impf.

bugle n горн.

build n (of person) телосложе́ние; vt стро́ить impf, по~ pf; ~ on пристра́ивать impf, пристро́ить pf (to +dat); ~ up vt (vi) накопля́ть impf; накопи́ть pf. **builder** n строи́тель m. **building** n (edifice) зда́ние; (action) строи́тельство; ~ site стро́йка; ~ society жили́щно-строи́тельный кооперати́в.

built-up area n застро́енный райо́н.

bulb n лу́ковица; (electric) ла́мпочка. **bulbous** adj лу́ковичный.

Bulgaria n Болга́рия. **Bulgarian** n болга́рин, -га́рка; adj болга́рский.

bulge n вы́пуклость; vi выпя́чиваться impf, вы́пятиться impf. **bulging** adj разбу́хший, оттопы́ривающийся.

bulk n (size) объём; (greater part) бо́льшая часть; in ~ гурто́м. **bulky** adj громо́здкий.

bull n бык; (male) саме́ц. **bulldog** n бульдо́г.

vt расчища́ть *impf*, расчи́стить *pf* бульдо́зером. **bulldozer** *n* бульдо́зер. **bullfinch** *n* снеги́рь *m*. **bullock** *n* вол. **bull's-eye** *n* я́блоко.

bullet *n* пу́ля. **bullet-proof** *adj* пулесто́йкий.

bulletin *n* бюллете́нь *m*.

bullion *n*: gold ~ зо́лото в сли́тках.

bully *n* зади́ра *m* & *f*; *vt* запу́гивать *impf*, запуга́ть *pf*.

bum *n* зад.

bumble-bee *n* шмель *m*.

bump *n* (*blow*) уда́р, толчо́к; (*swelling*) ши́шка; (*in road*) уха́б; *vi* ударя́ться *impf*, уда́риться *pf*; ~ **into** ната́лкиваться *impf*, натолкну́ться *pf* на+*acc*. **bumper** *n* ба́мпер.

bumpkin *n* дереве́нщина *m* & *f*.

bumptious *adj* самоуве́ренный.

bumpy *adj* уха́бистый.

bun *n* сдо́бная бу́лка; (*hair*) пучо́к.

bunch *n* (*of flowers*) буке́т; (*grapes*) гроздь; (*keys*) свя́зка.

bundle *n* у́зел; *vt* связывать *impf*, связа́ть *pf* в у́зел; ~ **off** спрова́живать *impf*, спрова́дить *pf*.

bungalow *n* бу́нгало *neut indecl.*

bungle *vt* по́ртить *impf*, ис~ *pf*.

bunk *n* ко́йка.

bunker *n* бу́нкер.

buoy *n* буй. **buoyancy** *n* плаву́честь; (*fig*) бо́дрость. **buoyant** *adj* плаву́чий; (*fig*) бо́дрый.

burden *n* бре́мя *neut*; *vt* обременя́ть *impf*, обремени́ть *pf*.

bureau *n* бюро́ *neut indecl.* **bureaucracy** *n* бюрокра́тия. **bureaucrat** *n* бюрокра́т. **bureaucratic** *adj* бюрократи́ческий.

burger *n* котле́та.

burglar *n* взло́мщик. **burglary** *n* кра́жа со взло́мом. **burgle** *vt* гра́бить *impf*, о~ *pf*.

burial *n* погребе́ние.

burlesque *n* бурле́ск.

burly *adj* здорове́нный.

burn *vt* жечь *impf*, с~ *pf*; *vt* & *i* (*injure*) обжига́ть(ся) *impf*, обже́чь(ся) *pf*; *vi* горе́ть *impf*, с~ *pf*; (*by sun*) загора́ть *impf*, загоре́ть *pf*; *n* ожо́г. **burner** *n* горе́лка.

burnish *vt* полирова́ть *impf*, от~ *pf*.

burp *vi* рыга́ть *impf*, рыгну́ть *pf*.

burrow *n* нора́; *vi* рыть *impf*, вы́~ *pf* нору́; (*fig*) ры́ться *impf*.

bursar *n* казначе́й. **bursary** *n* стипе́ндия.

burst *n* разры́в, вспы́шка; *vi* разрыва́ться *impf*, разорва́ться *pf*; (*bubble*) ло́паться *impf*, ло́пнуть *pf*; *vt* разрыва́ть *impf*, разорва́ть *pf*; ~ **into tears** распла́каться *pf*.

bury *vt* (*dead*) хорони́ть *impf*, по~ *pf*; (*hide*) зарыва́ть *impf*, зары́ть *pf*.

bus *n* авто́бус.

bush *n* куст. **bushy** *adj* густо́й.

busily *adv* энерги́чно.

business *n* (*affair*, *dealings*) де́ло; (*firm*) предприя́тие; **mind your own** ~ не ва́ше де́ло; **on** ~ по де́лу. **businesslike** *adj* делово́й. **businessman** *n* бизнесме́н.

busker *n* у́личный музыка́нт.
bust *n* бюст; (*bosom*) грудь.
bustle *n* суета́; *vi* суети́ться *impf*.
busy *adj* занято́й; *vt*: ~ **o.s.** занима́ться *impf*, заня́ться *pf* (**with** +*instr*). **busybody** *n* назо́йливый челове́к.
but *conj* но, а; ~ **then** зато́; *prep* кро́ме+*gen*.
butcher *n* мясни́к; *vt* ре́зать *impf*, за~ *pf*; ~**'s shop** мясна́я *sb*.
butler *n* дворе́цкий *sb*.
butt[1] *n* (*cask*) бо́чка.
butt[2] *n* (*of gun*) прикла́д; (*cigarette*) оку́рок.
butt[3] *n* (*target*) мише́нь.
butt[4] *vt* бода́ть *impf*, за~ *pf*; ~ **in** вме́шиваться *impf*, вмеша́ться *pf*.
butter *n* (сли́вочное) ма́сло; *vt* нама́зывать *impf*, нама́зать *pf* ма́слом; ~ **up** льстить *impf*, по~+*gen*. **buttercup** *n* лю́тик. **butterfly** *n* ба́бочка.
buttock *n* я́годица.
button *n* пу́говица; (*knob*) кно́пка; *vt* застёгивать *impf*, застегну́ть *pf*. **buttonhole** *n* пе́тля.
buttress *n* контрфо́рс; *vt* подпира́ть *impf*, подпере́ть *pf*.
buxom *adj* полногру́дая.
buy *n* поку́пка; *vt* покупа́ть *impf*, купи́ть *pf*. **buyer** *n* покупа́тель *m*.
buzz *n* жужжа́ние; *vi* жужжа́ть *impf*.
buzzard *n* каню́к.
buzzer *n* зу́ммер.
by *adv* ми́мо; *prep*: (*near*) о́коло+*gen*, у+*gen*; (*beside*) ря́дом c+*instr*; (*past*) ми́мо+*gen*; (*time*) к+*dat*; (*agent*) often not translated *with out prep*; ~ **and large** в це́лом.
bye *int* пока́!

by-election *n* дополни́тельные вы́боры *m pl*.
Byelorussian *see* **Belorussian**
bygone *adj* мину́вший; **let** ~**s be** ~ что прошло́, то прошло́. **by-law** *n* постановле́ние. **bypass** *n* обхо́д; *vt* обходи́ть *impf*, обойти́ *pf*. **by-product** *n* побо́чный проду́кт. **byroad** *n* небольша́я доро́га. **bystander** *n* свиде́тель *m*. **byway** *n* просёлочная доро́га. **byword** *n* олицетворе́ние (**for** +*gen*).
Byzantine *adj* византи́йский.

C

cab *n* (*taxi*) такси́ *neut indecl*; (*of lorry*) каби́на.
cabaret *n* кабаре́ *neut indecl*.
cabbage *n* капу́ста.
cabin *n* (*hut*) хи́жина; (*aeron*) каби́на; (*naut*) каю́та.
cabinet *n* шкаф; (*Cabinet*) кабине́т; ~**-maker** краснодере́вец; ~**-minister** мини́стр-член кабине́та.
cable *n* (*rope*) кана́т; (*electric*) ка́бель *m*; (*cablegram*) телегра́мма; *vt* и *i* телеграфи́ровать *impf & pf*.
cache *n* пота́йный склад.
cackle *vi* куда́хтать *impf*.
cactus *n* ка́ктус.
caddy *n* (*box*) ча́йница.
cadet *n* новобра́нец.
cadge *vt* стреля́ть *impf*, стрельну́ть *pf*.
cadres *n pl* ка́дры *m pl*.
Caesarean (section) *n* ке́сарево-сече́ние.
cafe *n* кафе́ *neut indecl*. **cafeteria** *n* кафете́рий.
caffeine *n* кофеи́н.
cage *n* кле́тка.

cajole vt задábривать impf, задóбрить pf.

cake n (large) торт, (small) пирóжное sb; (fruit-~) кекс; vt: **~d** облéпленный (in +instr).

calamitous adj бéдственный. **calamity** n бéдствие.

calcium n кáльций.

calculate vt вычислять impf, вычислить pf; vi рассчитывать impf, рассчитáть pf (on на+acc). **calculation** n вычислéние, расчёт. **calculator** n калькуля́тор.

calendar n календáрь m.

calf[1] n (cow) телёнок.

calf[2] n (leg) икрá.

calibrate vt калибровáть impf. **calibre** n калибр.

call v звать impf, по~ pf; (name) называ́ть impf, назвáть pf, (cry) кричáть impf, крúкнуть pf; (wake) будúть impf, раз~ pf; (visit) заходúть impf, зайтú pf (on к+dat; at в+acc); (stop at) остáнавливаться impf, останови́ться pf (at в, на, +prep); (summon) вызывáть impf, вызвать pf; (ring up) звонúть impf, по~ pf +dat; ~ **for** (require) трéбовать impf, по~ pf +gen; (fetch) заходúть impf, зайтú pf за+instr; ~ **off** отменя́ть impf, отменúть pf; ~ **out** вскрúкивать impf, вскрúкнуть pf; ~ **up** призывáть impf, призвáть pf; n (cry) крик; (summons) зов, призы́в; (telephone) (телефóнный) вызов, разговóр; (visit) визúт; (signal) сигнáл; **~-box** телефóн-автомáт; **~-up** призы́в. **caller** n посетúтель m, **-ница**; (tel) позвонúвший sb. **calling** n (voca-

tion) призвáние.

callous adj (person) чёрствый.

callus n мозóль.

calm adj спокóйный; n спокóйствие; vt & i (~ down) успокáивать(ся) impf, успокóить(ся) pf.

calorie n калóрия.

camber n скат.

camcorder n камкóрдер.

camel n верблю́д.

camera n фотоаппарáт. **cameraman** n кинооператóр.

camouflage n камуфля́ж; vt маскировáть impf, за~ pf.

camp n лáгерь m; vi (set up ~) располагáться impf, расположи́ться pf лáгерем; (go camping) жить impf в палáтках; **~-bed** раскладýшка; **~-fire** костёр.

campaign n кампáния; vi проводúть impf, провестú pf кампáнию.

campsite n лáгерь m, кéмпинг.

campus n университéтский городóк.

can[1] n бáнка; vt консервúровать impf, за~ pf.

can[2] v aux (be able) мочь impf, с~ pf +inf; (know how) умéть impf, с~ pf +inf.

Canada n Канáда. **Canadian** n канáдец, -дка; adj канáдский.

canal n канáл.

canary n канарéйка.

cancel vt (make void) аннулúровать impf & pf; (call off) отменя́ть impf, отменúть pf; (stamp) гасúть impf, по~ pf. **cancellation** n аннулúрование; отмéна.

cancer n рак; (C~) Рак. **cancerous** adj рáковый.

candelabrum n канделя́бр.

candid *adj* открове́нный.

candidate *n* кандида́т.

candied *adj* заса́харенный.

candle *n* свеча́. **candlestick** *n* подсве́чник.

candour *n* открове́нность.

candy *n* сла́дости *f pl*.

cane *n* (*plant*) тростни́к; (*stick*) трость, па́лка; *vt* бить *impf*, по~ *pf* па́лкой.

canine *adj* соба́чий; *n* (*tooth*) клык.

canister *n* ба́нка, коро́бка.

canker *n* рак.

cannabis *n* гаши́ш.

cannibal *n* людое́д. **cannibalism** *n* людое́дство.

cannon *n* пу́шка; ~-ball пу́шечное ядро́.

canoe *n* кано́э *neut indecl*; *vi* пла́вать *indet*, плыть *det* на кано́э.

canon *n* кано́н; (*person*) кано́ник. **canonize** *vt* канонизова́ть *impf & pf*.

canopy *n* балдахи́н.

cant *n* (*hypocrisy*) ха́нжество; (*jargon*) жарго́н.

cantankerous *adj* сварли́вый.

cantata *n* канта́та.

canteen *n* столо́вая *sb*.

canter *n* лёгкий гало́п; *vi* (*rider*) е́здить *indet*, е́хать *det* лёгким гало́пом; (*horse*) ходи́ть *indet*, идти́ *det* лёгким гало́пом.

canvas *n* (*art*) холст, (*naut*) паруси́на; (*tent material*) брезе́нт.

canvass *vi* агити́ровать *impf*, с~ *pf* (**for** за+*acc*); *n* собира́ние голосо́в; агита́ция. **canvasser** *n* собира́тель *m* голосо́в.

canyon *n* каньо́н.

cap *n* (*of uniform*) фура́жка; (*cloth*) ке́пка; (*woman's*) че-

пе́ц; (*lid*) кры́шка; *vt* превосходи́ть *impf*, превзойти́ *pf*.

capability *n* спосо́бность. **capable** *adj* спосо́бный (**of** на+*acc*).

capacious *adj* вмести́тельный. **capacity** *n* ёмкость; (*ability*) спосо́бность; **in the ~ of** в ка́честве +*gen*.

cape¹ *n* (*geog*) мыс.

cape² *n* (*cloak*) наки́дка.

caper *vi* скака́ть *impf*.

capers¹ *n pl* (*cul*) ка́персы *m pl*.

capillary *adj* капилля́рный.

capital *adj* (*letter*) прописно́й; ~ **punishment** сме́ртная казнь; *n* (*town*) столи́ца; (*letter*) прописна́я бу́ква; (*econ*) капита́л. **capitalism** *n* капитали́зм. **capitalist** *n* капитали́ст; *adj* капиталисти́ческий. **capitalize** *vt* извлека́ть *impf*, извле́чь *pf* вы́году (**on** из+*gen*).

capitulate *vi* капитули́ровать *impf & pf*. **capitulation** *n* капитуля́ция.

caprice *n* капри́з. **capricious** *adj* капри́зный.

Capricorn *n* Козеро́г.

capsize *vt & i* опроки́дывать(ся) *impf*, опроки́нуть(ся) *pf*.

capsule *n* ка́псула.

captain *n* капита́н; *vt* быть капита́ном +*gen*.

caption *n* по́дпись; (*cin*) титр.

captious *adj* приди́рчивый.

captivate *vt* пленя́ть *impf*, плени́ть *pf*. **captivating** *adj* плени́тельный. **captive** *n* & *adj* пле́нный. **captivity** *n* нево́ля; (*esp mil*) плен. **capture** *n* взя́тие, захва́т, пои́мка; *vt* (*person*) брать *impf*, взять *pf* в плен; (*seize*) захва́тывать

impf, захвати́ть *pf*.
car *n* маши́на; автомоби́ль *m*; ~ стоя́нка.
carafe *n* графи́н.
caramel(s) *n* караме́ль.
carat *n* кара́т.
caravan *n* фурго́н; (*convoy*) карава́н.
caraway (seeds) *n* тмин.
carbohydrate *n* углево́д. **carbon** *n* углеро́д; ~ **copy** ко́пия; ~ **dioxide** углекислота́; ~ **monoxide** о́кись углеро́да; ~ **paper** копирова́льная бума́га.
carburettor *n* карбюра́тор.
carcass *n* ту́ша.
card *n* (*stiff paper*) карто́н; (*visiting* ~) ка́рточка; (*playing* ~) ка́рта; (*greetings* ~) откры́тка; (*ticket*) биле́т. **cardboard** *n* карто́н; *adj* карто́нный.
cardiac *adj* серде́чный.
cardigan *n* кардига́н.
cardinal *adj* кардина́льный; ~ **number** коли́чественное числи́тельное *sb*; *n* кардина́л.
care *n* (*trouble*) забо́та; (*caution*) осторо́жность; (*tending*) ухо́д; **in the** ~ **of** на попече́нии +*gen*; **take** ~ осторо́жно!; **~**! смотри́(те)!; **take** ~ **of** забо́титься *impf*, по~ *pf* о+*prep*; *vi*: **I don't** ~ мне всё равно́; ~ **for** (*look after*) уха́живать *impf* за+*instr*; (*like*) нра́виться *impf*, по~ *pf impers +dat*.
career *n* карье́ра.
carefree *adj* беззабо́тный.
careful *adj* (*cautious*) осторо́жный; (*thorough*) тща́тельный. **careless** *adj* (*negligent*) небре́жный; (*incautious*) неосторо́жный

caress *n* ла́ска; *vt* ласка́ть *impf*.
caretaker *n* смотри́тель *m*, ~ница; *attrib* вре́менный.
cargo *n* груз.
caricature *n* карикату́ра; *vt* изобража́ть *impf*, изобрази́ть *pf* в карикату́рном ви́де.
carnage *n* резня́.
carnal *adj* пло́тский.
carnation *n* гвозди́ка.
carnival *n* карнава́л.
carnivorous *adj* плотоя́дный.
carol *n* (рожде́ственский) гимн.
carouse *vi* кути́ть *impf*, кутну́ть *pf*.
carp¹ *n* карп.
carp² *vi* придира́ться *impf*, придра́ться *pf* (**at** к+*dat*).
carpenter *n* пло́тник. **carpentry** *n* пло́тничество.
carpet *n* ковёр; *vt* покрыва́ть *impf*, покры́ть *pf* ковро́м.
carping *adj* приди́рчивый.
carriage *n* (*vehicle*) каре́та; (*rly*) ваго́н; (*conveyance*) перево́зка; (*bearing*) оса́нка. **carriageway** *n* прое́зжая часть доро́ги. **carrier** *n* (*on bike*) бага́жник; (*firm*) тра́нспортная кампа́ния; (*med*) бациллоноси́тель *m*.
carrot *n* морко́вка; *pl* морко́вь (collect).
carry *vt* (*by hand*) носи́ть *indet*, нести́ *det*; переноси́ть *impf*, перенести́ *pf*; (*in vehicle*) вози́ть *indet*, везти́ *det*; (*sound*) передава́ть *impf*, переда́ть *pf*, *vi* (*sound*) быть слы́шен; **be carried away** увлека́ться *impf*, увле́чься *pf*; ~ **on** (*continue*) продолжа́ть *impf*; ~ **out** выполня́ть *impf*, вы́полнить *pf*; ~ **over** переноси́ть *impf*, перенести́ *pf*.

cart n телёга; vt (lug) тащи́ть impf.

cartilage n хрящ.

carton n карто́нка.

cartoon n карикату́ра; (cin) мультфи́льм. **cartoonist** n карикатури́ст, ~ка.

cartridge n патро́н; (of record player) звукоснима́тель m.

carve vt ре́зать impf по+dat; (in wood) выреза́ть impf, вы́резать pf; (in stone) высека́ть impf, вы́сечь pf; (slice) нареза́ть impf, наре́зать pf. **carving** n резьба́; ~ **knife** нож для нареза́ния мя́са.

cascade n каска́д; vi па́дать impf.

case[1] n (instance) слу́чай; (law) де́ло; (med) больно́й sb; (gram) паде́ж; in ~ (в слу́чае) е́сли; in any ~ во вся́ком слу́чае; in no ~ не в ко́ем слу́чае; just in ~ на вся́кий слу́чай.

case[2] n (box) я́щик; (suitcase) чемода́н; (small box) футля́р; (cover) чехо́л; (display ~) витри́на.

cash n нали́чные sb; (money) де́ньги pl; ~ **on delivery** нало́женным платежо́м; ~ **desk, register** ка́сса; vt: ~ **a cheque** получа́ть impf, получи́ть pf де́ньги по че́ку. **cashier** n касси́р.

casing n (tech) кожу́х.

casino n казино́ neut indecl.

cask n бо́чка.

casket n шкату́лка.

casserole n (pot) ла́тка; (stew) рагу́ neut indecl.

cassette n кассе́та; ~ **recorder** кассе́тный магнитофо́н.

cassock n ря́са.

cast vt (throw) броса́ть impf, бро́сить pf; (shed) сбра́сы-

вать impf, сбро́сить pf; (theat) распределя́ть impf, распредели́ть pf ро́ли +dat; (found) лить impf, с~ pf; (knitting) спуска́ть impf, спусти́ть pf пе́тли; (naut) отплыва́ть impf, отплы́ть pf; ~ **on** (knitting) набира́ть impf, набра́ть pf пе́тли; n (of mind etc.) склад; (mould) фо́рма; (moulded object) сле́пок; (med) ги́псовая повя́зка; (theat) де́йствующие ли́ца (-ц pl. **castaway** n потерпе́вший sb кораблекруше́ние. **cast iron** n чугу́н. **cast-iron** adj чугу́нный. **cast-offs** n pl но́шеное пла́тье.

castanet n кастанье́та.

caste n ка́ста.

castigate vt и бичева́ть impf.

castle n за́мок; (chess) ладья́.

castor n (wheel) ро́лик; ~ **sugar** са́харная пу́дра.

castrate vt кастри́ровать impf & pf. **castration** n кастра́ция.

casual adj (chance) случа́йный; (offhand) небре́жный; (clothes) обы́денный; (unofficial) неофициа́льный; (informal) лёгкий; (labour) подённый; ~ **labourer** подё́нщик, -ица. **casualty** n (wounded) ра́неный sb; (killed) уби́тый sb; pl поте́ри (-рь) pl; ~ **ward** пала́та ско́рой по́мощи.

cat n ко́шка; (tom) кот; ~**'s-eye** (on road) (доро́жный) рефле́ктор.

catalogue n катало́г; (price list) прейскура́нт; vt катало-гизи́ровать impf & pf.

catalyst n катализа́тор. **catalytic** adj каталити́ческий.

catapult n (toy) рога́тка; (hist, aeron) катапу́льта; vt & i катапульти́ровать(ся) *impf & pf.*

cataract *n* (*med*) катара́кта.

catarrh *n* ката́р.

catastrophe *n* катастро́фа. **catastrophic** *adj* катастрофи́ческий.

catch *vt* (*ball, fish, thief*) лови́ть *impf*, пойма́ть *pf*; (*surprise*) застава́ть *impf*, заста́ть *pf*; (*disease*) заража́ться *impf*, зарази́ться *pf* +*instr*; (*be in time for*) успева́ть *impf*, успе́ть *pf* на+*acc*; *vt & i* (*snag*) зацепля́ть(ся) *impf*, зацепи́ть(ся) *pf* (*on* за+*acc*); ~ **on** (*become popular*) прививаться *impf*, приви́ться *pf*; ~ **up with** догоня́ть *impf*, догна́ть *pf*; *n* (*of fish*) уло́в; (*trick*) уло́вка; (*on door etc.*) задёлка. **catching** *adj* зара́зный. **catchword** *n* мо́дное слове́чко. **catchy** *adj* прили́пчивый.

categorical *adj* категори́ческий. **category** *n* катего́рия.

cater *vi*: ~ **for** поставля́ть *impf*, поста́вить *pf* прови́зию для+*gen*; (*satisfy*) удовлетворя́ть *impf*, удовлетвори́ть *pf*. **caterer** *n* поставщи́к (прови́зии).

caterpillar *n* гу́сеница.

cathedral *n* собо́р.

catheter *n* кате́тер.

Catholic *adj* католи́ческий; *n* като́лик, -и́чка. **Catholicism** *n* католи́чество.

cattle *n* скот.

Caucasus *n* Кавка́з.

cauldron *n* котёл.

cauliflower *n* цветна́я капу́ста.

cause *n* причи́на, по́вод; (*law etc.*) де́ло; *vt* причиня́ть *impf*, причини́ть *pf*; вызыва́ть *impf*, вы́звать *pf*; (*induce*) заста-

вля́ть *impf*, заста́вить *pf*.

caustic *adj* е́дкий.

cauterize *vt* прижига́ть *impf*, приже́чь *pf*.

caution *n* осторо́жность; (*warning*) предостереже́ние; *vt* предостерега́ть *impf*, предостере́чь *pf*. **cautious** *adj* осторо́жный. **cautionary** *adj* предостерега́ющий.

cavalcade *n* кавалька́да. **cavalier** *adj* бесцеремо́нный.

cavalry *n* кавале́рия.

cave *n* пеще́ра; *vi*: ~ **in** обва́ливаться *impf*, обвали́ться *pf*; (*yield*) сдава́ться *impf*, сда́ться *pf*. **caveman** *n* пеще́рный челове́к. **cavern** *n* пеще́ра. **cavernous** *adj* пеще́ристый.

caviare *n* икра́.

cavity *n* впа́дина, по́лость; (*in tooth*) дупло́.

cavort *vi* скака́ть *impf*.

caw *vi* ка́ркать *impf*, ка́ркнуть *pf*.

CD *abbr* (*of* **compact disc**) компа́кт-ди́ск; ~ **player** прои́грыватель *n* компа́кт-ди́сков.

cease *vt & i* прекраща́ть(ся) *impf*, прекрати́ть(ся) *pf*; *vi* перестава́ть *impf*, переста́ть *pf* (+*inf*); ~**-fire** прекраще́ние огня́. **ceaseless** *adj* непреста́нный.

cedar *n* кедр.

cede *vt* уступа́ть *impf*, уступи́ть *pf*.

ceiling *n* потоло́к; (*fig*) макси́мальный у́ровень *m*.

celebrate *vt* пра́здновать *impf*, от~ *pf*; (*extol*) прославля́ть *impf*, просла́вить *pf*. **celebrated** *adj* знамени́тый. **celebration** *n* пра́зднование. **celebrity** *n* знамени́тость.

celery n сельдере́й.

celestial adj небе́сный.

celibacy n безбра́чие. **celibate** adj холосто́й; n холостя́к.

cell n (prison) ка́мера; (biol) кле́тка.

cellar n подва́л.

cello n виолонче́ль.

cellophane n целлофа́н. **cellular** adj кле́точный. **celluloid** n целлуло́ид.

Celt n кельт. **Celtic** adj ке́льтский.

cement n цеме́нт; vt цементи́ровать impf, за~ pf.

cemetery n кла́дбище.

censor n це́нзор; vt подверга́ть impf, подве́ргнуть pf цензу́ре. **censorious** adj сверхкрити́ческий. **censorship** n цензу́ра. **censure** n порица́ние; vt порица́ть impf.

census n пе́репись.

cent n цент; per ~ проце́нт.

centenary n столе́тие. **centennial** adj столе́тний. **centigrade** adj: 10° ~ 10° по Це́льсию. **centimetre** n сантиме́тр. **centipede** n сороконо́жка.

central adj центра́льный; ~ **heating** центра́льное отопле́ние. **centralization** n централиза́ция. **centralize** vt централизова́ть impf & pf. **centre** n центр; середи́на; ~ **forward** центр нападе́ния; vi & i: ~ **on** сосредото́чивать(ся) impf, сосредото́чить(ся) pf на+prep. **centrifugal** adj центробе́жный. **century** n столе́тие, век.

ceramic adj керами́ческий. **ceramics** n pl кера́мика.

cereals n pl хле́бные зла́ки m pl; breakfast ~ зерновы́е

хло́пья (-ев) pl.

cerebral adj мозгово́й.

ceremonial adj церемониа́льный; n церемониа́л. **ceremonious** adj церемо́нный. **ceremony** n церемо́ния.

certain adj (confident) уве́рен (-нна); (undoubted) несомне́нный; (unspecified) изве́стный; (inevitable) ве́рный; **for** ~ наверняка́. **certainly** adv (of course) коне́чно, безусло́вно; (without doubt) несомне́нно; ~ **not!** ни в ко́ем слу́чае. **certainty** n (conviction) уве́ренность; (fact) несомне́нный факт.

certificate n свиде́тельство; сертифика́т. **certify** vt удостоверя́ть impf, удостове́рить pf.

cervical adj ше́йный. **cervix** n ше́йка ма́тки.

cessation n прекраще́ние.

cf. abbr ср., сравни́.

CFCs abbr (of chlorofluorocarbons) хлори́рованные фторуглеро́ды m pl.

chafe vt (rub) тере́ть impf; (rub sore) натира́ть impf, натере́ть pf.

chaff n (husks) мяки́на; (straw) се́чка.

chaffinch n зя́блик.

chagrin n огорче́ние.

chain n цепь; ~ **reaction** цепна́я реа́кция; ~ **smoker** зая́длый кури́льщик.

chair n стул, (armchair) кре́сло; (univ) ка́федра; vt (preside) председа́тельствовать impf на+prep. **chairman**, **-woman** n председа́тель m, -ница.

chalice n ча́ша.

chalk n мел. **chalky** adj мелово́й.

challenge n (summons, fig)

вы́зов; (*sentry's*) о́клик; (*law*) отво́д; *vt* вызыва́ть *impf*, вы́звать *pf*; (*sentry*) оклика́ть *impf*, окли́кнуть *pf*; (*law*) отводи́ть *impf*, отвести́ *pf*. **challenger** *n* претенде́нт. **challenging** *adj* интригу́ющий.

chamber *n* (*cavity*) ка́мера; (*hall*) зал; (*polit*) пала́та; *pl* (*law*) адвока́тская конто́ра; (*judge's*) кабине́т (судьи́); ~ **music** ка́мерная му́зыка; ~ **pot** ночно́й горшо́к. **chambermaid** *n* го́рничная *sb*.

chameleon *n* хамелео́н.

chamois *n* (*animal*) се́рна; (~*leather*) за́мша.

champagne *n* шампа́нское *sb*.

champion *n* чемпио́н, ~ка; (*upholder*) побо́рник, -ица; *vt* боро́ться *impf* за +*acc*. **championship** *n* пе́рвенство, чемпиона́т.

chance *n* случа́йность; (*opportunity*) возмо́жность, (*favourable*) слу́чай; (*likelihood*) шанс (*usu pl*); **by** ~ случа́йно; *adj* случа́йный; *vi*: ~ **it** рискну́ть *pf*.

chancellery *n* канцеля́рия. **chancellor** *n* ка́нцлер; (*univ*) ре́ктор; **C~ of the Exchequer** ка́нцлер казначе́йства.

chancy *adj* риско́ванный.

chandelier *n* лю́стра.

change *n* переме́на, измене́ние; (*of clothes etc.*) сме́на; (*money*) сда́ча; (*of trains etc.*) переса́дка; **for a** ~ для разнообра́зия; *vt* & *i* меня́ть(ся) *impf*, изменя́ть(ся) *impf*, измени́ть(ся) *pf*; *vi* (*one's clothes*) переодева́ться *impf*, переоде́ться *pf*; (*trains etc.*) переса́живаться *impf*, пере-се́сть *pf*; *vt* (*a baby*) пере-пелёнывать *impf*, пере-

лена́ть *pf*; (*money*) проли́в-ва́ть *impf*, обменя́ть *pf*; (*give* ~ *for*) разме́нивать *impf*, разменя́ть *pf*; ~ **into** превраща́ть *impf*, преврати́ть *pf* в+*acc*; ~ **over to** переходи́ть *impf*, перейти́ *pf* на+*acc*. **changeable** *adj* изме́нчивый.

channel *n* (*water*) прото́в; (*also TV*) кана́л; (*fig*) путь *m*; **the (English) C~** Ла-Ма́нш; *vt* (*fig*) направля́ть *impf*.

chant *n* (*eccl*) песнопе́ние; *vt* & *i* петь *impf*; (*slogans*) сканди́ровать *impf* & *pf*.

chaos *n* ха́ос. **chaotic** *adj* хаоти́чный.

chap *n* (*person*) па́рень *m*.

chapel *n* часо́вня; (*Catholic*) капе́лла.

chaperone *n* компаньо́нка.

chaplain *n* капелла́н.

chapped *adj* потреска́вшийся.

chapter *n* глава́.

char *vt* & *i* обу́гливать(ся) *impf*, обу́глить(ся) *pf*.

character *n* хара́ктер; (*theat*) де́йствующее лицо́; (*letter*) бу́ква; (*Chinese etc.*) иеро́глиф. **characteristic** *adj* характе́рный, ~ свойство; (*of person*) черта́ хара́ктера. **characterize** *vt* характеризова́ть *impf* & *pf*.

charade *n* шара́да.

charcoal *n* древе́сный у́голь *m*.

charge *n* (*for gun*; *electr*) заря́д; (*fee*) пла́та; (*person*) пито́мец, -мица; (*accusation*) обвине́ние; (*mil*) ата́ка; **be in** ~ **of** заве́довать *impf* +*instr*; **in the** ~ **of** на попече́нии +*gen*; *vt* (*gun*; *electr*) заряжа́ть *impf*, заряди́ть *pf*; (*accuse*) обвиня́ть *impf*, обвини́ть *pf* (**with** в+*prep*); (*mil*) атакова́ть *impf & pf*; *vi* броса́ться *impf*, бро́ситься *pf* в ата́ку; ~ (for) брать *impf*, взять *pf* (за+*acc*); ~ to (the account of) запи́сывать *impf*, записа́ть *pf* на счёт+*gen*.

chariot *n* колесни́ца.

charisma *n* обая́ние. **charismatic** *adj* обая́тельный.

charitable *adj* благотвори́тельный; (*kind, merciful*) милосе́рдный. **charity** *n* (*kindness*) милосе́рдие; (*organization*) благотвори́тельная организа́ция.

charlatan *n* шарлата́н.

charm *n* очарова́ние, пре́лесть; (*spell*) за́говор; *pl* ча́ры (чар) *pl*; (*amulet*) талисма́н; (*trinket*) брело́к; *vt* очаро́вывать *impf*, очарова́ть *pf*. **charming** *adj* очарова́тельный, преле́стный.

chart *n* (*naut*) морска́я ка́рта; (*table*) гра́фик; *vt* наноси́ть *impf*, нанести́ *pf* на гра́фик.

charter *n* (*document*) ха́ртия; (*statutes*) уста́в; *vt* нанима́ть *impf*, наня́ть *pf*.

charwoman *n* приходя́щая убо́рщица.

chase *vt* гоня́ться *indet*, гна́ться *det* за+*instr*; *n* пого́ня; (*hunting*) охо́та.

chasm *n* (*abyss*) бе́здна.

chassis *n* шасси́ *neut indecl*.

chaste *adj* целому́дренный.

chastise *vt* кара́ть *impf*, по~ *pf*.

chastity *n* целому́дрие.

chat *n* бесе́да; *vi* бесе́довать *impf*; ~-**show** телевизио́нная бесе́да-интервью́ *f*.

chatter *n* болтовня́; *vi* болта́ть *impf*; (*teeth*) стуча́ть *impf*. **chatterbox** *n* болту́н.

chatty *adj* разгово́рчивый.

chauffeur *n* шофёр.

chauvinism *n* шовини́зм. **chauvinist** *n* шовини́ст; *adj* шовинисти́ческий.

cheap *adj* дешёвый. **cheapen** *vt* (*fig*) опошля́ть *impf*, опошли́ть *pf*. **cheaply** *adv* дёшево.

cheat *vt* обма́нывать *impf*, обману́ть *pf*; *vi* плутова́ть *impf*, на~, с~ *pf*; *n* (*person*) обма́нщик, -ица; плут; (*act*) обма́н.

check[1] *n* контро́ль *m*, прове́рка; (*chess*) шах; ~**mate** шах и мат; *vt* (*examine*) проверя́ть *impf*, прове́рить *pf*, контроли́ровать *impf*, про~ *pf*; (*restrain*) сде́рживать *impf*, сдержа́ть *pf*; ~ **in** регистри́роваться *impf*, за~ *pf*; ~ **out** выпи́сываться *impf*, вы́писаться *pf*; ~-**out** ка́сса; ~-**up** осмо́тр.

check[2] *n* (*pattern*) кле́тка. **check(ed)** *adj* кле́тчатый.

cheek *n* щека́; (*impertinence*) на́глость. **cheeky** *adj* на́глый.

cheep *vi* пища́ть *impf*, пи́скнуть *pf*.

cheer *n* ободря́ющий во́зглас; ~**s!** за (ва́ше) здоро́вье!; *vt* (*applaud*) приве́тствовать *impf & pf*; ~ **up** ободря́ть(ся) *impf*, ободри́ть(ся) *pf*. **cheerful** *adj* весёлый. **cheerfully** *adv* ве́село. **cheerfulness** *n*... **cheerio** *int* пока́.

cheerless *adj* уны́лый.

cheese *n* сыр; ~-**cake** ватру́шка.

cheetah *n* гепа́рд.

chef *n* (шеф-)по́вар.

chemical *adj* хими́ческий; *n* химика́т. **chemist** *n* хи́мик; (*druggist*) апте́карь *m*; ~**'s** (*shop*) апте́ка. **chemistry** *n* хи́мия.

cheque *n* чек; **~-book** чёковая книжка.

cherish *vt* (*foster*) лелеять *impf*; (*hold dear*) дорожить *impf* +*instr*; (*love*) нежно любить *impf*.

cherry *n* вишня; *adj* вишнёвый.

cherub *n* херувим.

chess *n* шахматы (-т) *pl*; **~-board** шахматная доска; **~-men** шахматы (-т) *pl*.

chest *n* сундук; (*anat*) грудь; **~ of drawers** комод.

chestnut *n* каштан; (*horse*) гнедая *sb*.

chew *vt* жевать *impf*. **chewing-gum** *n* жевательная резинка.

chic *adj* элегантный.

chick *n* цыплёнок. **chicken** *n* курица; цыплёнок; *adj* трусливый; **~ out** трусить *impf*, с~ *pf*. **chicken-pox** *n* ветрянка.

chicory *n* цикорий.

chief *n* глава *m* & *f*; (*boss*) начальник; (*of tribe*) вождь *m*; *adj* главный. **chiefly** *adv* главным образом. **chieftain** *n* вождь *m*.

chiffon *n* шифон.

child *n* ребёнок; дитя *neut*; (-дов) *pl*. **childhood** *n* детство. **childish** *adj* детский. **childless** *adj* бездетный. **childlike** *adj* детский. **childrens'** *adj* детский.

chill *n* стручковый перец.

chill *n* холод; (*ailment*) простуда; *vt* охлаждать *impf*, охладить *pf*. **chilly** *adj* прохладный.

chime *n* (*set of bells*) набор колоколов; *pl* (*sound*) перезвон; (*of clock*) бой; *vt* & *i* (*clock*) бить *impf*, про~ *pf*; *vi*

(*bell*) звонить *impf*, по~ *pf*.

chimney *n* труба; **~-sweep** трубочист.

chimpanzee *n* шимпанзе *m indecl*.

chin *n* подбородок.

china *n* фарфор. **China** *n* Китай. **Chinese** *n* китаец, -аянка; *adj* китайский.

chink[1] *n* (*sound*) звон; *vi* звенеть *impf*, про~ *pf*.

chink[2] *n* (*crack*) щель.

chintz *n* ситец.

chip *vt* & *i* откалывать(ся) *impf*, отколоть(ся) *pf*; *n* (*of wood*) щепка; (*in cup*) щербина; (*in games*) фишка; *pl* картофель-соломка (*collect*); (*electron*) чип, микросхема.

chiropodist *n* человек, занимающийся педикюром. **chiropody** *n* педикюр.

chirp *vi* чирикать *impf*.

chisel *n* (*wood*) стамеска; (*masonry*) зубило; *vt* высекать *impf*, высечь *pf*.

chit *n* (*note*) записка.

chivalrous *adj* рыцарский. **chivalry** *n* рыцарство.

chlorine *n* хлор. **chloroform** *n* хлороформ. **chlorophyll** *n* хлорофилл.

chock-full *adj* битком набитый.

chocolate *n* шоколад; (*sweet*) шоколадка.

choice *n* выбор; *adj* отборный.

choir *n* хор *m*; **~-boy** певчий *sb*.

choke *n* (*valve*) дроссель *m*; *vi* давиться *impf*, по~ *pf*; (*with anger etc.*) задыхаться *impf*, задохнуться *pf* (**with** от+*gen*); *vt* (*suffocate*) душить *impf*, за~ *pf*; (*of plants*) заглушать, глушить *impf*, за~

cholera n холе́ра.
cholesterol n холестери́н.
choose vt (select) выбира́ть impf, вы́брать pf; (decide) реша́ть impf, реши́ть pf.
choosy adj разбо́рчивый.
chop vt (also ~ down) руби́ть impf, руба́ну́ть pf; ~ off отруба́ть impf, отруби́ть pf; n (cul) отбивна́я котле́та.
chopper n топо́р. **choppy** adj бурли́вый.
chop-sticks n па́лочки f pl для еды́.
choral adj хорово́й. **chorale** n хора́л.
chord n (mus) акко́рд.
chore n обя́занность.
choreographer n хорео́граф. **choreography** n хореогра́фия.
chorister n пе́вчий sb.
chortle vi фы́ркать impf, фы́ркнуть pf.
chorus n хор; (refrain) припе́в.
christen vt крести́ть impf & pf. **Christian** n христиани́н, -а́нка; adj христиа́нский; ~ name и́мя neut. **Christianity** n христиа́нство. **Christmas** n Рождество́; ~ **Day** пе́рвый день Рождества́; ~ **Eve** соче́льник; ~ **tree** ёлка.
chromatic adj хромати́ческий. **chrome** n хром. **chromium** n хром. **chromosome** n хромосо́ма.
chronic adj хрони́ческий.
chronicle n хро́ника, ле́топись.
chronological adj хронологи́ческий.
chrysalis n ку́колка.
chrysanthemum n хризанте́ма.

chubby adj пу́хлый.
chuck vt броса́ть impf, бро́сить pf; ~ **out** вышиба́ть impf, вы́шибить pf.
chuckle vi посме́иваться impf.
chum n това́рищ.
chunk n ломо́ть m.
church n це́рковь. **churchyard** n кла́дбище.
churlish adj гру́бый.
churn n масло́бойка; vt сбива́ть impf, сбить pf; vi (foam) пе́ниться impf, вс~ pf; (stomach) крути́ть impf; vi ~ **out** выпека́ть impf, вы́печь pf; ~ **up** взбить pf.
chute n жёлоб.
cider n сидр.
cigar n сига́ра. **cigarette** n сигаре́та; папиро́са; ~ **lighter** зажига́лка.
cinder n шлак; pl зола́.
cine-camera n киноаппара́т.
cinema n кино́ neut indecl.
cinnamon n кори́ца.
cipher n нуль m; (code) шифр.
circle n круг; (theatre) я́рус; vi кружи́ться impf; vt (walking) обходи́ть impf, обойти́ pf; (flying) облета́ть impf, облете́ть pf. **circuit** n кругооборо́т; объе́зд, обхо́д; (electron) схе́ма; (electr) цепь.
circuitous adj окру́жный.
circular adj кру́глый; (moving in a circle) кругово́й; n циркуля́р. **circulate** vi циркули́ровать impf; vt распространя́ть impf, распространи́ть pf. **circulation** n (air) циркуля́ция; (distribution) распростране́ние; (of newspaper) тира́ж; (med) кровообраще́ние.
circumcise vt обреза́ть impf, обре́зать pf. **circumcision** n обреза́ние.

circumference n окру́жность.
circumspect adj осмотри́тельный.
circumstance n обстоя́тельство; **under the ~s** при да́нных обстоя́тельствах, в тако́м слу́чае; **under no ~s** ни при каки́х обстоя́тельствах, ни в ко́ем слу́чае.
circumvent vt обходи́ть impf, обойти́ pf.
circus n цирк.
cirrhosis n цирро́з.
CIS abbr (of Commonwealth of Independent States) СНГ.
cistern n бачо́к.
citadel n цитаде́ль.
cite vt ссыла́ться impf, сосла́ться pf на+acc.
citizen n граждани́н, -а́нка.
citizenship n гражда́нство.
citrus n ци́трус; adj ци́трусовый.
city n го́род.
civic adj гражда́нский. **civil** adj гражда́нский; (polite) ве́жливый; **~ engineer** гражда́нский инжене́р; **~ engineering** гражда́нское строи́тельство; **C~ Servant** госуда́рственный слу́жащий sb; чино́вник; **C~ Service** госуда́рственная слу́жба. **civilian** n шта́тский sb; adj шта́тский. **civility** n ве́жливость. **civilization** n цивилиза́ция. **civilize** vt цивилизова́ть impf & pf. **civilized** adj цивилизо́ванный.
clad adj оде́тый.
claim n (demand) тре́бование, притяза́ние; (assertion) утвержде́ние; vt (demand) тре́бовать impf +gen; (assert) утвержда́ть impf, утверди́ть pf. **claimant** n претенде́нт.
clairvoyant n ясновиде́ц, -ди́ца;

adj ясновидя́щий.
clam n моллю́ск; vi: **~ up** отка́зываться impf, отказа́ться pf разгова́ривать.
clamber vi кара́бкаться impf, вс~ pf.
clammy adj вла́жный.
clamour n шум; vi: **~ for** шу́мно тре́бовать impf, по~ pf +gen.
clamp n зажи́м; vt скрепля́ть impf, скрепи́ть pf; **~ down on** прижа́ть pf.
clan n клан.
clandestine adj та́йный.
clang, clank n лязг; vt & i ля́згать impf, ля́згнуть pf (+instr).
clap n & i хлопа́ть impf, хло́пнуть pf +dat; n хлопо́к; (thunder) уда́р.
claret n бордо́ neut indecl.
clarification n (explanation) разъясне́ние. **clarify** vt разъясня́ть impf, разъясни́ть pf.
clarinet n кларне́т.
clarity n я́сность.
clash n (conflict) столкнове́ние; (disharmony) дисгармо́ния; vi ста́лкиваться impf, столкну́ться pf; (coincide) совпада́ть impf, совпа́сть pf; не гармони́ровать impf.
clasp n застёжка; (embrace) объя́тие; vt обхва́тывать impf, обхвати́ть pf; **~ one's hands** сплести́ pf па́льцы рук.
class n класс; **~-room** класс; vt классифици́ровать impf & pf.
classic adj класси́ческий; n кла́ссик; pl (literature) кла́ссика; (Latin and Greek) класси́ческие языки́ m pl. **classical** adj класси́ческий.
classification n классифика́-

ция. **classified** adj засекре́ченный. **classify** vt классифици́ровать impf & pf.

classy adj кла́ссный.

clatter n стук; vi стуча́ть impf, по~ pf.

clause n статья́; (gram) предложе́ние.

claustrophobia n клаустрофо́бия.

claw n ко́готь; vt цара́пать impf когтя́ми.

clay n гли́на; adj гли́няный.

clean adj чи́стый; adv (fully) соверше́нно; ~-shaven гла́дко вы́бритый; vt чи́стить impf, вы́~ pf. **cleaner** n убо́рщик, -ица. **cleaner's** n химчи́стка. **clean(li)ness** n чистота́. **cleanse** vt очища́ть impf, очи́стить pf. **clear** adj я́сный; (transparent) прозра́чный; (distinct) отчётливый; (free) свобо́дный (of от+gen); (pure) чи́стый; vt & i очища́ть(ся) impf, очи́стить(ся) pf; vt (jump over) перепры́гивать impf, перепры́гнуть pf; (acquit) опра́вдывать impf, оправда́ть pf; ~ **away** убира́ть impf, убра́ть pf со стола́; ~ **off** (go away) убира́ться impf, убра́ться pf; ~ **out** (vt) вычища́ть impf, вы́чистить pf; (vi) (make off) убира́ться impf, убра́ться pf; ~ **up** (tidy away) убира́ть impf, убра́ть pf; (weather) проясня́ться impf, проясни́ться pf; (explain) выясня́ть impf, вы́яснить pf. **clearance** n расчи́стка; (permission) разреше́ние. **clearing** n (glade) поля́на. **clearly** adv я́сно.

cleavage n разре́з груди́.

clef n (mus) ключ.

cleft n тре́щина.

clemency n милосе́рдие.

clench vt (fist) сжима́ть impf, сжать pf; (teeth) сти́скивать impf, сти́снуть pf.

clergy n духове́нство. **clergyman** n свяще́нник. **clerical** adj (eccl) духо́вный; (of clerk) канцеля́рский. **clerk** n конто́рский слу́жащий sb.

clever adj у́мный. **cleverness** n уме́ние.

cliche n клише́ neut indecl.

click vi щёлкать impf, щёлкнуть pf +instr.

client n клие́нт. **clientele** n клиенту́ра.

cliff n утёс.

climate n кли́мат. **climatic** adj климати́ческий.

climax n кульмина́ция.

climb vt & i ла́зить indet, лезть det на+acc; влеза́ть impf, влезть pf на+acc; поднима́ться impf, подня́ться pf на+acc; ~ **down** (tree) слеза́ть impf, слезть pf (с+gen); (mountain) спуска́ться impf, спусти́ться pf (с+gen); (give in) отступа́ть impf, отступи́ть pf и подъём. **climber** n альпини́ст, ~ка; (plant) вью́щееся расте́ние. **climbing** n альпини́зм.

clinch vt: ~ **a deal** закрепи́ть pf сде́лку.

cling vi (stick) прилипа́ть impf, прили́пнуть pf (**to** к+dat); (grasp) цепля́ться impf, цепи́ться pf (**to** за+acc).

clinic n кли́ника. **clinical** adj клини́ческий.

clink vt & i звене́ть impf, про~ pf (+instr); ~ **glasses** чо́каться impf, чо́кнуться pf; n звон.

clip[1] n скре́пка; зажи́м; vt

скрепля́ть *impf*, скрепи́ть *pf*.

clip² *vt* (*cut*) подстрига́ть *impf*, подстри́чь *pf*; **clippers** *n pl* но́жницы *f pl*. **clipping** *n* (*extract*) вы́резка.

clique *n* кли́ка.

cloak *n* плащ. **cloakroom** *n* гардеро́б; (*lavatory*) убо́рная *sb*.

clock *n* часы́ *m pl*; ~**wise** *n* по часово́й стре́лке; ~~**work** часово́й механи́зм; *vi*: ~ **in, out** отмеча́ться *impf*, отме́титься *pf* прихода́ на рабо́ту/уходя́ с рабо́ты.

clod *n* ком.

clog *vt*: ~ **up** засоря́ть *impf*, засори́ть *pf*.

cloister *n* арка́да.

close *adj* (*near*) бли́зкий; (*stuffy*) ду́шный; *vt & i* (*also* ~ **down**) закрыва́ть(ся) *impf*, закры́ть(ся) *pf*; (*conclude*) зака́нчивать *impf*, зако́нчить *pf*; *adv* бли́зко (**to** от+*gen*). **closed** *adj* закры́тый. **closeted** *adj*: be ~ **together** совеща́ться *impf* наедине́. **close-up** *n* фотогра́фия сня́тая кру́пным пла́ном. **closing** *n* закры́тие; *adj* заключи́тельный. **closure** *n* закры́тие.

clot *n* сгу́сток; *vi* сгуща́ться *impf*, сгусти́ться *pf*.

cloth *n* ткань; (*duster*) тря́пка; (*table-~*) ска́терть.

clothe *vt* одева́ть *impf*, оде́ть (**in** +*instr*, в+*acc*) *pf*. **clothes** *n pl* оде́жда, пла́тье.

cloud *n* о́блако; (*rain ~*) ту́ча; *vt* затемня́ть *impf*, затемни́ть *pf*; омрача́ть *impf*, омрачи́ть *pf*; ~ **over** покрыва́ться *impf*, покры́ться *pf* облака́ми, ту́чами. **cloudy** *adj* о́блачный; (*liquid*) му́тный.

clout *vt* ударя́ть *impf*, уда́рить *pf*; *n* затре́щина; (*fig*) влия́ние.

clove *n* гвозди́ка; (*of garlic*) зубо́к.

cloven *adj* раздвоённый.

clover *n* кле́вер.

clown *n* кло́ун.

club *n* (*stick*) дуби́нка; *pl* (*cards*) тре́фы (треф) *pl*; (*association*) клуб; *vt* колоти́ть *impf*, по~ *pf* дуби́нкой; *vi*: ~ **together** скла́дываться *impf*, сложи́ться *pf*.

cluck *vi* куда́хтать *impf*.

clue *n* (*evidence*) ули́ка; (*to puzzle*) ключ; (*hint*) намёк.

clump *n* гру́ппа.

clumsiness *n* неукло́жесть. **clumsy** *adj* неукло́жий.

cluster *n* гру́ппа; *vi* соби́раться *impf*, собра́ться *pf* гру́ппами.

clutch *n* (*grasp*) хва́тка; ко́гти *m pl*; (*tech*) сцепле́ние; *vt* зажима́ть *impf*, зажа́ть *pf*; *vi*: ~ **at** хвата́ться *impf*, хвати́ться *pf* за+*acc*.

clutter *n* беспоря́док; *vt* загроможда́ть *impf*, загроможда́ть *pf*.

c/o *abbr* (*of care of*) по а́дресу +*gen*; че́рез+*acc*.

coach *n* (*horse-drawn*) каре́та; (*rly*) ваго́н; (*bus*) авто́бус; (*tutor*) репети́тор; (*sport*) тре́нер; *vt* репети́ровать *impf*; тренирова́ть *impf*, на~ *pf*.

coagulate *vi* сгуща́ться *impf*, сгусти́ться *pf*.

coal *n* у́голь *m*; ~**mine** у́гольная ша́хта.

coalition *n* коали́ция.

coarse *adj* гру́бый.

coast *n* побере́жье, бе́рег; ~**guard** берегова́я охра́на; *vi* (*move without power*) дви́гаться *impf*, дви́нуться *pf* по ине́рции. **coastal** *adj* берегово́й, прибре́жный.

coat *n* пальто́ *neut indecl*; (*layer*) слой; (*animal*) мех; ~ **of arms** герб; *vt* покрыва́ть *impf*, покры́ть *pf*.

coax *vt* угова́ривать *impf*, уговори́ть *pf*.

cob *n* (*corn-~*) поча́ток кукуру́зы.

cobble *n* булы́жник (*also collect*). **cobbled** *adj* булы́жный.

cobbler *n* сапо́жник.

cobweb *n* паути́на.

Coca-Cola *n* (*propr*) ко́ка-ко́ла.

cocaine *n* кокаи́н.

cock *n* (*bird*) пету́х; (*tap*) кран; (*of gun*) куро́к; *vt* (*gun*) взводи́ть *impf*, взвести́ *pf* куро́к+*gen*.

cockerel *n* петушо́к.

cockle *n* сердцеви́дка.

cockpit *n* (*aeron*) каби́на.

cockroach *n* тарака́н.

cocktail *n* кокте́йль *m*.

cocky *adj* чва́нный.

cocoa *n* кака́о *neut indecl*.

coco(a)nut *n* коко́с.

cocoon *n* ко́кон.

cod *n* треска́.

code *n* (*of laws*) ко́декс; (*cipher*) код; *vt* шифрова́ть *impf*, за~ *pf*. **codify** *vt* кодифици́ровать *impf* & *pf*.

co-education *n* совме́стное обуче́ние.

coefficient *n* коэффицие́нт.

coerce *vt* принужда́ть *impf*, прину́дить *pf*. **coercion** *n* принужде́ние.

coexist *vi* сосуществова́ть *impf*. **coexistence** *n* сосуществова́ние.

coffee *n* ко́фе *m indecl*; ~-**mill** *n* кофе́йница; ~-**pot** *n* кофе́йник.

coffer *n pl* казна́.

coffin *n* гроб.

cog *n* зубе́ц. **cogwheel** *n* зубча́тое колесо́.

cogent *adj* убеди́тельный.

cohabit *vi* сожи́тельствовать *impf*.

coherent *adj* свя́зный. **cohesion** *n* сплочённость. **cohesive** *adj* сплочённый.

coil *vt* & *i* свёртывать(ся) *impf*, сверну́ть(ся) *pf* кольцо́м; *n* кольцо́; (*electr*) кату́шка.

coin *n* моне́та; *vt* чека́нить *impf*, от~ *pf*.

coincide *vi* совпада́ть *impf*, совпа́сть *pf*. **coincidence** *n* совпаде́ние. **coincidental** *adj* случа́йный.

coke *n* кокс.

colander *n* дуршла́г.

cold *n* хо́лод; (*med*) просту́да, на́сморк; *adj* холо́дный; ~-**blooded** *adj* жесто́кий; (*zool*) холоднокро́вный.

colic *n* ко́лики *f pl*.

collaborate *vi* сотру́дничать *impf*. **collaboration** *n* сотру́дничество. **collaborator** *n* сотру́дник, -ица; (*traitor*) коллаборациони́ст, -и́стка.

collapse *vi* ру́хнуть *pf*; *n* паде́ние; круше́ние.

collar *n* воротни́к; (*dog's*) оше́йник; ~-**bone** ключи́ца.

colleague *n* колле́га *m & f*.

collect *vt* собира́ть *impf*, собра́ть *pf*; (*as hobby*) коллекциони́ровать *impf*; (*fetch*) забира́ть *impf*, забра́ть *pf*. **collected** *adj* (*calm*) со́бранный; ~ **works** собра́ние сочине́ний. **collection** *n* (*stamps etc.*) колле́кция; (*church etc.*) сбор; (*post*) вы́емка. **collective** *n* коллекти́в; *adj* коллекти́вный; ~ **farm** колхо́з; ~ **noun** собира́тельное существи́тельное *sb*. **collectivization** *n* коллективиза́ция. **collector** *n* сбо́рщик; коллекционе́р.

college *n* колле́дж, учи́лище. **collide** *vi* ста́лкиваться *impf*, столкну́ться *pf*. **collision** *n* столкнове́ние.

colliery *n* каменноуго́льная ша́хта.

colloquial *adj* разгово́рный. **colloquialism** *n* разгово́рное выраже́ние.

collusion *n* та́йный сго́вор.

colon[1] *n* (*anat*) то́лстая кишка́. **colon**[2] *n* (*gram*) двоето́чие. **colonel** *n* полко́вник.

colonial *adj* колониа́льный. **colonialism** *n* колониали́зм. **colonize** *vt* колонизова́ть *impf* & *pf*. **colony** *n* коло́ния. **colossal** *adj* колосса́льный.

colour *n* цвет, кра́ска; (*pl*) (*flag*) знамя *neut*; ~**-blind** страда́ющий дальтони́змом; ~ **film** цветна́я плёнка; *vt* раскра́шивать *impf*, раскра́сить *pf*; *vi* красне́ть *impf*, по~ *pf*. **coloured** *adj* цветно́й. **colourful** *adj* я́ркий. **colourless** *adj* бесцве́тный.

colt *n* жеребёнок.

column *n* (*archit*, *mil*) коло́нна; (*of smoke etc.*) столб; (*of print*) столбе́ц. **columnist** *n* журнали́ст.

coma *n* ко́ма.

comb *n* гребёнка; *vt* причёсывать *impf*, причеса́ть *pf*.

combat *n* бой; *vt* боро́ться *impf* c+*instr*, про́тив+*gen*.

combination *n* сочета́ние; комбина́ция. **combine** *n* комбина́т; (~-*harvester*) комба́йн; *vt* & *i* совмеща́ть(ся)

impf, совмести́ть(ся) *pf*. **combined** *adj* совме́стный.

combustion *n* горе́ние.

come *vi* (*on foot*) приходи́ть *impf*, прийти́ *pf*; (*by transport*) приезжа́ть *impf*, прие́хать *pf*; ~ **about** случа́ться *impf*, случи́ться *pf*; ~ **across** случа́йно ната́лкиваться *impf*, натолкну́ться *pf* на+*acc*; ~ **back** возвраща́ться *impf*, возврати́ться *pf*; ~ **in** входи́ть *impf*, войти́ *pf*; ~ **out** выходи́ть *impf*, вы́йти *pf*; ~ **round** (*revive*) приходи́ть *impf*, прийти́ *pf* в себя́; (*visit*) заходи́ть *impf*, зайти́ *pf*; (*agree*) соглаша́ться *impf*, согласи́ться *pf*; ~ **up to** (*approach*) подходи́ть *impf*, подойти́ *pf* к+*dat*; (*reach*) доходи́ть *impf*, дойти́ *pf* до+*gen*. **come-back** *n* возвраще́ние.

comedian *n* комедиа́нт. **comedy** *n* коме́дия.

comet *n* коме́та.

comfort *n* комфо́рт; (*convenience*) удо́бство; (*consolation*) утеше́ние; *vt* утеша́ть *impf*, уте́шить *pf*. **comfortable** *adj* удо́бный.

comic *adj* коми́ческий; *n* ко́мик; (*magazine*) ко́микс. **comical** *adj* смешно́й.

coming *adj* сле́дующий.

comma *n* запята́я *sb*.

command *n* (*order*) прика́з; (*order*, *authority*) кома́нда; **have** ~ *of* (*master*) владе́ть *impf* +*instr*; *vt* прика́зывать *impf*, приказа́ть *pf* +*dat*; (*mil*) кома́ндовать *impf*, с~ *pf* +*instr*. **commandant** *n* коменда́нт. **commandeer** *vt* реквизи́ровать *impf* & *pf*. **commander** *n* команди́р; ~-**in**-

chief главнокома́ндующий *sb*. **commandment** *n* за́поведь. **commando** *n* деса́нтник.

commemorate *vt* ознаме́новывать *impf*, ознамено́вать *pf*. **commemoration** *n* ознамено́вание. **commemorative** *adj* па́мятный.

commence *vt* & *i* начина́ть(ся) *impf*, нача́ть(ся) *pf*. **commencement** *n* нача́ло.

commend *vt* хвали́ть *impf*, по~ *pf*; (*recommend*) рекомендова́ть *impf* & *pf*. **commendable** *adj* похва́льный. **commendation** *n* похвала́.

commensurate *adj* соразме́рный.

comment *n* замеча́ние; *vi* де́лать *impf*, с~ *pf* замеча́ния; ~ **on** комменти́ровать *impf* & *pf*, про~ *pf*. **commentary** *n* коммента́рий. **commentator** *n* коммента́тор.

commerce *n* комме́рция. **commercial** *adj* торго́вый; *n* рекла́ма.

commiserate *vi*: ~ **with** соболе́зновать *impf* +*dat*. **commiseration** *n* соболе́знова́ние.

commission *n* (*order for work*) зака́з; (*agent's fee*) комиссио́нные *sb*; (*of inquiry etc.*) коми́ссия; (*mil*) офице́рское зва́ние; *vt* зака́зывать *impf*, заказа́ть *pf*. **commissioner** *n* швейца́р. **commissioner** *n* комисса́р.

commit *vt* соверша́ть *impf*, соверши́ть *pf*; ~ **o.s.** обя́зываться *impf*, обяза́ться *pf*. **commitment** *n* обяза́тельство.

committee *n* комите́т.

commodity *n* това́р.

commodore *n* (*officer*) коммодо́р.

common *adj* о́бщий; (*ordinary*) просто́й; *n* о́бщинная земля́; ~ **sense** здра́вый смысл. **commonly** *adv* обы́чно. **commonplace** *adj* бана́льный. **commonwealth** *n* содру́жество.

commotion *n* сумато́ха.

communal *adj* о́бщинный, коммуна́льный. **commune** *n* комму́на; *vi* обща́ться *impf*.

communicate *vt* передава́ть *impf*, переда́ть *pf*; сообща́ть *impf*, сообщи́ть *pf*. **communication** *n* сообще́ние; связь. **communicative** *adj* разгово́рчивый.

communion *n* (*eccl*) прича́стие.

communiqué *n* коммюнике́ *neut indecl*.

Communism *n* коммуни́зм. **Communist** *n* коммуни́ст, ~ка; *adj* коммунисти́ческий.

community *n* общи́на.

commute *vt* заменя́ть *impf*, замени́ть *pf*; (*travel*) добира́ться *impf*, добра́ться *pf* тра́нспортом. **commuter** *n* регуля́рный пассажи́р.

compact[1] *n* (*agreement*) соглаше́ние.

compact[2] *adj* компа́ктный; ~ **disc** компа́кт-ди́ск; *n* пу́дреница.

companion *n* това́рищ; (*handbook*) спра́вочник. **companionable** *adj* общи́тельный. **companionship** *n* дру́жеское обще́ние. **company** *n* о́бщество, (*also firm*) компа́ния; (*theat*) тру́ппа; (*mil*) ро́та.

comparable *adj* сравни́мый. **comparative** *adj* сравни́ тельный; *n* сравни́тельная сте́пень. **compare** *vt* & *i* сра́внивать(ся) *impf*, сравни́ть(ся) *pf* (**to, with** c+*instr*).

comparison *n* сравне́ние.

compartment *n* отделе́ние; (*rly*) купе́ *neut indecl*.

compass *n* ко́мпас; *pl* ци́ркуль *m*.

compassion *n* сострада́ние. **compassionate** *adj* сострада́тельный.

compatibility *n* совмести́мость. **compatible** *adj* совмести́мый.

compatriot *n* соотече́ственник, -ица.

compel *vt* заставля́ть *impf*, заста́вить *pf*.

compensate *vt* компенси́ровать *impf* & *pf* (**for** за+*acc*). **compensation** *n* компенса́ция.

compete *vi* конкури́ровать *impf*; соревнова́ться *impf*.

competence *n* компете́нтность. **competent** *adj* компете́нтный.

competition *n* (*contest*) соревнова́ние, состяза́ние; (*rivalry*) конкуре́нция. **competitive** *adj* (*comm*) конкурентоспосо́бный. **competitor** *n* конкуре́нт, ~ка.

compilation *n* (*result*) компиля́ция; (*act*) составле́ние. **compile** *vt* составля́ть *impf*, соста́вить *pf*. **compiler** *n* состави́тель *m*, ~ница.

complacency *n* самодово́льство. **complacent** *adj* самодово́льный.

complain *vi* жа́ловаться *impf*, по~ *pf*. **complaint** *n* жа́лоба.

complement *n* дополне́ние; (*full number*) (ли́чный) со-

ста́в; *vt* дополня́ть *impf*, допо́лнить *pf*. **complementary** *adj* дополни́тельный.

complete *vt* заверша́ть *impf*, заверши́ть *pf*; *adj* (*entire, thorough*) по́лный; (*finished*) зако́нченный. **completion** *n* заверше́ние.

complex *adj* сло́жный; *n* ко́мплекс. **complexity** *n* сло́жность.

complexion *n* цвет лица́.

compliance *n* усту́пчивость. **compliant** *adj* усту́пчивый.

complicate *vt* осложня́ть *impf*, осложни́ть *pf*. **complicated** *adj* сло́жный. **complication** *n* осложне́ние.

complicity *n* соуча́стие.

compliment *n* комплиме́нт; *pl* приве́т; *vt* говори́ть *impf* комплиме́нт(ы) +*dat*; хвали́ть *impf*, по~ *pf*. **complimentary** *adj* ле́стный; (*free*) беспла́тный.

comply *vi*: ~ **with** (*fulfil*) исполня́ть *impf*, испо́лнить *pf*; (*submit to*) подчиня́ться *impf*, подчини́ться *pf* +*dat*.

component *n* дета́ль; *adj* составно́й.

compose *vt* (*music etc.*) сочиня́ть *impf*, сочини́ть *pf*; (*draft, constitute*) составля́ть *impf*, соста́вить *pf*. **composed** *adj* споко́йный; **be ~ of** состоя́ть *impf* из+*gen*. **composer** *n* компози́тор. **composition** *n* сочине́ние; (*make-up*) соста́в.

compost *n* компо́ст.

composure *n* самооблада́ние.

compound[1] *n* (*chem*) соедине́ние; *adj* сло́жный.

compound[2] *n* (*enclosure*) огоро́женное ме́сто.

comprehend *vt* понима́ть *impf*.

понять *pf.* **comprehensible** *adj* понятный. **comprehension** *n* понимание. **comprehensive** *adj* всеобъемлющий; ~ **school** общеобразовательная школа.

compress *vt* сжимать *impf*, сжать *pf.* **compressed** *adj* сжатый. **compression** *n* сжатие. **compressor** *n* компрессор.

comprise *vt* состоять *impf* из+*gen*.

compromise *n* компромисс; *vt* компрометировать *impf*, с~ *pf*; идти *impf*, пойти *pf* на компромисс.

compulsion *n* принуждение. **compulsory** *adj* обязательный.

compunction *n* угрызение совести.

computer *n* компьютер.

comrade *n* товарищ. **comradeship** *n* товарищество.

con[1] *see* **pro**[1]

con[2] *vt* надувать *impf*, надуть *pf*.

concave *adj* вогнутый.

conceal *vt* скрывать *impf*, скрыть *pf.*

concede *vt* уступать *impf*, уступить *pf*; (*admit*) признавать *impf*, признать *pf*; (*goal*) пропускать *impf*, пропустить *pf.*

conceit *n* самомнение. **conceited** *adj* самовлюблённый.

conceivable *adj* мыслимый. **conceive** *vt* (*plan, imagine*) задумывать *impf*, задумать *pf*; (*biol*) зачинать *impf*, зачать *pf*; *vi* забеременеть *pf.*

concentrate *vt & i* сосредоточивать(ся) *impf*, сосредоточить(ся) *pf* (он на+*prep*); *vt* (*also chem*) концентри-

ровать *impf*, с~ *pf.* **concentration** *n* сосредоточенность, концентрация.

concept *n* понятие. **conception** *n* понятие; (*biol*) зачатие.

concern *n* (*worry*) забота; (*comm*) предприятие; *vt* касаться *impf* +*gen*; ~ **o.s. with** заниматься *impf*, заняться *pf* +*instr*. **concerned** *adj* озабоченный; **as far as I'm** ~ что касается меня. **concerning** *prep* относительно+*gen.*

concert *n* концерт. **concerted** *adj* согласованный.

concertina *n* гармоника.

concession *n* уступка; (*econ*) концессия. **concessionary** *adj* концессионный.

conciliation *n* примирение. **conciliatory** *adj* примирительный.

concise *adj* краткий. **conciseness** *n* сжатость, краткость.

conclude *vt* заключать *impf*, заключить *pf.* **concluding** *adj* заключительный. **conclusion** *n* заключение; (*deduction*) вывод. **conclusive** *adj* решающий.

concoct *vt* стряпать *impf*, со~ *pf.* **concoction** *n* стряпня.

concourse *n* зал.

concrete *n* бетон; *adj* бетонный; (*fig*) конкретный.

concur *vi* соглашаться *impf*, согласиться *pf.* **concurrent** *adj* одновременный.

concussion *n* сотрясение.

condemn *vt* осуждать *impf*, осудить *pf*; (*as unfit for use*) браковать *impf*, за~ *pf.* **condemnation** *n* осуждение.

condensation *n* конденсация.

condense vt (liquid etc.) конденси́ровать impf & pf; (text etc.) сокраща́ть impf, сократи́ть pf. **condensed** adj сжа́тый; (milk) сгущённый. **condenser** n конденса́тор.

condescend vi снисходи́ть impf, снизойти́ pf. **condescending** adj снисходи́тельный. **condescension** n снисхожде́ние.

condiment n припра́ва.

condition n усло́вие; (state) состоя́ние; vt (determine) обусло́вливать impf, обусло́вить pf; (psych) приуча́ть impf, приучи́ть pf. **conditional** adj усло́вный.

condolence n: pl соболе́знование.

condom n презервати́в.

condone vt закрыва́ть impf, закры́ть pf глаза́ на+acc.

conducive adj способствующий (to +dat).

conduct n (behaviour) поведе́ние; vt вести́ impf, по~, про~ pf; (mus) дирижи́ровать impf +instr; (phys) проводи́ть impf. **conduction** n проводи́мость. **conductor** n (bus) конду́ктор; (phys) прово́дник; (mus) дирижёр.

conduit n трубопрово́д.

cone n ко́нус; (bot) ши́шка.

confectioner n конди́тер; ~'s (shop) конди́терская sb. **confectionery** n конди́терские изде́лия neut pl.

confederation n конфедера́ция.

confer vt присужда́ть impf, присуди́ть (on +dat) pf; vi совеща́ться impf. **conference** n совеща́ние; конфере́нция.

confess vt & i (acknowledge) признава́ть(ся) impf, призна́ть(ся) pf (to в+prep); (eccl) испове́довать impf & pf. **confession** n призна́ние; и́споведь. **confessor** n духовни́к.

confidant(e) n бли́зкий собесе́дник. **confide** vt доверя́ть impf, дове́рить pf; ~ in дели́ться impf, по~ pf c+instr. **confidence** n (trust) дове́рие; (certainty) уве́ренность; (self~) самоуве́ренность. **confident** adj уве́ренный. **confidential** adj секре́тный.

confine vt ограни́чивать impf, ограни́чить pf; (shut in) заключа́ть impf, заключи́ть pf. **confinement** n заключе́ние. **confines** n pl преде́лы m pl.

confirm vt подтвержда́ть impf, подтверди́ть pf. **confirmation** n подтвержде́ние; (eccl) конфирма́ция. **confirmed** adj закоренéлый.

confiscate vt конфискова́ть impf & pf. **confiscation** n конфиска́ция.

conflict n конфли́кт; противоре́чие; vi: ~ with противоре́чить impf +dat. **conflicting** adj противоречи́вый.

conform vi: ~ to подчиня́ться impf, подчини́ться pf +dat. **conformity** n соотве́тствие; (compliance) подчине́ние.

confound vt сбива́ть impf, сбить pf с то́лку. **confounded** adj прокля́тый.

confront vt стоя́ть impf лицо́м к лицу́ c+instr; ~ (person) with ста́вить impf, по~ pf лицо́м к лицу́ c+instr. **confrontation** n конфронта́ция.

confuse vt смуща́ть impf, смути́ть pf; (also mix up) пу́тать impf, за~ pf. **confusion** n смуще́ние; пу́таница.

congeal vt густе́ть impf, за~ pf; (blood) свёртываться impf, сверну́ться pf.

congenial adj прия́тный.

congenital adj врождённый.

congested adj перепо́лненный. **congestion** n (traffic) зато́р.

congratulate vt поздравля́ть impf, поздра́вить pf (on c+instr) поздравле́ние; ~s! поздравля́ю!

congregate vi собира́ться impf, собра́ться pf. **congregation** n (eccl) прихожа́не (-н) pl.

congress n съезд. **Congressman** n конгрессме́н.

conic(al) adj кони́ческий.

conifer n хво́йное де́рево. **coniferous** adj хво́йный.

conjecture n дога́дка; vt гада́ть impf.

conjugal adj супру́жеский.

conjugate vt спряга́ть impf, про~ pf. **conjugation** n спряже́ние.

conjunction n (gram) сою́з; in ~ with совме́стно c+instr.

conjure vi: ~ up (in mind) вызыва́ть impf, вы́звать pf в воображе́нии. **conjurer** n фо́кусник. **conjuring trick** n фо́кус.

connect vt & i свя́зывать(ся) impf, связа́ть(ся) pf; соединя́ть(ся) impf, соедини́ть(ся) pf. **connected** adj свя́зный. **connection, -exion** n связь; (rly etc.) переса́дка.

connivance n попусти́тельство. **connive** vi: ~ at попу-

стительствовать impf +dat.

connoisseur n знато́к.

conquer vt (country) завоёвывать impf, завоева́ть pf; (enemy) побежда́ть impf, победи́ть pf; (habit) преодолева́ть impf, преодоле́ть pf. **conqueror** n завоева́тель m. **conquest** n завоева́ние.

conscience n со́весть. **conscientious** adj добросо́вестный. **conscious** adj созна́тельный; predic в созна́нии; be ~ of сознава́ть impf +acc. **consciousness** n созна́ние.

conscript vt призыва́ть impf, призва́ть pf на вое́нную слу́жбу; n призывни́к. **conscription** n во́инская пови́нность.

consecrate vt освяща́ть impf, освяти́ть pf. **consecration** n освяще́ние.

consecutive adj после́довательный.

consensus n согла́сие.

consent vi соглаша́ться impf, согласи́ться pf (to +inf, на+acc); n согла́сие.

consequence n после́дствие; of great ~ большо́го значе́ния; of some ~ дово́льно ва́жный. **consequent** adj вытека́ющий. **consequential** adj ва́жный. **consequently** adv сле́довательно.

conservation n сохране́ние; (of nature) охра́на приро́ды. **conservative** adj консервати́вный; n консерва́тор. **conservatory** n оранже́рея. **conserve** vt сохраня́ть impf, сохрани́ть pf.

consider vt (think over) обду́мывать impf, обду́мать pf; (examine) рассма́тривать impf, рассмотре́ть pf; (regard) as, be of opinion that) счита́ть impf, счесть pf +instr, за+acc, что; (take into account) счита́ться impf c+instr. **considerable** adj значи́тельный. **considerate** adj внима́тельный. **consideration** n рассмотре́ние; внима́ние; (factor) фа́ктор; take into ~ принима́ть impf, приня́ть pf во внима́ние. **considering** prep принима́я +acc во внима́ние.

consign vt передава́ть impf, переда́ть pf. **consignment** n (goods) па́ртия; (consigning) отпра́вка това́ров.

consist vi: ~ of состоя́ть impf из+gen. **consistency** n (density) после́довательность; консисте́нция. **consistent** adj после́довательный; ~ with совмести́мый c+instr.

consolation n утеше́ние. **console**[1] vt утеша́ть impf, уте́шить pf.

console[2] n (control panel) пульт управле́ния.

consolidate vt укрепля́ть impf, укрепи́ть pf. **consolidation** n укрепле́ние.

consonant n согла́сный sb.

consort n супру́г, ~а.

conspicuous adj заме́тный. **conspiracy** n за́говор. **conspirator** n загово́рщик, ~ица. **conspiratorial** adj загово́рщицкий. **conspire** vi устра́ивать impf, устро́ить pf за́говор.

constable n полице́йский sb.

constancy n постоя́нство. **constant** adj постоя́нный. **constantly** adv постоя́нно.

constellation n созве́здие.

consternation n трево́га.

constipation n запо́р.

constituency n избира́тель-

ный о́круг. **constituent** n (component) составна́я часть; (voter) избира́тель m; adj составно́й. **constitute** vt составля́ть impf, соста́вить pf. **constitution** n (polit, med) конститу́ция; (composition) составле́ние. **constitutional** adj (polit) конституцио́нный.

constrain vt принужда́ть impf, прину́дить pf. **constrained** adj (inhibited) стесне́нный. **constraint** n принужде́ние; (inhibition) стесне́ние.

constrict vt (compress) сжима́ть impf, сжать pf; (narrow) су́живать impf, су́зить pf. **constriction** n сжа́тие; суже́ние.

construct vt стро́ить impf, по~ pf. **construction** n строи́тельство; (also gram) констру́кция; (interpretation) истолкова́ние; ~ site стро́йка. **constructive** adj конструкти́вный.

construe vt истолко́вывать impf, истолкова́ть pf.

consul n ко́нсул. **consulate** n ко́нсульство.

consult vt сове́товаться impf, по~ pf c+instr. **consultant** n консульта́нт. **consultation** n консульта́ция.

consume vt потребля́ть impf, потреби́ть pf; (eat or drink) съеда́ть impf, съесть pf. **consumer** n потреби́тель m; ~ goods това́ры m pl широ́кого потребле́ния.

consummate vt заверша́ть impf, заверши́ть pf; ~ a marriage осуществля́ть impf, осуществи́ть pf бра́чные отноше́ния. **consummation** n заверше́ние; (of marriage) осуществле́ние.

consumption *n* потребле́ние.

contact *n* конта́кт; (*person*) связь; ~ **lens** конта́ктная ли́нза; *vt* свя́зываться *impf*, связа́ться *pf* c+*instr*.

contagious *adj* зара́зный.

contain *vt* содержа́ть *impf*; (*restrain*) сде́рживать *impf*, сдержа́ть *pf*. **container** *n* (*vessel*) сосу́д; (*transport*) конте́йнер.

contaminate *vt* загрязня́ть *impf*, загрязни́ть *pf*. **contamination** *n* загрязне́ние.

contemplate *vt* (*gaze*) созерца́ть *impf*; размышля́ть *impf*; (*consider*) предполага́ть *impf*, предположи́ть *pf*. **contemplation** *n* созерца́ние; размышле́ние. **contemplative** *adj* созерца́тельный.

contemporary *n* совреме́нник; *adj* совреме́нный.

contempt *n* презре́ние; ~ **of court** неуваже́ние к суду́; **hold in** ~ презира́ть *impf*. **contemptible** *adj* презре́нный. **contemptuous** *adj* презри́тельный.

contend *vi* (*compete*) состяза́ться *impf*; ~ **for** оспа́ривать *impf*; ~ **with** справля́ться *impf*, спра́виться *pf* c+*instr*; *vt* утвержда́ть *impf*. **contender** *n* прете́нде́нт.

content[1] *n* содержа́ние; *pl* содержи́мое *sb*; (*table of*) ~**s** содержа́ние.

content[2] *predic* дово́лен (-льна); *vt*: ~ **o.s. with** дово́льствоваться *impf*, у~ *pf* +*instr*. **contented** *adj* дово́льный.

contention *n* (*claim*) утвержде́ние. **contentious** *adj* спо́рный.

contest *n* состяза́ние; *vt* (*dispute*) оспа́ривать *impf*, оспо́-

рить *pf*. **contestant** *n* уча́стник, -ица, состяза́ния.

context *n* конте́кст.

continent *n* матери́к. **continental** *adj* материко́вый.

contingency *n* возмо́жный слу́чай; ~ **plan** вариа́нт пла́на. **contingent** *adj* случа́йный; *n* континге́нт.

continual *adj* непреста́нный. **continuation** *n* продолже́ние. **continue** *vt & i* продолжа́ть(ся) *impf*, продо́лжить(ся) *pf*. **continuous** *adj* непреры́вный.

contort *vt* искажа́ть *impf*, искази́ть *pf*. **contortion** *n* искаже́ние.

contour *n* ко́нтур; ~ **line** горизонта́ль.

contraband *n* контраба́нда.

contraception *n* предупрежде́ние зача́тия. **contraceptive** *n* противозача́точное сре́дство; *adj* противозача́точный.

contract *n* контра́кт, догово́р; *vi* (*make a* ~) заключа́ть *impf*, заключи́ть *pf* контра́кт; *vt & i* (*shorten, reduce*) сокраща́ть(ся) *impf*, сократи́ть(ся) *pf*; *vt* (*illness*) заболева́ть *impf*, заболе́ть *pf* +*instr*. **contraction** *n* сокраще́ние; (*pl med*) схва́тки *f pl*. **contractor** *n* подря́дчик.

contradict *vt* противоре́чить *impf* +*dat*. **contradiction** *n* противоре́чие. **contradictory** *adj* противоречи́вый.

contraflow *n* встре́чное движе́ние.

contralto *n* контра́льто (*voice*) *neut & (person*) *f indecl*.

contraption *n* приспособле́ние.

contrary *adj* (*opposite*) про-

contrast *n* (*perverse*) противополо́жный; капри́зный; ~ **to** вопреки́ +*dat*; *n*: **on the** ~ наоборо́т.

contrast *n* контра́ст, противополо́жность; *vt* противопоста́вить *impf*, противопоста́вить *pf* (**with** +*dat*); *vi* контрасти́ровать *impf*.

contravene *vt* наруша́ть *impf*, нару́шить *pf*. **contravention** *n* наруше́ние.

contribute *vt* (*to fund etc.*) же́ртвовать *impf*, по~ *pf* (**to** в+*acc*); ~ **to** (*further*) соде́йствовать *impf* & *pf*, по~ *pf* (+*dat*); *vi* (*write for*) сотру́дничать *impf* в+*prep*. **contribution** *n* (*money*) поже́ртвование; (*fig*) вклад. **contributor** *n* (*donor*) же́ртвователь *m*; (*writer*) сотру́дник.

contrite *adj* ка́ющийся.

contrivance *n* приспособле́ние. **contrive** *vt* ухитря́ться *impf*, ухитри́ться *pf* +*inf*.

control *n* (*mastery*) контро́ль *m*; (*operation*) управле́ние; *pl* управле́ния *pl*; *vt* (*dominate*; *verify*) контроли́ровать *impf*, про~ *pf*; (*regulate*) управля́ть *impf* +*instr*; ~ **o.s.** сде́рживаться *impf*, сдержа́ться *pf*.

controversial *adj* спо́рный. **controversy** *n* спор.

convalesce *vi* выздора́вливать *impf*. **convalescence** *n* выздоровле́ние.

convection *n* конве́кция. **convector** *n* конве́ктор.

convene *vt* созыва́ть *impf*, созва́ть *pf*.

convenience *n* удо́бство; (*public* ~) убо́рная *sb*. **convenient** *adj* удо́бный.

convent *n* же́нский монасты́рь *m*.

convention *n* (*assembly*) съезд; (*agreement*) конве́нция; (*custom*) обы́чай; (*conventionality*) усло́вность. **conventional** *adj* общепри́нятый; (*also mil*) обы́чный.

converge *vi* сходи́ться *impf*, сойти́сь *pf*. **convergence** *n* схо́димость.

conversant *predic*: ~ **with** знако́м с+*instr*.

conversation *n* разгово́р. **conversational** *adj* разгово́рный. **converse**[1] *vi* разгова́ривать *impf*.

converse[2] *n* обра́тное. **conversely** *adv* наоборо́т. **conversion** *n* (*change*) превраще́ние; (*of faith*) обраще́ние; (*of building*) перестро́йка. **convert** *vt* (*change*) превраща́ть *impf*, преврати́ть *pf* (**into** в+*acc*); (*to faith*) обраща́ть *impf*, обрати́ть *pf* (**to** в+*acc*); (*a building*) перестра́ивать *impf*, перестро́ить *pf*. **convertible** *adj* обрати́мый; *n* автомоби́ль *m* со снима́ющейся кры́шей.

convex *adj* вы́пуклый.

convey *vt* (*transport*) перевози́ть *impf*, перевезти́ *pf*; (*communicate*) передава́ть *impf*, переда́ть *pf*. **conveyance** *n* перево́зка; переда́ча. **conveyancing** *n* нотариа́льная переда́ча. **conveyor belt** *n* транспортёрная ле́нта.

convict *n* осуждённый *sb*; *vt* осужда́ть *impf*, осуди́ть *pf*. **conviction** *n* (*law*) осужде́ние; (*belief*) убежде́ние. **convince** *vt* убежда́ть *impf*, убеди́ть *pf*. **convincing** *adj* убеди́тельный.

convivial *adj* весёлый.

convoluted *adj* извилистый; *(fig)* запу́танный.

convoy *n* конво́й.

convulse *vt*: be ~d with содрога́ться *impf*, содрогну́ться *pf* от+*gen*. **convulsion** *n* (*med*) конву́льсия.

cook *n* куха́рка, по́вар; *vt* гото́вить *impf*; *vi* вари́ться *impf*; с~ *pf*. **cooker** *n* плита́, печь. **cookery** *n* кулина́рия.

cool *adj* прохла́дный; *(calm)* хладнокро́вный; *(unfriendly)* холо́дный; *vt* охлажда́ть *impf*, охлади́ть *pf*; ~ **down, off** остыва́ть *impf*, осты́(ну)ть *pf*. **coolness** *n* прохла́да; *(calm)* хладнокро́вие; *(manner)* хо́лодность.

coop *n* куря́тник; *vt*: ~ **up** держа́ть *impf* взаперти́.

cooperate *vi* сотру́дничать *impf*. **cooperation** *n* сотру́дничество. **cooperative** *n* коопера́тив; *adj* кооперати́вный; *(helpful)* услу́жливый.

co-opt *vt* коопти́ровать *impf* & *pf*.

coordinate *vt* координи́ровать *impf* & *pf*; *n* координа́та. **coordination** *n* координа́ция.

cope *vi*: ~ **with** справля́ться *impf*, спра́виться *pf* с+*instr*.

copious *adj* оби́льный.

copper *n* (*metal*) медь; *adj* ме́дный.

coppice, copse *n* ро́ща.

copulate *vi* совокупля́ться *impf*, совокупи́ться *pf*.

copy *n* ко́пия; *(book)* экземпля́р; *vt* *(reproduce)* копи́ровать *impf*, с~ *pf*; *(transcribe)* перепи́сывать *impf*, переписа́ть *pf*, *(imitate)* подража́ть *impf* +*dat*. **copyright** *n* а́вторское пра́во.

coral *n* кора́лл.

cord *n* *(string)* верёвка; *(electr)* шнур.

cordial *adj* серде́чный.

corduroy *n* ру́бчатый вельве́т.

core *n* сердцеви́на; *(fig)* суть.

cork *n* *(material; stopper)* про́бка; *(float)* поплаво́к. **corkscrew** *n* што́пор.

corn¹ *n* зерно́; *(wheat)* пшени́ца; *(maize)* кукуру́за. **cornflakes** *n pl* кукуру́зные хло́пья (-пьев) *pl*. **cornflour** *n* кукуру́зная мука́. **corny** *adj* *(coll)* бана́льный.

corn² *n* *(med)* мозо́ль.

cornea *n* рогова́я оболо́чка.

corner *n* у́гол; *(sport)* краеуго́льный ка́мень *m*; *vt* загоня́ть *impf*, загна́ть *pf* в у́гол.

cornet *n* *(mus)* корне́т; *(ice-cream)* рожо́к.

cornice *n* карни́з.

coronary (thrombosis) *n* коронаротромбо́з. **coronation** *n* корона́ция. **coroner** *n* ме́дик суде́бной эксперти́зы.

corporal¹ *n* капра́л.

corporal² *adj* теле́сный; ~ **punishment** теле́сное наказа́ние.

corporate *adj* корпорати́вный. **corporation** *n* корпора́ция.

corps *n* ко́рпус.

corpse *n* труп.

corpulent *adj* ту́чный.

corpuscle *n* кровяно́й ша́рик.

correct *adj* пра́вильный; *(conduct)* корре́ктный; *vt* исправля́ть *impf*, испра́вить *pf*. **correction** *n* исправле́ние.

correlation *n* соотноше́ние.

correspond *vi* соотве́тствовать *impf* (**to, with** +*dat*); *(by letter)* перепи́сываться *impf*.

correspondence n соотве́тствие; (letters) корреспонде́нция. **correspondent** n корреспонде́нт. **corresponding** adj соотве́тствующий (to +dat).

corridor n коридо́р.

corroborate vt подтвержда́ть impf, подтверди́ть pf.

corrode vt разъеда́ть impf, разъе́сть pf. **corrosion** n корро́зия. **corrosive** adj е́дкий.

corrugated iron n рифлёное желе́зо.

corrupt adj (person) развращённый; (government) прода́жный; vt развраща́ть impf, разврати́ть pf. **corruption** n развраще́ние; корру́пция.

corset n корсе́т.

cortège n корте́ж.

cortex n кора́.

corundum n кору́нд.

cosmetic adj космети́ческий. **cosmetics** n pl косме́тика.

cosmic adj косми́ческий. **cosmonaut** n космона́вт.

cosmopolitan adj космополити́ческий.

cosmos n ко́смос.

Cossack n каза́к, -а́чка.

cosset vt не́жить impf.

cost n сто́имость, цена́; vt сто́ить impf.

costly adj дорого́й.

costume n костю́м.

cosy adj ую́тный.

cot n де́тская крова́тка.

cottage n котте́дж; ~ cheese творо́г.

cotton n хло́пок; (cloth) хлопчатобума́жная ткань; (thread) ни́тка; ~ wool ва́та; adj хлопковый; хлопчатобума́жный.

couch n дива́н.

couchette n спа́льное ме́сто.

cough n ка́шель m; vi ка́шлять impf.

council n сове́т; ~ tax ме́стный нало́г; ~ house жильё из обще́ственного фо́нда. **councillor** n член сове́та.

counsel n (advice) сове́т; (lawyer) адвока́т; vt сове́товать impf, по~ pf +dat.

count[1] vt счита́ть impf, со~, счесть pf; ~ on рассчи́тывать impf на+acc; n счёт. **countdown** n отсчёт вре́мени.

count[2] n (title) граф.

countenance n лицо́; vt одобря́ть impf, одо́брить pf.

counter n прила́вок; (token) фи́шка; adv: run ~ to идти́ impf вразре́з с+instr; vt пари́ровать impf, от~ pf. **counteract** vt противоде́йствовать impf+dat. **counterbalance** n противове́с; vt уравнове́шивать impf, уравнове́сить pf. **counterfeit** adj подде́льный. **counterpart** n соотве́тственная часть. **counterpoint** n контрапу́нкт. **counter-revolutionary** n контрреволюционе́р; adj контрреволюцио́нный. **countersign** vt ста́вить impf, по~ pf втору́ю по́дпись на+prep.

countess n графи́ня.

countless adj бесчи́сленный.

country n (nation) страна́; (native land) ро́дина; (rural areas) дере́вня; adj дереве́нский, се́льский. **countryman** n (compatriot) сооте́чественник; се́льский житель m. **countryside** n приро́дный ландша́фт.

county n гра́фство.

coup n (polit) переворо́т.

couple n пара; (a few) несколько +gen; vt сцеплять impf, сцепить pf.
coupon n купон; талон; ваучер.
courage n храбрость. **courageous** adj храбрый.
courier n (messenger) курьер; (guide) гид.
course n курс; (process) ход, течение; (of meal) блюдо; **of ~** конечно.
court n двор; (sport) корт, площадка; (law) суд; **~ martial** военный суд; vt ухаживать impf за+instr. **courteous** adj вежливый. **courtesy** n вежливость. **courtier** n придворный sb. **courtyard** n двор.
cousin n двоюродный брат, -ная сестра.
cove n бухточка.
covenant n договор.
cover n (covering; lid) покрышка; (shelter) укрытие; (chair ~; soft case) чехол; (bed) покрывало n; (book) переплёт, обложка; **under separate ~** в отдельном конверте; vt покрывать impf, покрыть pf; (hide, protect) закрывать impf, закрыть pf. **coverage** n освещение. **covert** adj скрытый.
covet n пожелать pf +gen.
cow¹ n корова. **cowboy** n ковбой. **cowshed** n хлев.
cow² vt запугивать impf, запугать pf.
coward n трус. **cowardice** n трусость. **cowardly** adj трусливый.
cower vi съёживаться impf, съёжиться pf.
cox(swain) n рулевой m.
coy adj жеманно стыдливый.

crab n краб.
crack n (in cup, ice) трещина; (in wall) щель; (noise) треск; adj первоклассный; vt (break) колоть impf, рас~ pf; (china) делать impf, с~ pf трещину в+acc; vi треснуть pf. **crackle** vi потрескивать impf.
cradle n колыбель.
craft n (trade) ремесло; (boat) судно. **craftiness** n хитрость. **craftsman** n ремесленник. **crafty** adj хитрый.
crag n утёс. **craggy** adj скалистый.
cram vt (fill) набивать impf, набить pf; (stuff in) впихивать impf, впихнуть pf; vi (study) зубрить impf.
cramp¹ n (med) судорога.
cramp² vt стеснять impf, стеснить pf. **cramped** adj тесный.
cranberry n клюква.
crane n (bird) журавль m; (machine) кран; vt (one's neck) вытягивать impf, вытянуть pf (шею).
crank¹ n заводная ручка; **~ shaft** коленчатый вал; vt заводить impf, завести pf.
crank² n (eccentric) чудак m. **cranky** adj чудаческий.
cranny n щель.
crash n (noise) грохот, треск; (accident) авария; (financial) крах; **~ course** ускоренный курс; **~ helmet** защитный шлем; **~ landing** аварийная посадка; vi (~ into) врезаться impf, врезаться pf в+acc; (aeron) разбиваться impf, разбиться pf; (fall with ~) грохнуться pf; vt (bang down) грохнуть pf.
crass adj грубый.
crate n ящик.

crater n кра́тер.

crave vi: ~ **for** жа́ждать impf +gen. **craving** n стра́стное жела́ние.

crawl vi по́лзать indet, ползти́ det; ~ **with** кише́ть+instr; n (sport) кроль m.

crayon n цветно́й каранда́ш.

craze n ма́ния. **crazy** adj помеша́нный (**about** на+prep).

creak n скрип; vi скрипе́ть impf.

cream n сли́вки (-вок) pl; (cosmetic; cul) крем; ~ **cheese** сли́вочный сыр; ~ **soured** смета́на; vt сбива́ть impf, сбить pf; adj (of cream) сли́вочный; (colour) кре́мовый. **creamy** adj сли́вочный, кре́мовый.

crease n скла́дка; vt мять impf, из~, с~ pf. **creased** adj мя́тый.

create vt создава́ть impf, созда́ть pf. **creation** n созда́ние. **creative** adj тво́рческий. **creator** n созда́тель m. **creature** n созда́ние.

crèche n (де́тские) я́сли (-лей) pl.

credence n ве́ра; **give** ~ ве́рить impf (**to** +dat). **credentials** n pl удостовере́ние; (diplomacy) вери́тельные гра́моты f pl. **credibility** n правдоподо́бие; (of person) спосо́бность вызыва́ть дове́рие. **credible** adj (of thing) правдоподо́бный; (of person) заслу́живающий дове́рия.

credit n дове́рие; (comm) креди́т; (honour) честь; **give** ~ кредитова́ть impf & pf +acc; отдава́ть impf, отда́ть pf до́лжное+dat; ~ **card** креди́тная ка́рточка; vt: ~ **with**

припи́сывать impf, приписа́ть pf +dat. **creditable** adj похва́льный. **creditor** n кредито́р.

credulity n легкове́рие. **credulous** adj легкове́рный.

creed n убежде́ния neut pl; (eccl) вероиспове́дание.

creep vi по́лзать indet, ползти́ det. **creeper** n (plant) по́лзучее расте́ние.

cremate vt крема́ровать impf & pf. **cremation** n крема́ция. **crematorium** n кремато́рий.

crêpe n креп.

crescendo adv, adj, & n креще́ндо indecl.

crescent n полуме́сяц.

crest n гре́бень m; (heraldry) герб.

crevasse, **crevice** n расще́лина, рассе́лина.

crew n брига́да; (of ship, plane) экипа́ж.

crib n (bed) де́тская крова́тка; vi спи́сывать impf, списа́ть pf.

crick n растяже́ние мышц.

cricket[1] n (insect) сверчо́к.

cricket[2] n (sport) крике́т; ~ **bat** бита́.

crime n преступле́ние.

Crimea n Крым. **Crimean** adj кры́мский.

criminal n престу́пник; adj престу́пный; (of crime) уголо́вный.

crimson adj мали́новый.

cringe vi (cower) съёживаться impf, съёжиться pf.

crinkle n морщи́на; vt & i мо́рщить(ся) impf, на~, с~ pf.

cripple n кале́ка m & f; vt кале́чить impf, ис~ pf; (fig) расша́тывать impf, расша́тать pf.

crisis n кри́зис.

crisp adj (brittle) хрустя́щий; (fresh) све́жий. crisps n pl хрустя́щий карто́фель m.

criss-cross adv крест-на́крест.

criterion n крите́рий.

critic n кри́тик. critical adj крити́ческий. critically adv (ill) тяжело́. criticism n кри́тика. criticize vt критикова́ть impf. critique n кри́тика.

croak vi ква́кать impf, ква́кнуть pf; хрипе́ть impf.

Croat n хорва́т, ~ка. Croatia n Хорва́тия. Croatian adj хорва́тский.

crochet n вяза́ние крючко́м; vt вяза́ть impf, с~ pf (крючко́м).

crockery n посу́да.

crocodile n крокоди́л.

crocus n кро́кус.

crony n закады́чный друг.

crook n (staff) по́сох; (swindler) моше́нник. crooked adj криво́й; (dishonest) нече́стный.

crop n (yield) урожа́й; pl культу́ры f pl; (bird's) зоб; vt (cut) подстрига́ть impf, подстри́чь pf; ~ up возника́ть impf, возни́кнуть pf.

croquet n кроке́т.

cross n крест; (biol) по́месь; adj (angry) злой; vt пересека́ть impf, пересе́чь pf; (biol) скре́щивать impf, скре́сти́ть pf; ~ off, out вычёркивать impf, вы́черкнуть pf. ~ o.s. крести́ться impf, пере~ pf. ~ over переходи́ть impf, перейти́ pf (че́рез) +acc. ~bar n поперечи́на. ~breed по́месь; ~country race кросс; ~examination перекрёстный допро́с; ~examine, ~question подверга́ть impf, подве́ргнуть pf пере-

крёстному допро́су; ~-eyed косогла́зый; ~-legged: sit ~ сиде́ть impf по-туре́цки; ~reference перекрёстная ссы́лка; ~road(s) перекрёсток; (fig) распу́тье; ~-section n перекрёстное сече́ние; ~wise adv крест-на́крест; ~word (puzzle) кроссво́рд. crossing n (intersection) перекрёсток; (foot) перехо́д; (transport) rly) перее́зд.

crotch n (anat) проме́жность.

crotchet n (mus) четвертна́я но́та.

crotchety adj раздражи́тельный.

crouch vi приседа́ть impf, присе́сть pf.

crow n воро́на; as the ~ flies по прямо́й ли́нии; vi кука́рекать impf. crowbar n лом.

crowd n толпа́; vi тесни́ться impf, с~ pf; ~ into втя́скиваться impf, втисну́ться pf. crowded adj перепо́лненный.

crown n коро́на; (tooth) коро́нка; (head) те́мя; (hat) тулья́; vt коронова́ть impf & pf.

crucial adj (important) о́чень ва́жный; (decisive) реша́ющий; (critical) крити́ческий.

crucifix n, crucifixion n распя́тие. crucify vt распина́ть impf, распя́ть pf.

crude adj (rude) гру́бый; (raw) сыро́й. crudeness, crudity n гру́бость.

cruel adj жесто́кий. cruelty n жесто́кость.

cruise n круи́з; vi крейси́ровать impf. cruiser n кре́йсер.

crumb n кро́шка.

crumble vt кроши́ть impf, рас~ pf; vi обва́ливаться impf, обвали́ться pf. crumbly adj рассы́пчатый.

crumple vt мять impf, c~ pf; (intentionally) кóмкать impf, c~ pf.

crunch n (fig) решáющий момéнт, vt грызть impf, раз~ pf; vi хрустéть impf, хрустнуть pf.

crusade n крестóвый похóд; (fig) кампáния. **crusader** n крестонóсец; (fig) борéц (for за+acc).

crush n дáвка; (infatuation) сильное увлечéние; vt давить impf, раз~ pf; (crease) мять impf, c~ pf; (fig) подавлять impf, подавить pf.

crust n (of earth) корá; (bread etc.) кóрка.

crutch n костыль m.

crux n: ~ of the matter суть дéла.

cry n крик; **a far** ~ **from** далекó от+gen; vi (weep) плáкать impf; (shout) кричáть impf.

crypt n склеп. **cryptic** adj загáдочный.

crystal n кристáлл; (glass) хрустáль m. **crystallize** vt & i кристаллизовать(ся) impf & pf.

cub n детёныш; bear ~ медвежóнок; fox ~ лисёнок; lion ~ львёнок; wolf ~ волчóнок.

cube n куб. **cubic** adj кубический.

cubicle n кабина.

cuckoo n кукушка.

cucumber n огурéц.

cuddle vt ласкáть impf, об-нять pf; vi обнимáться impf, обняться pf; ~ up прижимáться impf, прижáться pf (to k+dat).

cudgel n дубинка.

cue[1] n (theat) рéплика.

cue[2] n (billiards) кий.

cuff[1] n манжéта; **off the** ~ экспрóмтом; ~**-link** зáпонка.

cuff[2] vt (hit) шлёпать impf, шлёпнуть pf.

cul-de-sac n тупик.

culinary adj кулинáрный.

cull vt (select) отбирáть impf, отобрáть pf; (slaughter) бить impf.

culminate vi кончáться impf, кóнчиться pf (in +instr). **culmination** n кульминациóнный пункт.

culpability n винóвность. **culpable** adj винóвный. **culprit** n винóвник.

cult n культ.

cultivate vt (land) обрабáтывать impf, обрабóтать pf; (crops) вырáщивать impf, вырастить impf; (develop) развивáть impf, развить pf.

cultural adj культýрный. **culture** n культýра. **cultured** adj культýрный.

cumbersome adj громóздкий.

cumulative adj кумулятивный.

cunning n хитрость; adj хитрый.

cup n чáшка; (prize) кýбок.

cupboard n шкаф.

cupola n кýпол.

curable adj излечимый.

curative adj целéбный.

curator n хранитель m.

curb vt обуздывать impf, обуздáть pf.

curd (cheese) n творóг. **curdle** vt & i свёртывать(ся) impf, свернýть(ся) pf.

cure n срéдство (for прóтив+gen); vt вылéчивать impf, вылечить pf; (smoke) коптить impf, за~ pf; (salt) солить impf, по~ pf.

curfew n комендáнтский час.

curiosity n любопытство.

curious adj любопы́тный.
curl n ло́кон; vt завива́ть impf, зави́ть pf; ~ **up** свёртываться impf, сверну́ться pf.
curly adj кудря́вый.
currants n pl (dried) изю́м (collect).
currency n валю́та; (prevalence) хожде́ние. **current** adj теку́щий; n тече́ние. (air) струя́; (water; electr) ток.
curriculum n курс обуче́ния; ~ **vitae** автобиогра́фия.
curry[1] n кэ́рри neut indecl.
curry[2] vt: ~ **favour with** зайскивать impf пе́ред+instr, у+gen.
curse n прокля́тие; (oath) руга́тельство; vt проклина́ть impf, прокля́сть pf; vi руга́ться impf, по~ pf.
cursory adj бе́глый.
curt adj ре́зкий.
curtail vt сокраща́ть impf, сократи́ть pf.
curtain n занаве́ска.
curts(e)y n реверанс; vi де́лать impf, с~ pf реверанс.
curve n изги́б; (line) крива́я sb; vi изгиба́ться impf, изогну́ться pf.
cushion n поду́шка; vt смягча́ть impf, смягчи́ть pf.
custard n сла́дкий заварно́й крем.
custodian n храни́тель m.
custody n опе́ка; (of police) аре́ст; **to take into** ~ арестова́ть pf.
custom n обы́чай; (comm) клиенту́ра; pl (duty) тамо́женные по́шлины f pl; **go through** ~**s** проходи́ть impf, пройти́ pf тамо́женный осмо́тр; ~**house** тамо́жня; ~ **officer** тамо́женник.
customary adj обы́чный.

customer n клие́нт; покупа́тель m.
cut vt ре́зать impf, по~ pf; (hair) стричь impf, о~ pf; (mow) коси́ть impf, с~ pf; (price) снижа́ть impf, сни́зить pf; (cards) снима́ть impf, снять pf коло́ду; ~ **back** (prune) подреза́ть impf, подре́зать pf; (reduce) сокраща́ть impf, сократи́ть pf; ~ **down** сруба́ть impf, сруби́ть pf; ~ **off** отреза́ть impf, отре́зать pf; (interrupt) прерыва́ть impf, прерва́ть pf; (disconnect) отключа́ть impf, отключи́ть pf; ~ **out** выреза́ть impf, вы́резать pf; ~ **out for** созданный для+gen; ~ **up** разреза́ть impf, разре́зать pf; n (gash) поре́з; (clothes) покро́й; (reduction) сниже́ние; ~ **glass** хруста́ль m.
cute adj симпати́чный.
cutlery n ножи́, ви́лки и ло́жки pl.
cutlet n отбивна́я котле́та.
cutting n (press) вы́резка; (plant) черено́к; adj ре́зкий.
CV abbr (of **curriculum vitae**) автобиогра́фия.
cycle n цикл; (bicycle) велосипе́д; vi е́здить impf на велосипе́де. **cyclic(al)** adj цикли́ческий. **cyclist** n велосипеди́ст.
cylinder n цили́ндр. **cylindrical** adj цилиндри́ческий.
cymbals n pl таре́лки f pl.
cynic n ци́ник. **cynical** adj цини́чный. **cynicism** n цини́зм.
cypress n кипари́с.
Cyrillic n кири́ллица.
cyst n киста́.
Czech n чех, че́шка; adj че́шский; ~ **Republic** Че́шская Респу́блика.

D

dab n мазо́к; vt (eyes etc.) прикла́дывать impf платок к+dat; ~ **on** накла́дывать impf, наложи́ть pf мазка́ми.

dabble vi: ~ **in** пове́рхностно занима́ться impf, заня́ться pf +instr.

dachshund n та́кса.

dad, daddy n па́па; ~**long-legs** n долгоно́жка.

daffodil n жёлтый нарци́сс.

daft adj глу́пый.

dagger n кинжа́л.

dahlia n гео́ргин.

daily adv ежедне́вно; adj ежедне́вный; n (charwoman) приходя́щая убо́рщица; (newspaper) ежедне́вная газе́та.

dainty adj изя́щный.

dairy n маслобо́йня; (shop) моло́чная sb; adj моло́чный.

dais n помо́ст.

daisy n маргари́тка.

dale n доли́на.

dally vi (dawdle) ме́шкать impf; (toy) игра́ть impf +instr; (flirt) флиртова́ть impf.

dam n (barrier) плоти́на; vt запру́живать impf, запруди́ть pf.

damage n поврежде́ние; pl убы́тки m pl; vt поврежда́ть impf, повреди́ть pf.

damn n (curse) проклина́ть impf, прокля́сть pf (censure) осужда́ть impf, осуди́ть pf; int чёрт возьми́!; **I don't give a** ~ мне наплева́ть. **damnation** n прокля́тие. **damned** adj прокля́тый.

damp n сы́рость; adj сыро́й; vt (also **dampen**) сма́чивать impf, смочи́ть pf; (fig) охла-

жда́ть impf, охлади́ть pf.

dance vi танцева́ть impf; n та́нец; (party) танцева́льный ве́чер. **dancer** n танцо́р, ~ка; (ballet) танцо́вщик, -ица; балери́на.

dandelion n одува́нчик.

dandruff n пе́рхоть.

Dane n датча́нин, -а́нка; **Great** ~ дог. **Danish** adj да́тский.

danger n опа́сность. **dangerous** adj опа́сный.

dangle vt &i пока́чивать(ся) impf.

dank adj промо́зглый.

dapper adj выхоленный.

dare vi (have courage) осме́ливаться impf, осме́литься pf; (have impudence) сметь impf, по~ pf; vt вызыва́ть impf, вы́звать pf; в э́том. **daredevil** n лиха́ч, adj отча́янный. **daring** n отва́га; adj отча́янный.

dark adj тёмный; ~ **blue** тёмно-си́ний; n темнота́. **darken** vt затемня́ть impf, затемни́ть pf; vi темне́ть impf, по~ pf. **darkly** adv мра́чно. **darkness** n темнота́.

darling n дорого́й sb, ми́лый sb; adj дорого́й.

darn n што́пать impf, за~ pf.

dart n стрела́; (for game) мета́тельная стрела́; (tuck) вы́тачка; vi бро́ситься pf.

dash n (hyphen) тире́ neut indecl; (admixture) при́месь; vt швыря́ть impf, швырну́ть pf; vi броса́ться impf, бро́ситься pf. **dashboard** n прибо́рная доска́. **dashing** adj лихо́й.

data n pl да́нные sb pl. **database** n ба́за да́нных.

date[1] n (fruit) фи́ник.

date[2] n число́, да́та; (engage-

ment) свида́ние; *out of* ~ устаре́лый; *up to* ~ совреме́нный; *в* ку́рсе де́ла; *vt* дати́ровать *impf & pf*; (*go out with*) встреча́ться *impf c+instr*; *vi* (*originate*) относи́ться *impf* (*from* s+instr).

dative *adj* (*n*) да́тельный (паде́ж).

daub *vt* ма́зать *impf*, на~ *pf* (*with* +instr).

daughter *n* дочь; ~-**in-law** неве́стка (*in relation to mother*), сноха́ (*in relation to father*).

daunting *adj* угрожа́ющий.

dawdle *vi* ме́шкать *impf*.

dawn *n* рассве́т; (*also fig*) заря́; *vi* (*day*) рассвета́ть *impf*, рассвести́ *pf impers*; ~ (**up**)**on** осеня́ть *impf*, осени́ть *pf*; *it* ~ed on me меня́ осени́ло.

day *n* день *m*; (*24 hours*) су́тки *pl*; *pl* (*period*) пери́од, вре́мя *neut*; ~ *after* ~ изо дня́ в день; ~ *the* ~ *after* to-**morrow** послеза́втра; *the* ~ *before* накану́не; *the* ~ *before yesterday* позавчера́; *the other* ~ на дня́х; *by* ~ днём; *every other* ~ че́рез день; ~ *off* выходно́й день *m*; *one* ~ одна́жды; *these* ~s в на́ши дни. **daybreak** *n* рассве́т. **day-dreams** *n pl* мечты́ *f pl*. **daylight** *n* дневно́й свет; *in broad* ~ средь бе́ла дня. **daytime** *n*: *in the* ~ днём.

daze *vt*: *in a* ~, **dazed** *adj* оглушён (-ена́).

dazzle *vt* ослепля́ть *impf*, ослепи́ть *pf*.

deacon *n* дья́кон.

dead *adj* мёртвый; (*animals*) до́хлый; (*plants*) увя́дший; (*numb*) онеме́вший; *n*: *the* ~ мёртвые *sb pl*; *at* ~ *of night*

глубо́кой но́чью; *adv* соверше́нно; ~ *end* тупи́к; ~ *heat* одновреме́нный фи́ниш; ~*line* преде́льный срок; ~*lock* тупи́к.

deaden *vt* заглуша́ть *impf*, заглуши́ть *pf*.

deadly *adj* смерте́льный.

deaf *adj* глухо́й; ~ *and dumb* глухонемо́й. **deafen** *vt* оглуша́ть *impf*, оглуши́ть *pf*. **deafness** *n* глухота́.

deal[1] *n*: *a great, good,* ~ мно́го (+*gen*); (*with comp*) гора́здо.

deal[2] *n* (*bargain*) сде́лка; (*cards*) сда́ча; *vt* (*cards*) сдава́ть *impf*, сдать *pf*; (*blow*) наноси́ть *impf*, нанести́ *pf*; ~ *in* торгова́ть *impf* +instr; ~ *out* распределя́ть *impf*, распредели́ть *pf*; ~ *with* (*take care of*) занима́ться *impf*, заня́ться *pf* +instr; (*handle a person*) поступа́ть *impf*, поступи́ть *pf* c+instr; (*treat a subject*) рассма́тривать *impf*, рассмотре́ть *pf*; (*cope with*) справля́ться *impf*, спра́виться *pf* c+instr. **dealer** *n* торго́вец (*in* +instr).

dean *n* дека́н.

dear *adj* дорого́й; (*also n*) ми́лый (*sb*).

dearth *n* недоста́ток.

death *n* смерть; *put to* ~ казни́ть *impf & pf*; ~*bed n* сме́ртное ло́же; ~ *certificate* свиде́тельство о сме́рти; ~ *penalty* сме́ртная казнь. **deathly** *adj* смерте́льный.

debar *vt*: ~ *from* не допуска́ть *impf* до+gen.

debase *vt* унижа́ть *impf*, уни́зить *pf*; (*coinage*) понижа́ть *impf*, пони́зить *pf* ка́чество +gen.

debatable adj спо́рный. **debate** n пре́ния (-ий) pl; vt обсужда́ть impf, обсуди́ть pf.

debauched adj развращённый. **debauchery** n разврат.

debilitate vt ослабля́ть impf, осла́бить pf. **debility** n сла́бость.

debit n де́бет; vt дебетова́ть impf & pf.

debris n обло́мки m pl.

debt n долг. **debtor** n должни́к.

début n дебю́т; **make one's ~** дебюти́ровать impf & pf.

decade n десятиле́тие.

decadence n декаде́нтство. **decadent** adj декаде́нтский.

decaffeinated adj без кофеи́на.

decant vt перелива́ть impf, перели́ть pf. **decanter** n графи́н.

decapitate vt обезгла́вливать impf, обезгла́вить pf.

decay vi гнить impf, c~ pf; (tooth) разруша́ться impf, разру́шиться pf; n гние́ние; (tooth) разруше́ние.

decease n кончи́на. **deceased** adj поко́йный; n поко́йник, -ица.

deceit n обма́н. **deceitful** adj лжи́вый. **deceive** vt обма́нывать impf, обману́ть pf.

deceleration n замедле́ние.

December n дека́брь m; adj дека́брьский.

decency n прили́чие. **decent** adj прили́чный.

decentralization n децентрализа́ция. **decentralize** vt децентрализова́ть impf & pf.

deception n обма́н. **deceptive** adj обма́нчивый.

decibel n деци́бел.

decide vt реша́ть impf, ре-

ши́ть pf. **decided** adj реши́тельный.

deciduous adj листопа́дный.

decimal n десяти́чная дробь; adj десяти́чный; ~ **point** запята́я sb.

decimate vt (fig) коси́ть impf, c~.

decipher vt расшифро́вывать impf, расшифрова́ть pf.

decision n реше́ние. **decisive** adj (firm) реши́тельный, (deciding) реша́ющий.

deck n па́луба; (bus etc.) эта́ж; **~-chair** n шезло́нг; vt: **~ out** украша́ть impf, укра́сить pf.

declaim vt деклами́ровать impf, про~ pf.

declaration n объявле́ние; (document) деклара́ция. **declare** vt (proclaim) объявля́ть impf, объяви́ть pf; (assert) заявля́ть impf, заяви́ть pf.

declension n склоне́ние. **decline** n упа́док; vi приходи́ть impf, прийти́ pf в упа́док; vt отклоня́ть impf, отклони́ть pf; (gram) склоня́ть impf, про~ pf.

decode vt расшифро́вывать impf, расшифрова́ть pf.

decompose vi разлага́ться impf, разложи́ться pf.

décor n эстети́ческое оформле́ние. **decorate** vt украша́ть impf, укра́сить pf; (room) ремонти́ровать impf, от~ pf; (with medal etc.) награжда́ть impf, награди́ть pf. **decoration** n украше́ние; (medal) о́рден. **decorative** adj декорати́вный. **decorator** n маля́р.

decorous adj прили́чный. **decorum** n прили́чие.

decoy n (bait) прима́нка; vt зама́нивать impf, замани́ть pf.

decrease vt & i уменьша́ть(ся) impf, уме́ньшить(ся) pf, n уменьше́ние.

decree n ука́з; vt постановля́ть impf, постанови́ть pf.

decrepit adj дря́хлый.

dedicate vt посвяща́ть impf, посвяти́ть pf. **dedication** n посвяще́ние.

deduce vt заключа́ть impf, заключи́ть pf.

deduct vt вычита́ть impf, вы́честь pf. **deduction** n (subtraction) вы́чет; (inference) вы́вод.

deed n посту́пок; (heroic) по́двиг; (law) акт.

deem vt счита́ть impf, счесть pf +acc & instr.

deep adj глубо́кий; (colour) тёмный; (sound) ни́зкий; ~ **freeze** морози́льник. **deepen** vt & i углубля́ть(ся) impf, углуби́ть(ся) pf.

deer n оле́нь m.

deface vt обезобра́живать impf, обезобра́зить pf.

defamation n диффама́ция. **defamatory** adj клеветни́ческий.

default n (failure to pay) неупла́та; (failure to appear) нея́вка; (comput) автомати́ческий вы́бор; vi не выполня́ть свои́х обяза́тельств.

defeat n пораже́ние; vt побежда́ть impf, победи́ть pf. **defeatism** n пораже́нчество. **defeatist** n пораже́нец; adj пораже́нческий.

defecate vi испражня́ться impf, испражни́ться pf.

defect n дефе́кт; vi перебега́ть impf, перебежа́ть pf. **defective** adj неиспра́вный. **defector** n перебе́жчик.

defence n защи́та. **defenceless** adj беззащи́тный. **defend** vt защища́ть impf, защити́ть pf. **defendant** n подсуди́мый sb. **defender** n защи́тник. **defensive** adj оборони́тельный.

defer[1] vt (postpone) отсро́чивать impf, отсро́чить pf.

defer[2] vi: ~ **to** подчиня́ться impf +dat. **deference** n уваже́ние. **deferential** adj почти́тельный.

defiance n неповинове́ние; **in** ~ **of** вопреки́+dat. **defiant** adj вызыва́ющий.

deficiency n недоста́ток. **deficient** adj недоста́точный. **deficit** n дефици́т.

defile vt оскверня́ть impf, оскверни́ть pf.

define vt определя́ть impf, определи́ть pf. **definite** adj определённый **definitely** adv несомне́нно. **definition** n определе́ние. **definitive** adj оконча́тельный.

deflate vt & i спуска́ть impf, спусти́ть pf; vt (person) сбива́ть impf, сбить pf спесь c+gen. **deflation** n дефля́ция.

deflect vt отклоня́ть impf, отклони́ть pf.

deforestation n обезле́сение.

deformed adj уро́дливый. **deformity** n уро́дство.

defraud vt обма́нывать impf, обману́ть pf; ~ **of** выма́нивать impf, вы́манить pf +acc & y+gen (of person).

defray vt опла́чивать impf, оплати́ть pf.

defrost vt размора́живать impf, разморо́зить pf.

deft adj ло́вкий.

defunct adj бо́льше не существу́ющий.

defy vt (challenge) вызыва́ть

impf, вы́звать *pf*; (*disobey*) идти́ *impf*, по~ *pf* про́тив+*acc*; (*fig*) не поддава́ться *impf* +*dat*.

degenerate *vi* вырожда́ться *impf*, вы́родиться *pf*; *adj* вы́родившийся.

degradation *n* униже́ние. **degrade** *vt* унижа́ть *impf*, уни́зить *pf*. **degrading** *adj* унизи́тельный.

degree *n* сте́пень; (*math etc.*) гра́дус; (*univ*) учёная сте́пень.

dehydrate *vt* обезво́живать *impf*, обезво́дить *pf*. **dehydration** *n* обезво́живание.

deign *vi* снисходи́ть *impf*, снизойти́ *pf*.

deity *n* божество́.

dejected *adj* удручённый.

delay *n* заде́ржка; **without** ~ неме́дленно; *vt* заде́рживать *impf*, задержа́ть *pf*.

delegate *n* делега́т; *vt* делеги́ровать *impf* & *pf*. **delegation** *n* делега́ция.

delete *vt* вычёркивать *impf*, вы́черкнуть *pf*.

deliberate *adj* (*intentional*) преднаме́ренный; (*careful*) осторо́жный; *vt* & *i* размышля́ть *impf*, размы́слить *pf* (o+*prep*); (*discuss*) совеща́ться *impf* (o+*prep*). **deliberation** *n* размышле́ние; (*discussion*) совеща́ние.

delicacy *n* (*tact*) делика́тность; (*dainty*) ла́комство.

delicate *adj* то́нкий; (*tactful*, *needing tact*) делика́тный; (*health*) боле́зненный.

delicatessen *n* гастроно́м.

delicious *adj* о́чень вку́сный.

delight *n* наслажде́ние; (*delightful thing*) пре́лесть. **delightful** *adj* преле́стный.

delinquency *n* престу́пность.

delinquent *n* правонаруши́тель *m*, ~ница *f*; *adj* вино́вный.

delirious *adj*: **be** ~ бре́дить *impf*. **delirium** *n* бред.

deliver *vt* (*goods*) доставля́ть *impf*, доста́вить *pf*; (*save*) избавля́ть *impf*, изба́вить *pf* (*from* от+*gen*); (*lecture*) прочита́ть *impf*, проче́сть *pf*; (*letters*) разноси́ть *impf*, разнести́ *pf*; (*speech*) произноси́ть *impf*, произнести́ *pf*; (*blow*) наноси́ть *impf*, нанести́ *pf*. **deliverance** *n* избавле́ние. **delivery** *n* доста́вка.

delta *n* де́льта.

delude *vt* вводи́ть *impf*, ввести́ *pf* в заблужде́ние.

deluge *n* (*flood*) пото́п; (*rain*) ли́вень *m*; (*fig*) пото́к.

delusion *n* заблужде́ние; ~s **of grandeur** ма́ния вели́чия.

de luxe *adj* -люкс (*added to noun*).

delve *vi* углубля́ться *impf*, углуби́ться *pf* (*into* в+*acc*).

demand *n* тре́бование; (*econ*) спрос (*for* на+*acc*); *vt* тре́бовать *impf*, по~ *pf* +*gen*. **demanding** *adj* тре́бовательный.

demarcation *n* демарка́ция.

demean *vt*: ~ **o.s.** унижа́ться *impf*, уни́зиться *pf*.

demeanour *n* мане́ра вести́ себя́.

demented *adj* сумасше́дший.

dementia *n* слабоу́мие.

demise *n* кончи́на.

demobilize *vt* демобилизова́ть *impf* & *pf*.

democracy *n* демокра́тия.

democrat *n* демокра́т. **democratic** *adj* демократи́ческий. **democratization** *n* демократиза́ция.

demolish vt (destroy) разруша́ть impf, разру́шить pf; (building) сноси́ть impf, снести́ pf; (refute) опроверга́ть impf, опрове́ргнуть pf. **demolition** n разруше́ние; снос.

demon n де́мон.

demonstrable adj доказу́емый. **demonstrably** adv нагля́дно. **demonstrate** vt демонстри́ровать impf & pf; vi уча́ствовать impf в демонстра́ции. **demonstration** n демонстра́ция. **demonstrative** adj экспанси́вный; (gram) указа́тельный. **demonstrator** n демонстра́тор; (polit) демонстра́нт.

demoralize vt деморализова́ть impf & pf.

demote vt понижа́ть impf, пони́зить в до́лжности.

demure adj скро́мный.

den n берло́га.

denial n отрица́ние; (refusal) отка́з.

denigrate vt черни́ть impf, о~ pf.

denim adj джинсо́вый; n джинсо́вая ткань.

Denmark n Да́ния.

denomination n (money) досто́инство; (relig) вероиспове́дание. **denominator** n знамена́тель m.

denote vt означа́ть impf, озна́чить pf.

denounce vt (condemn) осужда́ть impf, осуди́ть pf; (inform on) доноси́ть impf, донести́ pf на+acc.

dense adj густо́й; (stupid) тупо́й. **density** n пло́тность.

dent n вмя́тина; vt вдавля́ть impf, с~ pf вмя́тину в+prep.

dental adj зубно́й. **dentist** n зубно́й врач. **dentures** n pl зубно́й проте́з.

denunciation n (condemnation) осужде́ние; (informing) доно́с.

deny vt отрица́ть impf; (refuse) отка́зывать impf, отказа́ть pf +dat (person) в+prep.

deodorant n дезодора́нт.

depart vi отбыва́ть impf, отбы́ть pf; (deviate) отклоня́ться impf, отклони́ться pf (from от+gen).

department n отде́л; (univ) ка́федра; ~ store универма́г.

departure n отбы́тие; (deviation) отклоне́ние.

depend vi зави́сеть impf (on от+gen); (rely) полага́ться impf, положи́ться pf (on на+acc). **dependable** adj надёжный. **dependant** n иждиве́нец. **dependence** n зави́симость. **dependent** adj зави́симый.

depict vt изобража́ть impf, изобрази́ть pf.

deplete vt истоща́ть impf, истощи́ть pf. **depleted** adj истощённый. **depletion** n истоще́ние.

deplorable adj плаче́вный. **deplore** vt сожале́ть impf о+prep.

deploy vt развёртывать impf, разверну́ть pf. **deployment** n развёртывание.

deport vt депорти́ровать impf & pf; высыла́ть impf, вы́слать pf. **deportation** n депорта́ция; высылка.

deportment n оса́нка.

depose vt сверга́ть impf, све́ргнуть pf. **deposit** n (econ) вклад; (advance) зада́ток; (sediment) оса́док; (coal etc.) месторожде́ние; vt (econ) вноси́ть impf, внести́ pf.

depot n (transport) депо́ neut

indecl; (*store*) склад.

deprave vt развраща́ть *impf*, разврати́ть *pf*. **depraved** *adj* развращённый. **depravity** *n* разврат.

deprecate vt осужда́ть *impf*, осуди́ть *pf*.

depreciate vt & *i* (*econ*) обесце́нивать(ся) *impf*, обесце́нить(ся) *pf*. **depreciation** *n* обесце́нение.

depress vt (*dispirit*) удруча́ть *impf*, удручи́ть *pf*. **depressed** *adj* удручённый. **depressing** *adj* угнета́ющий. **depression** *n* (*hollow*) впа́дина; (*econ, med, meteorol, etc.*) депре́ссия.

deprivation *n* лише́ние. **deprive** vt лиша́ть *impf*, лиши́ть *pf* (*of* +gen).

depth *n* глубина́; **in the** ~ **of winter** в разга́ре зимы́.

deputation *n* депута́ция. **deputize** vi замеща́ть *impf*, замести́ть *pf* (*for* +acc). **deputy** *n* замести́тель m; (*parl*) депута́т.

derail vt: **be derailed** сходи́ть *impf*, сойти́ *pf* с ре́льсов. **derailment** *n* схо́д с ре́льсов.

deranged *adj* сумасше́дший.

derelict *adj* забро́шенный.

deride vt высме́ивать *impf*, вы́смеять *pf*. **derision** *n* высме́ивание. **derisive** *adj* (*mocking*) насме́шливый. **derisory** *adj* (*mocking*) смехотво́рный.

derivation *n* происхожде́ние. **derivative** *n* произво́дное *sb*; *adj* произво́дный. **derive** vt извлека́ть *impf*, извле́чь *pf*; vi: ~ **from** происходи́ть *impf*, произойти́ *pf* от+gen.

derogatory *adj* отрица́тельный.

descend vi (& *t*) (*go down*)

спуска́ться *impf*, спусти́ться *pf* (+gen); **be descended from** происходи́ть *impf*, произойти́ *pf* из, от, +gen. **descendant** *n* пото́мок. **descent** *n* спуск; (*lineage*) происхожде́ние.

describe vt опи́сывать *impf*, описа́ть *pf*. **description** *n* описа́ние. **descriptive** *adj* описа́тельный.

desecrate vt оскверня́ть *impf*, оскверни́ть *pf*. **desecration** *n* оскверне́ние.

desert¹ *n* (*waste*) пусты́ня.

desert² vt покида́ть *impf*, поки́нуть *pf*; (*mil*) дезерти́ровать *impf* & *pf*. **deserter** *n* дезерти́р. **desertion** *n* дезерти́рство.

deserts *n pl* заслу́ги *f pl*. **deserve** vt заслу́живать *impf*, заслужи́ть *pf*. **deserving** *adj* досто́йный (*of* +gen).

design *n* (*pattern*) узо́р; (*of car etc.*) констру́кция, прое́кт; (*industrial*) диза́йн; (*aim*) у́мысел; vt проекти́ровать *impf*, с~ *pf*; (*intend*) предназнача́ть *impf*, предназна́чить *pf*.

designate vt (*indicate*) обознача́ть *impf*, обозна́чить *pf*; (*appoint*) назнача́ть *impf*, назна́чить *pf*.

designer *n* (*tech*) констру́ктор; (*industrial*) диза́йнер; (*of clothes*) модельер.

desirable *adj* жела́тельный. **desire** *n* жела́ние; vt жела́ть *impf*, по~ *pf* +gen. **desist** vi (*refrain*) возде́рживаться *impf*, воздержа́ться *pf* (*from* от+gen).

desk *n* пи́сьменный стол; (*school*) па́рта. **desolate** *adj* забро́шенный.

desolation n заброшенность.
despair n отчаяние; vi отчаиваться impf, отчаяться pf.
desperate adj отчаянный.
desperation n отчаяние.
despicable adj презренный.
despise vt презирать impf, презреть pf.
despite prep несмотря на+acc.
despondency n уныние. **despondent** adj унылый.
despot n деспот.
dessert n десерт.
destination n (of goods) место назначения; (of journey) цель. **destiny** n судьба.
destitute adj без всяких средств.
destroy vt разрушать impf, разрушить pf. **destroyer** n (naut) эсминец. **destruction** n разрушение. **destructive** adj разрушительный.
detach vt отделять impf, отделить pf. **detached** adj отдельный; (objective) беспристрастный; ~ **house** особняк. **detachment** n (objectivity) беспристрастие; (mil) отряд.
detail n деталь, подробность; **in detail** подробно; vt подробно рассказывать impf, рассказать pf. **detailed** adj подробный.
detain vt задерживать impf, задержать pf. **detainee** n задержанный sb.
detect vt обнаруживать impf, обнаружить pf. **detection** n обнаружение; (crime) расследование. **detective** n детектив; ~ **film, story, etc**. детектив. **detector** n детектор.
detention n задержание; (school) задержка в наказание.
deter vt удерживать impf,

detergent n моющее средство.
deteriorate vi ухудшаться impf, ухудшиться pf. **deterioration** n ухудшение.
determination n решимость. **determine** vt (ascertain) устанавливать impf, установить pf; (be decisive factor) определять impf, определить pf; (decide) решать impf, решить pf. **determined** adj решительный.
deterrent n средство устрашения.
detest vt ненавидеть impf. **detestable** adj отвратительный.
detonate vt & i взрывать(ся) impf, взорвать(ся) pf. **detonator** n детонатор.
detour n объезд.
detract vi: ~ **from** умалять impf, умалить pf +acc.
detriment n ущерб. **detrimental** adj вредный.
deuce n (tennis) равный счёт.
devaluation n девальвация. **devalue** vt девальвировать impf & pf.
devastate vt опустошать impf, опустошить pf. **devastated** adj потрясённый. **devastating** adj уничтожающий. **devastation** n опустошение.
develop vt & i развивать(ся) impf, развить(ся) pf; vt (phot) проявлять impf, проявить pf. **developer** n (of land etc.) застройщик. **development** n развитие.
deviant adj ненормальный. **deviate** vi отклоняться impf, отклониться pf (**from** от+gen). **deviation** n отклонение.
device n прибор.

devil n чёрт. **devilish** adj чертовский.

devious adj (circuitous) окружной; (person) непорядочный.

devise vt придумывать impf, придумать pf.

devoid adj лишённый (of +gen).

devolution n передача (власти).

devote vt посвящать impf, посвятить pf. **devoted** adj преданный. **devotee** n поклонник. **devotion** n преданность.

devour vt пожирать impf, пожрать pf.

devout adj набожный.

dew n роса.

dexterity n ловкость. **dext(e)rous** adj ловкий.

diabetes n диабет. **diabetic** n диабетик; adj диабетический.

diabolic(al) adj дьявольский.

diagnose vt диагностировать impf & pf. **diagnosis** n диагноз.

diagonal n диагональ; adj диагональный. **diagonally** adv по диагонали.

diagram n диаграмма.

dial n (clock) циферблат; (tech) шкала; vt набирать impf, набрать pf.

dialect n диалект.

dialogue n диалог.

diameter n диаметр. **diametric(al)** adj диаметральный; ~ly opposed диаметрально противоположный.

diamond n алмаз; (shape) ромб; pl (cards) бубны (-бён, -бнам) pl.

diaper n пелёнка.

diaphragm n диафрагма.

diarrhoea n понос.

diary n дневник.

dice see die¹

dicey adj рискованный.

dictate vt диктовать impf, про~ pf. **dictation** n диктовка. **dictator** n диктатор. **dictatorial** adj диктаторский. **dictatorship** n диктатура.

diction n дикция.

dictionary n словарь m.

didactic adj дидактический.

die¹ n (pl dice) игральная кость; (pl dies) (stamp) штамп.

die² vi (person) умирать impf, умереть pf; (animal) дохнуть impf, из~, по~ pf; (plant) вянуть impf, за~ pf; **be dying to** очень хотеть impf; ~ **down** (fire, sound) угасать impf, угаснуть pf; ~ **out** вымирать impf, вымереть pf.

diesel n (engine) дизель m; attrib дизельный.

diet n; (habitual food) пища; vi быть на диете. **dietary** adj диетический.

differ vi отличаться impf; различаться impf; (disagree) расходиться impf, разойтись pf. **difference** n разница; (disagreement) разногласие. **different** adj различный, разный. **differential** n (math, tech) дифференциал; (difference) разница. **differentiate** vt различать impf, различить pf.

difficult adj трудный. **difficulty** n трудность; (difficult situation) затруднение; **without** ~ без труда.

diffidence n неуверенность в себе. **diffident** adj неуверенный в себе.

diffused adj рассе́янный.

dig n (archaeol) раско́пки f pl; (poke) тычо́к; (gibe) шпи́лька; pl (lodgings) кварти́ра; **give a ~ in the ribs** ткнуть pf ло́ктем под ребро́; vt копа́ть impf, вы́~ pf; рыть impf, вы́~ pf; ~ **up** (bone) выка́пывать impf, вы́копать pf; (land) вска́пывать impf, вскопа́ть pf.

digest vt перева́ривать impf, перевари́ть pf. **digestible** adj удобовари́мый. **digestion** n пищеваре́ние.

digger n (tech) экскава́тор.

digit n (math) знак.

dignified adj велича́вый. **dignitary** n сано́вник. **dignity** n досто́инство.

digress vi отклоня́ться impf, отклони́ться pf. **digression** n отклоне́ние.

dike n да́мба; (ditch) ров.

dilapidated adj ве́тхий.

dilate vt & i расширя́ть(ся) impf, расши́рить(ся) pf.

dilemma n диле́мма.

dilettante n дилета́нт.

diligence n приле́жа́ние. **diligent** adj приле́жный.

dilute vt разбавля́ть impf, разба́вить pf.

dim adj (not bright) ту́склый; (vague) сму́тный; (stupid) тупо́й.

dimension n (pl) разме́ры n pl; (math) измере́ние. **-dimensional** in comb -ме́рный; **three-~** трёхме́рный.

diminish vt & i уменьша́ть(ся) impf, уме́ньшить(ся) pf. **diminutive** adj ма́ленький; n уменьши́тельное sb.

dimness n ту́склость.

dimple n я́мочка.

din n гро́хот; (voices) гам.

dine vi обе́дать impf, по~ pf. **diner** n обе́дающий sb.

dinghy n шлю́пка; (rubber ~) надувна́я ло́дка.

dingy adj (drab) ту́склый; (dirty) гря́зный.

dining-car n ваго́н-рестора́н. **dining-room** n столо́вая sb. **dinner** n обе́д; ~**-jacket** смо́кинг.

dinosaur n диноза́вр.

diocese n епа́рхия.

dip vt (immerse) окуна́ть impf, окуну́ть pf; (partially) обма́кивать impf, обмакну́ть pf; vi (slope) понижа́ться impf, пони́зиться pf; n (depression) впа́дина; (slope) укло́н; **have a ~** (bathe) купа́ться impf, вы́~ pf.

diphtheria n дифтери́я.

diphthong n дифто́нг.

diploma n дипло́м. **diplomacy** n диплома́тия. **diplomat** n диплома́т. **diplomatic** adj дипломати́ческий.

dire adj стра́шный; (ominous) злове́щий.

direct adj прямо́й; ~ **current** постоя́нный ток; vt направля́ть impf, напра́вить pf; (guide, manage) руководи́ть impf +instr; (film) режисси́ровать impf. **direction** n направле́ние; (guidance) руково́дство; (instruction) указа́ние; (film) режиссу́ра; **stage ~** рема́рка. **directive** n дире́ктива. **directly** adv пря́мо; (at once) сра́зу. **director** n дире́ктор; (film etc.) режиссёр (-постано́вщик). **directory** n спра́вочник, указа́тель m; (tel) телефо́нная кни́га.

dirt n грязь. **dirty** adj гря́зный; vt па́чкать impf, за~ pf.

disability n физи́ческий/пси-хи́ческий недоста́ток; (*ablement*) инвали́дность. **disabled** *adj*: he is ~ он инвали́д.

disadvantage n невы́годное положе́ние; (*defect*) недоста́ток. **disadvantageous** *adj* невы́годный.

disaffected *adj* недово́льный.

disagree *vi* не соглаша́ться *impf*, согласи́ться *pf*; (*not correspond*) не соотве́тствовать *impf* +*dat*. **disagreeable** *adj* неприя́тный. **disagreement** n разногла́сие; (*quarrel*) ссо́ра.

disappear *vi* исчеза́ть *impf*, исче́знуть *pf*. **disappearance** n исчезнове́ние.

disappoint *vt* разочаро́вывать *impf*, разочарова́ть *pf*. **disappointed** *adj* разочаро́ванный. **disappointing** *adj* разочаро́вывающий. **disappointment** n разочарова́ние.

disapproval n неодобре́ние. **disapprove** *vt & i* не одобря́ть *impf*.

disarm *vt* (*mil*) разоружа́ть *impf*, разоружи́ть *pf*; (*criminal; also fig*) обезору́живать *impf*, обезору́жить *pf*. **disarmament** n разоруже́ние.

disarray n беспоря́док.

disaster n бе́дствие. **disastrous** *adj* катастрофи́ческий.

disband *vt* распуска́ть *impf*, распусти́ть *pf*; *vi* расходи́ться *impf*, разойти́сь *pf*.

disbelief n неве́рие.

disc, disk n диск; ~ **jockey** веду́щий *sb* переда́чу.

discard *vt* отбра́сывать *impf*, отбро́сить *pf*.

discern *vt* различа́ть *impf*, различи́ть *pf*. **discernible** *adj* различи́мый. **discerning**

adj проница́тельный.

discharge *vt* (*ship etc.*) разгружа́ть *impf*, разгрузи́ть *pf*; (*gun; electr*) разряжа́ть *impf*, разряди́ть *pf*; (*dismiss*) увольня́ть *impf*, уво́лить *pf*; (*prisoner*) освобожда́ть *impf*, освободи́ть *pf*; (*debt; duty*) выполня́ть *impf*, вы́полнить *pf*; (*from hospital*) выпи́сывать *impf*, вы́писать *pf*; n разгру́зка; (*electr*) разря́д; увольне́ние; освобожде́ние; выполне́ние; (*matter discharged*) выделе́ния *neut pl*.

disciple n учени́к.

disciplinarian n сторо́нник дисципли́ны. **disciplinary** *adj* дисциплина́рный. **discipline** n дисципли́на; *vt* дисциплини́ровать *impf & pf*.

disclaim *vt* (*deny*) отрица́ть *impf*; ~ **responsibility** слага́ть *impf*, сложи́ть *pf* с себя́ отве́тственность.

disclose *vt* обнару́живать *impf*, обнару́жить *pf*. **disclosure** n обнаруже́ние.

discoloured *adj* обесцве́ченный.

discomfit *vt* смуща́ть *impf*, смути́ть *pf*. **discomfiture** n смуще́ние.

discomfort n неудо́бство.

disconcert *vt* смуща́ть *impf*, смути́ть *pf*.

disconnect *vt* разъединя́ть *impf*, разъедини́ть *pf*; (*switch off*) выключа́ть *impf*, вы́ключить *pf*. **disconnected** *adj* (*incoherent*) бессвя́зный.

disconsolate *adj* неуте́шный.

discontent n недово́льство. **discontented** *adj* недово́льный.

discontinue *vt* прекраща́ть *impf*, прекрати́ть *pf*.

discord n разногла́сие; (mus) диссона́нс. **discordant** adj несогласу́ющийся; диссони́рующий.

discotheque n дискоте́ка.

discount n ски́дка; vt (disregard) не принима́ть impf, приня́ть pf в расчёт.

discourage vt обескура́живать impf, обескура́жить pf; (dissuade) отгова́ривать impf, отговори́ть pf.

discourse n речь.

discourteous adj неве́жливый.

discover vt открыва́ть impf, откры́ть pf; (find out) обнару́живать impf, обнару́жить pf. **discovery** n откры́тие.

discredit n позо́р; vt дискреди́тировать impf & pf.

discreet adj такти́чный. **discretion** n (judgement) усмотре́ние; (prudence) благоразу́мие; **at one's ~** по своему́ усмотре́нию.

discrepancy n несоотве́тствие.

discriminate vt различа́ть impf, различи́ть pf; **~ against** дискримини́ровать impf & pf. **discrimination** n (taste) разбо́рчивость; (bias) дискримина́ция.

discus n диск.

discuss vt обсужда́ть impf, обсуди́ть pf. **discussion** n обсужде́ние.

disdain n презре́ние. **disdainful** adj презри́тельный.

disease n боле́знь. **diseased** adj больно́й.

disembark vi выса́живаться impf, вы́садиться pf.

disenchantment n разочарова́ние.

disengage vt освобожда́ть impf, освободи́ть pf; (clutch) отпуска́ть impf, отпусти́ть pf.

disentangle vt распу́тывать impf, распу́тать pf.

disfavour n неми́лость.

disfigure vt уро́довать impf, из~ pf.

disgrace n позо́р; (disfavour) неми́лость; vt позо́рить impf, о~ pf. **disgraceful** adj позо́рный.

disgruntled adj недово́льный.

disguise n маскиро́вка; vt маскирова́ть impf, за~ pf; (conceal) скрыва́ть impf, скрыть pf. **disguised** adj замаскиро́ванный.

disgust n отвраще́ние; vt внуша́ть impf, внуши́ть pf отвраще́ние +dat. **disgusting** adj отврати́тельный.

dish n блю́до; pl посу́да collect; **~-washer** (посу́до)мо́ечная маши́на; vt: **~ up** подава́ть impf, пода́ть pf.

dishearten vt обескура́живать impf, обескура́жить pf.

dishevelled adj растрёпанный.

dishonest adj нече́стный. **dishonesty** n нече́стность. **dishonour** n бесче́стье; vt бесче́стить impf, о~ pf. **dishonourable** adj бесче́стный.

disillusion vt разочаро́вывать impf, разочарова́ть pf. **disillusionment** n разочаро́ванность.

disinclination n нескло́нность, неохо́та. **disinclined** adj be ~ не хоте́ться impers +dat.

disinfect vt дезинфици́ровать impf & pf. **disinfectant** n дезинфици́рующее сре́дство.

disingenuous adj нейскре́нный.

disinherit vt лиша́ть impf, лиши́ть pf насле́дства.

disintegrate vi распада́ться impf, распа́сться pf. **disintegration** n распа́д.

disinterested adj бескоры́стный.

disjointed adj бессвя́зный.

disk see disc

dislike n нелюбо́вь (for k+dat); vt не люби́ть impf.

dislocate vt (med) вы́вихнуть pf.

dislodge vt смеща́ть impf, смести́ть pf.

disloyal adj нелоя́льный. **disloyalty** n нелоя́льность.

dismal adj мра́чный.

dismantle vt разбира́ть impf, разобра́ть pf.

dismay vt смуща́ть impf, смути́ть pf; n смуще́ние.

dismiss vt (sack) увольня́ть impf, уво́лить pf; (disband) распуска́ть impf, распусти́ть pf. **dismissal** n увольне́ние; ро́спуск.

dismount vi спе́шиваться impf, спе́шиться pf.

disobedience n непослуша́ние. **disobedient** adj непослу́шный. **disobey** vt не слу́шаться impf +gen.

disorder n беспоря́док. **disorderly** adj (untidy) беспоря́дочный; (unruly) бу́йный.

disorganized adj неорганизо́ванный.

disorientation n дезориента́ция. **disoriented** adj: I am/ was ~ я потеря́л(а) направле́ние.

disown vt отка́зываться impf, отказа́ться pf от+gen.

disparaging adj оскорби́тельный.

disparity n нера́венство.

dispassionate adj беспристра́стный.

dispatch vt (send) отправля́ть impf, отпра́вить pf; (deal with) распра́вля́ться impf, распра́виться pf c+instr; n отпра́вка; (message) донесе́ние; (rapidity) быстрота́; ~rider мотоцикли́ст свя́зи.

dispel vt рассе́ивать impf, рассе́ять pf.

dispensable adj необяза́тельный.

dispensary n апте́ка.

dispensation n (exemption) освобожде́ние (от обяза́тельства). **dispense** vt (distribute) раздава́ть impf, разда́ть pf; ~ with обходи́ться impf, обойти́сь pf без+gen.

dispersal n распростране́ние. **disperse** vt (drive away) разгоня́ть impf, разогна́ть pf; (scatter) рассе́ивать impf, рассе́ять pf; vi расходи́ться impf, разойти́сь pf.

dispirited adj удручённый.

displaced adj: ~ persons переме́щённые ли́ца neut pl.

display n пока́з; vt пока́зывать impf, показа́ть pf.

displeased predic недово́лен (-льна). **displeasure** n недово́льство.

disposable adj однора́зовый.

disposal n удале́ние; **at your** ~ в ва́шем распоряже́нии.

dispose vi: ~ of избавля́ться impf, изба́виться pf от+gen. **disposed** predic: ~ to располо́жен (-ена) k+dat or +inf. **disposition** n расположе́ние; (temperament) нрав.

disproportionate adj непропорциона́льный.

disprove vt опроверга́ть impf, опрове́ргнуть pf.

dispute n (*debate*) спор; (*quarrel*) ссо́ра; vt оспа́ривать *impf*, оспо́рить *pf*.

disqualification n дисквалифика́ция. **disqualify** vt дисквалифици́ровать *impf & pf*.

disquieting *adj* трево́жный.

disregard n пренебреже́ние +*instr*; vt игнори́ровать *impf & pf*; пренебрега́ть *impf*, пренебре́чь *pf* +*instr*.

disrepair n неиспра́вность.

disreputable *adj* по́льзующийся дурно́й сла́вой. **disrepute** n дурна́я сла́ва.

disrespect n неуваже́ние. **disrespectful** *adj* непочти́тельный.

disrupt vt срыва́ть *impf*, сорва́ть *pf*. **disruptive** *adj* подрывно́й.

dissatisfaction n недово́льство. **dissatisfied** *adj* недово́льный.

dissect vt разреза́ть *impf*, разре́зать *pf*; (*med*) вскрыва́ть *impf*, вскрыть *pf*.

disseminate vt распространя́ть *impf*, распространи́ть *pf*; **dissemination** n распростране́ние.

dissension n раздо́р. **dissent** n расхожде́ние; (*eccl*) раско́л.

dissertation n диссерта́ция.

disservice n плоха́я услу́га.

dissident n диссиде́нт.

dissimilar *adj* несхо́дный.

dissipate vt (*dispel*) рассе́ивать *impf*, рассе́ять *pf*; (*squander*) прома́тывать *impf*, промота́ть *pf*. **dissipated** *adj* распу́тный.

dissociate vt: ~ o.s. отмежёвываться *impf*, отмежева́ться *pf* (**from** +*gen*).

dissolute *adj* распу́тный. **dissolution** n расторже́ние;

(*parl*) ро́спуск. **dissolve** vt & i (*in liquid*) растворя́ть(ся) *impf*, раствори́ть(ся) *pf*; (*annul*) расторга́ть *impf*, расто́ргнуть *pf*; (*parl*) распуска́ть *impf*, распусти́ть *pf*.

dissonance n диссона́нс. **dissonant** *adj* диссони́рующий.

dissuade vt отгова́ривать *impf*, отговори́ть *pf*.

distance n расстоя́ние; **from a** ~ и́здали; **in the** ~ вдалеке́. **distant** *adj* далёкий; (*also of relative*) да́льний; (*reserved*) сде́ржанный.

distaste n отвраще́ние. **distasteful** *adj* проти́вный.

distended *adj* наду́тый.

distil vt (*whisky*) перегоня́ть *impf*, перегна́ть *pf*; (*water*) дистилли́ровать *impf & pf*. **distillation** n перего́нка; дистилля́ция. **distillery** n перего́нный заво́д.

distinct *adj* (*different*) отли́чный; (*clear*) отчётливый; (*evident*) заме́тный. **distinction** n (*difference*) отли́чие; (*discrimination*) разли́чие. **distinctive** *adj* отличи́тельный. **distinctly** *adv* я́сно.

distinguish vt различа́ть *impf*, различи́ть *pf*; ~ o.s. отлича́ться *impf*, отличи́ться *pf*. **distinguished** *adj* выдаю́щийся.

distort vt искажа́ть *impf*, искази́ть *pf*; (*misrepresent*) извраща́ть *impf*, изврати́ть *pf*. **distortion** n искаже́ние; извраще́ние.

distract vt отвлека́ть *impf*, отвле́чь *pf*. **distraction** n (*amusement*) развлече́ние; (*madness*) безу́мие.

distraught *adj* обезу́мевший;

distress n (suffering) огорче́ние; (danger) бе́дствие; vt огорча́ть impf, огорчи́ть pf.

distribute vt распределя́ть impf, распредели́ть pf. **distribution** n распределе́ние. **distributor** n распредели́тель m.

district n райо́н.

distrust n недове́рие; vt не доверя́ть impf. **distrustful** adj недове́рчивый.

disturb vt беспоко́ить impf, о~ pf. **disturbance** n наруше́ние поко́я; pl (polit etc.) беспоря́дки m pl.

disuse n неупотребле́ние; **fall into** ~ выходи́ть impf, вы́йти pf из употребле́ния. **disused** adj вы́шедший из употребле́ния.

ditch n кана́ва, ров.

dither vi колеба́ться impf.

ditto n то же са́мое; adv так же.

divan n дива́н.

dive vi ныря́ть impf, нырну́ть pf; (aeron) пики́ровать impf & pf; n ныро́к, прыжо́к в во́ду. **diver** n водола́з.

diverge vi расходи́ться impf, разойти́сь pf. **divergent** adj расходя́щийся.

diverse adj разнообра́зный. **diversification** n расшире́ние ассортиме́нта. **diversify** vt разнообра́зить impf. **diversion** n (detour) объе́зд; (amusement) развлече́ние. **diversity** n разнообра́зие.

divert vt отклоня́ть impf, отклони́ть pf; (amuse) развлека́ть impf, развле́чь pf. **diverting** adj заба́вный.

divest vt (deprive) лиша́ть impf, лиши́ть pf (of +gen); ~ **o.s.** отка́зываться impf, от-

каза́ться pf (of от+gen).

divide vt (share; math) дели́ть impf, по~ pf; (separate) разделя́ть impf, раздели́ть pf. **dividend** n дивиде́нд.

divine adj боже́ственный.

diving n ныря́ние; ~-**board** трампли́н.

divinity n (quality) боже́ственность; (deity) божество́; (theology) богосло́вие.

divisible adj дели́мый. **division** n (dividing) деле́ние, разделе́ние; (section) отде́л; (mil) диви́зия.

divorce n разво́д; vi разводи́ться impf, развести́сь pf. **divorced** adj разведённый.

divulge vt разглаша́ть impf, разгласи́ть pf.

DIY abbr (of **do-it-yourself**): **he is good at** ~ у него́ золоты́е ру́ки; ~ **shop** магази́н «сде́лай сам».

dizziness n головокруже́ние.

dizzy adj (causing dizziness) головокружи́тельный; **I am** ~ у меня́ кружи́тся голова́.

DNA abbr (of **deoxyribonucleic acid**) ДНК.

do vt де́лать impf, с~ pf; vi (be suitable) годи́ться impf; (suffice) быть доста́точным; ~-**it-yourself** see **DIY**; **that will** ~ хва́тит!; **how** ~ **you** ~? здра́вствуйте!; **как вы пожива́ете?**; ~ **away with** (abolish) уничтожа́ть impf, уничто́жить pf; ~ **in** (kill) убива́ть impf, уби́ть pf; ~ **up** (restore) ремонти́ровать impf, от~ pf; (wrap up) завёртывать impf, заверну́ть pf; (fasten) застёгивать impf, застегну́ть pf; ~ **without** обходи́ться impf, обойти́сь pf без+gen.

docile adj покорный. **docility** n покорность.

dock[1] n (naut) док; vt ставить impf, по~ pf в док; vi входить impf, войти pf в док; vi (spacecraft) стыковаться impf, со~ pf. **docker** n докер. **dockyard** n верфь.

dock[2] n (law) скамья подсудимых.

docket n квитанция; (label) ярлык.

doctor n врач; (also univ) доктор; vt (castrate) кастрировать impf & pf; (spay) удалять impf, удалить pf яичники y+gen; (falsify) фальсифицировать impf & pf. **doctorate** n степень доктора.

doctrine n доктрина.

document n документ; vt документировать impf & pf. **documentary** n документальный фильм. **documentation** n документация.

doddery adj дряхлый.

dodge n увёртка; vt уклоняться impf, уклониться pf от+gen; (jump to avoid) отскакивать impf, отскочить pf (от+gen). **dodgy** adj каверзный.

doe n самка.

dog n собака, пёс; (fig) преследовать impf. **dog-eared** adj захватанный.

dogged adj упорный.

dogma n догма. **dogmatic** adj догматический.

doings n pl дела neut pl.

doldrums n: be in the ~ хандрить impf.

dole n пособие по безработице; vt (~ out) выдавать impf, выдать pf.

doleful adj скорбный.

doll n кукла.

dollar n доллар.

dollop n солидная порция.

dolphin n дельфин.

domain n (estate) владение; (field) область.

dome n купол.

domestic adj (of household; animals) домашний; (of family) семейный; (polit) внутренний; n прислуга. **domesticate** vt приручать impf, приручить pf. **domesticity** n домашняя, семейная, жизнь.

domicile n местожительство.

dominance n господство. **dominant** adj преобладающий; господствующий. **dominate** vt господствовать impf над+instr. **domineering** adj властный.

dominion n владычество; (realm) владение.

domino n кость домино; pl (game) домино neut indecl.

don vt надевать impf, надеть pf.

donate vt жертвовать impf, по~ pf. **donation** n пожертвование.

donkey n осёл.

donor n жертвователь m; (med) донор.

doom n (ruin) гибель; vt обрекать impf, обречь pf.

door n дверь. **doorbell** n (дверной) звонок. **doorman** n швейцар. **doormat** n половик. **doorstep** n порог. **doorway** n дверной проём.

dope n (drug) наркотик; vt дурманить impf, о~ pf.

dormant adj (sleeping) спящий; (inactive) бездействующий.

dormer window n слуховое окно.

dormitory n общая спальня.

dormouse *n* со́ня.

dorsal *adj* спинно́й.

dosage *n* дозиро́вка. **dose** *n* до́за.

dossier *n* досье́ *neut indecl.*

dot *n* то́чка; *vt* ста́вить *impf,* по~ *pf* то́чки над+*acc;* (*scatter*) усе́ивать *impf,* усе́ять *pf* (with +*instr*); ~**ted line** пункти́р.

dote *vi:* ~ **on** обожа́ть *impf.*

double *adj* двойно́й; (*doubled*) удво́енный; ~**-bass** контраба́с; ~ **bed** двуспа́льная крова́ть; ~**-breasted** двубо́ртный; ~**-cross** обма́нывать *impf,* обману́ть *pf;* ~**-dealer** двуру́шник; ~**-dealing** двуру́шничество; ~**-decker** двухэта́жный авто́бус; ~**-edged** обоюдоо́стрый; ~ **glazing** двойны́е ра́мы *f pl;* ~ **room** ко́мната на двои́х; *adv* вдво́е; (*two together*) вдвоём; *n* двойно́е коли́чество; (*person's*) двойни́к; *pl* (*sport*) па́рная игра́; *vt & i* удва́ивать(ся) *impf,* удво́ить(ся) *pf;* ~ **back** возвраща́ться *impf,* верну́ться *pf* наза́д; ~ **up** (*in pain*) скрю́чиваться *impf,* скрю́читься *pf;* (*share a room*) помеща́ться *impf,* помести́ться *pf* вдвоём в одно́й ко́мнате; (~ *up as*) рабо́тать *impf* + *instr* по совмести́тельству.

doubt *n* сомне́ние; *vt* сомнева́ться *impf* в+*prep.* **doubtful** *adj* сомни́тельный. **doubtless** *adv* несомне́нно.

dough *n* те́сто. **doughnut** *n* по́нчик.

douse *vt* (*drench*) залива́ть *impf,* зали́ть *pf.*

dove *n* го́лубь *m.* **dovetail** *n* ла́сточкин хвост.

dowdy *adj* неэлега́нтный.

down¹ *n* (*fluff*) пух.

down² *adv* (*motion*) вниз; (*position*) внизу́; *adj:* **be** ~ **with** (*ill*) боле́ть *impf* +*instr; prep* (*down*) с+*gen,* по+*dat;* (*along*) (вдоль) по+*dat; vt* (*gulp*) опроки́дывать *impf,* опроки́нуть *pf;* ~**-and-out** бродя́га *m;* ~**cast,** ~**hearted** уны́лый. **downfall** *n* ги́бель. **downhill** *adv* под го́ру. **downpour** *n* ли́вень *m.* **downright** *adj* я́вный; *adv* соверше́нно. **downstairs** *adv* (*motion*) вниз; (*position*) внизу́. **downstream** *adv* вниз по тече́нию. **down-to-earth** *adj* реалисти́ческий. **downtrodden** *adj* угнетённый.

dowry *n* прида́ное *sb.*

doze *vi* дрема́ть *impf.*

dozen *n* дю́жина.

drab *adj* бесцве́тный; (*boring*) ску́чный.

draft *n* (*outline, rough copy*) набро́сок; (*document*) прое́кт; (*econ*) тра́тта; *see also* **draught;** *vt* составля́ть *impf,* соста́вить *pf* план, прое́кт, +*gen.*

drag *vt* тащи́ть *impf;* (*river etc.*) драги́ровать *impf & pf;* ~ **on** (*vi*) затя́гиваться *impf,* затяну́ться *pf; n* (*burden*) обу́за; (*on cigarette*) затя́жка; **in** ~ в же́нской оде́жде.

dragon *n* драко́н. **dragonfly** *n* стрекоза́.

drain *n* водосто́к; (*leakage; fig*) уте́чка; *vt* осуша́ть *impf,* осуши́ть *pf; vi* спуска́ться *impf,* спусти́ться *pf.* **drainage** *n* дрена́ж; (*system*) канализа́ция.

drake *n* се́лезень *m.*

drama *n* дра́ма; (*quality*) драмати́зм. **dramatic** *adj*

драмати́ческий. **dramatist** *n*
драмату́рг. **dramatize** *vt*
драматизи́ровать *impf & pf*.
drape *vt* драпирова́ть *impf*,
за~ *pf*; *n* драпиро́вка.
drastic *adj* радика́льный.
draught *n* (*air*) сквозня́к; (*trac-tion*) тя́га; *pl* (*game*) ша́шки *f
pl*; *see also* draft; there is a ~
сквози́т; ~ **beer** пи́во из
бо́чки. **draughtsman** *n* черт-
ёжник. **draughty** *adj*: it is
~ here здесь ду́ет.
draw *n* (*in lottery*) ро́зыгрыш;
(*attraction*) прима́нка; (*drawn
game*) ничья́; *vt* (*pull*) тяну́ть
impf, по~ *pf*; таска́ть *indet*,
тащи́ть *det*; (*curtains*) задёргивать *impf*, задёрнуть *pf*
(занаве́ски); (*attract*) при-
влека́ть *impf*, привле́чь *pf*;
(*pull out*) выта́скивать *impf*,
вы́тащить *pf*; (*sword*) обна-
жа́ть *impf*, обнажи́ть *pf*; (*lots*)
броса́ть *impf*, бро́сить *pf*
(жре́бий); (*water; inspiration*)
че́рпать *impf*, черпну́ть *pf*;
(*evoke*) вызыва́ть *impf*, вы́-
звать *pf*; (*conclusion*) выво-
ди́ть *impf*, вы́вести *pf* (за-
ключе́ние); (*diagram*) чер-
ти́ть *impf*, на~ *pf*; (*picture*)
рисова́ть *impf*, на~ *pf*; *vi*
(*sport*) сыгра́ть *pf* вничью́;
~ **aside** отводи́ть *impf*, от-
вести́ *pf* в сто́рону; ~ **back**
(*withdraw*) отступа́ть *impf*,
отступи́ть *pf*; ~ **in** втя́ги-
вать *impf*, втяну́ть *pf*; (*train*)
входи́ть *impf*, войти́ *pf* в
ста́нцию; (*car*) подходи́ть
impf, подойти́ *pf* (**to** к + *dat*);
(*days*) станови́ться *impf* ко-
ро́че; ~ **out** выта́гивать *impf*,
вы́тянуть *pf*; (*money*) вы́-
пи́сывать *impf*, вы́писать *pf*;
(*train/car*) выходи́ть *impf*,

вы́йти *pf* (со ста́нции/на до-
ро́гу); ~ **up** (*car*) подходи́ть
impf, подойти́ *pf* (**to** к + *dat*);
(*document*) составля́ть *impf*,
соста́вить *pf*. **drawback** *n*
недоста́ток. **drawbridge** *n*
подъёмный мост. **drawer** *n*
я́щик. **drawing** *n* (*action*)
рисова́ние, черче́ние; (*object*)
рису́нок, чертёж; ~**board**
черте́жная доска́; ~**pin**
кно́пка; ~**room** гости́ная *sb*.
drawl *n* протя́жное произно-
ше́ние.
dread *n* страх; *vt* боя́ться *impf*
+*gen*. **dreadful** *adj* ужа́сный.
dream *n* сон; (*fantasy*) мечта́;
vi ви́деть *impf*, у~ *pf* сон; ~
of ви́деть *impf*, у~ *pf* во сне́; ~
(*fig*) мечта́ть *impf* о+*prep*.
dreary *adj* (*weather*) па́смур-
ный; (*boring*) ску́чный.
dredge *vt* (*river etc.*) драги́-
ровать *impf & pf*. **dredger** *n*
дра́га.
dregs *n pl* оса́дки (-ков) *pl*.
drench *vt* прома́чивать *impf*,
промочи́ть *pf*; **get ~ed** про-
мока́ть *impf*, промо́кнуть *pf*.
dress *n* пла́тье; (*apparel*)
оде́жда; ~ **circle** бельэта́ж;
~**maker** портни́ха; ~ **rehearsal** генера́льная репе-
ти́ция; *vt & i* одева́ть(ся)
impf, оде́ть(ся) *pf*; *vt* (*cul*)
приправля́ть *impf*, припра́-
вить *pf*; (*med*) перевя́зывать
impf, перевяза́ть *pf*; ~ **up**
наряжа́ться *impf*, наряди́ть-
ся *pf* (**as** + *instr*).
dresser *n* ку́хонный шкаф.
dressing *n* (*cul*) припра́ва;
(*med*) перевя́зка; ~**-gown**
хала́т; ~**-room** убо́рная *sb*;
~**-table** туале́тный сто́лик.
dribble *vi* (*person*) пуска́ть
impf, пусти́ть *pf* слю́ни;

(sport) вести *impf* мяч.

dried *adj* сушёный. **drier** *n* сушилка.

drift *n* *(meaning)* смысл; *(snow)* сугроб; *vi* плыть *impf* по течению; *(naut)* дрейфовать *impf*; *(snow etc.)* скопляться *impf*, скопиться *pf*; ~ **apart** расходиться *impf*, разойтись *pf*.

drill[1] *n* сверло; *(dentist's)* бур; *vt* сверлить *impf*, про~ *pf*.

drill[2] *vt* *(mil)* обучать *impf*, обучить *pf* строю; *vi* проходить *impf*, пройти *pf* строевую подготовку; *n* строевая подготовка.

drink *n* напиток; *vt* пить *impf*, вы~ *pf*; ~**-driving** вождение в нетрезвом состоянии.

drinking-water *n* питьевая вода.

drip *n* *(action)* капанье; *(drop)* капля; *vi* капать *impf*, капнуть *pf*.

drive *n* *(journey)* езда; *(excursion)* прогулка; *(campaign)* поход, кампания; *(energy)* энергия; *(tech)* привод; *(driveway)* подъездная дорога; *vt* *(urge, chase)* гонять *indet*, гнать *det*; *(vehicle)* водить *impf* +*instr*; *(convey)* возить *indet*, везти *det*, по~ *pf*; *vi* *(travel)* ездить *indet*, ехать *det*, по~ *pf*; доводить *impf*, довести *pf* **(to** до+*gen)*; *(nail etc.)* вбивать *impf*, вбить *pf* **(into** в+*acc)*; ~ **away** *vt* прогонять *impf*, прогнать *pf*; *vi* уезжать *impf*, уехать *pf*; ~ **up** подъезжать *impf*, подъехать *pf* **(to** к+*dat)*.

driver *n* *(of vehicle)* водитель *m*, шофёр. **driving** *adj* *(force)* движущий; *(rain)* проливной; ~**-licence** водительские права *neut pl*; ~**-test** экзамен на получение водительских прав; ~**-wheel** ведущее колесо.

drizzle *n* мелкий дождь *m*; *vi* моросить *impf*.

drone *n* *(bee; idler)* трутень *m*; *(of voice)* жужжание; *(of engine)* гул; *vi* *(buzz)* жужжать *impf*; *(~ on)* бубнить *impf*.

drool *vi* пускать *impf*, пустить *impf* слюни.

droop *vi* поникать *impf*, поникнуть *pf*.

drop *n* *(of liquid)* капля; *(fall)* падение, понижение; *vt & i* *(price)* снижать(ся) *impf*, снизить(ся) *pf*; *vi* *(fall)* падать *impf*, упасть *pf*; *vt* *(let fall)* ронять *impf*, уронить *pf*; *(abandon)* бросать *impf*, бросить *pf*; ~ **behind** отставать *impf*, отстать *pf*; ~ **in** заходить *impf*, зайти *pf* **(on** к+*dat)*; ~ **off** *(fall asleep)* засыпать *impf*, заснуть *pf*; *(from car)* высаживать *impf*, высадить *pf*; ~ **out** выбывать *impf*, выбыть *pf* **(of** из +*gen)*. **droppings** *n pl* помёт.

drought *n* засуха.

droves *n pl*: **in** ~ толпами.

drown *vt* топить *impf*, у~ *pf*; *(sound)* заглушать *impf*, заглушить *pf*; *vi* тонуть *impf*, у~ *pf*.

drowsy *adj* сонливый.

drudgery *n* нудная работа.

drug *n* медикамент; *(narcotic)* наркотик; ~ **addict** наркоман, ~ка; *vt* давать *impf*, дать *pf* наркотик+*dat*.

drum *n* барабан; *vi* бить *impf* в барабан; барабанить *impf*; ~ **sth into s.o.** вдалбливать *impf*, вдолбить *pf* + *dat of*

person в го́лову. **drummer** *n*
бараба́нщик.

drunk *adj* пья́ный. **drunkard** *n*
пья́ница *m & f.* **drunken** *adj*
пья́ный; ~ **driving** вожде́ние
в нетре́звом состоя́нии.
drunkenness *n* пья́нство.

dry *adj* сухо́й; ~ **land** су́ша; *vt*
суши́ть *impf,* вы́~ *pf*; (*wipe
dry*) вытира́ть *impf,* вы́тереть *pf*; *vi* со́хнуть *impf,* вы́~,
про~ *pf*. **dry-cleaning** *n* хими́-
чи́стка. **dryness** *n* су́хость.

dual *adj* двойно́й; (*joint*) сов-
ме́стный; ~**purpose** двойно́-
го назначе́ния.

dub[1] *vt* (*nickname*) прозы-
ва́ть *impf,* прозва́ть *pf*.

dub[2] *vt* (*cin*) дубли́ровать *impf*
& *pf*.

dubious *adj* сомни́тельный.

duchess *n* герцоги́ня. **duchy**
n ге́рцогство.

duck[1] *n* (*bird*) у́тка.

duck[2] *vt* (*immerse*) окуна́ть
impf, окуну́ть *pf*; (*one's head*)
нагну́ть *pf*; (*evade*) увёртываться *impf,* уверну́ться *pf*
от+*gen*; *vi* (~ **down**) накло-
ня́ться *impf,* наклони́ться *pf*.

duckling *n* утёнок.

duct *n* прохо́д; (*anat*) прото́к.

dud *n* (*forgery*) подде́лка;
(*shell*) неразорва́вшийся сна-
ря́д; *adj* подде́льный; (*worthless*) него́дный.

due *n* (*credit*) до́лжное *sb*; *pl*
взно́сы *m pl*; *adj* (*proper*) до́-
лжный, надлежа́щий; *predic*
(*expected*) до́лжен (-жна́); *in*
course со вре́менем; ~ **south**
пря́мо на юг; ~ **to** благо-
даря́+*dat*.

duel *n* дуэ́ль.

duet *n* дуэ́т.

duke *n* ге́рцог.

dull *adj* (*tedious*) ску́чный;

(*colour*) ту́склый, (*weather*)
па́смурный; (*not sharp; stupid*) тупо́й; *vt* притупля́ть
impf, притупи́ть *pf*.

duly *adv* надлежа́щим о́бра-
зом; (*punctually*) своевре́-
менно.

dumb *adj* немо́й. **dumb-
founded** *adj* ошара́шенный.

dummy *n* (*tailor's*) манеке́н;
(*baby's*) со́ска; ~ **run** испы-
та́тельный рейс.

dump *n* сва́лка; *vt* сва́ливать
impf, свали́ть *pf*.

dumpling *n* клёцка.

dumpy *adj* приземи́стый.

dune *n* дю́на.

dung *n* наво́з.

dungarees *n pl* комбинезо́н.

dungeon *n* темни́ца.

dunk *vt* мака́ть *impf,* макну́ть
pf.

duo *n* па́ра; (*mus*) дуэ́т.

dupe *vt* надува́ть *impf,* на-
ду́ть *pf*; *n* простофи́ля *m & f.*

duplicate *n* ко́пия; **in** ~ в
двух экземпля́рах; *adj* (*double*) двойно́й; (*identical*) иден-
ти́чный; *vt* размножа́ть *impf,*
размно́жить *pf* **duplicity** *n*
двули́чность.

durability *n* про́чность. **durable** *adj* про́чный. **duration**
n продолжи́тельность.

duress *n* принужде́ние; **under**
~ под давле́нием.

during *prep* во вре́мя +*gen*;
(*throughout*) в тече́ние +*gen*.

dusk *n* су́мерки (-рек) *pl*.

dust *n* пыль; ~**bin** *n* мусо́рный
я́щик; ~**jacket** суперобло́ж-
ка; ~**man** мусорщик; ~**pan**
совок; *vt & i* (*clean*) стира́ть
impf, стере́ть *pf* пыль (с+*gen*);
(*sprinkle*) посыпа́ть *impf,* по-
сы́пать *pf sth +acc,* **with** +*instr.*

duster *n* пы́льная тря́пка.

dusty adj пы́льный.
Dutch adj голла́ндский; n: the ~ голла́ндцы m pl. **Dutchman** n голла́ндец. **Dutchwoman** n голла́ндка.
dutiful adj послу́шный. **duty** n (obligation) долг; обяза́нность; (office) дежу́рство; (tax) по́шлина; be on ~ дежу́рить impf; ~-free adj беспо́шлинный.
dwarf n ка́рлик; vt (tower above) возвыша́ться над+instr, возвы́ситься pf над+instr.
dwell vi обита́ть impf; ~ upon остана́вливаться impf на+prep. **dweller** n жи́тель m. **dwelling** n жили́ще.
dwindle vi убыва́ть impf, убы́ть pf.
dye n краси́тель m; vt окра́шивать impf, окра́сить pf.
dynamic adj динами́ческий.
dynamics n pl дина́мика.
dynamite n динами́т.
dynamo n дина́мо neut indecl.
dynasty n дина́стия.
dysentery n дизентери́я.
dyslexia n дисле́ксия. **dyslexic** adj: he is ~ он дисле́ктик.

E

each adj & pron ка́ждый; ~ other друг дру́га (dat -гу, etc.).
eager adj (pupil) усе́рдный; I am ~ to мне не те́рпится +inf; о́чень жела́ю +inf. **eagerly** adv с нетерпе́нием; жа́дно. **eagerness** n си́льное жела́ние.
eagle n орёл.
ear[1] n (corn) ко́лос.
ear[2] n (anat) у́хо; (sense) слух; ~-ache боль в у́хе; ~drum бараба́нная перепо́нка; ~mark

(assign) предназнача́ть impf, предназна́чить pf; ~phone нау́шник; ~ring серьга́; (clip-on) клипс; ~shot: within ~ в преде́лах слы́шимости; out of ~ вне преде́лов слы́шимости.
earl n граф.
early adj ра́нний; adv ра́но.
earn vt зараба́тывать impf, зарабо́тать pf; (deserve) заслу́живать impf, заслужи́ть pf. **earnings** n pl за́работок.
earnest adj серьёзный; n: in ~ всерьёз.
earth n земля́; (soil) по́чва; vt заземля́ть impf, заземли́ть pf. **earthenware** adj гли́няный. **earthly** adj земно́й. **earthquake** n землетрясе́ние. **earthy** adj земли́стый; (coarse) грубый.
earwig n уховёртка.
ease n (facility) лёгкость; (unconstraint) непринуждённость; with ~ легко́; vt облегча́ть impf, облегчи́ть pf; vi успока́иваться impf, успоко́иться pf.
easel n мольбе́рт.
east n восто́к; (naut) ост; adj восто́чный. **easterly** adj восто́чный. **eastern** adj восто́чный. **eastward(s)** adv на восто́к, к восто́ку.
Easter n Па́сха.
easy adj лёгкий; (unconstrained) непринуждённый; ~-going ужи́вчивый.
eat vt есть impf, съ~ pf; ку́шать impf, по~, съ~ pf; ~ away разъеда́ть impf, разъе́сть pf; ~ into въеда́ться impf, въе́сться pf в+acc; ~ up дое́дать impf, дое́сть pf. **eatable** adj съедо́бный.
eaves n pl стреха́. **eavesdrop**

vi подслу́шивать *impf*.

ebb *n* (*tide*) отли́в; (*fig*) упа́док.

ebony *n* чёрное де́рево.

ebullient *adj* кипу́чий.

EC *abbr* (*of* **European Community**) Европе́йское соо́бщество.

eccentric *n* чуда́к; *adj* экцентри́чный.

ecclesiastical *adj* церко́вный.

echo *n* э́хо; *vi* (*resound*) отража́ться *impf*, отрази́ться *pf*; *vt* (*repeat*) повторя́ть *impf*, повтори́ть *pf*.

eclipse *n* затме́ние; *vt* затмева́ть *impf*, затми́ть *pf*.

ecological *adj* экологи́ческий. **ecology** *n* эколо́гия.

economic *adj* экономи́ческий. **economical** *adj* эконо́мный. **economist** *n* экономи́ст. **economize** *vt & i* эконо́мить *impf*, с~ *pf*. **economy** *n* эконо́мика; (*saving*) эконо́мия.

ecstasy *n* экста́з. **ecstatic** *adj* экстати́ческий.

eddy *n* водоворо́т.

edge *n* край; (*blade*) ле́звие; **on** ~ в не́рвном состоя́нии; **have the** ~ **on** име́ть *impf* преиму́щество на+*instr*; *vt* (*border*) окаймля́ть *impf*, окайми́ть *pf*; *vi* пробира́ться *impf*, пробра́ться *pf*. **edging** *n* кайма́. **edgy** *adj* раздражи́тельный.

edible *adj* съедо́бный.

edict *n* ука́з.

edifice *n* зда́ние. **edifying** *adj* назида́тельный.

edit *vt* редакти́ровать *impf*, от~ *pf*; (*cin*) монти́ровать *impf*, с~ *pf*. **edition** *n* изда́ние; (*number of copies*) тира́ж. **editor** *n* реда́ктор.

editorial *n* передова́я статья́; *adj* реда́кторский, редакцио́нный.

educate *vt* дава́ть *impf*, дать *pf* образова́ние +*dat*; **where was he educated?** где он получи́л образова́ние? **educated** *adj* образо́ванный. **education** *n* образова́ние. **educational** *adj* образова́тельный; (*instructive*) уче́бный.

eel *n* у́горь *m*.

eerie *adj* жу́ткий.

effect *n* (*result*) сле́дствие; (*validity*; *influence*) де́йствие; (*impression*; *theat*) эффе́кт; **in** ~ факти́чески; **take** ~ вступа́ть *impf*, вступи́ть *pf* в си́лу; (*medicine*) начина́ть *impf*, нача́ть *pf* де́йствовать; *vt* производи́ть *impf*, произвести́ *pf*. **effective** *adj* эффекти́вный; (*striking*) эффе́ктный; (*actual*) факти́ческий. **effectiveness** *n* эффекти́вность.

effeminate *adj* женоподо́бный.

effervesce *vi* пузы́риться *impf*. **effervescent** *adj* (*fig*) искря́щийся.

efficiency *n* эффекти́вность. **efficient** *adj* эффекти́вный; (*person*) организо́ванный.

effigy *n* изображе́ние.

effort *n* уси́лие.

effrontery *n* на́глость.

effusive *adj* экспанси́вный.

e.g. *abbr* напр.

egalitarian *adj* эгалита́рный.

egg¹ *n* яйцо́; ~**cup** рю́мка для яйца́; ~**shell** яи́чная скорлупа́.

egg² *vt*: ~ **on** подстрека́ть *impf*, подстрекну́ть *pf*.

ego *n* «Я». **egocentric**

эгоцентри́ческий. **egoism** n
эгои́зм. **ego(t)ist** n эгои́ст.
~ка. **ego(t)istical** adj эгоцен-
три́ческий. **egotism** n эго-
ти́зм.

Egypt n Еги́пет. **Egyptian** n
египтя́нин, -я́нка; adj еги́-
петский.

eiderdown n пухо́вое одея́ло.

eight adj & n во́семь; (number
8) восьмёрка. **eighteen** adj
& n восемна́дцать. **eighteenth** adj & n восемна́д-
цатый. **eighth** adj & n вось-
мо́й; (fraction) восьма́я sb.
eightieth adj & n восьми-
деся́тый. **eighty** adj & n во́-
семьдесят; pl (decade) вось-
мидеся́тые го́ды (-до́в) m pl.

either adj & pron (one of two)
оди́н из двух, тот и́ли дру-
го́й; (both) и тот, и друго́й;
о́ба; (one or other) любо́й;
adv & conj: ~ ... **or** и́ли... и́ли,
ли́бо... ли́бо.

eject vt выбра́сывать impf,
вы́бросить pf; vi (pilot) ка-
тапульти́роваться impf & pf.

eke vt: ~ **out a living** переби-
ва́ться impf, переби́ться
pf ко́е-как.

elaborate adj (ornate) вити-
ева́тый; (detailed) подро́б-
ный; vt разраба́тывать impf,
разрабо́тать pf; (detail)
уточня́ть impf, уточни́ть pf.

elapse vi проходи́ть impf,
пройти́ pf; (expire) истека́ть
impf, исте́чь pf.

elastic n рези́нка; adj эласти́-
чный; ~ **band** рези́нка.
elasticity n эласти́чность.

elated adj в восто́рге. **elation**
n восто́рг.

elbow n ло́коть m; vt: ~ (**one's
way**) **through** прота́лкивать-
ся impf, протолкну́ться pf

че́рез+acc.

elder[1] n (tree) бузина́.

elder[2] n (person) ста́рец; pl
ста́ршие sb; adj ста́рший.
elderly adj пожило́й. **eldest**
adj ста́рший.

elect adj и́збранный; vt избира́ть impf, избра́ть pf. **election** n вы́боры m pl. **elector**
n избира́тель m. **electoral**
adj избира́тельный. **electo-
rate** n избира́тели m pl.

electric(al) adj электри́че-
ский; ~ **shock** уда́р электри́-
ческим то́ком. **electri-
cian** n эле́ктрик. **electricity**
n электри́чество. **electrify** vt
(convert to electricity) элек-
трифици́ровать impf & pf;
(charge with electricity; fig)
электризова́ть impf, на~ pf.
electrode n электро́д. **electron** n электро́н. **electronic**
adj электро́нный. **electronics** n электро́ника.

electrocute vt убива́ть impf,
уби́ть pf электри́ческим то́-
ком; (execute) казни́ть impf &
pf на электри́ческом сту́ле.
electrolysis n электро́лиз.

elegance n элега́нтность. **elegant** adj элега́нтный.

elegy n эле́гия.

element n элеме́нт; (earth,
wind, etc.) стихи́я; **be in one's
~** быть в свое́й стихи́и. **elemental** adj стихи́йный. **elementary** adj элемента́рный;
(school etc.) нача́льный.

elephant n слон.

elevate vt поднима́ть impf,
подня́ть pf. **elevated** adj
возвы́шенный. **elevation** n
(height) высота́. **elevator** n
(lift) лифт.

eleven adj & n оди́ннадцать.
eleventh adj & n оди́ннад-

цатый; **at the ~ hour** в послéднюю минýту.

elf n эльф.

elicit vt (obtain) выявля́ть impf, вы́явить pf; (evoke) вызыва́ть impf, вы́звать pf.

eligible adj имéющий прáво (for на+acc); (bachelor) подходя́щий.

eliminate vt (do away with) устраня́ть impf, устрани́ть pf; (rule out) исключа́ть impf, исключи́ть pf.

élite n эли́та.

ellipse n э́ллипс. **elliptic(al)** adj эллипти́ческий.

elm n вяз.

elocution n орáторское искýсство.

elongate vt удлиня́ть impf, удлини́ть pf.

elope vi бежáть det (с возлю́бленным).

eloquence n краснорéчие. **eloquent** adj краснорéчивый.

else adv (besides) ещё; (instead) другóй; (with neg) бóльше; **nobody ~** никтó бóльше; **or ~** инáче; a (не) то; и́ли же; **s.o. ~** ктó-нибýдь другóй; **something ~?** ещё чтó-нибудь? **elsewhere** adv (place) в другóм мéсте; (direction) в другóе мéсто.

elucidate vt разъясня́ть impf, разъясни́ть pf.

elude vt избегáть impf +gen. **elusive** adj неулови́мый.

emaciated adj истощённый.

emanate vi исходи́ть impf (from из, от, +gen).

emancipate vt эмансипи́ровать impf & pf. **emancipation** n эмансипáция.

embankment n (river) нáбережная sb; (rly) нáсыпь.

embargo n эмбáрго neut indecl.

embark vi сади́ться impf, сесть pf на корáбль; **~ upon** предпринимáть impf, предприня́ть pf. **embarkation** n посáдка (на корáбль).

embarrass vt смущáть impf, смути́ть pf; **be ~ed** чýвствовать impf себя́ неудóбно. **embarrassing** adj неудóбный. **embarrassment** n смущéние.

embassy n посóльство.

embedded adj врéзанный.

embellish vt (adorn) украшáть impf, укрáсить pf; (story) прикрáшивать impf, прикрáсить pf. **embellishment** n украшéние.

embers n pl тлéющие уголькú m pl.

embezzle vt растрáчивать impf, растрáтить pf. **embezzlement** n растрáта.

embitter vt ожесточáть impf, ожесточи́ть pf.

emblem n эмблéма.

embodiment n воплощéние. **embody** vt воплощáть impf, воплоти́ть pf.

emboss vt чекáнить impf, от~ pf.

embrace n объя́тие; vi обнимáться impf, обня́ться pf; vt обнимáть impf, обня́ть pf; (accept) принимáть impf, приня́ть pf; (include) охвáтывать impf, охвати́ть pf.

embroider vt вышивáть impf, вы́шить pf; (story) прикрáшивать impf, прикрáсить pf. **embroidery** n вы́шивка.

embroil vt впýтывать impf, впýтать pf.

embryo n эмбриóн.

emerald n изумрýд.

emerge vi появля́ться impf, появи́ться pf. **emergence**

появле́ние. **emergency** *n* кра́йняя необходи́мость; **state of** ~ чрезвыча́йное положе́ние; ~ **exit** запасно́й вы́ход.

emery paper *n* нажда́чная бума́га.

emigrant *n* эмигра́нт, ~ка. **emigrate** *vi* эмигри́ровать *impf* & *pf*. **emigration** *n* эмигра́ция.

eminence *n* (*fame*) знамени́тость. **eminent** *adj* выдаю́щийся. **eminently** *adv* чрезвыча́йно.

emission *n* испуска́ние. **emit** *vt* испуска́ть *impf*, испусти́ть *pf*; (*light*) излуча́ть *impf*, излучи́ть *pf*; (*sound*) издава́ть *impf*, изда́ть *pf*.

emotion *n* эмо́ция, чу́вство. **emotional** *adj* эмоциона́льный.

empathize *vt* сопережива́ть *impf*, сопережи́ть *pf*. **empathy** *n* эмпа́тия.

emperor *n* импера́тор.

emphasis *n* ударе́ние. **emphasize** *vt* подчёркивать *impf*, подчеркну́ть *pf*. **emphatic** *adj* вырази́тельный; категори́ческий.

empire *n* импе́рия.

empirical *adj* эмпири́ческий.

employ *vt* (*use*) по́льзоваться *impf* +*instr*; (*person*) нанима́ть *impf*, наня́ть *pf*. **employee** *n* сотру́дник, рабо́чий *sb*. **employer** *n* работода́тель *m*. **employment** *n* рабо́та, слу́жба; (*use*) испо́льзование.

empower *vt* уполномо́чивать *impf*, уполномо́чить *pf* (**to** на+*acc*)

empress *n* императри́ца.

emptiness *n* пустота́. **empty**

adj пусто́й; ~**-headed** пустоголо́вый; ~**s** (*container*) поро́жняя та́ра; *vt* (*solid*) высыпа́ть *impf*, вы́сыпать *pf*; (*liquid*) вылива́ть *impf*, вы́лить *pf*; *vi* пусте́ть *impf*, о~ *pf*.

emulate *vt* достига́ть *impf*, дости́гнуть, дости́чь *pf* +*gen*; (*copy*) подража́ть *impf* +*dat*.

emulsion *n* эму́льсия.

enable *vt* дава́ть *impf*, дать *pf* возмо́жность +*dat* & *inf*.

enact *vt* (*law*) принима́ть *impf*, приня́ть *pf*; (*theat*) разы́грывать *impf*, разыгра́ть *pf*. **enactment** *n* (*law*) постановле́ние; (*theat*) игра́.

enamel *n* эма́ль; *adj* эма́левый; *vt* эмали́ровать *impf* & *pf*.

encampment *n* ла́герь *m*.

enchant *vt* очаро́вывать *impf*, очарова́ть *pf*. **enchanting** *adj* очарова́тельный. **enchantment** *n* очарова́ние.

encircle *vt* окружа́ть *impf*, окружи́ть *pf*.

enclave *n* анкла́в.

enclose *vt* огора́живать *impf*, огороди́ть *pf*; (*in letter*) прикла́дывать *impf*, приложи́ть *pf*; **please find** ~**d** прилага́ется (-а́ются) +*nom*. **enclosure** *n* огоро́женное ме́сто; (*in letter*) приложе́ние.

encode *vt* шифрова́ть *impf*, за~ *pf*.

encompass *vt* (*encircle*) окружа́ть *impf*, окружи́ть *pf*; (*contain*) заключа́ть *impf*, заключи́ть *pf*.

encore *int* бис!; *n* вы́зов на бис.

encounter *n* встре́ча; (*in combat*) столкнове́ние; *vt* встреча́ть *impf*, встре́тить *pf*; *(fig)* ста́лкиваться *impf*, столкну́ться *pf* c+*instr*.

encourage *vt* ободря́ть *impf*, ободри́ть *pf*. **encouragement** *n* ободре́ние. **encouraging** *adj* ободри́тельный.

encroach *vi* вторга́ться *impf*, вто́ргнуться *pf* (on в+*acc*). **encroachment** *n* вторже́ние.

encumber *vt* обременя́ть *impf*, обремени́ть *pf*. **encumbrance** *n* обу́за.

encyclopaedia *n* энциклопе́дия. **encyclopaedic** *adj* энциклопеди́ческий.

end *n* коне́ц; *(death)* смерть; *(purpose)* цель; **an ~ in itself** самоце́ль; **in the ~** в конце́ концо́в; **make ~s meet** своди́ть *impf*, свести́ *pf* концы́ с конца́ми; **no ~ of** ма́сса+*gen*; **on ~** *(upright)* стоймя́, дыбо́м; *(continuously)* подря́д; **put an ~to** класть *impf*, положи́ть *pf* коне́ц +*dat*; *vt* конча́ть *impf*, ко́нчить *pf*; *(halt)* прекраща́ть *impf*, прекрати́ть *pf*; *vi* конча́ться *impf*, ко́нчиться *pf*.

endanger *vt* подверга́ть *impf*, подве́ргнуть *pf* опа́сности.

endearing *adj* привлека́тельный. **endearment** *n* ла́ска.

endeavour *n* попы́тка; *(exertion)* уси́лие; *(undertaking)* де́ло; *vi* стара́ться *impf*, по~ *pf*.

endemic *adj* эндеми́ческий.

ending *n* оконча́ние. **endless** *adj* бесконе́чный.

endorse *vt (document)* надпи́сывать *impf*, надписа́ть *pf*; *(support)* подде́рживать *impf*, поддержа́ть *pf*. **endorsement** *n* по́дпись; подде́ржка; *(on driving licence)* прокол.

endow *vt* обеспе́чивать *impf*, обеспе́чить *pf* постоя́нным дохо́дом; *(fig)* одаря́ть *impf*, одари́ть *pf*. **endowment** *n* поже́ртвование; *(talent)* дарова́ние.

endurance *n (of person)* выно́сливость; *(of object)* про́чность. **endure** *vt* выноси́ть *impf*, вы́нести *pf*; терпе́ть *impf*, по~ *pf*; *vi* продолжа́ться *impf*, продо́лжиться *pf*.

enemy *n* враг; *adj* вра́жеский.

energetic *adj* энерги́чный. **energy** *n* эне́ргия; *pl* си́лы *f pl*.

enforce *vt (law etc.)* следи́ть *impf* за выполне́нием +*gen*. **enforcement** *n* наблюде́ние за выполне́нием +*gen*.

engage *vt (hire)* нанима́ть *impf*, наня́ть *pf*; *(tech)* зацепля́ть *impf*, зацепи́ть *pf*. **engaged** *adj (occupied)* за́нятый; **be ~ in** занима́ться *impf*, заня́ться *pf* +*instr*; **become ~** обруча́ться *impf*, обручи́ться *pf* (to c+*instr*). **engagement** *n (appointment)* свида́ние; *(betrothal)* обруче́ние; *(battle)* бой; **~ ring** обруча́льное кольцо́. **engaging** *adj* привлека́тельный.

engender *vt* порожда́ть *impf*, породи́ть *pf*.

engine *n* дви́гатель *m*; *(rly)* локомоти́в; **~-driver** *(rly)* маши́ни́ст. **engineer** *n* инжене́р; *vt (fig)* организова́ть *impf & pf*. **engineering** *n* инжене́рное де́ло, те́хника.

England *n* А́нглия. **English** *adj* англи́йский; *n:* **the ~** *pl* англича́не (-н) *pl*. **Englishman, -woman** *n* англича́нин, -а́нка.

engrave vt гравирова́ть impf, вы́~ pf; (fig) вреза́ть impf, вре́зать pf. **engraver** n гравёр. **engraving** n гравю́ра.

engross vt поглоща́ть impf, поглоти́ть pf; **be ~ed in** быть поглощённым +instr.

engulf vt поглоща́ть impf, поглоти́ть pf.

enhance vt увели́чивать impf, увели́чить pf.

enigma n зага́дка. **enigmatic** adj зага́дочный.

enjoy vt получа́ть impf, получи́ть pf удово́льствие от+gen; наслажда́ться impf, наслади́ться pf +instr; (health etc.) облада́ть impf +instr; ~ o.s. хорошо́ проводи́ть impf, провести́ pf вре́мя. **enjoyable** adj прия́тный. **enjoyment** n удово́льствие.

enlarge vt увели́чивать impf, увели́чить pf; ~ **upon** распространя́ться impf, распространи́ться pf o+prep. **enlargement** n увеличе́ние.

enlighten vt просвеща́ть impf, просвети́ть pf. **enlightenment** n просвеще́ние.

enlist vi поступа́ть impf, поступи́ть pf на вое́нную слу́жбу; vt (mil) вербова́ть impf, за~ pf; (support etc.) заруча́ться impf, заручи́ться pf +instr.

enliven vt оживля́ть impf, оживи́ть pf.

enmity n вражда́.

ennoble vt облагора́живать impf, облагоро́дить pf.

ennui n тоска́.

enormity n чудо́вищность. **enormous** adj огро́мный. **enormously** adv чрезвыча́йно.

enough adj доста́точно +gen; adv доста́точно, дово́льно; **be ~** хвата́ть impf, хвати́ть pf impers+gen.

enquire, enquiry see inquire, inquiry

enrage vt беси́ть impf, вз~ pf.

enrapture vt восхища́ть impf, восхити́ть pf.

enrich vt обогаща́ть impf, обогати́ть pf.

enrol vt & i запи́сывать(ся) impf, записа́ть(ся) pf. **enrolment** n за́пись.

en route adv по пути́ (to, for в+acc).

ensconce vt: ~ o.s. заса́живаться impf, засе́сть pf (with за+acc).

ensemble n (mus) анса́мбль m.

enshrine vt (fig) охраня́ть impf, охрани́ть pf.

ensign n (flag) флаг.

enslave vt порабоща́ть impf, поработи́ть pf.

ensue vi сле́довать impf. **ensuing** adj после́дующий.

ensure vt обеспе́чивать impf, обеспе́чить pf.

entail vt (necessitate) влечь impf за собо́й.

entangle vt запу́тывать impf, запу́тать pf.

enter vt & i входи́ть impf, войти́ pf в+acc; (by transport) въезжа́ть impf, въе́хать pf в+acc; vt (join) поступа́ть impf, поступи́ть pf в, на, +acc; (competition) вступа́ть impf, вступи́ть pf в+acc; (in list) вноси́ть impf, внести́ pf в+acc.

enterprise n (undertaking) предприя́тие; (initiative) предприи́мчивость. **enterprising** adj предприи́мчивый.

entertain vt (amuse) развлека́ть impf, развле́чь pf;

(*guests*) принима́ть *impf*, приня́ть *pf*; угоща́ть *impf*, угости́ть *pf* (**to** +*instr*); (*hopes*) пита́ть *impf*. **entertaining** *adj* занима́тельный. **entertainment** *n* развлече́ние; (*show*) представле́ние.

enthral *vt* порабоща́ть *impf*, поработи́ть *pf*.

enthusiasm *n* энтузиа́зм. **enthusiast** *n* энтузиа́ст, ~ка. **enthusiastic** *adj* восто́рженный; по́лный энтузиа́зма.

entice *vt* зама́нивать *impf*, замани́ть *pf*. **enticement** *n* прима́нка. **enticing** *adj* зама́нчивый.

entire *adj* по́лный, це́лый, весь. **entirely** *adv* вполне́, соверше́нно; (*solely*) исключи́тельно. **entirety** *n*: **in its ~** по́лностью.

entitle *vt* (*authorize*) дава́ть *impf*, дать *pf* пра́во+*dat* (**to** на+*acc*); **be ~d** (*book*) называ́ться *impf*; **be ~d to** име́ть *impf* пра́во на+*acc*.

entity *n* объе́кт; фено́мен.

entomology *n* энтомоло́гия.

entourage *n* сви́та.

entrails *n pl* вну́тренности (-тей) *pl*.

entrance[1] *n* вход, въезд; (*theat*) вы́ход; **~ exam** вступи́тельный экза́мен; **~ hall** вестибю́ль *m*.

entrance[2] *vt* (*charm*) очаро́вывать *impf*, очарова́ть *pf*. **entrancing** *adj* очарова́тельный.

entrant *n* уча́стник (for +*gen*).

entreat *vt* умоля́ть *impf*, умоли́ть *pf*. **entreaty** *n* мольба́.

entrench *vt* **be, become ~ed** (*fig*) укореня́ться *impf*, укорени́ться *pf*.

entrepreneur *n* предпринима́тель *m*.

entrust *vt* (*secret*) вверя́ть *impf*, вве́рить *pf* (**to** +*dat*); (*object*; *person*) поруча́ть *impf*, поручи́ть *pf* (**to** +*dat*).

entry *n* вход, въезд; вступле́ние; (*theat*) вы́ход; (*note*) за́пись; (*in reference book*) статья́.

entwine *vt* (*interweave*) сплета́ть *impf*, сплести́ *pf*; (*wreathe*) обвива́ть *impf*, обви́ть *pf*.

enumerate *vt* перечисля́ть *impf*, перечи́слить *pf*.

enunciate *vt* (*express*) излага́ть *impf*, изложи́ть *pf*; (*pronounce*) произноси́ть *impf*, произнести́ *pf*. **enunciation** *n* изложе́ние; произноше́ние.

envelop *vt* оку́тывать *impf*, оку́тать *pf*. **envelope** *n* конве́рт.

enviable *adj* зави́дный. **envious** *adj* зави́стливый.

environment *n* среда́; (**the ~**) окружа́ющая среда́. **environs** *n pl* окре́стности *f pl*.

envisage *vt* предусма́тривать *impf*, предусмотре́ть *pf*.

envoy *n* посла́нник, аге́нт.

envy *n* за́висть; *vt* зави́довать *impf*, по~ *pf* +*dat*.

enzyme *n* энзи́м.

ephemeral *adj* эфеме́рный.

epic *n* эпопе́я; *adj* эпи́ческий.

epidemic *n* эпиде́мия.

epilepsy *n* эпиле́псия. **epileptic** *n* эпиле́птик; *adj* эпилепти́ческий.

epilogue *n* эпило́г.

episode *n* эпизо́д. **episodic** *adj* эпизоди́ческий.

epistle *n* посла́ние.

epitaph *n* эпита́фия.

epithet *n* эпи́тет.

epitome *n* воплоще́ние. **epitomize** *vt* воплоща́ть *impf*, воплоти́ть *pf*.

epoch *n* эпо́ха.

equal *adj* ра́вный, одина́ко-
вый; (*capable of*) спосо́бный
(**to** на+*acc*, +*inf*); *n* ра́вный
sb; *vt* равня́ться *impf* +*dat*.
equality *n* ра́венство. **equal-
ize** *vt* ура́внивать *impf*, уравня́ть *pf*; *vi* (*sport*) равня́ть
impf, с~ *pf* счёт. **equally** *adv*
равно́, ра́вным о́бразом.

equanimity *n* хладнокро́вие.

equate *vt* прира́внивать *impf*,
приравня́ть *pf* (**with** к+*dat*).
equation *n* (*math*) уравне́ние.

equator *n* эква́тор. **equat-
orial** *adj* экваториа́льный.

equestrian *adj* ко́нный.

equidistant *adj* равносто-
я́щий. **equilibrium** *n* равно-
ве́сие.

equip *vt* обору́довать *impf* &
pf; (*person*) снаряжа́ть *impf*,
снаряди́ть *pf*; (*fig*) воору-
жа́ть *impf*, вооружи́ть *pf*.
equipment *n* обору́дование,
снаряже́ние.

equitable *adj* справедли́вый.

equity *n* справедли́вость; *pl*
(*econ*) обыкнове́нные а́кции
f pl.

equivalent *adj* эквивале́нт-
ный; *n* эквивале́нт.

equivocal *adj* двусмы́слен-
ный.

era *n* э́ра.

eradicate *vt* искореня́ть *impf*,
искорени́ть *pf*.

erase *vt* стира́ть *impf*, сте-
ре́ть *pf*; (*from memory*) вычёркивать *impf*, вы́черк-
нуть *pf* (из па́мяти). **eraser**
n ла́стик.

erect *adj* прямо́й; *vt* сооружа́ть *impf*, сооруди́ть *pf*.
erection *n* сооруже́ние; (*biol*)
эре́кция.

erode *vt* разруша́ть *impf*,
разру́шить *pf*. **erosion** *n*
эро́зия; (*fig*) разруше́ние.

erotic *adj* эроти́ческий.

err *vi* ошиба́ться *impf*, оши-
би́ться *pf*; (*sin*) греши́ть
impf, со~ *pf*.

errand *n* поруче́ние; **run ~s**
быть на посы́лках (**for**
y+*gen*).

erratic *adj* неро́вный.

erroneous *adj* оши́бочный.
error *n* оши́бка.

erudite *adj* учёный. **erudition**
n эруди́ция.

erupt *vi* взрыва́ться *impf*,
взорва́ться *pf*; (*volcano*) из-
верга́ться *impf*, изве́ргнуть-
ся *pf*. **eruption** *n* изверже́-
ние.

escalate *vi* возраста́ть *impf*,
возрасти́ *pf*; *vt* интенсифи-
ци́ровать *impf* & *pf*.

escalator *n* эскала́тор.

escapade *n* вы́ходка. **escape**
n (*from prison*) побе́г; (*from
danger*) спасе́ние; (*leak*) утё́ч-
ка; **have a narrow ~** едва́
спасти́сь; *vi* (*flee*) бежа́ть *impf*
& *pf*; убега́ть *impf*, убежа́ть
pf; (*save o.s.*) спаса́ться *impf*,
спасти́сь *pf*; (*leak*) утека́ть
impf, уте́чь *pf*; *vt* избега́ть
impf, избежа́ть *pf* +*gen*;
(*groan*) вырыва́ться *impf*,
вы́рваться *pf* из, у, +*gen*.

escort *n* (*mil*) эско́рт; (*of
lady*) кавале́р; *vt* сопрово-
жда́ть *impf*, сопроводи́ть *pf*;
(*mil*) эскорти́ровать *impf* &
pf.

Eskimo *n* эскимо́с, ~ка.

esoteric *adj* эзотери́ческий.

especially *adv* осо́бенно.

espionage *n* шпиона́ж.

espousal *n* подде́ржка. **es-
pouse** *vt* (*fig*) подде́рживать

impf, поддержа́ть *pf*.

essay *n* о́черк.

essence *n* (*philos*) су́щность; (*gist*) суть; (*extract*) эссе́нция. **essential** *adj* (*fundamental*) существенный; (*necessary*) необходи́мый; *n pl* (*necessities*) необходи́мое *sb*; (*crux*) суть; (*fundamentals*) осно́вы *f pl*. **essentially** *adv* по существу́.

establish *vt* (*set up*) учрежда́ть *impf*, учреди́ть *pf*; (*fact etc.*) устана́вливать *impf*, установи́ть *pf*. **establishment** *n* (*action*) учрежде́ние, устано́вле́ние; (*institution*) учрежде́ние.

estate *n* (*property*) име́ние; (*after death*) насле́дство; (*housing* ~) жило́й масси́в; ~ **agent** аге́нт по прода́же недви́жимости; ~ **car** автомоби́ль *m* с ку́зовом «универса́л».

esteem *n* уваже́ние; *vt* уважа́ть *impf*. **estimate** *n* (*of quality*) оце́нка; (*of cost*) сме́та; *vt* оце́нивать *impf*, оцени́ть *pf*. **estimation** *n* оце́нка, мне́ние.

Estonia *n* Эсто́ния. **Estonian** *n* эсто́нец, -нка; *adj* эсто́нский.

estranged *adj* отчуждённый. **estrangement** *n* отчужде́ние.

estuary *n* у́стье.

etc. *abbr* и т.д. **etcetera** и так да́лее.

etch *vt* трави́ть *impf*, вы́- *pf*. **etching** *n* (*action*) травле́ние; (*object*) офо́рт.

eternal *adj* ве́чный. **eternity** *n* ве́чность.

ether *n* эфи́р. **ethereal** *adj* эфи́рный.

ethical *adj* эти́ческий,

эти́чный. **ethics** *n* э́тика.

ethnic *adj* этни́ческий.

etiquette *n* этике́т.

etymology *n* этимоло́гия.

EU *abbr* (*of* **European Union**) ЕС.

eucalyptus *n* эвка́липт.

Eucharist *n* прича́стие.

eulogy *n* похвала́.

euphemism *n* эвфеми́зм. **euphemistic** *adj* эвфемисти́ческий.

Europe *n* Евро́па. **European** *n* европе́ец; *adj* европе́йский; ~ **Community** Европе́йское соо́бщество; ~ **Union** Европе́йский сою́з.

evacuate *vt* (*person, place*) эвакуи́ровать *impf & pf*. **evacuation** *n* эвакуа́ция.

evade *vt* уклоня́ться *impf*, уклони́ться *pf* от+*gen*.

evaluate *vt* оце́нивать *impf*, оцени́ть *pf*. **evaluation** *n* оце́нка.

evangelical *adj* ева́нгельский. **evangelist** *n* евангели́ст.

evaporate *vt & i* испаря́ть(ся) *impf*, испари́ть(ся) *pf*. **evaporation** *n* испаре́ние.

evasion *n* уклоне́ние (*of* от+*gen*). **evasive** *adj* укло́нчивый.

eve *n* кану́н; **on the** ~ накану́не.

even *adj* ро́вный; (*number*) чётный; **get** ~ расквита́ться *pf* (**with** с+*instr*); *adv* да́же; (*just*) как раз; (*with comp*) ещё; ~ **if** да́же е́сли; ~ **though** хотя́; ~ **so** всё-таки; **not** ~ да́же не; *vt* выра́внивать *impf*, вы́ровнять *pf*.

evening *n* ве́чер; *adj* вече́рний; ~ **class** вече́рние ку́рсы *m pl*.

evenly *adv* по́ровну, ро́вно,

evenness *n* ро́вность.

·vent *n* собы́тие, происше́ствие; **in the ~ of** в слу́чае+*gen*; **in any ~** во вся́ком слу́чае; **in the ~** в коне́чном счёте. **eventful** *adj* по́лный собы́тий. **eventual** *adj* коне́чный. **eventuality** *n* возмо́жность. **eventually** *adv* в конце́ концо́в.

ever *adv* (*at any time*) когда́-либо, когда́-нибудь; (*always*) всегда́; (*emph*) же; **~ since** с тех пор (как); **~ so** о́чень; **for ~** навсегда́; **hardly ~** почти́ никогда́. **evergreen** *adj* вечнозелёный; *n* вечнозелёное расте́ние. **everlasting** *adj* ве́чный. **evermore** *adv*: **for ~** навсегда́.

every *adj* ка́ждый, вся́кий, все (*pl*); **~ now and then** вре́мя от вре́мени; **~ other** ка́ждый второ́й; **~ other day** че́рез день. **everybody, everyone** *pron* ка́ждый, все (*pl*). **everyday** *adj* (*daily*) ежедне́вный; (*commonplace*) повседне́вный. **everything** *pron* всё. **everywhere** *adv* всю́ду, везде́.

·vict *vt* выселя́ть *impf*, вы́селить *pf*. **eviction** *n* выселе́ние.

evidence *n* свиде́тельство, доказа́тельство; **give ~** свиде́тельствовать *impf* (о+*prep*; +*acc*; +что). **evident** *adj* очеви́дный.

evil *n* зло; *adj* злой.

evoke *vt* вызыва́ть *impf*, вы́звать *pf*.

evolution *n* эволю́ция. **evolutionary** *adj* эволюцио́нный. **evolve** *vt & i* развива́ть(ся) *impf*, разви́ть(ся) *pf*.

ewe *n* овца́.

ex- *in comb* бы́вший.

exacerbate *vt* обостря́ть *impf*, обостри́ть *pf*.

exact *adj* то́чный; *vt* взы́скивать *impf*, взыска́ть *pf* (**from, of** с+*gen*). **exacting** *adj* тре́бовательный. **exactitude, exactness** *n* то́чность. **exactly** *adv* то́чно; (*just*) как раз; (*precisely*) и́менно.

exaggerate *vt* преувели́чивать *impf*, преувели́чить *pf*. **exaggeration** *n* преувеличе́ние.

exalt *vt* возвыша́ть *impf*, возвы́сить *pf*; (*extol*) превозноси́ть *impf*, превознести́ *pf*.

examination *n* (*inspection*) осмо́тр; (*exam*) экза́мен; (*law*) допро́с. **examine** *vt* (*inspect*) осма́тривать *impf*, осмотре́ть *pf*; (*test*) экзаменова́ть *impf*, про— *pf*; (*law*) допра́шивать *impf*, допроси́ть *pf*. **examiner** *n* экзамена́тор.

example *n* приме́р; **for ~** наприме́р.

exasperate *vt* раздража́ть *impf*, раздражи́ть *pf*. **exasperation** *n* раздраже́ние.

excavate *vt* раска́пывать *impf*, раскопа́ть *pf*. **excavations** *n pl* раско́пки *f pl*. **excavator** *n* экскава́тор.

exceed *vt* превыша́ть *impf*, превы́сить *pf*. **exceedingly** *adv* чрезвыча́йно.

excel *vt* превосходи́ть *impf*, превзойти́ *pf*; *vi* отлича́ться *impf*, отличи́ться *pf* (**at, in** в+*prep*). **excellence** *n* превосхо́дство. **excellency** *n* превосходи́тельство. **excellent** *adj* отли́чный.

except *vt* исключа́ть *impf*, исключи́ть *pf*; *prep* кро́ме+*gen*. **exception** *n* исключе́ние; **take ~ to** возража́ть *impf* возрази́ть *pf* про́тив+*gen*. **exceptional** *adj* исключи́тельный.

excerpt *n* отры́вок.

excess *n* избы́ток. **excessive** *adj* чрезме́рный.

exchange *n* обме́н (of +*instr*); (of currency) разме́н; (building) би́ржа; (telephone) центра́льная телефо́нная ста́нция; ~ rate курс; *vt* обме́нивать *impf*, обменя́ть *pf* (for на+*acc*); обме́ниваться *impf*, обменя́ться *pf* +*instr*.

Exchequer *n* казначе́йство.

excise[1] *n* (duty) акци́з(ный сбор).

excise[2] *vt* (cut out) выреза́ть *impf*, вы́резать *pf*.

excitable *adj* возбуди́мый. **excite** *vt* (cause, arouse) возбужда́ть *impf*, возбуди́ть *pf*; (thrill, agitate) волнова́ть *impf*, вз~ *pf*. **excitement** *n* возбужде́ние; волне́ние.

exclaim *vi* восклица́ть *impf*, воскли́кнуть *pf*. **exclamation** *n* восклица́ние; ~ mark восклица́тельный знак.

exclude *vt* исключа́ть *impf*, исключи́ть *pf*. **exclusion** *n* исключе́ние. **exclusive** *adj* исключи́тельный.

excommunicate *vt* отлуча́ть *impf*, отлучи́ть *pf* (от це́ркви).

excrement *n* экскреме́нты (-тов) *pl*.

excrete *vt* выделя́ть *impf*, вы́делить *pf*. **excretion** *n* выделе́ние.

excruciating *adj* мучи́тельный.

excursion *n* экску́рсия.

excusable *adj* прости́тельный. **excuse** *n* оправда́ние; (pretext) отгово́рка; *vt* (for-

give) извиня́ть *impf*, извини́ть *pf*; (justify) опра́вдывать *impf*, оправда́ть *pf*; (release) освобожда́ть *impf*, освободи́ть *pf* (from от+*gen*); ~ me извини́те!; прости́те!

execute *vt* исполня́ть *impf*, испо́лнить *pf*; (criminal) казни́ть *impf* & *pf*. **execution** *n* исполне́ние; казнь. **executioner** *n* пала́ч. **executive** *adj* исполни́тельный о́рган; (person) руководи́тель *m*; *adj* исполни́тельный.

exemplary *adj* приме́рный. **exemplify** *vt* (illustrate by example) приводи́ть *impf*, привести́ *pf* приме́р +*gen*; (serve as example) служи́ть *impf*, по~ *pf* приме́ром +*gen*.

exempt *adj* освобождённый; *vt* освобожда́ть *impf*, освободи́ть *pf* (from от+*gen*). **exemption** *n* освобожде́ние.

exercise *n* (use) примене́ние; (physical ~; task) упражне́ние; take ~ упражня́ться *impf*; ~ book тетра́дь; *vt* (use) применя́ть *impf*, примени́ть *pf*; (dog) прогу́ливать *impf*; (train) упражня́ть *impf*.

exert *vt* ока́зывать *impf*, оказа́ть *pf*; ~ o.s. стара́ться *impf*, по~ *pf*. **exertion** *n* напряже́ние.

exhale *vt* выдыха́ть *impf*, вы́дохнуть *pf*.

exhaust *n* вы́хлоп; ~ fumes выхлопны́е га́зы *m pl*; ~ pipe выхлопна́я труба́; *vt* (use up) истоща́ть *impf*, истощи́ть *pf*; (person) изнуря́ть *impf*, изнури́ть *pf*; (subject) исче́рпывать *impf*, исче́рпать *pf*. **exhausted** *adj*: be ~ (person) быть изможённым. **exhausting** *adj* изнури́тельный.

exhibit 441 **explicit**

exhaustion n изнуре́ние; (depletion) истоще́ние. **exhaustive** adj исче́рпывающий.

exhibit n экспона́т; (law) веще́ственное доказа́тельство; vt (manifest) проявля́ть impf, прояви́ть pf; (publicly) выставля́ть impf, вы́ставить pf. **exhibition** n проявле́ние; (public ~) вы́ставка. **exhibitor** n экспоне́нт.

exhilarated adj в припо́днятом настрое́нии. **exhilarating** adj возбужда́ющий. **exhilaration** n возбужде́ние.

exhort vt увещева́ть impf. **exhortation** n увещева́ние.

exhume vt выка́пывать impf, вы́копать pf.

exile n изгна́ние; (person) изгна́нник; vt изгоня́ть impf, изгна́ть pf.

exist vi существова́ть impf. **existence** n существова́ние. **existing** adj существу́ющий.

exit n вы́ход; (theat) ухо́д (со сце́ны); vi уходи́ть impf, уйти́ pf. **~ visa** выездна́я ви́за.

exonerate vt опра́вдывать impf, оправда́ть pf.

exorbitant adj непоме́рный.

exorcize vt (spirits) изгоня́ть impf, изгна́ть pf.

exotic adj экзоти́ческий.

expand vt & i расширя́ть(ся) impf, расши́рить(ся) pf; **~ on** распространя́ться impf, распространи́ться pf o+prep.

expanse n простра́нство. **expansion** n расшире́ние. **expansive** adj экспанси́вный.

expatriate n экспатриа́нт, ~ка.

expect vt (await) ожида́ть impf +gen; ждать impf +gen, что; (suppose) полага́ть impf; (require) тре́бовать impf +gen, что́бы. **expectant** adj выжида́тельный; **~ mother** бере́менная же́нщина. **expectation** n ожида́ние.

expediency n целесообра́зность. **expedient** n приём; adj целесообра́зный. **expedite** vt ускоря́ть impf, уско́рить pf. **expedition** n экспеди́ция. **expeditionary** adj экспедицио́нный.

expel vt (drive out) выгоня́ть impf, вы́гнать pf; (from school etc.) исключа́ть impf, исключи́ть pf; (from country etc.) изгоня́ть impf, изгна́ть pf.

expend vt тра́тить impf, ис~, по~ pf. **expendable** adj необяза́тельный. **expenditure** n расхо́д. **expense** n расхо́д; pl расхо́ды m pl, at the **~ of** за счёт+gen; (fig) цено́ю+gen. **expensive** adj дорого́й.

experience n о́пыт; (incident) пережива́ние; vt испы́тывать impf, испыта́ть pf; (undergo) пережива́ть impf, пережи́ть pf. **experienced** adj о́пытный.

experiment n экспериме́нт; vi эксперименти́ровать impf (on, with над, с+instr). **experimental** adj эксперимента́льный.

expert n экспе́рт; adj о́пытный. **expertise** n специа́льные зна́ния neut pl.

expire vi (period) истека́ть impf, исте́чь pf. **expiry** n исте́чение.

explain vt объясня́ть impf, объясни́ть pf. **explanation** n объясне́ние. **explanatory** adj объясни́тельный.

expletive n (oath) бра́нное сло́во.

explicit adj я́вный; (of person) прямо́й.

explode vt & i взрыва́ть(ся) impf, взорва́ть(ся) pf; vt (discredit) опроверга́ть impf, опрове́ргнуть pf; vi (with anger etc.) разража́ться impf, разрази́ться pf.

exploit n по́двиг; vt эксплуати́ровать impf; (use to advantage) испо́льзовать impf & pf. **exploitation** n эксплуата́ция. **exploiter** n эксплуата́тор.

exploration n иссле́дование. **exploratory** adj иссле́довательский. **explore** vt иссле́довать impf & pf. **explorer** n иссле́дователь m.

explosion n взрыв. **explosive** n взры́вчатое вещество́; adj взры́вчатый; (fig) взрывно́й.

exponent n (interpreter) истолкова́тель m; (advocate) сторо́нник.

export n (выво́з, э́кспорт; vt вывози́ть impf, вы́везти pf; экспорти́ровать impf & pf. **exporter** n экспортёр.

expose vt (bare) раскрыва́ть impf, раскры́ть pf; (subject) подверга́ть impf, подве́ргнуть pf (to +dat); (discredit) разоблача́ть impf, разоблачи́ть pf; (phot) экспони́ровать impf & pf.

exposition n изложе́ние.

exposure n подверга́ние (to +dat); (phot) вы́держка; (unmasking) разоблаче́ние; (med) хо́лод.

expound vt излага́ть impf, изложи́ть pf.

express n (train) экспре́сс; adj (clear) то́чный; (purpose) специа́льный; (urgent) сро́чный; vt выража́ть impf, вы́разить pf. **expression** n выраже́ние; (expressiveness) вырази-

тельность. **expressive** adj вырази́тельный. **expressly** adv (clearly) я́сно; (specifically) специа́льно.

expropriate vt экспроприи́ровать impf & pf. **expropriation** n экспроприа́ция.

expulsion n (from school etc.) исключе́ние; (from country etc.) изгна́ние.

exquisite adj утончённый.

extant adj сохрани́вшийся.

extempore adv экспро́мптом. **extemporize** vt & i импровизи́ровать impf, сымпровизи́ровать pf.

extend vt (stretch out) протя́гивать impf, протяну́ть pf; (enlarge) расширя́ть impf, расши́рить pf; (prolong) продлева́ть impf, продли́ть pf; vi простира́ться impf, простере́ться pf. **extension** n (enlarging) расшире́ние; (time) продле́ние; (to house) пристро́йка; (tel) доба́вочный. **extensive** adj обши́рный. **extent** n (degree) сте́пень.

extenuating adj: ~ circumstances смягча́ющие вину́ обстоя́тельства neut pl.

exterior n вне́шность; adj вне́шний.

exterminate vt истребля́ть impf, истреби́ть pf. **extermination** n истребле́ние.

external adj вне́шний.

extinct adj (volcano) поту́хший; (species) вы́мерший; **become** ~ вымира́ть impf, вы́мереть pf. **extinction** n вымира́ние.

extinguish vt гаси́ть impf, по-~ pf. **extinguisher** n огнетуши́тель m.

extol vt превозноси́ть impf.

превознести́ pf.

extort vt вымога́ть impf (**from** y+gen). **extortion** n вымога́тельство. **extortionate** adj вымога́тельский.

extra n (theat) стати́ст, ~ка; (payment) приплата; adj дополни́тельный; (special) осо́бый; adv дополни́тельно.

extract n экстра́кт; (from book etc.) вы́держка; vt извлека́ть impf, извле́чь pf. **extraction** n извлече́ние; (origin) происхожде́ние. **extradite** vt выдава́ть impf, вы́дать pf. **extradition** n вы́дача.

extramarital adj внебра́чный.

extraneous adj посторо́нний.

extraordinary adj чрезвыча́йный.

extrapolate vt & i экстраполи́ровать impf & pf.

extravagance n расточи́тельность. **extravagant** adj расточи́тельный; (fantastic) сумасбро́дный.

extreme n кра́йность; adj кра́йний. **extremity** n (end) край; (adversity) кра́йность; pl (hands & feet) коне́чности f pl.

extricate vt выпу́тывать impf, вы́путать pf.

exuberance n жизнера́достность. **exuberant** adj жизнера́достный.

exude vt & i выделя́ть(ся) impf, вы́делить(ся) pf; (fig) излуча́ть(ся) impf, излучи́ть(ся) pf.

exult vi ликова́ть impf. **exultant** adj лику́ющий. **exultation** n ликова́ние.

eye n глаз; (needle etc.) ушко́; vt разгля́дывать impf, разгляде́ть pf. **eyeball** n глазно́е я́блоко. **eyebrow** n бровь.

eyelash n ресни́ца. **eyelid** n ве́ко. **eyeshadow** n те́ни f pl для век. **eyesight** n зре́ние. **eyewitness** n очеви́дец.

F

fable n ба́сня.

fabric n (structure) структу́ра; (cloth) ткань. **fabricate** vt (invent) выду́мывать impf, вы́думать pf. **fabrication** n вы́думка.

fabulous adj ска́зочный.

façade n фаса́д.

face n лицо́; (expression) выраже́ние; (grimace) грима́са; (side) сторона́; (surface) пове́рхность; (clock etc.) цифербла́т; **make ~s** ко́рчить pf ро́жи; **~ down** лицо́м вниз; **~ to ~** лицо́м к лицу́; **in the ~ of** пе́ред лицо́м+gen, вопреки́+dat; **on the ~ of it** на пе́рвый взгляд; vt (be turned towards) быть обращённым к+dat; (of person) стоя́ть impf лицо́м к+dat; (meet danger) смотре́ть impf в лицо́+dat; (cover) облицо́вывать impf, облицева́ть pf; **I can't ~ it** я не ду́маю об э́том и мочь. **faceless** adj безли́чный.

facet n грань; (fig) аспе́кт.

facetious adj шутли́вый.

facial adj лицево́й.

facile adj пове́рхностный. **facilitate** vt облегча́ть impf, облегчи́ть pf. **facility** n (ease) лёгкость; (ability) спосо́бность; pl (conveniences) удо́бства neut pl, (opportunities) возмо́жности f pl.

facing n облицо́вка; (of garment) отде́лка.

facsimile n факси́миле neut indecl.

fact n факт; the ~ is that ... де́ло в том, что...; as a matter of ~ со́бственно говоря́; in ~ на са́мом де́ле.

faction n фра́кция.

factor n фа́ктор.

factory n фа́брика, заво́д.

factual adj факти́ческий.

faculty n спосо́бность; (univ) факульте́т.

fade vi (wither) вя́нуть impf, за~ pf; (colour) выцвета́ть impf, вы́цвести pf; (sound) замира́ть impf, замере́ть pf.

faeces n pl кал.

fag n (cigarette) сигаре́та.

fail n: without ~ обяза́тельно; vi (weaken) слабе́ть impf, (break down) отка́зывать impf, отказа́ть pf; (not succeed) терпе́ть impf, по~ pf неуда́чу; не удава́ться impf, удаться pf impers+dat; vt & i (exam) прова́ливать(ся) impf, провали́ть(ся) pf; vt (disappoint) подводи́ть impf, подвести́ pf; **failing** n недоста́ток; prep за неиме́нием +gen.

failure n неуда́ча; (person) неуда́чник, -ица.

faint n о́бморок; adj (weak) сла́бый; (pale) бле́дный; I feel ~ мне ду́рно; ~-hearted малоду́шный; vi па́дать impf, упа́сть pf в о́бморок.

fair[1] n я́рмарка.

fair[2] adj (hair, skin) све́тлый; (weather) я́сный; (just) справедли́вый; (average) сно́сный; a ~ amount дово́льно мно́го +gen. **fairly** adv дово́льно.

fairy n фе́я; ~-tale ска́зка.

faith n ве́ра; (trust) дове́рие. **faithful** adj ве́рный; yours ~ly с уваже́нием.

fake n подде́лка; vt подде́лывать impf, подде́лать pf.

falcon n со́кол.

fall n паде́ние; vi па́дать impf, (у)па́сть pf; ~ **apart** распада́ться impf, распа́сться pf; ~ **asleep** засыпа́ть impf, засну́ть pf; ~ **back on** прибега́ть impf, прибе́гнуть pf к+dat; ~ **down** упа́сть pf; (building) разва́ливаться impf, развали́ться pf; ~ **in love with** влюбля́ться impf, влюби́ться pf в+acc; ~ **off** отпада́ть impf, отпа́сть pf; ~ **out** выпада́ть impf, вы́пасть pf; (quarrel) поссо́риться pf; ~ **over** опроки́дываться impf, опроки́нуться pf; ~ **through** прова́ливаться impf, провали́ться pf; **~out** радиоакти́вные оса́дки (-ков) pl.

fallacy n оши́бка.

fallible adj подве́рженный оши́бкам.

fallow n: lie ~ лежа́ть impf под па́ром.

false adj ло́жный; (teeth) иску́сственный; ~ **start** неве́рный старт. **falsehood** n ложь. **falsification** n фальсифика́ция. **falsify** vt фальсифици́ровать impf & pf. **falsity** n ло́жность.

falter vi спотыка́ться impf, споткну́ться pf; (stammer) запина́ться impf, запну́ться pf.

fame n сла́ва. **famed** adj изве́стный.

familiar adj (well known) знако́мый; (usual) обы́чный; (informal) фамилья́рный. **familiarity** n знако́мство; фамилья́рность. **familiarize** vt ознакомля́ть impf, ознако́мить pf (with c+instr).

family n семья; *attrib* семейный; ~ **tree** родословная *sb.*

famine n голод. **famished** *adj*: **be** ~ голодать *impf*.

famous *adj* знаменитый.

fan¹ n веер; (*ventilator*) вентилятор; ~**-belt** ремень *m* вентилятора; *vt* обмахивать *impf*, обмахнуть *pf*; (*flame*) раздувать *impf*, раздуть *pf*.

fan² n поклонник, -ица; (*sport*) болельщик. **fanatic** n фанатик. **fanatical** *adj* фанатический.

fanciful *adj* причудливый. **fancy** *adj* фантазия; (*whim*) причуда; **take a** ~ **to** увлекаться *impf*, увлечься *pf* +*instr*; *adj* витиеватый; *vt* (*imagine*) представлять *impf*, представить *pf* себе; (*suppose*) полагать *impf*, по~ *pf*; (*like*) нравиться *impf*, по~ *pf impers*+*dat*; ~ **dress** маскарадный костюм; ~**-dress** костюмированный.

fanfare n фанфара.

fang n клык; (*serpent's*) ядовитый зуб.

fantasize *vi* фантазировать *impf*. **fantastic** *adj* фантастический. **fantasy** n фантазия.

far *adj* дальний; **Russia is** ~ **away** Россия очень далеко; *adv* далеко; **as** ~ **as** (*prep*) до+*gen*; (*conj*) поскольку; **by** ~ намного; (**in**) **so** ~ **as** поскольку; ~ **do сих пор**; ~**-fetched** притянутый за волосы; ~**-reaching** далеко идущий; ~**-sighted** дальнозоркий.

farce n фарс. **farcical** *adj* смехотворный.

fare n (*price*) проездная плата; (*food*) пища; *vi* поживать *impf*. **farewell** *int* прощай(те)!; n прощание; *attrib* прощальный; **bid** ~ прощаться *impf*, проститься *pf* (**to** c+*instr*).

farm n ферма. **farmer** n фермер. **farming** n сельское хозяйство.

fart (*vulg*) n пукание; *vi* пукать *impf*, пукнуть *pf*.

farther *see* **further**. **farthest** *see* **furthest**.

fascinate *vt* очаровывать *impf*, очаровать *pf*. **fascinating** *adj* очаровательный. **fascination** n очарование.

Fascism n фашизм. **Fascist** n фашист, ~ка; *adj* фашистский.

fashion n мода; (*manner*) манера; **after a** ~ некоторым образом; *vt* придавать *impf*, придать *pf* форму +*dat*. **fashionable** *adj* модный.

fast¹ n пост; *vi* поститься *impf*.

fast² *adj* (*rapid*) скорый, быстрый; (*colour*) стойкий; (*shut*) плотно закрытый; **be** ~ (*timepiece*) спешить *impf*.

fasten *vt* (*attach*) прикреплять *impf*, прикрепить *pf* (**to** к+*dat*); (*tie*) привязывать *impf*, привязать *pf* (**to** к+*dat*); (*garment*) застёгивать *impf*, застегнуть *pf*. **fastener**, **fastening** n запор, задвижка; (*on garment*) застёжка.

fastidious *adj* брезгливый.

fat n жир; *adj* (*greasy*) жирный; (*plump*) толстый; **get** ~ толстеть *impf*, по~ *pf*.

fatal *adj* роковой; (*deadly*) смертельный. **fatalism** n фатализм. **fatality** n (*death*) смертельный случай. **fate** n судьба. **fateful** *adj* роковой.

father n отец; ~**-in-law** (*husband's* ~) свёкор; (*wife's* ~) тесть *m*. **fatherhood** n отцо́вство. **fatherland** *n* оте́чество. **fatherly** *adj* оте́ческий.

fathom *n* морска́я са́жень; *vt* (*fig*) понима́ть *impf*, поня́ть *pf*.

fatigue *n* утомле́ние; *vt* утомля́ть *impf*, утоми́ть *pf*.

fatten *vt* отка́рмливать *impf*, откорми́ть *pf*; *vi* толсте́ть *impf*, по~ *pf*. **fatty** *adj* жи́рный.

fatuous *adj* глу́пый.

fault *n* недоста́ток; (*blame*) вина́; (*geol*) сброс. **faultless** *adj* безупре́чный. **faulty** *adj* дефе́ктный.

fauna *n* фа́уна.

favour *n* (*kind act*) любе́зность; (*goodwill*) благоскло́нность; **in** (*s.o.'s*) ~ в по́льзу +*gen*; **be in** ~ of быть за+*acc*; *vt* (*support*) благоприя́тствовать *impf* +*dat*; (*treat with partiality*) ока́зывать *impf*, оказа́ть *pf* предпочте́ние +*dat*. **favourable** *adj* (*propitious*) благоприя́тный; (*approving*) благоскло́нный. **favourite** *n* люби́мец, -мица; (*also sport*) фавори́т, ~ка; *adj* люби́мый.

fawn[1] *n* оленёнок; *adj* желтова́то-кори́чневый.

fawn[2] *vi* подли́зываться *impf*, подлиза́ться *pf* (**on** к+*dat*).

fax *n* факс; *vt* посыла́ть *impf*, посла́ть *pf* по фа́ксу.

fear *n* страх, боя́знь, опасе́ние; *vt* & *i* боя́ться *impf* +*gen*; опаса́ться *impf* +*gen*. **fearful** *adj* (*terrible*) стра́шный; (*timid*) пугли́вый. **fearless** *adj* бесстра́шный. **fearsome** *adj* гро́зный.

feasibility *n* осуществи́мость. **feasible** *adj* осуществи́мый.

feast *n* (*meal*) пир; (*festival*) пра́здник; *vi* пирова́ть *impf*.

feat *n* по́двиг.

feather *n* перо́.

feature *n* черта́; (*newspaper*) (темати́ческая) статья́; ~ **film** худо́жественный фильм; *vt* помеща́ть *impf*, помести́ть *pf* на ви́дном ме́сте; (*in film*) пока́зывать *impf*, показа́ть *pf*; *vi* игра́ть *impf* сыгра́ть *pf* роль.

February *n* февра́ль *m*; *adj* февра́льский.

feckless *adj* безала́берный. **federal** *adj* федера́льный. **federation** *n* федера́ция.

fee *n* гонора́р; (*entrance* ~ *etc.*) взнос; *pl* (*regular payment, school, etc.*) пла́та.

feeble *adj* сла́бый.

feed *n* корм; *vt* корми́ть *impf*, на~, по~ *pf*; *vi* корми́ться *impf*, по~ *pf*; ~ **up** отка́рмливать *impf*, откорми́ть *pf*; **I am fed up with** мне надое́л (-а, -о; -и) +*nom*. **feedback** *n* обра́тная связь.

feel *n* чу́вствовать *impf*, по~ *pf*; (*think*) счита́ть *impf*, счесть *pf*; *vi* (~ *bad etc.*) чу́вствовать *impf*, по~ *pf* себя́ +*adv, +instr*; ~ **like** хоте́ться *impf impers+dat*. **feeling** *n* (*sense*) ощуще́ние; (*emotion*) чу́вство; (*impression*) впечатле́ние; (*mood*) настрое́ние.

feign *vt* притворя́ться *impf*, притвори́ться *pf* +*instr*. **feigned** *adj* притво́рный.

feline *adj* коша́чий.

fell *vt* (*tree*) сруба́ть *impf*, сруби́ть *pf*; (*person*) сбива́ть *impf*, сбить *pf* с ног.

fellow *n* па́рень *m*; (*of society etc.*) член; ~ **countryman** соотéчественник. **fellowship**

това́рищество.

felt n фетр; adj фе́тровый; ~
tip pen фломáстер.

female n (animal) сáмка; (person) же́нщина; adj же́нский.
feminine adj же́нский, же́нственный; (gram) же́нского
ро́да. **femininity** n же́нственность. **feminism** n феми-
ни́зм. **feminist** n фемини́ст,
~ка; adj феминíстский.

fence n забо́р; vi: ~ in ого-
рáживать impf, огороди́ть
pf; ~ **off** отгорáживать impf,
отгороди́ть pf; vi (sport)
фехтова́ть impf, vt квасить impf,
фехтова́льщик, -ица. **fencing** n (enclosure) забо́р; (sport)
фехтова́ние.

fend vt: ~ **off** отражáть impf,
отрази́ть pf; vi: ~ **for o.s.**
забо́титься impf, по~ pf о
себе́. **fender** n решётка.

fennel n фе́нхель m.

ferment n броже́ние; vi бро-
ди́ть impf, vt квасить impf,
за~ pf; (excite) возбуждáть
impf, возбуди́ть pf. **fermentation** n броже́ние; (excitement) возбужде́ние.

fern n пáпоротник.

ferocious adj свире́пый. **ferocity** n свире́пость.

ferret n хорёк; vt: ~ **out** (search
out) разню́хивать impf, раз-
ню́хать pf; vi: ~ **about** (rummage) ры́ться impf.

ferry n паро́м; vt перевози́ть
impf, перевезти́ pf.

fertile adj плодоро́дный. **fertility** n плодоро́дие. **fertilize**
vt (soil) удобря́ть impf, удо-
бри́ть pf; (egg) оплодотворя́ть
impf, оплодотвори́ть
pf. **fertilizer** n удобре́ние.

fervent adj горя́чий. **fervour**
n жар.

fester vi гнои́ться impf.

festival n прáздник, (music
etc.) фестивáль m. **festive**
adj прáздничный. **festivities**
n pl торжествá neut pl.

festoon vt украшáть impf,
украси́ть pf.

fetch vt (carrying) приноси́ть
impf, принести́ pf; (leading)
приводи́ть impf, привести́
pf; (go and come back with)
(on foot) идти́ impf, по~ pf
за+instr; (by vehicle) заезжáть
impf, зае́хать pf за+instr;
(price) выручáть impf, выручить pf. **fetching** adj при-
влекáтельный.

fetid adj зловóнный.

fetish n фети́ш.

fetter vt скóвывать impf, скó-
вать pf; n pl кандалы́ (-лóв)
pl; (fig) окóвы (-в) pl.

fettle n состоя́ние.

feud n крóвная месть.

feudal adj феодáльный. **feudalism** n феодали́зм.

fever n лихорáдка. **feverish**
adj лихорáдочный.

few adj & pron немнóгие pl;
мáло+gen; **a** ~ нéсколько
+gen; **quite a** ~ немáло +gen.

fiancé n жени́х. **fiancée** n
невéста.

fiasco n провáл.

fib n враньё; vi привирáть
impf, приврáть pf.

fibre n волокнó. **fibreglass** n
стекловолокнó. **fibrous** adj
волокни́стый.

fickle adj непостоя́нный.

fiction n худо́жественная ли-
терату́ра; (invention) вы́дум-
ка. **fictional** adj беллетри-
сти́ческий. **fictitious** adj вы́-
мышленный.

fiddle n (violin) скри́пка;
(swindle) обмáн; vi: ~ **about**

безде́льничать *impf*; ~ with
верте́ть *impf*; *vt* (falsify) пере-
де́лывать *impf*, подде́лать *pf*;
(cheat) жи́лить *impf*, у~ *pf*.
fidelity *n* ве́рность.
fidget *n* непосе́да *m & f*; *vi* ёрзать *impf*; не́рвничать *impf*.
fidgety *adj* непосе́дливый.
field *n* по́ле; (sport) пло-
ща́дка; (sphere) о́бласть; ~
glasses полево́й бино́кль *m*.
~**work** полевы́е рабо́ты *pl*.
fiend *n* дья́вол. **fiendish** *adj*
дья́вольский.
fierce *adj* свире́пый; (strong)
си́льный.
fiery *adj* о́гненный.
fifteen *adj & n* пятна́дцать.
fifteenth *adj & n* пятна́дца-
тый. **fifth** *adj & n* пя́тый;
(fraction) пя́тая *sb*. **fiftieth** *adj
& n* пятидеся́тый. **fifty** *adj &
n* пятьдеся́т; *pl* (decade) пяти-
деся́тые го́ды (-до́в) *pl*.
fig *n* инжи́р.
fight *n* дра́ка; (battle) бой; (fig)
борьба́; *vt* боро́ться *impf*
c+*instr*; *vi* дра́ться *impf*; *vt &
i* (wage war) воева́ть *impf*
c+*instr*. **fighter** *n* бое́ц; (aeron)
истреби́тель *m*. **fighting** *n*
бой *m pl*.
figment *n* плод воображе́ния.
figurative *adj* перено́сный. **figure** *n* (form, body, person) фи-
гу́ра; (number) ци́фра; (diagram) рису́нок; (image) изо-
браже́ние; (of speech) оборо́т
ре́чи; ~**head** (naut) носово́е
украше́ние; (person) номи-
на́льная глава́; *vt* (think) пола-
га́ть *impf*; *vi* фигури́ровать
impf; ~ **out** вычисля́ть *impf*,
вы́числить *pf*.
filament *n* волокно́; (electr)
нить.
file[1] *n* (tool) напи́льник; *vt* под-

пи́ливать *impf*, подпили́ть *pf*.
file[2] *n* (folder) па́пка; (comput)
файл; *vt* подшива́ть *impf*,
подши́ть *pf*; (complaint)
пода́ть *pf*.
file[3] *n* (row) ряд; **in** (single) ~
гусько́м.
filigree *n* филигра́нь; *adj* фи-
лигра́нный.
fill *vt & i* (also ~ **up**) на-
полня́ть(ся) *impf*, напо́л-
нить(ся) *pf*; *vt* заполня́ть
impf, запо́лнить *pf*; (tooth)
пломбирова́ть *impf*, за~ *pf*;
(occupy) занима́ть *impf*, за-
ня́ть *pf*; (satiate) насыща́ть
impf, насы́тить *pf*; ~ **in** (vt)
заполня́ть *impf*, запо́лнить
pf; (vi) замеща́ть *impf*, за-
мести́ть *pf*.
fillet *n* (cul) филе́ *neut indecl*.
filling *n* (tooth) пло́мба; (cul)
начи́нка.
filly *n* кобы́лка.
film *n* (layer; phot) плёнка; (cin)
фильм; ~ **star** кинозвезда́; *vt*
снима́ть *impf*, снять *pf*.
filter *n* фильтр; *vt* фильтро-
ва́ть *impf*, про~ *pf*; ~
through, out проса́чиваться
impf, просочи́ться *pf*.
filth *n* грязь. **filthy** *adj* гря́з-
ный.
fin *n* плавни́к.
final *n* фина́л; *pl* выпускны́е
экза́мены *m pl*; *adj* после́д-
ний; (decisive) оконча́тель-
ный. **finale** *n* фина́л. **final-
ist** *n* финали́ст. **finality** *n*
зако́нченность. **finalize** *vt*
(complete) заверша́ть *impf*,
заверши́ть *pf*; (settle) ула́жи-
вать *impf*, ула́дить *pf*. **finally**
adv наконе́ц.
finance *n* фина́нсы (-сов) *pl*;
vt финанси́ровать *impf & pf*.
financial *adj* фина́нсовый.

financier n финанси́ст.

finch n see comb, e.g. bullfinch

find n нахо́дка; vt находи́ть impf, найти́ pf; (person) застава́ть impf, заста́ть pf; **~ out** узнава́ть impf, узна́ть pf; **~ fault with** придира́ться impf, придра́ться pf k+dat. **finding** n pl (of inquiry) вы́воды m pl.

fine¹ n (penalty) штраф; vt штрафова́ть impf, о~ pf.

fine² adj (weather) я́сный; (excellent) прекра́сный; (delicate) то́нкий; (of sand etc.) ме́лкий; **~ arts** изобрази́тельное иску́сства neut pl; adv хорошо́.

finery n наря́д. **finesse** n то́нкость.

finger n па́лец; **~-nail** но́готь; **~-print** отпеча́ток па́льца; **~-tip** ко́нчик па́льца; **have at (one's) ~s** знать impf как свои́ пять па́льцев; vt щу́пать impf, по~ pf.

finish n коне́ц; (polish) отде́лка; (sport) фи́ниш; vt & i конча́ть(ся) impf, ко́нчить(ся) pf; vt ока́нчивать impf, око́нчить pf.

finite adj коне́чный.

Finland n Финля́ндия. **Finn** n финн, фи́нка. **Finnish** adj фи́нский.

fir n ель, пи́хта.

fire vt (bake) обжига́ть impf, обже́чь pf; (excite) воспламеня́ть impf, воспламени́ть pf; (gun) стреля́ть impf из+gen (at в+acc, по+dat); (dismiss) увольня́ть impf, уво́лить pf; n ого́нь m; (grate) ками́н; (conflagration) пожа́р; (bonfire) костёр; (fervour) пыл; **be on ~** горе́ть impf; **catch ~** загора́ться impf, загоре́ться pf; **set ~ to, set on ~** поджига́ть impf, поджэ́чь pf; **~-alarm** пожа́рная трево́га; **~-arm(s)** огнестре́льное ору́жие; **~-brigade** пожа́рная кома́нда; **~-engine** пожа́рная маши́на; **~-escape** пожа́рная ле́стница; **~-extinguisher** огнетуши́тель m; **~-guard** ками́нная решётка; **~-man** пожа́рный sb; **~-place** ками́н; **~-side** ме́сто у ками́на; **~-station** пожа́рное депо́ neut indecl; **~-wood** дрова́ (-в) pl; **~-work** фейерве́рк. **firing** n (shooting) стрельба́.

firm¹ n (business) фи́рма.

firm² adj твёрдый. **firmness** n твёрдость.

first adj пе́рвый; n пе́рвый sb; adv сперва́, снача́ла; (for the ~ time) впервы́е; **in the ~ place** во-пе́рвых; **~ of all** пре́жде всего́; **at ~** сперва́ на пе́рвый взгляд; **~ aid** пе́рвая по́мощь; **~-class** первокла́сный; **~-hand** из пе́рвых рук; **~-rate** первокла́сный.

fiscal adj фина́нсовый.

fish n ры́ба; adj ры́бный; vi лови́ть impf ры́бу; **~ for** (compliments etc.) напра́шиваться impf, напроси́ться pf на+acc; **~ out** выта́скивать impf, вы́таскать pf. **fisherman** n рыба́к. **fishery** n ры́бный про́мысел. **fishing** n ры́бная ло́вля; **~-boat** рыболо́вное су́дно; **~-line** леса́; **~-rod** у́дочка. **fish-monger** n торго́вец ры́бой. **fishy** adj ры́бный; (dubious) подозри́тельный.

fissure n тре́щина.

fist n кула́к.

fit¹ n **be a good ~** хорошо́ сиде́ть impf; adj (suitable) подходя́щий, го́дный; (healthy)

fit здоро́вый; vt (be suitable) годи́ться impf +dat, на+acc, для+gen; vt & i (be the right size for)) подойти́ impf, подойти́ pf (+dat); (adjust) прила́живать impf, прила́дить pf (to k+dat); (be small enough for) входи́ть impf, войти́ pf в+acc; ~ out снабжа́ть impf, снабди́ть pf.

fit² n (attack) припа́док; (fig) поры́в; **fitful** adj поры́вистый.

fitter n монтёр. **fitting** n (of clothes) приме́рка; pl армату́ра; adj подходя́щий.

five adj & n пять; (number 5) пятёрка; **~-year plan** пятиле́тка.

fix n (dilemma) переде́лка; (drugs) уко́л; vt (repair) чини́ть impf, по~ pf; (settle) назнача́ть impf, назна́чить pf; (fasten) укрепля́ть impf, укрепи́ть pf; **~ up** (organize) организова́ть impf & pf; (install) устана́вливать impf, установи́ть pf. **fixation** n фикса́ция. **fixed** adj устано́вленный. **fixture** n (sport) предстоя́щее спорти́вное мероприя́тие; (fitting) приспособле́ние.

fizz, fizzle vi шипе́ть impf; **fizzle out** выдыха́ться impf, вы́дохнуться pf. **fizzy** adj шипу́чий.

flabbergasted adj ошеломлённый.

flabby adj дря́блый.

flag¹ n флаг, зна́мя neut; vt: **~ down** остана́вливать impf, останови́ть pf.

flag² vi (weaken) ослабева́ть impf, ослабе́ть pf.

flagon n кувши́н.

flagrant adj вопию́щий.

flagship n фла́гман.

flagstone n плита́.

flair n чутьё.

flake n (of; pl хло́пья (-ьев) pl; vi шелуши́ться impf. **flaky** adj сло́истый.

flamboyant adj цвети́стый.

flame n пла́мя neut, ого́нь m; vi пыла́ть impf.

flange n фла́нец.

flank n (of body) бок; (mil) фланг; vt быть сбо́ку +gen.

flannel n флане́ль; (for face) моча́лка для лица́.

flap n (board) откидна́я доска́; (pocket, tent) кла́пан; (panic) па́ника; vt взма́хивать impf, взмахну́ть pf +instr; vi развева́ться impf.

flare n вспы́шка; (signal) сигна́льная раке́та; vi вспы́хивать impf, вспы́хнуть pf; **~ up** (fire) возгора́ться impf, возгоре́ться pf; (fig) вспыли́ть pf.

flash n вспы́шка; **in a ~** ми́гом; vi сверка́ть impf, сверкну́ть pf. **flashback** n ретроспе́кция. **flashy** adj показно́й.

flask n фля́жка.

flat¹ n (dwelling) кварти́ра.

flat² n (mus) бемо́ль m; (tyre) спу́щенная ши́на; **on the ~** на пло́скости; adj пло́ский; **~-fish** ка́мбала. **flatly** adv наотре́з. **flatten** vt & i выра́внивать(ся) impf, вы́ровнять(ся) pf.

flatmate n сосе́д, **~ка** по кварти́ре.

flatter vt льстить impf, по~ pf +dat. **flattering** adj льсти́вый. **flattery** n лесть.

flaunt vt щеголя́ть impf, щегольну́ть pf +instr.

flautist n флейти́ст.

flavour n вкус; (fig) при́вкус; vt приправля́ть impf, припра́вить pf.

flaw n изъя́н.

flax n лён. **flaxen** adj (colour) соло́менный.

flea n блоха́; ~ **market** барахо́лка.

fleck n кра́пинка.

flee vi бежа́ть impf & pf (from от+gen); vt бежа́ть impf из+gen.

fleece n руно́; vt (fig) обдира́ть impf, ободра́ть pf. **fleecy** adj шерсти́стый.

fleet n флот; (vehicles) парк.

fleeting adj мимолётный.

flesh n (as opposed to mind) плоть; (meat) мя́со; in the ~ во плоти́. **fleshy** adj мяси́стый.

flex n шнур; vt сгиба́ть impf, согну́ть pf. **flexibility** n ги́бкость. **flexible** adj ги́бкий.

flick vt & i щёлкать impf, щёлкнуть pf (+instr); ~ **through** пролиста́ть pf.

flicker n мерца́ние; vi мерца́ть impf.

flier see **flyer**

flight[1] n (fleeing) бе́гство; **put (take) to** ~ обраща́ть(ся) impf, обрати́ть(ся) pf в бе́гство.

flight[2] n (flying) полёт; (trip) рейс; ~ **of stairs** ле́стничный марш. **flighty** adj ве́треный.

flimsy adj (fragile) непро́чный; (dress) лёгкий; (excuse) сла́бый.

flinch vi (recoil) отпря́дывать impf, отпря́нуть pf; (avoid) уклоня́ться impf, уклони́ться pf (from от+gen).

fling vt швыря́ть impf, швырну́ть pf; vi (also ~ o.s.) броса́ться impf, бро́ситься pf.

flint n креме́нь m.

flip vt щёлкать impf, щёлкнуть pf +instr.

flippant adj легкомы́сленный.

flipper n ласт.

flirt n коке́тка; vi флиртова́ть impf (with c+instr). **flirtation** n флирт.

flit vi порха́ть impf, порхну́ть pf.

float n поплаво́к; vi пла́вать indet, плыть det; vt (company) пуска́ть impf, пусти́ть pf в ход.

flock n (animals) ста́до; (birds) ста́я; vi стека́ться impf, сте́чься pf.

flog vt сечь impf, вы́~ pf.

flood n наводне́ние; (bibl) пото́п; (fig) пото́к; vi (river etc.) выступа́ть impf, вы́ступить pf из берего́в; vt за-топля́ть impf, затопи́ть pf. **floodgate** n шлюз. **floodlight** n проже́ктор.

floor n пол; (storey) эта́ж; ~**board** полови́ца; vt (confound) ста́вить impf, по~ pf в тупи́к.

flop vi (fall) плю́хаться impf, плю́хнуться pf; (fail) прова́ливаться impf, провали́ться pf.

flora n фло́ра. **floral** adj цвето́чный.

florid adj цвети́стый; (ruddy) румя́ный. **florist** n торго́вец цвета́ми.

flounce[1] vi броса́ться impf, бро́ситься pf.

flounce[2] n (of skirt) обо́рка.

flounder[1] n (fish) ка́мбала.

flounder[2] vi бара́хтаться impf.

flour n мука́.

flourish n (movement) разма́хивание (+instr); (of pen) ро́счерк; vi (thrive) процвета́ть *impf*; *vt* (*wave*) разма́хивать *impf*, размахну́ть *pf* +*instr*.

flout *vt* попира́ть *impf*, попра́ть *pf*.

flow *vi* течь *impf*; ли́ться *impf*; *n* тече́ние.

flower *n* цвето́к; ~**bed** клу́мба; ~**pot** цвето́чный горшо́к; *vi* цвести́ *impf*. **flowery** *adj* цвети́стый.

fluctuate *vi* колеба́ться *impf*, по~ *pf*. **fluctuation** *n* колеба́ние.

flue *n* дымохо́д.

fluent *adj* бе́глый. **fluently** *adv* свобо́дно.

fluff *n* пух. **fluffy** *adj* пуши́стый.

fluid *n* жи́дкость; *adj* жи́дкий.

fluke *n* случа́йная уда́ча.

fluorescent *adj* флюоресце́нтный.

fluoride *n* фтори́д.

flurry *n* (*squall*) шквал; (*fig*) волна́.

flush *n* (*redness*) румя́нец; *vi* (*redden*) красне́ть *impf*, по~ *pf*; *vi* спуска́ть *impf*, спусти́ть *pf* во́ду в+*acc*.

flustered *adj* сконфу́женный.

flute *n* фле́йта.

flutter *vi* (*flit*) порха́ть *impf*, порхну́ть *pf*; (*wave*) развева́ться *impf*.

flux *n*: **in a state of ~** в состоя́нии измене́ния.

fly[1] *n* (*insect*) му́ха.

fly[2] *vi* лета́ть *indet*, лете́ть *det*, по~ *pf*; (*flag*) развева́ться *impf*; (*hasten*) нести́сь *impf*, по~ *pf*; *vt* (*aircraft*) управля́ть *impf* +*instr*; (*transport*) перевози́ть *impf*, перевезти́ *pf* (самолётом) *pf*; (*flag*) поднима́ть *impf*, подня́ть *pf*.

flyer, flier *n* лётчик. **flying** *n* полёт.

foal *n* (*horse*) жеребёнок.

foam *n* пе́на; ~ **plastic** пенопла́ст; ~ **rubber** пенорези́на; *vi* пе́ниться *impf*, вс~ *pf*. **foamy** *adj* пе́нистый.

focal *adj* фо́кусный. **focus** *n* фо́кус; (*fig*) центр; *vt* фокуси́ровать *impf*, с~ *pf*; (*concentrate*) сосредото́чивать *impf*, сосредото́чить *pf*.

fodder *n* корм.

foe *n* враг.

foetus *n* заро́дыш.

fog *n* тума́н. **foggy** *adj* тума́нный.

foible *n* сла́бость.

foil[1] *n* (*metal*) фольга́; (*contrast*) контра́ст.

foil[2] *vt* (*thwart*) расстра́ивать *impf*, расстро́ить *pf*.

foil[3] *n* (*sword*) рапи́ра.

foist *vt* навя́зывать *impf*, навяза́ть *pf* (**on** +*dat*).

fold[1] *n* (*sheep-*) овча́рня.

fold[2] *n* скла́дка, сгиб; *vt* скла́дывать *impf*, сложи́ть *pf*. **folder** *n* па́пка. **folding** *adj* складно́й.

foliage *n* листва́.

folk *n* наро́д, лю́ди *pl*; *pl* (*relatives*) родня́ *collect*; *attrib* наро́дный. **folklore** *n* фолькло́р.

follow *vt* сле́довать *impf*, по~ *pf* +*dat*, за+*instr*; (*walk behind*) идти́ *det* за+*instr*; (*fig*) следи́ть *impf* за+*instr*. **follower** *n* после́дователь *m*. **following** *adj* сле́дующий.

folly *n* глу́пость.

fond *adj* не́жный; **be ~ of** люби́ть *impf* +*acc*.

fondle *vt* ласка́ть *impf*.

fondness *n* любо́вь.

font *n* (*eccl*) купе́ль.

food *n* пи́ща, еда́. **foodstuff** *n* пищево́й проду́кт.

fool *n* дура́к; *vt* дура́чить

impf, о~ *pf*; *vi*: ~ about дура́читься *impf*. **foolhardy** *adj* безрассу́дно хра́брый. **foolish** *adj* глу́пый. **foolishness** *n* глу́пость. **foolproof** *adj* абсолю́тно надёжный.

foot *n* нога́; (*measure*) фут; (*of hill etc.*) подно́жие; **on** ~ пешко́м; **put one's ~ in it** сесть *pf* в лу́жу. **football** *n* футбо́л; *attrib* футбо́льный. **footballer** *n* футболи́ст. **foothills** *n pl* предго́рье. **footing** *n* (*fig*) ба́зис; **lose one's** ~ оступи́ться *pf*; **on an equal** ~ на ра́вной ноге́. **footlights** *n pl* ра́мпа. **footman** *n* лаке́й. **footnote** *n* сно́ска. **footpath** *n* (*pavement*) тропи́нка; (*pavement*) тротуа́р. **footprint** *n* след. **footstep** *n* (*sound*) шаг; (*footprint*) след. **footwear** *n* о́бувь.

for *prep* (*of time*) в тече́ние +*gen*, на+*acc*; (*of purpose*) для+*gen*, за+*acc*, +*instr*; (*price*) за+*acc*; (*on account of*) из-за +*gen*; (*in place of*) вме́сто+*gen*; ~ **the sake of** ра́ди+*gen*; **as** ~ что каса́ется+*gen*; *conj* так как.

forage *n* фура́ж; *vi*: ~ **for** разы́скивать *impf*.

foray *n* набе́г.

forbearance *n* возде́ржанность.

forbid *vt* запреща́ть *impf*, запрети́ть *pf* (+dat (*person*) & *acc* (*thing*)). **forbidding** *adj* гро́зный.

force *n* (*strength, validity*) си́ла; (*meaning*) смысл; (*armed* ~) вооружённые си́лы *f pl*; **by** ~ си́лой; *vt* (*compel*) заставля́ть *impf*, заста́вить *pf*; (*lock etc.*) взла́мывать *impf*, взлома́ть *pf*. **forceful** *adj* си́льный; (*speech*) убеди-

тельный. **forcible** *adj* наси́льственный.

forceps *n* щипцы́ (-цо́в) *pl*.

ford *n* брод; *vt* переходи́ть *impf*, перейти́ *pf* вброд+*acc*.

fore *n*: **come to the** ~ выдвига́ться *impf*, вы́двинуться *pf* на пере́дний пла́н.

forearm *n* предпле́чье. **foreboding** *n* предчу́вствие. **forecast** *n* предсказа́ние; (*of weather*) прогно́з; *vt* предска́зывать *impf*, предсказа́ть *pf*. **forecourt** *n* пере́дний двор. **forefather** *n* пре́док. **forefinger** *n* указа́тельный па́лец. **forefront** *n* (*foreground*) пере́дний план; (*leading position*) аванга́рд. **foregone** *adj*: ~ **conclusion** предрешённый исхо́д. **foreground** *n* пере́дний план. **forehead** *n* лоб.

foreign *adj* (*from abroad*) иностра́нный; (*alien*) чужда́й; (*external*) вне́шний; ~ **body** иноро́дное те́ло; ~ **currency** валю́та. **foreigner** *n* иностра́нец, -нка.

foreman *n* ма́стер.

foremost *adj* выдаю́щийся; **first and** ~ пре́жде всего́.

forename *n* и́мя.

forensic *adj* суде́бный.

forerunner *n* предве́стник. **foresee** *vt* предви́деть *impf*. **foreshadow** *vt* предвеща́ть *impf*. **foresight** *n* предви́дение; (*caution*) предусмотри́тельность.

forest *n* лес.

forestall *vt* предупрежда́ть *impf*, предупреди́ть *pf*. **forester** *n* лесни́чий *sb*. **forestry** *n* лесово́дство.

foretaste *n* предвкуше́ние; *vt* предвкуша́ть *impf*,

предвкуси́ть pf. **foretell** vt предска́зывать impf, предсказа́ть pf. **forethought** n предусмотри́тельность. **forewarn** vt предостерега́ть impf, предостере́чь pf. **foreword** n предисло́вие.

forfeit n (in game) фант; vt лиша́ться impf, лиши́ться pf +gen.

forge[1] n (smithy) ку́зница; (furnace) горн; vt кова́ть impf, вы́~ pf; (fabricate) подде́лывать impf, подде́лать pf.

forge[2] vi: ~ ahead продвига́ться impf, продви́нуться pf вперёд.

forger n фальшивомоне́тчик. **forgery** n подде́лка.

forget vt забыва́ть impf, забы́ть pf. **forgetful** adj забы́вчивый.

forgive vt проща́ть impf, прости́ть pf. **forgiveness** n проще́ние.

forgo vt возде́рживаться impf, воздержа́ться pf от+gen.

fork n (eating) ви́лка; (digging) ви́лы (-л) pl; (in road) разветвле́ние; vi (road) разветвля́ться impf, разветви́ться pf.

forlorn adj жа́лкий.

form n (shape; kind) фо́рма; (class) класс; (document) анке́та; vt (make, create) образо́вывать impf, образова́ть pf; (develop; make up) составля́ть impf, соста́вить pf; vi образо́вываться impf, образова́ться pf. **formal** adj форма́льный; (official) официа́льный. **formality** n форма́льность. **format** n форма́т. **formation** n образова́ние. **formative** adj: ~ years молоды́е го́ды (-до́в) m pl.

former adj (earlier) пре́жний; (ex) бы́вший; the ~ (of two) пе́рвый. **formerly** adv пре́жде.

formidable adj (dread) гро́зный; (arduous) тру́дный.

formless adj бесфо́рменный.

formula n фо́рмула. **formulate** vt формули́ровать impf, с~ pf. **formulation** n формулиро́вка.

forsake vt (desert) покида́ть impf, поки́нуть pf; (renounce) отка́зываться impf, отказа́ться pf от+gen.

fort n форт.

forth adv вперёд, да́льше; **back and** ~ взад и вперёд; **and so** ~ и так да́лее. **forthcoming** adj предстоя́щий; **be** ~ (available) поступа́ть impf, поступи́ть pf. **forthwith** adv неме́дленно.

fortieth adj & n сороково́й.

fortification n укрепле́ние. **fortify** vt укрепля́ть impf, укрепи́ть pf; (fig) подкрепля́ть impf, подкрепи́ть pf. **fortitude** n сто́йкость.

fortnight n две неде́ли f pl. **fortnightly** adj двухнеде́льный; adv раз в две неде́ли.

fortress n кре́пость.

fortuitous adj случа́йный.

fortunate adj счастли́вый. **fortunately** adv к сча́стью. **fortune** n (destiny) судьба́; (good ~) сча́стье; (wealth) состоя́ние.

forty adj & n со́рок; pl (decade) сороковы́е го́ды (-до́в) m pl.

forward adj пере́дний; (presumptuous) развя́зный; n (sport) напада́ющий sb; adv вперёд; vt (letter) пересыла́ть impf, пересла́ть pf.

fossil n ископа́емое sb; adj

ископа́емый. **fossilized** adj
ископа́емый.

foster vt (child) приюти́ть pf;
(idea) выка́шивать impf, вы́-
носить pf; (create) создава́ть
impf, созда́ть pf; (cherish) ле-
ле́ять impf; ~**child** приёмыш.

foul adj (dirty) гря́зный; (repulsive) отврати́тельный;
(obscene) непристо́йный; n
(sport) наруше́ние пра́вил;
vt (dirty) па́чкать impf, за-
ис~ pf; (entangle) запу́ты-
вать impf, запу́тать pf.

found vt осно́вывать impf,
основа́ть pf.

foundation n (of building)
фунда́мент; (basis) осно́ва;
(institution) учрежде́ние;
(fund) фонд. **founder**¹ n ос-
нова́тель m.

founder² vi (naut, fig) тону́ть
impf, по~ pf.

foundry n лите́йная sb.

fountain n фонта́н; ~**-pen**
автору́чка.

four adj & n четы́ре; (number
4) четвёрка; on all ~s на чет-
вере́ньках. **fourteen** adj & n
четы́рнадцать. **fourteenth** adj
& n четы́рнадцатый. **fourth**
adj & n четвёртый; (quarter)
че́тверть.

fowl n (domestic) дома́шняя
пти́ца; (wild) дичь indecl.

fox n лиса́, лиси́ца; vt озада́-
чивать impf, озада́чить pf.

foyer n фойе́ neut indecl.

fraction n (math) дробь; (portion) части́ца.

fractious adj раздражи́тель-
ный.

fracture n перело́м; vt & i
лома́ть(ся) impf, с~ pf.

fragile adj ло́мкий.

fragment n обло́мок; (of conversation) отры́вок; (of writ-

ing) фрагме́нт. **fragmentary**
adj отры́вочный.

fragrance n арома́т. **fragrant**
adj арома́тный, души́стый.

frail adj хру́пкий.

frame n о́стов; (build) тело-
сложе́ние; (picture) ра́ма;
(cin) кадр; ~ **of mind** настро-
е́ние; vt (devise) создава́ть
impf, созда́ть pf; (formulate)
формули́ровать impf, с~ pf;
(picture) вставля́ть impf,
вста́вить pf в ра́му; (incriminate) фабрикова́ть impf, с~
pf обвине́ние про́тив+gen.

framework n о́стов; (fig)
ра́мки f pl.

franc n франк.

France n Фра́нция.

franchise n (comm) приви-
ле́гия; (polit) пра́во го́лоса.

frank¹ adj открове́нный.

frank² vt (letter) франки́ро-
вать impf & pf.

frantic adj нейстовый.

fraternal adj бра́тский. **fraternity** n бра́тство.

fraud n обма́н; (person) об-
ма́нщик. **fraudulent** adj об-
ма́нный.

fraught adj: ~ **with** чрева́тый
+instr.

fray¹ vt & i обтрёпывать(ся)
impf, обтрепа́ть(ся) pf.

fray² n дра́ка.

freak n уро́д; attrib необы́ч-
ный.

freckle n весну́шка. **freckled**
adj весну́шчатый.

free adj свобо́дный; (gratis)
беспла́тный; ~ **kick** штраф-
но́й уда́р; ~ **speech** свобо́да
сло́ва; vt освобожда́ть impf,
освободи́ть pf. **freedom** n
свобо́да. **freehold** n неогра-
ни́ченное пра́во со́бственно-
сти на недви́жимость.

freelance *adj* внешта́тный. **Freemason** *n* франкмасо́н.

freeze *vi* замерза́ть *impf*, мёрзнуть *impf*, замёрзнуть *pf*; *vt* замора́живать *impf*, заморо́зить *pf*. **freezer** *n* морози́льник; (*compartment*) морози́лка. **freezing** *adj* моро́зный; **below** ~ ни́же нуля́.

freight *n* фрахт. **freighter** *n* (*ship*) грузово́е су́дно.

French *adj* францу́зский; ~ **bean** фасо́ль; ~ **horn** валто́рна; ~ **windows** двуство́рчатое окно́ до́ полу. **Frenchman** *n* францу́з. **Frenchwoman** *n* францу́женка.

frenetic *adj* нейсто́вый.

frenzied *adj* нейсто́вый. **frenzy** *n* нейсто́вство.

frequency *n* частота́. **frequent** *adj* ча́стый; *vt* ча́сто посеща́ть *impf*.

fresco *n* фре́ска.

fresh *adj* све́жий; (*new*) но́вый; ~ **water** пре́сная вода́. **freshen** *vt* освежа́ть *impf*, освежи́ть *pf*; *vi* свеже́ть *impf*, по~ *pf*. **freshly** *adv* свежо́; (*recently*) неда́вно. **freshness** *n* све́жесть. **freshwater** *adj* пресново́дный.

fret¹ *vi* му́читься *impf*. **fretful** *adj* раздражи́тельный.

fret² *n* (*mus*) лад.

fretsaw *n* ло́бзик.

friar *n* мона́х.

friction *n* тре́ние; (*fig*) тре́ния *neut pl*.

Friday *n* пя́тница.

fridge *n* холоди́льник.

fried *adj*: ~ **egg** яи́чница.

friend *n* друг, подру́га; прия́тель *m*, ~ница. **friendly** *adj* дру́жеский. **friendship** *n* дру́жба.

frieze *n* фриз.

frigate *n* фрега́т.

fright *n* испу́г. **frighten** *vt* пуга́ть *impf*, ис~, на~ *pf*. **frightful** *adj* стра́шный.

frigid *adj* холо́дный.

frill *n* обо́рка.

fringe *n* бахрома́; (*of hair*) чёлка; (*edge*) край.

frisk *vi* (*frolic*) резви́ться *impf*; *vt* (*search*) шмона́ть *impf*. **frisky** *adj* ре́звый.

fritter *vt*: ~ **away** растра́чивать *impf*, растра́тить *pf*.

frivolity *n* легкомы́сленность. **frivolous** *adj* легкомы́сленный.

fro *adv*: **to and** ~ взад и вперёд.

frock *n* пла́тье.

frog *n* лягу́шка.

frolic *vi* резви́ться *impf*.

from *prep* от+*gen*; (~ **off**, **down** ~ *in time*) с+*gen*; (*out of*) из+*gen*; (*according to*) по+*dat*; (*because of*) из-за+*gen*; **above** ~ све́рху; ~ **abroad** из-за грани́цы; ~ **afar** и́здали; ~ **among** из числа́+*gen*; ~ **behind** из-за+*gen*; ~ **day to day** изо дня́ в день; ~ **everywhere** отовсю́ду; ~ **here** отсю́да; ~ **memory** по па́мяти; ~ **now on** отны́не; ~ **there** отту́да; ~ **time to time** вре́мя от вре́мени; ~ **under** из-под+*gen*.

front *n* фаса́д; (*mil*) фронт; **in** ~ **of** впереди́+*gen*, пе́ред+*instr*; *adj* пере́дний; (*first*) пе́рвый.

frontier *n* грани́ца.

frost *n* моро́з; ~**-bite** отмороже́ние; ~**-bitten** отморо́женный. **frosted** *adj*: ~ **glass** ма́товое стекло́. **frosty** *adj* моро́зный; (*fig*) ледяно́й.

froth *n* пе́на; *vi* пе́ниться *impf*.

вс~ *pf.* **frothy** *adj* пе́нистый.

frown *n* хму́рый взгляд; *vi* хму́риться *impf*, на~ *pf.*

frugal *adj* (*careful*) бережли́вый; (*scanty*) ску́дный.

fruit *n* плод; *collect* фру́кты *m pl*; *adj* фрукто́вый. **fruitful** *adj* плодотво́рный. **fruition** *n*: come to ~ осуществи́ться *pf.* **fruitless** *adj* беспло́дный.

frustrate *vt* фрустри́ровать *impf & pf.* **frustrating** *adj* фрустри́рующий. **frustration** *n* фрустра́ция.

fry[1] *n* small ~ мелюзга́.

fry[2] *vt & i* жа́рить(ся) *impf*, за~, из~ *pf.* **frying-pan** *n* сковорода́.

fuel *n* то́пливо.

fugitive *n* бегле́ц.

fulcrum *n* то́чка опо́ры.

fulfil *vt* (*perform*) выполня́ть *impf*, вы́полнить *pf*; (*dreams*) осуществля́ть *impf*, осуществи́ть *pf.* **fulfilling** *adj* удовлетворя́ющий. **fulfilment** *n* выполне́ние; осуществле́ние; удовлетворе́ние.

full *adj* по́лный (of +*gen, instr*); (*replete*) сы́тый; ~ stop то́чка; ~ time: I work ~ time я рабо́таю на по́лную ста́вку; *n*: in ~ по́лностью; to the ~ в по́лной ме́ре. **fullness** *n* полнота́. **fully** *adv* вполне́.

fulsome *adj* чрезме́рный.

fumble *vi*: ~ for нащу́пывать *impf* +*acc*; ~ with вози́ться *impf* c+*instr*.

fume *vi* (*with anger*) кипе́ть *impf*, вс~ *pf* гне́вом. **fumes** *n* испаре́ния *neut pl.* **fumigate** *vt* оку́ривать *impf*, окури́ть *pf.*

fun *n* заба́ва; it was ~ бы́ло

заба́вно; have ~ забавля́ться *impf*; make ~ of смея́ться *impf*, по~ *pf* над+*instr.*

function *n* фу́нкция; (*event*) ве́чер; *vi* функциони́ровать *impf*; де́йствовать *impf.* **functional** *adj* функциона́льный. **functionary** *n* чино́вник.

fund *n* фонд; (*store*) запа́с.

fundamental *adj* основно́й; *n*: *pl* осно́вы *f pl.*

funeral *n* по́хороны (-о́н, -она́м) *pl.*

fungus *n* гриб.

funnel *n* воро́нка; (*chimney*) дымова́я труба́.

funny *adj* смешно́й; (*odd*) стра́нный.

fur *n* мех; ~ coat шу́ба.

furious *adj* бе́шеный.

furnace *n* горн, печь.

furnish *vt* (*provide*) снабжа́ть *impf*, снабди́ть *pf* (with *c*+*instr*); (*house*) обставля́ть *impf*, обста́вить *pf.* **furniture** *n* ме́бель.

furrow *n* борозда́.

furry *adj* пуши́стый.

further, farther *comp adj* да́льнейший; *adv* да́льше; *vt* продвига́ть *impf*, продви́нуть *pf.* **furthermore** *adv* к тому́ же. **furthest, farthest** *superl adj* са́мый да́льний.

furtive *adj* скры́тый, та́йный.

fury *n* я́рость.

fuse[1] *n & i* (of metal) сплавля́ть(ся) *impf*, спла́вить(ся) *impf.*

fuse[2] *n* (in bomb) запа́л; (detonating device) взрыва́тель *m.*

fuse[3] *n* (electr) про́бка, ~ перегора́ть *impf*, перегоре́ть *pf.*

fuselage *n* фюзеля́ж.

fusion *n* пла́вка, слия́ние.

fuss *n* суета́; *vi* суети́ться

impf. **fussy** *adj* суетли́вый; *(fastidious)* разбо́рчивый.

futile *adj* тще́тный. **futility** *n* тще́тность.

future *n* бу́дущее *sb*; *(gram)* бу́дущее вре́мя *neut*; *adj* бу́дущий. **futuristic** *adj* футуристи́ческий.

fuzzy *adj (hair)* пуши́стый; *(blurred)* расплы́вчатый.

G

gabble *vi* тарато́рить *impf.*

gable *n* щипе́ц.

gad *vi*: ~ **about** шата́ться *impf.*

gadget *n* приспособле́ние.

gaffe *n* опло́шность.

gag *n* кляп; *vt* засо́вывать *impf*, засу́нуть *pf* кляп +в рот+*dat.*

gaiety *n* весёлость. **gaily** *adv* ве́село.

gain *n* при́быль; *pl* дохо́ды *m pl*; *(increase)* приро́ст; *vt (acquire)* получа́ть *impf*, получи́ть *pf*; ~ **on** нагоня́ть *impf*, нагна́ть *pf.*

gait *n* похо́дка.

gala *n* пра́зднество; *adj* пра́здничный.

galaxy *n* гала́ктика; *(fig)* плея́да.

gale *n* бу́ря, шторм.

gall¹ *n (bile)* жёлчь; *(cheek)* на́глость; ~**bladder** жёлчный пузы́рь *m.*

gall² *vt (vex)* раздража́ть *impf*, раздражи́ть *pf.*

gallant *adj (brave)* хра́брый; *(courtly)* гала́нтный. **gallantry** *n* хра́брость; гала́нтность.

gallery *n* галере́я.

galley *n (ship)* гале́ра; *(kitchen)* ка́мбуз.

gallon *n* галло́н.

gallop *n* гало́п; *vi* галопи́ровать *impf.*

gallows *n pl* ви́селица.

gallstone *n* жёлчный ка́мень *m.*

galore *adv* в изоби́лии.

galvanize *vt* гальванизи́ровать *impf & pf.*

gambit *n* гамби́т.

gamble *n (undertaking)* риско́ванное предприя́тие; *vi* игра́ть *impf* в аза́ртные и́гры; *(fig)* рискова́ть *impf* (**with** +*instr*); ~ **away** прои́грывать *impf*, проигра́ть *pf.* **gambler** *n* игро́к. **gambling** *n* аза́ртные и́гры *f pl.*

game *n* игра́; *(single ~)* па́ртия; *(collect, animals)* дичь; *adj (ready)* гото́вый. **gamekeeper** *n* лесни́к.

gammon *n* о́корок.

gamut *n* га́мма.

gang *n* ба́нда; *(workmen)* брига́да.

gangrene *n* гангре́на.

gangster *n* га́нгстер.

gangway *n (passage)* прохо́д; *(naut)* схо́дни (-ней) *pl.*

gaol *n* тюрьма́; *vt* заключа́ть *impf*, заключи́ть *pf* в тюрьму́. **gaoler** *n* тюре́мщик.

gap *n (empty space; deficiency)* пробе́л; *(in wall etc.)* брешь; *(fig)* разры́в.

gape *vi (person)* зева́ть *impf (at* на+*acc)*; *(chasm)* зия́ть *impf.*

garage *n* гара́ж.

garb *n* одея́ние.

garbage *n* му́сор.

garbled *adj* искажённый.

garden *n* сад; *attrib* садо́вый. **gardener** *n* садо́вник. **gardening** *n* садово́дство.

gargle *vi* полоска́ть

про~ *pf* гóрло.

gargoyle *n* горгýлья.

garish *adj* кричáщий.

garland *n* гирля́нда.

garlic *n* чеснóк.

garment *n* предмéт одéжды.

garnish *n*; *vt* гарни́ровать *impf* & *pf*.

garret *n* мансáрда.

garrison *n* гарнизóн.

garrulous *adj* болтли́вый.

gas *n* газ; *attrib* гáзовый; *vt* отравля́ть *impf*, отрави́ть *pf* гáзом. **gaseous** *adj* газообрáзный.

gash *n* порéз; *vt* порéзать *pf*.

gasket *n* проклáдка.

gasp *vi* задыхáться *impf*, задохнýться *pf*.

gastric *adj* желýдочный.

gate *n* (*large*) ворóта (-т) *pl*; (*small*) калúтка. **gateway** *n* (*gate*) ворóта (-т) *pl*; (*entrance*) вход.

gather *vt* & *i* собирáть(ся) *impf*, собрáть(ся) *pf*; *vt* заключáть *impf*, заключи́ть *pf*. **gathering** *n* (*assembly*) собрáние.

gaudy *adj* кричáщий.

gauge *n* (*measure*) мéра; (*instrument*) калúбр, измери́тельный прибóр; (*rly*) колея́; (*criterion*) критéрий; *vt* измеря́ть *impf*, измéрить *pf*; (*estimate*) оцéнивать *impf*, оцени́ть *pf*.

gaunt *adj* тóщий.

gauntlet *n* рукави́ца.

gauze *n* мáрля.

gay *adj* весёлый; (*bright*) пёстрый; (*homosexual*) гомосексуáльный.

gaze *n* пристáльный взгляд; *vt* пристáльно глядéть *impf* (**at** на+*acc*).

gazelle *n* газéль.

GCSE *abbr* (*of General Certificate of Secondary Education*) аттестáт о срéднем образовáнии.

gear *n* (*equipment*) принадлéжности *f pl*; (*in car*) скóрость; ~ **lever** рычáг; *vt* приспособля́ть *impf*, приспосóбить *pf* (**to** к+*dat*). **gearbox** *n* корóбка передáч.

gel *n* космети́ческое желé *neut indecl*. **gelatine** *n* желати́н.

gelding *n* мéрин.

gelignite *n* гелигни́т.

gem *n* драгоцéнный кáмень *m*. **Gemini** *n* Близнецы́ *m pl*.

gender *n* род.

gene *n* ген.

genealogy *n* генеалóгия.

general *n* генерáл; *adj* óбщий; (*nationwide*) всеóбщий; **in** ~ вообщé. **generalization** *n* обобщéние. **generalize** *vi* обобщáть *impf*, обобщи́ть *pf*. **generally** *adv* (*usually*) обы́чно; (*in general*) вообщé. **generate** *vt* порождáть *impf*, породи́ть *pf*. **generation** *n* (*in descent*) поколéние. **generator** *n* генерáтор. **generic** *adj* родовóй; (*general*) óбщий.

generosity *n* (*magnanimity*) великодýшие; (*munificence*) щéдрость. **generous** *adj* великодýшный; щéдрый.

genesis *n* происхождéние; (**G**~) Кни́га Бытия́.

genetic *adj* генети́ческий. **genetics** *n* генéтика.

genial *adj* (*of person*) добродýшный.

genital *adj* половóй. **genitals** *n pl* половы́е óрганы *m pl*.

genitive *adj* (*n*) роди́тельный (падéж).

genius n (*person*) ге́ний; (*ability*) гениа́льность.

genocíde n геноци́д.

genre n жанр.

genteel adj благовоспи́танный.

gentile adj невре́йский; n невре́й, ~ка.

gentility n благовоспи́танность.

gentle adj (*mild*) мя́гкий; (*quiet*) ти́хий; (*light*) лёгкий.

gentleman n джентльме́н.

gentleness n мя́гкость. **gents** n pl мужска́я убо́рная sb.

genuine adj (*authentic*) по́длинный; (*sincere*) и́скренний.

genus n род.

geographical adj географи́ческий. **geography** n геогра́фия. **geological** adj геологи́ческий. **geologist** n гео́лог. **geology** n геоло́гия. **geometric(al)** adj геометри́ческий. **geometry** n геоме́трия.

Georgia n Гру́зия. **Georgian** n грузи́н, ~ка; adj грузи́нский.

geranium n гера́нь.

geriatric adj гериатри́ческий.

germ m микро́б.

German n не́мец, не́мка; adj неме́цкий; ~ **measles** красну́ха.

germane adj уме́стный.

Germanic adj герма́нский.

Germany n Герма́ния.

germinate vi прораста́ть impf, прорасти́ pf.

gesticulate vi жестикули́ровать impf. **gesture** n жест.

get vt (*obtain*) достава́ть impf, доста́ть pf; (*receive*) получа́ть impf, получи́ть pf; (*understand*) понима́ть impf, поня́ть pf; (*disease*) заража́ться impf, зарази́ться pf +instr;

(*induce*) угова́ривать impf, уговори́ть pf (**to do** +inf); (*fetch*) приноси́ть impf, принести́ pf, vi (*become*) станови́ться impf, стать pf +instr; **have got** (*have*) име́ть impf; **have got to** быть до́лжен (-жна́) +inf; ~ **about** (*spread*) распространя́ться impf, распространи́ться pf; (*move around*) передвига́ться impf; (*travel*) разъезжа́ть impf; ~ **at** (*mean*) хоте́ть impf сказа́ть; ~ **away** (*slip off*) ускольза́ть impf, ускользну́ть pf; (*escape*) убега́ть impf, убежа́ть pf; (*leave*) уезжа́ть impf, уе́хать pf; ~ **away with** избега́ть impf, избежа́ть pf отве́тственности за+acc; ~ **back** (*recover*) получа́ть impf, получи́ть pf обра́тно; (*return*) возвраща́ться impf, верну́ться pf; ~ **by** (*manage*) справля́ться impf, спра́виться pf; ~ **down** сходи́ть impf, сойти́ pf; ~ **down to** принима́ться impf, приня́ться pf за+acc; ~ **off** слеза́ть impf, слезть pf c+gen; ~ **on** сади́ться impf, сесть pf в, на, +acc; (*prosper*) преуспева́ть impf; ~ **on with** (*person*) ужива́ться impf, ужи́ться pf c+instr; ~ **out of** (*avoid*) избавля́ться impf, изба́виться pf от+gen; (*car*) выходи́ть impf, вы́йти pf из+gen; ~ **round to** успева́ть impf, успе́ть pf; ~ **to** (*reach*) достига́ть impf, дости́гнуть & дости́чь pf +gen; ~ **up** (*from bed*) встава́ть impf, встать pf.

geyser n (*spring*) ге́йзер; (*water-heater*) коло́нка.

ghastly adj ужа́сный.

gherkin n огурец.
ghetto n гетто neut indecl.
ghost n привидение. **ghostly** adj призрачный.
giant n гигант; adj гигантский.
gibberish n тарабарщина.
gibbet n виселица.
gibe n насмешка; vi насмехаться (at над+instr).
giblets n pl потроха (-хов) pl.
giddiness n головокружение. **giddy** predic: **I feel** ~ у меня кружится голова.
gift n (present) подарок; (donation; ability) дар. **gifted** adj одарённый.
gig n (theat) выступление.
gigantic adj гигантский.
giggle n хихиканье; vi хихикать impf, хихикнуть pf.
gild vt золотить impf, вы~, по~ pf.
gill n (of fish) жабра.
gilt n позолота; adj золочёный.
gimmick n трюк.
gin n (spirit) джин.
ginger n имбирь m; adj (colour) рыжий.
gingerly adv осторожно.
gipsy n цыган, ~ка.
giraffe n жираф.
girder n балка. **girdle** n пояс.
girl n (child) девочка; (young woman) девушка. **girlfriend** n подруга. **girlish** adj девичий.
girth n обхват; (on saddle) подпруга.
gist n суть.
give vt давать impf, дать pf; ~ **away** выдавать impf, выдать pf; ~ **back** возвращать impf, возвратить pf; ~ **in** (yield, vi) уступать impf, уступить pf (**to** +dat); (hand in, vt) вручать impf, вручить pf; ~ **out** (emit) издавать

impf, издать pf; (distribute) раздавать impf, раздать pf; ~ **up** отказываться impf, отказаться pf от+gen; (habit etc.) бросать impf, бросить pf; ~ **o.s. up** сдаваться impf, сдаться pf; **given** predic (inclined) склонен (-онна, -онно) (**to** к+dat).
glacier n ледник.
glad adj радостный; predic рад. **gladden** vt радовать impf, об~ pf.
glade n поляна.
gladly adv охотно.
glamorous adj яркий; (attractive) привлекательный.
glamour n яркость; привлекательность.
glance n (look) беглый взгляд; vi: ~ **at** взглядывать impf, взглянуть pf на+acc.
gland n железа. **glandular** adj железистый.
glare n (light) ослепительный блеск; (look) свирепый взгляд; vi свирепо смотреть impf (at на+acc). **glaring** adj (dazzling) ослепительный; (mistake) грубый.
glasnost n гласность.
glass n (substance) стекло; (drinking vessel) стакан; (wine ~) рюмка; (mirror) зеркало; pl (spectacles) очки (-ков) pl; attrib стеклянный. **glassy** adj (look) тусклый.
glaze n глазурь; vt (with glass) застеклять impf, застеклить pf; (pottery) глазуровать impf & pf; (cul) глазировать impf & pf. **glazier** n стекольщик.
gleam n проблеск; vi светиться impf.
glean vt собирать impf, собрать pf по крупицам.

glee *n* весе́лье. **gleeful** *adj* лику́ющий.

glib *adj* бо́йкий.

glide *vi* скользи́ть *impf*; (*aeron*) плани́ровать *impf*, с~ *pf*. **glider** *n* планёр.

glimmer *n* мерца́ние; *vi* мерца́ть *impf*.

glimpse *n* мелько́м ви́деть *impf*, y~ *pf*.

glint *n* блеск; *vi* блесте́ть *impf*.

glisten, glitter *vi* блесте́ть *impf*.

gloat *vi* злора́дствовать *impf*.

global *adj* (*world-wide*) мирово́й; (*total*) всео́бщий. **globe** *n* (*sphere*) шар; (*the earth*) земно́й шар; (*chart*) гло́бус. **globule** *n* ша́рик.

gloom *n* мрак. **gloomy** *adj* мра́чный.

glorify *vt* прославля́ть *impf*, просла́вить *pf*. **glorious** *adj* сла́вный; (*splendid*) великоле́пный. **glory** *n* сла́ва; *vi* торжествова́ть *impf*.

gloss *n* лоск; *vi*: ~ **over** зама́зывать *impf*, зама́зать *pf*. **glossary** *n* глосса́рий.

glove *n* перча́тка.

glow *n* за́рево; (*of cheeks*) румя́нец; *vi* (*incandesce*) накаля́ться *impf*, накали́ться *pf*; (*shine*) сия́ть *impf*.

glucose *n* глюко́за.

glue *n* клей; *vt* прикле́ивать *impf*, прикле́ить *pf* (**to** к+*dat*).

glum *adj* угрю́мый.

glut *n* избы́ток.

glutton *n* обжо́ра *m* & *f*. **gluttonous** *adj* обжо́рливый. **gluttony** *n* обжо́рство.

gnarled *adj* (*hands*) шишкова́тый; (*tree*) сучкова́тый.

gnash *vt* скрежета́ть *impf* +*instr*.

gnat *n* кома́р.

gnaw *vt* грызть *impf*.

gnome *n* гном.

go *n* (*energy*) эне́ргия; (*attempt*) попы́тка; **be on the** ~ быть в движе́нии; **have a** ~ пыта́ться *impf*, по~ *pf*; *vi* (*on foot*) ходи́ть *indet*, идти́ *det*, пойти́ *pf*; (*by transport*) е́здить *indet*, е́хать *det*, по~ *pf*; (*work*) рабо́тать *impf*; (*become*) станови́ться *impf*, стать *pf*+*instr*; (*belong*) идти́ *impf*; **be ~ing** (**to do**) собира́ться *impf*, собра́ться *pf* (+*inf*); ~ **about** (*set to work at*) бра́ться *impf*, взя́ться *pf* за+*acc*; (*wander*) броди́ть *indet*; ~ **away** (*on foot*) уходи́ть *impf*, уйти́ *pf*; (*by transport*) уезжа́ть *impf*, уе́хать *pf*; ~ **down** спуска́ться *impf*, спусти́ться *pf* (+*gen*); ~ **in(to)** (*enter*) входи́ть *impf*, войти́ *pf* в+*acc*; (*investigate*) рассле́довать *impf* & *pf*; ~ **off** (*go away*) уходи́ть *impf*, уйти́ *pf*; (*deteriorate*) по́ртиться *impf*, ис~ *pf*; ~ **on** (*continue*) продолжа́ть(ся) *impf*, продо́лжить(ся) *pf*; ~ **out** выходи́ть *impf*, вы́йти *pf*; (*flame etc.*) га́снуть *impf*, по~ *pf*; ~ **over** (*inspect*) пересма́тривать *impf*, пересмотре́ть *pf*; (*rehearse*) повторя́ть *impf*, повтори́ть *pf*; (*change allegiance etc.*) переходи́ть *impf*, перейти́ *pf* (**to** в, на, +*acc*, к+*dat*); ~ **through** (*scrutinize*) разбира́ть *impf*, разобра́ть *pf*; (*through with*) доводи́ть *impf*, довести́ *pf* до конца́; ~ **without** обходи́ться *impf* без+*gen*; ~ **ahead** предприи́мчивый; ~ **between** посре́дник.

goad vt (instigate) подстрекать impf, подстрекнуть pf (into k+dat); (taunt) раздражать impf.

goal n (aim) цель; (sport) ворота (-т) pl; (point won) гол.

goalkeeper n вратарь m.

goat n коза; (male) козёл.

gobble vt (eat) жрать impf; ~ up пожирать impf, пожрать pf.

goblet n бокал, кубок.

god n бог; (G~) Бог. **godchild** n крёстник, -ица. **goddaughter** n крёстница. **goddess** n богиня. **godfather** n крёстный sb. **God-fearing** adj богобоязненный. **godless** adj безбожный. **godly** adj набожный. **godmother** n крёстная sb. **godparent** n крёстный sb. **godsend** n божий дар. **godson** n крёстник.

goggle vi таращить impf глаза (at на+acc); n: pl защитные очки (-ко́в) pl.

going adj действующий. **goings-on** n pl дела neut pl.

gold n золото; adj золотой. ~-plated adj накладного золота. ~-smith золотых дел мастер.

golden adj золотой. ~ **eagle** беркут. **goldfish** n золотая рыбка.

golf n гольф; ~ **club** (implement) клюшка; ~ **course** площадка для гольфа. **golfer** n игрок в гольф.

gondola n гондола.

gong n гонг.

gonorrhoea n триппер.

good n добро; pl (wares) товар(ы); do ~ (benefit) идти impf, пойти pf на пользу +dat; adj хороший, добрый; ~-humoured добродушный; ~-looking красивый; ~ morning доброе утро!; ~ night спокойной ночи! **goodbye** int прощай(те)!; до свидания! **goodness** n доброта.

goose n гусь m; ~-flesh гусиная кожа.

gooseberry n крыжовник.

gore¹ n (blood) запёкшаяся кровь.

gore² vt (pierce) бодать impf, за~ pf.

gorge n (geog) ущелье; vi & t объедаться impf, объесться pf (on +instr).

gorgeous adj великолепный.

gorilla n горилла.

gorse n утёсник.

gory adj кровавый.

gosh int боже мой!

Gospel n Евангелие.

gossip n сплетня; (person) сплетник, -ица; vi сплетничать impf, на~ pf.

Gothic готический.

gouge vt: ~ **out** выдалбливать impf, выдолбить pf; (eyes) выкалывать impf, выколоть pf.

goulash n гуляш.

gourmet n гурман.

gout n подагра.

govern vt править impf +instr; (determine) определять impf, определить pf. **governess** n гувернантка. **government** n правительство. **governmental** adj правительственный. **governor** n губернатор; (of school etc.) член правления.

gown n платье; (official's) мантия.

grab vt захватывать impf, захватить pf.

grace n (gracefulness) грация; (refinement) изящество; (favour) милость; (at meal) молитва; have the ~ to быть насто́лько такти́чен, что; **with bad** ~ нелюбе́зно; **with good** ~ с досто́инством; vt (adorn) украша́ть impf, укра́сить pf; (favour) удоста́ивать impf, удосто́ить pf (with +gen). **graceful** adj грацио́зный.

gracious adj ми́лостивый.

gradation n града́ция.

grade n (level) сте́пень; (quality) сорт; vt сортирова́ть impf, рас~ pf.

gradient n укло́н.

gradual adj постепе́нный.

graduate n око́нчивший sb университе́т, вуз; vi конча́ть impf, око́нчить pf (университе́т, вуз); vt градуи́ровать impf & pf.

graffiti n на́дписи f pl.

graft n (bot) черено́к; (med) переса́дка (живо́й тка́ни); vt (bot) прививать impf, приви́ть pf (to +dat); (med) переса́живать impf, пересади́ть pf.

grain n (seed; collect) зерно́; (particle) крупи́нка; (of sand) песчи́нка; (of wood) (древе́сное) волокно́; **against the** ~ не по нутру́.

gram(me) n грамм.

grammar n грамма́тика; ~ **school** гимна́зия. **grammatical** adj граммати́ческий.

gramophone n проигрыва́тель m; ~ **record** грампласти́нка.

granary n амба́р.

grand adj великоле́пный; ~ **piano** роя́ль m. **grandchild** n внук, внука. **granddaughter** n вну́чка. **grandfather** n де́душка m. **grandmother** n ба́бушка. **grandparents** n ба́бушка и де́душка. **grandson** n внук. **grandstand** n

трибу́на.

grandeur n вели́чие.

grandiose adj грандио́зный.

granite n грани́т.

granny n ба́бушка.

grant n (financial) дота́ция; (univ) стипе́ндия; vt дарова́ть impf & pf; (concede) допуска́ть impf, допусти́ть pf; **take for** ~ed (assume) счита́ть impf, счесть pf само́ собо́й разуме́ющимся; (not appreciate) принима́ть impf как до́лжное.

granular adj зерни́стый.

granulated adj: ~ **sugar** са́харный песо́к.

granule n зёрнышко.

grape n виногра́д. **grapefruit** n гре́йпфрут.

graph n гра́фик.

graphic adj графи́ческий; (vivid) я́ркий.

graphite n графи́т.

grapple vi (struggle) боро́ться impf (with c+instr).

grasp n (grip) хва́тка; (comprehension) понима́ние; vt (clutch) хвата́ть impf, схвати́ть pf; (comprehend) понима́ть impf, поня́ть pf. **grasping** adj жа́дный.

grass n трава́. **grasshopper** n кузне́чик. **grassy** adj травяни́стый.

grate¹ n (in fireplace) решётка.

grate² vt (rub) тере́ть impf, на~ pf; vi (sound) скрипе́ть impf; ~ (up)on (irritate) раздража́ть impf, раздражи́ть pf.

grateful adj благода́рный.

grater n тёрка.

gratify vt удовлетворя́ть impf, удовлетвори́ть pf.

grating n решётка.

gratis adv беспла́тно.

gratitude *n* благода́рность.
gratuitous *adj* (*free*) дарово́й; (*motiveless*) беспричи́нный.
gratuity *n* (*tip*) чаевы́е *sb pl*.
grave[1] *n* моги́ла. **gravedigger** *n* моги́льщик. **gravestone** *n* надгро́бный ка́мень *m*. **graveyard** *n* кла́дбище.
grave[2] *adj* серьёзный.
gravel *n* гра́вий.
gravitate *vi* тяготе́ть *impf* (**towards** к+*dat*). **gravitational** *adj* гравитацио́нный. **gravity** *n* (*seriousness*) серьёзность; (*force*) тя́жесть.
gravy *n* (*мясна́я*) подли́вка.
graze[1] *vi* (*feed*) пасти́сь *impf*.
graze[2] *n* (*abrasion*) цара́пина; *vt* (*touch*) задева́ть *impf*, заде́ть *pf*; (*abrade*) цара́пать *impf*, о~ *pf*.
grease *n* жир; (*lubricant*) сма́зка; ~**paint** грим; *vt* сма́зывать *impf*, сма́зать *pf*. **greasy** *adj* жи́рный.
great *adj* (*large*) большо́й; (*eminent*) вели́кий; (*splendid*) замеча́тельный; **to a** ~ **extent** в большо́й сте́пени; **a** ~ **deal** мно́го (+*gen*); **a** ~ **many** мно́гие; ~**aunt** двою́родная ба́бушка; ~**granddaughter** пра́внучка; ~**grandfather** пра́дед; ~**grandmother** праба́бка; ~**grandson** пра́внук; ~**uncle** двою́родный де́душка *m*. **greatly** *adv* о́чень.
Great Britain *n* Великобрита́ния.
Greece *n* Гре́ция.
greed *n* жа́дность (**for** к+*dat*). **greedy** *adj* жа́дный (**for** к+*dat*).
Greek *n* грек, греча́нка; *adj* гре́ческий.
green *n* (*colour*) зелёный цвет; (*piece of land*) лужо́к; *pl*

зе́лень *collect*; *adj* зелёный; (*inexperienced*) неопы́тный.
greenery *n* зе́лень. **greenfly** *n* тля. **greengrocer** *n* зеленщи́к. **greenhouse** *n* тепли́ца; ~ **effect** парнико́вый эффе́кт.
greet *vt* здоро́ваться *impf*, по~ *pf* с+*instr*; (*meet*) встреча́ть *impf*, встре́тить *pf*. **greeting** *n* приве́т(ствие).
gregarious *adj* общи́тельный.
grenade *n* грана́та.
grey *adj* се́рый; (*hair*) седо́й.
greyhound *n* борза́я *sb*.
grid *n* (*grating*) решётка; (*electr*) сеть; (*map*) координа́тная се́тка.
grief *n* го́ре; **come to** ~ терпе́ть *impf*, по~ *pf* неуда́чу.
grievance *n* жа́лоба, оби́да.
grieve *vt* огорча́ть *impf*, огорчи́ть *pf*; *vi* горева́ть *impf* (**for** o+*prep*).
grievous *adj* тя́жкий.
grill *n* ра́шпер; *vt* (*cook*) жа́рить *impf*, за~, из~ *pf* (на ра́шпере); (*question*) допра́шивать *impf*, допроси́ть *pf*.
grille *n* (*grating*) решётка.
grim *adj* (*stern*) суро́вый; (*unpleasant*) неприя́тный.
grimace *n* грима́са; *vi* грима́сничать *impf*.
grime *n* грязь. **grimy** *adj* гря́зный.
grin *n* усме́шка; *vi* усмеха́ться *impf*, усмехну́ться *pf*.
grind *vt* (*flour etc.*) моло́ть *impf*, с~ *pf*; (*axe*) точи́ть *impf*, на~ *pf*; ~ **one's teeth** скрежета́ть *impf* зуба́ми.
grip *n* хва́тка; *vt* схва́тывать *impf*, схвати́ть *pf*.
gripe *vi* ворча́ть *impf*.
gripping *adj* захва́тывающий.

grisly *adj* жу́ткий.

gristle *n* хрящ.

grit *n* песо́к; (*for building*) гра́вий; (*firmness*) вы́держка.

grizzle *vi* хны́кать *impf*.

groan *n* стон; *vi* стона́ть *impf*.

grocer *n* бакале́йщик; ~'**s** (**shop**) бакале́йная ла́вка, гастроно́м. **groceries** *n pl* бакале́я *collect*.

groggy *adj* разби́тый.

groin *n* (*anat*) пах.

groom *n* ко́нюх; (*bridegroom*) жени́х; *vt* (*horse*) чи́стить *impf*, по~ *pf*; (*prepare*) гото́вить *impf*, под~ *pf* (**for** к+*dat*); **well-groomed** хорошо́ вы́глядящий.

groove *n* желобо́к.

grope *vi* нащу́пывать *impf* (**for, after** +*acc*).

gross[1] *n* (*12 dozen*) гросс.

gross[2] *adj* (*fat*) ту́чный; (*coarse*) гру́бый; (*total*) валово́й; ~ **weight** вес бру́тто.

grotesque *adj* гроте́скный.

grotto *n* грот.

ground *n* земля́; (*earth*) по́чва; *pl* (*dregs*) гу́ща; (*sport*) площа́дка; *pl* (*of house*) парк; (*reason*) основа́ние; ~ **floor** пе́рвый эта́ж; *vt* (*instruct*) обуча́ть *impf*, обучи́ть *pf* осно́вам (**in** +*gen*); (*aeron*) запреща́ть *impf*, запрети́ть *pf* полёты +*gen*; *vi* (*naut*) сади́ться *impf*, сесть *pf* на мель. **groundless** *adj* необосно́ванный. **groundwork** *n* фунда́мент.

group *n* гру́ппа; *vt* & *i* группирова́ть(ся) *impf*, с~ *pf*.

grouse[1] *n* шотла́ндская куропа́тка.

grouse[2] *vi* (*grumble*) ворча́ть *impf*.

grove *n* ро́ща.

grovel *vi* пресмыка́ться *impf* (**before** пе́ред+*instr*).

grow *vi* расти́ *impf*; (*become*) станови́ться *impf*, стать *pf* +*instr*; *vt* (*cultivate*) выра́щивать *impf*, вы́растить *pf*; (*hair*) отра́щивать *impf*, отрасти́ть *pf*; ~ **up** (*person*) выраста́ть *impf*, вы́расти *pf*; (*custom*) возника́ть *impf*, возни́кнуть *pf*.

growl *n* ворча́ние; *vi* ворча́ть *impf* (**at** на+*acc*).

grown-up *adj* взро́слый *sb*.

growth *n* рост; (*med*) о́пухоль.

grub *n* (*larva*) личи́нка; (*food*) жратва́; *vi*: ~ **about** ры́ться *impf*. **grubby** *adj* запа́чканный.

grudge *n* зло́ба; **have a** ~ **against** име́ть *impf* зуб про́тив+*gen*; *vt* жале́ть *impf*, по~ *pf* +*acc*, +*gen*. **grudgingly** *adv* неохо́тно.

gruelling *adj* изнури́тельный.

gruesome *adj* жу́ткий.

gruff *adj* (*surly*) грубова́тый; (*voice*) хри́плый.

grumble *vi* ворча́ть *impf* (**at** на+*acc*).

grumpy *adj* брюзгли́вый.

grunt *n* хрю́канье; *vi* хрю́кать *impf*, хрю́кнуть *pf*.

guarantee *n* гара́нтия; *vt* гаранти́ровать *impf* & *pf* (**against** от+*gen*). **guarantor** *n* поручи́тель *m*.

guard *n* (*device*) предохрани́тель; (*watch*; *soldiers*) карау́л; (*sentry*) часово́й *sb*; (*watchman*) сто́рож; (*rly*) кондукто́р; *pl* (*prison*) надзира́тель *m*; *vt* охраня́ть *impf*, охрани́ть *pf*; *vi*: ~ **against** остерега́ться *impf*, остере́чься *pf* +*gen, inf*.

guardian *n* храни́тель *m*;

guer(r)illa *n* (*law*) опеку́н.

guer(r)illa *n* партиза́н; ~ **warfare** партиза́нская война́.

guess *n* дога́дка; *vt* & *i* дога́дываться *impf*, догада́ться *pf* (о+*prep*); *vt* (~ *correctly*) уга́дывать *impf*, угада́ть *pf*. **guesswork** *n* дога́дки *f pl*.

guest *n* гость *m*; ~ **house** ма́ленькая гости́ница.

guffaw *n* хо́хот; *vi* хохота́ть *impf*.

guidance *n* руково́дство. **guide** *n* проводни́к, гид; (*guidebook*) путеводи́тель *m*; *vt* води́ть *indet*, вести́ *det*; (*direct*) руководи́ть *impf* +*instr*; ~**d missile** управля́емая раке́та. **guidelines** *n pl* инстру́кции *f pl*; (*advice*) сове́т.

guild *n* ги́льдия, цех.

guile *n* кова́рство. **guileless** *adj* простоду́шный.

guillotine *n* гильоти́на.

guilt *n* вина́; (*guiltiness*) вино́вность. **guilty** *adj* (*of crime*) вино́вный (**of** в+*prep*); (*of wrong*) винова́тый.

guinea-pig *n* морска́я сви́нка; (*fig*) подо́пытный кро́лик.

guise *n*: **under the** ~ **of** под ви́дом+*gen*.

guitar *n* гита́ра. **guitarist** *n* гитари́ст.

gulf *n* (*geog*) зали́в; (*chasm*) про́пасть.

gull *n* ча́йка.

gullet *n* (*oesophagus*) пищево́д; (*throat*) го́рло.

gullible *adj* легкове́рный.

gully *n* (*ravine*) овра́г.

gulp *n* глото́к; *vt* жа́дно глота́ть *impf*.

gum[1] *n* (*anat*) десна́.

gum[2] *n* каме́дь; (*glue*) клей; *vt* скле́ивать *impf*, скле́ить *pf*.

gumption *n* инициати́ва.

gun *n* (*piece of ordnance*) ору́дие, пу́шка; (*rifle etc.*) ружьё; (*pistol*) пистоле́т; *vt*: ~ **down** расстре́ливать *impf*, расстреля́ть *pf*. **gunner** *n* артиллери́ст. **gunpowder** *n* по́рох.

gurgle *vi* бу́лькать *impf*.

gush *vi* хлыну́ть *pf*.

gusset *n* клин.

gust *n* поры́в. **gusty** *adj* поры́вистый.

gusto *n* смак.

gut *n* кишка́; *pl* (*entrails*) кишки́ *f pl*; *pl* (*bravery*) му́жество; *vt* потроши́ть *impf*, вы~ *pf*; (*devastate*) опустоша́ть *impf*, опустоши́ть *pf*.

gutter *n* (*of roof*) (водосто́чный) жёлоб; (*of road*) сто́чная кана́ва.

guttural *adj* горта́нный.

guy[1] *n* (*rope*) оття́жка.

guy[2] *n* (*fellow*) па́рень *m*.

guzzle *vt* (*food*) пожира́ть *impf*, пожра́ть *pf*; (*liquid*) хлеба́ть *impf*, хлебну́ть *pf*.

gym *n* (*gymnasium*) гимнасти́ческий зал; (*gymnastics*) гимна́стика. **gymnasium** *n* гимнасти́ческий зал. **gymnast** *n* гимна́ст. **gymnastic** *adj* гимнасти́ческий. **gymnastics** *n* гимна́стика.

gynaecologist *n* гинеко́лог. **gynaecology** *n* гинеколо́гия.

gyrate *vi* враща́ться *impf*.

H

haberdashery *n* галантере́я; (*shop*) галантере́йный магази́н.

habit *n* привы́чка; (*monk's*) ря́са.

habitable *adj* приго́дный для

жилья́. **habitat** n есте́ственная среда́. **habitation** n: **unfit for** ~ неприго́дный для жилья́.

habitual adj привы́чный.

hack[1] vt руби́ть impf; ~**saw** ножо́вка.

hack[2] n (hired horse) наёмная ло́шадь; (writer) халту́рщик.

hackneyed adj изби́тый.

haddock n пи́кша.

haemophilia n гемофили́я.

haemorrhage n кровотече́ние. **haemorrhoids** n pl геморро́й collect.

hag n ка́рга.

haggard adj изможде́нный.

haggle vi торгова́ться impf, с~ pf.

hail[1] n град; vi **it is ~ing** идёт град. **hailstone** n гра́дина.

hail[2] vt (greet) приве́тствовать impf (& pf in past); (taxi) подзыва́ть impf, подозва́ть pf.

hair n (single ~) во́лос; collect (human) во́лосы pl (-о́с, -оса́м) pl; (animal) шерсть. **hairbrush** n щётка для воло́с. **haircut** n стри́жка; **have a ~** постри́чься pf. **hair-do** n причёска. **hairdresser** n парикма́хер. **hairdresser's** sb. **hairdryer** n фен. **hairstyle** n причёска. **hairy** adj волоса́тый.

hale adj: ~ **and hearty** здоро́вый и бо́дрый.

half n полови́на; (sport) тайм; adj полови́нный; **in ~** попола́м; **one and a ~** полтора́; ~ **past** (one etc.) полови́на (второ́го и т.д.); ~**hearted** равноду́шный; ~ **an hour** полчаса́; ~**time** переры́в ме́жду та́ймами; ~**way** на полпути́; ~**witted** слабоу́мный.

hall n (large room) зал; (entrance ~) холл, вестибю́ль m; (~ of residence) общежи́тие. **hallmark** n пробирное клеймо́; (fig) при́знак.

hallo int здра́сте, приве́т; (on telephone) алло́.

hallucination n галлюцина́ция.

halo n (around Saint) нимб; (fig) орео́л.

halt n остано́вка; vt & i остана́вливать(ся) impf, останови́ть(ся) pf; int (mil) стой(те)! **halting** adj запина́ющий.

halve vt дели́ть impf, раз~ pf попола́м.

ham n (cul) ветчина́.

hamlet n дереву́шка.

hammer n молото́к; vt бить impf молотко́м.

hammock n гама́к.

hamper[1] n (basket) корзи́на с кры́шкой.

hamper[2] vt (hinder) меша́ть impf, по~ pf +dat.

hamster n хомя́к.

hand n рука́; (worker) рабо́чий sb; (writing) по́черк; (clock ~) стре́лка; at ~ под руко́й; **on ~s and knees** на четвере́ньках; vt передава́ть impf, переда́ть pf; ~ **in** подава́ть impf, пода́ть pf; ~ **out** раздава́ть impf, разда́ть pf. **handbag** n су́мка. **handbook** n руково́дство. **handcuffs** n pl нару́чники m pl. **handful** n горсть.

handicap n (sport) гандика́п; (hindrance) поме́ха. **handicapped** adj: ~ **person** инвали́д.

handicraft n ремесло́.

handiwork n ручна́я рабо́та.

handkerchief n носово́й плато́к.

handle n рýчка, рукоя́тка; vt (people) обраща́ться impf c+instr; (situations) справля́ться impf, спра́виться pf c+instr; (touch) тро́гать impf, тро́нуть pf руко́й, рука́ми. **handlebar(s)** n руль m.

handmade adj ручно́й рабо́ты.

handout n пода́чка; (document) листо́к.

handrail n пери́ла (-л) pl.

handshake n рукопожа́тие.

handsome adj краси́вый; (generous) ще́дрый.

handwriting n по́черк.

handy adj (convenient) удо́бный; (skilful) ло́вкий; **come in ~** пригоди́ться pf.

hang vt ве́шать impf, пове́сить pf и висе́ть impf; **~ about** слоня́ться impf; **~ on** (cling) держа́ться impf; (tel) не ве́шать impf тру́бку; (persist) упо́рствовать impf; **~ out** выве́шивать impf, вы́весить pf; (spend time) болта́ться impf; **~ up** ве́шать impf, пове́сить pf; (tel) ве́шать impf, пове́сить pf тру́бку. **hanger** n ве́шалка. **hanger-on** n прилипа́ла m & f. **hangman** n пала́ч.

hangar n анга́р.

hangover n похме́лье.

hang-up n ко́мплекс.

hanker vi: **~ after** мечта́ть impf о+prep.

haphazard adj случа́йный.

happen vi (occur) случа́ться impf, случи́ться pf; происходи́ть impf, произойти́ pf; (~ to be somewhere) ока́зываться impf, оказа́ться pf; **~ upon** натáлкиваться impf, натолкну́ться pf на+асс.

happiness n сча́стье. **happy**

adj счастли́вый; **~-go-lucky** беззабо́тный.

harass vt (pester) дёргать impf; (persecute) пресле́довать impf. **harassment** n тра́вля; пресле́дование.

harbinger n предве́стник.

harbour n га́вань, порт; vt (person) укрыва́ть impf, укры́ть pf; (thoughts) затаи́ть impf, затаи́ть pf.

hard adj твёрдый; (difficult) тру́дный; (difficult to bear) тяжёлый; (severe) суро́вый; **~-boiled egg** яйцо́ вкруту́ю; **~-headed** практи́чный; **~-hearted** жестокосе́рдный; **~-up** стеснённый в сре́дствах; **~-working** трудолюби́вый. **hardboard** n строи́тельный карто́н.

harden vi затвердева́ть impf, затверде́ть pf; (fig) ожесточа́ться impf, ожесточи́ться pf.

hardly adv едва́ (ли).

hardship n (privation) нужда́.

hardware n скобяны́е изде́лия neut pl; (comput) аппарату́ра.

hardy adj (robust) выно́сливый; (plant) морозосто́йкий.

hare n за́яц.

hark vi: **~ back to** возвраща́ться impf, верну́ться pf к+dat; int слу́шай(те)!

harm n вред; vt вреди́ть impf, по~ pf +dat. **harmful** adj вре́дный. **harmless** adj безвре́дный.

harmonic adj гармони́ческий. **harmonica** n губна́я гармо́ника. **harmonious** adj гармони́чный. **harmonize** vi гармони́ровать impf (with c+instr). **harmony** n гармо́ния.

harness n у́пряжь; vt запрягáть *impf*, запрячь *pf*; (*fig*) испóльзовать *impf* & *pf*.

harp *n* áрфа; *vi*: ~ **on** твердить *impf* о+*prep*.

harpoon *n* гарпýн.

harpsichord *n* клавесин.

harrow *n* борона. **harrowing** *adj* душераздирáющий.

harsh *adj* (*sound, colour*) рéзкий; (*cruel*) суро́вый.

harvest *n* жáтва, сбор (урожáя); (*yield*) урожáй; (*fig*) плоды́ *m pl*; *vt & abs* собирáть *impf*, собрáть *pf* (урожáй).

hash *n*: make a ~ of напýтать *pf* +*acc*, в+*prep*.

hashish *n* гаши́ш.

hassle *n* беспокóйство.

hassock *n* подýшечка.

haste *n* спéшка. **hasten** *vi* спешить *impf*, по~ *pf*; *vi & t* торопи́ть(ся) *impf*, по~ *pf*; *vt* ускоря́ть *impf*, ускóрить *pf*. **hasty** *adj* (*hurried*) поспéшный; (*quick-tempered*) вспы́льчивый.

hat *n* шáпка; (*stylish*) шля́па.

hatch[1] *n* люк; ~**-back** маши́на-пикáп.

hatch[2] *vt* вылýпливаться, вылупля́ться *impf*, вылупиться *pf*.

hatchet *n* топóрик.

hate *n* нéнависть; *vt* ненави́деть *impf*. **hateful** *adj* ненави́стный. **hatred** *n* нéнависть.

haughty *adj* надмéнный.

haul *n* (*fish*) улóв; (*loot*) добы́ча; (*distance*) éзда; *vt* (*drag*) тянýть *impf*, таскáть *indet*, тащить *det* **haulage** *n* перевóзка.

haunt *n* люби́мое мéсто; *vt* (*ghost*) обитáть *impf*; (*memory*) преслéдовать *impf*. **haunted** *adj*: ~ **house** дом с приве-

дéниями. **haunting** *adj* навя́зчивый.

have *vt* имéть *impf*; I ~ (*possess*) у меня́ (есть; был, -á, -о) +*nom*; I ~ **not** у меня́ нет (*past* нé было) +*gen*; I ~ (**got**) to я дóлжен +*inf*; **you had better** вам лýчше бы +*inf*; ~ **on** (*wear*) быть одéтым в +*prep*; (*be engaged in*) быть зáнятым +*instr*.

haven *n* (*refuge*) убéжище.

haversack *n* рюкзáк.

havoc *n* (*devastation*) опустошéние; (*disorder*) беспоря́док.

hawk[1] *n* (*bird*) я́стреб.

hawk[2] *vt* (*trade*) торговáть *impf* вразнóс+*instr*. **hawker** *n* разнóсчик.

hawser *n* трос.

hawthorn *n* боя́рышник.

hay *n* сéно. **make** ~ коси́ть *impf*, с~ *pf* сéно. ~ **fever** сéнная лихорáдка. **haystack** *n* стог.

hazard *n* риск; *vt* рисковáть *impf* +*instr*. **hazardous** *adj* риско́ванный.

haze *n* ды́мка.

hazel *n* лещи́на. **hazelnut** *n* леснóй орéх.

hazy *adj* тумáнный; (*vague*) смýтный.

he *pron* он.

head *n* головá; (*mind*) ум; (~ *of coin*) лицевáя сторонá монéты; ~**s or tails**? орёл и́ли рéшка?; (*chief*) главá *m*, начáльник; *attrib* глáвный; *vt* (*lead*) возглавля́ть *impf*, возглáвить *pf*; (*ball*) забивáть *impf*, заби́ть *pf* головóй; *vi*: ~ **for** направля́ться *impf*, напрáвиться *pf* в, на, +*acc*, к+*dat*. **headache** *n* головнáя боль. **head-dress** *n* *n* головно́й убо́р. **header** *n* уда́р голово́й. **heading** *n* (*title*) заголо́вок. **headland** *n* мыс. **headlight** *n* фа́ра. **headline** *n* заголо́вок. **headlong** *adv* стремгла́в. **headmaster**, **-mistress** *n* дире́ктор шко́лы. **head-on** *adj* голово́й; *adv* в лоб. **headphone** *n* нау́шник. **headquarters** *n* штаб-кварти́ра. **headscarf** *n* косы́нка. **headstone** *n* надгро́бный ка́мень *m.* **headstrong** *adj* своево́льный. **headway** *n* движе́ние вперёд. **heady** *adj* опьяня́ющий.

heal *vt* излечи́ть *impf,* излечи́ть *pf,* *vi* зажива́ть *impf,* зажи́ть *pf.* **healing** *adj* целе́бный.

health *n* здоро́вье; ~ **care** здравоохране́ние. **healthy** *adj* здоро́вый; (*beneficial*) поле́зный.

heap *n* ку́ча; *vt* нагроможда́ть *impf,* нагромозди́ть *pf.*

hear *vt* слы́шать *impf,* y~ *pf;* (*listen to*) слу́шать *impf,* по~ *pf;* ~ **out** вы́слушивать *impf,* вы́слушать *pf.* **hearing** *n* слух; (*law*) слу́шание. **hearsay** *n* слух.

hearse *n* катафа́лк.

heart *n* се́рдце; (*essence*) суть; *pl* (*cards*) че́рви (-ве́й) *pl;* **by** ~ наизу́сть; ~ **attack** серде́чный при́ступ. **heartburn** *n* изжо́га. **hearten** *vt* ободря́ть *impf,* ободри́ть *pf.* **heartfelt** *adj* серде́чный. **heartless** *adj* бессерде́чный. **heart-rending** *adj* душераздира́ющий. **hearty** *adj* (*cordial*) серде́чный; (*vigorous*) здоро́вый.

hearth *n* оча́г.

heat *n* жара́; (*phys*) теплота́; (*of feeling*) пыл; (*sport*) забе́г, заéзд; *vt & i* (*heat up*) нагрева́ть(ся) *impf,* нагре́ть(ся) *pf;* *vt* (*house*) топи́ть *impf.* **heater** *n* нагрева́тель *m.* **heating** *n* отопле́ние.

heath *n* пу́стошь.

heathen *n* язы́чник; *adj* язы́ческий.

heather *n* ве́реск.

heave *vt* (*lift*) поднима́ть *impf,* подня́ть *pf;* (*pull*) тяну́ть *impf,* по~ *pf.*

heaven *n* (*sky*) не́бо; (*paradise*) *pl* небеса́ neut *pl.* **heavenly** *adj* небе́сный; (*divine*) боже́ственный.

heavy *adj* тяжёлый; (*strong, intense*) си́льный. **heavyweight** *n* тяжелове́с.

Hebrew *adj* (дре́вне)евре́йский.

heckle *vt* пререка́ться *impf* c+*instr.*

hectic *adj* лихора́дочный.

hedge *n* жива́я и́згородь. **hedgerow** *n* шпале́ра.

hedgehog *n* ёж.

heed *vt* обраща́ть вни- мание́ на+*acc.* **heedless** *adj* небре́жный.

heel[1] *n* (*of foot*) пята́; (*of foot, sock*) пя́тка; (*of shoe*) каблу́к.

heel[2] *vt* крени́ться *impf,* на~ *pf.*

hefty *adj* дю́жий.

heifer *n* тёлка.

height *n* высота́; (*of person*) рост. **heighten** *vt* (*strengthen*) усиливать *impf,* уси́лить *pf.*

heinous *adj* гну́сный.

heir *n* насле́дник. **heiress** *n* насле́дница. **heirloom** *n* фами́льная вещь.

helicopter *n* вертолёт.

helium *n* ге́лий.

hell *n* ад. **hellish** *adj* áдский.

hello *see* **hallo**

helm *n* руль.

helmet *n* шлем.

help *n* пóмощь; *vt* помогáть *impf*, помóчь *pf +dat*; (*can't* ~) не мочь *impf* не *+inf*; ~ **o.s.** брать *impf*, взять *pf* себé; ~ **yourself!** берите! **helpful** *adj* полéзный; (*obliging*) услýжливый. **helping** *n* (*of food*) пóрция. **helpless** *adj* беспóмощный.

helter-skelter *adv* как попáло.

hem *n* рубéц; *vt* подрубáть *impf*, подрубить *pf*; ~ **in** окружáть *impf*, окружить *pf*.

hemisphere *n* полушáрие.

hemp *n* (*plant*) конопля; (*fibre*) пенька.

hen *n* (*female bird*) сáмка; (*domestic fowl*) курица.

hence *adv* (*from here*) отсюда; (*as a result*) слéдовательно; **3 years** ~ чéрез три гóда. **henceforth** *adv* отныне.

henchman *n* приспéшник.

henna *n* хна.

hepatitis *n* гепатит.

her *poss pron* её; свой.

herald *n* вéстник; *vt* возвещáть *impf*, возвестить *pf*.

herb *n* травá. **herbaceous** *adj* травяной; ~ **border** цветóчный бордюр. **herbal** *adj* травяной.

herd *n* стáдо; (*people*) толпиться *impf*, с~ *pf*; *vt* (*tend*) пасти *impf*; (*drive*) загонять *impf*, загнáть *pf* в стáдо.

here *adv* (*position*) здесь, тут; (*direction*) сюда; ~ **is** ... вот (*+nom*); ~ **and there** там и сям; ~ **you are!** пожáлуйста. **hereabout(s)** *adv* поблизости. **hereafter** *adv* в будущем. **hereby** *adv* этим. **here-**

upon *adv* (*in consequence*) вслéдствие этого; (*after*) пóсле этого. **herewith** *adv* при сём.

hereditary *adj* наслéдственный. **heredity** *n* наслéдственность.

heresy *n* éресь. **heretic** *n* еретик. **heretical** *adj* еретический.

heritage *n* наслéдие.

hermetic *adj* герметический.

hermit *n* отшельник.

hernia *n* грыжа.

hero *n* герóй. **heroic** *adj* геройческий.

heroin *n* геройн.

heroine *n* героиня. **heroism** *n* геройзм.

heron *n* цáпля.

herpes *n* лишáй.

herring *n* сельдь; (*food*) селёдка.

hers *poss pron* её; свой.

herself *pron* (*emph*) (онá) самá; (*refl*) себя.

hertz *n* герц.

hesitant *adj* нерешительный. **hesitate** *vi* колебáться *impf*, по~ *pf*; (*in speech*) запинáться *impf*, запнýться *pf*. **hesitation** *n* колебáние.

hessian *n* мешковина.

heterogeneous *adj* разнорóдный.

heterosexual *adj* гетеросексуáльный.

hew *vt* рубить *impf*.

hexagon *n* шестиугóльник.

hey *int* эй!

heyday *n* расцвéт.

hi *int* привéт!

hiatus *n* пробéл.

hibernate *vi* быть *impf* в спячке; впадáть *impf*, впасть *pf* в спячку. **hibernation** *n* спячка.

hiccup *vi* ика́ть *impf*, икну́ть *pf*; *n* ико́та.

hide[1] *n* (*skin*) шку́ра.

hide[2] *vt & i* (*conceal*) пря́тать(ся) *impf*, с~ *pf*; скрыва́ть(ся) *impf*, скрыть(ся) *pf*.

hideous *adj* отврати́тельный.

hideout *n* укры́тие.

hiding *n* (*flogging*) по́рка.

hierarchy *n* иера́рхия.

hieroglyphics *n pl* иеро́глифы *m pl*.

hi-fi *n* прои́грыватель *m* с высокока́чественным воспроизведе́нием зву́ка за́писи.

higgledy-piggledy *adv* как придётся.

high *adj* высо́кий; (*wind*) си́льный; (*on drugs*) в наркоти́ческом дурма́не; ~**er education** вы́сшее образова́ние; ~**-handed** своево́льный; ~**-heeled** на высо́ких каблука́х; ~**jump** прыжо́к в высоту́; ~**-minded** благоро́дный; иде́йный; ~**-pitched** высо́кий; ~**-rise** высо́тный.

highbrow *adj* интеллектуа́льный. **highland(s)** *n* го́рная страна́; ~~ вы́сшая то́чка; *vt* обраща́ть *impf*, обрати́ть внима́ние на+*acc*.

highly *adv* весьма́; ~**-strung** легко́ возбужда́емый. **highness** *n* (*title*) высо́чество. **highstreet** *n* гла́вная у́лица. **highway** *n* магистра́ль.

hijack *vt* похища́ть *impf*, похи́тить *pf*. **hijacker** *n* похити́тель *m*.

hike *n* похо́д.

hilarious *adj* умори́тельный. **hilarity** *n* весе́лье.

hill *n* холм. **hillock** *n* хо́лмик. **hillside** *n* склон холма́. **hilly** *adj* холми́стый.

hilt *n* рукоя́тка.

himself *pron* (*emph*) (он) сам; (*refl*) себя́.

hind *adj* (*rear*) за́дний.

hinder *vt* меша́ть *impf*, по~ *pf*+*dat*. **hindrance** *n* поме́ха.

Hindu *n* инду́с; *adj* инду́сский.

hinge *n* шарни́р; *vi* (*fig*) зави́сеть *impf* от+*gen*.

hint *n* намёк; *vi* намека́ть *impf*, намекну́ть *pf* (**at** на+*acc*)

hip *n* (*anat*) бедро́.

hippie *n* хи́ппи *neut indecl*.

hippopotamus *n* гиппопота́м.

hire *n* наём, прока́т; ~**purchase** поку́пка в рассро́чку; *vt* нанима́ть *impf*, наня́ть *pf*; ~**out** сдава́ть *impf*, сдать *pf* напрока́т.

his *poss pron* его́; свой.

hiss *n* шипе́ние; *vi* шипе́ть *impf*; *vt* (*performer*) освисты́вать *impf*, освиста́ть *pf*.

historian *n* исто́рик. **historic(al)** *adj* истори́ческий. **history** *n* исто́рия.

histrionic *adj* театра́льный.

hit *n* (*blow*) уда́р; (*on target*) попада́ние (в цель); (*success*) успе́х; *vt* (*strike*) ударя́ть *impf*, уда́рить *pf*; (*target*) попада́ть *impf*, попа́сть *pf* (в цель); ~(**up**)**on** находи́ть *impf*, найти́ *pf*.

hitch *n* (*stoppage*) заде́ржка; *vt* (*fasten*) привя́зывать *impf*, привяза́ть *pf*; ~**up** подтя́гивать *impf*, подтяну́ть *pf*; ~**-hike** е́здить *indet*, е́хать *det*, по~ *pf* автосто́пом.

hither *adv* сюда́. **hitherto** *adv* до сих пор.

HIV *abbr* (*of human immuno-deficiency virus*) ВИЧ.

hive *n* у́лей.

hoard *n* запа́с; *vt* ска́пливать *impf*, скопи́ть *pf*.

hoarding *n* рекла́мный щит.

hoarse adj хри́плый.

hoax n надува́тельство.

hobble vi ковыля́ть impf.

hobby n хо́бби neut indecl.

hock n (wine) рейнве́йн.

hockey n хокке́й.

hoe n моты́га; vt моты́жить impf.

hog n бо́ров.

hoist n подъёмник; vt поднима́ть impf, подня́ть pf.

hold[1] n (naut) трюм.

hold[2] n (grasp) захва́т; (influence) влия́ние (on на+acc); **catch ~ of** ухвати́ться pf за+acc; (grasp) держа́ть impf; (contain) вмеща́ть impf, вмести́ть pf; (possess) владе́ть impf +instr; (conduct) проводи́ть impf, провести́ pf; (consider) счита́ть impf, счесть pf (+acc & instr, за+acc); vi держа́ться impf; (weather) проде́рживаться impf, продержа́ться pf; **~ back** сде́рживать(ся) impf, сдержа́ть(ся) pf; **~ forth** разглаго́льствовать impf; **~ on** (wait) подожда́ть pf; (tel) не ве́шать impf тру́бку; (grip) держа́ться (то за+acc); **~ out** (stretch out) протя́гивать impf, протяну́ть pf; (resist) не сдава́ться impf; **~ up** (support) подде́рживать impf, поддержа́ть pf; (impede) заде́рживать impf, задержа́ть pf. **holdall** n су́мка. **hold-up** n (robbery) налёт; (delay) заде́ржка.

hole n дыра́; (animal's) нора́; (golf) лу́нка.

holiday n (day off) выходно́й день; (festival) пра́здник; (annual leave) о́тпуск; pl (school) кани́кулы (-л) pl; **~-maker** тури́ст; **on ~** в о́тпуске.

holiness n свя́тость.

Holland n Голла́ндия.

hollow n впа́дина; (valley) лощи́на; adj пусто́й; (sunken) впа́лый; (sound) глухо́й; (~ out) выда́лбливать impf, вы́долбить pf.

holly n остроли́ст.

holocaust n ма́ссовое уничтоже́ние.

holster n кобура́.

holy adj свято́й, свяще́нный.

homage n почте́ние; **pay ~ to** преклоня́ться impf, преклони́ться pf пе́ред+instr.

home n дом; (native land) ро́дина; **at ~** до́ма; **feel at ~** чу́вствовать impf себя́ как до́ма; adj дома́шний; (native) родно́й; **H~ Affairs** вну́тренние дела́ neut pl; adv (direction) домо́й; (position) до́ма. **homeland** n ро́дина. **homeless** adj бездо́мный. **homemade** adj (food) дома́шний; (object) самоде́льный. **homesick** adj: **be ~** скуча́ть impf по до́му, восвоя́си. **homewards** adv домо́й.

homely adj просто́й.

homicide n (action) уби́йство.

homogeneous adj одноро́дный.

homosexual n гомосексуали́ст; adj гомосексуа́льный.

honest adj че́стный. **honesty** n че́стность.

honey n мёд. **honeymoon** n медо́вый ме́сяц. **honeysuckle** n жи́молость.

honk vi гуде́ть impf.

honorary adj почётный.

honour n честь; vt (respect) почита́ть impf, почти́ть impf, уста́ивать impf, удосто́ить pf (with +gen); (fulfil) выполня́ть impf, вы́полнить pf.

honourable *adj* че́стный.

hood *n* капюшо́н; (*tech*) капо́т.

hoodwink *vt* обма́нывать *impf*, обману́ть *pf*.

hoof *n* копы́то.

hook *n* крючо́к; *vt* (*hitch*) зацепля́ть *impf*, зацепи́ть *pf*; (*fasten*) застёгивать *impf*, застегну́ть *pf*.

hooligan *n* хулига́н.

hoop *n* о́бруч.

hoot *vi* (*owl*) у́хать *impf*, у́хнуть *pf*; (*horn*) гуде́ть *impf*. hooter *n* гудо́к.

hop¹ *n* (*plant; collect*) хмель *m*.

hop² *n* (*jump*) прыжо́к; *vi* пры́гать *impf*, пры́гнуть *pf* (на одно́й ноге́).

hope *n* наде́жда; *vi* наде́яться *impf*, по~ *pf* (for +acc). hopeful *adj* (*promising*) обнадёживающий; I am ~ я наде́юсь. hopefully *adv* с наде́ждой; (*it is hoped*) на́до наде́яться. hopeless *adj* безнадёжный.

horde *n* (*hist; fig*) орда́.

horizon *n* горизо́нт. horizontal *adj* горизонта́льный.

hormone *n* гормо́н.

horn *n* рог; (*French horn*) валто́рна; (*car*) гудо́к.

hornet *n* ше́ршень *m*.

horny *adj* (*calloused*) мозо́листый.

horoscope *n* гороско́п.

horrible, horrid *adj* ужа́сный. horrify *vt* ужаса́ть *impf*, ужасну́ть *pf*. horror *n* ужа́с.

hors-d'oeuvre *n* заку́ска.

horse *n* ло́шадь. horse-chestnut *n* ко́нский кашта́н. horseman, -woman *n* вса́дник, -ица. horseplay *n* возня́. horsepower *n* лошади́ная си́ла. horse-racing *n* ска́чки (-чек) *pl.* horse-radish *n*

хрен. horseshoe *n* подко́ва.

horticulture *n* садово́дство.

hose *n* (~-pipe) шланг.

hosiery *n* чуло́чные изде́лия *neut pl.*

hospitable *adj* гостеприи́мный.

hospital *n* больни́ца.

hospitality *n* гостеприи́мство.

host¹ *n* (*multitude*) мно́жество.

host² *n* (*entertaining*) хозя́ин.

hostage *n* зало́жник.

hostel *n* общежи́тие.

hostess *n* хозя́йка; (*air* ~) стюарде́сса.

hostile *adj* вражде́бный. hostility *n* вражде́бность; *pl* вое́нные де́йствия *neut pl.*

hot *adj* горя́чий, жа́ркий; (*pungent*) о́стрый; ~-headed вспы́льчивый; ~-water bottle гре́лка. hotbed *n* (*fig*) оча́г. hothouse *n* тепли́ца. hotplate *n* пли́тка.

hotel *n* гости́ница.

hound *n* охо́тничья соба́ка; *vt* трави́ть *impf*, за~ *pf.*

hour *n* час. hourly *adj* ежеча́сный.

house *n* дом; (*parl*) пала́та; *attrib* дома́шний; *vt* помеща́ть *impf*, помести́ть *pf.* household *n* семья́; *adj* хозя́йственный; дома́шний. housekeeper *n* эконо́мка. housewarming *n* новосе́лье. housewife *n* хозя́йка. housework *n* дома́шняя рабо́та. housing (*accommodation*) жильё; (*casing*) ко́жух; ~ estate жило́й масси́в.

hovel *n* лачу́га.

hover *vi* (*bird*) пари́ть *impf*; (*helicopter*) висе́ть *impf*; (*person*) мая́чить *impf*. hovercraft *n* су́дно на возду́шной поду́шке, СВП.

how *adv* как, каки́м о́бразом; ~ **do you do?** здра́вствуйте!; ~ **many**, ~ **much** ско́лько (+*gen*). **however** *adv* как бы ни (+*past*); *conj* одна́ко, тем не ме́нее; ~ **much** ско́лько бы ни (+*gen* & *past*).

howl *n* вой; *vi* выть *impf*.

howler *n* грубе́йшая оши́бка.

hub *n* (*of wheel*) ступи́ца; (*fig*) центр, средото́чие.

hubbub *n* шум, гам.

huddle *vi*: ~ **together** прижима́ться *impf*, прижа́ться *pf* друг к дру́гу.

hue *n* (*tint*) отте́нок.

huff *n*: **in a** ~ оскорблённый.

hug *n* объя́тие; *vt* (*embrace*) обнима́ть *impf*, обня́ть *pf*.

huge *adj* огро́мный.

hulk *n* ко́рпус (корабля́).

hulking *adj* (*bulky*) грома́дный; (*clumsy*) неуклю́жий.

hull *n* (*of ship*) ко́рпус.

hum *n* жужжа́ние; *n* (*buzz*) жужжа́ть *impf*; *vt* & *i* (*person*) напева́ть *impf*.

human *adj* челове́ческий, людско́й; *n* челове́к. **humane**, **humanitarian** *adj* челове́чный. **humanity** *n* (*human race*) челове́чество; (*humaneness*) гума́нность; **the Humanities** гуманита́рные нау́ки *f pl*.

humble *adj* (*person*) смире́нный; (*abode*) скро́мный; *vt* унижа́ть *impf*, уни́зить *pf*.

humdrum *adj* однообра́зный.

humid *adj* вла́жный; **humidity** *n* вла́жность.

humiliate *vt* унижа́ть *impf*, уни́зить *pf*. **humiliation** *n* униже́ние.

humility *n* смире́ние.

humorous *adj* юмористи́ческий. **humour** *n* ю́мор; (*mood*) настрое́ние; *vt* пота-

ка́ть *impf* +*dat*.

hump *n* горб; (*of earth*) буго́р. **humus** *n* перегно́й.

hunch *n* (*idea*) предчу́вствие; *vt* го́рбить *impf*, с~ *pf*. **hunchback** *n* (*person*) горбу́н, ~ка. **hunchbacked** *adj* горба́тый.

hundred *adj* & *n* сто; ~**s of** со́тни *f pl* +*gen*; **two** ~ две́сти; **three** ~ три́ста; **four** ~ четы́реста; **five** ~ пятьсо́т. **hundredth** *adj* & *n* со́тый.

Hungarian *n* венгр, венге́рка; *adj* венге́рский. **Hungary** *n* Ве́нгрия.

hunger *n* го́лод; (*fig*) жа́жда (**for** +*gen*); ~ **strike** голодо́вка; *vi* голода́ть *impf*; ~ **for** жа́ждать *impf* +*gen*. **hungry** *adj* голо́дный.

hunk *n* ломо́ть *m*.

hunt *n* охо́та; (*fig*) по́иски *m pl* (**for** +*gen*); *vt* охо́титься *impf* на+*acc*, за+*instr*; (*persecute*) трави́ть *impf*, за~ *pf*; ~ **down** вы́следить *pf*; ~ **for** иска́ть *impf* +*acc or gen*; ~ **out** отыска́ть *pf*. **hunter** *n* охо́тник. **hunting** *n* охо́та.

hurdle *n* (*sport*; *fig*) барье́р. **hurdler** *n* барьери́ст. **hurdles** *n pl* (*sport*) барье́рный бег.

hurl *vt* швыря́ть *impf*, швырну́ть *pf*.

hurly-burly *n* сумато́ха.

hurrah, **hurray** *int* ура́!

hurricane *n* урага́н.

hurried *adj* торопли́вый. **hurry** *n* спе́шка; **be in a** ~ спеши́ть *impf*; *vt* & *i* торопи́ть(ся) *impf*, по~ *pf*; *vi* спеши́ть *impf*, по~ *pf*.

hurt *n* вред; *vi* боле́ть *impf*; *vt* повреди́ть *impf*, повреди́ть *pf*; (*offend*) обижа́ть *impf*, оби́деть *pf*.

hurtle vi нести́сь impf, по~ pf.

husband n муж.

hush n тишина́; vt: ~ up замина́ть impf, замя́ть pf; int ти́ше!

husk n шелуха́.

husky adj (voice) хри́плый.

hustle n толкотня́; vt (push) затолка́ть impf, затолкну́ть pf; (herd people) загоня́ть impf, загна́ть pf; vt & i (hurry) торопи́ть(ся) impf, по~ pf.

hut n хи́жина.

hutch n кле́тка.

hyacinth n гиаци́нт.

hybrid n гибри́д; adj гибри́дный.

hydrangea n горте́нзия.

hydrant n гидра́нт.

hydraulic adj гидравли́ческий.

hydrochloric acid n соля́ная кислота́. **hydroelectric** adj гидроэлектри́ческий; ~ **power station** гидроэлектроста́нция, ГЭС f indecl. **hydrofoil** n су́дно на подво́дных кры́льях, СПК.

hydrogen n водоро́д.

hyena n гие́на.

hygiene n гигие́на. **hygienic** adj гигиени́ческий.

hymn n гимн.

hyperbole n гипе́рбола.

hyphen n дефи́с. **hyphen(ate)** vt писа́ть impf, на~ pf че́рез дефи́с.

hypnosis n гипно́з. **hypnotic** adj гипноти́ческий. **hypnotism** n гипноти́зм. **hypnotist** n гипнотизёр. **hypnotize** vt гипнотизи́ровать impf, за~ pf.

hypochondria n ипохо́ндрия. **hypochondriac** n ипохо́ндрик.

hypocrisy n лицеме́рие. **hypo-**

crite n лицеме́р. **hypocritical** adj лицеме́рный.

hypodermic adj подко́жный.

hypothesis n гипо́теза. **hypothesize** vi стро́ить impf, по~ pf гипоте́зу. **hypothetical** adj гипотети́ческий.

hysterectomy n гистерэктоми́я, удале́ние ма́тки.

hysteria n истери́я. **hysterical** adj истери́ческий. **hysterics** n pl исте́рика.

I

I pron я.

ibid(em) adv там же.

ice n лёд; ~**-age** леднико́вый пери́од; ~**axe** ледору́б; ~ **cream** моро́женое sb; ~ **hockey** хокке́й (с ша́йбой); ~ **rink** като́к; ~ **skate** конёк; vi ката́ться impf на конька́х; vt (chill) замора́живать impf, заморо́зить pf, (cul) глазирова́ть impf & pf; vi: ~ **over, up** обледене́ть impf, обледене́ть pf. **iceberg** n а́йсберг. **icicle** n сосу́лька. **icing** n (cul) глазу́рь f. **icy** adj ледяно́й.

icon n ико́на.

ID abbr (of **identification**) удостовере́ние ли́чности.

idea n иде́я, мысль; (conception) поня́тие.

ideal n идеа́л; adj идеа́льный. **idealism** n идеали́зм. **idealist** n идеали́ст. **idealize** vt идеализи́ровать impf & pf. **identical** adj тожде́ственный, одина́ковый. **identification** n (recognition) опозна́ние; (of person) установле́ние ли́чности. **identify** vt опознава́ть impf, опозна́ть pf. **identity** n (*of person*) ли́чность; ~ **card** удостовере́ние ли́чности.

ideological *adj* идеологи́ческий. **ideology** *n* идеоло́гия.

idiom *n* идио́ма. **idiomatic** *adj* идиомати́ческий.

idiosyncrasy *n* идиосинкра́зия.

idiot *n* идио́т. **idiotic** *adj* идио́тский.

idle *adj* (*unoccupied; lazy; purposeless*) пра́здный; (*vain*) тще́тный; (*empty*) пусто́й; (*machine*) недействующий; *vi* безде́льничать *impf*; (*engine*) рабо́тать *impf* вхолосту́ю; *vt*: ~ **away** пра́здно проводи́ть *impf*, провести́ *pf*. **idleness** *n* пра́здность.

idol *n* и́дол. **idolatry** *n* идолопокло́нство; (*fig*) обожа́ние. **idolize** *vt* боготвори́ть *impf*.

idyll *n* иди́ллия. **idyllic** *adj* идилли́ческий.

i.e. *abbr* т.е., то есть.

if *conj* е́сли, (*if, whether*) ли; **as** ~ как бу́дто; **even** ~ да́же е́сли; ~ **only** е́сли бы то́лько.

ignite *vt* зажига́ть *impf*, заже́чь *pf*; *vi* загора́ться *impf*, загоре́ться *pf*. **ignition** *n* зажига́ние.

ignoble *adj* ни́зкий.

ignominious *adj* позо́рный.

ignoramus *n* неве́жда *m*. **ignorance** *n* неве́жество, (*of certain facts*) неве́дение. **ignorant** *adj* неве́жественный; (*uninformed*) несве́дущий (*of* в+*prep*).

ignore *vt* не обраща́ть *impf* внима́ния на+*acc*; игнори́ровать *impf* & *pf*.

ilk *n*: **of that** ~ тако́го ро́да.

ill *n* (*evil*) зло; (*harm*) вред; *pl* (*misfortunes*) несча́стья (-тий)

pl; *adj* (*sick*) больно́й; (*bad*) дурно́й; *adv* пло́хо, ду́рно; **fall** ~ заболе́ть *impf*, заболе́ть *pf*; ~**-advised** неблагоразу́мный; ~**-mannered** неве́жливый; ~**-treat** *vt* пло́хо обраща́ться *impf* c+*instr*.

illegal *adj* нелега́льный. **illegality** *n* незако́нность, нелега́льность.

illegible *adj* неразбо́рчивый.

illegitimacy *n* незако́нность, (*of child*) незаконнорождённость. **illegitimate** *adj* незако́нный; незаконнорождённый.

illicit *adj* незако́нный, недозво́ленный.

illiteracy *n* негра́мотность. **illiterate** *adj* негра́мотный.

illness *n* боле́знь.

illogical *adj* нелоги́чный.

illuminate *vt* освеща́ть *impf*, освети́ть *pf*. **illumination** *n* освеще́ние.

illusion *n* иллю́зия. **illusory** *adj* иллюзо́рный.

illustrate *vt* иллюстри́ровать *impf* & *pf*, про~ *pf*. **illustration** *n* иллюстра́ция. **illustrative** *adj* иллюстрати́вный.

illustrious *adj* знамени́тый.

image *n* (*phys; statue etc.*) изображе́ние; (*optical* ~) отраже́ние; (*likeness*) ко́пия; (*metaphor; conception*) о́браз; (*reputation*) репута́ция. **imagery** *n* о́бразность.

imaginable *adj* вообрази́мый. **imaginary** *adj* вообража́емый. **imagination** *n* воображе́ние. **imagine** *vt* вообража́ть *impf*, вообрази́ть *pf*; (*conceive*) представля́ть *impf*, предста́вить *pf* себе́.

imbecile *n* слабоу́мный *sb*; (*fool*) глупе́ц.

imbibe vt (absorb) впитывать impf, впитать pf.

imbue vt внушать impf, внушить pf +dat and +acc (with +acc).

imitate vt подражать impf +dat. **imitation** n подражание (of +dat); attrib искусственный. **imitative** adj подражательный.

immaculate adj безупречный.

immaterial adj (unimportant) несущественный.

immature adj незрелый.

immeasurable adj неизмеримый.

immediate adj (direct) непосредственный; (swift) немедленный. **immediately** adv тотчас, сразу.

immemorial adj: from time ~ с незапамятных времён.

immense adj огромный.

immerse vt погружать impf, погрузить pf. **immersion** n погружение.

immigrant n иммигрант, ~ка. **immigration** n иммиграция.

imminent adj надвигающийся; (danger) грозящий.

immobile adj неподвижный. **immobilize** vt парализовать impf & pf.

immoderate adj неумеренный.

immodest adj нескромный.

immoral adj безнравственный. **immorality** n безнравственность.

immortal adj бессмертный. **immortality** n бессмертие. **immortalize** vt обессмертить pf.

immovable adj неподвижный; (fig) непоколебимый.

immune adj (to illness) невосприимчивый (to к+dat); (free from) свободный (from от+gen). **immunity** n имму-

нитет (from к+dat); освобождение (from от+gen). **immunize** vt иммунизировать impf & pf.

immutable adj неизменный.

imp n бесёнок.

impact n удар; (fig) влияние.

impair vt вредить impf, по~ pf.

impale vt протыкать impf, проткнуть pf.

impart vt делиться impf, по~ pf +instr (to c+instr).

impartial adj беспристрастный.

impassable adj непроходимый; (for vehicles) непроезжий.

impasse n тупик.

impassioned adj страстный.

impassive adj бесстрастный.

impatience n нетерпение. **impatient** adj нетерпеливый.

impeach vt обвинять impf, обвинить pf (for в+prep).

impeccable adj безупречный.

impecunious adj безденежный.

impedance n полное сопротивление. **impede** vt препятствовать impf, вос~ pf +dat. **impediment** n препятствие; (in speech) заикание.

impel vt побуждать impf, побудить pf (to +inf, к+dat).

impending adj предстоящий.

impenetrable adj непроницаемый.

imperative adj необходимый; n (gram) повелительное наклонение.

imperceptible adj незаметный.

imperfect n имперфект; adj несовершенный. **imperfection** n несовершенство; (fault) недостаток. **imperfective** adj (n) несовершенный (вид).

imperial adj имперский.

imperialism n империали́зм.
imperialist n империали́ст; attrib империалисти́ческий.
imperil vt подверга́ть impf, подве́ргнуть pf опа́сности.
imperious adj вла́стный.
impersonal adj безли́чный.
impersonate vt (imitate) подража́ть impf; (pretend to be) выдава́ть impf, вы́дать pf себя́ за+acc. **impersonation** n подража́ние.
impertinence n де́рзость. **impertinent** adj де́рзкий.
imperturbable adj невозмути́мый.
impervious adj (fig) глухо́й (to к+dat).
impetuous adj стреми́тельный.
impetus n дви́жущая си́ла.
impinge vi: ~ (up)on ока́зывать impf, оказа́ть pf отрица́тельный эффе́кт на+acc.
implacable adj неумоли́мый.
implant vt вводи́ть impf, ввести́ pf; (fig) се́ять impf, по~ pf.
implement[1] n ору́дие, инструме́нт.
implement[2] vt (fulfil) выполня́ть impf, вы́полнить pf.
implicate vt впу́тывать impf, впу́тать pf. **implication** n (inference) намёк; pl значе́ние.
implicit adj подразумева́емый; (absolute) безогово́рочный.
implore vt умоля́ть impf.
imply vt подразумева́ть impf.
impolite adj неве́жливый.
imponderable adj неопределённый.
import n (meaning) значе́ние; (of goods) и́мпорт; vt импорти́ровать impf & pf. **importer** n импортёр.
importance n ва́жность. **im-**

portant adj ва́жный.
impose vt (tax) облага́ть impf, обложи́ть pf +instr (on +acc); (obligation) налага́ть impf, наложи́ть pf (on на+acc); ~ (o.s.) on налега́ть impf на+acc. **imposing** adj внуши́тельный. **imposition** n обложе́ние, наложе́ние.
impossibility n невозмо́жность. **impossible** adj невозмо́жный.
impostor n самозва́нец.
impotence n бесси́лие; (med) импоте́нция. **impotent** adj бесси́льный; (med) импоте́нтный.
impound vt (confiscate) конфискова́ть impf & pf.
impoverished adj обедне́вший.
impracticable adj невыполни́мый.
imprecise n нето́чный.
impregnable adj непристу́пный.
impregnate vt (fertilize) оплодотворя́ть impf, оплодотвори́ть pf; (saturate) пропи́тывать impf, пропита́ть pf.
impresario n аге́нт.
impress vt производи́ть impf, произвести́ pf (како́е-либо) впечатле́ние на+acc; ~ upon (s.o.) внуша́ть impf, внуши́ть pf (+dat). **impression** n впечатле́ние; (imprint) отпеча́ток; (reprint) стереоти́пное изда́ние.
impressionism n импрессиони́зм. **impressionist** n импрессиони́ст.
impressive adj впечатля́ющий.
imprint n отпеча́ток; vt отпеча́тывать impf, отпеча́тать pf; (on memory) запеча́тл-

ва́ть *impf*, запечатле́ть *pf*.
imprison *vt* заключа́ть *impf*, заключи́ть *pf* (в тюрьму́). **imprisonment** *n* тюре́мное заключе́ние.
improbable *adj* невероя́тный.
impromptu *adj* импровизи́рованный; *adv* без подгото́вки, экспро́мтом.
improper *adj* (*incorrect*) непра́вильный; (*indecent*) неприли́чный. **impropriety** *n* неуме́стность.
improve *vt & i* улучша́ть(ся) *impf*, улу́чшить(ся) *pf*. **improvement** *n* улучше́ние.
improvisation *n* импровиза́ция. **improvise** *vt* импровизи́ровать *impf*, сымпровизи́ровать *pf*.
imprudent *adj* неосторо́жный.
impudence *n* на́глость. **impudent** *adj* на́глый.
impulse *n* толчо́к, и́мпульс; (*sudden tendency*) поры́в. **impulsive** *adj* импульси́вный.
impunity *n*: with ~ безнака́занно.
impure *adj* нечи́стый.
impute *vt* припи́сывать *impf*, приписа́ть *pf* (**to** +*dat*).
in *prep* (*place*) в+*prep*, на+*prep*; (*into*) в+*acc*, на+*acc*; (*point in time*) в+*prep*, на+*prep*; **in the morning** (*etc.*) у́тром (*instr*); **in spring** (*etc.*) весно́й (*instr*); (*at some stage in*; *throughout*) во вре́мя +*gen*; (*duration*) за+*acc*; (*after interval of*) че́рез+*acc*; (*during course of*) в тече́ние +*gen*; (*circumstance*) в+*prep*, при+*prep*; *adv* (*place*) внутри́; (*motion*) внутрь; (*at home*) до́ма; (*in fashion*) в мо́де; **in here, there** (*place*) здесь, там; (*motion*) сюда́, туда́; *adj* вну́тренний; (*fash-*

ionable) мо́дный; *n*: **the ins and outs** все хо́ды и вы́ходы.
inability *n* неспосо́бность.
inaccessible *adj* недосту́пный.
inaccurate *adj* нето́чный.
inaction *n* безде́йствие. **inactive** *adj* безде́йственный. **inactivity** *n* безде́йственность.
inadequate *adj* недоста́точный.
inadmissible *adj* недопусти́мый.
inadvertent *adj* неча́янный.
inalienable *adj* неотъе́млемый.
inane *adj* глу́пый.
inanimate *adj* неодушевлённый.
inappropriate *adj* неуме́стный.
inarticulate *adj* (*person*) косноязы́чный; (*indistinct*) невня́тный.
inasmuch *adv*: ~ **as** так как; ввиду́ того́, что.
inattentive *adj* невнима́тельный.
inaudible *adj* неслы́шный.
inaugural *adj* вступи́тельный. **inaugurate** *vt* (*admit to office*) торже́ственно вводи́ть *impf*, ввести́ *pf* в до́лжность; (*open*) открыва́ть *impf*, откры́ть *pf*; (*introduce*) вводи́ть *impf*, ввести́ *pf*. **inauguration** *n* введе́ние в до́лжность; откры́тие; нача́ло.
inauspicious *adj* неблагоприя́тный.
inborn, inbred *adj* врождённый.
incalculable *adj* неисчисли́мый.
incandescent *adj* накалённый.
incantation *n* заклина́ние.
incapability *n* неспосо́бность. **incapable** *adj* неспосо́бный (**of** к+*dat*, на+*acc*).

incapacitate vt де́лать impf, с~ pf неспосо́бным. **incapacity** n неспосо́бность.

incarcerate vt заключа́ть impf, заключи́ть pf (в тюрьму́). **incarceration** n заключе́ние (в тюрьму́).

incarnate adj воплощённый. **incarnation** n воплоще́ние.

incendiary adj зажига́тельный.

incense¹ n фимиа́м, ла́дан.

incense² vt разгнева́ть pf.

incentive n побужде́ние.

inception n нача́ло.

incessant adj непреста́нный.

incest n кровосмеше́ние.

inch n дюйм; ~ by ~ ма́лопома́лу; vi ползти́ impf.

incidence n (phys) паде́ние; (prevalence) распростране́ние. **incident** n слу́чай, инциде́нт. **incidental** adj (casual) случа́йный; (inessential) несуще́ственный. **incidentally** adv ме́жду про́чим.

incinerate vt испепеля́ть impf, испепели́ть pf. **incinerator** n мусоросжига́тельная печь.

incipient adj начина́ющийся.

incision n надре́з (in на+acc). **incisive** adj (fig) о́стрый. **incisor** n резе́ц.

incite vt подстрека́ть impf, подстрекну́ть pf (to к+dat). **incitement** n подстрека́тельство.

inclement adj суро́вый.

inclination n (slope) накло́н; (propensity) скло́нность (for, to к+dat). **incline** n накло́н; vt & i склоня́ть(ся) impf, склони́ть(ся) pf. **inclined** predic (disposed) скло́нен (-о́нна, -о́нно) (to к+dat).

include vt включа́ть impf, включи́ть pf (in в+acc; (con-

tain) заключа́ть impf, заключи́ть pf в себе́. **including** prep включа́я+acc. **inclusion** n включе́ние. **inclusive** adj включа́ющий (в себе́); adv включи́тельно.

incognito adv инко́гнито.

incoherent adj бессвя́зный.

income n дохо́д; ~ tax подохо́дный нало́г.

incommensurate adj несоразме́рный.

incomparable adj несравни́мый (to, with c+instr); (matchless) несравне́нный.

incompatible adj несовмести́мый.

incompetence n некомпете́нтность. **incompetent** adj некомпете́нтный.

incomplete adj непо́лный, незако́нченный.

incomprehensible adj непоня́тный.

inconceivable adj невообрази́мый.

inconclusive adj (evidence) недоста́точный; (results) неопределённый.

incongruity n несоотве́тствие. **incongruous** adj несоотве́тствующий.

inconsequential adj незначи́тельный.

inconsiderable adj незначи́тельный.

inconsiderate adj невнима́тельный.

inconsistency n непосле́довательность. **inconsistent** adj непосле́довательный.

inconsolable adj безуте́шный.

inconspicuous adj незаме́тный.

incontinence n (med) недержа́ние. **incontinent** adj: be ~ страда́ть impf недержа́нием.

incontrovertible *adj* неопровержи́мый.

inconvenience *n* неудо́бство; *vt* затрудня́ть *impf*, затрудни́ть *pf*. **inconvenient** *adj* неудо́бный.

incorporate *vt* (*include*) включа́ть *impf*, включи́ть *pf*; (*unite*) объединя́ть *impf*, объедини́ть *pf*.

incorrect *adj* непра́вильный.

incorrigible *adj* неисправи́мый.

incorruptible *adj* неподку́пный.

increase *n* рост, увеличе́ние; (*in pay etc.*) приба́вка; *vt & i* увели́чивать(ся) *impf*, увели́чить(ся) *pf*.

incredible *adj* невероя́тный.

incredulous *adj* недове́рчивый.

increment *n* приба́вка.

incriminate *vt* изоблича́ть *impf*, изобличи́ть *pf*.

incubate *vt* (*eggs*) выводи́ть *impf*, вы́вести *pf* (в инкуба́торе). **incubator** *n* инкуба́тор.

inculcate *vt* внедря́ть *impf*, внедри́ть *pf*.

incumbent *adj* (*in office*) стоя́щий у вла́сти; **it is ~** (*up)on* **you** вы на обя́заны.

incur *vt* навлека́ть *impf*, навле́чь *pf* на себя́.

incurable *adj* неизлечи́мый.

incursion *n* (*invasion*) вторже́ние; (*attack*) набе́г.

indebted *predic* в долгу́ (**to** у+*gen*).

indecency *n* неприли́чие. **indecent** *adj* неприли́чный.

indecision *n* нереши́тельность. **indecisive** *adj* нереши́тельный.

indeclinable *adj* несклоня́емый.

indeed *adv* в са́мом де́ле, действи́тельно; (*interrog*) неуже́ли?

indefatigable *adj* неутоми́мый.

indefensible *adj* не име́ющий оправда́ния.

indefinable *adj* неопредели́мый. **indefinite** *adj* неопределённый.

indelible *adj* несмыва́емый.

indemnify *vt*: **~ against** страхова́ть *impf*, за~ *pf* от+*gen*; **~ for** (*compensate*) компенси́ровать *impf & pf*. **indemnity** *n* (*against loss*) гара́нтия от убы́тков; (*compensation*) компенса́ция.

indent *vt* (*printing*) писа́ть *impf*, с~ *pf* с о́тступом. **indentation** *n* (*notch*) зубе́ц; (*printing*) о́тступ.

independence *n* незави́симость, самостоя́тельность. **independent** *adj* незави́симый, самостоя́тельный.

indescribable *adj* неопису́емый.

indestructible *adj* неразруши́мый.

indeterminate *adj* неопределённый.

index *n* (*alphabetical*) указа́тель *m*; (*econ*) и́ндекс; (*pointer*) стре́лка; **~ finger** указа́тельный па́лец.

India *n* Индия. **Indian** *n* инди́ец, индиа́нка; (*American*) инде́ец, индиа́нка; *adj* инди́йский; (*American*) инде́йский; **~ summer** ба́бье ле́то.

indicate *vt* ука́зывать *impf*, указа́ть *pf*; (*be a sign of*) свиде́тельствовать *impf* о+*prep*. **indication** *n* указа́ние; (*sign*) при́знак. **indicative** *adj* ука́зывающий; (*gram*) изъяви́тельный; *n* изъяви́тельное наклоне́ние. **indicator** *n* указа́тель *m*.

indict *vt* обвиня́ть *impf*, обвини́ть *pf* (**for** в+*prep*).

indifference *n* равноду́шие. **indifferent** *adj* равноду́шный; (*mediocre*) посре́дственный.

indigenous *adj* тузе́мный.

indigestible *adj* неудобовари́мый. **indigestion** *n* несваре́ние желу́дка.

indignant *adj* негоду́ющий; **be ~** негодова́ть *impf* (**with** на+*acc*). **indignation** *n* негодова́ние.

indignity *n* оскорбле́ние.

indirect *adj* непрямо́й; (*econ*; *gram*) ко́свенный.

indiscreet *adj* нескро́мный. **indiscretion** *n* нескро́мность.

indiscriminate *adj* неразбо́рчивый. **indiscriminately** *adv* без разбо́ра.

indispensable *adj* необходи́мый.

indisposed *predic* (*unwell*) нездоро́в.

indisputable *adj* бесспо́рный.

indistinct *adj* нея́сный.

indistinguishable *adj* неразличи́мый.

individual *n* ли́чность; *adj* индивидуа́льный. **individualism** *n* индивидуали́зм. **individualist** *n* индивидуали́ст. **individualistic** *adj* индивидуалисти́ческий. **individuality** *n* индивидуа́льность.

indivisible *adj* недели́мый.

indoctrinate *vt* внуша́ть *impf*, внуши́ть *pf* +*dat* (**with** +*acc*).

indolence *n* ле́ность. **indolent** *adj* лени́вый.

indomitable *adj* неукроти́мый.

Indonesia *n* Индоне́зия.

indoor *adj* ко́мнатный. **indoors** *adv* (*position*) в до́ме; (*motion*) в дом.

induce *vt* (*prevail on*) убежда́ть *impf*, убеди́ть *pf*; (*bring about*) вызыва́ть *impf*, вы́звать *pf*. **inducement** *n* побужде́ние.

induction *n* (*logic*, *electr*) инду́кция; (*in post*) введе́ние в до́лжность.

indulge *vt* потво́рствовать *impf* +*dat*; *vi* предава́ться *impf*, преда́ться *pf* (**in** +*dat*). **indulgence** *n* потво́рство; (*tolerance*) снисходи́тельность. **indulgent** *adj* снисходи́тельный.

industrial *adj* промы́шленный. **industrialist** *n* промы́шленник. **industrious** *adj* трудолюби́вый. **industry** *n* промы́шленность; (*zeal*) трудолю́бие.

inebriated *adj* пья́ный.

inedible *adj* несъедо́бный.

ineffective, ineffectual *adj* безрезульта́тный; (*person*) неспосо́бный.

inefficiency *n* неэффекти́вность. **inefficient** *adj* неэффекти́вный.

ineligible *adj* не име́ющий пра́во (**for** на+*acc*).

inept *adj* неуме́лый.

inequality *n* нера́венство.

inert *adj* ине́ртный. **inertia** *n* (*phys*) ине́рция; (*sluggishness*) ине́ртность.

inescapable *adj* неизбе́жный.

inevitability *n* неизбе́жность. **inevitable** *adj* неизбе́жный.

inexact *adj* нето́чный.

inexcusable *adj* непрости́тельный.

inexhaustible *adj* неистощи́мый.

inexorable *adj* неумоли́мый.

inexpensive *adj* недорого́й.

inexperience *n* нео́пытность. **inexperienced** *adj* нео́пытный.

inexplicable *adj* необъясни́мый.

infallible *adj* непогреши́мый.

infamous *adj* позо́рный. **infamy** *n* позо́р.

infancy *n* младе́нчество. **infant** *n* младе́нец. **infantile** *adj* де́тский.

infantry *n* пехо́та.

infatuate *vt* вскружи́ть *pf* го́лову +*dat*. **infatuation** *n* увлече́ние.

infect *vt* заража́ть *impf*, зарази́ть *pf* (**with** +*instr*). **infection** *n* зара́за, инфе́кция. **infectious** *adj* зара́зный; (*fig*) заразительный.

infer *vt* заключа́ть *impf*, заключи́ть *pf*. **inference** *n* заключе́ние.

inferior *adj* (*in rank*) ни́зший; (*in quality*) ху́дший, плохо́й; *n* подчинённый *sb*. **inferiority** *n* бо́лее ни́зкое ка́чество; **~ complex** ко́мплекс неполноце́нности.

infernal *adj* а́дский. **inferno** *n* ад.

infertile *adj* неплодоро́дный.

infested *adj*: **be ~ with** кише́ть *impf* +*instr*.

infidelity *n* неве́рность.

infiltrate *vt* постепе́нно проника́ть *impf*, прони́кнуть *pf* в+*acc*.

infinite *adj* бесконе́чный. **infinitesimal** *adj* бесконе́чно ма́лый. **infinitive** *n* инфинити́в. **infinity** *n* бесконе́чность.

infirm *adj* не́мощный. **infirmary** *n* больни́ца. **infirmity** *n* не́мощь.

inflame *vt & i* (*excite*) возбужда́ть(ся) *impf*, возбуди́ть(ся) *pf*; (*med*) воспаля́ть(ся) *impf*, воспали́ть(ся) *pf*. **inflammable** *adj* огнеопа́сный. **inflammation** *n* воспале́ние. **inflammatory** *adj* подстрека́тельский.

inflate *vt* надува́ть *impf*, наду́ть *pf*. **inflation** *n* (*econ*) инфля́ция.

inflection *n* (*gram*) фле́ксия.

inflexible *adj* неги́бкий; (*fig*) непрекло́нный.

inflict *vt* (*blow*) наноси́ть *impf*, нанести́ *pf* (**up**)**on** +*dat*; (*suffering*) причиня́ть *impf*, причини́ть *pf* (**up**)**on** +*dat*; (*penalty*) налага́ть *impf*, наложи́ть *pf* (**up**)**on** на+*acc*; **~ o.s.** (**up**)**on** навя́зываться *impf*, навяза́ться *pf* +*dat*.

inflow *n* втека́ние, прито́к.

influence *n* влия́ние; *vt* влия́ть *impf*, по~ *pf* на+*acc*. **influential** *adj* влия́тельный.

influenza *n* грипп.

influx *n* (*fig*) наплы́в.

inform *vt* сообща́ть *impf*, сообщи́ть *pf* (**of**, **about** +*about*, о+*prep*); *vi* доноси́ть *impf*, донести́ *pf* (**against** на+*acc*).

informal *adj* (*unofficial*) неофициа́льный; (*casual*) обы́денный.

informant *n* осведоми́тель *m*. **information** *n* информа́ция. **informative** *adj* поучи́тельный. **informer** *n* доно́счик.

infra-red *adj* инфракра́сный.

infrequent *adj* ре́дкий.

infringe *vt* (*violate*) наруша́ть *impf*, нару́шить *pf*; *vi*: **~ (up)on** посяга́ть *impf*, посягну́ть *pf* на+*acc*. **infringement** *n* наруше́ние; посяга́тельство.

infuriate vt разъярять impf, разъярить pf.

infuse vt (fig) внушать impf, внушить pf (into +dat). **infusion** n (fig) внушение; (herbs etc) настой.

ingenious adj изобретательный. **ingenuity** n изобретательность.

ingenuous adj бесхитростный.

ingot n слиток.

ingrained adj закоренелый.

ingratiate vt ~ o.s. вкрадываться impf, вкрасться pf в милость (with +dat).

ingratitude n неблагодарность.

ingredient n ингредиент, составляющее sb.

inhabit vt жить impf в, на, +prep; обитать impf в, на, +prep. **inhabitant** n житель m, ~ница.

inhalation n вдыхание. **inhale** vt вдыхать impf, вдохнуть pf.

inherent adj присущий (in +dat).

inherit vt наследовать impf & pf, y~ pf. **inheritance** n наследство.

inhibit vt стеснять impf, стеснить pf. **inhibited** adj стеснительный. **inhibition** n стеснение.

inhospitable adj негостеприимный; (fig) недружелюбный.

inhuman(e) adj бесчеловечный.

inimical adj враждебный; (harmful) вредный.

inimitable adj неподражаемый.

iniquity n несправедливость.

initial adj (перво)начальный; n начальная буква; pl инициалы m pl; vt ставить impf, по~ pf инициалы на+acc.

initially adv в начале.

initiate vt вводить impf, ввести pf (into в+acc). **initiation** n введение.

initiative n инициатива.

inject vt вводить impf, ввести pf (person +dat, substance +acc). **injection** n укол; (fig) инъекция.

injunction n (law) судебный запрет.

injure vt повреждать impf, повредить pf. **injury** n рана.

injustice n несправедливость.

ink n чернила (-л).

inkling n представление.

inland adj внутренний; adv (motion) внутрь страны; (place) внутри страны; I~ Revenue управление налоговых сборов.

in-laws n pl родственники m pl супруга, -ги.

inlay n инкрустация; vt инкрустировать impf & pf.

inlet n (of sea) узкий залив.

inmate n (prison) заключённый sb; (hospital) больной sb.

inn n гостиница.

innate adj врождённый.

inner adj внутренний. **innermost** adj глубочайший; (fig) сокровенный.

innocence n невинность; (guiltlessness) невиновность. **innocent** adj невинный; (not guilty) невиновный (of в+prep).

innocuous adj безвредный.

innovate vi вводить impf, ввести pf нововведения. I~ **novation** n нововведение. **innovative** adj новаторский. **innovator** n новатор.

innuendo n намёк, инсинуа́ция.

innumerable adj бесчи́сленный.

inoculate vt прививать impf, привить pf +dat (against +acc). **inoculation** n приви́вка.

inoffensive adj безоби́дный.

inopportune adj несвоевре́менный.

inordinate adj чрезме́рный.

inorganic adj неоргани́ческий.

in-patient n стациона́рный больно́й sb.

input n ввод.

inquest n суде́бное сле́дствие, дозна́ние.

inquire vt спра́шивать impf, спроси́ть pf; vi справля́ться impf, спра́виться pf (about о+prep); рассле́довать impf & pf (into +acc). **inquiry** n вопро́с, спра́вка; (investigation) рассле́дование.

inquisition n инквизи́ция. **inquisitive** adj пытли́вый, любозна́тельный.

inroad n (attack) набе́г; (fig) посяга́тельство (on, into на+acc).

insane adj безу́мный. **insanity** n безу́мие.

insatiable adj ненасы́тный.

inscribe vt надпи́сывать impf, надписа́ть pf; (engrave) выреза́ть impf, вы́резать pf. **inscription** n на́дпись.

inscrutable adj непостижи́мый, непроница́емый.

insect n насеко́мое sb. **insecticide** n инсектици́д.

insecure adj (unsafe) небезопа́сный; (not confident) неуве́ренный (в себе́).

insemination n оплодотворе́ние.

insensible adj (unconscious) потеря́вший созна́ние.

insensitive adj нечувстви́тельный.

inseparable adj неотдели́мый; (people) неразлу́чный.

insert vt вставля́ть impf, вкла́дывать impf, вложи́ть pf; (coin) опуска́ть impf, опусти́ть pf. **insertion** n (inserting) вставле́ние, вкла́дывание; (thing inserted) вста́вка.

inshore adj прибре́жный; adv бли́зко к бе́регу.

inside n вну́тренняя часть; pl (anat) вну́тренности f pl; turn ~ out вывёртывать impf, вы́вернуть pf наизна́нку; adj вну́тренний; adv (place) внутри́; (motion) внутрь; prep (place) внутри́+gen, в+prep; (motion) внутрь+gen, в+acc.

insidious adj кова́рный.

insight n проница́тельность.

insignia n зна́ки m pl разли́чия.

insignificant adj незначи́тельный.

insincere adj неи́скренний.

insinuate vt (hint) намека́ть impf, намекну́ть pf на+acc. **insinuation** n инсинуа́ция.

insipid adj пре́сный.

insist vt & i наста́ивать impf, настоя́ть pf (on на+prep). **insistence** n насто́йчивость. **insistent** adj насто́йчивый.

insolence n на́глость. **insolent** adj на́глый.

insoluble adj (problem) неразреши́мый; (in liquid) нераствори́мый.

insolvent adj несостоя́тельный.

insomnia n бессо́нница.

inspect vt инспекти́ровать impf, про~ pf. **inspection** n инспе́кция. **inspector** n инспе́ктор; (ticket ~) контролёр.

inspiration n вдохнове́ние. **inspire** vt вдохновля́ть impf, вдохнови́ть pf; внуша́ть impf, внуши́ть pf +dat (with +acc).

instability n неусто́йчивость; (of character) неуравнове́шенность.

install vt (person in office) вводи́ть impf, ввести́ pf в до́лжность; (apparatus) устана́вливать impf, установи́ть pf. **installation** n введе́ние в до́лжность; устано́вка; pf сооруже́ния neut pl.

instalment n (comm) взнос; (publication) вы́пуск; часть; **by ~s** в рассро́чку.

instance n (example) приме́р; (case) слу́чай; **for ~** наприме́р.

instant n мгнове́ние, моме́нт; adj неме́дленный; (coffee etc.) раствори́мый. **instantaneous** adj мгнове́нный. **instantly** adv неме́дленно, то́тчас.

instead adv вме́сто (of +gen); **~ of going** вме́сто того́, что́бы пойти́.

instep n подъём.

instigate vt подстрека́ть impf, подстрекну́ть pf (to к+dat). **instigation** n подстрека́тельство. **instigator** n подстрека́тель m, ~ница.

instil vt (ideas etc.) внуша́ть impf, внуши́ть pf (into +dat).

instinct n инсти́нкт. **instinctive** adj инстинкти́вный.

institute n институ́т; vt (establish) устана́вливать impf, установи́ть pf; (introduce) вводи́ть impf, ввести́ pf; (reforms) проводи́ть impf, про-

вести́ pf. **institution** n учрежде́ние.

instruct vt (teach) обуча́ть impf, обучи́ть pf (in +dat); (inform) сообща́ть impf, сообщи́ть pf +dat; (command) прика́зывать impf, приказа́ть pf +dat. **instruction** n (pl) инстру́кция; (teaching) обуче́ние. **instructive** adj поучи́тельный. **instructor** n инстру́ктор.

instrument n ору́дие, инструме́нт. **instrumental** adj (mus) инструмента́льный; (gram) твори́тельный; **be ~** in спосо́бствовать impf, по~ pf +dat; n (gram) твори́тельный паде́ж. **instrumentation** n (mus) инструмено́вка.

insubordinate adj неподчиня́ющийся.

insufferable adj невыноси́мый.

insular adj (fig) ограни́ченный.

insulate vt изоли́ровать impf & pf. **insulation** n изоля́ция. **insulator** n изоля́тор.

insulin n инсули́н.

insult n оскорбле́ние; vt оскорбля́ть impf, оскорби́ть pf. **insulting** adj оскорби́тельный.

insuperable adj непреодоли́мый.

insurance n страхова́ние; attrib страхово́й. **insure** vt страхова́ть impf, за~ pf (against от+gen).

insurgent n повста́нец.

insurmountable adj непреодоли́мый.

insurrection n восста́ние.

intact adj це́лый.

intake n (of persons) набо́р; (consumption) потребле́ние.

intangible adj неосязáемый.

integral adj неотъéмлемый.
integrate vt & i интегрúроваться impf & pf. **integration** n интегрáция.

integrity n (honesty) чéстность.

intellect n интеллéкт. **intellectual** n интеллигéнт; adj интеллектуáльный.

intelligence n (intellect) ум; (information) свéдения neut pl; (~ service) развéдка. **intelligent** adj ýмный.

intelligentsia n интеллигéнция.

intelligible adj понятный.
intemperate adj невоздéржанный.

intend vt собирáться impf, собрáться pf; (design) предназначáть impf, предназнáчить pf (for для+gen, на+acc).
intense adj сúльный. **intensify** vt & i усúливать(ся) impf, усúлить(ся) pf. **intensity** n интенсúвность, сúла.
intensive adj интенсúвный.

intent n намéрение; adj (resolved) стремящийся (on к+dat); (occupied) погружённый (on в+acc); (earnest) внимáтельный. **intention** n намéрение. **intentional** adj намéренный.

inter vt хоронúть impf, по~ pf.
interact vi взаимодéйствовать impf. **interaction** n взаимодéйствие.

intercede vi ходáтайствовать impf, по~ pf (for за+acc; with пéред+instr).
intercept vt перехвáтывать impf, перехватúть pf. **interception** n перехвáт.

interchange n обмéн (of +instr); (junction) трáнспортная развязка; vt обмéниваться impf, обменяться pf +instr. **interchangeable** adj взаимозаменяемый.

inter-city adj междугорóдный.

intercom n внутренняя телефóнная связь.
interconnected adj взаимосвязанный. **interconnection** n взаимосвязь.

intercourse n (social) общéние; (trade; sexual) сношéния neut pl.

interdisciplinary adj межотраслевóй.

interest n интерéс (in к+dat); (econ) процéнты m pl; vt интересовáть impf; (~ person) заинтересóвывать impf, заинтересовáть pf (in +instr); be ~ed in интересовáться impf +instr. **interesting** adj интерéсный.

interfere vi вмéшиваться impf, вмешáться pf (in в+acc). **interference** n вмешáтельство; (radio) помéхи f pl.

interim n: in the ~ тем врéменем; adj промежýточный; (temporary) врéменный.

interior n внýтренность; adj внýтренний.

interjection n восклицáние; (gram) междомéтие.

interlock vt & i сцепля́ть(ся) impf, сцепúть(ся) pf.
interloper n незвáный гость m.
interlude n (theat) антрáкт; (mus, fig) интерлюдия.

intermediary n посрéдник.
intermediate adj промежýточный.

interminable adj бесконéчный.
intermission n перерыв; (theat) антрáкт.

intermittent adj прерывистый.

intern vt интернировать impf & pf.

internal adj внутренний; ~ **combustion engine** двигатель m внутреннего сгорания.

international adj международный; n (contest) международные состязания neut pl.

internment n интернирование.

interplay n взаимодействие.

interpret vt (explain) толковать impf; (understand) истолковывать impf, истолковать pf; vi переводить impf, перевести pf. **interpretation** n толкование. **interpreter** n переводчик, -ица.

interrelated adj взаимосвязанный. **interrelationship** n взаимная связь.

interrogate vt допрашивать impf, допросить pf. **interrogation** n допрос. **interrogative** adj вопросительный.

interrupt vt прерывать impf, прервать pf. **interruption** n перерыв.

intersect vt & i пересекать(ся) impf, пересечь(ся) pf. **intersection** n пересечение.

intersperse vt (scatter) рассыпать impf, рассыпать pf (**between, among** между+instr, среди+gen).

intertwine vt & i переплетать(ся) impf, переплести(сь) pf.

interval n интервал; (theat) антракт.

intervene vi (occur) происходить impf, произойти pf; (**in** вмешиваться impf, вмешаться pf в+acc. **intervention** n вмешательство; (polit) интервенция.

interview n интервью neut

indecl; vt интервьюировать impf & pf, про-, pf. **interviewer** n интервьюер.

interweave vt воткать pf.

intestate adj без завещания.

intestine n кишка; pl кишечник.

intimacy n интимность. **intimate**[1] adj интимный.

intimate[2] vt (hint) намекать impf, намекнуть pf на+acc. **intimation** n намёк.

intimidate vt запугивать impf, запугать pf.

into prep в, во+acc, на+acc.

intolerable adj невыносимый.

intolerance n нетерпимость. **intolerant** adj нетерпимый.

intonation n интонация.

intoxicated adj пьяный. **intoxication** n опьянение.

intractable adj неподатливый.

intransigent adj непримиримый.

intransitive adj непереходный.

intrepid adj неустрашимый.

intricacy n запутанность. **intricate** adj запутанный.

intrigue n интрига; vi интриговать impf; vt интриговать impf, за- pf.

intrinsic adj присущий; (value) внутренний.

introduce vt вводить impf, ввести pf; (person) представлять impf, представить pf. **introduction** n введение; представление; (to book) предисловие. **introductory** adj вступительный.

introspection n интроспекция.

intrude vi вторгаться impf, вторгнуться pf (**into** в+acc); (disturb) мешать impf, по- pf. **intruder** n (burglar) грабитель m. **intrusion** n вторжение.

intuition n интуи́ция. **intuitive** adj интуити́вный.

inundate vt наводня́ть impf, наводни́ть pf. **inundation** n наводне́ние.

invade vt вторга́ться impf, вто́ргнуться pf в+acc. **invader** n захва́тчик.

invalid[1] n (person) инвали́д.

invalid[2] adj недействи́тельный. **invalidate** vt де́лать impf, с~ pf недействи́тельным.

invaluable adj неоцени́мый.

invariable adj неизме́нный.

invasion n вторже́ние.

invective n брань.

invent vt изобрета́ть impf, изобрести́ pf; (think up) выду́мывать impf, вы́думать pf. **invention** n изобрете́ние; вы́думка. **inventive** adj изобрета́тельный. **inventor** n изобрета́тель m.

inventory n инвента́рь m.

inverse adj обра́тный; n противополо́жность. **invert** vt перевора́чивать impf, переверну́ть pf. **inverted commas** n pl кавы́чки f pl.

invest vt & i (econ) вкла́дывать impf, вложи́ть pf (де́ньги) (in в+acc)

investigate vt иссле́довать impf & pf; (law) рассле́довать impf & pf. **investigation** n иссле́дование; рассле́дование.

investment n (econ) вклад. **investor** n вкла́дчик.

inveterate adj закорене́лый.

invidious adj оскорби́тельный.

invigorate vt оживля́ть impf, оживи́ть pf.

invincible adj непобеди́мый.

inviolable adj неруши́мый.

invisible adj неви́димый.

invitation n приглаше́ние. **invite** vt приглаша́ть impf, пригласи́ть pf. **inviting** adj привлека́тельный.

invoice n факту́ра.

invoke vt обраща́ться impf, обрати́ться pf к+dat.

involuntary adj нево́льный.

involve vt (entangle) вовлека́ть impf, вовле́чь pf; (entail) влечь impf за собо́й. **involved** adj сло́жный.

invulnerable adj неуязви́мый.

inward adj вну́тренний. **inwardly** adv внутри́. **inwards** adv внутрь.

iodine n йод.

iota n: not an ~ ни на йо́ту.

IOU n долгова́я распи́ска.

Iran n Ира́н. **Iranian** n ира́нец, -нка; adj ира́нский.

Iraq n Ира́к. **Iraqi** n жи́тель m, -ница Ира́ка; adj ира́кский.

irascible adj раздражи́тельный.

irate adj гне́вный.

Ireland n Ирла́ндия.

iris n (anat) ра́дужная оболо́чка; (bot) каса́тик.

Irish adj ирла́ндский. **Irishman** n ирла́ндец. **Irishwoman** n ирла́ндка.

irk vt раздража́ть impf, раздражи́ть pf +dat. **irksome** adj раздражи́тельный.

iron n желе́зо; (for clothes) утю́г; adj желе́зный; vt гла́дить impf, вы́~ pf.

ironic(al) adj ирони́ческий. **irony** n иро́ния.

irradiate vt (subject to radiation) облуча́ть impf, облучи́ть pf. **irradiation** n облуче́ние.

irrational adj неразу́мный.

irreconcilable *adj* непримири́мый.

irrefutable *adj* неопроверж́имый.

irregular *adj* нерегуля́рный; (*gram*) непра́вильный; (*not even*) неро́вный.

irrelevant *adj* неуме́стный.

irreparable *adj* непоправ́имый.

irreplaceable *adj* незамен́имый.

irrepressible *adj* неудерж́имый.

irreproachable *adj* безупре́чный.

irresistible *adj* неотраз́имый.

irresolute *adj* нереш́ительный.

irrespective *adj*: ~ **of** несмотря на+*acc*.

irresponsible *adj* безотве́тственный.

irretrievable *adj* непоправ́имый.

irreverent *adj* непочт́ительный.

irreversible *adj* необрат́имый.

irrevocable *adj* неотмен́яемый.

irrigate *vt* ороша́ть *impf*, орос́ить *pf*. **irrigation** *n* ороше́ние.

irritable *adj* раздраж́ительный. **irritate** *vt* раздража́ть *impf*, раздраж́ить *pf*. **irritation** *n* раздраже́ние.

Islam *n* исла́м. **Islamic** *adj* мусульма́нский.

island, **isle** *n* о́стров. **islander** *n* острови́тянин, -я́нка.

isolate *vt* изоли́ровать *impf* & *pf*. **isolation** *n* изоля́ция.

Israel *n* Изра́иль *m*. **Israeli** *n* израильтя́нин, -я́нка; *adj* изра́ильский.

issue *n* (*question*) спо́рный

вопро́с; (*of bonds etc.*) вы́пуск; (*of magazine*) но́мер; *vi* выходи́ть *impf*, вы́йти *pf*; (*flow*) течь *impf*; *vt* выпуска́ть *impf*, вы́пустить *pf*; (*give out*) выдава́ть *impf*, вы́дать *pf*.

isthmus *n* переше́ек.

it *pron* он, она́, оно́; -его́.

Italian *n* италья́нец, -нка; *adj* италья́нский.

italics *n pl* курси́в; **in ~** курси́вом. **italicize** *vt* выделя́ть *impf*, вы́делить *pf* курси́вом.

Italy *n* Ита́лия.

ITAR-Tass *abbr* ИТАР-ТАСС.

itch *n* зуд; *vi* чеса́ться *impf*.

item *n* (*on list*) предме́т; (*in account*) статья́; (*on agenda*) пункт; (*in magazine*) но́мер. **itemize** *vt* перечисля́ть *impf*, перечи́слить *pf*.

itinerant *adj* стра́нствующий. **itinerary** *n* маршру́т.

its *poss pron* его́, её; свой.

itself *pron* (*emph*) (он)о́ сам(о́), (она́) сама́; (*refl*) себя́, -ся (*suffixed to vt*).

ivory *n* слоно́вая кость.

ivy *n* плющ.

J

jab *n* толчо́к; (*injection*) уко́л; *vt* ты́кать *impf*, ткнуть *pf*.

jabber *vi* тарато́рить *impf*.

jack *n* (*cards*) вале́т; (*lifting device*) домкра́т; *vt* (~ **up**) поднима́ть *impf*, подня́ть *pf* домкра́том.

jackdaw *n* га́лка.

jacket *n* (*tailored*) пиджа́к; (*anorak*) ку́ртка; (*on book*) (супер)обло́жка.

jackpot *n* банк.

jade n (mineral) нефри́т.

jaded adj утомлённый.

jagged adj зазу́бренный.

jaguar n ягуа́р.

jail see **gaol**

jam¹ n (crush) да́вка; (in traffic) про́бка; vt (thrust) впи́хивать impf, впихну́ть pf (into в+acc); (wedge open; block) закли́нивать impf, закли́нить pf; (radio) заглуша́ть impf, заглуши́ть pf; vi (machine) закли́нивать impf, закли́нить pf impers+acc.

jam² n (conserve) варе́нье, джем.

jangle vi (& t) звя́кать (+instr).

janitor n привра́тник.

January n янва́рь; adj янва́рский.

Japan n Япо́ния. **Japanese** n япо́нец, -нка; adj япо́нский.

jar¹ n (container) ба́нка.

jar² vi (irritate) раздража́ть impf, раздражи́ть pf (upon +acc).

jargon n жарго́н.

jasmin(e) n жасми́н.

jaundice n желту́ха. **jaundiced** adj (fig) цини́чный.

jaunt n прогу́лка.

jaunty adj бо́дрый.

javelin n копьё.

jaw n че́люсть; pl пасть, рот.

jay n со́йка.

jazz n джаз; adj джа́зовый.

jealous adj ревни́вый; (envious) зави́стливый; be ~ of (person) ревнова́ть impf; (thing) зави́довать impf, по~ pf+dat; (rights) ревни́во оберега́ть impf, обере́чь pf. **jealousy** n ре́вность; за́висть.

jeans n pl джи́нсы (-сов) pl.

jeer n насме́шка; vt & i насмеха́ться impf (at над+instr).

jelly n (sweet) желе́ neut

indecl; (aspic) сту́день m. **jellyfish** n меду́за.

jeopardize vt подверга́ть impf, подве́ргнуть pf опа́сности. **jeopardy** n опа́сность.

jerk n рыво́к; vt дёргать impf +instr; (twitch) дёргаться impf, дёрнуться pf. **jerky** adj нерво́ный.

jersey n (garment) джемпер; (fabric) джерси́ neut indecl.

jest n шу́тка; **in** ~ в шу́тку; vi шути́ть impf, по~ pf. **jester** n шут.

jet¹ n (stream) струя́; (nozzle) сопло́; ~ engine реакти́вный дви́гатель m; ~ plane реакти́вный самолёт.

jet² n (mineralogy) гага́т; ~ **black** чёрный как смоль.

jettison vt выбра́сывать impf, вы́бросить pf за́ борт.

jetty n при́стань.

Jew n евре́й, евре́йка. **Jewish** adj евре́йский.

jewel n драгоце́нность, драгоце́нный ка́мень m. **jeweller** n ювели́р. **jewellery** n драгоце́нности f pl.

jib n (naut) кли́вер; vi: ~ at уклоня́ться impf от+gen.

jigsaw n (puzzle) моза́ика.

jingle n звя́канье; vi (& t) звя́кать impf, звя́кнуть pf (+instr).

job n (work) рабо́та; (task) зада́ние; (position) ме́сто. **jobless** adj безрабо́тный.

jockey n жоке́й; vi отти́рать impf друг дру́га.

jocular adj шутли́вый.

jog n (push) толчо́к; vt подта́лкивать impf, подтолкну́ть pf; vi бе́гать impf труско́й. **jogger** n занима́ющийся оздорови́тельным бе́гом. **jogging** n оздорови́тельный бег.

join vt & i соединя́ть(ся) impf, соедини́ть(ся) pf; vt (a group of people) присоединя́ться impf, присоедини́ться pf k+dat; (as member) вступа́ть impf, вступи́ть pf в+acc; vi: ~ in принима́ть impf, приня́ть pf уча́стие (в+prep); ~ up вступа́ть impf, вступи́ть pf в а́рмию.

joiner n столя́р.

joint n соедине́ние; (anat) суста́в; (meat) кусо́к; adj совме́стный; (common) о́бщий.

joist n перекла́дина.

joke n шу́тка; vi шути́ть impf, по~ pf. **joker** n шутни́к; (cards) джо́кер.

jollity n весе́лье. **jolly** adj весёлый; adv о́чень.

jolt n толчо́к; vt & i трясти́(сь) impf.

jostle vt & i толка́ть(ся) impf, толкну́ть(ся) pf.

jot n йо́та; not a ~ ни на йо́ту; vt (~ down) запи́сывать impf, записа́ть pf.

journal n журна́л; (diary) дневни́к. **journalese** n газе́тный язы́к. **journalism** n журнали́стика. **journalist** n журнали́ст.

journey n путеше́ствие; vi путеше́ствовать impf.

jovial adj весёлый.

joy n ра́дость. **joyful**, **joyous** adj ра́достный. **joyless** adj безра́достный. **joystick** n рыча́г управле́ния; (comput) джо́йстик.

jubilant adj лику́ющий; be ~ ликова́ть impf. **jubilation** n ликова́ние.

jubilee n юбиле́й.

Judaism n юдаи́зм.

judge n судья́ m; (connoisseur) цени́тель m; vt & i суди́ть

impf. **judgement** n (legal decision) реше́ние; (opinion) мне́ние; (discernment) рассуди́тельность.

judicial adj суде́бный. **judiciary** n судьи́ m pl. **judicious** adj здравомы́слящий.

judo n дзюдо́ neut indecl.

jug n кувши́н.

juggernaut n (lorry) многото́нный грузови́к; (fig) неумоли́мая си́ла.

juggle vi жонгли́ровать impf. **juggler** n жонглёр.

jugular n яре́мная ве́на.

juice n сок. **juicy** adj со́чный.

July n ию́ль m; adj ию́льский.

jumble n (disorder) беспоря́док; (articles) барахло́; vt перепу́тывать impf, перепу́тать pf.

jump n прыжо́к, скачо́к; vi прыга́ть impf, пры́гнуть pf, скака́ть impf; (from shock) вздра́гивать impf, вздро́гнуть pf; vt (~ over) перепры́гивать impf, перепры́гнуть pf; at (offer) ухва́тываться impf, ухвати́ться pf за+acc; ~ up вска́кивать impf, вскочи́ть pf.

jumper n джемпер.

jumpy adj не́рвный.

junction n (rly) у́зел; (roads) перекрёсток.

juncture n: at this ~ в э́тот моме́нт.

June n ию́нь m; adj ию́ньский.

jungle n джу́нгли (-лей) pl.

junior adj мла́дший; ~ school нача́льная шко́ла.

juniper n можжеве́льник.

junk n (rubbish) барахло́.

jurisdiction n юрисди́кция.

jurisprudence n юриспруде́нция.

juror n прися́жный sb. **jury**

присяжные sb; (in competition) жюри neut indecl.

just adj (fair) справедли́вый; (deserved) заслу́женный; adv (exactly) как раз, и́менно; (simply) про́сто; (barely) едва́; (very recently) то́лько что; ~ **in case** на вся́кий слу́чай.

justice n (proceedings) правосу́дие; (fairness) справедли́вость; **do ~ to** отдава́ть impf, отда́ть pf до́лжное +dat.

justify vt опра́вдывать impf, оправда́ть pf. **justification** n оправда́ние.

jut vi (~ **out**) выдава́ться impf, вы́ступать impf.

juvenile n & adj несовершенноле́тний sb & adj.

juxtapose vt помеща́ть impf, помести́ть pf ря́дом; (for comparison) сопоставля́ть impf, сопоста́вить pf (**with** c+instr).

K

kaleidoscope n калейдоско́п.

kangaroo n кенгуру́ m indecl.

Kazakhstan n Казахста́н.

keel n киль m; vi: ~ **over** опроки́дываться impf, опроки́нуться pf.

keen adj (enthusiastic) по́лный энтузиа́зма; (sharp) о́стрый; (strong) си́льный; **be ~ on** увлека́ться impf, увле́чься pf +instr; (want to do) о́чень хоте́ть impf +inf.

keep[1] n (tower) гла́вная ба́шня; (maintenance) содержа́ние.

keep[2] vt (possess, maintain) держа́ть impf; храни́ть impf; (observe) соблюда́ть impf, соблюсти́ pf (the law); (сде́рживать impf, сдержа́ть impf,

(one's word); (family) содержа́ть impf; (diary) вести́ impf; (detain) заде́рживать impf, задержа́ть pf; (retain, reserve) сохраня́ть impf, сохрани́ть pf; vi (remain) остава́ться impf, оста́ться pf; (of food) не по́ртиться impf; ~ **back** (vt) (hold back) уде́рживать impf, удержа́ть pf; (vi) держа́ться pf сза́ди; ~ **doing sth** всё +verb: **she ~s** giggling она́ всё хихи́кает; ~ **from** уде́рживаться impf, удержа́ться pf от+gen; ~ **on** продолжа́ть impf, продо́лжить pf (+inf); ~ **up (with)** (vi) не отстава́ть impf (от+gen).

keepsake n пода́рок на па́мять.

keg n бочо́нок.

kennel n конура́.

kerb n край тротуа́ра.

kernel n (nut) ядро́; (grain) зерно́; (fig) суть.

kerosene n кероси́н.

kettle n ча́йник.

key n ключ; (piano, typewriter) кла́виш(а); (mus) тона́льность; attrib веду́щий, ключево́й. **keyboard** n клавиату́ра. **keyhole** n замо́чная сква́жина.

KGB abbr КГБ.

khaki n & adj ха́ки neut, adj indecl.

kick n уда́р ного́й, пино́к; vt ударя́ть impf, уда́рить pf ного́й; пина́ть impf, пнуть pf; vi (of horse etc.) ляга́ться impf. **kick-off** n нача́ло (игры́).

kid[1] n (goat) козлёнок; (child) малы́ш.

kid[2] vt (deceive) обма́нывать impf, обману́ть pf; vi (joke) шути́ть impf, по~ pf.

kidnap vt похищать impf, похитить pf.

kidney n почка.

kill vt убивать impf, убить pf. **killer** n убийца m & f. **killing** n убийство; adj (murderous, fig) убийственный; (amusing) уморительный.

kiln n обжиговая печь.

kilo n кило neut indecl. **kilohertz** n килогерц. **kilogram(me)** n килограмм. **kilometre** n километр. **kilowatt** n киловатт.

kilt n шотландская юбка.

kimono n кимоно neut indecl.

kin n (family) семья; (collect, relatives) родня.

kind[1] n сорт, род; a ~ of что-то вроде+gen; this ~ of такой; what ~ of что (это, он, etc.) за +nom; ~ of (adv) как будто, как-то.

kind[2] adj добрый.

kindergarten n детский сад.

kindle vt зажигать impf, зажечь pf. **kindling** n растопка.

kindly adj добрый; adv любезно; (with imper) (request) будьте добры, +imper. **kindness** n доброта.

kindred adj: ~ spirit родная душа.

kinetic adj кинетический.

king n король m (also chess, cards, fig); (draughts) дамка. **kingdom** n королевство; (fig) царство. **kingfisher** n зимородок.

kink n перегиб.

kinship n родство; (similarity) сходство. **kinsman, -woman** n родственник, -ица.

kiosk n киоск; (telephone) будка.

kip n сон; vi дрыхнуть impf.

kipper n копчёная селёдка.

Kirghizia n Киргизия.

kiss n поцелуй; vt & i целовать(ся) impf, по~ pf.

kit n (clothing) снаряжение; (tools) набор, комплект; vt: ~ out снаряжать impf, снарядить pf. **kitbag** n вещевой мешок.

kitchen n кухня; attrib кухонный; ~ garden огород.

kite n (toy) змей.

kitsch n дешёвка.

kitten n котёнок.

knack n сноровка.

knapsack n рюкзак.

knead vt месить impf, с~ pf.

knee n колено. **kneecap** n коленная чашка.

kneel vi стоять impf на коленях; (~ down) становиться impf, стать pf на колени.

knickers n pl трусики (-ов) pl.

knick-knack n безделушка.

knife n нож; vt колоть impf, за~ ножом.

knight n (hist) рыцарь m; (holder of order) кавалер; (chess) конь m. **knighthood** n рыцарское звание.

knit vt (garment) вязать impf, с~ pf; (bones) срастаться impf, срастись pf; ~ one's brows хмурить impf, на~ pf брови. **knitting** n (action) вязание; (object) вязанье; ~-needle спица. **knitwear** n трикотаж.

knob n шишка, кнопка; (door handle) ручка. **knobb(l)y** adj шишковатый.

knock n (noise) стук; (blow) удар; vt & i (strike) ударять impf, ударить impf; (strike door etc.) стучать impf, по~ pf (at v+acc); ~ about (treat roughly) колотить impf, по~ pf

(*wander*) шата́ться *impf*; ~
down (*person*) сбива́ть *impf*,
сбить *pf* с ног; (*building*)
сноси́ть *impf*, снести́ *pf*; ~
off сбива́ть *impf*, сбить *pf*;
(*stop work*) шаба́шить *impf*
(рабо́ту); (*deduct*) сбавля́ть
impf, сба́вить *pf*; ~ **out**
выбива́ть *impf*, вы́бить *pf*;
(*sport*) нокаути́ровать *impf*
& *pf*; ~**-out** нока́ут; ~ **over**
опроки́дывать *impf*, опроки́-
нуть *impf*. **knocker** *n* двер-
но́й молото́к.

knoll *n* буго́р.
knot *n* у́зел; *vt* завя́зывать
impf, завяза́ть *pf* узло́м.
knotty *adj* (*fig*) запу́танный.
know *vt* знать *impf*; (~ *how
to*) уме́ть *impf*, с~ *pf* +*inf*;
~**-how** уме́ние. **knowing** *adj*
многозначи́тельный. **know-
ingly** *adv* созна́тельно.
knowledge *n* зна́ние; **to my
~** наско́лько мне изве́стно.
knuckle *n* суста́в па́льца; *vi*:
~ **down to** впряга́ться *impf*,
впря́чься *pf* в+*acc*; ~ **under**
уступа́ть *impf*, уступи́ть *pf*
(**to** +*dat*).

Korea *n* Коре́я.
ko(w)tow *vi* (*fig*) раболе́п-
ствовать *impf* (**to** пе́ред+*instr*).
Kremlin *n* Кремль *m*.
kudos *n* сла́ва.

L

label *n* этике́тка, ярлы́к; *vt*
прикле́ивать *impf*, при-
кле́ить *pf* ярлы́к к+*dat*.
laboratory *n* лаборато́рия.
laborious *adj* кропотли́вый.
labour *n* труд; (*med*) ро́ды
(-дов) *pl*; *attrib* трудово́й; ~-
force рабо́чая си́ла; ~**-inten-**

sive трудоёмкий; **L~ Party**
лейбори́стская па́ртия; *vi*
труди́ться *impf*; *vt*: **a point**
входи́ть *impf*, войти́ *pf* в
изли́шние подро́бности. **la-
boured** *adj* затруднённый;
(*style*) вы́мученный. **labourer**
n чернорабо́чий *sb*. **labourite** *n* лейбори́ст.
labyrinth *n* лабири́нт.
lace *n* (*fabric*) кру́жево; (*cord*)
шнуро́к; *vt* (~ *up*) шнуро-
ва́ть *impf*, за~ *pf*.
lacerate *vt* (*also fig*) терза́ть
impf, ис~ *pf*. **laceration** *n*
(*wound*) рва́ная ра́на.
lack *n* недоста́ток (**of** +*gen*,
в+*prep*), отсу́тствие; *vt* & *i*
не хвата́ть *impf*, хвати́ть *pf*
impers +*dat* (*person*), +*gen*
(*object*).
lackadaisical *adj* то́мный.
laconic *adj* лакони́чный.
lacquer *n* лак; *vt* лакирова́ть
impf, от~ *pf*.
lad *n* па́рень *m*.
ladder *n* ле́стница.
laden *adj* нагру́женный.
ladle *n* (*spoon*) поло́вник; *vt*
че́рпать *impf*, черпну́ть *pf*.
lady *n* да́ма, ле́ди *f indecl*.
ladybird *n* бо́жья коро́вка.
lag[1] *vi*: ~ **behind** отстава́ть
impf, отста́ть *pf* (от+*gen*).
lag[2] *vt* (*insulate*) изоли́ровать
impf & *pf*.
lagoon *n* лагу́на.
lair *n* ло́говище.
laity *n* (*in religion*) миря́не
(-н) *pl*.
lake *n* о́зеро.
lamb *n* ягнёнок.
lame *adj* хромо́й; **be ~** хро-
ма́ть *impf*; **go ~** хроме́ть
impf, о~ *pf*; *vt* кале́чить
impf, о~ *pf*.
lament *n* плач; *vt* сожале́ть

impf о+*prep*. **lamentable** *adj* приско́рбный.

laminated *adj* слои́стый.

lamp *n* ла́мпа; (*in street*) фона́рь *m*. **lamp-post** *n* фона́рный столб. **lampshade** *n* абажу́р.

lance *n* пи́ка; *vt* (*med*) вскрыва́ть *impf*, вскрыть *pf* (ланце́том).

land *n* земля́; (*dry ~*) су́ша; (*country*) страна́; *vi* (*naut*) прича́ливать *impf*, прича́лить *pf*; *vt* & *i* (*aeron*) приземля́ть(ся) *impf*, приземли́ть(ся) *pf*; (*find o.s.*) попада́ть *impf*, попа́сть *pf*. **landing** *n* (*aeron*) поса́дка; (*on stairs*) площа́дка; **~-stage** *n* при́стань. **landlady** *n* хозя́йка. **landlord** *n* хозя́ин. **landmark** *n* (*conspicuous object*) ориенти́р; (*fig*) ве́ха. **landowner** *n* землевладе́лец. **landscape** *n* ландша́фт; (*also picture*) пейза́ж. **landslide** *n* о́ползень *m*.

lane *n* (*in country*) доро́жка; (*street*) переу́лок; (*passage*) прохо́д; (*on road*) ряд; (*in race*) доро́жка.

language *n* язы́к; (*style, speech*) речь.

languid *adj* то́мный.

languish *vi* томи́ться *impf*.

languor *n* то́мность.

lank *adj* (*hair*) гла́дкий. **lanky** *adj* долговя́зый.

lantern *n* фона́рь *m*.

lap[1] *n* (*of person*) коле́ни (-ней) *pl*; (*sport*) круг.

lap[2] *vt* (*drink*) лака́ть *impf*, вы́~ *pf*; (*water*) плеска́ться *impf*.

lapel *n* отворо́т.

lapse *n* (*mistake*) оши́бка; (*interval*) промежу́ток; (*expiry*)

lapwing *n* чи́бис.

larch *n* ли́ственница.

lard *n* свино́е са́ло.

larder *n* кладова́я *sb*.

large *adj* большо́й; *n*: **at ~** (*free*) на свобо́де; **by and ~** вообще́ говоря́. **largely** *adj* в значи́тельной сте́пени. **largesse** *n* ще́дрость.

lark[1] *n* (*bird*) жа́воронок.

lark[2] *n* прока́за; *vi* (*~ about*) резви́ться *impf*.

larva *n* личи́нка.

laryngitis *n* ларинги́т. **larynx** *n* горта́нь.

lascivious *adj* похотли́вый.

laser *n* ла́зер.

lash *n* (*blow*) уда́р пле́тью; (*eyelash*) ресни́ца; *vt* (*beat*) хлеста́ть *impf*, хлестну́ть *pf*; (*tie*) привя́зывать *impf*, привя́зать *pf* (к к+*dat*).

last[1] *n* (*cobbler's*) коло́дка.

last[2] *adj* (*final*) после́дний; (*most recent*) про́шлый; **the year** (*etc.*) про́шлый год; **~ but one** предпосле́дний; **~ night** вчера́ ве́чером; *at* **~** наконе́ц; *adv* (*after all others*) по́сле всех; (*on the last occasion*) в после́дний раз; (*lastly*) наконе́ц.

last[3] *vi* (*go on*) продолжа́ться *impf*, продо́лжиться *pf*; дли́ться *impf*, про~ *pf*; (*be preserved*) сохраня́ться *impf*, сохрани́ться *pf*; (*suffice*) хвата́ть *impf*, хвати́ть *pf*. **lasting** *adj* (*permanent*) постоя́нный; (*durable*) про́чный.

lastly *adv* в заключе́ние; наконе́ц.

latch n щеколда.

late adj поздний; (recent) недавний; (dead) покойный; be ~ for опаздывать impf, опоздать pf за + acc; это поздно; n: за последнее время. lately adv за последнее время.

latent adj скрытый.

lateral adj боковой.

lath n рейка, дранка (also collect).

lathe n токарный станок.

lather n (мыльная) пена; vt i & мылить(ся) impf, на~ pf.

Latin n латинский; ~ский язык; ~-American латиноамериканский.

latitude n свобода; (geog) широта.

latter adj последний; ~-day современный. latterly adv за последнее время.

lattice n решётка.

Latvia n Латвия. Latvian n латвиец, -ийка; латыш, ~ка; adj латвийский, латышский.

laud vt хвалить impf, по~ pf. laudable adj похвальный.

laugh n смех; vi смеяться impf (at над + instr); ~ it off отшучиваться impf, отшутиться pf; ~ing-stock посмешище. laughable adj смешной. laughter n смех.

launch¹ vt (ship) спускать impf, спустить pf на воду; (rocket) запускать impf, запустить pf; (undertake) начинать impf, начать pf; n спуск на воду; запуск. launcher n (for rocket) пусковая установка. launching pad n пусковая площадка.

launch² n (naut) катер.

launder vt стирать impf, вы~ pf. laund(e)rette n прачеч-

ная sb самообслуживания.

laundry n (place) прачечная sb; (articles) бельё.

laurel n лавр(овое дерево).

lava n лава.

lavatory n уборная sb.

lavender n лаванда.

lavish adj щедрый; (abundant) обильный; vt расточать impf (upon + dat).

law n закон; (system) право; ~ and order правопорядок.

law-court n суд. lawful adj законный. lawless adj беззаконный.

lawn n газон; ~-mower газонокосилка.

lawsuit n процесс.

lawyer n адвокат, юрист.

lax adj слабый. laxative n слабительное sb. laxity n слабость.

lay¹ adj (non-clerical) светский.

lay² vt (place) класть impf, положить pf; (cable, pipes) прокладывать impf, проложить pf; (carpet) стлать impf, по~ pf; (trap etc.) устраивать impf, устроить pf; (eggs) класть impf, положить pf; v abs (lay eggs) нестись impf, с~ pf; ~ aside откладывать impf, отложить pf; ~ bare раскрывать impf, раскрыть pf; ~ a bet держать impf пари (on на + acc); ~ down (relinquish) отказываться impf, отказаться pf от + gen; (rule etc.) устанавливать impf, установить pf; ~ off (workmen) увольнять impf, уволить pf; ~ out (spread) выкладывать impf, выложить pf; (garden) разбивать impf, разбить pf; ~ the table накрывать impf, накрыть pf стол (for (meal) k+*dat*); ~ **up** запасáть *impf*, запастú *pf* +*acc*, +*gen*; **be laid up** быть прикóванным к постéли. **layabout** *n* бездéльник. **layer** *n* слой, пласт.

layman *n* мирянúн; (*non-expert*) неспециалúст.

laze *vi* бездéльничать *impf*. **laziness** *n* лень. **lazy** *adj* ленúвый; **~-bones** лентя́й, ~ка.

lead[1] *n* (*example*) примéр; (*leadership*) руковóдство; (*position*) пéрвое мéсто; (*theat*) главная роль; (*electr*) провóд; (*dog's*) повóдок; *vt* водúть *indet*, вестú *det*; (*be in charge of*) руководúть *impf* +*instr*; (*induce*) побуждáть *impf*, побудúть *pf*; *vi* & *i* (*cards*) ходúть *impf* (c+*gen*); *vi* (*sport*) занимáть *impf*, заня́ть *pf* пéрвое мéсто; ~ **away** уводúть *impf*, увестú *pf*; ~ **to** (*result in*) приводúть *impf*, привестú *pf* к+*dat*.

lead[2] *n* (*metal*) свинéц. **leaden** *adj* свинцóвый.

leader *n* руководúтель *m*, ~ница, лúдер; (*mus*) пéрвая скрúпка; (*editorial*) передовáя статья́. **leadership** *n* руковóдство.

leading *adj* ведýщий, выдаю́щийся; ~ **article** передовáя статья́.

leaf *n* лист; (*of table*) откиднáя доскá; *vi*: ~ **through** перелúстывать *impf*, перелистáть *pf*. **leaflet** *n* листóвка.

league *n* лúга; **in** ~ **with** в сою́зе с+*instr*.

leak *n* течь, утéчка; *vi* (*escape*) течь *impf*, (*allow water to* ~) пропускáть *impf* вóду; ~ **out** просáчиваться *impf*,

просочúться *pf*.

lean[1] *adj* (*thin*) худóй; (*meat*) пóстный.

lean[2] *vt* & *i* прислоня́ть(ся) *impf*, прислонúть(ся) *pf* (**against** к+*dat*); *vi* (~ **on, rely on**) опирáться *impf*, опе-рéться *pf* (**on** на+*acc*); (*be inclined*) быть склóнным (**to**(**wards**) к+*dat*); ~ **back** откúдываться *impf*, откúнуться *pf*; ~ **out of** высóвываться *impf*, высунуться *pf* в +*acc*. **leaning** *n* склóнность.

leap *n* прыжóк, скачóк; *vi* прыгать *impf*, прыгнуть *pf*; скакáть *impf*; ~ **year** висо-кóсный год.

learn *vt* учúться *impf*, об~ *pf* +*dat*; (*find out*) узнавáть *impf*, узнáть *pf*. **learned** *adj* учёный. **learner** *n* ученúк, -úца. **learning** *n* (*studies*) учéние; (*erudition*) учёность.

lease *n* арéнда; *vt* (*of owner*) сдавáть *impf*, сдать *pf* в арéнду; (*of tenant*) брать *impf*, взять *pf* в арéнду. **leaseholder** *n* аренáтор.

leash *n* привя́зь.

least *adj* наимéньший, малéйший; *adv* мéнее всегó; **at** ~ по крáйней мéре; **not in the** ~ ничýть.

leather *n* кóжа; *attrib* кóжаный.

leave[1] *n* (*permission*) разрешéние; (*holiday*) óтпуск; **on** ~ в óтпуске; **take** (**one's**) ~ прощáться *impf*, простúться *pf* (**of** c+*instr*).

leave[2] *vt* & *i* оставля́ть *impf*, остáвить *pf*; (*abandon*) покидáть *impf*, покúнуть *pf*; (*go away*) уходúть *impf*, уйтú *pf* (**from** от+*gen*); уезжáть *impf*, уéхать *pf* (**from** от+*gen*);

(go out of) выходи́ть impf, вы́йти pf из+gen; (entrust) предоставля́ть impf, предоста́вить pf (to +dat); ~ out пропуска́ть impf, пропусти́ть pf.

lecherous adj развра́тный.

lectern n анало́й; (in lecture room) пюпи́тр.

lecture n (discourse) ле́кция; (reproof) нота́ция; vi (deliver ~(s)) чита́ть impf, про~ pf ле́кцию (-ии) (on по+dat); vt (admonish) чита́ть impf, про~ pf нота́цию+dat; ~ room аудито́рия. **lecturer** n ле́ктор; (univ) преподава́тель m, ~ница.

ledge n вы́ступ; (shelf) по́лочка.

ledger n гла́вная кни́га.

lee n защи́та; adj подве́тренный.

leech n (worm) пия́вка.

leek n лук-поре́й.

leer vi криви́ться impf, с~ pf.

leeward n подве́тренная сторона́; adj подве́тренный.

leeway n (fig) свобо́да де́йствий.

left n ле́вая сторона́; (the L~; polit) ле́вые sb pl; adj ле́вый; adv нале́во, сле́ва (of +gen); ~-hander левша́ m & f; ~-wing ле́вый.

left-luggage office n ка́мера хране́ния.

leftovers n pl оста́тки m pl; (food) объе́дки (-ков) pl.

leg n нога́; (of furniture etc.) но́жка; (of journey etc.) эта́п.

legacy n насле́дство.

legal adj (of the law) правово́й; (lawful) лега́льный. **legality** n лега́льность. **legalize** vt легализи́ровать impf & pf.

legend n леге́нда. **legendary** adj легенда́рный.

leggings n pl вя́заные рейту́зы (-з) pl.

legible adj разбо́рчивый.

legion n легио́н.

legislate vi издава́ть impf, изда́ть pf зако́ны. **legislation** n законода́тельство. **legislative** adj законода́тельный. **legislator** n законода́тель m. **legislature** n законода́тельные учрежде́ния neut pl.

legitimacy n зако́нность; (of child) законорождённость. **legitimate** adj зако́нный; (child) законорождённый. **legitimize** vt узако́нивать impf, узако́нить pf.

leisure n свобо́дное вре́мя, досу́г; at ~ на досу́ге. **leisurely** adj неторопли́вый.

lemon n лимо́н. **lemonade** n лимона́д.

lend vt дава́ть impf, дать pf взаймы́ (to +dat); ода́лживать impf, одолжи́ть pf (to +dat).

length n длина́; (of time) продолжи́тельность; (of cloth) отре́з; at ~ подро́бно. **lengthen** vt & i удлиня́ть(ся) impf, удлини́ть(ся) pf. **lengthways** adv в длину́, вдоль. **lengthy** adj дли́нный.

leniency n снисходи́тельность. **lenient** adj снисходи́тельный.

lens n ли́нза; (phot) объекти́в; (anat) хруста́лик.

Lent n вели́кий пост.

lentil n чечеви́ца.

Leo n Лев.

leopard n леопа́рд.

leotard n трико́ neut indecl.

leper n прокажённый sb. **leprosy** n прока́за.

lesbian n лесбия́нка; adj лесби́йский.

lesion n поврежде́ние.

less adj ме́ньший; adv ме́ньше, ме́нее; prep за вы́четом +gen.

lessee n аренда́тор.

lessen vt & i уменьша́ть(ся) impf, уме́ньшить(ся) pf.

lesser adj ме́ньший.

lesson conj уро́к.

lest conj (in order that not) чтобы не; (that) как бы не.

let n (lease) сда́ча в наём; vt (allow) позволя́ть impf, позво́лить pf +dat; разреша́ть impf, разреши́ть pf +dat; (rent out) сдава́ть impf, сдать pf внаём (**to** +dat); v aux (imperative) (1st person) дава́й(те); (3rd person) пусть; ~ **alone** не говоря́ уже́ о+prep; ~ **down** (lower) опуска́ть impf, опусти́ть pf; (fail) подводи́ть impf, подвести́ pf; (disappoint) разочаро́вывать impf, разочарова́ть pf; ~ **go** выпуска́ть impf, вы́пустить pf; ~'**s go** пойдёмте!; по- шли́! поéхали!; ~ **in(to)** (admit) впуска́ть impf, впусти́ть pf в+acc; (into secret) посвяща́ть impf, посвяти́ть pf в+acc; ~ **know** дава́ть impf, дать pf знать +dat; ~ **off** (gun) вы́стрелить pf из+gen; (not punish) отпуска́ть impf, отпусти́ть pf без наказа́ния; ~ **out** (release, loosen) выпуска́ть impf, вы́пустить pf; ~ **through** пропуска́ть impf, пропусти́ть pf; ~ **up** затиха́ть impf, зати́хнуть pf.

lethal adj (fatal) смерте́льный; (weapon) смертоно́сный.

lethargic adj летарги́ческий.

lethargy n летарги́я.

letter n письмо́; (symbol) бу́ква; (printing) ли́тера; ~ **box** почто́вый я́щик. **lettering** n шрифт.

lettuce n сала́т.

leukaemia n лейкеми́я.

level n ýровень; adj ро́вный; ~ **crossing** (железнодоро́жный) перее́зд; ~**headed** уравнове́шенный; vt (make ~) выра́внивать impf, вы́ровнять pf; (sport) сра́внивать impf, сравни́ть pf; (gun) наводи́ть impf, навести́ pf (**at** в, на, +acc); (criticism) направля́ть impf, напра́вить pf (**at** про́тив+gen).

lever n рыча́г. **leverage** n де́йствие рычага́; (influence) влия́ние.

levity n легкомы́слие.

levy n (tax) сбор; vt (tax) взима́ть impf (**from** c+gen).

lewd adj (lascivious) похотли́вый; (indecent) са́льный.

lexicon n слова́рь m.

liability n (responsibility) отве́тственность (**for** за+acc); (burden) обу́за. **liable** adj отве́тственный (**for** за+acc); (susceptible) подве́рженный (**to** +dat).

liaise vi подде́рживать impf связь (с+instr). **liaison** n связь; (affair) любо́вная связь.

liar n лгун, ~ья.

libel n клевета́; vt клевета́ть impf, на~ pf на+acc. **libellous** adj клеветни́ческий.

liberal n либера́л; adj либера́льный; (generous) ще́дрый.

liberate vt освобожда́ть impf, освободи́ть pf. **liberation** n освобожде́ние. **liberator** n освободи́тель m.

libertine n распу́тник.

liberty n свобо́да; **at** ~ **in**

свобо́де.

Libra n Весы́ (-со́в) pl.

librarian n библиоте́карь m.

library n библиоте́ка.

libretto n либре́тто neut indecl.

licence[1] n (permission, permit) разреше́ние, лице́нзия; (liberty) (изли́шняя) во́льность.

license, -ce[2] vt (allow) разреша́ть impf, разреши́ть pf +dat; дава́ть impf, дать pf пра́во +dat.

licentious adj распу́щенный.

lichen n лиша́йник.

lick n лиза́ние; vt лиза́ть impf, лизну́ть pf.

lid n кры́шка; (eyelid) ве́ко.

lie[1] n (untruth) ложь; vi лгать impf, со∼ pf.

lie[2] n: ∼ of the land (fig) положе́ние веще́й; vi лежа́ть impf; (be situated) находи́ться impf; ∼ down ложи́ться impf, лечь pf; ∼ in остава́ться impf в посте́ли.

lieu n: in ∼ of вме́сто+gen.

lieutenant n лейтена́нт.

life n жизнь; (way of ∼) о́браз жи́зни; (energy) жи́вость.

lifebelt n спаса́тельный по́яс.

lifeboat n спаса́тельная ло́дка. **lifebuoy** n спаса́тельный круг. **lifeguard** n спаса́тель m, -ница. **life-jacket** n спаса́тельный жиле́т. **lifeless** adj безжи́зненный. **lifelike** adj реалисти́чный. **lifeline** n спаса́тельный коне́ц. **lifelong** adj пожи́зненный. **lifesize(d)** adj в натура́льную величину́. **lifetime** n жизнь.

lift n (machine) лифт, подъёмник; (force) подъёмная си́ла; give s.o. a ∼ подвози́ть impf, подвезти́ pf; vt & i поднима́ть(ся) impf, подня́ть(ся) pf.

ligament n свя́зка.

light[1] n свет, освеще́ние; (source of ∼) ого́нь m, ла́мпа, фона́рь m; pl (traffic ∼) светофо́р; can I have a ∼? мо́жно прикури́ть?; ∼-bulb ла́мпочка; adj (bright) све́тлый; (pale) бле́дный; vt & i (ignite) зажига́ть(ся) impf, заже́чь(ся) pf; vt (illuminate) освеща́ть impf, освети́ть pf; ∼ up освеща́ть(ся) impf, освети́ть(ся) pf; (begin to smoke) заку́рить pf.

light[2] adj (not heavy) лёгкий; ∼-hearted беззабо́тный.

lighten[1] vt (make lighter) облегча́ть impf, облегчи́ть pf; (mitigate) смягча́ть impf, смягчи́ть pf.

lighten[2] vt (illuminate) освеща́ть impf, освети́ть pf; vi (grow bright) светле́ть impf, по∼ pf.

lighter n зажига́лка.

lighthouse n мая́к.

lighting n освеще́ние.

lightning n мо́лния.

lightweight n (sport) легкове́с; adj легкове́сный.

like[1] adj (similar) похо́жий (на+acc); what is he ∼? что он за челове́к?

like[2] vt нра́виться impf, по∼ pf impers+dat; I ∼ him он мне нра́вится; люби́ть impf; vi (wish) хоте́ть impf; if you ∼ е́сли хоти́те; I should ∼ я хоте́л бы; мне хоте́лось бы.

likeable adj симпати́чный.

likelihood n вероя́тность.

likely adj (probable) вероя́тный; (suitable) подходя́щий.

liken vt уподобля́ть impf, уподо́бить pf (to +dat).

likeness n (resemblance) схо́дство; (portrait) портре́т.

likewise adv (similarly) подо́бно; (also) то́же, та́кже.

liking n вкус (for к+dat).

lilac n сире́нь; adj сире́невый.

lily n ли́лия; ~ of the valley ла́ндыш.

limb n член.

limber vi: ~ up размина́ться impf, размя́ться pf.

limbo n (fig) состоя́ние неопределённости.

lime[1] n (mineralogy) и́звесть.

limelight n: in the ~ (fig) в це́нтре внима́ния. **limestone** n известня́к.

lime[2] n (fruit) лайм.

lime[3] n (~-tree) ли́па.

limit n грани́ца, преде́л; vt ограни́чивать impf, ограни́чить pf. **limitation** n ограниче́ние. **limitless** adj безграни́чный.

limousine n лимузи́н.

limp[1] n хромота́; vi хрома́ть impf.

limp[2] adj мя́гкий; (fig) вя́лый.

limpid adj прозра́чный.

linchpin n чека́.

line[1] n (long mark) ли́ния, черта́; (transport, tel) ли́ния; (cord) верёвка; (wrinkle) морщи́на; (limit) грани́ца; (row) ряд; (of words) строка́; (of verse) стих; vt (paper) линова́ть impf, раз~ pf; vt & i (~ up) выстра́ивать(ся) impf, вы́строить(ся) pf в ряд.

line[2] vt (clothes) класть impf, положи́ть pf на подкла́дку.

lineage n происхожде́ние.

linear adj лине́йный.

lined[1] adj (paper) линова́нный; (face) морщи́нистый.

lined[2] adj (garment) на подкла́дке.

linen n полотно́; collect бельё.

liner n ла́йнер.

linesman n боково́й судья́ m.

linger vi заде́рживаться impf, задержа́ться pf.

lingerie n да́мское бельё.

lingering adj (illness) затяжно́й.

lingo n жарго́н.

linguist n лингви́ст. **linguistic** adj лингвисти́ческий. **linguistics** n лингви́стика.

lining n (clothing etc.) подкла́дка; (tech) облицо́вка.

link n (of chain) звено́; (connection) связь; vt соединя́ть impf, соедини́ть pf; связывать impf, связа́ть pf.

lino(leum) n линоле́ум.

lintel n перемы́чка.

lion n лев. **lioness** n льви́ца.

lip n губа́; (of vessel) край. **lipstick** n губна́я пома́да.

liquefy vt & i превраща́ть(ся) impf, преврати́ть(ся) pf в жи́дкое состоя́ние.

liqueur n ликёр.

liquid n жи́дкость; adj жи́дкий.

liquidate vt ликвиди́ровать impf & pf. **liquidation** n ликвида́ция; go into ~ ликвиди́роваться impf & pf.

liquor n (спиртно́й) напи́ток.

liquorice n лакри́ца.

list[1] n спи́сок; vt составля́ть impf, соста́вить pf спи́сок +gen; (enumerate) перечисля́ть impf, перечи́слить pf.

list[2] vi (naut) накреня́ться impf, крени́ться impf, накрени́ться pf.

listen vi слу́шать impf, по~ pf (to +acc). **listener** n слу́шатель m.

listless adj апати́чный.

litany n лита́ния.

literacy n гра́мотность.

literal adj буква́льный.

literary adj литерату́рный.
literate adj гра́мотный.
literature n литерату́ра.
lithe adj ги́бкий.
lithograph n литогра́фия.
Lithuania n Литва́. **Lithuanian** n лито́вец, -вка; adj лито́вский.
litigation n тя́жба.
litre n литр.
litter n (rubbish) сор; (brood) помёт; vt (make untidy) сори́ть impf, на~ pf (with +instr).
little n немно́гое; ~ by ~ ма́ло-пома́лу; a ~ немно́го +gen; adj ма́ленький, небольшо́й; (in height) небольшо́го ро́ста; (in distance, time) коро́ткий; adv ма́ло, немно́го.
liturgy n литурги́я.
live[1] adj живо́й; (coals) горя́щий; (mil) боево́й; (electr) под напряже́нием; (broadcast) прямо́й.
live[2] vi жить impf, ~ down загла́живать impf, загла́дить pf; ~ on (feed on) пита́ться impf +instr; ~ through пережи́ть pf; ~ until, to see дожива́ть impf, дожи́ть pf до+gen; ~ up to жить impf согла́сно +dat.
livelihood n сре́дства neut pl к жи́зни.
lively adj живо́й.
liven (up) vt & i оживля́ть(ся) impf, оживи́ть(ся) pf.
liver n пе́чень; (cul) печёнка.
livery n ливре́я.
livestock n скот.
livid adj (angry) взбешённый.
living n сре́дства neut pl к жи́зни; **earn a** ~ зараба́тывать impf, зарабо́тать на жизнь; adj живо́й; ~-**room** гости́ная sb.

lizard n я́щерица.
load n груз; (also fig) бре́мя neut; (electr) нагру́зка; n (lots) ку́ча; vt (goods) грузи́ть impf, по~ pf; (vehicle) грузи́ть impf, на~ pf; (fig) обременя́ть impf, обремени́ть pf; (gun, camera) заряжа́ть impf, заряди́ть pf.
loaf[1] n буха́нка.
loaf[2] vi безде́льничать impf.
loafer n безде́льник.
loan n заём; vt дава́ть impf, дать pf взаймы́.
loath, loth predic: **be** ~ **to** не хоте́ть impf +inf.
loathe vt ненави́деть impf.
loathing n отвраще́ние.
loathsome adj отврати́тельный.
lob vt высоко́ подбра́сывать impf, подбро́сить pf.
lobby n вестибю́ль m; (parl) кулуа́ры (-ров) pl.
lobe n (of ear) мо́чка.
lobster n ома́р.
local adj ме́стный.
locality n ме́стность.
localized adj локализо́ванный.
locate vt (place) помеща́ть impf, помести́ть pf; (find) находи́ть impf, найти́ pf; **be** ~**d** находи́ться impf.
location n (position) местонахожде́ние; **on** ~ (cin) на нату́ре.
locative adj (n) ме́стный (паде́ж).
lock[1] n (of hair) ло́кон; pl во́лосы (-о́с, -оса́м) pl.
lock[2] n замо́к; (canal) шлюз; vt & i запира́ть(ся) impf, запере́ть(ся) pf; ~ **out** не впуска́ть impf; ~ **up** (imprison) сажа́ть impf, посади́ть pf; (close) закрыва́ть(ся) impf, закры́ть(ся) pf.

locker n шка́фчик.
locket n медальо́н.
locksmith n слеса́рь m.
locomotion n передвиже́ние.
locomotive n локомоти́в.
lodge n (hunting) (охо́тничий) до́мик; (porter's) сторо́жка; (Masonic) ло́жа; vt (accommodate) помеща́ть impf, помести́ть pf; (complaint) пода́вать impf, пода́ть pf; vi (reside) жить impf (with y+gen); (stick) заса́живать impf, засе́сть pf. **lodger** n жиле́ц, жили́ца. **lodging** n (also pl) кварти́ра, (снима́емая) ко́мната.
loft n (attic) черда́к.
lofty adj о́чень высо́кий; (elevated) возвы́шенный.
log n бревно́; (for fire) поле́но; vt (naut) ва́хтенный журна́л.
logarithm n логари́фм.
loggerhead n: be at ~s быть в ссо́ре.
logic n ло́гика. **logical** adj (of logic) логи́ческий; (consistent) логи́чный.
logistics n pl материа́льно-техни́ческое обеспе́чение; (fig) пробле́мы f pl организа́ции.
logo n эмбле́ма.
loin n (pl) поясни́ца; (cul) филе́йная часть.
loiter vi слоня́ться impf.
lone, lonely adj одино́кий. **loneliness** n одино́чество.
long[1] vi (want) стра́стно жела́ть impf, по~ pf (for +gen); (miss) тоскова́ть impf (for по+dat).
long[2] adj (space) дли́нный; (time) до́лгий; (in measurements) длино́й в+acc; in the ~ run в коне́чном счёте; ~-

sighted дальнозо́ркий; ~-**suffering** долготерпели́вый; ~-**term** долгосро́чный; ~-**winded** многоречи́вый; adv до́лго; ~ **ago** (уже́) давно́; as ~ **as** пока́; ~ **before** задо́лго до+gen.
longevity n долгове́чность.
longing n стра́стное жела́ние (for +gen); тоска́ (for по+dat); adj тоску́ющий.
longitude n долгота́.
longways adv в длину́.
look n (glance) взгляд; (appearance) вид; (expression) выраже́ние; vi смотре́ть impf, по~ pf (at на, в, +acc); (appear) вы́глядеть impf +instr; (face) выходи́ть impf (towards, onto на+acc); ~ **about** осма́триваться impf, осмотре́ться pf; ~ **after** (attend to) присма́тривать impf, присмотре́ть pf (attend to) присма́тривать impf, присмотре́ть pf за+instr; ~ **down on** презира́ть impf; ~ **for** иска́ть impf +acc, +gen; ~ **forward to** предвкуша́ть impf, предвкуси́ть pf; ~ **in on** загля́дывать impf, загляну́ть pf k+dat; ~ **into** (investigate) рассма́тривать impf, рассмотре́ть pf; ~ **like** быть похо́жим на+acc; **it** ~s **like rain** похо́же на (то, что бу́дет) дождь; ~ **on** (regard) счита́ть impf, счесть pf (as +instr, за+instr); ~ **out** выгля́дывать impf, вы́глянуть pf (в окно́); быть насторо́же; imper осторо́жно!; ~ **over, through** просма́тривать impf, просмотре́ть pf; ~ **round** (inspect) осма́тривать impf, осмотре́ть pf; ~ **up** (raise eyes) поднима́ть impf, подня́ть pf глаза́; (in dictionary etc.) иска́ть impf; (improve) улучша́ться impf,

улу́чшиться pf; ~ up to уважа́ть impf.

loom¹ n тка́цкий стано́к.

loom² vi вырисо́вываться impf, вы́рисоваться pf; (fig) надвига́ться impf.

loop n пе́тля; vi образо́вывать impf, образова́ть pf пе́тлю; (fasten with loop) закрепля́ть impf, закрепи́ть pf пе́тлей; (wind) обма́тывать impf, обмота́ть pf (around вокру́г+gen).

loophole n бойни́ца; (fig) лазе́йка.

loose adj (free; not tight) свобо́дный; (not fixed) непри-креплённый; (connection, screw) сла́бый; (lax) распу́щенный; at a ~ end без де́ла.

loosen vt и ослабля́ть(ся) impf, осла́бить(ся) pf.

loot n добы́ча; vt гра́бить impf, о~ pf.

lop vt (tree) подреза́ть impf, подре́зать pf; (~ off) обруба́ть impf, обруби́ть pf.

lope vi бе́гать indet, бежа́ть det вприпры́жку.

lopsided adj кривобо́кий.

loquacious adj болтли́вый.

lord n (master) господи́н; (eccl) Госпо́дь; (title) лорд; vt: ~ it over помыка́ть impf +instr. lordship n (title) све́тлость.

lore n зна́ния neut pl.

lorry n грузови́к.

lose vt теря́ть impf, по~ pf; vt и i (game etc.) прои́грывать impf, проигра́ть pf; vi (clock) отстава́ть impf, отста́ть pf. loss n поте́ря; (monetary) убы́ток; (in game) про́игрыш.

lot n жре́бий; (destiny) уча́сть; (of goods) па́ртия; a ~, ~s

мно́го; the ~ всё, все pl.

loth see loath

lotion n лосьо́н.

lottery n лотере́я.

loud adj (sound) гро́мкий; (noisy) шу́мный; (colour) крича́щий; out ~ вслух. loud-speaker n громкоговори́тель m.

lounge n гости́ная sb; vi сиде́ть impf разваля́сь; (idle) безде́льничать impf.

louse n вошь. lousy adj (coll) парши́вый.

lovable adj ми́лый. love n любо́вь (of, for к≥+dat); in ~ with влюблённый в+acc; vt люби́ть impf. lovely adj прекра́сный; (delightful) преле́стный. lover n любо́вник, -ица.

low adj ни́зкий, невысо́кий; (quiet) ти́хий.

lower¹ vt опуска́ть impf, опусти́ть pf; (price, voice, standard) понижа́ть impf, пони́зить pf.

lower² adj ни́жний.

lowland n ни́зменность.

lowly adj скро́мный.

loyal adj ве́рный. loyalty n ве́рность.

LP abbr (of long-playing record) долгоигра́ющая пласти́нка.

Ltd. abbr (of Limited) с ограни́ченной отве́тственностью.

lubricant n сма́зка. lubricate vt сма́зывать impf, сма́зать pf. lubrication n сма́зка.

lucid adj я́сный. lucidity n я́сность.

luck n (chance) слу́чай; (good ~) сча́стье, уда́ча; (bad ~) неуда́ча. luckily adv к сча́стью. lucky adj счастли́вый; be ~ везти́ imp, по~ pf impers +dat: I was ~ мне повезло́.

lucrative adj при́быльный.
ludicrous adj смехотво́рный.
lug vt таска́ть indet, тащи́ть det.
luggage n бага́ж.
lugubrious adj печа́льный.
lukewarm adj теплова́тый; (fig) прохла́дный.
lull n (in storm) зати́шье; (interval) переры́в; vt (to sleep) убаю́кивать impf, убаю́кать pf; (suspicions) усыпля́ть impf, усыпи́ть pf.
lullaby n колыбе́льная пе́сня.
lumbar adj поясни́чный.
lumber[1] vi (move) брести́ impf.
lumber[2] n (domestic) рухля́дь; vt обременя́ть impf, обремени́ть pf. **lumberjack** n лесору́б.
luminary n свети́ло.
luminous adj светя́щийся.
lump n ком; (swelling) о́пухоль; vt: ~ **together** сме́шивать impf, смеша́ть pf (в одно́).
lunacy n безу́мие.
lunar adj лу́нный.
lunatic adj (n) сумасше́дший (sb).
lunch n обе́д; ~-**hour**, ~-**time** обе́денный переры́в; vi обе́дать impf, по~ pf.
lung n лёгкое sb.
lunge vi де́лать impf, с~ pf вы́пад (at про́тив+gen).
lurch[1] n: **leave in the** ~ покида́ть impf, поки́нуть pf в беде́.
lurch[2] vi (stagger) ходи́ть indet, идти́ det шата́ясь.
lure n прима́нка; vt прима́нивать impf, примани́ть pf.
lurid adj (gaudy) крича́щий; (details) жу́ткий.
lurk vi зата́иваться impf, зата́иться pf.
luscious adj со́чный.

lush adj пы́шный, со́чный.
lust n по́хоть (of, for к+dat); vi стра́стно жела́ть impf, по~ pf (for +gen). **lustful** adj похотли́вый.
lustre n гля́нец. **lustrous** adj глянцеви́тый.
lusty adj (healthy) здоро́вый; (lively) живо́й.
lute n (mus) лю́тня.
luxuriant adj пы́шный.
luxuriate vi наслажда́ться impf, наслади́ться pf (in +instr).
luxurious adj роско́шный. **luxury** n ро́скошь.
lymph attrib лимфати́ческий.
lynch vt линчева́ть impf & pf.
lyric n ли́рика; pl слова́ neut pl пе́сни. **lyrical** adj лири́ческий.

M

MA abbr (of Master of Arts) маги́стр гуманита́рных нау́к.
macabre adj жу́ткий.
macaroni n макаро́ны (-н) pl.
mace n (of office) жезл.
machination n махина́ция.
machine n маши́на; (state ~) аппара́т; attrib маши́нный; ~-**gun** пулемёт; ~ **tool** стано́к; vt обраба́тывать impf, обрабо́тать pf на станке́; (sew) шить impf, с~ pf на маши́не). **machinery** n (machines) маши́ны f pl; (of state) аппара́т. **machinist** n машини́ст; (sewing) шве́йник, -ица, швея́.
mackerel n ску́мбрия, макре́ль.
mackintosh n плащ.
mad adj сумасше́дший. **mad-**

den vt беси́ть impf, вз~ pf.
madhouse n сумасше́дший дом. **madly** adv безу́мно.
madman n сумасше́дший sb.
madness n сумасше́ствие.
madwoman n сумасше́дшая sb.

madrigal n мадрига́л.
maestro n маэ́стро m indecl.
Mafia n ма́фия.
magazine n журна́л; (of gun) магази́н.
maggot n личи́нка.
magic n ма́гия, волшебство́; adj (also **magical**) волше́бный. **magician** n волше́бник; (conjurer) фо́кусник.
magisterial adj авторите́тный.
magistrate n судья́ m.
magnanimity n великоду́шие.
magnanimous adj великоду́шный.
magnate n магна́т.
magnesium n ма́гний.
magnet n магни́т. **magnetic** adj магни́тный; (attractive) притяга́тельный. **magnetism** n магнети́зм; притяга́тельность. **magnetize** vt намагни́чивать impf, намагни́тить pf.
magnification n увеличе́ние.
magnificence n великоле́пие. **magnificent** adj великоле́пный.
magnify vt увели́чивать impf, увели́чить pf; (exaggerate) преувели́чивать impf, преувели́чить pf. **magnifying glass** n увеличи́тельное стекло́.
magnitude n величина́; (importance) ва́жность.
magpie n соро́ка.
mahogany n кра́сное де́рево.
maid n прислу́га. **maiden** adj (aunt etc.) незаму́жняя; (first)

пе́рвый; ~ **name** де́вичья фами́лия.
mail n (letters) по́чта; ~ **order** почто́вый зака́з; vt посыла́ть impf, посла́ть pf по по́чте.
maim vt кале́чить impf, ис~ pf.
main n (gas ~; pl) магистра́ль; **in the** ~ в основно́м; adj основно́й, гла́вный; (road) магистра́льный. **mainland** n матери́к. **mainly** adv в основно́м. **mainstay** n (fig) гла́вная опо́ра.
maintain vt (keep up) подде́рживать impf, поддержа́ть pf; (family) содержа́ть impf; (machine) обслу́живать impf, обслужи́ть pf; (assert) утвержда́ть impf. **maintenance** n подде́ржка; содержа́ние; обслу́живание.
maize n кукуру́за.
majestic adj вели́чественный.
majesty n вели́чественность; (title) вели́чество.
major¹ n (mil) майо́р.
major² adj (greater) бо́льший; (more important) бо́лее ва́жный; (main) гла́вный; (mus) мажо́рный; (mus) мажо́р.
majority n большинство́; (full age) совершенноле́тие.
make vt де́лать impf, с~ pf; (produce) производи́ть impf, произвести́ pf; (prepare) гото́вить impf, при~ pf; (amount to) равня́ться impf +dat; (earn) зараба́тывать impf, зарабо́тать pf; (compel) заставля́ть impf, заста́вить pf; (reach) добира́ться impf, добра́ться pf до+gen; (be in time for) успева́ть impf, успе́ть pf на+acc; **be made of** состоя́ть impf из+gen;

~ **as if, though** де́лать *impf,* с~ *pf* вид, что; ~ **a bed** сте-ли́ть *impf,* по~ *pf* посте́ль; ~ **believe** притворя́ться *impf,* притвори́ться *pf;* ~**-believe** притво́рство; ~ **do with** дово́льствоваться *impf,* у~ *pf +instr;* ~ **off** удира́ть *impf,* удра́ть *pf;* ~ **out** (*cheque*) выпи́сывать *impf,* вы́писать *pf;* (*assert*) утвержда́ть *impf,* утверди́ть *pf;* (*understand*) разбира́ть *impf,* разобра́ть *pf;* ~ **over** передава́ть *impf,* переда́ть *pf;* ~ **up** (*form, compose, complete*) составля́ть *impf,* соста́вить *pf;* (*invent*) выду́мывать *impf,* вы́думать *pf;* (*theat*) грими-рова́ть(ся) *impf,* за~ *pf;* ~-**up** (*theat*) грим; (*cosmetics*) косме́тика; (*composition*) соста́в; ~ **it up** мири́ться *impf,* по~ *pf* (**with** с+*instr*); ~ **up for** возмеща́ть *impf,* возме-сти́ть *pf;* ~ **up one's mind** реша́ться *impf,* реши́ться *pf.* **make** *n* ма́рка. **makeshift** *adj* вре́менный.

malady *n* боле́знь.

malaise *n* (*fig*) беспоко́йство.

malaria *n* маля́рия.

male *n* (*animal*) саме́ц; (*person*) мужчи́на *m; adj* мужско́й.

malevolence *n* недоброжела́-тельность. **malevolent** *adj* недоброжела́тельный.

malice *n* зло́ба. **malicious** *adj* зло́бный.

malign *vt* клевета́ть *impf,* на~ *pf* на+*acc.* **malignant** *adj* (*harmful*) зловре́дный; (*malicious*) зло́бный; (*med*) зло-ка́чественный.

malinger *vi* притворя́ться *impf,* притвори́ться *pf* больны́м.

malingerer *n* симуля́нт.

mallard *n* кря́ква.

malleable *adj* ко́вкий; (*fig*) податли́вый.

mallet *n* (*деревя́нный*) молото́к.

malnutrition *n* недоеда́ние.

malpractice *n* престу́пная не-бре́жность.

malt *n* со́лод.

maltreat *vt* пло́хо обраща́ть-ся *impf* с+*instr.*

mammal *n* млекопита́ющее *sb.*

mammoth *adj* грома́дный.

man *n* (*human, person*) чело-ве́к; (*human race*) челове́че-ство; (*male*) мужчи́на *m;* (*labourer*) рабо́чий *sb; pl* (*soldiers*) солда́ты *m pl; vt* (*furnish with men*) укомплекто́-вывать *impf,* укомплекто-ва́ть *pf* ли́чным соста́вом; ста́вить *impf* людéй к+*dat;* (*stall etc.*) обслу́жи-вать *impf,* обслужи́ть *pf;* (*gate, checkpoint*) стоя́ть *impf* на+*prep.*

manacle *n* нару́чник; *vt* надева́ть *impf,* наде́ть *pf* нару́чники на+*acc.*

manage *vt* (*control*) упра-вля́ть *impf +instr, vi(&t)* (*cope*) справля́ться *impf,* спра́вить-ся *pf* (с+*instr*); (*succeed*) суме́ть *pf.* **management** *n* управле́ние (*of +instr*); (*the* ~) администра́ция. **manager** *n* управля́ющий *sb* (*of +instr*); ме́неджер. **managerial** *adj* администрати́вный. **managing director** *n* дире́ктор-рас-поряди́тель *m.*

mandarin *n* мандари́н.

mandate *n* манда́т. **mandated** *adj* подманда́тный. **mandatory** *adj* обяза́тельный.

mane *n* гри́ва.

manful *adj* му́жественный.

manganese *n* ма́рганец.

manger *n* я́сли (-лей) *pl*; dog in the ~ соба́ка на се́не.

mangle *vt* (*mutilate*) кале́чить *impf*, ис~ *pf*.

mango *n* ма́нго *neut indecl.*

manhandle *vt* гру́бо обраща́ться *impf* с+*instr*.

manhole *n* смотрово́й коло́дец.

manhood *n* возмужа́лость.

mania *n* ма́ния. maniac *n* манья́к, -я́чка. manic *adj* маниака́льный.

manicure *n* маникю́р; *vt* де́лать *impf*, с~ *pf* маникю́р +*dat*. manicurist *n* маникю́рша.

manifest *adj* очеви́дный, *vt* (*display*) проявля́ть *impf*, прояви́ть *pf*; *n* манифе́ст. manifestation *n* проявле́ние. manifesto *n* манифе́ст.

manifold *adj* разнообра́зный.

manipulate *vt* манипули́ровать *impf* +*instr*. manipulation *n* манипуля́ция.

manly *adj* му́жественный.

mankind *n* челове́чество.

manner *n* (*way*) о́браз; (*behaviour*) мане́ра; *pl* мане́ры *f pl*. mannerism *n* мане́ра.

mannish *adj* мужеподо́бный.

manoeuvrable *adj* манёвренный. manoeuvre *n* манёвр; *vt* & *i* маневри́ровать *impf*.

manor *n* поме́стье. (*house*) поме́щичий дом.

manpower *n* челове́ческие ресу́рсы *m pl*.

manservant *n* слуга́ *m*.

mansion *n* особня́к.

manslaughter *n* непредумы́шленное уби́йство.

mantelpiece *n* ками́нная

доска́.

manual *adj* ручно́й; *n* руково́дство. manually *adv* вручну́ю.

manufacture *n* произво́дство; *vt* производи́ть *impf*, произвести́ *pf*. manufacturer *n* фабрика́нт.

manure *n* наво́з.

manuscript *n* ру́копись.

many *adj* & *n* мно́го +*gen*, мно́гие *pl*; how ~ ско́лько +*gen*.

map *n* ка́рта; (*of town*) план; *vt*: ~ out намеча́ть *impf*, наме́тить *pf*.

maple *n* клён.

mar *vt* по́ртить *impf*, ис~ *pf*.

marathon *n* марафо́н.

marauder *n* мародёр. marauding *adj* мародёрский.

marble *n* мра́мор; (*toy*) ша́рик; *attrib* мра́морный.

March *n* март; *adj* ма́ртовский.

march *vi* марширова́ть *impf*, про~ *pf*; *n* марш.

mare *n* кобы́ла.

margarine *n* маргари́н.

margin *n* (*on page*) по́ле; (*edge*) край; profit ~ при́быль; safety ~ запа́с про́чности.

marigold *n* ноготки́ (-ко́в) *pl*.

marijuana *n* марихуа́на.

marina *n* мари́на.

marinade *n* марина́д; *vt* мринова́ть *impf*, за~ *pf*.

marine *adj* морско́й; *n* (*soldier*) солда́т морско́й пехо́ты; *pl* морска́я пехо́та. mariner *n* моря́к.

marionette *n* марионе́тка.

marital *adj* супру́жеский, бра́чный.

maritime *adj* морско́й; (*near sea*) примо́рский.

mark[1] *n* (*coin*) ма́рка.

mark[2] *n* (*for distinguishing*)

ме́тка; (*sign*) знак; (*school*) отме́тка; (*trace*) след; **on your ~s** на старт!; *vt* (*indicate*, *celebrate*) отмеча́ть *impf*, отме́тить *pf*; (*school etc.*) проверя́ть *impf*, прове́рить *pf*; (*stain*) па́чкать *impf*, за~ *pf*; (*sport*) закрыва́ть *impf*, закры́ть *pf*; **~ my words** попо́мни(те) мои́ слова́!; *vt* размеча́ть *impf*, разме́тить *pf*. **marker** *n* знак; (*in book*) закла́дка.

market *n* ры́нок; **~ garden** огоро́д; **~-place** база́рная пло́щадь; *vt* продава́ть *impf*, прода́ть *pf*.

marksman *n* стрело́к.

marmalade *n* апельси́новый джем.

maroon[1] *adj* (*n*) (*colour*) тёмно-бордо́вый (цвет).

maroon[2] *vt* (*put ashore*) выса́живать *impf*, вы́садить *pf* (на необита́емом о́строве); (*cut off*) отреза́ть *impf*, отре́зать *pf*.

marquee *n* тэнт.

marquis *n* марки́з.

marriage *n* брак; (*wedding*) сва́дьба; *attrib* бра́чный. **marriageable** *adj*: **~ age** бра́чный во́зраст. **married** *adj* (*man*) жена́тый; (*woman*) заму́жняя, за́мужем; (*to each other*) жена́тые; (*of persons*) супру́жеский.

marrow *n* ко́стный мозг; (*vegetable*) кабачо́к.

marry *vt* (*of man*) жени́ться *impf* & *pf* на +*prep*; (*of woman*) выходи́ть *impf*, вы́йти *pf* за́муж за +*acc*; *vi* (*of couple*) пожени́ться *pf*.

marsh *n* боло́то. **marshy** *adj* боло́тистый.

marshal *n* ма́ршал; *vt* вы-

стра́ивать *impf*, вы́строить *pf*; (*fig*) собира́ть *impf*, собра́ть *pf*.

marsupial *n* су́мчатое живо́тное *sb*.

martial *adj* вое́нный; **~ law** вое́нное положе́ние.

martyr *n* му́ченик, -ица; *vt* му́чить *impf*, за~ *pf*. **martyrdom** *n* му́ченичество.

marvel *n* чу́до; *vi* изумля́ться *impf*, изуми́ться *pf*. **marvellous** *adj* чуде́сный.

Marxist *n* маркси́ст; *adj* маркси́стский. **Marxism** *n* маркси́зм.

marzipan *n* марципа́н.

mascara *n* тушь.

mascot *n* талисма́н.

masculine *adj* мужско́й; (*gram*) мужско́го ро́да; (*of woman*) мужеподо́бный.

mash *n* карто́фельное пюре́ *neut indecl*; *vt* размина́ть *impf*, размя́ть *pf*.

mask *n* ма́ска; *vt* маскиро́вать *impf*, за~ *pf*.

masochism *n* мазохи́зм. **masochist** *n* мазохи́ст. **masochistic** *adj* мазохи́стский.

mason *n* ка́менщик; (*M*~) масо́н. **Masonic** *adj* масо́нский. **masonry** *n* ка́менная кла́дка.

masquerade *n* маскара́д; *vi*: **~ as** выдава́ть *impf*, вы́дать *pf* себя́ за+*acc*.

Mass *n* (*eccl*) ме́сса.

mass *n* ма́сса; (*majority*) большинство́; *attrib* ма́ссовый; **~ media** сре́дства *neut pl* ма́ссовой информа́ции; **~-produced** ма́ссового произво́дства; **~ production** ма́ссовое произво́дство; *vt* масси́ровать *impf* & *pf*.

massacre *n* резня́; *vt* ре́зать *impf*, вы́резать *pf*.

massage *n* масса́ж; *vt* масси́ровать *impf* & *pf.* **masseur, -euse** *n* массажи́ст, -ка.

massive *adj* масси́вный.

mast *n* ма́чта.

master *n* (*owner*) хозя́ин; (*of ship*) капита́н; (*teacher*) учи́тель *m*; (M∼, *univ*) маги́стр; (*workman*; *artist*) ма́стер; (*original*) по́длинник, оригина́л; be ∼ of владе́ть *impf* +*instr*; ∼-**key** отмы́чка; *vt* (*overcome*) преодолева́ть *impf*, преодоле́ть *pf*; справля́ться *impf*, спра́виться *pf* с+*instr*; (*a subject*) овладева́ть *impf*, овладе́ть *pf* +*instr*. **masterful** *adj* вла́стный. **masterly** *adj* мастерско́й. **masterpiece** *n* шеде́вр. **mastery** *n* (*of a subject*) владе́ние (of +*instr*).

masturbate *vi* мастурби́ровать *impf*.

mat *n* ко́врик, (*at door*) полови́к; (*on table*) подста́вка.

match[1] *n* спи́чка. **matchbox** *n* спи́чечная коро́бка.

match[2] *n* (*equal*) ро́вня *m* & *f*; (*contest*) матч, состяза́ние; (*marriage*) па́ртия; *vi* & *t* (*go well* (*with*)) гармони́ровать *impf* (c+*instr*); подходи́ть *impf*, подойти́ *pf* (к+*dat*).

mate[1] *n* (*chess*) мат.

mate[2] *n* (*one of pair*) саме́ц, са́мка; (*fellow worker*) това́рищ; (*naut*) помо́щник капита́на; *vi* (*of animals*) спа́риваться *impf*, спа́риться *pf*.

material *n* материа́л; (*cloth*) мате́рия; *pl* (*necessary articles*) принадле́жности *f pl*. **materialism** *n* материали́зм. **materialistic** *adj* материалисти́ческий. **materialize** *vi* осуществля́ться *impf*, осуществи́ться *pf*.

maternal *adj* матери́нский; ∼ **grandfather** де́душка с матери́нской стороны́. **maternity** *n* матери́нство; ∼ **leave** декре́тный о́тпуск; ∼ **ward** роди́льное отделе́ние.

mathematical *adj* математи́ческий. **mathematician** *n* матема́тик. **mathematics, maths** *n* матема́тика.

matinée *n* дневно́й спекта́кль *m*.

matriarchal *adj* матриарха́льный. **matriarchy** *n* матриарха́т.

matriculate *vi* быть при́нятым в вуз. **matriculation** *n* зачисле́ние в вуз.

matrimonial *adj* супру́жеский. **matrimony** *n* брак.

matrix *n* ма́трица.

matron *n* (*hospital*) ста́ршая сестра́.

matt *adj* ма́товый.

matted *adj* спу́танный.

matter *n* (*affair*) де́ло; (*question*) вопро́с; (*substance*) вещество́; (*philos*; *med*) мате́рия; (*printed*) материа́л; a ∼ **of life and death** вопро́с жи́зни и сме́рти; a ∼ **of opinion** спо́рное де́ло; a ∼ **of taste** де́ло вку́са; **as a** ∼ **of fact** факти́чески; со́бственно говоря́; **what's the** ∼? в чём де́ло?; **what's the** ∼ **with him**? что с ним?; **it doesn't** ∼ э́то не име́ет значе́ния; **it** ∼**s a lot to me** для меня́ э́то о́чень ва́жно; ∼-**of-fact** прозаи́чный; *vi* име́ть *impf* значе́ние; **it doesn't** ∼ э́то не име́ет значе́ния.

matting *n* рого́жа.

mattress *n* матра́с.

mature *adj* зре́лый; *vi* зреть *impf*, со∼ *pf.* **maturity** *n* зре́лость.

maul vt терза́ть impf.

mausoleum n мавзоле́й.

mauve adj (n) розова́то-лило́вый (цвет).

maxim n сенте́нция.

maximum n ма́ксимум; adj максима́льный.

may v aux (possibility, permission) мочь impf, c~ pf; (possibility) возмо́жно, что +indicative; (wish) пусть +indicative.

May n (month) май; adj ма́йский; ~ **Day** Пе́рвое sb ма́я.

maybe adv мо́жет быть.

mayonnaise n майоне́з.

mayor n мэр. **mayoress** n жена́ мэ́ра; же́нщина-мэр.

maze n лабири́нт.

meadow n луг.

meagre adj ску́дный.

meal[1] n еда́; at ~times по вре́мя еды́.

meal[2] n (grain) мука́. **mealy** adj: ~-mouthed сладкоре́чи́вый.

mean[1] adj (average) сре́дний; n (middle point) середи́на; pl (method) сре́дство, спо́соб; pl (resources) сре́дства neut pl; by all ~s коне́чно, пожа́луйста; by ~s of при по́мощи +gen, посре́дством +gen; by no ~s совсе́м не; ~s test прове́рка нужда́емости.

mean[2] adj (ignoble) по́длый; (miserly) скупо́й; (poor) убо́гий.

mean[3] vt (have in mind) име́ть impf в виду́; (intend) намерева́ться impf +inf; (signify) зна́чить impf.

meander vi (stream) вить-ся impf; (person) броди́ть impf. **meandering** adj изви́листый.

meaning n значе́ние. **meaningful** adj (много)значи́-тельный. **meaningless** adj бессмы́сленный.

meantime, meanwhile adv ме́жду тем.

measles n корь. **measly** adj ничто́жный.

measurable adj измери́мый. **measure** n ме́ра; made to ~ сши́тый по ме́рке; сде́ланный на зака́з; vt измеря́ть impf, изме́рить pf; (for clothes) снима́ть impf, снять pf ме́рку c+gen; vi име́ть impf +acc: the room ~s 30 feet in length ко́мната име́ет три́дцать фу́тов в длину́; ~ off, out отмеря́ть impf, отме́рить pf; ~ up to соотве́тствовать impf +dat. **measured** adj (rhythmical) ме́рный. **measurement** n (action) измере́ние; pl (dimensions) разме́ры m pl.

meat n мя́со. **meatball** n котле́та. **meaty** adj мяси́стый; (fig) содержа́тельный.

mechanic n меха́ник. **mechanical** adj механи́ческий; (fig; automatic) машина́льный; ~ engineer инжене́р-меха́ник; ~ engineering машинострое́ние. **mechanics** n меха́ника. **mechanism** n механи́зм. **mechanization** n механиза́ция. **mechanize** vt механизи́ровать impf & pf.

medal n меда́ль. **medallion** n медальо́н. **medallist** n медали́ст.

meddle vi вме́шиваться impf, вмеша́ться pf (in, with в+acc).

media pl of **medium**

mediate vi посре́дничать impf. **mediation** n посре́дничество. **mediator** n посре́дник.

medical adj медици́нский; ~ student ме́дик, -и́чка. med-

icated adj (impregnated) пропи́танный лека́рством. **medicinal** adj (of medicine) лека́рственный; (healing) целе́бный. **medicine** n медици́на; (substance) лека́рство.

medieval adj средневеко́вый.

mediocre adj посре́дственный. **mediocrity** n посре́дственность.

meditate vi размышля́ть impf. **meditation** n размышле́ние. **meditative** adj заду́мчивый.

Mediterranean adj средиземномо́рский; n Средизе́мное мо́ре.

medium n (means) сре́дство; (phys) среда́; (person) ме́диум; pl (mass media) сре́дства neut pl ма́ссовой информа́ции; adj сре́дний; **happy ~** золота́я середи́на.

medley n смесь; (mus) попурри́ neut indecl.

meek adj кро́ткий.

meet vt & i встреча́ть(ся) impf, встре́тить(ся) pf; vt (make acquaintance) знако́миться impf, по~ pf c+instr; vi (assemble) собира́ться impf, собра́ться pf. **meeting** n встре́ча; (of committee) заседа́ние, ми́тинг.

megalomania n мегалома́ния.

megaphone n мегафо́н.

melancholic adj меланхоли́ческий. **melancholy** n грусть; adj уны́лый, гру́стный.

mellow adj (colour, sound) со́чный; (person) доброду́шный; vi смягча́ться impf, смягчи́ться pf.

melodic adj мелоди́ческий. **melodious** adj мелоди́чный. **melody** n мело́дия.

melodrama n мелодра́ма.

melodramatic adj мелодрама́тический.

melon n ды́ня; (water-~) арбу́з.

melt vt & i раста́пливать(ся) impf, растопи́ть(ся) pf; (smelt) пла́вить(ся) impf, рас~ pf; (dissolve) растворя́ть(ся) impf, раствори́ть(ся) pf; vi (thaw) та́ять impf, рас~ pf; **~ing point** то́чка плавле́ния.

member n член. **membership** n чле́нство; (number of ~) коли́чество чле́нов; attrib чле́нский.

membrane n перепо́нка.

memento n сувени́р. **memoir** n pl мемуа́ры (-ров) pl; воспомина́ния neut pl. **memorable** adj достопа́мятный.

memorandum n запи́ска.

memorial adj мемориа́льный; n па́мятник. **memorize** vt запомина́ть impf, запо́мнить pf. **memory** n па́мять; (recollection) воспомина́ние.

menace n угро́за; vt угрожа́ть impf +dat. **menacing** adj угрожа́ющий.

menagerie n звери́нец.

mend vt чини́ть impf, по~ pf; (clothes) што́пать impf, за~ pf; **~ one's ways** исправля́ться impf, испра́виться pf.

menial adj ни́зкий, чёрный.

meningitis n менинги́т.

menopause n кли́макс.

menstrual adj менструа́льный. **menstruation** n менструа́ция.

mental adj у́мственный; (of illness) психи́ческий; **~ arithmetic** счёт в уме́. **mentality** n ум; (character) склад ума́.

mention vt упомина́ть impf, упомяну́ть pf; **don't ~** не за что!; **not to ~** не говоря́ уже́ о+prep.

menu n меню́ neut indecl.

mercantile adj торго́вый.

mercenary adj коры́стный; (hired) наёмный; n наёмник.

merchandise n това́ры m pl.

merchant n купе́ц; торго́вец; ~ **navy** торго́вый флот.

merciful adj милосе́рдный. **mercifully** adv к сча́стью. **merciless** adj беспоща́дный.

mercurial adj (person) изме́нчивый. **mercury** n ртуть.

mercy n милосе́рдие; **at the** ~ **of** во вла́сти +gen.

mere adj просто́й; **a** ~ £40 всего́ лишь со́рок фу́нтов. **merely** adv то́лько, про́сто.

merge vt & i слива́ть(ся) impf, слить(ся) pf. **merger** n объедине́ние.

meridian n меридиа́н.

meringue n меренга.

merit n заслу́га, досто́инство; vt заслу́живать impf, заслужи́ть pf +gen.

mermaid n руса́лка.

merrily adv ве́село. **merriment** n весе́лье. **merry** adj весёлый; ~-**go-round** карусе́ль; ~-**making** весе́лье.

mesh n сеть; vi сцепля́ться impf, сцепи́ться pf.

mesmerize vt гипнотизи́ровать impf, за- pf.

mess n (disorder) беспоря́док; (trouble) беда́; (eating-place) столо́вая sb; vi: ~ **about** вози́ться impf; ~ **up** по́ртить impf, ис- pf.

message n сообще́ние. **messenger** n курье́р.

Messiah n месси́я m. **Messianic** adj месси́анский.

Messrs abbr господа́ (gen -д) m pl.

messy adj (untidy) беспоря́дочный; (dirty) гря́зный.

metabolism n обме́н веще́ств.

metal n мета́лл; adj металли́ческий. **metallic** adj металли́ческий. **metallurgy** n металлу́ргия.

metamorphosis n метаморфо́за.

metaphor n мета́фора. **metaphorical** adj метафори́ческий.

metaphysical adj метафизи́ческий. **metaphysics** n метафи́зика.

meteor n метео́р. **meteoric** adj метеори́ческий. **meteorite** n метеори́т. **meteorological** adj метеорологи́ческий. **meteorology** n метеороло́гия.

meter n счётчик; vt измеря́ть impf, изме́рить pf.

methane n мета́н.

method n ме́тод. **methodical** adj методи́чный.

Methodist n методи́ст; adj методи́стский.

methodology n методоло́гия.

methylated adj: ~ **spirit(s)** денатура́т.

meticulous adj тща́тельный.

metre n метр. **metric(al)** adj метри́ческий.

metronome n метроно́м.

metropolis n столи́ца. **metropolitan** adj столи́чный; n (eccl) митрополи́т.

mettle n хара́ктер.

Mexican adj мексика́нский; n мексика́нец, -а́нка. **Mexico** n Ме́ксика.

mezzanine n антресо́ли f pl.

miaow int мя́у; n мя́уканье; vi мя́укать impf, мя́укнуть pf.

mica n слюда́.

microbe n микро́б. **microchip** n чип, микросхе́ма. **microcomputer** n микрокомпью́тер. **microcosm** n микро-

ко́см. microfilm *n* микрофи́льм. **micro-organism** *n* микрооргани́зм. **microphone** *n* микрофо́н. **microscope** *n* микроско́п. **microscopic** *adj* микроскопи́ческий. **microwave** *n* микроволна́; ~ **oven** микроволно́вая печь.

mid *adj*: ~ **May** середи́на ма́я. **midday** *n* по́лдень *m*; *attrib* полу́денный. **middle** *n* середи́на; *adj* сре́дний; ~-**aged** сре́дних лет; **M~ Ages** сре́дние века́ *m pl*; ~-**class** буржуа́зный; ~-**man** посре́дник; ~-**sized** сре́днего разме́ра. **middleweight** *n* сре́дний вес. **midge** *n* мо́шка. **midget** *n* ка́рлик, -ица. **midnight** *n* по́лночь; *attrib* полу́ночный. **midriff** *n* диафра́гма. **midst** *n* середи́на. **midsummer** *n* середи́на ле́та. **midway** *adv* на полпути́. **midweek** *n* середи́на неде́ли. **midwinter** *n* середи́на зимы́. **midwife** *n* акуше́рка. **midwifery** *n* акуше́рство.

might *n* мощь; **with all one's** ~ и́зо всех сил. **mighty** *adj* мо́щный.

migraine *n* мигре́нь.

migrant *n* кочу́ющий; (*bird*) перелётный; *n* (*person*) пересе́ленец; (*bird*) перелётная пти́ца. **migrate** *vi* мигри́ровать *impf* & *pf*. **migration** *n* мигра́ция. **migratory** *adj* кочу́ющий; (*bird*) перелётный.

mike *n* микрофо́н.

mild *adj* мя́гкий.

mildew *n* пле́сень.

mile *n* ми́ля. **mileage** *n* расстоя́ние в ми́лях; (*of car*) пробе́г. **milestone** *n* верстово́й столб; (*fig*) ве́ха.

militancy *n* вои́нственность.

militant *adj* вои́нствующий; *n* активи́ст. **military** *adj* вое́нный; *n* вое́нные sb *pl* m. **militate** *vi*: ~ **against** говори́ть *impf* про́тив+*gen*. **militia** *n* мили́ция. **militiaman** *n* милиционе́р.

milk *n* молоко́; *attrib* моло́чный; *vt* дои́ть *impf*, по~ *pf*. **milkman** *n* продаве́ц молока́. **milky** *adj* моло́чный; **M~ Way** Мле́чный Путь *m*.

mill *n* ме́льница; (*factory*) фа́брика; *vt* (*grain etc.*) моло́ть *impf*, с~ *pf*; (*metal*) фрезерова́ть *impf*, от~ *pf*; (*coin*) гурти́ть *impf*; *vi*: ~ **around** толпи́ться *impf*. **miller** *n* ме́льник.

millennium *n* тысячеле́тие.

millet *n* (*plant*) про́со; (*grain*) пшено́.

milligram(me) *n* миллигра́мм. **millimetre** *n* миллиме́тр. **million** *n* миллио́н. **millionaire** *n* миллионе́р. **millionth** *adj* миллио́нный.

millstone *n* жёрнов; (*fig*) ка́мень *m* на ше́е.

mime *n* мим; (*dumb-show*) пантоми́ма; *vt* изобража́ть *impf*, изобрази́ть *pf* мими́чески. **mimic** *n* ми́мист; *vt* передра́знивать *impf*, передрази́ть *pf*. **mimicry** *n* имита́ция.

minaret *n* минаре́т.

mince *n* (*meat*) фарш; *vt* руби́ть *impf*; (*in machine*) пропуска́ть *impf*, пропусти́ть *pf* че́рез мясору́бку; *vi* (*walk*) семени́ть *impf*; **not** ~ **matters** говори́ть *impf* без обиняко́в. **mincemeat** *n* начи́нка из изю́ма, минда́ля и т.д.

mind *n* ум; **bear in** ~ — име́ть *impf* в виду́; **change one's** ~

переду́мывать *impf*, переду́мать *pf*; **make up one's ~** реша́ться *impf*, реши́ться *pf*; **you're out of your ~** вы с ума́ сошли́; *vt* (*give new point to*) обраща́ть *impf*, обрати́ть *pf* внима́ние на+*acc*; (*look after*) присма́тривать *impf*, присмотре́ть *pf* за+*instr*; **i don't ~** я ничего́ не име́ю про́тив; **don't ~ me** не обраща́й(те) внима́ния на меня́!; **~ you don't forget** смотри́ не забу́дь!; **~ your own business** не вме́шивайтесь в чужи́е дела́!; **never ~** ничего́! **mindful** *adj* по́мнящий. **mindless** *adj* бессмы́сленный.

mine¹ *poss pron* мой, свой.

mine² *n* ша́хта, рудни́к; (*fig*) исто́чник; (*mil*) ми́на; *vt* (*obtain from ~*) добыва́ть *impf*, добы́ть *pf*; (*mil*) мини́ровать *impf* & *pf*. **minefield** *n* ми́нное по́ле. **miner** *n* шахтёр.

mineral *n* минера́л; *adj* минера́льный; **~ water** минера́льная вода́. **mineralogy** *n* минерало́гия.

mingle *vt* & *i* сме́шивать(ся) *impf*, смеша́ть(ся) *pf*.

miniature *n* миниатю́ра; *adj* миниатю́рный.

minibus *n* микроавто́бус.

minim *n* (*mus*) полови́нная но́та. **minimal** *adj* минима́льный. **minimize** *vt* (*reduce*) доводи́ть *impf*, довести́ *pf* до ми́нимума. **minimum** *n* ми́нимум; *adj* минима́льный.

mining *n* го́рное де́ло.

minister *n* мини́стр; (*eccl*) свяще́нник. **ministerial** *adj* министе́рский. **ministration** *n* по́мощь. **ministry** *n* (*polit*) министе́рство; (*eccl*) духове́нство.

mink *n* но́рка; *attrib* но́рковый.

minor *adj* (*unimportant*) незначи́тельный; (*less important*) второстепе́нный; (*mus*) мино́рный; *n* (*person under age*) несовершенноле́тний *n*; (*mus*) мино́р. **minority** *n* меньшинство́; (*age*) несовершенноле́тие.

minstrel *n* менестре́ль *m*.

mint¹ *n* (*plant*) мя́та; (*peppermint*) пере́чная мя́та.

mint² *n* (*econ*) моне́тный двор; **in ~ condition** но́венький; *vt* чека́нить *impf*, от~, вы́~ *pf*.

minuet *n* менуэ́т.

minus *prep* ми́нус+*acc*; без+*gen*; *n* ми́нус.

minuscule *adj* малю́сенький.

minute¹ *n* мину́та; *pl* протоко́л.

minute² *adj* ме́лкий. **minutiae** *n pl* ме́лочи (-че́й) *f pl*.

miracle *n* чу́до. **miraculous** *adj* чуде́сный.

mirage *n* мира́ж.

mire *n* (*mud*) грязь; (*swamp*) боло́то.

mirror *n* зе́ркало; *vt* отража́ть *impf*, отрази́ть *pf*.

mirth *n* весе́лье.

misadventure *n* несча́стный слу́чай.

misapprehension *n* недопонима́ние. **misappropriate** *vt* незако́нно присва́ивать *impf*, присво́ить *pf*. **misbehave** *vi* ду́рно вести́ *impf* себя́. **misbehaviour** *n* дурно́е поведе́ние.

miscalculate *vt* непра́вильно рассчи́тывать *impf*, рассчита́ть *pf*; (*fig*, *abs*) просчи́тываться *impf*, просчита́ться *pf*. **miscalculation** *n* просчёт. **miscarriage** *n* (*med*) вы́кидыш; **~ of justice** судебная оши́бка. **miscarry** vi (med) име́ть impf вы́кидыш.

miscellaneous adj ра́зный, разнообра́зный. **miscellany** n смесь.

mischief n (harm) вред; (naughtiness) озорство́. **mischievous** adj озорно́й. **misconception** n непра́вильное представле́ние. **misconduct** n дурно́е поведе́ние. **misconstrue** vt непра́вильно истолко́вывать impf, истолкова́ть pf.

misdeed, misdemeanour n просту́пок. **misdirect** vt непра́вильно направля́ть impf, напра́вить pf; (letter) непра́вильно адресова́ть impf & pf.

miser n скупе́ц. **miserable** adj (unhappy, wretched) несча́стный, жа́лкий; (weather) скве́рный. **miserly** adj скупо́й. **misery** n страда́ние.

misfire vi дава́ть impf, дать pf осе́чку. **misfit** n (person) неуда́чник. **misfortune** n несча́стье. **misgiving** n опасе́ние. **misguided** adj обма́нутый.

mishap n неприя́тность. **misinform** vt непра́вильно информи́ровать impf & pf. **misinterpret** vt неве́рно истолко́вывать impf, истолкова́ть pf. **misjudge** vt неве́рно оце́нивать impf, оцени́ть pf. **misjudgement** n неве́рная оце́нка. **mislay** vt затеря́ть pf. **mislead** vt вводи́ть impf, ввести́ pf в заблужде́ние. **mismanage** vt пло́хо управля́ть impf +instr. **mismanagement** n плохо́е управле́ние. **misnomer** n непра́вильное назва́ние.

misogynist n женоненави́ст-

ник. **misogyny** n женоненави́стничество.

misplaced adj неуме́стный. **misprint** n опеча́тка. **misquote** vt непра́вильно цити́ровать impf, про~ pf. **misread** vt (fig) непра́вильно истолко́вывать impf, истолкова́ть pf. **misrepresent** vt искажа́ть impf, искази́ть pf. **misrepresentation** n искаже́ние.

Miss n (title) мисс.

miss n про́мах; vi прома́хиваться impf, промахну́ться pf; vt (fail to hit, see, hear) пропуска́ть impf, пропусти́ть pf; (train) опа́здывать impf, опозда́ть pf к+dat; (regret absence of) скуча́ть impf по+dat; ~ **out** пропуска́ть impf, пропусти́ть pf; ~ **the point** не понима́ть impf, поня́ть pf су́ти.

misshapen adj уро́дливый. **missile** n снаря́д, раке́та. **missing** adj отсу́тствующий, недоста́ющий; (person) пропа́вший без ве́сти. **mission** n ми́ссия; командиро́вка. **missionary** n миссионе́р. **missive** n посла́ние.

misspell vt непра́вильно писа́ть impf, на~ pf. **misspelling** n непра́вильное написа́ние.

mist n тума́н; vt & i затума́нивать(ся) impf, затума́нить(ся) pf.

mistake vt непра́вильно понима́ть impf, поня́ть pf; ~ **for** принима́ть impf, приня́ть pf за+acc, n оши́бка; **make a** ~ оши́ба́ться impf, оши́би́ться pf. **mistaken** adj оши́бочный; **be** ~ оши́ба́ться impf, оши́би́ться pf.

mister n ми́стер, господи́н.

mistletoe n оме́ла.

mistress n хозя́йка; (teacher) учи́тельница; (lover) любо́вница.

mistrust vt не доверя́ть impf +dat; n недове́рие. **mistrustful** adj недове́рчивый.

misty adj тума́нный.

misunderstand vt непра́вильно понима́ть impf, поня́ть pf. **misunderstanding** n недоразуме́ние.

misuse vt непра́вильно употребля́ть impf, употреби́ть pf; (ill treat) ду́рно обраща́ться impf c+instr; n непра́вильное употребле́ние.

mite n (insect) клещ; (child) кро́шка; **widow's ~** ле́пта вдови́цы; **not a ~** ничу́ть.

mitigate vt смягча́ть impf, смягчи́ть pf. **mitigation** n смягче́ние.

mitre n ми́тра.

mitten n рукави́ца.

mix vt меша́ть impf, c~ pf; vi сме́шиваться impf, смеша́ться pf; (associate) обща́ться impf; **~ up** (confuse) пу́тать impf, c~ pf; **get ~ed up in** замеша́ться impf, заме́шаться pf в+acc; n смесь. **mixer** n смеси́тель m; (cul) ми́ксер. **mixture** n смесь; (medicine) миксту́ра.

moan n стон; vi стона́ть impf, про~ pf.

moat n (крепостно́й) ров.

mob n толпа́; vt (attack) напада́ть impf, напа́сть pf толпо́й на+acc. **mobster** n банди́т.

mobile adj подвижно́й, передвижно́й. **mobility** n подви́жность. **mobilization** n мобилиза́ция. **mobilize** vt & i мобилизова́ть(ся) impf & pf.

moccasin n мокаси́н (gen pl -н).

mock vt & i издева́ться impf над+instr; adj (sham) поде́льный; (pretended) мни́мый; **~-up** n маке́т. **mockery** n издева́тельство; (travesty) паро́дия.

mode n (manner) о́браз; (method) ме́тод.

model n (representation) моде́ль; (pattern, ideal) образе́ц; (artist's) нату́рщик, -ица; (fashion) манеке́нщик, -ица; (make) моде́ль; adj образцо́вый; vt лепи́ть impf, вы́~, c~ pf; (clothes) демонстри́ровать impf & pf; vi (act as ~) быть нату́рщиком, -ицей; быть манеке́нщиком, -ицей; **~ after, on** создава́ть impf, созда́ть pf по образцу́ +gen.

moderate adj (various senses; polit) уме́ренный; (medium) сре́дний; vt умеря́ть impf, уме́рить pf; vi стиха́ть impf, сти́хнуть pf. **moderation** n уме́ренность; **in ~** уме́ренно.

modern adj совреме́нный; (language, history) но́вый. **modernization** n модерниза́ция. **modernize** vt модернизи́ровать impf & pf.

modest adj скро́мный. **modesty** n скро́мность.

modification n модифика́ция. **modify** vt модифици́ровать impf & pf.

modish adj мо́дный.

modular adj мо́дульный. **modulate** vt модули́ровать impf. **modulation** n модуля́ция. **module** n мо́дуль m.

mohair n мохе́р.

moist adj вла́жный. **moisten** vt & i увлажня́ть(ся) impf, увлажни́ть(ся) pf. **moisture** n вла́га.

molar n (*tooth*) коренно́й зуб.

mole[1] n (*on skin*) ро́динка.

mole[2] n (*animal; agent*) крот.

molecular adj молекуля́рный. **molecule** n моле́кула.

molest vt пристава́ть impf, приста́ть pf +dat.

mollify vt смягча́ть impf, смягчи́ть pf.

mollusc n моллю́ск.

molten adj распла́вленный.

moment n моме́нт, миг; at the ~ сейча́с; at the last ~ в после́днюю мину́ту; just a ~! сейча́с! **momentarily** adv на мгнове́ние. **momentary** adj мгнове́нный. **momentous** adj ва́жный. **momentum** n коли́чество движе́ния; (*impetus*) дви́жущая си́ла; gather ~ набира́ть impf, набра́ть pf ско́рость.

monarch n мона́рх. **monarchy** n мона́рхия.

monastery n монасты́рь m. **monastic** adj мона́шеский.

Monday n понеде́льник.

monetary adj де́нежный. **money** n де́ньги (-нег, -нья́м) pl; ~-lender ростовщи́к.

mongrel n дворня́жка.

monitor n (*naut; TV*) монито́р; vt проверя́ть impf, прове́рить pf.

monk n мона́х.

monkey n обезья́на.

mono n мо́но neut indecl. **monochrome** adj одноцве́тный. **monogamous** adj единобра́чный. **monogamy** n единобра́чие. **monogram** n моногра́мма. **monograph** n моногра́фия. **monolith** n моноли́т. **monolithic** adj моноли́тный. **monologue** n моноло́г. **monopolize** vt монополизи́ровать impf & pf. **monopoly**

n монопо́лия. **monosyllabic** adj односло́жный. **monosyllable** n односло́жное сло́во.

monotone n моното́нность; in a ~ моното́нно. **monotonous** adj моното́нный. **monotony** n моното́нность.

monsoon n (*wind*) муссо́н; (*rainy season*) дождли́вый сезо́н.

monster n чудо́вище. **monstrosity** n чудо́вищность. **monstrous** adj чудо́вищный; (*huge*) грома́дный.

montage n монта́ж.

month n ме́сяц. **monthly** adj ме́сячный; n ежеме́сячник; adv ежеме́сячно.

monument n па́мятник. **monumental** adj монумента́льный.

moo vi мыча́ть impf.

mood[1] n (*gram*) наклоне́ние. **mood**[2] n настрое́ние. **moody** adj капри́зный.

moon n луна́. **moonlight** n лу́нный свет; vi халту́рить impf. **moonlit** adj лу́нный.

moor[1] n ме́стность, поро́сшая ве́реском. **moorland** n ве́ресковая пу́стошь.

moor[2] vt & i швартова́ть(ся) impf, при~ pf. **mooring** n (*place*) прича́л; pl (*cables*) шварто́вы m pl.

Moorish adj маврита́нский.

moose n америка́нский лось m.

moot adj спо́рный.

mop n шва́бра; vt протира́ть impf, протере́ть pf (шва́брой); ~ one's brow вытира́ть impf, вы́тереть pf лоб; ~ up вытира́ть impf, вы́тереть pf.

mope vi хандри́ть impf.

moped n мопе́д.

moraine *n* море́на.
moral *adj* мора́льный; *n* мора́ль; *pl* нра́вы *m pl.* **morale** *n* мора́льное состоя́ние.
morality *n* нра́вственность, мора́ль. **moralize** *vi* морализи́ровать *impf.*
morass *n* боло́то.
moratorium *n* морато́рий.
morbid *adj* боле́зненный.
more *adj* (*greater quantity*) бо́льше +*gen*; (*additional*) ещё; *adv* бо́льше; (*forming comp*) бо́лее; **and what is ~** и бо́льше того́; **~ or less** бо́лее и́ли ме́нее; **once ~** ещё раз. **moreover** *adv* сверх того́; кро́ме того́.
morgue *n* морг.
moribund *adj* умира́ющий.
morning *n* у́тро; **in the ~** у́тром; **in the ~s** по утра́м; *attrib* у́тренний.
moron *n* слабоу́мный *sb.*
morose *adj* угрю́мый.
morphine *n* мо́рфий.
Morse (code) *n* а́збука Мо́рзе.
morsel *n* кусо́чек.
mortal *adj* сме́ртный; (*fatal*) смерте́льный; *n* сме́ртный *sb.* **mortality** *n* сме́ртность.
mortar *n* (*vessel*) сту́п(к)а; (*cannon*) миномёт; (*cement*) (известко́вый) раство́р.
mortgage *n* ссу́да на поку́пку до́ма; *vt* закла́дывать *impf*, заложи́ть *pf.*
mortify *vt* унижа́ть *impf*, уни́зить *pf.*
mortuary *n* морг.
mosaic *n* моза́ика; *adj* моза́ичный.
mosque *n* мече́ть.
mosquito *n* кома́р.
moss *n* мох. **mossy** *adj* мши́стый.
most *adj* наибо́льший; *n* наи-

бо́льшее коли́чество; *adj & n* (*majority*) большинство́ +*gen*; бо́льшая часть +*gen*; *adv* бо́льше всего́, наибо́лее; (*forming superl*) са́мый. **mostly** *adv* гла́вным о́бразом.
MOT (test) *n* техосмо́тр.
motel *n* моте́ль *m.*
moth *n* мотылёк; (*clothes-~*) моль.
mother *n* мать; *vt* относи́ться *impf* по-матери́нски к +*dat*; **~-in-law** (*wife's ~*) тёща; (*husband's ~*) свекро́вь; **~-of-pearl** *adj* перламу́тровый; **~ tongue** родно́й язы́к. **motherhood** *n* матери́нство. **motherland** *n* ро́дина. **motherly** *adj* матери́нский.
motif *n* моти́в.
motion *n* движе́ние; (*gesture*) жест; (*proposal*) предложе́ние; *vt* пока́зывать *impf*, показа́ть *pf* +*dat* же́стом, что́бы +*past.* **motionless** *adj* неподви́жный. **motivate** *vt* побужда́ть *impf*, побуди́ть *pf.* **motivation** *n* побужде́ние. **motive** *n* моти́в; *adj* дви́жущий.
motley *adj* пёстрый.
motor *n* дви́гатель *m*, мото́р; **~ bike** мотоци́кл; **~ boat** мото́рная ло́дка; **~ car** автомоби́ль *m*; **~ cycle** мотоци́кл; **~-cyclist** мотоцикли́ст; **~ racing** автомоби́льные го́нки *f pl*; **~ scooter** мотороллер; **~ vehicle** автомаши́на. **motoring** *n* автомобили́зм. **motorist** *n* автомобили́ст, **~ка.** **motorize** *vt* моторизова́ть *impf & pf.* **motorway** *n* автостра́да.
mottled *adj* кра́пчатый.

motto n девиз.

mould[1] n (shape) фо́рма, фо́рмочка; vt формова́ть impf, c~ pf. **moulding** n (archit) лепно́е украше́ние.

mould[2] n (fungi) пле́сень. **mouldy** adj запле́сневелый.

moulder vi разлага́ться impf, разложи́ться pf.

moult vi линя́ть impf, вы́~ pf.

mound n холм; (heap) на́сыпь.

Mount n (in names) гора́.

mount vt (ascend) поднима́ться impf, подня́ться pf на+acc; (~ a horse etc.) сади́ться impf, сесть pf на+acc; (picture) накле́ивать impf, накле́ить pf на карто́н; (gun) устана́вливать impf, установи́ть pf; ~ **up** (accumulate) нака́пливаться impf, накопи́ться pf, n (for picture) карто́н; (horse) верхова́я ло́шадь.

mountain n гора́; attrib го́рный. **mountaineer** n альпини́ст, ~ка. **mountaineering** n альпини́зм. **mountainous** adj гори́стый.

mourn vt опла́кивать impf, опла́кать pf; vi скорбе́ть impf (over o+prep). **mournful** adj скорбный. **mourning** n тра́ур.

mouse n мышь.

mousse n мусс.

moustache n усы́ (усо́в) pl.

mousy adj мыши́ный; (timid) ро́бкий.

mouth n рот; (poetical) уста́ (-т) pl; (entrance) вход; (of river) у́стье; to ~ говори́ть, сказа́ть pf одни́ми губа́ми. **mouthful** n глото́к. **mouth-organ** n губна́я гармо́ника. **mouthpiece** n мундшту́к; (person) ру́пор.

movable adj подвижно́й.

move n (in game) ход; (change of residence) перее́зд; (movement) движе́ние; (step) шаг; vt & i дви́гать(ся) impf, дви́нуть(ся) pf; vt (affect) тро́гать impf, тро́нуть pf; вноси́ть impf, внести́ pf; vi (develop) развива́ться impf, разви́ться pf; (~ house) переезжа́ть impf, перее́хать pf; ~ **away** (vt & i) удаля́ть(ся) impf, удали́ть(ся) pf; (vi) уезжа́ть impf, уе́хать pf; ~ **in** въезжа́ть impf, въе́хать pf; ~ **on** идти́ impf, пойти́ pf да́льше; ~ **out** съезжа́ть impf, съе́хать pf (of c+gen). **movement** n движе́ние; (mus) часть. **moving** n дви́жущий-ся; (touching) тро́гательный.

mow vt (also ~ **down**) коси́ть impf, c~ pf. **mower** n коси́лка.

MP abbr (of **Member of Parliament**) член парла́мента.

Mr abbr ми́стер, господи́н.

Mrs abbr ми́ссис f indecl, госпожа́.

Ms n миз, госпожа́.

much adj & n мно́го +gen; мно́гое sb; adv о́чень; (with comp adj) гора́здо.

muck n (dung) наво́з; (dirt) грязь; ~ **about** вози́ться impf; ~ **out** чи́стить impf, вы́~ pf; ~ **up** изга́живать impf, изга́дить pf.

mucous adj сли́зистый. **mucus** n слизь.

mud n грязь. **mudguard** n крыло́.

muddle vt пу́тать impf, c~ pf; vi: ~ **through** ко́е-ка́к справля́ться impf, спра́виться pf, n беспоря́док.

muddy adj гря́зный; vt обры́згивать impf, обры́згать pf гря́зью.

muff *n* муфта.

muffle *vt* (*for warmth*) закутывать *impf*, закутать *pf*; (*sound*) глушить *impf*, за~ *pf*.

mug *n* (*vessel*) кружка; (*face*) морда.

muggy *adj* сырой и тёплый.

mulch *n* мульча; *vt* мульчировать *impf* & *pf*.

mule *n* мул.

mull *vt*: ~ **over** обдумывать *impf*, обдумать *pf*. **mulled** *adj*: ~ **wine** глинтвейн.

mullet *n* (*grey* ~) кефаль; (*red* ~) барабулька.

multicoloured *adj* многокрасочный. **multifarious** *adj* разнообразный. **multilateral** *adj* многосторонний. **multimillionaire** *n* мультимиллионер. **multinational** *adj* многонациональный.

multiple *adj* составной; (*numerous*) многочисленный; ~ **sclerosis** рассеянный склероз; *n* кратное число; **least common** ~ общее наименьшее кратное *sb*. **multiplication** *n* умножение. **multiplicity** *n* многочисленность. **multiply** *vt* (*math*) умножать *impf*, умножить *pf*; *vi* размножаться *impf*, размножиться *pf*.

multi-storey *adj* многоэтажный.

multitude *n* множество; (*crowd*) толпа.

mum[1] *adj*: **keep** ~ молчать *impf*.

mum[2] *n* (*mother*) мама.

mumble *vt* & *i* бормотать *impf*, про~ *pf*.

mummy[1] *n* (*archaeol*) мумия.

mummy[2] *n* (*mother*) мама, мамочка.

mumps *n* свинка.

munch *vt* жевать *impf*.

mundane *adj* земной.

municipal *adj* муниципальный. **municipality** *n* муниципалитет.

munitions *n pl* военное имущество.

mural *n* стенная роспись.

murder *n* убийство; *vt* убивать *impf*, убить *pf*; (*language*) коверкать *impf*, ис~ *pf*. **murderer, murderess** *n* убийца *m* & *f*. **murderous** *adj* убийственный.

murky *adj* тёмный, мрачный.

murmur *n* шёпот; *vt* & *i* шептать *impf*, шепнуть *pf*.

muscle *n* мускул. **muscular** *adj* мышечный; (*person*) мускулистый.

Muscovite *n* москвич, ~ка.

muse *vi* размышлять *impf*.

museum *n* музей.

mush *n* каша.

mushroom *n* гриб.

music *n* музыка; (*sheet* ~) ноты *f pl*; ~-**hall** мюзик-холл; ~ **stand** пюпитр. **musical** *adj* музыкальный; *n* оперетта. **musician** *n* музыкант.

musk *n* мускус.

musket *n* мушкет.

Muslim *n* мусульманин, -анка; *adj* мусульманский.

muslin *n* муслин.

mussel *n* мидия.

must *v aux* (*obligation*) должен (-жна) *predic+inf*; надо *impers+dat* & *inf*; (*necessity*) нужно *impers+dat* & *inf*; ~ **not** (*prohibition*) нельзя *impers+dat* & *inf*.

mustard *n* горчица.

muster *n* собирать *impf*, собрать *pf*; (*courage etc.*) собираться *impf*, собраться *pf* с+*instr*.

musty *adj* за́тхлый.

mutation *n* мута́ция.

mute *adj* немо́й; *n* немо́й *sb*; (*mus*) сурди́нка. **muted** *adj* приглушённый.

mutilate *vt* уве́чить *impf*, из~ *pf*. **mutilation** *n* уве́чье.

mutineer *n* мяте́жник. **mutinous** *adj* мяте́жный. **mutiny** *n* мяте́ж; *vi* бунтова́ть *impf*, взбунтова́ться *pf*.

mutter *vi* бормота́ть *impf*; *impf*; *impf*; *impf* бормота́ние.

mutton *n* бара́нина.

mutual *adj* взаи́мный; (*common*) о́бщий.

muzzle *n* (*animal's*) мо́рда; (*on animal*) намо́рдник; (*of gun*) ду́ло; *vt* надева́ть *impf*, наде́ть *pf* намо́рдник на+*acc*; (*fig*) заставля́ть *impf*, заста́вить *pf* молча́ть.

my *poss pron* мой; свой.

myopia *n* близору́кость. **myopic** *adj* близору́кий.

myriad *n* мириа́ды (-д) *pl*; *adj* бесчи́сленный.

myrtle *n* мирт; *attrib* ми́ртовый.

myself *pron* (*emph*) (я) сам, сама́; (*refl*) себя́, -ся (*suffixed to vt*).

mysterious *adj* таи́нственный. **mystery** *n* та́йна.

mystic(al) *adj* мисти́ческий; *n* ми́стик. **mysticism** *n* мистици́зм. **mystify** *vt* озада́чивать *impf*, озада́чить *pf*.

myth *n* миф. **mythical** *adj* мифи́ческий. **mythological** *adj* мифологи́ческий. **mythology** *n* мифоло́гия.

N

nag¹ *n* (*horse*) ло́шадь.

nag² *vt* (*also* ~ **at**) пили́ть *impf* +*acc*; *vi* (*of pain*) ныть *impf*.

nail *n* (*finger-, toe-*~) но́готь *m*; (*metal spike*) гвоздь *m*; ~ **varnish** лак для ногте́й; *vt* прибива́ть *impf*, приби́ть *pf* (гвоздя́ми).

naive *adj* наи́вный. **naivety** *n* наи́вность.

naked *adj* го́лый; ~ **eye** невооружённый глаз. **nakedness** *n* нагота́.

name *n* назва́ние; (*forename*) и́мя *neut*; (*surname*) фами́лия; (*reputation*) репута́ция; **what is his** ~? как его́ зову́т?; ~**plate** доще́чка с фами́лией; ~**sake** тёзка *m & f*; *vt* называ́ть *impf*, назва́ть *pf*; (*appoint*) назнача́ть *impf*, назна́чить *pf*. **nameless** *adj* безымя́нный. **namely** *adv* (а) и́менно; то есть.

nanny *n* ня́ня.

nap *n* коро́ткий сон; *vi* вздремну́ть *pf*.

nape *n* загри́вок.

napkin *n* салфе́тка.

nappy *n* пелёнка.

narcissus *n* нарци́сс.

narcotic *adj* наркоти́ческий; *n* нарко́тик.

narrate *vt* расска́зывать *impf*, рассказа́ть *pf*. **narration** *n* расска́з. **narrative** *n* расска́з; *adj* повествова́тельный. **narrator** *n* расска́зчик.

narrow *adj* у́зкий; *vt & i* су́живать(ся) *impf*, су́зить(ся) *pf*. **narrowly** *adv* (*hardly*) чуть, е́ле-е́ле; **he** ~ **escaped drown-**

ing он чуть не утону́л. **narrow-minded** adj ограни́ченный. **narrowness** n у́зость.

nasal adj носово́й; (voice) гнуса́вый.

nasturtium n настурция.

nasty adj неприя́тный, проти́вный; (person) злой.

nation n (people) наро́д; (country) страна́. **national** adj национа́льный, наро́дный; (of the state) госуда́рственный; n по́дданный sb. **nationalism** n национали́зм. **nationalist** n националист, ~ка. **nationalistic** adj националисти́ческий. **nationality** n национа́льность; (citizenship) гражда́нство, по́дданство. **nationalization** n национализа́ция. **nationalize** vt национализи́ровать impf & pf.

native n (~ of) уроже́нец, -нка (+gen); (aborigine) тузе́мец, -мка; adj (innate) приро́дный; (of one's birth) родно́й; (indigenous) тузе́мный; ~ **land** ро́дина; ~ **language** родно́й язы́к; ~ **speaker** носи́тель m языка́.

nativity n Рождество́ (Христо́во).

natter vi болта́ть impf.

natural adj есте́ственный, приро́дный; ~ **resources** приро́дные бога́тства neut pl; ~ **selection** есте́ственный отбо́р; n (mus) бека́р. **naturalism** n натурали́зм. **naturalist** n натурали́ст. **naturalistic** adj натуралисти́ческий. **naturalization** n натурализа́ция. **naturalize** vt натурализи́ровать impf & pf. **naturally** adv есте́ственно. **nature** n приро́да;

(character) хара́ктер; by ~ по приро́де.

naught n: **come to** ~ своди́ться impf, свести́сь pf к нулю́.

naughty adj шаловли́вый.

nausea n тошнота́. **nauseate** vt тошни́ть impf impers от +gen. **nauseating** adj тошнотво́рный. **nauseous** adj: **I feel** ~ меня́ тошни́т.

nautical adj морско́й.

naval adj (вое́нно-)морско́й.

nave n неф.

navel n пупо́к.

navigable adj судохо́дный. **navigate** vt (ship) вести́ impf; (sea) пла́вать impf по+dat. **navigation** n навига́ция. **navigator** n штурман.

navvy n землеко́п.

navy n вое́нно-морско́й флот; ~ **blue** тёмно-си́ний.

Nazi n наци́ст, ~ка; adj наци́стский. **Nazism** n наци́зм.

NB abbr нотабе́не.

near adv бли́зко; ~ **at hand** под руко́й; ~ **by** ря́дом; prep во́зле+gen, о́коло+gen, y+gen; adj бли́зкий; ~**-sighted** близору́кий; vt & i приближа́ться impf, прибли́зиться pf к+dat. **nearly** adv почти́.

neat adj (tidy) опря́тный, аккура́тный; (clear) чёткий; (undiluted) неразба́вленный.

nebulous adj нея́сный.

necessarily adv обяза́тельно. **necessary** adj необходи́мый; (inevitable) неизбе́жный. **necessitate** vt де́лать impf, с~ pf необходи́мым. **necessity** n (object) необходи́мость; (inevitability) неизбе́жность; (object) предме́т пе́рвой необходи́мости.

neck n ше́я; (of garment) вы́рез; ~ **and** ~ голова́ в го́ло-

ву. **necklace** n ожере́лье.
neckline n вы́рез.
nectar n некта́р.
née adj урождённая.

need n нужда́; vt нужда́ться impf в+prep; I (etc.) ~ мне (dat) ну́жен (-жна́, -жно, -жны́) +nom; I ~ five roubles мне ну́жно пять рубле́й.

needle n игла́, ~ка; (knitting) спи́ца; (pointer) стре́лка; vt придира́ться impf, придра́ться pf к+dat.

needless adj нену́жный; ~ to say разуме́ется. **needy** adj нужда́ющийся.

negation n отрица́ние. **negative** adj отрица́тельный; n отрица́ние; (phot) негати́в.

neglect vt пренебрега́ть impf, пренебре́чь pf +instr; не забо́титься impf o+prep; n пренебреже́ние; (condition) забро́шенность. **neglectful** adj небре́жный, невнима́тельный (of к+dat). **negligence** n небре́жность. **negligent** adj небре́жный. **negligible** adj незначи́тельный.

negotiate vi вести́ impf перегово́ры; vt (arrange) заключа́ть impf, заключи́ть pf; (overcome) преодолева́ть impf, преодоле́ть pf. **negotiation** n (discussion) перегово́ры m pl.

Negro n негр; adj негритя́нский.

neigh n ржа́ние; vi ржать impf.
neighbour n сосе́д, ~ка. **neighbourhood** n ме́стность; in the ~ of о́коло+gen. **neighbouring** adj сосе́дний. **neighbourly** adj добрососе́дский.
neither adv та́кже не, то́же не; pron ни тот, ни друго́й; ~ ... nor ни ... ни.

neon n нео́н; attrib нео́новый.

nephew n племя́нник.
nepotism n кумовство́.
nerve n нерв; (courage) сме́лость; (impudence) на́глость; get on the ~s of де́йствовать impf, по— pf +dat на не́рвы. **nervous** adj не́рвный; ~ breakdown не́рвное расстро́йство. **nervy** adj нерво́зный.

nest n гнездо́; ~ egg сбереже́ния neut pl; vi гнезди́ться impf. **nestle** vi льнуть impf, при— pf.

net[1] n сеть, се́тка; vt (catch) лови́ть impf, пойма́ть pf сетя́ми.

net[2], **nett** adj чи́стый; vt получа́ть impf, получи́ть pf ... чи́стого дохо́да.

Netherlands n Нидерла́нды (-ов) pl.

nettle n крапи́ва.

network n сеть.

neurologist n невро́лог. **neurology** n невроло́гия. **neurosis** n невро́з. **neurotic** adj невроти́ческий.

neuter adj сре́дний, сре́днего ро́да; n сре́дний род; vt кастри́ровать impf & pf. **neutral** adj нейтра́льный; n (gear) нейтра́льная ско́рость. **neutrality** n нейтралите́т. **neutralize** vt нейтрализова́ть impf & pf. **neutron** n нейтро́н.

never adv никогда́; ~ again никогда́ бо́льше; ~ mind ничего́!; всё равно́!; ~ once ни ра́зу. **nevertheless** conj, adv тем не ме́нее.

new adj но́вый; (moon, potatoes) молодо́й. **new-born** adj новорождённый. **newcomer** n прише́лец. **newfangled** adj новомо́дный. **newly** adv то́лько что, неда́вно. **newness** n новизна́.

news n но́вость, -ти pl, изве́стие, -ия pl. **newsagent** n продаве́ц газе́т. **newsletter** n информацио́нный бюллете́нь m. **newspaper** n газе́та. **newsprint** n газе́тная бума́га. **newsreel** n кинохро́ника.

newt n трито́н.

New Zealand n Но́вая Зела́ндия; adj новозела́ндский.

next adj сле́дующий, бу́дущий; adv (~ time) в сле́дующий раз; (then) пото́м, зате́м; ~ **door** (house) в сосе́днем до́ме; (flat) в сосе́дней кварти́ре; ~ **of kin** ближа́йший ро́дственник; **to** ря́дом c+instr; (fig) почти́. **next-door** adj сосе́дний; **neighbour** ближа́йший сосе́д.

nib n перо́.

nibble vt & i грызть impf; vt обгрыза́ть impf, обгры́зть pf; (grass) щипа́ть impf; (fish) клева́ть impf.

nice adj (pleasant) прия́тный, хоро́ший; (person) ми́лый. **nicety** n то́нкость.

niche n ни́ша; (fig) своё ме́сто.

nick n (scratch) цара́пина; (notch) зару́бка; **in the ~ of time** в са́мый после́дний моме́нт; vt (scratch) цара́пать impf, o~ pf; (steal) стибри́ть pf.

nickel n ни́кель m.

nickname n про́звище; vt прозыва́ть impf, прозва́ть pf.

nicotine n никоти́н.

niece n племя́нница.

niggardly adj скупо́й.

niggling adj ме́лочный.

night n ночь; (evening) ве́чер; **at ~** но́чью; **last ~** вчера́ но́чью; attrib ночно́й; ~ **club** ночно́й клуб. **nightcap** n ночно́й колпа́к; (drink)

стака́нчик спиртно́го на́ ночь. **nightdress** n ночна́я руба́шка. **nightfall** n наступле́ние но́чи. **nightingale** n солове́й. **nightly** adj ежено́щный; adv ежено́щно. **nightmare** n кошма́р. **nightmarish** adj кошма́рный.

nil n нуль m.

nimble adj прово́рный.

nine adj & n де́вять; (number 9) девя́тка. **nineteen** adj & n девятна́дцать. **nineteenth** adj & n девятна́дцатый. **ninetieth** adj & n девяно́стый. **ninety** adj & n девяно́сто; pl (decade) девяно́стые го́ды (-до́в) m pl. **ninth** adj & n девя́тый.

nip vt (pinch) щипа́ть impf, щипну́ть pf; (bite) куса́ть impf, укуси́ть pf; ~ **in the bud** пресека́ть impf, пресе́чь pf в заро́дыше; n щипо́к; уку́с; **there's a ~ in the air** во́здух па́хнет моро́зцем. **nipple** n сосо́к.

nirvana n нирва́на.

nit n гни́да.

nitrate n нитра́т. **nitrogen** n азо́т.

no adj (not any) никако́й, не оди́н; (not a fool etc.) (совсе́м) не; adv нет; (нисколько) не+comp; n отрица́ние, отка́з; (in vote) го́лос „про́тив"; ~ **doubt** коне́чно, несомне́нно; ~ **longer** уже́ не, бо́льше не; **no one** никто́; ~ **wonder** не удиви́тельно.

Noah's ark n Но́ев ковче́г.

nobility n (class) дворя́нство; (quality) благоро́дство. **noble** adj дворя́нский; благоро́дный. **nobleman** n дворяни́н.

nobody pron никто́; n ничто́жество.

nocturnal *adj* ночно́й.

nod *vi* кива́ть *impf*, кивну́ть *pf* голово́й; *n* киво́к.

nodule *n* узело́к.

noise *n* шум. **noiseless** *adj* бесшу́мный. **noisy** *adj* шу́мный.

nomad *n* коче́вник. **nomadic** *adj* кочево́й.

nomenclature *n* номенклату́ра. **nominal** *adj* номина́льный. **nominate** *vt* (*propose*) выдвига́ть *impf*, вы́двинуть *pf*; (*appoint*) назнача́ть *impf*, назна́чить *pf*. **nomination** *n* выдвиже́ние; назначе́ние. **nominative** *adj* (*n*) имени́тельный (паде́ж). **nominee** *n* кандида́т.

non-alcoholic *adj* безалкого́льный. **non-aligned** *adj* неприсоедини́вшийся.

nonchalance *n* беззабо́тность. **nonchalant** *adj* беззабо́тный.

non-commissioned *adj*: ~ **officer** у́нтер-офице́р. **non-committal** *adj* укло́нчивый. **non-conformist** *n* нонконформи́ст; *adj* нонконформи́стский.

nondescript *adj* неопределённый.

none *pron* (*no one*) никто́; (*nothing*) ничто́; (*not one*) не оди́н; *adv* ниско́лько не; ~ **the less** тем не ме́нее.

nonentity *n* ничто́жество.

non-existent *adj* несуществу́ющий. **non-fiction** *n* документа́льный. **non-intervention** *n* невмеша́тельство. **non-party** *adj* беспарти́йный. **non-payment** *n* неплатёж.

nonplus *vt* ста́вить *impf*, поста́вить *pf* в тупи́к.

non-productive *adj* непроизво́дительный. **non-resident**

adj не прожива́ющий (где́-нибудь).

nonsense *n* ерунда́. **nonsensical** *adj* бессмы́сленный.

non-smoker *n* (*person*) неку́ря́щий *sb*; (*compartment*) купе́ *neut indecl*, для неку́рящих.

non-stop *adj* безостано́вочный; (*flight*) беспоса́дочный; *adv* без остано́вок; без поса́док. **non-violent** *adj* ненаси́льственный.

noodles *n pl* лапша́.

nook *n* уголо́к.

noon *n* по́лдень *m*.

no one *see* **no**

noose *n* пе́тля.

nor *conj* и не; то́же; neither ... ~ ни... ни.

norm *n* но́рма. **normal** *adj* норма́льный. **normality** *n* норма́льность. **normalize** *vt* нормализова́ть *impf & pf*.

north *n* се́вер; (*naut*) норд; *adj* се́верный; *adv* к се́веру, на се́вер; ~**-east** се́веро-восто́к; ~**easterly**, **-eastern** се́веро-восто́чный; ~**-west** се́веро-за́пад; ~**-westerly**, **-western** се́веро-за́падный. **northerly** *adj* се́верный. **northern** *adj* се́верный. **northerner** *n* северя́нин, -я́нка. **northward(s)** *adv* на се́вер, к се́веру.

Norway *n* Норве́гия. **Norwegian** *adj* норве́жский; *n* норве́жец, -жка.

nose *n* нос; *vt*: ~ **about, out** разню́хивать *impf*, разню́хать *pf*. **nosebleed** *n* кровотече́ние из носу. **nosedive** *n* пике́ *neut indecl*.

nostalgia *n* ностальги́я. **nostalgic** *adj* ностальги́ческий.

nostril *n* ноздря́.

not *adv* не; нет; ни; ~ **at all** ниско́лько, ничу́ть; (*reply to* thanks) не сто́ит (благода́рности); ~ once ни ра́зу; ~ that не то, что́бы; too дово́льно +neg; to say что́бы не сказа́ть; to make no ~ of не говоря́ уже́ о+prep.

notable adj заме́тный; (remarkable) замеча́тельный. **notably** adv (especially) осо́бенно; (perceptibly) заме́тно.

notary (public) n нота́риус.

notation n нота́ция; (mus) но́тное письмо́.

notch n зару́бка; vt: ~ up вый́грывать impf, вы́играть pf. **note** n (record) заме́тка, за́пись; (annotation) примеча́ние; (letter) запи́ска; (banknote) банкно́т; (mus) но́та; (tone) тон; (attention) внима́ние; vt отмеча́ть impf, отме́тить pf; ~ down запи́сывать impf, записа́ть pf. **notebook** n записна́я кни́жка. **noted** adj знамени́тый; изве́стный (for +instr). **notepaper** n почто́вая бума́га. **noteworthy** adj досто́йный внима́ния.

nothing n ничто́, ничего́; ~ but ничего́ кро́ме+gen, то́лько; ~ of the kind ничего́ подо́бного; come to ~ конча́ться impf, ко́нчиться pf ниче́м; for ~ (free) да́ром; (in vain) зря, напра́сно; have ~ to do with не име́ть impf никако́го отноше́ния к+dat; there is (was) ~ for it (but) to ничего́ друго́го не остаётся (оста́лось) (как); to say ~ of не говоря́ уже́ о+prep.

notice n (sign) объявле́ние; (warning) предупрежде́ние; (attention) внима́ние; (review) о́тзыв; give (in) one's ~ подава́ть impf, пода́ть pf заявле́ние об ухо́де с рабо-

ты; give s.o. ~ предупрежда́ть impf, предупреди́ть pf об увольне́нии; take ~ of обраща́ть impf, обрати́ть pf внима́ние на+acc; ~-board доска́ для объявле́ний; vt замеча́ть impf, заме́тить pf. **noticeable** adj заме́тный. **notification** n извеще́ние. **notify** vt извеща́ть impf, извести́ть pf (of o+prep).

notion n поня́тие.

notoriety n дурна́я сла́ва. **notorious** adj пресловутый.

notwithstanding prep несмотря́ на+acc; adv тем не ме́нее.

nought n (nothing) see **naught**; (zero) нуль m; (figure 0) ноль m.

noun n (имя neut) существи́тельное sb.

nourish vt пита́ть impf, напита́ть pf. **nourishing** adj пита́тельный. **nourishment** n пита́ние.

novel adj но́вый; (unusual) необыкнове́нный; n рома́н. **novelist** n романи́ст. **novelty** n (newness) новизна́; (new thing) нови́нка.

November n ноя́брь m; adj ноя́брьский.

novice n (eccl) по́слушник, -ица; (beginner) новичо́к.

now adv тепе́рь, сейча́с; (immediately) то́тчас же; (next) тогда́; conj: ~ (that) раз, когда́; (every) ~ and again, then вре́мя от вре́мени; by ~ уже́; from ~ on впредь; ~ ... ~ то ... то. **nowadays** adv в на́ше вре́мя.

nowhere adv (place) нигде́; (direction) никуда́; pron: I have ~ to go мне не́куда пойти́.

noxious adj вре́дный.

nozzle n сопло́.

nuance n нюа́нс.

nuclear adj я́дерный. **nucleus** n ядро́.

nude adj обнажённый, наго́й; n обнажённая фигу́ра.

nudge vt подта́лкивать impf, подтолкну́ть pf ло́ктем; n толчо́к ло́ктем.

nudity n нагота́.

nugget n саморо́док.

nuisance n доса́да; (person) раздража́ющий челове́к.

null adj: ~ **and void** недействи́тельный. **nullify** vt аннули́ровать impf & pf. **nullity** n недействи́тельность.

numb adj онемéлый; (from cold) окоченéлый; **go** ~ онемéть pf; (from cold) окоченéть pf.

number n (total) коли́чество; (total; symbol; math; gram) число́; (identifying numeral; item) но́мер; ~-**plate** номерна́я доще́чка; vt (assign a ~) нумерова́ть impf, за~, про~ pf; (contain) насчи́тывать impf; ~ **among** причисля́ть impf, причи́слить pf k+dat; **his days are ~ed** его́ дни сочтены́.

numeral n ци́фра; (gram) (и́мя neut) числи́тельное sb.

numerical adj числово́й. **numerous** adj многочи́сленный; (many) мно́го +gen pl.

nun n мона́хиня. **nunnery** n (же́нский) монасты́рь m.

nuptial adj сва́дебный; n: pl сва́дьба.

nurse n (child's) ня́ня; (medical) медсестра́; vt (suckle) корми́ть impf, на~, по~ pf; (tend sick) уха́живать impf за+instr; **nursing home** санато́рий; дом престаре́лых.

nursery n (room) де́тская sb; (day ~) я́сли (-лей) pl; (for

plants) пито́мник; ~ **rhyme** де́тские прибау́тки f pl; ~ **school** де́тский сад.

nut n орéх; (for bolt etc.) га́йка; (for) **in a** ~ **in two words** в двух слова́х.

nutmeg n муска́тный орéх.

nutrient n пита́тельное вещество́. **nutrition** n пита́ние. **nutritious** adj пита́тельный.

nylon n нейло́н; pl нейло́новые чулки́ (-ло́к) pl.

nymph n ни́мфа.

O

O int о!; ах!

oaf n неуклю́жий челове́к.

oak n дуб; attrib дубо́вый.

oar n весло́. **oarsman** n гребе́ц.

oasis n оа́зис.

oath n прися́га; (expletive) руга́тельство.

oatmeal n овся́нка. **oats** n pl овёс (овса́) collect.

obdurate adj упря́мый.

obedience n послуша́ние. **obedient** adj послу́шный.

obese adj ту́чный. **obesity** n ту́чность.

obey vt слу́шаться impf, по~ pf +gen; (law, order) подчиня́ться impf, подчини́ться pf +dat.

obituary n некроло́г.

object n (thing) предме́т; (aim) цель; (gram) дополне́ние; vi возража́ть impf, возрази́ть pf (to про́тив+gen); **I don't** ~ я не про́тив. **objection** n возраже́ние; **I have no** ~ я не возража́ю. **objectionable** adj неприя́тный. **objective** adj объекти́вный; n цель. **objectivity** n объекти́вность.

objector *n* возража́ющий *sb.*

obligation *n* обяза́тельство; **I am under an ~** я обя́зан(а).

obligatory *adj* обяза́тельный.

oblige *vt* обя́зывать *impf*, обяза́ть *pf*; **be ~d to** (*grateful*) быть обя́занным+*dat*.

obliging *adj* услу́жливый.

oblique *adj* косо́й; (*fig; gram*) ко́свенный.

obliterate *vt* (*efface*) стира́ть *impf*, стере́ть *pf*; (*destroy*) уничтожа́ть *impf*, уничто́жить *pf*. **obliteration** *n* стира́ние; уничтоже́ние.

oblivion *n* забве́ние. **oblivious** *adj* (*forgetful*) забы́вчивый; **to be ~ of** не замеча́ть+*gen*.

oblong *adj* продолгова́тый.

obnoxious *adj* проти́вный.

oboe *n* гобо́й.

obscene *adj* непристо́йный. **obscenity** *n* непристо́йность.

obscure *adj* (*unclear*) нея́сный; (*little known*) малоизве́стный; *vt* затемня́ть *impf*, затемни́ть *pf*; (*make*) де́лать *impf*, с~ *pf* нея́сным. **obscurity** *n* нея́сность; неизве́стность.

obsequious *adj* подобостра́стный.

observance *n* соблюде́ние; (*rite*) обря́д. **observant** *adj* наблюда́тельный. **observation** *n* наблюде́ние; (*remark*) замеча́ние. **observatory** *n* обсервато́рия. **observe** *vt* (*law etc.*) соблюда́ть *impf*, соблюсти́ *pf*; (*watch*) наблюда́ть *impf*; (*remark*) замеча́ть *impf*, заме́тить *pf*. **observer** *n* наблюда́тель *m*.

obsess *vt* пресле́довать *impf*. **obsessed by** одержи́мый +*instr*. **obsession** *n* одержи́мость; (*idea*) навя́зчивая

иде́я. **obsessive** *adj* навя́зчивый.

obsolete *adj* устаре́лый, вы́шедший из употребле́ния.

obstacle *n* препя́тствие.

obstetrician *n* акуше́р. **obstetrics** *n* акуше́рство.

obstinacy *n* упря́мство. **obstinate** *adj* упря́мый.

obstreperous *adj* бу́йный.

obstruct *vt* загражда́ть *impf*, загради́ть *pf*; (*hinder*) препя́тствовать *impf*, вос~ *pf* +*dat*. **obstruction** *n* загражде́ние; (*obstacle*) препя́тствие. **obstructive** *adj* загражда́ющий; препя́тствующий.

obtain *vt* получа́ть *impf*, получи́ть *pf*; достава́ть *impf*, доста́ть *pf*.

obtrusive *adj* навя́зчивый; (*thing*) броса́ющийся в глаза́.

obtuse *adj* тупо́й.

obviate *vt* устраня́ть *impf*, устрани́ть *pf*.

obvious *adj* очеви́дный.

occasion *n* слу́чай; (*cause*) по́вод; (*occurrence*) собы́тие; *vt* причиня́ть *impf*, причини́ть *pf*. **occasional** *adj* ре́дкий. **occasionally** *adv* иногда́, вре́мя от вре́мени.

occult *adj* оккульти́ст; **n: the ~** окку́льт.

occupancy *n* заня́тие. **occupant** *n* жи́тель *m*, ~ница.

occupation *n* заня́тие; (*military ~*) оккупа́ция; (*profession*) профе́ссия. **occupational** *adj* профессиона́льный; **~ therapy** трудотерапи́я. **occupy** *vt* занима́ть *impf*, заня́ть *pf*; (*mil*) оккупи́ровать *impf* & *pf*.

occur *vi* (*happen*) случа́ться *impf*, случи́ться *pf*; (*be found*) встреча́ться *impf*; **~**

to приходи́ть *impf*, прийти́
pf в го́лову+*dat*. **occurrence**
n слу́чай, происше́ствие.

ocean *n* океа́н. **oceanic** *adj*
океани́ческий.

o'clock *adv*: (at) six ~ (в)
шесть часо́в.

octagonal *adj* восьмиуго́ль-
ный.

octave *n* (*mus*) окта́ва.

October *n* октя́брь *m*; *adj*
октя́брьский.

octopus *n* осьмино́г.

odd *adj* (*strange*) стра́нный;
(*not in a set*) разро́зненный;
(*number*) нечётный; (*not
paired*) непа́рный; (*casual*)
случа́йный; **five hundred** ~
пятьсо́т с ли́шним; ~ **job**
случа́йная рабо́та. **oddity** *n*
стра́нность; (*person*) чуда́к, -
а́чка. **oddly** *adv* стра́нно; ~
enough как э́то ни стра́нно.
oddment *n* оста́ток. **odds** *n
pl* ша́нсы *m pl*; **be at** ~ **with**
(*person*) не ла́дить с+*instr*;
(*things*) не соотве́тствовать
impf +*dat*; **long** (**short**) ~
нера́вные (почти́ ра́вные)
ша́нсы *m pl*; **the** ~ **are that**
вероя́тнее всего́, что; ~ **and
ends** обры́вки *m pl*.

ode *n* о́да.

odious *adj* ненави́стный.

odour *n* за́пах.

oesophagus *n* пищево́д.

of *prep expressing* 1. *origin*:
из+*gen*: **he comes** ~ **a work-
ing-class family** он из рабо́-
чей семьи́; 2. *cause*: **he died**
~ **hunger** он у́мер от
го́лода; 3. *authorship*: *gen*: **the
works** ~ **Pushkin** сочине́ния
Пу́шкина; 4. *material*: из+*gen*:
made ~ **wood** сде́ланный из
де́рева; 5. *reference*: о+*prep*:
he talked ~ **Lenin** он гово-

ри́л о Ле́нине; 6. *partition*:
gen (*often in* -у́(-ю)): **a glass**
~ **milk, tea** стака́н молока́,
ча́ю; из+*gen*: **one** ~ **them**
оди́н из них; 7. *belonging*: *gen*:
the capital ~ **England** столи́ца
А́нглии.

off *adv*: *in phrasal vv, see v, e.g.*
clear ~ убира́ться; *prep* (*from
surface of*) c+*gen*; (*away from*)
от+*gen*; ~ **and on** вре́мя от
вре́мени; ~-**white** не совсе́м
бе́лый.

offal *n* требуха́.

offence *n* (*insult*) оби́да;
(*against law*) просту́пок, пре-
ступле́ние; **take** ~ обижа́ться *impf*, оби́деться *pf*
(**at** на+*acc*). **offend** *vt* обижа́ть *impf*, оби́деть *pf*; ~
against наруша́ть *impf*, нару́шить *pf*. **offender** *n* право-
наруши́тель *m*, ~ница. **offensive** *adj* (*attacking*) на-
ступа́тельный; (*insulting*)
оскорби́тельный; (*repulsive*)
проти́вный; *n* нападе́ние.

offer *vt* предлага́ть *impf*, предложи́ть *pf*; *n* предложе́ние;
on ~ в прода́же.

offhand *adj* бесцеремо́нный.

office *n* (*position*) до́лжность;
(*place, room etc.*) бюро́ *neut
indecl*, конто́ра, канцеля́рия.
officer *n* должностно́е лицо́;
(*mil*) офице́р. **official** *adj*
служе́бный; (*authorized*) официа́льный; *n* должностно́е
лицо́. **officiate** *vi* (*eccl*) соверша́ть *impf*, соверши́ть *pf*
богослуже́ние. **officious** *adj*
(*intrusive*) навя́зчивый.

offing *n*: **be in the** ~ предстоя́ть *impf*.

off-licence *n* ви́нный магази́н. **off-load** *vt* разгружа́ть *impf*, разгрузи́ть *pf*. **off-**

putting adj отта́лкивающий.

offset vt возмеща́ть impf, возмести́ть pf. **offshoot** n о́тпрыск. **offshore** adj прибре́жный. **offside** the игры́. **offspring** n пото́мок; (collect) пото́мки m pl.

often adv ча́сто.

ogle vt & i смотре́ть impf с вожделе́нием на+acc.

ogre n велика́н-людое́д.

oh int о!; ах!

ohm n ом.

oil n ма́сло; (petroleum) нефть; (paint) ма́сло, масляные кра́ски f pl; vt сма́зывать impf, сма́зать pf; ~-painting карти́на, напи́санная масляными кра́сками; ~ rig нефтяна́я вы́шка; ~-tanker та́нкер; ~-well нефтяна́я сква́жина. **oilfield** n месторожде́ние не́фти. **oilskin** n клеёнка; pl непромока́емый костю́м. **oily** adj масляни́стый.

ointment n мазь.

OK adv & adj хорошо́, норма́льно; int ла́дно!; vt одобря́ть impf, одобрить pf.

old adj ста́рый; (ancient; of long standing) стари́нный; (former) бы́вший; how ~ are you? ско́лько тебе́, вам, (dat) лет?; ~ age ста́рость; ~-age pension пе́нсия по ста́рости; old-fashioned старомо́дный; ~ maid ста́рая де́ва; ~ man (also father, husband) стари́к; ~-time стари́нный; ~ woman стару́ха; (coll) стару́шка.

olive n (fruit) оли́вка; (colour) оли́вковый цвет; adj оли́вковый; ~ oil оли́вковое ма́сло.

Olympic adj олимпи́йский; ~

games Олимпи́йские и́гры f pl.

omelette n омле́т.

omen n предзнаменова́ние. **ominous** adj злове́щий.

omission n про́пуск; (neglect) упуще́ние. **omit** vt (leave out) пропуска́ть impf, пропусти́ть pf; (neglect) упуска́ть impf, упусти́ть pf.

omnibus n (bus) авто́бус; (collection) колле́кция. **omnipotence** n всемогу́щество. **omnipotent** adj всемогу́щий. **omnipresent** adj вездесу́щий. **omniscient** adj всеве́дущий.

on prep (position) на+prep; (direction) на+acc; (time) в+acc; ~ the next day на сле́дующий день; ~ Mondays (repeated action) по понеде́льникам (dat pl); ~ the first of June пе́рвого ию́ня (gen); (concerning) по+prep, о+prep, на+acc; adv да́льше, вперёд; in phrasal vv, see vv, e.g. move ~ идти́ да́льше; and so ~ и так да́лее, и т.д.; be ~ (film etc.) идти́ impf; further ~ да́льше; later ~ по́зже.

once adv (one occasion) раз; (on past occasion) одна́жды; (formerly) не́когда; all at ~ неожи́данно; at ~ сра́зу, неме́дленно; (if, when) как то́лько; ~ again, more раз; ~ and for all раз и навсегда́; ~ or twice не́сколько раз; ~ upon a time there lived ... жи́л-бы́л... .

oncoming adj: ~ traffic встре́чное движе́ние.

one adj оди́н (одна́, -но́); (only, single) еди́нственный; n оди́н; pron: not usu translated; *v* translated in 2nd pers sg or by impers construction: ~ **never knows** никогда́ не зна́ешь; **where can ~ buy this book?** где мо́жно купи́ть э́ту кни́гу?; ~ **after another** оди́н за други́м; ~ **and all** все до одного́; все как оди́н; ~ **and only** еди́нственный; ~ **and the same** оди́н и тот же; ~ **another** друг дру́га (*dat* -гу, *etc.*); ~ **fine day** в оди́н прекра́сный день; **~ o'clock** час; **~-parent family** семья́ с одни́м роди́телем; **~-sided, -track, -way** односторо́нний; **~-time** бы́вший; **~-way street** у́лица односторо́ннего движе́ния.

onerous *adj* тя́гостный.

oneself *pron* себя́; -ся (*suffixed to vt*).

onion *n* (*plant; pl collect*) лук; (*single* ~) лу́ковица.

onlooker *n* наблюда́тель *m*.

only *adj* еди́нственный; *adv* то́лько; **if ~** е́сли бы то́лько; ~ **just** то́лько что; *conj* но.

onset *n* нача́ло.

onslaught *n* на́тиск. ~.

onus *n* отве́тственность.

onward(s) *adv* вперёд.

ooze *n* ил; *i* сочи́ться *impf*.

opal *n* опа́л.

opaque *adj* непрозра́чный.

open *adj* откры́тый; (*frank*) открове́нный; **in the ~ air** на откры́том во́здухе; **~-minded** *adj* непредубеждённый; *vt & i* открыва́ть(ся) *impf*, откры́ть(ся) *pf*, *vi* (*begin*) начина́ть *impf*, нача́ться *impf* (*flowers*) распуска́ться *impf*, распусти́ться *pf*. **opening** *n* (*aperture*) отве́рстие; (*beginning*) нача́ло; *adj* нача́льный, пе́рвый; (*intro-*

ductory) вступи́тельный.

opera *n* о́пера; *attrib* о́перный; **~-house** *n* о́перный теа́тр.

operate *vi* де́йствовать *impf* (**upon** на+*acc*); (*med*) опери́ровать *impf* & *pf* (**on** +*acc*); *vt* управля́ть *impf* +*instr.*

operatic *adj* о́перный.

operating-theatre *n* операцио́нная *sb.* **operation** *n* де́йствие; (*med;* *mil*) опера́ция. **operational** *adj* (*in use*) де́йствующий; (*mil*) операти́вный. **operative** *adj* де́йствующий. **operator** *n* опера́тор; (*telephone*) телефони́ст, ~ка.

operetta *n* опере́тта.

ophthalmic *adj* глазно́й.

opinion *n* мне́ние; **in my ~** по-мо́ему; **~ poll** опро́с обще́ственного мне́ния. **opinionated** *adj* догмати́чный.

opium *n* о́пиум.

opponent *n* проти́вник.

opportune *adj* своевре́менный. **opportunism** *n* оппортуни́зм. **opportunist** *n* оппортуни́ст. **opportunistic** *n* оппортунисти́ческий. **opportunity** *n* слу́чай, возмо́жность.

oppose *vt* (*resist*) проти́виться *impf*, вос— *pf* +*dat*; (*speak etc. against*) выступа́ть *impf*, вы́ступить *pf* про́тив+*gen*. **opposed** *adj* про́тив (**to** +*gen*); **as ~ to** в противополо́жность+*dat*. **opposing** *adj* проти́вный. (*opposite*) противополо́жный. **opposite** *adj* противополо́жный; (*reverse*) обра́тный; *n* противополо́жность; **just the ~** как раз наоборо́т; *adv* напро́тив; *prep* (на)про́тив+*gen*. **opposition**

n (*resistance*) сопротивле́ние; (*polit*) оппози́ция.

oppress *vt* угнета́ть *impf*. **oppression** *n* угнете́ние. **oppressive** *adj* угнета́ющий. **oppressor** *n* угнета́тель *m*.

opt *vi* выбира́ть *impf*, вы́брать *pf* (for +*acc*); ~ **out** не принима́ть *impf* уча́стия (of в+*prep*).

optic *adj* зри́тельный. **optical** *adj* опти́ческий. **optician** *n* о́птик. **optics** *n* о́птика.

optimism *n* оптими́зм. **optimist** *n* оптими́ст. **optimistic** *adj* оптимисти́ческий. **optimum** *adj* оптима́льный.

option *n* вы́бор. **optional** *adj* необяза́тельный.

opulence *n* бога́тство. **opulent** *adj* бога́тый.

opus *n* о́пус.

or *conj* и́ли; ~ **else** ина́че; ~ **so** приблизи́тельно.

oracle *n* ора́кул.

oral *adj* у́стный; *n* у́стный экза́мен.

orange *n* (*fruit*) апельси́н; (*colour*) ора́нжевый цвет; *attrib* апельси́новый; (*colour*) ора́нжевый.

oration *n* речь. **orator** *n* ора́тор.

oratorio *n* орато́рия.

oratory *n* (*speech*) красноре́чие.

orbit *n* орби́та; *vt* враща́ться *impf* по орби́те вокру́г+*gen*. **orbital** *adj* орбита́льный.

orchard *n* фрукто́вый сад.

orchestra *n* орке́стр. **orchestral** *adj* орке́стровый. **orchestrate** *vt* оркестрова́ть *impf* & *pf*. **orchestration** *n* оркестро́вка.

orchid *n* орхиде́я.

ordain *vt* предпи́сывать *impf*, предписа́ть *pf*; (*eccl*) посвя-

ща́ть *impf*, посвяти́ть *pf* (в духо́вный сан).

ordeal *n* тяжёлое испыта́ние.

order *n* поря́док; (*command*) прика́з; (*for goods*) зака́з; (*insignia, medal, fraternity*) о́рден; (*archit*) ряд; *pl* (*holy* ~) духо́вный сан; **in ~ to** (для того́) что́бы +*inf*; *vt* (*command*) прика́зывать *impf*, приказа́ть *pf* +*dat*; (*goods etc.*) зака́зывать *impf*, заказа́ть *pf*. **orderly** *adj* аккура́тный; (*quiet*) ти́хий; *n* (*med*) санита́р; (*mil*) ордина́рец.

ordinance *n* декре́т.

ordinary *adj* обыкнове́нный, обы́чный.

ordination *n* посвяще́ние.

ore *n* руда́.

organ *n* о́рган; (*mus*) орга́н. **organic** *adj* органи́ческий. **organism** *n* органи́зм. **organist** *n* органи́ст. **organization** *n* организа́ция. **organize** *vt* организо́вывать *impf* (*pres not used*), организова́ть *impf* (*in pres*) & *pf*; устра́ивать *impf*, устро́ить *pf*. **organizer** *n* организа́тор.

orgy *n* о́ргия.

Orient *n* Восто́к. **oriental** *adj* восто́чный.

orient, orientate *vt* ориенти́ровать *impf* & *pf* (**o.s.** ~**ся**). **orientation** *n* ориента́ция.

orifice *n* отве́рстие.

origin *n* происхожде́ние, нача́ло. **original** *adj* оригина́льный; (*initial*) первонача́льный; (*genuine*) по́длинный; *n* оригина́л. **originality** *n* оригина́льность. **originate** *vt* порожда́ть *impf*, породи́ть *pf*; *vi* брать *impf*, взять *pf* нача́ло (**from, in** в+*prep*, от+*gen*); (*arise*) возника́ть *impf*, возни́кнуть *pf*. **originator** *n* а́втор, инициа́тор.

ornament *n* украше́ние; *vt* украша́ть *impf*, укра́сить *pf*. **ornamental** *adj* декорати́вный.

ornate *adj* витиева́тый.

ornithologist *n* орнито́лог. **ornithology** *n* орнитоло́гия.

orphan *n* сирота́ *m & f*; *vt*: be ~ed сироте́ть *impf*, o~ *pf*. **orphanage** *n* сиро́тский дом. **orphaned** *adj* осироте́лый.

orthodox *adj* ортодокса́льный; (*eccl*, O~) правосла́вный. **orthodoxy** *n* ортодо́ксия; (O~) правосла́вие.

orthopaedic *adj* ортопеди́ческий.

oscillate *vi* колеба́ться *impf*, по~ *pf*. **oscillation** *n* колеба́ние.

osmosis *n* о́смос.

ostensible *adj* мни́мый. **ostensibly** *adv* я́кобы.

ostentation *n* выставле́ние напока́з. **ostentatious** *adj* показно́й.

osteopath *n* остеопа́т. **osteopathy** *n* остеопа́тия.

ostracize *vt* подверга́ть *impf*, подве́ргнуть *pf* остраки́зму.

ostrich *n* стра́ус.

other *adj* друго́й, ино́й; тот; every ~ ка́ждый второ́й; every ~ day че́рез день; on the ~ hand с друго́й стороны́; on the ~ side на той стороне́, по ту сто́рону; one or the ~ тот и́ли ино́й; the ~ day на днях, неда́вно; the ~ way round наоборо́т; the ~s остальны́е *sb pl*. **otherwise** *adv & conj* и́на́че, а то.

otter *n* вы́дра.

ouch *int* ой!, ай!

ought *v aux* до́лжен (-жна́)

(бы) +*inf*.

ounce *n* у́нция.

our, **ours** *poss pron* наш; свой. **ourselves** *pron* (*emph*) (мы) са́ми; (*refl*) себя́, -ся (*suffixed to vt*).

oust *vt* вытесня́ть *impf*, вы́теснить *pf*.

out *adv* 1. *in phrasal vv often rendered by pref* вы-; 2.: to be ~ *in various senses*: he is ~ (*not at home*) его́ нет до́ма; (*not in office etc.*) он вы́шел; (*sport*) выходи́ть *impf*, вы́йти *pf* из игры́; (*of fashion*) вы́йти *pf* из мо́ды; (*be published*) вы́йти *pf* из печа́ти; (*of candle etc.*) поту́хнуть *pf*; (*of flower*) распусти́ться *pf*; (*be unconscious*) потеря́ть *pf* созна́ние; 3.: ~ and-~ отъя́вленный; 4.: ~ of из+*gen*, вне+*gen*; ~ of date устаре́лый, старомо́дный; ~ of doors на откры́том во́здухе; ~ of work безрабо́тный.

outbid *vt* предлага́ть *impf*, предложи́ть *pf* бо́лее высо́кую це́ну, чем+*nom*. **outboard** *adj*: ~ motor подвесно́й мото́р *m*. **outbreak** *n* (*of anger, disease*) вспы́шка; (*of war*) нача́ло. **outbuilding** *n* надво́рная постро́йка. **outburst** *n* взрыв. **outcast** *n* изгна́нник. **outcome** *n* результа́т. **outcry** *n* (шу́мные) проте́сты *m pl*. **outdated** *adj* устаре́лый. **outdo** *vt* превосходи́ть *impf*, превзойти́ *pf*. **outdoor** *adj*, **outdoors** *adv* на откры́том во́здухе, на у́лице.

outer *adj* (*external*) вне́шний, нару́жный; (*far from centre*) да́льний. **outermost** *adj* са́мый да́льний.

outfit n (*equipment*) снаряже́ние; (*set of things*) набо́р; (*clothes*) наря́д. **outgoing** adj уходя́щий; (*sociable*) общи́тельный. **outgoings** n pl изде́ржки f pl. **outgrow** vt выраста́ть impf, вы́расти pf из+gen. **outhouse** n надво́рная постро́йка.

outing n прогу́лка, экску́рсия.

outlandish adj дико́винный. **outlaw** n лицо́ вне зако́на; банди́т; vt объяви́ть impf, объяви́ть pf вне зако́на. **outlay** n изде́ржки f pl. **outlet** n выходно́е отве́рстие; (*fig*) вы́ход; (*market*) ры́нок; (*shop*) торго́вая то́чка. **outline** n очерта́ние, ко́нтур; (*sketch, summary*) набро́сок; vt очерти́ть impf, очерти́ть pf; (*plans etc.*) набра́сывать impf, наброса́ть pf. **outlive** vt пережи́ть pf. **outlook** n перспекти́ва f pl; (*attitude*) кругозо́р. **outlying** adj перифери́йный. **outmoded** adj старомо́дный. **outnumber** vt чи́сленно превосходи́ть impf, превзойти́ pf. **out-patient** n амбулато́рный больно́й sb. **outpost** n форпо́ст. **output** n вы́пуск, проду́кция.

outrage n безобра́зие; (*indignation*) возмуще́ние; vt оскорбля́ть impf, оскорби́ть pf. **outrageous** adj возмути́тельный.

outright adv (*entirely*) вполне́; (*once for all*) раз (и) навсегда́; (*openly*) откры́то; adj прямо́й. **outset** n нача́ло; at the ~ внача́ле; from the ~ с са́мого нача́ла.

outside n нару́жная сторона́;

at the ~ са́мое бо́льшее; from the ~ извне́; on the ~ снару́жи; adj нару́жный, вне́шний; (*sport*) кра́йний; adv (*on the ~*) снару́жи; (*to the ~*) нару́жу; (*out of doors*) на откры́том во́здухе, на у́лице; prep вне+gen; за преде́лами+gen. **outsider** n посторо́нний sb; (*sport*) аутса́йдер.

outsize adj бо́льше станда́ртного разме́ра. **outskirts** n pl окра́ина. **outspoken** adj прямо́й. **outstanding** adj (*remarkable*) выдаю́щийся; (*unpaid*) неупла́ченный. **outstay** vt: ~ one's welcome заси́живаться impf, засиде́ться pf. **outstretched** adj распростёртый. **outstrip** vt обгоня́ть impf, обогна́ть pf. **outward** adj (*external*) вне́шний, нару́жный. **outwardly** adv вне́шне, на вид. **outwards** adv нару́жу.

outweigh vt переве́шивать impf, переве́сить pf. **outwit** vt перехитри́ть pf.

oval adj ова́льный; n ова́л.

ovary n яи́чник.

ovation n ова́ция.

oven n (*industrial*) печь; (*domestic*) духо́вка.

over adv & prep with vv: see vv; prep (*above*) над+instr; (*through; covering*) по+dat; (*concerning*) о+prep; (*across*) че́рез+acc; (*on the other side of*) по ту сто́рону+gen; (*more than*) свы́ше+gen; бо́лее+gen; (*with age*) за+acc; all ~ (*finished*) всё ко́нчено; (*everywhere*) повсю́ду; all ~ the country по все́й стране́; ~ again ещё раз; ~ against по сравне́нию с+instr; ~ and above не говоря́ уже́ о+*prep*; ~ **the telephone** по телефо́ну; ~ **there** вон там.

overall *n* хала́т; *pl* комбинезо́н; *adj* о́бщий. **overawe** *vt* внуша́ть *impf*, внуши́ть *pf* благогове́йный страх+*dat*. **overbalance** *vi* теря́ть *impf*, по~ *pf* равнове́сие. **overbearing** *adj* вла́стный. **overboard** *adv* (*motion*) за́ борт; (*position*) за бо́ртом. **overcast** *adj* о́блачный. **overcoat** *n* пальто́ *neut indecl*. **overcome** *vt* преодолева́ть *impf*, преодоле́ть *pf*; *adj* охва́ченный. **overcrowded** *adj* перепо́лненный. **overcrowding** *n* перенаселе́ние. **overdo** *vt* (*cook*) пережа́ривать *impf*, пережа́рить *pf*; ~ **it, things** (*work too hard*) переутомля́ться *impf*, переутоми́ться *pf*; (*go too far*) переба́рщивать *impf*, переборщи́ть *pf*. **overdose** *n* чрезме́рная до́за. **overdraft** *n* превыше́ние креди́та; (*amount*) долг ба́нку. **overdraw** *vi* превыша́ть *impf*, превы́сить *pf* креди́т в ба́нке. **overdue** *adj* просро́ченный; **be** ~ (*late*) запа́здывать *impf*, запозда́ть *pf*. **overestimate** *vt* переоце́нивать *impf*, переоцени́ть *pf*. **overflow** *vi* перелива́ться *impf*, перели́ться *pf*; (*river etc.*) разлива́ться *impf*, разли́ться *pf*; (*outlet*) водосли́в. **overgrown** *adj* заро́сший. **overhang** *vt & i* выступа́ть *impf* над+*instr*, в свес, вы́ступ. **overhaul** *vt* ремонти́ровать *impf* & *pf*; *n*: ремо́нт. **overhead** *adv* наверху́, над голово́й; *adj* возду́шный, подвес-

но́й; *n*: *pl* накладны́е расхо́ды *m pl*. **overhear** *vt* услы́шать *impf*, у-*pf*. **overheat** *vt & i* перегрева́ть(ся) *impf*, перегре́ть(ся) *pf*. **overjoyed** *adj* в восто́рге (**at** от+*gen*). **overland** *adj* сухопу́тный; *adv* по су́ше. **overlap** *vi* части́чно покрыва́ть, покры́ть *pf*; *vi* части́чно совпада́ть *impf*, совпа́сть *pf*. **overleaf** *adv* на оборо́те. **overload** *vt* перегружа́ть *impf*, перегрузи́ть *pf*. **overlook** *vt* (*look down on*) смотре́ть *impf* све́рху на+*acc*; (*of window*) выходи́ть *impf* на, в, +*acc*; (*not notice*) не замеча́ть *impf*, заме́тить *pf* +*gen*; (~ *offence etc.*) проща́ть *impf*, прости́ть *pf*.

overly *adv* сли́шком.

overnight *adv* (*during the night*) за́ ночь; (*suddenly*) неожи́данно; **stay** ~ ночева́ть *impf*, пере~ *pf*; *adj* ночно́й. **overpay** *vt* перепла́чивать *impf*, переплати́ть *pf*. **over-populated** *adj* перенаселённый. **over-population** *n* перенаселённость. **overpower** *vt* одолева́ть *impf*, одоле́ть *pf*. **overpriced** *adj* завы́шенный в цене́. **overproduction** *n* перепроизво́дство. **overrate** *vt* переоце́нивать *impf*, переоцени́ть *pf*. **override** *vt* (*fig*) отверга́ть *impf*, отве́ргнуть *pf*. **overriding** *adj* гла́вный, реша́ющий. **overrule** *vt* отверга́ть *impf*, отве́ргнуть *pf*. **overrun** *vt* (*conquer*) завоёвывать *impf*, завоева́ть *pf*; **be** ~ **with** кише́ть *impf* +*instr*.

overseas *adv* за мо́рем,

че́рез мо́ре; adj замо́рский.
oversee vt надзира́ть impf
за+instr. **overseer** n надзира́-
тель m, -ница. **overshadow**
vt затмева́ть impf, затми́ть
pf. **overshoot** vi переходи́ть
impf, перейти́ за грани́цу.
oversight n случа́йный не-
досмо́тр. **oversleep** vi про-
сыпа́ть impf, проспа́ть pf.
overspend vi тра́тить impf
сли́шком мно́го. **overstate**
vt преувели́чивать impf, пре-
увели́чить pf. **overstep** vt
переступа́ть impf, переступи́ть
пи́ть pf +acc, че́рез+acc.

overt adj я́вный, откры́тый.
overtake vt обгоня́ть impf,
обогна́ть pf. **overthrow** vt
сверга́ть impf, све́ргнуть pf.
overtime n (work) сверх-
уро́чная рабо́та; (payment)
сверхуро́чное sb; adv сверх-
уро́чно.

overtone n скры́тый намёк.
overture n предложе́ние;
(mus) увертю́ра.

overturn vt & i опроки́ды-
вать(ся) impf, опроки́нуть-
(ся) pf. **overwhelm** vt подав-
ля́ть impf, подави́ть pf.
overwhelming adj подавля́-
ющий. **overwork** vt & i пере-
утомля́ть(ся) impf, переуто-
ми́ть(ся) pf; n переутомле́-
ние.

owe vt (~ money) быть до́л-
жным +acc & dat; (be indebted) быть обя́занным +instr &
dat; he, she, ~s me three roubles он до́лжен, она́ должна́,
мне три рубля́; she ~s him
her life она́ обя́зана ему́
жи́знью. **owing** adj: be ~
причита́ться impf (to +dat); ~
to из-за+gen, по причи́не+gen.

owl n сова́.

own adj свой; (свой) со́бствен-
ный; **on one's** ~ самостоя́-
тельно; (alone) оди́н; vt (possess) владе́ть impf +instr; (admit) признава́ть impf, при-
зна́ть pf; ~ **up** признава́ть-
ся impf, призна́ться pf. **owner** n
владе́лец. **ownership** n владе́-
ние (of +instr), со́бственность.

ox n вол.

oxidation n окисле́ние. **oxide**
n о́кись. **oxidize** vt & i оки-
сля́ть(ся) impf, окисли́ть(ся)
pf. **oxygen** n кислоро́д.

oyster n у́стрица.

ozone n озо́н.

P

pace n шаг; (fig) темп; **keep**
~ **with** идти́ impf в но́гу
c+instr; **set the** ~ задава́ть
impf, зада́ть pf темп; vi; ~
up and down ходи́ть indet
взад и вперёд. **pacemaker** n
(med) электро́нный стиму́ля́-
тор.

pacifism n пацифи́зм. **pacifist** n пацифи́ст. **pacify** vt
усмиря́ть impf, усмири́ть pf.

pack n у́зел, вьюк; (soldier's)
ра́нец; (hounds) сво́ра; (wolves)
ста́я; (cards) коло́да; vt (& i)
упако́вывать(ся) impf, упа-
кова́ть(ся) pf; (cram) наби-
ва́ть impf, наби́ть pf. **package**
n посы́лка, паке́т; ~ **holiday**
организо́ванная туристи́че-
ская пое́здка. **packaging** n
упако́вка. **packet** n паке́т;
па́чка; (large sum of money)
ку́ча де́нег. **packing-case** n
я́щик.

pact n пакт.

pad n (cushion) поду́шечка;
(shin- etc.) щито́к; (of paper)

блокно́т; vt подбива́ть impf, подби́ть pf. **padding** n наби́вка.

paddle¹ n (oar) весло́; vi (row) грести́ impf.

paddle² n (wade) ходи́ть indet, идти́ det, пойти́ pf босико́м по воде́.

paddock n вы́гон.

pagan n язы́чник, -ица; adj язы́ческий. **paganism** n язы́чество.

page¹ n (~-boy) паж; vt (summon) вызыва́ть impf, вы́звать pf.

page² n (of book) страни́ца.

pageant n пы́шная проце́ссия. **pageantry** n пы́шность.

pail n ведро́.

pain n боль; pl (efforts) уси́лия neut pl; ~-killer болеутоля́ющее сре́дство; vt (fig) огорча́ть impf, огорчи́ть pf. **painful** adj боле́зненный; be ~ (part of body) боле́ть impf. **painless** adj безболе́зненный. **painstaking** adj стара́тельный.

paint n кра́ска; vt кра́сить impf, по~ pf; (portray) писа́ть impf, на~ pf кра́сками. **paintbrush** n кисть. **painter** n (artist) худо́жник, -ица (decorator) маля́р. **painting** n (art) жи́вопись; (picture) карти́на.

pair n па́ра; often not translated with nn denoting a single object, e.g. a ~ of scissors но́жницы (-ц) pl; a ~ of trousers па́ра брюк; vt спари-

вать impf, спа́рить pf; ~ off разделя́ться impf, разделя́ться pf по па́рам.

Pakistan n Пакиста́н. **Pakistani** n пакиста́нец, -а́нка; adj пакиста́нский.

pal n прия́тель m, ~ница.

palace n дворе́ц.

palatable adj вку́сный; (fig) прия́тный. **palate** n нёбо; (fig) вкус.

palatial adj великоле́пный.

palaver n (trouble) беспоко́йство; (nonsense) чепуха́.

pale¹ n (stake) кол; **beyond the** ~ невообрази́мый.

pale² adj бле́дный; vi бледне́ть impf, по~ pf.

palette n пали́тра.

pall¹ n покро́в.

pall² vi: ~ **on** надоеда́ть impf, надое́сть pf +dat.

palliative adj паллиати́вный; n паллиати́в.

pallid adj бле́дный. **pallor** n бле́дность.

palm¹ n (tree) па́льма; P~ Sunday Ве́рбное воскресе́нье.

palm² n (of hand) ладо́нь; vt: ~ **off** всу́чивать impf, всучи́ть pf (**on** +dat).

palpable adj осяза́емый.

palpitations n pl сердцебие́ние.

paltry adj ничто́жный.

pamper vt балова́ть impf, из~ pf.

pamphlet n брошю́ра.

pan¹ n (saucepan) кастрю́ля; (frying-~) сковорода́; (of scales) ча́шка; vt: ~ **out** промыва́ть impf, промы́ть pf; (fig) выходи́ть impf, вы́йти pf.

pan² vi (cin) панорами́ровать impf & pf.

panacea n панаце́я.

panache n рисо́вка.

pancake n блин.

pancreas n поджелу́дочная железа́.

panda n па́нда.

pandemonium n гвалт.

pander vi: ~ **to** потво́рствовать impf +dat.

pane n око́нное стекло́.

panel n пане́ль; (control-~) щит управле́ния; (of experts) гру́ппа специали́стов; (of judges) жюри́ neut indecl. **panelling** n пане́льная обши́вка.

pang n pl му́ки (-к) pl.

panic n па́ника; ~**-stricken** охва́ченный па́никой; vi впада́ть impf, впасть pf в па́нику. **panicky** adj пани́ческий.

pannier n корзи́на.

panorama n панора́ма. **panoramic** adj панора́мный.

pansy n аню́тины гла́зки (-зок) pl.

pant vi дыша́ть impf с оды́шкой.

panther n панте́ра.

panties n pl тру́сики (-ков) pl.

pantomime n рожде́ственское представле́ние; (dumb show) пантоми́ма.

pantry n кладова́я sb.

pants n pl трусы́ (-со́в) pl; (trousers) брю́ки (-к) pl.

papal adj па́пский.

paper n бума́га; pl докуме́нты m pl; (newspaper) газе́та; (wallpaper) обо́и (-о́ев) pl; (treatise) докла́д; adj бума́жный; vt окле́ить pf обо́ями. **paperback** n кни́га в бума́жной обло́жке. **paperclip** n скре́пка. **paperwork** n канцеля́рская

par n: **feel below** ~ чу́вствовать impf себя́ нева́жно;

on a ~ **with** наравне́ c+instr.

parable n при́тча.

parabola n пара́бола.

parachute n парашю́т; vi спуска́ться impf, спусти́ться pf с парашю́том. **parachutist** n парашюти́ст.

parade n пара́д; vi шество́вать impf; vt (show off) выставля́ть impf, вы́ставить pf напока́з.

paradigm n паради́гма.

paradise n рай.

paradox n парадо́кс. **paradoxical** adj парадокса́льный.

paraffin n (~ oil) кероси́н.

paragon n образе́ц.

paragraph n абза́ц.

parallel adj паралле́льный; n паралле́ль; vt соотве́тствовать impf +dat.

paralyse vt парализова́ть impf & pf. **paralysis** n парали́ч.

parameter n пара́метр.

paramilitary adj полувое́нный.

paramount adj первостепе́нный.

paranoia n парано́йя. **paranoid** adj: **he is** ~ он парано́ик.

parapet n (mil) бру́ствер.

paraphernalia n принадле́жности f pl.

paraphrase n переска́з; vt переска́зывать impf, пересказа́ть pf.

parasite n парази́т. **parasitic** adj паразити́ческий.

parasol n зо́нтик.

paratrooper n парашюти́ст-деса́нтник.

parcel n паке́т, посы́лка.

parch vt иссуша́ть impf, иссуши́ть pf; **become** ~**ed** пересыха́ть impf, пересо́хнуть pf.

parchment n перга́мент.

pardon n проще́ние; (law) поми́лование; vt проща́ть

impf, прости́ть *pf*; (*law*) поми́ловать *pf*.

pare *vt* (*fruit*) чи́стить *impf*, о~ *pf*; ~ **away**, **down** урѣзывать *impf*, урѣзать *pf*.

parent *n* роди́тель *m*, -ница.

parentage *n* происхожде́ние.

parental *adj* роди́тельский.

parentheses *n pl* (*brackets*) ско́бки *f pl*.

parish *n* прихо́д. **parishioner** *n* прихожа́нин, -а́нка.

parity *n* ра́венство.

park *n* парк; (*for cars etc.*) стоя́нка; *vt & abs* ста́вить *impf*, по~ *pf* (маши́ну). **parking** *n* стоя́нка.

parliament *n* парла́мент. **parliamentarian** *n* парламента́рий. **parliamentary** *adj* парла́ментский.

parlour *n* гости́ная *sb*.

parochial *adj* прихо́дский; (*fig*) ограни́ченный. **parochialism** *n* ограни́ченность.

parody *n* паро́дия; *vt* паро́дировать *impf & pf*.

parole *n* че́стное сло́во; **on** ~ освобождённый под че́стное сло́во.

paroxysm *n* парокси́зм.

parquet *n* парке́т; *attrib* парке́тный.

parrot *n* попуга́й.

parry *vt* пари́ровать *impf & pf*, от~ *pf*.

parsimonious *adj* скупо́й.

parsley *n* петру́шка.

parsnip *n* пастерна́к.

parson *n* свяще́нник.

part *n* часть *f*; (*in play*) роль; (*mus*) па́ртия; **for the most** ~ бо́льшей ча́стью; **in** ~ ча́стью; **for my** ~ что каса́ется меня́; **take** ~ **in** уча́ствовать *impf* в+*prep*; ~**time** (за́нятый) непо́лный рабо́-

чий день; *vt & i* (*divide*) разделя́ть(ся) *impf*, раздели́ть(ся) *pf*; *vi* (*leave*) расстава́ться *impf*, расста́ться *pf* (**from**, **with** c+*instr*); ~ **one's hair** де́лать *impf*, c~ *pf* себе́ пробо́р.

partake *vi* принима́ть *impf*, приня́ть *pf* уча́стие (**in**, **of** в+*prep*); (*eat*) есть *impf*, съ~ *pf* (**of** +*acc*).

partial *adj* части́чный; (*biased*) пристра́стный; ~ **to** неравноду́шный к+*dat*. **partiality** *n* (*bias*) пристра́стность. **partially** *adv* части́чно.

participant *n* уча́стник, -ица (**in** +*gen*). **participate** *vi* уча́ствовать *impf* (**in** в+*prep*). **participation** *n* уча́стие.

participle *n* прича́стие.

particle *n* части́ца.

particular *adj* осо́бый, осо́бенный; (*fussy*) разбо́рчивый; *n* подро́бность; **in** ~ в ча́стности.

parting *n* (*leave-taking*) проща́ние; (*of hair*) пробо́р.

partisan *n* (*adherent*) сторо́нник; (*mil*) партиза́н; *attrib* (*biased*) пристра́стный; (*mil*) партиза́нский.

partition *n* (*wall*) перегоро́дка; (*polit*) разде́л; *vt* разделя́ть *impf*, раздели́ть *pf*; ~ **off** отгора́живать *impf*, отгороди́ть *pf*.

partly *adv* части́чно.

partner *n* (*in business*) компаньо́н; (*in dance*, *game*) партнёр, ~ша. **partnership** *n* това́рищество.

partridge *n* куропа́тка.

party *n* (*polit*) па́ртия; (*group*) гру́ппа; (*social gathering*) вечери́нка; (*law*) сторона́; **be a** ~ **to** принима́ть *impf*,

приня́ть *pf* уча́стие в+*prep*; ~
attrib партийный; ~ **line**
(*polit*) ли́ния па́ртии; (*telephone*) о́бщий телефо́нный
про́вод; ~ **wall** о́бщая стена́.
pass *vt & i* (*go past, of time*)
проходи́ть *impf*, пройти́ *pf*
(*by* ми́мо+*gen*); (*travel past*)
проезжа́ть *impf*, прое́хать
pf (*by* ми́мо+*gen*); (*examination*) сдава́ть *impf*, сдать
pf (*экза́мен*); (*sport*) пасо-
ва́ть *impf*, пасну́ть *pf*; (*overtake*) обгоня́ть *impf*, обо-
гна́ть *pf*; (*time*) проводи́ть
impf, провести́ *pf*; (*hand on*)
передава́ть *impf*, переда́ть
pf; (*law, resolution*) утвер-
жда́ть *impf*, утверди́ть *pf*;
(*sentence*) выноси́ть *impf*,
вы́нести *pf* (*upon* +*dat*); ~
as, for слыть *impf*, про~ *pf*
+*instr*, за+*acc*; ~ **away** (*die*)
сконча́ться *pf*; ~ **o.s. off as**
выдава́ть *impf*, вы́дать *pf* за
себя́ за+*acc*; ~ **out** теря́ть
impf, по~ *pf* созна́ние; ~
over (*in silence*) обходи́ть
impf, обойти́ *pf* молча́нием;
~ **round** передава́ть *impf*,
переда́ть *pf*; ~ **up** подава́ть
impf, пода́ть *pf*; (*miss*) про-
пуска́ть *impf*, пропусти́ть *pf*;
n (*permit*) про́пуск; (*sport*)
пас; (*geog*) перева́л; **come to**
~ случа́ться *impf*, случи́ть-
ся *pf*; **make a** ~ **at** приста-
ва́ть *impf*, приста́ть *pf* к+*dat*.
passable *adj* проходи́мый,
прое́зжий; (*not bad*) непло-
хо́й.
passage *n* (*in prison*) прохо́д; (*of time*)
тече́ние; (*sea trip*) рейс; (*in
house*) коридо́р; (*in book*)
отры́вок; (*mus*) пасса́ж.
passenger *n* пассажи́р.
passer-by *n* прохо́жий *sb*.

passing *adj* (*transient*) мимолётный; *n*: **in** ~ мимохо́дом.
passion *n* страсть (*for* к+*dat*).
passionate *adj* стра́стный.
passive *adj* пасси́вный; (*gram*)
страда́тельный; *n* страда́-
тельный зало́г. **passivity** *n*
пасси́вность.
Passover *n* евре́йская Па́сха.
passport *n* па́спорт.
password *n* паро́ль *m*.
past *adj* про́шлый; (*gram*)
проше́дший; *n* про́шлое *sb*;
(*gram*) проше́дшее вре́мя
neut; *prep* ми́мо+*gen*; (*beyond*) за+*instr*; *adv* ми́мо.
pasta *n* макаро́нные изде́лия
neut pl.
paste *n* (*of flour*) те́сто; (*creamy mixture*) па́ста; (*glue*)
клей; (*jewellery*) страз; *vt* на-
кле́ивать *impf*, накле́ить *pf*.
pastel *n* (*crayon*) пасте́ль;
(*drawing*) рису́нок пасте́лью;
attrib пасте́льный.
pasteurize *vt* пастеризова́ть
impf & pf.
pastime *n* времяпрепровож-
де́ние.
pastor *n* па́стор. **pastoral** *adj*
(*bucolic*) пастора́льный; (*of
pastor*) па́сторский.
pastry *n* (*dough*) те́сто; (*cake*)
пиро́жное *sb*.
pasture *n* (*land*) па́стбище.
pasty[1] *n* пирожо́к.
pasty[2] *adj* (~-*faced*) бле́д-
ный.
pat *n* шлепо́к; (*of butter etc.*)
кусо́к; *vt* хло́пать *impf*, по~
pf.
patch *n* (*over eye*)
повя́зка (на глазу́); (*spot*)
пятно́; (*of land*) уча́сток
земли́; *vt* ста́вить *impf*, по~
pf запла́ту на+*acc*; ~ **up** (*fig*)
ула́живать *impf*, ула́дить *pf*.

patchwork n лоску́тная рабо́та; attrib лоску́тный. **patchy** adj неро́вный.

pâté n паште́т.

patent adj я́вный; ~ leather лакиро́ванная ко́жа; n пате́нт; vt патентова́ть impf, за~ pf.

paternal adj отцо́вский. **paternity** n отцо́вство.

path n тропи́нка, тропа́; (way) путь m.

pathetic adj жа́лкий.

pathological adj патологи́ческий. **pathologist** n пато́лог.

pathos n па́фос.

pathway n тропи́нка, тропа́.

patience n терпе́ние; (cards) пасья́нс. **patient** adj терпели́вый; n больно́й sb, пацие́нт, ~ка.

patio n терра́са.

patriarch n патриа́рх. **patriarchal** adj патриарха́льный.

patriot n патрио́т, ~ка. **patriotic** adj патриоти́ческий. **patriotism** n патриоти́зм.

patrol n патру́ль m; on ~ на дозо́ре; vt i патрули́ровать impf.

patron n покрови́тель m; (of shop) клие́нт. **patronage** n покрови́тельство. **patroness** n покрови́тельница. **patronize** vt (treat condescendingly) снисходи́тельно относи́ться impf, к+dat. **patronizing** adj покрови́тельственный.

patronymic n о́тчество.

patter[1] n (sound) бараба́нить impf, vi постуки́вание.

patter[2] n (speech) скорогово́рка.

pattern n (design) узо́р; (model) образе́ц; (sewing) вы́кройка.

paunch n брюшко́.

pauper n бедня́к.

pause n па́уза, переры́в; (mus) ферма́та; vi остана́вливаться impf, останови́ться pf.

pave vt мости́ть impf, вы́~ pf; ~ the way подгото́вить impf, подгото́вить pf по́чву (for для+gen). **pavement** n тротуа́р.

pavilion n павильо́н.

paw n ла́па; vt тро́гать impf ла́пой; (horse) бить impf копы́том.

pawn[1] n (chess) пе́шка.

pawn[2] n: in ~ в закла́де; vt закла́дывать impf, заложи́ть pf. **pawnbroker** n ростовщи́к. **pawnshop** n ломба́рд.

pay vt плати́ть impf, за~, у~ pf (for за+acc); (bill etc.) опла́чивать impf, оплати́ть pf; vi (be profitable) окупа́ться impf, окупи́ться pf; n жа́лованье, зарпла́та; ~ packet получка, ~roll платёжная ве́домость. **payable** adj подлежа́щий упла́те. **payee** n получа́тель m. **payload** n поле́зная нагру́зка. **payment** n упла́та, платёж.

pea n (also pl, collect) горо́х.

peace n мир; in ~ в поко́е; ~ and quiet мир и тишина́. **peaceable**, **peaceful** adj ми́рный.

peach n пе́рсик.

peacock n павли́н.

peak n (of cap) козырёк; (summit; fig) верши́на; ~ hour часы́ m pl пик.

peal n (sound) звон, трезво́н; (of laughter) взрыв.

peanut n ара́хис.

pear n гру́ша.

pearl n (also fig) жемчу́жина; pl (collect) же́мчуг.

peasant n крестья́нин, -я́нка; attrib крестья́нский.

peat n торф.

pebble n га́лька.

peck vt & i клева́ть impf, клю́нуть pf; n клево́к.

pectoral adj грудно́й.

peculiar adj (distinctive) своеобра́зный; (strange) стра́нный; ~ **to** свойственный +dat. **peculiarity** n осо́бенность; стра́нность.

pecuniary adj де́нежный.

pedagogical adj педагоги́ческий.

pedal n педа́ль; vi нажима́ть impf, нажа́ть pf педа́ль; (ride bicycle) е́хать impf, по~ pf на велосипе́де.

pedant n педа́нт. **pedantic** adj педанти́чный.

peddle vt торгова́ть impf вразно́с+instr.

pedestal n пьедеста́л.

pedestrian adj пешехо́дный; (prosaic) прозаи́ческий; n пешехо́д; ~ **crossing** перехо́д.

pedigree n родосло́вная sb; adj поро́дистый.

pedlar n разно́счик.

pee n пи-пи́ neut indecl; vi мочи́ться impf, по~ pf.

peek vi (~ in) загля́дывать impf, загляну́ть pf; (~ out) выгля́дывать impf, вы́глянуть pf.

peel n кожура́; vt очища́ть impf, очи́стить pf; vi (skin) шелуши́ться impf; (paint, ~ off) сходи́ть impf, сойти́ pf. **peelings** n pl очи́стки (-ков) pl.

peep vi (~ in) загля́дывать impf, загляну́ть pf; (~ out) выгля́дывать impf, вы́глянуть pf; n (glance) бы́стрый взгляд; ~**hole** глазо́к.

peer¹ vi всма́триваться impf,

всмотре́ться pf (**at** в+acc).

peer² n (noble) пэр; (person one's age) све́рстник.

peeved adj раздражённый.

peevish adj раздражи́тельный.

peg n ко́лышек; (clothes ~) крючо́к; (for hat etc.) ве́шалка; **off the** ~ гото́вый; vt прикрепля́ть impf, прикрепи́ть pf ко́лышком, -ками.

pejorative adj уничижи́тельный.

pelican n пелика́н.

pellet n ша́рик; (shot) дроби́на.

pelt¹ n (skin) шку́ра.

pelt² vt забра́сывать impf, заброса́ть pf; vi (rain) бараба́нить impf.

pelvis n таз.

pen¹ n (for writing) ру́чка; ~**friend** друг по перепи́ске.

pen² n (enclosure) заго́н.

penal adj уголо́вный. **penalize** vt штрафова́ть impf, о~ pf. **penalty** n наказа́ние; (sport) штраф; ~ **area** штрафна́я площа́дка; ~ **kick** штрафно́й уда́р. **penance** n епитимья́.

penchant n скло́нность (**for** к+dat).

pencil n каранда́ш; ~**sharpener** точи́лка.

pendant n подве́ска.

pending adj (awaiting decision) ожида́ющий реше́ния; prep (until) в ожида́нии +gen, до+gen.

pendulum n ма́ятник.

penetrate vt проника́ть impf, прони́кнуть pf в+acc. **penetrating** adj проница́тельный; (sound) пронзи́тельный. **penetration** n проникнове́ние; (insight) проница́тельность.

penguin n пингви́н.

penicillin n пеницилли́н.

peninsula n полуо́стров.

penis n пе́нис.

penitence n раска́яние. **penitent** adj раска́ивающийся; n ка́ющийся гре́шник.

penknife n перочи́нный нож.

pennant n вы́мпел.

penniless adj без гроша́.

penny n пе́нни neut indecl, пенс.

pension n пе́нсия; vt: ~ off увольня́ть impf, уво́лить pf на пе́нсию. **pensionable** (age) пенсио́нный. **pensioner** n пенсионе́р, ~ка.

pensive adj заду́мчивый.

pentagon n пятиуго́льник; the P~ Пентаго́н.

Pentecost n Пятидеся́тница.

penthouse n шика́рная кварти́ра на ве́рхнем этаже́.

pent-up adj (anger etc.) сде́рживаемый.

penultimate adj предпосле́дний.

penury n нужда́.

peony n пио́н.

people n pl (persons) лю́ди pl; sg (nation) наро́д; vt населя́ть impf, насели́ть pf.

pepper n пе́рец; vt перчи́ть impf, на~ pf. **peppercorn** n перчи́нка.

peppermint n пе́речная мя́та; (sweet) мя́тная конфе́та.

per prep (for each) (person) на+acc; **as** ~ согла́сно+dat; ~ **annum** в год; ~ **capita** на челове́ка; ~ **hour** в час; ~ **se** сам по себе́.

perceive vt воспринима́ть impf, восприня́ть pf.

per cent adv в n проце́нт. **percentage** n проце́нт; (part) часть.

perceptible adj заме́тный. **perception** n восприя́тие; (quality) понима́ние. **perceptive** adj то́нкий.

perch[1] n (fish) о́кунь m.

perch[2] n (roost) насе́ст; vi сади́ться impf, сесть pf. **perched** adj высоко́ сидя́щий, располо́женный.

percussion n (~ instruments) уда́рные инструме́нты m pl.

peremptory adj повели́тельный.

perennial adj (enduring) ве́чный; n (bot) многоле́тнее расте́ние.

perestroika n перестро́йка.

perfect adj соверше́нный; (gram) перфе́ктный; n перфе́кт; vt соверше́нствовать impf, y~ pf. **perfection** n соверше́нство. **perfective** adj (n) соверше́нный (вид).

perforate vt перфори́ровать impf & pf. **perforation** n перфора́ция.

perform vt (carry out) исполня́ть impf, испо́лнить pf; (theat, mus) игра́ть impf, сыгра́ть pf; vi выступа́ть impf, вы́ступить pf; (function) рабо́тать impf. **performance** n исполне́ние; (of person, device) де́йствие; (of play etc.) представле́ние, спекта́кль m; (of engine etc.) эксплуатацио́нные ка́чества neut pl. **performer** n исполни́тель m.

perfume n духи́ (-хо́в) pl; (smell) арома́т.

perfunctory adj пове́рхностный.

perhaps adv мо́жет быть.

peril n опа́сность, риск. **perilous** adj опа́сный, риско́ванный.

perimeter n вне́шняя грани́ца; (geom) пери́метр.

period n пери́од; (epoch) эпо́ха; (menstrual) ме́сячные sb pl.

periodic adj периоди́ческий.

periodical adj периоди́ческий; n периоди́ческое изда́ние.

peripheral adj перифери́йный. **periphery** n перифери́я.

periscope n периско́п.

perish vi погиба́ть impf, поги́бнуть pf; (spoil) по́ртиться impf, ис~ pf. **perishable** adj скоропо́ртящийся.

perjure v: ~ o.s. наруша́ть impf, нару́шить pf кля́тву. **perjury** n лжесвиде́тельство.

perk[1] n льго́та.

perk[2] vi: ~ up оживля́ться impf, оживи́ться pf. **perky** adj бо́йкий.

perm n перманент. **permanence** n постоя́нство. **permanent** adj постоя́нный.

permeable adj проница́емый. **permeate** vi проника́ть impf, прони́кнуть pf в+acc.

permissible adj допусти́мый. **permission** n разреше́ние. **permissive** adj (сли́шком) либера́льный; ~ **society** о́бщество вседозво́ленности. **permissiveness** n вседозво́ленность. **permit** vt разреша́ть impf, разреши́ть pf +dat; n про́пуск.

permutation n перестано́вка.

pernicious adj па́губный.

perpendicular adj перпендикуля́рный; n перпендикуля́р.

perpetrate vt соверша́ть impf, соверши́ть pf. **perpetrator** n вино́вник.

perpetual adj ве́чный. **perpetuate** vt увекове́чивать impf, увекове́чить pf. **perpetuity** n ве́чность; in ~ навсегда́, наве́чно.

perplex vt озада́чивать impf, озада́чить pf. **perplexity** n озада́ченность.

persecute vt пресле́довать impf. **persecution** n пресле́дование.

perseverance n насто́йчивость. **persevere** vi насто́йчиво, продолжа́ть impf at etc. +acc, inf).

Persian n перс, ~ия́нка; adj перси́дский.

persist vi упо́рствовать (in в+prep); насто́йчиво продолжа́ть impf (in +acc, inf). **persistence** n упо́рство. **persistent** adj упо́рный.

person n челове́к; (in play; gram) лицо́; in ~ ли́чно. **personable** adj привлека́тельный. **personage** n ли́чность. **personal** adj ли́чный. **personality** n ли́чность. **personally** adv ли́чно. **personification** n олицетворе́ние. **personify** vt олицетворя́ть impf, олицетвори́ть pf.

personnel n ка́дры (-ров) pl, персона́л; ~ **department** отде́л ка́дров.

perspective n перспекти́ва.

perspiration n пот. **perspire** vi поте́ть impf, вс~ pf.

persuade vt (convince) убежда́ть impf, убеди́ть pf (of в+prep); (induce) угова́ривать impf, уговори́ть pf. **persuasion** n убежде́ние. **persuasive** adj убеди́тельный.

pertain vi: ~ **to** относи́ться impf отнести́сь pf к+dat.

pertinent adj уме́стный.

perturb vt трево́жить impf, вс~ pf.

peruse *vt* (*read*) внима́тельно чита́ть *impf*, про~ *pf*; (*fig*) рассма́тривать *impf*, рассмотре́ть *pf*.

pervade *vt* наполня́ть *impf*. **pervasive** *adj* распространённый.

perverse *adj* капри́зный. **perversion** *n* извраще́ние. **pervert** *vt* извраща́ть *impf*, изврати́ть *pf*; *n* извращённый челове́к.

pessimism *n* пессими́зм. **pessimist** *n* пессими́ст. **pessimistic** *adj* пессимисти́ческий.

pest *n* вреди́тель *m*; (*fig*) зану́да. **pester** *vt* пристава́ть *impf*, приста́ть *pf* к+*dat*. **pesticide** *n* пестици́д.

pet *n* (*animal*) дома́шнее живо́тное *sb*; (*favourite*) люби́мец, -мица; ~ **shop** зоомагази́н; *vt* ласка́ть *impf*.

petal *n* лепесто́к.

peter *vi*: ~ **out** (*road*) исчеза́ть *impf*, исче́знуть *pf*; (*stream*; *enthusiasm*) иссяка́ть *impf*, исся́кнуть *pf*.

petite *adj* ма́ленькая.

petition *n* пети́ция; *vt* подава́ть *impf*, пода́ть *pf* проше́ние +*dat*. **petitioner** *n* проси́тель *m*.

petrified *adj* окамене́лый; **be** ~ (*fig*) оцепене́ть *pf* (**with** от+*gen*).

petrol *n* бензи́н; ~ **pump** бензоколо́нка; ~ **station** бензозапра́вочная ста́нция; ~ **tank** бензоба́к. **petroleum** *n* нефть.

petticoat *n* ни́жняя ю́бка.

petty *adj* ме́лкий; ~ **cash** де́ньги (де́нег, -ньга́м) *pl* на ме́лкие расхо́ды.

petulant *adj* раздражи́тельный.

pew *n* (церко́вная) скамья́.

phallic *adj* фалли́ческий. **phallus** *n* фа́ллос.

phantom *n* фанто́м.

pharmaceutical *adj* фармацевти́ческий. **pharmacist** *n* фармаце́вт. **pharmacy** *n* фармаци́я; (*shop*) апте́ка.

phase *n* фа́за; *vt*: ~ **in, out** постепе́нно вводи́ть *impf*, упраздня́ть *impf*.

Ph.D. *abbr* (*of* **Doctor of Philosophy**) кандида́т нау́к.

pheasant *n* фаза́н.

phenomenal *adj* феномена́льный. **phenomenon** *n* феноме́н.

phial *n* пузырёк.

philanderer *n* воло́кита *m*.

philanthropic *adj* филантропи́ческий. **philanthropist** *n* филантро́п. **philanthropy** *n* филантро́пия.

philately *n* филатели́я.

philharmonic *adj* филармони́ческий.

Philistine *n* (*fig*) фили́стер.

philosopher *n* фило́соф. **philosophical** *adj* филосо́фский. **philosophize** *vi* филосо́фствовать *impf*. **philosophy** *n* филосо́фия.

phlegm *n* мокрота́. **phlegmatic** *adj* флегмати́чный.

phobia *n* фо́бия.

phone *n* телефо́н; *vt* & *i* звони́ть *impf*, по~ *pf* +*dat*. See also **telephone**

phonetic *adj* фонети́ческий. **phonetics** *n* фоне́тика.

phoney *n* подде́льный.

phosphorus *n* фо́сфор.

photo *n* фо́то *neut indecl*. **photocopier** *n* копирова́льная маши́на. **photocopy** *n* фотоко́пия; *vt* де́лать *impf*, с~ *pf* фотоко́пию +*gen*. **photogenic** *adj* фотогени́чный.

photograph n фотогра́фия; vt фотографи́ровать impf, c~ pf. **photographer** n фото́граф. **photographic** adj фотографи́ческий. **photography** n фотогра́фия.

phrase n фра́за; vt формули́ровать impf, c~ pf.

physical adj физи́ческий; ~ **education** физкульту́ра; ~ **exercises** заря́дка. **physician** n врач. **physicist** n физик. **physics** n фи́зика.

physiological adj физиологи́ческий. **physiologist** n физио́лог. **physiology** n физиоло́гия. **physiotherapist** n физиотерапе́вт. **physiotherapy** n физиотерапи́я.

physique n телосложе́ние.

pianist n пиани́ст, ~ка. **piano** n фортепья́но neut indecl; (grand) роя́ль m; (upright) пиани́но neut indecl.

pick¹ vt (flower) срыва́ть impf, сорва́ть pf; (gather) собира́ть impf, собра́ть pf; (select) выбира́ть impf, вы́брать pf; ~ **one's nose, teeth** ковыря́ть impf, ковырну́ть pf в носу́, в зуба́х; ~ **a quarrel** иска́ть impf ссо́ры (with c+instr); ~ **one's way** выбира́ть impf, вы́брать pf доро́гу; ~ **on** (nag) придира́ться impf к+dat; ~ **out** отбира́ть impf, отобра́ть pf; ~ **up** (lift) поднима́ть impf, подня́ть pf; (acquire) приобрета́ть impf, приобрести́ pf; (fetch) (on foot) заходи́ть impf, зайти́ pf за+instr; (in vehicle) заезжа́ть impf, зае́хать pf за+instr; (a cold; a girl) подцепля́ть impf, подцепи́ть pf; ~ **o.s. up** поднима́ться impf, подня́ться pf;

~**up** (truck) пика́п; (electron) звукоснима́тель m.

pick² n вы́бор; (best part) лу́чшая часть; **take your** ~ выбира́й(те)!

pick³, pickaxe n кирка́.

picket n (person) пике́тчик, -ница; (collect) пике́т; vt пикети́ровать impf.

pickle n соле́нье; vt соли́ть impf, по~ pf. **pickled** adj солёный.

pickpocket n карма́нник.

picnic n пикни́к.

pictorial adj изобрази́тельный; (illustrated) иллюстри́рованный. **picture** n карти́на; (of health etc.) воплоще́ние; (film) фильм; the ~s кино́ neut indecl; vt (to o.s.) представля́ть impf, предста́вить pf себе́. **picturesque** adj живопи́сный.

pie n пиро́г.

piece n кусо́к, часть; (one of set) шту́ка; (of paper) листо́к; (mus, literature) произведе́ние; (chess) фигу́ра; (coin) моне́та; **take to** ~s разбира́ть impf, разобра́ть pf (на ча́сти); ~ **of advice** сове́т; ~ **of information** све́дение; ~ **of news** но́вость; ~-**work** сде́льщина; ~-**worker** сде́льщик; vt: ~ **together** воссоздава́ть impf, воссозда́ть pf карти́ну +gen. **piecemeal** adv поштучно.

pier n (mole) мол; (projecting into sea) пирс; (between windows etc.) просте́нок.

pierce vt пронза́ть impf, пронзи́ть pf; (ears) прока́лывать impf, проколо́ть pf. **piercing** adj пронзи́тельный.

piety n на́божность.

pig n свинья́. **pigheaded** adj упря́мый. **piglet** n поросё́нок. **pigsty** n свина́рник. **pigtail** n коси́чка.

pigeon n го́лубь; **~-hole** отделе́ние для бума́г.

pigment n пигме́нт. **pigmentation** n пигмента́ция.

pike n (fish) щу́ка.

pilchard n сарди́н(к)а.

pile[1] n (heap) ку́ча, ки́па; vt: ~ **up** сва́ливать impf, свали́ть pf в ку́чу; (load) нагружа́ть impf, нагрузи́ть pf (with +instr); vi: ~ **in(to)**, **on** забира́ться impf, забра́ться pf в+acc; ~ **up** накопля́ться impf, нака́пливаться impf, накопи́ться pf.

pile[2] n (on cloth etc.) ворс.

piles n pl геморро́й collect.

pilfer vt ворова́ть impf.

pilgrim n пилигри́м. **pilgrimage** n пало́мничество.

pill n пилю́ля; **the ~** противозача́точная пилю́ля.

pillage vt гра́бить impf, о~ pf; v abs мародёрствовать impf.

pillar n столб; **~-box** стоя́чий почто́вый я́щик.

pillion n за́днее сиде́нье (мотоци́кла).

pillory n позо́рный столб; vt (fig) пригвожда́ть impf, пригвозди́ть pf к позо́рному столбу́.

pillow n поду́шка. **pillowcase** n на́волочка.

pilot n (naut) ло́цман; (aeron) пило́т; adj о́пытный, про́бный; vt пилоти́ровать impf.

pimp n сво́дник.

pimple n прыщ.

pin n була́вка; (peg) па́лец; **~-point** то́чно определя́ть impf, определи́ть pf, **~-stripe**

то́нкая поло́ска; vt прика́лывать impf, приколо́ть pf; (press) прижима́ть impf, прижа́ть pf (against к+dat).

pinafore n пере́дник.

pincers n pl (tool) кле́щи (-ще́й) pl, пинце́т; (claw) клешня́ f pl.

pinch vt щипа́ть impf, (у)щипну́ть pf, (finger in door etc.) прищемля́ть impf, прищеми́ть pf; (of shoe) жать impf; (steal) стяну́ть pf в щипо́к; (of salt) щепо́тка; **at a ~** в кра́йнем слу́чае.

pine[1] vi томи́ться impf; ~ **for** тоскова́ть impf по+dat, prep.

pine[2] n (tree) сосна́.

pineapple n анана́с.

ping-pong n пинг-по́нг.

pink n (colour) ро́зовый цвет; adj ро́зовый.

pinnacle n верши́на.

pint n пи́нта.

pioneer n пионе́р, ~ка; vt прокла́дывать impf, проложи́ть pf путь к+dat.

pious adj на́божный.

pip[1] n (seed) зёрнышко.

pip[2] n (sound) бип.

pipe n труба́; (mus) ду́дка; (for smoking) тру́бка; **~-dream** пуста́я мечта́; vt пуска́ть impf, пусти́ть pf по трубе́; vi ~ **down** затиха́ть impf, зати́хнуть pf. **pipeline** n трубопрово́д; (oil ~) нефтепрово́д. **piper** n волы́нщик. **piping** adj: ~ **hot** с пы́лу.

piquant adj пика́нтный.

pique n: **in a fit of ~** в поры́ве раздраже́ния.

pirate n пира́т.

pirouette n пируэ́т; vi де́лать impf, с~ pf пируэ́т(ы).

Pisces n Ры́бы f pl.

pistol n пистолет.

piston n поршень m.

pit n яма; (mine) шахта; (orchestra ~) оркестр; (motor-racing) заправочно-ремонтный пункт; vt: ~ against выставлять impf, выставить pf против+gen.

pitch[1] n (resin) смола; ~-**black** чёрный как смоль; ~-**dark** очень тёмный.

pitch[2] vt (camp, tent) разбивать impf, разбить pf; (throw) бросать impf, бросить pf; vi (fall) падать impf, (у)пасть pf; (ship) качать impf, n (football ~ etc.) площадка; (degree) уровень m; (mus) высота; (slope) уклон.

pitcher n (vessel) кувшин.

pitchfork n вилы (-л) pl.

piteous adj жалкий.

pitfall n западня.

pith n сердцевина; (essence) суть; **pithy** adj (fig) содержательный.

pitiful adj жалкий. **pitiless** adj безжалостный.

pittance n жалкие гроши (-шей) pl.

pity n жалость; it's a ~ жалко, жаль; **take** ~ on сжалиться pf над+instr; **what a** ~ как жалко!; **what a** ~ жалеть impf, по~ pf; I ~ **you** мне жаль тебя.

pivot n стержень m; (fig) центр m; vi вращаться impf.

pixie n эльф.

pizza n пицца.

placard n афиша, плакат.

placate vt умиротворять impf, умиротворить pf.

place n место; in ~ of вместо+gen; in the first, second, ~ во-первых, во-вторых; out of ~ не на месте; (un-

suitable) неуместный; **take** ~ случаться impf, случиться pf; (pre-arranged event) состояться pf; **take the** ~ **of** заменять impf, заменить pf; vt (stand) ставить impf, по~ pf; (lay) класть impf, положить pf; (an order etc.) помещать impf, поместить pf.

placenta n плацента.

placid adj спокойный.

plagiarism n плагиат. **plagiarize** vt заимствовать impf & pf.

plague n чума; vt мучить impf, за~, из~ pf.

plaice n камбала.

plain n равнина; adj (clear) ясный; (simple) простой; (ugly) некрасивый; ~-**clothes policeman** переодетый полицейский sb.

plaintiff n истец, истица.

plaintive adj жалобный.

plait n коса; vt плести impf, с~ pf.

plan n план; vt планировать impf, за~, с~ pf; (intend) намереваться impf +inf.

plane[1] n (tree) платан.

plane[2] n (tool) рубанок; vt строгать impf, вы~ pf.

plane[3] n (surface) плоскость; (level) уровень m; (aeroplane) самолёт.

planet n планета.

plank n доска.

plant n растение; (factory) завод; vt сажать impf, посадить pf; (fix firmly) прочно ставить impf, по~ pf; (garden etc.) засаживать impf, засадить pf (with +instr).

plantation n (of trees) (лесо)-насаждение; (of cotton etc.) плантация.

plaque n дощечка.

plasma n пла́зма.

plaster n пла́стырь m; (for walls etc.) штукату́рка; (of Paris) гипс; vt (wall) штукату́рить impf, от~, о~ pf; (cover) обле́пливать impf, облепи́ть pf сухая штукату́рка. **plasterboard** n сухая штукату́рка. **plasterer** n штукату́р.

plastic n пластма́сса; adj (malleable) пласти́чный; (made of ~) пластма́ссовый; ~ surgery пласти́ческая хирурги́я.

plate n таре́лка; (metal sheet) лист; (in book) (вкладна́я) иллюстра́ция; (name ~ etc.) доще́чка.

plateau n плато́ neut indecl.

platform n платфо́рма; (rly) перро́н.

platinum n пла́тина.

platitude n бана́льность.

platoon n взвод.

plausible adj правдоподо́бный.

play vt & i игра́ть impf, сыгра́ть pf (game) в+acc, (instrument) на+prep, (record) ста́вить impf, по~ pf; ~ down преуменьша́ть impf, преуме́ньшить pf; ~ a joke, trick, on подшу́чивать impf, подшути́ть pf над+instr; ~ off игра́ть impf, сыгра́ть pf реша́ющую па́ртию; ~ safe де́йствовать impf наверняка́; n игра́; (theat) пье́са. **player** n игро́к; (actor) актёр, актри́са; (musician) музыка́нт. **playful** adj игри́вый. **playground** n площа́дка для игр. **playgroup, playschool** n де́тский сад. **playing** n: ~-card игра́льная ка́рта; ~-field игрова́я площа́дка. **playmate** n друг де́тства. **play-

thing** n игру́шка. **playwright** n драмату́рг.

plea n (entreaty) мольба́; (law) заявле́ние. **plead** vi умоля́ть (with +acc; for o+prep); vt (offer as excuse) ссыла́ться impf, сосла́ться pf на+acc; ~ (not) guilty (не) признава́ть impf, призна́ть pf себя́ вино́вным.

pleasant adj прия́тный. **pleasantry** n любе́зность. **please** vt нра́виться impf, по~ pf +dat; imper пожа́луйста; бу́дьте добры́; **pleased** adj дово́льный; predic рад. **pleasing, pleasurable** adj прия́тный. **pleasure** n удово́льствие.

pleat n скла́дка; vt плиссиро́вать impf.

plebiscite n плебисци́т.

plectrum n плектр.

pledge n (security) зало́г; (promise) заро́к, обеща́ние; vt отдава́ть impf, отда́ть pf в зало́г; ~ o.s. обя́зываться impf, обяза́ться pf; ~ one's word дава́ть impf, дать pf сло́во.

plentiful adj оби́льный. **plenty** n изоби́лие; ~ of мно́го+gen.

plethora n (fig) изоби́лие.

pleurisy n плеври́т.

pliable adj ги́бкий.

pliers n pl плоскогу́бцы (-цев) pl.

plight n незави́дное положе́ние.

plimsolls n pl спорти́вные та́почки f pl.

plinth n плинтус.

plod vi тащи́ться impf.

plonk vt плю́хнуть pf.

plot n (of land) уча́сток; (of book etc.) фа́була; (conspiracy) за́говор; vt (on graph, map, *etc.*) наносить *impf*, нанести на график, на карту; *v abs* (*conspire*) составлять *impf*, составить *pf* заговор.

plough *n* плуг; *vt* вспахивать, вс~ *pf*; *vi:* ~ **through** пробиваться *impf*, пробиться *pf* сквозь+*acc*.

ploy *n* уловка.

pluck *n* (*courage*) смелость; *vt* (*chicken*) щипать *impf*, об~ *pf*; (*mus*) щипать *impf*; (*flower*) срывать *impf*, сорвать *pf*; ~ **up courage** собираться *impf*, собраться *pf* с духом; *vi:* ~ **at** дёргать *impf*, дёрнуть *pf*. **plucky** *adj* смелый.

plug *n* (*stopper*) пробка; (*electr*) вилка; (*electr socket*) розётка; *vt* (~ **up**) затыкать *impf*, заткнуть *pf*; ~ **in** включать *impf*, включить *pf*.

plum *n* слива.

plumage *n* оперение.

plumb *n* лот; *adv* вертикально; (*fig*) точно; *vt* измерять *impf*, измерить *pf* глубину+*gen*; (*fig*) проникать *impf*, проникнуть *pf* в+*acc*; ~ **in** подключать *impf*, подключить *pf*.

plumber *n* водопроводчик. **plumbing** *n* водопровод.

plume *n* (*feather*) перо; (*on hat etc.*) султан.

plummet *n* падать *impf*, (у)пасть *pf*.

plump[1] *adj* пухлый.

plump[2] *vi:* ~ **for** выбирать *impf*, выбрать *pf*.

plunder *vt* грабить *impf*, о~ *pf*; *n* добыча.

plunge *vt* & *i* (*immerse*) погружать(ся) *impf*, погрузить(ся) *pf*; (*into* в+*acc*); *vi* (*dive*) нырять *impf*, нырнуть

pf; (*rush*) бросаться *impf*, броситься *pf*. **plunger** *n* плунжер.

pluperfect *n* давнопрошедшее время *neut*.

plural *n* множественное число. **pluralism** *n* плюрализм. **pluralistic** *adj* плюралистический.

plus *prep* плюс+*acc*; *n* (*знак*) плюс.

plushy *adj* шикарный.

plutonium *n* плутоний.

ply *vt* (*tool*) работать *impf* +*instr*; (*task*) заниматься *impf* +*instr*; (*keep supplied*) потчевать *impf* (*with* +*instr*); ~ **with questions** засыпать *impf*, засыпать *pf* вопросами.

plywood *n* фанера.

p.m. *adv* после полудня.

pneumatic *adj* пневматический; ~ **drill** отбойный молоток.

pneumonia *n* воспаление лёгких.

poach[1] *vt* (*cook*) варить *impf*; ~**ed egg** яйцо-пашот.

poach[2] *vi* браконьерствовать *impf*. **poacher** *n* браконьер.

pocket *n* карман; **out of** ~ в убытке; ~ **money** карманные деньги (-нег, -ньгам) *pl*; *vt* класть *impf*, положить *pf* в карман.

pock-marked *adj* рябой.

pod *n* стручок.

podgy *adj* толстенький.

podium *n* трибуна; (*conductor's*) пульт.

poem *n* стихотворение; (*longer* ~) поэма. **poet** *n* поэт. **poetess** *n* поэтесса. **poetic(al)** *adj* поэтический. **poetry** *n* поэзия, стихи *m pl*.

pogrom *n* погром.

poignancy *n* остротá. **poignant** *adj* óстрый.

point[1] *n* тóчка; (*place*; *in list*) пункт; (*in score*) очкó; (*in time*) момéнт; (*in space*) мéсто; (*essence*) суть; (*sense*) смысл; (*sharp*) остриё; (*tip*) кóнчик; (*power*) штéпсель *m*; *pl* (*rly*) стрéлка; **be on the ~ of** (*doing*) собирáться *impf*, собрáться *pf* +inf; **beside, off, the ~** нeкстáти; **that is the ~** в э́том и дéло; **the ~ is that** дéло в том, что; **there is no ~** (*in doing*) не имéет смы́сла (+inf); **to the ~** кстáти; **~-blank** прямóй; **~ of view** тóчка зрéния.

point[2] *vt* (*wall*) расшивáть *impf*, расшить *pf* швы+gen; (*gun etc.*) наводить *impf*, навести́ *pf* (**at** на+acc); *vi* по-, у-, кáзывать *impf*, по-, казáть *pf* (**at, to** на+acc).

pointed *adj* (*sharp*) óстрый. **pointer** *n* указáтель *m*, стрéлка. **pointless** *adj* бессмы́сленный.

poise *n* уравновéшенность. **poised** *adj* (*composed*) уравновéшенный; (*ready*) готóвый (**to** к+dat).

poison *n* яд; *vt* отравля́ть *impf*, отрави́ть *pf*. **poisonous** *adj* ядови́тый.

poke *vt* (*prod*) ты́кать *impf*, ткнуть *pf*; **~ fun at** подшýчивать *impf*, подшути́ть *pf* над+instr; (*thrust*) совáть *impf*, сýнуть *pf*; **~ the fire** мешáть *impf*, по~ *pf* у́голь в ками́не; *vi* ты́чок. **poker**[1] *n* (*rod*) кочергá.

poker[2] *n* (*cards*) пóкер. **poky** *adj* тéсный.

Poland *n* Пóльша.

polar *adj* поля́рный; **~ bear** бéлый медвéдь *m*. **polarity** *n* поля́рность. **polarize** *vt* поляризовáть *impf* & *pf*. **pole**[1] *n* (*geog*; *phys*) пóлюс; **~-star** Поля́рная звездá.

pole[2] *n* (*rod*) столб, шест; **~-vaulting** прыжóк с шестóм.

Pole *n* поля́к, пóлька.

polecat *n* хорёк.

polemic *adj* полеми́ческий; *n* полéмика.

police *n* поли́ция; (*as pl*) полицéйские *sb*; (*in Russia*) мили́ция; **~ station** полицéйский учáсток. **policeman** *n* полицéйский *sb*, полисмéн; (*in Russia*) милиционéр. **policewoman** *n* жéнщина-полицéйский *sb*; (*in Russia*) жéнщина-милиционéр.

policy[1] *n* поли́тика.

policy[2] *n* (*insurance*) пóлис.

polio *n* полиомиели́т.

Polish *adj* пóльский.

polish *n* (*gloss*, *process*) полирóвка; (*substance*) политýра; (*fig*) лоск; *vt* полировáть *impf*, от~ *pf*; **~ off** расправля́ться *impf*, распрáвиться *pf* с+instr. **polished** *adj* отточенный.

polite *adj* вéжливый. **politeness** *n* вéжливость.

politic *adj* полити́чный. **political** *adj* полити́ческий; **~ economy** политэконóмика; **~ prisoner** политзаключённый *sb*. **politician** *n* поли́тик. **politics** *n* поли́тика.

poll *n* (*voting*) голосовáние; (*opinion*) опрóс; **go to the ~s** голосовáть *impf*, про~ *pf* vi получáть *impf*, получи́ть *pf*.

pollen *n* пыльцá. **pollinate** *vt* опыля́ть *impf*, опыли́ть *pf*.

polling *attrib*: **~ booth** каби́на

для голосова́ния; ~ **station** избира́тельный уча́сток.

pollutant n загрязни́тель m. **pollute** vt загрязня́ть impf, загрязни́ть pf. **pollution** n загрязне́ние.

polo n по́ло neut indecl; ~ **neck sweater** водола́зка.

polyester n полиэфи́р. **polyethylene** n полиэтиле́н. **polyglot** n полигло́т; adj многоязы́чный. **polygon** n многоуго́льник. **polymer** n полиме́р. **polystyrene** n полистиро́л. **polytechnic** n техни́ческий вуз. **polythene** n полиэтиле́н. **polyunsaturated** adj: ~ **fats** полиненасы́щенные жиры́ m pl. **polyurethane** n полиурета́н.

pomp n пы́шность. **pomposity** n напы́щенность. **pompous** adj напы́щенный.

pond n пруд.

ponder vt обду́мывать impf, обду́мать pf; vi размышля́ть impf, размы́слить pf. **ponderous** adj тяжелове́сный.

pony n по́ни m indecl. **poodle** n пу́дель m.

pool¹ n (of water) пруд; (puddle) лу́жа; (swimming ~) бассе́йн.

pool² n (collective stakes) совоку́пность ста́вок; (common fund) о́бщий фонд; vt объединя́ть impf, объедини́ть pf.

poor adj бе́дный; (bad) плохо́й; n: **the** ~ бедняки́ m pl. **poorly** predic нездоро́в.

pop¹ vi хло́пать impf, хло́пнуть pf; vt (put) бы́стро всу́нуть pf (into в+acc); **on** забега́ть impf, забежа́ть pf к+dat; n хлопо́к.

pop² adj поп-; ~ **concert** поп-

конце́рт; ~ **music** поп-му́зыка.

pope n Па́па m.

poplar n то́поль m.

poppy n мак.

populace n просто́й наро́д. **popular** adj наро́дный; (liked) популя́рный. **popularity** n популя́рность. **popularize** vt популяризи́ровать impf & pf. **populate** vt населя́ть impf, насели́ть pf. **population** n населе́ние. **populous** adj (мно́го)лю́дный.

porcelain n фарфо́р.

porch n крыльцо́.

porcupine n дикобра́з.

pore¹ n по́ра.

pore² vi: ~ **over** погружа́ться impf, погрузи́ться pf в+acc.

pork n свини́на.

pornographic adj порнографи́ческий. **pornography** n порногра́фия.

porous adj по́ристый.

porpoise n морска́я свинья́.

porridge n овся́ная ка́ша.

port¹ n (harbour) порт; (town) портово́й го́род.

port² n (naut) ле́вый борт.

port³ n (wine) портве́йн.

portable adj порта́тивный.

portend vt предвеща́ть impf. **portent** n предзнаменова́ние. **portentous** adj злове́щий.

porter¹ n (at door) швейца́р.

porter² n (carrier) носи́льщик.

portfolio n портфе́ль m; (artist's) па́пка.

porthole n иллюмина́тор.

portion n часть, до́ля; (of food) по́рция.

portly adj доро́дный.

portrait n портре́т. **portray** vt изобража́ть impf, изобрази́ть pf. **portrayal** n изображе́ние.

Portugal n Португа́лия. **Portuguese** n португа́лец, -лка; adj португа́льский.

pose n по́за; vt (question) ста́вить impf, по~ pf; (a problem) представля́ть impf, предста́вить pf; vi пози́ровать impf; ~ **as** выдава́ть impf, вы́дать pf себя́ за+acc.

posh adj шика́рный.

posit vt постули́ровать impf & pf.

position n положе́ние, пози́ция; **in a** ~ **to** в состоя́нии +inf; vt ста́вить impf, по~ pf.

positive adj положи́тельный; (convinced) уве́ренный; (proof) несомне́нный; n (phot) позити́в.

possess vt облада́ть impf +instr; владе́ть impf +instr; (of feeling etc.) овладева́ть impf, овладе́ть pf +instr. **possessed** adj одержи́мый. **possession** n владе́ние (of +instr); pl со́бственность. **possessive** adj со́бственнический. **possessor** n облада́тель m.

possibility n возмо́жность. **possible** adj возмо́жный; **as much as** ~ ско́лько возмо́жно; **as soon as** ~ как мо́жно скоре́е. **possibly** adv возмо́жно, мо́жет быть.

post[1] n (pole) столб; vt (~ up) выве́шивать impf, вы́весить pf.

post[2] n (station) пост; (job) до́лжность; vt (station) расставля́ть impf, расста́вить pf; (appoint) назнача́ть impf, назна́чить pf.

post[3] n (letters, ~ office) по́чта; by ~ по́чтой; attrib почто́вый; ~-**box** почто́вый я́щик; ~-**code** почто́вый и́ндекс; ~ **office** по́чта; vt (send by) отправля́ть impf, отпра́вить pf по по́чте; (put in ~-box) опуска́ть impf, опусти́ть pf в почто́вый я́щик. **postage** n почто́вый сбор, почто́вые расхо́ды m pl; ~ **stamp** почто́вая ма́рка.

postal adj почто́вый; ~-**order** почто́вый перево́д.

postcard n откры́тка.

poster n афи́ша, плака́т.

poste restante n до востре́бования.

posterior adj за́дний; n зад.

posterity n пото́мство.

post-graduate n аспира́нт.

posthumous adj посме́ртный.

postman n почтальо́н. **postmark** n почто́вый ште́мпель m.

post-mortem n вскры́тие тру́па.

postpone vt отсро́чивать impf, отсро́чить pf. **postponement** n отсро́чка.

postscript n постскри́птум.

postulate vt постули́ровать impf & pf.

posture n по́за, положе́ние.

post-war adj послевое́нный.

posy n буке́тик.

pot n горшо́к; (cooking ~) кастрю́ля; vt; ~**shot** вы́стрел наугад; (food) консерви́ровать impf, за~ pf; (plant) сажа́ть impf, посади́ть pf в горшо́к; (billiards) загоня́ть impf, загна́ть pf в лу́зу.

potash n пота́ш. **potassium** n ка́лий.

potato n (also collect) карто́шка (no pl); (plant; also collect) карто́фель m (no pl).

potency n си́ла. **potent** adj си́льный.

potential *adj* потенциа́льный; *n* потенциа́л. **potentiality** *n* потенциа́льность.

pot-hole *n* (*in road*) вы́боина.

potion *n* зе́лье.

potter¹ *vi*: ~ **about** вози́ться *impf*.

potter² *n* гонча́р. **pottery** *n* (*goods*) гонча́рные изде́лия *neut pl*; (*place*) гонча́рная *f*.

potty¹ *adj* (*crazy*) поме́шанный (**about** на+*prep*).

potty² *n* ночно́й горшо́к.

pouch *n* су́мка.

poultry *n* дома́шняя пти́ца.

pounce *vi*: ~ (**up**)**on** набра́сываться *impf*, набро́ситься *pf* на+*acc*.

pound¹ *n* (*measure*) фунт; ~ **sterling** фунт сте́рлингов.

pound² *vt* (*strike*) колоти́ть *impf*, по~ *pf* по+*dat*, в+*acc*; *vi* (*heart*) колоти́ться *impf*; ~ **along** (*run*) мча́ться *impf* с гро́хотом.

pour *vt* лить *impf*, на~; ~ **out** налива́ть *impf*, нали́ть *pf*; *vi* ли́ться *impf*; it is ~**ing** (**with rain**) дождь льёт как из ведра́.

pout *vi* ду́ть(ся) *impf*, на~.

poverty *n* бе́дность; ~-**stricken** убо́гий.

POW *abbr* военнопле́нный *sb*.

powder *n* порошо́к; (*cosmetic*) пу́дра; *vt* и пу́дрить *impf*, на~ *pf*. **powdery** *adj* порошкообра́зный.

power *n* (*vigour*) си́ла; (*might*) могу́щество; (*ability*) спосо́бность; (*control*) власть; (*authorization*) полномо́чие; (*State*) держа́ва; ~ **cut** переры́в электропита́ния; ~ **point** розе́тка; ~ **station** электроста́нция. **powerful** *adj* си́льный. **powerless** *adj* бесси́льный.

practicable *adj* осуществи́мый. **practical** *adj* практи́ческий. **practically** *adv* практи́чески. **practice** *n* пра́ктика; (*custom*) обы́чай; (*mus*) заня́тия *neut pl*; **in** ~ на пра́ктике; **put into** ~ осуществля́ть *impf*, осуществи́ть *pf*. **practise** *vt* (*also abs of doctor etc.*) практикова́ть *impf*; упражня́ться *impf* в+*prep*; (*mus*) занима́ться *impf*, заня́ться *pf* на+*prep*. **practised** *adj* о́пытный. **practitioner** *n* (*doctor*) практику́ющий врач; **general** ~ врач о́бщей пра́ктики.

pragmatic *adj* прагмати́ческий. **pragmatism** *n* прагмати́зм. **pragmatist** *n* прагма́тист.

prairie *n* пре́рия.

praise *vt* хвали́ть *impf*, по~ *pf*; *n* похвала́. **praiseworthy** *adj* похва́льный.

pram *n* де́тская коля́ска.

prance *vi* (*horse*) гарцева́ть *impf*; (*fig*) задава́ться *impf*.

prank *n* вы́ходка.

prattle *vi* лепета́ть *impf*; *n* ле́пет.

prawn *n* креве́тка.

pray *vi* моли́ться *impf*, по~ *pf* (**to** +*dat*; **for** о+*prep*). **prayer** *n* моли́тва.

preach *vt & i* пропове́дывать *impf*. **preacher** *n* пропове́дник.

preamble *n* преа́мбула.

pre-arrange *vt* зара́нее организо́вывать *impf*, организова́ть *pf*.

precarious *adj* ненадёжный; опа́сный.

precaution *n* предосторо́жность. **precautionary** *adj*: ~ **measures** ме́ры предосторо́жности.

precede vt предшéствовать impf +dat. **precedence** n предпочтéние. **precedent** n прецедéнт. **preceding** adj предыдущий.

precept n наставлéние.

precinct n двор; pl окрéстности f pl. **pedestrian** ~ учáсток для пешехóдов; shopping ~ торгóвый пассáж.

precious adj драгоцéнный; (style) манéрный; adv очень.

precipice n обрыв. **precipitate** adj (person) опромéтчивый; vt (throw down) низвергáть impf, низвéргнуть pf; (hurry) ускорять impf, ускóрить pf. **precipitation** n (meteorol) осáдки m pl. **precipitous** adj обрывистый.

précis n конспéкт.

precise adj тóчный. **precisely** adv тóчно; (in answer) имéнно. **precision** n тóчность.

preclude vt предотвращáть impf, предотвратить pf.

precocious adj рáно развивáшийся.

preconceived adj предвзятый. **preconception** n предвзятое мнéние.

pre-condition n предпосылка.

precursor n предшéственник.

predator n хищник. **predatory** adj хищный.

predecessor n предшéственник.

predestination n предопределéние.

predetermine vt предрешáть impf, предрешить pf.

predicament n затруднительное положéние.

predicate n (gram) сказýемое sb. **predicative** adj предикативный.

predict vt предскáзывать impf, предсказáть pf. **predictable** adj предсказýемый. **prediction** n предскáзание.

predilection n пристрáстие (for к+dat).

predispose vt предрасполагáть impf, предрасположить pf (to к+dat). **predisposition** n предрасположéние (to к+dat).

predominance n преоблáдание. **predominant** adj преоблáдающий. **predominate** vi преоблáдать impf.

pre-eminence n превосхóдство. **pre-eminent** adj выдающийся.

pre-empt vt (fig) завладевáть impf, завладéть pf +instr прéжде других. **pre-emptive** adj (mil) упреждáющий.

preen vt (of bird) чистить impf, по~ pf клювом; ~ o.s. (be proud) гордиться impf собóй.

pre-fab n сбóрный дом. **pre-fabricated** adj сбóрный.

preface n предислóвие.

prefect n префéкт; (school) стáроста m.

prefer vt предпочитáть impf, предпочéсть pf. **preferable** adj предпочтительный. **preference** n предпочтéние. **preferential** adj предпочтительный.

prefix n пристáвка.

pregnancy n берéменность. **pregnant** adj берéменная.

prehistoric adj доисторический.

prejudice n предубеждéние; (detriment) ущéрб; vt наносить impf, нанести pf ущéрб+dat; ~ against предубеждáть impf, предубедить pf прóтив+gen; be ~d against имéть impf предубеждёние прóтив +gen.

preliminary adj предварѝ-
тельный.

prelude n прелюдия.

premarital adj добрáчный.

premature adj преждеврé-
менный.

premeditated adj преднамéренный.

premier adj пéрвый; n премь-
éр-минѝстр. **première** n
премьéра.

premise, premiss n (logic)
(пред)посылка. **premises** n
pl помещéние.

premium n прéмия.

premonition n предчýвствие.

preoccupation n озабóчен-
ность; (absorbing subject) за-
бóта. **preoccupied** adj оза-
бóченный. **preoccupy** vt по-
глощáть impf, поглотѝть pf.

preparation n приготовлéние;
pl подготóвка (for к+dat);
(substance) препарáт. **preparatory** adj подготовѝтель-
ный. **prepare** vt & i при-,
под-, готáвливать(ся) impf,
при-, под-, готóвить(ся) pf
(for к+dat). **prepared** adj
готóвый.

preponderance n перевéс.

preposition n предлóг.

prepossessing adj привлекá-
тельный.

preposterous adj нелéпый.

prerequisite n предпосылка.

prerogative n прерогатѝва.

presage vt предвещáть impf.

Presbyterian n пресвитериá-
нин, -áнка; adj пресвитериá-
нский.

prescribe vt предпѝсывать
impf, предписáть pf; (med)
пропѝсывать impf, пропи-
сáть pf. **prescription** n (med)
рецéпт.

presence n присýтствие; ~
of mind присýтствие дýха. **present** adj присýтствую-
щий; (being dealt with) дáн-
ный; (existing now) нынéшний; (also gram) настоящий;
predic налицó; be ~ при-
сýтствовать impf (at на+prep);
~-day нынéшний; n: the ~
настоящее sb; (gram) настоящее врéмя neut; (gift) по-
дáрок; at ~ в настоящее
врéмя neut; for the ~ покá;
vt (introduce) представлять
impf, представить pf (to
+dat); (award) вручáть impf,
вручить pf; (a play) стáвить
impf, по~ pf; (a gift) пре-
поднóсить impf, препод-
нестѝ pf +dat (with +acc); ~
o.s. являться impf, явиться
pf. **presentable** adj прилѝч-
ный. **presentation** n (in-
troducing) представлéние;
(awarding) подношéние.

presentiment n предчýвствие.

presently adv вскóре.

preservation n сохранéние.
preservative n консервáнт.
preserve vt (keep safe) со-
хранять impf, сохранить pf;
(maintain) хранѝть impf;
(food) консервѝровать impf,
за~ pf; n (for game etc)
заповéдник; (jam) варéнье.

preside vi председáтель-
ствовать impf (at на+prep).

presidency n президéнт-
ство. **president** n прези-
дéнт. **presidential** adj пре-
зидéнтский. **presidium** n
президиум.

press n (machine) пресс;
(printing firm) типографѝя;
(publishing house) издáтель-
ство; (the ~) прéсса, печáть;
~ **conference** пресс-кон-

фере́нция; vt (button etc) нажима́ть impf, нажа́ть pf; (clasp) прижима́ть impf, прижа́ть pf (to k+dat); (iron) гла́дить impf, вы́~ pf; (insist on) наста́ивать impf, насто́ять pf на+prep; (urge) угова́ривать impf; ~ on (make haste) потора́пливаться impf.

pressing adj неотло́жный. **pressure** n давле́ние; ~cooker скорова́рка; ~ group инициати́вная гру́ппа. **pressurize** vt (fig) ока́зывать impf, оказа́ть pf давле́ние на+acc. **pressurized** adj гермети́ческий.

prestige n прести́ж. **prestigious** adj прести́жный.

presumably adv предположи́тельно. **presume** vt полага́ть impf; (venture) позволя́ть impf, позво́лить pf себе́. **presumption** n предположе́ние; (arrogance) самонаде́янность. **presumptuous** adj самонаде́янный.

presuppose vt предполага́ть impf.

pretence n притво́рство. **pretend** vt притворя́ться impf, притвори́ться pf (to be +instr); де́лать impf, с~ pf вид (что); vi: ~ to претендова́ть impf на+acc. **pretender** n претенде́нт. **pretension** n прете́нзия. **pretentious** adj претенцио́зный.

pretext n предло́г.

prettiness n милови́дность. **pretty** adj хоро́шенький; adv дово́льно.

prevail vi (predominate) преобла́дать impf; ~ (up)on угова́ривать impf, уговори́ть pf. **prevalence** n распро-

стране́ние. **prevalent** adj распространённый.

prevaricate vi увя́ливать impf увя́льнуть pf.

prevent vt (stop from happening) предупрежда́ть impf, предупреди́ть pf; (stop from doing) меша́ть impf, по~ pf +dat. **prevention** n предупрежде́ние. **preventive** adj предупреди́тельный.

preview n предвари́тельный просмо́тр.

previous adj предыду́щий; adv: to +gen; пре́жде чем +inf. **previously** adv ра́ньше.

pre-war adj дово́енный.

prey n (animal) добы́ча; (victim) же́ртва (to +gen); bird of ~ хи́щная пти́ца; vi: ~ (up)on (emotion etc.) му́чить impf.

price n цена́; ~list прейскура́нт; vt назнача́ть impf, назна́чить pf це́ну +gen. **priceless** adj бесце́нный.

prick vt коло́ть impf, у~ pf; (conscience) му́чить impf; ~ up one's ears навостри́ть pf у́ши; n уко́л. **prickle** n (thorn) колю́чка; (spine) игла́. **prickly** adj колю́чий.

pride n го́рдость; ~ o.s. on горди́ться impf +instr.

priest n свяще́нник; (non-Christian) жрец.

prig n педа́нт.

prim adj чо́порный.

primarily adv первонача́льно; (above all) пре́жде всего́. **primary** adj основно́й; ~ school нача́льная шко́ла. **prime** n: in one's ~ в расцве́те сил; adj (chief) гла́вный; ~ minister премье́р-мини́стр; vt (engine) заправля́ть impf, запра́вить pf;

(*bomb*) активизи́ровать *impf* & *pf*; (*with facts*) инструкти́ровать *impf* & *pf*; (*with paint etc.*) грунтова́ть *impf*, за~ *pf*. грунт. **prim(a)eval** *adj* первобы́тный. **primitive** *adj* первобы́тный; (*crude*) примити́вный. **primordial** *adj* иско́нный.

primrose *n* первоцве́т; (*colour*) бле́дно-жёлтый цвет.

prince *n* принц; (*in Russia*) князь. **princely** *adj* кня́жеский; (*sum*) огро́мный. **princess** *n* принце́сса; (*wife*) княги́ня; (*daughter*) княжна́.

principal *adj* гла́вный; *n* дире́ктор. **principality** *n* кня́жество. **principally** *adv* гла́вным о́бразом.

principle *n* при́нцип; **in ~ в** при́нципе; **on ~** принципиа́льно. **principled** *adj* принципиа́льный.

print *n* (*mark*) след; (*also phot*) отпеча́ток; (*printing*) печа́ть; (*picture*) о́ттиск; **in ~** в прода́же; **out of ~** распро́данный; *vt* (*impress*) запечатлева́ть *impf*, запечатле́ть *pf*; (*book etc.*) печа́тать *impf*, на~ *pf*; (*write*) писа́ть *impf*, на~ *pf* печа́тными бу́квами; (*phot*: *~ out*, *off*) отпеча́тывать *impf*, отпеча́тать *pf*; (*of computer etc.*) распеча́тывать *impf*, распеча́тать *pf*; **~out** распеча́тка. **printer** *n* (*person*) печа́тник, типо́граф; (*of computer*) при́нтер. **printing** *n* печа́тание; **~-press** печа́тный стано́к.

prior *adj* пре́жний; *adv*: **~ to** до+*gen*. **priority** *n* приорите́т. **priory** *n* монасты́рь *m*.

prise *vt*: **~ open** взла́мывать

impf, взлома́ть *pf*.

prism *n* при́зма.

prison *n* тюрьма́; *attrib* тюре́мный; **~ camp** ла́герь *m*. **prisoner** *n* заключённый *sb*; (**~ of war**) (военно)пле́нный *sb*.

pristine *adj* нетро́нутый.

privacy *n* уедине́ние; (*private life*) ча́стная жизнь. **private** *adj* (*personal*) ча́стный, ли́чный; (*confidential*) конфиденциа́льный; **in ~** наедине́ в ча́стной жи́зни; *n* рядово́й *sb*.

privation *n* лише́ние.

privilege *n* привиле́гия. **privileged** *adj* привилегиро́ванный.

privy *adj*: **~ to** посвящённый в+*acc*.

prize *n* пре́мия, приз; **~-winner** призёр; *vt* высоко́ цени́ть.

pro¹ *n*: **~s and cons** до́воды *m pl* за и про́тив.

pro² *n* (*professional*) профессиона́л.

probability *n* вероя́тность. **probable** *adj* вероя́тный. **probably** *adv* вероя́тно.

probate *n* утвержде́ние завеща́ния.

probation *n* испыта́тельный срок; (*law*) усло́вный пригово́р; **got two years** получи́л два го́да усло́вно. **probationary** *adj* испыта́тельный.

probe *n* (*med*) зонд; *vt* рассле́дование; *vt* зонди́ровать *impf*; (*fig*) рассле́довать *impf* & *pf*.

probity *n* че́стность.

problem *n* пробле́ма, вопро́с; (*math*) зада́ча. **problematic** *adj* проблемати́чный.

procedural adj процеду́рный.
procedure n процеду́ра.
proceed vi (go further) идти́ impf, пойти́ pf да́льше; (act) поступа́ть impf, поступи́ть pf; (abs, ~ to say; continue) продолжа́ть impf, продо́лжить pf; (of action) продолжа́ться impf, продо́лжиться pf; ~ from исходи́ть impf. из, от+gen; ~ to (begin to) принима́ться impf, приня́ться pf +inf. **proceedings** n pl (activity) де́ятельность; (legal ~) судопроизво́дство; (published report) труды́ m pl; (publ. fl pl. **proceeds** n pl вы́ручка. **process** n проце́сс; vt обраба́тывать impf, обрабо́тать pf. **procession** n проце́ссия, ше́ствие.
proclaim vt провозглаша́ть impf, провозгласи́ть pf. **proclamation** n провозглаше́ние.
procure vt достава́ть impf, доста́ть pf.
prod vt ты́кать impf, ткнуть pf; n тычо́к.
prodigal adj расточи́тельный.
prodigious adj огро́мный.
prodigy n: child ~ вунде́ркинд.
produce vt (evidence etc.) представля́ть impf, предста́вить pf; (ticket etc.) предъявля́ть impf, предъяви́ть pf; (play etc.) ста́вить impf, по~ pf; (manufacture; cause) производи́ть impf, произвести́ pf, n (collect) проду́кты m pl.
producer n (econ) производи́тель m; (of play etc.) режиссёр. **product** n проду́кт; (result) результа́т. **production** n произво́дство; (of play etc.) постано́вка. **productive** adj продукти́вный; (fruitful)

плодотво́рный. **productivity** n производи́тельность.
profane adj све́тский; (blasphemous) богоху́льный. **profanity** n богоху́льство.
profess vt (pretend) притворя́ться impf, притвори́ться pf (to be +instr); (declare) заявля́ть impf, заяви́ть pf; (faith) испове́довать impf. **profession** n (job) профе́ссия. **professional** adj профессиона́льный; n профессиона́л. **professor** n профе́ссор.
proffer vt предлага́ть impf, предложи́ть pf.
proficiency n уме́ние. **proficient** adj иску́сный.
profile n про́филь m.
profit n (benefit) по́льза; (monetary) при́быль; vt приноси́ть impf, принести́ pf по́льзу +dat; vi: ~ from по́льзоваться impf, вос~ pf +instr; (financially) получа́ть impf, получи́ть pf при́быль на +prep. **profitable** adj (lucrative) при́быльный; (beneficial) поле́зный. **profiteering** n спекуля́ция.
profligate adj распу́тный.
profound adj глубо́кий.
profuse adj оби́льный. **profusion** n изоби́лие.
progeny n пото́мство.
prognosis n прогно́з.
program(m)e n програ́мма; vt программи́ровать impf, за~ pf. **programmer** n программи́ст.
progress n прогре́сс; (success) успе́хи m pl; make ~ де́лать impf, с~ pf успе́хи; vi продвига́ться impf, продви́нуться pf вперёд. **progression** n продвиже́ние.

progressive adj прогресси́в-
ный.

prohibit vt запреща́ть impf,
запрети́ть pf. **prohibition** n
запреще́ние; (on alcohol)
сухо́й зако́н. **prohibitive** adj
запрети́тельный; (price) не-
досту́пный.

project vt (plan) проекти́-
ровать impf, c~ pf; (a film)
демонстри́ровать impf, про~
pf; vi (jut out) выступа́ть
impf; n прое́кт. **projectile** n
снаря́д. **projection** n (cin)
прое́кция; (protrusion) вы́-
ступ; (forecast) прогно́з. **projector** n прое́ктор.

proletarian adj пролета́рский.
proletariat n пролетариа́т.

proliferate vi распростра-
ня́ться impf, распростра-
ни́ться pf. **proliferation** n
распростране́ние.

prolific adj плодови́тый.

prologue n проло́г.

prolong vt продлева́ть impf,
продли́ть pf.

promenade n ме́сто для гу-
ля́нья; (at seaside) на́береж-
ная sb; vi прогу́ливаться
impf, прогуля́ться pf.

prominence n изве́стность.
prominent adj выступа́ю-
щий; (distinguished) выдаю́-
щийся.

promiscuity n лёгкое пове-
де́ние. **promiscuous** adj лёг-
кого поведе́ния.

promise n обеща́ние; vt обе-
ща́ть impf & pf. **promising**
adj многообеща́ющий.

promontory n мыс.

promote vt (in rank) продви-
га́ть impf, продви́нуть pf;
(assist) спосо́бствовать impf
& pf +dat; (publicize) рекла-
ми́ровать impf. **promoter** n

(of event etc.) аге́нт. **promotion** n (in rank) продвиже́ние;
(comm) рекла́ма.

prompt adj бы́стрый, неме́д-
ленный; adv ро́вно; vt (incite) побужда́ть impf, побу-
ди́ть pf (to к+dat; +inf);
(speaker; also fig) подска́зы-
вать impf, подсказа́ть pf +dat;
(theat) суфли́ровать impf
+dat; n подска́зка. **prompter**
n суфлёр.

prone adj (лежа́щий) ничко́м;
predic: ~ to скло́нен (-онна́,
-о́нно) к+dat.

prong n зубе́ц.

pronoun n местоиме́ние.

pronounce vt (declare) объ-
явля́ть impf, объяви́ть pf;
(articulate) произноси́ть impf,
произнести́ pf. **pronounced**
adj я́вный; заме́тный. **pronouncement** n заявле́ние.
pronunciation n произно-
ше́ние.

proof n доказа́тельство; (printing) корректу́ра; **~-reader**
n корре́ктор; adj (impenetrable) непроница́емый (against
для+gen); (not yielding) не-
поддаю́щийся (against +dat).

prop¹ n (support) подпо́рка;
(fig) опо́ра; vt (~ open, up)
подпира́ть impf, подпере́ть
pf; (fig) подде́рживать impf,
поддержа́ть pf.

prop² n (theat) see props

propaganda n пропага́нда.

propagate vt & i размножа́ть-
(ся) impf, размно́жить(ся) pf;
(disseminate) распространя́ть-
(ся) impf, распространи́ть(ся)
pf. **propagation** n размноже́-
ние; распростране́ние.

propel vt приводи́ть impf,
привести́ pf в движе́ние.
propeller n винт.

propensity n накло́нность (to к+dat; +inf).

proper adj (correct) пра́вильный; (suitable) подходя́щий; (decent) присто́йный; ~ noun и́мя со́бственное. **properly** adv как сле́дует.

property n (possessions) со́бственность, иму́щество; (attribute) сво́йство; pl (theat) реквизи́т.

prophecy n проро́чество. **prophesy** vt проро́чить impf, на~ pf. **prophet** n проро́к. **prophetic** adj проро́ческий.

propitious adj благоприя́тный.

proponent n сторо́нник.

proportion n пропо́рция; (due relation) соразме́рность; pl разме́ры m pl. **proportional** adj пропорциона́льный. **proportionate** adj соразме́рный (to +dat; c+instr).

proposal n предложе́ние. **propose** vt предлага́ть impf, предложи́ть pf; (intend) предполага́ть impf; vi (~ marriage) де́лать impf, с~ pf предложе́ние (to +dat). **proposition** n предложе́ние.

propound vt предлага́ть impf, предложи́ть pf на обсужде́ние.

proprietor n со́бственник, хозя́ин.

propriety n прили́чие.

props n pl (theat) реквизи́т.

propulsion n движе́ние вперёд.

prosaic adj прозаи́ческий.

proscribe vt (forbid) запреща́ть impf, запрети́ть pf.

prose n про́за.

prosecute vt пресле́довать impf. **prosecution** n суде́бное пресле́дование; (pro-

secuting party) обвине́ние. **prosecutor** n обвини́тель m.

prospect n вид; (fig) перспекти́ва; vi: ~ for иска́ть impf. **prospective** adj бу́дущий. **prospector** n разве́дчик. **prospectus** n проспе́кт.

prosper vi процвета́ть impf. **prosperity** n процвета́ние. **prosperous** adj процвета́ющий; (wealthy) зажи́точный.

prostate (gland) n проста́та.

prostitute n проститу́тка. **prostitution** n проститу́ция.

prostrate adj распростёртый, (лежа́щий) ничко́м; (exhausted) обесси́ленный; (with grief) уби́тый (with +instr).

protagonist n гла́вный геро́й; (in contest) протагони́ст.

protect vt защища́ть impf, защити́ть pf. **protection** n защи́та. **protective** adj защи́тный. **protector** n защи́тник.

protégé(e) n протеже́ m & f indecl.

protein n бело́к.

protest n проте́ст; vi проте́стовать impf; vt (affirm) утвержда́ть impf.

Protestant n протеста́нт, ~ка; adj протеста́нтский.

protestation n (торже́ственное) заявле́ние (o+prep; что); (protest) проте́ст.

protocol n протоко́л.

proton n прото́н.

prototype n прототи́п.

protract vt тяну́ть impf. **protracted** adj дли́тельный.

protrude vi выдава́ться impf, вы́даться pf.

proud adj го́рдый; be ~ of горди́ться impf +instr.

prove vt дока́зывать impf, доказа́ть pf; vi ока́зываться *impf*, оказа́ться *pf* (**to be** +*instr*). **proven** *adj* дока́занный.

provenance *n* происхожде́ние.
proverb *n* посло́вица. **proverbial** *adj* воше́дший в погово́рку; (*well-known*) общеизве́стный.

provide *vt* (*supply person*) снабжа́ть *impf*, снабди́ть *pf* (**with** +*instr*); (*supply thing*) предоставля́ть *impf*, предоста́вить *pf* (**to, for** +*dat*); дава́ть *impf*, дать *pf* (**to, for** +*dat*); *vi*: ~ **for** предусма́тривать *impf*, предусмотре́ть *pf* +*acc*; (~ *for family etc.*) содержа́ть *impf* +*acc*. **provided (that)** *conj* при усло́вии, что; е́сли то́лько. **providence** *n* провиде́ние; (*foresight*) предусмотри́тельность. **provident** *adj* предусмотри́тельный. **providential** *adj* сча́стливый. **providing** *see* **provided (that)**

province *n* о́бласть; *pl* (*the* ~) прови́нция. **provincial** *adj* провинциа́льный.
provision *n* снабже́ние; *pl* (*food*) прови́зия; (*in agreement etc.*) положе́ние; **make** ~ **against** принима́ть *impf*, приня́ть *pf* ме́ры про́тив+*gen*. **provisional** *adj* вре́менный. **proviso** *n* усло́вие.
provocation *n* провока́ция. **provocative** *adj* провокацио́нный. **provoke** *vt* провоци́ровать *impf*, с~ *pf*; (*call forth, cause*) вызыва́ть *impf*, вы́звать *pf*.
prow *n* нос.
prowess *n* уме́ние.
prowl *vi* ры́скать *impf*.
proximity *n* бли́зость.
proxy *n* полномо́чие; (*person*)

уполномо́ченный *sb*, замести́тель *m*; **by** ~ по дове́ренности; **stand** ~ **for** быть *impf* замести́телем +*gen*.
prudence *n* благоразу́мие. **prudent** *adj* благоразу́мный.
prudery *n* притво́рная стыдли́вость. **prudish** *adj* ни в ме́ру стыдли́вый.
prune[1] *n* (*plum*) черносли́в.
prune[2] *vt* (*trim*) об-, под-, реза́ть *impf*, об-, под-, ре́зать *pf*.
pry *vi* сова́ть *impf* нос (**into** в+*acc*).
PS *abbr* (*of postscript*) постскри́птум.
psalm *n* псало́м.
pseudonym *n* псевдони́м.
psyche *n* пси́хика. **psychiatric** *adj* психиатри́ческий. **psychiatrist** *n* психиа́тр. **psychiatry** *n* психиатри́я. **psychic** *adj* яснови́дящий. **psychoanalysis** *n* психоана́лиз. **psychoanalyst** *n* психоанали́тик. **psychoanalytic(al)** *adj* психоаналити́ческий. **psychological** *adj* психологи́ческий. **psychologist** *n* психо́лог. **psychology** *n* психоло́гия. **psychopath** *n* психопа́т. **psychopathic** *adj* психопати́ческий. **psychosis** *n* психо́з. **psychotherapy** *n* психотерапи́я.
PTO *abbr* (*of please turn over*) см. на об., смотри́ на оборо́те.
pub *n* пивна́я *sb*.
puberty *n* полова́я зре́лость.
public *adj* обще́ственный; (*open*) публи́чный, откры́тый; ~ **school** ча́стная сре́дняя шко́ла; *n* пу́блика, о́бщественность; **in** ~ откры́то, публи́чно. **publication** *n* из-

да́ние. **publicity** *n* рекла́ма. **publicize** *vt* реклами́ровать *impf* & *pf*. **publicly** *adv* публи́чно, откры́то. **publish** *vt* публикова́ть *impf*, о~ *pf*; (*book*) издава́ть *impf*, изда́ть *pf*. **publisher** *n* изда́тель *m*. **publishing** *n* (*business*) изда́тельское де́ло; (*house*) изда́тельство.

pucker *vt* & *i* мо́рщить(ся) *impf*, с~ *pf*.

pudding *n* пу́динг, запека́нка; (*dessert*) сла́дкое *sb*.

puddle *n* лу́жа.

puff *n* (*of wind*) поры́в; (*of smoke*) дымо́к; ~ **pastry** сло́ёное те́сто; *vi* пыхте́ть *impf*; ~ **at** (*pipe etc.*) попы́хивать *impf* +*instr*; *vt*: ~ **up, out** (*inflate*) надува́ть *impf*, наду́ть *pf*.

pugnacious *adj* драчли́вый.

puke *vi* рвать *impf*, вы́~ *pf* *impers*+*acc*.

pull *vt* тяну́ть *impf*, по~ *pf*; таска́ть *indet*, тащи́ть *impf*, по~ *pf*; (*a muscle*) растя́гивать *impf*, растяну́ть *pf*; *vt* & *i* дёргать *impf*, дёрнуть *pf* (**at** (за)+*acc*); ~ **s.o's leg** разы́грывать *impf*, разыгра́ть *pf*; ~ **the trigger** спуска́ть *impf*, спусти́ть *pf* куро́к; ~ **apart, to pieces** разрыва́ть *impf*, разорва́ть *pf*; (*fig*) раскритикова́ть *pf*; ~ **down** (*demolish*) сноси́ть *impf*, снести́ *pf*; ~ **in** (*of train*) прибыва́ть *impf*, прибы́ть *pf*; (*of vehicle*) подъезжа́ть *impf*, подъе́хать *pf* к обо́чине; (*fig*) раскритикова́ть *pf*; ~ **off** (*garment*) стя́гивать *impf*, стяну́ть *pf*; (*achieve*) успе́шно заверша́ть *impf*, заверши́ть *pf*; ~ **on** (*garment*) натя́гивать

impf, натяну́ть *pf*; ~ **out** (*vt*) (*remove*) выта́скивать *impf*, вы́тащить *pf*; (*vi*) (*withdraw*) отка́зываться *impf*, отказа́ться *pf* от уча́стия (**of** в+*prep*); (*of vehicle*) отъезжа́ть *impf*, отъе́хать *pf* от обо́чины (*dorógi*); (*of train*) отходи́ть *impf*, отойти́ *pf* (**from** (от ста́нции); ~ **through** *vi* ожива́ть *impf*, вы́жить *pf*; **o.s. together** брать *impf*, взять *pf* себя́ в ру́ки; ~ **up** (*vt*) подтя́гивать *impf*, подтяну́ть *pf*; (*vt* & *i*) (*stop*) остана́вливать(ся) *impf*, останови́ть(ся) *pf*; *n* тя́га; (*fig*) блат.

pulley *n* блок.

pullover *n* пуло́вер.

pulp *n* пу́льпа.

pulpit *n* ка́федра.

pulsate *vi* пульси́ровать *impf*.

pulse *n* пульс.

pulses *n pl* (*food*) бобо́вые *sb*.

pulverize *vt* размельча́ть *impf*, размельчи́ть *pf*.

pummel *vt* колоти́ть *impf*, по~ *pf*.

pump *n* насо́с; *vt* кача́ть *impf*; ~ **in(to)** вка́чивать *impf*, вкача́ть *pf*; ~ **out** выка́чивать *impf*, вы́качать *pf*; ~ **up** нака́чивать *impf*, накача́ть *pf*.

pumpkin *n* ты́ква.

pun *n* каламбу́р.

punch[1] *vt* (*with fist*) ударя́ть *impf*, уда́рить *pf* кулако́м; (*hole*) пробива́ть *impf*, проби́ть *pf*; (*a ticket*) компости́ровать *impf*, про~ *pf*; ~**up** дра́ка; *n* (*blow*) уда́р кулако́м; (*for tickets*) компо́стер; (*for piercing*) перфора́тор.

punch[2] *n* (*drink*) пунш.

punctilious *adj* щепети́льный.

punctual *adj* пунктуа́льный.
  punctuality *n* пунктуа́ль-
  ность.
punctuate *vt* ста́вить *impf*,
  по~ *pf* зна́ки препина́ния
  в+*acc*; (*fig*) прерыва́ть *impf*,
  прерва́ть *pf*. **punctuation** *n*
  пунктуа́ция; ~ **marks** зна́ки
  m pl препина́ния.
puncture *n* проко́л; *vt* прока́-
  лывать *impf*, проколо́ть *pf*.
pundit *n* (*fig*) знато́к.
pungent *adj* е́дкий.
punish *vt* нака́зывать *impf*,
  наказа́ть *pf*. **punishable** *adj*
  наказу́емый. **punishment** *n*
  наказа́ние. **punitive** *adj* ка-
  ра́тельный.
punter *n* (*gambler*) игро́к; (*client*) клие́нт.
puny *adj* хи́лый.
pupil *n* учени́к, -и́ца; (*of eye*)
  зрачо́к.
puppet *n* марионе́тка, ку́кла.
puppy *n* щено́к.
purchase *n* поку́пка; (*lever-
  age*) то́чка опо́ры; *vt* покупа́ть *impf*, купи́ть *pf*. **pur-
  chaser** *n* покупа́тель *m*.
pure *adj* чи́стый.
purée *n* пюре́ *neut indecl*.
purely *adv* чи́сто.
purgatory *n* чисти́лище; (*fig*)
  ад. **purge** *vt* очища́ть *impf*,
  очи́стить *pf*; *n* очище́ние;
  (*polit*) чи́стка.
purification *n* очи́стка. **purify**
  vt очища́ть *impf*, очи́стить *pf*.
purist *n* пури́ст.
puritan, Р., *n* пурита́нин,
  -а́нка. **puritanical** *adj* пури-
  та́нский.
purity *n* чистота́.
purple *adj* (*n*) пу́рпу́рный,
  фиоле́товый (цвет).
purport *vi* претендова́ть *impf*.
purpose *n* цель, наме́рение;

on ~ наро́чно; **to no** ~ на-
  пра́сно. **purposeful** *adj* целеустремлённый. **purposeless**
  adj бесце́льный. **purposely**
  adv наро́чно.
purr *vi* мурлы́кать *impf*.
purse *n* кошелёк; *vt* поджи-
  ма́ть *impf*, поджа́ть *pf*.
pursue *vt* пресле́довать *impf*.
  pursuit *n* пресле́дование;
  (*pastime*) заня́тие.
purveyor *n* поставщи́к.
pus *n* гной.
push *vt* толка́ть *impf*, толк-
  ну́ть *pf*; (*press*) нажима́ть
  impf, нажа́ть *pf*; (*urge*) под-
  та́лкивать *impf*, подтолк-
  ну́ть *pf*; *vi* толка́ться *impf*;
  be ~**ed for** име́ть *impf* ма́ло+*gen*; **he is** ~**ing fifty** ему́
  ско́ро сту́кнет пятьдеся́т; ~
  one's way проти́скиваться
  impf, проти́снуться *pf*; ~
  around (*person*) помыка́ть
  impf +*instr*; ~ **aside** (*also fig*)
  отстраня́ть *impf*, отстрани́ть
  pf; ~ **away** отта́лкивать *impf*,
  оттолкну́ть *pf*; ~ **off** (*vi*) (*in
  boat*) отта́лкиваться *impf*,
  оттолкну́ться *pf* (от берега);
  (*go away*) убира́ться *impf*,
  убра́ться *pf*; ~ **on** (*vi*)
  продолжа́ть *impf* путь; ~
  толчо́к; (*energy*) эне́ргия
pushchair *n* коля́ска. **pusher**
  n (*drugs*) продаве́ц нарко́ти-
  ков. **pushy** *adj* напо́ристый.
puss, **pussy(-cat)** *n* ки́ска.
put *vt* класть *impf*, положи́ть
  pf; (*upright*) ста́вить *impf*,
  по~ *pf*; помеща́ть *impf*,
  помести́ть *pf*; (*into specified
  state*) приводи́ть *impf*, при-
  вести́ *pf*; (*express*) выража́ть
  impf, вы́разить *pf*; (*a question*) задава́ть *impf*, зада́ть
  pf; ~ **an end**, **a stop**, **to**

кла́сть *impf*, положи́ть *pf* коне́ц +*dat*; ~ o.s. in another's place ста́вить *impf*, по~ *pf* себя́ на ме́сто +*gen*; ~ about (*rumour etc.*) распространя́ть *impf*, распространи́ть *pf*; ~ away (*tidy*) убира́ть *impf*, убра́ть *pf*; (*save*) откла́дывать *impf*, отложи́ть *pf*; ~ back (*in place*) ста́вить *impf*, по~ *pf* на ме́сто; (*clock*) переводи́ть *impf*, перевести́ *pf* наза́д; ~ by (*money*) откла́дывать *impf*, отложи́ть *pf*; ~ down кла́сть *impf*, положи́ть *pf*; (*suppress*) подавля́ть *impf*, подави́ть *pf*; (*write down*) запи́сывать *impf*, записа́ть *pf*; (*passengers*) выса́живать *impf*, вы́садить *pf*; (*attribute*) припи́сывать *impf*, приписа́ть *pf* (to +*dat*); ~ forward (*proposal*) предлага́ть *impf*, предложи́ть *pf*; (*clock*) переводи́ть *impf*, перевести́ *pf* вперёд; ~ in (*install*) устана́вливать *impf*, установи́ть *pf*; (*a claim*) предъявля́ть *impf*, предъяви́ть *pf*; (*interpose*) вставля́ть *impf*, вста́вить *pf*; ~ in an appearance появля́ться *impf*, появи́ться *pf*; ~ off (*postpone*) откла́дывать *impf*, отложи́ть *pf*; (*repel*) отта́лкивать *impf*, оттолкну́ть *pf*; (*dissuade*) отгова́ривать *impf*, отговори́ть *pf* от+*gen*, +*inf*; ~ on (*clothes*) надева́ть *impf*, наде́ть *pf*; (*kettle, a record, a play*) ста́вить *impf*, по~ *pf*; (*turn on*) включа́ть *impf*, включи́ть *pf*; (*add to*) прибавля́ть *impf*, приба́вить *pf*; ~ on airs ва́жничать *impf*; ~ on weight толсте́ть *impf*, по~ *pf*; ~ out

(*vex*) обижа́ть *impf*, оби́деть *pf*; (*inconvenience*) затрудня́ть *impf*, затрудни́ть *pf*; (*a fire etc.*) туши́ть *impf*, по~ *pf*; ~ through (*tel*) соединя́ть *impf*, соедини́ть *pf* по телефо́ну; ~ up (*building*) стро́ить *impf*, по~ *pf*; (*hang up*) ве́шать *impf*, пове́сить *pf*; (*price*) повыша́ть *impf*, повы́сить *pf*; (*a guest*) дава́ть *impf*, дать *pf* ночле́г +*dat*; (*as guest*) ночева́ть *impf*, пере~ *pf*; ~ up to (*instigate*) подбива́ть *impf*, подби́ть *pf* на+*acc*; ~ up with терпе́ть *impf*.

putative *adj* предполага́емый.
putrefy *vi* гнить *impf*, с~ *pf*.
putrid *adj* гнило́й.
putty *n* зама́зка.
puzzle *n* (*enigma*) зага́дка; (*toy etc.*) головоло́мка; (*jigsaw*) моза́ика; *vt* озада́чивать *impf*, озада́чить *pf*; ~ out разга́дывать *impf*, разгада́ть *pf*; *vi*: ~ over лома́ть *impf* себе́ го́лову над+*instr*.
pygmy *n* пигме́й.
pyjamas *n pl* пижа́ма.
pylon *n* пило́н.
pyramid *n* пирами́да.
pyre *n* погреба́льный костёр.
python *n* пито́н.

Q

quack[1] *n* (*sound*) кря́канье; *vi* кря́кать *impf*, кря́кнуть *pf*.
quack[2] *n* шарлата́н.
quad *n* (*court*) четырёхуго́льный двор; *pl* (*quadruplets*) че́тверо близнецо́в. **quadrangle** *n* (*figure*) четыреху́гольник; (*court*) четырёхуго́льный двор. **quadrant** *n* квадра́нт.

quadruped n четвероно́гое живо́тное sb. **quadruple** adj четверно́й, в четы́ре ра́за бо́льший; vt & i учетверя́ть(ся) impf, учетвери́ть(ся) pf. **quadruplets** n pl че́тверо близнецо́в.

quagmire n боло́то.

quail n (bird) пе́репел.

quaint adj причу́дливый.

quake vi дрожа́ть impf (with от+gen).

Quaker n ква́кер, ~ка.

qualification n (for post etc.) квалифика́ция; (reservation) огово́рка. **qualified** adj компете́нтный; (limited) ограни́ченный. **qualify** vt & i (prepare for job) гото́вить(ся) impf (for к+dat; +inf); vt (render fit) де́лать impf, с~ pf приго́дным; (entitle) дава́ть impf, дать pf пра́во +dat (to на+acc); (limit): ~ what one says сде́лать pf огово́рку; vi получа́ть impf, получи́ть pf диплом; ~ for (be entitled to) име́ть impf пра́во на+acc.

qualitative adj ка́чественный. **quality** n ка́чество.

qualm n сомне́ние; (of conscience) угрызе́ние со́вести.

quandary n затрудни́тельное положе́ние.

quantify vt определя́ть impf, определи́ть pf коли́чество +gen. **quantitative** adj коли́чественный. **quantity** n коли́чество.

quarantine n каранти́н.

quarrel n ссо́ра; vi ссо́риться impf, по~ pf (with c+instr; about, for из-за+gen). **quarrelsome** adj вздо́рный.

quarry[1] n (for stone etc.) каменоло́мня; vt добыва́ть impf, добы́ть pf.

quarry[2] n (prey) добы́ча.

quart n ква́рта. **quarter** n че́тверть; (of year; of town) кварта́л; pl кварти́ры f pl; a ~ to one без че́тверти час; ~-final четверть-фина́л; vt (divide) дели́ть impf, раз~ pf на четы́ре ча́сти; (lodge) расквартиро́вывать impf, расквартирова́ть pf. **quarterly** adj кварта́льный; adv раз в кварта́л. **quartet** n кварте́т.

quartz n кварц.

quash vt (annul) аннули́ровать impf & pf; (crush) подавля́ть impf, подави́ть pf.

quasi- in comb ква́зи-.

quaver vi дрожа́ть impf; n (mus) восьма́я sb но́ты.

quay n на́бережная sb.

queasy adj: **I feel** ~ меня́ тошни́т.

queen n короле́ва; (cards) да́ма; (chess) ферзь m.

queer adj стра́нный.

quell vt подавля́ть impf, подави́ть pf.

quench vt (thirst) утоля́ть impf, утоли́ть pf; (fire, desire) туши́ть impf, по~ pf.

query n вопро́с; vt (express doubt) выража́ть impf выра́зить pf сомне́ние в+prep.

quest n по́иски m pl; in ~ of в по́исках+gen. **question** n вопро́с; **beyond** ~ вне сомне́ния; **it is a** ~ **of** э́то вопро́с+gen; **it is out of the** ~ об э́том не мо́жет быть и ре́чи; **the person in** ~ челове́к, о кото́ром идёт речь; **is this** де́ло в э́том; ~ **mark** вопроси́тельный знак; vt расспра́шивать impf, расспроси́ть pf; (interrogate) допра́шивать impf допроси́ть pf; (doubt) сомнева́ться impf в+prep. **questionable** adj сомни́тельный. **question-naire** *n* вопро́сник.

queue *n* о́чередь; *vi* стоя́ть *impf* в о́череди.

quibble *n* софи́зм; (*minor criticism*) приди́рка; *vi* придира́ться *impf*; (*argue*) спо́рить *impf*.

quick *adj* ско́рый, бы́стрый; ~**-tempered** вспы́льчивый; ~**-witted** находчивый; *n*: to the ~ за живо́е; *adv* ско́ро, бы́стро; *as imper* скоре́е! **quicken** *vt* & *i* ускоря́ть(ся) *impf*, ускори́ть(ся) *pf*. **quickness** *n* быстрота́. **quicksand** *n* зыбу́чий песо́к. **quicksilver** *n* ртуть.

quid *n* фунт.

quiet *n* (*silence*) тишина́; (*calm*) споко́йствие; (*tranquillity*) споко́йный *и*т спокойствие; *int* ти́ше!; *vt* & *i* успока́ивать(ся) *impf*, успоко́ить(ся) *pf*.

quill *n* перо́; (*spine*) игла́.

quilt *n* (стёганое) одея́ло; *vt* стега́ть *impf*, вы́~ *pf*. **quilted** *adj* стёганый.

quintessential *adj* наибо́лее суще́ственный.

quintet *n* квинте́т. **quins, quintuplets** *pl* пять близнецо́в.

quip *n* острота́; остри́ть *impf*, с~ *pf*.

quirk *n* причу́да. **quirky** *adj* с причу́дами.

quit *vt* (*leave*) покида́ть *impf*, поки́нуть *pf*; (*stop*) перестава́ть *impf*, переста́ть *pf*; (*give up*) броса́ть *impf*, бро́сить *pf*; (*resign*) уходи́ть *impf*, уйти́ *pf* с+*gen*.

quite *adv* (*wholly*) совсе́м; (*rather*) дово́льно; ~ **a few** дово́льно мно́го.

quits *predic*: **we are** ~ мы с тобо́й кви́ты; **I am** ~ **with him**

я расквита́лся (*past*) с ним.

quiver *vi* (*tremble*) трепета́ть *impf*; *n* тре́пет.

quiz *n* виктори́на. **quizzical** *adj* насме́шливый.

quorum *n* кво́рум.

quota *n* но́рма.

quotation *n* цита́та; (*of price*) цена́; ~ **marks** кавы́чки (-чек) *pl*. **quote** *vt* цити́ровать *impf*, про~ *pf*; ссыла́ться *impf*, сосла́ться *pf* на+*acc*; (*price*) назнача́ть *impf*, назна́чить *pf*.

R

rabbi *n* равви́н.

rabbit *n* кро́лик.

rabble *n* сброд.

rabid *adj* бе́шеный. **rabies** *n* бе́шенство.

race[1] *n* (*ethnic* ~) ра́са; род.

race[2] *n* (*contest*) (*on foot*) бег; (*of cars etc.*; *fig*) го́нка, го́нки *f pl*; (*of horses*) ска́чки *f pl*; ~**-track** трек; (*for horse* ~) скакова́я доро́жка; *vi* (*compete*) состяза́ться *impf* в ско́рости; (*rush*) мча́ться *impf*; *vt* бежа́ть *impf* наперегонки́ с+*instr*. **racecourse** *n* ипподро́м. **racehorse** *n* скакова́я ло́шадь.

racial *adj* ра́совый. **rac(ial)ism** *n* раси́зм. **rac(ial)ist** *n* раси́ст, ~ка; *adj* раси́стский.

racing *n* (*horses*) ска́чки *f pl*; (*cars*) го́нки *f pl*; ~ **car** го́ночный автомоби́ль *m*; ~ **driver** го́нщик.

rack *n* (*for hats etc.*) ве́шалка; (*for plates etc.*) стелла́ж; (*in train etc.*) се́тка; *vt*: ~ **one's brains** лома́ть *impf* себе́ го́лову.

racket[1] *n* (*bat*) раке́тка.

racket² n (uproar) шум; (illegal activity) рэ́кет. **racketeer** n рэкети́р.

racy adj колори́тный.

radar n (system) радиолока́ция; (apparatus) радиолока́тор, рада́р; (attrib) рада́рный.

radiance n сия́ние. **radiant** adj сия́ющий. **radiate** vt & i излуча́ть(ся) impf, излучи́ться pf. **radiation** n излуче́ние. **radiator** n батаре́я; (in car) радиа́тор.

radical adj радика́льный; n радика́л.

radio n ра́дио neut indecl; (set) радиоприёмник; vt ради́ровать impf & pf +dat.

radioactive adj радиоакти́вный. **radioactivity** n радиоакти́вность. **radiologist** n радио́лог; рентгено́лог. **radiotherapy** n радиотерапи́я.

radish n реди́ска.

radius n ра́диус.

raffle n лотере́я; vt разы́грывать impf, разыгра́ть pf в лотере́е.

raft n плот.

rafter n (beam) стропи́ло.

rag n тря́пка; pl (clothes) лохмо́тья (-ьев) pl.

rage n я́рость; all the ~ после́дний крик мо́ды; vi беси́ться impf; (storm etc.) бушева́ть impf.

ragged adj (jagged) зазу́бренный; (of clothes) рва́ный.

raid n налёт; (by police) обла́ва; vt де́лать impf, с~ pf налёт на+acc.

rail n пери́ла (-л) pl; (rly) рельс; by ~ по́ездом. **railing** n пери́ла (-л) pl.

railway n желе́зная доро́га; attrib железнодоро́жный. **railwayman** n железно-

доро́жник.

rain n дождь m; v impers: it is (was) ~ing идёт (шёл) дождь; vt rain impf, осыпа́ть pf +instr (upon +acc); vi осыпа́ться impf, осыпа́ться pf.

rainbow n ра́дуга. **raincoat** n плащ. **raindrop** n дождева́я ка́пля. **rainfall** n (amount of rain) коли́чество оса́дков. **rainy** adj дождли́вый; ~ day чёрный день n.

raise vt (lift) поднима́ть impf, подня́ть pf; (heighten) повыша́ть impf, повы́сить pf; (provoke) вызыва́ть impf, вы́звать pf; (money) собира́ть impf, собра́ть pf; (children) расти́ть impf.

raisin n изю́минка; pl (collect) изю́м.

rake n (tool) гра́бли (-бель & -блей) pl; vt грести́ impf; (~ together, up) сгреба́ть impf, сгрести́ pf.

rally vt & i спла́чивать(ся) impf, сплоти́ть(ся) pf; vi (after illness etc.) оправля́ться impf, опра́виться pf; n (meeting) слёт; ми́тинг; (motoring ~) (авто)ра́лли neut indecl; (tennis) обме́н уда́рами.

ram n (sheep) бара́н; vt (beat down) трамбова́ть impf, у~ pf; (drive in) вбива́ть impf, вбить pf.

ramble vi (walk) прогу́ливаться impf, прогуля́ться pf; (speak) буби́ть impf; n прогу́лка. **rambling** adj (incoherent) бессвя́зный.

ramification n (fig) после́дствие.

ramp n скат.

rampage vi бу́йствовать impf.

rampant adj (plant) бу́йный; (unchecked) безу́держный.

rampart n вал.

ramshackle *adj* вéтхий.

ranch *n* рáнчо *neut indecl.*

rancid *adj* прогóрклый.

rancour *n* злóба.

random *adj* случáйный; **at ~** науда́чу.

range *n* (*of mountains*) цепь; (*artillery ~*) полигóн; (*of voice*) диапазóн; (*scope*) круг, предéлы *m pl*; (*operating distance*) да́льность; *vi* (*vary*) колебáться *impf*, по~ *pf*; (*wander*) бродúть *impf*; **~ over** (*include*) охвáтывать *impf*, охватúть *pf*.

rank[1] *n* (*row*) ряд; (*taxi ~*) стоя́нка таксú; (*grade*) звáние, чин, ранг; *vt* (*classify*) классифицúровать *impf* & *pf*; (*consider*) считáть *impf* (*as* +*instr*); *vi*: **~** быть в числé+*gen.*

rank[2] *adj* (*luxuriant*) бýйный; (*in smell*) зловóнный; (*gross*) я́вный.

rankle *vi* болéть *impf.*

ransack *vt* (*search*) обша́ривать *impf*, обша́рить *pf*; (*plunder*) грáбить *impf*, о~ *pf.*

ransom *n* вы́куп; *vt* выкупáть *impf*, вы́купить *pf.*

rant *vi* вопúть *impf.*

rap *n* стук; *vt* (*rézko*) ударя́ть *impf*, удáрить *pf*; *vi* стучáть *impf*, стýкнуть *pf.*

rape[1] *vt* насúловать *impf*, из~ *pf*; *n* изнасúлование.

rape[2] *n* (*plant*) рапс.

rapid *adj* бы́стрый; *n*: *pl* поро́г, быстринá. **rapidity** *n* быстротá.

rapt *adj* восхищённый; (*absorbed*) поглощённый. **rapture** *n* востóрг. **rapturous** *adj* востóрженный.

rare[1] *adj* (*of meat*) недожáренный.

rare[2] *adj* рéдкий. **rarity** *n* рéдкость.

rascal *n* плут.

rash[1] *n* сыпь.

rash[2] *adj* опромéтчивый.

rasher *n* лóмтик (бекóна).

rasp *n* (*file*) рáшпиль *m*; (*sound*) скрéжет; *vt*: **~ out** гáркнуть *pf.*

raspberry *n* малúна (*no pl*; *usu collect*).

rasping *adj* (*sound*) скрипýчий.

rat *n* кры́са; **~ race** гóнка за успéхом.

ratchet *n* храповúк.

rate *n* нóрма, стáвка; (*speed*) скóрость; *pl* мéстные налóги *m pl*; **at any ~** во вся́ком слýчае; *vt* оцéнивать *impf*, оценúть *pf*; (*consider*) считáть *impf*; *vi* считáться *impf* (*as* +*instr*).

rather *adv* скорéе; (*somewhat*) довóльно; **he (she) had (would) ~** он (онá) предпочёл (-члá) бы+*inf.*

ratification *n* ратификáция. **ratify** *vt* ратифицúровать *impf* & *pf.*

rating *n* оцéнка.

ratio *n* пропóрция.

ration *n* паёк, рациóн; *vt* нормúровать *impf* & *pf*; **be ~ed** выдавáться *impf*, вы́даться *pf* по кáрточкам.

rational *adj* разýмный. **rationalism** *n* рационалúзм. **rationality** *n* разýмность. **rationalize** *vt* обоснóвывать *impf*, обосновáть *pf*; (*industry etc.*) рационализúровать *impf* & *pf.*

rattle *vi* & *t* (*sound*) гремéть *impf* (+*instr*); **~ along** (*move*) грохотáть *impf*; **~ off** (*utter*) отбарабáнить *pf*; *n* (*sound*) треск, грóхот; (toy) погремýшка. **rattlesnake** n гремýчая змея.

raucous adj рéзкий.

ravage vt опустошáть impf, опустошúть pf; n: pl разрушúтельное дéйствие.

rave vi брéдить impf; ~ **about** быть в востóрге от+gen.

raven n вóрон.

ravenous adj голóдный как волк.

ravine n ущéлье.

ravishing adj восхитúтельный.

raw adj сырóй; (inexperienced) неóпытный; ~ **material**; сырьё (no pl).

ray n луч.

raze vt: ~ **to the ground** ровнять impf, с~ pf с землёй.

razor n брúтва; ~-**blade** лéзвие.

reach vt (attain, extend to, arrive at) достигáть impf, достúчь & достúгнуть pf +gen, до+gen; доходúть impf, дойтú pf до+gen; (with hand) дотя́гиваться impf, дотянýться pf до+gen; vi (extend) простирáться impf & досягáемость; (pl, of river) течéние.

react vi реагúровать impf, от~, про~ pf (**to** на+acc). re**action** n реáкция. reaction**ary** adj реакцибнный; n реакционéр. **reactor** n реáктор.

read vt читáть impf, про~, прочéсть pf; (mus) разыгрáть impf, разобрáть pf; (~ a meter etc.) снимáть impf, снять pf показáния +gen; (univ) изучáть impf; (interpret) толковáть impf. **readable** adj интерéсный. **reader** n читáтель m, ~ница; (book) хрестомáтия.

readily adv (willingly) охóтно; (easily) легкó. **readiness** n готóвность.

reading n чтéние; (on meter) показáние.

ready adj готóвый (**for** к+dat, на+acc); **get** ~ готóвиться impf; ~-**made** готóвый; ~ **money** налúчные дéньги (-нег, -ньгáм) pl.

real adj настоя́щий, реáльный; ~ **estate** недвúжимость. **realism** n реалúзм. **realist** n реалúст. **realistic** adj реалистúчный, -úческий. **reality** n действúтельность; **in** ~ действúтельно. **realization** n (of plan etc.) осуществлéние; (of assets) реализáция; (understanding) осознáние. **realize** vt (plan etc.) осуществля́ть impf, осуществúть pf; (assets) реализовáть impf & pf; (apprehend) осознавáть impf, осознáть pf. **really** adv действúтельно, в сáмом дéле.

realm n (kingdom) королéвство; (sphere) óбласть.

reap vt жать impf, сжать pf; (fig) пожинáть impf, пожáть pf.

rear[1] vt (lift) поднимáть impf, подня́ть pf; (children) воспúтывать impf, воспитáть pf; vi (of horse) становúться impf, стать pf на дыбы́.

rear[2] n зáдняя часть; (mil) тыл; **bring up the** ~ замыкáть impf, замкнýть pf шéствие; adj зáдний; (also mil) ты́льный. **rearguard** n арьергáрд; ~ **action** арьергáрдный бой.

rearmament n перевооружéние.

rearrange vt меня́ть impf.

reason n (cause) причи́на, основа́ние; (intellect) ра́зум, рассу́док; vi рассужда́ть impf; ~ **with** (person) угова́ривать impf +acc. **reasonable** adj разу́мный; (inexpensive) недорого́й.

reassurance n успока́ивание. **reassure** vt успока́ивать impf, успоко́ить pf.

rebate n ски́дка.

rebel n повста́нец; vi восстава́ть impf, восста́ть pf. **rebellion** n восста́ние. **rebellious** adj мяте́жный.

rebound vi отска́кивать impf, отскочи́ть pf; n рикоше́т.

rebuff n отпо́р; vt дава́ть impf, дать pf +dat отпо́р.

rebuild vt перестра́ивать impf, перестро́ить pf.

rebuke vt упрека́ть impf, упрекну́ть pf; n упрёк.

rebuttal n опроверже́ние.

recalcitrant adj непоко́рный.

recall vt (an official) отзыва́ть impf, отозва́ть pf; (remember) вспомина́ть impf, вспо́мнить pf; n о́тзыв; (memory) па́мять.

recant vi отрека́ться impf, отре́чься pf.

recapitulate vt резюми́ровать impf & pf.

recast vt переде́лывать impf, переде́лать pf.

recede vi отходи́ть impf, отойти́ pf.

receipt n (receiving) получе́ние; pl (amount) вы́ручка; (written ~) квита́нция. **receive** vt (admit, entertain) принима́ть impf, приня́ть pf; (get, be given) получа́ть impf, получи́ть pf. **receiver** n (radio, television) приёмник; (tel) тру́бка.

recent adj неда́вний; (new)

но́вый. **recently** adv неда́вно.

receptacle n вмести́лище. **reception** n приём; ~ **room** приёмная sb. **receptionist** n секрета́рь m, -рша, в приёмной. **receptive** adj восприи́мчивый.

recess n (parl) кани́кулы (-л) pl; (niche) ни́ша. **recession** n спад.

recipe n реце́пт.

recipient n получа́тель m.

reciprocal adj взаи́мный. **reciprocate** vt отвеча́ть impf (взаи́мностью) на+acc.

recital n (sólный) конце́рт. **recitation** n публи́чное чте́ние. **recite** vt деклами́ровать impf, про~ pf; (list) перечисля́ть impf, перечи́слить pf.

reckless adj (rash) опроме́тчивый; (careless) неосторо́жный.

reckon vt подсчи́тывать impf, подсчита́ть pf; (also regard as) счита́ть impf, счесть pf (**to be** +instr); vi: ~ **on** рассчи́тывать impf, рассчита́ть pf на+acc; ~ **with** счита́ться impf c+instr. **reckoning** n счёт; **day of** ~ час распла́ты.

reclaim vt тре́бовать impf, по~ pf обра́тно; (land) осва́ивать impf, осво́ить pf.

recline vi полулежа́ть impf.

recluse n затво́рник.

recognition n узнава́ние; (acknowledgement) призна́ние. **recognize** vt узнава́ть impf, узна́ть pf; (acknowledge) признава́ть impf, призна́ть pf.

recoil vi отпря́дывать impf, отпря́нуть pf.

recollect vt вспомина́ть impf, вспо́мнить pf. **recollection** n воспомина́ние.

recommend *vt* рекомендовать *impf & pf*. recommendation *n* рекомендация.

recompense *n* вознаграждение; *vt* вознаграждать *impf*, вознаградить *pf*.

reconcile *vt* примирять *impf*, примирить *pf*; ~ o.s. примиряться *impf*, примириться *pf* (to c+*instr*). reconciliation *n* примирение.

reconnaissance *n* разведка.

reconnoitre *vt* разведывать *impf*, разведать *pf*.

reconstruct *vt* перестраивать *impf*, перестроить *pf*. reconstruction *n* перестройка.

record *vt* записывать *impf*, записать *pf* в запись; (*minutes*) протокол; (*gramophone* ~) грампластинка; (*sport etc.*) рекорд; off the ~ неофициально; *adj* рекордный; ~breaker, -holder рекордсмен, ~ка; ~player проигрыватель *m*. recorder *n* (*mus*) блок-флейта. recording *n* запись.

recount¹ *vt* (*narrate*) пересказывать *impf*, пересказать *pf*.

re-count² *vt* (*count again*) пересчитывать *impf*, пересчитать *pf*; *n* пересчёт.

recoup *vt* возвращать *impf*, вернуть *pf* (losses потерянное).

recourse *n*: have ~ to прибегать *impf*, прибегнуть *pf* к+*dat*.

recover *vt* (*regain possession*) получать *impf*, получить *pf* обратно; вернуть *pf*; *vi* (~ *health*) поправляться *impf*, поправиться *pf* (from после+*gen*). recovery *n* возвращение; выздоровление.

recreate *vt* воссоздавать *impf*, воссоздать *pf*.

recreation *n* развлечение, отдых.

recrimination *n* взаимное обвинение.

recruit *n* новобранец; *vt* вербовать *impf*, за~ *pf*. recruitment *n* вербовка.

rectangle *n* прямоугольник. rectangular *adj* прямоугольный.

rectify *vt* исправлять *impf*, исправить *pf*.

rector *n* (*priest*) приходский священник; (*univ*) ректор. rectory *n* дом приходского священника.

rectum *n* прямая кишка.

recuperate *vi* поправляться *impf*, поправиться *pf*. recuperation *n* выздоровление.

recur *vi* повторяться *impf*, повториться *pf*. recurrence *n* повторение. recurrent *adj* повторяющийся.

recycle *vt* перерабатывать *impf*, переработать *pf*.

red *adj* красный; (of hair) рыжий; *n* красный цвет; (*polit*) красный *sb*; in the ~ в долгу; ~handed с поличным; ~ herring ложный след; ~hot раскалённый докрасна; R~ Indian индеец, индианка; ~ tape волокита. redcurrant *n* красная смородина (*no pl*; *usu collect*). redden *vt* окрашивать *impf*, окрасить *pf* в красный цвет; *vi* краснеть *impf*, по~ *pf*. reddish *adj* красноватый; (hair) рыжеватый.

redecorate *vt* отделывать *impf*, отделать *pf*.

redeem *vt* (buy back) выкупать *impf*, выкупить *pf*.

(from sin) искупа́ть *impf*, искупи́ть *pf*. **redeemer** *n* искупи́тель *m*. **redemption** *n* вы́куп; искупле́ние.

redeploy *vt* передислоци́ровать *impf & pf*.

redo *vt* переде́лывать *impf*, переде́лать *pf*.

redouble *vt* удва́ивать *impf*, удво́ить *pf*.

redress *vt* исправля́ть *impf*, испра́вить *pf*; ~ **the balance** восстана́вливать *impf*, восстанови́ть *pf* равнове́сие; *n* возмеще́ние.

reduce *vt* (*decrease*) уменьша́ть *impf*, уме́ньшить *pf*; (*lower*) снижа́ть *impf*, сни́зить *pf*; (*shorten*) сокраща́ть *impf*, сократи́ть *pf*; (*bring to*) доводи́ть *impf*, довести́ *pf* (**to** в+*acc*). **reduction** *n* уменьше́ние, сниже́ние, сокраще́ние; (*discount*) ски́дка.

redundancy *n* (*dismissal*) увольне́ние. **redundant** *adj* изли́шний; **make** ~ увольня́ть *impf*, уво́лить *pf*.

reed *n* (*plant*) тростни́к; (*in oboe etc.*) язычо́к.

reef *n* риф.

reek *n* вонь; *vi*: ~ (**of**) воня́ть *impf* (+*instr*).

reel[1] *n* кату́шка; *vt*: ~ **off** (*story etc.*) отбараба́нить *pf*. **reel**[2] *vi* (*stagger*) пошатыва́ться *impf*, пошатну́ться *pf*.

refectory *n* (*monastery*) тра́пезная *sb*; (*univ*) столо́вая *sb*.

refer *vt* (*direct*) отсыла́ть *impf*, отосла́ть *pf* (**to** к+*dat*); *vi*: ~ **to** (*cite*) ссыла́ться *impf*, сосла́ться *pf* на+*acc*; (*mention*) упомина́ть *impf*, упомяну́ть *pf* +*acc*. **referee** *n* судья́ *m*; *vt* суди́ть *impf*. **reference** *n* (*to book etc.*)

ссы́лка; (*mention*) упомина́ние; (*testimonial*) характери́стика; ~ **book** спра́вочник. **referendum** *n* рефере́ндум.

refine *vt* очища́ть *impf*, очи́стить *pf*. **refined** *adj* (*in style etc.*) утончённый; (*in manners*) культу́рный. **refinement** *n* утончённость. **refinery** *n* (*oil* ~) нефтеочисти́тельный заво́д.

refit *vt* переобору́довать *impf & pf*.

reflect *vt* отража́ть *impf*, отрази́ть *pf*; *vi* размышля́ть *impf*, размы́слить *pf* (**on** o+*prep*). **reflection** *n* отраже́ние; размышле́ние; **on** ~ поду́мав. **reflective** *adj* (*thoughtful*) заду́мчивый. **reflector** *n* рефле́ктор. **reflex** *n* рефле́кс; *adj* рефле́кторный. **reflexive** *adj* (*gram*) возвра́тный.

reform *vt* реформи́ровать *impf & pf*; *vt & i* (*of people*) исправля́ть(ся) *impf*, испра́вить(ся) *pf*; *n* рефо́рма; исправле́ние. **Reformation** *n* Реформа́ция.

refract *vt* преломля́ть *impf*, преломи́ть *pf*.

refrain[1] *n* припе́в.

refrain[2] *vi* возде́рживаться *impf*, воздержа́ться *pf* (**from** от+*gen*).

refresh *vt* освежа́ть *impf*, освежи́ть *pf*. **refreshments** *n pl* напи́тки *m pl*.

refrigerate *vt* охлажда́ть *impf*, охлади́ть *pf*. **refrigeration** *n* охлажде́ние. **refrigerator** *n* холоди́льник.

refuge *n* убе́жище; **take** ~ находи́ть *impf*, найти́ *pf* убе́жище. **refugee** *n* бе́женец, -нка.

refund vt возвраща́ть impf, возврати́ть pf; (expenses) возмеща́ть impf, возмести́ть pf; n возвраще́ние (де́нег); возмеще́ние.

refusal n отка́з. **refuse**[1] vt отка́зывать impf, отказа́ть pf.

refuse[2] n му́сор.

refute vt опроверга́ть impf, опрове́ргнуть pf.

regain vt возвраща́ть impf, верну́ть pf.

regal adj короле́вский.

regale vt угоща́ть impf, угости́ть pf (with +instr).

regalia n pl рега́лии f pl.

regard vt смотре́ть impf, по~ pf на+acc; (take into account) счита́ться impf с+instr; **as** ~ счита́ть impf +instr, за+instr; **as** ~s что каса́ется+gen; n (esteem) уваже́ние; (attention) внима́ние; pl приве́т. **regarding** prep относи́тельно+gen. **regardless** adv не обраща́я внима́ния; ~ **of** не счита́ясь с+instr.

regatta n рега́та.

regenerate vt перерожда́ть impf, переродить pf. **regeneration** n перерожде́ние.

regent n ре́гент.

régime n режи́м.

regiment n полк. **regimental** adj полково́й. **regimentation** n регламента́ция.

region n регио́н. **regional** adj региона́льный.

register n реѐстр; (also mus) реги́стр; vt & i регистри́ровать impf, за~ pf; (a letter) отправля́ть impf, отпра́вить pf заказны́м. **registered** adj (letter) заказно́й. **registrar** n регистра́тор. **registration** n регистра́ция; ~ **number** но́мер маши́ны. **registry** n реги-

страту́ра; ~ **office** загс.

regression n регре́сс. **regressive** adj регресси́вный.

regret vt сожале́ть impf o+prep; n сожале́ние. **regretful** adj по́лный сожале́ния. **regrettable** adj приско́рбный. **regrettably** adv к сожале́нию.

regular adj регуля́рный; (also gram) пра́вильный; n (coll) завсегда́тай. **regularity** n регуля́рность. **regulate** vt регули́ровать impf, у~ pf. **regulation** n регули́рование; pl пра́вила neut pl.

rehabilitate vt реабилити́ровать impf & pf. **rehabilitation** n реабилита́ция.

rehearsal n репети́ция. **rehearse** vt репети́ровать impf, от~ pf.

reign n ца́рствование; vi ца́рствовать impf; (fig) цари́ть impf.

reimburse vt возмеща́ть impf, возмести́ть pf (+dat of person). **reimbursement** n возмеще́ние.

rein n по́вод.

reincarnation n перевоплоще́ние.

reindeer n се́верный оле́нь m.

reinforce vt подкрепля́ть impf, подкрепи́ть pf. **reinforcement** n (also pl) подкрепле́ние.

reinstate vt восстана́вливать impf, восстанови́ть pf. **reinstatement** n восстановле́ние.

reiterate vt повторя́ть impf, повтори́ть pf.

reject vt отверга́ть impf, отве́ргнуть pf; (as defective) бракова́ть impf, за~ pf; n брак. **rejection** n отка́з от+gen).

rejoice vi рáдоваться impf, об~ pf (in, at +dat). **rejoicing** n рáдость.

rejoin vt (вновь) присоединя́ться impf, присоедини́ться pf k+dat.

rejuvenate vt омола́живать impf, омолоди́ть pf.

relapse n рециди́в; vi снóва впадáть impf, впасть pf (into в+acc); (into illness) снóва заболевáть impf, заболéть pf. **relate** vt (tell) расска́зывать impf, рассказáть pf; (connect) свя́зывать impf, связáть pf; vi относи́ться impf к to+dat. **related** adj рóдственный. **relation** n отношéние; (person) рóдственник, -ица. **relationship** n (connection; liaison) связь; (kinship) родствó. **relative** adj относи́тельный; n рóдственник, -ица. **relativity** n относи́тельность.

relax vt ослабля́ть impf, ослáбить pf; vi (rest) расслабля́ться impf, расслáбиться pf. **relaxation** n ослаблéние; (rest) óтдых.

relay n (shift) смéна; (sport) эстафéта; (electr) релé neut indecl; vt передавáть impf, передáть pf.

release vt (set free) освобождáть impf, освободи́ть pf; (unfasten, let go) отпускáть impf, отпусти́ть pf; (film etc.) выпускáть impf, вы́пустить pf; n освобождéние; (film etc.) вы́пуск.

relegate vt переводи́ть impf, перевести́ pf в (ни́зшую грýппу). **relegation** n перевóд (в ни́зшую грýппу).

relent vi смягчáться impf, смягчи́ться pf. **relentless** adj непрестáнный.

relevance n умéстность. **relevant** adj относя́щийся к дéлу; умéстный.

reliability n надёжность. **reliable** adj надёжный. **reliance** n довéрие. **reliant** adj: **be ~ upon** зави́сеть impf от+gen.

relic n остáток, рели́квия.

relief[1] n (art, geol) рельéф.

relief[2] n (alleviation) облегчéние; (assistance) пóмощь; (in duty) смéна. **relieve** vt (alleviate) облегчáть impf, облегчи́ть pf; (replace) сменя́ть impf, смени́ть pf; (unburden) освобождáть impf, освободи́ть pf (of от+gen).

religion n рели́гия. **religious** adj религиóзный.

relinquish vt оставля́ть impf, остáвить pf; (right etc.) отка́зываться impf, отказáться pf от+gen.

relish n (enjoyment) смак; (cul) припрáва; vt смаковáть impf.

relocate vt & i перемещáть(ся) impf, перемести́ть(ся) pf.

reluctance n неохóта. **reluctant** adj неохóтный; **be ~ to** не желáть impf +inf.

rely vi полагáться impf, положи́ться pf (on на+acc).

remain vi оставáться impf, остáться pf. **remainder** n остáток. **remains** n pl остáтки pl; (human ~) остáнки (-ков) pl.

remand vt содержáть impf под стрáжей; **be on ~** содержáться impf под стрáжей.

remark vt замечáть impf, замéтить pf; n замечáние. **remarkable** adj замечáтельный.

remarry vi вступáть impf, вступи́ть pf в нóвый брак.

remedial adj лече́бный. **remedy** n сре́дство (**for** от, про́тив+gen); vt исправля́ть impf, испра́вить pf.

remember vt по́мнить impf, вспомина́ть impf, вспо́мнить pf; (greet) передава́ть impf, переда́ть pf приве́т от+gen (**to** +dat). **remembrance** n па́мять.

remind vt напомина́ть impf, напо́мнить pf +dat (**of** +acc, о+prep). **reminder** n напомина́ние.

reminiscence n воспомина́ние. **reminiscent** adj напомина́ющий.

remiss predic небре́жный. **remission** n (pardon) отпуще́ние; (med) реми́ссия. **remit** vt пересыла́ть impf, пересла́ть pf. **remittance** n перево́д де́нег; (money) де́нежный перево́д.

remnant n оста́ток.

remonstrate vi: ~ **with** увеща́ть impf +acc.

remorse n угрызе́ния neut pl со́вести. **remorseful** adj по́лный раска́яния. **remorseless** adj безжа́лостный.

remote adj отдалённый; ~ **control** дистанцио́нное управле́ние.

removal n (taking away) удале́ние; (of obstacles) устране́ние. **remove** vt (take away) убира́ть impf, убра́ть pf; (get rid of) устраня́ть impf, устрани́ть pf.

remuneration n вознагражде́ние. **remunerative** adj вы́годный.

renaissance n возрожде́ние; the R~ Возрожде́ние.

render n воздава́ть impf, возда́ть pf; (help etc.) ока́зы-

вать impf, оказа́ть pf; (role etc.) исполня́ть impf, испо́лнить pf; (stone) штукату́рить impf, о~, от~ pf. **rendering** n исполне́ние.

rendezvous n (meeting) свида́ние.

renegade n ренега́т, ~ка.

renew vt (extend; continue) возобновля́ть impf, возобнови́ть pf; (replace) обновля́ть impf, обнови́ть pf. **renewal** n (воз)обновле́ние.

renounce vt отверга́ть impf, отве́ргнуть pf; (claim) отка́зываться impf, отказа́ться pf от+gen.

renovate vt ремонти́ровать impf, от~ pf. **renovation** n ремо́нт.

renown n сла́ва. **renowned** adj изве́стный; **be** ~ **for** сла́виться impf +instr.

rent n (for home) квартпла́та; (for premises) (аре́ндная) пла́та; vt (of tenant) аре́ндовать impf & pf, (of owner) сдава́ть impf, сдать pf.

renunciation n (repudiation) отрица́ние; (of claim) отка́з.

rep n (comm) аге́нт.

repair vt ремонти́ровать impf, от~ pf; n (also pf) ремо́нт (only sg); почи́нка; **in good/ bad** ~ в хоро́шем/плохо́м состоя́нии.

reparations n pl репара́ции f pl.

repatriate vt репатрии́ровать impf & pf. **repatriation** n репатриа́ция.

repay vt отпла́чивать impf, отплати́ть pf (person +dat). **repayment** n отпла́та.

repeal vt отменя́ть impf, отмени́ть pf; n отме́на.

repeat vt & i повторя́ть(ся)

impf, повтори́ть(ся) *pf*; *n* повторе́ние. **repeatedly** *adv* неоднокра́тно.

repel *vt* отта́лкивать *impf*, оттолкну́ть *pf*; (*enemy*) отража́ть *impf*, отрази́ть *pf*.

repent *vi* раска́иваться *impf*, раска́яться *pf*. **repentance** *n* раска́яние. **repentant** *adj* раска́ивающийся.

repercussion *n* после́дствие.

repertoire *n* репертуа́р. **repertory** *n* (*store*) запа́с; (*repertoire*) репертуа́р; ~ **company** постоя́нная тру́ппа.

repetition *n* повторе́ние. **repetitious, repetitive** *adj* повторя́ющийся.

replace *vt* (*put back*) класть *impf*, положи́ть *pf* обра́тно; (*substitute*) заменя́ть *impf*, замени́ть *pf* (*by +instr*). **replacement** *n* заме́на.

replay *n* переигро́вка.

replenish *vt* пополня́ть *impf*, попо́лнить *pf*.

replete *adj* насы́щенный; (*sated*) сы́тый.

replica *n* ко́пия.

reply *vt* & *i* отвеча́ть *impf*, отве́тить *pf* (*to* на+*acc*); *n* отве́т.

report *vt* сообща́ть *impf*, сообщи́ть *pf*; *vi* докла́дывать *impf*, доложи́ть *pf*; (*present o.s.*) явля́ться *impf*, яви́ться *pf*; *n* сообще́ние; докла́д; (*school*) та́бель *m*; (*sound*) звук взры́ва, вы́стрела. **reporter** *n* корреспонде́нт.

repose *n* (*rest*) о́тдых; (*peace*) поко́й.

repository *n* храни́лище.

repossess *vt* изыма́ть *impf*, изъя́ть *pf* за непла́тёж.

reprehensible *adj* предосуди́тельный.

represent *vt* представля́ть *impf*, (*portray*) изобража́ть *impf*, изобрази́ть *pf*. **representation** *n* (*being represented*) представи́тельство; (*statement of case*) представле́ние; (*portrayal*) изображе́ние. **representative** *adj* изобража́ющий (*of +acc*); (*typical*) типи́чный; *n* представи́тель *m*.

repress *vt* подавля́ть *impf*, подави́ть *pf*. **repression** *n* подавле́ние, репре́ссия. **repressive** *adj* репресси́вный.

reprieve *vt* отсро́чивать *impf*, отсро́чить *pf +dat* приведе́ние в исполне́ние (сме́ртного) пригово́ра; *n* отсро́чка приведе́ния в исполне́ние (сме́ртного) пригово́ра; (*fig*) переды́шка.

reprimand *n* вы́говор; *vt* де́лать *impf*, с~ *pf* вы́говор +*dat*.

reprint *vt* переиздава́ть *impf*, переизда́ть *pf*; *n* переизда́ние.

reprisal *n* отве́тная ме́ра.

reproach *vt* упрека́ть *impf*, упрекну́ть *pf* (*with* в+*prep*). **reproachful** *adj* укори́зненный.

reproduce *vt* воспроизводи́ть *impf*, воспроизвести́ *pf*; *vi* размножа́ться *impf*, размно́житься *pf*. **reproduction** *n* (*action*) воспроизведе́ние; (*object*) репроду́кция; (*offspring*) размноже́ние. **reproductive** *adj* воспроизводи́тельный.

reproof *n* вы́говор. **reprove** *vt* де́лать *impf* с~ *pf* вы́говор +*dat*.

reptile *n* пресмыка́ющееся *sb*.

republic *n* респу́блика. **republican** *adj* республика́нский; *n* республика́нец, -нка.

repudiate vt (*renounce*) отка́зываться *impf*, отказа́ться *pf* от+*gen*; (*reject*) отверга́ть *impf*, отве́ргнуть *pf*. **repudiation** n отка́з (*of* от+*gen*).

repugnance n отвраще́ние. **repugnant** *adj* проти́вный.

repulse vt отража́ть *impf*, отрази́ть *pf*. **repulsion** n отвраще́ние. **repulsive** *adj* отврати́тельный.

reputable *adj* по́льзующийся хоро́шей репута́цией. **reputation, repute** n репута́ция. **reputed** *adj* предполага́емый. **reputedly** *adv* по о́бщему мне́нию.

request n про́сьба; **by, on, ~** по про́сьбе; vt проси́ть *impf*, по~ *pf* +*acc*, +*gen* (*person* +*acc*).

requiem n ре́квием.

require vt (*demand; need*) тре́бовать *impf*, по~ *pf* +*gen*; (*need*) нужда́ться *impf* в+*prep*. **requirement** n тре́бование; (*necessity*) потре́бность. **requisite** *adj* необходи́мый; n необходи́мая вещь. **requisition** n реквизи́ция; vt реквизи́ровать *impf & pf*.

resale n перепрода́жа.

rescind vt отменя́ть *impf*, отмени́ть *pf*.

rescue vt спаса́ть *impf*, спасти́ *pf*; n спасе́ние. **rescuer** n спаси́тель m.

research n иссле́дование (+*gen*); (*occupation*) иссле́довательская рабо́та; vi: **~ into** иссле́довать *impf & pf* +*acc*. **researcher** n иссле́дователь m.

resemblance n схо́дство. **resemble** vt похо́дить *impf* на+*acc*.

resent vt возмуща́ться *impf*,

возмути́ться *pf*. **resentful** *adj* возмущённый. **resentment** n возмуще́ние.

reservation n (*doubt*) огово́рка; (*booking*) предвари́тельный зака́з; (*land*) резерва́ция.

reserve vt (*keep*) резерви́ровать *impf & pf*; (*book*) зака́зывать *impf*, заказа́ть *pf*; n (*stock; mil*) запа́с, резе́рв; (*sport*) запасно́й игро́к; (*nature — etc.*) запове́дник; (*proviso*) огово́рка; (*self-restraint*) сде́ржанность; *attrib* запасно́й. **reserved** *adj* (*person*) сде́ржанный. **reservist** n резерви́ст. **reservoir** n (*for water*) водохрани́лище; (*for other fluids*) резервуа́р.

resettle vt переселя́ть *impf*, пересели́ть *pf*. **resettlement** n переселе́ние.

reshape vt видоизменя́ть *impf*, видоизмени́ть *pf*.

reshuffle n перестано́вка.

reside vi прожива́ть *impf*. **residence** n (*residing*) прожива́ние; (*abode*) местожи́тельство; (*official — etc.*) резиде́нция. **resident** n (*постоя́нный*) жи́тель m, ~ница; *adj* прожива́ющий; (*population*) посто́янный. **residential** *adj* жило́й.

residual *adj* остато́чный. **residue** n оста́ток.

resign vt отка́зываться *impf*, отказа́ться *pf* от+*gen*; vi уходи́ть *impf*, уйти́ *pf* в отста́вку; **~ o.s. to** покоря́ться *impf*, покори́ться *pf* +*dat*. **resignation** n отста́вка, заявле́ние об отста́вке; (*being resigned*) поко́рность. **resigned** *adj* поко́рный.

resilient *adj* выно́сливый.

resin n смола́.

resist vt сопротивля́ться impf +dat; (temptation) устоя́ть pf пе́ред+instr. **resistance** n сопротивле́ние. **resistant** adj сто́йкий.

resolute adj реши́тельный. **resolution** n (character) реши́тельность; (vow) заро́к; (at meeting etc.) резолю́ция; (of problem) разреше́ние. **resolve** vt (decide) реша́ть impf, реши́ть pf; (settle) разреша́ть impf, разреши́ть pf; n реши́тельность; (decision) реше́ние.

resonance n резона́нс. **resonant** adj зву́чный.

resort vi: ~ to прибега́ть impf, прибе́гнуть pf к+dat; n (place) куро́рт; **in the last ~** в кра́йнем слу́чае.

resound vi (of sound etc.) раздава́ться impf, разда́ться pf; (of place) оглаша́ться impf, огласи́ться pf (with +instr).

resource n (usu pl) ресу́рс. **resourceful** adj нахо́дчивый.

respect n (relation) отноше́ние; (esteem) уваже́ние; **with ~ to** что каса́ется+gen; vt уважа́ть impf. **respectability** n респекта́бельность. **respectable** adj прили́чный. **respectful** adj почти́тельный. **respective** adj свой. **respectively** adv соотве́тственно.

respiration n дыха́ние. **respirator** n респира́тор. **respiratory** adj дыха́тельный.

respite n переды́шка.

resplendent adj блиста́тельный.

respond vi: ~ to отвеча́ть impf, отве́тить pf на+acc; (react) реаги́ровать impf, про~, от~ pf на+acc. **response** n отве́т; (reaction)

о́тклик. **responsibility** n отве́тственность; (duty) обя́занность. **responsible** adj отве́тственный (to пе́ред+instr; for за+acc); (reliable) надёжный. **responsive** adj отзы́вчивый.

rest[1] vi отдыха́ть impf, отдохну́ть pf; vt (place) класть impf, положи́ть pf; (allow to ~) дава́ть impf, дать pf о́тдых+dat; n (repose) о́тдых; (peace) поко́й; (mus) па́уза; (support) опо́ра.

rest[2] n (remainder) оста́ток; (the others) остальны́е sb pl.

restaurant n рестора́н.

restful adj успока́ивающий.

restitution n возвраще́ние.

restive adj беспоко́йный.

restless adj беспоко́йный.

restoration n реставра́ция; (return) восстановле́ние. **restore** vt реставри́ровать impf & pf; (return) восстана́вливать impf, восстанови́ть pf.

restrain vt уде́рживать impf, удержа́ть pf (from от+gen). **restraint** n сде́ржанность.

restrict vt ограни́чивать impf, ограни́чить pf. **restriction** n ограниче́ние. **restrictive** adj ограничи́тельный.

result vi сле́довать impf; происходи́ть impf, произойти́ pf (from из+gen); ~ **in** конча́ться impf, ко́нчиться pf +instr; n результа́т; **as a ~** в результа́те (of +gen).

resume vt & i возобновля́ть(ся) impf, возобнови́ть(ся) pf. **résumé** n резюме́ neut indecl. **resumption** n возобновле́ние.

resurrect vt (fig) воскреша́ть impf, воскреси́ть pf. **resurrection** n (of the dead) воскресе́ние; (fig) воскреше́ние.

resuscitate vt приводи́ть impf, привести́ pf в созна́ние.

retail n ро́зничная прода́жа; attrib ро́зничный; adv в ро́зницу; vt продава́ть impf, прода́ть pf в ро́зницу; vt продава́ться impf в ро́зницу. **retailer** n ро́зничный торго́вец.

retain vt уде́рживать impf, удержа́ть pf.

retaliate vi отпла́чивать impf, отплати́ть pf тем же. **retaliation** n отпла́та, возме́здие.

retard vt замедля́ть impf, заме́длить pf. **retarded** adj отста́лый.

retention n удержа́ние. **retentive** adj (memory) хоро́ший.

reticence n сде́ржанность. **reticent** adj сде́ржанный.

retina n сетча́тка.

retinue n сви́та.

retire vi (withdraw) удаля́ться impf, удали́ться pf; (from office etc.) уходи́ть impf, уйти́ pf в отста́вку. **retired** adj в отста́вке. **retirement** n отста́вка. **retiring** adj скро́мный.

retort[1] vt отвеча́ть impf, отве́тить pf ре́зко; n возраже́ние.

retort[2] n (vessel) рето́рта.

retrace vt: ~ one's steps возвраща́ться impf, возврати́ться pf.

retract vt (draw in) втя́гивать impf, втяну́ть pf; (take back) брать impf, взять pf наза́д.

retreat vi отступа́ть impf, отступи́ть pf; n отступле́ние; (withdrawal) уедине́ние; (place) убе́жище.

retrenchment n сокраще́ние расхо́дов.

retrial n повто́рное слу́шание де́ла.

retribution n возме́здие.

retrieval n возвраще́ние; (comput) по́иск (информа́ции); vt брать impf, взять pf обра́тно.

retrograde adj (fig) реакцио́нный. **retrospect** n: in ~ ретроспекти́вно. **retrospective** adj (law) име́ющий обра́тную си́лу.

return vt & i (give back; come back) возвраща́ть(ся) impf, возврати́ть(ся) pf; верну́ть(ся) pf; vt (elect) избира́ть impf, избра́ть pf; n возвраще́ние; возвра́т; (profit) при́быль; by ~ обра́тной по́чтой; in ~ взаме́н (for +gen); many happy ~s! с днём рожде́ния!; ~ match отве́тный матч; ~ ticket обра́тный биле́т.

reunion n встре́ча (друзе́й и т. п.); family ~ сбор всей семьи́. **reunite** vt воссоединя́ть impf, воссоедини́ть pf.

reuse vt сно́ва испо́льзовать impf & pf.

rev n оборо́т; vt & i: ~ up рвану́ть(ся) pf.

reveal vt обнару́живать impf, обнару́жить pf. **revealing** adj показа́тельный.

revel vi пирова́ть impf; ~ in наслажда́ться impf +instr.

revelation n открове́ние.

revenge vt: ~ o.s. мстить impf, ото~ pf (for за+acc; on +dat); n месть.

revenue n дохо́д.

reverberate vi отража́ться impf. **reverberation** n отраже́ние; (fig) о́тзвук.

revere vt почита́ть impf. **reverence** n почте́ние. **Reverend** adj (in title) (его́) преподо́бие. **reverent(ial)** adj почти́тельный.

reverie n мечта́ние.

reversal n (change) измене́ние; (of decision) отме́на. **reverse** adj обра́тный; ~ gear за́дний ход; vt (change) изменя́ть impf, измени́ть pf; (decision) отменя́ть impf, отмени́ть pf; дать pf за́дний ход; n (the ~) обра́тное sb, противополо́жное sb; (~ gear) за́дний ход; (~ side) обра́тная сторона́. **reversible** adj обрати́мый; (cloth) двусторо́нний. **reversion** n возвраще́ние. **revert** vi возвраща́ться impf (to в+acc, к+dat); (law) переходи́ть impf, перейти́ pf (to к+dat).

review n (re-examination) пересмо́тр; (mil) пара́д; (survey) обзо́р; (criticism) реце́нзия; vt (re-examine) пересма́тривать impf, пересмотре́ть pf; (survey) обозрева́ть impf, обозре́ть pf; (troops etc.) принима́ть impf, приня́ть pf пара́д+gen; (book etc.) рецензи́ровать impf, про~ pf. **reviewer** n реце́нзент.

revise vt пересма́тривать impf, пересмотре́ть pf; исправля́ть impf, испра́вить pf; vi (for exam) гото́виться impf (for к+dat). **revision** n пересмо́тр, исправле́ние.

revival n возрожде́ние; (to life etc.) оживле́ние. **revive** vt возрожда́ть impf, возроди́ть pf; (resuscitate) оживля́ть impf, оживи́ть pf; vi ожива́ть impf, ожи́ть pf.

revoke vt отменя́ть impf, отмени́ть pf.

revolt n бунт; vt вызыва́ть impf, вы́звать pf отвраще́-

ние y+gen; vi бунтова́ть impf, взбунтова́ться pf. **revolting** adj отврати́тельный.

revolution n (single turn) оборо́т; (polit) револю́ция. **revolutionary** adj революцио́нный; n революционе́р. **revolutionize** vt революциони́зировать impf & pf. **revolve** vt & i враща́ть(ся) impf. **revolver** n револьве́р.

revue n ревю́ neut indecl.

revulsion n отвраще́ние.

reward n вознагражде́ние; vt (воз)награжда́ть impf, (воз)награди́ть pf.

rewrite vt перепи́сывать impf, переписа́ть pf; (recast) переде́лывать impf, переде́лать pf.

rhapsody n рапсо́дия.

rhetoric n рито́рика. **rhetorical** adj риторический.

rheumatic adj ревмати́ческий. **rheumatism** n ревмати́зм.

rhinoceros n носоро́г.

rhododendron n рододе́ндрон.

rhubarb n реве́нь n.

rhyme n ри́фма; pl (verse) стихи́ m pl; vt & i рифмова́ть(ся) impf.

rhythm n ритм. **rhythmic(al)** adj ритми́ческий, -чный.

rib n ребро́.

ribald adj непристо́йный.

ribbon n ле́нта.

rice n рис.

rich adj бога́тый; (soil) тучный; (food) жи́рный. **riches** n pl бога́тство. **richly** adv (fully) вполне́.

rickety adj (shaky) расша́танный.

ricochet vi рикошети́ровать impf & pf.

rid vt освобожда́ть impf, освободи́ть pf (of от+gen);

get ~ of избавля́ться *impf*, изба́виться *pf* от+*gen*. **riddance** *n*: good ~! ска́тертью доро́га!

riddle *n* (*enigma*) зага́дка.

riddled *adj*: ~ **with** изрешечённый, (*fig*) прони́занный.

ride *vi* е́здить *indet*, е́хать *det*, по~ *pf* (**on horseback** верхо́м); *vt* е́здить *indet*, е́хать *det*, по~ *pf* в, на+*prep*; *n* пое́здка, езда́. **rider** *n* вса́дник, -ица; (*clause*) дополне́ние.

ridge *n* хребе́т; (*on cloth*) рубчик; (*of roof*) конёк.

ridicule *n* насме́шка; *vt* осме́ивать *impf*, осмея́ть *pf*. **ridiculous** *adj* смешно́й.

riding *n* (*horse-~*) (верхова́я) езда́.

rife *predic* распространённый.

riff-raff *n* подо́нки (-ков) *pl*.

rifle *n* винто́вка; *vt* (*search*) обы́скивать *impf*, обыска́ть *pf*.

rift *n* тре́щина (*also fig*).

rig *vt* оснаща́ть *impf*, оснасти́ть *pf*; ~ **out** наряжа́ть *impf*, наряди́ть *pf*; ~ **up** скола́чивать *impf*, сколоти́ть *pf*; *n* бурова́я устано́вка. **rigging** *n* такела́ж.

right *adj* (*position*; *justified*; *polit*) пра́вый; (*correct*) пра́вильный; (*the one wanted*) тот; (*suitable*) подходя́щий; ~ **angle** прямо́й у́гол; *vt* исправля́ть *impf*, испра́вить *pf*; *n* пра́во; (*what is just*) справедли́вость; (~ *side*) пра́вая сторона́; (*the R~*) *polit* пра́вые *sb pl*: **be in the** ~ быть пра́вым; **by** ~**s** по пра́ву; ~ **of way** пра́во прохо́да, прое́зда; *adv* (*straight*) пря́мо; (*exactly*) то́чно, как

раз; (*to the full*) соверше́нно; (*correctly*) пра́вильно; как сле́дует; (*on the* ~) спра́ва (*of* от+*gen*); (*to the* ~) напра́во; ~ **away** напра́во.

righteous *adj* (*person*) пра́ведный; (*action*) справедли́вый.

rightful *adj* зако́нный.

rigid *adj* жёсткий; (*strict*) стро́гий. **rigidity** *n* жёсткость; стро́гость.

rigmarole *n* каните́ль.

rigorous *adj* стро́гий. **rigour** *n* стро́гость.

rim *n* (*of wheel*) о́бод; (*spectacles*) опра́ва. **rimless** *adj* без опра́вы.

rind *n* кожура́.

ring[1] *n* кольцо́; (*circle*) круг; (*boxing*) ринг; (*circus*) цирко́вая аре́на; ~ **road** кольцева́я доро́га; *vt* (*encircle*) окружа́ть *impf*, окружи́ть *pf*.

ring[2] *vi* (*sound*) звони́ть *impf*, по~ *pf*; (*ring out*; *of shot etc.*) раздава́ться *impf*, разда́ться *pf*; (*of place*) оглаша́ться *impf*, огласи́ться *pf* (**with** +*instr*); *vt* звони́ть *impf*, по~ *pf* в+*acc*; ~ **back** перезва́нивать *impf*, перезвони́ть *pf*; ~ **off** пове́сить *pf* тру́бку; ~ **up** звони́ть *impf*, по~ *pf* +*dat*; *n* звон, звоно́к.

ringleader *n* глава́рь *m*.

rink *n* като́к.

rinse *vt* полоска́ть *impf*, вы́~ *pf*; *n* полоска́ние.

riot *n* бунт; **run** ~ бу́йствовать *impf*; (*of plants*) бу́йно разраста́ться *impf*, разрасти́сь *pf*; *vi* бунтова́ть *impf*, взбунтова́ться *pf*. **riotous** *adj* бу́йный.

rip *vt & i* рва́ть(ся) *impf*, разо~ *pf*; ~ **up** разрыва́ть *impf*, разорва́ть *pf*; *n* проре́ха, разре́з.

ripe *adj* зре́лый, спе́лый.

ripen *vt* де́лать *impf*, с~ *pf* зре́лым; *vi* созрева́ть *impf*, созре́ть *pf*. **ripeness** *n* зре́лость.

ripple *n* рябь; *vt & i* покрыва́ть(ся) *impf*, покры́ть(ся) *pf* ря́бью.

rise *vi* поднима́ться *impf*, подня́ться *pf*; повыша́ться *impf*, повы́ситься *pf*; (*get up*) встава́ть *impf*, встать *pf*; (*rebel*) восстава́ть *impf*, восста́ть *pf*; (*sun etc.*) в(о)сходи́ть *impf*, взойти́ *pf*; *n* подъём, возвыше́ние; (*in pay*) приба́вка; (*of sun etc.*) восхо́д. **riser** *n*: **he is an early** ~ он ра́но встаёт. **rising** *n* (*revolt*) восста́ние.

risk *n* риск; *vt* рискова́ть *impf*, рискну́ть *pf* +*instr*. **risky** *adj* риско́ванный.

risqué adj непристо́йный.

rite *n* обря́д. **ritual** *n* ритуа́л; *adj* ритуа́льный.

rival *n* сопе́рник, -ица; *adj* сопе́рничающий; *vt* сопе́рничать *c+instr*. **rivalry** *n* сопе́рничество.

river *n* река́. **riverside** *attrib* прибре́жный.

rivet *n* заклёпка; *vt* заклёпывать *impf*, заклепа́ть *pf*; (*fig*) прико́вывать *impf*, прикова́ть (*on* к+*dat*).

road *n* доро́га; (*street*) у́лица; ~**block** загражде́ние на доро́ге; ~**map** доро́жная ка́рта; ~ **sign** доро́жный знак. **roadside** *n* обо́чина; *attrib* придоро́жный. **roadway** *n* мостова́я *sb*.

roam *vt & i* броди́ть *impf* (по+*dat*).

roar *n* (*animal's*) рёв; *vi* реве́ть *impf*.

roast *vt & i* жа́рить(ся) *impf*, за~, из~ *pf*; *adj* жа́реный; ~ **beef** ро́стбиф; *n* жарко́е *sb*.

rob *vt* гра́бить *impf*, о~ *pf*; красть *impf*, у~ *pf* у+*gen* (*of* +*acc*); (*deprive*) лиша́ть *impf*, лиши́ть *pf* (*of* +*gen*). **robber** *n* граби́тель *m*. **robbery** *n* грабёж.

robe *n* (*also pl*) ма́нтия.

robin *n* малино́вка.

robot *n* ро́бот.

robust *adj* кре́пкий.

rock[1] *n* (*geol*) (го́рная) поро́да; (*cliff etc.*) скала́; (*large stone*) большо́й ка́мень *m*; **on the** ~**s** (*in difficulty*) на мели́; (*drink*) со льдом.

rock[2] *vt & i* кача́ть(ся) *impf*, качну́ть(ся) *pf*; *n* (*mus*) рок; ~**ing-chair** кача́лка; ~ **and roll** рок-н-ро́лл.

rockery *n* альпина́рий.

rocket *n* раке́та; *vi* подска́кивать *impf*, подскочи́ть *pf*.

rocky *adj* скали́стый; (*shaky*) ша́ткий.

rod *n* (*stick*) прут; (*bar*) сте́ржень *m*; (*fishing-*~) у́дочка.

rodent *n* грызу́н.

roe[1] *n* икра́; (*soft*) моло́ки (-ло́к) *pl*.

roe[2] (**-deer**) *n* косу́ля.

rogue *n* плут.

roll[1] *n* (*cylinder*) руло́н; (*register*) рее́стр; (*bread*) бу́лочка; ~**call** переклн́чка.

roll[2] *vt & i* ката́ть(ся) *indet*, кати́ть(ся) *det*, по~ *pf*; (~ *up*) свёртывать(ся) *impf*, сверну́ть(ся) *pf* (*vt* ~ *out* (*dough*) раска́тывать *impf*, раската́ть *pf*; *vi* (*sound*) греме́ть *impf*; ~ **over**

перевора́чиваться *impf*, переверну́ться *pf*; *n* (*of drums*) бараба́нная дробь; (*of thunder*) раска́т.

roller *n* (*small*) ро́лик; (*large*) като́к; (*for hair*) бигуди́ *neut indecl*; ~**skates** коньки́ *m pl* на ро́ликах.

rolling *adj* холми́стый; ~**pin** ска́лка. ~**stock** подвижно́й соста́в.

Roman *n* ри́млянин, -я́нка; *adj* ри́мский; (*in phrases*) *n* ~ **Catholic** (*n*) като́лик, -и́чка; (*adj*) ри́мско-католи́ческий.

romance *n* (*tale*; *love affair*) рома́н; (*quality*) рома́нтика. **Romanesque** *adj* рома́нский. **Romania** *n* Румы́ния. **Romanian** *n* румы́н, ~ка; *adj* румы́нский.

romantic *adj* романти́чный, -ческий. **romanticism** *n* романти́зм.

romp *vi* вози́ться *impf*.

roof *n* кры́ша; ~ **of the mouth** нёбо; *vt* крыть *impf*, покры́ть *pf*.

rook[1] *n* (*chess*) ладья́.

rook[2] *n* (*bird*) грач.

room *n* ко́мната; (*in hotel*) но́мер; (*space*) ме́сто. **roomy** *adj* просто́рный.

roost *n* насе́ст.

root[1] *n* ко́рень *m*; **take** ~ укореня́ться *impf*, укорени́ться *pf*; *vi* пуска́ть *impf*, пусти́ть *pf* ко́рни; ~ **out** вырыва́ть *impf*, вы́рвать *pf* с ко́рнем; ~**ed to the spot** прико́ванный к ме́сту.

root[2] *vi* (*rummage*) ры́ться *impf*; ~ **for** боле́ть *impf* за +*acc*.

rope *n* верёвка; ~**ladder** верёвочная ле́стница; *vt*: ~ **in** (*enlist*) втя́гивать *impf*,

втяну́ть *pf*; ~ **off** о(т)гора́живать *impf*, о(т)городи́ть *pf* верёвкой.

rosary *n* чётки (-ток) *pl*.

rose *n* ро́за; (*nozzle*) се́тка.

rosemary *n* розмари́н.

rosette *n* розе́тка.

rosewood *n* ро́зовое де́рево.

roster *n* расписа́ние дежу́рств.

rostrum *n* трибу́на.

rosy *adj* ро́зовый; (*cheeks*) румя́ный.

rot *n* гниль; (*nonsense*) вздор; *vi* гнить *impf*, с~ *pf*; *vt* гнои́ть *impf*, с~ *pf*.

rota *n* расписа́ние дежу́рств.

rotary *adj* враща́тельный, ротацио́нный. **rotate** *vt & i* враща́ть(ся) *impf*. **rotation** *n* враще́ние; **in** ~ по о́череди.

rote *n*: **by** ~ наизу́сть.

rotten *adj* гнило́й; (*fig*) отврати́тельный.

rotund *adj* (*round*) кру́глый; (*plump*) по́лный.

rouble *n* рубль *m*.

rough *adj* (*uneven*) неро́вный; (*coarse*) грубый; (*sea*) бу́рный; (*approximate*) приблизи́тельный; ~ **copy** черновик; **the** ~ **it** жить *impf* без удобств. **roughage** *n* грубая пища. **roughly** *adv* грубо; (*approximately*) приблизи́тельно.

roulette *n* руле́тка.

round *adj* кру́глый; ~**shouldered** суту́лый; *n* (*object*) круг; (*circuit*; *also pl*) обхо́д; (*sport*) тур, ра́унд; (*series*) ряд; (*ammunition*) патро́н; (*of applause*) взрыв; *adv* вокру́г; (*in a circle*) по кру́гу; **all** ~ кругом; **all the year** ~ кру́глый год; *prep* вокру́г+*gen*; кругом+*gen*; по+*dat*; ~ **the**

corner (*motion*) зá угол, (*position*) за углóм; *vt* (*go ~*) огибáть *impf*, обогнýть *pf*; **~ off** (*complete*) завершáть *impf*, завершить *pf*; **~ up** сгонять *impf*, согнáть *pf*; **~ up** загóн; (*raid*) облáва.

roundabout *n* (*merry-go-round*) карусéль; (*road junction*) кольцевáя трáнспортная развязка; *adj* окóльный.

rouse *vt* будить *impf*, разбудить *pf*; (*to action etc.*) побуждáть *impf*, побудить *pf* (**to** +*dat*). **rousing** *adj* востóрженный.

rout *n* (*defeat*) разгрóм.

route *n* маршрýт, путь *m*.

routine *n* заведённый порядок, режим; *adj* установленный; очередной.

rove *vi* скитáться *impf*.

row[1] *n* (*line*) ряд.

row[2] *vi* (*in boat*) грести *impf*.

row[3] *n* (*dispute*) ссóра; (*noise*) шум; *vi* ссóриться *impf*, по~ *pf*.

rowdy *adj* буйный.

royal *adj* королéвский; (*majestic*) великолéпный. **royalist** *n* роялист; *adj* роялистский. **royalty** *n* член, члены *pl* королéвской семьи; (*fee*) áвторский гонорáр.

rub *vt & i* терéть(ся) *impf*; (*polish; chafe*) натирáть *impf*, натерéть *pf*; (**~ dry**) вытирáть *impf*, вытереть *pf*; **~ in, on** втирáть *impf*, втерéть *pf*; **~ out** стирáть *impf*, стерéть *pf*; **~ it in** растрáвливать *impf*, растравить *pf* рáну.

rubber *n* резина; (*eraser, also* **~ band**) резинка; *attrib* резиновый; **~-stamp** (*fig*) штамповáть *impf*.

rubbish *n* мýсор; (*nonsense*) чепухá.

rubble *n* щéбень *m*.

rubella *n* краснýха.

ruby *n* рубин.

ruck *vt* (**~ up**) мять *impf*, из~, с~ *pf*.

rucksack *n* рюкзáк.

rudder *n* руль *m*.

ruddy *adj* (*face*) румяный; (*damned*) проклятый.

rude *adj* грýбый. **rudeness** *n* грýбость.

rudimentary *adj* рудиментáрный. **rudiments** *n* *pl* основы *f* *pl*.

rueful *adj* печáльный.

ruff *n* (*frill*) брыжи (-жéй) *pl*; (*of feathers, hair*) кольцó (пéрьев, шéрсти) вокрýг шéи.

ruffian *n* хулигáн.

ruffle *n* обóрка; *vt* (*hair*) ерóшить *impf*, взъ~ *pf*; (*water*) рябить *impf*; (*person*) смущáть *impf*, смутить *pf*.

rug *n* (*mat*) ковёр; (*wrap*) плед.

rugby *n* рéгби *neut indecl*.

rugged *adj* (*rocky*) скалистый.

ruin *n* (*downfall*) гибель *f*; (*building, ruins*) развáлины *pl*, руины *f* *pl*; *vt* губить *impf*, по~ *pf*. **ruinous** *adj* губительный.

rule *n* прáвило; (*for measuring*) линéйка; (*government*) правлéние; **as a ~** как прáвило; *vt & i* прáвить *impf* (+*instr*); (*decree*) постановлять *impf*, постановить *pf*; **~ out** исключáть *impf*, исключить *pf*. **ruled** *adj* линóванный. **ruler** *n* (*person*) правитель *m*, ~ница; (*object*) линéйка. **ruling** *n* (*of court etc.*) постановлéние.

rum *n* (*drink*) ром.

Rumania(n) see **Romania(n)**

rumble vi громыха́ть impf; n громыха́ние.

ruminant n жва́чное (живо́тное) sb. **ruminate** vi (fig) размышля́ть impf (**over, on** o+prep).

rummage vi ры́ться impf.

rumour n слух; vt: **it is ~ed that** хо́дят слу́хи (pl), что.

rump n крестец; **~ steak** ромште́кс.

rumple vt мять impf, из~, с~ pf; (hair) еро́шить impf, взъ~ pf.

run vi бе́гать indet, бежа́ть det, по~ pf; (work, of machines) рабо́тать impf; (of bus etc.) ходи́ть indet, идти́ det; (seek election) выставля́ть impf, вы́ставить pf свою́ кандидату́ру; (of play etc.) идти́ impf; (of ink, dye) расплыва́ться impf, расплы́ться pf; (flow) течь impf; (of document) гласи́ть impf; vt (manage; operate) управля́ть impf +instr; (a business etc.) вести́ impf; **~ dry, low** исса́кать impf, исся́кнуть pf; **~ risks** рискова́ть impf; **~ across, into** (meet) встреча́ться impf, встре́титься pf с+instr; **~ away** (flee) убега́ть impf, убежа́ть pf; **~ down** (knock down) задави́ть pf; (disparage) принижа́ть impf, прини́зить pf; **be ~ down** (of person) переутоми́ться pf (in past tense); **~down** (decayed) запу́щенный; **~ in** (engine) обка́тывать impf, обка́тать pf; **~ into** see **~ across**; **~ out** конча́ться impf, ко́нчиться pf; **~ out of** истоща́ть impf, истощи́ть pf свой запа́с +gen; **~ over** (glance over)

бе́гло просма́тривать impf, просмотре́ть pf; (injure) задави́ть pf; **~ through** (pierce) прока́лывать impf, проколо́ть pf; (money) прома́тывать impf, промота́ть pf; (review) повторя́ть impf, повтори́ть pf; **~ to** (reach) (of money) хвата́ть impf, хвати́ть pf impers+gen на+acc: **the money won't ~ to a car** э́тих де́нег не хва́тит на маши́ну; **~ up against** ната́лкиваться impf, натолкну́ться pf на+acc; n бег; (sport) перебе́жка; (journey) пое́здка; (period) полоса́; **at a ~** бего́м; **on the ~** в бега́х; **~ on** большо́й спрос на+acc; **in the long ~** в конце́ концо́в.

rung n ступе́нька.

runner n (also tech) бегу́н; (of sledge) по́лоз; (bot) побе́г; **~ bean** фасо́ль; **~up** уча́стник, заня́вший второ́е ме́сто. **running** n бег; (management) управле́ние (of +instr); **be in the ~** име́ть impf ша́нсы; adj бегу́щий; (of~) бегово́й; (after pl n, in succession) подря́д; **~ commentary** репорта́ж; **~ water** водопрово́д. **runway** n взлётно-поса́дочная полоса́.

rupee n ру́пия.

rupture n разры́в; vt & i прорыва́ть(ся) impf, прорва́ть(ся) pf.

rural adj се́льский.

ruse n уло́вка.

rush[1] n (bot) тростни́к.

rush[2] vt & i (hurry) торопи́ть(ся) impf, по~ pf; vi (dash) броса́ться impf, бро́ситься pf; (of water) нести́сь impf, по~ pf; vt (to hospital etc.) умча́ть pf; n (of blood etc.) прили́в; (hurry) спе́шка; **be**

in a ~ торопи́ться *impf*; ~-hour(s) час(ы́) *m pl* пик.

Russia *n* Росси́я. **Russian** *sb*; *adj (of ~ nationality, culture)* ру́сский; *(of ~ State)* росси́йский.

rust *n* ржа́вчина; *vi* ржаве́ть *impf*, за~, по~ *pf*.

rustic *adj* дереве́нский.

rustle *n* ше́лест, шо́рох, шурша́ние; *vi & t* шелесте́ть *impf* (+*instr*); ~ **up** раздобыва́ть *impf*; раздобы́ть *pf*.

rusty *adj* ржа́вый.

rut *n* колея́.

ruthless *adj* безжа́лостный.

rye *n* рожь; *attrib* ржаной.

S

Sabbath *n (Jewish)* суббо́та; *(Christian)* воскресе́нье. **sabbatical** *n* годи́чный о́тпуск.

sable *n* со́боль.

sabotage *n* диве́рсия; *vt* саботи́ровать *impf & pf*. **saboteur** *n* диверса́нт.

sabre *n* са́бля.

sachet *n* упако́вка.

sack¹ *vt (plunder)* разгра́бить *pf*.

sack² *n* мешо́к; *(dismissal)*: **get the ~** быть уво́ленным; *vt* увольня́ть *impf*, уво́лить *pf*. **sacking** *n (hessian)* мешкови́на.

sacrament *n* та́инство; *(Eucharist)* прича́стие. **sacred** *adj* свяще́нный, свято́й. **sacrifice** *n* же́ртва; *vt* же́ртвовать *impf*, по~ *pf* +*instr*. **sacrilege** *n* святота́тство. **sacrosanct** *adj* свяще́нный.

sad *adj* печа́льный, гру́стный. **sadden** *vt* печа́лить *impf*, о~ *pf*.

saddle *n* седло́; *vt* седла́ть *impf*, о~ *pf*; *(burden)* обременя́ть *impf*, обремени́ть *pf* (**with** +*instr*).

sadism *n* сади́зм. **sadist** *n* сади́ст. **sadistic** *adj* сади́стский.

sadness *n* печа́ль, грусть.

safe *n* сейф; *adj (unharmed)* невреди́мый; *(out of danger)* в безопа́сности; *(secure)* безопа́сный; *(reliable)* надёжный; **~ and sound** цел и невреди́м. **safeguard** *n* предохрани́тельная ме́ра; *vt* предохраня́ть *impf*, предохрани́ть *pf*. **safety** *n* безопа́сность; **~-belt** реме́нь *m* безопа́сности; **~ pin** англи́йская була́вка; **~-valve** предохрани́тельный кла́пан.

sag *vi (of rope, curtain)* провиса́ть *impf*, прови́снуть *pf*; *(of ceiling)* прогиба́ться *impf*, прогну́ться *pf*.

saga *n* са́га.

sage¹ *n (herb)* шалфе́й.

sage² *n (person)* мудре́ц; *adj* му́дрый.

Sagittarius *n* Стреле́ц.

sail *n* па́рус; *vt (a ship)* управля́ть *impf* +*instr*; *vi* пла́вать *indet*, плыть *det*; *(depart)* отплыва́ть *impf*, отплы́ть *pf*. **sailing** *n (sport)* па́русный спорт; **~-ship** па́русное су́дно. **sailor** *n* матро́с, моря́к.

saint *n* свято́й *sb*. **saintly** *adj* свято́й.

sake *n*: **for the ~ of** ра́ди+*gen*.

salad *n* сала́т; **~-dressing** припра́ва к сала́ту.

salami *n* саля́ми *f indecl*.

salary *n* жа́лованье.

sale *n* прода́жа; *(also amount sold)* сбыт *(no pl)*; *(with reduced prices)* распрода́жа; **be**

for ~ продава́ться *impf*. **saleable** *adj* хо́дкий. **salesman** *n* продаве́ц. **saleswoman** *n* продавщи́ца.

salient *adj* основно́й.

saliva *n* слюна́.

sallow *adj* желтова́тый.

salmon *n* лосо́сь *m*.

salon *n* сало́н. **saloon** *n* (*on ship*) сало́н; (*car*) седа́н; (*bar*) бар.

salt *n* соль; ~**cellar** соло́нка; ~ **water** морска́я вода́; ~ **water** морско́й; (*fig*) солёный; *vt* соли́ть *impf*, по-~ *pf*. **salty** *adj* солёный.

salutary *adj* благотво́рный.

salute *n* отда́ча че́сти; (*with guns*) салю́т; *vt & i* отдава́ть *impf*, отда́ть *pf* честь (+*dat*).

salvage *n* спасе́ние; *vt* спаса́ть *impf*, спасти́ *pf*.

salvation *n* спасе́ние; S~ **Army** А́рмия спасе́ния.

salve *n* мазь; *vt*: ~ **one's conscience** успока́ивать *impf*, успоко́ить *pf* со́весть.

salvo *n* залп.

same *adj*: **the ~** тот же (са́мый); (*applying to both or all*) оди́н; (*identical*) одина́ковый; *pron*: **the ~** одно́ и то́ же, то же са́мое; *adv*: **the ~** таки́м же о́бразом, так же; **all the ~** всё-таки, тем не ме́нее. **sameness** *n* однообра́зие.

samovar *n* самова́р.

sample *n* образе́ц; *vt* про́бовать *impf*, по-~ *pf*.

sanatorium *n* санато́рий.

sanctify *vt* освяща́ть *impf*, освяти́ть *pf*. **sanctimonious** *adj* ха́нжеский. **sanction** *n* са́нкция; *vt* санкциони́ровать *impf & pf*. **sanctity** *n* (*holiness*) свя́тость; (*sacred-*

ness) свяще́нность. **sanctuary** *n* святи́лище; (*refuge*) убе́жище; (*for wild life*) запове́дник.

sand *n* песо́к; *vt* (~ **down**) шку́рить *impf*, по-~ *pf*; ~ **dune** дю́на.

sandal *n* санда́лия.

sandalwood *n* санда́ловое де́рево.

sandbank *n* о́тмель.

sandpaper *n* шку́рка; *vt* шлифова́ть *impf*, от-~ *pf* шку́ркой.

sandstone *n* песча́ник.

sandwich *n* бутербро́д; *vt*: ~ **between** втя́скивать *impf*, втя́снуть *pf* ме́жду+*instr*.

sandy *adj* (*of sand*) песча́ный; (*like sand*) песо́чный; (*hair*) рыжева́тый.

sane *adj* норма́льный; (*sensible*) разу́мный.

sang-froid *n* самооблада́ние.

sanguine *adj* оптимисти́ческий.

sanitary *adj* санита́рный; гигиени́ческий; ~ **towel** гигиени́ческая поду́шка. **sanitation** *n* (*conditions*) санита́рные усло́вия *neut pl*; (*system*) водопрово́д и канализа́ция.

sanity *n* психи́ческое здоро́вье; (*good sense*) здра́вый смысл.

sap *n* (*bot*) сок; *vt* (*exhaust*) истоща́ть *impf*, истощи́ть *pf*.

sapling *n* са́женец.

sapphire *n* сапфи́р.

sarcasm *n* сарка́зм. **sarcastic** *adj* саркасти́ческий.

sardine *n* сарди́на.

sardonic *adj* сардони́ческий.

sash[1] *n* (*scarf*) куша́к. **sash**[2] *n* (*frame*) скользя́щая ра́ма; ~-**window** подъёмное окно́.

satanic adj сатани́нский.

satchel n ра́нец, су́мка.

satellite n спу́тник, сателли́т (also fig); ~ **dish** параболи́ческая анте́нна; таре́лка (coll); ~ **TV** спу́тниковое телеви́дение.

satiate vt насыща́ть impf, насы́тить pf.

satin n атла́с.

satire n сати́ра. **satirical** adj сатири́ческий. **satirist** n сати́рик. **satirize** vt высме́ивать impf, вы́смеять pf.

satisfaction n удовлетворе́ние. **satisfactory** adj удовлетвори́тельный. **satisfy** vt удовлетворя́ть impf, удовлетвори́ть pf; (hunger, curiosity) утоля́ть impf, утоли́ть pf.

saturate vt насыща́ть impf, насы́тить pf; **I got ~d** (by rain) я промо́к до ни́тки. **saturation** n насыще́ние.

Saturday n суббо́та.

sauce n (cul); (cheek) на́глость. **saucepan** n кастрю́ля. **saucer** n блю́дце. **saucy** adj на́глый.

Saudi n сау́довец, -вка; adj сау́довский. **Saudi Arabia** n Сау́довская Ара́вия.

sauna n фи́нская ба́ня.

saunter vi прогу́ливаться impf.

sausage n соси́ска; (salami-type) колбаса́.

savage adj ди́кий; (fierce) свире́пый; (cruel) жесто́кий; n дика́рь m; vt иска́лечить pf. **savagery** n ди́кость; жесто́кость.

save vt (rescue) спаса́ть impf, спасти́ pf; (money) копи́ть impf, на~ pf; (put aside, keep) бере́чь impf; (avoid using) эконо́мить impf, с~ pf; vi: ~

up копи́ть impf, на~ pf де́ньги. **savings** n pl сбереже́ния neut pl; ~ **bank** сберега́тельная ка́сса. **saviour** n спаси́тель m.

savour vt смакова́ть impf. **savoury** adj пика́нтный; (fig) поря́дочный.

saw n пила́; vt пили́ть impf; ~ **up** распи́ливать impf, распили́ть pf. **sawdust** n опи́лки (-лок) pl.

saxophone n саксофо́н.

say vt говори́ть impf, сказа́ть pf; **to ~ nothing of** не говоря́ уже́ о+prep; **that is to** ~ то есть; (let us) ~ ска́жем; **it is said (that)** говоря́т; n (opinion) мне́ние; (influence) влия́ние; **have one's ~** вы́сказаться pf. **saying** n погово́рка.

scab n (on wound) струп; (polit) штрейкбре́хер.

scabbard n но́жны (gen -жен) pl.

scaffold n эшафо́т. **scaffolding** n леса́ (-со́в) pl.

scald vt обва́ривать impf, обвари́ть pf.

scale n (ratio) масшта́б; (grading) шкала́; (mus) га́мма; vt (climb) взбира́ться impf, взобра́ться pf на+acc; ~ **down** понижа́ть impf, пони́зить pf.

scales[1] n pl (of fish) чешуя́ (collect).

scales[2] n pl весы́ (-со́в) pl.

scallop n гребешо́к; (decoration) фесто́н.

scalp n ко́жа головы́.

scalpel n ска́льпель m.

scaly adj чешу́йчатый; (of boiler etc.) покры́тый на́кипью.

scamper vi бы́стро бе́гать impf; (frolic) резви́ться impf.

scan vt & i (verse) скандировать(ся) impf; vt (intently) рассматривать impf; (quickly) просматривать impf, просмотреть pf; (med) просвечивать impf, просветить pf; n просвечивание.

scandal n скандал; (gossip) сплетни (-тен) pl. **scandalize** vt шокировать impf & pf. **scandalous** adj скандальный.

Scandinavia n Скандинавия. **Scandinavian** adj скандинавский.

scanty adj скудный.

scapegoat n козёл отпущения.

scar n шрам; vt оставлять impf, оставить pf шрам на+prep.

scarce adj дефицитный; (rare) редкий. **scarcely** adv едва. **scarcity** n дефицит; редкость.

scare vt пугать impf, ис~, на~ pf; ~ away, off отпугивать impf, отпугнуть pf; n паника. **scarecrow** n пугало.

scarf n шарф.

scarlet adj (n) алый (цвет).

scathing adj уничтожающий.

scatter vt & i рассыпать(ся) impf, рассыпать(ся) pf; (disperse) рассеивать(ся) impf, рассеять(ся) pf; ~-brained ветреный. **scattered** adj разбросанный; (sporadic) отдельный.

scavenge vi рыться impf в отбросах. **scavenger** n (person) мусорщик; (animal) животное sb, питающееся падалью.

scenario n сценарий. **scene** n (place of disaster etc.)

место; (place of action) место действия; (view) пейзаж; (picture) картина; (theat) сцена, явление; (incident) сцена; **behind the ~s** за кулисами; **make a ~** устраивать impf, устроить pf сцену. **scenery** n (theat) декорация; (landscape) пейзаж. **scenic** adj живописный.

scent n (smell) аромат; (perfume) духи (-хов) pl; (trail) след. **scented** adj душистый.

sceptic n скептик. **sceptical** adj скептический. **scepticism** n скептицизм.

schedule n (timetable) расписание; vt составлять impf, составить pf расписание +gen.

schematic adj схематический.

scheme n (plan) проект; (intrigue) махинация; vi интриговать impf.

schism n раскол.

schizophrenia n шизофрения. **schizophrenic** adj шизофренический; n шизофреник.

scholar n учёный sb; **scholarly** adj учёный. **scholarship** n учёность; (payment) стипендия.

school n школа; attrib школьный; vt (train) приучать impf, приучить pf (**to** к+dat, +inf). **school-book** n учебник. **schoolboy** n школьник. **schoolgirl** n школьница. **schooling** n обучение. **school-leaver** n выпускник, -ица. **school teacher** n учитель m, ~ница.

schooner n шхуна.

sciatica n ишиас.

science n наука; ~ **fiction** научная фантастика. **scientific** adj научный. **scientist**

n учёный *sb.*

scintillating *adj* блиста́тельный.

scissors *n pl* но́жницы (-ц) *pl.*

scoff *vi* (*mock*) смея́ться *impf* (**at** над+*instr*).

scold *vt* брани́ть *impf*, вы~ *pf.*

scoop *n* (*large*) черпа́к; (*ice-cream* ~) ло́жка для моро́женого; *vt* (~ *out, up*) вычёрпывать *impf*, вы́черпать *pf.*

scooter *n* (*motor* ~) мото-ро́ллер.

scope *n* (*range*) преде́лы *m pl*; (*chance*) возмо́жность.

scorch *vt* (*fingers*) обжига́ть *impf*, обже́чь *pf*; (*clothes*) сжига́ть *impf*, сжечь *pf.*

score *n* (*of points etc.*) счёт; (*mus*) партиту́ра; *pl* (*great numbers*) мно́жество; (*notch*) де́лать *impf*, с~ *pf* зару́бки на+*prep*; (*points etc.*) получа́ть *impf*, получи́ть *pf*; (*mus*) оркестрова́ть *impf* & *pf*; *vi* (*keep* ~) вести́ *impf*, с~ *pf* счёт. **scorer** *n* счётчик.

scorn *n* презре́ние; *vt* презира́ть *impf*, презре́ть *pf*. **scornful** *adj* презри́тельный.

Scorpio *n* Скорпио́н.

scorpion *n* скорпио́н.

Scot *n* шотла́ндец, -дка. **Scotch** *n* (*whisky*) шотла́ндское ви́ски *neut indecl.* **Scotland** *n* Шотла́ндия. **Scots, Scottish** *adj* шотла́ндский.

scoundrel *n* подле́ц.

scour[1] *vt* (*cleanse*) отчища́ть *impf*, отчи́стить *pf.*

scour[2] *vt* & *i* (*rove*) ры́скать *impf* (по+*dat*).

scourge *n* бич.

scout *n* разве́дчик; (**S**~) бой-

ска́ут; *vi*: ~ **about** разы́скивать *impf* (**for** +*acc*).

scowl *vi* хму́риться *impf*, на~ *pf*; *n* хму́рый взгляд.

scrabble *vi*: ~ **about** ры́ться *impf.*

scramble *vi* кара́бкаться *impf*, вс~ *pf*; (*struggle*) дра́ться *impf* (**for** за+*acc*); ~**d eggs** яи́чница-болту́нья.

scrap[1] *n* (*fragment etc.*) кусо́чек; *pl* оста́тки *m pl*; *pl* (*of food*) объе́дки (-ков) *pl*; ~ **metal** металло́м; *vt* сдава́ть *impf*, сдать *pf* в утиль.

scrap[2] *n* (*fight*) дра́ка; *vi* дра́ться *impf.*

scrape *vt* скрести́ *impf*; (*graze*) цара́пать *impf*, о~ *pf*; ~ **off** отскреба́ть *impf*, отскрести́ *pf*; ~ **through** (*exam*) с трудо́м выде́рживать *impf*, вы́держать *pf*; ~ **together** наскреба́ть *impf*, наскрести́ *pf.*

scratch *vt* цара́пать *impf*, о~ *pf*; *vt* & *i* (*when itching*) чеса́ть(ся) *impf*, по~ *pf*; *n* цара́пина.

scrawl *n* кара́кули *f pl*; *vt* писа́ть *impf*, на~ *pf* кара́кулями.

scrawny *adj* сухопа́рый.

scream *n* крик; *vi* крича́ть *impf*, кри́кнуть *pf.*

screech *n* визг; *vi* визжа́ть *impf.*

screen *n* ши́рма; (*cin, TV*) экра́н; *vt* (*protect*) защища́ть *impf*, защити́ть *pf*; (*hide*) укрыва́ть *impf*, укры́ть *pf*; (*show film etc.*) демонстри́ровать *impf* & *pf*; (*check on*) проверя́ть *impf*, прове́рить *pf*; ~ **off** отгора́живать *impf*, отгороди́ть *pf* ши́рмой.

screw n винт; vt (~ on) привинчивать impf, привинтить pf; (~ up) завинчивать impf, завинтить pf; (crumple) комкать impf, с~ pf; ~ up one's eyes щуриться impf, со~ pf. **screwdriver** n отвёртка.

scribble vt строчить impf, на~ pf; n карáкули f pl.

script n (of film etc.) сценáрий; (of speech etc.) текст; (writing system) письмо; ~writer n сценарист. **Scripture** n священное писание.

scroll n свиток; (design) завиток.

scrounge vt (cadge) стрелять impf, стрельнуть pf; vi попрошайничать impf.

scrub[1] n (brushwood) кустáрник; (area) зáросли f pl.

scrub[2] vt мыть impf, вы~ pf щёткой.

scruff n: by the ~ of the neck за шиворот.

scruffy adj обóрванный.

scrum n схвáтка вокрýг мячá.

scruple n (also pl) колебáния neut pl; угрызéния neut pl сóвести. **scrupulous** adj скрупулёзный.

scrutinize vt рассмáтривать impf. **scrutiny** n рассмотрéние.

scuffed adj поцарáпанный.

scuffle n потасóвка.

sculpt vt вая́ть impf, из~ pf. **sculptor** n скýльптор. **sculpture** n скульптýра.

scum n нáкипь.

scurrilous adj непристóйный.

scurry vi поспéшно бéгать indet, бежáть impf.

scuttle[1] n (coal ~) ведёрко для угля́.

scuttle[2] vi (run away) удирáть impf, удрáть pf.

scythe n косá.

sea n мóре; attrib морскóй; ~ front нáбережная sb; ~-gull чáйка; ~-level ýровень m мóря; ~-lion морскóй лев; ~-shore побережье. **seaboard** n побережье. **seafood** n продýкты n pl мóря.

seal[1] n (on document etc.) печáть; vt скрепля́ть impf, скрепить pf печáтью; (close) запечáтывать impf, запечáтать pf; ~ up заде́лывать impf, задéлать pf

seal[2] n (zool) тюлéнь m; (fur~) кóтик.

seam n шов; (geol) пласт.

seaman n моря́к, матрóс.

seamless adj без швá.

seamstress n швея́.

seance n спиритический сеáнс.

seaplane n гидросамолёт.

searing adj паля́щий.

search vt обы́скивать impf, обыскáть pf; vi искáть impf (for +acc); n пóиски m pl; óбыск; ~-party пóисковая грýппа. **searching** adj (look) испы́тующий. **searchlight** n прожéктор.

seasick adj: I was ~ меня́ укачáло. **seaside** n бéрег мóря.

season n сезóн; (one of four) врéмя neut гóда; ~ ticket сезóнный билéт; vt (flavour) приправля́ть impf, припрáвить pf. **seasonable** adj по сезóну; (timely) своеврéменный. **seasonal** adj сезóнный. **seasoning** n припрáва.

seat n (place) мéсто; (of chair) сиде́нье; (chair) стул; (bench) скамéйка; (of trousers) зад; ~ belt привязнóй ремéнь m pl.

vt сажа́ть *impf*, посади́ть *pf*; *(of room etc.)* вмеща́ть *impf*, вмести́ть *pf*; **be ~ed** сади́ться *impf*, сесть *pf*.

seaweed *n* морска́я во́доросль.

secateurs *n pl* сека́тор.

secede *vi* отка́лываться *impf*, отколо́ться *pf*. **secession** *n* отко́л.

secluded *adj* укро́мный. **seclusion** *n* укро́мность.

second[1] *adj* второ́й; **~-class** второкла́ссный; **~-hand** поде́ржанный; *(of information)* из вторы́х рук; **~-rate** второразря́дный; **~ sight** ясновиде́ние; on **~** thoughts взве́сив всё ещё раз; have **~ thoughts** переду́мать *impf*, переду́мать *pf (about* +*acc)*; *n* второ́е *sb*; *(time)* секу́нда; *pl (comm)* това́р второ́го со́рта; **~ hand** *(of clock)* секу́ндная стре́лка; *vt (support)* подде́рживать *impf*, поддержа́ть *pf*; *(transfer)* откомандиро́вывать *impf* откомандирова́ть *impf* **secondary** *adj* втори́чный, второстепе́нный; *(education)* сре́дний. **secondly** *adv* во-вторы́х.

secrecy *n* секре́тность. **secret** *n* та́йна, секре́т; *adj* та́йный, секре́тный; *(hidden)* потайно́й.

secretarial *adj* секрета́рский. **secretariat** *n* секретариа́т. **secretary** *n* секрета́рь *m*, -рша; *(minister)* мини́стр.

secrete *vt (conceal)* укрыва́ть *impf*, укры́ть *pf*; *(med)* выделя́ть *impf*, вы́делить *pf*. **secretion** *n* укрыва́ние; *(med)* выделе́ние.

secretive *adj* скры́тный.

sect *n* се́кта. **sectarian** *adj* секта́нтский.

section *n* се́кция; *(of book)* разде́л; *(geom)* сече́ние. **sector** *n* се́ктор.

secular *adj* све́тский. **secularization** *n* секуляриза́ция.

secure *adj (safe)* безопа́сный; *(firm)* надёжный; *(emotionally)* уве́ренный; *vt (fasten)* закрепля́ть *impf*, закрепи́ть *pf*; *(guarantee)* обеспе́чивать *impf*, обеспе́чить *pf*; *(obtain)* достава́ть *impf*, доста́ть *pf*. **security** *n* безопа́сность; *(guarantee)* зало́г; *pl* це́нные бума́ги *f pl*.

sedate *adj* степе́нный.

sedation *n* успокое́ние. **sedative** *n* успока́ивающее сре́дство.

sedentary *adj* сидя́чий.

sediment *n* оса́док.

seduce *vt* соблазня́ть *impf*, соблазни́ть *pf*. **seduction** *n* обольще́ние. **seductive** *adj* соблазни́тельный.

see *vt & i* ви́деть *impf*, у~ *pf*; *vt (watch, look)* смотре́ть *impf*, по~ *pf*; *(find out)* узнава́ть *impf*, узна́ть *pf*; *(understand)* понима́ть *impf*, поня́ть *pf*; *(meet)* ви́деться *impf*, у~ *pf* с+*instr*; *(imagine)* представля́ть *impf*, предста́вить *pf* себе́; *(escort,* **~ off)** провожа́ть *impf*, проводи́ть *pf*; **~ about** *(attend to)* забо́титься *impf*, по~ *pf* о+*prep*; **~ through** *(fig)* ви́деть *impf*, наскво́зь+*acc*.

seed *n* се́мя *neut*. **seedling** *n* се́янец; *pl* расса́да. **seedy** *adj (shabby)* потрёпанный.

seeing (that) *conj* ввиду́ того́, что.

seek *vt* иска́ть *impf* +*acc, gen*.

seem vi каза́ться impf, по~ pf (+instr). **seemingly** adv по-ви́димому.

seemly adj прили́чный.

seep vi проса́чиваться impf, просочи́ться pf.

seethe vi кипе́ть impf, вс~ pf.

segment n отре́зок; (of orange etc.) до́лька; (geom) сегме́нт.

segregate vt отделя́ть impf, отдели́ть pf. **segregation** n сегрега́ция.

seismic adj сейсми́ческий.

seize vt хвата́ть impf, схвати́ть pf; vi: ~ up заеда́ть impf, зае́сть pf impers+acc; ~ upon ухва́тываться impf, ухвати́ться pf за+acc. **seizure** n захва́т; (med) припа́док.

seldom adv ре́дко.

select adj и́збранный; vt отбира́ть impf, отобра́ть pf. **selection** n (choice) вы́бор. **selective** adj разбо́рчивый.

self n со́бственное «я» neut indecl.

self- in comb само-; ~absorbed эгоцентри́чный; ~assured самоуве́ренный; ~catering (accommodation) жилье́ с ку́хней; ~centred эгоцентри́чный; ~confessed открове́нный; ~confidence самоуве́ренность; ~confident само-уве́ренный; ~conscious засте́нчивый; ~contained (person) незави́симый; (flat etc.) отде́льный; ~control самооблада́ние; ~defence самозащи́та; ~denial самоотрече́ние; ~determination самоопределе́ние; ~effacing скро́мный; ~employed person незави́симый предпринима́тель m; ~esteem

самоуваже́ние; ~evident очеви́дный; ~governing самоуправля́ющий; ~help самопо́мощь; ~importance самомне́ние; ~imposed доброво́льный; ~indulgent избало́ванный; ~interest со́бственный интере́с; ~pity жа́лость к себе́; ~portrait автопортре́т; ~preservation самосохране́ние; ~reliance самостоя́тельность; ~respect самоуваже́ние; ~righteous adj ха́нжеский; ~sacrifice самопоже́ртвование; ~satisfied самодово́льный; ~service самообслу́живание (attrib in gen after n); ~styled самозва́нный; ~sufficient самостоя́тельный.

selfish adj эгоисти́чный. **selfless** adj самоотве́рженный.

sell vt & i продава́ть(ся) impf, прода́ть(ся) pf; vt (deal in) торгова́ть impf +instr; ~ out распродава́ть impf, распрода́ть pf. **seller** n прода́вец. **selling** n прода́жа. **sell-out** n: the play was a ~ пье́са прошла́ с аншла́гом.

Sellotape n (propr) ли́пкая ле́нта.

semantic adj семанти́ческий. **semantics** n сема́нтика.

semblance n ви́димость.

semen n се́мя neut.

semi- in comb полу-; ~detached house дом, разделён-ный о́бщей стено́й. **semibreve** n це́лая но́та. **semicircle** n полукру́г. **semicircular** adj полукру́глый. **semicolon** n то́чка с запято́й. **semiconductor** n полупроводни́к. **semifinal** n полуфина́л.

seminar n семина́р. **seminary**

n семина́рия.

semiquaver *n* шестна́дцатая но́та.

semitone *n* полуто́н.

senate *n* сена́т; (*univ*) сове́т. **senator** *n* сена́тор.

send *vt* посыла́ть *impf*, посла́ть *pf* (**for** за+*instr*); ~ **off** отправля́ть *impf*, отпра́вить *pf*; ~**off** про́воды (-дов) *pl*. **sender** *n* отправи́тель *m*.

senile *adj* ста́рческий. **senility** *n* ста́рческое слабоу́мие.

senior *adj* (*n*) ста́рший (*sb*); ~ **citizen** стари́к, стару́ха. **seniority** *n* старшинство́.

sensation *n* сенса́ция; (*feeling*) ощуще́ние. **sensational** *adj* сенсацио́нный.

sense *n* чу́вство; (*good* ~) здра́вый смысл; (*meaning*) смысл; *pl* (*sanity*) ум; *vt* чу́вствовать *impf*. **senseless** *adj* бессмы́сленный.

sensibility *n* чувстви́тельность; *pl* самолю́бие. **sensible** *adj* благоразу́мный. **sensitive** *adj* чувстви́тельный; (*touchy*) оби́дчивый. **sensitivity** *n* чувстви́тельность.

sensory *adj* чувстви́тельный.

sensual, sensuous *adj* чу́вственный.

sentence *n* (*gram*) предложе́ние; (*law*) пригово́р; *vt* пригова́ривать *impf*, приговори́ть *pf* (**to** к+*dat*).

sentiment *n* (*feeling*) чу́вство; (*opinion*) мне́ние. **sentimental** *adj* сентимента́льный. **sentimentality** *n* сентимента́льность.

sentry *n* часово́й *sb*.

separable *adj* отдели́мый. **separate** *adj* отде́льный; *vt* & *i* отделя́ть(ся) *impf*, отдели́ть(ся) *pf*. **separation** *n* отделе́ние. **separatism** *n* сепарати́зм. **separatist** *n* сепарати́ст.

September *n* сентя́брь *m*; *adj* сентя́брьский.

septic *adj* септи́ческий.

sepulchre *n* моги́ла.

sequel *n* (*result*) после́дствие; (*continuation*) продолже́ние.

sequence *n* после́довательность; ~ **of events** ход собы́тий.

sequester *vt* секвестрова́ть *impf* & *pf*.

serenade *n* серена́да.

serene *adj* споко́йный. **serenity** *n* споко́йствие.

serf *n* крепостно́й *sb*. **serfdom** *n* крепостно́е пра́во.

sergeant *n* сержа́нт.

serial *adj*: ~ **number** сери́йный но́мер; *n* (*story*) рома́н с продолже́нием; (*broadcast*) сери́йная постано́вка. **serialize** *vt* ста́вить *impf*, по-~ *pf* в не́сколько частя́х.

series *n* (*succession*) ряд; (*broadcast*) се́рия переда́ч.

serious *adj* серьёзный. **seriousness** *n* серьёзность.

sermon *n* про́поведь.

serpent *n* змея́.

serrated *adj* зазу́бренный.

serum *n* сы́воротка.

servant *n* слуга́ *m*, служа́нка. **serve** *vt* служи́ть *impf*, по-~ *pf* +*dat* (**as, for** +*instr*); (*attend to*) обслу́живать *impf*, обслужи́ть *pf*; (*food; ball*) подава́ть *impf*, пода́ть *pf*; (*sentence*) отбыва́ть *impf*, отбы́ть *pf*;

(*writ etc.*) вруча́ть *impf*, вручи́ть *pf* (on +*dat*); *vi* (*be suitable*) годи́ться (**for** на +*acc*, для+*gen*); (*sport*) подава́ть *impf*, пода́ть *pf* мяч; **it ~s him right** подело́м *pf* (*dat*). **service** *n* (*act of serving*; *branch of public work*; *eccl*) слу́жба; (*quality of ~*) обслу́живание; (*of car etc.*) техобслу́живание; (*set of dishes*) серви́з; (*sport*) пода́ча; (*transport*) сообще́ние; **at your ~** к ва́шим услу́гам; *vt* (*car*) проводи́ть *impf*, провести́ *pf* техобслу́живание +*gen*; **~ charge** пла́та за обслу́живание; **~ station** ста́нция обслу́живания. **serviceable** *adj* (*useful*) поле́зный; (*durable*) про́чный. **serviceman** *n* военнослу́жащий *sb*. **serviette** *n* салфе́тка. **servile** *adj* рабо́лепный. **session** *n* заседа́ние, се́ссия. **set**[1] *vt* (*put*; **~ clock, trap**) ста́вить *impf*, по- *pf*; (*table*) накрыва́ть *impf*, накры́ть *pf*; (*bone*) вправля́ть *impf*, впра́вить *pf*; (*hair*) укла́дывать *impf*, уложи́ть *pf*; (*gem*) оправля́ть *impf*, опра́вить *pf*; (*bring into state*) приводи́ть *impf*, привести́ *pf* (**in, to** в+*acc*); (*example*) подава́ть *impf*, пода́ть *pf*; (*task*) задава́ть *impf*, зада́ть *pf*; *vi* (*solidify*) тверде́ть *impf*, за- *pf*; застыва́ть *impf*, засты́-(ну)ть *pf*; (*sun etc.*) заходи́ть *impf*, зайти́ *pf*; сади́ться *impf*, сесть *pf*; **~ about** (*begin*) начина́ть *impf*, нача́ть *pf*; (*attack*) напада́ть *impf*, напа́сть *pf* на+*acc*; **~ back** (*impede*) препя́тствовать *impf*, вос- *pf* +*dat*; **~ back** неуда́-

ча; **~ in** наступа́ть *impf*, наступи́ть *pf*; **~ off** (*on journey*) отправля́ться *impf*, отпра́виться *pf*; (*enhance*) оттеня́ть *impf*, оттени́ть *pf*; **~ out** (*state*) излага́ть *impf*, изложи́ть *pf*; (*on journey*) *see* **~ off**; **~ up** (*business*) осно́вывать *impf*, основа́ть *pf*. **set**[2] *n* набо́р, компле́кт; (*of dishes*) серви́з; (*radio*) приёмник; (*television*) телеви́зор; (*tennis*) сет; (*theat*) декора́ция; (*cin*) съёмочная площа́дка. **set**[3] *adj* (*established*) устано́вленный. **settee** *n* дива́н. **setting** *n* (*frame*) опра́ва; (*surroundings*) обстано́вка; (*of mechanism etc.*) устано́вка; (*of sun etc.*) захо́д. **settle** *vt* (*decide*) реша́ть *impf*, реши́ть *pf*; (*reconcile*) ула́живать *impf*, ула́дить *pf*; (*a bill etc.*) опла́чивать *impf*, оплати́ть *pf*; (*calm*) успока́ивать *impf*, успоко́ить *pf*; *vi* поселя́ться *impf*, посели́ться *pf*; (*subside*) оседа́ть *impf*, осе́сть *pf*; **~ down** уса́живаться *impf*, усе́сться *pf* (**to** за+*acc*). **settlement** *n* поселе́ние; (*agreement*) согла́шение; (*payment*) упла́та. **settler** *n* поселе́нец. **seven** *adj & n* семь; (*number 7*) семёрка. **seventeen** *adj & n* семна́дцать. **seventeenth** *adj & n* семна́дцатый. **seventh** *adj & n* седьмо́й; (*fraction*) седьма́я *sb*. **seventieth** *adj & n* семидеся́тый. **seventy** *adj & n* се́мьдесят; (*decade*) семидеся́тые го́ды (-до́в) *m pl*. **sever** *vt* (*cut off*) отреза́ть *impf*, отрéзать *pf*; (*relations*) разрывáть *impf*, разорвáть *pf*.

several *pron* (*adj*) нéсколько (+*gen*).

severance *n* разры́в; ~ **pay** выходнóе пособие.

severe *adj* стрóгий, сурóвый; (*pain, frost*) си́льный; (*illness*) тяжёлый. **severity** *n* стрóгость, суровость.

sew *vt* шить *impf*, с~ *pf*; ~ **on** пришивáть *impf*, приши́ть *pf*; ~ **up** зашивáть *impf*, заши́ть *pf*.

sewage *n* стóчные вóды *f pl*; ~**-farm** поля́ *neut pl* орошéния. **sewer** *n* стóчная трубá. **sewerage** *n* канализáция.

sewing *n* шитьё; ~**-machine** швéйная маши́на.

sex *n* (*gender*) пол; (*sexual activity*) секс; **have** ~ имéть *impf* сношéние. **sexual** *adj* половóй, сексуáльный; ~ **intercourse** половóе сношéние. **sexuality** *n* сексуáльность. **sexy** *adj* эроти́ческий.

sh *int* ти́ше!; тсс!

shabby *adj* вéтхий.

shack *n* лачýга.

shackles *n pl* окóвы (-в) *pl*.

shade *n* тень; (*of colour, meaning*) оттéнок; (*lamp-*) абажýр; **a** ~ чуть-чýть; *vt* затеня́ть *impf*, затени́ть *pf*; (*eyes etc.*) заслоня́ть *impf* (*drawing*) тушевáть *impf*, за~ *pf*. **shadow** *n* тень; *vt* (*follow*) тáйно следи́ть *impf* за+*instr*. **shadowy** *adj* тёмный. **shady** *adj* тени́стый; (*suspicious*) подозри́тельный.

shaft *n* (*of spear*) дрéвко; (*arrow*, *fig*) стрелá; (*of light*) луч; (*of cart*) оглóбля; (*axle*) вал; (*mine, lift*) шáхта.

shaggy *adj* лохмáтый.

shake *vt & i* трясти́(сь) *impf*; *vi* (*tremble*) дрожáть *impf*; *vt* (*weaken*) колебáть *impf*, по~ *pf*; (*shock*) потрясáть *impf* потрясти́ *pf*; ~ **hands** пожимáть *impf*, пожáть *pf* рýку (**with** +*dat*); ~ **one's head** покачáть *pf* головóй; ~ **off** стря́хивать *impf*, стряхнýть *pf*; (*fig*) избавля́ться *impf*, избáвиться *pf* от+*gen*. **shaky** *adj* шáткий.

shallow *adj* мéлкий; (*fig*) повéрхностный.

sham *vt & i* притворя́ться *impf*, притвори́ться *pf* +*instr*; *n* притвóрство; (*person*) притвóрщик, -ица; *adj* притвóрный.

shambles *n* хáос.

shame *n* (*guilt*) стыд; (*disgrace*) позóр; **what a** ~! как жаль!; *vt* стыди́ть *impf*, при~ *pf*. **shameful** *adj* позóрный. **shameless** *adj* бессты́дный.

shampoo *n* шампýнь *m*.

shanty[1] *n* (*hut*) хибáрка; ~ **town** трущóба.

shanty[2] *n* (*song*) матрóсская пéсня.

shape *n* фóрма; *vt* придавáть *impf*, придáть *pf* фóрму+*dat*; *vi*: ~ **up** склáдываться *impf*, сложи́ться *pf*. **shapeless** *adj* бесфóрменный. **shapely** *adj* стрóйный.

share *n* дóля; (*econ*) áкция; *vt* дели́ть *impf*, по~ *pf*; (*opinion etc.*) разделя́ть *impf*, раздели́ть *pf*. **shareholder** *n* акционéр.

shark *n* акýла.

sharp *adj* óстрый; (*steep*) крутóй; (*sudden; harsh*) рéзкий; *n* (*mus*) диéз; *adv* (*with time*)

ро́вно; (of angle) кру́то.
sharpen vt точи́ть impf, на~ pf.
shatter vt & i разбива́ть(ся) impf, разби́ть(ся) pf вдре́безги; vt (hopes etc.) разруша́ть impf, разру́шить pf.
shave vt & i бри́ть(ся) impf, по~ pf, в бритьё. **shaver** n электри́ческая бри́тва.
shawl n шаль.
sheaf n сноп; (of papers) свя́зка.
shear vt стричь impf, о~ pf. **shears** n pl но́жницы (-ц) pl.
sheath n но́жны (gen -жен) pl.
shed¹ n сара́й.
shed² vt (tears, blood, light) пролива́ть impf, проли́ть pf; (skin, clothes) сбра́сывать impf, сбро́сить pf.
sheen n блеск.
sheep n овца́. **sheepish** adj сконфу́женный. **sheepskin** n овчи́на; ~ **coat** дублёнка.
sheer adj (utter) су́щий; (textile) прозра́чный; (rock etc.) отве́сный.
sheet n (on bed) простыня́; (of glass, paper, etc.) лист.
sheikh n шейх.
shelf n по́лка.
shell n (of mollusc etc.) ра́ковина; (of tortoise) щит; (of egg, nut) скорлупа́; (of building etc.) о́стов; (explosive ~) снаря́д; vt (peas etc.) лущи́ть impf, об~ pf; (bombard) обстре́ливать impf, обстреля́ть pf.
shellfish n (mollusc) моллю́ск; (crustacean) ракообра́зное sb.
shelter n убе́жище; vt (provide with refuge) приюти́ть pf; vt & i укрыва́ть(ся) impf, укры́ть(ся) pf.

shelve¹ vt (defer) откла́дывать impf, отложи́ть pf.
shelve² vi (slope) отло́го спуска́ться impf.
shelving n (shelves) стелла́ж.
shepherd n пасту́х; vt проводи́ть impf, провести́ pf.
sherry n хе́рес.
shield n щит; vt защища́ть impf, защити́ть pf.
shift vt & i (change position) перемеща́ть(ся) impf, перемести́ть(ся) pf; (change) меня́ть(ся) impf, pf; n переме́ще́ние; переме́на; (of workers) сме́на; ~ **work** сме́нная рабо́та. **shifty** adj ско́льзкий.
shimmer vi мерца́ть impf; n мерца́ние.
shin n го́лень.
shine vi свети́ть(ся) impf; (glitter) блесте́ть impf; (excel) блиста́ть impf; (sun, eyes) сия́ть impf; vt (a light) освеща́ть impf, освети́ть pf фонарём (on +acc); n гля́нец.
shingle n (pebbles) га́лька.
shingles n опоя́сывающий лиша́й.
shiny adj блестя́щий.
ship n кора́бль m; су́дно; (transport) перевози́ть impf, перевезти́ pf; (dispatch) отправля́ть impf, отпра́вить pf. **shipbuilding** n судострои́тельство. **shipment** n (dispatch) отпра́вка; (goods) па́ртия. **shipping** n суда́ (-до́в) pl. **shipshape** adv в по́лном поря́дке. **shipwreck** n кораблекруше́ние; **be ~ed** терпе́ть impf, по~ pf кораблекруше́ние. **shipyard** n верфь.
shirk vt уви́ливать impf, увильну́ть pf от+gen.
shirt n руба́шка.

shit (*vulg*) n говно́; vi срать *impf*, по~ *pf*.

shiver vi (*tremble*) дрожа́ть *impf*; n дрожь.

shoal n (*of fish*) ста́я.

shock n (*emotional*) потрясе́ние; (*impact*) уда́р, толчо́к; (*electr*) уда́р то́ком; (*med*) шок; vt шоки́ровать *impf*. **shocking** *adj* (*outrageous*) сканда́льный; (*awful*) ужа́сный.

shoddy *adj* халту́рный.

shoe n ту́фля; vt подко́вывать *impf*, подкова́ть *pf*. **shoe-lace** n шнуро́к. **shoe-maker** n сапо́жник. **shoe-string** n: on a ~ с небольши́ми сре́дствами.

shoo int кш!; vt прогоня́ть *impf*, прогна́ть *pf*.

shoot vt & i (*discharge*) стреля́ть *impf* в+*acc* из+*gen*; at в+*acc*, по+*dat*); (*arrow*) пуска́ть *impf*, пусти́ть *pf*; (*execute*) расстре́ливать *impf*, расстреля́ть *pf*; (*hunt*) охо́титься *impf* на+*acc*; (*football*) бить *impf* (по воро́там); (*cin*) снима́ть *impf*, снять *pf* (фильм); vi (*go swiftly*) проноси́ться *impf*, пронести́сь *pf*; ~ down (*aircraft*) сбива́ть *impf*, сбить *pf*; ~ up (*grow*) бы́стро расти́ *impf*, по~ *pf*; (*prices*) подска́кивать *impf*, подскочи́ть *pf*; n (*branch*) росто́к, побе́г; (*hunt*) охо́та. **shooting** n стрельба́; (*hunting*) охо́та; ~-gallery тир.

shop n магази́н; (*workshop*) мастерска́я *sb*; ~ assistant продаве́ц, -вщи́ца; ~-lifter магази́нный вор; ~-lifting воровство́ в магази́нах;

~ steward цехово́й ста́роста m; ~-window витри́на; vi де́лать *impf*, с~ *pf* поку́пки (f *pl*). **shopkeeper** n ла́вочник. **shopper** n покупа́тель m, -ница. **shopping** n поку́пки f *pl*; go, do one's ~ де́лать *impf*, с~ *pf* поку́пки; ~ centre торго́вый центр.

shore[1] n бе́рег.

shore[2] vt: ~ up подпира́ть *impf*, подпере́ть *pf*.

short *adj* коро́ткий; (*not tall*) ни́зкого ро́ста; (*deficient*) недоста́точный; be ~ of испы́тывать *impf*, испыта́ть *pf* недоста́ток в+*prep*; (*curt*) ре́зкий; in ~ одни́м сло́вом; ~-change обсчи́тывать *impf*, обсчита́ть *pf*; ~ circuit коро́ткое замыка́ние; ~ cut коро́ткий путь m; ~ list оконча́тельный спи́сок; ~-list включа́ть *impf*, включи́ть *pf* в оконча́тельный спи́сок; ~-lived недолгове́чный; ~-sighted близору́кий; (*fig*) недальнови́дный; ~ story расска́з; in ~ supply дефици́тный; ~-tempered вспы́льчивый; ~-term краткосро́чный; ~-wave коротково́лновый. **shortage** n недоста́ток. **shortcoming** n недоста́ток. **shorten** vt & i укора́чивать(ся) *impf*, укороти́ть(ся) *pf*. **shortfall** n дефици́т. **shorthand** n стеногра́фия; ~ typist машини́стка-стенографи́стка. **shortly** *adv*: ~ after вско́ре (по́сле+*gen*); ~ before незадо́лго (до+*gen*). **shorts** n *pl* шо́рты (-т) *pl*.

shot n (*discharge of gun*) вы́стрел; (*pellets*) дробь; (*person*) стрело́к; (*attempt*) попы́тка; (*phot*) сни́мок;

кадр; (*sport*) (*stroke*) уда́р; (*throw*) бросо́к; **like a ~** немéдленно; **~-gun** дробови́к.

should *v aux* (*ought*) до́лжен (бы) +*inf:* **you ~ know that** вы должны́ зна́ть э́то что́; **I ~ be here soon** он до́лжен бы быть тут ско́ро; (*conditional*) бы +*past:* **I ~ say** я бы сказа́л(а); **I ~ like** я бы хотéл(а).

shoulder *n* плечо́; **~-blade** лопа́тка; **~-strap** бретéлька; взва́ливать *impf*, взвали́ть *pf* на пле́чи; (*fig*) брать *impf*, взять *pf* на себя́.

shout *n* крик; *vi* крича́ть *impf*, кри́кнуть *pf;* **~ down** перекри́кивать *impf*, перекрича́ть *pf.*

shove *n* толчо́к; *vt & i* толка́ть(ся) *impf*, толкну́ть *pf;* **~ off** (*coll*) убира́ться *impf*, убра́ться *pf.*

shovel *n* лопа́та; *vt* (**~ up**) сгреба́ть *impf*, сгрести́ *pf.*

show *vt* пока́зывать *impf*, показа́ть *pf;* (*exhibit*) выставля́ть *impf*, вы́ставить *pf;* (*film etc.*) демонстри́ровать *impf*, про~ *pf;* *vi* (*also ~ up*) быть ви́дным, заме́тным; **~ off** (*vi*) привлéчь *pf* к себе́ внима́ние; **~ up** *see vi;* (*appear*) появля́ться *impf*, появи́ться *pf;* *n* (*exhibition*) вы́ставка; (*theat*) спекта́кль *m;* (*effect*) ви́димость; **~ of hands** голосова́ние подня́тием руки́; **~-case** витри́на; **~-jumping** соревнова́ние по ска́чкам; **~-room** сало́н. **showdown** *n* развя́зка.

shower *n* (*rain*) до́ждик; (*hail, fig*) град; (**~-bath**) душ; *vt* осыпа́ть *impf*, осы́пать *pf* +*instr* (**on** +*acc*); *vi* прини-

ма́ть *impf*, приня́ть *pf* душ. **showery** *adj* дождли́вый.

showpiece *n* образе́ц. **showy** *adj* показно́й.

shrapnel *n* шрапне́ль.

shred *n* клочо́к; **not a ~** ни ка́пли; *vt* мельчи́ть *impf*, из~ *pf.*

shrewd *adj* проница́тельный.

shriek *vi* визжа́ть *impf;* взви́гнуть *pf.*

shrill *adj* пронзи́тельный.

shrimp *n* креве́тка.

shrine *n* святы́ня.

shrink *vi* сади́ться *impf*, сесть *pf;* (*recoil*) отпря́нуть *pf;* *vt* вызыва́ть *impf*, вы́звать *pf* уса́дку +*gen;* **~ from** избега́ть *impf* +*gen.* **shrinkage** *n* уса́дка.

shrivel *vi* смо́рщиваться *impf*, смо́рщиться *pf.*

shroud *n* са́ван; *vt* (*fig*) оку́тывать *impf*, оку́тать *pf* (**in** +*instr*).

Shrove Tuesday вто́рник на ма́сленой неде́ле.

shrub *n* куст. **shrubbery** *n* куста́рник.

shrug *vt & i* пожима́ть *impf*, пожа́ть *pf* (плеча́ми).

shudder *n* содрога́ние; *vi* содрога́ться *impf*, содрогну́ться *pf.*

shuffle *vt & i* (*one's feet*) ша́ркать *impf* (нога́ми); *vt* (*cards*) тасова́ть *impf*, с~ *pf;* *n* тасо́вка.

shun *vt* избега́ть *impf* +*gen.*

shunt *vi* (*rly*) маневри́ровать *impf*, с~ *pf;* *vt* (*rly*) переводи́ть *impf*, перевести́ *pf* на запасно́й путь.

shut *vt & i* (*also ~ down*) закрыва́ть(ся) *impf*, закры́ть(ся) *pf;* **~ out** (*exclude*) исключа́ть *impf*, исключи́ть pf; (fence off) загора́живать impf, загороди́ть pf; (keep out) не пуска́ть impf, пусти́ть pf; ~ up (imper) заткни́сь!

shutter n ста́вень m; (phot) затво́р.

shuttle n челно́к.

shy¹ adj засте́нчивый.

shy² vi (in alarm) отпря́дывать impf, отпря́нуть pf.

Siberia n Сиби́рь. **Siberian** adj сиби́рский; n сибиря́к, -я́чка.

sick adj больно́й; be ~ (vomit) рвать impf, вы~ pf impers +acc: he was ~ его́ вы́рвало; feel ~ тошни́ть impf impers +acc; be ~ of надоеда́ть impf, надое́сть pf +nom (object) & dat (subject): I'm ~ of her она́ мне надое́ла; ~-leave о́тпуск по боле́зни. **sicken** vt вызыва́ть impf, вы́звать pf тошноту́, (disgust) отвраще́ние, y+gen; vi заболева́ть impf, заболе́ть pf. **sickening** adj отврати́тельный.

sickle n серп.

sickly adj боле́зненный; (nauseating) тошнотво́рный. **sickness** n боле́знь; (vomiting) тошнота́.

side n сторона́; (of body) бок; ~ by ~ ря́дом (with c+instr); on the ~ на стороне́; vi: ~ with встава́ть impf, встать pf на сто́рону+gen; ~-effect побо́чное де́йствие; ~-step (fig) уклоня́ться impf, уклони́ться pf от+gen; ~-track (distract) отвлека́ть impf, отвле́чь pf. **sideboard** n буфе́т; pl ба́ки (-к) pl. **sidelight** n боково́й фона́рь m. **sideline** n (work) побо́чная рабо́та. **sidelong** adj (glance) косо́й.

sideways adv бо́ком.

siding n запасно́й путь m.

sidle vi: ~ up to подходи́ть impf, подойти́ pf к (+dat) бочко́м.

siege n оса́да; lay ~ to оса́ждать impf, осади́ть pf; raise the ~ of снима́ть impf, снять pf оса́ду c+gen.

sieve n си́то; vt просе́ивать impf, просе́ять pf.

sift vt просе́ивать impf, просе́ять pf; (fig) тща́тельно рассма́тривать impf, рассмотре́ть pf.

sigh vi вздыха́ть impf, вздохну́ть pf; n вздох.

sight n (faculty) зре́ние; (view) вид; (spectacle) зре́лище; pl достопримеча́тельности f pl; (on gun) прице́л; at first ~ с пе́рвого взгля́да; catch ~ of уви́деть pf; know by ~ знать impf в лицо́; lose ~ of теря́ть impf, по~ pf из ви́ду, (fig) упуска́ть impf, упусти́ть pf из ви́ду.

sign n знак; (indication) при́знак; (~board) вы́веска; vt & abs подпи́сывать(ся) impf, подписа́ть(ся) pf; vi (give~) подава́ть impf, пода́ть pf знак; ~ on (as unemployed) запи́сываться impf, записа́ться pf в списки́ безрабо́тных; ~ up нанима́ться impf, наня́ться pf.

signal n сигна́л; vt & i сигнализи́ровать impf & pf. **signal-box** n сигна́льная бу́дка. **signalman** n сигна́льщик. **signatory** n подписа́вший sb; (of treaty) сторона́, подписа́вшая догово́р. **signature** n по́дпись. **significance** n значе́ние. **significant** adj значи́тельный.

signify vt означа́ть impf.

signpost n указа́тельный столб.

silage n си́лос.

silence n молча́ние, тишина́; vt заста́вить pf замолча́ть.

silencer n глуши́тель m. **silent** adj (not speaking) безмо́лвный; (of film) немо́й; (without noise) ти́хий; be ~ молча́ть impf.

silhouette n силуэ́т; vt: be ~d вырисо́вываться impf, вы́рисоваться pf (against на фо́не+gen).

silicon n кре́мний. **silicone** n силико́н.

silk n шёлк; attrib шёлковый. **silky** adj шелкови́стый.

sill n подоко́нник.

silly adj глу́пый.

silo n си́лос.

silt n ил.

silver n серебро́; (cutlery) столо́вое серебро́; (of ~) сере́бряный; (silvery) серебри́стый; ~-plated посере́брённый; **silversmith** n сере́бряных дел ма́стер. **silverware** n столо́вое серебро́. **silvery** adj серебри́стый.

similar adj подо́бный (to +dat). **similarity** n схо́дство. **similarly** adv подо́бным о́бразом.

simile n сравне́ние.

simmer vi кипяти́ть impf на ме́дленном огне́; vi кипе́ть impf на ме́дленном огне́; ~ down успока́иваться impf, успоко́иться pf.

simper vi жема́нно улыба́ться impf, улыбну́ться pf.

simple adj просто́й; ~-minded тупова́тый. **simplicity** n простота́. **simplify** vt упроща́ть impf, упрости́ть pf. **simply** adv про́сто.

simulate vt притворя́ться impf, притвори́ться pf +instr; (conditions etc.) модели́ровать impf & pf (pearls etc.) иску́сственный.

simultaneous adj одновре́ме́нный.

sin n грех; vi греши́ть impf, co~ pf.

since adv с тех пор; prep c+gen; conj с тех пор как; (reason) так как.

sincere adj и́скренний. **sincerely** adv и́скренне; **yours** ~ и́скренне Ваш. **sincerity** n и́скренность.

sinew n сухожи́лие.

sinful adj гре́шный.

sing vt & i петь impf, про~, c~ pf.

singe vt пали́ть impf, o~ pf.

singer n певе́ц, -ви́ца.

single adj оди́н; (unmarried) (of man) нежена́тый; (of woman) незаму́жняя; (bed) односпа́льный; ~-handed без посторо́нней по́мощи; ~-minded целеустремлённый; ~ parent мать/оте́ц-одино́чка; ~ room ко́мната на одного́; n (ticket) биле́т в оди́н коне́ц; (tennis etc.) одино́чная игра́ vt: ~ out выделя́ть impf, вы́делить pf. **singly** adv по-одному́.

singular n еди́нственное число́; adj еди́нственный; (unusual) необыча́йный. **singularly** adv необыча́йно.

sinister adj злове́щий.

sink vi (descend slowly) опуска́ться impf, опусти́ться pf; (in mud etc.) погружа́ться impf, погрузи́ться pf; (in water) тону́ть impf, по~ pf; vt (ship) топи́ть impf, по~ pf, *(pipe, post)* вка́пывать *impf*, вкопа́ть *pf*; *n* ра́ковина.

sinner *n* гре́шник, -ица.

sinus *n* па́зуха.

sip *vt* пить *impf*, ма́ленькими глотка́ми; *n* ма́ленький глото́к.

siphon *n* сифо́н; ~ **off** *impf*, *fig*) перека́чивать *impf*, перекача́ть *pf*.

sir *n* сэр.

siren *n* сире́на.

sister *n* сестра́; ~**-in-law** *(husband's sister)* золо́вка; *(wife's sister)* своя́ченица; *(brother's wife)* неве́стка.

sit *vi (be sitting)* сиде́ть *impf*; *(~ down)* сади́ться *impf*, сесть *pf*; *(parl, law)* заседа́ть *impf*; *vt* уса́живать *impf*, усади́ть *pf*; *(exam)* сдава́ть *impf*; ~ **back** отки́дываться *impf*, отки́нуться *pf*; ~ **down** сади́ться *impf*, сесть *pf*; ~ **up** припод[у]нима́ться *impf*, приподня́ться *pf*; *(not go to bed)* не ложи́ться *impf* спать.

site *n (where a thing takes place)* ме́сто; *(where a thing is)* местоположе́ние.

sitting *n (parl etc.)* заседа́ние; *(for meal)* сме́на; ~**-room** гости́ная *sb*.

situated *adj*: be ~ находи́ться *impf*. **situation** *n* местоположе́ние; *(circumstances)* положе́ние; *(job)* ме́сто.

six *adj & n* шесть; *(number 6)* шестёрка. **sixteen** *adj & n* шестна́дцать. **sixteenth** *adj & n* шестна́дцатый. **sixth** *adj & n* шесто́й; *(fraction)* шеста́я *sb*. **sixtieth** *adj & n* шестидеся́тый. **sixty** *adj & n* шестьдеся́т; *pl (decade)* шестидеся́тые го́ды (-до́в) *m pl*.

size *n* разме́р; *vt*: ~ **up** оце́нивать *impf*, оцени́ть *pf*. **sizeable** *adj* значи́тельный.

sizzle *vi* шипе́ть *impf*.

skate[1] *n (fish)* скат.

skate[2] *n (ice~)* конёк; *(roller~)* конёк на ро́ликах; *vi* ката́ться *impf* на конька́х; **skating-rink** като́к.

skeleton *n* скеле́т.

sketch *n* зарисо́вка; *(theat)* скетч; *vt & i* зарисо́вывать *impf*, зарисова́ть *pf*. **sketchy** *adj* схемати́ческий; *(superficial)* пове́рхностный.

skew *adj* косо́й; **on the ~** ко́со.

skewer *n* ве́ртел.

ski *n* лы́жа; ~**-jump** трампли́н; *vi* ходи́ть *impf* на лы́жах.

skid *n* зано́с; *vi* заноси́ть *impf*, занести́ *pf impers+acc*.

skier *n* лы́жник. **skiing** *n* лы́жный спорт.

skilful *adj* иску́сный. **skill** *n* мастерство́; *(countable)* поле́зный на́вык. **skilled** *adj* иску́сный; *(trained)* квалифици́рованный.

skim *vt* снима́ть *impf*, снять *pf (cream* сли́вки *pl, scum* на́кипь) c+*gen*; *vi* скользи́ть *impf (over, along* по+*dat)*; ~ **through** бе́гло просма́тривать *impf*, просмотре́ть *pf*; *adj*: ~ **milk** снято́е молоко́.

skimp *vt & i* скупи́ться *impf* (на+*acc*). **skimpy** *adj* ску́дный.

skin *n* ко́жа; *(hide)* шку́ра; *(of fruit etc.)* кожура́; *(on milk)* пёнка; *vt* сдира́ть *impf*, содра́ть *pf* ко́жу, шку́ру, c+*gen*; *(fruit)* снима́ть *impf*, снять *pf* кожуру́ c+*gen*. **skinny** *adj* то́щий.

skip[1] *vi* скака́ть *impf*; *(with rope)* пры́гать *impf* че́рез скака́лку; *vt* (*omit*) пропуска́ть *impf*, пропусти́ть *pf*.

skip[2] *n* (*container*) скип.

skipper *n* (*naut*) шки́пер.

skirmish *n* схва́тка.

skirt *n* ю́бка; *vt* обходи́ть *impf*, обойти́ *pf* стороно́й; **~ing-board** пли́нтус.

skittle *n* ке́гля; *pl* ке́гли *f pl*.

skulk *vi* (*hide*) скрыва́ться *impf*; (*creep*) кра́сться *impf*.

skull *n* че́реп.

skunk *n* скунс.

sky *n* не́бо. **skylark** *n* жа́воронок. **skylight** *n* окно́ в кры́ше. **skyline** *n* горизо́нт. **skyscraper** *n* небоскрёб.

slab *n* плита́; (*of cake etc.*) кусо́к.

slack *adj* (*loose*) сла́бый; (*sluggish*) вя́лый; (*negligent*) небре́жный; *n* (*of rope*) слабина́; *pl* брю́ки (-к) *pl*. **slacken** *vt* ослабля́ть *impf*, осла́бить *pf*; *vt & i* (*slow down*) заmedля́ть(ся) *impf*, заме́длить(ся) *pf*; *vi* ослабева́ть *impf*, осла́беть *pf*.

slag *n* шлак.

slam *vt & i* захло́пывать(ся) *impf*, захло́пнуть(ся) *pf*.

slander *n* клевета́; *vt* клевета́ть *impf*, на~ *pf* на+*acc*. **slanderous** *adj* клеветни́ческий.

slang *n* жарго́н. **slangy** *adj* жарго́нный.

slant *vt & i* наклоня́ть(ся) *impf*, наклони́ть(ся) *pf*; *n* укло́н. **slanting** *adj* косо́й.

slap *vt* шлёпать *impf*, шлёпнуть *pf*; *n* шлепо́к; *adv* пря́мо. **slapdash** *adj* небре́жный. **slapstick** *n* фарс.

slash *vt* (*cut*) поро́ть *impf*, рас~ *pf*; (*fig*) уре́зывать *impf*, уре́зать *pf*; *n* разре́з.

(*sign*) дробь.

slat *n* пла́нка.

slate[1] *n* сла́нец; (*for roofing*) (крове́льная) пли́тка.

slate[2] *vt* (*criticize*) разноси́ть *impf*, разнести́ *pf*.

slaughter *n* (*of animals*) убо́й; (*massacre*) резня́; *vt* (*animals*) ре́зать *impf*, за~ *pf*; (*people*) убива́ть *impf*, уби́ть *pf*. **slaughterhouse** *n* бо́йня.

Slav *n* славяни́н, -я́нка; *adj* славя́нский.

slave *n* раб, рабы́ня; *vi* рабо́тать *impf* как раб. **slavery** *n* ра́бство.

Slavic *adj* славя́нский.

slavish *adj* ра́бский.

Slavonic *adj* славя́нский.

slay *vt* убива́ть *impf*, уби́ть *pf*.

sleazy *adj* убо́гий.

sledge *n* са́ни (-не́й) *pl*.

sledge-hammer *n* кува́лда.

sleek *adj* гла́дкий.

sleep *n* сон; **go to ~** засыпа́ть *impf*, засну́ть *pf*; *vi* спать *impf*; (*spend the night*) ночева́ть *impf*, пере~ *pf*. **sleeper** *n* спя́щий *sb*; (*on track*) шпа́ла; (*sleeping-car*) спа́льный ваго́н. **sleeping** *adj* спя́щий; **~-bag** спа́льный мешо́к; **~-car** спа́льный ваго́н; **~-pill** снотво́рная табле́тка. **sleepless** *adj* бессо́нный. **sleepy** *adj* со́нный.

sleet *n* мо́крый снег.

sleeve *n* рука́в; (*of record*) конве́рт.

sleigh *n* са́ни (-не́й) *pl*.

sleight-of-hand *n* ло́вкость рук.

slender *adj* (*slim*) то́нкий; (*meagre*) ску́дный; (*of hope etc.*) сла́бый.

sleuth *n* сы́щик.

slice n кусо́к; vt (~ up) наре́зать impf, наре́зать impf.
slick adj (dextrous) ло́вкий; (crafty) хи́трый; n нефтяна́я плёнка.
slide vi скользи́ть impf; vt (drawer etc.) задвига́ть impf, задви́нуть pf; n (children's ~) го́рка; (microscope ~) предме́тное стекло́; (phot) диапозити́в, слайд; (for hair) зако́лка. **sliding** (door) задвижно́й.
slight[1] adj (slender) то́нкий; (inconsiderable) небольшо́й; (light) лёгкий; not the ~est ни мале́йший, -шей (gen); not in the ~est ничу́ть.
slight[2] vt пренебрега́ть impf, пренебре́чь pf +instr; n оби́да.
slightly adv слегка́, немно́го.
slim adj то́нкий; (chance etc.) сла́бый; vi худе́ть impf, по~ pf.
slime n слизь. **slimy** adj сли́зистый; (person) ско́льзкий.
sling vt (throw) швыря́ть impf, швырну́ть pf; (suspend) подве́шивать impf, подве́сить pf; n (med) перевя́зь.
slink vi кра́сться impf.
slip n (mistake) оши́бка; (garment) комбина́ция; (pillow-case) на́волочка; (paper) листо́чек; ~ of the tongue обмо́лвка; give the ~ ускользну́ть pf от+gen; vi скользи́ть impf, скользну́ть pf; (fall over) поскользну́ться pf; (from hands etc.) выска́льзывать impf, вы́скользнуть pf; vt (insert) сова́ть impf, су́нуть pf; ~ off (depart) ускольза́ть impf, ускользну́ть pf; ~ up (make mistake) ошиба́ться impf, ошиби́ться pf. **slipper** n та́пка. **slippery** adj ско́льзкий.

slit vt разреза́ть impf, разре́зать pf; (throat) перере́зать pf; n щель; (cut) разре́з.
slither vi скользи́ть impf.
sliver n ще́пка.
slob n неря́ха m & f.
slobber vi пуска́ть impf, пусти́ть pf слю́ни.
slog n: (hit) си́льно ударя́ть impf, уда́рить pf; (work) упо́рно рабо́тать impf.
slogan n ло́зунг.
slop n: pl помо́и (-ев) pl; vt & i выплёскивать impf, вы́плескать(ся) pf.
slope n (artificial) накло́н; (geog) склон; vi име́ть impf накло́н. **sloping** adj накло́нный.
sloppy adj (work) неря́шливый; (sentimental) сентимента́льный.
slot n отве́рстие; ~-machine автома́т; vt: ~ in вставля́ть impf, вста́вить pf.
sloth n лень.
slouch vi (stoop) суту́литься impf.
slovenly adj неря́шливый.
slow adj ме́дленный; (tardy) медли́тельный; (stupid) тупо́й; (business) вя́лый; the (clock) отстава́ть impf, отста́ть pf; adv ме́дленно; vt & i (~ down, up) замедля́ть(ся) impf, заме́длить(ся) pf.
sludge n (mud) грязь; (sediment) отсто́й.
slug n (zool) слизня́к.
sluggish adj вя́лый.
sluice n шлюз.
slum n трущо́ба.
slumber n сон; vi спать impf.
slump n спад; vi ре́зко па́дать impf, (у)па́сть pf; (of person) сва́ливаться impf, свали́ться pf.

slur vt говори́ть impf невня́тно; n (stigma) пятно́.

slush n сля́коть.

slut n (sloven) неря́ха; (trollop) потаску́ха.

sly adj хи́трый; on the ~ тайко́м.

smack[1] vi: ~ of па́хнуть impf +instr.

smack[2] n (slap) шлепо́к; vt шлёпать impf, шлёпнуть pf.

small adj ма́ленький, небольшо́й, ма́лый; (of agent, particles; petty) ме́лкий; ~ change ме́лочь; ~-scale мелкомасшта́бный; ~ talk све́тская бесе́да.

smart[1] vi сади́ть impf impers.

smart[2] adj элега́нтный; (brisk) бы́стрый; (cunning) ло́вкий; (sharp) смека́листый (coll).

smash vt & i разбива́ть(ся) impf, разби́ть(ся) pf; vi: ~ into вреза́ться impf, вре́заться pf в+acc; n (crash) гро́хот; (collision) столкнове́ние; (blow) си́льный уда́р.

smattering n поверхностное зна́ние.

smear vt сма́зывать impf, сма́зать pf; (dirty) па́чкать impf, за~, ис~ pf; (discredit) порочи́ть impf, о~ pf; n (spot) пятно́; (slander) клевета́; (med) мазо́к.

smell n (sense) обоня́ние; (odour) за́пах; vt чу́вствовать impf за́пах+gen; (sniff) ню́хать impf, по~ pf; vi: ~ of па́хнуть impf +instr. **smelly** adj воню́чий.

smelt vt (ore) пла́вить impf; (metal) выпла́вля́ть impf, вы́плавить pf.

smile vi улыба́ться impf, улыбну́ться pf; n улы́бка.

smirk vi ухмыля́ться impf,

ухмыльну́ться pf; n ухмы́лка.

smith n кузне́ц.

smithereens n: (in)to ~ вдре́безги.

smithy n ку́зница.

smock n блу́за.

smog n тума́н (с ды́мом).

smoke n дым; ~-screen дымова́я заве́са; vt & i (cigarette etc.) кури́ть impf, по~ pf; vt (cure; colour) копти́ть impf, за~ pf; vi (abnormally) дыми́ть impf; (of fire) дыми́ться impf, за~ pf. **smoker** n кури́льщик, -ица, куря́щий sb. **smoky** adj ды́мный.

smooth adj (surface etc.) гла́дкий; (movement etc.) пла́вный; vt прила́живать impf, пригла́дить pf; ~ over сгла́живать impf, сгла́дить pf.

smother vt (stifle, also fig) души́ть impf, за~ pf; (cover) покрыва́ть impf, покры́ть pf.

smoulder vi тлеть impf.

smudge n пятно́; vt сма́зывать impf, сма́зать pf.

smug adj самодово́льный.

smuggle vt провози́ть impf, провезти́ pf контраба́ндой; (convey secretly) проноси́ть impf, пронести́ pf. **smuggler** n контрабанди́ст. **smuggling** n контраба́нда.

smut n са́жа; (indecency) непристо́йность. **smutty** adj гря́зный; непристо́йный.

snack n заку́ска; ~ bar заку́сочная sb; (within institution) буфе́т.

snag n (fig) загво́здка; vt зацепля́ть impf, зацепи́ть pf.

snail n ули́тка.

snake n змея́.

snap vi (of dog or person)

snare *n* лову́шка.

snarl *vi* рыча́ть *impf*, за- *pf*; *n* рыча́ние.

snatch *vt* хвата́ть *impf*, (с)хвати́ть *pf*; *vi*: ~ at хвата́ться *impf*, (с)хвати́ться *pf* за+*acc*; *n* (*fragment*) обры́вок.

sneak *vi* (*slink*) кра́сться *impf*; *vt* (*steal*) стащи́ть *pf*; *n* я́бедник, -ица (*coll*). **sneaking** *adj* та́йный. **sneaky** *adj* лука́вый.

sneer *vi* насмеха́ться *impf* (at над+*instr*).

sneeze *vi* чиха́ть *impf*, чихну́ть *pf*; *n* чиха́нье.

snide *adj* ехи́дный.

sniff *vi* шмы́гать *impf*, шмыгну́ть *pf* но́сом; *vt* ню́хать *impf*, по~ *pf*.

snigger *n* отрезок; *n* хихи́кать *impf*, хихи́кнуть *pf*; *n* хихи́канье.

snip *vt* ре́зать *impf* (но́жницами); ~ off среза́ть *impf*, сре́зать *pf*.

snipe *vi* стреля́ть *impf* из укры́тия (at в+*acc*); (*fig*) напада́ть *impf* на+*acc*. **sniper** *n* сна́йпер.

snippet *n* отре́зок; *pl* (*of news etc.*) обры́вки *m pl*.

snivel *vi* (*run at nose*) распуска́ть *impf*, распусти́ть *pf* со́пли; (*whimper*) хны́кать *impf*.

snob *n* сноб. **snobbery** *n* сно-бизм. **snobbish** *adj* снобистский.

snoop *vi* шпио́нить *impf*; ~ about разню́хивать *impf*, разню́хать *pf*.

snooty *adj* чва́нный.

snooze *vi* вздремну́ть *pf*; *n* коро́ткий сон.

snore *vi* храпе́ть *impf*.

snorkel *n* шно́ркель *m*.

snort *vi* фы́ркать *impf*, фы́ркнуть *pf*.

snot *n* со́пли (-ле́й) *pl*.

snout *n* ры́ло, мо́рда.

snow *n* снег; ~-white белосне́жный; *it is* ~*ing*, it snows идёт снег; ~ed under зава́ленный рабо́той; we were ~ed up в нас занесло́ сне́гом. **snowball** *n* снежо́к. **snowdrop** *n* подсне́жник. **snowflake** *n* снежи́нка. **snowman** *n* сне́жная ба́ба. **snowstorm** *n* мете́ль. **snowy** *adj* сне́жный; (*snow-white*) белосне́жный.

snub *vt* игнори́ровать *impf* & *pf*.

snuff[1] *n* (*tobacco*) ню́хательный таба́к.

snuff[2] *vt*: ~ out туши́ть *impf*, по~ *pf*.

snuffle *vi* сопе́ть *impf*.

snug *adj* ую́тный.

snuggle *vi*: ~ up to прижима́ться *impf*, прижа́ться *pf* к+*dat*.

so *adv* так; (*in this way*) так, таки́м о́бразом; (*thus, at beginning of sentence*) ита́к; (*also*) та́кже, то́же; *conj* (*therefore*) поэ́тому; and ~ on и так да́лее; if ~ в тако́м слу́чае; ~ ... as так (ой)...; как; ~ as to с тем что́бы; ~-called так называ́емый; (in) ~ far as насто́лько;

long! пока́!; ~ long as поско́льку; ~ **much** насто́лько; ~ **much** до тако́й сте́пени; ~ **much the better** тем лу́чше; ~ **that** что́бы; ... that так... что; ~ **to say, speak** так сказа́ть; ~ **what?** ну и что?

soak *vt* мочи́ть *impf*, на~ *pf*; (*drench*) прома́чивать *impf*, промочи́ть *pf*; ~ **up** впи́тывать *impf*, впита́ть *pf*; *vi*: ~ **through** проса́чиваться *impf*, просочи́ться *pf*; **get ~ed** промока́ть *impf*, промо́кнуть *pf*.

soap *n* мы́ло; *vt* мы́лить *impf*, на~ *pf*; ~ **opera** многосери́йная переда́ча; ~ **powder** стира́льный порошо́к. **soapy** *adj* мы́льный.

soar *vi* пари́ть *impf*; (*prices*) подска́кивать *impf*, подскочи́ть *pf*.

sob *vi* рыда́ть *impf*; *n* рыда́ние.

sober *adj* трéзвый; *vt & i*: ~ **up** отрезвля́ть(ся) *impf*, отрезви́ть(ся) *pf*. **sobriety** *n* трéзвость.

soccer *n* футбо́л.

sociable *adj* общи́тельный.

social *adj* обще́ственный, социа́льный; **S~ Democrat** социа́л-демокра́т; ~ **sciences** обще́ственные нау́ки *pl*; ~ **security** социа́льное обеспе́чение. **socialism** *n* социали́зм. **socialist** *n* социали́ст; *adj* социалисти́ческий. **socialize** *vi* обща́ться *impf*. **society** *n* о́бщество. **sociological** *adj* социологи́ческий. **sociologist** *n* социо́лог. **sociology** *n* социоло́гия.

sock *n* носо́к.

socket *n* (*eye*) впа́дина; (*electr*)

штéпсель *m*; (*for bulb*) патро́н.

soda *n* со́да; ~**-water** содо́вая вода́.

sodden *adj* промо́кший.

sodium *n* на́трий.

sodomy *n* педера́стия.

sofa *n* дива́н.

soft *adj* мя́гкий; (*sound*) ти́хий; (*colour*) нея́ркий; (*malleable*) ко́вкий; (*tender*) нéжный; ~ **drink** безалкого́льный напи́ток. **soften** *vt & i* смягча́ть(ся) *impf*, смягчи́ть(ся) *pf*. **softness** *n* мя́гкость. **software** *n* програ́ммное обеспе́чение.

soggy *adj* сыро́й.

soil[1] *n* по́чва.

soil[2] *vt* па́чкать *impf*, за~, ис~ *pf*.

solace *n* утеше́ние.

solar *adj* со́лнечный.

solder *n* припо́й; *vt* пая́ть *impf*; (*together*) спа́ивать *impf*, спая́ть *pf*. **soldering iron** *n* пая́льник.

soldier *n* солда́т.

sole[1] *n* (*of foot, shoe*) подо́шва.

sole[2] *n* (*fish*) морско́й язы́к.

sole[3] *adj* еди́нственный.

solemn *adj* торже́ственный. **solemnity** *n* торже́ственность.

solicit *vt* проси́ть *impf*, по~ *pf* +*acc, gen,* о+*prep*; *vi* (*of prostitute*) пристава́ть *impf* к мужчи́нам. **solicitor** *n* адвока́т. **solicitous** *adj* забо́тливый.

solid *adj* (*not liquid*) твёрдый; (*not hollow; continuous*) сплошно́й; (*firm*) про́чный; (*pure*) чи́стый; *n* твёрдое тéло; *pl* твёрдая пи́ща. **solidarity** *n* солида́рность. **solidify** *vi* затвердева́ть *impf*, затверде́ть *pf.* **solidity** *n* твёрдость; про́чность.

soliloquy *n* моноло́г.

solitary *adj* одино́кий, уединённый; **~ confinement** одино́чное заключе́ние. **solitude** *n* одино́чество, уедине́ние.

solo *n* со́ло *neut indecl*; *adj* со́льный; *adv* со́ло. **soloist** *n* соли́ст, -ка.

solstice *n* солнцестоя́ние.

soluble *adj* раствори́мый. **solution** *n* раство́р; *(of puzzle etc.)* реше́ние. **solve** *vt* реша́ть *impf*, реши́ть *pf.* **solvent** *adj* растворя́ющий; *(financially)* платёжеспосо́бный; *n* раствори́тель *m.*

sombre *adj* мра́чный.

some *adj & pron (any)* како́й-нибудь; *(a certain)* како́й-то; *(a certain amount or number of)* не́который, *or often expressed by noun in (partitive) gen;* *(several)* не́сколько+*gen;* *(~ people, things)* не́которые *pl;* **~ day** когда́-нибудь; **~ more** ещё; **~ ... others** одни́... други́е. **somebody, someone** *n, pron (def)* кто́-то; *(indef)* кто́-нибудь. **somehow** *adv* ка́к-то; ка́к-нибудь; *(for some reason)* почему́-то; **~ or other** так и́ли ина́че.

somersault *n* са́льто *neut indecl;* *vi* кувырка́ться *impf,* кувыр(к)ну́ться *pf.*

something *n & pron (def)* что́-то; *(indef)* что́-нибудь; **~ like** *(approximately)* приблизи́тельно; *(a thing like)* что́-то вро́де+*gen*. **sometime** *adv* не́когда; *adj* бы́вший. **sometimes** *adv* иногда́. **somewhat** *adv* не́сколько, дово́льно. **somewhere** *adv (po-*

sition) (def) где́-то; *(indef)* где́-нибудь; *(motion)* куда́-то; куда́-нибудь.

son *n* сын. **~-in-law** зять *m.*

sonata *n* сона́та.

song *n* пе́сня.

sonic *adj* звуково́й.

sonnet *n* соне́т.

soon *adv* ско́ро; *(early)* ра́но; **as ~ as** как то́лько; **as ~ as possible** как мо́жно скоре́е; **~er or later** ра́но и́ли по́здно; the **~er the better** чем ра́ньше, тем лу́чше.

soot *n* са́жа, ко́поть.

soothe *vt* успока́ивать *impf,* успоко́ить *pf; (pain)* облегча́ть *impf,* облегчи́ть *pf.*

sophisticated *adj (person)* иску́шённый; *(equipment)* сло́жный.

soporific *adj* снотво́рный.

soprano *n* сопра́но *(voice) neut & (person) f indecl.*

sorcerer *n* колду́н. **sorcery** *n* колдовство́.

sordid *adj* гря́зный.

sore *n* боля́чка; *adj* больно́й; **my throat is ~** у меня́ боли́т го́рло.

sorrow *n* печа́ль. **sorrowful** *adj* печа́льный. **sorry** *adj* жа́лкий; *predic:* **be ~** жале́ть *impf (about* о+*prep) (for* +*gen); ~!* извини́(те)!

sort *n* род, вид, сорт; *vt (also ~ out)* сортирова́ть *impf,* рас~ *pf; (also fig)* разбира́ть *impf,* разобра́ть *pf.*

sortie *n* вы́лазка.

SOS *n* (ра́дио)сигна́л бе́дствия.

soul *n* душа́.

sound[1] *adj (healthy, thorough)* здоро́вый; *(in good condition)* испра́вный; *(logical)* здра́вый, разу́мный; (of sleep) кре́пкий.

sound² n (noise) звук, шум; attrib звуково́й; ~ **effects** звуковы́е эффе́кты m pl; vi звуча́ть impf.

sound³ vt (naut) измеря́ть impf, изме́рить pf глубину́ +gen; ~ **out** зонди́ровать impf, по~ pf; n зонд.

sound⁴ n (strait) проли́в.

soup n суп; vt: ~**ed up** форси́рованный.

sour adj ки́слый; ~ **cream** смета́на; vt & i (fig) озлобля́ть(ся) impf, озло́бить(ся) pf.

source n исто́чник; (of river) исто́к.

south n юг; (naut) зюйд; adj ю́жный; adv к ю́гу, на юг; ~-**east** юго-восто́к; ~-**west** юго-за́пад. **southerly** adj ю́жный. **southern** adj ю́жный. **southerner** n южа́нин, -а́нка. **southward(s)** adv на юг, к ю́гу.

souvenir n сувени́р.

sovereign adj сувере́нный; n мона́рх. **sovereignty** n сувере́нитет.

soviet n сове́т; S~ **Union** Сове́тский Сою́з; adj (S~) сове́тский.

sow¹ n свинья́.

sow² vt (seed) се́ять impf, по~ pf; (field) засе́ивать impf, засе́ять pf.

soya n: ~ **bean** со́евый боб.

spa n куро́рт.

space n (place, room) ме́сто; (expanse) простра́нство; (interval) промежу́ток; (outer ~) ко́смос; attrib косми́ческий; vt расставля́ть impf, расста́вить pf с промежу́тками. **spacecraft**, **-ship** n

косми́ческий кора́бль m. **spacious** adj просто́рный.

spade n (tool) лопа́та; pl (cards) пи́ки (пик) pl.

spaghetti n спаге́тти neut indecl.

Spain n Испа́ния.

span n (of bridge) проле́т; (aeron) разма́х; vt (of bridge) соединя́ть impf, соедини́ть pf сторо́ны +gen; (river) берега́ +gen; (fig) охва́тывать impf, охвати́ть pf.

Spaniard n испа́нец, -нка. **Spanish** adj испа́нский.

spank vt шлёпать impf, шлёпнуть pf.

spanner n га́ечный ключ.

spar¹ n (aeron) лонжеро́н.

spar² vi бокси́ровать impf; (fig) препира́ться impf.

spare adj (in reserve) запасно́й; (extra, to ~) ли́шний; (of seat, time) свобо́дный; ~ **parts** запасны́е ча́сти f pl; ~ **room** ко́мната для госте́й; n: pl запча́сти f pl; vt (grudge) жале́ть impf, по~ pf +acc, gen; **he ~d no pains** он не жале́л трудо́в; (do without) обходи́ться impf, обойти́сь pf без+gen; (time) уделя́ть impf, удели́ть pf; (show mercy towards) щади́ть impf, по~ pf; (save from) избавля́ть impf, изба́вить pf от+gen: ~ **me the details** изба́вьте меня́ от подро́бностей.

spark n и́скра; ~-**plug** запа́льная свеча́; vt (~ off) вызыва́ть impf, вы́звать pf.

sparkle vi сверка́ть impf.

sparrow n воробе́й.

sparse adj ре́дкий.

Spartan adj спарта́нский.

spasm n спазм. **spasmodic** adj спазмоди́ческий.

spastic n паралитик.

spate n разлив; (fig) поток.

spatial adj пространственный.

spatter, splatter vt (liquid) брызгать impf & pf (with +instr; person etc.) забрызгивать impf, забрызгать pf (with +instr); vi плескать(ся) impf, плеснуть pf.

spatula n шпатель m.

spawn vt & i метать impf (икру); vt (fig) порождать impf, породить pf.

speak vt & i говорить impf, сказать pf; vi (make speech) выступать impf, выступить pf (с речью); (~ out) высказываться impf, высказаться pf (for за+acc; against против+gen). **speaker** n говорящий sb; (giving speech) выступающий sb; (orator) оратор; (S~, parl) спикер; (loud-~) громкоговоритель m.

spear n копьё; vt пронзать impf, пронзить pf копьём. **spearhead** n vt возглавлять impf, возглавить pf.

special adj особый, специальный. **specialist** n специалист, ~ка. **speciality** n специальность n специализация. **specialize** vt & i специализировать(ся) impf & pf. **specially** adv особенно.

species n вид.

specific adj особенный. **specification(s)** n спецификация.

specify vt уточнять impf, уточнить pf.

specimen n образец, экземпляр.

speck n крапинка, пятнышко. **speckled** adj крапчатый.

spectacle n зрелище; pl очки

(-ков) pl.

spectacular adj эффектный; (amazing) потрясающий

spectator n зритель m.

spectre n призрак.

spectrum n спектр.

speculate vi (meditate) размышлять impf, размыслить pf (on о+prep); (conjecture) гадать impf; (comm) спекулировать impf. **speculation** n (conjecture) догадка; (comm) спекуляция. **speculative** adj гипотетический; (comm) спекулятивный. **speculator** n спекулянт

speech n речь. **speechless** adj (fig) онемевший.

speed n скорость; vi мчаться impf, про~ pf, (illegally) превышать impf, превысить pf скорость; vt: ~ **up** ускорять impf, ускорить pf. **speedboat** n быстроходный катер.

speedometer n спидометр.

speedy adj быстрый, скорый.

spell[1] n (charm) заговор.

spell[2] vt (say) произносить impf, произнести pf по буквам; (write) правильно писать impf, на~ pf; **how do you** ~ **that word?** как пишется это слово?

spell[3] n (period) период.

spellbound adj зачарованный.

spelling n правописание.

spend vt (money; effort) тратить impf, ис~, по~ pf; (time) проводить impf, провести pf.

sperm n сперма.

sphere n сфера; (ball) шар. **spherical** adj сферический.

spice n пряность; vt приправлять impf, приправить pf.

spicy adj пря́ный; (fig) пика́нтный.

spider n пау́к.

spike n (point) остриё; (on fence) зубе́ц; (on shoes) шип.

spill vt & i (liquid) пролива́ть(ся) impf, проли́ть(ся) pf; (dry substance) рассыпа́ть(ся) impf, рассы́пать(ся) pf.

spin vt (thread etc.) прясть impf, с~ pf; (coin) подбра́сывать impf, подбро́сить pf; vt & i (turn) кружи́ть(ся) impf, ~ **out** (prolong) затя́гивать impf, затяну́ть pf.

spinach n шпина́т.

spinal adj спинно́й; ~ **column** спинно́й хребе́т; ~ **cord** спинно́й мозг.

spindle n ось m. **spindly** adj дли́нный и то́нкий.

spine n (anat) позвоно́чник, хребе́т; (prickle) игла́; (of book) корешо́к. **spineless** adj (fig) бесхара́ктерный.

spinning n пряде́ние; ~ **wheel** пря́лка.

spinster n незаму́жняя же́нщина.

spiral adj спира́льный; (staircase) винтово́й; n спира́ль; vi (rise sharply) ре́зко возраста́ть impf, возрасти́ pf.

spire n шпиль m.

spirit n дух, душа́; pl (mood) настрое́ние; pl (drinks) спиртно́е sb; ~**level** ватерпа́с; vt: ~ **away** та́йно уноси́ть impf, унести́ pf. **spirited** adj живо́й. **spiritual** adj духо́вный. **spiritualism** n спиритуали́зм. **spiritualist** n спири́т.

spit[1] n (skewer) ве́ртел.

spit[2] vi (of person) плева́ть impf, плю́нуть pf; (of rain) мороси́ть impf; (of fire) разбры́згивать impf, разбры́згать pf и́скры;

(sizzle) шипе́ть impf; vt: ~ **out** выплёвывать impf, вы́плюнуть pf; ~**ing image** то́чная ко́пия; n слюна́.

spite n зло́ба; **in** ~ **of** несмотря́ на+acc. **spiteful** adj зло́бный.

spittle n слюна́.

splash vt (person) забры́згивать impf, забры́згать pf (**with** +instr); (~ liquid) бры́згать impf +instr; vi плеска́ть(ся) impf, плесну́ть pf; (move) шлёпать impf, шлёпнуть pf (**through** по+dat); n (act, sound) плеск; (mark made) пятно́.

splatter see **spatter**

spleen n селезёнка.

splendid adj великоле́пный.

splendour n великоле́пие.

splice vt (ropes etc.) сра́щивать impf, срасти́ть pf; (film, tape) скле́ивать impf, скле́ить pf концы́+gen.

splint n ши́на.

splinter n оско́лок; (in skin) зано́за; vt & i расщепля́ть(ся) impf, расщепи́ть(ся) pf.

split n расще́лина, расще́п; (schism) раско́л; pf шпага́т; vt & i расщепля́ть(ся) impf, расщепи́ть(ся) pf, раска́лывать(ся) impf, расколо́ть(ся) pf; (divide) дели́ть impf, раз~ pf; ~ **second** мгнове́ние о́ка; ~ **up** (part company) расходи́ться impf, разойти́сь pf.

splutter vi бры́згать impf слюно́й; (utter) говори́ть impf захлёбываясь.

spoil n (booty) добы́ча; vt & i (damage; decay) по́ртить(ся) impf, ис~ pf; vt (indulge) балова́ть impf, из~ pf.

spoke n спи́ца.

spokesman, -woman n представитель m, ~ница.

sponge n губка; ~ **cake** бисквит; vt (wash) мыть impf, вы~, по~ pf губкой; vi: ~ **on** жить impf на счёт+gen.

sponger n приживальщик.

spongy adj губчатый.

sponsor n спонсор; vt финансировать impf & pf.

spontaneity n спонтанность.

spontaneous adj спонтанный.

spoof n пародия.

spooky adj жуткий.

spool n катушка.

spoon n ложка; vt черпать impf, черпнуть pf ложкой. **spoonful** n ложка.

sporadic adj спорадический.

sport n спорт; ~ **s car** спортивный автомобиль m; vt щеголять impf, щегольнуть pf +instr. **sportsman** n спортсмен. **sporty** adj спортивный.

spot n (place) место; (mark) пятно; (pimple) прыщик; **on the** ~ на месте; (at once) сразу; ~ **check** выборочная проверка; vt (notice) замечать impf, заметить pf. **spotless** adj абсолютно чистый. **spotlight** n прожектор; (fig) внимание. **spotty** adj прыщеватый.

spouse n супруг, ~a.

spout vi бить impf струёй; хлынуть pf (pontificate) ораторствовать impf; vt извергать impf, извергнуть pf (verses etc.) декламировать impf, про~ pf; n (tube) носик; (jet) струя.

sprain vt растягивать impf, растянуть pf; n растяжение.

sprawl vi (of person) развали-

ваться impf, развалиться pf; (of town) раскидываться impf, раскинуться pf.

spray[1] n (flowers) вет(оч)ка.

spray[2] n брызги (-г) pl; (atomizer) пульверизатор; vt опрыскивать impf, опрыскать pf (with +instr); (cause to scatter) распылять impf, распылить pf.

spread vt & i (news, disease, etc.) распространять(ся) impf, распространить(ся) pf; vt (lay out) расстилать impf, разостлать pf; (unfurl, unroll) развёртывать impf, развернуть pf; (bread etc. +acc; butter etc. +instr) намазывать impf, намазать pf; n (expansion) распространение; (span) размах; (feast) пир; (paste) паста.

spree n кутёж; **go on a** ~ кутить impf, кутнуть pf.

sprig n веточка.

sprightly adj бодрый.

spring vi (jump) прыгать impf, прыгнуть pf; vt (tell unexpectedly) неожиданно сообщать impf, сообщить pf (on +dat); ~ **a leak** давать impf, дать pf течь; ~ **from** (originate) происходить impf, произойти pf из+gen; n (jump) прыжок; (season) весна, attrib весенний; (water) источник; (elasticity) упругость; (coil) пружина; ~**clean** генеральная уборка. **springboard** n трамплин.

sprinkle vt (with liquid) опрыскивать impf, опрыскать pf (with +instr); (with solid) посыпать impf, посыпать pf (with +instr). **sprinkler** n разбрызгиватель m.

sprint vi бежать impf на

коро́ткую диста́нцию; (*rush*)
рвану́ться *pf*; *n* спринт.
sprinter *n* спри́нтер.
sprout *vi* пуска́ть *impf*, пу-
сти́ть *pf* ростки́; *n* росто́к;
pl брюссе́льская капу́ста.
spruce[1] *adj* наря́дный, эле-
га́нтный; *vt*: ~ **o.s. up** приво-
ди́ть *impf*, привести́ *pf* себя́
в поря́док.
spruce[2] *n* ель.
spur *n* шпо́ра; (*fig*) сти́мул;
on the ~ of the moment под
влия́нием мину́ты; *vt*: ~ **on**
подхлёстывать *impf*, под-
хлестну́ть *pf*.
spurious *adj* подде́льный.
spurn *vt* отверга́ть *impf*, от-
ве́ргнуть *pf*.
spurt *n* (*jet*) струя́; (*effort*)
рыво́к; *vi* бить *impf* струёй;
(*make an effort*) де́лать *impf*,
с~ *pf* рыво́к.
spy *n* шпио́н; *vi* шпио́нить
impf (**on** за+*instr*). **spying** *n*
шпиона́ж.
squabble *n* перебра́нка; *vi*
вздо́рить *impf*, по~ *pf*.
squad *n* кома́нда, гру́ппа.
squadron *n* (*mil*) эскадро́н;
(*naut*) эска́дра; (*aeron*) эскад-
ри́лья.
squalid *adj* убо́гий.
squall *n* шквал.
squalor *n* убо́жество.
squander *vt* растра́чивать
impf, растра́тить *pf*.
square *n* (*shape*) квадра́т; (*in
town*) пло́щадь; (*on paper,
material*) кле́тка; (*instrument*)
науго́льник; *adj* квадра́т-
ный; (*meal*) пло́тный; *vt*
~ **root** квадра́тный ко́рень *m*; *vt*
(*accounts*) своди́ть *impf*, све-
сти́ *pf*; (*math*) возводи́ть
impf, возвести́ *pf* в квадра́т;
vi (*correspond*) соотве́тство-

вать *impf* (**with** +*dat*).
squash *n* (*crowd*) толку́чка;
(*drink*) сок; *vt* разда́вливать
impf, раздави́ть *pf*, (*suppress*)
подавля́ть *impf*, подави́ть
pf; *vi* вти́скиваться *impf*,
вти́снуться *pf*.
squat *adj* призе́мистый; *vi*
сиде́ть *impf* на ко́рточках;
~ **down** сади́ться *impf*, сесть
pf на ко́рточки.
squatter *n* незако́нный жиле́ц.
squawk *n* клёкот; *vi* клеко-
та́ть *impf*.
squeak *n* писк; (*of object*)
скрип; *vi* пища́ть *impf*, пи́ск-
нуть *pf*; (*of object*) скрипе́ть
impf, скри́пнуть *pf*. **squeaky**
adj пискли́вый, скрипу́чий.
squeal *n* визг; *vi* визжа́ть
impf, ви́згнуть *pf*.
squeamish *adj* брезгли́вый.
squeeze *n* (*crush*) да́вка;
(*pressure*) сжа́тие; (*hand*) по-
жа́тие; *vt* дави́ть *impf*; сжи-
ма́ть *impf*, сжать *pf*; ~ **in**
впи́хивать(ся) *impf*, впих-
ну́ть(ся) *pf*; вти́скивать(ся)
impf, вти́снуть(ся) *pf*; ~ **out**
выжима́ть *impf*, вы́жать *pf*;
~ **through** проти́скивать(ся)
impf, проти́снуть(ся) *pf*.
squelch *vi* хлю́пать *impf*,
хлю́пнуть *pf*.
squid *n* кальма́р.
squint *n* косогла́зие; *vi* ко-
си́ть *impf*; (*screw up eyes*)
щу́риться *impf*.
squire *n* сквайр, поме́щик.
squirm *vi* (*wriggle*) извива́ть-
ся *impf*, изви́ться *pf*.
squirrel *n* бе́лка.
squirt *n* струя́; *vi* бить *impf*
струёй; *vi* пуска́ть *impf*, пу-
сти́ть *pf* струю́ (*substance*
+*gen*; **at** на+*acc*).
St. *abbr* (*of Street*) ул., у́лица.

(of Saint) св., Свято́й, -а́я.

stab *n* уда́р (ножо́м *etc.*); *(pain)* внеза́пная о́страя боль; *vt* наноси́ть *impf*, нанести́ *pf* уда́р (ножо́м *etc.*) (*person* +*dat*).

stability *n* усто́йчивость, стаби́льность. **stabilize** *vt* стабилизи́ровать *impf & pf*. **stable** *adj* усто́йчивый, стаби́льный; *(psych)* уравнове́шенный; *n* коню́шня.

staccato *n* стакка́то *neut indecl*; *adv* стакка́то; *adj* отры́вистый.

stack *n* ку́ча; *vt* скла́дывать *impf*, сложи́ть *pf* в ку́чу.

stadium *n* стадио́н.

staff *n (personnel)* штат, сотру́дники *m pl*; *(stick)* по́сох, жезл; *adj* шта́тный; *(mil)* штабно́й.

stag *n* саме́ц-оле́нь *m*.

stage *n (theat)* сце́на; *(period)* ста́дия; *vt (theat)* ста́вить *impf*, по~ *pf*; *(organize)* организо́вывать *impf & pf*; ~-**manager** режиссёр.

stagger *vi* шата́ться *impf*, шатну́ться *pf*; *vt (hours of work etc.)* распределя́ть *impf*, распредели́ть *pf*. **be staggered** *vt* поража́ться *impf*, порази́ться *pf*. **staggering** *adj* потряса́ющий.

stagnant *adj (water)* стоя́чий; *(fig)* засто́йный. **stagnate** *vi* заста́иваться *impf*, застоя́ться *pf*, *(fig)* косне́ть *impf*, за~ *pf*.

staid *adj* степе́нный.

stain *n* пятно́; *(dye)* кра́ска; *vt* па́чкать *impf*, за~, ис~ *pf*; *(dye)* окра́шивать *impf*, окра́сить *pf*; ~**ed glass** цветно́е стекло́. **stainless** *adj*: ~ **steel** нержаве́ющая сталь.

stair *n* ступе́нька. **staircase**, **stairs** *n pl* ле́стница.

stake *n (stick)* кол; *(bet)* ста́вка; *(comm)* до́ля; **be at** ~ быть поста́вленным на ка́рту; *vt (mark out)* огора́живать *impf*, огороди́ть *pf* ко́льями; *(support)* укрепля́ть *impf*, укрепи́ть *pf* ко́лом; *(risk)* ста́вить *impf*, по~ *pf* на ка́рту.

stale *adj* несве́жий; *(musty, damp)* за́тхлый; *(hackneyed)* изби́тый.

stalemate *n* пат; *(fig)* тупи́к.

stalk *n* сте́бель *m*; *vt* высле́живать *impf*; *vi (& t) (stride)* ше́ствовать *impf* (по+*dat*).

stall *n* сто́йло; *(booth)* ларёк; *pl (theat)* парте́р; *vi (of engine)* гло́хнуть *impf*, за~ *pf*; *(play for time)* оття́гивать *impf*, оттяну́ть *pf* вре́мя; *vt (engine)* неча́янно заглуша́ть *impf*, заглуши́ть *pf*.

stallion *n* жеребе́ц.

stalwart *adj* сто́йкий; *n* сто́йкий приве́рженец.

stamina *n* выно́сливость.

stammer *vi* заика́ться *impf*; *n* заика́ние.

stamp *n* печа́ть; *(postage)* (почто́вая) ма́рка; *vt* штампова́ть *impf*; *vi* то́пать *impf*, то́пнуть *pf* (нога́ми); ~ **out** поборо́ть *pf*.

stampede *n* пани́ческое бе́гство; *vi* обраща́ть *impf* в пани́ческое бе́гство.

stance *n* пози́ция.

stand *n (hat, coat)* ве́шалка; *(music)* пюпи́тр; *(umbrella, support)* подста́вка; *(booth)* ларёк; *(taxi)* стоя́нка; *(at stadium)* трибу́на; *(position)* пози́ция; *(resistance)* сопротивле́ние; *vi* стоя́ть *impf*; ~ **up**

вставать *impf*, встать *pf*; (*remain in force*) оставаться *impf*, остаться в силе; *vt* (*put*) ставить *impf*, по~ *pf*; (*endure*) терпеть *impf*, по~ *pf*; ~ **back** отходить *impf*, отойти *pf* (**from** от+*gen*); (*not go forward*) держаться *impf* позади; ~ **by** (*vi*) (*not interfere*) не вмешиваться *impf*, вмешаться *pf*; (*be ready*) быть *impf* на готове; (*vt*) (*support*) поддерживать *impf*, поддержать *pf*; (*stick to*) придерживаться *impf* +*gen*; ~ **down** (*resign*) уходить *impf*, уйти *pf* с поста (**as** +*gen*); ~ **for** (*signify*) означать *impf*; (*tolerate*): **I shall not** ~ **for it** я не потерплю; ~**in** заместитель *m*; ~ **in** (*for*) замещать *impf*, заместить *pf*; ~ **out** выделяться *impf*, выделиться *pf*; ~ **up** вставать *impf*, встать *pf*; ~ **up for** (*defend*) отстаивать *impf*, отстоять *pf*; ~ **up to** (*endure*) выдерживать *impf*, выдержать *pf*; (*not give in to*) противостоять *impf* +*dat*. **standard** *n* (*norm*) стандарт, норм; (*flag*) знамя *neut*; ~ **of living** жизненный уровень *m*; *adj* нормальный, стандартный. **standardization** *n* нормализация, стандартизация. **standardize** *vt* стандартизировать *impf* & *pf*; нормализовать *impf* & *pf*. **standing** *n* положение; *adj* (*upright*) стоячий; (*permanent*) постоянный. **standpoint** *n* точка зрения. **standstill** *n* остановка, застой, пауза; **be at a** ~ стоять *impf* на мёртвой точке; **bring (come) to a** ~ остана́вли-

ва́ть(ся) *impf*, останови́ть(ся) *pf*.
stanza *n* строфа́.
staple[1] *n* (*metal bar*) скоба́; (*for paper*) скре́пка; *vt* скрепля́ть *impf*, скрепи́ть *pf*.
staple[2] *n* (*product*) гла́вный проду́кт; *adj* основно́й.
star *n* звезда́; (*asterisk*) звёздочка; *vi* игра́ть *impf*, сыгра́ть *pf* гла́вную роль. **starfish** *n* морска́я звезда́.
starboard *n* пра́вый борт.
starch *n* крахма́л; *vt* крахма́лить *impf*, на~ *pf*. **starchy** *adj* крахма́листый; (*prim*) чо́порный.
stare *n* при́стальный взгляд; *vi* при́стально смотре́ть *impf* (**at** на+*acc*).
stark *adj* (*bare*) го́лый; (*desolate*) пусты́нный; (*sharp*) ре́зкий; *adv* соверше́нно.
starling *n* скворе́ц.
starry *adj* звёздный.
start *n* нача́ло; (*sport*) старт; *vi* начина́ться *impf*, нача́ться *pf*; (*engine*) заводи́ться *impf*, завести́сь *pf*; (*set out*) отправля́ться *impf*, отпра́виться *pf*; (*shudder*) вздра́гивать *impf*, вздро́гнуть *pf*; (*sport*) стартова́ть *impf* & *pf*; *vt* начина́ть *impf*, нача́ть *pf* (*gerund, inf,* +*inf*; **by**, +*gerund* с того́, что…; **with** +*instr*, с+*gen*); (*car, engine*) заводи́ть *impf*, завести́ *pf* (*fire, rumour*) пуска́ть *impf*, пусти́ть *pf*; (*found*) осно́вывать *impf*, основа́ть *pf*. **starter** *n* (*tech*) стартёр; (*cul*) заку́ска. **starting-point** *n* отправно́й пункт.
startle *vt* испуга́ть *pf*.
starvation *n* го́лод. **starve** *vi* голода́ть *impf*; (*to death*) умира́ть *impf*, умере́ть *pf* с

го́лоду; *vt* мори́ть *impf*, по~, у~ *pf* го́лодом. **starving** *adj* голода́ющий; (*hungry*) о́чень голо́дный.

state *n* (*condition*) состоя́ние; (*polit*) госуда́рство, *attrib adj* (*ceremonial*) торже́ственный; пара́дный; (*polit*) госуда́рственный; *vt* (*announce*) заявля́ть *impf*, заяви́ть *pf*; (*expound*) излага́ть *impf*, изложи́ть *pf*. **stateless** *adj* не име́ющий гражда́нства. **stately** *adj* вели́чественный. **statement** *n* заявле́ние; (*comm*) отчёт. **statesman** *n* госуда́рственный де́ятель *m*.

static *adj* неподви́жный.

station *n* (*rly*) вокза́л, ста́нция; (*social*) обще́ственное положе́ние; (*meteorological, hydro-electric power, radio etc.*) ста́нция; (*post*) пост; *vt* размеща́ть *impf*, размести́ть *pf*. **stationary** *adj* неподви́жный.

stationery *n* канцеля́рские принадле́жности *f pl*; (*writing-paper*) почто́вая бума́га; ~ **shop** канцеля́рский магази́н.

statistic *n* статисти́ческое да́нное. **statistical** *adj* статисти́ческий. **statistician** *n* стати́стик. **statistics** *n* стати́стика.

statue *n* ста́туя. **statuette** *n* статуэ́тка.

stature *n* рост; (*merit*) кали́бр.

status *n* ста́тус. **status quo** *n* ста́тус-кво *neut indecl*.

statute *n* стату́т. **statutory** *adj* устано́вленный зако́ном.

staunch *adj* ве́рный.

stave *vt*: ~ **off** предотвраща́ть *impf*, предотврати́ть *pf*.

stay *n* (*time spent*) пребыва́ние; *vi* (*remain*) остава́ть-

ся *impf*, оста́ться *pf* (**to dinner** обе́дать); (*put up*) остана́вливаться *impf*, останови́ться *pf* (**at** (*place*) в+*prep*; **at** (*friends' etc.*) у+*gen*); (*live*) жить; ~ **behind** остава́ться *impf*, оста́ться *pf*; ~ **in** остава́ться *impf*, оста́ться *pf* до́ма; ~ **up** не ложи́ться *impf* спать; (*trousers*) держа́ться *impf*. **staying-power** *n* выно́сливость.

stead *n*: **stand s.o. in good** ~ ока́зываться *impf*, оказа́ться *pf* поле́зным кому́-л. **steadfast** *adj* сто́йкий, непоколеби́мый.

steady *adj* (*firm*) усто́йчивый; (*continuous*) непреры́вный; (*wind, temperature*) ро́вный; (*speed*) постоя́нный; (*unshakeable*) непоколеби́мый; *vt* (*boat etc.*) приводи́ть *impf*, привести́ *pf* в равнове́сие.

steak *n* бифште́кс.

steal *vt & abs* ворова́ть *impf*, с~ *pf*; красть *impf*, у~ *pf*; *vi* (*creep*) кра́сться *impf*, подкра́дываться *impf*, подкра́сться *pf*. **stealth** *n*: **by** ~ укра́дкой. **stealthy** *adj* ворова́тый, та́йный, скры́тый.

steam *n* пар; **at full** ~ на всех пара́х; **let off** ~ (*fig*) дава́ть *impf*, дать *pf* вы́ход свои́м чу́вствам; *vt* па́рить *impf*, по~ *pf*; (*vessel*) ходи́ть *indet*, идти́ *det* на пара́х; ~ **up** (*mist over*) запотева́ть *impf*, запоте́ть *pf*; поте́ть *impf*, за~, от~ *pf*; **engine** парова́я маши́на. **steamer**, **steamship** *n* парохо́д. **steamy** *adj* напо́лненный па́ром; (*passionate*) горя́чий.

steed n конь m.

steel n сталь; adj стально́й; vt:
~ **o.s.** ожесточа́ться impf,
ожесточи́ться pf; ~ **works**
сталелите́йный заво́д. **steely**
adj стально́й.

steep[1] adj круто́й; (excessive)
чрезме́рный.

steep[2] vt (immerse) погружа́ть impf, погрузи́ть pf (in
in+acc); (saturate) пропи́тывать impf, пропита́ть pf (in
+instr).

steeple n шпиль m. **steeple-
chase** n ска́чки f pl с препя́тствиями.

steer vt управля́ть impf, пра́
вить impf +instr; vi abs рули́ть impf; ~ **clear of** избега́ть impf, избежа́ть pf +gen.
steering-wheel n руль m.

stem[1] n стёбель m; (of wineglass) но́жка; (ling) осно́ва;
vi: ~ **from** происходи́ть impf,
произойти́ pf от+gen.

stem[2] vt (stop) остана́вливать impf, останови́ть pf.

stench n злово́ние.

stencil n трафаре́т; (tech)
шабло́н; vt наноси́ть impf,
нанести́ pf по трафаре́ту.
stencilled adj трафаре́тный.

step n (pace, action) шаг;
(dance) па neut indecl; (of
stairs, ladder) ступе́нь; by
~ шаг за ша́гом; in ~ в но́гу;
out of ~ не в но́гу; **take** ~s
принима́ть impf, приня́ть pf
ме́ры vi шага́ть impf, шагну́ть pf ступа́ть impf, ступи́ть pf; ~ **aside** сторони́ться impf, по~ pf; ~ **back**
отступа́ть impf, отступи́ть
pf; ~ **down** (resign) уходи́ть
impf, уйти́ pf в отста́вку; ~
forward выступа́ть impf, вы́
ступить pf; ~ **in** (intervene)

вме́шиваться impf, вмеша́ться pf; ~ **on** наступа́ть
impf, наступи́ть pf на+acc
(s.o.'s foot кому́-л. на́ ногу);
~ **over** переша́гивать impf,
перешагну́ть pf +acc, че́
рез+acc; ~ **up** (increase) повыша́ть impf, повы́сить pf.
step-ladder n стремя́нка.
stepping-stone n ка́мень m
для перехо́да; (fig) сре́дство. **steps** n pl ле́стница.
stepbrother n сво́дный брат.
stepdaughter n па́дчерица.
stepfather n о́тчим. **stepmother** n ма́чеха. **stepsister**
n сво́дная сестра́. **stepson** n
па́сынок.

steppe n степь f.

stereo n (system) стереофони́ческая систе́ма; (stereo-
phony) стереофо́ния; adj (re-
corded in ~) сте́рео indecl.
stereophonic adj стереофони́ческий. **stereotype** n
стереоти́п. **stereotyped** adj
стереоти́пный.

sterile adj стери́льный. **sterility** n стери́льность. **steri-
lization** n стерилиза́ция. **sterilize** vt стерилизова́ть impf &
pf.

sterling n сте́рлинг; **pound** ~
фунт сте́рлингов; adj стерлинговый.

stern[1] n корма́.

stern[2] adj суро́вый, стро́гий.

stethoscope n стетоско́п.

stew n (cul) мя́со тушёное
вме́сте с овоща́ми; vt & i
(cul) туши́ть(ся) impf, с~ pf;
(fig) томи́ть(ся) impf, с~ pf.

steward n бортпроводни́к.
stewardess n стюарде́сса.

stick[1] n па́лка; (of chalk etc.)
па́лочка; (hockey) клю́шка.

stick[2] vt (spear) зака́лывать

impf, заколо́ть *pf;* (*make adhere*) прикле́ивать *impf,* прикле́ить *pf* (**to** к+*dat*); (*coll*) (*put*) ста́вить *impf,* по~ *pf;* (*lay*) класть *impf,* положи́ть *pf;* (*endure*) терпе́ть *impf,* вы́~ *pf; vi* (*adhere*) ли́пнуть *impf* (**to** к+*dat*); прилипа́ть *impf,* прили́пнуть *pf* (**to** к+*dat*); ~ **in** (*thrust in*) втыка́ть *impf,* воткну́ть *pf* (*into opening*) всо́вывать *impf,* всу́нуть *pf;* ~ **on** (*glue on*) накле́ивать *impf,* накле́ить *pf;* ~ **out** (*thrust out*) высо́вывать *impf,* вы́сунуть *pf* (*from* из+*gen*); (*project*) торча́ть *impf;* ~ **to** (*keep to*) приде́рживаться *impf,* приде́ржаться *pf* +*gen;* (*remain at*) не отвлека́ться *impf* от+*gen;* ~ **together** держа́ться *impf* вме́сте; ~ **up for** заступа́ть *impf,* заступи́ть *pf;* **be, get, stuck** застрева́ть *impf,* застря́ть *pf.* **sticker** *n* накле́йка.

sticky *adj* ли́пкий.

stiff *adj* жёсткий, неги́бкий; (*prim*) чо́порный; (*difficult*) тру́дный; (*penalty*) суро́вый; **be** ~ (*ache*) боле́ть *impf.* **stiffen** *vt* де́лать *impf,* с~ *pf* жёстким; *vi* станови́ться *impf,* стать *pf* жёстким. **stiffness** *n* жёсткость; (*primness*) чо́порность.

stifle *vt* души́ть *impf,* за~ *pf;* (*suppress*) подавля́ть *impf,* подави́ть *pf;* (*sound*) заглуша́ть *impf,* заглуши́ть *pf; vi* зады́хаться *impf,* задохну́ться *pf.* **stifling** *adj* уду́шливый.

stigma *n* клеймо́.

stile *n* перела́з (*coll*).

stilettos *n pl* ту́фли *f pl* на шпи́льках.

still *adv* (всё) ещё; (*nevertheless*) тем не ме́нее; (*motionless*) неподви́жно; **stand** ~ не дви́гаться *impf,* дви́нуться *pf; n* (*quiet*) тишина́; *adj* ти́хий; (*immobile*) неподви́жный. **still-born** *adj* мертворождённый. **still life** *n* натюрмо́рт. **stillness** *n* тишина́.

stilted *adj* ходу́льный.

stimulant *n* возбужда́ющее сре́дство. **stimulate** *vt* возбужда́ть *impf,* возбуди́ть *pf.* **stimulating** *adj* возбуди́тельный. **stimulation** *n* возбужде́ние. **stimulus** *n* сти́мул.

sting *n* (*wound*) уку́с; (*stinger; fig*) жа́ло; *vt* жа́лить *impf,* у~ *pf; vi* (*burn*) жечь *impf.* **stinging** *adj* (*caustic*) язви́тельный.

stingy *adj* скупо́й.

stink *n* вонь; *vi* воня́ть *impf* (*of* +*instr*). **stinking** *adj* воню́чий.

stint *n* срок; *vi:* ~ **on** скупи́ться *impf,* по~ *pf* на+*acc.*

stipend *n* (*salary*) жа́лование; (*grant*) стипе́ндия.

stipulate *vt* обусло́вливать *impf,* обусло́вить *pf.* **stipulation** *n* усло́вие.

stir *n* (*commotion*) шум; *vt* (*mix*) меша́ть *impf,* по~ *pf;* (*excite*) волнова́ть *impf,* вз~ *pf; vi* (*move*) шевели́ться *impf,* шевельну́ться *pf;* ~ **up** возбужда́ть *impf,* возбуди́ть *pf.* **stirring** *adj* волну́ющий.

stirrup *n* стре́мя *neut.*

stitch *n* стежо́к; (*knitting*) пе́тля; (*med*) шов; (*pain*) ко́лики *f pl; vt* (*embroider, make line of* ~es) строчи́ть *impf,* про~ *pf;* (*join by sewing, make, suture*) сшива́ть *impf*, сшить *pf*; ~ **up** зашива́ть *impf*, заши́ть *pf*. **stitching** *n* (*stitches*) стро́чка.

stoat *n* горноста́й.

stock *n* (*store*) запа́с; (*of shop*) ассортиме́нт; (*live-*) скот; (*cul*) бульо́н; (*lineage*) семья́; (*fin*) а́кции *f pl*; **in** ~ в нали́чии; **out of** ~ распро́дан; **take** ~ **of** крити́чески оце́нивать *impf*, оцени́ть *pf*; *adj* станда́ртный; *vt* име́ть в нали́чии; ~ **up** запаса́ться *impf*, запасти́сь *pf* (**with** +*instr*). **stockbroker** *n* биржево́й ма́клер. **stock-exchange** *n* би́ржа. **stockpile** *n* запа́с; *vt* нака́пливать *impf*, накопи́ть *pf*. **stock-taking** *n* переучёт.

stocking *n* чуло́к.

stocky *adj* призе́мистый.

stodgy *adj* тяжёлый.

stoic(al) *adj* сто́йческий. **stoicism** *n* стоици́зм.

stoke *vt* топи́ть *impf*.

stolid *adj* флегмати́чный.

stomach *n* желу́док, (*also surface of body*) живо́т; *vt* терпе́ть *impf*, по~ *pf*. **stomach ache** *n* боль в животе́.

stone *n* ка́мень *m*; (*of fruit*) ко́сточка; *adj* ка́менный; *vt* побива́ть *impf*, поби́ть *pf* камня́ми; (*fruit*) вынима́ть *impf*, вы́нуть *pf* ко́сточки из+*gen*. **Stone Age** *n* ка́менный век. **stone-deaf** *adj* соверше́нно глухо́й. **stone-mason** *n* ка́менщик. **stonily** *adv* с ка́менным выраже́нием, хо́лодно. **stony** *adj* камени́стый; (*fig*) ка́менный.

stool *n* табуре́т, табуре́тка.

stoop *n* суту́лость; *vi* & *t* суту́лить(ся) *impf*, с~ *pf*; (*bend* (*down*)) наклоня́ть(ся) *impf*, наклони́ть(ся) *pf*; ~ **to**

(*abase o.s.*) унижа́ться *impf*, уни́зиться *pf* до+*gen*; (*condescend*) снисходи́ть *impf*, снизойти́ *pf* до+*gen*. **stooped, stooping** *adj* суту́лый.

stop *n* остано́вка; **put a** ~ **to** положи́ть *pf* коне́ц +*dat*; *vt* остана́вливать *impf*, останови́ть *pf*; (*discontinue*) прекраща́ть *impf*, прекрати́ть *pf*; (*restrain*) уде́рживать *impf*, удержа́ть *pf* (**from** от+*gen*); *vi* остана́вливаться *impf*, останови́ться *pf*; (*discontinue*) прекраща́ться *impf*, прекрати́ться *pf*; (*cease*) перестава́ть *impf*, переста́ть *pf* (+*inf*); ~ **up** *vt* затыка́ть *impf*, заткну́ть *pf*. **stoppage** *n* остано́вка; (*strike*) заба́стовка. **stopper** *n* про́бка. **stop-press** *n* экстренное сообще́ние в газе́те. **stopwatch** *n* секундоме́р.

storage *n* хране́ние. **store** *n* запа́с; (*storehouse*) склад; (*shop*) магази́н; **set** ~ **by** цени́ть *impf*; **what is in** ~ **for me?** что ждёт меня́ впереди́?; *vt* запаса́ть *impf*, запасти́ *pf*; (*put into storage*) сдава́ть *impf*, сдать *pf* на хране́ние. **storehouse** *n* склад. **store-room** *n* кладова́я *sb*.

storey *n* эта́ж.

stork *n* а́ист.

storm *n* бу́ря, (*thunder* ~) гроза́; *vt* (*mil*) штурмова́ть *impf*; *vi* бушева́ть *impf*. **stormy** *adj* бу́рный.

story *n* расска́з, по́весть; (*anecdote*) анекдо́т; (*plot*) фа́була; ~-**teller** расска́зчик.

stout *adj* (*strong*) кре́пкий; (*staunch*) сто́йкий; (*portly*) доро́дный.

stove *n* (*with fire inside*) печь,

(*cooker*) плита́.

stow *vt* укла́дывать *impf*, уложи́ть *pf*. **stowaway** *n* безбиле́тный пассажи́р.

straddle *vt* (*sit astride*) сиде́ть *impf* верхо́м на+*prep*; (*stand astride*) стоя́ть *impf*, расста́вив но́ги над+*instr*.

straggle *vi* отстава́ть *impf*, отста́ть *pf*. **straggler** *n* отста́вший *sb*. **straggling** *adj* разбро́санный. **straggly** *adj* растрёпанный.

straight *adj* прямо́й; (*undiluted*) неразба́вленный; *predic* (*in order*) в поря́дке; *adv* пря́мо; ~ **away** сра́зу. **straighten** *vt* & *i* выпрямля́ть(ся) *impf*, вы́прямить(ся) *pf*; *vt* (*put in order*) поправля́ть *impf*, попра́вить *pf*. **straightforward** *adj* прямо́й; (*simple*) просто́й.

strain[1] *n* (*tension*) натяже́ние; (*sprain*) растяже́ние; (*effort, exertion*) напряже́ние; (*tendency*) скло́нность; (*sound*) звук; *vt* (*stretch*) натя́гивать *impf*, натяну́ть *pf*; (*sprain*) растя́гивать *impf*, растяну́ть *pf*; (*exert*) напряга́ть *impf*, напря́чь *pf*; (*filter*) проце́живать *impf*, процеди́ть *pf*; *vi* (*also exert o.s.*) напряга́ться *impf*, напря́чься *pf*. **strained** *adj* натя́нутый. **strainer** *n* (*tea ~*) си́течко; (*sieve*) си́то.

strain[2] *n* (*breed*) поро́да.

strait(s) *n* (*geog*) проли́в. **straitjacket** *n* смири́тельная руба́шка. **straits** *n pl* (*difficulties*) затрудни́тельное положе́ние.

strand[1] *n* (*hair, rope*) прядь; (*thread, also fig*) нить.

strand[2] *vt* сажа́ть *impf*, посади́ть *pf* на мель. **stranded** *adj* на мели́.

strange *adj* стра́нный; (*unfamiliar*) незнако́мый; (*alien*) чужо́й. **strangely** *adv* стра́нно. **strangeness** *n* стра́нность. **stranger** *n* незнако́мец.

strangle *vt* души́ть *impf*, за~ *pf*. **stranglehold** *n* мёртвая хва́тка. **strangulation** *n* удуше́ние.

strap *n* реме́нь *m*; *vt* (*tie up*) стя́гивать *impf*, стяну́ть *pf* ремнём. **strapping** *adj* ро́слый.

stratagem *n* хи́трость. **strategic** *adj* стратеги́ческий. **strategist** *n* страте́г. **strategy** *n* страте́гия.

stratum *n* слой.

straw *n* соло́ма; (*drinking*) соло́минка; **the last ~** после́дняя ка́пля; *adj* соло́менный.

strawberry *n* клубни́ка (*no pl; usu collect*); (*wild*) земляни́ка (*no pl; usu collect*).

stray *vi* сбива́ться *impf*, сби́ться *pf*; (*digress*) отклоня́ться *impf*, отклони́ться *pf*; *adj* (*lost*) заблуди́вшийся; (*homeless*) бездо́мный; *n* (*from flock*) отби́вшееся от ста́да живо́тное *sb*; ~ **bullet** шальна́я пу́ля.

streak *n* полоса́ (*of luck* везе́ния); (*tendency*) жи́лка; *vi* (*rush*) проноси́ться *impf*, пронести́сь *pf* с полоса́ми (*with* +*gen*). **streaked** *adj* с поло́сами. **streaky** *adj* полоса́тый; (*meat*) с просло́йками жи́ра.

stream *n* (*brook, tears*) ручéй; (*brook, flood, tears, people etc.*) пото́к; (*current*) тече́ние; **up/down** ~ вверх/вниз по тече́нию; *vi* течь *impf*, струи́ться *impf*; (*rush*) проноси́ться *impf*, пронести́сь

pf; (blow) развева́ться impf.
streamer n вы́мпел. **stream-lined** adj обтека́емый; (fig) хорошо́ нала́женный.
street n у́лица; adj у́личный; ~ **lamp** у́личный фона́рь m.
strength n си́ла; (numbers) чи́сленность; **on the ~ of** в си́лу+gen. **strengthen** vt уси́ливать impf, уси́лить pf.
strenuous adj (work) тру́дный; (effort) напряжённый.
stress n напряже́ние; (mental) стресс; (emphasis) ударе́ние; vt (accent) ста́вить impf, по~ pf ударе́ние на+acc; (emphasize) подчёркивать impf подчеркну́ть pf. **stressful** adj стрессовый.
stretch n (expanse) отре́зок; **at a ~** (in succession) подря́д; vt & i (widen, spread out) растя́гивать(ся) impf, растяну́ть(ся) pf; (in length, ~ out limbs) вытя́гивать(ся) impf, вы́тянуть(ся) pf; (tauten) натя́гивать(ся) impf, натяну́ть(ся) pf; (extend, e.g. rope, forth limbs) протя́гивать(ся) impf, протяну́ть(ся) pf; vi (material, land) тяну́ться impf; ~ **one's legs** (coll) размина́ть impf, размя́ть pf но́ги.
stretcher n носи́лки (-лок) pl.
strew vt разбра́сывать impf, разброса́ть pf; ~ **with** посыпа́ть impf, посы́пать pf +instr.
stricken adj поражённый.
strict adj стро́гий. **stricture(s)** n (стро́гая) кри́тика.
stride n (большо́й) шаг; pl (fig) успе́хи m pl; **to take in in one's ~** преодолева́ть impf, преодоле́ть pf что-л. без уси́лий; vi шага́ть impf.
strident adj ре́зкий.
strife n раздо́р.

strike n (refusal to work) забасто́вка; (mil) уда́р; **be on ~** бастова́ть impf; (go on ~) забастова́ть impf; (attack) ударя́ть impf, уда́рить pf; (the hour) бить impf, про~ pf; vt (hit) ударя́ть impf, уда́рить pf; (impress) поража́ть impf, порази́ть pf; (discover) открыва́ть impf, откры́ть pf; (match) зажига́ть impf, заже́чь pf; (the hour) бить impf, про~ pf; (occur to) приходи́ть impf, прийти́ pf в го́лову+dat; ~ **off** вычёркивать impf, вы́черкнуть pf; ~ **up** начина́ть impf, нача́ть pf. **striker** n забасто́вщик. **striking** adj порази́тельный.
string n бечёвка; (mus) струна́; (series) ряд; pl (mus) стру́нные инструме́нты m pl; ~ **bag**, ~ **vest** се́тка; vt (thread) низа́ть impf, на~ pf; ~ **along** (coll) води́ть impf за нос; ~ **out** (prolong) растя́гивать impf, растяну́ть pf; **strung up** (tense) напряжённый. **stringed** adj стру́нный.
stringy adj (fibrous) волокни́стый; (meat) жи́листый.
stringent adj стро́гий.
strip[1] n полоса́, поло́ска.
strip[2] vt (undress) раздева́ть impf, разде́ть pf; (deprive) лиша́ть impf, лиши́ть pf (of +gen); ~ **off** (tear off) сдира́ть impf, содра́ть pf; vi раздева́ться impf, разде́ться pf. **strip-tease** n стрипти́з.
stripe n полоса́. **striped** adj полоса́тый.
strive vi (endeavour) стреми́ться impf (for к+dat); (struggle) боро́ться impf (for за+acc; against про́тив+gen).

stroke n (blow, med) уда́р; (of oar) взмах; (swimming) стиль m; (of pen etc.) штрих; (piston) ход; vt гла́дить impf, по~ pf.

stroll n прогу́лка; vi прогу́ливаться impf, прогуля́ться pf.

strong adj си́льный; (stout) кре́пкий; (of drinks) кре́пкий; (healthy) здоро́вый; (opinion etc.) твёрдый. **stronghold** n кре́пость. **strong-minded, strong-willed** adj реши́тельный.

structural adj структу́рный. **structure** n структу́ра; (building) сооруже́ние; vt организова́ть impf & pf.

struggle n борьба́; vi боро́ться impf (for за+acc; against про́тив+gen); (writhe, ~ with fig) би́ться (with над+instr).

strum vt бренча́ть impf (on на+prep).

strut¹ n (vertical) сто́йка; (horizontal) распо́рка.

strut² vi ходи́ть indet, идти́ det го́голем.

stub n огры́зок; (cigarette) оку́рок; (counterfoil) коре́шо́к; vt: ~ one's toe уда́ря́ться impf, уда́риться pf ного́й (on на+acc); ~ out гаси́ть impf, по~ pf.

stubble n жнивьё; (hair) щети́на.

stubborn adj упря́мый. **stubbornness** n упря́мство.

stucco n штукату́рка.

stud¹ n (collar, cuff) за́понка; (nail) гвоздь m с большо́й шля́пкой; vt (bestrew) усе́ивать impf, усе́ять pf (with +instr).

stud² n (horses) ко́нный заво́д.

student n студе́нт, ~ка.

studied adj напускно́й.

studio n сту́дия.

studious adj лю́бящий нау́ку; (diligent) стара́тельный.

study n изуче́ние; pl заня́тия neut pl; (investigation) иссле́дование; (art, mus) этю́д; (room) кабине́т; vt изуча́ть impf, изучи́ть pf; учи́ться impf, об~ pf +dat; (scrutinize) рассма́тривать impf, рассмотре́ть pf; vi (take lessons) учи́ться impf, об~ pf; (do one's studies) занима́ться impf.

stuff n (material) материа́л; (things) ве́щи f pl; vt набива́ть impf, наби́ть pf; (cul) начиня́ть impf, начини́ть pf; (cram into) запи́хивать impf, запиха́ть pf (into в+acc); (shove into) сова́ть impf, су́нуть pf (into в+acc); vi (overeat) объеда́ться impf, объе́сться pf. **stuffiness** n духота́. **stuffing** n наби́вка; (cul) начи́нка. **stuffy** adj ду́шный.

stumble vi (also fig) спотыка́ться impf, споткну́ться pf (over о+acc); ~ upon натыка́ться impf, наткну́ться pf на+acc. **stumbling-block** n ка́мень m преткнове́ния.

stump n (tree) пень m; (pencil) огры́зок; (limb) культя́; vt (perplex) ста́вить impf, по~ pf в тупи́к.

stun vt (also fig) оглуша́ть impf, оглуши́ть pf. **stunning** adj потряса́ющий.

stunt¹ n трюк.

stunt² vt заде́рживать impf, задержа́ть pf рост+gen. **stunted** adj низкоро́слый.

stupefy vt оглуша́ть impf, оглуши́ть pf. **stupendous** adj колосса́льный. **stupid** adj глу́пый. **stupidity** n глу́пость. **stupor** n оцепене́ние.

sturdy adj крепкий.

stutter n заикание; vi заикаться impf.

sty¹ n (pig~) свинарник.

sty² n (on eye) ячмень n.

style n стиль m; (taste) вкус; (fashion) мода; (sort) род; (of hair) причёска. **stylish** adj модный. **stylist** n (of hair) парикмахер. **stylistic** adj стилистический. **stylize** vt стилизовать impf & pf.

stylus n игла звукоснимателя.

suave adj обходительный.

subconscious adj подсознательный; n подсознание. **subcontract** vt давать impf, дать pf подрядчику. **subcontractor** n подрядчик. **subdivide** vt подразделять impf, подразделить pf. **subdivision** n подразделение. **subdue** vt покорять impf, покорить pf; subdued adj (suppressed, dispirited) подавленный; (soft) мягкий; (indistinct) приглушённый. **sub-editor** n помощник редактора.

subject n (theme) тема; (discipline, theme) предмет; (question) вопрос; (thing on to which action is directed) объект; (gram) подлежащее sb; (national) подданный sb; adj: ~ to (susceptible to) подверженный+dat; (on condition that) при условии, что...; если; be ~ to (change etc.) подлежать impf +dat; vt: ~ to подвергнуть impf, подвергнуть pf +dat. **subjection** n подчинение. **subjective** adj субъективный. **subjectivity** n субъективность. **subject-matter** n (of book, lecture) содержание, тема; (of discussion) предмет.

subjugate vt покорять impf, покорить pf. **subjugation** n покорение.

subjunctive (mood) n сослагательное наклонение.

sublet vt передавать impf, передать pf в субаренду.

sublimate vt сублимировать impf & pf. **sublimation** n сублимация. **sublime** adj возвышенный.

subliminal adj подсознательный. **sub-machine-gun** n автомат. **submarine** n подводная лодка. **submerge** vt погружать impf, погрузить impf. **submission** n подчинение; (for inspection) представление. **submissive** adj покорный. **submit** vi подчиняться impf, подчиниться pf (to +dat); vt представлять impf, представить pf. **subordinate** n подчинённый sb; adj подчинённый; (secondary) второстепенный; (gram) придаточный; vt подчинять impf, подчинить pf. **subscribe** vi подписываться impf, подписаться pf (to на+acc); ~ to (opinion) присоединяться impf, присоединиться pf к+dat. **subscriber** n подписчик; абонент. **subscription** n подписка, абонемент; (fee) взнос. **subsection** n подраздел. **subsequent** adj последующий. **subsequently** adv впоследствии. **subservient** adj раболепный. **subside** vi убывать impf, убыть pf; (soil) оседать impf, осесть pf. **subsidence** n (soil) оседание. **subsidiary** adj вспомогательный; (secondary) второстепенный; n филиал. **subsidize** vt субсидировать *impf* & *pf*. **subsidy** *n* субси́дия. **subsist** *vi* (live) жить *impf* (on +*instr*). **substance** *n* вещество́; (essence) су́щность, суть; (content) содержа́ние. **substantial** *adj* (durable) про́чный; (considerable) значи́тельный; (food) пло́тный. **substantially** *adv* (basically) в основно́м; (considerably) значи́тельно. **substantiate** *vt* обосно́вывать *impf*, обоснова́ть *pf*. **substitute** *n* (person) замести́тель *m*; (thing) заме́на; *vt* заменя́ть *impf*, замени́ть *pf* +*instr* (for +*acc*); I ~ water for milk заменя́ю молоко́ водо́й. **substitution** *n* заме́на. **subsume** *vt* относи́ть *impf*, отнести́ *pf* к како́й-л. катего́рии. **subterfuge** *n* уве́ртка. **subterranean** *adj* подзе́мный. **subtitle** *n* подзаголо́вок; (cin) субти́тр.

subtle *adj* то́нкий. **subtlety** *n* то́нкость.

subtract *vt* вычита́ть *impf*, вы́честь *pf*. **subtraction** *n* вычита́ние. **suburb** *n* при́город. **suburban** *adj* при́городный. **subversion** *n* подрывна́я де́ятельность. **subversive** *adj* подрывно́й. **subway** *n* подзе́мный перехо́д.

succeed *vi* удава́ться *impf*, уда́ться *pf*; the plan will ~ план уда́ется; he ~ed in buying the book ему́ удало́сь купи́ть кни́гу; (be successful) преуспева́ть *impf*, преуспе́ть *pf* (in +*prep*); (follow) сменя́ть *impf*, смени́ть *pf*; (be heir) насле́довать *impf* & *pf* (to +*dat*). **succeeding** *adj* после́дующий. **success** *n* успе́х. **successful** *adj* успе́шный,

succession *n* (series) ряд; (to throne) престолонасле́дие; right of ~ пра́во насле́дования; in ~ подря́д, оди́н за други́м. **successive** *adj* (consecutive) после́довательный. **successor** *n* прее́мник.

succinct *adj* сжа́тый.

succulent *adj* со́чный.

succumb *vi* (to pressure) уступа́ть *impf*, уступи́ть *pf* (to +*dat*); (to temptation) поддава́ться *impf*, подда́ться *pf* (to +*dat*).

such *adj* тако́й; ~ people таки́е лю́ди; ~ as (for example) так наприме́р; (of a kind as) тако́й как; ~ beauty as yours така́я красота́ как ва́ша; (that which) тот, кото́рый; I shall read ~ books as I like я бу́ду чита́ть те кни́ги, кото́рые мне нра́вятся; ~ as тако́й, что́бы; his illness was not ~ as to cause anxiety его́ боле́знь была́ не тако́й (серьёзной), что́бы вы́звать беспоко́йство; ~ and ~ тако́й-то; *pron* тако́в; ~ was his character тако́в был его́ хара́ктер; as ~ сам по себе́; ~ is not the case э́то не так. **suchlike** *pron* (inanimate) тому́ подо́бное; (people) таки́е лю́ди *pl*.

suck *vt* соса́ть *impf*; ~ in вса́сывать, всоса́ть *pf*; (engulf) заса́сывать *impf*, засоса́ть *pf*; ~ out выса́сывать *impf*, вы́сосать *pf*; ~ up to (coll) подли́зываться *impf*, подлиза́ться *pf* к+*dat*. **sucker** *n* (biol, rubber device) присо́ска; (bot) корнево́й побе́г. **suckle** *vt* корми́ть *impf*, на *pf* гру́дью. **suction** *n* вса́сывание.

sudden adj внеза́пный. **suddenly** adv вдруг. **suddenness** n внеза́пность.

sue vt & i подава́ть impf, пода́ть pf в суд (на+acc); ~ **s.o. for damages** предъявля́ть impf, предъяви́ть pf (к) кому́-л. иск о возмеще́нии уще́рба.

suede n за́мша; adj за́мшевый.

suet n нутряно́е са́ло.

suffer vi страда́ть impf, по~ pf +instr, от+gen; (loss, defeat) терпе́ть impf, по~ pf; (tolerate) терпе́ть impf, по~ pf; vt (from +instr, от+gen). **sufferance** n: he is here on ~ его́ здесь те́рпят. **suffering** n страда́ние.

suffice vi & t быть доста́точным (для+gen); хвата́ть impf, хвати́ть pf impers+gen (+dat). **sufficient** adj доста́точный.

suffix n су́ффикс.

suffocate vt удуша́ть impf, удуши́ть pf; vi задыха́ться impf, задохну́ться pf. **suffocating** adj удушли́вый. **suffocation** n удуше́ние.

suffrage n избира́тельное пра́во.

suffuse vt залива́ть impf, зали́ть pf (with +instr).

sugar n са́хар; adj са́харный; vt подсла́щивать impf, подсласти́ть pf; ~ **basin** са́харница; ~ **beet** са́харная свёкла; ~ **cane** са́харный тро́стник. **sugary** adj (fig) слаща́вый.

suggest vt предлага́ть impf, предложи́ть pf; (evoke) напомина́ть impf, напо́мнить pf; (imply) намека́ть impf,

намекну́ть pf на+acc; (indicate) говори́ть impf о+prep. **suggestion** n предложе́ние; (psych) внуше́ние. **suggestive** adj вызыва́ющий мысли (of o+prep); (indecent) собла зни́тельный.

suicidal adj самоуби́йствен ный; (fig) губи́тельный. **suicide** n самоуби́йство; **commit** ~ соверша́ть impf, соверши́ть pf самоуби́йство.

suit n (clothing) костю́м; (law) иск; (cards) масть; **follow** ~ (fig) сле́довать impf, по~ pf приме́ру; vt (be convenient for) устра́ивать impf устро́ить pf; (adapt) приспо са́бливать impf, приспосо́ бить pf; (be able for, match) подходи́ть impf, подойти́ pf (+dat); (look attractive on) идти́ impf +dat. **suitability** n приго́дность. **suitable** ad (fitting) подходя́щий; (convenient) удо́бный. **suitably** adv соотве́тственно. **suit case** n чемода́н.

suite n (retinue) сви́та; (furni ture) гарниту́р; (rooms) апар та́менты m pl; (mus) сюи́та.

suitor n покло́нник.

sulk vi ду́ться impf. **sulky** adj наду́тый.

sullen adj угрю́мый.

sully vt пятна́ть impf, за~ pf.

sulphur n се́ра. **sulphuric** ~ **acid** се́рная кислота́.

sultana n (raisin) изю́минка pl кишми́ш (collect).

sultry adj зно́йный.

sum n су́мма; (arithmetica problem) арифмети́ческая за да́ча; pl арифме́тика; v: ~ u vi & t (summarize) подводи́ть impf, подвести́ pf ито́ги (+gen) vt (appraise) оце́нивать impf

оцени́ть pf.
summarize vt сумми́ровать impf & pf. **summary** n резюме́ neut indecl, сво́дка; adj сумма́рный; (dismissal) бесцеремо́нный.
summer n ле́то; attrib ле́тний.
summer-house n бесе́дка.
summit n верши́на; ~ meeting встре́ча на верха́х.
summon vt вызыва́ть impf, вы́звать pf; ~ up one's courage собира́ться impf, собра́ться pf с ду́хом. **summons** n вы́зов; (law) пове́стка в суд; vt вызыва́ть impf, вы́звать pf в суд.
sumptuous adj роско́шный.
sun n со́лнце; in the ~ на со́лнце. **sunbathe** vi загора́ть impf. **sunbeam** n со́лнечный луч. **sunburn** n зага́р; (inflammation) со́лнечный ожо́г. **sunburnt** adj загоре́лый; become ~ загора́ть impf, загоре́ть pf.
Sunday n воскресе́нье.
sundry adj ра́зный; all and ~ всё и вся.
sunflower n подсо́лнечник. **sun-glasses** n pl очки́ (-ко́в) pl от со́лнца.
sunken adj (cheeks, eyes) впа́лый; (submerged) погружённый; (ship) зато́пленный; (below certain level) ни́же (како́го-л. у́ровня).
sunlight n со́лнечный свет. **sunny** adj со́лнечный. **sunrise** n восхо́д со́лнца. **sunset** n зака́т. **sunshade** n (parasol) зо́нтик; (awning) наве́с. **sunshine** n со́лнечный свет. **sunstroke** n со́лнечный уда́р. **suntan** n зага́р. **sun-tanned** adj загоре́лый.
super adj замеча́тельный.

superb adj превосхо́дный. **supercilious** adj высокоме́рный. **superficial** adj пове́рхностный. **superficiality** n пове́рхностность. **superfluous** adj ли́шний. **superhuman** adj сверхчелове́ческий. **superintendent** n заве́дующий sb (of +instr); (police) ста́рший полице́йский офице́р. **superior** adj ста́рший sb; (better) превосхо́дный; (in rank) ста́рший; (haughty) высокоме́рный. **superiority** n превосхо́дство. **superlative** adj превосхо́дный; n (gram) превосхо́дная сте́пень. **superman** n сверхчелове́к. **supermarket** n универса́м. **supernatural** adj сверхъесте́ственный. **superpower** n сверхдержа́ва. **supersede** vt заменя́ть impf, замени́ть pf. **supersonic** adj сверхзвуково́й. **superstition** n суеве́рие. **superstitious** adj суеве́рный. **superstructure** n надстро́йка. **supervise** vt наблюда́ть impf за+instr. **supervision** n надзо́р. **supervisor** n нача́льник; (of studies) руководи́тель m.
supper n у́жин; have ~ у́жинать impf, по~ pf.
supple adj ги́бкий. **suppleness** n ги́бкость.
supplement n (to book) дополне́ние; (to periodical) приложе́ние; vt дополня́ть impf, допо́лнить pf. **supplementary** adj дополни́тельный.
supplier n поставщи́к. **supply** n (stock) запа́с; (econ) предложе́ние; pl (mil) припа́сы (-ов) pl; vt снабжа́ть impf, снабди́ть pf (with +instr).

support n поддержка; vt поддерживать impf, поддержать pf; (family) содержать impf. **supporter** n сторонник; (sport) болельщик. **supportive** adj участливый.

suppose vt (think) полагать impf; (presuppose) предполагать impf, предположить pf; (assume) допускать impf, допустить pf. **supposed** adj (assumed) предполагаемый. **supposition** n предположение.

suppress vt подавлять impf, подавить pf. **suppression** n подавление.

supremacy n господство. **supreme** adj верховный.

surcharge n наценка.

sure adj уверенный (of в+prep; that что); (reliable) верный; ~ enough действительно; he is ~ to come он обязательно придёт; make ~ of (convince o.s.) убеждаться impf, убедиться pf в+prep; make ~ that (check up) проверять impf, проверить pf что. **surely** adv наверняка. **surety** n порука; **stand ~ for** ручаться impf, поручиться pf за+acc.

surf n прибой; vi заниматься impf, заняться pf сёрфингом. **surface** n поверхность; (exterior) внешность; **on the** ~ (fig) внешне; **under the** ~ (fig) по существу; adj поверхностный; vi всплывать impf, всплыть pf.

surfeit n (surplus) излишек.

surge n волна; vi (rise, heave) вздыматься impf; (emotions) нахлынуть pf; ~ **forward** ринуться pf вперёд.

surgeon n хирург. **surgery** n (treatment) хирургия; (place)

кабинет; (~ hours) приёмные часы m pl (врача). **surgical** adj хирургически

surly adj (morose) угрюмый; (rude) грубый.

surmise vt & i предполагать impf, предположить pf.

surmount vt преодолевать impf, преодолеть pf.

surname n фамилия.

surpass vt превосходить impf, превзойти pf.

surplus n излишек; adj лишний.

surprise n (astonishment) удивление; (surprising thing) сюрприз; vt удивлять impf, удивить pf; (come upon suddenly) заставать impf, застать pf врасплох; **be** ~ (at) удивляться impf, удивиться pf (+dat). **surprising** adj удивительный.

surreal adj сюрреалистический. **surrealism** n сюрреализм. **surrealist** n сюрреалист; adj сюрреалистический.

surrender n сдача; (renunciation) отказ; vt сдавать impf, сдать pf; (give up) отказываться impf, отказаться pf от+gen; vi сдаваться impf, сдаться pf; ~ **o.s. to** предаваться impf, предаться pf +dat.

surreptitious adj тайный.

surrogate n заменитель m.

surround vt окружать impf, окружить pf (with +instr). **surrounding** adj окружающий. **surroundings** n (environs) окрестности f pl; (milieu) среда.

surveillance n надзор.

survey n (review) обзор; (inspection) инспекция; (poll) опрос; vt (review) обозре ва́ть *impf*, обозре́ть *pf*; (*inspect*) инспекти́ровать *impf*, про~ *pf*; (*poll*) опра́шивать *impf*, опроси́ть *pf*. **surveyor** *n* инспе́ктор.

survival *n* (*surviving*) выжива́ние; (*relic*) пережи́ток. **survive** *vt* пережива́ть *impf*, пережи́ть *pf*; *vi* выжива́ть *impf*, вы́жить *pf*. **survivor** *n* уцеле́вший *sb*; (*fig*) боре́ц.

susceptible *adj* подве́рженный (**to** влия́нию +*gen*); (*sensitive*) чувстви́тельный (**to** к+*dat*); (*impressionable*) впечатли́тельный.

suspect *n* подозрева́емый *sb*; *adj* подозри́тельный; *vt* подозрева́ть *impf* (**of** в+*prep*); (*assume*) полага́ть *impf* (**that** что).

suspend *vt* (*hang up*) подве́шивать *impf*, подве́сить *pf*; приостана́вливать *impf*, приостанови́ть *pf*; (*debar temporarily*) вре́менно отстраня́ть *impf*, отстрани́ть *pf*; **~ed sentence** усло́вный пригово́р. **suspender** *n* (*stocking*) подвя́зка. **suspense** *n* неизве́стность. **suspension** *n* (*halt*) приостано́вка; (*of car*) рессо́ры *f pl*; **~ bridge** вися́чий мост.

suspicion *n* подозре́ние; **on ~** по подозре́нию (**of** в+*loc*); (*trace*) отте́нок. **suspicious** *adj* подозри́тельный.

sustain *vt* (*support*) подде́рживать *impf*, поддержа́ть *pf*; (*suffer*) потерпе́ть *pf*. **sustained** *adj* (*uninterrupted*) непреры́вный. **sustenance** *n* пи́ща.

swab *n* (*mop*) шва́бра; (*med*) тампо́н; (*specimen*) мазо́к.

swagger *vi* расха́живать *impf*

с ва́жным ви́дом.

swallow[1] *n* глото́к; *vt* прогла́тывать *impf*, проглоти́ть *pf*; **~ up** поглоща́ть *impf*, поглоти́ть *pf*.

swallow[2] *n* (*bird*) ла́сточка.

swamp *n* боло́то; *vt* залива́ть *impf*, зали́ть *pf*; (*fig*) зава́ливать *impf*, завали́ть *pf* (**with** +*instr*). **swampy** *adj* боло́тистый.

swan *n* ле́бедь *m*.

swap *n* обме́н; *vt* (*for different thing*) меня́ть *impf*, об~, по~ *pf* (**for** на+*acc*); (*for similar thing*) обме́ниваться *impf*, обменя́ться *pf* +*instr*.

swarm *n* (*of bees*) рой; (*crowd*) толпа́; *vi* рои́ться *impf*, толпи́ться *impf*; (*teem*) кише́ть *impf* (**with** +*instr*).

swarthy *adj* сму́глый.

swastika *n* сва́стика.

swat *vt* прихло́пывать *impf*, прихло́пнуть *pf*.

swathe *n* (*expanse*) простра́нство; *vt* (*wrap*) заку́тывать *impf*, заку́тать *pf*.

sway *n* (*influence*) влия́ние; (*power*) власть *vt* & *i* кача́ть(ся) *impf*, качну́ть(ся) *pf*; *vt* (*influence*) име́ть *impf* влия́ние на+*acc*.

swear *vi* (*vow*) кля́сться *impf*, по~ *pf*; (*curse*) руга́ться *impf*, ругну́ться *pf*; **~-word** руга́тельство.

sweat *n* пот; *vi* поте́ть *impf*, вс~ *pf*. **sweater** *n* сви́тер. **sweaty** *adj* по́тный.

swede *n* брю́ква. **Swede** *n* шве́д, ~дка. **Sweden** *n* Шве́ция. **Swedish** *adj* шве́дский.

sweep *n* (*span*) разма́х; (*chimney-~*) трубочи́ст; *vt* подмета́ть *impf*, подмести́ *pf*; *vi* *(go majestically)* ходи́ть *indet*, идти́ *det*, пойти́ *pf* велича́во; *(move swiftly)* мча́ться *impf*; ~ **away** смета́ть *impf*, смести́ *pf*. **sweeping** *n (changes)* радика́льный; *(statement)* огу́льный.

sweet *n (sweetmeat)* конфе́та; *(dessert)* сла́дкое *sb*; *adj* сла́дкий; *(fragrant)* души́стый; *(dear)* ми́лый. **sweeten** *vt* подсла́щивать *impf*, подсласти́ть *pf*. **sweetheart** *n* возлюбленный, -нная *sb*. **sweetness** *n* сла́дость.

swell *vi (up)* опуха́ть *impf*, опу́хнуть *pf*; *vt & i (a sail)* надува́ть(ся) *impf*, наду́ть(ся) *pf*; *vt (increase)* увели́чивать *impf*, увели́чить *pf*; *n (of sea)* зыбь. **swelling** *n* о́пухоль.

swelter *vi* изнемога́ть *impf* от жары́. **sweltering** *adj* зно́йный.

swerve *vi* ре́зко свёртывать, свора́чивать *impf*, сверну́ть *pf*.

swift *adj* бы́стрый.

swig *n* глото́к; *vt* хлеба́ть *impf*.

swill *n* по́йло; *vt (rinse)* полоска́ть *impf*, вы́- *pf*.

swim *vi* пла́вать *indet*, плыть *det*; *vt (across)* переплыва́ть *impf*, переплы́ть *pf* +*acc*, че́рез+*acc*. **swimmer** *n* плове́ц, пловчи́ха. **swimming** *n* пла́вание. **swimming-pool** *n* бассе́йн для пла́вания. **swimsuit** *n* купа́льный костю́м.

swindle *vt* обма́нывать *impf*, обману́ть *pf*; *n* обма́н. **swindler** *n* моше́нник.

swine *n* свинья́.

swing *vi* кача́ться *impf*, качну́ться *pf*; *vt* кача́ть *impf*, качну́ть *pf* +*acc*, *instr*; *(arms)* разма́хивать *impf* +*instr*;

(go majestically) ходи́ть *indet*, идти́ *det*, пойти́ *pf* велича́во; *(move swiftly)* мча́ться *impf*; ~ **away** смета́ть *impf*, смести́ *pf*. **sweeping** *n (changes)* радика́льный; *(statement)* огу́льный.

кача́ние; *(shift)* крен; *(seat)* каче́ли (-лей) *pl*; **in full** ~ в по́лном разга́ре.

swingeing *adj (huge)* грома́дный; *(forcible)* си́льный.

swipe *n* си́льный уда́р; *vt* с си́лой ударя́ть *impf*, уда́рить *pf*.

swirl *vi* крути́ться *impf*; *n (of snow)* вихрь *m*.

swish *vi (cut the air)* рассека́ть *impf*, рассе́чь *pf* во́здух со сви́стом; *(rustle)* шелесте́ть *impf*; *vt (tail)* взма́хивать *impf*, взмахну́ть *pf* +*instr*; *(brandish)* разма́хивать *impf* +*instr*; *n (of whip)* свист; *(rustle)* ше́лест.

Swiss *n* швейца́рец, -ца́рка; *adj* швейца́рский.

switch *n (electr)* выключа́тель *m*; *(change)* измене́ние; *vt & i (also* ~ **over)** переключа́ть(ся) *impf*, переключи́ть(ся) *pf*; *vt (swap)* меня́ться *impf*, об—, по— *pf* +*instr*; ~ **off** выключа́ть *impf*, вы́ключить *pf*; ~ **on** включа́ть *impf*, включи́ть *pf*. **switchboard** *n* коммута́тор.

Switzerland *n* Швейца́рия.

swivel *vt & i* враща́ть(ся) *impf*.

swollen *adj* взду́тый.

swoon *n* о́бморок; *vi* па́дать *impf*, упа́сть *pf* в о́бморок.

swoop *vi:* ~ **down** налета́ть *impf*, налете́ть *pf (on* на+*acc*); *n* налёт; **at one fell** ~ одни́м уда́ром.

sword *n* меч.

sycophant *adj* льсти́вый.

syllable *n* слог.

syllabus *n* програ́мма.

symbol *n* си́мвол. **symbolic(al)** *adj* символи́ческий. **symbolism** *n* символи́зм. **symbolize** *vt* символизи́ровать *impf*.

symmetrical adj симметри́ческий. **symmetry** n симметрия. **sympathetic** adj сочу́вственный. **sympathize** vi сочу́вствовать impf (with +dat). **sympathizer** n сторо́нник. **sympathy** n сочу́вствие. **symphony** n симфо́ния. **symposium** n симпо́зиум. **symptom** n симпто́м. **symptomatic** adj симптомати́чный. **synagogue** n синаго́га. **synchronization** n синхрониза́ция. **synchronize** vt синхронизи́ровать impf & pf. **syndicate** n синдика́т. **syndrome** n синдро́м. **synonym** n сино́ним. **synonymous** adj синоними́ческий. **synopsis** n конспе́кт. **syntax** n си́нтаксис. **synthesis** n си́нтез. **synthetic** adj синтети́ческий. **syphilis** n си́филис. **Syria** n Си́рия. **Syrian** n сири́ец, сири́йка; adj сири́йский. **syringe** n шприц; vt спринцева́ть impf. **syrup** n сиро́п; (treacle) па́тока. **system** n систе́ма; (network) сеть; (organism) органи́зм. **systematic** adj системати́ческий. **systematize** vi систематизи́ровать impf & pf.

T

tab n (loop) пе́телька; (on uniform) петли́ца; (of boot) ушко́; **keep ~s on** следи́ть impf за+instr. **table** n стол; (chart) табли́ца; **~cloth** ска́терть; **~spoon** столо́вая ло́жка; **~ tennis** насто́льный те́ннис; vt (for

discussion) предлага́ть impf, предложи́ть pf на обсужде́ние. **tableau** n жива́я карти́на. **tablet** n (pill) табле́тка; (of stone) плита́; (memorial ~) мемориа́льная доска́; (name plate) доще́чка. **tabloid** n (newspaper) малоформа́тная газе́та; (derog) бульва́рная газе́та. **taboo** n табу́ neut indecl; adj запрещённый. **tacit** n молчали́вый. **taciturn** adj неразгово́рчивый. **tack¹** n (nail) гво́здик; (stitch) намётка; (naut) галс; (fig) курс; vt (fasten) прикрепля́ть impf, прикрепи́ть pf гво́здиками; (stitch) смётывать impf, смета́ть pf на живу́ю ни́тку; (fig) добавля́ть impf, доба́вить pf ((on)to +dat); vi (naut; fig) лави́ровать impf. **tack²** n (riding) сбру́я (collect). **tackle** n (requisites) снасть (collect); (sport) блокиро́вка; vt (problem) бра́ться impf, взя́ться pf за+acc; (sport) блоки́ровать impf & pf. **tacky** adj ли́пкий. **tact** n такт(и́чность). **tactful** adj такти́чный. **tactical** adj такти́ческий. **tactics** n pl та́ктика. **tactless** adj беста́ктный. **tadpole** n голова́стик. **Tadzhikistan** n Таджикиста́н. **tag** n (label) ярлы́к; (of lace) наконе́чник; vt (label) прикрепля́ть impf, прикрепи́ть pf ярлы́к на+acc; vi: **~ along** (follow) тащи́ться impf сза́ди; **may I ~ along?** мо́жно с ва́ми? **tail** n хвост; (of shirt) ни́жний коне́ц; (*of coat*) фа́лда; (*of coin*) обра́тная сторона́ моне́ты; heads or ~s? орёл и́ли ре́шка?; *pl* (*coat*) фрак; *vt* (*shadow*) выслѐживать *impf*; *vi*: ~ away, off постепе́нно уменьша́ться *impf*; (*grow silent, abate*) затиха́ть *impf*. **tailback** *n* хвост. **tailcoat** *n* фрак.

tailor *n* портно́й *sb*; **~-made** сши́тый на зака́з; (*fig*) сде́ланный индивидуа́льно.

taint *vt* по́ртить *impf*, ис~ *pf*.

Taiwan *n* Тайва́нь *m*.

take *vt* (*various senses*) брать *impf*, взять *pf*; (*also seize, capture*) захва́тывать *impf*, захвати́ть *pf*; (*receive, accept*; *breakfast*; *medicine*; *steps*) принима́ть *impf*, приня́ть *pf*; (*convey, escort*) провожа́ть *impf*, проводи́ть *pf*; (*public transport*) е́здить *indet*, е́хать *det*, по~ *pf* +*instr*, на+*prep*; (*photograph*) снима́ть *impf*, снять *pf*; (*occupy*; ~ *time*) занима́ть *impf*, заня́ть *pf*; (*impers*) how long does it ~? ско́лько вре́мени ну́жно?; (*size in clothing*) носи́ть *impf*; (*exam*) сдава́ть *impf*; *vi* (*be successful*) име́ть *impf* успе́х (*of injection*) привива́ться *impf*, приви́ться *pf*; ~ after походи́ть *impf* на+*acc*; ~ away (*remove*) убира́ть *impf*, убра́ть *pf*; (*subtract*) вычита́ть *impf*, вы́честь *pf*; ~away магази́н, где продаю́т на вы́нос; ~ back (*return*) возвраща́ть *impf*, возврати́ть *pf*; (*retrieve, retract*) брать *impf*, взять *pf* наза́д; ~ down (*in writing*) запи́сывать *impf*, записа́ть *pf*; (*remove*) снима́ть *impf*, снять

pf; ~ s.o., sth for, to be принима́ть *impf*, приня́ть *pf* за+*acc*; ~ from отнима́ть *impf*, отня́ть *pf* у, от+*gen*; ~ in (*carry in*) вноси́ть *impf*, внести́ *pf*; (*lodgers*; *work*) брать *impf*, взять *pf*; (*clothing*) ушива́ть *impf*, уши́ть *pf*; (*understand*) понима́ть *impf*, поня́ть *pf*; (*deceive*) обма́нывать *impf*, обману́ть *pf*; ~ off (*clothing*) снима́ть *impf*, снять *pf*; (*mimic*) передра́знивать *impf*, передразни́ть *pf*; (*aeroplane*) взлета́ть *impf*, взлете́ть *pf*; ~-off (*imitation*) подража́ние; (*aeron*) взлёт; ~ on (*undertake*; *hire*) брать *impf*, взять *pf* на себя́; (*acquire*) приобрета́ть *impf*, приобрести́ *pf*; (*at game*) сража́ться *impf*, срази́ться *pf* с+*instr* (at в+*acc*); ~ out вынима́ть *impf*, вы́нуть *pf*; (*dog*) выводи́ть *impf*, вы́вести *pf* (for a walk на прогу́лку); (*to theatre, restaurant etc.*) приглаша́ть *impf*, пригласи́ть *pf* (to в+*acc*); we took them out every night мы приглаша́ли их куда́-нибудь ка́ждый ве́чер; ~ it out on срыва́ть *impf*, сорва́ть *pf* всё на+*prep*; ~ over принима́ть *impf*, приня́ть *pf* руково́дство +*instr*; ~ to (*thing*) пристрасти́ться *pf* к+*dat*; (*person*) привя́зываться *impf*, привяза́ться *pf* к+*dat*; (*begin*) станови́ться *impf*, стать *pf* +*inf*; ~ up (*interest oneself in*) занима́ться *impf*, заня́ться *pf* (*with an official etc.*) обраща́ться *impf*, обрати́ться *pf* с+*instr*, к+*dat*; (*challenge*) принима́ть *impf*, приня́ть *pf*; (*time, space*) занима́ть *impf*, заня́ть *pf*; ~ **up with** (*person*) свя́зываться *impf*, связа́ться *pf* c+*instr*; *n* (*cin*) дубль *m*.

taking *adj* привлека́тельный.

takings *n pl* сбор.

talcum powder *n* тальк.

tale *n* расска́з.

talent *n* тала́нт. **talented** *adj* тала́нтливый.

talk *vi* разгова́ривать *impf* (**to**, **with** c+*instr*); (*gossip*) спле́тничать *impf*, на~ *pf*; *vt & i* говори́ть *impf*, по~ *pf*; ~ **down to** говори́ть *impf* свысока́ c+*instr*; ~ **into** угова́ривать *impf*, уговори́ть *pf* +*inf*; ~ **out of** отгова́ривать *impf*, отговори́ть *pf* +*inf*, от+*gen*; ~ **over** (*discuss*) обсужда́ть *impf*, обсуди́ть *pf*; ~ **round** (*persuade*) переубежда́ть *impf*, переубеди́ть *pf*; *n* (*conversation*) разгово́р; (*lecture*) бесе́да; *pl* перегово́ры (-ров) *pl*. **talkative** *adj* разгово́рчивый; (*derog*) болтли́вый. **talker** *n* говоря́щий *sb*; (*chatterer*) болту́н (*coll*); (*orator*) ора́тор. **talking-to** (*coll*) вы́говор.

tall *adj* высо́кий; (*in measurements*) ро́стом в+*acc*.

tally *n* (*score*) счёт; *vi* соотве́тствовать (**with** +*dat*).

talon *n* ко́готь *m*.

tambourine *n* бу́бен.

tame *adj* ручно́й; (*insipid*) пре́сный; *vt* приуча́ть *impf*, приручи́ть *pf*. **tamer** *n* укроти́тель *m*.

tamper *vi*: ~ **with** (*meddle*) тро́гать *impf*, тро́нуть *pf*; (*forge*) подде́лывать *impf*, подде́лать *pf*.

tampon *n* тампо́н.

tan *n* (*sun~*) зага́р; *adj* жел-

това́то-кори́чневый; *vt* (*hide*) дуби́ть *impf*, вы́~ *pf*; (*beat*) (*coll*) дуба́сить *impf*, от~ *pf*; *vi* загора́ть *impf*, загоре́ть *pf*; (*of sun*): **tanned** загоре́лый.

tang *n* (*taste*) ре́зкий при́вкус; (*smell*) о́стрый за́пах.

tangent *n* (*math*) каса́тельная *sb*; (*trigonometry*) та́нгенс; **go off at a** ~ отклоня́ться *impf*, отклони́ться *pf* от те́мы.

tangerine *n* мандари́н.

tangible *adj* осяза́емый.

tangle *vt & i* запу́тывать(ся) *impf*, запу́таться *pf*; *n* пу́таница.

tango *n* та́нго *neut indecl*.

tangy *adj* о́стрый; ре́зкий.

tank *n* бак; (*mil*) танк.

tankard *n* кру́жка.

tanker *n* (*sea*) та́нкер; (*road*) автоцисте́рна.

tantalize *vt* дразни́ть *impf*.

tantamount *predic* равноси́лен (-льна) (**to** +*dat*).

tantrum *n* при́ступ раздраже́ния.

tap[1] *n* кран; *vt* (*resources*) испо́льзовать *impf & pf*; (*telephone conversation*) подслу́шивать *impf*.

tap[2] *n* (*knock*) стук; *vt* сту́ча́ть *impf*, по~ *pf* в+*acc*, по+*dat*; ~-**dance** (*vi*) отбива́ть *impf*, отби́ть *pf* чечётку; (*n*) чечётка; ~-**dancer** чечёточник, -ица.

tape *n* (*cotton strip*) тесьма́; (*adhesive, magnetic, measuring, etc.*) ле́нта; ~-**measure** руле́тка; ~ **recorder** магнитофо́н; ~ **recording** за́пись; *vt* (*seal*) закле́ивать *impf*, закле́ить *pf*; (*record*) запи́сывать *impf*, записа́ть *pf* на ле́нту.

taper *vt & i* су́живать(ся) *impf*, су́зить(ся) *pf*.

tapestry *n* гобеле́н.

tar *n* дёготь *m*.

tardy *adj* (*slow*) медли́тельный; (*late*) запозда́лый.

target *n* мише́нь, цель.

tariff *n* тари́ф.

tarmac *n* (*material*) гудро́н; (*road*) гудрони́рованное шоссе́ *neut indecl*; (*runway*) бетони́рованная площа́дка; *vt* гудрони́ровать *impf & pf*.

tarnish *vt* де́лать *impf*, с~ *pf* ту́склым; (*fig*) пятна́ть *impf*, за~ *pf*; *vi* тускне́ть *impf*, по~ *pf*.

tarpaulin *n* брезе́нт.

tarragon *n* эстраго́н.

tart[1] *adj* (*taste*) ки́слый; (*fig*) ко́лкий.

tart[2] *n* (*pie*) сла́дкий пиро́г.

tart[3] *n* (*prostitute*) шлю́ха.

tartan *n* шотла́ндка.

tartar *n* ви́нный ка́мень *m*.

task *n* зада́ча; **take to** ~ де́лать *impf*, с~ *pf* вы́говор+*dat*; ~ **force** операти́вная гру́ппа.

Tass *abbr* ТАСС, Телегра́фное аге́нтство Сове́тского Сою́за.

tassel *n* ки́сточка.

taste *n* (*also fig*) вкус; **take a** ~ **of** про́бовать *impf*, по~ *pf*; *vt* чу́вствовать *impf*, по~ *pf* вкус+*gen*; (*sample*) про́бовать *impf*, по~ *pf*; (*fig*) вкуша́ть *impf*, вкуси́ть *pf*; (*wine etc.*) дегусти́ровать *impf & pf*; *vi* име́ть *impf* вкус, привку́с (**of** +*gen*). **tasteful** *adj* (сде́ланный) со вку́сом. **tasteless** *adj* безвку́сный. **tasting** *n* дегуста́ция. **tasty** *adj* вку́сный.

tatter *n pl* лохмо́тья (-ьев) *pl*. **tattered** *adj* обо́рванный.

tattoo *n* (*design*) татуиро́вка; *vt* татуи́ровать *impf & pf*.

taunt *n* насме́шка; *vt* насмеха́ться *impf* над+*instr*.

Taurus *n* Теле́ц.

taut *adj* ту́го натя́нутый; туго́й.

tavern *n* таве́рна.

tawdry *adj* мишу́рный.

tawny *adj* рыжева́то-кори́чневый.

tax *n* нало́г; ~-**free** освобождённый от нало́га; *vt* облага́ть *impf*, обложи́ть *pf* нало́гом; (*strain*) напряга́ть *impf*, напря́чь *pf*; (*patience*) испы́тывать *impf*, испыта́ть *pf*. **taxable** *adj* подлежа́щий обложе́нию нало́гом. **taxation** *n* обложе́ние нало́гом. **taxing** *adj* утоми́тельный. **taxpayer** *n* налогоплате́льщик.

taxi *n* такси́ *neut indecl*; ~-**driver** води́тель *m* такси́; ~-**rank** стоя́нка такси́; *vi* (*aeron*) рули́ть *impf*.

tea *n* чай; ~-**bag** паке́тик с сухи́м ча́ем; ~-**cloth**, ~-**towel** полоте́нце для посу́ды; ~-**cosy** чехо́льчик (для ча́йника); ~-**cup** ча́йная ча́шка; ~-**leaf** ча́йный лист; ~-**pot** ча́йник; ~-**spoon** ча́йная ло́жка; ~-**strainer** ча́йное си́течко.

teach *vt* учи́ть *impf*, на~ *pf* (*person* +*acc*; *subject* +*dat*, *inf*); преподава́ть *impf* (*subject* +*acc*); (*coll*) проучи́ть *impf*, проучи́ть *pf*. **teacher** *n* учи́тель *m*, ~ница; преподава́тель *m*, ~ница. **teaching college** педагоги́ческий институ́т. **teaching** *n* (*instruction*) обуче́ние; (*doctrine*) уче́ние.

teak *n* тик; *attrib* ти́ковый.

team *n* (*sport*) кома́нда; (*of people*) брига́да; (*of horses etc.*) упря́жка; **~mate** член той же кома́нды; **~work** сотру́дничество; *vi* (~ *up*) объединя́ться *impf*, объедини́ться *pf*.

tear¹ *n* (*rent*) проре́ха; *vt* (*also* ~ *up*) рвать *impf*; (*also* ~ *up*) разрыва́ть *impf*, разорва́ть *pf*; *vi* рва́ться *impf*; (*rush*) мча́ться *impf*; **~ down, off** срыва́ть *impf*, сорва́ть *pf*; **~ out** вырыва́ть *impf*, вы́рвать *pf*.

tear² *n* (~*drop*) слеза́; **~gas** слезоточи́вый газ. **tearful** *adj* слезли́вый.

tease *vt* дразни́ть *impf*.

teat *n* сосо́к.

technical *adj* техни́ческий; **~ college** техни́ческое учи́лище. **technicality** *n* форма́льность. **technically** *adv* (*strictly*) форма́льно. **technician** *n* те́хник. **technique** *n* те́хника; (*method*) ме́тод. **technology** *n* техноло́гия, те́хника. **technological** *adj* технологи́ческий. **technologist** *n* техно́лог.

teddy-bear *n* медвежо́нок.

tedious *adj* ску́чный. **tedium** *n* ску́ка.

teem¹ *vi* (*swarm*) кише́ть *impf* (*with* +*instr*).

teem² *vi*: it is ~ing (*with rain*) дождь льёт как из ведра́.

teenage *adj* ю́ношеский. **teenager** *n* подро́сток. **teens** *n pl* во́зраст от трина́дцати до девятна́дцати лет.

teeter *vi* кача́ться *impf*, качну́ться *pf*.

teethe *vi*: the child is teething у ребёнка проре́зываются

зу́бы; **teething troubles** (*fig*) нача́льные пробле́мы *f pl*.

teetotal *adj* тре́звый. **teetotaller** *n* тре́звенник.

telecommunication(s) *n* да́льняя связь. **telegram** *n* телегра́мма. **telegraph** *n* телегра́ф; **~ pole** телегра́фный столб. **telepathic** *adj* телепати́ческий. **telepathy** *n* телепа́тия. **telephone** *n* телефо́н; *vt* (*message*) телефони́ровать *impf* & *pf* +*acc*, о+*prep*; (*person*) звони́ть *impf*, по~ *pf* (по телефо́ну) +*dat*; **~ box** телефо́нная бу́дка; **~ directory** телефо́нная кни́га; **~ exchange** телефо́нная ста́нция; **~ number** но́мер телефо́на. **telephonist** *n* телефони́ст, **~ка**. **telephoto lens** *n* телеобъекти́в. **telescope** *n* телеско́п. **telescopic** *adj* телескопи́ческий. **televise** *vt* пока́зывать *impf*, показа́ть *pf* по телеви́дению. **television** *n* телеви́дение; (*set*) телеви́зор; *attrib* телевизио́нный.

telex *n* те́лекс.

tell *vt* & *i* (*relate*) расска́зывать *impf*, рассказа́ть *pf* (*thing told* +*acc*, о+*prep*; *person told* +*dat*); *vt* (*utter, inform*) говори́ть *impf*, сказа́ть *pf* (*thing uttered* +*acc*; *thing informed about* о+*prep*; *person informed* +*dat*); (*order*) веле́ть *impf* & *pf* +*dat*; **~ one thing from another** отлича́ть *impf*, отличи́ть *pf* +*acc* от+*gen*; *vi* (*have an effect*) сказа́ться *impf*, сказа́ться *pf* (*on* на+*prep*); **~ off** отчи́тывать *impf*, отчита́ть *pf*; **~ on, tales about** я́бедничать *impf*, на~ *pf* на+*acc*.

teller n (of story) расска́з-
чик; (of votes) счётчик; (in
bank) касси́р. **telling** adj (effective) эффекти́вный; (significant) многозначи́тельный.
telltale n спле́тник; adj преда́-
да́тельский.

temerity n де́рзость.

temp n рабо́тающий sb вре́-
менно; vi рабо́тать impf вре́-
менно.

temper n (character) нрав;
(mood) настрое́ние; (anger)
гнев; lose one's ~ выходи́ть
impf, вы́йти pf из себя́; vt
(fig) смягча́ть impf, смяг-
чи́ть pf.

temperament n темпера́мент.
temperamental adj темпера́-
ментный.

temperance n (moderation)
уме́ренность; (sobriety) тре́з-
венность.

temperate adj уме́ренный.

temperature n температу́ра;
(high ~) повы́шенная тем-
перату́ра; take s.o.'s ~ из-
меря́ть impf, изме́рить pf
температу́ру +dat.

tempest n бу́ря. **tempestuous** adj бу́рный.

template n шабло́н.

temple¹ n (religion) храм.

temple² n (anat) висо́к.

tempo n темп.

temporal adj (of time) вре́-
менно́й; (secular) мирско́й.

temporary adj вре́менный.

tempt vt соблазня́ть impf, со-
блазни́ть pf; ~ fate искуша́ть
impf, испыта́ть pf судь-
бу́. **temptation** n собла́зн.
tempting adj соблазни́тель-
ный.

ten adj & n де́сять; (number
10) деся́тка. **tenth** adj & n
деся́тый.

tenable adj (logical) разу́м-
ный.

tenacious adj це́пкий. **tenacity** n це́пкость.

tenancy n (renting) наём
помеще́ния; (period) аре́нды.
tenant n аренда́тор.

tend¹ vi (be apt) име́ть склон-
ность (to к+dat, +inf).

tend² vt (look after) уха́жи-
вать impf за+instr.

tendency n тенде́нция. **ten-
dentious** adj тенденцио́з-
ный.

tender¹ vt (offer) предлага́ть
impf, предложи́ть pf; vi (make
~ for) подава́ть impf заявку́
pf заявку́ (на торга́х); n пред-
ложе́ние; **legal ~** зако́нное
платёжное сре́дство.

tender² adj (delicate, affectionate) не́жный. **tenderness** n
не́жность.

tendon n сухожи́лие.

tendril n у́сик.

tenement n (dwelling-house)
жило́й дом; **~-house** много-
кварти́рный дом.

tenet n до́гмат, при́нцип.

tennis n те́ннис.

tenor n (direction) направле́-
ние; (purport) смысл; (mus)
те́нор.

tense¹ n вре́мя neut.

tense² vt напряга́ть impf, на-
пря́чь pf; adj напряжённый.
tension n напряже́ние.

tent n пала́тка.

tentacle n щу́пальце.

tentative adj (experimental)
про́бный; (preliminary) пред-
вари́тельный.

tenterhooks n pl: be on ~ си-
де́ть impf как на иго́лках.

tenth see ten

tenuous adj (fig) неубеди́-
тельный.

tenure n (of property) владе́ние; (of office) пребыва́ние в до́лжности; (period) срок; (guaranteed employment) несменя́емость.

tepid adj теплова́тый.

term n (period) срок; (univ) семе́стр; (school) че́тверть; (technical word) те́рмин; (expression) выраже́ние; pl (conditions) усло́вия neut pl; (relations) отноше́ния neut pl; **on good ~s** в хоро́ших отноше́ниях; **come to ~s with** (resign o.s. to) покоря́ться impf, покори́ться pf k+dat; vt называ́ть impf, назва́ть pf.

terminal adj коне́чный; (med) сме́ртельный; n (electr) зажи́м; (computer, aeron) термина́л; (terminus) коне́чная остано́вка.

terminate vt & i конча́ть(ся) impf, ко́нчить(ся) pf (in +instr). **termination** n прекраще́ние.

terminology n терминоло́гия.

terminus n коне́чная остано́вка.

termite n терми́т.

terrace n терра́са; (houses) ряд домо́в.

terracotta n террако́та.

terrain n ме́стность.

terrestrial adj земно́й.

terrible adj ужа́сный. **terribly** adv ужа́сно.

terrier n терье́р.

terrific adj (huge) огро́мный; (splendid) потряса́ющий. **terrify** vt ужаса́ть impf, ужасну́ть pf.

territorial adj территориа́льный. **territory** n террито́рия.

terror n у́жас; (person; polit) терро́р. **terrorism** n террори́зм. **terrorist** n террори́ст,

~ка. **terrorize** vt терроризи́ровать impf & pf.

terse adj кра́ткий.

tertiary adj тре́тичный; (education) вы́сший.

test n испыта́ние, про́ба; (exam) экза́мен; контро́льная рабо́та; (analysis) ана́лиз; n ~ **tube** проби́рка; vt (try out) испы́тывать impf, испыта́ть pf; (check up on) проверя́ть impf, прове́рить pf; (give exam to) экзаменова́ть impf, про~ pf.

testament n завеща́ние; Old, New T~ Ве́тхий, Но́вый заве́т.

testicle n яи́чко.

testify vi свиде́тельствовать impf (to в по́льзу+gen); against про́тив+gen); vt (declare) заявля́ть impf, заяви́ть pf; (be evidence of) свиде́тельствовать o+prep.

testimonial n рекоменда́ция, характери́стика. **testimony** n свиде́тельство.

tetanus n столбня́к.

tetchy adj раздражи́тельный.

tête-à-tête n adv тет-а-те́т.

tether n: be at, come to the end of one's ~ дойти́ pf до то́чки; vt привя́зывать impf, привяза́ть pf.

text n текст. **textbook** n уче́бник.

textile adj тексти́льный; n ткань; pl тексти́ль m (collect).

textual adj текстово́й.

texture n тексту́ра.

than conj (comparison) чем; other ~ (except) кро́ме+gen.

thank vt благодари́ть impf, по~ pf (for за+acc); ~ God сла́ва Бо́гу; ~ you спаси́бо; благодарю́ вас; n pl благода́рность; ~s to (good value) благодаря +*dat*; (*bad result*) из-за+*gen*. **thankful** *adj* благода́рный. **thankless** *adj* неблагода́рный. **thanksgiving** *n* благодаре́ние.

that *demonstrative adj & pron* тот; ~ **which** тот кото́рый; *rel pron* кото́рый; *conj* что; (*purpose*) что́бы; *adv* так, до тако́й сте́пени.

thatched *adj* соло́менный.

thaw *vt* раста́пливать *impf*, растопи́ть *pf*; *vi* та́ять *impf*, рас~ *pf*.

the *def article, not translated; adv* тем; **the … the …** чем … тем; ~ **more** ~ **better** чем бо́льше, тем лу́чше.

theatre *n* теа́тр; (*lecture ~*) аудито́рия; (*operating ~*) операцио́нная *sb*; ~**-goer** театра́л. **theatrical** *adj* театра́льный.

theft *n* кра́жа.

their, theirs *poss pron* их; свой.

theme *n* те́ма.

themselves *pron* (*emph*) (они́) са́ми; (*refl*) себя́, -ся (*suffixed to vt*).

then *adv* (*at that time*) тогда́; (*after that*) пото́м; **now and** ~ вре́мя от вре́мени; *conj* в тако́м слу́чае, тогда́; *adj* тогда́шний; **by** ~ к тому́ вре́мени; **since** ~ с тех пор.

thence *adv* отту́да. **thenceforth, -forward** *adv* с того́/э́того вре́мени.

theologian *n* тео́лог. **theological** *adj* теологи́ческий. **theology** *n* теоло́гия.

theorem *n* теоре́ма. **theoretical** *adj* теорети́ческий. **theorize** *vi* теоретизи́ровать *impf*. **theory** *n* тео́рия.

therapeutic *adj* терапевти-

ческий. **therapist** *n* (*psychotherapist*) психотерапе́вт. **therapy** *n* терапи́я.

there *adv* (*place*) там; (*direction*) туда́; *int* вот!; ну!; ~ **is**, **are** есть, име́ется (-е́ются); ~ **you are** (*on giving sth*) пожа́луйста. **thereabouts** *adv* (*near*) побли́зости; (*approximately*) приблизи́тельно. **thereafter** *adv* по́сле э́того. **thereby** *adv* таки́м о́бразом. **therefore** *adv* поэ́тому. **therein** *adv* в э́том. **thereupon** *adv* зате́м.

thermal *adj* теплово́й, терми́ческий; (*underwear*) тёплый.

thermometer *n* термо́метр, гра́дусник. **thermos** *n* те́рмос. **thermostat** *n* термоста́т.

thesis *n* (*proposition*) те́зис; (*dissertation*) диссерта́ция.

they *pron* они́.

thick *adj* то́лстый; (*in measurements*) толщино́й в+*acc*; (*dense*) густо́й; (*stupid*) тупо́й; ~**-skinned** толстоко́жий. **thicken** *vt & i* утолща́ть(ся) *impf*, утолсти́ть(ся) *pf*; (*make, become denser*) сгуща́ть(ся) *impf*, сгусти́ть(ся) *pf*; *vi* (*become more intricate*) усложня́ться *impf*, усложни́ться *pf*. **thicket** *n* ча́ща. **thickness** *n* (*also dimension*) толщина́; (*density*) густота́; (*layer*) слой. **thickset** *adj* корена́стый.

thief *n* вор. **thieve** *vi* ворова́ть *impf*. **thievery** *n* воровство́.

thigh *n* бедро́.

thimble *n* напёрсток.

thin *adj* (*slender; not thick*) то́нкий; (*lean*) худо́й; (*too liquid*) жи́дкий; (*sparse*) ре́д-

кий; vt & i де́лать(ся) impf,
с~ pf то́нким, жи́дким; vi
(also ~ out) реде́ть impf,
по~ pf; vt: ~ out прореза́ть
impf, проредить pf.

thing n вещь; (object) предме́т; (matter) де́ло.

think vt & i ду́мать impf, по~
pf (about, of +prep); (consider) счита́ть impf, счесть
pf (to be +instr +acc; that
что); vi (reflect, reason) мы́слить impf; (intend) намерева́ться impf (of doing +inf);
~ out проду́мывать impf,
проду́мать pf; ~ over обду́-
мывать impf, обду́мать pf;
~ up, of приду́мывать impf,
приду́мать pf. **thinker** n мысли́тель m. **thinking** adj мы́слящий; (reflection) размышле́ние; to my way of ~
по моему́ мне́нию.

third adj & n тре́тий; (fraction) треть; T~ **World**
страны́ pl тре́тьего ми́ра.

thirst n жа́жда (for +gen (fig));
vi (fig) жа́ждать impf (for
+gen). **thirsty** adj: be ~
хоте́ть impf пить.

thirteen adj & n трина́дцать.
thirteenth adj & n трина́дцатый.
thirtieth adj & n тридца́тый.
thirty adj & n три́дцать; pl
(decade) тридца́тые го́ды
(-до́в) m pl.

this demonstrative adj & pron
э́тот; like ~ вот так; ~
morning сего́дня у́тром.

thistle n чертополо́х.

thither adv туда́.

thorn n шип. **thorny** adj колю́чий; (fig) терни́стый.

thorough adj основа́тельный; (complete) соверше́нный. **thoroughbred** adj

чистокро́вный. **thoroughfare** n прое́зд; (walking) прохо́д. **thoroughgoing** adj
радика́льный. **thoroughly**
adv (completely) соверше́нно.
thoroughness n основа́тельность.

though conj хотя́; несмотря́
на то, что; as ~ как бу́дто;
adv одна́ко.

thought n мысль; (meditation)
размышле́ние; (intention) наме́рение; pl (opinion) мне́ние.
thoughtful adj заду́мчивый;
(considerate) внима́тельный.
thoughtless adj небре́жный;
(inconsiderate) невнима́тельный.

thousand adj & n ты́сяча.
thousandth adj & n ты́сячный.

thrash vt бить impf, по~ pf;
~ out (discuss) обстоя́тельно обсужда́ть impf, обсуди́ть pf; vi: ~ about мета́ться
impf. **thrashing** n (beating)
взбу́чка (coll).

thread n ни́тка, нить (also
fig); (of screw etc.) резьба́; vt
(needle) продева́ть impf, продеть pf ни́тку в+acc; (beads)
нани́зывать impf, низа́ть
pf; ~ one's way пробира́ться
impf, пробра́ться pf (through
че́рез+acc). **threadbare** adj
потёртый.

threat n угро́за. **threaten** vt
угрожа́ть impf, грози́ть impf,
при~ pf (person +dat; with
+instr; to do +inf).

three adj & n три; (number 3)
тро́йка; ~-dimensional трёхме́рный; ~-quarters три че́тверти; **threefold** adj тройно́й; adv втройне́. **threesome** n тро́йка.

thresh vt молоти́ть impf.

threshold n поро́г.

thrice adv три́жды.

thrift n бережли́вость. **thrifty** adj бережли́вый.

thrill n тре́пет; vt восхища́ть impf, восхити́ть pf; **be thrilled** быть в восто́рге. **thriller** n приключе́нческий, детекти́вный (novel) рома́н, (film) фильм. **thrilling** adj захва́тывающий.

throat n го́рло.

throb vi (heart) си́льно би́ться impf, пульси́ровать impf; n бие́ние; пульса́ция.

throes n pl: **in the ~** в мучи́тельных попы́тках.

thrombosis n тромбо́з.

throne n трон, престо́л; **come to the ~** вступа́ть impf, вступи́ть pf на престо́л.

throng n толпа́; vi толпи́ться impf; vt заполня́ть impf, запо́лнить pf.

throttle n (tech) дро́ссель m; vt (strangle) души́ть impf, за~ pf; (tech) дроссели́ровать impf & pf; **~ down** сбавля́ть impf, сба́вить pf газ.

through prep (across, via, ~ opening) че́рез+acc, ~ (esp ~ thick of) сквозь+acc; (air, streets etc.) по+dat; (agency) посре́дством+gen; (reason) из-за+gen; adv наскво́зь; (from beginning to end) до конца́; **be ~ with** (sth) ока́нчивать impf, око́нчить pf; (s.o.) порыва́ть impf, порва́ть pf с+instr; **put ~** (on telephone) соединя́ть impf, соедини́ть pf; **~ and ~** соверше́нно; adj (train) прямо́й; (traffic) сквозно́й. **throughout** adv повсю́ду, во всех от-

ноше́ниях; prep по всему́ (всей, всему́; pl всем)+dat; (from beginning to end) с нача́ла до конца́+gen.

throw n бросо́к; vt броса́ть impf, бро́сить pf; (confuse) смуща́ть impf, смути́ть pf; (rider) сбра́сывать impf, сбро́сить pf; (party) устра́ивать impf, устро́ить pf; **~ o.s. into** броса́ться impf, бро́ситься pf в+acc; **~ away, out** выбра́сывать impf, вы́бросить pf; **~ down** сбра́сывать impf, сбро́сить pf; **~ in** (add) добавля́ть impf, доба́вить pf; (sport) вбра́сывать impf, вбро́сить pf; **~-in** вбра́сывание мяча́; **~ off** сбра́сывать impf, сбро́сить pf; **~ open** распа́хивать impf, распахну́ть pf; **~ out** (see also **~ away**) (expel) выгоня́ть impf, вы́гнать pf; (reject) отверга́ть impf, отве́ргнуть pf; **~ over, ~ up** (abandon) броса́ть impf, бро́сить pf; **~ up** подбра́сывать impf, подбро́сить pf; (vomit) рвать impf, вы́~ pf impers; **he threw up** его́ вы́рвало.

thrush n (bird) дрозд.

thrust n (shove) толчо́к; (tech) тя́га; vt (shove) толка́ть impf, толкну́ть pf; (~ into, out of) give quickly, carelessly) сова́ть impf, су́нуть pf.

thud n глухо́й звук; vi па́дать impf, па́сть impf с глухи́м сту́ком.

thug n головоре́з (coll).

thumb n большо́й па́лец; **under the ~ of** под башмако́м у+gen; vt: **~ through** перели́стывать impf, перелиста́ть pf; **~ a lift** голосова́ть impf, про~ pf.

thump n (blow) тяжёлый

удáр; (thud) глухóй звук, стук; vi колотúть impf, по~ pf в+acc, по+dat; vi колотúться impf.

thunder n гром; vi гремéть impf; **it thunders** гром гремúт. **thunderbolt** n удáр мóлнии. **thunderous** adj громóвый. **thunderstorm** n грозá. **thundery** adj грозовóй.

Thursday n четвéрг.

thus adv так, такúм óбразом.

thwart vt мешáть impf, по~ pf +dat; (plans) расстрáивать impf, расстрóить pf.

thyme n тимьян.

thyroid n (~ gland) щитовúдная железá.

tiara n тиáра.

tick n (noise) тúканье; (mark) птúчка; vi тúкать impf, тúкнуть pf; vt отмечáть impf, отмéтить pf птúчкой; ~ **off** (scold) отдéлывать impf, отдéлать pf.

ticket n билéт; (label) ярлы́к; (season) ~ кáрточка; (cloakroom) ~ номерóк; (receipt) квитáнция; ~ **collector** контролёр; ~ **office** (билéтная) кáсса.

tickle n щекóтка; vt щекотáть impf, по~ pf; (amuse) веселúть impf, по~, раз~ pf; vi щекотáть impf, impers; **my throat ~s** у меня щекóчет в гóрле. **ticklish** adj (fig) щекотлúвый; **to be ~** боя́ться impf щекóтки.

tidal adj прúливо-отлúвный. ~ **wave** прилúвная волнá.

tide n прилúв и отлúв; **high ~** прилúв; **low ~** отлúв; (current, tendency) течéние; **the ~ turns** (fig) собы́тия принимáют другóй оборóт; vt: ~ **over** помогáть impf,

помóчь pf +dat of person спрáвиться (difficulty c+instr; **will this money ~ you over?** вы протя́нете с этими деньгáми?

tidiness n аккурáтность. **tidy** adj аккурáтный; (considerable) поря́дочный; vt убирáть impf, убрáть pf; приводúть impf, привестú pf в поря́док.

tie n (garment) гáлстук; (cord) завя́зка; (link; tech) связь; (equal points etc.) рáвный счёт; **end in a ~** закáнчиваться impf, закóнчиться pf вничью́; (burden) обýза, pl (bonds) ýзы (уз) pl; vt свя́зывать impf, связáть pf (also fig); (~ **up**) завя́зывать impf, завязáть pf; (restrict) огранúчивать impf, огранúчить pf; ~ **down** (fasten) привя́зывать impf, привязáть pf; (~ **up**) (tether) привя́зывать impf, привязáть pf; (parcel) перевя́зывать impf, перевязáть pf; vi (be ~d) завя́зываться impf, завязáться pf; (sport) сыгрáть pf вничью́; ~ **in, up with** совпадáть impf, совпáсть pf c+instr.

tier n ряд, я́рус.

tiff n размóлвка.

tiger n тигр.

tight adj (cramped) тéсный; (strict) стрóгий; (taut) тугóй; ~ **corner** (fig) трýдное положéние. **tighten** vt & i натя́гивать impf, натянýть pf; (clench, contract) сжимáть impf, сжать pf; **one's belt** потýже затя́гивать impf, затянýть pf пóяс (also fig); ~ **up** (discipline etc.) подтя́гивать impf, подтянýть pf (coll). **tightly**

(*strongly*) про́чно; (*closely, cramped*) те́сно. **tightrope** *n* натя́нутый кана́т. **tights** *n pl* колго́тки (-ток) *pl*.

tile *n* (*roof*) черепи́ца (*collect*; *decorative*) ка́фель *m* (*collect*); *vt* крыть *impf*, по~ *pf* черепи́цей, ка́фелем; (*floor*) ка́фельный. **tiled** *adj* (*roof*) черепи́чный; (*floor*) ка́фельный.

till¹ *prep* до+*gen*; not ~ то́лько (**Friday in пя́тницу**; **the next day на сле́дующий день**); *conj* пока́ не; **not ~** то́лько когда́.

till² *n* ка́сса.

till³ *vt* возде́лывать *impf*, возде́лать *pf*.

tiller *n* (*naut*) ру́мпель *m*.

tilt *n* накло́н; **at full ~** по́лным хо́дом; *vt & i* наклоня́ть(ся) *impf*, наклони́ть(ся) *pf*; (*heel* (*over*)) крени́ть(ся) *impf*, на~ *pf*.

timber *n* лесоматериа́л.

time *n* вре́мя *neut*; (*occasion*) раз; (*mus*) такт; (*sport*) тайм; *pl* (*period*) времена́ *pl*; (*in comparison*) раз; **five ~s as big в пять раз бо́льше**; (*multiplication*) **four ~s four четы́режды четы́ре; ~ and again, ~ after ~ не раз, ты́сячу раз; ~ a ~зом, одновре́менно; at this ~ в э́то вре́мя; at ~s времена́ми; at the same ~ в то же вре́мя; before my ~ до меня́; for a long ~ до́лго; (*up to now*) давно́; for the ~ being пока́; from ~ to ~ вре́мя от вре́мени; in ~ (*early enough*) во́-время; (*with ~*) со вре́менем; in good ~ заблаговре́менно; in ~ with в такт +*dat*; in no ~ момента́льно; on ~ во́-время; one

at a ~ по одному́; **be in ~** успева́ть *impf*, успе́ть *pf* (**for к**+*dat*, **на**+*acc*); **have ~ to** (*manage*) успева́ть *impf*, успе́ть *pf* +*inf*; **have a good ~** хорошо́ проводи́ть *impf*, провести́ *pf* вре́мя; **it is ~** пора́ (**to** +*inf*); **what is the ~?** кото́рый час?; **~ bomb** бо́мба заме́дленного де́йствия; **~-consuming** отнима́ющий мно́го вре́мени; **~ difference** ра́зница во вре́мени; **~-lag** отстава́ние во вре́мени; **~ zone** часово́й по́яс; *vt* (*choose ~*) выбира́ть *impf*, вы́брать *pf* вре́мя +*gen*; (*ascertain ~ of*) измеря́ть *impf*, изме́рить *pf* вре́мя +*gen*. **timeless** *adj* ве́чный. **timely** *adj* своевре́менный. **timetable** *n* расписа́ние; гра́фик.

timid *adj* ро́бкий.

tin *n* (*metal*) о́лово; (*container*) ба́нка; (*cake-~*) фо́рма; (*baking ~*) проти́вень *m*; **~ foil** оловя́нная фольга́; **~-opener** консе́рвный нож; **~ned food** консе́рвы (-вов) *pl*.

tinge *n* отте́нок; *vt* (*also fig*) слегка́ окра́шивать *impf*, окра́сить *pf*.

tingle *vi* (*sting*) коло́ть *impers*; **my fingers ~ у меня́ ко́лет па́льцы; his nose ~d with the cold моро́з пощи́пывал ему́ нос; (*burn*) горе́ть *impf*.

tinker *vi*: **~ with** вози́ться *impf c*+*instr*.

tinkle *n* звон, звя́канье; *vi* (*& t*) звене́ть *impf* (+*instr*).

tinsel *n* мишура́.

tint *n* отте́нок; *vt* подкра́шивать *impf*, подкраси́ть *pf*.

tiny *adj* кро́шечный.

tip¹ *n* (*end*) ко́нчик.

tip² n (money) чаевы́е (-ы́х) pl; (advice) сове́т; (dump) сва́лка; vt & i (tilt) наклоня́ть(ся) impf, наклони́ть(ся) pf; (give ~) дава́ть impf, дать pf (person +dat; money де́ньги на чай, information ча́стную информа́цию); ~ out выба́ливать impf, вы́валить pf; ~ over, up (vt & i) опроки́дывать(ся) impf, опроки́нуть(ся) pf.

Tippex n (propr) бели́ла.

tipple n напи́ток.

tipsy adj подвы́пивший.

tiptoe n: on ~ на цы́почках.

tip-top adj превосхо́дный.

tirade n тира́да.

tire vt (weary) утомля́ть impf, утоми́ть pf; vi утомля́ться impf, утоми́ться pf. **tired** adj уста́лый; be ~ of: I am ~ of him он мне надое́л; I am ~ of playing мне надое́ло игра́ть; ~ out изму́ченный. **tiredness** n уста́лость. **tireless** adj неутоми́мый. **tiresome** adj надое́дливый. **tiring** adj утоми́тельный.

tissue n ткань; (handkerchief) бума́жная салфе́тка. **tissue-paper** n папиро́сная бума́га.

tit¹ n (bird) сини́ца.

tit² n: ~ for tat зуб за́ зуб.

titbit n ла́комый кусо́к; (news) пика́нтная но́вость.

titillate vt щекота́ть impf, по-~ pf.

title n (of book etc.) загла́вие; (rank) зва́ние; (sport) зва́ние чемпио́на; ~-holder чемпио́н; ~-page ти́тульный лист; ~-role загла́вная роль. **titled** adj титуло́ванный.

titter n хихи́канье; vi хихи́кать impf, хихи́кнуть pf.

to prep (town, a country,

theatre, school, etc.) в+acc; (the sea, the moon, the ground, post-office, meeting, concert, north, etc.) на+acc; (the doctor; towards, up ~) к+dat; (the ~ one's surprise etc.) к+dat; (with accompaniment of) под+acc; (in toast) за+acc; (time): ten minutes ~ three без десяти́ три; (compared with) в сравне́нии с+instr; ~ one ~ ten — одно́ из десяти́; (in order to) что́бы +inf; adv: shut the door ~ закры́ть impf, приходи́ть impf, прийти́ pf в созна́ние; ~ and fro взад и вперёд.

toad n жа́ба. **toadstool** n пога́нка.

toast n (bread) поджа́ренный хлеб; (drink) тост; vt (bread) поджа́ривать impf, поджа́рить pf; (drink) пить impf, вы́-~ pf за здоро́вье +gen. **toaster** n то́стер.

tobacco n таба́к. **tobacconist's** n (shop) таба́чный магази́н.

toboggan n са́ни (-не́й) pl; vi ката́ться impf на саня́х.

today adv сего́дня; n сего́дняшний день; nowadays в на́ши дни; n сего́дняшний день m; ~'s newspaper сего́дняшняя газе́та.

toddler n малы́ш.

toe n па́лец ноги́; (of sock etc.) носо́к; vt: ~ the line (fig) ходи́ть indet по стру́нке.

toffee n (substance) ири́с; (a single ~) ири́ска.

together adv вме́сте; (simultaneously) одновреме́нно.

toil n тяжёлый труд; vi труди́ться impf.

toilet n туале́т; ~ paper туале́тная бума́га. **toiletries** n *pl* туале́тные принадле́жности *f pl*.

token *n* (sign) знак; (coin substitute) жето́н; **as a ~ of** в знак +gen; *attrib* символи́ческий.

tolerable *adj* терпи́мый; (satisfactory) удовлетвори́тельный. **tolerance** *n* терпи́мость. **tolerant** *adj* терпи́мый. **tolerate** *vt* терпе́ть *impf*, по~ *pf*; (allow) допуска́ть *impf*, допусти́ть *pf*. **toleration** *n* терпи́мость.

toll[1] *n* (duty) по́шлина; **take its ~** ска́зываться *impf*, сказа́ться *pf* (**on** на+*prep*).

toll[2] *vi* звони́ть *impf*, по~ *pf*.

tom(-cat) *n* кот.

tomato *n* помидо́р; *attrib* тома́тный.

tomb *n* моги́ла. **tombstone** *n* надгро́бный ка́мень *m*.

tomboy *n* сорване́ц.

tome *n* том.

tomorrow *adv* за́втра; *n* за́втрашний день *m*; **~ morning** за́втра у́тром; **the day after ~** послеза́втра; **see you ~** до за́втра.

ton *n* то́нна; (*pl, lots*) ма́сса.

tone *n* тон; *vt*: **~ down** смягча́ть *impf*, смягчи́ть *pf*; **~ up** тонизи́ровать *impf* & *pf*.

tongs *n* щипцы́ (-цо́в) *pl*.

tongue *n* язы́к; **~-in-cheek** с насме́шкой, ирони́чески; **~-tied** косноязы́чный; **~-twister** скорогово́рка.

tonic *n* (med) тонизи́рующее сре́дство; (mus) то́ника; (drink) напи́ток «то́ник».

tonight *adv* сего́дня ве́чером.

tonnage *n* тонна́ж.

tonsil *n* минда́лина. **tonsillitis** *n* тонзилли́т.

too *adv* сли́шком; (also) та́к-

же, то́же; (very) о́чень; (moreover) к тому́ же; **none ~** не сли́шком.

tool *n* инструме́нт, (fig) ору́дие.

toot *n* гудо́к; *vi* гуде́ть *impf*.

tooth *n* зуб; (tech) зубе́ц; *attrib* зубно́й; **~-brush** зубна́я щётка. **toothache** *n* зубна́я боль. **toothless** *adj* беззу́бый. **toothpaste** *n* зубна́я па́ста. **toothpick** *n* зубочи́стка. **toothy** *adj* зуба́стый (coll).

top[1] *n* (toy) волчо́к.

top[2] *n* (of object; fig) верх; (of hill etc.) верши́на; (of tree) верху́шка; (of head) маку́шка; (lid) кры́шка; (upper part) ве́рхняя часть; **~ hat** цили́ндр; **~-heavy** переве́шивающий в свое́й ве́рхней ча́сти; **~-secret** соверше́нно секре́тный; **on ~ of** (position) на+prep, сверх+gen; (on to) на+acc; **on ~ of everything** сверх всего́; **from ~ to bottom** све́рху до́низу; **at the ~ of one's voice** во весь го́лос; **at ~ speed** во весь опо́р; *adj* ве́рхний, вы́сший, са́мый высо́кий; (foremost) пе́рвый; *vt* (cover) покрыва́ть *impf*, покры́ть *pf*; (exceed) превосходи́ть *impf*, превзойти́ *pf*; (cut ~ off) обреза́ть *impf*, обре́зать *pf* верху́шку +gen; **~ up** (with liquid) долива́ть *impf*, доли́ть *pf*.

topic *n* те́ма, предме́т. **topical** *adj* актуа́льный.

topless *adj* с обнажённой гру́дью.

topmost *adj* са́мый ве́рхний; са́мый ва́жный.

topographical *adj* топографи́ческий. **topography** *n* топогра́фия.

topple vt & i опроки́дывать(ся) impf, опроки́нуть(ся) pf.
topsy-turvy adj повёрнутый вверх дном; (disorderly) беспоря́дочный; adv вверх дном.
torch n электри́ческий фона́рь m; (flaming) фа́кел.
torment n муче́ние; vt му́чить impf, за~, из~ pf.
tornado n торна́до neut indecl.
torpedo n торпе́да; vt торпеди́ровать impf & pf.
torrent n пото́к. **torrential** adj (rain) проливно́й.
torso n ту́ловище; (art) торс.
tortoise n черепа́ха. **tortoiseshell** n черепа́ха.
tortuous adj изви́листый.
torture n пы́тка; (fig) му́ка; vt пыта́ть impf; (torment) му́чить impf, за~, из~ pf.
toss n бросо́к; **win (lose) the ~** (не) выпада́ть impf, вы́пасть pf жре́бий impers (**I won the ~** мне вы́пал жре́бий); vt броса́ть impf, бро́сить pf; (coin) подбра́сывать impf, подбро́сить pf; (head) вски́дывать impf, вски́нуть pf; (salad) переме́шивать impf, перемеша́ть pf; vi (in bed) мета́ться impf; **~ aside, away** отбра́сывать impf, отбро́сить pf; **~ up** броса́ть impf, бро́сить pf жре́бий.
tot¹ n (child) малы́ш; (of liquor) глото́к.
tot²: **~ up** (vt) скла́дывать impf, сложи́ть pf; (vi) равня́ться impf (**to** +dat).
total n ито́г, су́мма; adj о́бщий; (complete) по́лный; **in ~** в це́лом, вме́сте; vt подсчи́тывать impf, подсчита́ть pf; vi равня́ться impf +dat.

totalitarian adj тоталита́рный. **totality** n вся су́мма целико́м; **the ~** of весь. **totally** adv соверше́нно.
totter vi шата́ться impf.
touch n прикоснове́ние; (sense) осяза́ние; (shade) отте́нок; (taste) при́вкус; (small amount) чу́точка; (of illness) лёгкий при́ступ; **get in ~ with** свя́зываться impf, связа́ться pf c+instr; **keep in (lose) ~ with** подде́рживать impf, поддержа́ть pf (теря́ть impf, по~ pf) связь, конта́кт c+instr; **put the finishing ~es** to отде́лывать impf, отде́лать pf; vi (lightly) прика́саться impf, прикосну́ться pf к+dat; каса́ться impf, косну́ться pf +gen; (also disturb; affect) тро́гать impf, тро́нуть pf; (be comparable with) идти́ impf в сравне́нии c+instr; vi (be contiguous; come into contact) соприкаса́ться impf, соприкосну́ться pf; **~ down** приземля́ться impf, приземли́ться pf; **~down** поса́дка; **~ (up)on** (fig) каса́ться impf, косну́ться pf +gen; **~ up** поправля́ть impf, попра́вить pf. **touched** adj тро́нутый.
touchiness n оби́дчивость.
touching adj трога́тельный.
touchstone n про́бный ка́мень m. **touchy** adj оби́дчивый.
tough adj жёсткий; (durable) про́чный; (difficult) тру́дный; (hardy) выно́сливый. **toughen** vt & i де́лать(ся) impf, с~ pf жёстким.
tour n (journey) путеше́ствие, пое́здка; (excursion) экску́рсия; (of artistes) гастро́ли f pl; (of duty) объе́зд; vt (& i

путешéствовать *impf* (по +*dat*); (*theat*) гастролировать *impf* (coll).
tourism *n* туризм.
tourist *n* турист, ~ка.
tournament *n* турнир.
tousle *vt* взъерошивать *impf*, взъерошить *pf* (coll).
tout *n* зазывáла *m*; (*ticket ~*) жучок.
tow *vt* букси́ровать *impf*; ~ **on** ~ на буксире.
towards *prep* к+*dat*.
towel *n* полотéнце.
tower *n* бáшня; *vi* выситься *impf*, возвышáться *impf* (*above* над+*instr*).
town *n* город; *attrib* городскóй; ~ **hall** рáтуша. **townsman** *n* горожáнин.
toxic *adj* токси́ческий.
toy *n* игрýшка; *vi*: ~ **with** (*sth in hands*) вертéть *impf* в рукáх; (*trifle with*) игрáть *impf* (с)+*instr*.
trace *n* след; *vt* (*track down*) выслéживать *impf*, выследить *pf*; (*copy*) кальки́ровать *impf*, с~ *pf*; ~ **out** (*plan*) набрáсывать *impf*, набросáть *pf*; (*map, diagram*) чертить *impf*.
tracing-paper *n* кáлька.
track *n* (*path*) дорóжка; (*mark*) след; (*rly*) путь *m*, (*sport, on tape*) дорóжка; (*on record*) зáпись; ~ **suit** тренирóвочный костюм; **off the beaten** ~ в глуши́; **go off the** ~ (*fig*) отклоняться *impf*, отклони́ться *pf* от тéмы; **keep** ~ **of** следи́ть *impf* за+*instr*; **lose** ~ **of** теря́ть *impf*, по~ *pf* след+*gen*; *vt* прослéживать *impf*, проследи́ть *pf*; ~ **down** выслéживать *impf*, выследить *pf*.
tract[1] *n* (*land*) прострáнство.

tract[2] *n* (*pamphlet*) брошюра.
tractor *n* трáктор.
trade *n* торгóвля; (*occupation*) профéссия, ремеслó; ~ **mark** фабри́чная мáрка; ~ **union** профсоюз; **~unionist** *n* член профсоюза; *vi* торговáть *impf* (*in* +*instr*); *vt* (*swap like things*) обмéниваться *impf*, обменя́ться *pf* +*instr*; (~ *for sth different*) обмéнивать *impf*, обменя́ть *pf* (*for* на+*acc*); ~ **in** сдавáть *impf*, сдать *pf* в счёт покýпки нóвого. **trader, tradesman** *n* торгóвец. **trading** *n* торгóвля.
tradition *n* тради́ция. **traditional** *adj* традициóнный. **traditionally** *adv* по тради́ции.
traffic *n* движéние; (*trade*) торгóвля; ~ **jam** прóбка; *vi* торговáть *impf* (*in* +*instr*).
trafficker *n* торгóвец (*in* +*instr*). **traffic-lights** *n pl* светофóр.
tragedy *n* трагéдия. **tragic** *adj* трагический.
trail *n* (*trace, track*) след; (*path*) тропи́нка; *vt* (*track*) выслéживать *impf*, выследить *pf*; *vt & i* (*drag*) таскáть(ся) *indet*, тащи́ть(ся) *det*. **trailer** *n* (*on vehicle*) прицéп; (*cin*) (кино)рóлик.
train *n* пóезд; (*of dress*) шлейф; *vt* (*instruct*) обучáть *impf*, обучи́ть *pf* (*in* +*dat*); (*prepare*) готóвить *impf* (*for* к+*dat*); (*sport*) тренирóвать *impf*, на~ *pf*; (*animals*) дрессирóвать *impf*, вы~ *pf*; (*aim*) наводи́ть *impf*, навести́ *pf*; (*plant*) направля́ть *impf*, напрáвить *pf* рост+*gen*; *vi* приготáвливаться *impf*,

приготóвиться *pf* (for k+dat); (sport) тренировáться *impf*, на~ *pf*. **trainee** *n* стажёр, практикáнт. **trainer** *n* (sport) трéнер; (of animals) дрессирóвщик; (shoe) кроссóвка.

training *n* обучéние; (sport) тренирóвка; (of animals) дрессирóвка; ~**-college** (teachers') педагогический институт.

traipse *vi* таскáться *indet*, тащиться *det*.

trait *n* чертá.

traitor *n* предáтель *m*, ~ница.

trajectory *n* траектóрия.

tram *n* трамвáй.

tramp *n* (vagrant) бродя́га *m*; *vi* (walk heavily) тóпать *impf*.

trample *vt* топтáть *impf*, по-, ис~ *pf*; ~ **down** выта́птывать *impf*, вы́топтать *pf*; ~ **on** (fig) попирáть *impf*, попрáть *pf*.

trampoline *n* батýт.

trance *n* транс.

tranquil *adj* спокóйный. **tranquillity** *n* спокóйствие. **tranquillize** *vt* успокáивать *impf*, успокóить *pf*. **tranquillizer** *n* транквилизáтор.

transact *vt* (business) вести́ *impf*; (a deal) заключáть *impf*, заключи́ть *pf*. **transaction** *n* дéло, сдéлка; *pl* (publications) трудý *m pl*.

transatlantic *adj* трансатланти́ческий.

transcend *vt* превосходи́ть *impf*, превзойти́ *pf*. **transcendental** *adj* (philos.) трансцендентáльный.

transcribe *vt* (copy out) перепи́сывать *impf*, переписáть *pf*. **transcript** *n* кóпия. **transcription** *n* (copy) кóпия.

transfer *n* (of objects) перенóс, перемещéние; (of money;

of people) перевóд; (of property) передáча; (design) переводнáя карти́нка; *vt* (objects) переноси́ть *impf*, перенести́ *pf*; перемещáть *impf*, перемести́ть *pf*; (money; people; design) переводи́ть *impf*, перевести́ *pf*; (property) передавáть *impf*, передáть *pf*; *vi* (to different job) переходи́ть *impf*, перейти́ *pf*; (change trains etc.) пересáживаться *impf*, пересéсть *pf*. **transferable** *adj* допускáющий передáчу.

transfix *vt* (fig) прикóвывать *impf*, прикову́ть *pf* к мéсту.

transform *vt* и преобразóвывать(ся) *impf*, преобразовáть(ся) *pf*; ~ **into** *vt* (i) превращáть(ся) *impf*, преврати́ть(ся) *pf* в+*acc*. **transformation** *n* преобразовáние; превращéние. **transformer** *n* трансформáтор.

transfusion *n* переливáние (крóви).

transgress *vt* нарушáть *impf*, нарýшить *pf*; *vi* (sin) греши́ть *impf*, за~ *pf*. **transgression** *n* нарушéние; (sin) грех.

transience *n* мимолётность. **transient** *adj* мимолётный.

transistor *n* транзи́стор; ~ **radio** транзи́сторный приёмник.

transit *n* транзи́т; **in** ~ (goods) при перевóзке; (person) по пути́; ~ **camp** транзи́тный лáгерь *m*. **transition** *n* перехóд. **transitional** *adj* перехóдный. **transitive** *adj* перехóдный. **transitory** *adj* мимолётный.

translate *vt* переводи́ть *impf*, перевести́ *pf*. **translation** *n* перево́д. **translator** n перево́дчик.

translucent adj полупрозра́чный.

transmission n переда́ча. **transmit** vt передава́ть impf, переда́ть pf. **transmitter** n (ра́дио)переда́тчик.

transparency n (phot) диапозити́в. **transparent** adj прозра́чный.

transpire vi (become known) обнару́живаться impf, обнару́житься pf; (occur) случа́ться impf, случи́ться pf.

transplant vt переса́живать impf, пересади́ть pf; (med) де́лать impf, с~ pf переса́дку+gen; n (med) переса́дка.

transport n (various senses) тра́нспорт; (conveyance) перево́зка; attrib тра́нспортный; vt перевози́ть impf, перевезти́ pf. **transportation** n тра́нспорт, перево́зка.

transpose vt переставля́ть impf, переста́вить pf; (mus) транспони́ровать impf & pf. **transposition** n перестано́вка; (mus) транспониро́вка.

transverse adj попере́чный.

transvestite n трансвести́т.

trap n лову́шка (also fig), западня́; vt (catch) лови́ть impf, пойма́ть pf в лову́шку; (jam) защемля́ть impf, защеми́ть pf. **trapdoor** n люк.

trapeze n трапе́ция.

trapper n звероло́в.

trappings n pl (fig) (exterior attributes) вне́шние атрибу́ты m pl; (adornments) украше́ния neut pl.

trash n дрянь (coll). **trashy** adj дрянно́й.

trauma n тра́вма. **traumatic**

adj травмати́ческий.

travel n путеше́ствие; ~ **agency** бюро́ neut indecl путеше́ствий; ~ **sick: be** ~ **sick** укача́ть impf; укача́ть pf impers +acc; **I am** ~ **sick in cars** меня́ в маши́не ука́чивает; vi путеше́ствовать impf; vt объезжа́ть impf, объе́хать pf. **traveller** n путеше́ственник; (salesman) коммивояжёр; ~'s **cheque** тури́стский чек.

traverse vt пересека́ть impf, пересе́чь pf.

travesty n паро́дия.

trawler n тра́улер.

tray n подно́с; in- (out-)~ корзи́нка для входя́щих (исходя́щих) бума́г.

treacherous adj преда́тельский; (unsafe) ненадёжный. **treachery** n преда́тельство.

treacle n па́тока.

tread n похо́дка; (stair) ступе́нька; (of tyre) протёктор; vi ступа́ть impf, ступи́ть pf; ~ **on** наступа́ть impf, наступи́ть pf на+acc; vt топта́ть impf.

treason n изме́на.

treasure n сокро́вище; vt высоко́ цени́ть impf. **treasurer** n казначе́й. **treasury** n (also fig) сокро́вищница; **the T**~ госуда́рственное казначе́йство.

treat n (pleasure) удово́льствие; (entertainment) угоще́ние; vt (have as guest) угоща́ть impf, угости́ть pf (to +instr); (med) лечи́ть impf (for от+gen; with +instr); (behave towards) обраща́ться impf c+instr; (process) обраба́тывать impf, обрабо́тать pf (with +instr); (discuss) трактова́ть *impf* o+*prep*; (*regard*) относи́ться *impf*, отнести́сь *pf* к+*dat* (**as** как к+*dat*). **treatise** *n* тракта́т.

treatment *n* (*behaviour*) обраще́ние; (*med*) лече́ние; (*processing*) обрабо́тка; (*discussion*) тракто́вка. **treaty** *n* догово́р.

treble *adj* тройно́й; (*trebled*) утро́енный; *adv* втро́е; *n* (*mus*) дискка́нт; *vt* & *i* утра́ивать(ся) *impf*, утро́ить(ся) *pf*.

tree *n* де́рево.

trek *n* (*migration*) переселе́ние; (*journey*) путеше́ствие; *vi* (*migrate*) переселя́ться *impf*, перес́ели́ться *pf*; (*journey*) путеше́ствовать *impf*.

trellis *n* шпале́ра; (*for creepers*) решётка.

tremble *vi* дрожа́ть *impf* (**with** от+*gen*); **trembling** *n* дрожь; **in fear and** ~ трепеща́.

tremendous *adj* (*huge*) огро́мный; (*excellent*) потряса́ющий.

tremor *n* дрожь; (*earthquake*) толчо́к. **tremulous** *adj* дрожа́щий.

trench *n* кана́ва, ров; (*mil*) око́п.

trend *n* направле́ние, тенде́нция. **trendy** *adj* мо́дный.

trepidation *n* тре́пет.

trespass *n* (*on property*) наруше́ние грани́ц; *vi* наруша́ть *impf*, нару́шить *pf* грани́цу (**on** +*gen*); (*fig*) вторга́ться *impf*, вто́ргнуться *pf* (**on** в+*acc*). **trespasser** *n* нару́шитель *m*.

trestle *n* ко́злы (-зел, -злам) *pl*; ~ **table** стол на ко́злах.

trial *n* (*test*) испыта́ние (*also ordeal*), про́ба; (*law*) проце́сс, суд; (*sport*) попы́тка;

on ~ (*probation*) на испыта́нии; (*of objects*) взя́тый на про́бу; (*law*) под судо́м; ~ **and error** ме́тод проб и оши́бок.

triangle *n* треуго́льник. **triangular** *adj* треуго́льный.

tribal *adj* племенно́й. **tribe** *n* пле́мя *neut*.

tribulation *n* го́ре, несча́стье.

tribunal *n* трибуна́л.

tributary *n* прито́к. **tribute** *n* дань; **pay** ~ (*fig*) отдава́ть *impf*, отда́ть *pf* дань (уваже́ния) (**to** +*dat*).

trice *n*: **in a** ~ мгнове́нно.

trick *n* (*ruse*) хи́трость; (*deception*) обма́н; (*conjuring*) фо́кус; (*stunt*) трюк; (*joke*) шу́тка; (*habit*) привы́чка; (*cards*) взя́тка; **play a** ~ **on** игра́ть *impf*, сыгра́ть *pf* шу́тку с+*instr*; *vt* обма́нывать *impf*, обману́ть *pf*. **trickery** *n* обма́н.

trickle *vi* сочи́ться *impf*.

trickster *n* обма́нщик. **tricky** *adj* сло́жный.

tricycle *n* трёхколёсный велосипе́д.

trifle *n* пустя́к; **a** ~ (*adv*) немно́го +*gen*; *vi* шути́ть *impf*, по— *pf* (**with** с+*instr*). **trifling** *adj* пустяко́вый.

trigger *n* (*of gun*) куро́к; *vt* ~ **off** вызыва́ть *impf*, вы́звать *pf*.

trill *n* трель.

trilogy *n* трило́гия.

trim *n* поря́док, гото́вность; **in fighting** ~ в боево́й гото́вности; **in good** ~ (*sport*) в хоро́шей фо́рме; (*haircut*) подстри́жка; *adj* опря́тный; *vt* (*cut, clip, cut off*) подреза́ть *impf*, подре́зать *pf*; (*hair*) подстрига́ть *impf*, подстри́чь *pf; (a dress etc.)* отде́лывать *impf*, отде́лать *pf* **trimming** *n (on dress)* отде́лка; *(to food)* гарни́р.

Trinity *n* Тро́ица.

trinket *n* безделу́шка.

trio *n* три́о *neut indecl; (of people)* тро́йка.

trip *n* пое́здка, путеше́ствие, экску́рсия; *(business ~)* командиро́вка; *vi (stumble)* спотыка́ться *impf*, споткну́ться *pf* (**over** o+*acc*); *vt (also ~ up)* подставля́ть *impf*, подста́вить *pf* но́жку +*dat (also fig); (confuse)* запу́тывать *impf*, запу́тать *pf*.

triple *adj* тройно́й; *(tripled)* утро́енный; *vt & i* утра́ивать(ся) *impf*, утро́ить(ся) *pf*. **triplet** *n (mus)* трио́ль; *(one of ~s)* близне́ц (из тро́йни); *pl* тро́йня.

tripod *n* трено́жник.

trite *adj* бана́льный.

triumph *n* торжество́, побе́да; *vi* торжествова́ть *impf*, вос~ *pf* (**over** над+*instr*). **triumphal** *adj* триумфа́льный. **triumphant** *adj (exultant)* торжеству́ющий; *(victorious)* победоно́сный.

trivia *n pl* ме́лочи *(-че́й) pl.*

trivial *adj* незначи́тельный. **triviality** *n* тривиа́льность.

trivialize *vt* опошля́ть *impf*, опошли́ть *pf*.

trolley *n* теле́жка; *(table on wheels)* сто́лик на колёсиках. **trolley-bus** *n* тролле́йбус.

trombone *n* тромбо́н.

troop *n* гру́ппа, отря́д; *(mil)* войска́ *neut pl; vi* идти́ *impf*, по~ *pf* стро́ем.

trophy *n* трофе́й; *(prize)* приз.

tropic *n* тро́пик. **tropical** *adj* тропи́ческий.

trot *n* рысь; *vi* рыси́ть *impf; (rider)* е́здить *indet*, е́хать *det*, по~ *pf* ры́сью; *(horse)* ходи́ть *indet*, идти́ *det*, пойти́ *pf* ры́сью.

trouble *n (worry)* беспоко́йство, трево́га; *(misfortune)* беда́; *(unpleasantness)* неприя́тности *f pl; (effort, pains)* труд; *(care)* забо́та; *(disrepair)* неиспра́вность (**with** в+*prep*); *(illness)* боле́знь; **heart ~** больно́е се́рдце; **~-maker** наруши́тель *m*, ~ница споко́йствия; **ask for ~** напра́шиваться *impf*, напроси́ться *pf* на неприя́тности; **be in ~** име́ть *impf* неприя́тности; **get into ~** попа́сть *pf* в беду́; **take ~** стара́ться *impf*, по~ *pf*; **take the ~** труди́ться *impf*, по~ *pf* (**to** +*inf*); **the ~ is (that)** беда́ в том, что; *vt (make anxious, disturb, give pain)* беспоко́ить *impf*, по~ *pf*; **may I ~ you for ...?** мо́жно попроси́ть у вас +*acc*?; *vi (take the ~)* труди́ться *impf*. **troubled** *adj* беспоко́йный. **troublesome** *adj (restless, fidgety)* беспоко́йный; *(capricious)* капри́зный; *(difficult)* тру́дный.

trough *n (for food)* корму́шка.

trounce *vt (beat)* поро́ть *impf*, вы́~ *pf; (defeat)* разбива́ть *impf*, разби́ть *pf*.

troupe *n* тру́ппа.

trouser-leg *n* штани́на *(coll).* **trousers** *n pl* брю́ки *(-к) pl*, штаны́ *(-но́в) pl.*

trout *n* форе́ль.

trowel *n (for building)* мастеро́к; *(garden ~)* садо́вый сово́к.

truancy *n* прогу́л. **truant** *n*

прогу́льщик; **play ~** прогу́ливать *impf*, прогуля́ть *pf*.

truce *n* переми́рие.

truck[1] *n*: **have no ~ with** не име́ть *impf* никаки́х дел с+*instr*.

truck[2] *n* (lorry) грузови́к; (rly) ваго́н-платфо́рма.

truculent *adj* свире́пый.

trudge *vi* уста́ло тащи́ться *impf*.

true *adj* (faithful, correct) ве́рный; (correct) пра́вильный; (story) правди́вый; (real) настоя́щий; **come ~** сбыва́ться *impf*, сбы́ться *pf*.

truism *n* трюи́зм. **truly** *adv* (sincerely) и́скренне; (really, indeed) действи́тельно; **yours ~** пре́данный Вам.

trump *n* ко́зырь *m*; *vt* бить *impf*, по~ *pf* ко́зырем; **~ up** фабрикова́ть *impf*, с~ *pf*.

trumpet *n* труба́; *vt* (proclaim) труби́ть *impf* о+*prep*. **trumpeter** *n* труба́ч.

truncate *vt* усека́ть *impf*, усе́чь *pf*.

truncheon *n* дуби́нка.

trundle *vt & i* кати́ть(ся) *indet*, кати́ть(ся) *det*, по~ *pf*.

trunk *n* (stem) ствол; (anat) ту́ловище; (elephant's) хо́бот; (box) сунду́к; *pl* (swimming) пла́вки *(-вок) pl*; (boxing etc.) трусы́ *(-со́в) pl*; **~ call** вы́зов по междугоро́дному телефо́ну; **~ road** магистра́льная доро́га.

truss *n* (girder) фе́рма; (med) грыжево́й банда́ж; *vt* (tie (up), bird) свя́зывать *impf*, связа́ть *pf*; (reinforce) укрепля́ть *impf*, укрепи́ть *pf*.

trust *n* дове́рие; (body of trustees) опе́ка; (property held in ~) дове́рительная со́бственность; (econ) трест; **take on ~** принима́ть *impf*, приня́ть *pf* на ве́ру; *vt* доверя́ть *impf*, дове́рить *pf* +*dat* (with +*acc*; **to** +*inf*); *vi* (hope) наде́яться *impf*, по~ *pf*. **trustee** *n* опеку́н. **trustful, trusting** *adj* дове́рчивый. **trustworthy, trusty** *adj* надёжный, ве́рный.

truth *n* пра́вда; **tell the ~** говори́ть *impf*, сказа́ть *pf* пра́вду; **to tell you the ~** по пра́вде говоря́. **truthful** *adj* правди́вый.

try *n* (attempt) попы́тка; (test, trial) испыта́ние, про́ба; *vt* (taste; sample) про́бовать *impf*, по~ *pf*; (patience) испы́тывать *impf*, испыта́ть *pf* (law) суди́ть *impf* (**for** за+*acc*); (endeavour) стара́ться *impf*, по~ *pf*; **~ on** (clothes) примеря́ть *impf*, приме́рить *pf*. **trying** *adj* тру́дный.

tsar *n* царь *m*. **tsarina** *n* цари́ца.

tub *n* ка́дка; (bath) ва́нна; (of margarine etc.) упако́вка.

tubby *adj* то́лстенький.

tube *n* тру́бка, труба́; (toothpaste etc.) тю́бик; (underground) метро́ *neut indecl*.

tuber *n* клу́бень *m*. **tuberculosis** *n* туберкулёз.

tubing *n* тру́бы *f pl*. **tubular** *adj* трубча́тый.

tuck *n* (in garment) скла́дка; *vt* (thrust into, ~ away) засо́вывать *impf*, засу́нуть *pf*; (hide away) пря́тать *impf*, с~ *pf*; **~ in** (shirt etc.) запра́вля́ть *impf*, запра́вить *pf*; **~ in, up** (blanket, skirt) подты́ка́ть *impf*, подоткну́ть *pf*; **~ up** (sleeves) засу́чивать *impf*, засучи́ть *pf*, (in bed) укрыва́ть *impf*, укры́ть *pf*.

Tuesday n вто́рник.

tuft n пучо́к.

tug vt тяну́ть impf, по~ pf; vi (sharply) дёргать impf, дёрнуть pf (at за+acc); n рыво́к; (tugboat) букси́р.

tuition n обуче́ние (in +dat).

tulip n тюльпа́н.

tumble vi (fall) па́дать impf, (у)па́сть pf; n паде́ние. **tumbledown** adj полуразру́шенный. **tumbler** n стака́н.

tumour n о́пухоль.

tumult n (uproar) сумато́ха; (agitation) волне́ние. **tumultuous** adj шу́мный.

tuna n туне́ц.

tundra n ту́ндра.

tune n мело́дия; **in ~** в тон, (of instrument) настро́енный; **out of ~** не в тон, фальши́вый, (of instrument) расстро́енный; **change one's ~** (пере)меня́ть impf, переме́нить pf тон; vt (instrument; radio) настра́ивать impf, настро́ить pf; (engine etc.) регули́ровать impf, от~ pf; **~ in** настра́ивать impf, настро́ить pf (radio) ра́дио (**to** на+acc); vi: **~ up** настра́ивать impf, настро́ить pf инструме́нт(ы). **tuneful** adj мело́дичный. **tuner** n (mus) настро́йщик; (receiver) приёмник.

tunic n туни́ка; (of uniform) ки́тель m.

tuning n настро́йка; (of engine) регулиро́вка; **~-fork** n камерто́н.

tunnel n тунне́ль m; vi прокла́дывать impf, проложи́ть pf тунне́ль m.

turban n тюрба́н.

turbine n турби́на.

turbulence n бу́рность; (aeron) турбуле́нтность. **turbulent** adj бу́рный.

tureen n су́пник.

turf n дёрн.

turgid adj (pompous) напы́щенный.

Turk n тру́ок, турча́нка. **Turkey** n Ту́рция.

turkey n инди́ок, f инде́йка; (dish) инди́юшка. **Turkish** adj туре́цкий. **Turkmenistan** n Туркмениста́н.

turmoil n (disorder) беспоря́док; (uproar) сумато́ха.

turn n (change of direction) поворо́т; (revolution) оборо́т; (service) услу́га; (change) измене́ние; (one's ~ to do sth) о́чередь; (theat) но́мер; **~ of phrase** оборо́т ре́чи; **at every ~** на ка́ждом шагу́; **by, in turn(s)** по о́череди; vt (handle, key, car around, etc.) повора́чивать impf, поверну́ть pf, (revolve, rotate) враща́ть impf; (page; on its face) перевёртывать impf, переверну́ть pf; (direct) направля́ть impf, напра́вить pf; (cause to become) де́лать impf, с~ pf +instr; (on lathe) точи́ть impf; vi (change direction) повора́чивать impf, поверну́ть pf, (rotate) враща́ться impf; (~ round) повора́чиваться impf, поверну́ться pf; (become) станови́ться impf, стать pf +instr; **~ against** ополча́ться impf, ополчи́ться pf на+acc; проти́в+gen; **~ around** see **~ round;** **~ away** (vt & i) отвора́чивать(ся) impf, отверну́ть(ся) pf; (refuse admittance) прогоня́ть impf, прогна́ть pf; **~ back** (vi) повора́чивать impf, поверну́ть pf наза́д; (vt) (bend back) отгибáть *impf*, отогнýть *pf*; ~ **down** (*refuse*) отклонять *impf*, отклонить *pf*; (*collar*) отгибáть *impf*, отогнýть *pf*; (*make quieter*) дéлать *impf*, с~ *pf* тише; ~ **grey** (*vi*) седéть *impf*, по~ *pf*; ~ **in** (*so as to turn inwards*) поворáчивать *impf*, повернýть *pf* вовнýть; ~ **inside out** выворáчивать *impf*, вы́вернуть *pf* наизнáнку; ~ **into** (*change into*) (*vt & i*) превращáть(ся) *impf*, превратить(ся) *pf* в+*acc*; (*street*) свора́чивать *impf*, сверну́ть *pf* на+*acc*; ~ **off** (*light, radio etc.*) выключáть *impf*, вы́ключить *pf*; (*tap*) закрывáть *impf*, закры́ть *pf*; (*vi*) (*branch off*) свора́чивать *impf*, сверну́ть *pf*; ~ **on** (*light, radio etc.*) включáть *impf*, включи́ть *pf*; (*tap*) открывáть *impf*, откры́ть *pf*; (*attack*) напада́ть *impf*, напáсть *pf* на+*acc*; ~ **out** (*light etc.*): *see* ~ **off**; (*prove to be*) окáзываться *impf*, оказáться *pf* (*to be* +*instr*); (*drive out*) выгоня́ть *impf*, вы́гнать *pf*; (*pockets*) вывёртывать *impf*, вы́вернуть *pf*; (*be present*) приходи́ть *impf*, прийти́ *pf*; (*product*) выпускáть *impf*, вы́пустить *pf*; ~ **over** (*page, on its face, roll over*) (*vt & i*) перевёртывать(ся) *impf*, переверну́ть(ся) *pf*; (*hand over*) передавáть *impf*, передáть *pf*; (*think about*) обдýмывать *impf*, обдýмать *pf*; (*overturn*) (*vt & i*) опроки́дывать(ся) *impf*; ~ **pale** бледнéть *impf*, по~ *pf*; ~ **red** краснéть *impf*, по~ *pf*; ~ **round** (*vi*

(*rotate*; ~ *one's back*; ~ *to face sth*) повёртываться *impf*, поверну́ться *pf*; (~ *to face*) оборáчиваться *impf*, оберну́ться *pf*; (*vt*) повёртывать *impf*, поверну́ть *pf*; ~ **sour** скисáть *impf*, скиснуть *pf*; ~ **to** обращáться *impf*, обрати́ться *pf* к+*dat* (*for* за+*instr*); ~ **up** (*appear*) появля́ться *impf*, появи́ться *pf*; (*be found*) находи́ться *impf*, найти́сь *pf*; (*shorten garment*) подшивáть *impf*, подши́ть *pf*; (*crop up*) подвёртываться *impf*, подверну́ться *pf*; (*bend up; stick up*) (*vt & i*) загибáть(ся) *impf*, загну́ть(ся) *pf*; (*make louder*) дéлать *impf*, с~ *pf* грóмче; ~ **up one's nose** воротить *impf* нос (**at** от+*gen*) (*coll*); ~ **upside down** повора́чивать *impf*, переверну́ть *pf* вверх дном. **turn-out** *n* количество приходя́щих.

turn-up *n* (*on trousers*) обшлáг.

turner *n* тóкарь *m*.

turning *n* (*road*) поворóт.

turning-point *n* поворóтный пункт.

turnip *n* рéпа.

turnover *n* (*econ*) оборóт; (*of staff*) текýчесть рабóчей си́лы.

turnpike *n* дорóжная застáва.

turnstile *n* турникéт.

turntable *n* (*rly*) поворóтный круг; (*gramophone*) диск.

turpentine *n* скипидáр.

turquoise *n* (*material, stone*) бирюзá; *adj* бирюзóвый.

turret *n* бáшенка.

turtle *n* черепáха.

turtle-dove *n* гóрлица.

tusk *n* би́вень *m*, клык.

tussle *n* дрáка; *vi* дрáться *impf* (**for** за+*acc*)

tutor n (*private teacher*) ча́стный дома́шний учи́тель m, ~ница; (*univ*) преподава́тель m, ~ница; (*primer*) уче́бник; vt (*instruct*) обуча́ть impf, обучи́ть pf (+in +dat); (*give lessons to*) дава́ть impf, дать pf уро́ки+dat; (*guide*) руководи́ть impf +instr. **tutorial** n консульта́ция.

tutu n (*ballet*) па́чка.

TV abbr (of television) ТВ, телеви́дение; (*set*) телеви́зор.

twang n (*of string*) ре́зкий звук (натя́нутой струны́); (*voice*) гнуса́вый го́лос.

tweak n щипо́к; vt щипа́ть impf, (у)щипну́ть pf.

tweed n твид.

tweezers n pl пинце́т.

twelfth adj & n двена́дцатый. **twelve** adj & n двена́дцать.

twentieth adj & n двадца́тый. **twenty** adj & n два́дцать; pl (*decade*) двадца́тые го́ды (-до́в) m pl.

twice adv два́жды; ~ **as** вдво́е, в два ра́за +comp.

twiddle vt (*turn*) верте́ть impf +acc, instr; (*toy with*) игра́ть impf +instr; ~ **one's thumbs** (*fig*) безде́льничать impf.

twig n ве́точка, прут.

twilight n су́мерки (-рек) pl.

twin n близне́ц; pl (*Gemini*) Близнецы́ m pl; ~ **beds** па́ра односпа́льных крова́тей; ~ **brother** брат-близне́ц; ~ **town** го́род-побрати́м.

twine n бечёвка, шпага́т; vt (*twist, weave*) вить impf, c~ pf; vt & i (~ **round**) обвива́ть(ся) impf, обви́ть(ся) pf.

twinge n при́ступ (бо́ли); (*of conscience*) угрызе́ние.

twinkle n мерца́ние; (*of eyes*) огонёк; vi мерца́ть impf,

сверка́ть impf. **twinkling** n мерца́ние; **in the** ~ **of an eye** в мгнове́ние о́ка.

twirl n & i (*twist, turn*) верте́ть(ся) impf; (*whirl, spin*) кружи́ть(ся) impf.

twist n (*bend*) изги́б, поворо́т; (~*ing*) круче́ние; (*in story*) поворо́т фа́булы; vt скру́чивать impf, крути́ть impf, c~ pf; (*distort*) искажа́ть impf, искази́ть pf; (*sprain*) подвёртывать impf, подверну́ть pf; vi (*climb, meander*) ви́ться impf. **twisted** adj искривлённый (*also fig*).

twit n дура́к.

twitch n подёргивание; vt & i дёргать(ся) impf, дёрнуть(ся) pf (at за+acc).

twitter n щебет; vi щебета́ть impf, чири́кать impf.

two adj & n два, две (f); (*collect; 2 pairs*) дво́е; (*number 2*) дво́йка; **in** ~ (*in half*) на́двое, попола́м; ~-**seater** двухме́стный (автомоби́ль); ~-**way** двусторо́нний. **twofold** adj двойно́й; adv вдво́йне. **twosome** n па́ра.

tycoon n магна́т.

type n тип, род; (*printing*) шрифт; vt писа́ть impf, на~ pf на маши́нке. **typescript** n маши́нопись. **typewriter** n пи́шущая маши́нка. **typewritten** adj машинопи́сный.

typhoid n брюшно́й тиф.

typical adj типи́чный. **typify** vt служи́ть impf, по~ pf типи́чным приме́ром +gen.

typist n машини́стка.

typography n книгопеча́тание; (*style*) оформле́ние.

tyrannical adj тирани́ческий. **tyrant** n тира́н.

tyre n ши́на.

U

ubiquitous adj вездесу́щий.
udder n вы́мя neut.
UFO abbr (of unidentified flying object) НЛО, неопо́знанный лета́ющий объе́кт.
ugh int тьфу!
ugliness n уро́дство. **ugly** adj некраси́вый, уро́дливый; (unpleasant) неприя́тный.
UK abbr (of United Kingdom) Соединённое Короле́вство.
Ukraine n Украи́на. **Ukrainian** n украи́нец, -нка; adj украи́нский.
ulcer n я́зва.
ulterior adj скры́тый.
ultimate adj (final) после́дний, оконча́тельный; (purpose) коне́чный. **ultimately** adv в коне́чном счёте, в конце́ концо́в. **ultimatum** n ультима́тум.
ultrasound n ультразву́к. **ultra-violet** adj ультрафиоле́товый.
umbilical adj: ~ cord пупови́на.
umbrella n зо́нтик, зонт.
umpire n судья́ m; vt & i суди́ть impf.
umpteenth adj: for the ~ time в кото́рый раз.
unabashed adj без вся́кого смуще́ния. **unabated** adj неосла́бленный. **unable** adj: be ~ to не мочь impf, c~ pf; быть не в состоя́нии; (not know how to) не уме́ть impf, c~ pf. **unabridged** adj несокращённый. **unaccompanied** adj без сопровожде́ния; (mus) без аккомпанеме́нта. **unaccountable** adj

необъясни́мый. **unaccustomed** adj (not accustomed) непривы́кший (to к+dat); (unusual) непривы́чный. **unadulterated** adj настоя́щий; (utter) чисте́йший. **unaffected** adj непринуждённый. **unaided** adj без по́мощи, самостоя́тельный. **unambiguous** adj недвусмы́сленный. **unanimity** n единоду́шие. **unanimous** adj единоду́шный. **unanswerable** adj (irrefutable) неопроверже́мый. **unarmed** adj невооружённый. **unashamed** adj бессо́вестный. **unassailable** adj непристу́пный; (irrefutable) неопроверже́мый. **unassuming** adj скро́мный. **unattainable** adj недосяга́емый. **unattended** adj без присмо́тра. **unattractive** adj непривлека́тельный. **unauthorized** adj неразрешённый. **unavailable** adj не име́ющийся в нали́чии, недосту́пный. **unavoidable** adj неизбе́жный. **unaware** predic: be ~ of не сознава́ть impf +acc; не знать про o+prep. **unawares** adv враспло́х.

unbalanced adj (psych) неуравнове́шенный. **unbearable** adj невыноси́мый. **unbeatable** adj (unsurpassable) не могу́щий быть превзойдённым; (invincible) непобеди́мый. **unbeaten** adj (undefeated) непокорённый; (unsurpassed) непревзойдённый. **unbelief** n неве́рие. **unbelievable** adj невероя́тный. **unbeliever** n неве́рующий sb. **unbiased** adj беспристра́стный. **unblemished** adj незапя́тнанный. **unblock**

прощати́ *impf*, прочи́стить *pf*. **unbolt** *vt* отпира́ть *impf*, отпере́ть *pf*. **unborn** *adj* ещё не рождённый. **unbounded** *adj* неограни́ченный. **unbreakable** *adj* небьющийся. **unbridled** *adj* разнузданный. **unbroken** *adj* (*intact*) неразби́тый, це́лый; (*continuous*) непреры́вный; (*unsurpassed*) непоби́тый; (*horse*) необъе́зженный. **unbuckle** *vt* расстёгивать *impf*, расстегну́ть *pf*. **unburden** *vt* расстёгивать *impf*, отвести́ *pf* ду́шу. **unbutton** *vt* расстёгивать *impf*, расстегну́ть *pf*.

ncalled-for *adj* неуме́стный. **uncanny** *adj* жу́ткий, сверхъесте́ственный. **unceasing** *adj* непреры́вный. **unceremonious** *adj* бесцеремо́нный. **uncertain** *adj* (*not sure, hesitating*) неуве́ренный; (*indeterminate*) неопределённый, нея́сный; be ~ (*not know for certain*) то́чно не знать *impf*; in no ~ terms недвусмы́сленно. **uncertainty** *n* неизве́стность; неопределённость. **unchallenged** *adj* не вызыва́ющий возраже́ний. **unchanged** *adj* неизме́нившийся. **unchanging** *adj* неизменя́ющийся. **uncharacteristic** *adj* нетипи́чный. **uncharitable** *adj* немилосе́рдный, жесто́кий. **uncharted** *adj* неиссле́дованный. **unchecked** *adj* (*unrestrained*) необу́зданный. **uncivilized** *adj* нецивилизо́ванный. **unclaimed** *adj* невостре́бованный.

uncle *n* дя́дя *m*.

unclean *adj* нечи́стый. **un-**

clear *adj* нея́сный. **uncomfortable** *adj* неудо́бный. **uncommon** *adj* необыкнове́нный; (*rare*) ре́дкий. **uncommunicative** *adj* неразгово́рчивый, сде́ржанный. **uncomplaining** *adj* безро́потный. **uncomplicated** *adj* несло́жный. **uncompromising** *adj* бескомпроми́ссный. **unconcealed** *adj* нескрыва́емый. **unconcerned** *adj* (*unworried*) беззабо́тный; (*indifferent*) равноду́шный. **unconditional** *adj* безогово́рочный, безусло́вный. **unconfirmed** *adj* неподтверждённый. **unconnected** *adj* ~ with свя́занный с+*instr*. **unconscious** *adj* (*also unintentional*) бессозна́тельный; (*predic*) без созна́ния; be ~ of не сознава́ть *impf* +*gen*; *n* подсозна́тельное *sb*. **unconsciousness** *n* бессозна́тельное состоя́ние. **unconstitutional** *adj* неконституцио́нный. **uncontrollable** *adj* неуде́ржи́мый. **uncontrolled** *adj* бесконтро́льный. **unconventional** *adj* необы́чный; оригина́льный. **unconvincing** *adj* неубеди́тельный. **uncooked** *adj* сыро́й. **uncooperative** *adj* неотзы́вчивый. **uncouth** *adj* гру́бый. **uncover** *vt* раскрыва́ть *impf*, раскры́ть *pf*. **uncritical** *adj* некрити́чный.

unctuous *adj* еле́йный. **uncut** *adj* неразре́занный; (*unabridged*) несокращённый. **undamaged** *adj* неповреждённый. **undaunted** *adj* бесстра́шный. **undecided** *adj* (*not settled*) нерешённый; (*irresolute*) нереши́тельный.

undefeated adj непокорённый. **undemanding** adj нетребовательный. **undemocratic** adj недемократи́ческий. **undeniable** adj неоспори́мый.

under prep (position) под+instr; (direction) под+acc; (fig) под +instr; (less than) ме́ньше+gen; (in view of, in the reign, time of) при+prep; **~age** несовершенноле́тний; **~ way** на ходу́; adv (position) вни́зу; (direction) вниз; (less) ме́ньше. **undercarriage** n шасси́ neut indecl. **underclothes** n pl ни́жнее бельё. **undercoat** n (of paint) грунто́вка. **undercover** adj та́йный. **undercurrent** n подво́дное тече́ние; (fig) скры́тая тенде́нция. **undercut** vt (price) назнача́ть impf, назна́чить pf бо́лее ни́зкую це́ну чем+nom. **underdeveloped** adj слаборазви́тый. **underdog** n неуда́чник. **underdone** adj недожа́ренный. **underemployment** n непо́лная за́нятость. **underestimate** vt недооце́нивать impf, недооцени́ть pf; n недооце́нка. **underfoot** adv под нога́ми.

undergo vt подверга́ться impf, подве́ргнуться pf +dat; (endure) переноси́ть impf, перенести́ pf. **undergraduate** n студе́нт, ~ка. **underground** n (rly) метро́ neut indecl; (fig) подпо́лье; adj подзе́мный; (fig) подпо́льный; adv под землёй; (fig) подпо́льно. **undergrowth** n подле́сок. **underhand** adj заку́лисный. **underlie** vt (fig) лежа́ть impf в осно́ве +gen. **underline** vt подчёркивать impf, под-

черкну́ть pf. **underlying** adj лежа́щий в осно́ве. **underling** n подчинённый sb.

undermine vt (authority) подрыва́ть impf, подорва́ть pf; (health) разруша́ть impf, разру́шить pf.

underneath adv (position) внизу́; (direction) вниз; prep (position) под+instr; (direction) под+acc; n ни́жняя часть; adj ни́жний.

undernourished adj исху́далый; **be ~** недоеда́ть impf.

underpaid adj низкоопла́чиваемый. **underpants** n pl трусы́ (-со́в) pl. **underpass** n прое́зд по полотно́м доро́ги; тонне́ль m. **underpin** vt подводи́ть impf, подвести́ pf фунда́мент под+acc; (fig) подде́рживать impf, поддержа́ть pf. **underprivileged** adj обделённый; (poor) бе́дный. **underrate** vt недооце́нивать impf, недооцени́ть pf. **underscore** vt подчёркивать impf, подчеркну́ть pf. **undersecretary** n замести́тель m мини́стра. **underside** n ни́жняя сторона́, низ. **undersized** adj малоро́слый. **understaffed** adj неукомплекто́ванный.

understand vt понима́ть impf, поня́ть pf; (have heard say) слы́шать impf. **understandable** adj поня́тный. **understanding** n понима́ние; (agreement) соглаше́ние; adj (sympathetic) отзы́вчивый. **understate** vt преуменьша́ть impf, преуме́ньшить pf. **understatement** n преуменьше́ние.

understudy n дублёр. **undertake** vt (enter upon)

предпринима́ть *impf*, предприня́ть *pf*; (*responsibility*) брать *impf*, взять *pf* на себя́; (+*inf*) обя́зываться *impf*, обяза́ться *pf*; (*pledge*) гаранти́ровать *impf*. **undertaker** *n* гробо́вщик. **undertaking** *n* предприя́тие; (*pledge*) гара́нтия. **undertone** *n* (*fig*) подте́кст; **in an ~** вполго́лоса. **underwater** *adj* подво́дный. **underwear** *n* ни́жнее бельё. **underweight** *adj* исхуда́лый. **underworld** *n* (*mythology*) преиспо́дняя *sb*; (*criminals*) престу́пный мир. **underwrite** *vt* (*guarantee*) гаранти́ровать *impf* & *pf*. **underwriter** *n* страхо́вщик.

undeserved *adj* незаслу́женный. **undesirable** *adj* нежела́тельный; *n* нежела́тельное лицо́. **undeveloped** *adj* нера́звитый; (*land*) незастро́енный. **undignified** *adj* недосто́йный. **undiluted** *adj* неразба́вленный. **undisciplined** *adj* недисциплини́рованный. **undiscovered** *adj* неоткры́тый. **undisguised** *adj* я́вный. **undisputed** *adj* беспо́рный. **undistinguished** *adj* заура́дный. **undisturbed** *adj* (*untouched*) нетро́нутый; (*peaceful*) споко́йный. **undivided** *adj*: **~ attention** по́лное внима́ние. **undo** *vt* (*open*) открыва́ть *impf*, откры́ть *pf*; (*untie*) развя́зывать *impf*, развяза́ть *pf*; (*unbutton*, *unhook*, *unbuckle*) расстёгивать *impf*, расстегну́ть *pf*; (*destroy*, *cancel*) уничтожа́ть *impf*, уничто́жить *pf*. **undoubted** *adj* несомне́нный. **undoubtedly** *adv* несомне́нно. **undress** *vt* & *i* раздева́ть(ся) *impf*, разде́ть(ся)

pf. **undue** *adj* чрезме́рный. **unduly** *adv* чрезме́рно.

undulating *adj* волни́стый; (*landscape*) холми́стый. **undying** *adj* (*eternal*) ве́чный.

unearth *vt* (*dig up*) выка́пывать *impf*, вы́копать *pf* из земли́; (*fig*) раска́пывать *impf*, раскопа́ть *pf*. **uneasiness** *n* (*anxiety*) беспоко́йство; (*awkwardness*) нело́вкость. **uneasy** *adj* беспоко́йный; нело́вкий. **uneconomic** *adj* нерента́бельный. **uneconomical** *adj* (*car etc.*) неэконо́мичный; (*person*) неэконо́мный. **uneducated** *adj* необразо́ванный. **unemployed** *adj* безрабо́тный. **unemployment** *n* безрабо́тица; **~ benefit** посо́бие по безрабо́тице. **unending** *adj* бесконе́чный. **unenviable** *adj* незави́дный. **unequal** *adj* нера́вный. **unequalled** *adj* непревзойдённый. **unequivocal** *adj* недвусмы́сленный. **unerring** *adj* безоши́бочный. **uneven** *adj* неро́вный. **uneventful** *adj* непримеча́тельный. **unexceptional** *adj* обы́чный. **unexpected** *adj* неожи́данный. **unexplored** *adj* неиссле́дованный.

unfailing *adj* неизме́нный; (*inexhaustible*) неисчерпа́емый. **unfair** *adj* несправедли́вый. **unfaithful** *adj* неве́рный. **unfamiliar** *adj* незнако́мый; (*unknown*) неве́домый. **unfashionable** *adj* немо́дный. **unfasten** *vt* (*detach*, *untie*) открепля́ть *impf*, открепи́ть *pf*; (*undo*, *unbutton*, *unhook*) расстёгивать *impf*, расстегну́ть *pf*; (*open*) открыва́ть *impf*, откры́ть *pf*. **unfavour-**

able adj неблагоприя́тный. **unfeeling** adj бесчу́вственный. **unfinished** adj незако́нченный. **unfit** adj него́дный; (unhealthy) нездоро́вый. **unflagging** adj неослабева́ющий. **unflattering** adj неле́стный. **unflinching** adj непоколеби́мый. **unfold** vt & i развёртывать(ся) impf, разверну́ть(ся) pf; vi (fig) раскрыва́ться impf, раскры́ться pf. **unforeseen** adj непредви́денный. **unforgettable** adj незабыва́емый. **unforgivable** adj непрости́тельный. **unforgiving** adj непроща́ющий. **unfortunate** adj несча́стный; (regrettable) неуда́чный; n неуда́чник. **unfortunately** adv к сожале́нию. **unfounded** adj необосно́ванный. **unfriendly** adj недружелю́бный. **unfulfilled** adj (hopes etc.) неосуществлённый; (person) неудовлетворённый. **unfurl** vt & i развёртывать(ся) impf, разверну́ть(ся) pf. **unfurnished** adj немеблиро́ванный.

ungainly adj неуклю́жий. **ungovernable** adj неуправля́емый. **ungracious** adj нелюбе́зный. **ungrateful** adj неблагода́рный. **unguarded** adj (incautious) неосторо́жный. **unhappiness** n несча́стье. **unhappy** adj несчастли́вый. **unharmed** adj невреди́мый. **unhealthy** adj нездоро́вый; (harmful) вре́дный. **unheard-of** adj неслы́ханный. **unheeded** adj незаме́ченный. **unheeding** adj невнима́тельный. **unhelpful** adj беспле́зный; (person) неотзы́вчивый. **unhesitating** adj пе-

ши́тельный. **unhesitating** adv без колеба́ния. **unhir dered** adj беспрепя́тственный. **unhinge** vt (fig) рас стра́ивать impf, расстро́ит pf. **unholy** adj (impious нечести́вый; (awful) ужа́с ный. **unhook** vt (undo hook of) расстёгивать impf, рас стегну́ть pf; (uncouple) рас цепля́ть impf, расцепи́ть p **unhurt** adj невреди́мый.

unicorn n единоро́г.

unification n объедине́ние. **uniform** n фо́рма; adj едино обра́зный; (unchanging) по стоя́нный. **uniformity** n еди нообра́зие.

unify vt объединя́ть impf объедини́ть pf.

unilateral adj односторо́нний **unimaginable** adj невообра зи́мый. **unimaginative** ad лишённый воображе́ния прозаи́чный. **unimportant** ad нева́жный. **uninformed** ad (ignorant) несве́дущий (about в+prep); (ill-informed) неосве домлённый. **uninhabited** adj необита́емый. **uninhibited** adj нестеснённый. **uninspired** adj бана́льный. **unintelligible** adj непоня́тный. **unintentional** adj неча́янный. **unintentionally** adv неча́янно. **uninterested** adj незаинте ресо́ванный. **uninteresting** adj неинтере́сный. **uninterrupted** adj непреры́вный.

union n (alliance) сою́з; (joining together, alliance) объедине́ние; (trade ~) проф сою́з. **unionist** n член проф сою́за; (polit) униони́ст. **unique** adj уника́льный. **unison** n: in ~ (mus) в уни со́н; (fig) в согла́сии.

unit n едини́ца; (mil) часть.
unite vt & i соединя́ть(ся) impf, соедини́ть(ся) pf; объединя́ть(ся) impf, объедини́ть(ся) pf. **united** adj соединённый, объединённый; U~ **Kingdom** Соединённое Короле́вство; U~ **Nations** Организа́ция Объединённых На́ций; U~ **States** Соединённые Шта́ты m pl Аме́рики. **unity** n еди́нство.
universal adj всео́бщий; (many-sided) универса́льный. **universe** n вселе́нная sb; (world) мир. **university** n университе́т; attrib университе́тский.
unjust adj несправедли́вый.
unjustifiable adj непрости́тельный. **unjustified** adj неопра́вданный.
unkempt adj нечёсаный. **unkind** adj недо́брый, злой. **unknown** adj неизве́стный.
unlawful adj незако́нный.
unleaded adj неэтили́рованный. **unleash** vt (also fig) развя́зывать impf, развяза́ть pf.
unless conj е́сли … не.
unlike adj непохо́жий (на+acc); (in contradistinction to) в отли́чие от+gen. **unlikely** adj малове́роятный; **it is ~ that** вряд ли. **unlimited** adj неограни́ченный. **unlit** adj неосвещённый. **unload** vt (vehicle etc.) разгружа́ть impf, разгрузи́ть pf; (goods etc.) выгружа́ть impf, вы́грузить pf. **unlock** vt отпира́ть impf, отпере́ть pf; открыва́ть impf, откры́ть pf. **unlucky** adj (number etc.) несчастли́вый; (unsuccessful) неуда́чный.
unmanageable adj тру́дный, непоко́рный. **unmanned** adj

автомати́ческий. **unmarried** adj холосто́й; (of man) жена́тый; (of woman) неза́мужняя. **unmask** vt (fig) разоблача́ть impf, разоблачи́ть pf. **unmentionable** adj упомина́емый. **unmistakable** adj несомне́нный, я́сный. **unmitigated** adj (thorough) отъя́вленный. **unmoved** adj: **be ~** оставля́ть impf, оста́ться pf равноду́шен, -шна.
unnatural adj неесте́ственный. **unnecessary** adj нену́жный. **unnerve** vt лиша́ть impf, лиши́ть pf му́жества. **unnoticed** adj незаме́ченный.
unobserved adj незаме́ченный. **unobtainable** adj недосту́пный. **unobtrusive** adj скро́мный, ненавя́зчивый. **unoccupied** adj незаня́тый, свобо́дный; (house) пусто́й. **unofficial** adj неофициа́льный. **unopposed** adj не встре́тивший сопротивле́ния. **unorthodox** adj неортодокса́льный.
unpack vt распако́вывать impf, распакова́ть pf. **unpaid** adj (bill) неупла́ченный; (person) не получа́ющий пла́ты; (work) беспла́тный. **unpalatable** adj невку́сный; (unpleasant) неприя́тный. **unparalleled** adj несравни́мый. **unpleasant** adj неприя́тный. **unpleasantness** n неприя́тность. **unpopular** adj непопуля́рный. **unprecedented** adj беспрецеде́нтный. **unpredictable** adj непредска́зуемый. **unprejudiced** adj беспристра́стный. **unprepared** adj неподгото́влен-

ный, неготóвый. unprepossessing adj непривлекáтельный. unpretentious adj
простóй, без претéнзий. unprincipled adj беспринцúпный. unproductive adj непродуктúвный. unprofitable
adj невыгодный. unpromising adj малообещáющий. unprotected adj незащищённый. unproven adj недокáзанный. unprovoked adj
непровоцúрованный. unpublished adj неопубликóванный, неúзданный. unpunished adj безнакáзанный.

unqualified adj неквалифицúрованный; (unconditional)
безоговóрочный. unquestionable adj несомнéнный,
неоспорúмый. unquestionably adv несомнéнно, бесспóрно.

unravel vt & i распýтывать
(ся) impf, распýтать(ся) pf;
vt (solve) разгáдывать impf,
разгадáть pf. unread adj
(book etc.) непрочúтанный.
unreadable adj (illegible) неразбóрчивый; (boring) неудобочитáемый. unreal adj
нереáльный. unrealistic adj
нереáльный. unreasonable
adj (person) неразýмный;
(behaviour, demand, price)
необоснóванный. unrecognizable adj неузнавáемый.
unrecognized adj непрúзнанный. unrefined adj (manners etc.) грýбый. unrelated adj не имéющий отношéния (to к+dat),
несвязанный (to c+instr); we
are ~ мы не рóдственники.
unrelenting adj (ruthless) нежáлостный; (unremitting) неослáбный. unreliable adj не

надёжный. unremarkable adj
невидáющийся. unremitting
adj неослáбный; (incessant)
беспрестáнный. unrepentant adj нераскáявшийся. unrepresentative adj нетипúный. unrequited adj: ~ love
неразделённая любóвь. unreserved adj (full) пóлный;
(open) откровéнный; (unconditional) безоговóрочный;
(seat) незаброни́рованный.
unresolved adj нерешённый.
unrest n беспокóйство; (polit)
волнéния neut pl. unrestrained adj несдéржанный.
unrestricted adj неограниченный. unripe adj незрéлый. unrivalled adj бесподóбный. unroll vt & i развёртывать(ся) impf, развернýть(ся) pf. unruffled adj
(smooth) глáдкий; (calm) спокóйный. unruly adj непокóрный.

unsafe adj опáсный; (insecure)
ненадёжный. unsaid adj:
leave ~ молчáть impf о+prep.
unsaleable adj нехóдкий.
unsalted adj несолёный.
unsatisfactory adj неудовлетворúтельный. unsatisfied adj неудовлетворённый.
unsavoury adj (unpleasant)
неприя́тный; (disreputable)
сомнúтельный. unscathed
adj невредúмый; (predic) цел
и невредúм. unscheduled
adj (transport) внеочереднóй; (event) незаплани́рованный. unscientific adj ненаýчный. unscrew vt & i отвúнчивать(ся) impf, отвинтúть(ся) pf. unscrupulous
adj беспринцúпный. unseat
vt (of horse) сбрáсывать impf,
сбрóсить pf с седлá; (parl)

лиша́ть *impf*, лиши́ть *pf* парла́ментского манда́та.

unseemly *adj* неподоба́ющий. **unseen** *adj* неви́данный. **unselfconscious** *adj* непосре́дственный. **unselfish** *adj* бескоры́стный. **unsettle** *vt* выбива́ть *impf*, вы́бить *pf* из колеи́; (*upset*) расстра́ивать *impf*, расстро́ить *pf*. **unsettled** *adj* (*weather*) неусто́йчивый; (*unresolved*) нерешённый. **unsettling** *adj* волну́ющий. **unshakeable** *adj* непоколеби́мый. **unshaven** *adj* небри́тый. **unsightly** *adj* непригля́дный, уро́дливый. **unsigned** *adj* неподпи́санный. **unskilful** *adj* неуме́лый. **unskilled** *adj* неквалифици́рованный. **unsociable** *adj* необщи́тельный. **unsold** *adj* непро́данный. **unsolicited** *adj* непро́шеный. **unsolved** *adj* нерешённый. **unsophisticated** *adj* просто́й. **unsound** *adj* (*unhealthy, unwholesome*) нездоро́вый; (*not solid*) непро́чный; (*unfounded*) необосно́ванный; of ~ mind душевнобольно́й. **unspeakable** *adj* (*inexpressible*) невырази́мый; (*very bad*) отврати́тельный. **unspecified** *adj* то́чно не ука́занный, неопределённый. **unspoilt** *adj* неиспо́рченный. **unspoken** *adj* невы́сказанный. **unstable** *adj* неусто́йчивый; (*mentally*) неуравнове́шенный. **unsteady** *adj* неусто́йчивый. **unstuck** *adj*: come ~ откле́иваться *impf*, откле́иться *pf*; (*fig*) прова́ливаться *impf*, провали́ться *pf*. **unsuccessful** *adj* неуда́чный, безуспе́шный. **unsuitable** *adj* неподо-

ходя́щий. **unsuited** *adj* непригодный. **unsung** *adj* невоспе́тый. **unsupported** *adj* неподдержанный. **unsure** *adj* неуве́ренный (of o.s. в себе́). **unsurpassed** *adj* непревзойдённый. **unsurprising** *adj* неудиви́тельный. **unsuspected** *adj* (*unforeseen*) непредви́денный. **unsuspecting** *adj* неподозрева́ющий. **unsweetened** *adj* неподсла́щенный. **unswerving** *adj* непоколеби́мый. **unsympathetic** *adj* несочу́вствующий. **unsystematic** *adj* несистемати́ческий.

untainted *adj* неиспо́рченный. **untangle** *vt* распу́тывать *impf*, распу́тать *pf*. **untapped** *adj*: ~ resources неиспо́льзованные ресу́рсы *m pl*. **untenable** *adj* несостоя́тельный. **untested** *adj* неиспы́танный. **unthinkable** *adj* невообрази́мый. **unthinking** *adj* безду́мный. **untidiness** *n* неопря́тность; (*disorder*) беспоря́док. **untidy** *adj* неопря́тный; (*in disorder*) в беспоря́дке. **untie** *vt* развя́зывать *impf*, развяза́ть *pf*; (*set free*) освобожда́ть *impf*, освободи́ть *pf*.

until *prep* до+*gen*; not ~ не ра́ньше+*gen*; ~ then до тех пор; *conj* пока́, пока́... не; not ~ то́лько когда́.

untimely *adj* (*premature*) безвре́менный; (*inappropriate*) неуме́стный. **untiring** *adj* неутоми́мый. **untold** *adj* (*incalculable*) бессчётный, несме́тный; (*inexpressible*) невырази́мый. **untouched** *adj* нетро́нутый; (*indifferent*) равноду́шный. **untoward**

неблагоприя́тный. **untrained**
adj необу́ченный. **untried**
adj неиспы́танный. **untroubled**
adj споко́йный. **untrue**
adj неве́рный. **untrustworthy**
adj ненадёжный. **untruth** *n*
непра́вда, ложь. **untruthful**
adj лжи́вый.

unusable *adj* неприго́дный.
unused *adj* неиспо́льзован-
ный; (*unaccustomed*) непри-
вы́кший (к +*dat*); **I am ~
to this** я к э́тому не привы́к.
unusual *adj* необыкнове́н-
ный, необы́чный. **unusually**
adv необыкнове́нно. **un-
utterable** *adj* невырази́мый.

unveil *vt* (*statue*) торже́ст-
венно открыва́ть *impf*, от-
кры́ть *pf*; (*disclose*) обна-
ро́довать *impf* & *pf*.

unwanted *adj* нежела́нный.
unwarranted *adj* неопра́в-
данный. **unwary** *adj* неосто-
ро́жный. **unwavering** *adj* не-
поколеби́мый. **unwelcome**
adj нежела́тельный; (*unpleasant*) неприя́тный. **unwell** *adj*
нездоро́вый. **unwieldy** *adj*
громо́здкий. **unwilling** *adj*
несклóнный; **be ~** не хо-
те́ть *impf*, за~ *pf* (to +*inf*).
unwillingly *adv* неохо́тно.
unwillingness *n* неохо́та.
unwind *vt* & *i* разма́тывать-
(ся) *impf*, размота́ть(ся) *pf*;
(*rest*) отдыха́ть *impf*, отдох-
ну́ть *pf*. **unwise** *adj* не-
(благо)разу́мный. **unwitting**
adj нево́льный. **unwittingly**
adv нево́льно. **unworkable**
adj неприми́мый. **unworld-
ly** *adj* не от ми́ра сего́. **unworthy** *adj* недосто́йный.
unwrap *vt* развёртывать
impf, разверну́ть *pf*. **unwrit-
ten** *adj*: **~ law** непи́саный

зако́н.

unyielding *adj* упо́рный, не-
пода́тливый.
unzip *vt* расстёгивать *impf*,
расстегну́ть *pf* (мо́лнию+*gen*).
up *adv* (*motion*) наве́рх, вверх;
(*position*) наверху́, вверху́;
and down вверх и вниз; (*back
and forth*) взад и вперёд; **~
to** (*towards*) к+*dat*; (*as far as,
until*) до+*gen*; **to now** до
сих пор; **be ~ against** име́ть
impf де́ло с+*instr*; **it is ~ to
you**+*inf*, э́то вам+*inf*, вы
должны́+*inf*; **what's ~?** что
случи́лось?; в чём де́ло?;
your time is ~ ва́ше вре́мя
истекло́; **~ and about** на
нога́х; **he isn't ~ yet** он ещё
не встал; **he isn't ~ to this
job** он не го́дится для э́той
рабо́ты; *prep* вверх по+*dat*;
(*along*) (вдоль) по+*dat*; *vt*
повыша́ть *impf*, повы́сить,
vi (*leap up*) взять *pf*; *adj*: **~-
to-date** совреме́нный; (*fash-
ionable*) мо́дный; **~-and-com-
ing** многообеща́ющий; **~s
and downs** (*fig*) превра́т-
ности *f pl* судьбы́.
upbringing *n* воспита́ние.
update *vt* модернизи́ровать
impf & *pf*; (*a book etc.*) до-
полня́ть *impf*, допо́лнить *pf*.
upgrade *vt* повыша́ть *impf*,
повы́сить *pf* (по слу́жбе).
upheaval *n* потрясе́ние.
uphill (*fig*) тяжёлый; *adv* в
го́ру.
uphold *vt* подде́рживать *impf*,
поддержа́ть *pf*.
upholster *vt* обива́ть *impf*,
оби́ть *pf*. **upholsterer** *n* обо́й-
щик. **upholstery** *n* оби́вка.
upkeep *n* содержа́ние.
upland *n* гори́стая часть
страны́; *adj* наго́рный.

uplift vt поднима́ть impf, подня́ть pf.

up-market adj дорого́й.

upon prep (position) на+prep, (motion) на+acc; see on

upper adj ве́рхний; (socially, in rank) вы́сший; **gain the ~ hand** одержа́ть impf, одержа́ть pf верх (over над+instr); n передо́к. **uppermost** adj са́мый ве́рхний, вы́сший; **be ~ in person's mind** бо́льше всего́ занима́ть impf, заня́ть pf мы́сли кого́-л.

upright n сто́йка; adj вертика́льный; (honest) че́стный; **~ piano** пиани́но neut indecl.

uprising n восста́ние.

uproar n шум, гам.

uproot vt вырыва́ть impf, вы́рвать pf c ко́рнем; (people) выселя́ть impf, вы́селить pf.

upset vt расстра́ивать impf, расстро́ить pf; vi расстра́иваться impf, расстро́иться pf; (overturn) опроки́дывать impf, опроки́нуть pf; adj (miserable) расстро́енный; **~ stomach** расстро́йство желу́дка.

upshot n развя́зка, результа́т.

upside-down adj переве́рнутый вверх дном; adv вверх дном; (in disorder) в беспоря́дке.

upstairs adv (position) наверху́; (motion) наве́рх; n ве́рхний эта́ж; adj находя́щийся в ве́рхнем этаже́.

upstart n вы́скочка m & f.

upstream adv про́тив тече́ния; (situation) вверх по тече́нию.

upsurge n подъём, волна́.

uptake n: **be quick on the ~** бы́стро сообража́ть impf, сообрази́ть pf.

upturn n (fig) улучше́ние. **up-**

turned adj (face etc.) по́днятый кве́рху; (inverted) переверну́тый.

upward adj напра́вленный вверх. **upwards** adv вверх; **~ of** свы́ше+gen.

uranium n ура́н.

urban adj городско́й.

urbane adj ве́жливый.

urchin n мальчи́шка m.

urge n (incitement) побужде́ние; (desire) жела́ние; vt (impel, ~ on) подгоня́ть impf, подогна́ть pf; (warn) предупрежда́ть impf, предупреди́ть pf; (try to persuade) убежда́ть impf. **urgency** n сро́чность, ва́жность; **a matter of great ~** сро́чное де́ло. **urgent** adj сро́чный; (insistent) настоя́тельный. **urgently** adv сро́чно.

urinate vi мочи́ться impf, по~ pf. **urine** n моча́.

urn n у́рна.

US(A) abbr (of **United States of America**) США, Соединённые Шта́ты Аме́рики.

usable adj го́дный к употребле́нию. **usage** n употребле́ние; (treatment) обраще́ние. **use** n (utilization) употребле́ние, по́льзование; (benefit) по́льза; (application) примене́ние; **it is no ~ (-ing)** бесполе́зно (+inf); **make ~ of** испо́льзовать impf & pf; по́льзоваться impf +instr; vt употребля́ть impf, употреби́ть pf; по́льзоваться impf +instr; (apply) применя́ть impf, примени́ть pf; (treat) обраща́ться impf c+instr; **~d to see him often** я ча́сто его́ встреча́л; **be, get ~d to** привыка́ть impf, привы́кнуть pf (**to** k+dat); **~ up** расхо́довать *impf*, из~ *pf*. used *adj* (*second-hand*) ста́рый.

useful *adj* поле́зный; come in ~, prove ~ пригоди́ться *pf* (to +*dat*). useless *adj* бесполе́зный. user *n* потреби́тель *m*.

usher *n* (*theat*) биле́тёр; *vt* (*lead in*) вводи́ть *impf*, ввести́ *pf*; (*proclaim*: ~ in) возвеща́ть *impf*, возвести́ть *pf*. usherette *n* биле́тёрша.

USSR *abbr* (*of* Union of Soviet Socialist Republics) СССР, Сою́з Сове́тских Социалисти́ческих Респу́блик.

usual *adj* обыкнове́нный, обы́чный; as ~ как обы́чно. usually *adv* обыкнове́нно, обы́чно.

usurp *vt* узурпи́ровать *impf* & *pf*. usurper *n* узурпа́тор.

usury *n* ростовщи́чество.

utensil *n* инструме́нт; *pl* у́тварь, посу́да.

uterus *n* ма́тка.

utilitarian *adj* утилита́рный. utilitarianism *n* утилитари́зм. utility *n* поле́зность; *pl*: public utilities коммуна́льные услу́ги *f pl*. utilize *vt* испо́льзовать *impf* & *pf*.

utmost *adj* (*extreme*) кра́йний; this is of the ~ importance to me э́то для меня́ кра́йне ва́жно; *n*: do one's ~ де́лать *impf*, с~ *pf* всё возмо́жное.

Utopia *n* уто́пия. utopian *adj* утопи́ческий.

utter *attrib* по́лный, абсолю́тный; (*out-and-out*) отъя́вленный (*coll*); *vt* произноси́ть *impf*, произнести́ *pf*; (*let out*) издава́ть *impf*, изда́ть *pf*. utterance *n* (*uttering*) произнесе́ние; (*pronouncement*)

выска́зывание. utterly *adv* соверше́нно.

Uzbek *n* узбе́к, -е́чка. Uzbekistan *n* Узбекиста́н.

V

vacancy *n* (*for job*) вака́нсия, свобо́дное ме́сто; (*at hotel*) свобо́дный но́мер. vacant *adj* (*post*) вака́нтный; (*post: not engaged, free*) свобо́дный; (*empty*) пусто́й; (*look*) отсу́тствующий. vacate *vt* освобожда́ть *impf*, освободи́ть *pf*. vacation *n* кани́кулы (-л) *pl*; (*leave*) о́тпуск.

vaccinate *vt* вакцини́ровать *impf* & *pf*. vaccination *n* приви́вка (against *от*, про́тив +*gen*). vaccine *n* вакци́на.

vacillate *vi* колеба́ться *impf*. vacillation *n* колеба́ние.

vacuous *adj* пусто́й. vacuum *n* ва́куум; (*fig*) пустота́; ~ clean чи́стить *impf*, вы́-, по-~ *pf* пылесо́сом; ~ cleaner пылесо́с; ~ flask те́рмос.

vagabond *n* бродя́га *m*.

vagary *n* капри́з.

vagina *n* влага́лище.

vagrant *n* бродя́га *m*.

vague *adj* (*indeterminate, uncertain*) неопределённый; (*unclear*) нея́сный; (*dim*) сму́тный; (*absent-minded*) рассе́янный. vagueness *n* неопределённость, нея́сность; (*absent-mindedness*) рассе́янность.

vain *adj* (*futile*) тще́тный, напра́сный; (*empty*) пусто́й; (*conceited*) тщесла́вный; in ~ напра́сно.

vale *n* дол, доли́на.

valentine *n* (*card*) поздрави́тельная ка́рточка с днём

святого Валенти́на.

valet n камерди́нер.

valiant adj хра́брый.

valid adj действи́тельный; (weighty) ве́ский. **validate** vt (ratify) утвержда́ть impf, утверди́ть pf. **validity** n действи́тельность; (weightiness) ве́скость.

valley n доли́на.

valour n до́блесть.

valuable adj це́нный; n pl це́нности f pl. **valuation** n оце́нка. **value** n це́нность; (math) величина́; pl це́нности f pl; ~-added tax нало́г на доба́вленную сто́имость; ~ judgement субъекти́вная оце́нка; vt (estimate) оце́нивать impf, оцени́ть pf; (hold dear) цени́ть impf.

valve n (tech, med, mus) кла́пан; (tech) ве́нтиль m; (radio) электро́нная ла́мпа.

vampire n вампи́р.

van n фурго́н.

vandal n ванда́л. **vandalism** n вандали́зм. **vandalize** vt разруша́ть impf, разру́шить pf.

vanguard n аванга́рд.

vanilla n вани́ль.

vanish vi исчеза́ть impf, исче́знуть pf.

vanity n (futility) тщета́; (conceit) тщесла́вие.

vanquish vt побежда́ть impf, победи́ть pf.

vantage-point n (mil) наблюда́тельный пункт; (fig) вы́годная пози́ция.

vapour n пар.

variable adj изме́нчивый; (weather) неусто́йчивый, переме́нный; n (math) переме́нная (величина́). **variance** n: be at ~ with (contradict) проти́воречить impf +dat; (disa-

gree) расходи́ться impf, разойти́сь pf во мне́ниях c+instr.

variant n вариа́нт. **variation** n (varying) измене́ние; (variant) вариа́нт; (variety) разнови́дность; (mus) вариа́ция.

varicose adj: ~ veins расшире́ние вен.

varied adj разнообра́зный. **variegated** adj разноцве́тный, разнообра́зие; (sort) разнови́дность; (a number) ряд; ~ show варьете́ neut indecl. **various** adj ра́зный.

varnish n лак; vt лакирова́ть impf, от~ pf.

vary vt разнообра́зить impf, меня́ть impf; vi (change) меня́ться impf; (differ) ра́зниться impf.

vase n ва́за.

Vaseline n (propr) вазели́н.

vast adj грома́дный. **vastly** adv значи́тельно.

VAT abbr (of value-added tax) нало́г на доба́вленную сто́имость.

vat n чан, бак.

vaudeville n водеви́ль m.

vault¹ n (leap) прыжо́к; vt перепры́гивать impf, перепры́гнуть pf; vi пры́гать impf, пры́гнуть pf.

vault² n (arch, covering) свод; (cellar) по́греб; (tomb) склеп. **vaulted** adj сво́дчатый.

VDU abbr (of visual display unit) монито́р.

veal n теля́тина.

vector n (math) ве́ктор.

veer vi (change direction) меня́ть impf, измени́ть pf направле́ние; (turn) повора́чивать impf, повороти́ть pf.

vegetable n о́вощ; adj овощно́й. **vegetarian** n вегетари-

а́нец, -нка; *attrib* вегетари-
а́нский. **vegetate** *vi* (*fig*)
прозяба́ть *impf*. **vegetation**
n расти́тельность.

vehemence *n* (*force*) си́ла;
(*passion*) стра́стность. **vehe-
ment** *adj* (*forceful*) си́льный;
(*passionate*) стра́стный.

vehicle *n* тра́нспортное сре́д-
ство; (*motor* ~) автомоби́ль
m; (*medium* ~) сре́дство.

veil *n* вуа́ль; (*fig*) заве́са.
veiled *adj* скры́тый.

vein *n* ве́на; (*of leaf; streak*)
жи́лка; **in the same** ~ в том
же ду́хе.

velocity *n* ско́рость.

velvet *n* ба́рхат; *adj* ба́рхат-
ный. **velvety** *adj* бархати́-
стый.

vending-machine *n* торго́вый
автома́т. **vendor** *n* продаве́ц,
-вщи́ца.

vendetta *n* венде́тта.

veneer *n* фане́ра; (*fig*) лоск.

venerable *adj* почте́нный.
venerate *vt* благогове́ть *impf*
пе́ред+*instr*. **veneration** *n*
благогове́ние.

venereal *adj* венери́ческий.

venetian blind *n* жалюзи́ *neut
indecl*.

vengeance *n* месть; **take** ~
мсти́ть *impf*, ото— *pf* (on
+*dat*; **for** за+*acc*); **with a** ~
вовсю́. **vengeful** *adj* мсти́-
тельный.

venison *n* оле́нина.

venom *n* яд. **venomous** *adj*
ядови́тый.

vent[1] *n* (*opening*) вы́ход (*also
fig*), отве́рстие; *vt* (*feelings*)
дава́ть *impf*, дать *pf* вы́-
ход+*dat*; излива́ть *impf*, изли́ть *pf* (on на+*acc*).

vent[2] *n* (*slit*) разре́з.

ventilate *vt* прове́тривать *impf*,

прове́рить *pf*. **ventilation** *n*
вентиля́ция. **ventilator** *n*
вентиля́тор.

ventriloquist *n* чревовеща́-
тель *m*.

venture *n* предприя́тие; *vi*
(*dare*) осме́ливаться *impf*,
осме́литься *pf*; *vt* (*risk*)
рискова́ть *impf* +*instr*.

venue *n* ме́сто.

veranda *n* вера́нда.

verb *n* глаго́л. **verbal** *adj*
(*oral*) у́стный; (*relating to
words*) слове́сный; (*gram*)
отглаго́льный. **verbatim** *adj*
досло́вный; *adv* досло́вно.
verbose *adj* многосло́вный.

verdict *n* пригово́р.

verge *n* (*also fig*) край; (*of
road*) обо́чина; (*fig*) грань;
on the ~ **of** на гра́ни+*gen*; **he
was on the** ~ **of telling all** он
чуть не рассказа́л всё; *vi*: ~
on грани́чить *impf* c+*instr*.

verification *n* прове́рка; (*confirmation*) подтвержде́ние.
verify *vt* проверя́ть *impf*,
прове́рить *pf*; (*confirm*) под-
твержда́ть *impf*, подтвер-
ди́ть *pf*.

vermin *n* вреди́тели *m pl*.

vernacular *n* родно́й язы́к;
ме́стный диале́кт; (*homely
language*) разгово́рный язы́к.

versatile *adj* многосторо́нний.

verse *n* (*also bibl*) стих; (*stanza*)
строфа́; (*poetry*) стихи́ *m pl*.
versed *adj* о́пытный, све́ду-
щий (**in** в+*prep*).

version *n* (*variant*) вариа́нт;
(*interpretation*) ве́рсия; (*text*)
текст.

versus *prep* про́тив+*gen*.

vertebra *n*; *pl* позво́нок; *pl* по-
звоно́чник. **vertebrate** *n* позво-
но́чное живо́тное *sb*.

vertical *adj* вертика́льный; *n*

вертика́ль.

vertigo n головокруже́ние.

verve n жи́вость, энтузиа́зм.

very adj (that ~ same) тот са́мый; (this ~ same) э́тот са́мый; **at that ~ moment** в тот са́мый моме́нт; (precisely) как раз; **you are the ~ person I was looking for** как раз вас я иска́л; **the ~** (even the) да́же, оди́н; **the ~ thought frightens me** одна́, да́же, мысль об э́том меня́ пуга́ет; (the extreme) са́мый; **at the ~ end** в са́мом конце́; adv adv; **~ much** о́чень; **~ much +comp** гора́здо +comp; **~+superl, superl;** **~ first** са́мый пе́рвый; **~ well** (agreement) хорошо́, ла́дно; **not ~** не о́чень, дово́льно +neg.

vessel n сосу́д; (ship) су́дно.

vest[1] n ма́йка; (waistcoat) жиле́т.

vest[2] vt (with power) облека́ть impf, обле́чь pf (with +instr). **vested** adj: **~ interest** ли́чная заинтересо́ванность, **~ interests** (entrepreneurs) кру́пные предприни́матели m pl.

vestibule n вестибю́ль m.

vestige n (trace) след; (sign) при́знак.

vestments n pl (eccl) облаче́ние. **vestry** n ри́зница.

vet[2] n ветерина́р; vt (fig) проверя́ть impf, прове́рить pf.

veteran n ветера́н; adj

veterinary adj ветерина́рный. **~ветерина́р.**

veto n ве́то neut indecl; vt налага́ть impf, наложи́ть pf ве́то на+acc.

vex vt досажда́ть impf, досади́ть pf +dat. **vexation** n доса́да. **vexed** adj (annoyed)

серди́тый; (question) спо́рный. **vexatious, vexing** adj доса́дный.

via prep че́рез+acc.

viable adj (able to survive) жизнеспосо́бный; (feasible) осуществи́мый.

viaduct n виаду́к.

vibrant adj (lively) живо́й. **vibrate** vi вибри́ровать impf; vt (make) заставля́ть impf, заста́вить pf вибри́ровать. **vibration** n вибра́ция. **vibrato** n вибра́то neut indecl.

vicar n прихо́дский свяще́нник. **vicarage** n дом свяще́нника.

vicarious adj чужо́й.

vice[1] n (evil) поро́к.

vice[2] n (tech) тиски́ (-ко́в) pl.

vice[3] n comb combе- замести́тель m; **~-chairman** замести́тель m председа́теля; **~-chancellor** (univ) проре́ктор; **~-president** вице-президе́нт.

viceroy n вице-коро́ль m.

vice versa adv наоборо́т.

vicinity n окре́стность; **in the ~** побли́зости (of от+gen).

vicious adj зло́бный; **~ circle** поро́чный круг.

vicissitude n превра́тность.

victim n же́ртва; (of accident) пострада́вший sb. **victimization** n пресле́дование. **victimize** vt пресле́довать impf.

victor n победи́тель m, **~ница**.

Victorian adj викториа́нский.

victorious adj победоно́сный. **victory** n побе́да.

video n (~ recorder, ~ cassette, ~ film) ви́део neut indecl; **~ camera** видеока́мера; **~ cassette** видеокассе́та; (~ cassette) **recorder** видеомагнитофо́н; **~ game** видеоигра́; **~ tape** запи́сывать записа́ть pf на ви́део.

vie vi сопе́рничать impf (with c+instr; for в+prep).

Vietnam n Вьетна́м. **Vietnamese** n вьетна́мец, -мка; adj вьетна́мский.

view n (prospect, picture) вид; (opinion) взгляд; (viewing) просмо́тр; (inspection) осмо́тр; in ~ ввиду́+gen; on ~ вы́ставленный для обозре́ния; with a ~ to с це́лью+gen, +inf; vt (pictures etc.) рассма́тривать impf; (inspect) осма́тривать impf, осмотре́ть pf; (mentally) смотре́ть impf на+acc; **viewer** n зри́тель m, ~ница. **viewfinder** n видоиска́тель m. **viewpoint** n то́чка зре́ния.

vigil n бо́дрствование; keep ~ бо́дрствовать impf, дежу́рить impf. **vigilance** n бди́тельность. **vigilant** adj бди́тельный. **vigilante** n дружи́нник.

vigorous adj си́льный, энерги́чный. **vigour** n си́ла, эне́ргия.

vile adj гну́сный. **vilify** vt черни́ть impf, о~ pf.

villa n ви́лла.

village n дере́вня; attrib дереве́нский. **villager** n жи́тель m дере́вни.

villain n злоде́й.

vinaigrette n припра́ва из у́ксуса и оли́вкового ма́сла.

vindicate vt опра́вдывать impf, оправда́ть pf. **vindication** n оправда́ние.

vindictive adj мсти́тельный.

vine n виногра́дная лоза́.

vinegar n у́ксус.

vineyard n виногра́дник.

vintage n (year) год; (fig) вы́пуск; attrib (wine) ма́роч-

ный; (car) архаи́ческий.

viola n (mus) альт.

violate vt (treaty, privacy) наруша́ть impf, нару́шить pf; (grave) оскверня́ть impf, оскверни́ть pf. **violation** n наруше́ние; оскверне́ние.

violence n (physical coercion, force) наси́лие; (strength, force) си́ла. **violent** adj (person, storm, argument) свире́пый; (pain) си́льный; (death) наси́льственный. **violently** adv си́льно, о́чень.

violet n (bot) фиа́лка; (colour) фиоле́товый цвет; adj фиоле́товый.

violin n скри́пка. **violinist** n скрипа́ч, ~ка.

VIP abbr (of very important person) о́чень ва́жное лицо́.

viper n гадю́ка.

virgin n де́вственница, (male) де́вственник; V~ Mary де́ва Мари́я. **virginal** adj де́вственный. **virginity** n де́вственность. **Virgo** n Де́ва.

virile adj мужественный. **virility** n му́жество.

virtual adj факти́ческий. **virtually** adv факти́чески. **virtue** n (excellence) доброде́тель; (merit) досто́инство; by ~ of на основа́нии+gen. **virtuosity** n виртуо́зность. **virtuoso** n виртуо́з. **virtuous** adj доброде́тельный.

virulent adj (med) вируле́нтный; (fig) зло́бный.

virus n ви́рус.

visa n ви́за.

vis-à-vis prep (with regard to) по отноше́нию к+dat.

viscount n вико́нт. **viscountess** n викинте́сса.

viscous adj вя́зкий.

visibility n ви́димость. **visible**

adj ви́димый. **visibly** *adv* я́вно, заме́тно.

vision *n* (*sense*) зре́ние; (*apparition*) виде́ние; (*dream*) мечта́; (*insight*) проница́тельность. **visionary** *adj* (*unreal*) при́зрачный; (*impracticable*) неосуществи́мый; (*insightful*) проница́тельный; *n* (*dreamer*) мечта́тель *m*.

visit *n* посеще́ние, визи́т; *vt* посеща́ть *impf*, посети́ть *pf*; (*call on*) заходи́ть *impf*, зайти́ *pf* к+dat. **visitation** *n* официа́льное посеще́ние. **visitor** *n* гость *m*, посети́тель.

visor *n* (*of cap*) козырёк; (*in car*) солнцезащи́тный щито́к; (*of helmet*) забра́ло.

vista *n* перспекти́ва, вид.

visual *adj* (*of vision*) зри́тельный; (*graphic*) нагля́дный; ~ **aids** нагля́дные посо́бия *neut pl*. **visualize** *n* представля́ть *impf*, предста́вить *pf* себе́.

vital *adj* абсолю́тно необходи́мый (**to, for** для+gen); (*essential to life*) жи́зненный; **of ~ importance** первостепе́нной ва́жности. **vitality** *n* (*liveliness*) эне́ргия. **vitally** *adv* жи́зненно.

vitamin *n* витами́н.

vitreous *adj* стекля́нный.

vitriolic *adj* (*fig*) е́дкий.

vivacious *adj* живо́й. **vivacity** *n* живо́сть.

viva (voce) *n* у́стный экза́мен.

vivid *adj* (*bright*) я́ркий; (*lively*) живо́й. **vividness** *n* я́ркость; жи́вость.

vivisection *n* вивисе́кция.

vixen *n* лиси́ца-са́мка.

viz. *adv* то есть, а и́менно.

vocabulary *n* (*range, list, of words*) слова́рь *m*; (*range of words*) запа́с слов; (*of a lan-*

guage) слова́рный соста́в.

vocal *adj* голосово́й; (*mus*) вока́льный; (*noisy*) шу́мный; ~ **chord** голосова́я свя́зка.

vocalist *n* певе́ц, -ви́ца.

vocation *n* призва́ние. **vocational** *adj* профессиона́льный.

vociferous *adj* шу́мный.

vodka *n* во́дка.

vogue *n* мо́да; **in ~** в мо́де.

voice *n* го́лос; *vt* выража́ть *impf*, вы́разить *pf*.

void *n* пустота́; *adj* пусто́й; (*invalid*) недействи́тельный; ~ **of** лишённый +gen.

volatile *adj* (*chem*) лету́чий; (*person*) непостоя́нный, неусто́йчивый.

volcanic *adj* вулкани́ческий. **volcano** *n* вулка́н.

vole *n* (*zool*) полёвка.

volition *n* во́ля; **by one's own ~** по свое́й во́ле.

volley *n* (*missiles*) залп; (*fig*) град; (*sport*) уда́р с лёта; *vt* (*sport*) ударя́ть *impf*, уда́рить *pf* с лёта. **volleyball** *n* волейбо́л.

volt *n* вольт. **voltage** *n* напряже́ние.

voluble *adj* говорли́вый.

volume *n* (*book*) том; (*capacity, size*) объём; (*loudness*) гро́мкость. **voluminous** *adj* обши́рный.

voluntary *adj* доброво́льный. **volunteer** *n* доброво́лец; *vt* предлага́ть *impf*, предложи́ть *pf*; *vi* (*offer*) вызыва́ться *impf*, вы́зваться *pf* (*inf.* +inf; **for** в+acc); (*mil*) идти́ *impf*, пойти́ *pf* доброво́льцем.

voluptuous *adj* сластолюби́вый.

vomit *n* рво́та; *vt* (& *i*) рвать

impf, вы́рвать *pf impers* (+*instr*); he was ~ing blood его́ рва́ло кро́вью.

voracious *adj* прожо́рливый; (*fig*) ненасы́тный.

vortex *n* (*also fig*) водоворо́т, вихрь *m*.

vote *n* (*poll*) голосова́ние; (*individual* ~) го́лос; the ~ (*suffrage*) пра́во го́лоса; (*resolution*) во́тум *no pl*; ~ of no confidence во́тум недове́рия (in +*dat*); ~ of thanks выраже́ние благода́рности; *vi* голосова́ть *impf*, про~ *pf* (for за+*acc*; against про́тив+*gen*); *vt* (*allocate by vote*) ассигнова́ть *impf & pf*; (*deem*) признава́ть *impf*, призна́ть *pf*; the film was ~d a failure фильм был при́знан неуда́чным; ~ in избира́ть *impf*, избра́ть *pf* голосова́нием. **voter** *n* избира́тель *m*.

vouch *vi*: ~ for руча́ться *impf*, поручи́ться *pf* за+*acc*. **voucher** *n* (*receipt*) распи́ска; (*coupon*) тало́н.

vow *n* обе́т; *vt* кля́сться *impf*, по~ *pf* в+*prep*.

vowel *n* гла́сный *sb*.

voyage *n* путеше́ствие.

vulgar *adj* вульга́рный, гру́бый, по́шлый. **vulgarity** *n* вульга́рность, по́шлость.

vulnerable *adj* уязви́мый.

vulture *n* гриф; (*fig*) хи́щник.

W

wad *n* комо́к; (*bundle*) па́чка. **wadding** *n* ва́та; (*padding*) наби́вка.

waddle *vi* ходи́ть *indet*, идти́ *det*, пойти́ *pf* вперева́лку (*coll*).

wade *vt & i* (*river*) переходи́ть *impf*, перейти́ *pf* вброд; *vi*: ~ through (*mud etc.*) проби́раться *impf*, пробра́ться *pf* сквозь (*sth boring etc.*) одолева́ть *impf*, одоле́ть *pf*.

wafer *n* ва́фля.

waffle[1] *n* (*dish*) ва́фля.

waffle[2] *vi* трепа́ться *impf*.

waft *vt & i* нести́(сь) *impf*, по~ *pf*.

wag *vt & i* (*tail*) виля́ть *impf*, вильну́ть *pf* (+*instr*); *vt* (*finger*) грози́ть *impf*, по~ *pf* +*instr*.

wage[1] *n* (*pay*) see wages

wage[2] *vt*: ~ war вести́ *impf*, про~ *pf* войну́.

wager *n* пари́ *neut indecl*; *vi* держа́ть *impf* пари́ (that что); *vt* ста́вить *impf* по~ *pf*.

wages *n pl* за́работная пла́та.

waggle *vt & i* пома́хивать *impf*, помаха́ть *pf* (+*instr*).

wag(g)on *n* (*carriage*) пово́зка; (*cart*) теле́га; (*rly*) ваго́н-платфо́рма.

wail *n* вопль *m*; *vi* вопи́ть *impf*.

waist *n* та́лия; (*level of* ~) по́яс; ~-deep, high (*adv*) по по́яс. **waistband** *n* по́яс. **waistcoat** *n* жиле́т. **waistline** *n* та́лия.

wait *n* ожида́ние; lie in ~ (for) подстерега́ть *impf*, подстере́чь *pf*; *vi* (& *t*) (*also* ~ for) ждать *impf* (+*gen*); *vi* (*be a waiter, waitress*) быть официа́нтом, -ткой; ~ on обслу́живать *impf*, обслужи́ть *pf*. **waiter** *n* официа́нт. **waiting** *n*: ~-list спи́сок; ~-room приёмная *sb*; (*rly*) зал ожида́ния. **waitress** *n* официа́нтка.

waive *vt* отка́зываться *impf*, отказа́ться *pf* от+*gen*.

wake[1] *n* (*at funeral*) поми́нки (-нок) *pl*.

wake[2] *n* (*naut*) кильва́тер; **in the ~ of** по сле́ду +*gen*, за+*instr*.

wake[3] *vt* (*also* ~ **up**) буди́ть *impf*, раз~ *pf*; *vi* (*also* ~ **up**) просыпа́ться *impf*, просну́ться *pf*.

Wales *n* Уэ́льс.

walk *n* (*walking*) ходьба́; (*gait*) похо́дка; (*stroll*) прогу́лка; (*path*) тропа́; ~**out** (*strike*) забасто́вка; (*as protest*) демонстрати́вный ухо́д; ~**over** лёгкая побе́да; **ten minutes' ~ from here** де́сять мину́т ходьбы́ отсю́да; **go for a ~** идти́ *impf*, пойти́ *pf* гуля́ть; **from all ~s of life** всех слоёв о́бщества; *vi* ходи́ть *indet*, идти́ *det*, пойти́ *pf*; гуля́ть *impf*, по~ *pf*; ~ **away, off** уходи́ть *impf*, уйти́ *pf*; ~ **in** входи́ть *impf*, войти́ *pf*; ~ **out** выходи́ть *impf*, вы́йти *pf*; ~ **out on** броса́ть *impf*, бро́сить *pf*; ~ (*traverse*) обходи́ть *impf*, обойти́ *pf*; (*take for* ~) выводи́ть *impf*, вы́вести *pf* гуля́ть. **walker** *n* ходо́к. **walkie-talkie** *n* ра́ция. **walking** *n* ходьба́; ~**stick** трость.

Walkman *n* (*propr*) во́кмен.

wall *n* стена́; *vt* обноси́ть *impf*, обнести́ *pf* стено́й; ~ **up** (*door, window*) заде́лывать *impf*, заде́лать *pf*; (*brick up*) замуро́вывать *impf*, замурова́ть *pf*.

wallet *n* бума́жник.

wallflower *n* желтофио́ль.

wallop *n* си́льный уда́р; *vt* си́льно ударя́ть *impf*, уда́рить *pf*.

wallow *vi* валя́ться *impf*; **in**

wallpaper *n* обо́и (обо́ев) *pl*.

walnut *n* гре́цкий оре́х; (*wood, tree*) оре́ховое де́рево, оре́х.

walrus *n* морж.

waltz *n* вальс; *vi* вальси́ровать *impf*.

wan *adj* бле́дный.

wand *n* па́лочка.

wander *vi* броди́ть *impf*; (*also of thoughts etc.*) блужда́ть *impf*; ~ **from the point** отклоня́ться *impf*, отклони́ться *pf* от те́мы. **wanderer** *n* стра́нник.

wane *n*: **be on the ~** убыва́ть *impf*, убыва́ть *impf*, убы́ть *pf*; (*weaken*) ослабева́ть *impf*, ослабе́ть *pf*.

wangle *vt* заполуча́ть *impf*, заполучи́ть *pf*.

want *n* (*lack*) недоста́ток; (*requirement*) потре́бность; (*desire*) жела́ние; **for ~ of** за недоста́тком +*gen*; *vt* хоте́ть *impf*, за~ *pf* +*gen*, *acc*; (*need*) нужда́ться *impf* в+*prep*; **I you to come at six** я хочу́, что́бы ты пришёл в шесть; **wanting** *adj*: **be ~** недостава́ть *impf* (*impers*+*gen*); **experience is ~** недостаёт о́пыта.

wanton *adj* (*licentious*) распу́тный; (*senseless*) бессмы́сленный.

war *n* война́; (*attrib*) вое́нный; **at ~** в состоя́нии войны́; ~ **memorial** па́мятник па́вшим в войне́.

ward *n* (*hospital*) пала́та; (*child etc.*) подопе́чный; (*district*) райо́н; *vt*: ~ **off** отража́ть *impf*, отрази́ть *pf*.

warden *n* (*prison*) нача́льник; (*college*) ре́ктор; (*hostel* коменда́нт.

warder n тюре́мщик.

wardrobe n гардеро́б.

warehouse n склад. **wares** n pl изде́лия neut pl, това́ры m pl.

warfare n война́.

warhead n боева́я голо́вка.

warily adv осторо́жно.

warlike adj вои́нственный.

warm n тепло́; adj (also fig) тёплый; ~-**hearted** серде́чный; vt & i греть(ся) impf, согре́ть(ся) impf, согре́ть(ся) pf; ~ **up** (food etc.) подогрева́ть impf, подогре́ть pf; (liven up) оживля́ть(ся) impf, оживи́ть(ся) pf; (sport) размина́ться pf; (mus) разы́грываться impf, разыгра́ться pf. **warmth** n тепло́; (cordiality) серде́чность.

warn v предупрежда́ть impf, предупреди́ть pf (**about** o+prep). **warning** n предупрежде́ние.

warp n & i (wood) коро́биться(ся) impf, по~, с~ pf; vt (pervert) извраща́ть impf, изврати́ть pf.

warrant n (for arrest etc.) о́рдер; vt (justify) опра́вдывать impf, оправда́ть pf; (guarantee) гаранти́ровать impf & pf. **warranty** n гара́нтия.

warrior n во́ин.

warship n вое́нный кора́бль m.

wart n борода́вка.

wartime n: **in** ~ во вре́мя войны́.

wary adj осторо́жный.

wash n мытьё; (thin layer) го́нкий слой; (lotion) примо́чка; (surf) прибо́й; (back-

wash) попу́тная волна́; **at the** ~ в сти́рке; **have a** ~ мы́ться impf, по~ pf; vt & i мыть(ся) impf, вы~, по~ pf; vt (clothes) стира́ть impf, вы~ pf; (of sea) омыва́ть impf; ~ **away, off, out** смыва́ть impf, смыть(ся) pf; (carry away) сноси́ть impf, снести́ pf; ~ **out** (rinse) спола́скивать impf, сполосну́ть pf; ~ **up** (dishes) мыть impf, вы~, по~ pf (посу́ду); ~ **one's hands** (of it) умыва́ть impf, умы́ть pf ру́ки. **washed-out** adj (exhausted) утомлённый. **washer** n (tech) ша́йба. **washing** n (of clothes) сти́рка; (clothes) бельё; ~-**machine** стира́льная маши́на; ~-**powder** стира́льный порошо́к; ~-**up** (action) мытьё посу́ды; (dishes) гря́зная посу́да; ~-**up liquid** жи́дкое мы́ло для мытья́ посу́ды.

wasp n оса́.

wastage n уте́чка. **waste** n (desert) пусты́ня; (refuse) отбро́сы m pl; (of time, money, etc.) растра́та; **go to** ~ пропада́ть impf, пропа́сть pf да́ром; adj (desert) пусты́нный; (superfluous) нену́жный; (uncultivated) невозде́ланный; **lay** ~ опустоша́ть impf, опусто́шить pf; ~**land** пусты́рь m; ~ **paper** нену́жные бума́ги f pl; (for recycling) макулату́ра; ~ **products** отхо́ды (-дов) pl; ~-**paper basket** корзи́на для бума́ги; vt тра́тить impf, по~, ис~ pf; (time) теря́ть impf, по~ pf; vi: ~ **away** ча́хнуть impf, за~ pf.

wasteful *adj* расточи́тельный.

watch *n* (*timepiece*) часы́ (-о́в) *pl*; (*duty*) дежу́рство; (*naut*) ва́хта; **keep ~** see наблюда́ть *impf* за+*instr*; **~-dog** сторожево́й пёс; **~-tower** сторожева́я ба́шня; *vt* (*observe*) наблюда́ть *impf*; (*keep an eye on*) следи́ть *impf* за+*instr*; (*look after*) смотре́ть *impf*, по~ *pf* за+*instr*; **~ television, a film** смотре́ть *impf*, по~ *pf* телеви́зор, фильм; *vi* смотре́ть *impf*; **~ out!** (*be careful*) бере́чься *impf* (*for* +*gen*); **~ out for** ждать *impf* +*gen*; **~ out!** осторо́жно! **watchful** *adj* бди́тельный. **watchman** *n* (ночно́й) сто́рож. **watchword** *n* ло́зунг.

water *n* вода́; **~-colour** акваре́ль; **~-heater** кипяти́льник; **~-main** водопрово́дная магистра́ль; **~ melon** арбу́з; **~-pipe** водопрово́дная труба́; **~-ski** (*n*) во́дная лы́жа; **~-skiing** водолы́жный спорт; **~-supply** водоснабже́ние; **~-way** во́дный путь *m*; *vt* (*flowers etc.*) полива́ть *impf*, поли́ть *pf*; (*animals*) пои́ть *impf*, на~ *pf*; (*irrigate*) ороша́ть *impf*, ороси́ть *pf*; (*eyes*) слези́ться *impf*; (*mouth*): **my mouth ~s** у меня́ слю́нки теку́т; **~ down** разбавля́ть *impf*, разба́вить *pf*. **watercourse** *n* ру́сло. **watercress** *n* кресс водяно́й. **waterfall** *n* водопа́д. **waterfront** *n* часть го́рода примыка́ющая к бе́регу. **watering-can** *n* ле́йка. **waterlogged** *adj* заболо́ченный. **watermark** *n* водяно́й знак. **waterproof** *adj* непромока́емый; *n* непромока́е-

мый плащ. **watershed** *n* водоразде́л. **waterside** *n* бе́рег. **watertight** *adj* водонепроница́емый; (*fig*) неопрове́ржимый. **waterworks** *n pl* водопрово́дные сооруже́ния *neut pl*. **watery** *adj* водяни́стый.

watt *n* ватт.

wave *vt* (*hand etc.*) маха́ть *impf*, махну́ть *pf* +*instr*; (*flag*) разма́хивать *impf* +*instr*; **~ (~ hand)** маха́ть *impf*, по~ *pf* (*at* +*dat*); (*flutter*) разве-ва́ться *impf*; **~ aside** отма́хиваться *impf*, отмахну́ться *pf* от+*gen*; **~ down** остана́вливать *impf*, останови́ть *pf*; *n* (*in various senses*) волна́; (*of hand*) взмах; (*of hair*) зави́вка. **wavelength** *n* длина́ волны́. **waver** *vi* колеба́ться *impf*. **wavy** *adj* волни́стый.

wax *n* воск; (*in ear*) се́ра; *vt* вощи́ть *impf*, на~ *pf*. **waxen** *adj* восково́й. **waxwork** *n* восковая фигу́ра; *pl* музе́й восковы́х фигу́р.

way *n* (*road, path, route*) доро́га, путь *m*; (*direction*) сторона́; (*manner*) о́браз; (*method*) спо́соб; (*respect*) отноше́ние; (*habit*) привы́чка; **by the ~** (*fig*) кста́ти; **among** про́чим; **on the ~** по доро́ге, по пути́; **this ~** (*direction*) сюда́; (*in this ~*) таки́м о́бразом; **the other ~ round** наоборо́т; **under ~** на ходу́; **be in the ~** меша́ть *impf*; **get out of the ~** уходи́ть *impf*, уйти́ *pf* с доро́ги; **give ~** (*yield*) поддава́ться *impf*, подда́ться *pf* (*to* +*dat*); (*collapse*) обру́шиваться *impf*, обру́шиться *pf*; **go out of one's ~ to** стара́ться *impf* по~ *pf* изо всех сил +*inf*; **get, have, one's own** ~ добива́ться *impf*, доби́ться *pf* своего́; **make** ~ уступа́ть *impf*, уступи́ть *pf* доро́гу (**for** +*dat*). **waylay** *vt* (*lie in wait for*) подстерега́ть *impf*, подстере́чь *pf*; (*stop*) перехва́тывать *impf*, перехвати́ть *pf* по пути́. **wayside** *adj* придоро́жный; *n*: **fall by the** ~ выбыва́ть *impf*, вы́быть *pf* из стро́я.

wayward *adj* своенра́вный.

WC *abbr* (*of* water-closet) убо́рная *sb*.

we *pron* мы.

weak *adj* сла́бый. **weaken** *vt* ослабля́ть *impf*, осла́бить *pf*; *vi* слабе́ть *impf*, о~ *pf*. **weakling** *n* (*person*) сла́бый челове́к; (*plant*) сла́бое расте́ние. **weakness** *n* сла́бость.

weal *n* (*mark*) рубе́ц.

wealth *n* бога́тство; (*abundance*) изоби́лие. **wealthy** *adj* бога́тый.

wean *vt* отнима́ть *impf*, отня́ть *pf* от груди́; (*fig*) отуча́ть *impf*, отучи́ть *pf* (**of, from** от+*gen*).

weapon *n* ору́жие. **weaponry** *n* вооруже́ние.

wear *n* (*wearing*) но́ска; (*clothing*) оде́жда; (~ **and tear**) изно́с; *vt* носи́ть *impf* ~; быть в+*prep*; **what shall I** ~? что мне наде́ть?; *vi* носи́ться *impf*, ~ **off** *impf*, *prep*, *novelty*) проходи́ть *impf*, пройти́ *pf*; (*cease to have effect*) перестава́ть *impf*, переста́ть *pf* де́йствовать; ~ **out** (*clothes*) изна́шивать(ся) *impf*, износи́ть(ся) *pf*; (*exhaust*) изму́чивать *impf*, изму́чить *pf*. **weariness** *n* уста́лость. **wear-**

ing, **wearisome** *adj* утоми́тельный. **weary** *adj* уста́лый; *vt* & *i* утомля́ть(ся) *impf*, утоми́ть(ся) *pf*.

weasel *n* ла́ска.

weather *n* пого́да; **be under the** ~ нева́жно себя́ чу́вствовать *impf*; ~**-beaten** обве́тренный; ~**forecast** прогно́з пого́ды; *vt* (*storm etc.*) выде́рживать *impf*, вы́держать *pf*; (*expose to atmosphere*) подверга́ть *impf*, подве́ргнуть *pf* атмосфе́рным влия́ниям. **weather-cock, weathervane** *n* флю́гер. **weatherman** *n* метеоро́лог.

weave[1] *vt* & *i* (*fabric*) ткать *impf*, с~ *pf*; *vt* (*fig*; *also wreath etc.*) плести́ *impf*, с~ *pf*. **weaver** *n* ткач, ~и́ха.

weave[2] *vi* (*wind*) ви́ться *impf*.

web *n* (*cobweb*; *fig*) паути́на; (*fig*) сплете́ние. **webbed** *adj* перепо́нчатый. **webbing** *n* тка́ная ле́нта.

wed *vt* (*of man*) жени́ться *impf* & *pf* на+*prep*; (*of woman*) выходи́ть *impf*, вы́йти *pf* за́муж за+*acc*; (*unite*) сочета́ть *impf* & *pf*; *vi* пожени́ться *pf*. **wedded** *adj* супру́жеский; ~ **to** (*fig*) пре́данный +*dat*. **wedding** *n* сва́дьба, бракосочета́ние; ~**-cake** сва́дебный торт; ~**-day** день *m* сва́дьбы; ~**-dress** подвене́чное пла́тье; ~**-ring** обруча́льное кольцо́.

wedge *n* клин; *vt* (~ *open*) закли́нивать *impf*, закли́нить *pf*; *vt* & *i*: ~ **in(to)** вкли́нивать(ся) *impf*, вкли́нить(ся) *pf* (в+*acc*).

wedlock *n* брак; **born out of** ~ рождённый вне бра́ка, внебра́чный.

Wednesday *n* среда́.

weed n сорня́к; ~**-killer** герби́цид; vt поло́ть impf, вы́~ pf; ~ **out** удаля́ть impf, удали́ть pf. **weedy** adj (person)

week n неде́ля; ~**-end** суббо́та и воскресе́нье, выходны́е sb pl. **weekday** n бу́дний день m. **weekly** adj еженеде́льный; (wage) неде́льный; adv еженеде́льно; n еженеде́льник.

weep vi пла́кать impf. **weeping willow** n плаку́чая и́ва.

weigh vt (also fig) взве́шивать impf, взве́сить pf; (consider) обду́мывать impf, обду́мать pf; vt & i (so much) ве́сить impf; ~ **down** отягоща́ть impf, отяготи́ть pf; ~ **on** тяготи́ть impf; ~ **out** отве́шивать impf, отве́сить pf; ~ **up** (appraise) оце́нивать impf, оцени́ть pf. **weight** n (also authority) вес; (load, also fig) тя́жесть; (sport) шта́нга; (influence) влия́ние; lose ~ худе́ть impf, по~ pf; put on ~ толсте́ть impf, по~ pf. ~**lifter** штанги́ст. ~**lifting** n подня́тие тя́жестей; vt (make heavier) утяжеля́ть impf, утяжели́ть pf. **weightless** adj невесо́мый. **weighty** adj ве́ский.

weir n плоти́на.

weird adj (strange) стра́нный.

welcome n приём; adj жела́нный; (pleasant) прия́тный; you are ~ (don't mention it) пожа́луйста; you are ~ to use my bicycle мой велосипе́д к ва́шим услу́гам; you are ~ to stay the night вы мо́жете переночева́ть у меня́/нас; vt приве́тствовать impf (& pf in past tense); int добро́ пожа́ловать!

weld vt сва́ривать impf, свари́ть pf. **welder** n сва́рщик.

welfare n благосостоя́ние; **W~ State** госуда́рство всео́бщего благосостоя́ния.

well[1] n коло́дец; (for stairs) ле́стничная кле́тка.

well[2] vi: ~ **up** (anger etc.) вскипа́ть impf; (tears) ~**ed up** глаза́ напо́лнились слеза́ми.

well[3] adj (healthy) здоро́вый; feel ~ чу́вствовать impf, по~ pf себя́ хорошо́, здоро́вым; get ~ поправля́ться impf, попра́виться pf; look ~ хорошо́ вы́глядеть impf; all is ~ всё в поря́дке; int ну(!); adv хорошо́; (very much) о́чень; as ~ то́же; as ~ as (in addition to) кро́ме+gen; it may ~ be true вполне́ возмо́жно, что э́то так; very ~ хорошо́!; ~ **done!** молоде́ц! ~**-balanced** уравнове́шенный; ~**-behaved** (благо)воспи́танный; ~**-being** благополу́чие; ~**-bred** благовоспи́танный; ~**-built** кре́пкий; ~**-defined** чёткий; ~**-disposed** благоскло́нный; ~**-done** (cooked) (хорошо́) прожа́ренный; ~**-fed** отко́рмленный; ~**-founded** обосно́ванный; ~**-groomed** (person) хо́леный; ~**-heeled** состоя́тельный; ~**-informed** осведомлённый (about в+prep); ~**-known** изве́стный; ~**-meaning** де́йствующий из лу́чших побужде́ний; ~**-nigh** почти́; ~**-off** состоя́тельный; ~**-paid** хорошо́ опла́чиваемый; ~**-preserved** хорошо́ сохрани́вшийся; ~**-to-do** состоя́тельный; ~**-wisher** доброжела́тель m.

wellington (boot) *n* резиновый сапог.

Welsh *adj* уэльский. **Welshman** *n* валлиец. **Welshwoman** *n* валлийка.

welter *n* путаница.

wend *vt*: ~ **one's way** держать *impf* путь.

west *n* запад; (*naut*) вест; *adj* западный; *adv* на запад, к западу. **westerly** *adj* западный. **western** *adj* западный; *n* (*film*) вестерн. **westward(s)** *adv* на запад, к западу.

wet *adj* мокрый; (*paint*) непросохший; (*rainy*) дождливый; ~ **through** промокший до нитки; *n* (*dampness*) влажность; (*rain*) дождь *m*; *vt* мочить *impf*, на~ *pf*.

whack *n* (*blow*) удар; *vt* колотить *impf*, по~ *pf*. **whacked** *adj* разбитый.

whale *n* кит.

wharf *n* пристань.

what *pron* (*interrog*, *int*) что; (*how much*) сколько; (*rel*) (то,) что; ~ (...) **for** зачем; ~ **if** а что если; ~ **is your name** как вас зовут?; *adj* (*interrog*, *int*) какой; ~ **kind of** какой. **whatever, whatsoever** *pron* что бы ни+*past* (~ **you think** что бы вы ни думали); всё, что (**take** ~ **you want** возьми всё, что хотите); *adj* какой бы ни+*past* (~ **books he read**s) какие бы то ни книги он ни прочитал); (*at all*) ~ **no chance** ~ нет никакой возможности; **is there any chance** ~? есть ли хоть какая-нибудь возможность?

wheat *n* пшеница.

wheedle *vt* (*coax into doing*) уговаривать *impf*, угово-

рить *pf* с помощью лести; ~ **out of** выманивать *impf*, выманить *pf* y+*gen*.

wheel *n* колесо; (*steering* ~, *helm*) руль *m*; (*potter's*) гончарный круг; *vt* (*push*) катать *indet*, катить *det*, по~ *pf*; *vt* & *i* (*turn*) повёртывать(ся) *impf*, повернуть(ся) *pf*; *vi* (*circle*) кружиться *impf*. **wheelbarrow** *n* тачка. **wheelchair** *n* инвалидное кресло.

wheeze *vi* сопеть *impf*.

when *adv* когда; *conj* когда, в то время как; (*whereas*) тогда как; (*if*) если; (*although*) хотя. **whence** *adv* откуда. **whenever** *adv* когда же; *conj* (*every time*) всякий раз когда; (*at any time*) когда (*no matter when*) когда бы ни+*past*; **we shall have dinner** ~ **you arrive** во сколько бы вы ни приехали, мы пообедаем.

where *adv* & *conj* (*place*) где; (*whither*) куда; **from** ~ откуда. **whereabouts** *adv* где; *n* местонахождение. **whereas** *conj* тогда как; хотя. **whereby** *adv* & *conj* посредством чего. **wherein** *adv* & *conj* в чём. **wherever** *adv* & *conj* (*place*) где бы ни+*past*; (*whither*) куда бы ни+*past*; ~ **he goes** куда бы он ни пошёл; ~ **you like** где/куда хотите. **wherewithal** *n* средства *neut pl*.

whet *vt* (*sharpen*) точить *impf*, на~ *pf*; (*fig*) возбуждать *impf*, возбудить *pf*.

whether *conj* ли; **I don't know** ~ **he will come** я не знаю, придёт ли он; ~ **he comes or not** придёт (ли) он или нет.

which adj (interrog, rel) какóй; prn (interrog) какóй; (person) кто; (rel) котóрый; (rel to whole statement) что; ~ **is** ~? (persons) из них кто?; (things) что-что?; **whichever** adj & prn какóй бы ни+past (~ **book you choose** какýю бы кнúгу ты ни вы́брал); любóй (**take** ~ **book you want** возьмúте любýю кнúгу).

whiff n зáпах.

while n врéмя neut; **a little** ~ недóлго; **a long** ~ дóлго; **for a long** ~ (up to now) давнó; **for a** ~ на врéмя; **in a little** ~ скóро; **it is worth** ~ стóит э́то сдéлать; vt: ~ **away** проводúть impf, провестú pf; conj покá; **in the** ~ тем врéменем; (although) хотя́; (contrast) а; **we went to the cinema** ~ **they went to the theatre** мы ходúли в кинó, а онú в теáтр. **whilst** see **while**

whim n прúхоть, капрúз.

whimper vi хны́кать impf; (dog) скулúть impf.

whimsical adj капрúзный; (odd) причýдливый.

whine n (wail) вой; (whimper) хны́канье; vi (dog) скулúть impf; (wail) выть impf; (whimper) хны́кать impf.

whinny vi тúхо ржать impf.

whip n кнут, хлыст; vt (lash) хлестáть impf, хлестнýть pf; (cream) сбивáть impf, сбить pf; ~ **off** скúдывать impf, скúнуть pf; ~ **out** выхвáтывать impf, вы́хватить pf; ~ **round** бы́стро повёртываться impf, повернýться pf; ~ **round** сбор дéнег; ~ **up** (stir up) разжигáть impf, разжéчь pf.

whirl n кружéние; (of dust, fig) вихрь m; (turmoil) сумáтоха; vt & i кружúть(ся) impf, за~ pf. **whirlpool** n водоворóт. **whirlwind** n вихрь m.

whirr vi жужжáть impf.

whisk n (of twigs etc. бéничек; (utensil) мутóвка; (movement) помáхивание; vt (cream etc.) сбивáть impf, сбить pf; ~ **away, off** (brush off) смáхивать impf, смахнýть pf; (take away) бы́стро уносúть impf, унестú pf.

whisker n (human) вóлос на лицé; (animal) ус; pl (human) бакенбáрды f pl.

whisky n вúски neut indecl.

whisper n шёпот; vt & i шептáть impf, шепнýть pf.

whistle n (sound) свист; (instrument) свистóк; vi свистéть impf, свúстнуть pf; vt насвúстывать impf.

white adj бéлый; (hair) седóй; (pale) блéдный; (with milk) с молокóм; **paint** ~ крáсить impf, по~ pf в бéлый свет; ~**collar worker** слýжащий sb; ~ **lie** невúнная ложь; ~ (colour) бéлый свет; (egg, eye) белóк; (~ **person**) бéлый sb. **whiten** vt бе- лúть impf, на~, по~, вы́~ pf; vi бéлеть impf, по~ pf. **white- ness** n белизнá. **whitewash** n побéлка; vt белúть impf, по~ pf; (fig) обелять impf, обелúть pf.

whither adv & conj кудá.

Whitsun n Трóица.

whittle vt: ~ **down** уменьшáть impf, умéньшить pf.

whiz(z) vi: ~ **past** просвистéть

who pron (interrog) кто; (rel) котóрый.

hoever pron кто бы ни~past; (he who) тот, кто.

hole adj (entire) весь, це́лый; (intact, of number) це́лый; n (thing complete) це́лое sb; (all here is) весь sb; (sum) су́мма; on the ~ в о́бщем. **wholehearted** adj беззаве́тный. **whole-heartedly** adv от всего́ се́рдца. **wholemeal** adj из непросе́янной муки́. **wholesale** adj опто́вый; (fig) ма́ссовый; adv о́птом. **wholesaler** n опто́вый торго́вец. **wholesome** adj здоро́вый. **wholly** adv по́лностью.

hom pron (interrog) кого́ etc.; (rel) кото́рого etc.

hoop n крик; vi крича́ть impf, кри́кнуть pf: ~ it up бу́рно весели́ться impf; ~ing cough коклю́ш.

hore n проститу́тка.

hose pron (interrog, rel) чей; (rel) кото́рого.

hy adv почему́; int да ведь! **ick** n фити́ль m.

icked adj ди́кий. **wickedness** n ди́кость.

icker attrib плетёный.

icket n (cricket) воро́тца.

ide adj широ́кий; (extensive) обши́рный; (in measurements) в+acc ширино́й; ~ awake по́лный внима́ния; ~ open широ́ко откры́тый; adv (off target) ми́мо це́ли. **widely** adv широ́ко. **widen** vt & i расши́ря́ть(ся) impf, расши́рить(ся) pf. **widespread** adj распространённый.

idow n вдова́. **widowed** adj овдове́вший. **widower** n вдове́ц.

idth n ширина́; (fig) широта́; (of cloth) полотни́ще.

ield vt (brandish) разма́хи-

вать impf +instr; (power) по́льзоваться impf +instr.

wife n жена́.

wig n пари́к.

wiggle vt & i (move) шевели́ть(ся) impf, по~, шевельну́ть(ся) pf (+instr).

wigwam n вигва́м.

wild adj ди́кий; (flower) полево́й; (uncultivated) невозде́ланный; (tempestuous) бу́йный; (furious) неи́стовый; (ill-considered) необду́манный; be ~ about быть без ума́ от+gen: ~goose chase сумасбро́дная зате́я; n: pl де́бри (-рей) pl. **wildcat** adj (unofficial) неофициа́льный. **wilderness** n пусты́ня. **wildfire** n: spread like ~ распространя́ться impf, распространи́ться pf с молниено́сной быстрото́й. **wildlife** n жива́я приро́да. **wildness** n ди́кость.

wile n хи́трость.

wilful adj (obstinate) упря́мый; (deliberate) преднаме́ренный.

will n во́ля; (~power) си́ла во́ли; (at death) завеща́ние; against one's ~ про́тив во́ли; of one's own free ~ добро́во́льно; with a ~ с энтузиа́змом; good ~ до́брая во́ля; make one's ~ писа́ть impf, на~ pf завеща́ние; vt (want) хоте́ть impf, за~ pf +gen, acc; vt aux: he ~ be president он бу́дет президе́нтом; he ~ return tomorrow он вернётся за́втра; ~ you open the window? откро́йте окно́, пожа́луйста. **willing** adj гото́вый; (eager) стара́тельный. **willingly** adv охо́тно. **willingness** n гото́вность.

willow n и́ва.

willy-nilly adv во́лей-нево́лей.

wilt vi поника́ть impf, пони́кнуть pf.

wily adj хи́трый.

win n побе́да; vt & i вы́и́грывать impf, вы́играть pf; vt (obtain) добива́ться impf, доби́ться pf +gen; ~ over угова́ривать impf, уговори́ть pf; (charm) располага́ть impf, расположи́ть к себе́.

wince vi вздра́гивать impf, вздро́гнуть pf.

winch n лебёдка; поднима́ть impf, подня́ть pf с по́мощью лебёдки.

wind[1] n (air) ве́тер; (breath) дыха́ние; (flatulence) ве́тры m pl; ~ **instrument** духово́й инструме́нт; ~**-swept** откры́тый ветра́м; **get** ~ **of** прон́юхивать impf, пронюха́ть pf; vt (make gasp) заставля́ть impf, заста́вить pf задохну́ться.

wind[2] vi (meander) ви́ться impf; извива́ться impf; vt (coil) нама́тывать impf, намота́ть pf; (watch) заводи́ть impf, завести́ pf (wrap) уку́тывать impf, уку́тать pf; ~ **up** (vt) (reel) сма́тывать impf, смота́ть pf; (watch) see wind[2]; (vt & i) (end) конча́ть(ся) impf, ко́нчить(ся) pf; **winding** (meander) изви́листый; (staircase) винтово́й.

windfall n па́далица; (fig) золото́й дождь.

windmill n ветряна́я ме́льница.

window n окно́; (of shop) витри́на; ~**-box** нару́жный я́щик для цвето́в; ~**-cleaner** мо́йщик о́кон; ~**-dressing** оформле́ние витри́н; (fig)

показу́ха; ~**-frame** око́нная ра́ма; ~**-ledge** подоко́нник; ~**-pane** око́нное стекло́; ~**-shopping** рассма́тривание витри́н; ~**-sill** подоко́нник.

windpipe n дыха́тельное го́рло. **windscreen** n ветрово́е стекло́; ~ **wiper** дво́рник. **windsurfer** n виндсёрфинги́ст. **windsurfing** n виндсёрфинг. **windward** adj наве́тренный. **windy** adj ве́треный.

wine n вино́; ~ **bar** ви́нный погребо́к; ~ **bottle** ви́нная буты́лка; ~ **list** ви́нная ~**-tasting** дегуста́ция вин. **wineglass** n рю́мка. **winery** n ви́нный заво́д. **winy** adj ви́нный.

wing n (also polit) крыло́ (archit) фли́гель m; (sport фланг; pl (theat) кули́сы f pl. **winged** adj крыла́тый.

wink n (blink) морга́ние; (a sign) подми́гивание; vi мига́ть impf, мигну́ть pf; ~ **at** подми́гивать impf, подми́гнуть pf +dat; (fig) смотре́ть impf, по~ pf сквозь па́льцы на+acc.

winkle vt: ~ **out** выкови́ривать impf, вы́ковырять pf.

winner n победи́тель m ~**-ница**. **winning** adj (victorious) выи́грывающий; (shot решающий; (charming) привлека́тельный; n: pl выи́грыш ~**-post** фи́нишный столб.

winter n зима́; attrib зи́мний. **wintry** adj зи́мний; (cold холо́дный.

wipe vt (also ~ **out** inside or вытира́ть impf, вы́тереть p ~ **away**, **off** стира́ть imp стере́ть pf; ~ **out** (extern inate) уничтожа́ть impf, у

...róжить *pf*; (*cancel*) смы́-
...áть *impf*, смыть *pf*
...re *n* про́волока; (*carrying
...urrent*) про́вод; ~ **netting**
про́волочная се́тка. **wire-
...ss** *n* ра́дио *neut indecl*. **wir-
...ing** *n* электропрово́дка. **wiry**
adj жи́листый.

...sdom *n* му́дрость; ~ **tooth**
зуб му́дрости. **wise** *adj* му́д-
рый; (*prudent*) благоразу́м-
...

...sh *n* жела́ние; **with best
...es** всего́ хоро́шего, с наи-
...учшими пожела́ниями; *vt*
...оте́ть *impf*, за~ *pf* (I ~ I
...ould see him мне хоте́лось
...ы его́ ви́деть; I ~ **to go** я
...очу́ пойти́; I ~ **you to come
...arly** я хочу́, что́бы вы ра́но
...ришли́; I ~ **the day were
...ver** хорошо́ бы день уже́
...о́нчился); жела́ть *impf*
...gen (I ~ **you luck** жела́ю
...ам уда́чи); (*congratulate on*)
...ить *pf* (I ~ **you a happy
...irthday** поздравля́ю тебя́ с
...нём рожде́ния); *vi*: ~ **for**
...жела́ть *impf* +*gen*; мечта́ть
...*mpf* +*prep*. **wishful** *adj*: ~
- **thinking** самообольще́ние;
...приня́тие жела́емого за
...е́йствительное.

...sp *n* (*of straw*) пучо́к; (*hair*)
...ло́чок; (*smoke*) стру́йка.
...steria *n* глици́ния.
...stful *adj* тоскли́вый.
...t *n* (*mind*) ум; (*wittiness*)
...строу́мие; (*person*) остря́к;
...**be at one's ~'s end** не знать
...*mpf* что де́лать.
...tch *n* ве́дьма; **~-hunt** охо́та
...а ве́дьмами. **witchcraft** *n*
...олдовство́.

...th *prep* (*in company of, to-
...ether* ~) (*вме́сте*) с+*instr*;

(*as a result of*) от+*gen*; (*at
house of, in keeping of*) у+*gen*;
(*by means of*) +*instr*; (*in spite
of*) несмотря́ на+*acc*; (*including*) включа́я+*acc*; ~ **each/
one another** друг с дру́гом.

withdraw *vt* (*retract*) брать
impf, взять *pf* наза́д; (*hand*)
отдёргивать *impf*, отдёр-
нуть *pf*; (*cancel*) снима́ть *impf*,
снять *pf*; (*mil*) выводи́ть *impf*,
вы́вести *pf*; (*money from circulation*) изыма́ть *impf*, изъ-
я́ть *pf* из обраще́ния; (*diplomat
etc.*) отзыва́ть *impf*, ото-
зва́ть *pf*; (*from bank*) брать
impf, взять *pf*; *vi* удаля́ться
impf, удали́ться *pf*; (*drop out*)
выбыва́ть *impf*, вы́быть *pf*;
(*mil*) отходи́ть *impf*, отойти́
pf. **withdrawal** *n* (*retraction*)
взя́тие наза́д; (*cancellation*)
сня́тие; (*mil*) отхо́д; (*money
from circulation*) изъя́тие;
(*departure*) ухо́д. **withdrawn**
adj за́мкнутый.

wither *vi* вя́нуть *impf*, за~ *pf*.
withering *adj* (*fig*) уничто-
жа́ющий.

withhold *vt* (*refuse to grant*) не
дава́ть *impf*, дать *pf* +*gen*;
(*payment*) уде́рживать *impf*,
удержа́ть *pf*; (*information*)
ута́ивать *impf*, утаи́ть *pf*.

within *prep* (*inside*) внут-
ри́+*gen*, в+*prep*; (~ **the lim-
its of**) в преде́лах +*gen*; (*time*) в
тече́ние +*gen*; *adv* внутри́;
from ~ изнутри́.

without *prep* без+*gen*; ~ **saying good-bye** не проща́ясь; **do
**~ обходи́ться *impf*, обойти́сь
pf без+*gen*.

withstand *vt* выде́рживать
impf, вы́держать *pf*.

witness *n* (*person*) свиде́тель
m; (*eye-*~) очеви́дец; (*to sig-*

nature etc.) завери́тель m; bear ~ to свиде́тельствовать impf, за~ pf; ~box ме́сто для свиде́тельских показа́ний; vt быть свиде́телем+gen; (document etc.) заверя́ть impf, заве́рить pf.

witticism n остро́та. **witty** adj остроу́мный.

wizard n волше́бник, колду́н.

wizened adj морщи́нистый.

wobble vt & i шата́ть(ся) impf, шатну́ть(ся) pf; vi (voice) дрожа́ть impf. **wobbly** adj ша́ткий.

woe n го́ре; ~ is me! го́ре мне! **woeful** adj жа́лкий.

wolf n волк; vt пожира́ть impf, пожра́ть pf.

woman n же́нщина. **womanizer** n волоки́та. **womanly** adj же́нственный.

womb n ма́тка.

wonder n чу́до; (amazement) изумле́ние; (it's) no ~ не удиви́тельно; ~ интересова́ться impf (I ~ who will come интере́сно, кто придёт); vi: I shouldn't ~ if не удиви́тельно бу́дет, е́сли; ~ if you could help me не могли́ бы вы мне помо́чь?; ~ at удивля́ться impf, удиви́ться pf +dat. **wonderful**, **wondrous** adj замеча́тельный.

wont n: as is his ~ по своему́ обыкнове́нию; predic: be ~ to име́ть привы́чку+inf.

woo vt уха́живать impf за +instr.

wood n (forest) лес; (material) де́рево; (firewood) дрова́ pl. **woodcut** n гравю́ра на де́реве. **wooded** adj леси́стый. **wooden** adj (also fig) деревя́нный. **woodland** n леси-

стая ме́стность; attrib ле́сно́й. **woodpecker** n дя́те. **woodwind** n деревя́нные ду́ховые инструме́нты m p. **woodwork** n столя́рная р бо́та; (wooden parts) деревя́нные ча́сти (-те́й) pl. **woo worm** n жучо́к. **woody** (plant etc.) деревяни́стый. (wooded) леси́стый.

wool n шерсть. **woollen** a шерстяно́й. **woolly** adj ше сти́стый; (indistinct) нея́. ный.

word n сло́во; (news) изв стие; by ~ of mouth у́стн have a ~ with поговори́ть c+instr; in a ~ одни́м сл вом; in other ~s други́ми слова́ми; ~ for ~ сло́во сло́во; ~ processor ко пью́тер-изда́тель m; ~ выража́ть impf, вы́разит pf; формули́ровать impf, pf. **wording** n формул ро́вка.

work n рабо́та; (labour; t scholarly ~) труд; (occup tion) заня́тие; (studies) заня тия neut pl; (of art) про ведение; (book) сочине́н pl (factory) заво́д; (mech nism) механи́зм; at ~ (at ing~) за рабо́той; (at pl of ~) на рабо́те; out of безрабо́тный; ~-force рабо́ чая си́ла; ~-load нагрузь vi (also function) рабо́та impf (at, on над+instr; (stud занима́ться impf, заня́т pf; (also toil, labour) тр ди́ться impf; (have effe function) де́йствовать im (succeed) удава́ться im уда́ться pf; vt (operate) упр вля́ть impf; обраща́т ся impf c+instr; (wonde ворить *impf*, со~ *pf*; (soil) обрабатывать *impf*, обработать *pf*; (compel to ~) заставлять *impf*, заставить *pf*; ~ **in** вставлять *impf*, вставить *pf*; ~ **off** (debt) отрабатывать *impf*, отработать *pf*; (weight) сгонять *impf*, согнать *pf*; (energy) давать *impf*, дать *pf*; ~ **out** (solve) находить *impf*, найти *pf* решение +gen; (plans etc.) разрабатывать *impf*, разработать *pf*; (sport) тренироваться *impf*; **everything ~ed out well** всё кончилось хорошо; ~ **out at** (amount to) составлять *impf*, составить *pf*; ~ **up** (perfect) вырабатывать *impf*, выработать *pf*; (excite) возбуждать *impf*, возбудить *pf*; (appetite) нагуливать *impf*, нагулять *pf*. **workable** *adj* осуществимый, реальный. **workaday** *adj* будничный. **workaholic** *n* труженик. **worker** *n* работник; (manual) рабочий *sb*. **working** *adj*: ~ **class** рабочий класс; ~ **hours** рабочее время *neut*; ~ **party** комиссия. **workman** *n* работник. **workmanlike** *adj* искусный. **workmanship** *n* искусство, мастерство. **workshop** *n* мастерская *sb*.

world *n* мир, свет; *attrib* мировой; ~-**famous** всемирно известный; ~ **war** мировая война; ~-**wide** всемирный. **worldly** *adj* мирской; (person) опытный.

worm *n* червь *m*; (intestinal) глист; *vt*: ~ **o.s. into** вкрадываться *impf*, вкрасться *pf* +acc; ~ **out** выведывать

impf, выведать *pf* (of y+gen); ~ **one's way** пробираться *impf*, пробраться *pf*.

worry *n* (anxiety) беспокойство; (care) забота; *vt* беспокоить *impf*, о~ *pf*; *vi* беспокоиться *impf*, о~ *pf* (about o+prep).

worse *adj* худший; *adv* хуже; *n*: **from bad to** ~ всё хуже и хуже. **worsen** *vt* & *i* худшать(ся), ухудшать(ся) *pf*.

worship *n* поклонение (of +dat); (service) богослужение; *vt* поклоняться *impf* +dat; (adore) обожать *impf*. **worshipper** *n* поклонник, -ица.

worst *adj* наихудший, самый плохой; *adv* хуже всего; *n* самое плохое.

worth *n* (value) цена, ценность; (merit) достоинство; **give me a pound's** ~ **of petrol** дайте мне бензина на фунт; *adj*: **be** ~ (of equal value to) стоить *impf* (**what is it** ~? сколько это стоит?); (deserve) стоить *impf* +gen (**is this film** ~ **seeing?** стоит посмотреть этот фильм?). **worthless** *adj* ничего не стоящий; (useless) бесполезный. **worthwhile** *adj* стоящий. **worthy** *adj* достойный.

would *v aux* (conditional): **he would be angry if he found out** он бы рассердился, если бы узнал; (expressing wish) **she** ~ **like to know** она бы хотела знать; **I** ~ **rather** я бы предпочёл; (expressing indirect speech): **he said he** ~ **be late** он сказал, что придёт поздно.

would-be *adj*: ~ **actor** человек, мечтающий стать актёром.

wound n ра́на; vt ра́нить impf & pf. **wounded** adj ра́неный.

wrangle n пререка́ние; vi пререка́ться impf.

wrap n (shawl) шаль; vt (also ~ up) завёртывать impf, заверну́ть pf; ~ up (in wraps) заку́тывать(ся) impf, заку́тать(ся) pf; ~ped up in поглощённый +instr. **wrapper** n обёртка. **wrapping** n обёртка; ~ **paper** обёрточная бума́га.

wrath n гнев.

wreak vt: ~ **havoc on** разоря́ть impf, разори́ть pf.

wreath n вено́к.

wreck n (ship) оста́нки (-ов) корабля́; (vehicle, person, building, etc.) развали́на; vt (destroy, also fig) разруша́ть impf, разру́шить pf; **be** ~**ed** терпе́ть impf, по~ pf круше́ние; (of plans etc.) ру́хнуть pf. **wreckage** n обло́мки m pl круше́ния.

wren n крапи́вник.

wrench n (jerk) дёрганье; (tech) га́ечный ключ; (fig) боль; vt (snatch, pull out) вырыва́ть impf, вы́рвать pf (**from** y+gen); ~ **open** взла́мывать impf, взлома́ть pf.

wrest vt (wrench) вырыва́ть impf, вы́рвать pf (**from** y+gen).

wrestle vi боро́ться impf. **wrestler** n боре́ц. **wrestling** n борьба́.

wretch n несча́стный m; (scoundrel) него́дяй. **wretched** adj жа́лкий; (unpleasant) скве́рный.

wriggle vi извива́ться impf, изви́ться pf; (fidget) ёрзать impf; ~ **out of** увиливать impf, увильну́ть от+gen.

wring vt (also ~ out) выжи-

ма́ть impf, вы́жать pf; (extort) исторга́ть impf, исто́ргнуть pf (**from** y+gen); (neck) свёртывать impf, сверну́ть pf (of +dat); ~ **one's hands** лома́ть impf, с~ pf ру́ки.

wrinkle n морщи́на; vt & мо́рщить(ся) impf, с~ pf.

wrist n запя́стье; ~**watch** на ру́чные часы́ (-со́в) pl.

writ n повестка.

write vt & i писа́ть impf, на~ pf; ~ **down** запи́сывать impf, записа́ть pf; ~ **off** (cancel) спи́сывать impf, списа́ть pf; **the car was a** ~**off** маши́н была́ совсем испо́рчена; ~ **out** выпи́сывать impf, вы́писать pf (**in full** пол ностью); ~ **up** (account o) подро́бно описывать impf, описа́ть pf; (notes) переп сывать impf, переписа́ть p ~**up** (report) отчёт. **writer** писа́тель m, ~ница.

writhe vi ко́рчиться impf, pf.

writing n (handwriting) п черк; (work) произведе́ни in ~ в пи́сьменной фо́рм ~**paper** почто́вая бума́га.

wrong adj (incorrect) непра вильный, неве́рный; (th wrong ...) не тот (**I ha bought the** ~ **book** я купи́ не ту кни́гу; **you've got tl** ~ **number** (tel) вы не ту по́пали; (mistaken) непра́вь (**you are** ~ вы непра́в); (**u just**) несправедли́вый; (si ful) дурно́й; (out of orde нела́дный; (side of clo л́евый; ~ **side out** наизна ку; ~ **way round** наоборо́ n зло; (injustice) несправ ли́вость; **be in the** ~ б непра́вым; **do** ~ греши́ *impf*, со~ *pf*; *adv* не-пра́вильно, неве́рно; go ~ не получа́ться *impf*, получи́ться *pf*; *vt* обижа́ть *impf*, оби́деть *pf*; (*be unjust to*) быть несправедли́вым к+*dat*. **wrongdoer** *n* престу́пник, гре́шник, -ица. **wrongful** *adj* несправедли́вый. **wrongly** *adv* несправедли́во; (*unjustly*) несправедли́во.

wrought *adj*: ~ **iron** сва́рочное желе́зо.

wry *adj* (*smile*) криво́й; (*humour*) сухо́й, ирони́ческий.

X

xenophobia *n* ксенофо́бия.

X-ray *n* (*picture*) рентге́н-(овский сни́мок); *pl* (*radiation*) рентге́новы лучи́ *m pl*; *vt* (*photograph*) де́лать *impf*, с~ *pf* рентге́н +*gen*.

Y

yacht *n* я́хта. **yachting** *n* па́русный спорт. **yachtsman** *n* яхтсме́н.

yank *vt* рвану́ть *pf*.

yap *vi* тя́вкать *impf*, тя́вкнуть *pf*.

yard[1] *n* (*piece of ground*) двор.

yard[2] *n* (*measure*) ярд. **yard-stick** *n* (*fig*) мери́ло.

yarn *n* пря́жа; (*story*) расска́з.

yawn *n* зево́к; *vi* зева́ть *impf*, зевну́ть *pf*; (*chasm etc.*) зия́ть *impf*.

year *n* год; ~ **in**, ~ **out** из го́да в год. **yearbook** *n* ежего́дник. **yearly** *adj* ежего́дный, годово́й; *adv* ежего́дно.

yearn *vi* тоскова́ть *impf* (**for** по+*dat*). **yearning** *n* тоска́ (**for** по+*dat*).

yeast *n* дро́жжи (-же́й) *pl*.

yell *n* крик; *vi* крича́ть *impf*, кри́кнуть *pf*.

yellow *adj* жёлтый; *n* жёлтый цвет. **yellowish** *adj* желтова́тый.

yelp *n* визг; *vi* визжа́ть *impf*, взви́згнуть *pf*.

yes *adv* да; *n* утвержде́ние, согла́сие; (*in voting*) го́лос «за».

yesterday *adv* вчера́; *n* вчера́шний день *m*; ~ **morning** вчера́ у́тром; **the day before** ~ позавчера́; ~**'s newspaper** вчера́шняя газе́та.

yet *adv* (*still*) ещё; (*so far*) до сих пор; (*in questions*) уже́; (*nevertheless*) тем не ме́нее; **as** ~ пока́, до сих пор; **not** ~ ещё не; *conj* одна́ко, но.

yew *n* тис.

Yiddish *n* и́диш.

yield *n* (*harvest*) урожа́й; (*econ*) дохо́д; *vt* (*fruit, revenue, etc.*) приноси́ть *impf*, принести́ *pf*; дава́ть *impf*, дать *pf*; (*give up*) сдава́ть *impf*, сдать *pf*; *vi* (*give in*) (**to** *enemy etc.*) уступа́ть *impf*, уступи́ть *pf* (**to** +*dat*); (*give way*) поддава́ться *impf*, подда́ться *pf* (**to** +*dat*).

yoga *n* йо́га.

yoghurt *n* кефи́р.

yoke *n* (*also fig*) ярмо́; (*fig*) и́го; (*of dress*) коке́тка; *vt* впряга́ть *impf*, впрячь *pf* в ярмо́.

yolk *n* желто́к.

yonder *adv* вон там; *adj* вон тот.

you *pron* (*familiar sg*) ты; (*familiar pl, polite sg & pl*) вы; (*one*) *not usu translated*; *v translated in 2nd pers sg or by impers construction*: ~ **never**

know никогда́ не зна́ешь.
young adj молодо́й; **the ~** молодёжь; n (collect) детёныши m pl. **youngster** n ма́льчик, де́вочка.
your(s) poss pron (familiar sg; also in letter) твой; (familiar pl, polite sg & pl; also in letter) ваш; свой. **yourself** pron (emph) (familiar sg) (ты) сам (m), сама́ (f); (familiar pl, polite sg & pl) (вы) са́ми; (refl) себя́; -ся (suffixed to vt); **by ~** (independently) самостоя́тельно, сам; (alone) оди́н.
youth n (age) мо́лодость; (young man) ю́ноша m; (collect, as pl) молодёжь; **~ club** молодёжный клуб; **~ hostel** молодёжная турба́за. **youthful** adj ю́ношеский.
Yugoslavia n Югосла́вия.

Z

zany adj смешно́й.
zeal n рве́ние, усе́рдие. **zealot** n фана́тик. **zealous** adj ре́вностный, усе́рдный.
zebra n зе́бра.
zenith n зени́т.

zero n нуль m, ноль m.
zest n (piquancy) пика́нтность; (ardour) энтузиа́зм; **~ for life** жизнера́дость.
zigzag n зигза́г; adj зигзагообра́зный; vi де́лать impf, с~ pf зигза́ги; идти́ det зигза́гами.
zinc n цинк.
Zionism n сиони́зм. **Zionist** n сиони́ст.
zip n (~ fastener) (застёжка-) мо́лния; vt & i: **~ up** застёгивать(ся) impf, застегну́ть (ся) pf на мо́лнию.
zodiac n зодиа́к; **sign of the ~** знак зодиа́ка.
zombie n челове́к спя́щий на ходу́.
zone n зо́на; (geog) по́яс.
zoo n зоопа́рк. **zoological** adj зоологи́ческий; **~ garden(s)** зоологи́ческий сад. **zoologist** n зоо́лог. **zoology** n зооло́гия.
zoom vi (rush) мча́ться impf, ~ **in** (phot) де́лать impf, с~ pf наплы́в; **~ lens** объекти́в с переме́нным фо́кусным расстоя́нием.
Zulu adj зулу́сский; n зулу́~ка.

Appendix I Spelling Rules

It is assumed that the user is acquainted with the following spelling rules which affect Russian declension and conjugation.

ы, **ю**, and **я** do not follow **г**, **к**, **х**, **ж**, **ч**, **ш**, and **щ**; instead, **и**, **у**, and **а** are used, e.g. **ма́льчик**и, **кричу́**, **лежа́т**, **ноча́ми**; similarly, **ю** and **я** do not follow **ц**; instead, **у** or **а** are used.

Unstressed **о** does not follow **ж**, **ц**, **ч**, **ш**, or **щ**; instead, **е** is used, e.g. **му́ж**ем, **ме́сяц**ев, **хоро́ш**ее.

Appendix II Declension of Russian Adjectives

The following patterns are regarded as regular and are not shown in the dictionary entries.

singular	nom	acc	gen	dat	instr	prep
masculine	тёпл|ый	~ый	~ого	~ому	~ым	~ом
feminine	тёпл|ая	~ую	~ой	~ой	~ой	~ой
neuter	тёпл|ое	~ое	~ого	~ому	~ым	~ом

plural	nom	acc	gen	dat	instr	prep
masculine	тёпл|ые	~ые	~ых	~ым	~ыми	~ых
feminine	тёпл|ые	~ые	~ых	~ым	~ыми	~ых
neuter	тёпл|ые	~ые	~ых	~ым	~ыми	~ых

Appendix III Declension of Russian Nouns

The following patterns are regarded as regular and are
not shown in the dictionary entries. Forms marked
should be particularly noted.

1 Masculine

Singular	nom	acc	gen	dat	instr	prep
	обе́д	~	~а	~у	~ом	~е
	слу́ча|й	~й	~я	~ю	~ем	~е
	марш	~	~а	~у	~ем	~е
	каранда́ш	~	~а́	~у́	~о́м*	~е́
	сцена́ри|й	~й	~я	~ю	~ем	~и*
	портфе́л|ь	~ь	~я	~ю	~ем	~е

Plural	nom	acc	gen	dat	instr	prep
	обе́д|ы	~ы	~ов	~ам	~ами	~ах
	слу́ча|и	~и	~ев	~ям	~ями	~ях
	ма́рш|и	~и	~ей*	~ам	~ами	~ах
	каранда́ш|и	~и	~ей*	~а́м	~а́ми	~а́х
	сцена́ри|и	~и	~ев*	~ям	~ями	~ях
	портфе́л|и	~и	~ей*	~ям	~ями	~ях

2 Feminine

Singular	nom	acc	gen	dat	instr	prep
	газе́т|а	~у	~ы	~е	~ой	~е
	ба́н|я	~ю	~и	~е	~ей	~е
	ли́ни|я	~ю	~и	~и*	~ей	~и*
	ста́ту|я	~ю	~и	~е*	~ей	~е*
	бол|ь	~ь	~и	~и*	~ью*	~и

	nom	acc	gen	dat	instr	prep
газе́т|ы		~ы	~	~ам	~ами	~ах
ба́н|и		~и	~ь*	~ям	~ями	~ях
ли́ни|и		~и	~й*	~ям	~ями	~ях
ста́ту|и		~и	~й*	~ям	~ями	~ях
бо́л|и		~и	~ей*	~ям	~ями	~ях

Neuter

	nom	acc	gen	dat	instr	prep
чу́вств|о		~о	~а	~у	~ом	~е
учи́лищ|е		~е	~а	~у	~ем	~е
зда́ни|е		~е	~я	~ю	~ем	~и*
ущел|ье		~ье	~ья	~ью	~ьем	~ье

	nom	acc	gen	dat	instr	prep
чу́вств|а		~а	~	~ам	~ами	~ах
учи́лищ|а		~а	~	~ам	~ами	~ах
зда́ни|я		~я	~й*	~ям	~ями	~ях
ущел|ья		~ья	~ий*	~ьям	~ьями	~ьях

Appendix IV Conjugation of Russian Verbs

The following patterns are regarded as regular and a
not shown in the dictionary entries.

1. **-e-** conjugation

(a) **чита́|ть**	~ю	~ешь	~ет	~ем	~ете	~ю
(b) **сия́|ть**	~ю	~ешь	~ет	~ем	~ете	~ю
(c) **про́б|овать**	~ую	~уешь	~ует	~уем	~уете	~у
(d) **рис|ова́ть**	~у́ю	~у́ешь	~у́ет	~у́ем	~у́ете	~у́

2. **-и-** conjugation

(a) **говор|и́ть**	~ю́	~и́шь	~и́т	~и́м	~и́те	~я́
(b) **стро́|ить**	~ю	~ишь	~ит	~им	~ите	~я

Notes

1. Also belonging to the **-e-** conjugation are:

   i) most other verbs in **-ать** (but see Note 2(
below), e.g. **жа́ждать** (жа́жду, -ждешь); **пря́та**
(пря́чу, -чешь), **колеба́ть** (коле́блю, -блешь).

   ii) verbs in **-еть** for which the 1st pers sing **-ек**
given, e.g. **жале́ть**.

   iii) verbs in **-нуть** for which the 1st pers sing **-ну**
given (e.g. **вя́нуть**), **ю** becoming **у** in the 1st pers si
and 3rd pers pl.

   iv) verbs in **-ять** which drop the **я** in conjugatio
e.g. **ла́ять** (ла́ю, ла́ешь); **се́ять** (се́ю, се́ешь).

Also belonging to the **-и-** conjugation are:

i)   verbs in consonant + **-ить** which change the consonant in the first person singular, e.g. **досади́ть** (-ажу́, -ади́шь), or insert an **-л-**, e.g. **доба́вить** (доба́влю, -вишь).

ii)   other verbs in vowel + **-ить**, e.g. **затаи́ть, кле́ить** (as 2b above).

iii)   verbs in **-еть** for which the 1st pers sing is given as consonant + **ю** or **у**, e.g. **звене́ть** (-ню́, -ни́шь), **ви́деть** (ви́жу, ви́дишь).

iv)   two verbs in **-ять** (**стоя́ть, боя́ться**).

v)   verbs in **-ать** whose stem ends in **ч, ж, щ**, or **ш**, not changing between the infinitive and conjugation, e.g. **крича́ть** (-чу́, -чи́шь). Cf. Note 1(i).

Key to the Russian Alphabet

Capital	Lower-case	Approx. English Sour
А	а	a
Б	б	b
В	в	v
Г	г	g
Д	д	d
Е	е	ye
Ё	ё	yo
Ж	ж	zh (as in measure)
З	з	z
И	и	i
Й	й	y
К	к	k
Л	л	l
М	м	m
Н	н	n
О	о	o
П	п	p
Р	р	r
С	с	s
Т	т	t
У	у	oo
Ф	ф	f
Х	х	kh (as in lo*ch*)
Ц	ц	ts
Ч	ч	ch
Ш	ш	sh
Щ	щ	shch
Ъ	ъ	″ ('hard sign'; not pronounced as separate sound)
Ы	ы	y
Ь	ь	′ ('soft sign'; not pronounced as separate sound)
Э	э	e
Ю	ю	yu
Я	я	ya